Understanding the Bible

Understanding the Bible

SIXTH EDITION

Stephen L. Harris

California State University, Sacramento

Boston   Burr Ridge, IL   Dubuque, IA   Madison, WI   New York
San Francisco   St. Louis   Bangkok   Bogotá   Caracas   Kuala Lumpur
Lisbon   London   Madrid   Mexico City   Milan   Montreal   New Delhi
Santiago   Seoul   Singapore   Sydney   Taipei   Toronto

McGraw-Hill Higher Education

A Division of The **McGraw-Hill** Companies

1 2 3 4 5 6 7 8 9 0 DOC/DOC 0 9 8 7 6 5 4 3 2

Library of Congress Cataloging-in-Publication Data

Harris, Stephen L.
    Understanding the Bible / Stephen L. Harris.— 6th ed.
      p. cm.
    Includes bibliographical references and index.
    ISBN 0-7674-2916-8
    1. Bible—Introductions.   I. Title.
  BS475.3 .H32   2002
  220.6′1—dc21   2002075199

Publisher, Ken King; sponsoring editor, Jon-David Hague; production editor,
Holly Paulsen; manuscript editor, Beth T. Berkelhammer; design manager,
Sharon Spurlock; art editor, Emma Ghiselli; text designer, Claire Seng-
Niemoeller; cover designer, Susan Breitbard; illustrator, Carto-Graphics; photo
researcher, Brian Pecko; production supervisor, Rich DeVitto. The text was
set in 10/12 Adobe Caslon by G&S Typesetters and printed on acid-free 45#
Scholarly Matte, PMS 562U Green, by R. R. Donnelley.

Cover image: *Noah's Ark During the Flood* (fresco c. 1100). Abby Church, Saint-
Savin-sur-Gartempe, France. © Bridgeman Art Library/Giraudon/Lauros

www.mhhe.com

In memory of Glenn Edwin Harris

Preface

The only single-volume introductory text that places each book of the Hebrew Bible (Old Testament), the Apocrypha, and the Christian Greek Scriptures (New Testament) in its historical and cultural context, *Understanding the Bible* is designed for students undertaking their first systematic study of biblical literature. Like its predecessors, the sixth edition has two major goals: to make readers familiar with the Bible's contents and to acquaint them with the many ways in which contemporary scholarship helps to illuminate the biblical documents. Taking a consistently nonsectarian approach, this text both explores the sociopolitical and religious forces that shaped the individual biblical books and examines the enduring significance of their diverse messages. From Genesis to Revelation, each biblical document is studied on its own terms and is allowed to speak for itself, as free as humanly possible from ideological assumptions.

This new edition has been revised throughout, particularly in the opening chapters, which have been extensively reorganized to make it easier for readers to understand the complex process by which the Bible was formed. The Bible is not a single volume but rather a library of originally separate books written by many different authors during a span of more than a thousand years. Thus tracing the development of the Bible's ideas over time and through ever-changing historical circumstances is indispensable in order to appreciate both its di-

verse literary forms and its multiple religious functions. Abandoning the question-and-answer format of previous editions, the first chapter has been rewritten to provide a clearer and more comprehensive overview of the Bible's organizational structure, unifying themes, and literary transmission. The section also offers a more streamlined approach to such topics as the formation of the biblical canon, the translation of the Bible into English, and the role of modern scholarship in clarifying the nature and purpose of the biblical texts. Revisions in Chapter 2, "History and Geography of the Ancient Near East," now more explicitly emphasize connections between many biblical themes and older Near Eastern traditions, including stories about creation, the Flood, and speculations about the afterlife.

Because the Hebrew Bible (Old Testament) was created by and for the Jewish community of faith, this textbook generally follows the Jewish three-part division (the Tanak) of its contents: Torah (Law, or divine instruction), Nevi'im (Prophets), and Kethuvim (Writings). Besides reflecting the Hebrew Bible's chronological growth, this three-part division also embodies the evolving faith of Israel, the ancient Near Eastern people that produced the Bible. Emulating the tripartite Jewish Scriptures, Christian editors of the New Testament also arranged their sacred books into three distinct units that generally parallel the organization of the

Hebrew Bible, an ordering that illustrates only one of the innumerable links connecting Christianity with its parent faith, Judaism.

An entirely new chapter—Chapter 3, "The God of Israel: An Evolving Portrait"—explores the historical origins, composite character, and multiple roles of the biblical God. The Bible's single most important contribution to world religion, the concept of a single all-powerful Deity who created and sustains the universe has profoundly influenced all three of the monotheistic faiths, Judaism, Christianity, and Islam. The claim that the Israelite God—Yahweh—was the only God, however, is the product of a long, historical evolution in which Yahweh gradually assumed many of the attributes and functions of older Near Eastern deities. This process of assimilating different divine beings, such as El, head of the Canaanite pantheon, into a single God concept helps to explain Yahweh's paradoxical character, in which his creative and destructive impulses seem to war against each other. Contemporary Western theology has inherited the still unresolved problem of an omnipotent Deity who is all good but who tolerates injustice and undeserved suffering.

A second new chapter—Chapter 11, "Additional Portraits of Jesus: Noncanonical Gospels and the Quest for the Historical Jesus"—both examines early Christian accounts of Jesus' life and teachings that were not included in the New Testament and studies the ongoing scholarly attempts to recover the "real" Jesus of history, distinguishing his authentic voice from the theological views of the Gospel authors who interpreted him. This section analyzes some recently rediscovered works, such as the Gospel of Thomas, Secret Mark, and the Gospel of Peter, as well as the Gospels attributed to James and Thomas that allegedly describe Jesus' childhood and family background. The sixth edition also incorporates discussions of other early noncanonical writings, including the Didache (Teaching of the Twelve Apostles), 1 Clement (by the third bishop of Rome), the Epistle of Barnabas (supposedly by Paul's mentor), and the Apocalypse of Peter, a vision of sinners in hell. This edition of *Understanding the Bible* closes with a new survey of some historical events and innovative ideas, such as scientific rationalism, that influence our views of the biblical message in contemporary Western society.

In addition, the introductory essay on the Torah (Genesis–Deuteronomy) has been revised to present a more complete coverage of current scholarly theories about its composition and about its principal themes. The discussions of Genesis and Exodus (Chapter 4) have been similarly expanded, as has the section introducing Joshua and the historical origins of Israel (Chapter 5). Both the introduction to the Writings, the third part of the Hebrew Bible (Tanak), and the discussion of Job (Chapter 12) have been significantly rewritten. Virtually all parts of the text, including the bibliographies, have been updated to incorporate the insights of recent scholarship.

To make biblical history and literature as accessible to beginning students as possible, *Understanding the Bible* utilizes a variety of pedagogical aids. The discussion of each biblical topic or book is introduced with a "Key Topics/Themes" paragraph that highlights the main issues covered in that section. To help students remember the material presented, each section ends with two sets of questions: "Questions for Review" target essential facts about the biblical texts and historical background; and "Questions for Discussion and Reflection" invite readers to think about broader ideas and concepts relevant to the larger issues of ethical or religious meaning, often relating to the students' own concerns. Drawing readers' attention to particularly important information, the first occurrence of important biblical characters, events, or concepts in each section or chapter are printed in **boldface**. For readers' convenience, all boldfaced terms are listed in "Key Terms and Concepts" at the end of every chapter or section, and these terms are also succinctly defined in a comprehensive glossary at the back of the book. To assist students explore particular subjects more fully and to prepare research papers, each section of the book includes a list of "Recommend Reading" that features recent works by leading scholars.

A particularly helpful feature of this book is the inclusion of numerous maps, charts, tables, illustrations, and boxes that supplement the discussions in the main text. Several new boxes enhance the book's information value, discussing such topics as Moses' encounter with God on Sinai/Horeb, the origin of the Satan figure and the evolution of ideas about Sheol (the biblical Underworld), "milestone" events in the growth of early Christianity, and Paul's views on the origins of sin and death.

One new box, "Anthropomorphism, Patriarchy, and the Gender of God" (Chapter 4), addresses an issue that troubles many of today's Bible readers: the portrayal of the Deity as a male figure. In both the Old and New Testaments, biblical writers consistently employ the masculine pronoun when referring to supernatural beings, whether gods, angels, or demons. (This is partly a function of the nature of ancient Hebrew grammar, which has no pronoun to designate the neutral "it.") Exceptions include prophetic denunciations of female deities, such as Ishtar—the "Queen of Heaven"—Asherah (or Astarte), Baal's female consort (and, as some scholars believe, perhaps also the name of a feminine partner of Yahweh whose existence was excised from the official records by later biblical editors), as well as other fertility goddesses worshiped by Israel's neighbors. When dealing with the concept of divinity, a moment's reflection reminds us that a universal God cannot be limited by human gender (perhaps implicit in the Genesis statement that God formed both male and female in the divine "image"). Although this text avoids sexist language wherever possible, readers must distinguish between current ideas about gender-free spirituality and the presuppositions of the Near Eastern and Greco-Roman patriarchal society that produced the Judeo-Christian Scriptures. To respect the historical integrity of the biblical texts and minimize reader confusion, I use the same pronouns that appear in the passages under discussion. In the larger world of church liturgy, theology, philosophy, and the social history of religion, readers will recognize that the Being whose nature biblical writers seek to communicate transcends human attributes, including gender.

Among those who helped to make the sixth edition a reality, I particularly wish to thank the reviewers who have used this textbook in class and were able to offer practical advice on improving its usefulness as a teaching tool. The reviewers are Andrew Barnaby, University of Vermont; John Betlyon, Penn State University; Donald Chinula, Stillman College; Jonathan Greiser, Furman University; Jennifer Herdt, University of Notre Dame; and Paul Mirecki, University of Kansas.

I would also like to express my gratitude to this edition's sponsoring editor, Jon-David Hague; to the production editor, Holly Paulsen; and to the manuscript editor, Beth Berkelhammer. In addition, I would like to thank my friend and colleague Brad Nystrom for his fluent and readable translation of Cleanthes' "Hymn to Zeus."

Contents

Chapter 12   A Christian History and the Pauline Letters   511

Chapter 13   General Epistles and Some Visions of End Time   575

Boxes, Tables, and Illustrations

The Bible

An Overview

Key Topics/Themes

Divided into two main sections, the Old Testament and New Testament, the Bible is a diverse anthology of documents composed over a period of 1100 years. Written in the Hebrew language (hence the name *Hebrew Bible*), the first section is referred to in Hebrew as the *Tanak,* an acronym based on the first letter of each of its three major divisions: *Torah* (divine instruction), *Nevi'im* (Prophets), and *Kethuvim* (Writings). The three-part Tanak (Hebrew Bible) explores the relationship between God and Israel, his chosen people, with whom he concludes a series of covenants (pacts or agreements), including divine promises for a permanent homeland and other blessings. The New Testament is a collection of twenty-seven Greek books produced by the early Christian community between about 50 and 150 C.E. and added to a Greek edition of the Hebrew Bible, the Septuagint.

With no original texts by any biblical writer surviving, scholars must rely on copies of manuscripts made many centuries after the works were first composed. Before the Dead Sea Scrolls were discovered, beginning in 1947, the oldest biblical texts were the series of manuscripts edited by medieval Jewish scholars, the *masoretes* ("transmitters"). Known as the Masoretic Text (MT), it is the edition upon which most editions of the Old Testament (Hebrew Bible) are based. Dating from about 250 B.C.E. to the first century C.E., some of the Dead Sea Scrolls, mostly in fragmental form, are almost a thousand years older than the Masoretic Text. In the early fifth century C.E., a Christian scholar, Jerome, translated both the Hebrew Bible (Tanak) and the New Testament into Latin, creating the Vulgate Bible. Another millennium passed before the Bible began to be translated into English.

KEY QUESTIONS

What is the Bible? Where, when, and in what languages did it originate? How was the Bible formed, and how was it transmitted to us? How did the Bible come to be translated into contemporary English?

Why We Read the Bible

Sacred to two global religions, Judaism and Christianity, the Bible continues to shape the lives of 2 billion people, approximately a third of the global population. In the West, biblical teachings about the nature of God and the purpose of human life profoundly influence standards of behavior and assumptions about ultimate reality. In Western society, even people who do not belong to a church or synagogue typically express biblical attitudes in forming their personal views of life, judging their own and others' conduct according to biblical principles of social justice and ethical responsibility. From popular notions about angelic visitations to speculations about a future Day of Judgment and the end of history as we know it, most Westerners automatically echo ideas promulgated in the Bible.

Pervasive in the West, the biblical concept of God — Creator, Judge, and Ruler of the universe — extends far beyond the Western hemisphere to embrace the peoples of Islam. The world's third great monotheistic* faith, Islam (meaning "submission" or "surrender" to God) recognizes the same God worshiped by Jews and Christians. In the Qur'an (Koran), the sacred book of Islam, biblical characters such as Abraham, Moses, and Jesus are presented as God's prophets, predecessors of the ultimate prophet, Muhammad (Mohammed). To understand the dynamic interaction between these three world religions, an awareness of how the biblical views of God developed over time is essential (see Chapter 3).

Until a few generations ago, familiarity with biblical stories and expressions was part of most Westerners' life experience. Besides regularly hearing excerpts of the Bible read aloud in church or synagogue, people also attended chapel or other religious services in schools, where studying biblical subjects was an integral part of the curriculum. Almost every English poet, from Shakespeare and Milton to Eliot and Auden, could count on educated readers recognizing their numerous allusions to biblical phrases or characters. Intimately familiar with the Authorized (King James) Version or some other English translation, most people knew that the "apple of his eye" referred to God's love for **Israel** (his chosen people), and that Jacob's gift of a "coat of many colors" to his son Joseph incited murderous jealousy in Joseph's brothers.

Although many people in Jewish or Christian communities no longer can quote — or even recognize — biblical references, Western culture continues to follow many biblical precepts, including in its legal and judicial system. Western courts today are divided over issues raised by ancient Israel's prophets and lawmakers, controversies ranging from issues of capital punishment to the rights of women to society's obligations to the poor and powerless. Biblical statements made thousands of years ago — from taboos on homosexuality to prohibitions on divorce and remarriage — are still passionately debated. Because Western society, to an incalculable extent, is shaped by ancient Judeo-Christian religious traditions preserved in the Bible, a knowledge of the historical, social, and religious forces that prompted biblical authors to express their particular views helps us to understand better our own way of life.

What Is the Bible?

Known as the Good Book, as if it were a single volume, the Bible is in fact a collection of many individual books written over a period of 1100 years. Derived from the Greek *biblia,* the word *bible* means "little books," denoting its nature as an anthology or library of diverse compositions, ranging from poetry and narrative to law and prophecy.

Divided into two main sections, the Old Testament and the New Testament, the Bible's two distinct parts represent its origins in two different religious communities during different historical periods. The larger, older section — the Old Testament — was written by and for the Jewish community of faith and contains material composed be-

---

*Monotheism is the belief in a single God; **polytheism,** the belief in more than one god, characterized the religions of the ancient world, as it does such contemporary faiths as Hinduism.

tween about the twelfth and second centuries B.C.E.* Because most of its contents were composed in Hebrew, the language of ancient Israel, most contemporary scholars refer to the Old Testament as the Hebrew Bible.

Between about 50 and 150 C.E., well after all the books of the Hebrew Bible had been written, the early Christian movement produced a series of documents — Gospels, letters, and sermons — that were eventually collected to form the New Testament. The twenty-seven Greek books comprising the New Testament were then added to a Greek edition of the Hebrew Bible — the **Septuagint** — to form the two-part Christian Bible. The Christian church regards both the Hebrew Bible and the New Testament as Scripture, a term designating writings that a religious group considers to be sacred and authoritative in determining the group's belief and practice. In Judaism, only the Hebrew Bible has the authority of Scripture.

The Old Testament and the Hebrew Bible (Tanak)

Although the Old Testament and the Hebrew Bible are commonly regarded as synonymous, there are some significant differences between them. Most Protestant versions of the Old Testament have exactly the same books as the Hebrew Bible, albeit in a slightly different order. Catholic and Greek Orthodox versions, however, include about fourteen books or parts of books that early Jewish editors excluded from the Hebrew Bible. These additional books, known as the **Apocrypha,** were generally composed later than the Hebrew Scriptures and, beginning in the third century B.C.E., were gradually incorporated in the Septuagint, the Greek-language edition used in the early church. Following the Protestant Reformation in

the sixteenth century C.E., Protestant bibles, such as the King James Version, typically relegated the apocryphal books to a separate unit between the Old and New Testaments. By the early nineteenth century, most Protestant bibles deleted the Apocrypha altogether (Table 1.1). In some recent Protestant English translations, however, such as the Revised English Bible and the New Revised Standard Version, the apocryphal writings have been restored. In the Jerusalem Bible, the English edition of the Old Testament quoted in this textbook, the Apocrypha are integrated with the other books of the Hebrew Bible. (See Chapter 8 for a discussion of the Apocrypha.)

THE THREE-PART HEBREW BIBLE (TANAK)

Arrangement of Contents   In discussing the Hebrew Bible (Old Testament), this text observes the traditional arrangement of its contents made by ancient Jewish editors, which differs somewhat from most Christian editions of the Old Testament. Both Catholic and Protestant bibles divide the biblical documents into four major sections, grouping books together according to their literary category regardless of their original function or date of composition. The four-part Christian Old Testament begins with the **Pentateuch** (a Greek term meaning "five scrolls," the first five books of the Bible — Genesis, Exodus, Leviticus, Numbers, and Deuteronomy); it continues with a long list of historical books, from Joshua to Ezra and Nehemiah (or to 1 and 2 Maccabees in Catholic and Orthodox bibles); follows with works of Wisdom and poetry, such as Psalms, Proverbs, and Job; and concludes with books ascribed to individual prophets, such as Isaiah, Jeremiah, Ezekiel, Amos, and Malachi (the last document in the Christian Old Testament).

By contrast, the Hebrew Bible follows a three-part division — Torah, Prophets, and Writings — that more accurately reflects the chronological order in which the books were written and subsequently added to the **canon,** the official list of books that a religious community accepts as authentic and binding. (In Catholic and Orthodox

---

*B.C.E. is an abbreviation for "before the Common Era," corresponding to B.C. ("before Christ"); C.E. refers to the "Common Era"—a religiously neutral term many scholars use instead of "A.D." (*anno domini,* Latin for "in the year of the Lord").

Table 1.1 Order of Books in the Old Testament (Tanak)

Hebrew Bible (Masoretic Text)	Greek Septuagint Bible	Roman Catholic and Greek Orthodox Old Testament	Protestant Old Testament
Torah (Pentateuch)	*Pentateuch*	*Pentateuch*	*Pentateuch*
Genesis	Genesis	Genesis	Genesis
Exodus	Exodus	Exodus	Exodus
Leviticus	Leviticus	Leviticus	Leviticus
Numbers	Numbers	Numbers	Numbers
Deuteronomy	Deuteronomy	Deuteronomy	Deuteronomy
Nevi'im (Prophets)			
(Former Prophets)	*Historical Books*	*Historical Books*	*Historical Books*
Joshua	Joshua	Josue (Joshua)	Joshua
Judges	Judges	Judges	Judges
	Ruth	Ruth	Ruth
	1–2 Regnorum	1 and 2 Kings	
1–2 Samuel	(1–2 Samuel)	(1–2 Samuel)	1–2 Samuel
1–2 Kings	3–4 Regnorum (1–2 Kings)	3–4 Kings (1–2 Kings)	1–2 Kings
	1–2 Paralipomenon (1–2 Chronicles)	1–2 Paralipomenon (1–2 Chronicles)	1–2 Chronicles
	1 Esdras	1–2 Esdras (Ezra-Nehemiah)	Ezra Nehemiah
	2 Esdras (Ezra-Nehemiah)		Esther
	Esther	Tobias (Tobit)*	
	Judith	Judith*	
	Tobit	Esther (with additions)	
	1–4 Maccabees	1–2 Maccabees*	
	Poetry and Wisdom	*Poetry and Wisdom*	*Poetry and Wisdom*
	Psalms	Job	Job
	Odes	Psalms	Psalms
	Proverbs	Proverbs	Proverbs
	Ecclesiastes	Ecclesiastes	Ecclesiastes
	Song of Songs	Canticle of Canticles (Song of Solomon)	Song of Solomon
	Job		
	Wisdom of Solomon	Wisdom of Solomon*	
	Sirach (Ecclesiasticus)	Ecclesiasticus*	
	Psalms of Solomon	(Widsom of Jesus ben Sirach)	
(Latter Prophets)	*Prophetic Books*	*Prophetic Books*	*Prophetic Books*
Isaiah		Isaias (Isaiah)	Isaiah
Jeremiah		Jeremias (Jeremiah)	Jeremiah

Table 1.1 (continued)

Hebrew Bible (Masoretic Text)	Greek Septuagint Bible	Roman Catholic and Greek Orthodox Old Testament	Protestant Old Testament
		Lamentations	Lamentations
		Baruch (including the epistle of Jeremias)*	
Ezekiel		Ezechiel (Ezekiel)	Ezekiel
		Daniel (with additions; Prayer of Azariah and Song of the Three Young Men;* Susanna;* Bel and the Dragon*)	Daniel
Book of Twelve			
Hosea		Osee (Hosea)	Hosea
Amos		Joel	Joel
Micah		Amos	Amos
Joel		Abidas (Obadiah)	Obadiah
Obadiah		Jonas (Jonah)	Jonah
Jonah		Micheas (Micah)	Micah
Nahum		Nahum	Nahum
Habakkuk		Habucuc (Habakkuk)	Habakkuk
Zephaniah		Sophonias (Zephaniah)	Zephaniah
Haggai		Aggeus (Haggai)	Haggai
Zechariah		Zacharias (Zechariah)	Zechariah
Malachi		Malachias (Malachi)	Malachi
	Isaiah		
Kethuvim (Writings)	Jeremiah		
Psalms	Baruch		
Job	Lamentations		
Proverbs	Epistle of Jeremiah		
Ruth	Ezekiel		
Song of Solomon	Susanna		
Ecclesiastes	Daniel		
Lamentations	Bel and the Dragon		
Esther			
Daniel			
Ezra-Nehemiah			
1–2 Chronicles			

*Not in Jewish or most Protestant Bibles; considered deuterocanonical by Catholic scholars and relegated to the Apocrypha by Protestants.

churches, the apocryphal books, such as Tobit, Judith, and 1 and 2 Maccabees, are regarded as **deuterocanonical**, belonging to a second later canon; see Chapter 8.)

THE TANAK

During the last centuries B.C.E. and first century C.E., Jewish scholars gradually completed a long process of compiling and editing their sacred literature to form the present three-part Hebrew Bible. Among Jews, the Hebrew Bible is typically called the **Tanak** (also spelled **Tanakh**), an acronym derived from the initial consonants of the three sections into which the Scriptures are divided: Torah, Nevi'im, and Kethuvim (Box 1.1). Taken as a whole, the Tanak's three major divisions form a complex exploration of its two principal themes — the nature of God and God's ongoing relationship with Israel, the ancient Near Eastern people with whom he entered into a special partnership (Box 1.2).

The first part of the Tanak (Hebrew Bible), the five books of the Pentateuch, is called the **Torah**, which means "teaching" or "instruction." Because **Moses** is the leading human figure in four books of Torah (Exodus through Deuteronomy), the person through whom God conveys his legal commands and other instructions, this division is also known as the "Mosaic Law" or "Books of Moses" (see Chapter 4). The Hebrew Bible's second part, the **Nevi'im (Prophets),** is divided into two subsections: The first consists of narratives relating Israel's historical experience from its conquest of **Canaan**, the territory God had promised to the Israelites, to its loss of that land when the Near Eastern empire of **Babylon** destroyed the royal capital, **Jerusalem**, and took its ruling classes into exile. Recounted in the books of Joshua, Judges, 1 and 2 Samuel, and 1 and 2 Kings, this narrative section covers the period from about 1250 B.C.E. to 587 B.C.E., the latter date marking a crucial turning point in biblical history. (See Figure 1.1 for a map showing Israel's location between the great empires of Babylon and Egypt.) The long narrative that begins in Genesis with God's creation of the world and his promise of a permanent homeland to **Abraham**'s descendants (the people of Israel) thus ends tragically — and abruptly — in 2 Kings, with Abraham's progeny captive in Babylon.

The second subsection of the Nevi'im (Prophets) does not continue the narrative of Israel's history or describe its eventual return from exile to rebuild Jerusalem. The second subunit consists instead of collections of **oracles** (pronouncements believed to be divinely inspired) of Israel's prophets. The prophetic books include three "major" prophets — Isaiah, Jeremiah, and Ezekiel — and twelve "minor" prophets, including Amos, Hosea, Micah, Jonah, and Malachi. Most of these prophetic oracles relate to specific political crises in Israel's history, such as the threat from **Assyria**, an aggressive military power during the eighth and seventh centuries B.C.E., and the Babylonian invasion of the early sixth century B.C.E. (see Chapter 5). As arranged in the Hebrew Bible, the prophetic works immediately follow the historical narratives (Genesis through 2 Kings) and illustrate the issues — such as Israel's breaking its vow to worship God exclusively — that many biblical writers believed were the cause of Israel's ultimate defeat and loss of homeland.

The Hebrew Bible's third and final division, the **Kethuvim** (Writings), contains the most diverse material, including volumes of poetry, such as Psalms, Song of Songs, and Lamentations; short stories, such as Ruth and Esther; and books of Wisdom, such as Proverbs, Job, and Ecclesiastes. Whereas no biblical author produced a comprehensive account of Israel's history after the exile, a postexilic writer composed the books of Ezra and Nehemiah, historical narratives which offer brief glimpses of life in Jerusalem after the exile, when Israel was under the domination of **Persia**, the empire that had replaced Babylon as ruler of the ancient Near East.

The Kethuvim also includes Daniel, the only **apocalypse** admitted to the Tanak and, in the opinion of most scholars, the last-written book in the Hebrew Bible canon. *Apocalypse* means an "uncovering" or "revelation," a visionary composition that "unveils" hidden realities of the spirit world or the distant future (see Chapter 7). Many apocalyptic works were written during the last centuries

Box 1.1 Tanak—The Three-Part Hebrew Bible

A comparatively recent term for the Hebrew Bible, Tanak (also spelled Tanakh) is an acronym composed of consonants designating the first letter of the three major divisions of the Hebrew Scriptures. Vowel sounds are inserted between the consonants.

T Torah (the five books of Mosaic instruction)
- Genesis, Exodus, Leviticus, Numbers, Deuteronomy

N Nevi'im (the Prophets)
- The Former Prophets [Deuteronomistic History]: Joshua, Judges, 1 and 2 Samuel, 1 and 2 Kings
- The Latter Prophets [compiled in the prophets' names]: Isaiah, Jeremiah, Ezekiel, and the Scroll of the Twelve (Amos, Hosea, Micah, Joel, etc.)

K Kethuvim (the Writings)
- Psalms
- Job, Proverbs [Wisdom Books]

- Festival scrolls: Ruth, Song of Songs, Ecclesiastes, Lamentations, Esther
- Daniel [an apocalypse]
- Ezra-Nehemiah, 1 and 2 Chronicles [historical narratives]

In the traditional arrangement of books in the Hebrew Bible, the prophets are placed next to the historical narratives of Joshua through 2 Kings, juxtaposing the prophetic warnings about Israel's misconduct with the story of Israel's political rise and fall. Because 2 Kings ends with the overthrow of the Davidic dynasty and the people's exile to Babylon, it is appropriate to link historical events with the message of the prophets, the large majority of whom were active during or immediately after the period of the monarchy. The third section, the Kethuvim, contains works composed (mostly) after the exile, including reinterpretations of Israel's history, material focusing on the community's formal worship, and speculations about the nature of Wisdom and God's future plans for the world. (See also Table 1.1)

Box 1.2 Multiple Meanings of the Name "Israel"

In the Hebrew Bible, the name *Israel* has several meanings. As used by many biblical writers, it denotes collectively the descendants of **Jacob** (whose name was changed to Israel), the people bound to Yahweh in a special covenant relationship. It also refers historically to three different but related political entities: (1) the united twelve-tribe kingdom of Israel under kings Saul, David, and Solomon (roughly 1020–922 B.C.E.); (2) the northern ten-tribe kingdom that formed after Solomon's death (922 B.C.E.) and that was destroyed by Assyria two centuries later (many biblical writers also refer to the northern kingdom as **Ephraim**, the name of its most important tribe); and (3) Yahweh's covenant people

geneally, even after Assyria's destruction of Israel in 722/721 B.C.E.

Following the northern tribes' secession from the united kingdom in 922 B.C.E., the smaller southern state of **Judah** continued to be ruled by King David's successors and is commonly still alluded to figuratively as "Israel," in the sense of being Yahweh's covenant community — a practice observed in this text. Dominated successively by the empires of Babylon, Persia, Greece, and Rome, the inhabitants of Judah, or **Judeans**, eventually became known as **Jews**, a term that also included persons of Judean descent who lived in the **Diaspora** (the "scattering" of Jews living outside of their Palestinian homeland).

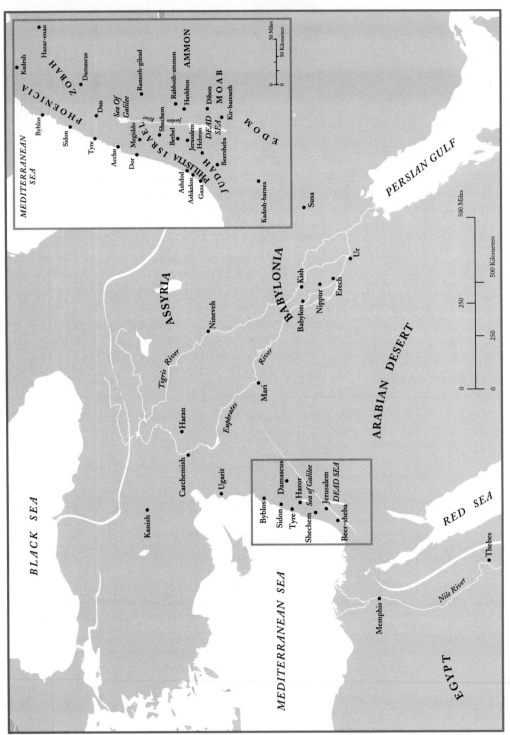

Figure 1.1 Map of Israel and the Ancient Near East. Located between the major powers of Mesopotamia (Assyria and Babylonia) and Egypt, the kingdom of Israel was repeatedly devastated by military invasions of its stronger neighbors, events that loom large in the biblical narratives. The inset shows Israel as it appeared between about 921 and 721 B.C.E., when it was divided into the southern kingdom of Judah and the northern kingdom of Israel. The northern state of Israel ceased to exist when the Assyrians destroyed it in 721 B.C.E. The smaller state of Judah, with its capital at Jerusalem, however, was partly restored about fifty years after the Babylonians destroyed it in 587 B.C.E.

B.C.E. and first centuries C.E., including the Book of Revelation, the final book of the New Testament.

The Tanak's Final Statement   Jewish editors closed the Kethuvim — and hence the Tanak itself — with 1 and 2 Chronicles. Although Ezra and Nehemiah relate events that occurred much later than those covered in the books of Chronicles, editors deliberately assigned Chronicles the important end position of the canonical Hebrew Bible. At the end of Chronicles, **Cyrus the Great** (reigned 558–530 B.C.E.), emperor of Persia and conqueror of Babylon, issues a decree encouraging the former Jewish exiles to return from Babylon to Jerusalem to rebuild its Temple, restoring the worship of Israel's God. By according Chronicles the final word in Israel's long partnership with God, the Tanak leaves its readers an open invitation to journey back to Jerusalem, where God is again present — and accessible — in his favored sanctuary. Whatever the future may bring, the Jewish Scriptures close with a confident assurance of the unique bond linking God to his chosen people.

By contrast, the Christian Old Testament, which places 1 and 2 Chronicles among the historical narratives immediately after 1 and 2 Kings, concludes with the minor prophets, ending with the oracles of Malachi. In the Christian arrangement, the Old Testament closes with Malachi's prophecy about an unnamed future "messenger" and the return of the prophet Elijah, who had previously been carried to heaven in a fiery chariot (Mal. 3:1, 22–24; cf. 2 Kings 1–2). By placing the prophetic books as the climax of God's revelation to Israel, Christian editors emphasized the supreme importance of prophetic oracles about a royal descendant of King David — the **Messiah** or **Christ** — which they believed were fulfilled in **Jesus** of Nazareth. Drawing extensively on Israelite prophecy to create their portraits of Jesus, the Gospel writers present Jesus' forerunner, **John the Baptist**, as Malachi's foretold "messenger" or "herald" and also identify John as the returned Elijah (Matt. 11:10–14; Luke 7:27–28). The Christian canonical order of books effectively transforms the Jewish Scriptures into a proto-Christian document.

The New Testament

TESTAMENT AND COVENANT

Whereas the Christian designation of the Hebrew Bible (Tanak) as the Old Testament was intended to contrast the Mosaic dispensation with that of Jesus in the Gospels, it also expresses the close relationship between the two sections of the Bible (Box 1.3). In biblical usage, *testament* is roughly synonymous with **covenant**, which means a vow, promise, agreement, treaty, or even contract. Throughout most of the Tanak, and parts of the New Testament as well, the making of covenants functions as God's principal means of relating to humanity. In Exodus, the second book of the Hebrew Bible, **Yahweh** (the personal name of Israel's God) forges a legal partnership with the Israelites, commanding them to obey all of the 600 laws and statutes he reveals at Mount **Sinai** (enumerated in Exodus, Leviticus, Numbers, and Deuteronomy). Because Moses serves as mediator between Yahweh and his people, this pact is called the **Mosaic Covenant**. According to Deuteronomy 28–29, if Israel faithfully adheres to all Yahweh's regulations, it will prosper economically, militarily, and politically. Failure to obey, however, will lead to national catastrophe. Invoking the natural elements, Yahweh informs Israel that its future success depends on the people's fidelity to him:

> "I call heaven and earth to witness against you today: I set before you life or death, blessing or curse. Choose life, then, so that you and your descendants may live in the love of Yahweh your God, obeying his voice, clinging to him . . ."
> Deut. 29:19–20

Centuries after the time of Moses, the Israelite prophet Jeremiah declared that Israel had been so disloyal to Yahweh and his Torah (instruction) that the Mosaic agreement was broken, resulting in the Babylonian overthrow of Jerusalem and deportation of the covenant people to Babylon. Jeremiah promised, however, that Yahweh would replace the old Mosaic pact with a "new covenant [testament]" (Jer. 31:31). The Gospel writers believed that Jesus instituted the promised New Covenant

Box 1.3   The Structure of the Bible: An Overview

The Bible is so diverse in literary form and content that many readers find it difficult to discern any principle of organizational structure that binds the whole together. Except for the very general theme of God's unfolding purpose and his often troubled relationship with the humans he created "in [his] image and likeness" (Gen. 1:26–27 cf. 5:1–3), this varied collection—written over a period of at least 1100 years and under ever-changing historical and cultural circumstances—seems to lack a coherent design. The Hebrew Bible's first book, Genesis, offers a definite beginning to the biblical story with its twofold description of God's creating heaven and earth (Gen. 1 and 2), and the final New Testament book, Revelation, provides an imaginative completion of the divine action, with its vision of "new heavens and a new earth" (Rev. 21:1–3). But the vast body of material lying between the framing narratives of the original creation and the future triumph of God's will seems devoid of any real unity.

THE HEBREW BIBLE (TANAK)

By carefully examining the Jewish editors' arrangement of the Hebrew Bible's contents, however, it is possible to discover a unifying structure that also expresses an important aspect of its meaning. Each major section of the three-part Tanak opens and/or closes with a statement about God's repeated promises to give Israel a national homeland. After a brief survey of human origins (Gen. 1–11), Genesis begins Israel's story with Yahweh's sudden appearance to Abraham, at which he unconditionally promises that Abraham's descendants will possess the land of Canaan "forever." Deuteronomy, the fifth book of the Torah, ends with Abraham's multitudinous descendants poised to enter Canaan. Their leader, Moses, is permitted to glimpse the Promised Land from afar but is not allowed to share his people's inheritance. That Moses dies before he personally can experience the culmination of Israel's national hopes introduces a theme of divine promise and deferred fulfillment that helps to shape the Tanak's structure as a whole.

The second part of the Hebrew Bible, the Prophets (Nevi'im), opens with a long prose narrative—the books of Joshua through 2 Kings—recounting more than 600 years of Israel's history (c. 1200–562 B.C.E.). In the Book of Joshua, Moses's

successor Joshua conducts a lightning-fast military conquest of Canaan, which gives Abraham's progeny seemingly full possession of that territory. (Judges, however, shows that the Israelites actually occupied very little of Canaan.) The narratives of 1 and 2 Samuel and 1 Kings describe the successful rise of Israel as a nation, culminating in the establishment of a monarchy under King David. Although Yahweh voluntarily swears to make David's heirs rule over Israel "forever" (2 Sam. 7; cf. Ps. 89), 2 Kings reports that the Davidic monarchy comes to a disastrous end when Babylon destroys Jerusalem and its Temple in 587 B.C.E.

Whereas the first books of the Prophets (Deuteronomistic History) tell how Israel acquired Canaan and then lost it, the second subunit in this division of the Hebrew Bible is a collection of books named for individual prophets, most of whom were active during the period of the Davidic monarchy. Observing Tanak order, this section begins with the Book of Isaiah, a prophet who advised Davidic kings when invading Assyrian armies seized most of Israel's northern territory. It closes with the short Book of Malachi, named for the messenger who warned that Yahweh threatens to afflict "the land" with yet another curse.

The third division of the Hebrew Bible, the Writings (Kethuvim), opens with an anthology of Psalms, devotional poetry sung during services at the Jerusalem Temple, the religious and geographical center of the Jewish state. The important end position of the Tanak—literally the final word of Israel's Scriptures—is given to the Book of 2 Chronicles. A late retelling of the history of Israel's monarchy and its fall to Babylon, 2 Chronicles ends on a note of hope. It concludes with a decree of Cyrus, emperor of Persia, who defeated Babylon in 539 B.C.E. and allowed exiled Jews to return to their homeland. The culminating event in the Hebrew Bible, Cyrus' order to rebuild the Jerusalem sanctuary, the only earthly shrine at which Yahweh was thought to be invisibly present, is thus open-ended and partly ambiguous. Like Deuteronomy's conclusion to the Torah, which leaves God's vows to Abraham largely unfulfilled, 2 Chronicles' final passages evoke the uncertain nature of the covenant community's future: Will Yahweh's scattered and demoralized people accept the invitation to repopulate their devastated

Box 1.3 *(continued)*

homeland? And what are Yahweh's intentions about keeping his promises to Israel's ancestors?

STRUCTURE OF THE NEW TESTAMENT

In wrestling with these and other questions about God's vows to Abraham and David, a small group of first-century Jews living under the dominion of the Roman Empire provided some distinctive answers that eventually separated them from the majority of their fellow Jews. This group, the early Christian community, believed that Yahweh's ancient promises given through Abraham, Moses, and David had been fulfilled in the life and death of Jesus of Nazareth, whom they viewed as David's ultimate heir, the Messiah (Hebrew, *Mashiah*, "Anointed One"; in Greek, *Christos* [English, "Christ"]). Whereas the Hebrew Bible emphasizes the partnership between God and Israel developing through space and time, the New Testament focuses almost exclusively on the role of God's human son, Jesus, who, Christians believed, inaugurated a "new covenant [testament]" with all humanity.

During the fourth and fifth centuries C.E., Christian editors arranged the New Testament's twenty-seven books in a way that roughly parallels the organization of the Hebrew Bible: The Gospels, in which Jesus presents his teachings and establishes a new "covenant," correspond to the Torah, in which Moses conveys divine instructions and mediates Israel's covenant with Yahweh; Acts, a narrative account of the early church, corresponds to the historical narratives of Joshua through Kings; Paul's letters correspond to the anthology of prophets (Nevi'im); and Hebrews, the catholic epistles, and Revelation, to the miscellaneous Writings (Kethuvim) (see Box 10.1). Placed first in the New Testament canon, the Gospel of Matthew highlights the close link between the Hebrew Bible and the Christian Scriptures by opening with a genealogy that connects Jesus with many of the Tanak's most prominent figures, such as Abraham, Jacob, David, and Josiah. For Matthew, as well as other New Testament writers, Jesus is the Davidic Messiah of whom Isaiah and the other prophets spoke. Quoting profusely from the Septuagint (Greek edition of the Hebrew Bible), Matthew repeatedly cites Jewish Scripture to demonstrate Jesus' Messianic credentials, a practice that is observed by virtually all New Testament authors, who typically underscore the continuity between ancient Israel and the nascent Christian community (see Chapter 10).

Perusing the New Testament book by book, from the Gospels to Revelation, readers travel from the alpha (first letter of the Greek alphabet) of Jesus' obscure arrival on earth to the omega (last letter of the Greek alphabet) of his universal reign. Two astronomical images in the first and last books of the New Testament canon impart a cosmic frame to the rest of the collection. In Matthew's nativity story, a mysterious star leads foreign astrologers to Jesus' birthplace, inadvertently inciting King Herod's attempts to kill the child (Matt. 2:1–12). In Revelation's description of the risen Jesus, the once vulnerable infant has become a gigantic figure dominating the sky and holding an entire constellation of stars in one hand (Rev. 1:8–2:1). Editors thus gave the New Testament contents a linear structure that begins with Matthew's genealogy linking Jesus with heroes from Israel's distant past and ends with images of a future new creation ruled by that same Jesus, now transformed into the cosmic Christ.

Bracketed between Matthew's account of Jesus' origins and Revelation's Big Bang vision of his global conquest are a disparate assortment of three additional Gospels, a theologically oriented church history, and twenty-one letters, sermons, and tracts. For all the theological variety encountered in these documents, they exhibit one overriding concern: the absolute centrality of Jesus' role in God's plan for human salvation. By placing four different versions of Jesus' biography at the head of the collection, Christian editors not only illustrated the divergent ways in which Jesus could be interpreted acceptably by four different Christian groups, but also affirmed the supreme importance of Jesus' ministry, death, and resurrection. The canonical order thus emphasizes the primacy of Jesus' story, the four Gospels together forming a composite foundation document for the Christian religion. No matter how influential the writings that appear later, such as Paul's letters with their radical declaration that salvation comes to Jew and Gentile alike through faith, they must always be weighed against the initial presentations of what Jesus said and did.

Whereas Yahweh looms as the central character in the Hebrew Bible, he rarely appears in the New Testament, usually as a disembodied voice. In the Christian Scriptures, it is his human son, Jesus of Nazareth, who represents him, serving as the divinely appointed agent who brings God's will to

(continued)

Box 1.3 *(continued)*

fruition. To a large extent, the books that follow the Gospels either explore the consequences of Jesus' redemptive career or offer interpretative meditations on it. The New Testament's second part, Acts, is a sequel to Luke's Gospel, showing how an idealized early church grew and prospered because it was led by the same Spirit that inspired Jesus. According to Luke-Acts, Jesus' later disciples imitate their master's example of service by perpetuating his activities throughout the Greco-Roman world.

Because Paul figures prominently in Acts, a collection of his letters follows naturally as the second part of the New Testament's second main division. Paul's correspondence with newly founded Christian congregations scattered throughout the Roman Empire offers close-up views of individual Christian groups and their difficulties in trying to follow Jesus in a sometimes hostile world. Written before the Gospels appeared, the authentic Pauline letters

vividly reflect early Christianity's struggle for unity of thought and purpose.

Corresponding to the Writings, the third part of the New Testament consists of a variety of letters, sermons, and an apocalypse, most of which were composed during the late first and early second century C.E. While Hebrews is anonymous, the catholic epistles are ascribed to leaders of the original Jerusalem church, the apostles Peter and John, and two of Jesus' kinsmen, James and Jude. Revelation, the last work in the canon, conveys little of the compassion and forgiveness that the Gospels attribute to Jesus, but its apocalyptic image of Christ as cosmic warrior assures readers that he exercises full control over human history. From a Christian perspective, Jesus, the victorious conqueror, permanently defeats Evil, compensates the faithful for their suffering, and gloriously renews all creation, completing the divine plan for humanity initiated in Genesis.

(New Testament) at the **Last Supper** he held with his disciples: "And he took the cup, and gave thanks, and gave it to them, saying Drink ye all of it. For this is my blood of the new testament . . ." (Matt. 26:27–28, King James Version). The adjective *new,* not present in the earliest manuscripts, was added later to emphasize the change in God's relationship with humankind (cf. Mark 14:24; 1 Cor. 11:25). Most contemporary English translations, including the New Revised Standard Version, the New Jerusalem Bible, and the Revised English Bible, omit the interpolated "new" and use "covenant" instead of "testament" in this passage.

Believing themselves to be the people of the New Covenant that Jesus inaugurated the night before his death, Christians eventually called their compilation of sacred writings the New Testament. Although the Hebrew Bible (Tanak), which dealt with the older Mosaic Covenant, became known as the Old Testament (cf. 2 Cor. 3:14; Gal. 3:15–18), many scholars suggest that it is more appropriate to call it the *First* Testament—the original covenant by which Yahweh irrevocably bound himself to Abraham's descendants forever. Because Christians believed that the ancient Tanak

promises made to Israel were fulfilled in Jesus and his followers (all members of the first-century C.E. Jewish community), they saw the international multiethnic Christian community as an extension and continuation of Yahweh's partnership with Israel. The church was convinced that Jesus and his mission could be fully understood only in the context of the Hebrew Bible (Box 1.3).

ORIGINAL BIBLICAL LANGUAGES

As its title implies, most of the Hebrew Bible was written in classical **Hebrew**, the Semitic tongue spoken in ancient Israel. Some later books were composed in **Aramaic**, an Aramean (Syrian) dialect closely related to Hebrew and probably also the native language of Jesus and his first disciples. By contrast, New Testament authors wrote entirely in *koinē* Greek, the international language of the workaday first-century world. *Koinē* originated from the fusion of classical Greek with the commercial vernacular of Near Eastern peoples conquered by **Alexander the Great** (reigned 336–323 B.C.E.). The blending of Oriental and Greek elements produced a cosmopolitan culture known as

Hellenism. Arbitrarily dated as beginning with the death of Alexander in 323 B.C.E., Hellenistic culture exerted considerable influence on the thinking of late biblical writers, especially the authors of the Apocrypha and the New Testament (see Chapter 8).

The Septuagint   So pervasive did Greek language and culture become throughout the eastern Mediterranean world in the last centuries B.C.E. that the large Jewish colony living in Alexandria, Egypt, resolved to translate their Scriptures from Hebrew and Aramaic into Greek. A wealthy port city established by Alexander, Alexandria was then one of the world's largest centers of literary and scientific research, an appropriate environment in which to undertake the first major translation of the Bible. Beginning in about 250 B.C.E. with a rendition of the Pentateuch into Greek, the Septuagint grew in discrete stages as historical, prophetic, and other books were added over time. According to a tradition preserved in the Letter of Aristias, a noncanonical Jewish document, the Septuagint was almost miraculously produced. In Aristias's legendary account, the Septuagint was the work of seventy-two Hebrew scholars (divided into twelve groups of six) who labored seventy-two days to create a set of identical translations, their remarkable agreement signifying divine guidance in the project. Abbreviated in informal usage to "the work of the seventy," the Septuagint (represented by the roman numerals **LXX**) became the standard biblical text for Jews throughout the Greco-Roman world and is the version quoted most frequently in the New Testament.

How the Bible Was Formed and Handed Down to Us

The Bible we read today — a printed bound volume that readers can hold in their hands — is a relatively modern development. For the first thousand years of its literary evolution, the Bible existed only as a slowly growing accumulation of individual manuscripts, each with its own compositional history. Biblical books were typically written on papyrus, paper-like sheets made from the papyrus plant, and then rolled around a small wooden stick to form a **scroll**. To accommodate longer books, such as the five volumes of the Pentateuch or the "major" prophets (Isaiah, Jeremiah, and Ezekiel), strips of papyrus about nine or ten inches long and five or six inches wide were stitched or glued together, forming scrolls up to twenty-five to thirty feet long. An almost perfectly preserved ancient manuscript of Isaiah, found among the Dead Sea Scrolls, consists of seventeen strips of sheepskin joined by linen thread and measures about twenty-four feet in length. The twelve "minor prophets" (so called because of their relative brevity) were fitted on a single scroll.

The manufacture of papyrus scrolls, which probably originated in Egypt shortly after 3000 B.C.E., was gradually replaced by the introduction of more durable materials, such as parchment, which is made from the dried and treated skins of sheep, calves, or goats. Vellum, a finer grade of parchment, was formed from the tanned hides of kids and calves and was used for particularly important documents. Jeremiah 36 offers a glimpse into the process of making and revising a prophetic scroll: After Jeremiah dictates his oracles to his secretary Baruch, the king to whom they are addressed, Jehoiakim, burns the manuscript. The prophet then dictates to Baruch a new version of his message, inserting additional material to form a longer scroll. Scrolls also figure prominently in prophetic visions from Ezekiel to Revelation (Ezek. 2:8–3:3; Zech. 5:1–4; Rev. 5:1–14; 10:1–11).

Although the stick or short wooden poles around which papyrus or parchment sheets were rolled were commonly fitted with handles, the process of unwinding a long scroll to find a particular passage made their use slow and cumbersome. (The task of finding specific texts was particularly difficult in ancient times, when Hebrew manuscripts were written without vowels, capitalizations, punctuation, or even spaces between words and sentences; it was not until the European Middle Ages that scholars, for greater ease of reference, divided biblical books into chapters and verses.) Because of the scroll's limitations, during

Roman times businessmen pioneered the use of the **codex**, a forerunner of the modern book in which individual papyrus or parchment leaves were sewn together to form a succession of easily turned pages featuring a continuous text. Christians quickly adopted the codex for their sacred writings. The oldest complete editions of the Christian Bible, dating from the fourth century, survive in such Greek manuscripts as the **Codex Sinaiticus** and Codex Vaticanus.

TRANSMITTING THE BIBLICAL TEXT

Our knowledge of the Bible's formation and transmission is severely limited by the fact that not a single scrap of any biblical author's original composition has survived. In many cases, hundreds of years separate a writer's original work from extant manuscript copies. The great chronological gap between a given book's date of composition and the oldest version we have of it is troubling—because it is precisely during a document's earliest stages of transmission, before it acquires the status of recognized Scripture, that a text is most fluid, subject to editorial additions, deletions, and other changes.

Ideally, one might think that once a particular book had been completed, a single master copy would be made and that all subsequent copies would faithfully reproduce it. In practice, however, it appears that many ancient **scribes** (persons who could read and write, an extremely rare skill in the ancient world) also acted as editors and commentators, adding explanatory phrases or otherwise modifying the text to reflect the covenant community's ever-changing circumstances. Many editorial changes were minor, mere errors in copying, but others produced notable differences in content; some manuscripts of Isaiah and Jeremiah, for example, are much shorter than what eventually became accepted as the standard version.

TEXTUAL CRITICISM

Because neither the author's manuscript nor copies made soon after a book first appeared survive, it is not possible to determine the full extent to which later copies differ from the writer's original version. By carefully comparing and analyzing all extant copies and early translations of a particular book, however, taking careful note of their similarities and differences, scholars attempt to determine the text's original wording, an academic discipline known as **textual criticism**. Textual critics have been able to detect clear evidence that some books of the Hebrew Bible underwent significant editing before they reached their present form. Close analysis of the **Deuteronomistic History** (abbreviated **DH**)—Deuteronomy and the sequence of narrative books from Joshua through 2 Kings that adopts Deuteronomy's distinctive view of history—indicates that these documents underwent extensive revision after the exile (see Chapters 4 and 5).

Most contemporary editions of the Hebrew Bible (Old Testament) rely primarily on the **Masoretic Text** (abbreviated **MT**), which takes its name from *Masorah* (Hebrew, "transmission"), a term referring to a school of medieval Jewish scholars who, during the ninth and tenth centuries C.E., produced a series of Hebrew manuscripts. Two representative examples of the Masoretic tradition, the Aleppo Codex and the Leningrad Codex, are among the most important manuscripts. Noted for their scrupulous care in copying each letter of the text, the Masoretic scholars also added vowel sounds and accent marks to the consonants of the Hebrew script. Their work, including marginal notes, remains an invaluable resource for modern translators (Figure 1.2).

The Dead Sea Scrolls   Until the mid-twentieth century, most scholars assumed that the Masoretic Text represented a single authoritative textual tradition going back to biblical times. Attempts to look behind the MT to earlier phases of the text's transmission were unsuccessful. Beginning in 1947, however, the situation changed dramatically. A series of manuscript discoveries near the Dead Sea (an area then controlled by the state of Jordan but now in possession of Israel) unexpectedly provided scholars with copies of biblical manuscripts up to a thousand years older than the Masoretic Text. Known collectively as the **Dead Sea Scrolls**, two

Figure 1.2 This page from the Book of Leviticus belongs to one of the oldest copies of the Hebrew Torah, the Masoretic (traditional) Text, dating from the mid-ninth century C.E.

groups of manuscript discoveries were particularly important: those found in caves near **Qumran**, dating from about 250 B.C.E. to 68 C.E., and a group of slightly younger texts recovered from sites bordering the Dead Sea south of Qumran. These two manuscript collections effectively illuminate a landmark change in the Hebrew Bible's textual development. Many of the almost 200 biblical scrolls found near Qumran, most in a highly fragmentary condition, showed significant differences from the Masoretic Text, including not only variations in wording but also in content, with some containing sentences and even whole paragraphs absent from the medieval texts. Other Qumran manuscripts lacked whole passages found in the MT; one manuscript of Jeremiah, for example, was considerably shorter than the MT edition, while one collection of the Psalms includes lyrics not present in the MT.

By contrast, the somewhat younger manuscripts recovered south of Qumran, written during the late first and early second centuries C.E., showed a striking agreement with the medieval Masoretic Text. The relative uniformity of this second group of manuscripts indicates that at some point after the Jewish revolt against Rome (66–73 C.E.) and the Roman destruction of Jerusalem (70 C.E.), Jewish scribes succeeded in producing a relatively standardized edition of the biblical text. A few recent Bible translations, such as the New Revised Standard Version (NRSV), have taken advantage of these manuscript finds to correct earlier readings of the Hebrew text. (The complete extant Dead Sea texts of the canonical Hebrew Bible, as well as some apocryphal documents, are available in a new English translation, *The Dead Sea Scrolls Bible;* see Martin Albegg, Jr., et al., in "Recommended Reading.") The contents of the Dead Sea Scrolls are discussed in Chapter 9.

The New Testament Text Establishing a standard Greek text for the New Testament also presents a formidable challenge. Although we have no fewer than 5000 ancient manuscript copies of the New Testament, no two are precisely alike. Variations among extant copies range from minor differences in wording to significant discrepancies involving interpolated passages and other editorial commentaries in the text. In addition to sometimes extensive differences between manuscripts, the attempt to establish a reliable standard text is complicated by the fact that our oldest transcriptions consist only of fragments dating from about 200 C.E., at least a century to a century and a half after they were first composed. A rare exception is a tiny scrap of the Gospel of John containing four verses from Chapter 18. On the basis of its calligraphy (form of handwriting), historians date it at approximately 125 C.E., about thirty years after the Gospel was written (Figure 1.3).

Most of these early manuscripts survive only in small pieces, and all were found in Egypt, where the dry climate aids preservation of the papyrus on which they were written. The oldest extant copies of the New Testament as a whole, the Codex Sinaiticus and Codex Vaticanus, were compiled

Figure 1.3 The oldest surviving manuscript of a New Testament book, these fragments of the Gospel of John date from about 125 C.E. Preserved for 1800 years in the dry sands of an Egyptian grave, these tiny scraps of papyrus contain four verses from John 18 (Rylands Greek Papyrus 457 [also known as P52]).

in the fourth century C.E. Written on expensive parchment, these famous codices reflect the new-found prosperity of the Christian church after it had been officially recognized by the Roman government. The production of Christian literature was encouraged by **Constantine I** (r. 306– 337 C.E.), the first Christian emperor, and contrasts sharply with conditions a few years earlier under the emperor Diocletian. During the "Great Persecution" (303–305 C.E.), Diocletian attempted to exterminate Christianity, ordering the imprisonment or execution of its leaders and the burning of their books. Diocletian's attacks on the church help to explain why we have no complete New Testament texts dating prior to Constantine's reign.

Problems in Transmission   The large gap between the time that most of the New Testament was composed (c. 50–100 C.E.) and the age of the oldest complete manuscript copies (fourth century C.E.) makes it impossible to be sure that we possess exact copies of letters that **Paul**, early Christianity's most effective missionary, dictated to the new congregations he founded, or of the Gospels as they originally circulated in their respective authors' communities. Some scholars believe that, besides making relatively minor errors of transmission, generations of Christian scribes who copied New Testament books may have edited various passages to make them conform more closely to evolving

doctrines of the church. Scribes also commonly modified the wording of one Gospel to make it conform to that in another—a practice known as *harmonization.* A number of scribal additions have long been recognized and omitted in modern translations—such as interpolated trinitarian passages in 1 John—but, in the absence of first- or second-century manuscripts, scholars can only speculate about the nature and degree of many copyists' modifications (Box 1.4). For a discussion of some probable scribal additions to the Gospels, such as the "long conclusion" to Mark and other passages that reinterpret Jesus according to later theological developments, see Chapter 10.

Creating a Standard Greek Text   The great fourth-century codex editions of the New Testament were written in unical characters. Also called "majuscules," unicals are large or capital letters written in continuous script without spaces between words and usually without accents. Later manuscripts, called "minuscules," were written in small cursive letters, with individual letters connected to form groups and syllables. The unical codices are the most important basis of the text from which modern translations into English or other languages are made. Of particular value is the Codex Sinaiticus, a mid-fourth-century manuscript discovered during the 1800s in the monastery of Saint Catherine at the foot of Mount Sinai.

Box 1.4 Copyists' Modifications of New Testament Manuscripts

No two ancient Greek manuscripts of New Testament books are precisely alike. Although most differences in the texts were probably caused by unintentional errors in copying, some textual variations seem to result from deliberate changes, many of which may have been motivated by theological considerations. A few of the oldest manuscripts, including the Codex Sinaiticus, do not contain the phrase "son of God" in Mark 1:1, leading some scholars to think that the phrase was inserted at the beginning of the Gospel to refute a belief that Jesus became God's adopted son at his baptism. Another possibly intentional change, made for the same purpose, may appear in Luke's account of Jesus' baptism; some early manuscripts have God declare, "You are my son; *this day* I have begotten you," a quotation from Psalm 2 (Luke 3:22; emphasis added). Most modern translations use an alternative phrasing that avoids the adoption issue, having God say, "in you I am well pleased" or "in you I delight" (New English Bible).

Similar concerns about an orthodox understanding of Jesus' origins apparently influenced manuscript changes in Luke's story of the youthful Jesus' being left behind in the Temple. Mary's reprimand to the child, "your father and I have been anxiously searching for you," was, in some manuscripts, changed to "*we* have been searching for you" (Luke 2:48; emphasis added), ostensibly to avoid any implication that Joseph was Jesus' real father. A theological belief in Jesus' omniscience may have prompted deletion of references to "the Son" from some copies of Matthew's statement that "about that day and hour [of the End] no one knows, . . . not even the Son; no one but the Father alone" (Matt. 24:36).

Perhaps the most striking New Testament interpolation appears in very late manuscripts of 1 John 5:7–8, where a scribe inserted the Bible's only explicit reference to the Christian doctrine of the Trinity; asserting that God exists in three persons and that "these three are one." This trinitarian statement occurs in no manuscript dating prior to the fourteenth century.

Some scholars argue that theological controversies over such issues as Christ's eternally divine nature and equality with God prompted some scribes to emend manuscripts so that they conformed to the orthodox position (see Ehrman in "Recommended Reading").

Besides the entire New Testament (including books not now in the canon), the Sinaiticus also contains most of the Greek Old Testament. Additional pages of the Codex Sinaiticus were discovered as late as 1975.

Even older is the Codex Vaticanus (early fourth century), but it lacks a number of canonical books, including Hebrews, several Pauline letters, and Revelation. Together with the slightly later unical editions — the Codex Alexandrinus and the Codex Bezae — these landmark editions provide scholars with the foundation on which to reconstruct the Greek texts of the New Testament. In constructing a reliable text for both the Old and New Testaments, scholars must consult many hundreds of manuscript fragments, abundant quotations from Jewish and Christian writers of the early centuries C.E., various minuscule editions, and scores of translations in Latin, Syriac, Coptic, and other languages spoken in the ancient world.

Contemporary translations are typically based on a variety of carefully edited Greek texts that incorporate the latest scholarship, including newly discovered manuscripts. In preparing the New English Bible (NEB), the edition of the New Testament quoted in this textbook, translators followed *The Greek New Testament,* edited by R. G. V. Tasker and published in 1964. After another major resource, the twenty-sixth edition of the *Novum Testamentum Graece,* was issued in 1979, scholars also consulted this text for the Revised English Bible (1989). Translators of the New Revised Standard Version of the Bible employed the third edition of *The Greek New Testament* (1983).

Thanks to recent manuscript discoveries and the work of modern linguists and textual critics, it is possible today to produce a much more accurate translation of the Bible than ever before, although absolute certainty remains elusive. Where modern translations differ from the long-familiar reading in the King James, or "Authorized," Version of the Bible, it is commonly because contemporary translators work from far better Hebrew and Greek texts than were available to the King James editors when their version was first published in 1611.

THE PROCESS OF CANONIZATION

The Hebrew Bible Canon   Scholars emphasize that the formation of the biblical canon—the list of books officially recognized as Scripture—was a slow and gradual process. At no time during the period of the Bible's formation did a religious council, either Jewish or Christian, explicitly determine its contents. The Hebrew Bible grew by degrees, adding new documents as Israel's writers, over many generations, recorded and interpreted the covenant community's political and spiritual experiences. The end result of a long period of literary development, canonization took place as **Judean*** priests, scribes, and other religious leaders gradually accepted the religious authority of a particular book or set of books.

Following their return from the Babylonian exile during the late sixth and fifth centuries B.C.E., Judean religious leaders assembled and edited their people's religious traditions, both oral and written—an essential task to strengthen and unify a largely dispirited group then undergoing a crisis in which their identity as Yahweh's chosen group was severely threatened (see Chapter 6). Encouraging the covenant community's sense of purpose and mission, postexilic leaders promoted the Mosaic legacy, sponsoring public readings of Torah at national festivals and worship services until familiarity with these teachings and their recognized place in communal identity made them by use and habit

an integral part of Judean life. Perhaps during the fourth century B.C.E., when Persian administrators actively encouraged the publication of Judean religious laws, Mosaic legal traditions were edited and reshaped into the five books of the Pentateuch and proclaimed as binding on all Jews (Neh. 8; Ezra 7). A compendium of narratives about Israel's ancestors and Mosaic legislation, the Pentateuch was the first part of the Hebrew Bible to achieve canonical status.

Although not all scholars agree, many believe that the second main division of the Tanak, the Prophets (Nevi'im), was generally accepted by about 200 B.C.E., at least by some influential groups within the Jewish community. The earliest reference to all three parts of the Tanak as authoritative occurs in the Wisdom book of Jesus Son of Sirach, in which the author's son and translator mentions "the Law [Torah] and the Prophets [Nevi'im] and the other books of our ancestors" (Ecclus. Prologue). Written in Egypt in about 132 B.C.E., the preface's allusion to the "other" books refers to the Tanak's third section, the Writings (Kethuvim), the last part to be canonized. Although some of the Writings, such as the Psalms, had been used in Judean worship for generations, this part of the Hebrew Bible may have remained open-ended well into the first centuries C.E., with some Jewish groups, such as those living in Egypt, accepting books that ultimately were not included in the Tanak. It was apparently not until after the Romans destroyed the Temple in Jerusalem (70 C.E.) that the Jewish community finally began to set a precise limit on the number of books comprising the Writings. Then the challenge facing Jewish scholars was not so much what to accept, considering the large number of religious compositions then circulating, as what to omit.

The Academy of Yavneh (Jamnia)   After the Roman destruction of the Jewish state, a group of distinguished **rabbis** (Hebrew, "teachers") assembled at the coastal town of Yavneh (Jamnia) to consolidate, unify, and preserve the teachings of postwar Judaism. The **Academy of Jamnia (Yavneh)**, founded in about 90 C.E., was once thought to have formally closed the canon, deciding exactly

---

Judean—refers to inhabitants of **Judea, a Greek term used after the exile to denote the territory surrounding Jerusalem, a part of the former southern kingdom of Judah. All members of the covenant community, as well as citizens of Judea, came to be known as "Jews."*

which books constituted genuine Scripture. Scholars now believe, however, that no such conclusive action was taken, although the rabbis did debate the merits of certain books, such as Ezekiel, which seems to contradict the Mosaic Torah; Ecclesiastes, which displays a skeptical attitude toward conventional piety; and the Song of Solomon, which celebrates erotic love. Even these last two books, perhaps because they were traditionally ascribed to King Solomon, were accorded scriptural status. Defining the precise limits of the Writings, however, may have been a function of the rabbis' labors in creating a standard biblical text — prototype of the later Masoretic Text — produced during the chaotic period between the two uprisings against Rome (66–73 C.E. and 132–135 C.E.).

Writing late in the first century C.E., the Jewish historian **Flavius Josephus** (c. 37–100 C.E.), seems to assume the existence of an established canon. In the work *Against Apion,* Josephus defends his tradition against Greco-Roman criticism, emphasizing the limited number of its sacred books:

> For we [the Jews] have not an innumerable multitude of books among us, disagreeing from and contradicting one another [as the Greeks have] but only *twenty-two books,* which contain the records of all past times; which are justly believed to be divine; and of them five belong to Moses, which contain his laws and the traditions of the origin of mankind until his death . . . the prophets, who were after Moses, wrote down what was done in their times in thirteen books. The remaining four books contain hymns to God and precepts for the conduct of human life.
>
> *Against Apion,* Bk. 1.8

Josephus's reference to a total of twenty-two volumes of Scripture probably corresponds to the twenty-four books into which the Tanak's present contents are divided. (The Tanak's twenty-four are precisely the same as the thirty-nine books in the Protestant Old Testament; the numerical difference comes from the fact that in the Hebrew Bible, 1 and 2 Samuel, 1 and 2 Kings, 1 and 2 Chronicles, etc., are counted as single books; the twelve "minor" prophets, fitting on a single scroll, figure as one volume; Ruth is considered an addendum to Judges and Lamentations to Jeremiah.) As noted

above, Catholic and Orthodox editions, which include the apocryphal books, feature a longer Old Testament.

New Testament Canonization   When the rabbis first met at Yavneh (Jamnia) in 90 C.E., much of the New Testament had not yet been written. A decade before the turn of the first century, it is likely that only Paul's letters, the Gospels of Mark and Matthew (and perhaps the two-volume Luke-Acts) had been composed. Although the latest works to be canonized were written by about 140–150 C.E., it was not until the late fourth century that a list of New Testament books corresponding exactly to the collection's present contents was published (Table 1.2). In 367 C.E., **Athanasius,** then bishop of Alexandria, Egypt, issued an Easter Letter listing the four Gospels, Acts, Pauline letters, Hebrews, seven **catholic epistles** (James; 1 and 2 Peter; 1, 2, and 3 John; and Jude), and Revelation in the same order we have them today. Even after Athanasius, however, Christians living in different parts of the Roman Empire continued to use many books not recognized in Athanasius's inventory — and to reject others, such as James, 2 Peter, and Revelation, that the bishop accepted in his canon.

During the four centuries separating the ministry of Jesus from the church's general acceptance of all twenty-seven books eventually included in the New Testament, Christians produced a host of other literature, most written in the same literary genres (categories) as the canonical books — Gospels, Acts of the Apostles, letters, apocalypses, sermons, and tracts (Box 1.5). As in the case of the Tanak's third division, the Writings, canonization involved not so much a process of what to accept but of what to leave out. The **Muratorian Canon,** which scholars once dated to the late second or early third century C.E. but now think was probably compiled in the fourth century, is typical of the mixed bag of canonical and noncanonical books found in different church catalogues. Listing twenty-four books (corresponding to the number of books in the Tanak), the Muratorian Canon includes the four Gospels, Acts, thirteen letters ascribed to Paul (but not Hebrews), Jude, 1 and 2

Table 1.2 Approximate Order of Composition of New Testament Books

APPROXIMATE DATE C.E.	TITLE OF BOOK	AUTHOR
50	1 Thessalonians	Paul
	2 Thessalonians (if by Paul)	
54–55	1 and 2 Corinthians	Paul
56	Galatians	Paul
56–57	Romans	Paul
61	Colossians (if by Paul)	Paul
61	Philippians	Paul
62	Philemon	Paul
66–70	Gospel of Mark	Anonymous
66–73	**Jewish War Against Rome: Destruction of Jerusalem and the Temple**	
80–85	Gospel of Matthew	Anonymous
85–90	Gospel of Luke and Acts	Anonymous
85–95	Hebrews, 1 Peter, Ephesians, James	Anonymous or pseudonymous
90–95	Gospel of John	Anonymous
95	Revelation (the Apocalypse)	John of Patmos
95–100	Letters of John	The Elder
110–30	1 and 2 Timothy, Titus	Pseudonymous
130–50	Jude, 2 Peter	Pseudonymous

(but not 3) John, the Wisdom of Solomon, Revelation, and the Apocalypse of Peter. The Muratorian list excludes five books that finally attained canonical rank, but it includes a Greek Wisdom book that was ultimately assigned to the Old Testament Apocrypha and an "apostolic" vision of hell that was not included in any canon.

The Codex Claromontanus is a sixth-century Greek-Latin manuscript that contains a list also thought to derive ultimately from the fourth century C.E. Besides enumerating most of the (ultimately) canonical works, this codex includes the Epistle of Barnabas, the Shepherd of Hermas, the Acts of Paul, and the Apocalypse of Peter—all four of which were eventually omitted from the canon. Even the Codex Sinaiticus, which contains all twenty-seven canonical books, also includes the Epistle of Barnabas and the Shepherd of Hermas. As late as the fifth century, a Greek manuscript known as the Codex Alexandrinus included both 1 and 2 Clement as part of the Christian Scriptures. Whereas 1 Clement is a letter written in around 96 C.E. by a bishop of Rome, 2 Clement is pseudonymous (composed by an unknown writer in the

name of a famous person). The practice of **pseudonmity** was extremely common among Jewish writers during the period from about 300 B.C.E. to 200 C.E., producing a veritable flood of literature incorrectly ascribed to figures from the Hebrew Bible, such as Enoch, Abraham, Moses, Isaiah, and Daniel. Beginning in the first century C.E., Christian authors also wrote pseudonymously, attributing Gospels, letters, and other documents to revered church leaders, including Peter, James, John, and Paul (See Chapters 8, 12, and 13).

Writing in the fourth century B.C.E., the church historian **Eusebius** observed that, even after Christianity had been legally validated by the Roman government, the New Testament canon was still not fixed. In describing the church's varied opinions about a given book's authenticity, Eusebius divided contenders for official canonization into three main categories. The universally "acknowledged" works number twenty-one, including the four Gospels, Acts, Paul's letters, and some of the catholic epistles. The "disputed" books accepted by some churches but not others include six that eventually entered the canon: Revelation,

Box 1.5 Abbreviations of Books of the Bible, in Alphabetical Order

THE HEBREW BIBLE (TANAK OR OLD TESTAMENT)

Amos	Amos
1 Chron.	1 Chronicles
2 Chron.	2 Chronicles
Dan.	Daniel
Deut.	Deuteronomy
Eccles.	Ecclesiastes
Esther	Esther
Exod.	Exodus
Ezek.	Ezekiel
Ezra	Ezra
Gen.	Genesis
Hab.	Habakkuk
Hag.	Haggai
Hos.	Hosea
Isa.	Isaiah
Jer.	Jeremiah
Job	Job
Joel	Joel
Jonah	Jonah
Josh.	Joshua
Judg.	Judges
1 Kings	1 Kings
2 Kings	2 Kings
Lam.	Lamentations
Lev.	Leviticus
Mal.	Malachi
Mic.	Micah
Nah.	Nahum
Neh.	Nehemiah
Num.	Numbers
Obad.	Obadiah
Prov.	Proverbs
Ps. (pl., Pss.)	Psalms
Ruth	Ruth
1 Sam.	1 Samuel
2 Sam.	2 Samuel
S. of S.	Song of Songs
Zech.	Zechariah
Zeph.	Zephaniah

DEUTEROCANONICAL (APOCRYPHAL) BOOKS

Add. to Dan.	Additions to Daniel
Add. to Esther	Additions to Esther
Bar.	Baruch (includes Letter of Jeremiah)
Ecclus.	Ecclesiasticus (Wisdom of Jesus ben Sirach)
1 Esd.	1 Esdras
2 Esd.	2 Esdras
Jth.	Judith
1 Macc.	1 Maccabees
2 Macc.	2 Maccabees
Tob.	Tobit
Wisd. of Sol.	Wisdom of Solomon

THE NEW TESTAMENT

Acts	Acts of the Apostles
Col.	Colossians
1 Cor.	1 Corinthians
2 Cor.	2 Corinthians
Eph.	Ephesians
Gal.	Galatians
Heb.	Hebrews
James	James
John	John (Gospel)
1 John	1 John (Epistle)
2 John	2 John (Epistle)
3 John	3 John (Epistle)
Jude	Jude
Luke	Luke (Gospel)
Mark	Mark (Gospel)
Matt.	Matthew (Gospel)
1 Pet.	1 Peter
2 Pet.	2 Peter
Phil.	Philippians
Philem.	Philemon
Rev.	Revelation (the Apocalypse)
Rom.	Romans
1 Thess.	1 Thessalonians
2 Thess.	2 Thessalonians
1 Tim.	1 Timothy
2 Tim.	2 Timothy
Titus	Titus

OTHER ABBREVIATIONS

B.C.E.	Before the common era. Dates correspond to dates B.C.
C.E.	Common era. Dates correspond to dates A.D.

(continued)

James, Jude, 2 Peter, and 2 and 3 John. Five other candidates for official inclusion failed to make the cut: the Acts of Paul, the Shepherd of Hermas, the Apocalypse of Peter, the Epistle of Barnabas, and the Didache, a treatise on early Christian rituals and ethics. Eusebius's "rejected" books are the Gospels ascribed to Peter, Thomas, and Matthias and the Acts attributed to Andrew, John, and other apostles.

Gospel of Thomas   As the author of canonical Luke notes in the formal preface to his Gospel, "many" other Christian writers before him had already composed Gospels. Today only fragments of a few of these noncanonical Gospels survive, most in the form of brief quotations from early church writers. Only one, discovered near the village of Nag Hammadi, Egypt, in 1945, exists in its entirety — the **Gospel of Thomas**. Containing no narrative or accounts of Jesus' miraculous works, death, or resurrection, the Gospel of Thomas consists entirely of 114 sayings of the risen and glorified Jesus. Some of these sayings include parables similar to those in the first three Gospels, but others seem to express ideas associated with one of the many variations in early Christianity, that known as **Gnosticism.**

Marcion and Christian Gnosticism   One of the first great debates about the contents of Christian Scripture — and hence of a viable canon — was precipitated by a Roman Christian named **Marcion**. By Marcion's day (c. 140 C.E.), Paul's letters had already been collected — the nucleus of the later New Testament — and the Gospels of Mark, Matthew, Luke, and John were also widely used in many Christian circles. Marcion, however, claimed that only one Gospel — an edited version of Luke — along with Paul's letters, was acceptable for Christian teaching. According to Marcion, Christians should completely reject the Hebrew Bible because it portrayed God (Yahweh) as an ethically inferior deity, a false God who created and was responsible for a physical world permeated by violence, disease, and death. In contrast to the biblical Yahweh, who was inseparable from his material creation, the true God was purely spiritual, a "higher" Being of light and love whom Jesus Christ had revealed. Marcion's radical ideas characterized a movement then widespread in the early church, Gnosticism. Taking its name from the Greek word *gnosis* (knowledge), **Gnosticism** is a general label applied to an extremely diverse set of beliefs and practices. Because the church later denounced Gnostic views as **heresy** (false teaching), most of our information about Marcion's teachings derives from church leaders' attacks against it.

In general, Gnosticism expresses a strongly mystical approach to human existence, emphasizing that an enlightened believer achieves salvation though attaining spiritual insight or "knowledge" of heavenly truths denied the average person. Following Plato's doctrine that humans consist of a duality — a perishable body and an immortal soul — Gnostics taught that reality consists of two distinct modes of being, an invisible heavenly realm to which the soul belongs and in which it originated and an inferior visible world to which the desire-filled and corruptible body belongs. The true God is the source of ultimate reality, the unseen generator of eternal spirit who sent Jesus into the physical world to impart a saving awareness of humanity's essentially divine nature. To benefit from Jesus' revelation of the Supreme God — so different from Yahweh — Gnostics urged Christians to disassociate themselves from what they regarded as the limited and "unspiritual" bonds of Old Testament "deceptions." In decisively repudiating Gnosticism's claims, the church affirmed its unbreakable connection with the heritage of Israel and its Scriptures. Accepting the Hebrew Bible as their Old Testament, Christians, however, significantly reinterpreted it, viewing it largely as a repository of prophecies and foreshadowings of Jesus' life and teachings. The intimate link between the two testaments is apparent on virtually every page of the New Testament, whose writers repeatedly cite its authority to demonstrate that Jesus was truly the long-awaited heir of King David predestined to rule kingdoms of both heaven and earth.

As with the Hebrew Bible, canonization of the New Testament books did not occur by any formal decree of the church, but came about gradually as many books — but not others — were found useful in teaching believers the essence of their faith. Read aloud in worship services from Syria to Italy to North Africa to Gaul (modern France), the Gospels, Acts, and Paul's letters demonstrated their long-term effectiveness in defining and regulating belief and behavior, helping to retain a strong connection with Christian origins. Gospels that preserved the accepted words and deeds of Jesus served the dual purpose of keeping the church anchored to its roots and of standardizing its chief doctrines. Documents that were thought to support what, over an extended period of time, came to be regarded as **orthodoxy** (correct teaching) earned canonical recognition. Books that were deemed to present heretical views were discarded and condemned. A universally accepted canon of authoritative books provided a unifying force for churches scattered throughout the Roman Empire, establishing widely acknowledged criteria for what eventually became mainstream Christianity.

How the Bible Became Available in English Translation

The Hebrew Bible had long been available in Greek translation when the Christian church first adopted the Septuagint as its preferred version of Scripture. The Septuagint and the New Testament (also a Greek work) commonly circulated together throughout the eastern half of the Roman Empire (later known as the Byzantine Empire), where *koinē* was universally spoken. In the west, however, where Latin was the dominant tongue, Latin translations of the Septuagint and the New Testament began to appear during the early centuries C.E. This movement culminated in Jerome's landmark translation, the famous **Vulgate**, a monumental work of biblical scholarship produced between about 385 and 405 C.E. Commissioned by the Bishop of Rome to make the Scriptures accessible to the Latin-speaking public, Jerome worked directly from Hebrew and Greek manuscripts, creating a Latin edition that became the official Bible of the Roman Catholic Church. Adhering to Athanasius's canon, Jerome included all seven catholic epistles, as well as the controversial Hebrews and Revelation. The Vulgate, however, did not include several other "disputed" writings, such as the Epistle of Barnabas or the Apocalypse of Peter, works that many Christians once regarded as virtually equal to what we think of as "genuine" New Testament books. Nor did Jerome's original edition of the Vulgate include most of the books appearing in the Septuagint but which rabbinical editors had rejected from the Tanak. Later Latin editions of the Old Testament, however, accepted as deuterocanonical the Septuagint books that Jerome labeled *Apocrypha,* an adjective meaning "hidden" or "obscure." (No one knows why Jerome used this term; some commentators suggest that the books were kept sequestered from the public, perhaps because some of their contents were considered unorthodox, or that their meaning was hidden from persons lacking perception.)

Following the collapse of the western Roman Empire in the late fifth century C.E. and the onset of the European Dark Ages, education and literacy rapidly declined. With the political fragmentation of Europe and the rise of new languages, Latin ceased to be understood by the majority of the European population. While Latin continued to be used in church services and by an international body of church scholars, for almost 1000 years no major new translation of the Bible appeared.

Isolated churchmen occasionally undertook to translate selected books of Scripture into one of the new European languages. The first person credited with doing so was the Venerable Bede, a Benedictine monk and historian of Anglo-Saxon England, who translated the Bible into his native tongue. In the 730s, Bede rendered part of Jerome's Latin Vulgate into Old English. During the tenth and eleventh centuries, a few other biblical books, including the Psalms and Gospels, also appeared in English. Not until the fourteenth century, however, did the entire Bible become available in English. This pioneering translation was the work of an English priest named John Wycliffe, who wished to make the Scriptures accessible to Christian laypeople who did not know Latin. Wycliffe finished his task of translating both the Old and New Testaments by about 1383. The national church, however, fearing the consequences of the Bible's being read and interpreted by ordinary persons, condemned Wycliffe's version in 1408 and forbade any further translation.

THE INVENTION OF PRINTING AND THE PROTESTANT REFORMATION

Two historical events ensured that the Bible would find a large reading public in English. The first was Johannes Gutenberg's invention of movable type in 1455, a revolutionary advance that made it possible to print books relatively quickly, rather than copying them laboriously by hand. The second was a religious movement known as the Protestant Reformation, begun in Germany in 1517. In that year a German monk named Martin Luther vigorously protested administrative corruption and other abuses within the Roman Catholic Church. Luther's German translation of the Bible (1522–

1534) was the first version in a modern European language based not on the Vulgate, but on the original Hebrew and Greek.

The first English translator to work directly from Hebrew and Greek manuscripts was William Tyndale; under the threat of church persecution, he fled to Germany, where his translation of the New Testament was published in 1525 (revised 1534). Official hostility to his work prevented him from completing his translation of the Old Testament, and in 1535–1536, he was betrayed, tried for heresy, and burned at the stake. Tyndale's vivid English phrasing of the New Testament has influenced almost every English translation since.

Although the church forbade the reading of Wycliffe's or Tyndale's translations, it nevertheless permitted free distribution of the first printed English Bible—the Coverdale Bible (1535),which relied heavily on Tyndale's work. Matthew's Bible (1537), containing additional sections of Tyndale's Old Testament, was revised by Coverdale, and the result was called the Great Bible (1539). The Bishop's Bible (1568) was a revision of the Great Bible, and the King James Version (KJV) was commissioned as a scholarly revision of the Bishop's Bible. The Geneva Bible (1560), which the English Puritans had produced in Switzerland, also significantly influenced the King James Bible.

THE KING JAMES BIBLE (AUTHORIZED VERSION)

By far the most popular English Bible of all time, the King James translation was authorized by James I, son of Mary, Queen of Scots, who appointed fifty-four scholars to make a new version of the Bishop's Bible for official use in the Anglican (English) Church. After seven years' labor, during which the oldest manuscripts then available were diligently consulted, the king's scholars produced in 1611 the Authorized, or King James, Version. One of the masterpieces of English literature, it was created at a time when the language was at its richest and most vivid. In the beauty of its rhythmic prose and colorful imagery, the King James Version remains unsurpassed in literary excellence. It has had a pervasive influence on subsequent English culture, with its phrasing of the Scriptures remarkably memorable and quotable.

Despite its wonderful poetic qualities, however, the King James Version has grave disadvantages as a text for studying the Bible. The very attributes that contribute to its linguistic elegance — the archaic diction, poetic rhythms, and Renaissance vocabulary — tend to obscure the explicit meaning of the text for many readers. Translated by scholars who grew up on the then-contemporary poetry of Edmund Spenser and William Shakespeare, the King James text presents real problems of comprehensibility to the average American student. Students who have difficulty undertaking *Hamlet* cannot expect to follow Paul's sometimes complex arguments when they are couched in terms that have been largely obsolete for centuries. Even more important for serious Bible students, its translators lacked access to ancient manuscripts that have since been discovered and to recent linguistic studies that have greatly increased our understanding of the Hebrew, Aramaic, and Greek languages and thought.

CHALLENGES IN TRANSLATING HEBREW AND GREEK INTO ENGLISH

In his preface to the Greek edition of Wisdom of Jesus Son of Sirach (also called Ecclesiasticus), the author's grandson bemoans the enormous difficulty translators face in trying to express the exact meaning of a text in a totally different language. Despite his "diligent labor in translating," he states, readers with a knowledge of the biblical Hebrew in which Sirach's Wisdom book was written may find that he has "rendered some phrases imperfectly."

> For what was originally expressed in Hebrew does not have exactly the same sense when translated into another language. Not only this book [Ecclesiasticus], but even the Law [Torah] itself, the Prophecies, and the rest of the books differ not a little when read in the original.
>
> Ecclus. Prologue

Even the best-equipped modern translators can experience the same kind of frustration that beset Sirach's grandson when attempting to render a Hebrew, Aramaic, or Greek text into contemporary English. In general, most of today's translators adopt one of two contrasting approaches to the problem. Whereas some Bible translators try to give the most literal translation possible (known as a formal equivalence) sometimes with awkward or almost unintelligible results, others seek to produce an English approximation of the original languages, a procedure known as dynamic equivalence. In dynamic equivalence, translators usually make little effort to reproduce the exact wording or sentence structure of the original, but only to convey the meaning of the text in a phrasing that is natural to English usage. (For some examples of both methods, see Box 1.6).

MODERN ENGLISH AND AMERICAN TRANSLATIONS

Realizing that language changes over the years and that words lose their original meanings and take on new connotations, Bible scholars have repeatedly updated and reedited the King James text. The first Revised Version of the King James was published in England between 1881 and 1885; a slightly modified text of this edition, the American Standard Revised Version, was issued in 1901. Using the (then) latest studies in archaeology and linguistics, the Revised Standard Version (RSV) appeared between 1946 and 1952. Because modern scholarship continues to advance in its understanding of biblical languages and textual history, an updated edition, the New Revised Standard, with the Apocrypha, was published in 1991.

Readers can now choose from a wide selection of modern translations, most of which incorporate the benefits of expert scholarship that draws on interdisciplinary fields of linguistic, historical, and literary studies. These include the Jerusalem Bible (JB) (1966), which transliterates several Hebrew terms for God — notably the personal name Yahweh and the title El Shaddai — into the English text. An updated edition, the New Jerusalem Bible,

Box 1.6 Comparison of Some Contemporary Old Testament Translations: God's Revelation of His Personal Name to Moses (Exodus 3:13–15)

Following Jewish custom, which considers the divine name too holy to pronounce, most contemporary translators render the four Hebrew consonants (YHWH), signifying God's personal name, as "the LORD," typically printing it in small capitals. To distinguish the sacred name (YHWH) from the general title "Lord" (Hebrew, *Adonai*), a generic term meaning "nobleman" or "master," English editions capitalize only the initial "L" in "Lord."

> And Moses said unto God, Behold, when I come unto the children of Israel, and shall say unto them, The God of your fathers hath sent me unto you; and they shall say to me, What is his name? what shall I say unto them? And God said unto Moses, I AM THAT I AM: and he said, Thus shalt thou say unto the children to Israel, I AM hath sent me unto you. And God said moreover unto Moses, the LORD [Yahweh] God of your fathers, the God of Abraham, the God of Isaac, and the God of Jacob, hath sent me unto you: this is my name forever and this is my memorial unto all generations.—King James Version (KJV).

> Moshe [Moses] said to God:
> Here, I will come to the Children of Israel and I will say to them:
> The God of your fathers has sent me to you,
> and they will say to me, What is his name?
> What shall I say to them?
> God said to Moshe:
> Ehyeh Asher Ehyeh/I will be-there howsoever I will be-there.
> And he said: Thus you will say to the Children of Israel:
> Ehyeh/I-Will Be-There sends me to you.
> And God said further to Moshe:
> Thus shall you say to the Children of Israel:
> YHWH [Yahweh],
> the God of your fathers,
> the God of Avraham [Abraham], the God of Yitzhak [Issac], and the God of Yaakov [Jacob], sends me to you.
> This is my name for the ages, that it my title (from) generation to generation.
> —*The Five Books of Moses,* translated by Everett Fox. [This recent translation of the Torah adheres closely to the structure and rhythms

of the original Hebrew, transliterating (giving equivalent English letters for the Hebrew consonants), as in the names of the patriarchs and in the key phrase of God's self-naming: Ehyeh Asher Ehyeh, which is commonly rendered as "I Am Who I Am," but which Fox translates as "I will-be-there howsoever I will be there," evoking the crucial theme of divine presence implied in God's words. In the third person, the divine name is "YHWH (Yahweh)."]

> Moses said to God, "Suppose I go to the Israelites and say to them, 'The God of your fathers has sent me to you,' and they ask me, 'What is his name?' Then what shall I tell them? God said to Moses, "I Am Who I Am. This is what you are to say to the Israelites: 'I Am has sent me to you." God also said to Moses, "Say to the Israelites, 'The LORD [Yahweh], the God of your fathers — the God of Abraham, the God of Isaac, and the God of Jacob — has sent me to you.' This is my name forever, the name by which I am to be remembered from generation to generation."— New International Version (NIV)

> Moses said to God, 'If I come to the Israelites and tell them that the God of their forefathers has sent me to them, and they ask me his name, what am I to say to them?' God answered, 'I am that I am. Tell them the I AM has sent you to them. He continued, 'You are to tell the Israelites, that it is the LORD [Yahweh], the God of their forefathers, the God of Abraham, the God of Isaac, and the God of Jacob, who has sent you to them. This is my name for ever; this is my title in every generation . . .'— The Revised English Bible (REB)

> Then Moses said to God, "I am to go, then, to the sons of Israel and say to them, 'The God of your fathers has sent me to you." But if they ask me what his name is, what am I to tell them?" And God said to Moses, "I Am Who I Am. This," he added, "is what you must say to the sons of Israel: 'I Am has sent me to you.'" And God also said to Moses, "You are to say to the sons of Israel: 'Yahweh, the God of your fathers,

Box 1.6 (continued)

the God of Abraham, the God of Isaac, and the God of Jacob, has sent me to you.' This is my name for all time, by this name I shall be invoked for all generations to come . . .."— The Jerusalem Bible.

But Moses said to God, "If I come to the Israelites and say to them, 'The God of your ancestors has sent me to you,' and they ask me, 'What is his name?' What shall I say to them?" God said

to Moses, "I AM WHO I AM." He said further, "Thus you shall say to the Israelites, 'I AM has sent me to you.'" God also said to Moses, "Thus you shall say to the Israelites, 'The LORD, the God of your ancestors, the God of Abraham, the God of Isaac, and the God of Jacob, has sent me to you.' This is my name forever, and this is my title for all generations. . . .."— New Revised Standard Version (NRSV)

appeared in 1989. The New English Bible (NEB) (1970, 1976), the product of an international body of Roman Catholic, Jewish, and Protestant scholars, was recently further refined and reissued as the Revised English Bible (1989). Unless otherwise indicated, all biblical citations in this textbook are from the NEB.

The widely used New International Version (NIV), completed in the 1970s, reflects a generally conservative Protestant viewpoint. A popular Roman Catholic translation, the New American Bible (NAB) (1970), is also highly readable. Like the Jerusalem Bible and the New (and Revised) English Bible, it includes fresh renderings of the deuterocanonical books (the Apocrypha). Most of these new translations are available in paperback editions, which contain extensive annotations, maps, and scholarly commentary. (Box 1.5 lists some useful abbreviations of all biblical books and other related terms.)

Some translations favored by many students need to be used with caution. Whereas the Good News Bible offers a fluent paraphrase of the original languages in informal English, many scholars think that the Living Bible strays so far from the original texts as to be unreliable and misleading. Some doctrinally oriented versions, such as the New World Translation published by the Watchtower Society (Jehovah's Witnesses), consistently tend to render controversial passages in a way that supports their distinctive beliefs.

The multivolume Doubleday Anchor Bible is an excellent study aid. A cooperative effort by Prot-

estant, Roman Catholic, and Jewish scholars, each volume in the series is the work of an individual translator, who provides extensive interpretative commentary. The Scholars Version (SV) is another in-progress multivolume translation with extensive annotation. Intended as an aid in discovering the historical Jesus, the Scholars Version of *The Five Gospels* (1993) (including the Gospel of Thomas) uses a color code to indicate the relative authenticity of sayings ascribed to Jesus. Sayings considered most likely to be accurate versions of Jesus' actual words are printed in red or pink, doubtful sayings in gray, and those deemed notto represent his authentic voice in black. Adopting an idiomatic, conversational style, the SV translators have also issued *The Complete Gospels,* which compiles all known canonical and noncanonical Gospel material from the first three centuries of Christianity, including the fragmentary Secret Mark and Gospel of Peter (see Chapter 11).

The Bible and Modern Scholarship

The variety of literary forms found in the Bible— genealogies, legal instructions, prophetic oracles, historical narratives, devotional lyrics, erotic poetry, proverbs, letters, parables, short stories, essays of skeptical Wisdom, and mystical visions of the future— is matched by the diversity of its religious thought. The Bible's overarching themes concern the nature of God and his relationship to humankind, but these themes are not expressed in a single monolithic viewpoint. Contributors to the biblical literature were many, and they wrote from an enormous range of personal, historical, and theological perspectives. Even in a single book, such as Psalms, for example, we find a wide spectrum of religious feeling, extending from praises of God's grandeur to heartfelt questioning of the Deity's fidelity to his word. The affirmation of divine goodness in Psalm 118 and the celebration of Yahweh's glorious creation in Psalm 19 contrast markedly with the complaints about the sufferings he unjustly inflicts upon those faithful to him in Psalm 44 (especially verses 19–22). In Psalm 89, the poet even accuses God of breaking his sworn oath to David (Ps. 89:20–45).

The tension between the theological certainties promoted in Deuteronomy and the Deuteronomistic History (Joshua–2 Kings)—obedience to the covenant brings life and prosperity whereas disobedience brings defeat and death (cf. Deut. 28–29)—and the criticism of these simplistic explanations presented in such Wisdom books as Job and Ecclesiastes is striking. In Job, the writer dramatizes the painful disconnection between conventional ideas about God's justice, his promised rewards to the faithful and punishment to the disobedient, and the painful realities of the real world, where the wicked often prosper at the expense of the good (see Chapter 7). For the author of Ecclesiastes, the problem of God's responsibility for evil and undeserved suffering is so unanswerable that he can only take refuge in profound skepticism, denying that even the wise can discover ethical meaning in a universe so riddled with apparently random acts of injustice.

> And I look on the work of God: plainly no one can discover what the work is that goes on under the sun or explain why [people] should toil to seek yet never discover. Not even a sage can discover it, though he may claim to know.
>
> Eccl. 8:17; cf. 3:11; 9:11; 11:5

For many contemporary readers, the extraordinarily diverse responses that different biblical writers make to lived experience, from thanksgiving for God's generosity to anger or despair at his apparent failure unequivocally to validate ethical behavior (Eccl. 4:1–3), is one of the Bible's greatest strengths. Instead of promoting a doctrinally rigid view of the divine-human relationship, such as those adopted by some religious institutions, different biblical authors offer a wide range of religious perceptions encompassing a broad spectrum of spiritual possibilities. The absolute certainty of divine justice in human history advocated by the authors of Deuteronomy and Joshua–2 Kings—that God's people suffered national disaster only because they had failed to worship him wholeheartedly—is balanced by counter-arguments in Psalms and the Wisdom literature that question the moral logic of this assumption (see Chapter 7).

The rich diversity of individual voices speaking to us in both the Hebrew Bible and New Testament is an intrinsic part of their enduring value. To grasp the importance of this diversity, it is necessary to let each individual biblical writer speak for himself, without trying to force one author's statements to conform to those of another. Only by recognizing the multiplicity of viewpoints raised in Scripture will readers begin to appreciate its power to illuminate the many dimensions and varieties of religious experience.

In approaching the Bible analytically, it is important to remember that studying Scripture in a college or university classroom necessarily differs from reading it in church as part of an act of worship. At a religious service, whether Jewish, Catholic, Orthodox, or Protestant, short excerpts to be read aloud usually are chosen to encourage listeners to behave ethically: Stories of biblical heroes or villains offer models for worshipers to emulate or avoid. In a devotional setting, the Bible speaks with largely undisputed authority.

In a university environment, however, the Bible is studied in the same way as any other literary document from the ancient world. Using techniques similar to those applied in the disciplines of history, anthropology, sociology, linguistics, and literary studies, students investigate such topics as the question of a document's date and authorship, the implied audience and social setting, the historical context, and the writer's apparent assumptions and goals. It is essential to read carefully to perceive what a text actually says (as opposed to what one may have been told about it elsewhere) and to compare it to similar works written at approximately the same time and under the same cultural influences. Comparative study of the Gospels, which were composed between 70 and 100 C.E., reveals much about their individual authors' distinctive theological concerns, helping to explain reasons for both similarities and differences in their accounts (see Box 10.2).

Since the eighteenth-century Age of Enlightenment, when scientists and other scholars developed analytical tools to clear away long-held misconceptions about both the natural and the social worlds, vitually all forms of traditional authority have been challenged. In physics, the work of Newton, Einstein, and other scientists revolutionized our understanding of the universe. In the political arena, rebels challenged the claim that kings ruled by divine right, triggering the American and French revolutions. In the social world, long-accepted institutions, such as slavery, exploitative child labor, and the subjugation of women, were questioned or replaced by more just practices. Religious claims, including authoritarian uses of the Bible, were similarly scrutinized. During the last two centuries, an international community of scholars—Jewish, Catholic, Protestant, and others—has developed innovative methods to illuminate the nature and growth of biblical documents. This cosmopolitan body of scholars, historians, textual experts, literary critics, linguists, anthropologists, sociologists, and theologians includes thousands of university faculty, clergy, seminary instructors, and academic researchers. Collectively, their efforts have provided us with an increasingly precise and well-documented study of the biblical literature and the environment out of which it grew. Virtually every textbook used in college and seminary courses today, including this one, draws heavily on these scholarly resources. (At the end of each chapter in this text, readers will find a list of publications by major biblical scholars, offering valuable references for further study.)

Some of the principal methods that scholars use to study the Gospels are summarized in Chapter 10; here, we briefly clarify the term *biblical criticism.* For some people, the term *criticism* may awaken negative feelings, perhaps implying fault-finding or a derogatory judgment. But in biblical studies, it is a positive means of understanding scriptural texts more accurately and objectively. *Criticism* derives from the Greek word *krino,* which means "to judge" or "to discern," to exercise rational analysis in evaluating something. In the field of art and literature, it involves the ability to recognize artistic worth and to distinguish the relative merits or defects of a given work. In biblical studies, various critical methods are used, ranging from techniques for investigating the oral traditions that preceded the written documents to literary analysis of their final form, content, and structure.

Because, for hundreds of millions of believers, the Bible embodies their deeply held convictions and spiritual aspirations, approaching it objectively is difficult. For some readers, the rigorous application of dispassionate logic to documents thought to reveal the divine will seems inappropriate. For many people, however, spirituality, reverence for concepts of divinity, love of the biblical tradition, and critical study are not incompatible; from this perspective, thinking analytically about religious texts and the cultural environment that helped shape them is both a tribute to the texts' intrinsic value and a means of understanding them more accurately. Many scholars believe that the scriptures of most world religions, including the Vedas, Hebrew Bible, New Testament, and Qur'an, were composed to express authentic human experiences of divine power—represented by such classic moments as Moses encountering God at a burning bush on the slopes of Mount Sinai, or Jesus hearing a heavenly voice after his baptism at the Jordan River, or Paul beholding the glorified Christ on the road to Damascus. These unique religious experiences. which seem to transcend the ordinary limits of human life, if they are to be preserved for others, must be articulated in human language that is ill-equipped to express unearthly realities. Writing of Jesus' apparently supernatural abilities and personal vision of God's kingdom, for example, the New Testament authors inevitably depicted them in terms of the prevailing culture, using then-current images and metaphors to approximate the inexpressible. Although scholarship cannot investigate the world of the spirit or the elusive dimension of religious transcendence the biblical authors explore, it offers enormous help in examining the means — cultural, social, historical, and literary — by which ancient writers conveyed these phenomena to us.

ASSUMPTIONS AND APPROACHES

The way we approach studying the Bible depends largely on our preconceptions about its historical origins and the kind of religious authority it embodies. Attitudes toward the Bible range from uncritical acceptance of every statement at face value to intense skepticism that denies it any historical credibility. Between these two extremes lies a great variety of viewpoints, each with its characteristic assumptions — ideas or beliefs that one takes for granted, assuming them to be true without first carefully examining their validity. These sometimes unconscious assumptions can profoundly influence the reader's understanding of the biblical text, predetermining its meaning.

In studying the Bible, it is helpful to clear away some common misconceptions that tend to inhibit thinking logically about it. One typical assumption is that, because the Bible contains sacred literature, revered by millions as conveying divine revelation, all its statements, whether scientific, historical, or theological, must be factually accurate in every respect. This view equates factuality with religious truth and is commonly expressed in an either-or formula: Either the Bible derives from God, and is therefore literally true, or it is of human origin and thus false. (This opinion assumes that human insight and creativity have little or no value.) Insisting that Scripture must be "inerrant" — entirely free from all error — if it is to have any real worth creates a false dilemma, forcing people to choose unnecessarily between two apparently unreconcilable extremes. This black-and-white fallacy, characteristic of some fundamentalists, is not supported by biblical writers, none of whom explicitly claims to be error-free.

A religious movement that began early in the twentieth century among conservative Protestants, chiefly in North America, **fundamentalism** arose partly in response to post-Enlightenment scientific rationalism, which was regarded as undermining the certainties of Christianity. Asserting that every biblical passage is inerrant, fundamentalists assume that, in the act of writing Scripture, biblical authors transcended the ordinary limitations of time, place, and culture to produce absolutely infallible documents. Most scholars, whether Jewish, Catholic, or Protestant, do not accept fundamentalism's "all or nothing" approach, which tends to make enemies of faith and intellect. Rather than fearing or ignoring the discoveries of science and other academic disciplines, they think it more productive to make use of analytical techniques that help to explain the process by which ancient writers and editors produced the Bible in its present form.

SOME METHODS OF BIBLICAL ANALYSIS

Historical Criticism   To help us understand the complex process by which biblical literature was created, contemporary scholarship attempts to analyze the texts as objectively as humanly possible, without imposing doctrinal or other presumptions about their nature. In general, biblical criticism falls into two major divisions, historical and literary. **Historical criticism** involves the analysis of documents that purport to record historical events, investigating the historical setting in which the texts originated. Using standards of evidence analogous to those in the social sciences, historical critics test a given account against several criteria, including such standards as factual accuracy, historical plausibility, and authorial presuppositions. Historians ask such questions as: Is this event likely to have occurred in the way the author presents it? Does it accord with what we already know about this particular historical situation from non-biblical sources, such as ancient Near Eastern archives or inscriptions from the Greco-Roman world? What is the writer's bias or personal agenda, and how does it affect what he reports? Historical critics investigate such issues as a document's authorship, date and place of composition, intended audience, and the social and cultural circumstances that produced it.

Some biblical documents present historians with almost insurmountable challenges because they report supernatural phenomena that by definition lie beyond the scope of ordinary history. According to one literary strand in Exodus, for example, God directly intervenes in history to part the waters of a great sea, allowing his people to escape the pursuing Egyptians, who are drowned when the divided waters suddenly converge (Ex. 14–15; see Box 4.6). In the same book, Yahweh appears on the "mountain of God," to inscribe stone tablets with the Ten Commandments and to permit Moses to see his "hand," "back," and "glory" (divine essence) (Ex. 24; 32–34). The account in Joshua contains many spectacular disruptions of the natural order, from the collapse of Jericho's walls to the sun's apparent "standing still" in its orbit (Josh. 6; 10:12–15). It is probably significant that most miraculous events in the Hebrew Bible are assigned to Israel's distant past, the remote periods of the Genesis ancestors and the Mosaic era when Israel first became a nation. These "historical" traditions were already a distant memory at the time they were written down, and they belonged to a special, unrepeatable epoch when God directly displayed his controlling presence in human affairs. Books written closer to the author's own time, however, such as Ezra, Nehemiah, Esther, and 1 Maccabees — and whose authors saw contemporary life operating according to familiar standards of probability — report no comparable divine interventions or manifestations of the supernatural.

Although many of the last-written documents in the Hebrew Bible, especially those describing events of the postexilic period, avoid depicting supernatural phenomena, the miraculous vigorously reasserts itself in the New Testament, particularly in the Gospel accounts of Jesus' life (composed between about 66 and 95 C.E.). Because the Gospel authors believed in Jesus' divinity — that he was qualitatively different from every other character in history — their presentation is colored by their faith. Like many of their Greco-Roman contemporaries, the **Evangelists** (Gospel writers) describe a world populated by supernatural beings, assigning speaking roles to both angels and devils. Jesus is shown on various occasions holding conversations with Satan or his "legion" of demons, malignant spirits who are identified as the unseen cause of disease and madness (cf. Matt. 4; Luke 4; Mark 1–3). Although many people in antiquity uncritically accepted the existence of such entities, they are not part of the universe as modern science defines it and as most people now experience the world in their daily lives.

Historical critics' recognition that many biblical writers embraced a worldview significantly different from our own and that their concerns were more religious than historical means that historians must interpret biblical narratives carefully, judiciously distinguishing between recoverable historical fact and religious claims that exceed the reach of historical investigation. Because the historian's sphere is necessarily restricted to the material realm, which operates according to widely agreed-upon laws of predictability, he or she cannot evaluate nonmaterial phenomena, alleged events that are not repeatable in the laboratory or otherwise open to scientific scrutiny. Using archaeological evidence, such as an inscription identifying **Pontius Pilate** as governor of Judea for the years equivalent to 26–36 C.E., historians can confirm that Pilate represented Rome during Jesus' lifetime. They cannot confirm, however, that the man whom Pilate crucified overcame death and rose from the grave.

For many readers, it is precisely these unrepeatable manifestations of supernatural power — God's rescue of Israel at a chaotic sea and Jesus' rising from the tomb — that give the biblical stories their incomparable value as guarantors of purpose and meaning in human life. The biblical narrators' assertions that God delivered a perfect law to Moses and that Jesus is the Son of God who promised a future return to establish his universal rule are, for countless believers, incontrovertible facts. However, such claims of faith, which posit a spiritual dimension of existence outside the physical world, are inaccessible to historical verification.

Although they can neither confirm nor deny the historicity of Israel's escape from Egypt or of Jesus' resurrection from the dead, historians can investigate the development of these traditions, analyzing the process by which they reached their present literary forms. In **source criticism**, scholars search for the sources, both oral and written, that the author(s) or editor(s) utilized to create their documents. An exhaustive analysis of the Pentateuch (Genesis–Deuteronomy) suggests to most scholars that it is a composite work, consisting of at least four major sources deriving from different periods of Israel's history. Following the Babylonian exile, Jewish editors eventually combined these sources into the complex collection of law, poetry, genealogy, and narrative that make up the Pentateuch we have today. The four different interwoven strands offer numerous clues to their separate origins, ranging from the different names for God used by different authors to the repetitions, contradictions, and other discrepancies that we find in the text. For a discussion of scholarly theories about the Pentateuch's composite nature, see the section "Who Wrote the 'Books of Moses'?" in Chapter 4.

A related method, **form criticism** (from the German *Formsgeschichte*) recognizes that in addition to extended oral and documentary sources, such as those used in the Pentateuch and the narratives of Joshua through 2 Kings, these longer accounts are made up of many smaller units — ancient folk tales, genealogies, anecdotes about distant ancestors, royal court archives, war hymns, battle stories, parables, formulas outlining priestly rituals, poems of lament or praise, short creeds traditionally recited at Israelite places of worship, such as Bethel or Jerusalem — that generally are self-contained, with clear-cut beginnings and endings, and that can stand alone. These individual units, such as the story of Abraham's near-sacrifice of his son Isaac (Gen. 22) or the two versions of Jacob's being renamed Israel (Gen. 32 and 35), are called **pericopes**. Each pericope had an independent existence in Israel's oral tradition before it was written down and eventually incorporated into a continuous narrative. Formerly independent pericopes are the building blocks out of which the present biblical text, from Pentateuch to Gospels, is constructed.

Form criticism looks behind the written form of a pericope to discover the older oral form in which it circulated before being written down. The form critic tries to ascertain the "life setting" (from the German *Sitz-im-Leben*), the social and historical circumstances in which an individual pericope, such as the two versions of God's disclosure of his personal name, Yahweh, to Moses (Ex. 3 and 6) or various anecdotes about Jesus' miraculous cures, originated. Oral traditions about Moses' role in inaugurating the covenant with Yahweh at Mount Sinai (also called **Horeb** in some literary strands) were probably repeated annually at various covenant-renewal ceremonies at holy sites such as Shechem or Jerusalem (cf. Josh. 24), gathering new interpretative meanings as Israel's political and religious situation changed over the years. Scholars believe that many generations of oral transmission passed before these recitations were permanently fixed in written form.

Whereas form criticism concentrates on the stages of development that orally transmitted traditions undergo before they are crystalized in writing, **redaction criticism** (from the German *Redaktions-geschichte*) emphasizes the role of the individual biblical author. Redaction critics point out that the author-editor (redactor) does not slavishly copy sources but commonly revises them, weaving together and shaping older documents according to his or her specific religious purpose. This discipline's emphasis on the author's crucial function in assembling, rearranging, and reinterpreting older material applies equally to the formation of both the Hebrew Bible and New Testament. Redaction analysis shows that the Gospel writers, like the compilers of the Pentateuch, were not simply recorders of historical fact or received tradition but also conscious interpreters of their subject. As different writers contributed different traditions about Moses that eventually were blended together in the Pentateuch, so each Gospel writer presented Jesus' life from a distinctive **theological** (from the Greek *theos* [God] and *logos* [word, or "study of"]) perspective consistent with his individual comprehension of Jesus' nature and teachings (see Chapter 10).

Literary Criticism   Whereas the historical-critical method attempts to uncover the historical circumstances in which a text originated and evolved, **literary criticism** tries to discover the significance of the text as we now have it. Knowing that the duplications and other discrepancies in the Pentateuch and the four different Gospels derive at least in part from these documents' incorporation of diverse sources, as well as from a long process of editing, helps us to understand their complex nature. The task of literary criticism is to examine the texts' final form, searching for ways to identify important themes and ideas and thus interpret their meaning. To a great extent, every experienced student is a literary critic, reading not only to acquire information but also to recognize the author's main interests, assumptions, and message. Readers automatically pick up clues—such as frequently repeated words, images, and phrases—that suggest the author's basic concerns.

A first step in literary analysis of the Bible is to identify its various literary genres or categories (Box 1.7). To begin with the most obvious, the Bible contains many prose **narratives**—literary compositions that tell a story, arranging the characters and events in a sequential order, typically to express a theme, a recurring topic or idea that permeates the work, making an implicit statement about the text's meaning. In the Genesis narrative about a global flood, for example, the detailed account of God's destructive actions embody a theme of divine judgment on disobedient humanity and a concurrent theme of redemption as God saves Noah's three sons and their wives to repopulate the post-flood earth (Gen. 6–8). In examining the Pentateuch as a whole, some critics have found a unifying theme that helps bind together its disparate contents—that of God's repeated promises to Israel for land, progeny, the divine presence, and other blessings, coupled with the theme of long-delayed fulfillment of these promises. (For a discussion of other literary forms and themes in the Pentateuch, see Chapter 4.)

The Tanak's first eleven books—Genesis through 2 Kings—consist largely of narrative, opening with the world's creation, continuing with tales of Israel's ancestors and the creation of Israel as a covenant community that eventually establishes itself in Canaan and forms a national state under such kings as Saul, David, and Solomon, and ending with Yahweh's abandonment of that community (Judah) to Babylonian destruction (587 B.C.E.). Commonly known as Israel's **national epic**, this long narration (interspersed with detailed passages of law and ritual) essentially recounts the formation and dissolution of a difficult partnership between Yahweh and his people. As shaped by postexilic editors deeply influenced by Deuteronomy's philosophy of history, this narrative presents a clear-cut theme: Obedience to Yahweh's covenant brings national success, while disobedience results in national annihilation. Narratives about the postexilic community's partial restoration, such as Ezra and Nehemiah, are less ambitious and comprehensive; they merely describe conditions under Persian rule, when the politically impotent covenant community focused on its Mosaic obligations to worship Yahweh exclusively and centered its worship at the rebuilt Jerusalem Temple. 1 and 2 Chronicles provide a revised version of material in 1 and 2 Kings according to a priestly viewpoint, reinterpreting Israel's history from the reign of Saul (c. 1020–1000 B.C.E.) to the end of the Babylonian exile (c. 538 B.C.E.). After Alexander the Great conquered the Persian Empire (332 B.C.E.), some of his successors attempted forcibly to impose Greek culture and religion on the Jewish community, resulting in the last-written biblical narratives, the apocryphal books of 1 and 2 Maccabees, which narrate a successful Jewish rebellion against foreign oppression and the temporary establishment of an autonomous Jewish state (140–63 B.C.E.).

Presenting an idealized and theologically oriented account of the early Christian movement from about 30 to 60 C.E., the Book of Acts (written in about 85–90 C.E.) is the New Testament's major narrative work. Using techniques resembling those found in Greco-Roman biographies, the Gospels also use narrative to portray Jesus' life and actions, although they also contain many subgenres, such as parables, genealogies, speeches,

Box 1.7 Some Representative Literary Genres in the Hebrew Bible

A library of ancient Israelite literature, the Hebrew Bible (Tanak) contains a remarkable variety of literary genres composed over a period of more than 1000 years. Scholars believe that ancient hymns celebrating Israel's military victories (late second millennium B.C.E. are among the oldest documents incorporated into the biblical text; mystical visions of future history, such as those found in Daniel, are thought to be among the last written (c. 165 B.C.E.). Scholars disagree on the dates of composition for most of the examples given below.

GENRE	REPRESENTATIVE EXAMPLE
Battle/Victory Hymns	"Song of the Sea" (Exod. 15:1–18) "Song of Deborah" (Judg. 5:1–31)
Fable	"Jotham's Fable of Kingship" (Judg. 9:8–15)
Historical Narrative	Prose Epic of Israel's Origins: from the call of Abraham to the Israelites' arrival at Mount Sinai/Horeb (Gen. 12:1–Exod. 19:25); from the formulation of the Mosaic Covenant to the forty-year wandering in the wilderness (Exod. 24:1–18; 32:1–34:35; Num. 10:11–26:4; 31:1–36:13); from the conquest of Canaan to the fall of Jerusalem to Babylon (Josh. 1:1–2; Kings 25:30).
Divine Commands and Statutes	The Ten Commandments (Exod. 20:1–17; Deut. 5:6–21). The Book of the Covenant (legal regulations) (Exod. 20:22–23:33); collections of divine decrees and ordinances (Exod. 35:1–40:33; Lev. 1:1–27:34; Num. 1:1–10:10; Deut. 4:44–30:20)
Genealogies	Tables of Descent: from Adam to Noah (Gen. 5:1–32); from Noah to Abraham (Gen. 10:1–32; 11:10–27); sons of Jacob (Israel) (Gen. 35:22–26; 46:8–27; cf. Exod. 1:1–5); from Adam to the family of Saul, first king of a united Israel (1 Chron. 1:1–9:35); list of returnees from the Babylonian exile (Ezra 2:1–63; Neh. 7:6–63)
Short Stories	Prose tale of a Moabite ancestress of King David (Ruth 1:1–4:22); nationalistic tale of a heroic queen (Esther 1:1–10:3).
Wisdom Books	Collection of practical advice (Prov. 1:1–31:31); poetic drama questioning divine justice (Job 1:1–42:8); skeptical meditations on life's futility (Ecclesiastes 1:1–12:14)
Devotional Poetry	Anthology of lyrics sung at Temple services, including songs of praise, bitter complaints, and appeals for help (Ps. 1:1–150:6).
Erotic Poetry	Compilation of passionate lyrics celebrating physical love (Song of Songs 1:1–8:14)
Prophetic Oracles	Collections of warnings and promises, commonly in poetry, by Israel's prophets (Isa. 1:1–66:24; Hosea 1:1–14:9; Micah 1:1–7:20; Joel 1:1–3:21, etc.)
Apocalypse (a "revelation" or "unveiling" of the spirit world and/or future events)	Mystical visions, in highly symbolic language, of God's long-term plans for Israel and the world (Daniel 2:1–45; 7:1–12:13)

moral pronouncements, miracle stories, and confrontation accounts in which Jesus confounds his opponents. Twenty-one of the New Testament's twenty-seven books take the form of letters, although some, such as 1 John, are actually tracts, and others, such as Hebrews, are elaborate sermons. Revelation, like Daniel, is an apocalypse, containing visions of the spirit world and a cosmic conflict between Good and Evil.

Although Israel probably developed its legal system gradually during the period of the monarchy (c. 1020–587 B.C.E.) and the Persian era (538–332 B.C.E.), biblical editors placed all Israelite laws, statutes, and ordinances within the framework of the Mosaic Covenant concluded at Mount Sinai. Large blocks of legal material are inserted into older narratives, interrupting the flow of events: Except for chapters 24 and 32–34, most of Exodus 20–50 consists of ethical, ritual, and social prescriptions. Ritual material, with a few ethical directives, occupies all of Leviticus and the first ten chapters of Numbers. After a prologue narrating Israel's experience at Sinai/Horeb, Deuteronomy is devoted to an extensive compilation of Mosaic decrees, some of which revise and modify earlier laws given in Exodus. For a discussion of some distinctive legal codes embedded in the Pentateuch, see Chapter 4.

The prophetic books of the Hebrew Bible, such as Isaiah, Jeremiah, Ezekiel, Amos, Hosea, and Micah, are primarily edited compilations of the prophets' spoken oracles—pronouncements from God typically introduced as the "word of the Lord." The prophetic anthologies encompass many subgenres, including riddles, parables, ethical counsel, and allegories (narratives in which each character, event, or object has a symbolic value). Although extremely heterogenous, the prophetic books feature some general themes: warnings of divine punishment for disloyalty to Yahweh and, to a lesser extent, additional promises of a future global transformation under Yahweh's universal rule. The apocalyptic sections, such as Isaiah 24–27 and the last part of Zechariah, are thought to have been added later during the postexilic era (see Chapter 6).

Other literary genres found in the Bible have already been mentioned in passing: the prose fiction of Ruth and Esther (as well as the apocryphal Tobit and Judith) are short stories that dramatize the great variety of means by which God guides individual human lives to accomplish his purpose. The pragmatic wisdom taught in Proverbs, a collection of prudent observations about achieving a successful life in harmony with the divine will, contrasts with another book traditionally ascribed to Solomon, the unabashedly sensual celebration of sexual love featured in the Song of Songs. Wisdom books such as Job and Ecclesiastes, which contain considerable poetry along with an astringent critique of traditional views about God, appeal not to the authoritative divine revelation promoted in the Pentateuch and the Prophets, but to an intellectual honesty willing to confront a painful paradox: the inherently baffling and contradictory quality of God's relationship to his human "image."

Biblical authors' use of a wide variety of literary forms, including their extensive use of poetry and other figurative language, implies a great deal about the subtle, almost intangible nature and function of religious communication. In composing the narratives of Joshua through 2 Kings, the authors do not attempt to write history in the modern sense, but selectively describe historical events for religious purposes, to exalt Yahweh as Lord of History, the God who expresses his will through what happens in the realm of human societies, on both the national and international level. By contrast, parables—used by Jesus and many of the prophets—are works of purely imaginative fiction that do not depend on any external events to make their psychological or spiritual impact. As Jesus' preferred mode of discourse in portraying the nature of God's rule and its implications for humanity, the parable does not depend on literal truth to make its point. When Jesus tells of a Samaritan traveler befriending a man who had been beaten and left for dead or of a father who cherishes his sinful son as much as he loves his righteous child, it does not matter that the characters and actions in the parable are entirely fictional

(Luke 10:29–37; 15:11–32). Expressing his ideas in brief comparisons, short stories, metaphors, and other figures of speech, Jesus conveys insights about human interconnectedness — including messages illustrating the practice of unconditional love — that do not need to be historically factual to be ethically "true." Like the theologically oriented narratives of the Hebrew Bible, the Gospel accounts in which Jesus' parables are embedded may function at times in a similar manner, reporting stories intended to highlight spiritual values, instead of merely reporting the happenings of a limited historical moment.

Biblical authors and characters employ many diverse literary strategies to convey their sense of the way that God communicates with people, using simile, metaphor, symbolism, allegory, hyperbole, and other rhetorical devices. Because writers necessarily use the limited resources of human language to convey perceptions of unseen realities that cannot be defined in finite human terms, they often rely on poetic figures of speech. When the Gospel authors show Jesus describing the kingdom of God, he uses the common devise of a **simile**, comparing divine rule to the growth of a tiny mustard seed. Whereas a simile uses "like" or "as" in likening one thing to another, a **metaphor** makes an implied comparison, as when the psalmists declare that Yahweh is a "shepherd," a "shield," or a "rock." **Symbolism**, which uses a physical object to signify something else, occurs throughout the Bible but is especially prevalent in apocalyptic works such as Daniel, where a huge idol made of gold, silver, bronze, iron, and clay represents a succession of Near Eastern empires, each inferior to its predecessor (Dan. 2). As noted above, in an allegorical narrative everything is symbolic, including the characters and incidents in the plot. In Revelation 12, the author creates an allegory in which an enormous red dragon pursues a pregnant woman into the desert, where she gives birth to a future king, after which the dragon wars against the woman's children, thereby rendering Rome's earthly persecution of the Christian church as a cosmic attack by Satan on God's Messiah.

Biblical writers also commonly exploit hyperbole — extreme exaggeration — to command readers' attention. The sayings of Jesus are rife with hyperbole. He suggests that we remove the rafter from our eye before criticizing our neighbor for the speck in his or that we cut off our right hand rather than use it in wrongful action. Dramatic irony, in which characters in a play or story speak or behave in ignorance of essential facts that the audience or reader already knows, is another common literary device. In 2 Samuel, after the prophet Nathan relates a parable to King David about a rich man's despicable conduct, and the king responds by indignantly condemning the wrongdoer, Nathan boldly identifies David as the rich miscreant. Unknowingly, David had judged himself. Mark's Gospel makes a similar use of irony in which demons recognize Jesus' identity, whereas all the human characters, including Jesus' family, friends, and disciples, fail to perceive his relationship to God. Many of the Bible's literary techniques underscore the lamentable human capacity to treasure our personal or cultural presuppositions, blinders that keep us from seeing truly. In this textbook, we will draw frequently on the insights of both historical and literary criticism, using whatever analytical methods are helpful in clarifying the Bible's diverse messages.

QUESTIONS FOR REVIEW

1. What does the word *bible* literally mean, and how does this definition express the nature of the Bible as an anthology of religious literature?

2. Explain the relationship of the Christian Old Testament to the Hebrew Bible; define the term *Tanak,* and name and describe the three main sections into which it is divided. In what way do Protestant editions of the Old Testament resemble the contents of the Tanak? How do Catholic and Orthodox editions of the Old Testament differ from the Tanak in content? Define the terms *canon, Apocrypha,* and *Deuterocanon.*

3. Define the terms *covenant* and *testament* and explain their use in the Bible. With what catastrophic event does the first narrative sequence of the Hebrew Bible (Genesis through 2 Kings) end? How does this disaster in 587 B.C.E. relate to the concept of a covenant relationship between Israel and God?

4. According to Christian belief, who introduced a "new" covenant with his followers, and under what circumstances?

5. In what languages was the Bible originally written? When and where was the first major edition of the Old Testament produced in a language other than its original? What edition of the Hebrew Bible was used by the early Christian community? Why was the New Testament written in Greek?

6. Describe the process by which the Hebrew Bible and New Testament were copied and transmitted to us. Define *textual criticism* and explain the difficulties scholars face in trying to create a reliable biblical text.

7. Explain the process by which the Hebrew Bible canon formed, including some of the major events that affected this development. How and when was the New Testament canon established? What role did Marcion's criticism of the Hebrew Bible play in the church's attitude toward the Old Testament? What was the significance of Jerome's Latin edition of the Bible, the Vulgate?

8. How did the Bible come to be translated into English? When did English versions first appear? What two historical developments ensured that the Bible would become available in modern European languages? Name some important recent translations of the Bible.

9. Describe some of the goals and methods of contemporary biblical scholarship, including *source criticism, form criticism, redaction criticism, historical criticism,* and *literary criticism.* In approaching the biblical texts objectively and analytically, what do scholars hope to achieve?

QUESTIONS FOR DISCUSSION AND REFLECTION

1. Most of today's Bible readers are not familiar with the ancient languages in which the Bible was written, nor are they usually aware of the enormous differences between the cultures of the ancient Near East, in which the biblical texts originated, and that of twenty-first century North America. Since all the extant copies of biblical documents were made many centuries after their authors first composed them, virtually all readers must depend on the work of linguists, text critics, and other scholars for their English editions of the Bible. How do you go about finding an English version of the Bible that you consider to

be relatively faithful to the original texts? What criteria do you use in evaluating the trustworthiness of a particular edition?

2. How do our unexamined assumptions and preconceptions influence our understanding of the Bible? Should we rely on the authority of a particular religious institution in trying to comprehend what individual writers say in different books? If we wish to read the texts objectively, how do we manage to attain that goal? How can the last 250 years of biblical scholarship help us break free of erroneous presuppositions and analyze each biblical document in the context of its individual author's place, time, and worldview? What are the advantages of letting each biblical work speak for itself without making its message necessarily conform to that of other writers who underwent different religious experiences?

TERMS AND CONCEPTS TO REMEMBER*

Abraham	historical criticism
Alexander the Great/Hellenism	Israel (people and nation-state)
apocalypse	Jerusalem
Apocrypha	Jesus of Nazareth/Last
approaches to studying the Bible	Supper and New Covenant
Athanasius, Easter Letter of	Jewish revolt against Rome (66–73 C.E.)
Babylon	John the Baptist
Bible in English, the	Judea/Judean
Canaan	*koinē*
canon and Deuterocanon	literary criticism
catholic epistles	Marcion/Gnosticism
Codex Sinaiticus/Codex Vaticanus	Masoretic Text (MT)
Cyrus the Great	Messiah (Anointed One), Christ
Dead Sea Scrolls	monotheism and
Deuteronomistic History (DH)	polytheism
Eusebius	Moses/Mosaic Covenant
Evangelists	Muratorian Canon
Flavius Josephus	narrative/theme
fundamentalism	orthodoxy/heresy
Gospel of Thomas	Paul
Hebrew/Aramaic	Pentateuch
Hebrew Bible	pericope

*All terms are defined in the Glossary at the back of this book.

Persia
Pontius Pilate
pseudonymity
rabbi/Academy of
  Yavneh (Jamnia)
Scripture
scroll/codex
Septuagint (LXX)
source criticism/form
  criticism
Sinai

Tanak: Torah, Nevi'im,
  and Kethuvim
textual criticism
theological orientation of
  biblical authors
uses of simile, metaphor,
  poetic images,
  parables, and other
  figures of speech
Vulgate Bible
Yahweh

RECOMMENDED READING

General Works

Achtemeier, Paul J., ed. *The HarperCollins Bible Dictionary*, rev. ed. San Francisco: HarperSanFrancisco, 1996. One of the best single-volume treatments of biblical topics.

Albright, W. F., and Freedman, D. N., eds. *The Anchor Bible.* New York: Doubleday, 1964–. A multivolume series featuring new translations of individual books of the Bible, with careful annotations by Jewish, Catholic, and Protestant scholars.

Brown, R. E., Fitzmeyer, J. A., and Murphy, R. E. *The New Jerome Biblical Commentary,* 2nd ed. Englewood Cliffs, N. J.: Prentice-Hall, 1990. Provides theological discussions of all books in the biblical canon by leading scholars.

Coogan, Michael D., ed. *The Oxford Dictionary of the Biblical World.* New York: Oxford University Press, 1998. Contains informative essays on the historical growth of both the Hebrew Bible and New Testament.

Freedman, David Noel, ed. *The Anchor Bible Dictionary,* Vols. 1–6. New York: Doubleday, 1992. An indispensable resource.

———, ed. *Eerdmans Dictionary of the Bible.* Grand Rapids, Mich.: William B. Eerdmans Publishing Company, 2000. An excellent and up-to-date reference.

Kee, Howard C., ed. *The Cambridge Companion to the Bible.* New York: Cambridge University Press, 1997. Places each biblical document in its sociohistorical context.

Metzger, Bruce M., ed. *The Oxford Companion to the Bible.* New York: Oxford University Press, 1993. Interpretative commentary on biblical texts by a group of mainly British scholars.

The New Interpreter's Bible. Nashville: Abingdon Press, 1996–. A multivolume extensively annotated edition of the entire Bible, including Apocrypha, featuring two parallel translations of the biblical texts (New International Version and the New Revised Standard Version).

Rogerson, John. *Atlas of the Bible.* New York: Facts on File, 1985. A well-illustrated resource on the geographical, historical, and archaeological background of both the Hebrew Bible and the New Testament.

Canon, Textual Transmission, and English Translations

Abegg, Martin, Jr., Flint, Peter, and Ulrich, Eugene, eds. *The Dead Sea Scrolls Bible.* San Francisco: HarperSanFrancisco, 1999. Translates into contemporary English all manuscript fragments of canonical books of the Hebrew Bible, plus 1 Enoch and Ben Sirach.

Barr, James. *Holy Scripture: Canon, Authority, Criticism.* Louisville, Ky.: Westminster, 1983.

Bobrick, Benson. *Wide As the Waters: The Story of the English Bible and the Revolution It Inspired.* Paperback ed. New York: Penguin USA, 2002.

Bruce, F. F. *History of the Bible in English,* 3rd edition. New York: Oxford University Press, 1978. A concise history and critical evaluation of all major English translations from Anglo-Saxon times to the late twentieth century.

Ehrman, Bart D. *The Orthodox Corruption of Scripture: The Effect of Early Christological Controversies on the Text of the New Testament.* New York: Oxford University Press, 1993. Provides detailed analysis of variations in ancient manuscripts, demonstrating that copyists' intentional changes are typically motivated by theological concerns.

Farmer, William R., and Farkasfalvy, D. M. *The Formation of the New Testament Canon: An Ecumenical Approach.* New York: Paulist Press, 1983.

Fox, Everett, ed. *The Five Books of Moses.* The Schocken Bible, Vol. 1. New York: Schocken Books, 1995. The first part of the Tanak in unusually vivid prose.

Fredricks, E. S., ed. *The Bible and Bibles in America.* Louisville, Ky.: John Knox, 1988.

Friedman, Richard Elliott. *The Hidden Book in the Bible: The Discovery of the First Prose Masterpiece.* San Francisco: HarperSanFrancisco, 1998. Includes a full translation of an early narrative (called "J") that editors later wove into the present biblical text.

Jewish Publication Society. *Tanakh: The Holy Scriptures.* Philadelphia: Jewish Publication Society, 1985. Authoritative English translation for the Jewish community.

Leiman, Sid Z. *The Canon and Masorah of the Hebrew Bible: An Introductory Reader.* New York: KTAV, 1974.

Lewis, Jack P. *The English Bible from KJV to NIV: A History and Evaluation.* Grand Rapids, Mich.: Baker

Book House, 1982. A scholarly review of major English translations from the King James Version to the New International Version.

Metzger, Bruce M., and Murphy, Roland E., eds. *The New Oxford Annotated Bible: New Revised Standard Version.* New York: Oxford University Press, 1991. Includes both Testaments and the Apocrypha.

The Revised English Bible with the Apocrypha. Oxford University Press, Cambridge University Press, 1989. A clear, readable translation utilizing recent scholarly research.

Rost, Leonard. *Judaism Outside the Hebrew Canon: An Introduction to the Documents.* Nashville: Abingdon Press, 1976. Surveys the Apocrypha and other books not included in the Tanak.

Sanders, James. *Torah and Canon.* Minneapolis: Fortress Press, 1972. A standard reference.

———. *From Sacred Story to Sacred Text: Canon in Paradigm.* Minneapolis: Fortress Press, 1986. An influential study.

Tucker, Gene M., Petersen, David L., and Wilson, Robert R., eds. *Canon, Theology, and Old Testament Interpretation.* Minneapolis: Fortress Press, 1988.

Vagnay, Leon, and Amphous, Christian-Bernard. *An Introduction to New Testament Textual Criticism,* 2nd ed. New York: Cambridge University Press, 1991.

von Campenhausen, Hans. *The Formation of the Christian Bible.* Translated by J. A. Baker. Philadelphia: Fortress Press, 1972.

Wegner, Paul D. *The Journey from Texts to Translations: The Origin and Development of the Bible.* Grand Rapids, Mich.: Baker Book House, 2000. A readable investigation of the Bible's literary evolution.

Wurthwein, Ernst. *The Text of the Old Testament.* Translated by E. F. Rhodes. Grand Rapids, Mich.: Eerdmans, 1979.

Criticism and Interpretation

Alter, Robert, and Kermode, Frank, eds. *The Literary Guide to the Bible.* Cambridge, Mass.: Belknap Press of Harvard University Press, 1987. A collection of helpful essays on books of both the Hebrew Bible and New Testament.

Fishbane, Michael. *Biblical Interpretation in Ancient Israel.* Oxford: Clarendon Press, 1985. For advanced students, a scholarly examination of how later biblical authors used and transformed older biblical traditions.

Gabel, John B.; Wheeler, Charles B.; and York, Anthony D. *The Bible as Literature: An Introduction,* 3rd ed. New York: Oxford University Press, 1996. An excellent book for the beginning student.

Gneuse, Robert, *The Authority of the Bible: Theories of Inspiration, Revelation, and the Canon of Scripture.* New York: Paulist Press, 1985. A brief but thoughtful review of biblical authority and the nature of divine inspiration.

Grant, R. M., with Tracy, D. *A Short History of the Interpretation of the Bible,* 2nd ed. Philadelphia: Fortress Press, 1985. A good survey.

Hirsh, E. D., Jr. *Validity in Interpretation.* New Haven, Conn.: Yale University Press, 1967.

Holladay, Carl R. "Contemporary Methods of Reading the Bible." In *The New Interpreter's Bible,* Vol. 1, pp. 125–149. Nashville, Tenn.: Abingdon Press, 1994. An introductory review of current scholarly approaches to studying the Bible.

Kugel, James L. *The Bible as It Was.* Cambridge, Mass.: Belknap Press of Harvard University Press, 1997. Examines ancient interpretations of the Hebrew Bible from the closing centuries B.C.E. and first centuries C.E.

Laffey, Alice L. *An Introduction to the Old Testament: A Feminist Perspective.* Philadelphia: Fortress Press, 1988. Surveys Hebrew Bible stories involving women's issues.

McKenzie, S. L., and Haynes, R., eds. *To Each Its Own Meaning: An Introduction to Biblical Criticisms and Their Applications.* Louisville, Ky.: Westminster/John Knox Press, 1993.

Morgan, R., with Barton, J. *Biblical Interpretation.* Oxford: Oxford University Press, 1988.

Newsome, Carol A., and Ringe, Sharon H., eds. *The Women's Bible Commentary.* Louisville, Ky.: Westminster/ John Knox Press, 1992. A one-volume commentary on both testaments utilizing feminist scholarship.

Schüssler Fiorenza, Elizabeth. *Bread Not Stone: The Challenge of Feminist Biblical Interpretation.* Boston: Beacon Press, 1985. An important contribution to modern scholarship.

———. *But She Said: Feminist Practices of Biblical Interpretation.* Boston: Beacon Press, 1992.

Silva, Moises. "Contemporary Theories of Biblical Interpretation." In *The New Interpreter's Bible,* Vol. 1, pp. 107–124. Nashville, Tenn.: Abingdon Press, 1994. Surveys theoretical methods, including structuralism and reader response theory.

PART ONE

The Hebrew Bible
Tanak, or Old Testament

History and Geography of the Ancient Near East

Key Topics/Themes

Archaeological evidence indicates that humans have inhabited the Near East for tens of thousands of years. Sites of prehistoric villages, small towns, and other settlements abound from central Anatolia (modern Turkey) to Syria to Mesopotamia (modern Iraq). It was not until about 3200 B.C.E., however, that the first large urban centers were established. Originating in southern Mesopotamia, the first urban civilization (Sumer) produced a written literature about the gods, the creation of the world, and the afterlife that significantly influenced the biblical worldview. Whereas Sumerian and later Babylonian city-states typically remained relatively small and autonomous, the Egyptians created the first unified national state in the mid-third millennium B.C.E. For most of its history, Israel, located geographically between powerful empires in Egypt and Mesopotamia, was dominated politically by a succession of Egyptian, Assyrian, Babylonian, Persian, and Greek invaders. Events recounted in the Hebrew Bible are set almost entirely in this ancient Near Eastern context.

KEY QUESTIONS

In what ways do aspects of ancient Egyptian and Mesopotamian culture anticpate ideas and beliefs that later appear in the Hebrew Bible? How does the New Testament reflect the Greco-Roman culture in which it originated?

A Prologue to the Biblical World

For thousands of years before Israel came into existence, the **Fertile Crescent**—a strip of arable land curving from the head of the Persian Gulf northwestward to Syria and then southward through Canaan into Egypt—was studded with tiny villages and other settlements (Figure 2.1). At **Jericho**, famous for its walls that tumbled before the blast of Joshua's trumpets, archaeologists have discovered evidence of human habitation dating back to 9000 B.C.E. Lying six miles west of the Jordan River, north of the Dead Sea, Jericho is the world's oldest known walled town. Archaeological excavations have uncovered the ruins of a circular stone

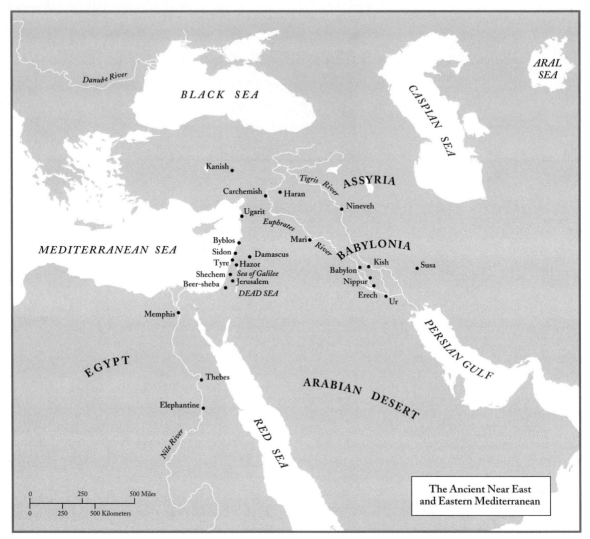

Figure 2.1 Map of the ancient Near East. The Fertile Crescent, which extends from the head of the Persian Gulf northwestward through Syria and then southwestward through Canaan into Egypt, was the location of the world's oldest urban civilizations. In Genesis, the itinerary of Abraham's travels — from Ur on the southern Euphrates River to Haran in northern Mesopotamia and thence into Canaan and Egypt — marks the boundaries of the biblical world.

tower thirty feet high, as well as plastered, painted skulls with eyes made from seashells. Like other figurines from the Stone Age, these reconstructions of human faces probably had a religious meaning that is now impossible to know.

Repeatedly abandoned and then resettled, perhaps because of invasions or fluctuations in the climate, Jericho's ruins now form a high mound of rubble called a **tell**. Composed of numerous layers of debris, each representing a different period of settlement, tells mark the sites of ancient cities throughout the Near East.

Only recently discovered, another important site, called Ain Ghazal (Arabic for "the spring of the gazelle") is located northeast of modern Amman, Jordan, near the Zarqa River (the biblical Jabbok).

Table 2.1 Some Major Events in the History of Biblical and Other World Religions

Approximate Date	Event	Biblical Reference
15,000 b.c.e.	Elaborate cave paintings are created at Lascaux, France; rituals of magic and religion evolve.	
10,000 b.c.e.	Pleistocene (Ice Age) glaciers retreat; Stone Age settlements are built in Canaan.	
9000 b.c.e.	The first permanent settlement occurs at Jericho.	
7000–5600 b.c.e.	Catal Huyuk, a town in south-central Turkey, is the apparent center of fertility cult, goddess worship.	
6000 b.c.e.	Neolithic pottery and figurines are crafted at Jericho.	
3500 b.c.e.	The wheel is invented in Mesopotamia; trade, commerce, and the communication of ideas expand.	
I. Early Bronze Age (c. 3400–2100 b.c.e.)		
3300 b.c.e.	Sumerian city-states form; cuneiform writing is invented; ancient Mesopotamian traditions about creation and divine-human relationships develop; temples are built to honor gods.	
3000 b.c.e.	The first nation-state forms in Egypt; traditions of creation and divine justice evolve.	
2500 b.c.e.	The Egyptian pyramids are built (First through Third dynasties); a powerful priestly class develops; rituals are encoded to ensure a happy afterlife.	
2500 b.c.e.	Pre-Hindu civilization flourishes in the Indus Valley.	
2330 b.c.e.	Sargon I conquers Mesopotamian city-states and creates the first empire; Sargon supports the worship of Sin, Akkadian moon god, for whom Mount Sinai is named.	
II. Middle Bronze Age (2100–1550 b.c.e.)		
2000–1450 b.c.e.	Minoan civilization flourishes on Crete; worship of goddess figures develops.	
1850–1700 b.c.e.	Nomadic Hebrews roam the Fertile Crescent in the age of biblical patriarchs.	Genesis 12–50
1700 b.c.e.	Hammurabi of Babylon produces a law code endorsed by the sun god Shamash, protector of justice.	
III. Late Bronze Age (1550–1200 b.c.e.)		
1500 b.c.e.	Compilation of Vedic literature begins in India; Stonehenge is built in England.	
1350 b.c.e.	Akhenaton orders the worship of one god, the sun, which briefly establishes the world's first monolatry.	
1250 b.c.e.	Moses leads Israelite slaves from Egypt and establishes the worship of Yahweh at Mount Sinai (formerly sacred to the moon god Sin).	Exodus 13–34
1250–1200 b.c.e.	Mycenaean Greeks besiege Troy in northwestern Turkey, the source event of Homer's *Iliad* and *Odyssey* (written eighth century b.c.e.).	
IV. Iron Age (c. 1200 b.c.e.)		
1200 b.c.e.	Israelite tribes settle in Canaan; Yahwism competes with the worship of Baal and Asherah.	Joshua 1–24; Judges 1–21
1000 b.c.e.	David becomes king of united Israel.	2 Samuel 2–21

(continued)

Table 2.1 *(continued)*

Approximate Date	Event	Biblical Reference
950 B.C.E.	Solomon builds Yahweh's Temple in Jerusalem; a Yahwist writer later composes the earliest account of Israel's history (J document).	1 Kings 3–11
922 B.C.E.	Israel splits into rival kingdoms of Judah (south) and Israel (north).	2 Kings 12–13
860–840 B.C.E.	The prophets Elijah and Elisha denounce Canaanite influences and promote Yahwism alone.	1 Kings 17–22; 2 Kings 9
850–750 B.C.E.	The Greek poets Homer and Hesiod describe forms, qualities, and functions of Greek gods.	
750 B.C.E.	The prophets Amos and Hosea are active in Israel; a northern Israelite storyteller compiles an account of Israelite history (E source).	Amos 1–9; Hosea 1–14
721 B.C.E.	Assyrian armies destroy the northern ten-tribe nation of Israel; the prophet Isaiah is active in Judah.	2 Kings 17–20; Isaiah 36–37; 2 Chronicles 32–34
621 B.C.E.	An early edition of Deuteronomy is discovered in Solomon's Temple; King Josiah's reforms centralize Yahwism in Jerusalem.	2 Kings 22–23
604 B.C.E.	Lao Tzu, founder of Taoism, is born.	
600 B.C.E.	The prophet Zoroaster, founder of the dualistic religion Zoroastrianism, which becomes Persia's state religion, is born; in Judah, the prophet Jeremiah advocates submission to Babylonian dominion.	Jeremiah 1–26
587 B.C.E.	The Babylonians under Nebuchadnezzar destroy Jerusalem, ending the royal Davidic dynasty.	2 Kings 24; Psalms 74, 89
587–538 B.C.E.	Babylonian captivity begins the Jewish Diaspora; in Babylon, Jewish priests begin the final process of compiling the Torah and revising the Deuteronomistic History.	
563–483 B.C.E.	In India, Siddhartha Gautama experiences mystical enlightenment, becoming the Buddha.	
551–479 B.C.E.	In China, Master Kung (Confucius) enunciates a religious philosophy that becomes the basis of the Chinese educational system.	
539 B.C.E. and after	After Cyrus the Great conquers Babylon in 539 B.C.E., the Jewish upper classes return to Jerusalem; the postexilic prophets Haggai and Zechariah urge the rebuilding of the Temple.	Ezra 1–6; Haggai 2
538–330 B.C.E.	Persia rules Judah; the influence of Zoroastrianism promotes a belief in cosmic dualism and angelology.	
515 B.C.E.	A new sanctuary is completed on the site of Solomon's Temple.	
500–400 B.C.E.	The great Hindu epics *Ramayana* and *Mahabharata* are composed.	
445 B.C.E.	Ezra brings an edition of the Torah from Babylon and promulgates reforms in Jerusalem.	Nehemiah 8
336–323 B.C.E.	Alexander the Great conquers most of the known world, bringing Greek culture and ideas to the ancient Near East.	1 Maccabees 1
167–164 B.C.E.	The Greek-Syrian king Antiochus IV attempts to eradicate Judaism; the Maccabean revolt begins; the Book of Daniel, adapting Zoroastrian dualism to Yahwism, predicts the final conflict between cosmic Good and Evil.	2 Maccabees 4; Daniel 1–12
142–63 B.C.E.	Hasmonean (Maccabean) kings rule Judah.	1 Maccabees
63 B.C.E.	Pompey makes Judea part of the Roman Empire.	
27–30 C.E.	Jesus of Nazareth preaches Torah reforms and is executed by the Roman governor Pontius Pilate.	

Table 2.1 (continued)

APPROXIMATE DATE	EVENT	BIBLICAL REFERENCE
30 C.E.	The first Christian community is formed in Jerusalem.	
35–62 C.E.	Paul, a Diaspora Jew who converted to Christianity, founds a series of non-Jewish Christian churches in Syria, Asia Minor, and Greece; he teaches that Gentile converts need not keep Torah ordinances, including circumcision and dietary restrictions.	
66–73 C.E.	The Jews revolt against Rome.	
66–70 C.E.	The first narrative of Jesus' life, the Gospel of Mark, is written.	
70 C.E.	Roman armies destroy Jerusalem and its Temple.	
80–90 C.E.	The Gospels of Matthew and Luke are written.	
90 C.E.	The Rabbinical Council at Jamnia leads the reconstruction of Judaism after the Roman destruction of the Jewish state.	
200 C.E.	The Mishnah, the first part of the Talmud, is compiled.	
313 C.E.	The Roman emperor Constantine issues the Edict of Milan, making Christianity a legally recognized religion.	
500 C.E.	Compilation of the Talmud is complete.	
570–632 C.E.	The Prophet Mohammed dictates the *Qur'an* and founds the religion of Islam.	
632–750 C.E.	Islam spreads rapidly through the Near East and into North Africa and Spain and France.	

Table 2.2 A Tentative Chronology of Tanak (Hebrew Bible) Writings

APPROXIMATE DATE	COMPOSITION
1200–900 B.C.E.	The oldest biblical poetry, such as the Song of Deborah (Judg. 5), Song of Miriam (Exod. 15:21), verses from the Book of Jashar (Josh. 10:13), and other poems hailing Yahweh as warrior (e.g., Num. 21), is orally composed.
950–850 B.C.E.	The first prose narrative of Israel's origins, the Yahwist (J) account, is composed in Judah; J's narrative is preserved in parts of the present editions of Genesis, Exodus, and Numbers. Some J passages may also survive in parts of the Deuteronomistic History (DH). The Court History (2 Sam. 9–24 and 1 Kings 1–2) may also be from J's hand.
950–587 B.C.E.	Royal archives are compiled at the courts of Israel and Judah, sources for the Deuteronomistic account of the monarchy (Samuel through Kings).
850–750 B.C.E.	The Elohist (E) account of Israel's origins is composed in the northern kingdom of Israel. E passages appear in parts of the Torah and (perhaps) DH.
750 B.C.E.	The prophet Amos delivers his message orally; his disciples commit Amos's oracles to writing at an unknown later date.
746–735? B.C.E.	Hosea delivers his oral message in Israel; disciples later compile his words in written form.
740–701 B.C.E.	Isaiah of Jerusalem delivers his prophetic oracles warning of Assyria's threat to Judah; disciples later preserve Isaiah's words in parts of Isaiah 1–39.
740–700 B.C.E.	Micah delivers prophetic oracles that are later recorded and preserved in the Jerusalem Temple (Jer. 26:16–18).
700–621 B.C.E.	The central part of Deuteronomy (Chs. 12–29) is composed.

(continued)

Table 2.2 (continued)

Approximate Date	Composition
630–609 B.C.E.	The prophetic oracles of Zephaniah are compiled.
621 B.C.E.	The prophetess Huldah begins the process of biblical canonization by affirming the authenticity of an early edition of Deuteronomy.
621–609 B.C.E.	The first edition of the Deuteronomistic History (Joshua through 2 Kings), incorporating older poetic and prose documents, is written (perhaps by the scribe Baruch in Jerusalem).
612 B.C.E.	Nahum delivers his oracles on Nineveh's fall.
609–598 B.C.E.	Habukkuk delivers his oracles on the Babylonian threat.
600–587 B.C.E.	Some prophetic oracles of Jeremiah are recorded by his secretary Baruch.
587 B.C.E.	Obadiah denounces Edom's part in Babylon's devastation of Judah and Jerusalem.
580 B.C.E.	Ezekiel's visions in the Babylonian captivity are recorded; Baruch compiles more of Jeremiah's oracles, adding biographical material.
550–500 B.C.E.	Collections of legal and ritual material by priestly writer(s) are inserted into JE narratives and preserved in parts of Exodus, Leviticus, and Numbers.
540s B.C.E.	Second Isaiah delivers oracles of hope in Babylon, which are recorded later in Isaiah 40–55.
520 B.C.E.	Postexilic prophets Haggai and Zechariah encourage rebuilding of Jerusalem Temple.
500 B.C.E.	Deuteronomistic and priestly reediting of older documents continues in postexilic Jerusalem.
500–450 B.C.E.	Third Isaiah delivers oracles that are later incorporated into Isaiah 56–66.
500–400 B.C.E.	The poetic dialogues in Job are composed and inserted into the framework of an old prose tale.
500–300 B.C.E.	Additional psalms are composed and used in worship at the Second Temple.
490–400 B.C.E.	The prophetic books of Malachi, Joel, and Jonah are compiled; an old folktale is rewritten, creating the Book of Ruth.
450–400 B.C.E.	Priestly editor(s) complete the revision of legal material in Exodus, Leviticus, Numbers, and Deuteronomy; Ezra returns from Babylon to Jerusalem with a revised edition of the Torah.
400 B.C.E.	The Book of Proverbs is compiled.
400–300 B.C.E.	The process of canonization of the Torah is completed; the Book of Esther is composed; disciples of a Jerusalem sage compile the Book of Ecclesiastes; the books of Chronicles and Ezra-Nehemiah are written.
250 B.C.E.	The Torah is translated into Greek, forming the first part of the Septuagint Bible.
200–100 B.C.E.	Collections of the prophets are canonized.
165 B.C.E.	The Book of Daniel is composed.
90–100 C.E.	Jewish scholars at the Academy of Jamnia preside over the compilation of the biblical texts, completing the final part of the Hebrew Bible.

Established in about 7200 B.C.E., Ain Ghazal was inhabited continuously for about 2000 years. At its height, the town covered thirty acres, about ten times the size of contemporaneous Jericho.

The contours of the biblical world are broadly outlined by the journeys of Abraham, whom Genesis depicts as the primary ancestor of Israel. According to Genesis, Abraham is born in Ur, one of the oldest cities of southern Mesopotamia, later moving to **Haran** in Syria. Following a divine sum-

mons, he and his family subsequently travel from northwest Mesopotamia through Canaan to Egypt and back again, their itinerary encompassing virtually the entire geographical region in which the biblical drama is staged. The tradition placing Israel's ultimate origins in Mesopotamia is significant, for much of the Hebrew Bible reflects Mesopotamian views about the nature and structure of the cosmos and the interrelationship of gods and mortals. Centuries of political domination by

Mesopotamian powers such as Assyria and Babylon climaxed in 587 B.C.E. when the covenant people were exiled in Babylon. Prolonged exposure to Babylonian cultural traditions, scholars believe, resulted in a strong Mesopotamian flavor to many biblical narratives, including the first eleven chapters of Genesis (see Chapter 4). (For an outline of major historical events, see Table 2.1 on p. 45. For a chronology of the Hebrew Bible, see Table 2.2 on p. 47.)

Mesopotamia, Site of the World's First Urban Civilization

Mesopotamia—the "land between the rivers"—is the name the Greeks assigned to a region at the head of the Persian Gulf in what is now southern Iraq. In this flat, swampy area near the mouths of the **Tigris** and **Euphrates** rivers, the world's first urban civilization was born. Shortly after 3500 B.C.E., a people called the **Sumerians** founded the earliest cities, such as **Ur**, Abraham's birthplace, and **Uruk**, home to King **Gilgamesh**, the first hero of Western literature (Figure 2.2). A remarkably innovative people, the Sumerians constructed elaborate irrigation systems, erected monumental temples to their gods, and devised the first law codes to protect property and foster social order. By inventing the wheel (fourth millennium B.C.E.),

they facilitated travel, trade, and economic prosperity (Figures 2.3 and 2.4). At an early date, Sumerian merchants exported goods to Egypt, which was simultaneously evolving a highly sophisticated civilization in northeast Africa.

In about 3200 B.C.E., the Sumerians devised a system of writing—known as **cuneiform**—that used wedge-shaped symbols inscribed with a metal stylus on clay tables. When dried or baked, these inscribed clay tablets proved almost indestructible, surviving to the present in the tens of thousands (Figure 2.5). Although cuneiform was invented primarily to record tax lists, inventories, and other business transactions, it was also used to record topics ranging from magical formulas to mythical tales about gods and heroes. Some cuneiform literature anticipates themes found in the Hebrew Bible, including traditions about the world's creation from a watery chaos and a devastating prehistoric flood.

Sumer's lasting contribution to subsequent cultures ranges from religion and literature to mathematics and architecture. Fashioning a numerical system based on sixty, symbol of the sky god **Anu**, head of their pantheon, the Sumerians introduced the practice of dividing the hour into sixty minutes and the circle into 360 degrees. Although less well known today than Egypt's pyramids, Sumerian building enterprises were no less impressive. Because the alluvial plain they occupied lacked the granite and limestone used by Egyptian builders, the Sumerians mass-produced clay bricks, typically

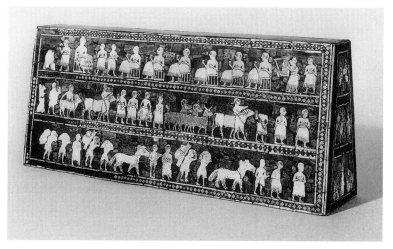

Figure 2.2 In the 1920s, archaeologists found remarkable works of art in the royal tombs of Ur's Third Dynasty (c. 2060–1950 B.C.E.), including this Standard of Ur, a decorative mosaic of inlaid shell and lapis lazuli. The bottom scene depicts men and animals carrying goods, perhaps from a military victory that the seated figures (top level) are celebrating. Note the musician entertaining the banqueters (top right).

Figure 2.3 The wealth and elegance of Ur's Third Dynasty are reflected in this splendid gold headdress found in Lady PuAbi's tomb, which Sir Leonard Woolley excavated in the 1920s.

Figure 2.4 Fashioned of limestone, this Sumerian figurine dates from about 2500 B.C.E. The shaved head and long flounced tunic were typically Sumerian styles of dress.

baked and glazed, with which they constructed massive walls around their cities, which also featured large temple complexes honoring the city's patron deity. Their most distinctive architectural form was the **ziggurat**, a towering, multitiered edifice that typically dominated the city's skyline (Figure 2.6). At the top level stood a chapel or shrine believed to house the divinity, such as Anu, to whom the building was dedicated. With broad staircases connecting its several levels, the ziggurat functioned like the spire of a Christian cathedral, a visible link symbolically connecting humans on earth with invisible deities inhabiting the sky.

The importance of the ziggurat, and the sacred urban site on which it stood, is expressed in Mesopotamian place names. *Babylon*, which eventually became the region's greatest city, means "the gate of the god," indicating its status as the holy place

of **Marduk**, creator of the universe and king of the gods. The significance of Marduk's Babylonian ziggurat is also suggested by its name, *Etemenanki,* "the house that is the foundation of heaven and earth."

When Jacob, Abraham's grandson, dreams of a vast staircase or "ladder" on which supernatural beings ascend to or descend from heaven, his vision conveys the ziggurat's religious function, providing a sacred zone at which the divine and human realms can intersect. Setting up a stone pillar to commemorate his glimpse of the spirit world, Jacob exclaims that Bethel, the "House of God" where he slept and communicated with Yahweh, is nothing less than "the gate of heaven" (Gen. 28:10–19), his personal Babylon. Jacob's percep-

Figure 2.5 One of the oldest—and most durable—documents of world history, this clay prism records a cuneiform list of Sumerian kings "from the time that kingship was lowered [to human society] from heaven." Probably derived from a Sumerian original composed about 2100 B.C.E., the purpose of this compilation was to demonstrate that the gods selected one city—Uruk, Ur, or another—to rule successively over its Mesopotamian neighbors. These citations of the lengths of each king's reign anticipate the genealogies of Genesis and the Israelite dynastic records of Kings and Chronicles.

tion of a ziggurat's transcendent purpose reveals a more plausible understanding of Mesopotamian religion than the equally famous story of the Tower of Babel in Genesis 11. In the Babel episode, the author represents humanity's prideful attempt to erect a structure high enough to "reach heaven" as an offense against Yahweh. Accordingly, Yahweh thwarts human ambition by overthrowing the ziggurat, scattering its builders abroad, and confusing their languages. Although this tale explains why earth's inhabitants are divided by both geographical distance and language barriers, some

commentators believe that it distorts the Mesopotamians' reasons for constructing their sacred towers.

THE AKKADIAN INVASION AND FORMATION OF THE FIRST EMPIRE

In about 2500 B.C.E., Sumer was invaded by a Semitic people known as the **Akkadians**. Assimilating the older Sumerian culture, including its cuneiform script, which they adapted to transcribe their own language, the Akkadians established the world's first empire. **Sargon I** of Akkad (c. 2334–2279 B.C.E.) rose from obscurity to become the earliest ruler to forge a union of previously independent city-states. After conquering Ur, he appointed his daughter as high priestess of the Akkadian moon god **Sin**. For the next 1800 years, Mesopotamian rulers followed Sargon's lead by appointing their daughters to officiate at the moon god's temple. According to many scholars, Sinai, the mountain where Moses encounters Yahweh, takes its name from Sin, the Akkadian lunar deity.

Sargon's most celebrated successor, his grandson **Naram-Sin**, proclaimed himself "king of the four quarters of the earth," indicating that he may have extended his rule over most of Mesopotamia (Figure 2.7). Among Naram-Sin's many exploits was his destruction of **Ebla**, a major city in northern Syria. In 1975, archaeologists excavated Ebla's royal archives, uncovering an extensive library written in cuneiform. Dating to the twenty-third century B.C.E., Ebla's collections of hymns, proverbs, myths, and rituals offer a fascinating glimpse into a highly sophisticated northwest Mesopotamian culture that flourished several centuries before Abraham. Shortly after Ebla's discovery, a few scholars made sweeping claims about its supposed connection to the Hebrew Bible. One proposed that Ebla's pantheon included a god named Ya, an abbreviated form of Yahweh, and that a king called Ebrum may have been a forefather of Abraham. The majority of scholars, however, have since rejected such assertions as premature and unverifiable. Although further study is necessary before Ebla's possible relevance to biblical traditions is understood, some early findings may be significant:

Figure 2.6 The Sumerians built the world's first skyscrapers, towers of sunbaked bricks known as ziggurats. In this artist's reconstruction of the ancient ziggurat at Ur, the chapel to Nanna, god of the moon, (predecessor of the Akkadian Sin) crowns the temple structure. These artificial mountains served as pedestals to which heavenly beings could descend to earth, treading the sacred stairways linking the human and divine worlds. Jacob's dream at Bethel (Gen. 28:2–11) envisions a similar "gateway to heaven."

One personal name appearing in the documents— *Ishra-il*—seems too similar to *Israel* to be merely coincidental. Genesis states that Jacob had his name changed to Israel after wrestling with a mysterious nocturnal visitor at Peniel. The Ebla text suggests, however, that the name existed long before it was bestowed on the progenitor of Israel's twelve tribes.

After dominating Mesopotamia for two centuries, Sargon's empire fell to a new invader, the **Amorites** (or "Westerners"), who swept through many parts of the Fertile Crescent. Merely raiding and looting in some areas, the Amorites settled in others, building new towns in northern and western Canaan. They also founded or greatly expanded two important city-states in Mesopotamia—**Mari** on the middle Euphrates and **Babylon** on the river's southern segment. Located near the modern border of Syria and Iraq, the Mari site has yielded more than 20,000 clay tablets approximately 4000 years old. Some of these cuneiform texts appear to contain information about Bronze Age social customs that would provide valuable background for the Genesis stories about Abraham, Isaac, and Jacob. A similar literary find at Nuzi on the upper Tigris River promised to illuminate legal and marital practices of the mid-second

millennium B.C.E., a period shortly after the traditional dates for the patriarchal age. Despite alleged parallels to the domestic arrangements of Abraham and Sarah or Jacob and his family, however, continued study of the Nuzi tablets suggests that the social mores they reflect are not those of the Genesis narratives. Although archaeologists can uncover material remains of vanished civilizations presumably contemporaneous with biblical characters and events, they have not been able to verify the historicity of Israel's ancestors.

THE EPIC OF GILGAMESH

In addition to innumerable legal and commercial documents, archaeologists have also discovered important works of Mesopotamian literature that contain many similarities to passages in the Hebrew Bible. During the mid-nineteenth century C.E., archaeologists uncovered the cuneiform library of the Assyrian emperor **Ashurbanipal IV** (668–627 B.C.E.). Ashurbanipal was one of the last powerful rulers of imperial **Assyria**, a war-like nation that dominated the Near East from the eleventh to the seventh centuries B.C.E. In the ruins of Ashurbanipal's palace at **Nineveh**, capital of the

Figure 2.7 In this stele commemorating a victory of Naram-Sin, grandson of the Akkadian empire-builder Sargon I, the king ascends a mountain whose peak reaches into heaven, while his enemies are crushed beneath his feet. During Naram-Sin's thirty-seven-year reign in the twenty-third century B.C.E., the Akkadian Empire reached its height.

edited the work had inserted into the hero's adventures a long narrative about a global deluge. Apparently borrowed from a previously independent flood myth featuring **Atrahasis**, another Akkadian hero, the Gilgamesh version of the deluge contains remarkably close parallels to the account in Genesis 6–8, in which Yahweh drowns the world's entire population except for a single family (see Box 2.1., cf. Box 4.1). Discovery of the Gilgamesh flood story made scholars aware, for the first time, that the Genesis authors had drawn on an older Mesopotamian tradition in composing the biblical text. Widely disseminated throughout the ancient Near East, tablets containing all or parts of the epic have been found in innumerable ancient libraries, including one at the Hittite capital in central Asia Minor. Gilgamesh's adventures were read even in Israel; a fragment was recovered at Megiddo in lower Galilee, and the hero is mentioned by name in the Dead Sea Scrolls, documents dating from about 250 B.C.E. to 68 C.E.

Gilgamesh's story has two distinct parts. In the first, he strongly bonds with a wild man, Enkidu, whom the gods created out of clay to be his life-partner. After the two friends slay such monsters as the fiery Humbaba and the ferocious "bull of heaven," a personification of drought and earthquake, Gilgamesh commits a grave offense by rejecting the sexual advances of **Ishtar**, goddess of love and war and divine patron of his city, Uruk. After Ishtar persuades the heavenly council to punish Gilgamesh by afflicting Enkidu with a fatal disease, Gilgamesh, overwhelmed by grief and terrified by his first personal encounter with death, experiences a crisis that changes his life. He determines, through sheer strength of will, to find a way to escape human mortality.

In the epic's second part, Gilgamesh leaves Uruk, embarking on a long and dangerous quest to find everlasting life. Abandoning the known world, he crosses the "waters of death" and journeys through a region of total darkness to find the remote island dwelling of his ancestor, **Utnapishtim**. Like the later figure of Noah, Utnapishtim is the only man to survive a great prehistoric flood and the only one to whom the gods have granted immortality. After enduring superhuman hardship,

Assyrian Empire, excavators found a large collection of ancient literary documents, including the most complete extant copy of the *Epic of Gilgamesh*. Although the Sumerians had composed stories about Gilgamesh, a legendary ruler of Uruk, as early as the second millennium B.C.E., the Akkadian version found in Ashurbanipal's royal library has greater significance to biblical scholars. On the eleventh of twelve tablets on which the poem is inscribed, the Akkadian scribes who translated and

Box 2.1 Excerpts from the Mesopotamian Flood Story in the Gilgamesh Epic

Living on a floodplain bordering the Euphrates and Tigris rivers, the ancient inhabitants of Mesopotamia repeatedly experienced severe floods, some of which destroyed early centers of civilization. Two Mesopotamian poems, the epics of Gilgamesh and Atrahasis, render ancient flood traditions in terms of a single catastrophic event that wipes out all of humanity, except for a single patriarch who survives by building an ark. In the Sumero-Babylonian epic of Gilgamesh, the title hero, seeking everlasting life, visits his ancestor Utnapishtim, the only man to survive the global deluge. Utnapishtim tells Gilgamesh that long ago, when the gods, led by Enlil, deity of storm and wind, determined to drown all humanity, Ea, the kindly god of wisdom, warned Utnapishtim of the coming disaster. Like the biblical Noah, Utnapishtim is ordered to construct a wooden ark, stock it with supplies, and take aboard animals and birds.

> Utnapishtim spoke to him, to Gilgamesh,
> Let me reveal to you a closely guarded matter,
>   Gilgamesh,
> And let me tell you the secret of the gods.
> Shuruppak is a city that you yourself know,
> Situated [on the bank of] the Euphrates.
> That city was already old when the gods within it
> Decided that the great gods should make a flood.
> There was Anu their father,
> Warrior Ellil their counsellor . . .
> Far-sighted Ea swore the oath (of secrecy) with
>   them,
> So he repeated their speech to a reed hut,
> "Reed hut, reed hut, brick wall, brick wall,
> Listen, reed hut, and pay attention, brick wall.
> (This is the message:)
> Man of Shuruppak, son of Ubara-Tutu,
> Dismantle your house, build a boat.
> Leave possessions, search out living things.

> Reject chattels and save lives!
> Put aboard the seed of all living things, into the
>   boat.
> The boat that you are to build
> Shall have her dimensions in proportion,
> Her width and length shall be in harmony,
> Roof her like the Apsu."
> I realized and spoke to my master Ea,
> "I have paid attention to the words that you spoke
>   in this way,
> My master, and I shall act upon them.
> But how can I explain myself to the city, the men
>   and the elders?"
> Ea made his voice heard and spoke,
> He said to me, his servant,
> "You shall speak to them thus:
> "I think that Ellil [Enlil] has rejected me,
> And so I cannot stay in your city,
> And I cannot set foot on Ellil's land again.
> I must go down to the Apsu and stay with my
>   master Ea . . ."
> I put on board the boat all my kith and kin.
> Put on board cattle from open country, wild
>   beasts from open country, all kinds of
>   craftsmen.
> Shāmash had fixed the hour:
> In the morning cakes/"darkness",
> In the evening a rain of wheat/"heaviness"
> (I) shall shower down:
> Enter into the boat and shut your door!"
> That hour arrived;
> In the morning cakes/"darkness," in the evening a
>   rain of wheat/"heaviness" showered down.
> I saw the shape of the storm,
> The storm was terrifying to see.
> I went aboard the boat and closed the door.
> To seal the boat I handed over the (floating) palace
>   with her cargo to Puzur-Amurru the
>   boatman. . . .

Gilgamesh arrives exhausted at Utnapishtim's "faraway" paradise. Scoffing at his descendant's ambition to live forever, Utnapishtim reminds Gilgamesh that his host's possession of eternal life stems from unique, unrepeatable circumstances: being selected by the wise divinity **Ea** to build an ark, take aboard pairs of animals, and thus survive a watery cataclysm that engulfs the rest of humanity (an abridged translation of the Gilgamesh flood story appears in Box 2.1). In pity at Gilgamesh's despair, Utnapishtim's wife persuades her husband to reveal that a plant capable of miraculously re-

Box 2.1 (continued)

[Storm gods bring the Flood, returning the world
    to a dark watery chaos.]
Everything light turned to darkness.
On the first day the tempest [rose up],
Blew swiftly and [brought (?) the flood-weapon],
Like a battle force [the destructive *kašūšu*-weapon]
    passed over [the people]
No man could see his fellow,
Nor could people be distinguished from the sky.
Even the gods were afraid of the flood-weapon.
They withdrew; they went up to the heaven of Anu.
The gods cowered, like dogs crouched by an out-
    side wall.
Ishtar screamed like a woman giving birth;
The Mistress of the Gods, sweet of voice, was
    wailing,
"Has that time really returned to clay,
Because I spoke evil in the gods' assembly?
How could I have spoken such evil in the gods' as-
    sembly?
I should have (?) ordered a battle to destroy my
    people;
I myself gave birth (to them), they are my own
    people,
Yet they fill the sea like fish spawn!"
The gods of the Anunnaki were weeping with her.
The gods, humbled, sat there weeping.
Their lips were closed and covered with scab.
For six days and [seven (?)] nights
The wind blew, flood and tempest overwhelmed
    the land;
When the seventh day arrived the tempest, flood
    and onslaught
Which had struggled like a woman in labour, blew
    themselves out (?).
The sea became calm, the *imhullu*-wind grew
    quiet, the flood held back.
I looked at the weather; silence reigned,
For all mankind had returned to clay.
The flood-plain was flat as a roof.

I opened a porthole and light fell on my cheeks.
I bent down, then sat. I wept.
My tears ran down my cheeks.
I looked for banks, for limits to the sea.
Areas of land were emerging everywhere (?).
The boat had come to rest on Mount Nimush.
The mountain Nimush held the boat fast and did
    not let it budge. . . .
When the seventh day arrived,
I put out and released a dove.
The dove went; it came back,
For no perching place was visible to it, and it
    turned round.
I put out and released a swallow.
The swallow went; it came back,
For no perching place was visible to it, and it
    turned round.
I put out and released a raven.
The raven went, and saw the waters receding.
And it ate, preened (?), lifted its tail and did not
    turn round.
Then I put (everything ?) out to the four winds,
    and I made a sacrifice. . . .
The gods smelt the fragrance,
The gods smelt the pleasant fragrance,
The gods like flies gathered over the sacrifice.
As soon as the Mistress of the Gods arrived
She raised the great flies which Anu had made to
    please her:
"Behold, O gods, I shall never forget (the
    significance of) my lapis lazuli necklace,
I shall remember these times, and I shall never
    forget.
[As in Genesis, the rainbow (Ishtar's jeweled neck-
    lace) serves to remind the gods of the con-
    sequences of their destructive impulses.]

storing youth grows at the bottom of the sea. After risking his life to obtain the rejuvenating plant, Gilgamesh begins his perilous return to Uruk, only to have the plant stolen from him and eaten by a snake. Ironically, the serpent is thus able to shed its skin, apparently renewing its life, whereas mortal humans tragically lack the ability to recapture lost youth.

On his journey to Utnapishtim, Gilgamesh meets Siduri, a wise barmaid and minor goddess, who tells him that he will never find the everlasting life he seeks, reminding him that the gods reserve it exclusively for themselves. Instead of wearing himself out trying to be a god, she advises him to accept the ordinary consolations of humanity's mortal state:

> As for you, Gilgamesh, fill your belly with good things; day and night, night and day, dance and be merry, feast and rejoice. Let your clothes be fresh, bathe yourself in water, cherish the little child that holds your hand, and make your wife happy in your embrace; for this too is the lot of man.
>
> *Epic of Gilgamesh*

Siduri's advice is echoed almost exactly in the biblical Ecclesiastes, where the author deplores the unacceptable fact that all human effort ends in death. Life's only comfort lies in the enjoyment of commonplace pleasures that God concedes to mortals:

> Go, eat your bread with joy and drink your wine with a glad heart; for what you do God has approved beforehand. Wear white [the garment of festivity] all the time, do not stint your head of oil. Spend your life with the woman you love, through all the fleeting days of the life God has given you under the sun.
>
> Eccles. 9:7–9

Ecclesiastes' emphasis on human mortality reflects the Bible's general agreement with ancient Mesopotamian beliefs about the gods' prerogatives: Humans do not share their immortality. In Genesis 3, Yahweh posts a cherub wielding a fiery sword to keep the first humans from eating of the "tree of life" that grows in Eden, the "garden of God." Humanity is barred from tasting the tree's fruit, lest they imitate divinity and "live forever" (Gen. 3:22–24).

THE LAW CODE OF HAMMURABI

The city of Babylon, which plays a pivotal role in biblical history, first achieved prominence when the Amorites founded a dynasty there. In the reign of **Hammurabi** (also spelled "Hammurapi"), sixth king in the Amorite line, the city became the center of a new Mesopotamian empire. Uniting all Mesopotamian city-states under his rule, Hammurabi created a broad dominion that rivaled that of Sargon I. Because of the enormous difficulties in

establishing a definitive chronology for events in the remote past, historians do not agree on Hammurabi's dates. Many scholars place his forty-two-year reign between 1792 and 1750 B.C.E., but another widely accepted chronology gives his dates as 1728 to 1686 B.C.E. An effective general and capable administrator, Hammurabi is best remembered for a code of law published later in his reign. Divided into 282 separate units by modern scholars, the **Code of Hammurabi** is inscribed on a solid **stele** of black diorite nearly eight feet tall (Figure 2.8). Originally erected for public reading in the Babylonian city of Sippar, the block was later carried off by Elamites to Susa, where archaeologists found it more than 3000 years later. At the top of the diorite column, a sculptor carved a bas-relief portrait of Hammurabi receiving the laws from the sun god **Shamash**, exactly as Moses is later represented as receiving the Torah from Yahweh at Mount Sinai (Figure 2.9).

Hammurabi's laws are expressed in the same literary structure and, in some instances, have the same content as Mosaic decrees. Both the Hammurabic and Mosaic legal formats employ the casuistic form: If such and such happens, then such and such will be the punishment. Part of the Mosaic legislation is also codified in a manner resembling the older Babylonian model, as in the section of Exodus known as the Book of the Covenant (Exod. 20:22–23, 33; 24:7). Babylonian, Egyptian, and Israelite traditions commonly reflect similar concepts of justice, including protection of society's poor and powerless members. Both the Hammurabic and Mosaic laws refer specifically to "widows and orphans" as representing a class of people who need to be shielded from exploitation.

Hammurabi declares that his purpose is to "promote the welfare of the people, . . . to cause justice to prevail in the land, to destroy the wicked and the evil, that the strong might not oppress the weak." As in earlier Mesopotamian law codes, however, Hammurabi's system did not offer equal protection to people belonging to different classes. In general, the nobility fared far better than the social classes beneath them: Whereas an aristocrat was allowed to pay a fine for manslaughter, a slave was automatically condemned to death. Merely injuring a person who stood higher in the social hier-

Figure 2.8 The legacy of Babylon's first important king, the Stele of Hammurabi — a basalt slab nearly eight feet tall — records an ancient Sumero-Babylonian legal code that contains statutes resembling laws found in the Mosaic Torah. Erected in the eighteenth century B.C.E., it reflects legal principles common to ancient Mesopotamia, the original home of the Israelite ancestors.

archy brought more severe penalties than would murdering a slave.

Both Mesopotamian and Mosaic laws levied the death penalty for numerous offenses, and both allowed physical mutilation of the condemned. Under Hammurabi, if a nobleman injured a social equal, he was to suffer an equivalent maiming:

> If a seignior [nobleman] has destroyed the eye of a member of the aristocracy, they shall destroy his eye.
> If he has broken another seignior's bone, they shall break his bone. . . .
> If a seignior has knocked out the tooth of a seignior of his own rank, they shall knock out his own tooth.
>   Code of Hammurabi, Sections 196, 197, 200

Using the same examples found in Hammurabi's code, the Mosaic Torah perpetuated the ancient Near Eastern demand for exact retaliation:

> If a man injures his neighbor, what he has done must be done to him: broken limb for broken limb, eye for eye, tooth for tooth. As the injury inflicted, so must the injury be suffered.
>   Lev. 24:19–20

Judges and executioners are to "show no pity" (Deut. 19:21) in enforcing the biblical *lex talionis*, the law of retaliation. This principle of inflicting precisely the same kind of injury that had been inflicted on a victim was central to the Israelite sense of justice. Biblical writers considered the *lex talionis* so important that they proclaimed it in three of the five books of Torah (Exod. 21:23–25; Lev. 24:19–21; Deut. 19:21).

In both the Mosaic and Hammurabic codes, the *lex talionis* serves to limit the degree of vengeance to which a wronged party is legally entitled: injured persons may not take an aggressor's life; they are restricted to inflicting wounds precisely equivalent to those they had received. Both codes agree,

Figure 2.9 In the ancient Near East, law codes — which kings and other leaders imposed on their people — were commonly ascribed to the nation's gods. In this scene at the top of the Stele of Hammurabi, Hammurabi (with hands clasped reverently) receives legal commands from the enthroned sun god, Shamash, just as Moses is represented as receiving Torah laws from Yahweh many centuries later.

however, that upper-class offenders may escape physical punishment by paying for injuries inflicted on social inferiors. According to Babylonian law, a nobleman who blinds or knocks out the tooth of a commoner must pay a fine; if he seriously harms another nobleman's slave, he must pay one-half of the slave's value (Hammurabi, Sections 199, 201, etc.).

While making similar distinctions between persons of differenet social rank, however, the Mosaic code introduces a more humane element: A master who injures his slave must set that slave free:

> When a man strikes the eye of his slave, male or female, and destroys the use of it, he must give him his freedom to compensate for the eye. If he knocks out the tooth of his slave, male or female, he must give him freedom to compensate for the tooth.
>
> Exod. 21:26–27

Although slaves are regarded as physical property throughout the ancient Near East, the biblical provision is innovative in recognizing slaves' humanity and granting the right to freedom in compensation for injury.

Egypt, the First National State

The name ***Egypt*** derives from *Aiguptos,* the Greek version of *Hut-Ptah,* the "Temple of Ptah," the term by which the Egyptians identified their country. The "temple," or holy dwelling place of Ptah, the Egyptian creator god, was the strip of fertile land bordering the Nile River. Beyond this narrow cultivated zone, watered by annual inundations of the Nile, stretched vast, inhospitable deserts that effectively isolated Egypt from its neighbors. Whereas the broad plains of Mesopotamia were easily—and frequently—invaded by foreign armies, Egypt's unique geographical features allowed it to develop independently of most foreign influences. Bordered on the east and west by arid wastes and on the south by a rugged terrain through which the Nile flowed in impassable cataracts, ancient Egypt enjoyed an uninterrupted period of stability and nation building.

FROM KINGDOM TO EMPIRE

Beginning as a coalition of small political districts called *nomes,* Egypt first evolved into two distinct kingdoms, known as Upper Egypt and Lower Egypt. In about 3100 B.C.E., the two kingdoms were merged under the rule of Narmer, king of Upper (southern) Egypt. From this point on, Egyptian pharaohs wore a headdress combining the white crown of Upper Egypt with the red crown of Lower Egypt.

Historians divide subsequent ancient Egyptian history into three major periods: the Old Kingdom, or Pyramid Age (Third to Sixth Pharaonic Dynasties, c. 2686–2160 B.C.E.); the Middle Kingdom, or Feudal Age (the Eleventh and Twelfth Dynasties, c. 2030–1720 B.C.E.); and the New

Kingdom, or Empire (the Eighteenth to Twentieth Dynasties, c. 1570–1075 B.C.E.). Under the Empire, New Kingdom pharaohs such as Thutmose I extended Egypt's dominion northeastward into Canaan. In about 1490 B.C.E., Egyptian forces defeated a coalition of more than one hundred rulers of Syrian and Canaanite city-states at the Battle of **Megiddo**, a site that in later history marked several decisive Israelite defeats. (Apparently regarded as of crucial significance in biblical history, sixteen centuries later Megiddo lent its name—*Har-Megiddo* [Armageddon]—to identify the place where cosmic Good and Evil would fight their ultimate battle [Rev. 16:16].) Until near the end of the New Kingdom, Egypt maintained a line of military fortresses in Canaan, guarding against unwanted incursions from Mesopotamia or Asia Minor.

EGYPT'S ENDURING LEGACY

The Egyptian system of writing in pictorial characters—**hieroglyphics**—developed at about the same time as, or shortly after, the invention of cuneiform script in Mesopotamia. The Egyptians also made spectacular advances in mathematics and astronomy, devising a calendar based on the solar year of 365 days. This calendar featured twelve months of thirty days each, to which five festival days were added to round out the year. The familiar practice of dividing the day into twenty-four hours and beginning a new day at midnight is also a legacy from ancient Egypt.

Egypt's numerous gifts to the modern world include the science of geometry. Devising methods to compute the areas and volumes of abstract geometric forms, Egyptian architects applied these skills to build the world's first large-scale structures in stone. An edifice of massive grandeur, the multitiered Step Pyramid was constructed for King Zoser (Djoser) about 2650 B.C.E. Erected shortly afterward, the enormous pyramids at Giza still tower hundreds of feet above the Nile valley, the sole survivors of the ancient world's Seven Wonders.

Egypt's great pyramids and colossal sphinx at al-Jizah were already many centuries old when Abraham's grandson Jacob and his eleven sons, driven by famine in Canaan, sought refuge in the prosperous Nile region. Because the Nile supplied Egypt's extensive irrigation system even in many drought years when crops in neighboring areas failed, Ptah's land attracted many nomadic peoples hoping to secure Egyptian grain. According to Genesis, Israel's ancestors—the tribes of Jacob (Israel)—were among many who settled temporarily in the delta region.

One popular theory holds that Semitic nomads were welcome in Egypt at the time Israelite tribes entered because Egypt was then ruled by foreigners known as the **Hyksos**. Although native Egyptian control of the country was rarely surrendered, in the seventeenth century B.C.E. the Semitic Hyksos infiltrated the population, eventually usurping pharaoh's throne. In 1560 B.C.E., an Egyptian revolt expelled the Hyksos rulers and established the Eighteenth Dynasty (see Chapter 4). This native royal line included some of Egypt's most famous rulers, including Queen Hatshepsut, the great military strategist Thutmose III, and Amenhotep IV.

Amenhotep IV, who changed his name to **Akhenaton** (1364–1347 B.C.E.), scandalized the Egyptian priesthood by ordering that only a single deity, the sun god **Aton** (Aten), be universally acknowledged. Whereas some historians believe that Akhenaton established the world's first monotheism, many think that his cult of Aton was really an example of **monolatry**—worship of a single god while conceding the existence of other deities. Although Akhenaton's religious experiment was brief—his youthful successor Tutankhamen revoked his reforms—it may have set a precedent that indirectly influenced Moses' concept of Yahweh's "jealousy." The revolutionary belief that a single god could require his devotees to honor no other gods is the cornerstone of the Mosaic religion.

Correspondence preserved in the ruined archives of Tell el-Amarna, the site to which Akhenaton moved his capital, gives a vivid picture of Egypt during the dominion of Aton. The **Amarna Age**, the period of Akhenaton's reign, and the exclusive cult of the sun were largely forgotten by 1306 B.C.E., when Rameses I founded a new royal dynasty, the nineteenth. Under Rameses II (1290–1224 B.C.E.), the Egyptian Empire reached its zenith in prosperity and prestige. Many historians

Figure 2.10 This granite statue of Rameses II (1290–1224 B.C.E.) only hints at the Egyptian ruler's enormous power. Appearing deceptively mild, Rameses wears the distinctive royal headdress and holds the scepter symbolizing his absolute control of the state. Many historians believe that Rameses II was the unnamed pharaoh of the Exodus.

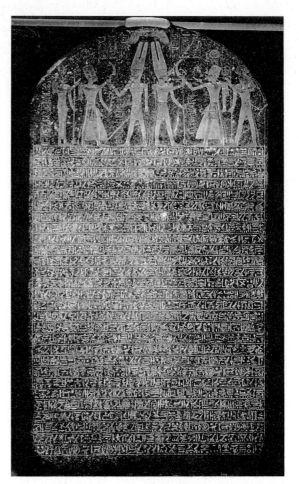

Figure 2.11 The Stele of Merneptah (c. 1224–1211 B.C.E.), son of and successor to Rameses II, contains the first extrabiblical reference to Israel's existence. Advertising his victories over various Canaanite states, Merneptah claims that he has so devastated Israel that its "seed [offspring] is not," a conventional military boast. A double figure of the god Amon appears at the top center, with Pharaoh Merneptah (also in double representation) standing on either side of the deity.

believe that **Rameses II**, a vigorous—and vainglorious—leader was the pharaoh of the Exodus (Figure 2.10). Rameses made a habit of recording his military defeats, as well as his genuine victories, as complete triumphs. If a band of Hebrew slaves did escape from Egypt during his long reign, it is not surprising that court scribes did not see fit to mention it.

The earliest known reference to Israel as a distinct people appears on a victory inscription of **Merneptah**, Rameses II's son and successor (Fig-

ure 2.11). Merneptah boasts of his conquests in Canaan, claiming to have laid Israel waste, indicating that the Israelites were already established in Canaan shortly after 1220 B.C.E., the approximate time of Merneptah's campaign. (See Box 2.2.)

One of the most important finds of modern archaeology is the justly famous **Rosetta Stone**, a large, flat slab of basalt inscribed with the same message in three different scripts—Greek, hiero-

Box 2.2 Some Non-Israelite Inscriptions Referring to Israel or Judah

Although characters such as Abraham and Moses and events such as the Exodus from Egypt loom large in the Hebrew Bible, we have no extrabiblical confirmation of their historical reality. The earliest extrabiblical reference to Israel's existence—Pharaoh Merneptah's inscription commemorating Egyptian victories in Canaan—dates to the late thirteenth century B.C.E. After Merneptah's inscription, which indicates that Israel was then an identifiable people, there is a gap of several centuries before another inscription mentions Israel. It is not until the ninth century B.C.E. that an imperfectly preserved inscription found at Tel Dan seems to allude to the "house of David," as does a stele erected by Mesha (c. 849–820 B.C.E.), king of **Moab**, a small state bordering Israel. For the entire time span from the Exodus through the conquest of Canaan, the period of the Judges, and the rise of the kingdom of David, the archaeological record is largely silent. Because we have only the biblical account of Israel's growth into a powerful political state in the tenth century B.C.E., a few scholars question the historicity of the Davidic kingdom, regarding it as a postexilic glorification of

Israel's distant past. While acknowledging the theological bias of biblical historians, however, the majority of scholars still accept the historicity of a united kingdom under David and Solomon.

Although relatively sparse, we have more extrabiblical data for the period of the divided kingdom, when Israel and Judah were separate nations. Omri, one of Israel's most militarily successful rulers, is mentioned in several ninth- and eighth-century B.C.E. inscriptions, including those of Mesha and the Assyrian emperors Tiglath-Pileser III and Sargon II. Assyrian archives also refer to several other Israelite kings, most of whom paid heavy tribute to their Assyrian overlords, including Jehu, Menahem, Pekah, and Hoshea.

Assyria also forced the tiny southern kingdom of Judah to pay over a large part of its income. Royal annals record that kings Uzziah, Ahaz, and Hezekiah poured money into Assyrian coffers. Following Assyria's decline, the Babylonian ruler Nebuchadnezzar conquered Judah, imprisoning one of Judah's last kings, Jehoiachim, in Babylon, where scribes kept a careful record of his rations.

---

glyphic, and demotic. In the 1820s, a French scholar, Jean-François Champollion, deciphered the inscriptions and thereby discovered the key to reading Egyptian hieroglyphics. Champollion's breakthrough allowed scholars for the first time to understand previously inaccessible works of Egyptian literature. Scholars have since translated many Egyptian documents related to the biblical text, finding several parallels to the Book of Proverbs, Job, and other examples of wisdom writing. (See Chapter 7.)

Egyptian–Israelite Affinities

Many similarities and affinities exist between ancient Egyptian and Israelite cultures. For example, Moses' name, like those of many subsequent Israelite priests, is Egyptian. His name is derived from the Egyptian verb *msw* (to be born) or the

noun *mesu* (child, son). The same root appears in such Egyptian names as Thutmose and Ahmose.

Some scholars believe that Egyptian ethical and religious motifs, such as the concept of **Maat**—which combined justice, truth, right thought, and conduct—helped shape ancient Israel's view of divine righteousness. Another possible connection between the Egyptian and Israelite religions appears in the way in which the two peoples housed their gods. In Egypt, statues of the gods—visible symbols of the divinity's invisible presence—were hidden away in windowless sanctuaries. Because the statues were protected from public gaze by massive stone walls, the god's holiness was enhanced by elements of secrecy and mystery. Only official priests and the pharaoh himself were allowed into the inner room that contained the deity's sacred image. In Israel, King Solomon built a similar kind of temple to house the Ark of the Covenant, on which Yahweh's *kavod* (glory) was

Box 2.3 Egyptian Myths Anticipating Biblical Concepts of Creation

In Mesopotamian, Egyptian, and Hebrew traditions, water is the primal substance out of which the universe developed. Ancient cosmogonies (stories about the birth or origin of the cosmos) typically pictured major elements composing the world — earth, sky, atmosphere — as gods, a means by which thinkers in a prescientific age could denote the superhuman forces that fashioned and sustained the universe. Thus, the Babylonian *Enuma Elish* depicts the pre-creation waste of limitless water as the deities Apsu (sweet or potable water) and Tiamat (saltwater). Similarly, the Egyptian creation account associated with Heliopolis (meaning "City of the Sun") postulates a primordial expanse of water, called Nu, that had to be separated and divided during the process of forming the world. According to the Heliopolis account, the sun god Atum arose out of Nu, standing on a primeval mound, a prototype of the inhabitable earth, surrounded by a vast watery chaos.

Atum, who in his divine being encompassed the totality of everything that exists, became the source of all other gods, the first two of whom he spewed forth in his semen. Producing Shu and Tefnut (thought to signify air and moisture, respectively) from his body, Atum initiated the proliferation of divine life that included Geb (the male principle, earth) and Nut (the female principle, sky). His progeny also included the gods who symbolized the divinely ordained structure of Egyptian society: Osiris, lord of the Underworld; his consort Isis, symbolizing the royal throne; Seth, Osiris's destructive brother, a personification of chaos; Nephthys, sister of Isis and wife of Seth; and Horus, son of Osiris and Isis, who represented the power of the reigning pharaoh.

Although Atum, the supreme creator god who embodies the life-giving energy of the sun, presides over an ordered, harmonious system (the cosmos), the Egyptians apparently feared an eventual return of the original watery chaos. In Egyptian cosmology (a philosophical view of the universe's nature and purpose), even after creation the primal waters continued to surround the world, separated from it by the vault of the sky (Nut) and confined to subterranean regions by the overlying earth (Geb). The Egyptian notion of waters gathered above the atmosphere and below the earth is essentially that presented in Genesis I, where Elohim (God) "divided the waters above the vault [sky, or "firmament"] from the waters under the vault" (Gen. 1:6–7). When God brings the flood, he simply releases the primal waters stored above the vault by activating the "sluices of heaven" (openings in the sky's broad dome) and by causing "the springs of the great deep [water-filled abyss beneath the earth]" to break through to the surface (Gen. 7:11–12). (See also Exod. 20:4, which refers to "the waters beneath the earth," the underground remnant of primeval sea on which the dry land is precariously balanced.) Interestingly, the Egyptians had no tradition of a global deluge, perhaps because they received very little rain and anticipated the annual inundations of the Nile as a natural blessing that ensured the regular fertilization of their fields.

Another Egyptian account, devised by the priests of Ptah at Memphis during the thirteenth century B.C.E., offers a creation by divine thought and speech, a concept employed not only in Genesis 1 but also in the Gospel of John. Ptah, after whom the nation of Egypt (the "Temple of Ptah") is named, was promoted by the Memphis priests as superior to all other deities, including Atum, the sun. According to a late version of the myth, inscribed on stone by order of Pharaoh Shabaka about 700 B.C.E., Ptah gave birth to all things, including the gods, by his "heart" and "tongue." Because many ancient languages, including biblical Hebrew, which has few abstract terms, used the word for heart to designate "mind" or "consciousness," Ptah created by thinking the universe into existence, fashioning it by the power of his word. When Ptah conceived an idea of something, he then pronounced its identity, causing it to be — a process that Elohim also follows in Genesis 1. The concept of a divine utterance or word (Greek, *logos*) as the means by which all creation exists, later elaborated by Greek philosophers, ultimately found expression in the opening hymn to the Logos (Word) in John's Gospel, where the writer identifies it with the prehuman Jesus, God's creative agent (John 1:1–5).

enthroned. In some biblical writers' judgment, however, Solomon allied himself too closely with Egypt, marrying the pharaoh's daughter and erecting shrines to the gods of his many foreign wives in the Temple precincts (1 Kings 9:16–18, 21; 11:1–8). Even after Solomon's time, the temple rituals continued to resemble those of Egypt: Only the hereditary high priest was permitted to enter the sanctuary's innermost chamber, the Holy of Holies that sheltered Yahweh's unseen presence. (See Box 2.3 for an account of possible links between Egyptian myths and biblical concepts of creation.)

The Egyptian Afterlife

Until relatively late in its history, the Israelite community did not adopt one of the Egyptian religion's central tenets: the expectation of a joyous afterlife. A firm conviction that the next world offered rewards for good behavior inspired the Egyptians' famous practice of embalming their beloved dead and placing them in richly decorated tombs. Whereas Egyptian, Greek, and other ancient cultures maintained a strong interest in the afterlife, it was not until the second century B.C.E. that apocalyptic visionaries such as the authors of Daniel and 1 Enoch began to express hope in future resurrection similar to that of the Egyptian religion. (See Chapter 8.)

The apocalyptic concept of postmortem judgment, which Egyptian faith had honored for millennia, was eventually passed on from Judaism to Christianity. The Christian Apocalypse (Revelation) pictures cosmic judgment, in which names are read from a "book of life," in terms echoing ancient Egyptian beliefs (Rev. 20). Egyptian artworks depicting **Osiris**, god of the dead, weighing the deceased's heart on a scale balanced by the feather of truth, anticipate Judeo-Christian doctrines about the afterlife and final judgment (see Rev. 20).

Perhaps Egypt's most lasting contribution to biblical religion was the ritual practice of **circumcision**. The surgical removal of the foreskin (prepuce) from the penis, circumcision was a physically

distinguishing mark on all Israelite males. According to the Greek historian Herodotus, this originally Egyptian practice spread to a few other nations, whereas the majority of men "leave their private parts as nature made them" (*The Histories*, Book 2, 37; cf. Josh. 5:2–6 and Jer. 9:25–26). In ancient Israel (and in modern Judaism), all male infants, when eight days old, routinely had the foreskin amputated (Gen. 17:12; Lev. 12:3; Luke 1:59; Phil. 3:5). This ancient Egyptian rite, in fact, is interpreted as the indelible "sign" of God's covenant with Abraham and all his descendants: "My Covenant shall be marked on your bodies as a Covenant in perpetuity" (Gen. 17:9–14).

Canaan and Israel

Located strategically between the great powers of Egypt and Mesopotamia (Figure 2.12), Israel and its Canaanite neighbors shared both a common culture and a vulnerability to foreign invasion. Excavations at the ancient Canaanite settlement of **Ugarit** (also known by its modern Arabic name **Ras Shamra**), uncovered a library of cuneiform texts that, like the epics of Gilgamesh and the Enuma Elish, anticipate ideas that appear later in the Hebrew Bible. Composed in a hitherto unknown Semitic language that, when deciphered, showed affinities with biblical Hebrew, the Ugaritic texts provided a major source of information about the Canaanite religion, including tales about conflicts between the gods and natural forces. Dating from about 1600–1400 B.C.E., these documents reveal that the chief Canaanite god, **El**—the general Semitic term for deity—was thought of in much the same way as early Israelite concepts of Yahweh (see Chapter 3). Called "Father of Years," "Compassionate," and "Father of Humankind," El is also referred to in epithets suggesting that he is the world creator and source of the watery abyss that precedes creation in Genesis 1:1.

Although Israel's religious leaders staunchly resisted any compromise with El's son **Baal**, the Canaanite god of storm, rain, and fecundity, many scholars believe that qualities and attributes of El

Figure 2.12 Map of Canaan, the land promised to Abraham's descendants. The map shows the areas occupied by Judah and Samaria after the fall of the northern kingdom of Israel in the late eighth century B.C.E.

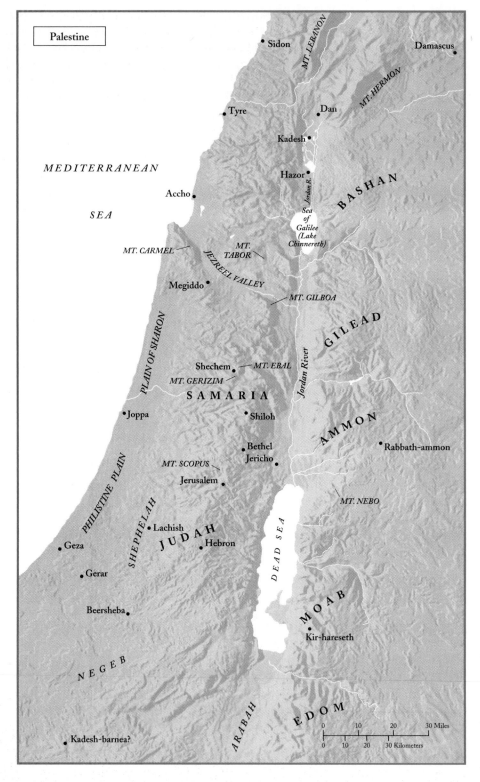

were assimilated into the biblical portrait of Yahweh. As they settled in Canaan, the Israelites gradually took over many older Canaanite shrines and sanctuaries, such as those at Bethel, Shechem, and Salem (Jerusalem). Comparative study of Canaanite and biblical literature indicates that the Israelites also adopted various Canaanite hymns, poems, and religious titles to apply to Yahweh's worship.

ISRAEL AND THE NEAR EASTERN POWERS

Although it was too small and its period of national unity too brief for Israel to play a dominant role in international politics, Israel's religious legacy accords it a significant place in Near Eastern history. A brief survey of Israel's story, including its conflicts with the empires of Egypt and Mesopotamia, is a necessary prerequisite to understanding the biblical account. According to the books of Samuel and Kings, the Israelite kingdom that David and Solomon built — extending from the borders of Egypt northward to the Euphrates River — was at first militarily successful, temporarily subjugating several smaller neighboring states, such as Moab, Ammon, and Edom. Little archaeological evidence of Solomon's reputed wealth has been uncovered, leading some historians to doubt the historicity of the biblical account (see Box 2.2). Nevertheless, many scholars believe that a united Israelite kingdom in the tenth century B.C.E. may have been successful politically, if only because the major powers of Mesopotamia and Egypt were then politically weak.

The Divided Kingdom   After Solomon's death in 922 B.C.E., the larger portion of his kingdom broke away to form the northern kingdom of Israel, with the much smaller territory of Judah still ruled by Davidic kings. According to an influential critical theory known as the Documentary Hypothesis, at some time during the period of the divided monarchy, oral traditions celebrating Israel's ancestors and the Davidic dynasty were first compiled into a continuous narrative. Called the Yahwist because he (or she) consistently used the divine name Yahweh, this anonymous writer is widely credited with composing an account that became the narrative framework for the Torah (for a discussion of theories about the Torah's authorship, see Chapter 4).

In the ninth century B.C.E., the **Assyrians**, a Mesopotamian people named for **Assur** (Asshur), their god of war, began a series of conquests that created perhaps the most feared of all ancient Near Eastern empires. Efficiently organized and ruthlessly aggressive, Assyrian armies terrorized the Near East with their iron war chariots and seemingly invincible cavalry. Walled cities that refused to surrender were mercilessly sacked and burned, with their inhabitants enslaved and deported to distant parts of the empire. Prisoners were routinely tortured, flayed alive, and otherwise hideously mutilated — an effective means of discouraging resistance.

By the eighth century B.C.E., the kingdoms of both Israel and Judah were essentially vassals of the Assyrian emperor, who extorted vast sums of tribute, impoverishing both states. During this troubled epoch, ancestral tales of northern Israel began to coalesce in a (possibly oral) narrative that provided a second major source of the Torah. Known as the Elohist, the narrator regularly uses "Elohim" as the preferred name for God. At about the same time, the prophets Amos and Hosea were active in the northern region, castigating the ruling classes for their exploitation of the poor and for adulterating Yahweh's cult with that of Baal. When Israel revolted against Assyrian oppression, **Sargon II** laid siege to the Israelite capital, **Samaria**, destroying it in 722–721 B.C.E. and deporting the urban upper classes. According to 2 Kings, the Assyrians settled foreigners in Israel's former territory who mixed with the remaining Israelites and adopted the worship of Yahweh. Their descendants came to be known as **Samaritans** and were harshly condemned for maintaining Yahweh's sanctuary near the ancient site of Shechem, denounced by southern writers as an illicit rival to the Jerusalem Temple. Some Israelite refugees, fleeing from the Assyrians, apparently settled in Judah, bringing with them the Elohist traditions, which Judean scribes substantially revised, combining them with and subordinating them to the

Yahwist's older account. This blending of sources produced a composite narrative known as JE, an epic celebration of Israel's past relationship with Yahweh.

Another Assyrian emperor, **Sennacherib**, invaded Judah and destroyed most of its fortified cities, although he failed to capture Jerusalem. The apparently miraculous deliverance of Judah's holy city appeared to confirm that the Davidic kings who ruled there would be protected by Yahweh's presence in the national sanctuary. During the Assyrian crisis, the prophet Isaiah urged King Hezekiah not to make foreign alliances against the invaders, but to rely solely on Yahweh's salvation. (The contemporary prophet Micah, however, predicted the eventual destruction of Jerusalem for its inhabitants' misdeeds.) For a time, Jerusalem escaped the fate of Samaria, but its rulers had to pay a humiliating tribute to keep the Assyrians at bay (2 Kings 18:13–16).

As the seventh century B.C.E. drew to a close, Assyria's growing weakness brought rapid change to the Near East. Taking advantage of Assyrian decline, the Judean king **Josiah** (ruled 640–609 B.C.E.) expanded Judah's territory, reconquering part of Israel's former land and conducting a major religious reform that revived Mosaic traditions, including a national celebration of the Passover. Josiah's sweeping reforms also banned sacrifice at any shrine except the Jerusalem Temple, a prohibition found only in one "book of the law," Deuteronomy. Scholars believe that the Deuteronomy scroll, "found" during Temple repairs, was probably composed during or shortly before Josiah's religious revival and served as the scriptural authority for his actions. Incorporating a variety of older oral and written sources, including royal archives, the first edition of the Deuteronomistic History encompassing Joshua through 2 Kings was also written at this time. After Judah's fall to Babylon, however, it was significantly re-edited to provide a theological explanation for the debacle.

When Nineveh, the Assyrian capital, fell in 612 B.C.E. to a coalition of Babylonians and Medes (an ancient Iranian people), a general sense of relief must have swept through the Near East. The brief oracles of Nahum reflects Judah's rejoicing at the prospect of a world freed from Assyrian violence (see Chapter 6). Judah's respite from foreign domination was short-lived, however. In 609 B.C.E., the Egyptian pharaoh **Necho** invaded Judah and killed Josiah at Megiddo, ending his revitalization of Judah's worship. Necho then faced Babylon's **Nebuchadnezzar** at the epochal Battle of **Carchemish**, a city in Syria (605 B.C.E.); Necho's defeat decisively ended Egypt's role as an international power, leaving Babylon as the Near East's new master.

THE FALL OF JERUSALEM AND THE BABYLONIAN EXILE

Reduced to vassalage under the Neo-Babylonian Empire, Judah rebelled in 597 B.C.E., resulting in the sacking of Jerusalem by Nebuchadnezzar and the deportation of its upper classes to Babylon. Among the exiles was the priest-prophet **Ezekiel** (see Chapter 6). More than a century earlier, Isaiah had assured King Hezekiah that Yahweh would not permit the Assyrians to desecrate the city where he had placed his name (2 Kings 19:32–34). By contrast, during Judah's Babylonian crisis both Ezekiel and **Jeremiah** preached a strikingly different message: Neither Yahweh's presence in the Temple nor his promise to maintain the Davidic dynasty would save Judah. Jeremiah urged **Zedekiah**, the last Davidic king, to submit to Babylon as Yahweh's rod of correction. When Zedekiah's advisors, hoping for aid from Egypt, persuaded the king to rebel in 587 B.C.E., Nebuchadnezzar promptly marched on Jerusalem, capturing and demolishing it along with Solomon's Temple. A large part of the population was removed to Babylon, with only the poor left behind.

The period of the **Babylonian exile** (587–538 B.C.E.) and the centuries immediately following, when **Persia** replaced Babylon as ruler of the Near East, were the most productive eras in terms of biblical composition. Scholars believe that much of the Hebrew Bible, including the Torah and the historical books (Joshua through 2 Kings), as well as the collections ascribed to various prophets, was thoroughly revised and re-edited during the late sixth, fifth, and fourth centuries B.C.E. The composite (JE) epic of Israel's origins, along with Deuteronomy and the Deuteronomistic History, was partly rewritten from the perspective of Judah's catastrophic defeat by Babylon. Without king, country, or sanctuary, the Jewish exiles in Babylon pondered on the national disaster that had robbed them of all the divine promises made to Abraham and David. In its final edition, the Torah thus does not end as one would expect, with Israel's possession of Canaan. Instead, it concludes with Moses' ultimate disappointment—seeing the Promised Land from afar and then dying before he can enter it. The divine promises remain in effect, but their fulfillment lies in the indefinite future.

Taken as a whole, the long historical account of Abraham's heirs, beginning in Genesis and extending through 2 Kings, ends on a similarly disquieting note, with the covenant people still not possessing the land, but only remembering it from their distant captivity in Babylon. At that low point in their history, it may have seemed to them as if God had entirely abandoned his people. During the exile and its aftermath, Judean writers produced varied works that dramatized their nation's misfortunes, including the Book of Job, in which a righteous man reexamines traditional concepts of God's character and divine justice. As Job, after almost unbearable suffering, is finally returned to divine favor, so Israel could hope for restoration.

THE RETURN FROM BABYLON AND THE DOMINANCE OF PERSIA

After Judah's former leaders had passed almost half a century in exile, a new prophet, Second Isaiah, proclaimed to his fellow Judeans that Yahweh had forgiven them and would soon stage a new Exodus, returning them to the Promised Land (Isa. 40–55). In 539 B.C.E., a new ruler of Persia, Cyrus the Great, captured Babylon. A year later, as part of a general policy to enlist the loyalty of Babylon's former subjects, Cyrus permitted the exiles to return to the ruins of Jerusalem and restore the worship of their God. Many Judean exiles, however, remained in Mesopotamia, where they continued to compile and edit legal and prophetic documents that eventually became part of the Hebrew Bible.

Although the Persians did not permit a reestablishment of Davidic kings, they did endorse the rebuilding of Yahweh's Jerusalem Temple, which was rededicated in about 515 B.C.E. The approximately six centuries following this reconstruction are known as the **Second Temple period**, during which the territory surrounding Jerusalem—henceforth known as **Judea**—was dominated by a series of foreign empires, including Persia, Greece, and Rome. Much of the Bible's third main division, the Writings, was composed under Persian rule, including the later historical books of 1 and 2 Chronicles, Ezra, and Nehemiah, which bring the postexilic story of the covenant people to the fourth century B.C.E. Although it contains some older material, the collection of Psalms, which is commonly designated a songbook for the Second Temple, was probably also compiled during the Persian era, as was an anthology of practical wisdom, the Book of Proverbs. Although it shows the Jews fighting for their survival against some hostile Persian administrators, the Book of Esther suggests a generally friendly treatment of the covenant people by Persia's rulers.

Alexander's Conquests and the Hellenistic Era

The biblical world changed swiftly and pervasively with the conquests of **Alexander the Great**, whose armies swept through the Persian Empire in the late fourth century B.C.E. Building a vast empire that stretched from Greece eastward to western India and as far south as Egypt, Alexander (reigned 336–323 B.C.E.) actively promoted **Hellenism**, the adoption of Greek language, literature, social customs, and ethical values, throughout the eastern Mediterranean region. Alexander's policies, perpetuated by his successors, created a new international culture known as **Hellenistic**. A fusion of classical Greek (Hellenic) civilization with Near Eastern cultures, the Hellenistic synthesis produced a creative flowering of Greek and Oriental motifs in art, architecture, philosophy, science, literature, and religion. Arbitrarily dated as beginning with Alexander's death in 323 B.C.E., the Hellenistic period chronologically overlaps the period of Roman expansion and continues into the early centuries C.E.

Along with a new form of the Greek language, the *koinē* spoken by Alexander's soldiers, Hellenistic culture introduced new ways of thought and expression into the eastern Mediterranean world. It also produced, among educated classes at least, a more open worldview in which Hellenistic peoples saw themselves as citizens not merely of a particular city-state (the *polis*) but of the world (*cosmos*) as a whole. This *cosmopolitan* outlook helped break down barriers between different traditions, allowing an integration of Greek with other ethnic customs, a widespread process by which even the Palestinian Jewish community became partly Hellenized, adopting Greek styles of education, dress, behavior, and other social practices. *Koinē* became so widely spoken that Jews living in Alexandria, Egypt's largest city, found it necessary to translate the Hebrew Bible into *koinē* Greek, beginning in about 250 B.C.E. This Greek translation, the Septuagint (see Chapter 1) was not only the edition used by many Jews who lived in the **Diaspora** (the "scattering" of Jews living outside the Jewish homeland), but also that adopted by the early Christian community, which wrote its own scriptures, the New Testament, in *koinē* Greek.

Following Alexander's death at Babylon (a city he planned to rebuild), his far-flung empire was divided among his most powerful generals, including **Ptolemy**, who took Egypt as his portion, and **Seleucus**, who ruled over Syria, which then also encompassed the territory of Mesopotamia. The tiny region of Judea initially was under Ptolemaic control, but after 199 B.C.E. it was ruled by the Seleucid dynasty. When the Seleucid king **Antiochus IV** (175–163 B.C.E.) attempted to unify the ethnically diverse peoples of his kingdom by forcibly imposing Hellenization, a band of Torah-observant Jews, the **Maccabees**, resisted violently. They waged guerrilla warfare against Antiochus's troops until the Syrian forces were eventually driven from Judea in 142 B.C.E. Two deuterocanonical histories, 1 and 2 Maccabees, vividly dramatize Antiochus's persecutions of the **hasidim**, Jews loyal to their national religion, and the Maccabean Revolt that followed. Most scholars believe that the Book of Daniel, with its mystical visions of Gentile empires rising and falling according to a divinely predestined plan and its promise that those who died faithful to their Torah obligations would be resurrected to future life, was composed during this exceptionally turbulent period (see Chapter 8).

Whereas the books of Daniel and Maccabees reject Jewish adoption of Greek or other foreign customs, the deuterocanonical Wisdom of Solomon offers an innovative assimilation of Greek ideas into the biblical tradition. Writing in Greek during the first century B.C.E., the author of this pseudonymous wisdom book accepts a variety of Greek philosophical notions, including the supreme value of cultivating ethical virtues and a belief in the soul's innate immortality and its preexistence before descending to earth to inhabit a human body. At the same time that he integrates Hellenic and Hebraic concepts, the writer also provides an extended denunciation of idolatry, making the common but erroneous assumption that non-Jews actually worshiped a god's physical image rather than the idea of divinity that it represented.

The Roman Occupation of Judea

As Rome, which had dominated the western Mediterranean basin since the third century B.C.E., expanded eastward, it gradually absorbed the Hellenistic kingdoms of Macedonia, Syria, and Egypt. Roman troops, led by **Pompey**, occupied Judea in 63 B.C.E., bringing to an end the briefly independent Jewish kingdom that had been ruled by the Maccabees' descendants, the **Hasmoneans** (142–63 B.C.E.). In 40 B.C.E., the Roman Senate appointed **Herod I**, an Idumean (Edomite) prince whose family had converted to Judaism, as king of Judea. Extremely unpopular with his prospective subjects, Herod had to take Jerusalem by force and thereafter ruled with a strange mixture of political cunning and open brutality. Almost 130 years after the Roman legions arrived in Judea, the Jews rebelled against Roman rule (66–73 B.C.E.). Whereas Jewish fighters under the Maccabees eventually had succeeded in expelling Seleucid occupation forces and gaining political autonomy, the revolt against Rome ended tragically. Roman armies led by **Titus**, son of the emperor **Vespasian** (reigned 69–79 C.E.), captured and destroyed Jerusalem, massacring tens of thousands of Jews and demolishing the great Temple that Herod had lavishly rebuilt (70 C.E.). In the aftermath of this disaster, which effectively ended the Jewish state, a more united form of Judaism arose, led by rabbis who reinterpreted Torah regulations for the Jewish community's radically changed circumstances.

Among the many diverse manifestations of Judaism during the first century C.E., a movement led by Jesus of Nazareth eventually had the greatest historical impact on Rome. Three centuries after Jesus was crucified by **Pontius Pilate**, appointed governor of Judea by the emperor **Tiberius** (14–37 C.E.), another Roman ruler, the emperor **Constantine** (307–337 C.E.), accorded Christianity official status. Before the end of the fourth century C.E., one of Constantine's successors, **Theodosius** (379–395 C.E.), officially banned all the older Greco-Roman religions, making Christianity the only legitimate faith of the Roman Empire.

Probably composed during the first Jewish revolt against Rome (66–73 C.E.), approximately forty years after Jesus' crucifixion, the Gospel of Mark was the earliest canonical account of Jesus' life to be written. At the time of Rome's destruction of Jerusalem (70 C.E.), less than half of the New Testament—Paul's letters (c. 50–62 C.E.) and Mark's Gospel—was in existence. Most of the New Testament, including the Gospels attributed to Matthew, Luke, and John, as well as Acts, the catholic epistles, and Revelation, had yet to be written. It was not until the mid-second century C.E. that the latest canonical document, 2 Peter, was produced. (For further discussion of Hellenistic culture, the Maccabean uprising, the Jewish wars with Rome, and the historical background of the New Testament, see Chapters 8 and 9.)

RECOMMENDED READING

Baines, J., and Malek, J. *Atlas of Ancient Egypt.* New York: Facts on File, 1980.

Coogan, Michael D. *Stories from Ancient Canaan.* Philadelphia: Westminster Press, 1978. A paperback collection of Canaanite myths and their biblical parallels.

———. *The Oxford History of the Biblical World.* New York: Oxford University Press, 1998. Provides the latest archaeological and historical background for each period of Israelite development, from the patriarchal to the Greco-Roman epoch.

Cross, Frank M., ed. *Canaanite Myth and Hebrew Epic, Essays in the History of the Religion of Israel.* Cambridge, Mass.: Harvard University Press, 1973.

Dalley, Stephanie. *Myths from Mesopotamia: Creation, the Flood, Gilgamesh, and Others.* New York: Oxford University Press, 1989.

Damrosch, David. *The Narrative Covenant: Transformations of Genre in the Growth of Biblical Literature.* San Francisco: Harper&Row, 1987.

Foster, Benjamin R. *From Distant Days: Myths, Tales, and Poetry of Ancient Mesopotamia.* Bethesda, Md.: CDL Press, 1995.

Foster, John L. *Hymns, Prayers, and Songs: An Anthology of Ancient Egyptian Lyric Poetry.* Atlanta: Scholars Press, 1995.

Gordon, Cyrus, and Rendsburg, Gary A. *The Bible and the Ancient Near East,* 4th ed. New York: Norton, 1997.

Gray, John. *Near Eastern Mythology.* New York: Peter Bedrick Books, 1982.

Hallo, William W., ed. *The Context of Scripture.* Vol. 1, *Canonical Compositions from the Biblical World.* Leiden, The Netherlands: Brill, 1997. The first in a new series of volumes on ancient Near Eastern literature.

Harris, Roberta L. *The World of the Bible.* London: Thames & Hudson, 1995. An illustrated survey of biblical history and archaeology.

Heidel, Alexander. *The Gilgamesh Epic and Old Testament Parallels.* Chicago: University of Chicago Press, 1949.

Hobson, Christine. *The World of the Pharaohs: A Complete Guide to Ancient Egypt.* New York: Thames & Hudson, 1987.

Ions, Veronica. *Egyptian Mythology.* New York: Peter Bedrick Books, 1982.

Jacobson, Thorkild. *The Treasures of Darkness: A History of Mesopotamian Religion.* New Haven, Conn.: Yale University Press, 1976.

Kramer, Samuel N. *History Begins at Sumer.* New York: Doubleday/Anchor Books, 1959.

———. *The Sumerians.* Chicago: University of Chicago Press, 1963.

———. *Cradle of Civilization.* New York: Time-Life Books, 1967.

Kuhrt, Amelie. *The Ancient Near East, c. 3000–330 B.C.* New York: Routledge, 1996. A Comprehensive and authoritative study.

Maier, John, ed. *Gilgamesh: A Reader.* Wauconda, Ill.: Bolchazy-Carducci, 1997. A collection of informative scholarly essays on the background and interpretation of the Gilgamesh epic.

Matthews, Victor H., and Benjamin, Don C. *Old Testament Parallels: Documents from the Ancient Near East*, rev. ed. New York: Paulist Press, 1997.

Murnane, William J. *Texts from the Amarna Period in Egypt.* Atlanta: Scholars Press, 1995.

O'Connor, David. *A Short History of Ancient Egypt.* Pittsburgh: Carnegie Museum of Natural History, 1990.

Parker, Simon B. "The Ancient Near Eastern Literary Background of the Old Testament." In *The New Interpreter's Bible*, Vol. 1, pp. 228–243. Nashville, Tenn.: Abingdon Press, 1994. An authoritative and readable overview.

————. *Ugaritic Narrative Poetry.* Atlanta: Scholars Press, 1997. Shows parallels between Canaanite and biblical views of divinity.

————. *Stories in Scripture and Inscriptions: Comparative Studies on Narratives in Northwest Semitic Inscriptions and the Hebrew Bible.* New York: Oxford University Press, 1997.

Pritchard, James B., ed. *The Ancient Near East: An Anthology of Texts and Pictures.* Princeton, N.J.: Princeton University Press, 1965. A less expensive work containing excerpts from the following book and *Ancient Near Eastern Texts.*

————, ed. *The Ancient Near East in Pictures Relating to the Old Testament.* Princeton, N.J.: Princeton University Press, 1965. A companion volume to *Ancient Near Eastern Texts.*

————, ed. *Ancient Near Eastern Texts Relating to the Old Testament*, 3rd ed., supp. Princeton, N.J.: Princeton University Press, 1969. Translations of relevant Egyptian, Babylonian, Canaanite, and other ancient literatures — the standard work.

Redford, Donald B. *Egypt, Canaan, and Israel in Ancient Times.* Princeton, N.J.: Princeton University Press, 1992. A recent scholarly study of the first civilizations in North Africa and western Asia.

Roaf, Michael. *Cultural Atlas of Mesopotamia and the Ancient Near East.* New York and Oxford: Facts on File, 1990.

Roth, Martha T. *Law Collections from Mesopotamia and Asia Minor.* Atlanta: Scholars Press, 1997.

Sandars, N. K. *Poems of Heaven and Hell from Ancient Mesopotamia.* New York and London: Penguin Books, 1971.

————. *The Epic of Gilgamesh.* Baltimore: Penguin Books, 1972. A freely translated version of the *Epic of Gilgamesh* with a scholarly introduction.

Sasson, Jack M., ed. *Civilizations of the Ancient Near East*, 4 vols. New York: Simon & Schuster/Macmillan, 1995. A compendium of scholarly essays on historical, cultural, and religious aspects of ancient Near Eastern life, many of which relate to the Hebrew Bible.

Wilson, John A. *The Culture of Ancient Egypt.* Chicago: University of Chicago Press, 1963.

Wolkstein, Diane, and Kramer, S. N. *Inanna: Queen of Heaven and Earth, Her Stories and Hymns from Sumer.* New York: Harper & Row, 1983.

The Promised Land

The land of Canaan (Palestine) probably has more religious associations for more people than any other part of the world, for it is the Holy Land to Catholic, Eastern Orthodox, Protestant, Jew, and Muslim alike. During the past 4000 years, more wars have been fought for its possession than for almost any other geographical area. From Egyptian, Amorite, and Israelite in the ancient world to Turk, Arab, Palestinian, and Israeli in modern times, millions have died attempting to gain or hold this small territory, which is roughly the size of Maryland. (The generalized map of Palestine in Figure 2.12 shows the location of some major sites mentioned in the Hebrew Bible.)

THE GEOGRAPHY OF CANAAN

Much of the area's importance arises from its location. A relatively narrow strip (roughly 150 miles long and 70 miles wide) between the eastern end of the Mediterranean Sea and the inland deserts, Canaan was a land bridge between the three great civilized centers of the ancient world. Egypt lay to the southwest, Asia Minor to the northwest, and Mesopotamia to the northeast. Except for brief periods when these areas were militarily weak, armies repeatedly marched through the Palestinian corridor, generally devastating the regions they occupied. During peaceful times, however, Canaan flourished, as traders and caravans bearing grain, spices, gold, hides, and textiles traveled along the three main trade routes that crossed the land. Control of these international commercial highways provided considerable wealth for which many nations contended.

One thinks of modern Palestine as dry and rather barren, but in biblical times it was at least partly forested and relatively well watered. Then as now, however, the climate varied considerably in the country's four major regions. The western region is a low coastal plain, twenty to thirty miles wide at most. This narrow strip, which provided the chief highway to Egypt, was under Egyptian rule when the Israelites first invaded Canaan following 1250 B.C.E., although the Philistines occupied it during most of Israel's history. (Ironically, the whole country came to be known as **Palestine**, a name derived from Philistia, the hated scourge of the Israelites.)

Inland, running roughly north-south, is the second major region, a limestone ridge of low mountains and small valleys. This central hill country, much less fertile than the coastal plain, extends from the Valley of **Beersheba** in the south to the mountains of Lebanon in the north. The hilly range is broken in the north by the broad Plain of Megiddo, formed by the Kishon River, which flows northwestward to the Mediterranean Sea just north of Mount Carmel, a precipitous rocky massif that juts into the sea and forms the northern boundary of the coastal plain.

Megiddo's level fields join the Valley of **Jezreel** to the east, near Mount Gilboa, forming an east-west–trending greenbelt, the most fertile part of the country. The site of several bloody and decisive battles in Israel's history, the Megiddo area is cited in Revelation 16:16 as the location of **Armageddon**, the final cosmic war between God and the devil. Not far to the north, where the limestone hills rise steeply to merge with the Lebanon Range, was the small village of Nazareth, where Jesus grew to manhood. A poor, rather bleak area, it afforded few attractions other than its southward view of Megiddo's gentle plains.

Between Palestine's mountainous backbone and the Transjordan hills to the east is the Great Rift Valley, which runs from north to south the full length of the country. This geological fault zone provides the channel for the **Jordan River**, which rises in the **Sea of Galilee** and flows sixty-five miles south to the **Dead Sea**, a great salt lake 1290 feet below sea level, the lowest point in the earth's land surface. Paralleling the Jordan on both sides is a lush band of vegetation; around the Dead Sea, however, nothing grows, making it a striking im-

age of utter desolation (Figure 2.13). According to local folktales, the sea now covers the remains of Sodom and Gomorrah, which had lain near its shores before the area was decimated by a natural catastrophe.

Located east of the Jordan River, the fourth general region, **Transjordan**, is a rugged mountainous terrain cut by deep canyons that flood during heavy rains. Extending from the plains of southern Syria east of Galilee to the Brook Zered at the southern end of the Dead Sea, Transjordan averages about 1500 feet above sea level, although many of its peaks rise to twice that height. Legend has it that Jesus' family fled to Transjordan when the Romans temporarily lifted their siege of Jerusalem. It is at least probable that some Palestinian Christians found refuge in this sparsely populated area during the Roman wars (66–73 C.E.).

But Palestine's division into four distinct regions is more meaningful than ordinary geographical sectioning might suggest. In terms of Israel's history, radical differences among areas meant that their inhabitants were relatively self-contained and somewhat culturally isolated from the inhabitants of adjacent but topographically dissimilar areas. Farmers cultivated the fertile plains, small valleys, and terraced hillsides, growing wheat, barley, olives, and grapes. On nearby stony ridges, shepherds pastured sheep or goats that subsisted on occasional tufts of grass. By contrast, Israel's chief cities, located in the central hill country, were trade centers open to considerable cultural exchange with itinerant traders from Egypt, Mesopotamia, Syria, Phoenicia, and other affluent urban civilizations.

Palestine's regional and economic diversity sometimes led to suspicion and distrust among the three main occupational groups — farmers, shepherds, and commercial city dwellers. Shepherds, living a seminomadic outdoor life, regarded the cities as sources of financial exploitation and corruption, and eighth-century B.C.E. prophets, such as Amos and Hosea, typically sided with the country people in this regard. City people, in turn, regarded farmers and villagers as backward and given to compromising their faith by the worship of agricultural and fertility deities. To a degree, then, Israel's class and religious conflicts emanated from

Figure 2.13 Photographed from a U.S. spacecraft, this view of the southeastern corner of the Mediterranean shows southern Palestine (top left) and the Sinai desert (center). The Gulf of Suez lies below the Sinai peninsula and the Gulf of Aqabah above it. The long troughlike depression extending northward from Aqabah holds the Dead Sea, Jordan Valley, and the Sea of Galilee.

the economic and cultural divergences caused by Palestine's unusually diverse geography.

Even more decisive than its diverse internal geography was Palestine's position between the great powers of the ancient world. Except for a few decades during the reigns of David and Solomon, this strategic land bridge joining Asia to Africa was continually trampled by other nations. Israel's successive military domination by Assyria, Babylon, Medo-Persia, Macedonian Greece, and Rome gave its thinkers a distinctive philosophy of history and of their God's will. The Bible writers saw in their nation's relentless sufferings not an accident

of geography, but the inevitable consequences of their national sins, a belief that will be discussed further in the summaries of Deuteronomy and the Deuteronomistic History. (See Chapter 5.)

THE BIBLE'S NORTH–SOUTH POLARITIES

Many important events in biblical history reflect a sharp division between the northern and southern parts of Israel. Just as the United States was divided between the North and South during the American Civil War (1861–1865), so Israel was split into two rival states for much of its history. United briefly under their first three kings, Saul, David, and Solomon, the twelve tribes of Israel divided into two hostile camps following Solomon's death in 922 B.C.E. The ten northern tribes, which controlled most of the nation's territory, formed the kingdom of Israel, while the tribes of Judah and Benjamin formed the much smaller kingdom of Judah.

The tension between north and south — with each of the two kingdoms claiming to represent Yahweh's covenant people — strongly influenced their respective religious traditions. Whereas Israel's kings established Yahwist shrines at Bethel and Dan, Judah's leaders insisted that Yahweh accepted worship only at the Jerusalem sanctuary. In the Books of Kings, Judean writers consistently condemn all of Israel's rulers for their failure to recognize the Jerusalem Temple's supremacy. After Assyria destroyed the northern capital of Samaria and deported much of Israel's population (721 B.C.E.), refugees from the northern kingdom fled south to Judah, bringing with them traditions of their nation's past, some of which Judean editors later revised and incorporated into the biblical text. (See Chapter 4.)

Even after Jerusalem's destruction by Babylon and partial restoration in 538 B.C.E., Judah's hostility toward Jews occupying Israel's former territories persisted. By New Testament times, inhabitants of this area were called Samaritans and regarded as violators of true Judaism. In the Gospel of Mark, which scholars believe was the first Gospel written, Jesus' life is arranged according to a geographical north–south division that is reminiscent of Israel's ancient polarities. In Mark (as well as Matthew and Luke), most of Jesus' ministry takes place in the northern region of Galilee, where he performs miracles, draws large crowds, and successfully proclaims the kingdom of God. In the second part of Mark's narrative, however, Jesus travels south to Judea and Jerusalem, where he is rejected, arrested, and executed. Although Mark reverses the traditional symbolism of the two districts — designating the north as the area in which Jesus flourishes and the south as the place of his suffering and death — his Gospel echoes the Hebrew Bible's emphasis on north–south geographical divisions and their significance in the working out of God's historical design.

Approaching the Bible

Before beginning a discussion of individual biblical books, it is helpful to review some of the major events of Bible history. In referring to Table 2.1, however, the reader is cautioned to remember that the dates are only roughly approximate and that scholars differ in their attempts to correlate events in Egypt, Mesopotamia, and Palestine with the biblical record. The ancient world had no common method of reckoning time; dating of events before the seventh or sixth centuries B.C.E. is especially conjectural.

It should be further noted that no attempt has been made in the following chapters to discuss every aspect of the contents of the thirty-nine books of the Hebrew Bible. The summaries provide introductory material necessary or helpful to understanding individual books but are no substitute for reading the Bible itself. In general, only those themes or events that the author thought most significant are included, and these are signaled by headnotes with corresponding key questions. Recommended readings at the end of each major section will direct the student to authoritative works that offer more thorough coverage of particular biblical topics.

QUESTIONS FOR REVIEW

1. Define the Fertile Crescent and the region of Mesopotamia. Describe some of ancient Sumer's contributions to civilization, including the invention of cuneiform and the religious function of the ziggurat.

2. Who were the Akkadians and Amorites? What political innovation did Sargon I introduce?

3. Summarize the story of Gilgamesh and its relationship to later biblical traditions. How does the flood account in Gilgamesh anticipate that in Genesis 6–8?

4. Enumerate some of the parallels between Hammurabi's legal code and some regulations and statutes found in the Mosaic Covenant. How did you explain the resemblance between Mesopotamian and biblical law?

5. From what god is the name "Egypt" derived? Describe some of the achievements of this first nation-state. What religious innovations did Akhenaton promote? Explain the importance of the Merneptah stele.

6. What discoveries were made at Ugarit (Ras Shamra), and what do they reveal about El, head of the Canaanite pantheon? Who was Baal?

7. After the United Kingdom under kings David and Solomon was split into two kingdoms — Israel in the north and Judah in the south — how were they affected by the rise of Assyria?

8. Who was Josiah, and what reforms did he bring to Judah? After the fall of Assyria, what new power dominated the Near East? What happened to Jerusalem and its upper classes under Nebuchadnezzar?

9. How did the policies of Cyrus the Great affect Judean exiles in Babylon? What new political power now ruled the Near East, including Judea?

10. Who was Alexander the Great, and what was his role in Hellenizing the Near East, including Judea? How did a descendant of one of Alexander's successors, Antiochus IV, attempt to destroy Judaism? What role did the Maccabees play in liberating their country?

11. How did Judea come under Roman rule, and what resulted when the Jews revolted against Rome (66–73 C.E.)?

QUESTIONS FOR DISCUSSION AND REFLECTION

1. As many historians have observed, ancient Israel — which produced the Hebrew Bible — did not exist in a cultural vacuum, but assimilated and transformed many of the ideas and practices of older Near Eastern civilizations. Describe some of the customs and religious concepts from ancient Egypt and Mesopotamia that, reinterpreted according to the Israelite faith in Yahweh, became part of the Hebrew Bible/Old Testament. How did biblical writers transform old traditions about a great flood to express their belief in a righteous God? What similarities can you see between Ptah's creation of the universe and the account of creation in Genesis 1? Why did Egyptian, Mesopotamian, and Israelite views of creation all postulate the existence of a primal watery abyss?

2. Ancient Israel's geographic location between the mighty empires of Egypt and Mesopotamia virtually ensured its repeated domination by superior military forces. Rather than view their history as the result of a vulnerable position and the realities of international aggression, however, most biblical writers interpreted Israel's rise and fall as a consequence of its failure to worship Yahweh alone. How do you interpret Judah's destruction by Babylon (587 B.C.E.) and again by Rome (70 C.E.)? Why did Yahweh not protect his covenant people from their enemies?

TERMS AND CONCEPTS TO REMEMBER

Akhenaton	Herod I
Akkadians	hieroglyphics
Alexander the Great	Hyksos
Amarna Age	Ishtar
Amorites	Jeremiah
Antiochus IV	Jericho
Anu	Jezreel
Armageddon	Jordan River
Ashurbanipal I	Josiah
Assur (Asshur)	Judea
Assyria	*lex talionis*
Aton (Aten)	Maat
Atrahasis	Maccabees
Baal	Marduk
Babylon	Mari
Babylonian exile	Megiddo
Beersheba	Merneptah
Carchemish, Battle of	Mesopotamia
circumcision	Moab
Code of Hammurabi	monolatry
Constantine	Naram-Sin
cuneiform	Nebuchadnezzar
Dead Sea	Nineveh
Diaspora	Osiris
Ea	Palestine
Ebla	Persia
Egypt	Pompey
El	Pontius Pilate
Ezekiel	Ptolemy
Fertile Crescent	Rameses II
Galilee, Sea of	Rosetta Stone
Gilgamesh	Samaria/Samaritans
Hammurabi	Sargon I
Haran (in Syria)	Sargon II
hasidim	Second Temple period
Hasmoneans	Seleucus
Hellenism/Hellenistic	Sennacherib

Shamash
Sin
stele
Sumerians
tell (tel)
Theodosius
Tiberius
Tigris and Euphrates
   rivers

Titus
Transjordan
Ugarit (Ras Shamra)
Ur
Uruk
Utnapishtim
Vespasian
Zedekiah
ziggurat

RECOMMENDED READING

Aharoni, Yohanan, ed. *The Macmillan Bible Atlas,* 3rd ed. New York: Macmillan, 1993. An extremely useful historical atlas, with 271 maps.

Baly, Denis. *Basic Biblical Geography.* Minneapolis: Fortress Press, 1987. A useful introduction.

Kark, Ruth. *The Land That Became Israel: Studies in Historical Geography.* Translated by Michael Gordon. New Haven, Conn.: Yale University Press, 1990. An informative study.

Pritchard, James B. *The Atlas of the Bible.* New York: Harper & Row, 1987. A lavishly illustrated guide to the archaeology and historical geography of Canaan and other biblical lands.

Roaf, Michael. *Cultural Atlas of Mesopotamia and the Ancient Near East.* New York: Facts on File, 1990. An excellent source.

Rogerson, John. *Atlas of the Bible.* Oxford: Phaidon, 1989. Useful maps and illustrations.

CHAPTER 3

The God of Israel
An Evolving Portrait

Key Topics/Themes

Although Israel ultimately proclaimed that Yahweh alone is God, the biblical concept of Deity, evolving slowly over time, incorporated many different cultural sources to create a composite portrait of divinity. Historically, biblical writers appear to have appropriated traditions about El, head of the Canaanite pantheon, as well as other Near Eastern deities. Some scholars believe that Yahweh, the personal name of Israel's divine patron, may have originated among the Kenites, a people of Midian with whom Moses was closely allied. A champion of cosmic justice who jealously demands exclusive devotion, Yahweh is variously portrayed as warrior, king, judge, holy being, and loving partner. Showing a theological continuity with the Tanak, the New Testament's portrayal of God manifests a similar tension between his beneficence and his severity.

KEY QUESTIONS

Explain how the biblical concepts of God draw on ancient Near Eastern views of divinity, such as the Canaanite El. What concepts of God are as-

sociated with the different names for the biblical Deity? In what different roles does Israel's God appear? How did the transition from polytheism and henotheism to monotheism affect the Bible's portrayal of God? How does the New Testament Deity resemble that of the Hebrew Bible?*

> Listen then, Israel: Yahweh our God is the one Yahweh. You shall love Yahweh your God with all your heart, with all your soul, with all your strength.
>
> Deut. 6:4

This famous command in Deuteronomy, known as the **Shema**, is the essential expression of Israel's faith, a passionate commitment to a single God, Yahweh. Like the Shema (named for the Hebrew verb "hear" or "listen"), the first of the Ten Commandments enjoins Israel to worship Yahweh exclusively, to "have no gods except [him]" (Exod.

---

*Before undertaking this discussion of the historical origins of the complex, even contradictory nature of the biblical God, it is helpful to read the presentation of God's character in Genesis 1–35; Exodus 1–20, 24, and 32–34; Numbers 11–14; and Deuteronomy 1–9 and 28–34.

20:3; cf. Deut. 5:7). Neither of these Torah demands for total loyalty to Yahweh, however, denies that divine rivals to Israel's God may exist.

Although some biblical writers, such as the prophet known as **Second Isaiah**, eventually created a genuine monotheism, unmistakable traces of polytheism in the Hebrew Bible indicate that, at least in its earlier stages, Israelite religion was not monotheistic but henotheistic. **Henotheism**, allegiance to one god while conceding that others also exist, characterizes numerous biblical passages scattered throughout the canon. In Moses' song celebrating Yahweh's miraculous deliverance of his people at a turbulent sea, the poet asks, "Who *among the gods* is your like, Yahweh?" (Exod. 15:11, emphasis added). Israel's God is "incomparable" in his justice and saving power, but he is not the only deity in the universe. In Israel's eyes, he is simply superior to the others: "For Yahweh is a great God, a greater King than all other gods" (Ps. 95:3); he is "exalted far above all gods" (Ps. 97:9). On its long path to formulating the world's first ethical monotheism, Israel not only conceived of its God as one among many but also borrowed titles and attributes of foreign gods that were subsequently applied to the Israelite Deity. The Bible's complex portrait of God — to whom biblical authors assign an astonishing variety of roles and functions — is thus a creative synthesis that draws on many different sources.

An important clue to some of the diverse elements that contributed to the Hebrew Bible's composite portrayal of the Deity appears in the multiplicity of names and titles given him in the Hebrew text. Many English translations, however, tend to obscure the biblical texts' distinctions between different divine names. Although occasionally employing such titles as "the Holy One of Israel" or other epithets, English Bibles commonly use only a few terms to designate the Deity — "God," "the Lord," "LORD," or "GOD," and, less frequently, "the Almighty." Such uniform use of "Lord" or "LORD God" disguises and misrepresents the variety of terms that the authors of the Tanak evoked to express their vision of divinity. The presence of these different names is significant, offering important insights into the historical evolution of Israel's ideas about the Deity and suggesting that the origin of Israel's God is as complex, and in some ways as mysterious, as the historical origins of Israel itself (see Chapter 5).

The Names of Israel's God

ELOHIM

Several biblical books, notably Genesis, Exodus, Psalms, and Job, employ a particularly large number of terms to identify God. The first chapter of Genesis uses the generic name **Elohim**, a plural form denoting "gods" or "divine powers." Depending on its literary context, the plural *Elohim* is translated either "gods" (when referring to non-Israelite deities) or "God" (a capitalized singular when alluding to the biblical God) (cf. Exod. 12:12; Josh. 24:15; Judg. 6:10). In Genesis 1, for example, *Elohim* takes a singular verb, indicating the writer's intent to focus on the uniqueness of Israel's God. The most common biblical term for God, the plural *Elohim* may have been used even by strictly monotheistic writers as a grammatical device to emphasize God's supreme excellence and majesty.

THE CANAANITE EL

The singular form, **El**, is the common word for "divine being" in several ancient Near Eastern languages, including Hebrew and Canaanite, the language of **Canaan**, the region in which the Israelite people settled. As a generic term, it designates divinity in general. As a proper noun, however, El is the name of the chief god of the Canaanite **pantheon**, the roster of a community's officially recognized gods. Regarded as a divine king who presided over a heavenly assembly of other gods, El was worshiped throughout Canaan and Syria both before and after the establishment of Israel in Canaan. At a very early stage of Israelite religion, it appears that the Canaanite El was also acknowledged as Israel's patron deity, with whom Yahweh, the God of the Covenant, was later identified.

According to Genesis 33:20, "El [is the] God of Israel" (see the New Revised Standard Version's

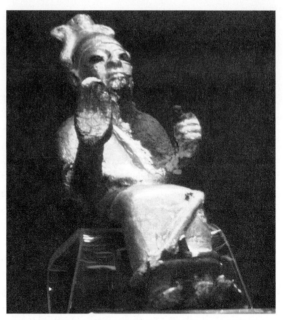

Figure 3.1 *Left:* The El stele from Ugarit. Scholars believe that the seated figure receiving homage represents the sky god El, head of the Canaanite pantheon and father of Baal, god of storm and earth's fertility. Whereas biblical writers consistently denounce Baal, they say nothing against El, who was widely worshiped as a celestial guarantor of justice throughout Syria and Canaan and was apparently identified with the Israelite Yahweh early in the development of the biblical concept of God. According to Genesis 33:20, "El [is the] God of Israel," a name that emphasizes Israel's pre-historic bond to El. *Right:* Seated figure of El. This statuette of bronze covered with gold depicts El, who was re-garded as an embodiment of divine wisdom and compassion, qualities also ascribed to Yahweh.

rendition of this statement: "El-Elohe-Israel"). The crucial importance of El in the evolution of biblical religion is clearly evident in Israel's name, which is a compound of El, meaning either "May El [God] contend" or "May El [God] rule." (For two differ-ent versions of God bestowing the name "Israel" on the patriarch Jacob, see Genesis 32:25–32 and 35:9–15.)

Beginning in the late 1920s, archaeologists ex-cavating at **Ugarit** (modern Ras Shamra in Syria) discovered an extensive Canaanite library, which included several texts preserving myths about El. Featured prominently in Ugaritic traditions from the fifteenth century B.C.E., in the myths of Aqhat, Keret, and Sahar and Salim, for example, El was viewed as the world's creator and the upholder of cosmic order. As divine sovereign who rules over both the celestial assembly and earthly political systems, El had a special relationship to the human king, who was called "son of El [God]." Known as

the "Father of Years" and revered for his merciful nature, El is depicted in Canaanite art as a dig-nified old man with a long beard, seated on a throne (Figure 3.1). This image of an aged divin-ity, serene and benevolent, may have influenced one of the Bible's best-known descriptions of God as the white-haired "Ancient of Days" in the Book of Daniel (Dan. 7:9–14).

The theory that the Canaanite El (a name oc-curring about two hundred times in the Tanak) was assimilated into the biblical concept of God at an early date is reinforced by the fact that no bibli-cal writer says a negative word about El. Despite the fact that El had altars and sanctuaries through-out the region, Israel's religious leaders apparently did not regard him as a threat. The opposite is true of El's son, **Baal**, the Canaanite god of storm and fertility. In book after book, Israelite prophets ve-hemently denounce the worship of Baal, who is consistently condemned as the chief rival of Yahweh. Baal, and his female consort **Asherah** (*Athirat* in Ugaritic), appear frequently as almost irresistibly attractive evils who lead Israel away from its covenant obligation to worship Yahweh alone. The prophets' total silence about Baal's parent indicates that by the time the prophetic literature was officially compiled, El had already merged with the figure of Yahweh, who assimilated many of the older Canaanite creator deity's qualities into his character.

In many biblical passages, El appears as part of a formulaic phrase, such as *El Shaddai, El Olam,* or *El Elyon,* or with other epithets that designate his special attributes. In Genesis, which preserves traditions about Israel's ancestors, Abraham, Isaac, and Jacob, wandering through the land of Canaan, the authors candidly indicate the evolutionary process by which some of El's traits were gradually assumed by Yahweh. When Abraham's Egyptian concubine, **Hagar**, unexpectedly receives Yahweh's promise that she will be blessed with countless descendants, she spontaneously identifies the unknown divine speaker as "El Roi," the "God of Seeing," realizing that she has "seen the one who sees me" (Gen. 16:7–14). At the Canaanite sanctuary of **Salem** (thought to be the future site of Jerusalem), Abraham is shown explicitly appropriating one of El's exalted titles, *El Elyon* ("God Most High") for his family deity, Yahweh (Gen. 14:17–23). At Beersheba, another Canaanite site, Abraham venerates *El Olam* (the "Everlasting God"), whom he commemorates by planting a tamarisk tree (Gen. 21:33). When Jacob dreams of a stairway to heaven, he names his God-haunted resting place "Bethel," the "House of El," a site that played an important part in Israel's later worship.

According to one tradition incorporated into the Book of Exodus, before the time of Moses the ancestral God was known to the Israelites only as **El Shaddai**, a phrase usually translated as "God Almighty," although many scholars believe that it means "God of the Mountain." The biblical Deity, like many other gods of Mesopotamia, Canaan, and Greece, was thought to dwell invisibly on a heavenly mountain, a cosmic peak such as that represented by the Greek Mount Olympus, celestial home of Zeus and the other Olympian gods. Exodus repeatedly refers to "the mountain of

God," which is given two different names, Sinai and Horeb, the place where God commissions Moses, where he identifies himself as *both* El Shaddai and Yahweh (cf. Exod. 3 and 6), and where he later communicates the Torah to his people (Exod. 19, 24, 34). (After Solomon's Temple was built on Mount Zion in Jerusalem, the sacred hill was seen as the earthly counterpart of Yahweh's heavenly abode [see Jon Levenson in "Recommended Reading"].)

Yahweh — Leader of the Divine Council

Some of the Hebrew Bible's oldest poetry depicts Israel's God as a member of the divine council, a heavenly assembly of divine beings. A belief that the gods who govern the cosmos regularly met to discuss their policies and formulate their plans for humankind permeates ancient Near Eastern thought. Apparently modeled on the practice of kings and emperors holding conferences with high-ranking advisers, the concept of a celestial assembly plays a prominent role not only in Canaanite myth, but also in such Mesopotamian works as the *Enuma Elish* creation story and the epics of Atrahasis and Gilgamesh. In the *Enuma Elish,* the Babylonian gods, threatened by Tiamat's aggression, meet to bestow supreme power on Marduk, acclaiming the young warrior god their champion against the dragon of chaos. In Gilgamesh, the gods hold council after the Flood to lament their destructive excesses; they also assemble to discuss ways to punish Gilgamesh for rejecting Ishtar's sexual advances. In the Atrahasis epic, they similarly confer after the great deluge, exploring less extreme options—such as plague, famine, and the assaults of wild beasts—for limiting human population growth (see Stephanie Dalley in "Recommended Reading").

In biblical parallels to these Near Eastern divine assemblies, Israel's God is distinguished from his divine peers by his ethical character, particularly his concern for humanity's poor and downtrodden. According to Psalm 82, God implicitly contrasts

his passion for justice with the other gods' misguided support of social and economic oppression:

> God stands in the divine assembly,
> among the gods he dispenses justice.
> "No more mockery of justice,
> no more favoring the wicked!
> Let the weak and the orphan have justice,
> be fair to the wretched and destitute,
> rescue the weak and the needy,
> save them from the clutches of the wicked."
>
> Ps. 82:1–4

Because his fellow divinities lack the biblical God's
compassion and sensitivity to human welfare, they
are "ignorant and senseless," acting "blindly," and
undermining the "very basis of earthly society,"
subverting divine justice (Ps. 82:5). Without the
capacity for ethical growth, the rival deities are
doomed to extinction, a prediction that forms the
poem's climax:

> I once said, "You too are gods,
> sons of the Most High [Elyon], all of you;
> but all the same, you shall die like [mortals]."
>
> Ps. 82:7

The notion that a god can die may startle modern
readers, but in the ancient world, defeated gods
may indeed cease to exist. After Marduk overthrows Tiamat's divine consort Kingu, he slays his
fallen opponent, later appointing Ea, Marduk's
father, to fashion humankind out of Kingu's clot-
ted blood. After her death, Marduk dismembers
Tiamat's corpse, utilizing part of her body to make
the earth and the remainder to shape the vault of
heaven.

Echoing traditions of El's heavenly court and
Canaanite polytheism, Psalm 89 also portrays Yahweh as a member of the "assembly of holy ones"
who is characterized by his unique "faithfulness":

> Who in the skies can compare with Yahweh?
> Which among the heaven-born can rival him?
> God, dreaded in the assembly of holy ones,
> great and terrible to all around him.
>
> Ps. 89:6–7

Empowered by his great wisdom and ethical superiority, Yahweh is eventually seen as reigning
supreme over other council members, known collectively as "the sons of the gods" (*bene ha elohim*).
Ultimately reduced to a dependant status as Yahweh's vassals and servants, the "sons of the gods"
become Yahweh's divine courtiers, running errands
and conveying orders to human recipients. It is
presumably these subjugated divine beings whom
Elohim addresses at creation when he proposes,
"Let us [plural] make man in our own image, in
the likeness of ourselves" (Gen. 1:26). God's associates in creation are also identified as the "stars of
the morning," the "Sons of God" who joyfully ac-
claim the universe's formation (Job 38:7). In the
second creation account, Yahweh similarly evokes
his supernatural retinue, observing that because
"the man has become like one of us"—acquired
godlike knowledge by eating of the forbidden
tree—he must be evicted from paradise before the
mortal human becomes fully divine by also ingest-
ing from the "tree of life" (Gen. 3:22). Yahweh
therefore posts **cherubim**, hybrid creatures with
the combined physical characteristics of humans,
animals, and birds (see Figure 6.7), to keep humanity from returning to its garden home, making
inaccessible the earthly source of immortality.

Although biblical writers rarely allude to Yahweh's hidden activities in heaven, three Tanak authors briefly lift the veil separating the spiritual
realm from our material world, showing Yahweh
holding court in heaven. In 1 Kings 22, the narrator portrays Yahweh seated on his throne and surrounded by "all the array of heaven"—the divine
courtiers and soldiers who constitute his invisible
"hosts [armies]." Yahweh's objective in calling this
assembly is to fashion a strategy by which Ahab,
king of Israel, can be lured into fighting a battle in
which he will be killed. After the council members
offer contradictory suggestions, one "spirit" volunteers to perform the deception:

> "How?" Yahweh asked him. He replied, "I will go
> and be a lying spirit in the mouths of all his
> prophets." "You shall trick him," Yahweh said,
> "you shall succeed. Go and do it."
>
> 1 Kings 22:19–22

In this brief glimpse of Yahweh's ordinarily hidden
manipulation of human actions, the writer depicts
the Deity using devious means to effect his pur-

pose, sending a "lying spirit" to inspire Ahab's court prophets with false assurances of victory and thus leading the unsuspecting king to his death.

A similar scene of Yahweh's exploitation of his courtiers' negative qualities implicitly lies behind the story in which one of God's supernatural agents afflicts **Saul**, Israel's first king, with madness. Having resolved to overthrow the man he had previously selected as king, Yahweh dispatches an "evil spirit" to torment Saul, intensifying his emotional instability and subverting his ability to reign effectively (1 Sam. 16:14–15). Because he has already decided to replace Saul with young David, Yahweh plans to bring David to prominence at Saul's court, for the youth's musical skills prove indispensable in calming Saul's mind:

> And whenever the [evil] spirit from God troubled Saul, David took the harp and played; then Saul grew calm, and recovered, and the evil spirit left him.
>
> 1 Sam. 16:23

Given some of the heavenly courtiers' willingness to lie, deceive, or torment, albeit on his own orders, it is not surprising that Yahweh is reluctant to trust them:

> In his own servants, God puts no trust,
> and even with his angels he has fault to find.
> Job 4:18

The prophet Zechariah offers a second portrayal of the heavenly court in session, envisioning Yahweh as rendering judgment between two opposing members of his retinue. One figure, "the **satan**," acts as Yahweh's prosecuting attorney whose function is to detect and expose humanity's errors, accusing them to the heavenly king. (In the Hebrew Bible, *satan*, which means "obstacle" or "adversary," is only humanity's enemy, not God's; Tanak writers do not grant him the cosmic authority he assumes in the New Testament. See Box 7.2). In Zechariah's account, Yahweh ignores his prosecutor's recommendation and decides in favor of the accused, Joshua the High Priest, whose case is represented by the second heavenly figure, an angel. Representing the covenant community on earth, Joshua is symbolically absolved of wrong-

doing, his "dirty" garments exchanged for clean raiment. Yahweh's **angel**—a term meaning "messenger"—who had defended Joshua against "the satan's" accusations, accordingly restores the priest to divine favor (Zech. 3:1–10).

The Book of Job describes two parallel meetings of the heavenly council. In the first, Yahweh summons all the "sons of God" before his throne, among whom is "the satan" (the Hebrew text uses the definite article to indicate that *satan* is not a proper name but merely a function). As in Zechariah's account, "the satan" is a regular member of the divine court, one whose job, like that of the secret police of an ancient Near Eastern emperor, involves his patrolling the earth to ferret out potentially disloyal subjects. Serving as the appointed officer through whom Yahweh identifies and punishes human misconduct, "the satan" introduces his deep distrust of humanity into the celestial proceedings. Apparently aware of his servant's cynicism, Yahweh brings Job, a person of exemplary righteousness, to his prosecutor's attention. "The satan" promptly accuses Job, and by implication all other mortals, of worshiping God for selfish reasons, seeking the protection from harm and the material rewards that the Deity accords his favorites. For unknown reasons, Yahweh accepts "the satan's" challenge, stripping Job of all he holds dear, including his children, health, reputation, and confidence in God's justice (Job 1–2; see Chapter 7).

YAHWEH'S ASSISTANTS

The authors of Samuel, Kings, and Job unveil deliberations of the divine council to portray God in seeming collusion with a "lying spirit," an "evil spirit," and "the satan" to accomplish his goals. Other biblical passages indicate that some members of the heavenly assembly also assisted Yahweh in his governance of the world. According to an old poem incorporated into Deuteronomy, when the "Most High [Elyon]" first assigned nations and peoples "according to the number of the sons of God," giving each deity a particular group to rule, Yahweh, who is here probably distinct from the "Most High," received Israel as his "portion" or "share of inheritance [from Elyon]" (Deut. 32:8–9). This ancient tradition apparently lies behind the Book of Daniel's depiction of different heavenly beings directing the activities of different nations. In Daniel, the only canonical book in the Hebrew Bible to provide names for individual angels, Gabriel, a conveyer of visions, informs Daniel that each of the empires that successively dominates the ancient Near East is ruled by a spirit prince, and that Israel's supernatural patron and protector is Michael, an archangel (Dan. 10:4–21; cf. 12:1).

YAHWEH'S GEOGRAPHICAL ASSOCIATIONS

Whereas El was well known throughout ancient Canaan and Syria long before Israel became a nation, Yahweh seems to have been much less widely recognized. When Moses appeared before Pharaoh to demand Israel's release from bondage, the Egyptian ruler implies that he has never heard of the Israelite God, or at least does not regard him as a power to be reckoned with: "Who is Yahweh," Pharaoh demands, "that I should listen to him and let Israel go? I know nothing of Yahweh" (Exod. 5:2–3). Indeed, Yahweh explicitly states that one of his primary reasons for staging all the spectacular "signs and wonders" involved in liberating Israel from Egyptian control is to enhance his public reputation. He instructs Moses to inform Pharaoh that Yahweh could easily have wiped Egypt from the face of the earth, but that he allowed Pharaoh to remain "to make [Pharaoh] see my power and to have my name published throughout all the earth" (Exod. 9:15–16).

Later in the Sinai wilderness, when Yahweh angrily threatens to exterminate a faithless Israel, Moses dissuades him, pointing out that Yahweh must realize that the international community will regard Israel's destruction as evidence of Yahweh's insufficient power. "If you destroy this people [Israel] now as if it were one man, then the nations who have heard about you [because of the plagues on Egypt] will say, 'Yahweh was *not able* to bring this people into the land he swore to give them and so he slaughtered them in the wilderness'" (Num. 14:15–16; emphasis added). Accepting Moses' argument, Yahweh determines that only the adult generation that left Egypt shall die; those under twenty will survive to enter Canaan.

Role of Jethro and the Kenites   Exodus' two different versions of how the divine name was first disclosed (Exod. 3 and 6) agree that God did not reveal himself as Yahweh until he did so to Moses at the burning thorn bush. How, then, did Moses experience a **theophany** (a manifestation or appearance of God) in which El Shaddai was identified with a previously unknown divinity named Yahweh? According to some scholars, the origins of Yahweh's worship are to be found in the culture of ancient **Midian**, a region east of the Gulf of Aqaba in northwestern Arabia (Figure 3.2). An early tradition integrated into the Exodus narrative places the "mountain of God," where Moses first encountered Yahweh, in or near Midian. Two of the older sources woven into the text of Exodus state that after Moses fled from Egypt, he came under the protection of a "priest of Midian," called **Jethro** in one strand (the Elohist) and Reuel in another (the Yahwist) (see Chapter 4 for a discussion of the documentary sources of the Pentateuch). Not only does Jethro/Reuel take Moses under his wing and give the fugitive his daughter **Zipporah** as a wife, he later presides over communal meals with Yahweh and acts as Moses' adviser in organizing Israel's judicial system. Although easy to overlook in the Torah's emphasis on Moses, Jethro's importance is evident at several crucial points in the story of Moses' relationship with Yahweh. It is while tending Jethro's flocks on Horeb, God's sacred mountain, that Moses receives the revelation of the divine name, Yahweh (Exod. 3–4). Immediately after that first theophany—and before carrying out Yahweh's orders to return to Egypt—Moses goes to Jethro to request permission to leave Midian (Exod. 4:18).

As Moses leads the people from Egypt back to the Midianite "mountain of God" for a second theophany—at which Yahweh's legal instructions for Israel will be disclosed—Jethro reappears in the narrative, his activities filling an entire chapter (Exod. 18). Again, Jethro's importance is highlighted, with Moses showing deference to his father-in-law by going out of the camp to meet him, bowing down before him, and personally

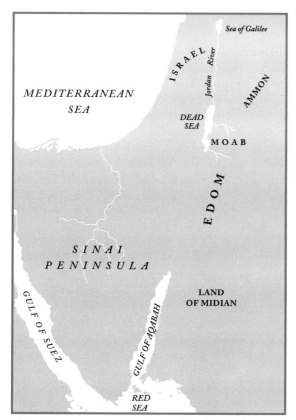

Figure 3.2 Map showing the location of Midian. The geographical region associated with Midian was the northwestern corner of the Arabian Peninsula, east of the Gulf of Aqabah and south of Edom. According to an ancient tradition now embedded in the Exodus narrative, Moses first encounters Yahweh while working for his father-in-law Jethro (also called Ruel), a "priest of Midian." Some scholars believe that the "mountain of God" (named "Sinai" in one literary strand and "Horeb" in another), was located in Midian rather than on the Sinai Peninsula. In this view, Yahweh was originally the god worshiped by Midianites and later identified with El, head of the Canaanite Pantheon (cf. Exod. 3:13–15; 6:2–4).

over the priestly rituals, offering sacrifices "in the presence of God" (Exod. 18:12). Moses then carries out Jethro's detailed instructions for establishing a hierarchy of magistrates to settle the people's legal disputes. In his last recorded service to Israel, Jethro is shown guiding Moses and the Ark of the Covenant as they leave "the mountain of God," where Yahweh had revealed his Torah, to begin the long wilderness journey to Canaan (Num. 10:29–32).

The old traditions associating Yahweh's sacred mountain and the commissioning of Moses with Jethro and Midianite territory is reenforced by some of Israel's earliest poetry. An archaic war hymn in Judges states that Yahweh traveled to Canaan, Israel's Promised Land, from regions south and east of Israel:

> Yahweh, when you set out from Seir,
> as you trod the land of Edom,
> earth shook, the heavens quaked,
>   and the heavens poured,
> the clouds dissolved into water.
> The mountains melted before Yahweh,
> before Yahweh, the God of Israel.
>   Judg. 5:4–5

Ancient verses appended to Deuteronomy agree that

> Yahweh came from Sinai,
>   For them, after Seir, he rose on the horizon,
> after Mount Paran he shone forth.
> For them he came, after the mustering at Kadesh,
> from his zenith as far as the foothills.
>   Deut. 33:2

A third reference, from the prophet Habakkuk, gives the same locale for Yahweh's mountain abode:

> Eloah [another "El" name for God] came from
>   Teman,
>   and the Holy One from Mount Paran.
> His majesty veils the heavens,
>   and the earth is filled with his glory . . .
> When he stands up he makes the earth tremble,
> with his glance he makes the nations quake.
> Then the ancient mountains are dislodged;
>   the everlasting hills sink down.
> I have seen the tents of Cushan terrified,
>   the pavilions of the land of Midian shuddering.
>   Hab. 3:3–7

bringing him up to date on Israel's escape from Egypt. Jethro's response to Yahweh's humiliation of Pharaoh serves to confirm that Yahweh's goal in publicizing his "name" among the nations has been accomplished: "Now I know that Yahweh is *greater than all the gods*" (Exod. 18:11, emphasis added; cf. Exod. 9:15–16). Even though Aaron, Israel's official High Priest, is present on this occasion, Jethro takes precedence over Aaron by presiding

Because these early traditions concur that Yahweh and his geographical homeland were to be found in Seir, Edom, Teman, Cushan, and Midian, all of which are located in the northwest Arabian Peninsula—Median territory—some scholars argue that Yahweh's worship originated there.

Jethro, the priest to whom even Moses and Aaron deferred, belonged to a subgroup of the Midianites known as the **Kenites,** famous for their skill in metal craft. The theory that the Mosaic cult of Yahweh originated in this branch of the Midianites is known as the **Kenite hypothesis.** First proposed about a century ago, this hypothesis has recently been revived and revised by such scholars as Frank M. Cross (see "Recommended Reading"). Although many scholars find the Kenite proposal suggestive, it has won only limited acceptance. Proponents of the theory point out, however, that the passages showing Jethro and the Midianites in a favorable light must be very early; by the time Israel was fully settled in Canaan, the Midianites had become political enemies (see Judges 6–8), and later Israelite writers are unlikely to have composed narratives in which the authority of a Midianite religious leader is recognized by both Moses and Aaron. Recent archaeological discoveries in northern Arabia indicate the presence of Midianites there before 1100 B.C.E. Egyptian inscriptions of the period refer to this group by the general term *Shasu;* a list by the pharaoh Amenhotep III mentions the "land of the Shasu: *S'rr,*" which probably designates Seir. Another list cites "the land of the Shasu: *Yhw3,*" an apparent reference to Yahweh (see Coogan in "Recommended Reading").

Roles and Characteristics of the Biblical God

Whatever the geographical origins of Yahweh, the diverse Near Eastern sources blended together in the biblical portrayal of God are reflected in the Deity's multifaceted character. The Hebrew Bible begins its composite portrait with a hymn to his creative might. In Genesis 1, Elohim first appears as the originator of light, methodically transforming the sterile darkness of primal chaos into a life-filled cosmos in which light and dark alternate. Surveying his completed work, Elohim pronounces the harmonious world order he has fashioned, including its human images of his divinity, "very good" (Gen. 1:31). Only six chapters later, however, Yahweh reverses Elohim's optimistic evaluation of humanity: "Yahweh regretted having made man on the earth and his heart was grieved. 'I will rid the earth's face of man, my own creation . . . and of animals also, reptiles too, and the birds of heaven; for I regret having made them'" (Gen. 6:6–8). Repelled by humankind's "wickedness," Yahweh then drowns all of earth's creatures, both human and animal, except for the few that he preserves in Noah's wooden boat.

The Bible's first eight chapters, in which God first creates life and then annihilates it, establish a tension between the Deity's creative and destructive tendencies that characterizes his behavior from Genesis to Revelation. Although capable of mercy and compassion, the biblical Deity possesses so lofty an ethical sense that he can rarely tolerate anything less than total adherence to the exacting standards he sets. In the biblical worldview, human misconduct inevitably invites divine punishment, often of a spectacularly violent nature, as when Yahweh incinerates entire cities with fire from heaven (Gen. 19), slays all of Egypt's firstborn sons (Exod. 14), or sends epidemics to wipe out tens of thousands of his own people.

The seeming paradox of God as both Creator and Destroyer of life stems partly from conflicting traditions about the gods that Israel inherited from older Near Eastern cultures. In the myths from ancient Mesopotamia, different gods played different roles in stories about creation and a prehistoric flood. In the *Enuma Elish,* one god—Marduk—subdues the forces of chaos and creates the world from Tiamat's body, after which he delegates the task of creating humankind to his father Ea, the god of wisdom. (Another tradition, found in the Atrahasis epic, states that a mother goddess, Nintu-Mami, is the divine potter who shapes humans out of clay.) In Mesopotamian tradition, however, none of these creator gods is responsible for destroying humanity in a global deluge. According to the Gilgamesh epic, it is Enlil, the ill-tempered god of storm and wind, who persuades the divine assembly to drown all humanity. A friend to humanity, the compassionate Ea subverts Enlil's destructive plan by secretly warning the man Utnapishim of the imminent disaster and instructing him to build an ark in which his family, as well as representative animals, reptiles, and birds, will be saved. The ancient polytheistic version of the Flood story, in which two opposing deities, Enlil and Ea, take opposite roles of destroyer and savior, thus makes reasonably good sense. When the Genesis writers revised and adapted the Mesopotamian traditions to fit their emerging monotheism, however, they assigned the actions of three different deities—Marduk, Enlil, and Ea—to a single divinity, Yahweh/Elohim. As the author of Joshua 24 observes, Israel's forebears were familiar with Mesopotamian gods and their worship (Josh. 24:14); during their captivity in Babylon, Israelite leaders become equally well acquainted with Babylonian traditions, including stories of creation and the Flood.

As a result of this merging of formerly separate divine personalities, the biblical God manifests seemingly contradictory qualities and is consequently represented as having to change his mind about his own creative work, "regretting" that he had made a flawed humanity (see Exod. 32:14 for another divine change of mind). In Genesis 6–8, which weaves together two originally independent deluge accounts from two different literary sources (see Box 2.1), God takes over both Enlil's role as violent destroyer and Ea's role as the savior of Noah and his three sons, survivors who will repopulate the post-Flood world. In monotheism—which ascribes all things to one Deity—light and dark, mercy and judgment, peace and violence, life and death, all must have a single divine source (see Isa. 45).

Although the biblical God may have assumed some of the conflicting traits of older Near Eastern deities that contribute to his somewhat paradoxical character, he also manifests qualities that radically distinguish him from other ancient gods. Yahweh is unique in his inflexible demand to be worshiped exclusively. Whereas all the major gods of polytheism expected suitable recognition and respect, they did not ask people to honor them alone. Yahweh, however, describes himself as a "jealous God,"

roused to fury when anyone in the covenant community prays or sacrifices to any of the innumerable other deities whom the Israelites are said to have worshiped along with Yahweh. (See Judges 10:6 for a partial list of Near Eastern nations whose gods the Israelites also revered.) In addition to his refusal to share Israel's allegiance with divine competitors, Yahweh also forbids any artistic representation of himself or of his material creation (Exod. 20:3–6; see Chapter 4 for an apparent exception to this rule, golden images of the cherubim that guard the Ark of the Covenant).

GOD AS DIVINE SOVEREIGN

In perhaps his most fundamental self-description, Yahweh outlines both the kindness and severity inherent in his character. Alone with Moses atop Mount Sinai/Horeb, Yahweh permits Moses to observe his back (to see his face is prohibited), while striding before his servant and reciting:

> Yahweh, Yahweh, a God of tenderness and compassion, slow to anger, rich in kindness and faithfulness; for thousands he maintains his kindness, forgives faults, transgressions, sin; yet he lets nothing go unchecked, punishing the father's fault in the sons and in the grandsons to the third and fourth generation.
>
> Exod 34:5–7

Yahweh thus informs Moses of the conflicting qualities, simultaneously beneficent and dangerous, that he will express in his relationship with Israel. Although he is gracious, merciful, loving, and patient, his perfect righteousness demands that human wrongdoing be punished. Yahweh's resolve to chastise any generation of Israel for the sins of its ancestors is an expression of his divine sovereignty—a function of his omnipotence and absolute freedom. It is this unlimited sovereignty that allows him to employ any means he wishes to accomplish his goals; he is not subject to human standards of fairness or ethical responsibility, as in his "hardening" of Pharaoh's "heart" or his use of "evil" or "lying" spirits to manipulate disobedient humans.

In time, Yahweh modifies the Torah principle of penalizing the entire covenant community for errors committed by previous generations. During

Box 3.1 Anthropomorphism, Patriarchy, and the Gender of God

Although numerous biblical writers insist on God's *transcendence*—his absolute freedom from earthly or other material limitations—others portray the Deity in anthropomorphic language. **Anthropomorphism**, ascribing human shape, form, and emotion to a divinity, characterizes most ancient religions, in which artists typically portrayed gods as idealized human beings, only larger and enormously more powerful. Rare in passages by priestly or Wisdom authors, anthropomorphism is relatively common in the Tanak's narrative and prophetic literature. In Genesis and Exodus, God is endowed with human characteristics and behaviors: He strolls through Eden to enjoy a cooling breeze (Gen. 3:8); he appears to Abraham in the guise of a traveler enjoying an hospitable meal (Gen. 18–19); he inscribes stone tablets with his "finger" (Deut. 9:10); he permits Moses to observe his "back," while shielding his "face" from view (Exod. 33:22–23); he even allows seventy Israelite leaders to look directly at him as if he were an object of physical sight (Exod. 24:9–11). In the Prophets and Psalms, writers make innumerable references to the divine anatomy, citing such appendages or features as his "feet," "hands," "mouth," or "nostrils" (characteristically dilated in anger). Daniel provides

what has become perhaps the most enduring popular image: God as the "Ancient One," with the "hair of his head like pure wool," and wearing "clothes white as snow" (Dan. 7:9). Although traditional interpreters regard these anthropomorphic features as literary metaphors, we cannot be certain that ancient poets consciously saw them as mere figures of speech.

The Genesis assertion that God fashioned humanity as an "image" and "likeness" of himself has invited considerable speculation about the nature of the divine-human affinity. Although traditional Judeo-Christian interpretation denies that Genesis implies a physical resemblance between God and humans, some biblical writers suggest a spiritual, psychological, or even political "likeness." Psalm 8, for example, states that Yahweh made "man" only a "little less than a god" and "crowned him with glory and splendor," installing him as "lord over the work of your hands" (Ps. 8:4–6). Mirroring God's sovereignty on an earthly level, humans, in their role as caretakers of creation, rank close to God himself when exercising wise governance of the terrestrial environment.

To many modern readers, one of biblical anthropomorphism's most troubling aspects is its consistent

---

the Babylonian exile (sixth century B.C.E.), he declares to the prophet Ezekiel that henceforth the Israelites will not be made to suffer for their predecessors' misconduct. Having punished Israel so thoroughly that it was virtually exterminated, Yahweh states that in the future he will deal with each new generation separately; those persons who faithfully keep Torah regulations will not be punished for the sins of either their ancestors or their descendants (Ezek. 18).

GOD AS WARRIOR

At different periods of its history, Israel emphasized different traits and functions of its God. We will discuss only a few of the biblical God's many roles: warrior, holy being, king, lord of history, loving partner, and ultimate reality (Box 3.1). Although both Canaanite and Israelite tradition generally depict El as a pacific figure, Yahweh appears to have emerged in Israel's consciousness first as a divine warrior, the powerful conqueror of Egypt's Pharaoh and the battle captain who led Israel's forces into Canaan. Long before priestly writers made their God the universal Creator, Israelite poets sang of Yahweh's prowess on the battlefield, praising him as *Yahweh Sabaoth*. Commonly translated "LORD of Hosts," this phrase actually refers to Yahweh as cosmic general, commander of invisible armies that he unleashes against Israel's Canaanite enemies (Josh. 5:13–15).

In most ancient societies, the earliest literature takes the form of oral poetry, such as war hymns commemorating a people's victories. Most scholars believe that some of the oldest passages in the Bible are based on archaic military songs that were

Box 3.1 *(continued)*

association of God with traditional male roles and its use of masculine pronouns when alluding to the Deity. Although a few writers evoke maternal images in describing Yahweh (Isa. 49:15), most portray God in decidedly masculine terms: He is a warrior, king, judge, or executioner who intimidates and dominates because of his enormous strength. He is also imagined in familial terms, as a father who laments the waywardness of his children (Hos. 11) or a husband who agonizes over the infidelity of his treacherous wife (Hos. 1–2). Because the power to control nature and intervene in human affairs is a prerequisite of divinity in almost every culture — and because ancient societies typically emphasized masculine values and attitudes — it is perhaps historically inevitable that Israel's God is regularly portrayed in masculine terms. Like most of its Near Eastern neighbors, ancient Israel was a **patriarchy**, a social organization marked by the supremacy of the father in a clan or family, a sociopolitical arrangement in which male leadership and standards constitute the prevailing norm and in which women and children are generally subject to patriarchal control.

   While espousing patriarchal values, however, the Genesis authors also suggest that God transcends common notions of gender: He creates *both* males and females "in his image" (Gen. 1:27). According to some commentators, this passage implies that the Creator is androgynous, encompassing both masculine and feminine qualities in the divine nature. It also reminds us that the Deity belongs to the *Other*, a dimension of reality profoundly different from the material realm to which humans are bound. Infinitely mysterious and undefinable, God by definition represents forces beyond human ability to emulate or comprehend. Although given anthropomorphic traits, the biblical Deity embodies a mode of existence intrinsically alien to that of humanity.

   Given the historical fact that both the Hebrew Bible and the New Testament were written by and for members of a thoroughly patriarchal society, today's readers may view the anthropomorphic and gender-biased portraits of the Deity as culture-bound. While respecting the integrity of the ancient texts in which God is invariably "he" — and the simple linguistic fact that the Hebrew language has no word for "it" — many contemporary believers, in both synagogue and church, acknowledge that the ineffable Being whom biblical authors seek to communicate cannot be contained in finite human categories, including those of gender.

composed and transmitted orally for centuries before they were crystallized in writing. Some of these songs were apparently collected in an anthology (now lost) known as the Book of Jashar (or the Book of the Just), which is cited in the canonical Joshua. A verse quoted from Jashar contains the famous command for sun and moon to "stand still over Gibeon," evoking nature's cooperation so that Israelite troops can take advantage of extended daylight to slaughter their opponents (Josh. 10:13).

   A similar poetic volume, the Book of the Wars of Yahweh, is quoted in Numbers 21, in which Yahweh supplies Israel's invading armies with fresh well water, enabling them to sweep like a "fire" over Sihon, an Amorite king who refuses to allow Israelite tribes to pass through his territory (Num. 21:15, 18, 28–30). Other ancient war poetry, incorporated into the Book of Judges, appears in the Song of Deborah, who extols the woman Jael for murdering Sisera, a Canaanite leader who took refuge in her tent. Deborah's poem applies to Yahweh's fierce advance from Edom (Seir) some of the same violent storm images that Canaanite poetry uses to describe Baal as warrior (Judg. 5:4–5).

   Yahweh's greatest military achievement is his defeat of the Egyptian army, which he drowns in a chaotic sea, a miraculous victory celebrated in the Song of Moses:

> Yahweh I sing: he has covered himself in glory, horse and rider he has thrown into the sea. . . .
> *Yahweh is a warrior;*
> Yahweh is his name.
>
> Exod. 15:1, 3, emphasis added

By briefly reviving the primal watery chaos that preceded creation (Gen. 1:1) to engulf his enemies,

Yahweh decisively answers Pharoah's earlier question: "Who is Yahweh that I should listen to him?" (Exod. 5:2).

When the Israelites are about to invade Canaan, Yahweh, or his agent, appears to assure their leader Joshua that his people enjoy the support of divine battalions. Joshua sees a mysterious figure who grasps a "naked sword" and who identifies himself as the "captain of the army of Yahweh," guaranteeing that an obedient Israel is invincible (Josh. 5:13–15). Centuries later, Yahweh's importance as warrior is again emphasized when young David, Israel's future king, tells the giant Goliath that "Yahweh is the lord of the battle" (1 Sam. 17:47). As late as the sixth century B.C.E., Second Isaiah, who envisions Yahweh leading his people on a "new exodus" out of Babylon, describes God as a mighty warrior (Isa. 42:13; cf. Isa. 45:1–6, 13).

GOD AS HOLY BEING

Whereas Israel's oldest conceptions of Yahweh may have presented him primarily as warrior, his supreme holiness is also a vital part of the composite biblical portrait. To the priestly writers who composed the elaborate instructions for ritual worship found in parts of Exodus, Leviticus, Numbers, and Ezekiel, their God was absolutely holy — set apart from ordinary life and approachable only through elaborate ceremonies that he himself prescribed. The vast gulf between the holy, ineffable God and ordinary Israelites could be bridged only through the ministrations of Israel's hereditary priests, who mediated between worshiper and Deity. After David's son Solomon centralized Israel's worship by building a new royal sanctuary in Jerusalem, officially delegated priests presided over the animal sacrifices believed necessary to atone for sin and reconcile God and his people.

While in the Jerusalem Temple, the prophet Isaiah had a vision of Yahweh's awe-inspiring holiness, with his heavenly throne surrounded by tens of thousands of celestial beings called *seraphs* (plural, *seraphim*) (Isa. 6:1–8). Mentioned only in this passage, the **seraphim**'s principal function is to praise God, whose incomparable holiness they extol. Possessing three pairs of wings, the seraphim

use one set for flying, one for covering their eyes (shielding them from the glare of God's blinding radiance), and one for covering their "feet," perhaps a euphemism for genitals (Isa. 6:1–8). Because the word appears several times associated with the serpents that attacked the Israelites in the wilderness (Num. 21:8; Deut. 8:15; Isa. 14:29; 30:6), many scholars believe that it refers to "fiery serpents." As the cherubim displayed the nonhuman features of birds and animals, so the seraphim may have been serpentine in form and radiated flame, a common symbol of the divine presence.

GOD AS KING

One of the Tanak's fundamental assumptions is that Yahweh invisibly reigned over Israel as king (Deut. 33:5; Judg. 8:23; Isa. 43:15). Several psalms also hail Israel's God as ruler of all nations (Pss. 22:28; 47:2, 7–8). A group of poems known as the "Enthronement Psalms" (Pss. 93, 95–99) emphasize his universal sovereignty, as well as his future intention to subdue all peoples (Pss. 96:13; 98:9; see Chapter 7). As heaven's king, Yahweh establishes a special relationship with Israel's royal family, authorizing the institution of monarchy and guaranteeing that David's heirs will rule over Israel "forever" (2 Sam. 7:8–17; 23:5; Ps. 89:19–37). When Davidic kings are crowned, Yahweh adopts them as "sons," echoing El's paternal relationship to Canaanite rulers (Ps. 2; 110). Because of the close bond between Yahweh and the Davidic dynasty, the authors of Chronicles can refer to the Davidic throne as God's "kingdom" (1 Chron. 17:14; 28:5; 29:11). As cosmic sovereign who administers earthly societies through kingly representatives, Yahweh, in some respects, resembles the idealized monarch of a Near Eastern empire — powerful and scrupulously just, but jealous of his supreme authority and easily provoked to punish insubordination.

GOD AS LORD OF HISTORY

The authors of Israel's national epic, Genesis through 2 Kings, present Yahweh as the Lord of history, the all-powerful director of human events who determines the fate of both Israel and its neighboring states. For some later writers, Yahweh also writes the script of global history. In Daniel, he is shown overseeing the succession of ancient Near Eastern powers, from Babylon and Persia, to Greece and the Hellenistic kingdoms (Dan. 2; 7–11). In this role, Yahweh is also cosmic Judge, the Being on whose will all persons and nations depend for justice. As the prophet Amos states, it was commonly believed that the biblical God controlled everything that happened, from Israel's military victories and defeats to great natural disasters (Amos 3:3–8).

GOD AS LOVING PARTNER

While emphasizing Yahweh's firm control of history, many of Israel's prophets also proclaimed his almost infinite capacity to love. Balancing the fear-inspiring aspects of divine power and holiness with divine *hesed*—which can be translated as "steadfast love" or "loyal affection"—several prophets designate this quality as one of God's most distinguishing characteristics. To illustrate God's passionate attachment to Israel, Hosea compares the Deity to a loving husband whose wife (Israel) is faithless and ungrateful. Hosea also uses the metaphor of a doting father and rebellious son, who, like an adulterous wife, could legally be condemned to death (Lev. 20:10; Deut. 21:18–21; 22:22). Although God's justice prompts him to execute Israel for its crimes, Hosea states that his *hesed* leads him to "recoil" from so harsh a judgment. He cannot bring himself to abandon "Ephraim" (a northern tribe standing for all Israel) to its enemies:

> When Israel was a child, I loved him,
> and I called my son out of Egypt.
> But the more I called to them, the further they
>   went from me;
> they have offered sacrifice to the Baals,
>   and set their offerings smoking before the idols.
> Yet I myself taught Ephraim to walk,
> I took them in my arms;
> yet they have not understood that I was the one
>   looking after them. . . .
> Ephraim, how could I part with you?
> Israel, how could I give you up?

> [God cannot bear to destroy his beloved.]
> My heart recoils from it,
>   my whole being trembles at the thought.
> I will not give rein to my fierce anger;
>   I will not destroy Ephraim again;
>   for I am God, not man;
>   I am the Holy One in your midst
>   and have no wish to destroy.
> Hos. 11:1–3, 8–9

Providing a rare glimpse into God's thought processes—an inner debate between conflicting emotions, righteous anger, and loving compassion—Hosea shows God's *hesed* winning out over his wrath. For he is God and not a fallible mortal who behaves according to merely human standards of retributive justice.

Because God loves Israel, he asks for Israel's love in return. Alone among the gods of antiquity, Yahweh asks his people not only to worship him exclusively but also to offer him unconditional love. The Shema's demand that the Israelites love Yahweh with all their hearts and souls, unparalleled in ancient religion, implies that Israel's God, as Hosea declared, feels a similar emotion for them (Deut. 6:4).

GOD AS ULTIMATE REALITY

Perhaps the most powerful declarations of God's unrivaled might and majesty occur in the pronouncements of Second Isaiah (Isa. 40–55). One of the greatest poets in the Hebrew Bible, Second Isaiah is an uncompromising monotheist who explicitly states that Yahweh alone is God, the incomparable Being whose will is irresistible in both earth and heaven. Categorically rejecting the existence of other divinities, the poet states that Yahweh is the source of all things, including both good and evil:

> I am Yahweh, unrivaled,
> I make the light and create the dark.
> I make good fortune and create calamity,
> It is I, Yahweh, who do all this.
> Isa. 45:6–7

In making Yahweh not only supreme, as other Bible writers did in asserting his superiority to other members of the divine assembly, but also the single universal Deity, Second Isaiah articulates an important new dimension in Israelite thought. When viewed as the sole source of everything that happens—light and dark, good and bad—the biblical God ultimately becomes even more problematic, his universal omnipotence raising ethical and theological issues with which Israel's Wisdom teachers would stage a long and creative struggle (see Chapter 7).

The biblical account of Israel's historical partnership with Yahweh—the central subject of the Tanak—features many memorable human figures, from Abraham and Sarah to Ruth and David. No matter how vividly realized, however, human actors in the biblical drama are always secondary to God, who is not only the object of Israel's worship but also the Hebrew Bible's undisputed protagonist. All that human participants do, all that they achieve by war, conquest, or any other means, is explicitly ascribed to Yahweh's actions. In the Exodus story, for example, Moses, his brother Aaron, his sister Miriam, and even Egypt's Pharaoh, are merely instruments that Yahweh maneuvers to achieve his long-term historical goals. Although biblical writers address only a limited segment of human history in one small part of the world, they nonetheless establish an enduring pattern of the divine-human relationship that remains the standard for both modern Judaism and Christianity.

God in the New Testament

The God depicted in the Hebrew Bible is also the God of the New Testament. Although some commentators argue that there is a major difference between Yahweh, the God of Israel, and the heavenly Father whom Jesus revealed, that stereotypical distinction is misleading. The alleged contrast between the Old Testament's legalistic, judgmental Deity and the New Testament's merciful God of grace does not bear up under scrutiny. God is both loving and vengeful in both the Jewish and Christian Scriptures, as the Gospel accounts of Jesus' suffering and death demonstrate. In presenting

Jesus' story, the Gospel writers maintain the tension between God's compassionate generosity and his unyielding demand for absolute submission to his will, no matter how painful to his human subjects. According to Matthew's Sermon on the Mount, Jesus portrays the Father as unconditionally loving, showering nature's blessings on both good and bad—a "perfect" altruism that humans should emulate (Matt. 5:43–48). Jesus urges people to trust implicitly in God's unlimited beneficence, to abandon themselves completely to his willingness to provide for all their needs (Matt. 6:25–34), for, like the generous father who does not distinguish between his worthy and unworthy children, God loves all people alike (Luke 15:11–32). Presenting a different aspect of the divine-human relationship, Mark's Gospel shows Jesus, on the night before his crucifixion, begging to be spared the humiliating and agonizing death that his Father apparently requires him to suffer (Mark 14:32–42). The God who demands his son's death is the same God who ordered Abraham to slay Isaac (Gen. 22). Like Isaac, or the millions of animals slaughtered at the Temple altar, Jesus is to be offered up as a blood sacrifice, a view expounded at length in the New Testament Book of Hebrews.

The complexity and paradox of the biblical Deity's ethical nature is also reflected in 1 John, in which the writer provides the Bible's only explicit definition of God. In studying this short document, readers find the author declaring that "God is light" and "God is love." But these confident assertions of God's essential goodness appear in the context of denigrating fellow believers who have split from his community. The author berates his former Christian brothers as "liars" and "Antichrist" (cf. 1 John 2, 4)—an attitude strikingly different from Jesus' vision of the Father's universal benevolence. In its portrayal of a vengeful and violent Deity, Revelation revives and perpetuates the image of Yahweh as warrior, annihilating most of the global population as he had once slain the Egyptian firstborn.

Although there is a strong theological continuity between the Old and New Testaments, the means by which God manifests himself in the Christian Scriptures differs significantly from the theophanies contained in the Pentateuch. With the exception of Revelation's images of the divine warrior, God is depicted in the New Testament primarily as an invisible presence, the power that brings about the birth — and death — of the Messiah and that guides the development of the Christian faith. God appears only as a disembodied heavenly "voice" in the first three Gospels, first to designate the newly baptized Jesus as his "beloved son" (Mark 1:11; Matt. 3:17; Luke 3:22) and again to affirm Jesus' authority at the Transfiguration, when Jesus suddenly appears to his disciples as a being of light (Mark 9:2–8; Matt. 17:1–8; Luke 9:28–36). As Moses spoke Yahweh's instructions to the assembled Israelites in Deuteronomy, so Jesus, presented as a "greater Moses," speaks for God, delivering authoritative interpretations of the divine requirements (cf. Matt. 5–7; Luke 6). New Testament writers, however, depict Jesus as far more than Israel's ultimate prophet and teacher: In the Fourth Gospel, John, Jesus is the divine Word (Greek, *Logos*), the principle of cosmic Wisdom, who descends from heaven to earth (John 1:1–3, 14). In the prologue to John's Gospel, the Deity — or his eternal attribute of creative Wisdom — takes on flesh as Jesus of Nazareth, bridging the gulf between holy Deity and imperfect humanity. The doctrine of the **Incarnation** — that God himself became the man Jesus — eventually led to orthodox Christianity's distinctive concept of a triune God — Father, Son, and Holy Spirit. Officially articulated at the church Council of Nicaea in 325 C.E., the doctrine of the Trinity, which makes Jesus co-equal with God, is probably the major factor dividing Christianity from its parent faith, Judaism.

QUESTIONS FOR REVIEW

1. What does the Shema ask of Israel?

2. Define "monotheism" and "henotheism." Judging by references to Yahweh and "other gods" in the biblical texts, was ancient Israel always fully monotheistic?

3. Who was El to the Canaanites? How was El identified with Israel's divine patron, Yahweh? What qualities do they have in common? How does the name "Israel" incoporate the concept of El?

4. What was the Divine Council in ancient Near Eastern religious thought, and how did Yahweh come to dominate it? What were the attributes that distinguished him from other deities?

5. Who were the cherubim and seraphim? What are angels? What roles do they play in the divine court?

6. Define and explain the Kenite hypothesis. Why do many historians think that the worship of Yahweh originated in Midian? How does the Exodus account link Jethro, priest of Midian, with Moses?

7. Describe the different roles that different biblical authors ascribe to Yahweh. How did Israel eventually come to envision Yahweh as both Israel's special patron and world sovereign?

8. List the anthropomorphic qualities you find in biblical portrayals of God.

QUESTIONS FOR DISCUSSION AND REFLECTION

1. Ancient Mesopotamian poets could explain the contradictory actions of divine beings by subscribing to the notion that the god who created the world (Marduk) was not the same god who subsequently drowned almost all humanity in a global deluge (Enlil). In adapting these traditions to Israel's faith in Yahweh, biblical authors combined both the creative and destructive aspects of divinity in a single God, one who creates out of beneficence and annihilates out of righteous indignation when his human creation behaves badly. This concept of a Deity who is both gracious and violently punitive — the consequence of melding two different divine functions into one — has dominated the monotheistic religions for more than two millennia. Defend or argue against this proposition: Divine benevolence (God as Loving Partner) and divine brutality (God as Warrior) are really compatible.

2. In what ways do New Testament writers accept and adapt the inherited concept of Israel's God? Describe some aspects of the Father whom Jesus knew; how does Jesus' life — faithfulness coupled with unjust suffering and death — illustrate the paradox of an All-Good and All-Powerful God? Given that both the Hebrew Bible and New Testament are the literary products of long-vanished cultures of antiquity, how should people today interpret the biblical portrayal of God? From the perspective of your personal views of

ethical goodness, how would you modify the character of God as it is depicted in the Pentateuch and in Revelation? Explain your answer.

TERMS AND CONCEPTS TO REMEMBER

angel	God as Ultimate Reality
anthropomorphism	God's chief attributes
Baal and Asherah	henotheism
Canaan	incarnation
cherubim	Jethro
Divine Council, the	Kenites/Kenite hypothesis
El	esis
Elohim	Midian
El Shaddai	pantheon
God as Divine Warrior	patriarchy
God as Holy Being	Salem
God as Lord of History	seraphim
God as Loving Partner	Shema, the
God as synthesis of Near	Saul
Eastern deities	Ugarit (Ras Shamra)

RECOMMENDED READING

Albright, William F. *Yahweh and the Gods of Canaan: A Historical Analysis of Two Contrasting Faiths.* New York: Doubleday/Anchor Books, 1969. A pioneering study of Israelite religion evolving in its ancient Canaanite context.

Anderson, Gary A. "Introduction to Israelite Religion." In *The New Interpreter's Bible,* Vol. 1, pp. 272–283. Nashville, Tenn.: Abingdon Press, 1994. A recent scholarly survey of the historical evolution of Israel's God concept.

Brueggemann, Walter. *Theology of the Old Testament: Testimony, Dispute, Advocacy.* Minneapolis: Fortress Press, 1997. A thorough and highly sophisticated study of the Hebrew Bible's paradoxical portrayal of God.

Coogan, Michael D., ed. *The Oxford History of the Biblical World.* New York: Oxford University Press, 1998. Includes discussion of the Kenite hypothesis, which traces the origins of Yahwism to ancient Midian.

Cross, Frank M. *Canaanite Myth and Hebrew Epic: Essays in the History of the Religion of Israel.* Cambridge, Mass.: Harvard University Press, 1975 (paperback reprint, 1997). An authoritative examination of parallels between Canaanite religion and the biblical concepts of God.

———. *From Epic to Canon: History and Literature in Ancient Israel.* Baltimore: Johns Hopkins University Press, 1998. Collection of essays on Near Eastern cultural influences on Israelite religion.

Dalley, Stephanie. *Myths from Mesopotamia: Creation, the Flood, Gilgamesh, and Others.* New York: Oxford University Press, 1989. Provides complete translations of the *Enuma Elish* and the epics of Atrahasis and Gilgamesh.

Friedman, Richard Elliott. *The Hidden Face of God.* San Francisco: HarperSanFrancisco, 1995. Traces the gradual disappearance of God from the biblical text, following the arrangement of books in the Tanak.

Frymer-Kensky, Tikva. *In the Wake of the Goddesses: Women, Culture, and the Biblical Transformation of Pagan Myth.* New York: Fawcett Columbine, 1992. A brilliant analysis of the cultural processes by which biblical authors eliminated or transformed ancient concepts of feminine divinity.

Gerstenberger, Erhard S. *Yahweh the Patriarch: Ancient Images of God and Feminist Theology.* Minneapolis: Fortress Press, 1986. Argues that Yahweh originally had a female consort, Ahserah, who was later purged from the postexilic cult.

Good, Robert M. "Asherah," "Baal," and "El." In P. J. Achtemeier, ed. *The HarperCollins Bible Dictionary,* pp. 82–83, 94–95, 275–276. San Francisco: HarperSanFrancisco, 1996. Concise descriptions of three major gods in the Canaanite pantheon.

Lang, Bernhard. *The Hebrew God: Portrait of an Ancient Diety.* New Haven: Yale University Press, 2002. Argues that Israel's God incorporates the roles and functions of many ancient Near Eastern divinities.

Levenson, Jon D. *Sinai and Zion: An Entry into the Jewish Bible.* San Francisco: HarperSanFrancisco, 1985. Includes discussion of Israelite henotheism.

Miles, Jack. *God: A Biography.* New York: Knopf, 1995. Analyzes the Israelite God as he appears as a literary character in the Hebrew Bible (Tanak).

Niditch, Susan. *Ancient Israelite Religion.* New York: Oxford University Press, 1997. Places Israel's evolving concepts of God in their historical, sociological, and archaeological contexts.

Parker, Simon B. *Ugaritic Narrative Poetry.* Atlanta: Scholars Press, 1997. Shows important parallels between Canaanite literature and biblical descriptions of God.

Rabinowitz, Jacob. *The Faces of God: Canaanite Mythology as Hebrew Theology.* Woodstock, CT: Spring Publications, 1998. Explores the influences of Canaanite myth on biblical concepts of God, particularly the relationship of El to Yahweh.

Rose, Martin. "Names of God in the Old Testament." In D. N. Freedman, ed., *The Anchor Bible Dictionary,* Vol. 4, pp. 1001–1011. New York: Doubleday, 1992. An excellent essay with which to begin a study of the biblical God.

Smith, Mark S. *The Early History of God: Yahweh and the Other Deities in Ancient Israel.* San Francisco: Harper & Row, 1990. An indispensable study.

————. *The Origins of Monotheism: Israel's Polytheistic Background and the Ugaritic Texts.* New York: Oxford University Press, 2001. Examines evolution of biblical concepts of God in the Near Eastern context.

————. *Untold Stories: The Bible and Ugaritic Studies in the Twentieth Century.* Peabody, Mass.: Hendrickson Publishers, 2001. Reviews scholarly discoveries and interpretations of the tablets found at Ugarit from the late 1920s on.

Terrien, Samuel. *The Elusive Presence: The Heart of Biblical Theology.* San Francisco: Harper & Row, 1978. A perceptive study of the biblical concept of God.

Thompson, Henry O. "Yahweh." In D. N. Freedman, ed., *The Anchor Bible Dictionary,* Vol. 6, pp. 1011–1012. New York: Doubleday, 1992. Discusses the significance of the personal name of God, Yahweh.

CHAPTER 4

The Torah

Five Books of Divine Instruction
(the Pentateuch)

Key Topics/Themes

Depicting human history as a progressive revelation of the divine will, the Torah emphasizes both the promises of future benefits that Yahweh makes to Israel's ancestors, Abraham, Isaac, and Jacob, and the obligation laid upon these patriarchs' descendants, the Israelites, to worship Yahweh exclusively and obey all his laws. Containing a diverse mixture of narrative, genealogy, poetry, law, etiology, folklore, and myth, the first five books of the Tanak (the Pentateuch) are not the work of a single author, such as Moses, but the product of a long process of composition, revision, and repeated editing by different writers and redactors (editors) spanning many different periods of Israel's history. Although some scholars have recently challenged this theory, a majority of scholars believe that the best explanation for the Pentateuch's duplications, contradictions, and other discrepancies is that it is a composite work consisting of at least four different literary and/or oral sources. According to

the documentary hypothesis, the four sources— identified as J, E, D, and P—were combined by postexilic redactors to create the Pentateuch we have today.

Too complex in both literary origin and theological content to be reduced to a single viewpoint, the Bible's first five books are nonetheless partly unified by an emphasis on Yahweh's covenant relationship with his people and the recurrent theme of divine promises that are only partially fulfilled. In its final form, the Torah addresses the questions and concerns of a community of exiles hoping to repossess the land God had vowed to give Abraham's progeny.

KEY QUESTIONS

Why do scholars think that the Pentateuch is a composite document, incorporating four discrete sources? What literary forms does it contain? How do the divine promises to Israel's ancestors help to unify this diverse material?

The Torah: An Overview

The first division of the three-part Hebrew Bible, the Torah opens with an account of God's creation of the world and early interaction with humanity as a whole (Gen. 1–11), but quickly shifts emphasis to focus on the creation of Israel. Beginning with the call of Abraham in Genesis 12, the five books of Torah tell the story of Israel's origins and its transformation from a band of slaves into a "holy nation" dedicated to the service of Yahweh. Virtually all events in Israel's story, including its escape from Egyptian bondage and miraculous deliverance at a chaotic sea, are merely a prelude to the grand culmination—Yahweh's theophany at Mount Sinai/Horeb. The heart and soul of Torah (divine instruction) lie in the vast body of laws, statutes, and precepts that Yahweh transmits through Moses to the Israelites, prescribing a way of life that qualitatively distinguishes them from all other peoples. Even though the series of divine promises repeated throughout Genesis are only partly realized at the conclusion of Deuteronomy, God's instruction to Israel is by then complete, a divinely authorized legacy to guide all future generations of Abraham's children.

Near the end of Deuteronomy, Israel is asked to choose between fidelity to Yahweh, which will bring abundant life and prosperity to the nation, and the worship of other gods, which will inevitably bring suffering and death (Deut. 27–30). Israel's response to Yahweh's challenge determines its subsequent history: the Deuteronomistic narratives (Joshua–2 Kings) that follow Deuteronomy illustrate the disastrous consequences of breaking the Sinai agreement.

Who Wrote the "Books of Moses"?

The ancient belief that Moses composed the Pentateuch is based partly on several passages in Exodus, Numbers, and Deuteronomy in which Yahweh orders Moses to write down some of God's specific instructions. According to Exodus 17:14, Yahweh tells Moses to "write [about the defeat of Amalek, a local king] in a book to keep the memory of it." After receiving from Yahweh a list of legal ordinances (Exod. 21–23), known as the **Book of the Covenant**, Moses "put all [these particular] commands of Yahweh into writing" (Exod. 24:4); he also writes down the ritual laws revealed in Exodus 34 (Exod. 34:27–28) and Israel's travel itinerary during its long journey from Egypt through the Sinai wilderness (Num. 33:2). In all of these texts, Moses is depicted as recording only specific events and particular legal codes, not the whole Pentateuch.

In Deuteronomy, however, Moses is pictured as compiling the entire law code contained in that book (Deut. 31:9), as well as lyrics to a "song" he taught Israel (Deut. 31:19, 22). According to Deuteronomy 31, he was responsible for "the words of this law [Torah] to the very end" (Deut. 31:24), composing "this book of the law," which he then entrusts to Israel's priests for safekeeping (Deut. 31:9, 24–26). Most scholars believe that this legal work is the same "book of the law [Torah]" found during repairs on the Jerusalem Temple during the late seventh century B.C.E., more than 600 years after the period when Moses supposedly lived (2 Kings 22:8–23:3). The validation of a sweeping religious reform by king **Josiah** (640–609 B.C.E.), this early edition of Deuteronomy (probably consisting of chapters 12–26) was subsequently expanded to become the fifth book of the Pentateuch. In time, not only the legal code embedded in Deuteronomy, but all of Israel's sacred laws contained in the Pentateuch were ascribed to Mosaic authorship, imbuing them with that leader's stature and authority.

PROBLEMS WITH MOSAIC AUTHORSHIP

In contrast to traditional views of Mosaic authorship, virtually all contemporary scholars are convinced that, in its present form, the Pentateuch could not have derived from Moses. Careful scrutiny of the text offers compelling evidence that the Bible's first five books are not the work of a single author, but the product of multiple authors and editors laboring over a span of many centuries.

Even casual readers commonly notice numerous repetitions, contradictions, and discrepancies of all kinds that point to the composite nature of the Pentateuch. If Moses is the presumed author, why is he always referred to in the third person, as an author writing *about* him would do? If Moses is truly the "most humble of men, the humblest man on earth" as Numbers 12:3 describes him, would he plausibly make such an immodest evaluation of his personal humility? Readers also note Deuteronomy's many repetitions of the phrase "until this day," clear indications that the writer looks back from his time to that of a distant past (Deut. 3:14; 34:6, etc.). Deuteronomy's account of Moses' death might be seen as a postscript by a later hand, were it not in exactly the same style as that of the rest of the book—and in language virtually identical to that in the historical books (Joshua through 2 Kings) that follow (see Chapter 5). Frequent anachronisms, the placing of persons or events out of their proper chronological order, also indicate post-Mosaic authorship. Many statements in Genesis, such as "At that time the Canaanites were in the land" (Gen. 12:6; 13:7), refer to an epoch centuries after Moses' time, when the original inhabitants of Canaan had been expelled or assimilated by the Israelite population. References to territories east of the Jordan River as lying "beyond the Jordan" presuppose a vantage point on the west side of the river, but Israel's tribes did not occupy this western region until long after Moses' era (Gen. 50:10; cf. Num. 21:1). Other anachronisms, such as the Genesis list of Edom's kings who ruled "before an Israelite king ruled" (Gen. 36:31), demonstrate that the author lived at a period after Israel's monarchy had been established, centuries after Moses' day.

Repetitions and Duplications Even when studying the Pentateuch for the first time, readers are commonly struck by the great number of duplications, passages in which the same story—or a close variant—is told a second time, sometimes with the same characters and sometimes with different characters involved. The phenomenon of duplication, present throughout both narrative and legal sections of the Pentateuch, begins with two different versions of creation. In Genesis 1, which has a lofty, majestic style, Elohim (God) creates all life forms, beginning with plants and animals and culminating in the appearance of human beings, male and female, made simultaneously in his own image. Beginning with Genesis 2, which has a more vivid, earthy style, it is *Yahweh Elohim* (Yahweh God) who fashions the first man and, only after creating a series of animals—none of which proves a suitable mate for the human male—models the first woman from the man's rib. Whereas biblical editors sometimes placed two different accounts of the same event side-by-side, as they did with Genesis's two distinct creation stories, at other times they interwove two originally separate narratives. In Genesis 6–8, editors combined two stories of a global deluge—Noah's Flood—that can easily be disentangled to produce two parallel flood stories that are fully complete in themselves (Box 4.1.)

A story that illustrated a particular theme—the irresistible beauty of some Israelite women and the threat this attraction had to fulfilling God's vow to multiply Abraham's descendants—was apparently particularly popular with biblical writers, who include in Genesis three variations of the same tale. While traveling in Egypt, Abraham fears that Pharaoh will kill him in order to possess Abraham's wife Sarah, whom he accordingly passes off as his sister. After Pharaoh places Sarah in his harem, compensating her "brother" with lavish gifts of livestock, Yahweh afflicts Egypt's royal household with plagues (foreshadowing the ten plagues brought on a later pharaoh). Chastened, Pharaoh returns Sarah to her husband, reproaching Abraham for having deceived him (Gen. 12:10–20). Seemingly unmindful of Pharaoh's just criticism, in Genesis 20 Abraham again represents Sarah as his sister, this time to **Abimelech,** a Canaanite king. Again, God is angry, appearing to Abimelech in a dream and threatening to kill him for appropriating Abraham's wife. As in the previous version, Abraham receives a rich reward in cattle and slaves for having deceived a foreign ruler (Gen. 20:1–18). In the third variation on this

Box 4.1 Two Versions of the Flood Story

The present text of Genesis relating the story of a universal deluge combines two Flood accounts, attributed, respectively, to the Yahwist writer (J) and the priestly writer (P). Each of the two accounts stands alone as a complete and independent narrative in this translation by Richard Friedman. Priestly text appears in boldface and J text appears in regular type.

*The Flood — Genesis 6:5 – 8:22**

GENESIS 6

5   And Yahweh saw that the evil of humans was great in the earth, and all the inclination of the thoughts of their heart was only evil all the day.

6   And Yahweh regretted that he had made humans in the earth, and he was grieved to his heart.

7   And Yahweh said, "I shall wipe out the humans which I have created from the face of the earth, from human to beast to creeping thing to bird of the heavens, for I regret that I have made them."

8   But Noah found favor in Yahweh's eyes.

9   **These are the generations of Noah: Noah was a righteous man, perfect in his generations. Noah walked with God.**

10   **And Noah sired three sons: Shem, Ham, and Japheth.**

11   **And the Earth was corrupted before God, and the earth was filled with violence.**

12   **And God saw the earth, and here it was corrupted, for all flesh had corrupted its way on the earth.**

13   **And God said to Noah, "The end of all flesh has come before me, for the earth is filled with violence because of them, and here I am going to destroy them with the earth.**

14   **Make yourself an ark of gopher wood, make rooms with the ark, and pitch it outside and inside with pitch.**

15   **And this is how you shall make it: Three hundred cubits the length of the ark, fifty cubits its width, and thirty cubits its height.**

16   **You shall make a window for the ark, and you shall finish it to a cubit from the top, and you shall make an entrance to the ark in its side. You shall make lower, second, and third stories for it.**

17   **And here I am bringing the flood, water over the earth, to destroy all flesh in which is the breath of life from under the heavens. Everything which is on the land will die.**

18   **And I shall establish my covenant with you. And you shall come to the ark, you and your sons and your wife and your sons' wives with you.**

19   **And of all the living, of all flesh, you shall bring two to the ark to keep alive with you, they shall be male and female.**

20   **Of the birds according to their kind, and of the beasts according to their kind, and of all the creeping things of the earth according to their kind, two of each will come to you to keep alive.**

21   **And you, take for yourself of all food which will be eaten and gather it to you, and it will be for you and for them for food."**

22   **And Noah did according to all that God commanded him — so he did.**

GENESIS 7

1   And Yahweh said to Noah, "Come, you and all your household, to the ark, for I have seen you as righteous before me in this generation.

2   Of all the clean beasts, take yourself seven pairs, man and his woman; and of the beasts which are not clean, two, man and his woman.

3   Also of the birds of the heavens seven pairs, male and female, to keep alive seed on the face of the earth.

4   For in seven more days I shall rain on the earth forty days and forty nights, and I shall wipe

*From *Who Wrote the Bible* by Richard Friedman. Reprinted with the permission of Simon and Schuster. Copyright © 1987 by Richard Friedman.

(continued)

Box 4.1 (continued)

out all the substance that I have made from upon the face of the earth."

5   And Noah did according to all that Yahweh had commanded him.

6   **And Noah was six hundred years old, and the flood was on the earth.**

7   And Noah and his sons and his wife and his sons' wives with him came to the ark from before the waters of the flood.

8   **Of the clean beasts and of the beasts which were not clean, and of the birds and of all those which creep upon the earth,**

9   **Two of each came to Noah to the ark, male and female, as God had commanded Noah.**

10   And seven days later the waters of the flood were on the earth.

11   **In the six hundredth year of Noah's life, in the second month, in the seventeenth day of the month, on this day all the fountains of the great deep were broken up, and the windows of the heavens were opened.**

12   And there was rain on the earth, forty days and forty nights.

13   **In this very day, Noah and Shem, Ham, and Japheth, the sons of Noah, and Noah's wife and his sons' three wives with them came to the ark,**

14   **They and all the living things according to their kind, and all the beasts according to their kind, and all the creeping things that creep on the earth according to their kind, and all the birds according to their kind, and every winged bird.**

15   **And they came to Noah to the ark, two of each, of all flesh in which is the breath of life.**

16   **And those which came were male and female, some of all flesh came, as God had commanded him.** And Yahweh closed it for him.

17   And the flood was on the earth for forty days and forty nights, and the waters multiplied and raised the ark, and it was lifted from the earth.

18   And the waters grew strong and multiplied greatly on the earth, and the ark went on the surface of the waters.

19   And the waters grew very very strong on the earth, and they covered all the high mountains that are under all the heavens.

20   Fifteen cubits above, the waters grew stronger, and they covered the mountains.

21   **And all flesh, those that creep on the earth, the birds, the beasts, and the wild animals, and all the swarming things that swarm on the earth, and all the humans expired.**

22   Everything that had the breathing spirit of life in its nostrils, everything that was on the dry ground, died.

23   And he wiped out all the substance that was on the face of the earth, from human to beast, to creeping thing, and to bird of the heavens, and they were wiped out from the earth, and only Noah and those who were with him in the ark were left.

24   **And the waters grew strong on the earth a hundred fifty days.**

GENESIS 8

1   **And God remembered Noah and all the living, and all the beasts that were with him in the ark, and God passed a wind over the earth, and the waters were decreased.**

2   **And the fountains of the deep and the windows of the heavens were shut**, and the rain was restrained from the heavens.

3   And the waters receded from the earth continually, **and the waters were abated at the end of a hundred fifty days.**

4   **And the ark rested, in the seventh month, in the seventeenth day of the month, on the mountains of Ararat.**

5   **And the waters continued receding until the tenth month; in the tenth month, on the first of the month, the tops of the mountains appeared.**

6   And it was at the end of forty days, and Noah opened the window of the ark which he had made.

7   **And he sent out a raven, and it went back and forth until the waters dried up from the earth.**

Box 4.1 (continued)

8   And he sent out a dove from him to see whether the waters had eased from the face of the earth.

9   And the dove did not find a resting place for its foot, and it returned to him to the ark, for waters were on the face of the earth, and he put out his hand and took it and brought it to him to the ark.

10   And he waited seven more days, and he again sent out a dove from the ark.

11   And the dove came to him at evening time, and here was an olive leaf torn off in its mouth, and Noah knew that the waters had eased from the earth.

12   And he waited seven more days, and he sent out a dove, and it did not return to him ever again.

13   **And it was in the six hundred and first year, in the first month, on the first of the month, the waters dried from the earth.** And Noah turned back the covering of the ark and looked, and here the face of the earth had dried.

14   **And in the second month, on the twenty-seventh day of the month, the earth dried up.**

15   **And God spoke to Noah, saying,**

16   **"Go out from the ark, you and your wife and your sons' wives with you.**

17   **All the living things that are with you, of all flesh, of the birds, and of the beasts, and of all the creeping things that creep on the earth, that go out with you, shall swarm in the earth and be fruitful and multiply in the earth."**

18   **And Noah and his sons and his wife and his sons' wives went out.**

19   **All the living things, all the creeping things and all the birds, all that creep on the earth, by their families, they went out of the ark.**

20   And Noah built an altar to Yahweh, and he took some of each of the clean beasts and of each of the clean birds, and he offered sacrifices on the altar.

21   And Yahweh smelled the pleasant smell, and Yahweh said to his heart, "I shall not again curse the ground on man's account, for the inclination of the human heart is evil from their youth, and I shall not again strike all the living as I have done.

22   All the rest of the days of the earth, seed and harvest, and cold and heat, and summer and winter, and day and night shall not cease."

theme, it is Isaac, son of Abraham, who deceives Abimelech—now identified as a "Philistine" ruler—by misrepresenting his wife Rebekah as his sister. Although Abimelech reprimands Isaac for lying about his relationship with Rebekah, Isaac is richly rewarded by God, who makes him a rich man (Gen. 26:1–14).

Genesis also includes two different versions of Jacob's encounter with God in which his name is changed to Israel, identifying him as the progenitor of the twelve Israelite tribes. In the first, Jacob wrestles all night at Peniel with a mysterious figure whom he later identifies as God and who confers the name change (Gen. 32:22–32). In the second, which occurs not at Peniel but Bethel, the Deity calls himself *El Shaddai* ("God Almighty" or "God of the [Cosmic] Mountain") and again announces that Jacob will henceforth be called Israel (Gen. 35:9–15). Similarly, Genesis records two contra-

dictory accounts of Joseph's descent into Egypt: In one, his brothers sell him to Ishmaelites, who take him to Egypt (Gen. 37:25–27); in the other, Midianites pull him out of a dry well where his jealous brothers had thrown him, and it is they who sell him to the Ishmaelites (Gen. 37:21–25, 28–30).

As in the deluge story, the Exodus account of the Israelites crossing a chaotic sea is a blend of two (or three) once separate traditions that now appear as a single narrative (Exod. 14–15; see Box 4.6). Exodus also includes two distinct versions of Yahweh's revelation of his sacred name to Moses. Three chapters after God's extended conversation with Moses at the burning bush in which he identifies himself as the "God [Elohim] of your father," whose previously hidden name is Yahweh (Exod. 3:1–4:17), he again appears to Moses, as if for the first time. In this second version of the commissioning of Moses, Yahweh states that he was formerly known to Israel's ancestors not as Elohim, as Exodus 3:6 states it, but as El Shaddai:

> I am Yahweh. To Abraham, Isaac, and Jacob I appeared as El Shaddai; I did not make myself known to them by my name Yahweh.
>
> Exod. 6:3

The Deity's unequivocal declaration that he had not revealed his personal name, Yahweh, before confiding it to Moses contrasts strikingly with another tradition in the Pentateuch that Yahweh's name was known and used long before the Genesis flood. Beginning in Genesis 2:4b where "Yahweh God made earth and heaven," one literary strand identifies God as Yahweh throughout the Pentateuch. According to this contributor to the composite biblical story, Enosh, grandson of Adam, was the "first [person] to invoke the name of Yahweh" (Gen. 4:26). These conflicting claims about when Yahweh first disclosed his name offer important clues to the different sources and authorship of the Pentateuch.

THE DOCUMENTARY HYPOTHESIS: FOUR SOURCES OF THE PENTATEUCH

As noted in Chapter 1, source criticism endeavors to isolate and identify the different sources, both oral and written, that redactors incorporate into a written document. In studying the compositional history of the Pentateuch, source criticism has proven enormously influential, providing a comprehensive theory that many scholars think best accounts for the duplications, anachronisms, and other discrepancies found in the "Books of Moses." Known as the **documentary hypothesis**, this theory holds that the Pentateuch can be understood most effectively by recognizing its composite nature. Although a minority of scholars has recently challenged it, the documentary hypothesis remains the standard model in Pentateuchal studies and serves as the point of departure even for those who disagree with it.

According to the documentary theory, the Torah is a literary patchwork in which at least four originally separate documents and/or oral traditions—dating from four different periods of Israelite history—have been stitched together to form the present text. The interweaving of our once-independent sources explains both the repetitions and the contradictions in the present text (Table 4.1).

J, the Yahwist Source   According to the documentary hypothesis, the earliest source is called **J** because the author typically uses the name Yahweh (in German, *Jahweh*) for God. Also known as the **Yahwist** writer, J is the first to compose a continuous narrative of Israel's origins. J's work incorporates ancient **oral traditions** about Israel's prehistory as well as tales of the ancestral fathers and mothers. Designating God as Yahweh from the outset of his account, J opens his narrative with the second creation story (Gen. 2:4b–25) and the parable of Adam and Eve's loss of Eden (Gen. 3:1–24), as well as one version of the flood story. Emphasizing the indispensable role of women such as Sarah, Rebekah, Leah, and Rachel in this saga of Israel's ancestors, J recounts the wanderings of Israel's forebears, their descent into Egypt, and Yahweh's rescuing them from Egyptian bondage and guiding them to Mount Sinai, where he reveals his Torah. Although some scholars believe that J's narrative—distinctive portions of which are embedded in Genesis, Exodus, and Numbers—originally extended into the story of the conquest of Canaan and the establishment of the Davidic monarchy (Joshua, Judges, 1 and 2 Samuel), many scholars find it difficult to determine exactly where J's narrative ends. Some have proposed that J's contribution to the biblical story includes the **Court History**, an account of David's rise to power as king of Israel that forms the basis for most of 2 Samuel and 1 Kings 1–2. (See Friedman in "Recommended Reading.")

Although most scholars recognize the existence of the J strand in the Pentateuch, controversy rages over the time of its composition. According to the classic version of the documentary hypothesis, J's narrative was produced, at least in part, as a justification or validation of the Davidic monarchy (established c. 1000 B.C.E.). After Davidic rulers had transformed Israel's formerly competing tribes

Table 4.1 The Documentary Hypothesis: Four Principal Sources of the Pentateuch

SOURCE	CHARACTERISTICS
J (Yahwist)	Uses personal name *Yahweh* for God; anthropomorphic portrayal of Deity; vivid, concrete style; dramatic storyline, beginning with creation (Gen. 2:4b) and extending at least to conclusion of Mosaic Covenant at Sinai; strong orientation toward traditions of Judah, setting many patriarchal tales in that region.
E (Elohist)	Uses generic plural *Elohim* for God; style less picturesque and view of Deity less anthropomorphic than J's; begins narrative with Abraham and concludes with Israelites at the "mountain of God," which E calls Horeb; strong orientation toward northern kingdom of Israel (Ephraim), where most patriarchal stories are set.
D (Deuteronomist)	Emphasizes conditional nature of the Mosaic Covenant and interprets Israel's military/political defeats as a direct result of the people's failure to worship Yahweh wholeheartedly; more elaborate rhetorical style than J or E; reflects policies of Josiah's religious reforms (c. 621 B.C.E.); insists that only one central sanctuary is acceptable to Yahweh; D's interpretation of Israel's history influenced writing of Joshua–2 Kings, the Deuteronomistic History (DH).
P (Priestly)	Focuses on priestly interests, particularly legalistic and ritual aspects of Israel's religion; precise, pedantic style, meticulously listing genealogies, censuses, dates, and instructions for the cult; thought to have been added to older JE epic during and after the Babylonian exile (following 587 B.C.E.); strong affinity with concepts expressed by the exilic prophet Ezekiel.

into a political unity—with both kings and priests recently centered at the new capital of Jerusalem—the Yahwist writer composed a literary affirmation of the new order, perhaps in the later tenth or ninth century B.C.E. (see Box 5.4). The J narrative, from the call of Abraham to the conquest of Canaan and the rise of Davidic kings, presumably functioned as a foundation document illustrating that Israel's social, political, and religious institutions were the outworking of Yahweh's historical purpose.

Certainly the J material woven into the Torah focuses on **Judah,** the name of both the tribe to which David belonged and the southern territory over which he and his heirs ruled. To emphasize the importance of Judah in Israel's past, J associates many of the patriarchs with geographical sites that are also significant to Judah's royal dynasty. Thus, in J's account Abraham dwells in Hebron or Mamre (Gen. 13:18; 18:1), the location of Judah's first capital city, where David's reign was first acclaimed (2 Sam. 2–5), and the hometown of Zadok, who served as high priest under David and Solomon (2 Sam. 8:17; cf. 1 Kings 1:32–45). J's description of the boundaries of the land that Yahweh promised to Abraham's progeny (Gen. 15:18)

corresponds to the political frontiers of the Davidic kingdom (cf. 1 Kings 4:21). By contrast, J gives a negative account of **Shechem** (Gen. 34), which in the late tenth century B.C.E. had become the capital of anti-Judean northern tribes that had seceded from the Davidic monarchy after Solomon's death. Because J emphasizes Judah's central role in Israel's story, he is regarded as a native of Judah, perhaps a member of the royal court living at Jerusalem, giving J's literary symbol a double meaning (Figure 4.1).

Whereas the standard documentary view holds that the Yahwist author wrote during the period of the monarchy, a few critics have recently argued that the Yahwist account is a relatively late work, composed some time *after* the Babylonian destruction of Judah brought the Davidic monarchy to an end. In this revisionist theory, the Tanak's first four books (Genesis–Numbers), were compiled by postexilic writers as a preface to Deuteronomy (see Rendtorff, van Seters, and Whybray in "Recommended Reading").

E, the Elohist Source According to the documentary hypothesis, the Pentateuch's second oldest narrative strand (which some scholars think was

Figure 4.1 The facial expression on this statuette of an ancient Egyptian scribe reveals the intelligence and consciousness of power characteristic of the literate professional class that controlled the preservation and interpretation of Egypt's history. In common with its Near Eastern neighbors, Israel developed a scribal class associated with the royal court that played a major role in creating the Bible.

oral rather than written) is that identified as **E**, the **Elohist** tradition, so named because this source characteristically uses *Elohim* rather than Yahweh as the preferred term for God. Of the four hypothetical pentateuchal sources, E is the least well preserved, although extended Elohist passages have been identified in Genesis and Exodus. According to the sequence of events postulated by the documentary hypothesis, after Israel's twelve tribes had split into the two rival kingdoms of Judah and Israel (following 921 B.C.E.), a writer in the northern kingdom of Israel produced a second narrative of his people's origins, or at least a collection of individual stories about Abraham, Isaac, Jacob, Esau, Joseph, and Moses. Perhaps consciously designed as a corrective to J's Judah-oriented account, the

Elohist material focuses on traditions associated with the northern part of Israel. E does not review early human history as J had done, beginning instead with tales of Abraham and his descendants. As Martin Noth has observed, E survives in the Pentateuch only as disconnected fragments, preserving very few traditions that are not duplicated in other sources (see "Recommended Reading"). Within Genesis, E contributes mainly to stories of sibling conflict, such as the rivalry between Jacob and Esau, as well as that between Joseph and his brothers. In Exodus, E provides an account of Jethro, Moses' father-in-law; the revelation of Yahweh's name to Moses; and Israel's encounter with God on his sacred mountain. The large majority of E material parallels narratives from J and other contributors, adding traditions, including Abraham's near-sacrifice of his son Isaac, to the end of the Abraham cycle (Gen. 20–22), as well as variant material to the Jacob–Esau and Joseph cycles.

Although some scholars view E as primarily supplemental oral material added to enrich J's narrative, E introduces some important differences in the biblical tradition. Whereas J specifies Mount Sinai as the sacred locale of Yahweh's revelation of the Torah to Israel, E calls it Horeb. J refers to the inhabitants of Palestine as Canaanites, whereas E labels them Amorites. J names Moses' father-in-law as Ruel or Hobab, whereas E knows him as Jethro, priest of Midian.

According to J, people worshiped Yahweh almost from the beginning of human history (Gen. 4:26), but E states that Yahweh kept his name secret until Moses' day (Exod. 3:15). Whereas J's portrait of God is strongly anthropomorphic, E paints a somewhat more abstract and remote Deity. J describes Yahweh strolling through Eden to enjoy a cooling breeze, dining with Abraham under the oaks of Mamre, personally wrestling with Jacob, and appearing directly to Moses. Elohist material tends to present God as transcendent, typically employing an angelic go-between when speaking to Abraham or Moses. Recounting Jacob's dream at Bethel, E depicts the invisible link between heaven and earth with the image of a celestial stairway trod by divine beings (Gen. 28:10–19). Whereas J sets many of the ancestral tales in

Judah's territory, E prefers geographical sites connected with the northern tribes, the most prominent of which was **Ephraim**, thus also giving the "E" symbol a twofold significance.

Because the E strand survives only in fragmental form, many scholars doubt that it originated as a continuous narrative, or that it was ever a separate written document. Some critics argue that E merely represents variations of ancient Israel's vast storehouse of oral traditions which redactors added to expand upon J's story of Israel's formation.

The JE Epic   Elohist material, whether oral or written, may have been integrated into J's account after 721 B.C.E., when the northern kingdom of Israel fell to the Assyrians. Israelite refugees fleeing south into Judah may have brought Elohist traditions with them to Jerusalem, where they eventually were incorporated into the Yahwist's narrative. If E was indeed a written source, it is not surprising that the unknown Judean scribe or editor who combined it with J rigorously subordinated E material to J's narrative framework, breaking it up into short fragments that supplemented the Yahwist document. The resultant composite work, **JE**, inevitably contained innumerable conflicts and repetitions, such as the three similar incidents in which a patriarch's wife is represented as his sister or desired by a foreign ruler (cf. Gen. 12:10–20; 20:1–18; 26:6–11). The JE redactor skillfully dovetailed these redundant passages, retaining even contradictory accounts as equally venerable.

D, the Deuteronomist Source   The third principal source of the Pentateuch is known as **D**, the **Deuteronomist**. Scholarly opinion is sharply divided about the extent to which the Deuteronomist's influence is present in the five Torah books. Some critics believe that whereas J and E passages appear throughout Genesis, Exodus, and Numbers, D's work is largely confined to the Book of Deuteronomy. Conversely, a growing number of scholars regard D as the dominant influence in the Pentateuch, with some maintaining that the core of Deuteronomy (12–26) may be the oldest part of the Torah, to which JE material was later added as an extended introduction. At the least,

recent scholarly trends find an increasing number of Deuteronomy-influenced passages incorporated into the JE narratives of Genesis, Exodus, and Numbers.

While differing about the relative ages and literary relationship of JE and D, most scholars agree that Deuteronomy, or at least its central section, was the "book of the law [Torah]" discovered in 621 B.C.E. during repairs on the Jerusalem Temple. Discovery of this allegedly Mosaic document helped fuel or validate a major reform of Israelite religion conducted by King Josiah, who zealously followed Deuteronomy's injunction to centralize Judah's worship "only in the place [Yahweh] himself will choose . . . to set his name there and give it a home" (Deut. 12:4–6). Acting on Deuteronomy's declaration that Yahweh would accept sacrifices only at the "place" designated—assumed to be Jerusalem—Josiah systematically destroyed all other altars and shrines, including those at Bethel and other sanctuaries associated with the Genesis patriarchs (2 Kings 22:3–23:25; cf. 2 Chron. 34–35). Josiah's other reforms, such as the celebration of a national Passover feast, also echo policies advocated in Deuteronomy.

Deuteronomy's insistence that Israel's national welfare was conditional upon the people's loyalty to Yahweh and their allegiance to Torah requirements determined the way in which subsequent writers presented Israel's story. The prose narratives that follow Deuteronomy—Joshua through 2 Kings—relate Israel's historical experience almost entirely in terms of deuteronomic theory. Because these books are so thoroughly permeated by Deuteronomy's equation of disobedience with national failure, this sequence is called the Deuteronomistic History. (In this text, the adjective "deuteronomic" refers to the Book of Deuteronomy and the philosophy of history it promotes. By contrast, the term "deuteronomistic" refers to material pertaining to the historical narratives, Joshua through Kings. The **Deuteronomistic History** is abbreviated as **DH** (see Chapter 5).)

In its major themes and theological viewpoint, Deuteronomy belongs with the deuteronomistic narratives that follow it and that promote exactly the same philosophy of history. Originally, it probably stood at the head of the series of books — Joshua, Judges, 1 and 2 Samuel, and 1 and 2 Kings — that together form a cohesive literary unit. In editing the Hebrew Bible, however, redactors separated Deuteronomy from the narratives that are largely shaped by its ideas and placed it as the fifth book of Torah. The Pentateuch thus concludes with Moses' warnings about the painful consequences of covenant breaking.

P, the Priestly Source   The fourth and final contribution to the Torah, according to the documentary hypothesis, was the work of **priestly** writers who lived during and after the Babylonian exile (from 587 to perhaps as late as the fourth century B.C.E.). Given the scholarly designation of **P**, this component of the Pentateuch represents the concerns of a postexilic school of priestly redactors who labored to collect, preserve, and edit Israel's religious heritage. The P school assembled several originally separate legal codes, encompassing hundreds of laws, statutes, and ordinances, and inserted them at various points in the JE epic of old Israel. Extensively revising the older material, the priestly editors compiled the vast body of legal material that extends from Exodus 35 through Leviticus to Numbers 10. Although the priestly contribution emphasizes ritual, purity laws, genealogies, and the minutiae of cult sacrifice, it also includes significant additions to the JE narrative. In addition to interpolating a priestly version of the Abrahamic Covenant (Gen. 17), P scribes wove their tradition of the Flood story into that of J, producing a considerably expanded (and self-contradictory) version of a global deluge. They also added another creation account (Gen. 1) and the narrative of Moses' death (Deut. 34), thus giving the Pentateuch its crucial opening and closing passages and determining its final shape and structure.

P's version of creation, which serves as a preface to the entire Hebrew Bible, emphasizes the distinctions and divisions that characterize the separations of pure and impure in Leviticus. Culminating in Elohim's establishment of the first Sabbath, P's creation account provides cosmic validation of that priest-regulated institution. P gives exhaustively detailed instructions for building Israel's portable shrine, the **Tabernacle**, a portable dwelling place for God that is rendered in terms similar to those that describe the creation (Exod. 25–31; 35–40). The elaborate machinery of the sacrificial cult, including animal offerings to expiate sin and guilt — also under priestly jurisdiction — occupies much of Leviticus.

SOME RECENT MODIFICATIONS OF THE DOCUMENTARY HYPOTHESIS

For more than a hundred years, most biblical scholars have endorsed some form of the documentary hypothesis, making it the standard model in studies of the Pentateuch's origins. It has never been without its critics, however; like any theory, the documentary hypothesis is useful only so long as it can successfully account for all the available facts, such as the repetitions, anachronisms, and innumerable inconsistencies found in the Torah. Although no scholarly consensus has thus far emerged, some recent critics have proposed alternate models, rejecting the classical assumption that the Tanak's initial five books represent the compilation of four originally independent sources, J, E, D, and P.

Some critics argue that P was not originally a separate document; instead, P material is a series of unconnected interpolations that postexilic redactors inserted into the older narratives. Some scholars view P as representing a long succession of priestly editors who, over a century or two, gradually reshaped Israel's ancient and sometimes conflicting traditions into a semblance of literary unity. By binding an expanded and edited version of Deuteronomy to the Yahwist-Elohist (JE) account, into which they had inserted their distinctive legal instructions, the P school eventually created the five-part Torah we have today.

Other scholars contend that the various strands of tradition woven into the Pentateuch do not derive from older written texts, such as J or E, but are based primarily on diverse oral traditions about Israel's national **cult** (formal system of worship), particularly oral recitations of allegiance to Yahweh, such as the statements preserved in Deuteronomy

6 and 26 and Joshua 24 (cf. Deut. 6:20–25; 26:5–9; Josh. 24:2–13). Before Josiah's reforms centralized worship at Jerusalem late in the seventh century B.C.E., public reiterations of the laws, rituals, and ancient lore were associated with numerous ritual sites mentioned in Genesis, Joshua, Judges, and 1 and 2 Samuel, including Bethel, Shechem, Kadesh, and Shiloh—as well as Jerusalem. Evolving differences between individual tribal stories and customs rehearsed at these different sanctuaries may have contributed to the different strata of theological beliefs found in the Pentateuch.

Despite wide scholarly disagreements about the dating and order of composition of various parts of the Torah, virtually all scholars recognize that the present work is a patchwork of multiple sources, its complex literary history betrayed by the many repetitions and inconsistencies apparent in the text. The current debate centers on how much—if any—of the Torah's sources existed as written documents before the exile (587–538 B.C.E.). Although it seems clear that extensive editing of both the Pentateuch and other biblical books took place following the exile, a large number of scholars offer persuasive evidence that Israel had produced many documents about its ongoing relationship with Yahweh long before the fall to Babylon (see works by Friedman, Nicholson, and Campbell and O'Brien in "Recommended Reading").

Major Themes of the Pentateuch

While recognizing the value of source criticism in discussing many passages in the Pentateuch, this book will focus on the present form of the text. Despite its multiple authorship and long history of editorial additions and revisions, the final version of the Pentateuch presents some recurring themes that help to provide some degree of coherence. Although they worked with diverse materials dating from different periods in Israel's history, the Pentateuch's final editors carefully arranged their various sources to highlight the historical evolution of Yahweh's unique partnership with Israel. Two themes in particular help to unify the Pentateuch's

rich compendium of ancestral tradition, genealogy, law and poetry: Yahweh's unsolicited promises to Abraham, Isaac, and Jacob, and Yahweh's ongoing relationship with these patriarchs' descendants, the Israelites. The divine promises (grouped together in Genesis 12–50) and Yahweh's binding demands upon his people (specified in the Torah's extensive legal requirements) not only shape the Pentateuch's general structure, but also the Deuteronomistic History that follows. Poised between the promises on one hand and the fearful necessity of consistently obeying all of Yahweh's exacting commands on the other, the covenant community struggles to find its way between the opposite poles of hope and retribution. Encompassing both the divine promises of blessing and threats of future loss, the Torah story prepares the reader for the account of Israel's bittersweet historical experience that lies ahead.

THEMES OF POTENTIAL BLESSINGS AND CURSES

The curses Deuteronomy specifies for a disobedient Israel—reflecting the redactors' awareness of Judah's fall to Babylon and subsequent exile—provide a counterpoint to the promised blessings (Deut. 28; cf. Lev. 26). Throughout the Pentateuch and Deuteronomistic History, the author/editors depict two powerful forces at work in human history: God's positive intentions for an obedient humanity and an opposing force of human rebelliousness that subverts the divine will. The conflict between Yahweh's intention for his human creation and humankind's resistance to it begins with the first human couple's disobedience in Eden (Gen. 3) and dominates the primeval history (Gen. 1–11). Human ingratitude for divine blessings persists in Israel's story, particularly the people's complaints about Moses' leadership and flagrant disloyalty to the God who had rescued them from Egyptian slavery. In Exodus and Numbers, the Israelites—apparently unmindful of the benefits of freedom and nationhood that Yahweh confers upon them—break virtually every commandment, violating the terms of their covenant bond at the very moment of its inception (Exod. 32; cf.

Num. 14). The Torah's description of Israel's wanton behavior at Sinai, in fact, sets the tone for the deeply troubled relationship between Yahweh and his people narrated in Judges through 2 Kings, as well in as the prophetic books.

In emphasizing Israel's repeated violation of its covenant obligations, the Torah narrative highlights the flaws in the Israelite community that will eventually result in its suffering the curses of political defeat, exile, and extreme suffering that Yahweh had enunciated as the inevitable consequences of disobedience. Viewing their past from the perspective of exile, the Torah editors also envision a restoration of the broken divine-human relationship, expressed in a return to the land promised Abraham's descendants (Deut. 30). In predicting Israel's future restoration, in fact, God makes perhaps his most astonishing promise: He will give the Israelites the ability to trust and worship him alone, effecting an inner change that enables the people to love him with all their "hearts . . . and souls" (Deut. 30:4–6).

Before examining the Torah's depiction of the partnership between Yahweh and Israel, we will consider the vows that Yahweh makes to Israel's ancestors. (For a more complete discussion of covenant themes, see the works by Clines and Scullion in "Recommended Reading.") The divine promises, all contained in Genesis, may be divided into six components: Yahweh swears to give Abraham and/or his grandson Jacob (1) a son; (2) descendants; (3) his presence; (4) land; (5) blessing; and (6) covenant. Although the partial fulfillment of these vows serves to tie together the patriarchal stories of Genesis with some of the later Torah narratives as well as the historical books that follow, it is important to remember that not all versions of the divine promises contain each of the six provisions. Because each source now embedded in the Torah had its own tradition of the divine oaths, no two of them are precisely alike.

A Son and Descendants The promise of a son occurs alone in Genesis 18, but it is usually linked with the more general promise of the patriarchs' descendants, which are to be as innumerable as the "stars of heaven" or the "sands of the sea." Abra-

ham will become the father of a "multitude of nations" (including Israel through Isaac and, according to another tradition, the Arab peoples through Ishmael), as well as a line of kings (the royal dynasty founded by David many centuries later). In Genesis, which is deeply concerned with issues of fertility and reproduction, the divine guarantee of progeny is opposed by repeated threats to its fulfillment, expressed in the theme of the "barren wife" (for most of their lives Abraham's wife Sarah and Jacob's wife Rachel are unable to bear children) and in Yahweh's own demand that Abraham sacrifice his son Isaac, the sole heir through whom Yahweh's promises were to be accomplished.

An interesting variation of the son motif appears in Torah stories about God's favoring younger sons. Although the principle of *primogeniture* (the practice of giving the right of inheritance to the eldest son) was common in the ancient Near East, several narratives feature the triumph of a younger son over his older brothers. This pattern is established early in Genesis when God accepts Abel's worship while rejecting that of his older brother Cain (Gen. 4:1–16). Abraham's firstborn son Ishmael is superseded by Isaac, as Esau is displaced by his younger twin Jacob (Gen. 21; 27). Later, Jacob confers his primary blessing on Judah, his fourth-born son, repudiating Reuben, his firstborn (Gen. 49). Joseph is preferred over his ten older brothers, anticipating David's precedence over his seven older siblings (1 Sam. 16) and Solomon's inheritance of Israel's throne, displacing his older fraternal rival (1 Kings 1–2). Some scholars think that the Torah's oft-repeated exaltation of younger men above their brothers was a device to help justify Solomon's kingship, an ascension that involved the killing of David's oldest son and presumed heir. If these stories (mostly found in J and the Court History) were intended to offer literary precedents for Solomon's actions, they may also provide a clue to the time of their composition (see Box 5.4).

Divine Presence Yahweh's pledge to be an invisible companion to his chosen worshipers figures most prominently in the Jacob story, where God states that he will accompany Jacob on his many journeys (Gen. 26:3, 24; 28:15; 31:3). The theme of divine presence reappears as a major feature of Yahweh's intimate relationship with Moses (Exod. 3–4) and is also the force that guides and protects Israel on its perilous trek through the Sinai wilderness. Demonstrating the crucial importance of housing the divine presence in Israel's midst, detailed instructions for constructing the Tabernacle and Ark of the Covenant take up almost eleven chapters in Exodus (Ex. 25–31; 35–40). Interestingly, it is David who later installs the Ark in Jerusalem, which he captures from a Canaanite tribe to make his capital, and it is David with whom the divine presence is said to figure most prominently (2 Sam. 5:1–8:18). David's heir, Solomon (perhaps the youngest of his many sons), is granted the privilege of building Yahweh's Temple in Jerusalem, the sanctuary at which God places his sacred "name," emblem of the divine presence (1 Kings 8; cf. Deut. 12).

Land The theme of descendants and nationhood is closely linked to the promise of land, the territory of Canaan that Yahweh swears to give Abraham and his offspring (Gen. 12:1–8; 13:14–17; 15:7–21), a pledge that is reiterated to Jacob and his sons (Gen. 26:3–4; 28:4; 35:12; 50:24) and which is fulfilled only in the United Kingdom of David and Solomon (1 Kings 4:21). The entire narrative sequence of Genesis through 2 Kings, in fact, is largely a theological claim for Israel's divinely granted right to wrest the land from its native inhabitants, the Canaanites, balanced by a theological argument explaining why Israel ultimately forfeited its possession of the land. Deuteronomy's recitation of Israel's religious and moral failings provides the rationale for the people's loss of its national heritage (Deut. 28–30; Lev. 26).

Universal Blessing Whereas the promise of land relates specifically to Israel's identity as a national state, Yahweh's assurance of blessing to Abraham and his descendants has a more universal application. At the outset of his personal relationship with Abraham, Yahweh offers assurance that not only Abraham's heirs but "all the tribes [families] of the earth shall bless themselves by you" (Gen. 12:3).

The theme of a divine blessing that will ultimately encompass all peoples emphasizes the importance of Israel's mission as a conveyer of Yahweh's favor to humankind (Gen. 18:18; 22:18; 26:3–4; 28:14).

Covenant As explained in Chapter 1, God's preferred means of defining his special relationship with Israel is through initiating a series of covenants contracting him to remain Israel's patron Deity forever. Whereas the Noachan Covenant (Gen. 9) is made with all humankind, the various covenants with Abraham (Gen. 12; 15; 17; and 22) relate exclusively to the chosen people. In Genesis 17, a priestly composition that brings together almost all the elements of the divine promises, God links together the assurance of countless descendants, divine presence, land, kingship, and blessing, combining all these elements in a "covenant in perpetuity, to be your God and the God of your descendants after you" (Gen. 17:4–10). In making this covenant (*berit*), a term repeated thirteen times in twenty-two verses, God emphasizes that he solemnly binds himself to Abraham's progeny not only in the present but also in the future, perpetuating the God–Israel association for all time to come (see Box 4.3).

Partial Fulfillments Different aspects of the Genesis promises are highlighted in the next four Torah books. In Exodus, the promise that Abraham would have multitudinous descendants is already partially fulfilled, with Egypt's ruler becoming alarmed at the Israelites' unprecedented fecundity. Exodus also extensively elaborates the theme of covenant, giving it a radical new twist. Whereas Genesis presents all God's promises as unilateral—voluntary pledges on the Deity's part that require few reciprocal obligations from the human recipients of the promises—Exodus makes God's vow to protect Israel explicitly dependent upon the people's obedience to the entire body of legal instruction given at Mount Sinai/Horeb. Underscoring the theme of Yahweh's presence, manifested visibly in a "pillar of cloud" by day and a "pillar of fire" by night, Exodus also makes provision for later generations' ongoing communion with God through constructing the Tabernacle, in which Yahweh's "glory" is enshrined (Exod. 40:34–36).

The Book of Leviticus, which prescribes regulations for Israelite behavior that will render them ritually pure in approaching Yahweh, further develops the themes of divine presence and Israel's special partnership with the Lord. Demanding that Israel must be as holy as its God (Lev. 11:44), Leviticus articulates a sacred ethic that grounds human interaction in a conception of the Deity's nature.

Numbers, emphasizing both the numerical increase of Abraham's progeny and their lack of gratitude to the Deity who had rescued them from Egyptian slavery, also recounts the Israelites' preparations for laying siege to the land of Canaan. The determination to enter the Promised Land further resounds through Deuteronomy, which stipulates Yahweh's specific requirements for a successful invasion of Canaan as well as dire warnings about the consequences of Israel's failure to adhere to deuteronomic law. Moses's admonition makes clear that the covenant community's actual possession of the land and growth to true nationhood depend entirely on the people's living up to Yahweh's exacting standards.

Some Literary Forms in the Pentateuch

Although the Torah is primarily regarded as sacred teaching, a theologically oriented account of Yahweh's unique relationship with Israel through space and time, it is also a composite document encompassing several distinct categories of literature. Among the literary genres it contains are narrative, genealogy, etiology (a subgenre of narrative), itinerary, cult legend, and legal code (see Box 1.7).

NARRATIVE

Much of the Torah is devoted to Yahweh's laws and ordinances, but stories are an equally important component. Genesis, most of Exodus, and much of Numbers consists of **narrative**—an account of characters and events arranged in sequential order to illustrate a major theme or concept. Following a generally chronological development—from the creation of the world to the creation of Israel—the Torah contains all the elements typical of a story, including setting (the locale varies from Mesopotamia to Canaan to Egypt); character (from Adam and Eve to Abraham and Sarah to Moses, Aaron, and Miriam); conflict (from the sibling rivalry of Cain and Abel to Yahweh's ambivalent relationship with Israel); and plot (the promises to Abraham advance through a series of connected incidents until their partial culmination in the formation of Israel, a step-by-step unfolding of the Deity's long-range historical plan).

Although editors divided the Torah into five individual books, each occupying a separate scroll, there is considerable overlap among them, with narratives and legal material carrying over from one volume to the next. The first continuous narrative unit, Genesis 1:1 to Exodus 19:3, moves from God's creation of the universe to his assembling of the Israelites at the foot of Mount Sinai/Horeb. This narrative sequence includes a large chronological gap between the descent of Jacob's sons into Egypt that concludes Genesis and the description of their descendants' Egyptian bondage that opens Exodus, but the entire Genesis–Exodus account functions as a coherent literary whole. From the call of Abraham in Genesis 12 to his progeny's arrival at Sinai, the extended narrative functions as a prelude to the Torah's climactic event—the giving of Yahweh's law and the formalizing of the covenant with Israel.

The second major segment of the Pentateuch, Exodus 19:4 through Numbers 10:10, subordinates narrative to large blocks of ethical, ritual, and legal material defining the terms of Yahweh's covenant with Israel. Beginning in Exodus 19, narrative movement comes to an almost complete halt as Yahweh issues orders to prepare the people ritually for his appearance among them; in Exodus 20, he personally delivers the Ten Commandments to a terrified people. The rest of Exodus, all of

Leviticus, and much of Numbers are largely devoted to the enumeration of more than 600 laws, ordinances, statutes, and rituals that make up the covenant alliance. Relatively short fragments of narrative are interspersed among several law-giving episodes, notably Exodus 24, which describes the formal ratification of the Mosaic Covenant, and Exodus 32–34, which relates the Israelites' violation of the covenant in the golden calf incident and Yahweh's graciousness in renewing the pact. Anchored at a single location, Sinai, this Torah section temporally occupies almost a year; it begins with the ritually purified Israelites vowing to obey Yahweh's laws (most of which they have not yet heard) and ends with the people's leaving Sinai to head toward Canaan.

The third part of Torah, also a mixture of narrative and legal instruction (Numbers 10:10–Deuteronomy 34:12), covers Israel's forty-year journey through the desert, where Yahweh continues to deliver still more laws at the Tabernacle; it closes on the plains of **Moab,** near the borders of Canaan, where Moses gives three farewell speeches, recounting Israel's adventures with Yahweh up to that moment and issuing an extensive revised edition of the law (Deut 1:1–33). After prophesying Israel's future exile, Moses dies and is buried at an unknown location, the last event recorded in the Torah (Deut. 34).

The Narrative Voices   As in other surviving ancient Near Eastern literature, such as the *Epic of Gilgamesh* and the *Enuma Elish,* the Torah has a narrator, the unidentified person who tells the story. In fact, as a result of its multiple sources, the Torah has multiple narrative voices, each of which assumes absolute knowledge of the subject related. Speaking in the third person, the narrators presume to report the precise events of creation, a global flood, the origins of different national and ethnic groups, and other events of the extremely remote past. Like the different poets who contributed to the composition of *Gilgamesh,* the Torah authors commonly advance the narrative through dialogue, recounting long conversations between two characters even when no third party was present to witness the exchange, such as the debates between Yahweh and Abraham over the ethical issue of Yahweh's destroying Sodom (Gen. 18) or between Moses and Yahweh over the Deity's proposal to exterminate Israel (Exod. 32; Num. 14).

As many Near Eastern texts demonstrate, it was common literary practice for ancient writers to create speeches for both long-dead heroes and their gods, such as Gilgamesh's dialogue with his divine patron Shamash in the bejeweled "garden of the gods." Torah writers thus present much of Yahweh's self-revelation on Sinai/Horeb through private conversations with Moses (Exod. 3; 24; 32–34). Other Tanak authors compose scenes set entirely in heaven, where divine beings speak among themselves, such as the portrayal of Yahweh's celestial court in Job (Job 1–2; cf. 1 Kings 22:18–28 and Zech. 3). The custom of fashioning dialogue for gods, prevalent in Mesopotamian and Egyptian literature, is well illustrated in Homer's *Iliad* and *Odyssey,* epic poems perhaps contemporaneous with some Torah sources, in which Zeus and his fellow Olympians meet in council to discuss their plans for directing human destiny.

Biblical Transformations of Myth   Although the Torah, definitively edited by monotheistic redactors during and after the Babylonian exile, contains no extended myths comparable to those in the Homeric epics, it does contain a number of mythological motifs. From the Greek word *mythos* (something uttered, a story), **myth** refers to traditional narratives about gods and heroes, typically involving stories of creation and/or origins of religious and social customs. Mythic language and imagery occur in such biblical passages as the angels' descent from heaven to mate with mortal women, producing a race of heroes and giants (Gen. 6). The notion that great men of the prehistoric era inherited their superhuman qualities from a divine parent permeates both Mesopotamian and Greek mythology; while including a brief allusion to the tradition, however, the Genesis narrator carefully avoids any description of the heroes' mythic exploits. Whereas Genesis provides only a cursory reference, the noncanonical Book of

1 Enoch offers an elaborate account of the fate of Genesis's "fallen" angels, who also taught humankind the arts and technologies of civilization (see Chapter 8). (For references to the mythological concept of a divine council, see Chapter 3.)

GENEALOGIES

The use of genealogies, a literary subgenre, to bind together individual narrative units and provide continuity, is largely a priestly contribution to the Pentateuch. Whereas the Yahwist writer in Genesis creatively interweaves brief genealogies with narrative, the priestly school inserts them into the narrative as relatively large blocks of material, using a rigid formula that lists a patriarch's age at the time he fathered his first son, the number of years he lived after his firstborn, his total age at the time of death, and the fact that "he died" (i.e., Gen. 5). Reenforcing the importance of male offspring, the priestly genealogies trace an unbroken line of descent from Adam to Abraham. A variation of the genealogical lists occurs in Genesis 49, where Jacob, in the form of prophecy, pronounces moral judgments on his twelve sons. Another extensive genealogy occupies the opening chapters of Numbers, along with lists of priestly functions.

ETIOLOGY

Some Torah passages take the form of **etiologies**— stories that explain the cause or origin of some natural phenomenon, social custom, or religious ritual. Genesis features several etiological anecdotes, such as the folk tale in which Lot's wife is changed into a pillar of salt, presumably to account for the unusual salt formations bordering the Dead Sea. The story of Jacob's wrestling with a mysterious nocturnal visitor is also given an etiological emphasis, according to which the Israelites do not eat part of an animal's hip "because [the wrestler] had struck Jacob in the socket of the hip on the sciatic nerve" (Gen. 32:25–33). Interestingly, this prohibition against consuming this part of an animal's anatomy does not appear in any of the Torah's several law codes.

In a broad sense, the divine speeches in which El Shaddai or Yahweh promises Canaan to Abraham's descendants function as etiologies, asserting that Israel's political claim to the territory originates in divine action. By placing the promises for land early in Israel's prehistory—centuries before Israelite tribes actually occupied Canaan—the Genesis authors show that Israel's right to possess the area was part of God's plan from the beginning. Genesis also explains why Israel became a sovereign state relatively late in Near Eastern history—although nationhood was its preordained birthright, it was God's pleasure to delay implementation of his promise.

ITINERARY

A literary category that characterizes nomadic societies, the **itinerary**—accounts of a people's movements from one geographical area to another—may represent one of the Torah's oldest strata. The Genesis account of Abraham's migration from Mesopotamia to Canaan follows a route marked by conventions of the genre, noting the place of departure, the destination, and specific place names, such as oases or camp sites, along the way, as well as other geographical features. Related to the itinerary genre, the journey motif dominates much of the Torah action. Abraham, Jacob, Joseph, Moses, and the people of Israel are almost constantly on the move, traveling to or from the Promised Land. While Exodus recounts the Israelites' journey from Egypt to meet Yahweh at Sinai, Numbers underscores their subsequent forty-year trek through the Sinai wilderness. The metaphor of homeless wanderers ever seeking a permanent resting place dominates the Torah story of Israel's early life.

CULT LEGENDS

Many tales of the patriarchs dramatize their religious experiences at a particular site, such as Bethel, Hebron, or Shechem, which later became important centers of Israelite worship. Known as **cult legends** because they serve to validate centers of worship, these stories may also have etiological purposes, explaining when and how the place became sacred through its association with one of Israel's ancestors. After Jacob has his visionary dream of ascending and descending divinities at Luz, he changes its name to Bethel ("House of God"), erecting a stone monument there to commemorate his experience (Gen. 28:10–19). A second version of Jacob's naming Bethel (and of God's changing Jacob's name to Israel) appears in Gen. 35, where Jacob again erects a stone monument. The ancient Canaanite sanctuary at Shechem, where Israel's tribes later held covenant-renewal ceremonies, had a similar cult legend. At Shechem Jacob buys property and erects an altar, which he calls "El, God of Israel" (33:18–20).

LEGAL CODES

The Torah's mixture of different literary genres, in which narrative and legal instruction figure most prominently, suggests not only its multiple sources but also its multiple purposes. From the poetic creation account in Genesis 1 to Moses' "song" deploring the Israelites' misconduct in Deuteronomy 32, the five Torah books utilize both storytelling and legal instruction to illustrate the complex nature of the divine-human relationship. Narrative, preserving ancient traditions about Israel's bond to Yahweh, demonstrates how God interacts with such characters as Abraham, Jacob, and Moses. These leaders who "listen" attentively to God's voice provide later readers with models for maintaining a dynamic bond with Israel's Deity.

Whereas the narratives of Genesis, Exodus, and Numbers focus on divine intervention and human response, the Torah's extensive legal codes present the means by which Yahweh wishes to regulate human life and worship. In its final form, the Torah incorporates at least five originally separate bodies of law, in addition to the Ten Commandments. Scholars believe that these formerly distinct codes derive from different groups within Israelite society; their inclusion in the Torah probably represented a compromise among the competing claims of rival priesthoods (Aaronic and Levite), as well as

those from circles who were deeply influenced by the prophetic tradition (see Friedman and Campbell and O'Brien in "Recommended Reading"). During the final process of editing the Torah, both the legal and narrative legacies treasured by discrete social groups were ultimately combined to provide Israel with its most comprehensive guide.

AUDIENCE FOR THE PENTATEUCH

If we knew at what particular historical periods the various parts of the Pentateuch were composed, and under what circumstances it received its final form, this information would not only help in tracing the evolution of Israel's religion, but also aid in understanding its presumed intent and meaning. When, for example, did the Genesis promises of land, nationhood, and a line of kings originate? Some scholars think that Yahweh's promises, probably in oral from, first served the interests of the Israelite tribes who occupied Canaan, providing a divinely mandated right to drive out the native inhabitants and take over the region. Other scholars argue that the promises derive from the later monarchy, a premise supported by the close verbal parallels between Yahweh's covenant with Abraham and his similarly unconditional pact with King David (cf. Gen. 12; 15; 17; 22; 2 Sam. 7; cf Box 5.3). In this view, the promises may already have been incorporated into the Yahwist's (J's) account, perhaps as early as the late ninth or eighth century B.C.E. A small number of scholars, however, date the first four books, called the **Tetrateuch**, long after the end of the Davidic monarchy, during the Persian or even Hellenistic period.

Whether the Pentateuch was composed entirely after the exile and primarily from oral traditions, as a few recent critics speculate, or whether it was simply revised and reedited from previously existing written sources, as the documentary hypothesis proposes, in its final form it was addressed to a community of exiles. The Genesis stories of wandering families, journeying rootlessly from Mesopotamia to Canaan to Egypt, would strike a responsive chord among exiles whom the Babylonian invasion had driven to these very locations. The theme of divine promises made to the peripatetic ancestors—yet to be fulfilled, and then only partially, at some unspecified future time—spoke directly to the exiles' homelessness and anxieties about the future. Like Abraham, Sarah, Jacob, Rachel, and Joseph and his eleven brothers, these expatriates longed to possess assurance of a secure homeland from an unimpeachable source, the ancestral God. Exiles could also closely identify with the Exodus story of miraculous deliverance from foreign bondage, particularly when an exilic prophet, Second Isaiah, compared repatriation from Babylon to a new exodus, evoking ancient tradition to envision a glorious future (Is. 40–55).

As finally redacted, the Pentateuch assures Yahweh's people that, true to his covenant with Abraham, God will take them under his protective wing, providing not only the blessings of prosperity and protection from enemies but also divine instruction that gives meaning to life. In these assurances, the completed Pentateuch embodies the ultimate goals of Israel's collective aspirations. It is not the hope of a posthumous reward—the Mosaic teachings do not even mention the idea of immortality or a future life in heaven—it is the hope for a fulfilling life in the here and now, in a material world that God had pronounced "very good" (Gen. 1:31), a divine evaluation of creation that Israel fully endorsed. Israel's goal of an abundant earthly life proves hauntingly elusive, however, as foreshadowed by the Pentateuch's highly inconclusive ending. In Deuteronomy's final chapter, most of the promises are still unrealized, the convenant people still outside the land of promise, their national leader, Moses, dead, and their future prospects profoundly uncertain. Such was the covenant people's situation in exile, when priestly editors shaped the Pentateuch into a form that gave its audience both a privileged identity and a lasting purpose.

QUESTIONS FOR REVIEW

1. What is the Pentateuch? Why are the first five books of the Bible traditionally called the Torah or the "Books of Moses"?

2. List some of the duplications and inconsistencies in the Torah that cause most scholars to doubt Mosaic authorship. Define the documentary hypothesis, including the significance of the letters J, E, D, and P in designating different sources now embedded in the composite text. Summarize the distinguishing characteristic of the Yahwist, Elohist, Deuteronomist, and priestly sources. Which of these do scholars believe was the first to write a continuous account of Israel's traditions?

3. What school or group of writers was responsible for the Torah's present form? How did their contributions shape the Torah's final form?

4. Describe several of the major themes that impart unity to the Torah. List the six elements in the promises that Yahweh makes to Israel's ancestors. How do these divine promises help shape the Torah narratives?

5. Define the terms *narrative* and *narrator*. What are some of the other literary components of the Torah?

QUESTIONS FOR DISCUSSION AND REFLECTION

1. If scholars are correct in assuming that the Torah is a composite document consisting of at least four different sources composed during different periods of Israel's history, how does this view affect your attitude toward the biblical text? Is a belief in traditional Mosaic authorship necessary to value the Torah as a meaningful religious document? Explain.

2. In your opinion, why does God make promises to the patriarchs and then delay their implementation for centuries? How do the unconditional promises made to Abraham (and later to David) contrast with the highly conditional promises of the Mosaic Covenant?

TERMS AND CONCEPTS TO REMEMBER

Abimelech	J (Yahwist)
cult legend	JE (Yahwist/Elohist)
D (Deuteronomist)	Josiah
Deuteronomistic	Judah
History (DH)	Mosaic Convenant
documentary hypothesis	narrative
E (Elohist)	oral tradition
Ephraim	P (priestly source)
etiology	patriarch
Ezra	Pentateuch
Horeb, Mount	redactor
itinerary	

RECOMMENDED READING

Alter, Robert. *The Art of Biblical Narrative.* New York: Basic Books, 1982. An influential study of the literary components of biblical narratives.

Anderson, Gary A. "Introduction to Israelite Religion." In *The New Interpreter's Bible,* Vol. 1, pp. 272–283. Nashville: Abingdon Press, 1994. An informative survey of important ideas in biblical religion.

Blenkinsopp, Joseph. *The Pentateuch: An Introduction to the First Five Books of the Bible.* New York: Doubleday, 1992.

———. "Introduction to the Pentateuch." In *The New Interpreter's Bible,* Vol. 1, pp. 305–318. Nashville: Abingdon Press, 1994. Helpful for beginning students.

Birch, Bruce C., Walter Brueggemann, Terence E. Fretheim, and David L. Peterson. *A Theological Introduction to the Old Testament.* Nashville: Abingdon press, 1999. Includes cogent discussions of the Pentateuch, including historical-critical and literary analysis, by leading biblical scholars.

Bright, John. *A History of Israel.* Louisville, Ky.: Westminster/John Knox Press, 2002. An update of a standard work.

Brueggemann, Walter. *Theology of the Old Testament.* Minneapolis: Fortress Press, 1997. One of the most important works in biblical theology, it focuses on the complex character of God.

Campbell, Anthony F., and Mark A. O'Brien. *Sources of the Pentateuch: Texts, Introductions, Annotations.* Minneapolis: Fortress Press, 1993. Identifies passages ascribed to the J, E, and P sources and prints them as separate blocks of material.

Clines, David J. A. *The Theme of the Pentateuch,* 2nd edition. Supplement Series 10. Sheffield, England: JSOT Press, 1997. Discusses literary themes that unify diverse Torah narratives.

Dorsey, David A. *The Literary Structure of the Old Testament: A Commentary on Genesis-Malachi.* Grand Rapids, Mich.: Baker Books, 1999. Detailed analysis of thematic continuities, organization, and literary units in each book of the Hebrew Bible.

Fox, Everett. *The Five Books of Moses.* The Schocken Bible, Vol. 1. New York: Schocken Books, 1995. This fresh new translation includes helpful interpretative commentary.

Fretheim, Terence E. *The Pentateuch.* Nashville: Abingdon, 1996. A concise discussion of unifying themes and theological motifs in the five books of Torah.

Friedman, Richard E. *Commentary on the Torah with a New English Translation.* San Francisco: HarperSanFrancisco, 2001. Providing both Hebrew text and a fresh translation, Friedman analyzes the Pentateuch as a unified literary unit.

———. *The Hidden Book in the Bible: The Discovery of the First Prose Masterpiece.* San Francisco: HarperSanFrancisco, 1998. Identifies J's once independent account, now embedded in the Torah and Deuteronomistic History, and translates it as a continuous narrative.

Gabel, John B., and Charles B. Wheeler. *The Bible as Literature: An Introduction,* 3rd ed. New York: Oxford University Press, 1996. Examines major literary elements of the biblical text.

Nicholson, Ernest. *The Pentateuch in the Twentieth Century: The Legacy of Julius Wellhausen.* Oxford: Clarendon Press, 1998. A detailed critique of recent attacks on the documentary hypothesis and a thoughtful defense of the classic theory.

Noth, Martin, *The Deuteronomistic History.* JSOT Supplement 15. Sheffield, England: JSOT, 1981. A standard work of scholarship.

Rendtorff, Rolf. *The Problem of the Process of the Transmission of the Pentateuch.* Translated by J. J. Scullion. Sheffield, England: JSOT, 1990. Questions the documentary hypothesis.

Schwartz, Regina M., ed. *The Book and the Text: The Bible and Literary Theory.* London: Blackwell, 1990.

Scullion, John J. "Genesis, the Narrative of." In D. N. Freedman, ed., *The Anchor Bible Dictionary,* Vol. 2, pp. 941–962. New York: Doubleday, 1992. Examines major themes and literary categories in Genesis.

Van Seters, John. *In Search of History: Historiography in the Ancient World and the Origins of Biblical History.* New Haven, Conn.: Yale University Press, 1983. Argues for the postexilic origin of the Pentateuch.

Westermann, Claus. *What Does the Old Testament Say About God?* John Knox, 1979.

Whybray, R. N. *The Making of the Pentateuch: A Methodological Study.* Sheffield, England: JSOT Press, 1987. Rejects the documentary hypothesis and views the Torah as a postexilic creation.

Genesis

KEY TOPICS/THEMES

Opening with a priestly hymn to God's creative majesty and an etiological tale dramatizing humanity's alienation from its Creator, Genesis introduces themes that will dominate most of the Hebrew Bible. The first of three parts into which the book is divided, the primeval history (Chs. 1–11), shows the Deity manifesting a profound ambivalence toward his flawed human creation. After expelling the first humans from their paradise home, Yahweh/Elohim then almost completely annihilates humankind in a global deluge, following which he permanently divides the population by erecting language barriers between peoples and scattering them over the face of the earth. In the second section, however—the cycle of ancestral stories (Chs. 12–36)—the divine-human relationship improves as the narrative focuses on God's series of promises to a specific group, the family of Abraham, Isaac, and Jacob, the progenitors of Israel. In the third section, the story of Joseph (Chs. 37–50), God utilizes the rivalry among brothers to further his purpose of making Abraham's descendants a source of universal blessing. Genesis concludes with the chosen people still few in number and settled in Egypt, far from their promised homeland.

KEY QUESTIONS

In compiling Genesis, how did the priestly editors universalize Israel's God as the world's creator? How did they apply older Near Eastern theologial ideas to their account of early humanity? How does Genesis assert Israel's right to possess Canaan?

The first book of the Torah, Genesis serves as a prologue to the story of Israel's formation narrated in the remaining four volumes of the Pentateuch. By identifying Yahweh/Elohim, the God of Israel, as the creator of the universe, the Torah narrator not only places Israel's history in a cosmic context but also introduces God as the Tanak's true protagonist, the principal actor in the biblical drama. The Genesis portrayal of the Deity, drawn from a variety of ancient sources, establishes a concept of God that prevails throughout the Hebrew Bible and continues to inform the theology of the world's monotheistic faiths (see Chapter 3).

Although in Genesis 1 God initially appears as a *transcendent,* distant Being who speaks the world into existence, in Genesis 2 he is also shown as *immanent,* stooping to mold the first human out of clay, and later frequently descending to earth, communicating with his chosen favorites. Both creator of the world and master of human history, the biblical God operates directly through visible materializations to human companions and indirectly, behind the scenes, to implement his future plans for Israel. By the end of Genesis, he has maneuvered Israel's ancestors into Egypt, where

Joseph foretells the next major event in the biblical epic, the Israelites' flight from Egypt and eventual possession of the Promised Land (Gen. 50:24–25).

SOURCES

The composite nature of Genesis becomes evident from a careful reading of the first two chapters, which present two very different versions of creation. Differences in style, vocabulary, and theology indicate that the first account is a priestly composition (Gen. 1:1–2:4a), but that the second (Gen. 2:4b–24) is the work of the Yahwist (J). Using the Deity's personal name, Yahweh, from the outset, the Yahwist provides the main story line for most of the book. Elohistic (E) material, which survives only in fragments integrated into J's continuous narrative, first appears in the cycle of stories about Abraham, most prominently in Genesis 20–22.

Next to the Yahwist, the priestly school (P) makes the largest contribution to Genesis. Besides the first creation account, the priestly source also includes its own version of the flood story, which later editors have intricately interwoven with the Yahwist's older deluge narrative (see Box 4.1). P is also responsible for the longest description of the Abrahamic Covenant (Gen. 17) and the episode in which Abraham purchases a burial cave, the only parcel of the Promised Land he is ever to own. For many readers, perhaps the most noticeable P sections are the genealogies, long lists of names that trace the descent of a person, family, or ethnic group from a given ancestor. Although readers often skip these elaborate family trees, their presence helps to tie together the various narrative segments in Genesis and impose a schematic order on the book's diverse contents. With the same concern for orderly sequence that characterizes P's creation hymn, the genealogies present human history in a highly symmetrical format, listing ten generations between Adam and Noah (Gen. 5) and ten generations between Noah and Abraham (Gen. 11). For P, the proliferation of humanity, in obedience to a divine command (1:28; cf. 9:1) can be expressed in a neat pattern.

THE PRIMEVAL HISTORY

The Priestly Account Whereas most of the Pentateuch concentrates on God's special relationship with Israel, Genesis begins with accounts of creation and human origins, giving a universal perspective to narratives about Israel's ancestors that follow. In the priestly story (Gen. 1:1–2:4a), Elohim transforms a dark, watery chaos into a **cosmos**, an orderly system characterized by predictability and harmony. Although some theologians interpret Genesis 1 as depicting creation *ex nihilo*—out of nothing—the Hebrew text does not unequivocally support that view. Elohim does not bring forth the cosmos out of emptiness, but uses pre-existing raw material—a boundless, formless abyss of water—to fashion the universe. The Jewish Publication Society thus translates the Bible's opening lines: "When God [Elohim] began to create the heaven and the earth—the earth being unformed and void, with darkness over the deep [*tehom*] and the wind from God sweeping over the waters. . . ." The English phrase, "the deep," translates the Hebrew *tehom*, which refers to the ancient Near Eastern concept of undifferentiated sea that existed before divine action brought the world into being (Figure 4.2). Working with this primordial substance, Elohim employs a six-step process by which the primal chaotic ocean is illuminated, divided, and shaped into a structured environment that will support life.

Highly methodical, the priestly source arranges the creative week into two sets of three related actions. On day one, Elohim creates light (the illuminating opposite of primal darkness, sterility, and death and thus a basic expression of the divine nature) and then separates light from darkness, initiating the regular alteration of day and night that governs human existence. On day two, he creates the "dome" or vault of heaven (*rakiah* in Hebrew and sometimes translated as "firmament"), a cosmic arch that divides the primal waters above the domed sky from those below, making room for subsequent life to flourish. On day three, God separates dry land from the surrounding sea, providing an environment for terrestrial animals that are created on day six (Box 4.2).

In the second three-day unit, Elohim creates birds, fish, and animals to inhabit the three regions—air, sea, and earth—he had previously separated and shaped from the primal watery element. The sky "dome" formed on the second day becomes the structure into which God fits astronomical bodies, the "lights" of sun, moon, and stars. Although sun and moon were commonly worshiped as divinities in the Near East, P does not even name them, stating that they exist only to "rule" or regulate the seasons, allowing humans to devise calendars. P's reluctance to name these "lights" may stem from the fact that the Hebrew word for sun, *shemesh*, is virtually identical to that for Shamash, the Babylonian solar deity.

On day five, Elohim generates creatures to swim through the lower sea and fly through the sky vault that had been separated from each other on day two. Days three and six also correspond: The dry land and plants created on the third day provide a sustaining environment for the animals and humans formed on the sixth.

The creation of humanity, male and female together, *both* in the divine "likeness" and "image," marks the climax of the priestly narrative. Immediately following his creative labors, which he pronounces "very good," God "rests." God's day of postcreation repose is later cited as justification for Israel's observing the **Sabbath**, the seventh day of the week in which all work ceases (cf. Exod. 20:8–11; Deuteronomy's version of this commandment, however, gives a different rationale for the Sabbath, declaring it an opportunity to remember Israel's escape from forced labor in Egypt (Deut. 5:12–15).

THE YAHWIST VERSION OF CREATION

Whereas the P source depicts an elevated, transcendent, and highly structured view of creation, the Yahwist (J) narrative brings creative events down to earth, portraying an anthropomorphic Yahweh and a humanity (in Hebrew: *adam*) composed of dust (*adamah*). P's creation emerges from an oceanic abyss, but J's precreation environment is a rainless, empty desert that Yahweh irrigates with subterranean waters (2:5–6).

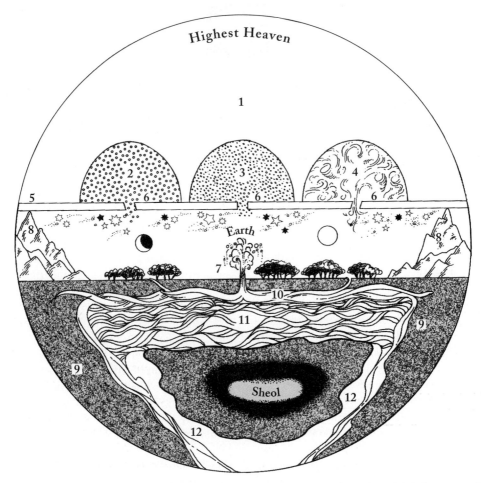

Figure 4.2 The artist's re-creation of the ancient biblical view of the universe shows (1 and 11) the waters above and below the earth; (2, 3, and 4) chambers or storehouses of hail, rain, and snow; (5 and 6) the firmament with its openings or sluices; (7) fountains of the deep; (8) the mountain pillars on which the firmament rests; (9) the pillars of the earth; (10) the navel of the earth; and (12) the watery abyss. Sheol, abode of the dead, is the dark cavern at the center of the lower hemisphere.

J also gives a different order to creation. Whereas P states that Elohim creates men and women simultaneously, at the end of a long sequence, J shows Yahweh fashioning the first human *before* animals, trees, or before the human creature is divided into two separate selves. Whereas P's humanity is imprinted with the divine image, J's is shaped of ordinary clay, which is then animated by Yahweh's "breath." After designing the human creature (*adam*), a mortal duality of earth and divine energy, Yahweh then plants a garden "in

Eden," where he causes vegetation to grow, including a tree of life and a tree of knowledge. (The term *adam* here means "humankind"; it is not used as the first man's personal name until later in the narrative.)

Only after placing the human alone in Eden, as gardener and caretaker, does Yahweh apparently notice that total solitude is "not good" for him. Resolving to "make him a helper as his partner," Yahweh then proceeds to create a variety of animals and birds, bringing them to *adam* to name.

Box 4.2 Parallels of Habitat and Inhabitants

In Genesis 1, the priestly writer divides Elohim's creative work into six distinct stages or "days." In this carefully arranged scheme, the element, region, or environment created on days two and three provide the place or sphere of existence for the objects or creatures created on days four, five, and six.

DAY	REGION OR HABITAT	DAY	INHABITANT
1	Light (day and night)		———
2	"Vault" of Sky (a)	4	Astronomical "lights"
	separated from Sea (b)	5	Birds and sea creatures
3 (a)	Dry land	6 (a)	Land animals
3 (b)	Plant life	6 (b)	Humanity

As if expecting *adam* to select a mate from this menagerie, Yahweh parades all his nonhuman species past the mortal, who can find no suitable companion among them. Perceiving that *adam* is qualitatively different from the other creatures he has made, Yahweh then puts *adam* to sleep, removing part of his body (the famous rib) and using it to fashion the first woman. The woman's appearance — she is not called **Eve** until Genesis 3:20 — inspires the first poetry: **Adam** rejoices that she is "bone of my bones and flesh of my flesh" (2:23). The affinity between the pair is expressed in the poem's wordplay on *ish* (Hebrew, man) and *ishah* (woman). Unlike the animal species, she is his true kin, an appropriate partner. (For Laban's use of the same poetic phrase to describe his blood kinship to Jacob, see Gen. 29:14).

Adam, Eve, and the Serpent   In J's tale of human origins and humanity's loss of paradise, the writer introduces one of the staples of global folklore, a talking animal. (The only other speaking animal in the Hebrew Bible appears in the story of Balaam's donkey [Num. 22–24].) Although the Genesis **serpent** is generally interpreted negatively and commonly identified with Satan, neither J nor any other Tanak writer does so. In the Yahwist's fable, the serpent is not called "evil," merely "subtle" or "crafty," possessing a skeptical intelligence that questions the way God runs things. It knows what God knows, that eating forbidden fruit will impart knowledge of "good and evil," giving humans a godlike perspective (Gen. 3:1–7). In fact, Yahweh confirms that the prohibited fruit has magically transformed humans into "one of us [beings of the heavenly council]," which prompts him to keep the pair from acquiring another prerogative of divinity, immortality (3:22). To prevent their eating from the "tree of life" and living "forever," Yahweh evicts Adam and Eve from **Eden**, putting this source of divinity permanently out of reach. The way back to their garden home is barred by **cherubim**, who wield flaming swords (3:22–24). Common figures in Mesopotamian art, the cherubim typically guard the entrances to temples and royal palaces; in Exodus 25–31, Yahweh orders that images of them be placed on either side of the Ark of the Covenant, symbolizing his celestial throne and its guardians.

J states that the effects of human disobedience — the deliberate breaking of God's command — are immediate and deeply painful. Losing their former innocence, Adam and Eve suddenly realize they are naked, perhaps implying a hitherto unknown sense of sexual shame. Like naive children, they attempt to hide from Yahweh, who, not yet informed of their misconduct, soon appears for his customary walk through the garden. Once aware of their betrayal, Yahweh's judgment is swift and severe: The "crafty" serpent who had pointed out that they could acquire divine knowledge is stripped of its limbs and reduced to an object of human fear (3:5, 14–15). Yahweh condemns the woman to pain in childbirth and domination by her husband—a reflection of women's subordination to men in J's patriarchal society, but not part of the original divine plan. For the man, Yahweh blights the soil, consigning males to the exhausting labor that peasant farmers experience in trying to wrest a living from arid Near Eastern fields.

The cost of knowledge without divine permission or guidance also includes a frightening consciousness of human mortality, and Yahweh reminds the pair that they must return to the soil from which they were formed. As the serpent had observed, they do not die in the same "day" that they disobeyed—Adam lives on for nearly 1000 years—but the huge gulf between mortal humanity and immortal divinity is clearly drawn. Although Israel's neighbors, particularly the civilizations of Egypt and Greece, developed elaborate traditions about the human soul and its posthumous rewards or punishments, the Hebrew Bible says little on the subject. It is not until the last-written part of the Tanak—the Book of Daniel—appears in the second century B.C.E. that a biblical writer explicitly introduces ideas about a future life, envisioning not an immortality of spirit but a resurrection of the physical body (Dan. 12:1–3; see Chapter 8).

THE CONSEQUENCES OF HUMAN DISOBEDIENCE

Cain and Abel Despite the severity of his judgment, J's Deity is capable of surprising tenderness and concern for the humans who failed to trust his governance. Before driving Adam and Eve out into the harsh world of adult experience, Yahweh makes clothes of animal skins to cover their nakedness. After the exile, his presence abides with the couple, enabling them to fulfill the earlier mandate of procreation: Eve bears the world's first child, **Cain**, "with the help of Yahweh" (4:2). Even while bearing sons and daughters, Adam and Eve soon learn the inescapable consequences of their disobedience,

which injects an element of lethal violence into the human predicament.

Introducing a theme of rivalry between brothers that disrupts family relationships throughout the Genesis narrative (and resurfaces in stories about King David's sons in 2 Samuel), J shows Cain bitterly envious of his younger brother **Abel**. When Yahweh prefers the animal sacrifices of Abel, a shepherd, to the grain offerings of Cain, a farmer, Cain reacts against this divine favoritism by killing Abel. Despite the seriousness of the crime—the first taking of a human life—Yahweh treats Cain with leniency, imprinting him with a special "mark" that prevents other people (of unexplained origin) from punishing the murderer (4:13–16). Once the shedding of human blood has begun, however, humanity's condition deteriorates rapidly. J's list of Cain's descendants culminates in **Lamech**, who savagely boasts that he avenges every wrong "seventy-sevenfold" (4:17–24), establishing a culture of violence that eventually leads to humanity's destruction.

THE FLOOD STORY

In the Genesis account of a global flood, God's response to human "wickedness" includes a profound sorrow. Observing humanity's violence, Yahweh's "heart [is] grieved" (Gen. 6:5–6). Regretting that he had made humankind, Yahweh resolves to wipe his failed experiment from the face of the earth. In P's version of the deluge, God brings back the chaotic sea that he had divided and tamed in Genesis 1, opening the "sluices of heaven" to release waters stored above the sky "dome" and causing subterranean "springs of the great deep [primal abyss]" to "break through" (6:11). Drawing upon Mesopotamian lore concerning a prehistoric deluge (Box 2.1), both J and P reproduce elements from the Atrahasis and Gilgamesh traditions, including a divine decision to spare a single human family (see Box 4.1). Like the Babylonian Utnapishtim, **Noah** is instructed to build an ark, a rectangular wooden chest, and stock it with all kinds of birds and animals. Unlike his violent contemporaries, Noah had "walked with God" (6:9; cf. 5:22), which results in his preservation, along with that of his three sons, Ham, Shem, and Japheth, and their respective wives.

The Noachan Covenant   Emphasizing that in God's purpose even global catastrophe involves a creative and saving element, Genesis 9 presents the postflood world as a new beginning for humanity. After repeating the command to "be fruitful" and repopulate the earth (9:7; cf. 1:28), God institutes the first of four biblical covenants. The covenant with Noah and his descendants is universal, encompassing the entire world population. Described as "everlasting," it includes a declaration of the sacredness of life, both human and animal, and a divine promise never again to drown the earth (9:1–11). Like the later agreements made through Abraham and Moses, the pact with Noah has a "sign"—the rainbow as a visible symbol of God's reconciliation with humankind.

The primeval history concludes by tracing the genealogies of Noah's sons, **Ham, Shem,** and **Japheth,** who represent the three principal branches of the human family known to the ancient Hebrews (Chs. 10–11). From Shem come the Semitic peoples, among them the Babylonians, Assyrians, Arabs, and Israelites. Ham was the **eponymous** (name-giving) ancestor of the Egyptians and their (then) political dependents, including the Canaanites, while Japheth was the supposed progenitor of the Aegean Sea peoples, including the Greeks.

Amid the lengthy genealogies—sometimes called the "table of nations"—editors inserted J's story of the Tower of Babel. An etiological account explaining the great diversity of languages spoken in different geographical areas, the story contains themes of human ambition and divine retribution that initially appeared in J's narrative about the expulsion from Eden. When humanity, united in language and purpose, attempts to build a tower "with its top reaching heavens" and thus "make a name for [themselves]," Yahweh realizes that "nothing will be too hard for [humans] to do." Accordingly, he overthrows the tower, "confuses" their speech so that they can no longer understand each other, and scatters a linguistically divided humanity throughout the earth (11:1–9). Deeply dis-

trustful of human culture, particularly when concentrated in cities, J regards the Babel incident as exemplifying an attitude the Greeks called *hubris,* a pride that offends the gods.

STORIES OF ISRAEL'S ANCESTORS

After surveying the human race as a whole, the Genesis account narrows to focus on the ancestors of a single nation, Israel. The remainder of Genesis (Chs. 12–50) is devoted to tracing the stories of Abraham and Sarah, progenitors of the future Israel, and their colorful descendants through four turbulent generations. Opening with God's call to Abraham in **Haran,** a major city in northwestern Mesopotamia, the action then shifts all over the map of the Fertile Crescent, ending with Abraham's great-grandchildren—Joseph and his eleven brothers, eponymous founders of the **Twelve Tribes of Israel**—settled in Egypt. The journeys of Abraham and his progeny, in fact, outline the geographical contours of the biblical world, from the valley of the Euphrates to that of the Nile (see Figure 2.1). In their wandering between the two Near Eastern centers of political power, Mesopotamia in the north and Egypt in the south, the patriarchal families also anticipate the later historical movements of the Israelite people.

The story of Abraham (Chs. 12–25) introduces a positive new phase in the divine-human partnership. In the primeval history, God's relationship with humanity as a whole had been largely adversarial, culminating in global judgment and destruction. By Genesis 12, however, Yahweh is apparently resigned to the inevitability of human wrongdoing (Gen. 8:21–22) and prepared to display great flexibility in anticipating and circumventing the results of human frailty.

In Genesis's second narrative cycle (Chs. 25–36), God utilizes the sibling rivalry between **Esau** and **Jacob,** twin sons of **Isaac** and **Rebekah,** to realize his goals. Drawing on the flawed personalities of both brothers—Jacob's calculating self-interest and Esau's crass impulsiveness—to achieve the desired outcome, God ensures that the Abrahamic promise is transmitted according to his long-range plan. Perhaps Genesis's most notable example of

God's transforming potentially lethal domestic strife into an occasion for fulfilling the divine will occurs in the third narrative cycle (Chs. 37–50), stories involving Joseph and his envious brothers (see page 126).

Divine Appearances   The biblical narrator typically expresses God's interaction with humanity by describing a **theophany**, a visible or otherwise perceptible appearance of the Deity to human beings. In Genesis, God appears more frequently to more individuals, and over a longer span of time, than in any other book of the Bible. After the primeval history, however, divine communication changes significantly in both content and purpose. Whereas before the flood, God's conversations with such figures as Adam, Eve, Cain, and Noah usually involve prohibitions, condemnations, or warnings, after the flood his speeches mostly take the form of vows and promises. Providing thematic coherence to the diverse ancestral tales, the divine promises to Abraham and his heirs—for multitudinous descendants, land, blessing, the divine presence, and a special covenant partnership—help to unify the entire Pentateuch.

THE STORY OF ABRAHAM AND SARAH

According to Joshua 24, neither Abraham nor his father Terah was originally a worshiper of Yahweh. As natives of Ur, one of Mesopotamia's oldest cities, they naturally "served other gods" (Josh. 24:2; cf. Gen. 11:26–31). Yahweh's reason for uniquely honoring Abraham, the product of a polytheistic society, is not explicitly stated but can be partly inferred from Abraham's behavior. In Genesis 12, when Yahweh suddenly breaks into Abraham's consciousness, ordering him to abandon his home in Haran, where Terah had transported his family, and journey to an unspecified destination, Abraham immediately complies. Throughout the narrative, whenever God speaks, Abraham *listens*—in the biblical sense of the verb, paying full attention to the divine summons and responding obediently. As Genesis 15 expresses it, Abraham "put his faith" in Yahweh's promises, and Yahweh "counted this [trust] as making him justified" (15:6).

In Genesis 14, Abraham takes on the unexpected role of warrior, rescuing his nephew **Lot**, son of his uncle Haran, from a coalition of Canaanite kings. After defeating the kings, he pays ten percent of his captured booty to **Melchizedek**, the king-priest of **Salem**, a Canaanite sanctuary thought to be the future site of Jerusalem (Gen. 14:18–22).

THE ABRAHAMIC COVENANT

When Yahweh next appears to Abraham, God conducts a mysterious nocturnal ritual, in which he passes between the two halves of a slaughtered animal, ratifying the covenant with his friend (15:1–18). The Abrahamic Covenant, four different versions of which are included in Genesis (12:2–3; 15:1–21; 17:1–22; 22:15–18), is a solemn contractual agreement by which Yahweh pledges to make Abraham the progenitor of nations (particularly Israel), to give his innumerable descendants the entire territory of Canaan, and to be their God forever (Box 4.3). The version outlined in Genesis 15 specifies the Promised Land's boundaries, which are to extend from the valley of the "great river" Euphrates to that of the Nile (15:18), from northwest Mesopotamia to the northeast border of Egypt. Because Israel's frontiers did not reach that extent until the reigns of David and Solomon—and then only briefly—scholars believe that this form of the promise can be dated no earlier than the period of the monarchy, many centuries after Abraham's time (cf. 1 Kings 4:21).

In Genesis 17, Yahweh introduces a ritual requirement for Abraham and all his male offspring, **circumcision**—surgically removing the foreskin of the penis. As a physical "sign" of an Israelite's Abrahamic descent (17:11), P regards circumcision as so important that he anachronistically ascribes it to the patriarchal epoch. Although incorporated into the Mosaic law (Lev. 12:1–5; cf. Exod. 12:44, 48), the ritual was probably not widely observed until much later in Israel's history, as indicated by conflicting traditions about its origin. Although presumably descended from Abraham, Moses apparently was unaware that Yahweh required circumcision, a lapse for which Yahweh threatens to kill him (Exod. 4:22–24). Although this puzzling

Box 4.3 The Covenants with Noah and Abraham

An extremely important biblical concept, a covenant (Hebrew, *berit*) is a vow, promise, contract, agreement, or pact. The biblical writers commonly use the term to express Yahweh's purposeful relationship with an individual or a nation. In the ancient Near Eastern culture out of which the Bible grew, there were two principal forms of covenant: (1) the *suzerainty covenant,* a political treaty between a superior party who dictated the terms of the arrangement and an inferior party who obeyed them, and (2) the *parity covenant,* an agreement between equals who were both obligated to observe its provisions.

In the Hebrew Bible, Yahweh, the great king or suzerain, initiates four major covenants — all an expression of divine graciousness in God's voluntarily binding himself to a person or a people. Genesis contains the texts of two formal covenants — the Noachan and Abrahamic — and some commentators believe that others are implied in the two creation accounts. Although *berit* is not mentioned in Genesis 1, some scholars believe that a covenant relationship is suggested when Elohim grants humanity dominion over the earth and issues a command to populate it (Gen. 1:26 – 31). A comparable legal implication occurs in Yahweh's directive to cultivate Eden and his prohibition against tasting the tree of knowledge (Gen. 2:16 – 17). The first explicitly stated covenant, a recapitulation of God's order to procreate, is promulgated through Noah (Gen. 9:1 – 17). Universal in scope, encompassing all living creatures, both human and animal, it emphasizes the sacredness of life and the faithfulness of God, who promises never again to inundate the world. Its "sign" is the rainbow.

The second formal covenant that Yahweh initiates in Genesis is with Abraham, whom the Deity promises a son, countless descendants, land, blessings, and a special covenant relationship — promises that shape the biblical narrative from Genesis through 2 Kings. Because ancient compilers apparently used a variety of sources, Genesis contains several versions or aspects of the Abrahamic Covenant. In Genesis 15, Yahweh, like a powerful king making a land grant to a favored subject, promises the land of Canaan (Palestine) to Abraham's progeny (the Israelites). The oath is ratified by an ancient ritual in which Yahweh passes between the two halves of a dismembered sacrificial animal. (A parallel covenant rite is described in Jer. 34:18 – 21.) A later priestly account of the covenant (Gen. 17) repeats Yahweh's pledge about Canaan;

states that Abraham will father a "multitude of nations," including a line of kings; and stresses circumcision of all Jewish males as a sign "in perpetuity" of the God's self-imposed bond with Israel. Yahweh also promises that "all the nations of the earth" will "bless themselves" because of Abraham (Gen. 12:3; 22:18).

The theme of kingly descendants anticipates the Davidic Covenant, in which Yahweh vows to keep King David's royal heirs on Judah's throne forever (2 Sam. 7:8 – 17; Ps. 89:19 – 37). The Deity's pacts with both Abraham and David are similarly unconditional, with the human beneficiaries required to do nothing in return, although circumcision functions as evidence that Abraham's progeny recognize their covenant status. Because the Genesis covenants assumed their literary form during and after the Davidic monarchy, many scholars believe that the Deity's oath to produce a royal line from Abraham is modeled on the pact with David. (See Chapter 5, Box 5.4.)

The Noachan, Abrahamic, and Davidic covenants differ strikingly in degree, if not entirely in kind, from the Mosaic Covenant articulated in Exodus. (See the discussion in Box 4.7, "The Mosaic Covenant," in the next section.) Although Noah, Abraham, and David display a trusting obedience to Yahweh's demands, which is presumably the reason for their being selected as covenant bearers, the Genesis and Davidic covenants place much less stress on reciprocal obligation from the human parties involved. According to the priestly rendition of the Abrahamic vow, the patriarch is to "bear himself blameless," implying a continuing moral relation between him and Yahweh (Gen. 17:1 – 2), but the Deity does not require an oath of obedience or a long list of legal stipulations comparable to that enunciated in the Mosaic pact. (The priestly reference to Abraham's keeping statutes and laws [Gen. 26:4 – 6] may be an effort to bring the Abrahamic tradition, at least partially, in line with the later Mosaic arrangement.) Throughout the historical narratives from Genesis to 2 Kings, and many of the prophetic books as well, a painful tension exists between the two different kinds of covenant. Yahweh's unconditional promises to Abraham (for descendants, land, presence, blessing, etc.) and to David (for an everlasting royal dynasty) seem to run counter to the conditional terms of the Mosaic Covenant, in which God's help and protection depend almost entirely on Israel's loyal obedience to divine law.

episode may have served an etiological purpose, highlighting the need for all Israelite males to be circumcised, another tradition, preserved in Joshua 5, provides a different account of Israelites' initiating the circumcision ritual. Before invading Canaan, Joshua orders his troops to submit to mass circumcision (Josh. 5:2–7), a practice with which they were apparently unfamiliar.

Abraham's Sons   At age eighty-six, eleven years after first receiving Yahweh's sworn oath to give him a son, Abraham finally has a child, **Ishmael**, not by his wife **Sarah**, but by **Hagar**, Sarah's slave. Another thirteen years pass, and Abraham is ninety-nine before Yahweh appears again, this time under the oak trees of Mamre (18:1), where Abraham is informed that within a year he and his wife will have a son. Overhearing the prophecy, Sarah laughs—both she and Abraham are long past the age of procreation (18:1–15). From the Genesis narrator's viewpoint, however, it is precisely *because* the couple has grown too old to reproduce that the divinely planned moment finally arrives. By the next year, Sarah and Abraham indeed have an heir of their "own flesh and blood"—**Isaac**, whose name (literally, "laughter") echoes his mother's mirth at hearing an "impossible" prediction.

Immediately after promising Abraham an heir, Yahweh announces that he is on his way to inspect the cities of **Sodom** and Gomorrah, for he has heard rumors of their wickedness. Perceiving Yahweh's intention to destroy the cities, Abraham questions God's justice in annihilating whole populations. "Will the Judge of all the earth not administer justice?" he asks. Submitting to his covenant partner's courteous but persistent questioning, Yahweh finally declares that he will not destroy the cities if even ten righteous people can be found in them (18:16–35). In some views, Yahweh's wrath against Sodom was ignited by its residents' homosexuality. Genesis 19, however, describes an attempted gang rape of two male visitors, not the sexual activity of mutually consenting adults. In contrast to Abraham's generous hospitality, the men of Sodom violently assault strangers, whom Near Eastern custom dictated they should welcome and protect. When alluding to Sodom's notoriety, later biblical authors do not mention sexual misconduct, emphasizing instead the city's failure to help the "poor and needy" and its deplorable lack of hospitality. (See Ezekiel's comparison of Sodom and Judah [Ezek. 16:48–58].)

National Etiologies   Before fire from heaven consumes Sodom and its sister cities, Yahweh, out of regard for Abraham, rescues Lot and his two daughters. Like Noah after an even greater cataclysm, Lot becomes drunk and—his wife having been changed into a pillar of salt—commits incest with his two daughters. The sons of this illicit union are the eponymous ancestors of **Moab** and **Ammon**, two small states that bordered ancient Israel. Commonly presenting a single individual as the progenitor of an entire people or nation, the Genesis authors claim that Jacob's brother Esau literally "is Edom" (36:1). Similarly, Jacob is identified as Israel (32:28; 35:10); his twelve sons are depicted as identical with the later twelve tribes that traditionally composed the kingdom of Israel (29:31; 30:24; 35:16–20; 49:16). In these legendary etiologies, Israel receives its name from God as a validation of its chosen status, whereas neighboring countries such as Amon and Moab are the products of unspeakable sin, while Edom, Israel's cultural "twin," derives from one whom God rejects as covenant bearer.

The Binding of Isaac   Whereas most of God's direct communications with Abraham take the form of assured blessings, God's abrupt order to offer Isaac as a human sacrifice is a startling contrast. Up to this point, the narrative had moved slowly toward Abraham's goal of having his own son and heir, the promised child that Yahweh himself now threatens to destroy in an episode (from the Elohist) known as the "binding of Isaac" (Ch. 22). Abraham's willingness to kill Isaac without pleading for the boy as he had pled for God to spare Sodom, and his silence in the face of this horrific demand have long troubled Bible readers (Box 4.4). With his knife raised to cut his son's throat, Abraham is stopped by the intervention of an angel,

Box 4.4 Yahweh and Child Sacrifice

Although the Genesis narrator interprets God's demand for human sacrifice as a mere test of Abraham's exemplary obedience, the episode raises many troubling issues about both the ethical nature of the biblical God and the character of ancient Israelite religion. According to the second Torah book, Exodus, Yahweh has the right to claim the life of all Israelite firstborn sons, who are to be "given" (sacrificed) to him as part of ritual worship, just as the firstborn of "flocks and herds" are (Exod. 22:29–30). Although Torah regulations also permit Israelites to "redeem" their sons by offering an animal substitute (Exod. 34:20), there are hints that Yahweh did not always discourage child sacrifice. In Judges, Jephthah is possessed by "the spirit of Yahweh" when he resolves that if Yahweh will grant him military victory, he will make a "holocaust" or "burnt offering" of the first person he meets after the battle. Ironically, the first to greet Jephthah upon his triumphal return home — for Yahweh has given him success — is his daughter, who then undergoes a rite of mourning for her unfulfilled life. The Judges author presents Jephthah's vow to sacrifice a human being as if it were not unusual (Judg. 11:29–40), perhaps because early Israelite society, to some extent, shared the practice with its immediate neighbors, the Canaanites. When the prophet Micah (eighth century B.C.E.) rhetorically asked, "Must I give my first born for what I have done wrong, the fruit of my body for my own sin?" he evidently expected that at least some in his audience would respond in the affirmative (Mic. 6:6).

How effective the offering of a royal child could be at a time of national crisis is illustrated in a story about Mesha, king of Moab (ninth century B.C.E.). When Israelite armies besiege Mesha's fortified city, the king, in desperation, brings out his firstborn son, the heir to his throne, and sacrifices him on the city wall, in full view of the attackers. The result of Mesha's act, presumably a last-ditch appeal for help to the Moabite god **Chemosh**, is the instant withdrawal of Israelite troops, thus delivering the Moabites from their enemies. The biblical text in this passage has apparently been edited, making what supposedly happened strangely ambiguous: We are told only that after Mesha offered his son, "great wrath came upon Israel" (2 Kings 3:26–27). The text does not indicate whether the "wrath" was that

of Yahweh or Chemosh, for whom King Solomon had built an altar near Jerusalem (1 Kings 11:7). The Israelites' failure to capture Mesha's stronghold is particularly notable because this episode immediately follows the prophet Elisha's prediction that Yahweh would "put Moab itself into [Israel's] power," allowing it to take "every fortified town" (2 Kings 3:18–19) — a prophecy ostensibly thwarted by Mesha's resorting to a supreme act of faith, child sacrifice.

The Bible's severest condemnation of child sacrifice occurs in the Book of Jeremiah (early sixth century B.C.E.), where the prophet denies that Yahweh ever ordered — or even thought of — such atrocities (Jer. 19:5–6). However, Jeremiah's contemporary, the priest-prophet Ezekiel, contends that Yahweh did indeed legislate child sacrifice — but as a bad law that he would then punish the Israelites for observing:

> I even gave them laws that were not good and observances by which they could never live; and I polluted them with their own offerings, *making them sacrifice all their firstborn;* which was to punish them, so that they would learn that I am Yahweh.
> Ezek. 20:25–26, italics added

According to Ezekiel, the Exodus command to offer firstborn sons as if they were animals (Exod. 22:30) was "not good," but was a snare that led Israel astray. Perhaps the prophet implies that the recipients of Yahweh's Torah should have had the ethical vision to discern between what was potentially good or evil in it, rejecting the latter even when a law purported to derive from God. In his recognition that Yahweh would prefer to accept a ram instead of Isaac — obeying the second voice that spared human life rather than the first that had ordered him to kill — Abraham proved decisively that he possessed the saving power of spiritual discernment. Noting that Yahweh's command to offer Isaac was unworthy, some later rabbinical commentators suggested that it was not God, but the Satan (the Deity's ethically undeveloped shadow self) who tempted Abraham to commit an abomination. (See Jon D. Levenson, *The Death and Resurrection of the Beloved Son: The Transformation of Child Sacrifice in Judaism and Christianity* [New Haven, Conn.: Yale University Press, 1993]).

who directs him to spare Isaac and offer instead a ram caught in a nearby thorn bush. Gratified at Abraham's remarkable display of obedience, Yahweh (in a J fragment?) then reaffirms his covenant vows, reiterating the promise made during his first appearance to Abraham ten chapters earlier, that his covenant partner will be the source of universal blessing (22:15–18; ct. 12:3).

"An old man who had lived his full span of years," Abraham dies at age 175 and is buried near Sarah's grave in Canaan (25:7–11). Ever sensitive to the divine presence, Abraham is the biblical model of supreme self-surrender, embodying an exemplary willingness to submit every part of one's life to the divine will. He also embodies the paradox inherent in the divine-human relationship: Divine favor invariably encompasses suffering as well as blessing. With most of God's promises to be realized only in the far distant future, he receives the only form of posthumous reward recognized in the Torah—vicarious survival through progeny and a reputation so "famous that it will be used as a blessing" to all (12:2).

THE STORY OF JACOB AND HIS FAMILY

Isaac and Rebekah   After devoting a dozen chapters to Abraham and Sarah, Genesis passes briefly over the career of Isaac, who emerges as an essentially passive figure. In his most memorable postures, Isaac is shown either as a hapless youth stretched out on a sacrificial altar (Ch. 22) or an aged man prone on his bed (Ch. 27), the victim of a deceitful conspiracy by his wife and younger son. (Although Isaac, old and feeble, appears near death in Genesis 27, he does not actually die until decades later, when he is allegedly 180; the Genesis narratives do not always follow a linear movement [35:27–29].) Isaac's wife Rebekah (Rebecca), a far more decisive character, first appears in Genesis 24 when Abraham's servant returns to the patriarch's Mesopotamian homeland to find Isaac a mate from among Abraham's kinfolk. Offering water from a well to Abraham's travel-weary emissary, Rebekah at once manifests the hospitality that marks admirable behavior. Then, as if recognizing a divinely presented opportunity, she coura-

geously volunteers to accept an unknown bridegroom and cast her lot in a strange land. After marrying Isaac and giving birth to twin sons, Esau (the firstborn) and Jacob, she plays a major part shaping Israel's destiny. Privately informed that Yahweh prefers the younger son (who is also her personal favorite), she not only initiates the plot to deceive Isaac into blessing Jacob rather than Esau, the firstborn, but also arranges for Jacob to escape his brother's vengeance by sending him from Canaan to her relatives in Mesopotamia. Considering Rebekah's assertiveness, it is not surprising that her husband has no other wives or concubines, making Isaac the only truly monogamous patriarch.

Jacob   A spiritual cousin of the quick-witted Greek hero Odysseus (Ulysses), Jacob is sometimes regarded as primarily a trickster. His function in the biblical narrative, however, is far more complex than that dismissive label implies, for Jacob's strengths, weaknesses, and dynamic relationship to God are presented as a paradigm for the character of Israel, the nation named after him. In the totality of his story, which extends from prenatal struggles with Esau in Rebekah's womb (25:21–28) to death bed evaluations of his twelve sons more than a century later (Ch. 49), Jacob undergoes a variety of powerful life-changing experiences. As a young man, he shrewdly exploits his older brother's demand for instant gratification, persuading Esau to sell him his birthright for a pot of stew (25:29–31). He then completes the theft of Esau's inheritance, his legal rights as firstborn, by appropriating his brother's identity, lying to his nearly blind father and deceiving Isaac into conferring the paternal blessing on him (Ch. 27).

After Rebekah learns that Esau plans to kill his usurping brother and sends Jacob fleeing northward to Mesopotamia, Yahweh begins a series of encounters with the fugitive that culminates in his bestowing a significant new identity upon Jacob. The first theophany occurs at Bethel, where Jacob stops overnight on his way to Haran. Sleeping outdoors with a stone for his pillow, he dreams of a "ladder," a ramp reaching from earth to heaven on which angels ascend and descend (as Mesopotamian deities invisibly tread the ceremonial stairway of a Babylonian ziggurat). Yahweh also appears in the dream and restates the familiar promise to Abraham, adding a vow to accompany Jacob on his journey. On awakening, Jacob behaves in characteristic fashion, combining reverence for the divine presence and a pragmatic concern for his personal welfare. Although impressed by the sanctity of the place, which he renames **Bethel** (literally, the "house of El") (28:10–22), Jacob is unwilling to commit himself to Yahweh on the basis of a mere dream, however "awesome." After anointing a stone pillar with oil to commemorate his unexpected contact with divinity, Jacob boldly adds his own terms to the covenant promises Yahweh had just enunciated: "*If* God goes with me and keeps me safe on this journey . . ., *if* he gives me bread to eat and clothes to wear, and *if* I return home safely to my father, *then* Yahweh shall be my God." Casting his covenant stipulations in the same "if . . . then" formula typical of the later Mosaic law, Jacob informs the Deity that allegiance to him will depend on how effectively divine promises are translated into the realities of food and security (28:18–22).

The Theophany at Peniel (Penuel)

Despite conflict with his uncle **Laban**, whose daughters **Leah** and **Rachel**, he marries, Jacob's sojourn in Mesopotamia is productive in almost every sense. Not only does he acquire great wealth in the form of sheep, goats, and cattle during his twenty-year stay (Figure 4.3), he also fathers eleven sons (some by his wives' maids) and a daugher, **Dinah**. (A twelfth son, Benjamin, is later born to Rachel.) Traveling back to Canaan to meet his estranged brother, Jacob has a second nocturnal theophany, this time by the river Jabbok, a tributary of the Jordan River. Alone in the dark and terrified of the next day's reunion with Esau, whose vengeance he has good reason to fear, Jacob suddenly finds himself attacked by an unknown entity. Wrestling all night, the two opponents are so evenly matched that neither can defeat the other. Only in the predawn twilight does Jacob recognize his mysterious assailant's identity, suddenly realizing that "I have seen God face to face" (32:30). Although a variant account of Jacob's encounter refers to his op-

Figure 4.3 A treasure from the Royal Cemetery of Ur, this ornamental goat stands on its hind legs, leaning against a golden plant. Probably a fertility icon, the goat has horns and eyes of lapis lazuli, with face, horns, and legs of wood overlaid with gold.

ponent as an "angel" (Hos. 12:4), one of the traditions incorporated into this passage implies that Jacob's adversary is God himself. If so, the Deity apparently assumes human form (and therefore only limited human strength) for this physical struggle with Jacob. When Jacob refuses to release him, the divine attacker bestows both blessing and a name change—henceforth Jacob is *Israel,* the one who has "striven with God and with humans, and [has] prevailed." Instead of being Jacob (meaning "supplanter" [cf. 25:26; 27:36]), the trickster who had stolen Esau's legal rights, he is now Israel, signaling a new identity as one who effectively struggles with both God and mortals— and survives. Although modern scholars think that "Israel" probably means "God [El] rules," the Genesis writer's interpretation is highly apporpriate to the biblical portrayal of Israel as a nation locked in a complex (and sometimes adversarial) relationship with God. Memorializing the encounter, Jacob renames the site Peniel (Penuel), which means "The Face of El [God]" (32:22–32).

After his reconciliation with Esau (Ch. 33), Jacob makes another pilgrimage to Bethel, where God again appears, this time identifying himself as El Shaddai and renewing his covenant vow, adding that Jacob's descendants will include kings (35:1–14). In this second (probably Elohist) version of Jacob's name change to Israel, Jacob again sets up a stone pillar, again anoints it, and again changes the site's name from Luz to Bethel (35; cf. 32). Although in Chapter 37 the narrative shifts from Jacob's adventures to concentrate on the conflict among his sons, Jacob again takes center stage near the end of Genesis, where the dying patriarch offers an extensive catalogue of "blessings" (including some curses and severe condemnations) for each of his twelve male offspring (Ch. 49). After his death, he is buried near Abraham's grave in Canaan.

THE STORY OF JOSEPH AND HIS BROTHERS

Although the final section of Genesis (Chs. 37–50) focuses on the story of **Joseph**, the Hebrew text labels it "the story of the family of Jacob" (37:2, New Revised Standard Version). This editorial emphasis on Jacob/Israel's family as a group highlights the narrative's larger purpose, the transition from God's relationship with individual ancestors, such as Abraham and Jacob, to the Deity's evolving partnership with a whole people. As the nucleus of a future nation, Jacob's twelve sons, with their wives and children, now form a corporate body, a development illustrated in Chapter 49, where Jacob describes each of his sons as distinctive tribal entities. "All these [Jacob's sons]," the narrator points out, "make up the tribes of Israel, twelve in number" (49:28). In moving from tales about individual family units to the portrayal of a much larger ethnic coalition, Genesis prepares for the emergence of Israelite nationhood described in the next book of Torah, Exodus.

The dramatic account of Joseph's rise from kidnap victim, slave, and prisoner to a powerful position at the Egyptian royal court — the subject of Chs. 37–50 — is thus set in the larger context of God's plans for Israelite nationhood. Although Joseph's personal story occupies the narrative foreground, God operates unobtrusively behind the scenes, using Joseph as his instrument who will ultimately reconcile Jacob's quarreling sons, forging them into a united people. In this section, God makes only one appearance, and then it is not to Joseph but to Jacob, in a nocturnal "vision" (46:2–4; cf. 48:3–4). Instead of direct theophanies, Joseph receives only dreams — and a divinely granted ability to interpret them.

Whereas the tales of Abraham, Isaac, and Jacob are highly episodic — consisting of loosely connected narrative units bound together only by repeated divine promises and travel itineraries — the Joseph story forms a coherent literary whole. (Chapter 38, an interpolated episode in which Tamar poses as a prostitute to claim her legal right to a child from Jacob's son Judah, is one of the few major digressions.) Often called a short story or novella, the self-contained Joseph section has a unified plot in which the consequences of fraternal strife lead to a climactic reversal of the brothers' initial status, with Joseph transformed from helpless victim to imperial vizier, and his bullying brothers into humble suppliants. As a longer and more structured narrative than those found earlier in Genesis, the Joseph saga resembles other short stories found in the Hebrew Bible, such as Ruth and Esther.

In the opening scenes of conflict between brothers, reminiscent of that between Cain and Abel or Jacob and Esau, Joseph is introduced as Jacob's favorite son, decked out in his father's gift of an elaborate garment, and antagonizing his siblings by telling them two dreams that foreshadow his future greatness. In the first dream, his ten brothers bow low before him, honoring his superiority; in the second, even the sun, moon, and stars (his two parents and their other children) do obeisance. Only seventeen years old, Joseph foresees future glory for himself, but is woefully insensitive to the feelings of his older brothers.

The JE text describing the brothers' conspiracy to punish Joseph's youthful arrogance combines two conflicting versions of the tale. In the Elohist source, the eldest brother, Reuben (representing a northern tribe) persuades the others not to kill Joseph, but merely to throw him into a dry well, where passing Midianites extricate him and take him to Egypt. In the Yahwist account, Judah (representing the most prominent southern tribe) intercedes for Joseph, suggesting that he not be harmed but be sold as a slave to a caravan of Ishmaelites, who then transport him to Egypt.

As a result of editors' bringing together two different literary strands, Joseph is twice sold into Egyptian slavery, first by E's Midianites (37:36) and then by J's Ishmaelites (39:1–2). In both versions, his Egyptian buyer and new master is **Potiphar**, an important official at Pharaoh's court. At this point, the biblical tradition apparently draws on an ancient Egyptian tale about a virtuous young man who resists the attempt of his brother's wife to seduce him and who, after many misadventures, subsequently rises to become Egypt's crown prince (see Pritchard in "Recommended Reading"). Although he rejects the sexual advances of Potiphar's wife, Joseph—like the hero of the Egyptian legend—is falsely accused of betraying his master and thrown into prison.

Even in disgrace, Joseph benefits from Yahweh's "kindness," receiving special favor from the chief jailer, who places the Hebrew in charge of the other prisoners. Joseph's ability to interpret the dream of two of Pharaoh's imprisoned courtiers eventually leads to his being released from jail and brought to Pharaoh's court, where he also practices the art of divination (foretelling future events). His fortune is made when he correctly relates that Pharaoh's two dreams about seven starving cows eating seven fat ones are prophetic—seven years of abundant crops will be followed by a severe, prolonged famine. Emphasizing that this foreknowledge is possible only because God chooses to reveal his intentions, Joseph is appointed Pharaoh's chief administrator. During the years of prosperity, Joseph governs Egypt shrewdly, filling its warehouses with surplus grain. When famine strikes, he controls the food supply, exchanging grain and seed for the people's money, livestock, and land, all of which then become Pharaoh's property. By the famine's end, the Egyptian population—excepting the priestly class, which retains its economic autonomy—has been reduced to mere "slaves," landless tenants working for Pharaoh, who is now Egypt's sole landowner (Chs. 41; 47).

As famine had driven Abraham from Canaan to Egypt (12:10), so Jacob's ten sons migrate from Canaan to the Nile region, seeking grain. (Jacob's twelfth son, Benjamin, stays home with his father.) There the brothers fall into Joseph's power, fulfilling Joseph's adolescent dream of being exalted above his older siblings (Chs. 42–45; cf. 37:2–11). Only after putting his now needy and dependant brothers through a series of humiliating manipulations, does Joseph—with impressive self-dramatization—reveal his identity, graciously forgiving them the wrongs they had done him. Although the Joseph story reaches its climax in the brothers' recognition that Egypt's preeminent governor is none other than their formerly despised sibling, the ultimate purpose of the Genesis narrative is not realized until Jacob is also brought into Egypt and the entire family is advantageously settled in the eastern Nile delta. The "story of the family of Jacob" (37:2, NRSV), riven by conflict and crisis that threaten to disrupt the Abrahamic lineage, at last achieves a peaceful resolution, with the previously divided group reunited and welcomed by Pharaoh as alien residents in Egypt (Ch. 50).

In a final speech to his brothers, Joseph tells them that although they intended to do him "evil," by "God's design" their intentions had "turned to good" (50:20). By seizing upon human weakness, such as the brothers' murderous jealousy, Yahweh had converted its consequences (Joseph's abduction to Egypt) into an opportunity for benefitting both Israelites and Egyptians. By Genesis's conclusion, the vow that Yahweh makes during his first appearance to Abraham (12:1–3)—that all earth's families would find blessing through Abraham's progeny—is already being fulfilled. Joseph's deathbed request to have his bones eventually taken for reburial in Canaan also points toward future developments in the divine plan, indicating that Israel's Egyptian sojourn will be only an extended detour in the long pilgrimage toward the Promised Land (50:24–26; cf. Exod 13:19).

QUESTIONS FOR REVIEW

1. Explain how the terms *Torah, law, instruction, Pentateuch,* and *"books of Moses"* are related.

2. Describe the various promises that Yahweh makes to Abraham and other figures in the Pentateuch. How do these promises serve to bind together or unify the five diverse parts of the Torah?

3. Describe some of the differences between the two creation accounts in Genesis 1 and 2. What issues concern the priestly author? Why do you suppose that in the Yahwist's account, Yahweh creates the animals *after* Adam (humanity) is already formed?

4. Reread the two separate versions of Noah's flood that are interwoven in Genesis 6–8. What differences do you find between the Yahwist and the priestly accounts?

5. Describe some of the personal qualities and attributes that typify the Yahwist's portrait of Yahweh. In what ways does the Yahwist combine both creative and destructive aspects of God's nature?

6. Who were Abraham and Sarah? Describe the terms of Yahweh's promises to Abraham (the Abrahamic Covenant). In what ways is God's vow to Abraham like the oath God made to Noah after the Flood? What test of Abraham's loyalty does Yahweh make of his servant? Does Abraham live to see the divine promises fulfilled?

7. What roles do Sarah, Rebekah, and Rachel play in the Genesis story of Israel's origins?

8. Describe Jacob's character. In what specific ways does his career depend upon trickiness or deceit? Why does he fear the anger of his brother Esau? How do Jacob's prayers to God change over time?

9. Explain how the twelve sons of Jacob come to dwell in Egypt. How does Joseph attain a position that allows him to fulfill his dream of lording it over his older brothers? At the end of Genesis, are Abraham's descendants any closer to possessing the Promised Land?

QUESTIONS FOR DISCUSSION AND REFLECTION

1. Biblical scholars assert that Genesis is a composite work in which the ancient Yahwist and Elohist narratives were later edited by priestly redactors to produce the present biblical text. If we accept that this canonical book is the product of multiple authors and priestly editors, how does this theory shape our readings of specific passages and sections of Genesis? Given the fact that ancient writers, from Egypt and Babylon to Homeric Greece, freely composed speeches for their gods, how are we to understand the biblical God's conversations with Eve or Abraham?

2. Most scholars think that biblical authors were less interested in achieving factual objectivity and more interested in presenting an ethical or religious interpretation of Israel's remote past. How does Genesis illustrate the authors' theological concerns about Israel as divinely chosen people and (later) as a political state? Explain how the biblical writers' approach does or does not fulfill a modern reader's expectations of reliable historicity.

3. Many readers see modern science and biblical faith as being in conflict. Whereas the priestly author of Genesis 1 drew on ancient Mesopotamian theories about how the cosmos was fashioned from a primeval sea during a single creative week, the modern sciences of astronomy and geology provide overwhelming evidence that the universe did not originate in a watery abyss and that it has been evolving for billions of years. Given the fact that biblical writers, completely unaware of the geological and paleontological record, were concerned primarily with asserting the cosmic supremacy of their God, how may we incorporate both biblical and scientific insights into a coherent worldview?

4. The Pentateuch is largely organized according to a series of divine promises to Abraham for descendants, land, blessings, the divine presence, and a special covenant relationship. Why do you think the biblical Deity chooses to interact with Israel's ancestors in this way? Why does he so long delay the fulfillment of his promises? With very few exceptions, most biblical writers view God as the patron and guide of Israel alone, to the exclusion of all other peoples, a view later adopted by Christianity and Islam, who similarly identify their respective religious communities as recipients of an exclusive revelation. How might we reconcile the concept of a universal God with the notion that the Deity relates only to one segment of the global population?

TERMS AND CONCEPTS TO REMEMBER

Abel	Babel
Adam	Bethel
Ammon	Cain
Ark, the	Chemosh

cherub, cherubim (pl.)
circumcision
Eden
Edom
Enoch
Enuma Elish
Esau
Eve
Fall, the
firmament
Flood, the
Hagar
Ham
Haran
Isaac
Ishmael
Jacob
Japheth
Joseph
Lamech

Levi
Leviathan
Lot
Melchizedek
Methuselah
Moab
Noah
Peniel (Penuel)
Rachel
Rahab
Rebekah (Rebecca)
Sabbath
Salem
Sarah
serpent
Shechem
Shem
Sodom
theophany
Twelve Tribes of Israel

RECOMMENDED READING

Alter, Robert. *Genesis.* New York: Norton, 1996. A fresh translation and commentary.

Anderson, Bernhard W. *Creation Versus Chaos: The Reinterpretation of Mythical Symbolism in the Bible.* New York: Association Press, 1967.

———, ed. *Creation in the Old Testament.* Philadelphia: Fortress Press, 1984.

Bailey, Lloyd R. *Genesis, Creation, and Creationism.* Mahwah, N.J.: Paulist Press, 1991. Examines the claims of fundamentalist creationists.

Clines, David J. A. *The Theme of the Pentateuch,* 2nd ed., Supplement Series 10. Sheffield, Eng.: JSOT Press, 1997. Discusses literary themes that unify diverse Torah narratives.

Coats, George W. *Genesis.* Grand Rapids, Mich.: Eerdmans, 1983.

Ellis, Peter. *The Yahwist: The Bible's First Theologian.* Notre Dame, Ind.: Fides, 1968.

Fox, Everett, ed. *The Five Books of Moses.* The Schocken Bible, Vol. 1. New York: Schocken Books, 1995. A superb new translation that captures the flavor of the original Hebrew.

Fretheim, Terence E. "The Book of Genesis." In *The New Interpreter's Bible.* Vol. 1, pp. 321–674. Nashville: Abingdon Press, 1994. Contains extensive scholarly commentary on the Genesis text.

Fukkelman, J. P. *Narrative Art in Genesis: Specimens of Stylistic and Structural Analysis.* Assen, Netherlands: Van Gorcum, 1975.

Hendel, Ronald S. "Genesis, Book of." In D. N. Freedman, ed., *The Anchor Bible Dictionary,* Vol. 2, pp. 933–941. New York: Doubleday, 1992.

Jeansonne, Sharon P. *The Women of Genesis: From Sarah to Potiphar's Wife.* Minneapolis: Fortress Press, 1990.

Kikawada, Isaac M. "Primeval History." In D. N. Freedman, ed., *The Anchor Bible Dictionary,* Vol. 5, pp. 461–466. New York: Doubleday, 1992. Examines Genesis 1–11, placing biblical narrative in the context of Near Eastern creation and flood myths.

Levenson, Jon D. *Creation and the Persistence of Evil: The Jewish Drama of Divine Omnipotence.* San Francisco: Harper & Row, 1988.

Niditch, Susan. *Chaos to Cosmos: Studies in Biblical Patterns of Creation.* Chico, Calif.: Scholars Press, 1985.

Pagels, Elaine. *Adam, Eve, and the Serpent.* New York: Random House, 1988. Critically examines the historical-political origins of the Christian doctrine of original sin.

Pritchard, James B., ed. *Ancient Near Eastern Texts Relating to the Old Testament,* 3rd ed. Princeton, N.J.: Princeton University Press, 1969. Contains "The Story of Two Brothers" that an Israelite author adapted for the Joseph story in Genesis.

Sailhamer, John H. *The Pentateuch as Narrative: A Biblical-Theological Commentary.* Library of Biblical Interpretation. Grand Rapids, Mich.: Zondervan, 1992. Examines the literary continuity of Torah stories.

Sarna, Nahum M. *Understanding Genesis.* New York: Schocken Books, 1970.

Scullion, John J. "Genesis, The Narrative of." In D. N. Freedman, ed., *The Anchor Bible Dictionary,* Vol. 2, pp. 941–962. New York: Doubleday, 1992.

Speiser, E. A., ed. *Genesis.* Anchor Bible. Garden City, N.Y.: Doubleday, 1964. A scholarly translation with extensive notes.

Trible, Phyllis. *God and the Rhetoric of Sexuality.* Philadelphia: Fortress Press, 1978. A close examination of Genesis 2–3 and other relevant biblical texts.

von Rad, Gerhard. *Genesis.* Philadelphia: Westminster Press, 1972. A standard work.

Westermann, Claus. *Genesis 1–11.* Minneapolis: Augsburg, 1984.

———. *Genesis 12–36.* Minneapolis: Augsburg, 1985.

———. *Genesis 37–50.* Minneapolis: Augsburg, 1986.

Exodus

KEY TOPICS/THEMES

In Exodus, God's promises to Abraham for multitudinous descendants, the divine presence, blessings, and a special relationship begin to be fulfilled. The families of Jacob and his twelve sons—numbering only seventy—who had settled in Egypt at the conclusion of Genesis have, after many generations, become a populous community and a perceived threat to Egypt's ruler. After a long silence, Yahweh at last "remembers" his vow to Abraham and commissions Moses to lead the Israelites from Egyptian oppression to freedom as the "people of God." Divided into two main sections, the deliverance from Egypt and journey to Sinai/Horeb (Chs.1–18) and the revelation of God's law at Sinai (Chs. 19–40), Exodus balances its initial theme of liberation from human tyranny with its later emphasis on Israel's ethical and legal responsibility to its divine liberator. In the Torah (instruction) which he communicates through Moses at Sinai, Yahweh introduces an entirely new dimension into his relationship with Abraham's progeny: Israel henceforth must adhere to a vast body of legal and ritual regulations if it is to benefit from Yahweh's patronage, its strict obedience a condition of divine favor. Major components of Exodus include the story of Moses (Chs. 2–6); Yahweh's war against Pharaoh and the institution of the Passover (Chs. 7–13); the miraculous sea crossing and desert journey to Sinai/Horeb (Chs. 14–18); the Sinai theophany, golden calf episode, and ratification of the Mosaic Covenant (Chs. 19–24; 32–34); and instructions for the tabernacle cult (Chs. 25–31; 35–40).

KEY QUESTIONS

What role does Moses play as Yahweh's agent in the creation of Israel? What are the terms of the covenant at Sinai/Horeb? How does Israel violate its bond to God, and how does Yahweh react to this disloyalty?

With the possible exception of Deuteronomy, Exodus expresses the core of Israelite faith more than any other book in the Hebrew Bible. In this dramatic account of Israel's escape from Egyptian bondage and sudden emergence as a society ruled directly by God—a **theocracy**—Exodus explicitly defines the nature of Yahweh's relationship to his chosen people. The narrative moves from the rigidly structured nation of Egypt, where Pharaoh reigns as a god-king, to an uninhabited desert, where Yahweh reveals that he alone is Israel's ruler.

Descending to the summit of Mount Sinai/Horeb like a lightning bolt from heaven, Yahweh discloses to an awe-struck people that he has rescued them from Pharaoh's control and given them freedom for one purpose: to worship and obey him. Unlike the Abrahamic Covenant, which makes few specific demands on the human partner, the pact that Yahweh concludes with Israel at Sinai is bilateral—the people must swear to observe a large body of law or he will reject them. Although the Mosaic Torah regulates a great variety of Israel's activities, including formal worship, sacrifice, civil order, some property rights, and the institution of human slavery, it does not govern every aspect of life in the covenant community (there are laws regulating divorce, for example, but none covering marriage). Despite its omissions, the Torah serves effectively to define the ethical and religious bonds linking Israel with its divine protector. Because observance of the *mitzvot* (divine commandments) is designed to permeate and shape many aspects of the Israelites' daily existence, it functions as a constant reminder of their obligation to Yahweh.

ISRAEL IN EGYPT

While in Egypt, the Israelites have grown so numerous that "they filled the land" (1:7), creating a population boom of foreign immigrants that alarms Egyptian authorities and results in the Israelites' enslavement. The blessings of fecundity, so prominent in Genesis' alternating tales of barrenness and childbearing, have inadvertently brought Israel into conflict with a new Egyptian dynasty, a pharaoh "who knew nothing of Joseph [and his contribution to Egyptian well-being]" (1:8). Although the narrative states that Israel's sojourn in Egypt lasted 430 years (Exod. 12:40), other passages imply that it was much shorter (only four generations according to Exodus 5:16–20), a time span that many historians regard as more plausible.

Problems of Historicity   To date, historians and archaeologists have not been able to verify any of the events described in Exodus (Figure 4.4). No known Egyptian records refer to the plagues that

NEUES REICH
Dyn.XVIII.

THEBEN
aus einem Grabe von Abd el Qurna.

Figure 4.4 This Egyptian tomb painting depicts slaves making bricks for the building enterprises of an Eighteenth Dynasty pharaoh. Although the work pictured is almost identical to that ascribed to Hebrew slaves in the book of Exodus, archaeologists — despite Egypt's wealth of extant inscriptions, archival records, and other artifacts — have been unable to find any physical evidence corroborating the Hebrews' presence there.

allegedly devastated Egypt, the flight of Hebrew slaves, or the drowning of an Egyptian army. Nor do Egypt's many surviving archives mention the biblical Moses (who bears an Egyptian name) or the contest between his deity, Yahweh, and the power of Pharaoh, who was believed to embody Horus, a form of the sun god. The earliest Egyptian reference to Israel's existence, Pharaoh Merneptah's victory stele, dates from the late thirteenth century B.C.E., when the Israelites were already settled in Canaan (see Chapter 2).

The fact that Exodus does not name either the pharaoh who oppressed Israel or the one whom Moses confronted creates a problem in dating the events it relates. Although the lack of references to specific historical figures increases the difficulty in establishing a reliable historical context for the Exodus, many scholars believe that the most probable setting for the story was Egypt's nineteenth dynasty (c. 1306–1200 B.C.E.). Many historians favor this period because the radical changes in Egyptian political leadership that had preceded the eighteenth and nineteenth dynasties provide a plausible background to events described in Exodus 1, particularly the shift in governmental attitude toward the Hebrews (a term commonly used for the Israelites before their establishment in Canaan). Although, for most of its long history, Egypt was

ruled by native kings, the succession of Egyptian pharaohs was interrupted between about 1750 and 1550 B.C.E. when non-Egyptian rulers dominated northern Egypt. Known as the **Hyksos** (an Egyptian term for "foreign princes"), this Semitic group is thought to have infiltrated Egypt from Syria and/or Canaan, roughly the same region in which the Israelite ancestors had lived. It was probably a Hyksos pharaoh who, sharing many of the same social customs as the Hebrews, welcomed Joseph and his family to Egypt. Resentful of these foreign rulers, however, native Egyptian leaders drove the Hyksos out of Egypt in about 1550 B.C.E., reestablishing Egyptian control of the state and (probably) adopting a hostile policy toward remaining immigrants from Canaan. If this reconstruction of events is correct, the pharaoh who enslaved the Israelites was probably Seti (Sesthos) I (c. 1305–1290 B.C.E.), and Moses' royal antagonist was most likely **Rameses II** (c. 1290–1224 B.C.E. (Figure 4.5).

Literary Sources Although some scholars argue that the Tetrateuch (first four books of the Pentateuch) were composed, perhaps by a single author, well after the exile, many scholars believe that the documentary hypothesis still best explains the internal contradictions and the diverse nature of the

Figure 4.5 The temple of Amon at Karnak, Egypt, has 134 gigantic columns bearing hieroglyphic inscriptions, one of which records Pharaoh Shiskak's invasion of Palestine (c. 918 B.C.E.). The massive structure was probably completed during the reign of Rameses II (c. 1290–1224 B.C.E.).

and 35–40 (see also Box 4.11). Priestly editors also injected numerous additions into the JE narrative, heightening the miraculous element of Israel's deliverance deliverance and providing a second version of Moses's reception of the divine name (6:3–13). (For an informed discussion of specific passages by J, E, D, or P, see *Sources of the Pentateuch* by Anthony Campbell and Mark O'Brien; see also *The Pentateuch in the Twentieth Century* by Ernest Nicholson in "Recommended Reading.")

MOSES AND YAHWEH

No figure looms larger in Israel's story than Moses, the man whom tradition credits with founding the Yahwist faith. Moses' agency both in forming the Israelite nation and in transmitting Yahweh's Torah to the covenant people is regarded as so crucial that later writers who contributed to the different literary strands in Exodus describe him in a dazzling variety of roles—lawgiver, prophet, judge, and even military leader. Described as initially reluctant to take on the tasks that Yahweh assigns him (Exod. 4:10–17), Moses becomes not only God's chief instrument in creating Israel but also God's intimate confidant, speaking with Yahweh "face to face, as a man speaks with his friend" (Exod. 33:11; cf. Deut. 34:10–11). Whereas Yahweh may commune indirectly with others by vision or dream, with Moses he speaks "plainly and not in riddles," even permitting him to see "the form of Yahweh" (Num. 12:8). So prestigious is Moses' reputation as a legislator that all of Israel's laws, even those that clearly date from much later periods, are ascribed to Mosaic origin and thus given his unimpeachable authority. As Yahweh himself describes Moses' role, this exceedingly meek man (Num. 12:3) with a debilitating speech impediment (Exod. 4:10–11) acts "as a god for Pharaoh" (Exod. 7:1), a human vehicle for conveying divine power.

Yahweh's Preeminent Servant In any other ancient Near Eastern tradition than that of Israel, Moses undoubtedly would be accorded superhuman status, made another Sargon or Gilgamesh—

material found in Exodus. As in Genesis, the disparate strands of the Yahwist, Elohist, priestly school, and as some scholars now propose, the Deuteronomist, are intricately interwoven. According to most scholarly analyses of the text, the Yahwist (J) supplies the main narrative, supplemented by excerpts from the Elohist source (E). The JE account apparently was reworked by both the Deuteronomist (the version of the Ten Commandments in Exodus 20 seems to be based on the commandments listed in Deuteronomy 5) and the postexilic priestly school, which added considerable genealogical, legal, and ritual material, including the Tabernacle instructions in Chapters 25–31

Box 4.5 The Endangered Child: A Pattern in Heroic Myth

Tales involving an infant who narrowly escapes death and later becomes a national hero are common in both world mythology and some biblical narratives. In Greek myth, numerous future heroes are abandoned and/or almost killed in their youth: The newborn Perseus is imprisoned in a chest with his mother and thrown into the sea, only to be rescued and live to avenge the wrongs done him; the baby Heracles (Hercules), who will grow up to earn glory by slaying monsters and redressing injustice, is almost strangled in his cradle by snakes; the infant Oedipus, who later becomes king of Thebes, is left out on a lonely hillside to be devoured by wild animals; even the young Dionysus, a future Olympian god, is torn to pieces by the Titans before his father Zeus, king of the gods, resurrects him to immortality. In Roman mythology, perhaps the most famous endangered children are the twins Romulus and Remus, the founders of Rome, who as babies are cast out and then adopted and nursed by a she-wolf.

In Near Eastern lore, the closest parallel to Moses' story is the Akkadian tale about **Sargon I**, who, like the future Hebrew leader, was cast adrift on a great river. When Sargon's mother places him in a pitch-sealed basket to float down the Euphrates River, he is rescued not by a princess but by an ordinary gardener who subsequently raised the boy as his own. From such humble origins, Sargon rose to displace the Sumerian monarch, Ur-Zababa as the ruler of Kish and to found the first Mesopotamian empire. By adding this element of deliverance to J's story of Moses, a later biblical redactor emphasizes the specialness of Moses' role, a variation of another biblical theme of the "barren wife" who unexpectedly bears a son chosen to become a leader of his people, such as Isaac, Jacob, Joseph, Samson, or Samuel — most of whom are selected before birth to serve the divine purpose. In the New Testament, the story of King Herod's attempt to kill the infant Jesus similarly fits the mythic pattern of the threatened hero (Matt. 2:1–18).

a glorious hero whose exploits elevate him to semi-divinity. As the man who successfully defies Egypt's tyrant, releases chaotic waters to drown pursuing armies, and leads his people through a dangerous wilderness to freedom and nationhood, Moses is without peer: "Never," states Deuteronomy, "has there been such a prophet in Israel as Moses, the man Yahweh knew face to face" (Deut. 34:10). While affirming Moses' unparalleled contribution to forging Israel's bond with Yahweh, however, the Torah writers are careful to subordinate him to the God he serves. Rather than a hero in his own right, Moses is always Yahweh's obedient spokesman. The priestly authors who prepared the final edition of the Torah took pains to explain why Yahweh did not allow his devoted servant to enter the Promised Land. "Because you did not believe that I could proclaim my holiness in the eyes of the sons of Israel," Yahweh tells Moses and Aaron, "you shall not lead this assembly into the

land I am giving them" (Num. 20:12). Although Moses' fatal error is not specified, some commentators assume that it is the lawgiver's failure to give Yahweh full credit when he brings water gushing from a rock (Num. 20:10). Considering Moses' self-sacrificing commitment to Yahweh and his people — including his refusal to accept Yahweh's offer to make the family of Moses, and not Israel, his chosen nation (Num. 14:12) — God's verdict may seem unduly harsh. For the Torah writers, however, Moses is both a model of humble service *and* a demonstration that even the greatest of human beings cannot measure up to Yahweh's standard of perfect righteousness.

Moses' Infancy   Most scholars recognize that the Torah combines too many strands of tradition to permit an accurate recovery of the "historical Moses." The problem of Moses' historicity is compounded by the presence of legend and folklore embedded in his story. According to Exodus 1–2, Moses is born under Pharaoh's decree that all Hebrew boys must be drowned, a fate he escapes when his mother secretly sets him adrift on the Nile in a watertight cradle. A childless daughter of Pharaoh — a princess who apparently does not fear to disobey her father's edict — finds the boy and raises him as her own, a near-death experience that characterizes stories about the infancy of future heroes in world myth (Box 4.5). Given an Egyptian name derived from the same root as pharaohs Thutmose and Ahmose, Moses becomes familiar with the royal court, presumably an advantage when he later appears before Pharaoh to demand Israel's release.

The Flight from Egypt to Midian   The incident that prompts the first of two major transitions in Moses' life foreshadows an important motif in the Pentateuch — his fellow Israelites' failure to value Moses' leadership. The day after killing an Egyptian whom he had found beating a Hebrew, Moses returns to the same location, where two Hebrews are now fighting. When Moses rebukes the aggressor for striking his fellow countryman, implying that the oppressed Hebrews should support each other, the assailant shows no gratitude for Moses' attempt to defend or make peace among his people. Instead, the bully frightens Moses by alluding to the murder of the Egyptian, an offense that could bring the death penalty.

After fleeing from Egypt, Moses settles in **Midian**, a desert region south of Edom, where he lives as a shepherd and marries the daughter of a local priest named **Jethro** in E's account and **Ruel** in J's version. (See Chapter 3 for a discussion of the "Kenite hypothesis" and the possible Midianite origin of Yahwism.) It is while tending sheep on "the mountain of God" in Midianite territory that Moses experiences the second great reversal of his life course.

TWO REVELATIONS OF THE DIVINE NAME

Although they derive from two separate sources, Exodus's two different accounts of the revelation of the divine name (Exod. 3 and Exod. 6) have similar purposes: to demonstrate that El, Elohim, or El Shaddai, the Deity worshiped by Israel's distant ancestors, and Yahweh, the divinity who speaks to Moses, are the same God. In his version of Israel's past, the Yahwist writer had already made this crucial identification, retrojecting Yahweh's worship as far back as the pre-Flood era and asserting that people had evoked the name "Yahweh" almost from the beginning of human history (Gen. 4:26). In contrast, the Elohist and priestly writers believe that the divine name, Yahweh, was not known until God revealed it to Moses (3:13–15; 6:2–4). Both Exodus 3 (E) and Exodus 6 (P), therefore, make a special point of insisting that El, the ancient Canaanite deity, and Yahweh, Israel's divine patron, are one.

The First Theophany   The first revelation of God's personal name occurs at a burning bush on Sinai/Horeb. Climbing the sacred mountain to investigate the phenomenon of a shrub that flames without being consumed, Moses unexpectedly encounters God, who announces that he is the same deity who had made promises to Moses' remote ancestors, vows that for centuries had gone unfulfilled. A voice from the midst of fire — the transforming element that symbolizes divinity — orders Moses to remove his sandals, for he treads on ground made holy by the divine presence. Identified as the *Elohim* of Abraham, Isaac, and Jacob, the voice states that God is now ready to act, not only to fulfill ancient vows to the ancestors, but also for the first time to intervene on the world stage of national politics. He proposes to crush one powerful national state in order to create another, a "holy nation," dedicated to his service. The revelation of the divine name not only serves to identify Yahweh with various manifestations of the ancestral El, but also to disclose God's future plans for both Israel and other "nations" who will speak of his saving actions (Exod. 3:1–16; cf. Exod. 32:11–14; Num. 14:19–21). (For a discussion of the significance of the divine name, see Chapter 3.)

The Second Theophany   Whereas E (and perhaps some D) material underlies Yahweh's self-disclosure in Exodus 3–4, a second revelation of the divine name comes from the priestly source. In P's version of Yahweh's initial appearance to Moses, God declares:

> I am Yahweh. To Abraham and Isaac and Jacob I appeared as El Shaddai. I did not make myself known to them by my name Yahweh. . . .
>
> Exod. 6:1–8

Like the author(s) of Exodus 3, the priestly writer insists that El Shaddai, known from ancient times, is really Yahweh.

YAHWEH'S WAR AGAINST PHARAOH

The Ten Plagues The Hebrews in Egypt at first openly doubt Moses' authority to lead them, a response that anticipates their future complaints and rebellions in the wilderness. Pharaoh also refuses to recognize the authority of either Moses or his God, declaring that he knows nothing of Yahweh. As he had informed Moses at the burning bush, Yahweh is prepared to deal with Pharaoh's stubbornness, inflicting a sequence of plagues calculated to break Egyptian resistance to his will. Beginning with a bloody pollution of the Nile and other Egyptian waters, the plagues gradually increase in severity. Swarms of frogs, then mosquitoes, then gadflies afflict the Egyptians, demonstrating Yahweh's control of nature. Pharaoh begs Moses to end the plagues but treacherously goes back on his word when the pests disappear.

The narrator attributes Pharaoh's obstinacy to Yahweh, who resolves to "harden" Pharaoh's heart even before the king has an opportunity to make up his own mind (4:21–23; cf. 7:3; 10:1, 20, 27; 14:8), thus forcing him to "sin" in refusing to let Israel go. God's apparent interference with the Egyptian ruler's free will may distress modern readers, but in the Exodus tradition, Pharaoh's resistance was necessary to the Deity's purpose. If Egypt had meekly submitted to Moses' request, there would have been no awesome plagues, no "signs and wonders" demonstrating the supremacy of Israel's God. In the biblical portrayals of God, the Deity is characteristically shown as focused on his public reputation, maneuvering

people and events to maximize general awareness of his hitherto unrecognized power (Exod. 9:15–16; cf. 10:1–2).

As Pharaoh consistently refuses to acknowledge the God of his slaves, the plagues increase in deadliness. From diseases of livestock, to devastating storms, to invasions of locusts, Egypt experiences the wrath of Yahweh. In the ninth plague, total darkness shrouds the entire land except where the Hebrews live, a frightening return to the primal darkness that engulfed earth before God created light. In comparing the J and P accounts of the calamities inflicted on Egypt, scholars have discovered that whereas the Yahwist recognizes only eight plagues, the priestly school added two others, the infestation of gnats (8:16–19) and the affliction of boils on humans and animals (9:8–12), making up the familiar ten. A separate tradition preserved in Psalm 105 reports only seven plagues and presents them in a different order (Ps. 105:26–38; cf. Ps. 78:43–51).

Death of the Firstborn In Genesis, God had utilized natural forces to punish disobedience, exterminating most of humanity in a flood and consuming all inhabitants of five cities in fire (Gen. 6–8; 19). For the climactic act of divine destruction in Exodus, however, Yahweh employs a supernatural agent, the Angel of Death (a lethal aspect of the Deity), and does not indiscriminately kill the entire affected population. An example of retributive justice—"eye for eye" and "life for life"—Yahweh's choice of Egyptian victims is a calculated response to an earlier pharaoh's policy of killing newborn Hebrew males (1:15–22).

According to Exodus 12:29, Yahweh himself carries out the death sentences, from the "firstborn of Pharaoh, heir to the throne," to the "firstborn of the prisoner in [Pharaoh's] dungeon." Today's readers may blanch at a divine execution of such people as the children of Pharaoh's prisoners who had nothing to do with their king's actions, but the narrator is concerned with the *thoroughness* of Yahweh's action, which encompasses all classes of Egyptian society. No one, guilty or innocent, is allowed to escape the divine judgment on the group to which he belongs.

The Passover   To make sure that the Angel of Death distinguishes between Egyptian and Israelite households and spares the latter, the Israelites are told to sacrifice a goat or lamb and smear the blood on their doorposts, prompting the divine executioner to "pass over" their dwellings. According to the priestly account in Exodus 12, the feast of **Passover** was initiated during the Hebrews' last night in Egypt, as, shadowed by the dread angel's wings, they gathered safely inside blood-marked houses to eat unleavened bread, bitter herbs, and the sacrificed lamb. In this section, the eating of unleavened bread is explained by the haste with which the Israelites had to flee — they had no time to allow yeast to leaven the bread. A major annual observance in both ancient Israel and modern Judaism, the Passover ceremony is described in several different Torah passages (Lev. 23:5–8; Num. 28:16–25). Whereas Exodus depicts Passover as a private family meal, with neither altar nor officiating priest, the Book of Deuteronomy transforms it into a public national festival. According to the deuteronomic code, all Israelites must leave their homes and travel to Jerusalem to observe Passover (Deut. 16:1–8), an ordinance reflecting King Josiah's late seventh century B.C.E. centralization of Yahweh's cult at his royal capital (2 Kings 23).

Although Exodus links the feast of unleavened bread with the ritual slaying of a young goat or lamb, many historians believe that these two rites originated separately and were later combined by priestly editors. The annual spring sacrifice of a year-old specimen from the flocks was probably developed from a pastoral (shepherd's) fertility ceremony, and the practice of consuming unleavened bread from a prehistoric festival of the new wheat harvest (cf. Exod. 5:1; 23:14–17; 34:18–25). Besides the Passover celebration, the tenth plague is also associated with the enriching of the former slaves: The terrified Egyptians urge the Israelites to leave, showering them with "jewelry of silver and gold," the "spoils" of Egypt that are the first material signs of the promised blessings to come (12:33–36).

THE ESCAPE FROM EGYPT

Deliverance at the Yam Suf   For the ultimate demonstration of Yahweh's might, Pharaoh is maneuvered into leading his army in pursuit of the Israelites. Trapped between Egyptian charioteers and a great sea, the Israelites seem doomed to an ignominious return to slavery. At this crucial moment, however, Yahweh intervenes to deliver his people in an act that forever after would be remembered as the pivotal event in the story of Israel's salvation. The two chief sources of the present text, J and P, agree on the miraculous character of Israel's deliverance but present two distinctly different versions of what happened (Box 4.6). According to J's tradition, the Israelites remained quietly on the shore while Yahweh employed a strong east wind that blew "all night," driving back the sea and leaving its bed dry. In the morning, after the wind has presumably died down and the waters have flowed back to their normal depth, Yahweh causes the Egyptian troops to panic and dash headlong into the sea, so that "Yahweh overthrew the Egyptians in the very middle of the sea" (14:13–14, 24, 25b, 27). In J's account, only the Egyptians enter the sea; the Israelites merely "keep still" and observe their former oppressors drown. J's story roughly approximates the version preserved in the "Song of Moses," an ancient poem that praises Yahweh as triumphant warrior: "Horse and rider he has thrown into the sea . . . the chariots and the army of Pharaoh he has hurled into the sea" (15:1, 4).

The priestly additions to J's narrative greatly intensify the miraculous element, asserting that when Moses stretches out his hand, the sea divides into two parts, enabling the Israelites to walk dryshod across the sea floor between two standing walls of water, one on their right and one on their left. When Moses raises his hand a second time, the walls of water collapse: "The returning waters overwhelmed the chariots and the horsemen of Pharaoh's whole army, which had followed the Israelites into the sea" (14:15–18; 21–23, 28).

A fragment from another tradition, perhaps the Elohist, suggests a more mundane turn of events, noting that Yahweh "so clogged [the Egyptians']

Box 4.6 Excerpts from the Yahwist and Priestly Accounts of Israel's Deliverance at the Great Sea

In this composite passage from Exodus 14, the Yahwist (J) narrative appears in boldface, and the priestly account (P) in roman type. (For economy, the text has been somewhat abbreviated.)

. . . [Pharaoh] **and his courtiers changed their minds about the people** [the Israelites]. **"What have we done," they said, "allowing Israel to leave our service?" So Pharaoh had his chariot harnessed and gathered his troops about him . . . So the Egyptians gave chase . . . the** [children] **of Israel looked around — and there were the Egyptians in pursuit of them! The** [children] **of Israel were terrified . . . Moses answered the people, "Have no fear! Stand firm and you will see what Yahweh will do to save you today: The Egyptians you see today, you will never see again. Yahweh will do the fighting for you: You have only to keep still** [Exod. 14:5b–6, 9, 10, 13–14].

Yahweh said to Moses, "Why do you cry to me so? Tell the sons of Israel to march on. For yourself, raise your staff and stretch out your hand over the sea and part it for the sons of Israel to walk through the sea on dry ground. I for my part will make the heart of the Egyptians stubborn that they will follow them. So shall I win myself glory at the expense of Pharaoh, of all his army, his chariots, his horsemen. And when I have won glory for myself, at the expense of Pharaoh, and his chariots, and his army, the Egyptians will learn that I am Yahweh" [Exod. 14:15–18].

. . . **The pillar of cloud changed station from the front to the rear of them, and remained there. It came between the camp of the Egyptians and the camp of Israel. The cloud was dark, and the night passed without the armies drawing any closer the whole night long** [Exod. 14:19b–20]. Moses stretched out his hand over the sea. **Yahweh drove back the sea with a strong easterly wind all night, and he made dry land of**

the sea. The waters parted and the sons of Israel went on dry ground right into the sea, walls of water to right and to left of them. The Egyptians gave chase: After them they went, right into the sea, all Pharaoh's horses, chariots, and his horsemen [Exod. 14:22–23]. **In the morning watch, Yahweh looked down on the army of the Egyptians from the pillar of fire and cloud, and threw the army into confusion.** [He so clogged their chariot wheels that they could scarcely make headway.] **"Let us flee from the Israelites," the Egyptians cried. "Yahweh is fighting for them against the Egyptians!"** "Stretch out your hand over the sea," Yahweh said to Moses, "that the waters may flow back on the Egyptians and their chariots and their horsemen." Moses stretched out his hand over the sea **and as day broke the sea returned to its bed. The fleeing Egyptians marched right into it, and Yahweh overthrew the Egyptians in the very middle of the sea** [Exod. 14:27]. The returning waters overwhelmed the chariots and the horsemen of Pharaoh's whole army, which had followed the Israelites into the sea; not a single one of them was left. But the [children] of Israel had marched through the sea on dry ground, walls of water to right and left of them [Exod. 14:28–29]. **That day Yahweh rescued Israel from the Egyptians, and Israel saw the Egyptians laying dead along the shore. Israel witnessed the great act that Yahweh had performed against the Egyptians, and the people venerated Yahweh; they put their faith in Yahweh and in Moses, his servant** [Exod. 14:30–31].

The redactor who fused together the originally separate Yahwist and priestly accounts retained most of both documents, skillfully blending the two into a narrative that, despite the discrepancies arising from its dissimilar sources, is a powerful testimony to Yahweh's saving action.

...hat they could scarcely make ...e Egyptians realize that Israel's ...ully opposing them, they lose ...ve up their pursuit (14:25). Al- ...ditions evoke a spectacularly well- ...e from Egyptian pursuers, the nu- mer... ...screpancies are almost impossible to reconcile. The narrative's main theological point is that, after witnessing their deliverance, the Is- raelites for the first time "put their faith in Yahweh and in Moses' (14:31).

The Yam Suf   In Hebrew, the location of Israel's dramatic sea rescue is called *yam suf,* which the Septuagint translates as the "Red Sea," a custom followed by the Vulgate and most English editions of the Hebrew Bible. With few sites mentioned in the Exodus narrative positively identified, neither the route the Israelites took from Egypt nor the body of water they encountered is known. If there is any historical basis to the Exodus tradition, the *yam suf* is unlikely to be the main channel of the Red Sea, which is an enormous rift valley, flooded by the Arabian Ocean, a geologic spreading center along which the continents of Africa and Asia are slowly pulling apart. Even if its waters were super- naturally divided to form a dry pathway, crossing its bed would require descending into, and ascend- ing from, a chasm deeper and more precipitous than Arizona's Grand Canyon.

Because *suf* commonly means "reed," as it does in the story of the infant Moses' being discovered among reeds of the Nile (Exod. 2:3–5), the Jerusalem Bible renders the phrase as "Reed Sea" or "Sea of Reeds," indicating the body of water may have been a large marsh or lake, perhaps the swampy region north of the Gulf of Suez. Other suggestions for the geographical location of the *yam suf* include Lake Sirbonis (Lake Bardawil) or a southern extension of the present Lake Menzaleh. In the absence of any hard evidence identifying the Israelites' travel itinerary from Egypt to the Sinai wilderness, scholars have suggested several possible routes; one plausible reconstruction of Israel's path across the Sinai Peninsula is shown in Figure 4.6. An alternate route, favored by some early Jewish

and Arabic traditions, places the "mountain of God," the goal of the Israelites' exodus from Egypt, near Edom or Midian, desert regions southeast of Canaan (see Figure 3.1).

THE THEOPHANY AT SINAI/HOREB

The Covenant with Yahweh   In Exodus 19, the long narrative that began with the call of Abraham (Gen. 12) reaches its culmination. As Abraham's descendants — allegedly numbering 600,000 men, plus women and children (Exod. 12:37) — assemble at the foot of Mount Sinai (Horeb), the literary character of the Pentateuch undergoes a marked change. Instead of narrative, which com- prises most of Genesis 1:1 through Exodus 19, the Torah henceforth consists primarily of the terms of the covenant between Yahweh and Israel (Box 4.7). Several important narrative passages appear, par- ticularly Exodus 24 and 32–34, but the entire cen- tral section of the Pentateuch — Exodus 20:1– Numbers 10 — is devoted to the enumeration of Yahweh's specific requirements for his people, who are to be a "kingdom of priests, a consecrated na- tion" (Exod. 19:6). The people remain camped at the "mountain of God" for almost a year while Yahweh's teaching — more than 600 commands, ordinances, and statutes — is conveyed in discrete stages through Moses (Exod. 19:1; Num. 10:11) (Figure 4.7.).

The Ten Commandments   God's instructions for Israel, the observance of which will identify the nation as truly his people, open with the famous **Ten Commandments**. Also called the **Decalogue** ("ten words"), this part of Torah has the distinction of being the only passage in the Hebrew Bible re- portedly written by Yahweh himself and spoken directly to the people (20:1; 24:12). Israel's first ob- ligation is to worship Yahweh alone and, second, to make no images of him. Although the narrative commonly portrays him anthropomorphically (in human form), the ineffable Deity cannot be rep- resented in any material way. Attempts to liken God to "anything" that lives in the three-tier uni- verse, "in heaven above, . . . on the earth be-

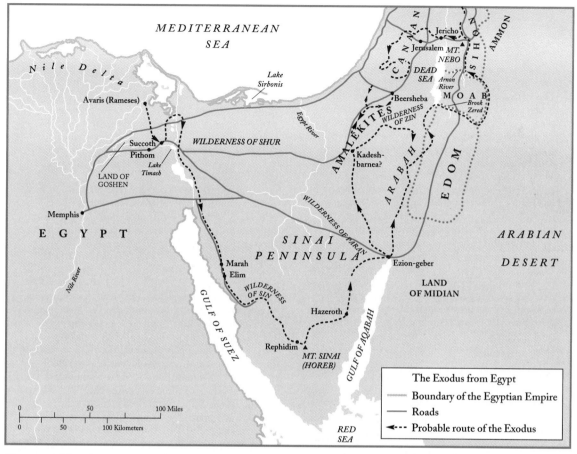

Figure 4.6 Map showing a plausible reconstruction of the Israelites' path across the Sinai Peninsula, from Egypt to the Promised Land.

neath, or in the waters under the earth [residue of the precreation sea]" are denounced as "idolatry" and expressly forbidden (20:4–6). Nor is Yahweh's personal name to be invoked unworthily, as in swearing false oaths or for magical purposes. (In the ancient world, knowledge of a deity's "hidden" or self-defining name was thought to give persons the ability to exert magical control.)

As Genesis 2:2–3 presents God's rest day—the **Sabbath**—as divinely instituted, so the Decalogue insists that Israel scrupulously observe the week's seventh day as a memorial, remembering that after completing his six-day creation, Elohim desisted from labor. All levels of Israelite society, including women, children, and slaves, are to be regularly granted this respite from work (20:8–10; cf. Gen. 2:2–3). The tenth commandment, not to "covet" or persist in desiring what is not rightfully one's own, goes beyond outward behavior to urge the people to reject feelings of envy that may lead not only to chronic discontent but also harmful action. The remaining commandments—honoring of parents and refraining from antisocial acts, such as murder, theft, adultery, or perjury—are paralleled in the legislation of other Near Eastern societies. Israel's resolve to recognize only one God, who permits no image of his divinity, however, is unique in the ancient world.

Box 4.7 The Mosaic Covenant

The central expression of Yahweh's partnership with Israel, the Mosaic Covenant consists of two unequal parts: the lengthy enumeration of God's ethical and legal requirements, encompassing all the laws in Exodus, Leviticus, Numbers, and Deuteronomy, and the people's brief collective pledge to obey them all. Many scholars believe that the Mosaic agreement is at least partly modeled on a treaty form common in ancient Near Eastern political alliances, the *suzerain treaty*. In such agreements, the suzerain — or great king — agrees to offer aid or protection to a less powerful vassal, who in turn pledges an oath of loyalty to his overlord. In the treaty concluded at Mount Sinai/Horeb, the sovereign Yahweh dictates the terms of the agreement to which the inferior party, Israel, must agree. A study of Near Eastern treaties from the first millennium B.C.E. particularly Hittite and Assyrian examples, shows that they typically included the following provisions:

1. A preamble
2. An account of historical circumstances leading to the treaty
3. Stipulations and requirements
4. Arrangements for public reading of the text and its safekeeping in a shrine

5. A list of divine witnesses to the treaty
6. A vivid catalog of blessings for abiding by its terms and curses for violating them

All these elements occur in the Torah, although they are found in widely scattered fragments throughout the biblical text.

After Yahweh arrives at Sinai/Horeb to conclude his treaty with Israel, he speaks directly to the people, reducing the traditional preamble and historical recapitulation to a brief statement identifying himself as suzerain and giving the reason for his vassal's submission to him: "I am Yahweh your God, who brought you out of the land of Egypt, out of the house of slavery." (Exod. 20:1–2). In fact, Yahweh's terse statement summarizes the entire Exodus narrative up to that point, the Torah story of Israel's deliverance from Egyptian bondage functioning as an elaborate preamble to the Sinai treaty-making.

Only one small part of Yahweh's covenant requirements — the Ten Commandments and the Book of the Covenant (Exod. 20–23) — are given before Israel's ratification of the treaty takes place. In Exodus 24, the Israelites are pictured as unanimously accepting their covenant obligations, "with one voice," swearing to abide by all Yahweh's demands (Exod.

The collection of statutes and ordinances that follows the Decalogue (Exod. 20:18–23:33) is known as the Book of the Covenant. Although the laws in this section presuppose a settled agrarian existence in Canaan, they may be among the oldest legislation in the Pentateuch. After the Decalogue's revolutionary commitment to worshiping a single God and total rejection of images, however, this section's laws validating and regulating human slavery may come as a shock. Considering that the Torah narratives had just recounted Israel's liberation from bondage — Yahweh had explicitly responded to "their appeal to be free of their slave drivers" (3:7) — it may seem inconsistent that Yahweh's law provides for Israelites to enslave their fellow citizens. Accepting the widespread practice of

selling people to pay off debt, the Book of the Covenant reflects the social norms of antiquity, safeguarding the rights of property owners (21:1–11; cf. Deut. 15:12–18). Because neither the Hebrew Bible nor the New Testament condemns the owning, buying, or selling of human beings, many Western slave holders later argued that the biblical Deity condones the institution of slavery, a position bitterly contested before, during, and even after the American Civil War.

The Golden Calf The Exodus narrative, interrupted by a long block of priestly material (Exod. 25–31), resumes in Chapter 32. While Moses spends forty days atop Sinai, listening to Yahweh's exhaustive instructions for the Tabernacle and re-

Box 4.7 (continued)

24:3). Moses then performs a binding ritual, slaughtering sacrificial animals and casting part of the blood on an altar representing Yahweh, thus sealing the treaty. After Moses reads from the Book of the Covenant and the people again vow to uphold all its provisions, he sprinkles the Israelites with the rest of the sacrificial blood, thereby confirming the people's commitment to the divine suzerain.

Although Moses calls upon no divine witnesses to the covenant, the twelve stone pillars he sets up to represent the twelve tribes of Israel (Exod. 24:4) may have served that function. When Moses' successor Joshua conducts a similar covenant ritual, he erects a memorial stone that "has heard all the words that Yahweh has spoken" to the Israelites and will be a "witness" against them if they default (Josh. 24:27). In Deuteronomy, Moses calls "heaven and earth" to testify against Israel if the people break their vows, invoking the whole cosmos as a sign of the seriousness of Israel's promise (Deut. 30:19). Observing the custom of recording and safeguarding Near Eastern treaties, both Moses and Joshua are shown preparing written documents that are then deposited in a shrine (Exod. 24:27; Josh. 24:25–26).

The blessings that will accrue from keeping the covenant and all the curses that will result from violating it are enumerated in Deuteronomy 28–30 and Leviticus 26. Echoing similar benefits promised for

loyalty or penalties for treachery contained in Near Eastern treaties, Yahweh's threat to trap covenant breakers in an unlivably harsh world, where the heavens are like "brass" and the earth is like "iron" (Deut. 28:23; Lev. 26:19), is almost identical to the metallic imagery of curses listed in a treaty that Esarhaddon, king of Assyria, concluded in 677 B.C.E.

Whereas some Torah commands—such as Yahweh's insistence on being worshiped exclusively and his prohibition against images—are unparalleled in anitquity, other Covenant regulations resemble those found in many Near Eastern legal codes. **Policy law** (also called **apodictic law**), such as the Ten Commandments, with their imperative absolutes ordering the people not to kill, steal, or bear false witness, is unusual in form, but the ethical principles expressed are commonly recognized in non-Israelite cultures. By contrast, **legal procedures** (also called **case law**), with its typical formula "if such and such is the case, then . . . must be done," characterize many Near Eastern laws. The *if-then* pattern appears throughout the famous Code of Hammurabi (about 1690 B.C.E.) and typifies many legal procedures outlined in the Torah (Exod. 20:22–23:5; Lev. 1–7, 12–15; etc.).

---

ceiving the Decalogue that God's "finger" has inscribed on two stone tablets, the people urge Aaron, Moses's brother and Israel's high priest, to create a **golden calf,** which they immediately identify as the "god" who "brought [them] out of Egypt" (32:1–6). Informing Moses that he has observed the Israelites's lapse into idolatry and that he plans to wipe them out, Yahweh offers to replace Israel with Moses and his family. After persuading Yahweh to "change his mind" for the sake of his reputation among the Egyptians, Moses descends from the mountain, smashes the two tablets God had inscribed (32:7–20), and calls on the Levites (members of his own tribe) to slaughter the golden calf worshipers. Again climbing Sinai (he makes at least eight ascents in the Exodus narra-

tive) to confer with God, Moses inscribes a second set of tablets, symbolizing Yahweh's reconciliation with a presumably repentant Israel (Chs. 33–34). (See Box 4.8.)

The Tabernacle Much of the remainder of Exodus is devoted to detailed provisions for providing Yahweh with a shelter as he accompanies Israel on the long journey to Canaan. By far the longest Torah passages concerning a single topic, Exodus 25–31 enumerates Yahweh's instructions for building the **Tabernacle**—the portable tent-shrine that he will symbolically inhabit—while Exodus 35–40 records its actual construction. Skilled artisans undertake the project from the inside out, first building the **Ark of the Covenant**, a rectangular

Figure 4.7 This rugged peak in the Sinai desert is the traditional site at which Yahweh communicated the Torah to Moses. Known as Mount Sinai in J's account, it is called Horeb in the E and D traditions. Although much of the Torah's action takes place in Sinai's shadow, where the Israelites camp for almost two years (Exod. 19:2 to Num. 10:12), archaeologists have been unable to find any physical evidence of the tribes' sojourn there — or at any other peak in the region.

chest, plated in gold leaf, on which Yahweh's "glory" will rest. The golden statues of cherubim, token representations of the supernatural courtiers that surround God's heavenly throne, are placed at each end of the Ark. Their wings extended, they shelter the *kapporeth* or Ark cover (later called the "mercy seat"), the place where the Deity is invisibly enthroned and from which he will henceforth issue his commands to Moses. Exodus reaches its climactic moment when Yahweh, shrouded in cloud, enters the completed Tabernacle, filling it with his "glory." Stipulating that Israel would not take a single step toward its promised destination unless the "cloud" lifted from Yahweh's tent home as a sign that the day's travels were to begin, Exodus concludes with an affirmation that the covenant people were at last being led directly by God himself. "For the cloud of Yahweh rested on the tabernacle by day, and a fire shone in the cloud by night, for all the house of Israel to see" (40:38). For the first time since he strolled through Eden, Yahweh will again dwell intimately with mortals, assuming the challenge of shaping Israel in his image.

QUESTIONS FOR REVIEW

1. How many members of Jacob's family settled in Egypt? Why did a new pharaoh enslave their descendants? What tasks were the Israelites forced to perform, and how did it affect their spirit?

2. Summarize the story of Moses from his infancy to his encounter with Yahweh at the "mountain of God." What aspect of himself does God reveal to Moses, and what does he commission Moses to do? Describe some of the difficulties Moses faces in carrying out Yahweh's orders, including Pharaoh's attitude.

3. Explain the problems that historians must deal with in examining the historicity of the Exodus narrative. How much does archaeology reveal about the presence of Israel in Egypt or in the Sinai wilderness? Who may have been the pharaoh of the Exodus?

4. Explain the Kenite hypothesis and the evidence for or against this theory. Describe Moses' association with Jethro, priest of Midian, and Jethro's role in the Exodus story.

5. Describe the Passover festival. According to Exodus, how was the first Passover instituted? What occurred during its initial observance, and how is that event of enormous significance to Israel?

6. How do biblical writers enhance the cosmic significance of Israel's deliverance at the *yum suf,* sometimes translated as the "Sea of Reeds"? What is the theological purpose of the Sea narrative?

7. Describe the theophany at Sinai/Horeb. What part of the Torah does Yahweh himself put in writing? What are the first commandments? What is the Book of the Covenant? What aspect of divine instruction does the priestly writer apparently regard as most important?

Box 4.8 Was God "Seen" at Mount Sinai?

The interweaving of multiple literary sources in the Exodus account of Yahweh's appearances on Mount Sinai/Horeb has resulted in the incorporation of radically contrasting ideas about the Deity's physical visibility. According to Exodus 33:20, God informs Moses that he is forbidden to see God's "face," because "man can not see me and live." A few verses earlier in the present text, however, we are told that Yahweh "would speak to Moses face to face, as a man speaks to a friend" (Exod. 33:11). Postulating an abstract, ineffable, and transcendent Deity, traditional religion usually emphasizes the first statement: Mortals cannot survive an unmediated experience of divinity. The anthromorphic concept of a deity who can be visible to human eyes, which is also embraced by the canonical text, is typically denied, or explained away.

The God who insists that his face not be seen remains essentially hidden during the disclosure of his "glory" to Moses. Placing Moses in a rocky cleft and shielding him with his "hand," Yahweh projects his "splendor" as if it were a separate entity traversing the mountaintop. When God finally removes his hand from obstructing Moses's vision, it is only to allow the prophet a glimpse of his "back," which is not described. This account of a Sinai theophany is paradoxically almost as much a concealment as a revelation, serving to deepen the divine mystery (Exod. 33:17–25).

By contrast, a different tradition embedded in Exodus indicates that mortals could look directly at God and survive. In Exodus 24, Moses, Aaron, and seventy Israelite "elders" climb Sinai to enjoy a meal with God, an event that may have been based on the ancient Near Eastern custom of holding banquets to commemorate a powerful tribal chief's acceptance of lesser clans into a status of kinship. According to this passage, Moses and the elders "saw the God of Israel," who did not strike down his guests, but permitted them to "eat and drink" as they "gazed on God" (Exod. 24:9–11). Remaining firmly in the flesh, they consume material food even while basking in the divine presence, as a group repeating the experience of Abraham who apparently dined with God under the oak trees near Hebron (Gen. 18).

The Torah's inclusion of both anthropomorphic imagery in which God may be visible to human eyes (as J and other traditions say he was to Abraham, Jacob, and Moses) and its seemingly contradictory proclamation that Israel's God does not appear in physical form conveys both the transcendence and immanance of the biblical Deity. The mystery of an unknowable Spirit who can create the universe and also stoop to break bread with his mortal creatures is maintained.

---

8. Describe the Ark of the Covenant and the Tabernacle that housed it. What purpose or function did these two sacred items serve? How are they related to the Genesis promise of the divine presence?

QUESTIONS FOR DISCUSSION AND REFLECTION

1. Describe and discuss the content of the divine teaching at Sinai. What does God require of Israel? Cite specific decrees and statutes. After delivering Israel from Egyptian slavery, why does Yahweh endorse the institution of slavery among his people? Explain the law of retaliation ("eye for eye") and its ethical implications.

2. How do you account for the presence of repetitions, discrepancies, and contradictions in Exodus, such as the two different versions of the revelation of Yahweh's name (Exod. 3 and 6), different versions of the *yam suf* deliverance, and different statements about whether God was visible during the Sinai theophany? (Compare Exod. 34:10–28; 24:9–11; 33:11; and 18–23 before making your answer).

3. Describe the nature of Israel's behavior that profoundly offends Yahweh. Why does the golden calf episode so enrage God that he threatens to destroy Israel? How does Moses persuade God to change his mind? How do you feel about Yahweh's "jealousy" and violence?

TERMS AND CONCEPTS TO REMEMBER

Aaron	Passover
Decalogue (Ten Com-	Rameses II
mandments)	Sabbath
golden calf	Sargon I
Jethro (Ruel)	Tabernacle
Midian	theocracy

RECOMMENDED READING

Albertz, Rainer. *A History of Israelite Religion in the Old Testament Period.* Vol. 1, *From the Beginnings to the End of the Monarchy.* Louisville, Ky.: Westminster/John Knox Press, 1994. Includes a detailed analysis of the historical and social contexts for the composition and redaction of Exodus.

Batto, Bernard F. *Slaying the Dragon: Mythmaking in the Biblical Tradition.* Louisville, Ky.: Westminster/John Knox Press, 1992. Discusses the priestly use of creation myth in P's narrative of the Reed Sea deliverance.

Beegle, Dewey M. "Moses." In D. N. Freedman, ed., *The Anchor Bible Dictionary,* Vol. 4, pp. 909–918. New York: Doubleday, 1992. An examination of the Torah's diverse strands of tradition regarding Moses' role.

Brueggemann, Walter. "The Book of Exodus." In *The New Interpreter's Bible.* Vol. 1, pp. 677–981. Nashville: Abingdon Press, 1994. Contains extensive scholarly commentary on the Exodus text.

Campbell, Antony F. and O'Brien, Mark A. *Sources of the Pentateuch: Texts, Introductions, Annotations.* Minneapolis: Fortress Press, 1993. Includes an identification of different sources of Exodus—primarily J, E, and P—and prints each source as a separate document.

Clifford, Richard J. "Exodus." In R. E. Brown et al., eds., *The New Jerome Biblical Commentary,* 2nd ed., pp. 44–60. Englewood Cliffs, N.J.: Prentice-Hall, 1990.

Coogan, Michael D., ed. *The Oxford History of the Biblical World.* New York: Oxford University Press, 1998. Discusses the Kenite hypothesis and possible Midianite origin of Yahwism.

Cross, Frank Moore. *Canaanite Myth and Hebrew Epic: Essays in the History of the Religion of Israel.* Cambridge, Mass.: Harvard University Press, 1973. A major scholar's investigation of historical origins of ancient Israelite beliefs.

———. *From Epic to Canon: History and Literature in Ancient Israel.* Baltimore: Johns Hopkins University Press, 1998. Essays on Near Eastern influences on Israelite religion, including the concept of the covenant relationship between Yahweh and Israel.

Crüsemann, Frank. *The Torah: Theology and Social History of Old Testament Law.* Minneapolis: Fortress Press, 1996. An exhaustive analysis of the historical and literary development of the biblical text.

Kitchen, K. A. "Exodus, The." In D. N. Freedman, ed., *The Anchor Bible Dictionary,* Vol. 2, pp. 700–708. New York: Doubleday, 1992.

Mendenhall, George E. *Law and Covenant in Israel and the Ancient Near East.* Pittsburgh: Biblical Colloquium, 1955. An influential study of correspondences between ancient treaty documents and the growth of Israel's covenant tradition.

Nicholson, Ernest. *The Pentateuch in the Twentieth Century: The Legacy of Julius Wellhausen.* Oxford: Clarendon Press, 1998. A persuasive defence of the documentary hypothesis.

Noth, Martin. *Exodus.* Philadelphia: Westminster Press, 1962.

Sarna, Nahum M. *Understanding Exodus.* New York: Schocken Books, 1987.

———. "Exodus, Book of." In D. N. Freedman, ed., *The Anchor Bible Dictionary,* Vol. 2, pp. 689–700. New York: Doubleday, 1992.

Leviticus

KEY TOPICS/THEMES

A vast collection of legal and liturgical material, Leviticus contains priestly instructions about maintaining the ritual and ethical purity of the Israelite community, an obligation necessitated by Yahweh's abiding presence in the tabernacle. Each individual Israelite must remain "holy," scrupulously observing priestly distinctions between "clean" and "unclean" in diet, private life, and public behavior, thus avoiding a contamination that offends the Deity and brings punishment on the entire community. The first section deals with laws of sacrifice (Chs. 1–7); the second, with the ordination of Aaron and his sons and the consecration of the tabernacle (Chs. 8–10); the third, with various kinds of defilement and cleansing (Chs. 11–15); the fourth, with the ritual of Yom Kippur, the Day of Atonement (Ch. 16); the fifth, with regulations concerning holiness in blood sacrifice, sexual activity, human relations, and priestly conduct (Chs. 17–21); the sixth, with the religious calendar and festivals, including the Jubilee Year (Chs. 22–25); the seventh, with curses for disobedience (Ch. 26); and the eighth, with miscellaneous holy things (Ch. 27).

KEY QUESTIONS

How are the priestly laws contained in Leviticus intended to make Israel a ritually "pure" and "holy" people? How did Israel become "at one" with Yahweh on the Day of Atonement?

Now one of the least read parts of the Bible, Leviticus nevertheless represents an important stage in the development of Israel's religion. Scholars believe that Israelite priests assembled the book during and shortly after the Babylonian exile (587–538 B.C.E.), when the entire Jewish nation lay in ruins and its upper classes were held captive in Babylon. Responding to a threatened loss of national and religious identity, the priests attempted to preserve and standardize Israel's forms of worship. The result is the enormous body of cult material cataloged in the Torah.

Although most of Leviticus's laws and regulations presuppose a return to the homeland and Temple, it also contains rules on circumcision and diet that could be observed even in exile. These rituals and legal stipulations, which begin in Exodus 25–31 and 35–40 and carry over into Numbers 1–10, belong almost exclusively to the Priestly document (P). Their purpose is to demonstrate that by conscientiously observing all the legal and liturgical requirements set forth by the priests, the Israelite people will remain distinct and different from the Gentile nations that endeavor to overwhelm or absorb them, thereby helping to maintain Israel's unique legacy. Presenting detailed regulations to ensure the sanctity of both the Tabernacle and everyday life, Leviticus spells out the implications of Exodus's definition of Israel's purpose as a covenant community: It must be a "kingdom of priests, a holy nation" (Exod. 19:6).

ISRAEL'S PURITY LAWS

Guidelines and Taboos Despite the Septuagint title, Leviticus has little to do with the **Levites** or their law; it concentrates almost exclusively on the descendants of Aaron and their priestly functions. The opening section (Chs. 1–7) regulates sacrificial offerings, both voluntary and required, to provide the means for Yahweh's worshipers to re-move guilt and sin, perceived as a disruption of divinely instituted order that defiles not only the individual offender but also the entire community and the land it inhabited (see also Lev. 18:26–30). Providing guidelines for laypeople on how to make proper sacrifices of animals or grain, this section covers procedures appropriate for the high priest (4:3–12), the community (4:13–26), and the individual (4:27–35; 5:1–13).

The second section (Chs. 8–10) describes the exacting ceremonies for installing the Aaronite priests. The third section (Chs. 11–15), which outlines rules to distinguish "clean" from "unclean" foods and practices, also defines ritual defilements and their expurgation. Because Israel's priests viewed the world as consisting of mutually exclusive categories separated by boundaries that it was a sin to violate, they are deeply concerned about keeping different kinds of things from being mixed. Thus, it is forbidden to weave wool and linen into a single garment or to boil a kid (young goat) in its mother's milk, thus wrongly blending two distinct kinds of fabric or combining meat with a different animal product. The priestly belief that everything must be of a single kind or nature also appears in the rules concerning leprosy. When a priest finds a man with mottled skin, partly flaky and white with leprosy and partly of normal color and texture, he must pronounce him "unclean" (13:9–11). But if the disease spreads over the entire body so that the skin is uniformly leprous, the priest may judge the man "clean": "Since it has all become white, he is clean" (13:12–17). It is not the disfiguring diseases, or the possibility that it may infect others, that contaminates; it is the leper's simultaneously manifesting two different conditions that belong in separate categories.

The priestly concern with sexual taboos reflects a similar abhorrence toward the mixing of kinds. A man may not have intercourse with a menstruating woman because life-giving semen should not mix with a flow of blood, which is associated with death. Any sexual contact also renders both partners "unclean" because the bodily fluids produced during intercourse have trespassed their natural boundaries within the body (15:16–24).

Women's biological functions are regarded as essentially "unclean." Merely touching an object

Box 4.9 The Year of Jubilee

According to Deuteronomy 15, every seventh year Israel was to observe a general remission of debts, forgiving loans and freeing Israelite slaves who, through inability to pay off their financial obligations, had sold themselves into slavery. Stating that there should be "no poor among you then [the time of remission]" (Deut. 15:4), the ordinance apparently was enacted to encourage a more equitable distribution of material possessions in Israelite society, limiting the accumulation of wealth by prosperous creditors and ensuring that the poor did not sink permanently into hopeless debt. During the Sabbatical Year, the land was to lie uncultivated, with neither sowing nor harvesting permitted, for Yahweh was to be acknowledged as the supreme landlord, and the human owners as merely "strangers and guests" (Lev. 25:1–2).

Leviticus 25 introduces the concept of a "super" Sabbatical Year, held in the fiftieth year as the culmination of seven Sabbatical cycles of seven years each,

when all land was to be returned to its ancestral owners and all Israelite slaves freed (Lev. 25:8–17; 23:55; 27:16–25; cf. Num. 36:4). This festival of wholesale land remission was proclaimed on the Day of Atonement by the blowing of a shofar (a trumpet made from a ram's horn). Called "Jubilee," this celebration takes its name from the Hebrew word for ram's horn. Many scholars believe that the Jubilee was introduced at the close of the Babylonian exile, which lasted exactly forty-nine years (587–538 B.C.E.), permitting exiles returning to their homeland to reclaim property they or their forbears had been forced to sell when they were deported to Babylon.

Although the Jubilee may have originated in a particular historical-economic context, the concept of Yahweh's endorsing a general remission of debt and freeing of slaves was later seen as prophetic of a future time of full liberation for the covenant people. An occasion for rejoicing, the Jubilee Year expresses the positive aspects of divine rule.

---

previously used by a menstruating woman contaminates a person (Lev. 15:19–32). Because birth produces a flow of blood, a woman who delivers a male child is considered unclean for seven days, and for another thirty-three days she cannot participate in the social or religious life of the community. If she delivers a female baby, the period of her ostracism is doubled, rendering her unclean for fourteen days and depriving her of normal activities for sixty-six days (12:1–8).

Chapter 18 lists many other sexual prohibitions that forbid a variety of erotic combinations, ranging from taking both a woman and her sister into a man's harem (Lev. 18:18), to making love to a menstruating wife (18:19), to lying "with a man as with a woman" (18:22), all of which transgress the priestly notion of acceptable boundaries. Leviticus also forbids a liaison with the wife of a brother, although Deuteronomy unequivocally states that an Israelite—to remain in good standing—must marry his brother's widow, presumably to perpetuate the deceased's name and consolidate family

property (Deut. 25:5–10). (Box 4.9 discusses another provision, the Year of Jubilee, which involves remitting debts and freeing slaves.)

Rituals of Atonement Chapter 16 describes one of Israel's most significant ceremonies, the **scapegoat** offering. Annually, on the **Day of Atonement (Yom Kippur)**, the high priest is instructed to prepare two goats for sacrifice. At the Tent of Meeting (another name for the Tabernacle), the priest draws lots for the goats, slaughtering one as a blood sacrifice to Yahweh and keeping the other alive as a symbolic bearer of the people's collective sins. Ritually laying hands on the live goat, the priest transfers the nation's guilt to the animal, which, metaphorically laden with Israel's misdeeds, is then led out into the desert "to **Azazel**." The scapegoat thus removes the punishable object of Yahweh's wrath from the community and transfers it to the uninhabited wilderness. (Scholars remain undecided whether Azazel is a place or a desert demon that destroys the "sinful" goat.)

The term *scapegoat* has come to mean any innocent person who suffers for the crimes of others; its fullest expression in the Hebrew Bible is found in Isaiah's Song of the Suffering Servant, a poem in which a guiltless man bears the sins of his people and, by so doing, wins forgiveness for them:

On him lies a punishment that brings us
   peace,
and through his wounds we are healed.
                                        Isa. 53:5

By taking away the people's collective offenses, the scapegoat ceremony lets them become "at one" with their God, effecting a reconciliation that restores harmony between Yahweh and the Israelites. Through such priestly rituals, the participants are cleansed or spiritually re-created and brought closer to the divine image in which humanity was originally formed.

Yahweh's Holy People Chapters 17–26, with their reiterated refrain "I am Yahweh," represent a distinctive body of material known as the **Holiness Code**. Covering a wide variety of human sins, sacrifices, seasonal festivals, and cleansing formulas, this portion of the book emphasizes Yahweh as the source of holiness and of the laws that Israel must observe to acquire a holiness appropriate for his special people. Despite the code's stress on ritual, it is important to remember that the P writers presuppose the worshiper's ethical integrity—sacrifice was no substitute for honorable behavior (cf. Mic. 6:6–8).

Amid rather dry priestly regulations for making burnt offerings, the reader will find passages of great ethical and psychological insight. On the matter of social justice, for example, we are told: "You must neither be partial to the little man, nor overawed by the great; you must pass judgment on your neighbor according to justice. . . . You must not bear hatred for your brother in your heart. . . . You must love your neighbor as yourself. I am Yahweh" (Lev. 19:15–18). Besides containing the only command in the Pentateuch to love one's neighbor as a religious duty, Leviticus also enjoins the Israelites to treat strangers and foreign residents with compassion, remembering that they themselves were once outsiders in a strange land (Lev. 19:34).

The Holiness Code concludes by placing Israel's laws and ceremonies in the general context of the covenant with Yahweh. In a passage reminiscent of the deuteronomic school of thought, Chapter 26 enumerates the respective blessings or curses that will follow obedience or disobedience to the laws contained in this book. Security, divine protection, military victory, and material prosperity are guaranteed if Israel keeps all God's commandments; drought, famine, disease, poverty, military defeat, and total ruin are predicted if the nation fails to honor these edicts (Lev. 26:3–43). Promising to remember his covenant with Abraham, the Deity also pledges to rescue his people from their enemies' power and restore them to Canaan. Although there was probably an ancient tradition that national disaster would befall a disobedient Israel, this description of the Babylonian exile and return indicates a relatively late date for this particular passage.

Noting similarities between the Holiness Code and legal material in the Book of Ezekiel, some critics believe that Leviticus dates from the time of Ezekiel or later, the sixth or fifth centuries B.C.E. Other scholars date the Levitical rituals governing sacrifices to the Second Temple period (roughly fifth through second centuries B.C.E.). A contemporary of Ezekiel, the prophet Jeremiah categorically denied that any of the sacrificial practices observed in his day actually originated during the Mosaic era. According to Jeremiah, Yahweh gave the Exodus generation "no orders about holocaust and sacrifice," implying that such elaborate ceremonies were a later priestly innovation (Jer. 7:22).

QUESTIONS FOR REVIEW

1. Describe the priestly school's concern with purity laws—distinguishing ceremonially "clean" and "unclean" objects and persons—and the religious concept of holiness. In what way does P envision Israel as a "holy nation of priests"?

2. What is the purpose of animal, grain, and other sacrifices prescribed in the Torah? What statement does the person offering sacrifice make to God?

3. Describe the scapegoat ritual on the annual Day of Atonement (Yom Kippur). How does this ceremony relate to later concepts of vicarious suffering and redemption, such as that presented in Isaiah 53?

QUESTIONS FOR DISCUSSION AND REFLECTION

1. Analyze the priestly tendency to separate and categorize all things according to their "kind," or intrinsic nature (a way of looking at the world that also was present in the first creation account [Gen. 1]). Why is a person whose skin is entirely leprous "clean," whereas a person only partly leprous is "unclean" (Lev. 13:9–17)?

2. How does the priestly attitude toward blood and women's menstrual cycles contribute toward a social devaluation of women? Is this ancient taboo behind some modern religious attempts to restrict women's roles in church or synagogue? Explain.

3. In what ways can ritual sacrifice function as an effective means for dealing with sinful conduct, for putting things right so as to free the worshiper for future service to God?

TERMS AND CONCEPTS TO REMEMBER

Azazel	Holiness Code
Day of Atonement	Levites
(Yom Kippur)	scapegoat

RECOMMENDED READING

Cross, Frank M., ed. "The Priestly Houses of Early Israel." In *Canaanite Myth and Hebrew Epic: Essays in the History and the Religion of Israel,* pp. 293–325. Cambridge, Mass.: Harvard University Press, 1973. An indispensable resource for understanding how the priests edited the Pentateuch.

de Vaux, Roland. *Studies in Old Testament Sacrifice.* Cardiff: University of Wales Press, 1964.

Gammie, John G. *Holiness in Israel.* OBT. Philadelphia: Fortress Press, 1989. In-depth study of Israel's concept of holiness.

Kaiser, Walter C., Jr. "The Book of Leviticus." In *The New Interpreter's Bible,* Vol. 1, pp. 985–1191. Nashville: Abingdon Press, 1994. A scholarly interpretation and reflection on Israel's liturgical codes.

Levine, B. A. "Priestly Writers." In G. A. Buttrick, ed., *The Interpreter's Dictionary of the Bible: Supplementary Volume,* pp. 683–687. Nashville: Abingdon Press, 1976.

Milgrom, Jacob. *Leviticus 1–16.* The Anchor Bible. New York: Doubleday, 1991. A masterful analysis of the priestly cult.

Noth, Martin. *Leviticus.* Philadelphia: Westminster Press, 1975. Provides information about the priestly tradition and Israel's cultic worship.

Numbers

KEY TOPICS/THEMES

A partial account of Israel's forty-year wandering in the Sinai wilderness, Numbers is a transitional work that links Yahweh's revelation of the Torah at Mount Sinai with Israel's subsequent long journey to Canaan. Beginning with a census of the twelve tribes, Numbers demonstrates that the promise to give Abraham multitudinous descendants is being fulfilled and that these descendants are being disciplined and prepared to take possession of the Promised Land. Whereas the first ten chapters record Israel's burgeoning population and additional laws Israelites must keep, the remaining chapters (Num. 10:11–36:13) describe Israel's itinerary as the people march from camp to desert camp, at last reaching the plains of Moab, near the Jordan River. Emphasizing that Canaan is soon to be theirs, Yahweh allocates specific territories to tribal leaders (Ch. 34) and appoints cities of refuge for certain criminals (Ch. 35). Brief conflicts with Edom and Moab, Israel's future neighbors, underscore the nearness of Israel's nationhood.

Intermixing narrative and legal material, Numbers focuses on issues of leadership and obedience as the people complain about their hardships and rebel against Moses. When the people fail to believe that Yahweh can drive out the Canaanites for them, God condemns the entire older generation—including Moses, Aaron, and Miriam—to die in the wilderness.

KEY QUESTIONS

Why does Yahweh prevent most adult Israelites from entering the Promised Land? How does Moses restrain God's anger?

THEMATIC UNITY

Although Numbers — which mixes genealogies, laws, rituals, legends, poetry, and narrative — may appear disorganized and difficult to follow, the book does have thematic unity. Numbers takes its title from its Greek name, *arithmoi,* referring to the census or "numbering" of the people described in the first four chapters. The Hebrew title, *bemidbar,* means "in the wilderness," designating the location of Israel's forty-year journey between Sinai and the borders of Canaan, the land Yahweh has promised to Abraham's descendants. The combined elements of numbering and wilderness travel suggest part of Numbers's meaning. Israel's male population is counted twice: at the beginning of the book while the people are still receiving the Sinai revelation and again years later after the older generation has perished for refusing to trust Yahweh (cf. Num. 1–4, 26). In between are narrative examples of the people's collective failure to appreciate the law Yahweh has given them or to cooperate with his appointed leader, Moses.

Whereas the early chapters are linked to the Sinai experience, Numbers's final section looks ahead to Israel's future military victories over the Canaanites and the allocation of different areas in the Promised Land to the twelve tribes (Num. 32–35). Besides connecting the Mosaic Torah with Israel's ultimate possession of Canaan, Numbers achieves thematic unity by emphasizing the importance of submitting to Yahweh's governing arrangements and ethical directions. Only a fully obedient Israel can expect to enjoy a consummation of the divine promises.

ISRAEL IN THE DESERT

Israel's Rebellions and Yahweh's Anger In Numbers, it is human failure that delays attainment of Yahweh's promises. Although blessed with the divine presence, the Israelites seem unable to recognize or honor Yahweh living in their midst. From the moment they leave Sinai and head into the wilderness, Yahweh visibly guides them, appearing as a columnar cloud by day and a towering flame by night (Num. 10:33–34; 14:14). Despite these phenomena that confirm Yahweh's nurturing presence, however, the people incessantly complain, their discontent culminating in a series of outright rebellions against Moses — and against the God he represents. Although Yahweh earlier had tolerated the people's grumbling, after having made them the gift of divine instruction at Sinai, he no longer restrains his anger at their ingratitude or lack of trust. His patience apparently exhausted, Israel's savior now threatens to become its destroyer.

Whereas Yahweh presumably had intended to lead the Israelites directly to Canaan, their cowardly dread of the land's inhabitants causes him to delay fulfilling his promises for an additional forty years. According to Numbers 13:25–14:38, ten of the twelve spies sent to reconnoiter Canaan return with discouraging reports of impregnably fortified cities and savage giants. Terrified, the people are ready to stone **Joshua** and **Caleb**, the only two spies who give a favorable view of their prospects. Provoked beyond endurance — do the people not remember his triumph as a warrior when he overthrew Pharaoh's troops? — Yahweh is ready to annihilate the entire nation. Acting as intercessor between the faithless people and their wrathful God, Moses pleads with Yahweh to change his mind, reminding him that the Gentile nations are watching his experiment with Israel and that he stands to lose face if he allows his people to perish in the desert. Yahweh must also recall his oath to Abraham, as well as his words to Moses on Mount Sinai:

> Yahweh is slow to anger and rich in
>   graciousness,
> forgiving faults and transgressions . . .
> Num. 14:18, 19

In the "abundance of his graciousness," then, Yahweh must not exterminate the people.

Yahweh's forgiveness is limited, however. He does not wipe them out completely, but decrees that no Israelite over the age of twenty will live to enter Canaan. Also, for every day that the spies reconnoiter the area, the Israelites must wander a year, until their "dead bodies . . . fall" in the desert. Practically speaking, the forty-year gap between leaving Egypt and settling in Canaan had its cultural and religious advantages. The older generation, imperfectly versed in the Yahwist faith and contaminated by their repeated lapses into idolatry, would be eliminated. Only those younger Israelites thoroughly indoctrinated in the Mosaic religion would be allowed to form the new nation. The two exceptions were Joshua and Caleb, who, alone among the elder group, had faith in Yahweh's ability to defeat the Canaanite militia.

Israel's Rebellion Against Moses Although Moses has repeatedly deflected Yahweh's wrath from smiting Israel, his protective role is unappreciated by the people he defends. Early in their wilderness trek, the Israelites complain bitterly about their restricted diet. Yahweh supplements the daily supply of **manna**—a powdery food that falls from heaven each night—by sending them quail to eat. But he also sends a plague to punish them for wanting more than he had volunteered to provide. Moses' authority is more seriously undermined in his own household when his brother Aaron and sister **Miriam** declare that their communication with God is as good as his. For her presumptuousness, Miriam (but not her equally presumptuous brother) is struck with leprosy (Num. 12). Moses, kind-hearted as always, intervenes with Yahweh, and after a seven-day excommunication from the camp, Miriam is cured.

Although Numbers portrays Miriam as guilty of inappropriate ambition, the prophet Micah cites a tradition in which Miriam, Moses, and Aaron were remembered as a trio of equals. Micah quotes Yahweh as endorsing the leadership of all three together: "I sent Moses to lead you, *with Aaron and Miriam*" (Mic. 6:4, italics added).

The principal challenge to Moses' position, however, comes from a respectable group of Israel's leaders, including **Korah**, who is a Levite, and Dathan, Abiram, and On of the tribe of Reuben, along with 250 other "men of repute." This group argues that because all Israel is consecrated to Yahweh's service, Moses and Aaron have no right to assume so much authority. During a confrontation between the rebels and Moses at the Tent of Meet-

ing, the earth opens up to swallow Korah and the others, including their wives, children, and possessions. The 250 men associated with the rebellion are consumed when Yahweh sends fire from heaven (Num. 16:28–35).

Balaam's Blessing Interpolated into the account of Israel's insurrections against Moses and Yahweh is an old folktale that illustrates how a Near Eastern fortune teller performed his job (Chs. 22–24). This is the humorous story of **Balaam**, a Canaanite prophet hired by King Balak of Moab to curse Israel, whose presence in the area he regards as a military threat. Although Balaam conscientiously tries to earn his fee by invoking the customary curses, Yahweh turns the curses into blessings. Even Balaam's donkey, which miraculously finds a voice to reprimand her master, plays a part in thwarting Balak's designs. Neither pagan king nor hired prophet can resist Yahweh's plans for Israel.

The Balaam story, in which even a foreign soothsayer involuntarily serves Israel's welfare, functions as an ironic counterpoint to the chosen people's scandalous behavior at Peor, a site in Moab. Here, Israelite men succumb to "the daughters of Moab," who persuade them to worship **Baal**, a Canaanite fertility god who becomes Yahweh's chief rival after his people settle in Canaan (Figure 4.8). This episode appears to blend disparate sources, adding the affair of Zimri, an Israelite who takes a **Midianite** wife. Outraged at this mixing with foreign women, the Aaronite priest Phinehas seizes a lance and stabs Zimri and his mate "right through the groin," an act that Yahweh interprets as zeal for his cause and that earns Phinehas's line the reward of an eternal priesthood. Although Moses himself had married a Midianite wife, Zipporah (Exod. 2:15–21), the editors of Numbers employ this incident to condemn intermarriage with Canaanite women, a practice they believe later corrupted Israelite worship of Yahweh. To demonstrate their God's displeasure at mixed marriages, the editors note that Yahweh sends a plague that kills 24,000 of his people, presumably the last contingent of the Exodus generation (Num. 25:1–18). The orgy at Peor is also used to justify the slaughter of all Midian-

progress. As in Exodus, it is Yahweh's awe-inspiring strength and determination to fulfill his pledge to Abraham that wholly absorb the writers' attention. In the fifth volume of the Torah, Deuteronomy, Yahweh pursues the same policy he had invoked against the Midianites—a holy war demanding the pitiless extermination of virtually every human being in Canaan.

QUESTIONS FOR REVIEW

1. According to Numbers, why does Yahweh condemn the Israelites to wander for forty years in the Sinai wilderness? In what ways would the new Mosaic religion benefit from an enforced isolation from other nations until all the people familiar with the older Egyptian culture died off?

2. Why does Yahweh threaten to exterminate Israel? How does Moses persuade him to relent? What does this episode in Chapter 14 say about Yahweh's character and manner of dealing with his chosen people?

3. Summarize the episodes involving Balaam and the Israelites' orgy at Peor. Why does the latter incident begin with Moabites and suddenly change to an involvement with Midianites? Do you think that two different sources or traditions have been combined?

QUESTIONS FOR DISCUSSION AND REFLECTION

1. In Numbers the theme of the Israelites' grumbling and discontent culminates in open rebellion against Moses. How does the narrator in Numbers show that the people's resistance to Mosaic leadership is really an attempted revolt against Yahweh?

2. In Exodus, Aaron led the people's worship of the golden calf while Moses was atop Mount Sinai receiving the Ten Commandments from Yahweh. Although Moses kills 3000 Israelites who had offended Yahweh, Aaron escapes punishment. In Numbers, when Aaron joins Miriam in asserting equal authority with Moses, the High Priest again escapes the consequences of his attempted leadership coup, whereas Miriam is afflicted with a dreaded skin disease and temporarily banished from the Israelites' camp. Why do you think that the biblical writers, particularly the priestly school, consistently exonerate Aaron, even when he takes the lead in committing idolatry and

Figure 4.8 This bronze statuette of a bull—seven inches long and five inches high—was found at a Palestinian cultic site dating from the period of Israel's judges (c. 1200 B.C.E.). Representing masculine strength and virility, the bull was commonly associated with both Baal and Yahweh.

ites (who are also descendants of Abraham [Gen. 25:1–2]), including women and children—except for Midianite virgins, who are seized to populate Israelite harems (Num. 31:1–24).

To most contemporary readers, the picture that Numbers paints of Yahweh is not altogether sympathetic. As pictured in the Midianite episode, the Deity seems little more than capricious, amoral, impatient, and destructive—a God who is easy to fear but difficult to love. Even after scribes and priestly editors extensively revised the text, these ancient narratives represented Yahweh as essentially the national God of Israel, a supernatural being who shows little concern for other peoples except to slaughter them when they impede Israel's

tries to undermine the authority of Yahweh's appointed leader?

TERMS AND CONCEPTS TO REMEMBER

Baal	Korah
Balaam	manna
Caleb	Midianites
Joshua	Miriam

RECOMMENDED READING

Crüsemann, Frank. *The Torah: Theology and Social History of Old Testament Law.* Minneapolis: Fortress Press, 1996. Includes discussion of legal material in Numbers.

Dozeman, Thomas B. "The Book of Numbers." In *The New Interpreter's Bible,* Vol. 2, pp. 3–268. Nashville: Abingdon Press, 1998. Extensive scholarly analysis.

Milgrom, Jacob. *Numbers.* Philadelphia: Jewish Publication Society, 1990. A standard commentary.

———. "Numbers, Book of." In D. N. Freedman, ed., *The Anchor Bible Dictionary,* Vol. 4, pp. 1146–1155. New York: Doubleday, 1992.

Deuteronomy

KEY TOPICS/THEMES

Cast in the form of Moses' three farewell speeches to a new generation of Israelites poised to enter the Promised Land, Deuteronomy presents an elaborate exposition of the ethical and religious standards Israel must meet if it is to enjoy a fruition of the divine promises. Scholars believe the book's core (Chs. 12–26) originated during the eighth century B.C.E. in the northern kingdom of Israel, after which it was brought to Judah, thoroughly revised, and "discovered" at the Jerusalem Temple during the time of King Josiah's religious reforms (c. 621 B.C.E.). Composed to meet Israel's political and religious crises, Deuteronomy provides a powerful criterion by which to interpret Israel's national successes and failures: Obedience to the Mosaic Torah ensures prosperity and divine protection; disobedience brings national defeat and death. This philosophy of history inspired the school of writers who produced the Deuteronomistic History (DH), the heavily edited narrative

of Israel's history from the conquest of Canaan in the Book of Joshua (c. 1200 B.C.E.) through the Babylonian destruction of Judah (587 B.C.E.) in 2 Kings. In Deuteronomy's opening section, Moses reviews Israel's historical experience from Mount Horeb (Sinai) through the wilderness (Chs. 1–4). In his second speech, Moses restates Yahweh's law, including the Ten Commandments (Chs. 5–26, 28). His third discourse emphasizes the "two ways" of life and destruction (Chs. 29–30). Chapter 27 describes a covenant-renewal ceremony at Shechem, and Chapters 32 and 33 contain ancient poetry about Yahweh and the twelve tribes. The book closes with a priestly appendix recounting Moses' death (Ch. 34).

KEY QUESTIONS

How does Deuteronomy differ, in both literary form and legal content, from the other books of the Pentateuch? What is its presumed connection to King Josiah's reforms?

THE DEUTERONOMIC TORAH

The Greek-speaking Jews from the third century B.C.E. onward called the Pentateuch's fifth book Deuteronomy (literally, "second law"), a misleading designation because the book nowhere describes itself as a supplement to the Torah given at Sinai. Deuteronomy contains much legal material largely independent of the Exodus–Numbers tradition (cf. Chs. 12, 17, 18, etc.). The Hebrew title *Eleh Hádevarim* (These are the words [of Moses]) is more accurate, because, unlike the other books of the Torah in which Yahweh directs his words to Moses, who then transmits them to Israel, Deuteronomy shows Moses speaking directly to the people. The book takes the form of three farewell sermons that Moses delivers shortly before his death. Whereas Exodus portrays Moses as so inarticulate that he needs Aaron to speak for him (Exod. 4:10–12), Deuteronomy depicts him as as overwhelmingly eloquent. Moses' speeches take place on the plains of Moab east of Jordan, along which the Israelites are massed just prior to their invasion of Canaan. Deuteronomy is thus pictured as a final recapitulation of Israel's covenant faith before Yahweh leads them into the land he had promised their ancestors.

Although canonized as the Torah's final book, Deuteronomy, in its literary history and origins, has little to do with the JE narratives that precede it. In style and theological outlook, Deuteronomy actually belongs to the historical books that follow it. The alert reader will notice, even in English translation, striking differences in style, phrasing, vocabulary, and theological assumptions between Deuteronomy and other parts of the Pentateuch. Because it purports to be a cycle of public addresses, the book is highly rhetorical, even florid, in style, and the hortatory tone prevails throughout in such phrases as "with all your heart and soul," "in order that it may go well with you," "be thankful," "in a place he himself will choose," "a land where milk and honey flow," and "if only you obey the voice of Yahweh your God."

Compared with earlier sections of the Torah, too, Deuteronomy commonly offers a more humane, sophisticated teaching, stressing both Yahweh's "steadfast love" for Israel and the people's moral obligation to "remember" his heroic acts on their behalf by loving him with their entire being. More than most other parts of the Pentateuch, Deuteronomy emphasizes social justice, personal ethics, and neighborly responsibilities, and it is therefore not surprising that later Jewish writers cite it frequently. In the New Testament, Jesus is shown employing Deuteronomy to refute the Devil himself (Matt. 4; Luke 4).

Josiah's Reforms   Most biblical historians agree that the Book of the Law that was found in 621 B.C.E. when King Josiah was conducting Temple repairs (2 Kings 22:3–10) was Deuteronomy, or at least its nucleus (Chs. 12–26). According to 2 Kings 22–23, this discovery reinforced Josiah's radical program to bring Judah's worship into strict conformity with the Mosaic tradition. Because Deuteronomy 12 demanded that Israel sacrifice only at a single (unnamed) sanctuary, which both king and priests took to be the Temple at Jerusalem, Josiah ordered the wholesale destruction of outlying altars, shrines, and cult sites at which the country people had worshiped for centuries.

Although it was officially published in Josiah's time, an early draft of Deuteronomy was probably compiled many years earlier. Many scholars believe that the deuteronomic core originated in the northern kingdom of Israel when a writer or group of writers attempted to curtail religious and social abuses by composing an appeal to the Mosaic heritage. The author(s) may have incorporated traditions stemming from covenant-renewal ceremonies such as the one that Joshua conducted at Shechem (cf. Deut. 27 and Josh. 24). Later transferred to the old tribal sanctuary at Shiloh during the period of the judges (c. 1200–1020 B.C.E.), these rites were preserved among the northern Israelites. According to this theory, the protodeuteronomic material was probably brought south to Jerusalem by refugees from the Assyrian destruction of Samaria in 721 B.C.E. Extensively reedited from a Judaean perspective, the book was kept underground during King Manasseh's reign, a period of foreign religious influence when devoted Yahwists were not encouraged to insist on Israel's strict allegiance to the Mosaic Torah (see 2 Kings 21). With Josiah's ascension to the Davidic throne and a decline in Assyrian power, however, a revival of the national religion made welcome the reappearance of Deuteronomy. Ironically, a text intended to enhance a cult center in the northern kingdom ultimately was used to support the preeminence of Solomon's Temple.

It seems likely that Deuteronomy was added to and reedited even after Josiah's reign. The book has two introductions, one of which may have been appended after the seventh century B.C.E. The miscellaneous poetry at the end, such as the Song of Moses (Ch. 32) and the Blessing of Moses (Ch. 33), seems to represent ancient traditions about the great lawgiver that later editors wished to preserve as part of the Mosaic legacy. When Deuteronomy was placed with the JE narratives as the concluding volume of the Torah, priestly scribes also added a tradition about Moses' death (Ch. 34).

Moses' First Two Speeches   In his first discourse, Moses reminds a new generation of Israelites (whose parents died in the wilderness) of all that has happened since the departure from Mount

Horeb (Sinai), pointing out that Yahweh has faithfully kept his covenant promises and urging the younger generation to honor their obligations by obeying Yahweh's laws (Deut. 1:1–4:44). Moses' second speech comprises the bulk of Deuteronomy (Chs. 5–26, 28), including an expanded version of the Decalogue (Deut. 5:6–21), the **Shema**—a classic definition of Israel's essential faith (Deut. 6:4–9; Box 4.10)—and the deuteronomic code, a long list of ordinances covering such diverse matters as the central place of worship, dietary restrictions, divorce, the role of prophets, and various social regulations (Chs. 12–26). Some of this resembles material found in Exodus 20–23 and parts of Leviticus and Numbers, but much is new material relating to the future institutions of monarchy (Ch. 17) and prophecy (Ch. 18).

In general, it appears that the Judean editors of Deuteronomy wished to update and revise Israel's ancient legal and sacrificial practices in the light of seventh-century B.C.E. understanding of the Mosaic heritage (Box 4.11). The emphasis on a central sanctuary (Ch. 12), which Josiah's policies enforce, necessitates a revolution in national worship. The abolition of sacrifices at all rural shrines, which throws many Levites out of work; a reduction in the number of yearly festivals; and an insistence that all Israelites must travel to Jerusalem to observe institutionalized holy days such as Passover—all profoundly disrupt old customs. The effect is political as well as religious: Centralization of the national religion in Jerusalem serves to augment the prestige and influence of the Davidic dynasty reigning there.

Much of the second discourse is devoted to laws regulating civil organization, marriage and divorce (which can be initiated only by men), social welfare, and criminal justice. Because the Torah makes no provisions for building prisons, convicted criminals must either pay fines, submit to ritual mutilation, or be executed. For persons committing involuntary manslaughter, cities of refuge are established, but Deuteronomy also recognizes the ancient right of the deceased's relatives to avenge a kinsman's death. If the "blood avengers" catch and kill the accidental slayer before that person reaches a designated place of asylum, they may legally do so.

Deuteronomy imposes the death penalty on many kinds of behavior, ranging from premeditated murder to juvenile delinquency and religious nonconformity. Idolatry, blasphemy, heresy, and the practice of magic or attempted communion with the dead are also capital offenses, commonly punished by stoning or burning. Deuteronomy's compilers repeat the *lex talionis*—law of retaliation—given in Exodus: "Life for life, eye for eye, tooth for tooth, hand for hand, foot for foot" (Deut. 19:21; Box 4.12). Although harsh according to modern sensibilities, this principle of retributive justice controls the extent to which an injured party can demand vengeance. One may not take a life to satisfy the loss of an eye; one must inflict only the precise equivalent of one's own injury (cf. Exod. 21:23–24 and Lev. 24:19–20). (For the commentary of a Jewish teacher of the first century C.E. concerning retaliation, see Matt. 5:38–48.)

After describing a covenant-renewal ceremony to be held at Mount Ebal in northern Israel once the people cross the Jordan River (Ch. 27), the book provides a list of material rewards (blessings) if Israel keeps the law and a much longer list of punishments (curses) if it disobeys the law (Ch. 28). This passage expresses the essence of what is known as the deuteronomic hypothesis of history. Briefly, it states that Israel's future is totally conditional on the Israelites' collective religious behavior. Obedience to the Torah will bring national prosperity; disobedience will result in national disaster, including military defeat and exile. This bleak vision closes Moses' second sermon.

Moses' Third Speech   The third and final speech (Chs. 29–30) seems more like a rhetorical conclusion to the second address than a separate discourse. Here, Moses enumerates additional sufferings destined to befall the Israelites if they sin. "In anger, in fury, in fierce wrath," Yahweh will devastate their land and inflict so much misery that even survivors will wish they had died. In common with the prophets, however, there is a promise that when the people repent their sins and return to Yahweh, he will forgive them and restore a small remnant of them to their homeland. The people

Box 4.10 Deuteronomy's Proclamations of Faith

Besides presenting its distinctive version of the Ten Commandments (5:6–21), the Book of Deuteronomy also contains several passages defining essential features of Israelite religion. The Shema, named for its opening imperative—"listen" or "hear"—proclaims the uniqueness of Yahweh and his demand for unconditional love (6:4–9). (Later tradition added passages from Deut. 11:13–21 and Num. 15:37–41 to form a prayer that was recited every morning and evening [Deut. 6:7].) Deuteronomy 26 highlights a recitation of Israel's reasons for its indebtedness to Yahweh, who had rescued his people from slavery and brought them to Canaan. Many scholars think that this creed—a brief formula stating authoritative religious belief—originated orally as part of Israelite worship at various shrines and, in a greatly expanded version, eventually formed the basis of the Torah's written narratives.

The Shema

Listen, Israel: Yahweh our God is the one Yahweh. You shall love Yahweh your God with all your heart, with all your soul, with all your strength. Let these words I urge on you today be written on your heart. You shall repeat them to your children and say them over to them whether at rest in your house or walking abroad, at your lying down or at your rising; you shall fasten them on your hand as a sign [signifying action] and on your forehead [signifying thought] as a circlet; you shall write them on the doorposts of your house and on your gates.

Deut. 6:4–9; see also Deut. 11:13–31 and Num. 15:37–41

The following creed, expressing Israel's historical experience of its God, was recited at the harvest festival of first fruits. Although it reviews events from the latter part of Genesis, the first half of Exodus, and Joshua, it makes no mention of covenant-making at Sinai or Horeb, which may have originated in a separate tradition.

My father [Jacob, progenitor of Israel] was a wandering Aramaean [Syrian]. He went down into Egypt to find refuge there, few in numbers, but there he became a nation, great, mighty, and strong. The Egyptians ill-treated us, they gave us no peace and inflicted harsh slavery on us. But we called on Yahweh the God of our fathers. Yahweh heard our voice and saw our misery, our toil, and our oppression, and Yahweh brought us out of Egypt with mighty hand and outstretched arm, with great terror, and with signs and wonders. He brought us here and gave us this land, a land where milk and honey flow. Here, then, I bring the first fruits of the produce of the soil that you, Yahweh, have given me.

Deut. 26:5–10

In addition to its concise declarations of faith, Deuteronomy also articulates a vision of the infinite continuity of Israel's bond to Yahweh: It is not only the generation led by Moses that hears God's call to absolute commitment, but also all future Israelite generations who figuratively experience Yahweh's presence. "Not with you alone do I make this covenant today and pronounce these sanctions, but with him also who is not here today, as well as with him who stands with us here in the presence of Yahweh our God" (Deut. 29:13–15).

Summarizing both the benefits and obligations of the covenant bond, Deuteronomy's editors insist that Torah obedience is fully obtainable and that Israel has the free will to choose its life-giving blessings:

For this Law [Torah] that I enjoin on you today is not beyond your strength or beyond your reach. It is not in heaven, so that you need to wonder, "Who will go up to heaven for us and bring it down to us, so that we may hear it and keep it?" Nor is it beyond the seas, so that you need to wonder, "Who will cross the seas for us and bring it back to us, so that we may hear it and keep it?" No, the Word is very near to you, it is in your mouth and in your heart for your observance. . . . I call heaven and earth to witness against you today: I set before you life or death, blessing or curse. Choose life, then, so that you and your descendants may live. . . .

Deut. 30:11–14, 19

Box 4.11 Six Distinct Legal Codes Embedded in the Torah

Although Mosaic commandments, statutes, and ordinances are commonly regarded as a single body of
law, the Torah actually contains at least six different
legal codes. Because each code appears separate and
distinct from the other codes, scholars believe that
each one originated independently among different
groups living at different periods in Israel's history.
These discrete legal documents may have been combined during and after the Babylonian exile (late
sixth and fifth centuries B.C.E.), when the covenant
community was part of the Persian Empire. According to the Book of Ezra, Persian administrators ordered the exiles who had returned to Jerusalem to
govern the restored community by producing a compilation of Israel's legal traditions that would then
become the official law of the land. Conformity to a
single sacred legal corpus derived from the Mosaic
heritage was enforced by imperial Persian authority:
"If anyone does not obey the Law [Torah] of your
God—which is the law of the king [Persian em-
peror]—let judgment be strictly executed for him:
death, banishment, confiscation, or imprisonment"
(Ezra 7:1–26). The Persian threat of financial loss or
capital punishment for those not practicing the divinely (and governmentally) sanctioned Torah was a
strong inducement for scribes to produce and for the
people to accept a definitive edition of Israel's legal
code. Whatever the time and place of its origin, all
Torah legislation was ultimately assigned to Moses
and thus given his prestige and authority. The discrete legal corpora finally incorporated into the Pentateuch include these six sources:

1. The Book of the Covenant, the Elohist's revision
   of an ancient legal code (Exod. 20:18–23:33)

2. The Ritual Decalogue, the Yahwist's compendium
   of henotheistic and cultic requirements (Exod.
   34:11–26)

3. The Deuteronomic Code, the core of canonical
   Deuteronomy, introduced during the reign of
   Josiah (late seventh century B.C.E.) (Deut. 12–26)

4. The Decalogue, the Ten "Sayings" or Commandments (Exod. 20:17; Deut. 5:6–21)

5. The Holiness Code, ritually separating and distinguishing Israel from surrounding peoples
   (Lev. 17–26)

6. The Priestly Code, formal liturgies and sacrificial
   rituals (Lev. 1–16, 27; Num 1–10) (See also the
   Tabernacle cult [Exod. 25–31, 35–40].)

---

are repeatedly reminded that the responsibility for
their future rests squarely on their own shoulders.

In truly "winged words," Yahweh emphasizes
the people's freedom of choice. Setting before
them "life and prosperity" or "death and disaster,"
he urges them to choose a life in which they and
their descendants can live to enjoy the love of their
God. The ancient song ascribed to Moses (Ch. 32)
is actually a hymn glorifying Yahweh and denouncing the people's misuse of their free will:

He [Yahweh] is the rock, his work is perfect,
for all his ways are Equity.
A God faithful, without unfairness,
Uprightness itself and Justice.
They [the people] have acted perversely,
those he begot without blemish,
a deceitful and underhand brood.

Is this the return you make to Yahweh?
O foolish, unwise people!

Deut. 32:4–6

Evil fortune, then, is directly the community's responsibility, for both Yahweh and his creation are
perfect.

Moses' Last Days and Death   After the Blessing
of Moses (Ch. 33), which strongly resembles
Jacob's blessing (Gen. 49), Deuteronomy records
Moses' death. Prohibited from entering the Promised Land for an unspecified reason (perhaps his
taking credit for bringing water from the rocks
at Meribah [Num. 20:2–13]), the 120-year-old
Moses glimpses Canaan from a high mountain
and dies alone, hidden from the people he has

Box 4.12 The Torah's Three Versions of the Law of Retaliation

A legal principle widely known in Mesopotamia long before the time of Moses, the *lex talionis* (law of retaliation) appears prominently in three books of the Torah. In Deuteronomy, it is placed in the context of bearing false witness — making untrue accusations against a fellow citizen that could result in his legal mutilation or execution. According to the Deuteronomic legal code, if a man is proved to have testified falsely against another Israelite, the magistrates must "deal with him as he would have dealt with his brother," making the liar's punishment an example to others who might be tempted to behave unjustly. Without pity, the judges are to exact "life for life, eye for eye, tooth for tooth, hand for hand, foot for foot" (Deut. 19:15–21).

Whereas Deuteronomy employs the *lex talionis* as an instrument of poetic justice — the wrong one person tries to inflict on another is instead visited on him — the Book of the Covenant in Exodus applies it to cases involving physical assault. In contrast to Deuteronomy, the Exodus legal code defines penalties levied against masters who beat, maim, or kill slaves and against men whose fighting injures a pregnant woman, causing her to miscarry. If a mistreated slave dies under a master's blows, the owner must "pay the penalty"; if, however, the injured slave survives "for one or two days, [the master] shall pay no penalty because the slave is his by right of purchase" (Exod. 21:20–21). In the case of quarreling men whose violence causes a pregnant woman to lose her child, the aggressor must pay her master or husband an appropriate monetary compensation; if the woman dies, however, the *lex talionis* applies: "you shall give life for life, eye for eye, tooth for tooth, . . . burn for burn, wound for wound, stroke for stroke" (Exod. 21:22–25).

According to the Leviticus legal code, the infliction of physical injuries must be repaid strictly in kind: "If a man injures his neighbor, what he has done must be done to him: broken bone for broken bone, eye for eye, tooth for tooth." Whereas persons who kill another's animal must make restitution for its value, those who commit homicide must die (Lev. 24:19–22). It is not known if Israelite officials regularly enforced the principle of exact retaliation — condemning persons who unintentionally damaged another's eye to undergo state-administered mutilation — but the *lex talionis* did serve to shield offenders from suffering death for causing accidental injuries.

---

guided for forty years. His unfulfilled career provides an effective symbol for his nation's future experience. As an awed commentator penned in conclusion: "Never has there been such a prophet in Israel as Moses, the man Yahweh knew face to face" (Deut. 34:10). No stronger argument could be given for the absolute necessity of adhering to the Mosaic teachings — as presented in Deuteronomy.

DEUTERONOMY'S POSITION IN THE PENTATEUCH

Scholars believe that Deuteronomy originated as a legal code distinct from the Yahwist, Elohist, and priestly sources that eventually were blended together to form the Pentateuch's narrative framework. In its earlier editions, Deuteronomy stood as a separate and independent repository of Mosaic traditions, although ultimately it was linked to a series of historical writings (Joshua through 2 Kings) that were deeply influenced by the deuteronomic theory of history. The deuteronomic formula, which attributes all of Israel's political and military defeats to covenant-breaking, consistently shapes the presentation of Israel's post-Mosaic story, from its initial conquest of Canaan to the catastrophic loss of its land to Babylon in 587 B.C.E. Unified by themes illustrating the disastrous results of disobedience, Deuteronomy and the narrative books following it once constituted a coherent literary unit.

After the Babylonian exile and its disappointing aftermath, in which Israel was not restored to its former glory, priestly writers reedited and rearranged their sacred books to reflect the new realities faced by a politically powerless covenant community. Thus, the Torah ends before the divine promises are truly fulfilled, with the people still outside their promised home. Although its style and content clearly belong to the Joshua–Kings narrative sequence, the postexilic priestly school separated Deuteronomy from the historical books it once headed, making it instead the fifth volume of the Pentateuch. By adding a new introduction and conclusion that featured an account of Moses' death, priestly editors attempted to make Deuteronomy an integral part of the JE version of Moses' story. By also inserting large blocks of legal instruction in the Exodus–Numbers narratives, including the entire Book of Leviticus, the priestly redactors elevated the whole of Israel's diverse legal codes and traditions to the status of Mosaic revelation.

In its present position, Deuteronomy functions as a capstone to the Pentateuch and a thematically appropriate introduction to the second major division of the Hebrew Bible, the books of Joshua through 2 Kings. Like the authors and editors of Deuteronomy, the Deuteronomistic interpreters of Israel's subsequent history are unswerving in their conviction that the covenant people freely chose their tragic fate by failing to honor their collective vow to worship Yahweh alone.

QUESTIONS FOR REVIEW

1. Describe how Deuteronomy differs from other books of the Torah in both form and content. How do scholarly theories about Deuteronomy's origins help explain its differences from other parts of the Pentateuch?

2. According to most contemporary scholars, when was Deuteronomy actually written, and under what circumstances was it "discovered" and published?

3. Define the deuteronomic hypothesis. According to Deuteronomy 28–29, on what kinds of behavior does the Israelites' national future depend? Explain the philosophy of history promulgated in the deuteronomic view of covenant-keeping or -breaking.

QUESTIONS FOR DISCUSSION AND REFLECTION

1. Why do you suppose Deuteronomy ends with Israel still outside the Promised Land and with Moses dying before he can experience the fulfillment of Yahweh's promises? Why do the biblical narratives repeatedly emphasize the theme of *deferred* realization of divine promises? According to Proverbs 13:12, "hope deferred makes the heart sick." Do Yahweh's delays have an adverse effect on the well-being of his people? Explain.

2. By the close of the Pentateuch, to what extent have the promises to Abraham and his descendants been realized?

TERMS AND CONCEPTS TO REMEMBER

lex talionis   Shema

RECOMMENDED READING

Clements, Ronald E. "The Book of Deuteronomy." In *The New Interpreter's Bible*, Vol. 2, pp. 271–538. Nashville: Abingdon Press, 1998. Contains extensive commentary.

Crüsemann, Frank. *The Torah: Theology and Social History of Old Testament Law*. Minneapolis: Fortress Press, 1996.

Fretheim, Terence E. *Deuteronomic History*. Nashville: Abingdon Press, 1983. A brief introduction to the DH compositions.

Friedman, Richard E. *Who Wrote the Bible?* New York: Harper & Row, 1987. A brilliant analysis of the historical and theological forces behind the compilation and reediting of Deuteronomy and the Deuteronomistic History.

McKenzie, Steven L. "Deuteronomistic History." In D. N. Freedman, ed., *The Anchor Bible Dictionary*, Vol. 2, pp. 160–168. New York: Doubleday, 1992. Examines the influence of Deuteronomy's view of history on the books of Joshua through Kings.

von Rad, Gerhard. *Studies in Deuteronomy*. Studies in Biblical Theology, No. 9. London: SCM Press, 1953. A form-critical approach.

———. *Deuteronomy*. Philadelphia: Westminster Press, 1966.

Weinfield, Moshe. "Deuteronomy, Book of." In D. N. Freedman, ed., *The Anchor Bible Dictionary*, Vol. 2, pp. 168–183. New York: Doubleday, 1992. Discusses the origin and content of the Torah's fifth book.

The Prophets (Nevi'im) I
The Deuteronomistic History

Key Topics/Themes

The long narrative of Israel's national origins that began in the Torah continues in the first part of the Tanak's second major division, the Prophets (*Nevi'im*). Known as the Deteronomistic History because it interprets Israel's historical experience strictly according to principles of divine retribution spelled out in Deuteronomy, this section—Joshua, Judges, 1 and 2 Samuel, and 1 and 2 Kings—essentially tells the story of how Israel first took possession of Canaan, the territory promised to Abraham's descendants, and then lost it. Written to illustrate the disastrous consequences of failure to worship Yahweh exclusively, the Deuteronomistic History (DH) neatly divides Israel's story into five distinct epochs: (1) the conquest of Canaan under Joshua; (20) the period of the judges; (3) the rise of the Israelite monarchy under Saul and David; (4) following Solomon's death, the division of the united monarchy into two separate kingdoms of Israel and Judah; and (5) Assyria's destruction of the northern kingdom of Israel (722 B.C.E.) and Babylon's destruction of the southern kingdom of

Judah (587 B.C.E.). Subordinating the complexities of history to a single theme, the DH drives home the point that when Israel's leaders, such as David, remained true to the covenant with Yahweh, the nation prospered, but when his successors, most notoriously King Manasseh, violated the Mosaic pact, Yahweh abandoned his people to their more powerful Near Eastern neighbors.

KEY QUESTIONS

How do the DH writers' theological assumptions shape their account of Israel's history? Why do they depict Israelite history as divided into several discrete eras? How do they reconcile their view of an all-powerful Yahweh with the national disasters that repeatedly befell his chosen people?

The second major section of the Hebrew Bible, the **Prophets** (Nevi'im), is divided into two distinct parts. The first part, traditionally known as the Former Prophets, but which scholars refer to as the Deuteronomistic History (DH), is a long prose narrative that traces a theologically oriented version of Israel's history from the conquest of Canaan in the late thirteenth century B.C.E. to the destruction of the Jewish state in the sixth century B.C.E. (The dating of the conquest, however, and even its historicity, are open to question.) The second part, called the Latter Prophets, is a collection—mostly in poetry—of fifteen prophetic books that bear the names of individual prophets, such as Isaiah, Jeremiah, and Hosea. The historical-theological accounts, Joshua through 2 Kings, provide necessary background for the teachings of Israel's prophets, who typically appear in times of political crisis to proclaim Yahweh's viewpoint in a particular historical situation. Isaiah, for example, serves as both prophet and political adviser to several Judean kings during the late eighth century B.C.E. When Assyrian armies overrun the northern kingdom of Israel and threaten to gobble up Judah as well, Isaiah of Jerusalem counsels King Hezekiah not to fear because Yahweh has resolved to protect Jerusalem, his holy city, from capture (2 Kings 19).

The Deuteronomistic Theory of History

Scholars refer to the Former Prophets as the **Deuteronomistic History** because these theologically oriented narratives rigorously interpret Israel's historical experience according to rules laid down in the Book of Deuteronomy. As noted previously, Deuteronomy's philosophy of history is inflexible: When Israel worships Yahweh alone and faithfully keeps all Torah regulations, the nation will win all its battles and prosper economically. But if the people—or their individual leaders—mix Yahweh's cult with Canaanite elements, the nation will suffer military defeat, financial ruin, and eventual enslavement to foreign masters (Deut. 28–30).

TWO EDITIONS OF THE DEUTERONOMISTIC HISTORY

Many scholars believe that there were two main editions of the Deuteronomistic History. The first version was composed during the reign of Josiah

(640–609 B.C.E.), the Judean king who zealously purged Yahwism of Canaanite influences and led the people in a renewal of their covenant vows. Josiah's sweeping reforms were conducted according to "everything that was said in the book of the covenant found in the Temple of Yahweh" (2 Kings 23:1–3). As explained in Chapter 4, most scholars think that the "book of the covenant" responsible for Josiah's revival of exclusive Yahwism was Deuteronomy, with its insistence on a single central sanctuary, directives for observing Passover, and a list of curses for disobedience (cf. Deut. 12–28; 2 Kings 22–23).

Composed at the high tide of Josiah's triumphant religious and military campaigns, the first edition of the Deuteronomistic History praised Josiah in terms accorded no other Davidic king. Not only did he please Yahweh "in every respect" (2 Kings 22:2), but Josiah "turned to Yahweh . . . with all his heart, all his soul, all his strength, in perfect loyalty to the law of Moses" (2 Kings 23:25). Josiah's total devotion to Yahweh, in fact, is rendered in terms that fulfill Deuteronomy's supreme command—to love Israel's God absolutely (Deut. 6:4–6).

In its original form, the Deuteronomistic History had a remarkable literary symmetry. The first edition began with an account of Joshua's stunning military and religious exploits and ended in 2 Kings with a summary of Josiah's Yahwist reforms and partial reconquest of the Promised Land. Backed by Yahweh's invisible armies, Joshua successfully led Israel in a holy war, capturing Canaanite strongholds, seizing large Canaanite territories, and overthrowing Canaanite shrines. At the conclusion of the narrative, Josiah performs similar feats, leading Judah's troops into northern territories that had been previously lost to Assyria and systematically demolishing illicit places of worship throughout his kingdom (cf. Josh. 1–11; 2 Kings 23). Both men are portrayed as national heroes who exemplify deuteronomistic piety in action. Joshua's gathering together of the tribes for a solemn covenant-renewal ceremony—witnessed by a stone monument that Joshua sets up to commemorate the event (Josh. 24)—is paralleled by Josiah's conducting a comparable ritual "beside the

[Temple] pillar." In both cases, the covenant terms are read aloud to the people, who then swear to uphold them (cf. Josh. 24:24–28; 2 Kings 23:3).

Probably written to help promote Josiah's crusade to honor Yahweh alone, this first version of the Deuteronomistic History could give Israel's story a happy outcome, including the complete fulfillment of all the divine promises. Although the 600-year-long period from Joshua to Josiah had witnessed many reversals, attributed to the people's covenant-breaking, in the long run Yahweh and his people finally were united under a king "like his father David"—one through whom God could rule effectively. Promulgating Deuteronomy's laws as his country's constitution, Josiah presided over a Judean theocracy.

After Josiah's early death (609 B.C.E.) and Judah's subsequent fall to Babylon, however, the Deuteronomistic historian(s) had to revise their neatly symmetrical presentation of Israel's history. Josiah's reign could no longer be seen as the climactic fulfillment of the covenant people's relationship to Yahweh, for this glorious moment was soon followed by national calamity (2 Kings 25). Viewing Israel's history from the perspective of exile in Babylon, the Deuteronomistic editors found a way to explain their nation's collapse and the extinction of the Davidic dynasty, which Yahweh had promised would govern his people forever (2 Sam. 7). It was one of Josiah's predecessors, King Manasseh, who was responsible for the catastrophe. Immediately following the passage in which they extolled Josiah's life-giving reforms, the editor(s) inserted this critical warning:

> Yet Yahweh did not renounce the heat of his great anger which blazed out against Judah because of the provocation Manasseh had offered him. Yahweh decreed, "I will thrust Judah away from me too, as I have already thrust Israel. I will cast away Jerusalem, this city I had chosen, and the Temple of which I had said: There my name shall be."
>
> 2 Kings 23:26–27

The fathers' sins would be visited upon their great-grandchildren, because "Yahweh would not forgive" (2 Kings 24:4).

Revised during the Babylonian exile to reflect a devastating historical reality, the books of Joshua through Kings now present Israel's history according to a single principle—the fatal consequences of disobedience to Yahweh. As the Deuteronomistic historian(s) saw it, the nation's survival was *always conditional* on the people's strict adherence to their covenant obligations. Josiah's heroic efforts were ultimately futile, because too many other kings, predominantly Manasseh, had flagrantly violated Torah commands. In the Deuteronomistic view, these ancient failures perfectly account for every lost battle, foreign invasion, crop failure, drought, famine, plague, or political humiliation. All historical figures and events in the Former Prophets are subordinated to that view. By scattering brief references to the coming national defeat and exile throughout the narrative, the reviser(s) transformed the Deuteronomistic History, their foreshadowings making the ultimate disaster appear inevitable (cf. Deut. 4:26–27; 28:36, 63–64; Josh. 23:16; 1 Kings 9:7; 11:35–36; 15:3–4; 2 Kings 8:18–19; 20:16–19, etc.).

IDENTITY OF THE DEUTERONOMISTIC AUTHORS

According to R. E. Friedman in *Who Wrote the Bible?*, a careful study of the Deuteronomistic History indicates that the First edition was compiled during Josiah's reign by a single priestly writer associated with the royal court. Friedman suggests further that the same person revised the text during the exile, adding the account of Josiah's unsatisfactory successors and the passages foreshadowing Judah's destruction. For Friedman, the most likely candidate is the prophet Jeremiah, who repeatedly warned Judah's last kings of the dire results of covenant-breaking, although Jeremiah's secretary **Baruch** probably did the actual writing. (See Chapter 6.) Archaeologists recently found a clay stamp used to seal documents; the stamp contains the inscription "Belonging to Baruch, son of Neriyah the scribe." Friedman speculates that this item may represent the author or editor of eight books of the Bible. Other scholars, however, maintain that the Deuteronomistic History was composed by a school or circle of anonymous Judean scribes.

SOURCES OF THE HISTORY

In compiling their account, the Deuteronomistic historian(s) drew upon both oral traditions, such as stories about the prophets Elijah and Elisha, and several written documents, including collections of archaic poetry, such as the Book of Jashar (Josh. 10:13; 2 Sam. 1:18). Royal archives that list the deeds of Israelite and Judean rulers were frequently cited, including the Book of the Acts of Solomon (1 Kings 11:41), the Book of the Annals of the Kings of Judah (1 Kings 14:29), and the Book of the Annals of the Kings of Israel (1 Kings 14:19). These court records would doubtless have provided more extensive coverage of the various rulers' economic, political, and social accomplishments than the Deuteronomistic author(s) cared to preserve. Unfortunately, none has survived.

Major Events and Their Meaning

Although the six books of Joshua through 2 Kings provide a sweeping overview of Israel's history, they do not contain all the factual information that a modern historian would consider essential. The Deuteronomistic writer(s)' goals are not those of a scientific investigator who seeks to assemble a complete and objective picture of the social, economic, cultural, and religious forces that created ancient Israel. Writing from a deliberately limited viewpoint, the Deuteronomistic author(s) proposed only one factor to account for Israel's rise and fall—its loyalty or disloyalty to Yahweh. Events that a contemporary historian would view as the natural consequences of specific political or military conditions, the Deuteronomistic writer(s) attributed solely to Israel's state of religious health. The rise of new, aggressive Mesopotamian empires that repeatedly invaded Canaan during the eighth and sixth centuries B.C.E. thus were considered not the inevitable result of imperialist expansionism, but the means that Yahweh used to punish his people. Assyria and Babylon were merely the instruments of his wrath.

Emphasizing the theological meaning rather than the mere facts of historical change, the Deuteronomistic History covers seven crucial periods or events:

1. The **conquest of Canaan** under Joshua's leadership
2. The twelve-tribe confederacy and its battles with assorted Canaanite city-states (Judg.)
3. The Philistine crisis leading to tribal unification and establishment of the monarchy, which reaches its apex under kings David and Solomon (1 and 2 Sam.; 1 Kings)
4. The secession of the northern ten tribes after Solomon's death and the development of two kingdoms of Judah and Israel (1 Kings)
5. The parallel dynastic histories of the divided kingdoms, culminating in Assyria's destruction of Israel and its capital, Samaria, in 721 B.C.E. (2 Kings)
6. King Josiah's religious reforms in Judah following 621 B.C.E.
7. Babylon's obliteration of Judah and the Jerusalem Temple in 587 B.C.E. (2 Kings)

Besides ascribing every military victory to Yahweh's pleasure at the people's loyalty and every defeat to his anger at their unfaithfulness, the Deuteronomistic History is characterized by these three motifs:

1. Yahwist prophets such as Elijah and Elisha are pictured as heroic crusaders against the cult of Baal and other Canaanite impurities. (Behaving as warriors as well as prophets, Elijah and Elisha attack and massacre practitioners of Baalism.)

2. The text emphasizes the preeminence of Jerusalem, the only site at which Yahweh accepts the sacrifices mandated by the Mosaic Torah. Because the northern kingdom (after 922 B.C.E.) maintained several rival sanctuaries, *all* of its kings were uniformly blacklisted.

3. Besides condemning every ruler in the northern kingdom, the DH also adversely judges every king of Judah who was not a thoroughgoing Yahwist. Painting David as the ideal monarch, the prototype of the God-favored ruler with whom Yahweh makes an "everlasting covenant," the Deuteronomistic narrative presents only two Davidic successors—Hezekiah and Josiah—as measuring up to Mosaic standards.

Although 1 and 2 Samuel appear to have been edited only slightly, the other books — Joshua, Judges, and Kings — reflect the heavy hand of the Deuteronomistic author(s), who appear to have shaped the narrative to underscore the moral causes of historical events.

Although its main thrust is to demonstrate that Israel had earned its tragic fall, the Deuteronomistic History ends with a glimmer of hope. After briefly describing the ruling class's exile to Babylon, the account concludes with a minor but possibly significant event: Following the death of Nebuchadnezzar, Judah's King Jehoiachin is released from prison and allowed to dine at the new Babylonian ruler's table (2 Kings 25:27–30). Did the final editor, after all, dare hope that, true to his word, Yahweh would perhaps restore the Davidic royal line?

Observing the Order of the Hebrew Bible

In the Hebrew Bible, the Deuteronomistic History and the prophetic books form a coherent unit separate from the third great division of the Tanak — the Writings (Kethuvim). This separation makes sense chronologically because most of the prophets were active during the historical period covered by the books of Kings (tenth through sixth centuries B.C.E.). Whereas Christian editions of the Old Testament place the prophets last in the canon, making them a thematic link to prophetic fulfillment in the New Testament, the Hebrew Bible places them next to the historical books, emphasizing the prophetic interpretation of Israel's covenant-breaking and illustrating the moral rationale for Israel's fall to Babylon. Rabbinical editors arrange narratives of Israel's later history — after the Babylonian exile — such as Ezra and Nehemiah, among the Writings. Following the order in the Tanak, we will first discuss the preexilic histories and then the individual prophets, in Chapter 6. In Chapter 7, we will resume tracing the course of Israel's history in the postexilic books of Chronicles, Ezra, and Nehemiah. Although the brief Book of Ruth appears after Judges in most Protestant and Catholic Bibles, we will observe the Jewish placement and discuss it among the Writings, in Chapter 7.

QUESTIONS FOR REVIEW

1. What part of the Hebrew Bible is traditionally called the "Former Prophets," and what kinds of books does it include?

2. What is the Deuteronomistic History, and how is it connected with the Book of Deuteronomy? With what events in Israel's history does the DH begin and end?

QUESTION FOR DISCUSSION AND REFLECTION

Why do scholars think that there were two editions of the Deuteronomistic History, one composed during the reign of Josiah and the other a revised version that appeared after 587 B.C.E.? How did the force of historical events necessitate a reevaluation of Israel's story?

TERMS AND CONCEPTS TO REMEMBER

Baruch	Deuteronomistic History
conquest of Canaan	Prophets

RECOMMENDED READING

Fretheim, Terence E. *Deuteronomic History.* Nashville: Abingdon Press, 1983.

Friedman, Richard E. *Who Wrote the Bible?* New York: Harper & Row, 1987.

McKenzie, Steven L. "Deuteronomistic History." In D. N. Freedman, ed., *The Anchor Bible Dictionary,* Vol. 2, pp. 160–168. New York: Doubleday, 1992. An excellent introduction to the topic.

Noth, Martin, *The Deuteronomistic History.* JSOT Supplement 15. Sheffield, England: JSOT, 1981. A groundbreaking and widely accepted study.

Joshua

KEY TOPICS/THEMES

Integrating a variety of older sources into a Deuteronomistic framework, Joshua presents Israel's conquest of Canaan as a direct result of its obedience to the Mosaic Covenant. After an introduction

Figure 5.1 Like many cities throughout Canaan, Lachish was attacked repeatedly by invading armies. This Assyrian bas-relief from the royal palace at Nineveh realistically portrays the armies of Sennacherib laying siege to Lachish (701 B.C.E.). Although Lachish, along with forty-six other Judean towns, was totally demolished (2 Kings 23:18), Jerusalem miraculously survived the Assyrian invasion. Note the assault ramp built against Lachish's gates and the civilian inhabitants fleeing by a side exit (right), while three naked captives are impaled on pointed wooden stakes (lower center).

emphasizing the link between Torah observance and military victory (Ch. 1), the book describes a rapid series of successful attacks on Canaanite centers (Chs. 2–12). The second half of the book lists the apportioning of land among the twelve tribes (Chs. 13–22), concluding with Joshua's farewell speech and an intertribal covenant-renewal ceremony (Chs. 23–24).

KEY QUESTIONS

What theological view does Joshua's narrator advance? How well does this picture of the conquest accord with the archaeological record?

The first unit of the Deuteronomistic History, the Bible's sixth book—Joshua—dramatizes the deuteronomic thesis in action. Rather than give an objective account of the twelve Israelite tribes' settlement in Canaan near the beginning of the Iron Age, Joshua presents history through the eyes of a zealous Yahwist. Using a variety of battle scenes to demonstrate its point, the book shows that Yahweh—portrayed as an invincible warrior-king—directs Israel's assault on the Canaanites, granting the tribes total victory when they are fully loyal to their covenant with him. (As Figure 5.1 shows, the cities of Canaan were repeatedly besieged by a number of invaders.)

The conviction that God will defeat all enemies of an obedient Israel is expressed in Joshua's vision

of the supernatural "captain" of Yahweh's army, who appears in human form, brandishing "a naked sword" (Josh. 5:13–15). Fighting invisibly alongside Israel's soldiers, the presence of this heavenly commander reveals that God has predetermined Israel's success. Whereas in Numbers the older Israelite generation had failed to believe that Yahweh could annihilate the Canaanites or capture Canaan's seemingly impregnable walled towns, Joshua's troops show an exemplary faith. The first military operation, the siege of Jericho, is accomplished without material weapons: Its defensive walls crumble at the sound of priestly trumpets and a "mighty war cry" shouted by the "whole people" (6:1–5, 14–16). By contrast, a temporary lapse into disobedience causes the Israelites to fail in their siege of the nearby town of 'Ai. Only after executing the guilty parties do they take the city (Ch. 7).

Like the Torah, this story of the conquest betrays a variety of sources, probably including fragments of the JE document. Perhaps even older are quotations from the now-lost **Book of Jashar**, which seems to have been a collection of early Israelite war hymns and other poems, some of which may have been contemporaneous with the victories they celebrate. Using both oral traditions and these written texts, the Deuteronomistic author(s) compiled Joshua's main narrative, creating their highly idealized version of a faithful Israel's military invincibility. The priestly writer(s) who produced the final edition during the Babylonian exile added some genealogical and other material, primarily to the book's second half. A composite work, Joshua thus includes material that spans a lengthy period—poetry that was first composed orally during the conquest and priestly commentary from the postexilic age.

THE CONQUEST OF CANAAN AS A CONTINUATION OF THE EXODUS

Joshua as Another Moses Despite repetitions and sometimes disjointed narratives that result from the authors' use of multiple sources, Joshua gives an exciting, if not historically accurate, picture of the conquest of Canaan. The charismatic leader of twelve tribes united by Yahwistic faith, Joshua is presented as a second Moses. Like Moses, he leads the people through parted waters—this time those of the Jordan River, which is held back at flood tide to permit Israel's crossing. Instead of Moses' staff, however, it is the Ark of the Covenant, carried by priests, that effects the miracle (Josh. 3–4). Like Moses, too, Joshua experiences a theophany, a vision of Yahweh's divine general whose participation guarantees victory over the Canaanites. He also resembles the great lawgiver in adding to the Book of the Covenant, in proclaiming Yahweh's commandments, and in presiding over a reenactment at **Shechem** of the pact that binds Israel to Yahweh (4:1–9; 23–24).

The Fall of Jericho After entering Canaan, the Israelites do not immediately begin their military campaign. Instead, all males born during the forty-year wandering assemble at **Gilgal** to be circumcised, an operation that incapacitates them for several days, though the threatened residents of nearby **Jericho** make no attempt to take advantage of their vulnerability (Josh. 5:1–12) (Figure 5.2). Now ritually acceptable, the warriors still do not attack the Canaanite stronghold. Instead, they follow Joshua's instructions to march silently around the city seven times until a signal is given, at which time they are to raise a loud shout, blow their

Figure 5.2 The world's "oldest walled town," Jericho was first occupied by prehistoric settlers in about 9000 B.C.E. The round tower, twenty-five feet high, dates from the earliest Neolithic (New Stone Age) period (8000–7000 B.C.E.). Erosion has removed most of Jericho's remains from the late Bronze Age period, the time of Israel's invasion of Canaan described in the Book of Joshua (c. 1200 B.C.E.).

trumpets, and charge Jericho's ramparts (Ch. 6). That is the earlier of two accounts of Jericho's fall that have been woven imperfectly into a single narrative. The second version emphasizes the priests' role in carrying the Ark of the Covenant and sounding ram's-horn trumpets during some thirteen circuits of the town (6:4, 8–9, 11–13).

On the final day, the city walls collapse except for that part supporting the house of **Rahab** the prostitute (perhaps the priestess of a Canaanite fertility cult), who had hidden Israelite spies when they had reconnoitered the city. The entire population is placed under the "sacred **ban**," which means that the people are massacred as an offering to Yahweh, a form of human sacrifice. The Israelites' belief that Yahweh required the deaths of all non-Hebrews in Canaan may shock modern

Box 5.1 The Deuteronomists' Concept of Holy War

In Genesis, Israel's ancestors generally live peaceably among the ethnically mixed inhabitants of Canaan, some of whom are presented as notably admirable characters. Melchizedek, who presides over a shrine for "God Most High [El Elyon]" at Salem, merits Abraham's respect (Gen. 14:17–24), and Abimelech, king of Canaanite Gezer, dreams of Abraham's God, who explicitly commends the ruler's "clear conscience" (Gen. 20:1–18). The stories of Abraham, Isaac, and Jacob show the patriarchs freely making alliances with or peacefully buying property from Canaanites at Salem, Gezer, and Shechem. In Deuteronomy and the Deuteronomistic History (Joshua through Kings), however, the Canaanites are never depicted as helpful allies or acceptable neighbors. Instead, they are consistently portrayed as dangerous to the Israelite faith, their very existence a threat to Israel's loyalty to Yahweh.

Deuteronomy and the historical books that follow propose only one solution to the Canaanites' presence in the land Yahweh had promised to Abraham's progeny: They must be exterminated without mercy. The deuteronomic portrait of Yahweh, characterized as "a consuming fire, a jealous God" (Deut.

4:24), is that of a ruthless warrior who, to benefit his one favored community, orders the slaughter of every man, woman, and child dwelling in Canaan. All Canaanites are placed "under ban," a component of holy war in which the enemy is consecrated to the attackers' God and, in effect, sacrificed to him. Allowing Canaanites to live would make them a source of religious corruption:

> You must lay them under ban. You must make no covenant with them nor show them any pity. You must not marry with them: you must not give a daughter of theirs to a son of yours, for this would turn your son away from following me to serving other gods, and the anger of Yahweh would blaze out against you and soon destroy you.
>
> Deut. 7:2–4

The reason given for God's animosity toward Israel's political enemies is their alleged practice of child sacrifice: "For Yahweh detests . . . and hates what they have done for their gods, even burning their sons and daughters in the fire for their gods" (Deut. 12:31). (In Deuteronomy, Yahweh's attitude toward

sensibilities, but the concept of holy war plays an important part throughout the history of the Near East, from ancient times to the present (Box 5.1).

After the spectacular victory at Jericho, the Israelites suffer a setback at 'Ai (Ch. 7). Inquiring of Yahweh why his people have been ignominiously routed, Joshua is told that Yahweh was not with them because an Israelite soldier violated the ban on Jericho by stealing and hiding some booty. Casting lots, Joshua eliminates all citizens except a man named Achan, who admits having taken some of Jericho's valuables for himself. Achan and his wife, children, and flocks are then stoned to death. After they have purged the sinner from their midst, the Israelites easily succeed in capturing 'Ai (Ch. 8).

The campaign is thereafter an uninterrupted series of Israelite triumphs. All enemies are defeated,

including the Anakim, a race of "giants" (formidable warriors), who had intimidated the Israelite spies forty years earlier (Num. 13:33). Thirty-one kings and their armies are vanquished, although large areas, such as the Philistine territory to the southwest, remain unconquered. Joshua divides the conquered country among the twelve tribes (Josh. 13–22), thus bringing to a satisfactory conclusion the first part of Yahweh's plan for the region.

JOSHUA AND THE HISTORICAL ORIGINS OF ISRAEL

According to Joshua, Israel became a political entity when it militarily conquered the land of Canaan, displacing and slaughtering its former inhabitants. Although the first part of the book depicts Israel's invasion of Canaan as lightning fast and to-

Box 5.1 (continued)

human sacrifice differs from that attributed to him by some other biblical authors. See the discussion of Isaac in the "Genesis" section of Chapter 4.) The inhabitants of towns conquered in geographically distant areas may be spared annihilation if the citizens submit to becoming Israelite slaves, but in nearby Canaanite settlements, Israel's armies must not "spare the life of any living thing" (Deut. 20:10–18).

According to Joshua, Israelite soldiers rigorously enforce Yahweh's "ban" when they capture Jericho, killing "men and women, young and old, even the oxen and sheep and donkeys, massacring them all" (Josh. 6:21). Pursuing a conscious policy of genocide, Joshua's troops treat all Canaanites as condemned criminals, "delivering every single soul over to the ban, as Yahweh the God of Israel had commanded" (Josh. 10:40; cf. Josh. 10:30–33, 39; 11:11–14). Yahweh, in fact, is pictured as inspiring Canaanite leaders to resist Joshua's invasion, "so that they might be mercilessly delivered over to the ban and be wiped out, as Yahweh had ordered Moses" (Josh. 11:20). After the Israelite tribes had formed a monarchy with Saul as king, political enemies placed under the ban continued to be slaughtered as offerings to Yahweh. When Saul spares the life of Agag, king of the neighboring Amalekites, the prophet

Samuel angrily denounces Saul's clemency and personally "butchered Agag before Yahweh at Gilgal" (1 Sam. 15:16–33). The phrase "before Yahweh" indicates that Samuel killed the prisoner of war at a Yahwistic shrine, making Agag a human sacrifice in the divine presence.

Modern readers may find the notion of exterminating entire human populations as blood sacrifices to Israel's God a puzzling contradiction to the Decalogue's prohibition against killing (Exod. 20:13; Deut. 5:17; cf. Gen. 9:5–6). But from the deuteronomic perspective, it apparently seemed the only way to protect Israelites from the snares and temptations of Canaanite religion. Writing from the conviction that Israel's historical failure to serve Yahweh wholeheartedly resulted from the people's attempts to combine the worship of Yahweh with that of the Canaanite Baal, the deuteronomic editors, in retrospect, believed that Israel should have eliminated all temptation from its midst. The possibility that Israel might have approached the problem less violently—by actively seeking to teach its neighbors the ethical superiority of Yahwism—is not entertained.

tally successful, a careful reading of specific passages gives a different impression. Most of Joshua's battle stories deal only with the central hill country, while Chapter 13 concedes that much of Canaan had yet to be captured (13:1–6). Historians believe that the second volume of the Deuteronomistic History, Judges, gives a more accurate picture, noting that long after Joshua's death, most of the Promised Land remained under native Canaanite control (Judg. 1:1–2:23). The Israelites "could not drive out the inhabitants of the [fertile central] plain, because they had iron chariots." The invaders also fail to capture Jerusalem from the Jebusites (Judg. 1:21), nor are their attacks on many other towns and villages successful (Judg. 1:27–35; cf. 2:20–23). To a great extent, the early Israelites lived in close proximity to their Canaanite neighbors, and may have been culturally indistinguishable from them.

For more than a century, archaeologists have performed extensive excavations of biblical sites mentioned in Joshua, such as Jericho, 'Ai, and Hazor. While some sites have yielded evidence that a few towns, such as Debir, Lachish, and Hazor, were attacked and burned in about 1200 B.C.E., thorough examination of other sites, including Jericho and 'Ai, does not confirm the biblical claims. Radiocarbon dating proves that Jericho had been destroyed centuries before Joshua's time and that if any settlement then existed at that location, it was insignificant, a far cry from the massively fortified city that Joshua describes. In Joshua's day, the town of 'Ai had been abandoned for an even longer period; its very name means "ruin."

Instead of finding evidence to support a sweeping conquest of Canaan, as Joshua depicts it, archaeologists have uncovered scores of small, unfortified sites in the hill country, away from the

Box 5.2 Three Models for the Historic Origins of Israel

The disparity between Joshua's account of rapid conquest of Canaan and the archaeological record, which indicates that only a few sites mentioned in the biblical narrative were actually destroyed during the late thirteenth century B.C.E., has led to increasing skepticism about Joshua's historical reliability. Drawing on both the biblical text and the available archaeological evidence, scholars presently offer three competing theories on Israelite origins: the traditional conquest model, the peaceful infiltration model, and the social revolution model. According to the first of these three hypothetical reconstructions of Israel's beginnings, the Exodus–Conquest tradition contains a residue of authentic historical memory. As proof that a band of Israelites *did* invade Canaan, the proponents of this conservative model point to the fact that excavated sites like Hazor and Debir seem to have undergone destruction at the end of the Bronze Age, although admittedly no evidence connects these destructions with the biblical Israelites. They also note that the Merneptah inscription acknowledges that Israel was already present in Canaan by the late thirteenth century B.C.E. and was identified as a people rather than a political state (see Chapter 2). Critics of this model, however, cite the

total absence of archaeological proof that hordes of Israelite slaves escaped from Egypt and subsequently overwhelmed Canaan. Joshua's emphasis on the importance of Jericho and 'Ai, moreover, is contradicted by the thorough excavations done at these sites, which had been abandoned long before the generally accepted dates for the Conquest. In fact, the story of 'Ai's capture looks suspiciously like an etiological narrative designed to explain the meaning and origin of the city's name ("ruin").

Noting the proliferation of small villages and farm communities in Canaan's previously unoccupied hills during the early Iron Age, proponents of the infiltration model argue that these newly established settlements represent Israel's earliest presence in the land. Rather than entering Canaan as violent warriors, these "proto-Israelites" immigrated gradually and peacefully, engaging primarily in pastoral and agricultural occupations. Although some immigrants may have come from Egypt, as a group they readily assimilated Canaanite culture, adopting Canaanite words such as *El* and *Elohim* to denote their Deity. This theory not only explains the enduring popularity of Canaanite gods — Baal and Asherah — among the Israelite masses, it also helps to account for Is-

---

major urban centers, that were established during the thirteenth and twelfth centuries B.C.E., indicating a sudden increase of that region's population (Box 5.2). Although little distinguishes the material remains in this area from the surrounding Canaanite culture, some scholars have proposed that these burgeoning settlements represent the emergence of new inhabitants — the Israelites.

In contrast to the official Exodus–Conquest tradition, which depicts the Israelites as outsiders — an ethnically distinct group of escaped slaves from Egypt — some biblical writers emphasize Israel's Canaanite origins. The prophet Ezekiel (early sixth century B.C.E.) describes his people as multinational foundlings:

> By origin and birth you belong to the land of Canaan. Your father was an Amorite and your mother a Hittite. At birth, the very day you were

> born . . . you were exposed in the open fields . . . you were unloved . . . I [Yahweh] saw you struggling in your blood as I was passing, and I said to you as you lay in your blood: Live, and grow. . . .
>
> Ezek. 16:3–6

In a ritual summation of the Exodus story, Deuteronomy similarly refers to Israel's "father" as a "wandering Aramean [Syrian]" (Deut. 26:5). Numerous other biblical texts cite Israel's close connection with neighboring states in Canaan, portraying Israel and Edom as brothers (cf. Gen. 25 and 26), and Moab and Amon also as blood relations (Gen. 19:30–38). Although none of these variant traditions accords well with the Exodus–Conquest story, many scholars think that these scattered references to Israel's Canaanite roots are historically suggestive.

Box 5.2 *(continued)*

rael's disunity after its settlement in Canaan, as well as its deep distrust toward the monarchy among tribal leaders (cf. 1 Samuel). If the immigrants were largely unrelated, they probably felt no inclination to unite under the leader from a single dominant tribe.

By contrast, the third—"revolutionary"—model assumes that the people who became the Israelites were native Canaanites who rebelled against an exploitative urban elite, overthrowing their former rulers and establishing a more egalitarian society. The rebels were composed of various indigenous Canaanite peoples who shared a common antipathy toward the feudal aristocracy that governed the area during a period of declining Egyptian influence. Some of these Canaanite revolutionaries are allegedly referred to in the Amarna letters as *Hapiru,* whom the Egyptians regarded as bandits (and sometimes employed as mercenaries) (see Chapter 2). It was these rebellious city-dwellers and peasant farmers who attacked several Canaanite cities, such as Hazor, undermining the ruling classes from within as well as without. Like the infiltration model, this theory also has the advantage of offering a plausible explanation for later Israelite dislike of the monarchy: The very idea of kingship was opposed to the revolutionaries' antiaristocratic bias. The social revolt model also explains archaeologists' discovery of the similarity be-

tween Israelite and Canaanite culture, for both groups belonged to the same ethnic category. Additionally, the weakening of Egyptian control over Canaan following the death of Rameses III in the mid-twelfth century B.C.E. would have made it easier for a peasant revolt to succeed, particularly if the catalyst for that uprising was the introduction of a new religious cult, that of Yahweh. The social revolutionary theory, however, fails to explain why successful rebels decided to cast themselves as former Egyptian slaves or why they adopted the worship of Yahweh, a "jealous God," who adamantly refused to share his cult with any Canaanite deity.

None of these three competing theories has won over a majority of scholars, largely because the available evidence is too inconclusive. Even today, we still know little about the ethnic composition and civilization of Canaan's diverse peoples, let alone about the nomadic peoples who wandered in and out of the region. There remains a huge gap between Merneptah's brief reference to Israel in the late thirteenth century B.C.E. and the much later inscriptions alluding to Israel's kings of the ninth century B.C.E. For almost 400 years, the archaeological record is virtually silent, leaving only the biblical text with which to reconstruct tentative theories about Israel's origins.

Some tantalizing clues alluding to the ethnically and religiously mixed nature of the peoples who eventually became known as Israel appear in Joshua 24, which describes the Israelite tribes assembling together at Shechem to renew their covenant vows to Yahweh. A careful reading of this crucial passage indicates that the assembled group consisted of a large variety of peoples with different cultural and religious affiliations. Rather than a single mass of recently liberated Egyptian slaves, the Shechem crowds included peoples of both Mesopotamian and Canaanite origins. Joshua begins his covenant renewal speech, which in style and diction resembles Moses' farewell address in Deuteronomy, by observing that "in ancient days" Israel's ancestors had "served other gods" and then asks his hearers to reject both the ancestral gods of Mesopotamia and the Canaanite deities they

presently worshiped, "the gods of the Amorites in whose land you are *now living*" (24:14–15, emphasis added). When the crowd swears that they will "serve Yahweh, for he is our God," Joshua questions their ability to do so. His audience of mixed ethnic groups has not fully understood the implications of Yahweh's "jealousy": An oath to worship Yahweh means that they cannot also honor Canaanite or other deities, for if they combine Yahwism with Baalism, Yahweh will destroy them (24:19–22). That the assembly of Shechem includes Canaanite groups—people who had not experienced the Exodus or previously been part of the Mosaic arrangement—is strongly indicated when Joshua orders his hearers to "cast away the alien gods among you and give your hearts to Yahweh." Joshua's plea seems incongruous to a people who had journeyed with Yahweh through the

Figure 5.3 Some archaeologists believe that this mono-
lith may be the stone that Joshua erected at Shechem
to hear and bear witness to Yahweh's covenant with
Israel (Josh. 24:26–28). Located forty-one miles
north of Jerusalem between Mount Ebal and Mount
Gerizim, Shechem was an ancient Canaanite sanctuary
that became the first religious center of Israel's tribal
confederacy.

wilderness, but it is understandable when applied
to groups unfamiliar with Yahweh's rigorous demands for exclusive devotion. Not only are the new
recruits to Yahwism "witnesses" against themselves
if they fail to live up to their commitment, a more
enduring "witness" is also invoked, the stone that
Joshua erects to testify "against [them] because it
has heard all the words that Yahweh has spoken"
(24:23–27) (Figure 5.3). Regardless of their ancestral roots, the entire company is henceforth obligated to revere Yahweh alone.

As many commentators have observed, the site
of Joshua's covenant ceremony is significant:
Shechem was an ancient Canaanite cult center of
Baal Berith (Lord of the Covenant); it was also a
site near which Jacob had built an altar to El, the

high God of Canaan with whom Yahweh was
identified (cf. Judg. 9:1–6, 37; 10:47; Gen. 35:1–
15). It thus had important associations with both
indigenous Canaanites and Israel's forebears. The
fact that Joshua shows the Israelites occupying this
area without having to fight for it suggests that the
native inhabitants were well disposed to the new-
comers, apparently ready to merge with them and
accept their God, whom they could envision as another manifestation of El.

In Joshua 22, the conflict between the tribes of
Gad, Reuben, and half of Manasseh, who settle in
territory east of the Jordan River, also indicates
that the people who eventually became Israel consisted of a mixed company, some of whom were
unsure that their membership in the covenant community would be permanently honored (Figure 5.4).
When these eastern tribes crossed Jordan, they set
up an altar to advertise their claim to be part of Israel, an action that would have been unnecessary if
they had been an integral part of the group that left
Egypt (22:1–34). In the opinion of many scholars,
historical Israel encompassed a variety of peoples
who achieved a tenuous unity under the banner
of worshiping Yahweh alone. If the Yahwist
movement was led by former Egyptian slaves, the
Canaanite groups who joined it apparently also
volunteered to make the Exodus story their own,
becoming by adoption children of Abraham and
followers of the Mosaic tradition. In this case, the
Exodus–Conquest story provided a unifying national theme that forcefully expressed a composite
Israel's collective partnership with God.

Although Joshua contains hints that Israel's occupation of Canaan involved both migrants from
Egypt and some elements of the indigenous population, its primary function in the Deuteronomistic History is to emphasize that a covenant people
faithful to their divine warrior will reap the rewards of Yahweh's promises to Abraham. Continued possession of the Promised Land, as Joshua's
final warnings at Shechem make clear, depends entirely on the people's resolve to resist the temptations posed by Baal and Asherah and to honor
Yahweh exclusively. All components of Israel were
to echo Joshua's famous vow: "As for me and my
house, we will serve Yahweh" (24:15).

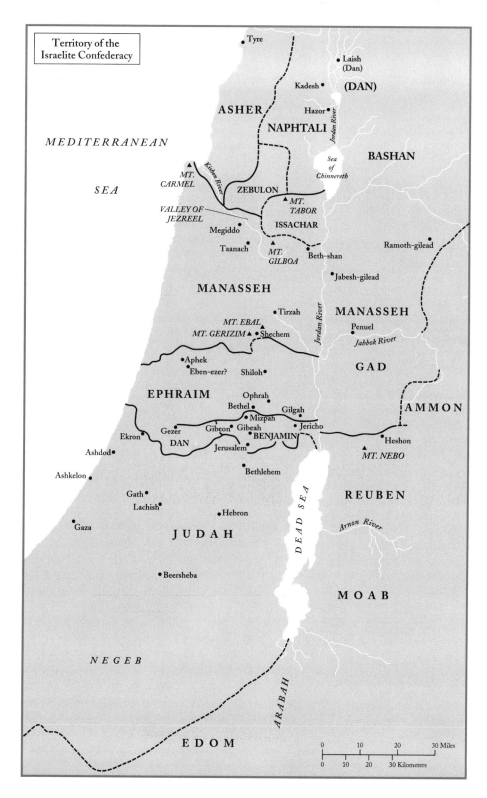

Territory of the
Israelite Confederacy

MEDITERRANEAN

SEA

Tyre

Laish
(Dan)

Kadesh

(DAN)

ASHER

Hazor

NAPHTALI

Jordan River

BASHAN

*Sea
of
Chinnereth*

MT.
CARMEL

Kishon River

ZEBULON

MT.
TABOR

VALLEY OF
JEZREEL

ISSACHAR

Megiddo

MT.
GILBOA

Ramoth-gilead

Taanach

Beth-shan

Jabesh-gilead

MANASSEH

Tirzah

MANASSEH

Jordan River

Penuel

MT. EBAL
MT. GERIZIM

Shechem

Jabbok River

Aphek

Eben-ezer?

Shiloh

GAD

EPHRAIM

Ophrah

Bethel

Gilgah

AMMON

Gezer

Mizpah

Gibeon

Gibeah

Jericho

Ekron

DAN

BENJAMIN

Heshon

Ashdod

Jerusalem

MT. NEBO

Ashkelon

Bethlehem

Gath

DEAD SEA

REUBEN

Lachish

Hebron

Gaza

Arnon River

JUDAH

Beersheba

MOAB

NEGEB

ARABAH

EDOM

0		10		20	30 Miles

0	10	20	30 Kilometers

Figure 5.4 Map of
the Israelite confed-
eracy. Traditionally,
Israelite territory
extended from Dan
(Laish) to Beersheba
in the south.

QUESTIONS FOR REVIEW

1. How does Joshua equate fidelity to Yahweh with military success? In what specific incidents, such as the capture of Jericho or the failed assault on 'Ai, does the book illustrate the Deuteronomic thesis?

2. In Joshua's idealized account of the Israelites' conquest of Canaan, how does Yahweh again function as divine warrior? By the end of Joshua, does Israel have full possession of the Promised Land?

QUESTIONS FOR DISCUSSION AND REFLECTION

1. The biblical writers' attitude toward the native inhabitants of Canaan changes radically between the accounts in Genesis and Joshua. In Genesis, Israel's ancestors mingle peacefully with the Canaanites, buying small parcels of land and entering into agreements with local princes. When Yahweh promises to give the region to Abraham's descendants, he says nothing about their having to engage in a prolonged and violent struggle to possess it. In Deuteronomy and the Deuteronomistic History, however, Yahweh commands that the Israelites annihilate the entire Canaanite population in order to fulfill the divine promise. What reasons do the Deuteronomist and the DH writers give to justify the mass extermination of whole populations?

2. Explain the concept of "holy war" and the practice of placing enemy cities "under the ban." If the entire population of a town, including children, is slaughtered because it is consecrated to the invaders' deity, does this amount to the Israelites' practicing human sacrifice? In what ways does the Bible's endorsement of religiously inspired genocide affect people's thinking today? How does the portrait of Yahweh's dividing humanity into two mutually exclusive groups — the "chosen" and the "condemned" — influence some contemporary ideas about the "saved" and the "damned"?

TERMS AND CONCEPTS TO REMEMBER

'Ai   Jericho
ban   Rahab
Book of Jashar   Shechem
Gilgal

RECOMMENDED READING

Ahlström, Gösta W. *The History of Ancient Palestine.* Minneapolis: Fortress Press, 1993. A comprehensive study of the archaeological record in Canaan.

Boling, Robert G. *Joshua.* Garden City, N.Y.: Doubleday, 1982.

————. "Joshua, Book of." In D. N. Freedman, ed., *The Anchor Bible Dictionary,* Vol. 3, pp. 1002–1015. New York: Doubleday, 1992.

Coote, Robert B. "The Book of Joshua." In *The New Interpreter's Bible,* Vol. 2, pp. 555–719. Nashville: Abingdon Press, 1998. Good analysis of parallel stories of Joshua and Josiah.

Curtis, Andrian H. *Joshua.* Sheffield, England: Sheffield Academic Press, 1994. Brief and balanced evaluation of historical and social issues in Joshua.

Dever, William G. *What Did the Biblical Writers Know and When Did They Know It?: What Archaeology Can Tell About the Reality of Ancient Israel.* Grand Rapids, Mich.: Eerdmans, 2001. Indispensable.

Gottwald, Norman K. *The Tribes of Yahweh: A Sociology of the Religion of Liberated Israel, 1250–1050 B.C.E.* Maryknoll, N.Y.: Orbis Books, 1979.

Redford, Donald B. *Egypt, Canaan, and Israel in Ancient Times.* Princeton, N.J.: Princeton University Press, 1992. Examines the pervasive Egyptian influence in Canaan, which is largely ignored by Bible writers.

Soggin, J. Alberto. *Joshua.* Philadelphia: Westminster Press, 1972.

Judges

KEY TOPICS/THEMES

A transitional book surveying the turbulent period between Joshua's death and the formation of the Israelite monarchy (c. 1200–1020 B.C.E. according to biblical reckoning), Judges is our principal source of information about Israel before it became organized into a national state. This composite narrative, a patchwork of folktales, victory hymns, and battle stories, portrays a weak and disunited people struggling on two fronts: to maintain their precarious toehold in Canaan and to discover their identity as a covenant community. The Deuteronomistic editors arrange their disparate material in a series of biographical sketches of charismatic military leaders, called judges, who sporadically direct a few Israelite tribes against their many enemies.

Because Israel has no central government during this period—and no king other than Yahweh—some of the leaders, such as Deborah and Gideon and his son Abimelech, are implicitly presented, respectively, as possible models to emulate or warnings of tyranny to avoid in the future Israelite state. After two separate introductions revealing how little of the Promised Land Israel as yet possesses and the lethal dangers of assimilation with the native peoples, Judges recounts the exploits of a dozen leaders, the most prominent of whom include Ehud (Ch. 3), Deborah and Barak (Chs. 4–5), Gideon and Abimelech (Chs. 6–9), Jephthah (Ch. 10), and Samson (Chs. 13–16). Concluding with miscellaneous anecdotes not integrated into the main narrative, such as the war against Benjamin (Chs. 19–21), the book presents a complex picture of Israel's premonarchic life.

KEY QUESTIONS

Describe the moral and military challenges Israel's leaders face. What moral and social anarchy leads to the desire for a king?

DRAMATIZING A CYCLIC VIEW OF ISRAEL'S EARLY HISTORY

Combining a wide variety of ancient poems, riddles, battle songs, military annals, and legendary anecdotes, the compilers of Judges create an ambivalent account of Israel's premonarchic period, a distant and perplexing time that was remembered as an era of both unprecedented freedom and frightening insecurity (Box 5.3). Without a king who could unite fiercely independent tribes into an effective army, Israel was forced repeatedly to defend its territorial claims in a series of inconclusive wars against encroaching neighbor states, such as Edom, Moab, and Ammon. Lacking a central sanctuary or a powerfully organized priesthood to enforce a uniformly observed Yahwism, the people, apparently unaware that the Torah (as previously described in the Pentateuch) even existed, tended to supplement the worship of Yahweh with that

of rival gods, particularly the Canaanite Baal. The compilers of Judges impose a theoretical unity on their extremely diverse sources by organizing Israel's premonarchic history into a cyclical pattern. When a judge loyal to Yahweh presides and the people worship Israel's God exclusively, the whole community prospers, winning battles against invading troops and reaping the benefits of their heritage. After the Yahwist judge dies, however, the people soon "prostitute themselves to Baal," arousing Yahweh's anger and causing him to deliver them over to enemy oppression. In their anguish, the people then cry out to Yahweh, who "feels pity" and raises up a new judge to overthrow their oppressors. After a generation of revived Yahwism, the people again backslide, and the whole cycle begins anew. This theory of history, which some scholars believe was applied by Deuteronomistic editors and which others believe already existed in an earlier edition of Judges, is clearly set forth in Judges 2:11–23. This crucial passage ends with a theological explanation of Israel's continuing inability to expel the Canaanites from the region promised to Abraham's descendants:

> Then Yahweh's anger flamed out against Israel, and he said, "Since this people has broken the covenant . . . I will not evict any of the nations that Joshua left in the land . . ."; this was to test them by means of these nations, to see whether Israel would or would not tread the paths of Yahweh as once their ancestors had trodden them.
> Judg. 2:20–22

The term **judge** (*shofet* in Hebrew) does not refer to judicial figures in the legal sense. With the exception of **Deborah**, who dispenses justice under her palm tree, settling her neighbors' disputes (4:4–5), the dozen judges do not preside over a court or usually render verdicts among contending parties. They are charismatic (literally, "spirit-filled") military leaders who spontaneously intervene in major crises, driving off the armies of petty princes engaged in raiding Israel's territory in the Canaanite hill country. Their significance typically derives from their memorable personalities and/or their success on the battlefield.

Box 5.3 Judges' Picture of the Emergence of Yahwism in Canaan

Although the Pentateuch states that *all* the diverse statutes and legal codes contained in the present Torah were revealed during Moses' lifetime, most scholars believe that the Torah is actually a composite body of law that incorporates material derived from many different periods of Israel's history. As the postexilic Book of Ezra suggests, comprehensive editions of the Torah probably did not exist until the Persian era (539–332 B.C.E.), when Persian rulers ordered that Judah's religious leaders produce a definitive version of their legal traditions (Ezra 7:11–26; cf. Neh. 8:1–18).

Editors of the Pentateuch and the Deuteronomistic History, however, present their nation's religious past as if the Israelites had possessed the complete Torah—and therefore knew their God's precise requirements—ever since their wanderings in the Sinai wilderness, making their repeated lapses from Yahwism inexcusable. In the official version of Israel's early history, the people are portrayed as either willfully rebellious or massively indifferent to Torah, even though Joshua 24 states that all the tribes gathered at Shechem had unanimously sworn to abide by "the Book of the Law of God."

In contrast to Joshua, which creates an idealized view of Israel's entry into Canaan, the Book of Judges shows how little of the land the tribes really possessed—and how little they seemed to know

of Yahweh. The narrative preserves brief but important glimpses of Israel's early religious practices, indicating that instead of having been imported complete and ready-made into Canaan, the religion of Yahweh emerged slowly and painfully in a thoroughly Canaanite context. Contrary to the later official record, biblical scholars believe that Yahwism probably evolved in a lengthy and complex process of **syncretism**, the gradual blending together of different religious traditions to create a new religion.

Joshua noted that even after they had supposedly lived for two generations under the Mosaic Covenant, the people still honored Egyptian and Mesopotamian gods (Josh. 24:14). Judges adds that in Canaan, the Israelites worshiped a diverse array of foreign gods: Baal, his female consort Astarte, and deities from almost every neighboring culture, including those of Moab, Ammon, Syria, Phoenicia, and Philistia (10:6). One of Judges' most prominent leaders, Gideon, is also named Jerubbaal, a name extolling Baal's role as his worshiper's defender. After Yahweh appears to him, however, Gideon becomes a convert to Yahwism, tearing down Baal's altar and constructing a new shrine to Yahweh on the spot (6:25–32), an action by which Yahweh not only replaces a rival deity but incorporates his attributes and powers. Foreshadowing this syncretism, Genesis

---

The total number of judges listed is twelve, suggesting to scholars that the book's compilers intended them to represent the whole of Israel's twelve tribes. This literary scheme, however, is undercut by the fact that the judges rarely, if ever, managed to muster more than a few tribes or clans for any enterprise. (Deborah, for example, complains bitterly about the tribes who were conspicuously absent when most needed [5:16–18].) Historically, the judges' individual activities probably overlapped, but the Deuteronomistic History presents them as appearing in chronological sequence in order to make each judge's story provide another example of the sin–punishment–restoration cycle.

About half the judges mentioned are associated with heroic exploits; the others are merely names on the page.

FROM A CYCLIC RETURN TO A DOWNWARD SPIRAL

Although tales about the various judges may seem placed in random order, the narrator subtly arranges his individual stories to illustrate a movement away from the cyclic fall-from-and-return-to divine favor in the first part of the book to a darker, less hopeful presentation of Israel's deteriorating

Box 5.3 *(continued)*

shows Abraham at Salem similarly appropriating the honorific titles of the Canaanite El Elyon (God Most High) for his patron Yahweh (Gen. 14:17–22). At Shechem, the place Joshua chose to ratify Yahweh's covenant, Jacob — progenitor and symbol of Israel — had purchased land and "erected an altar which he called, 'El, God of Israel'" (Gen. 33:18–20). According to Judges 9, a temple to "El-berith [El of the Covenant]" stood there in Abimelech's day (Judg. 9:46); it is the same shrine referred to in Judges 9:4 as the "temple of Baal-berith [Baal of the Covenant]." Yahweh, eventually known as "Lord of the Covenant," is thus preceded by older Canaanite divinities who once held the same title.

As discovered in the archives of Ugarit, an ancient Canaanite city, El, described as the "ancient of days," was the supreme Canaanite god and the father of Baal. Although Bible writers furiously denounce Baal, they never condemn El, undoubtedly because at a very early date El (which is also the generic term for divine being) became identified with Yahweh. As the name *Israel* demonstrates, the covenant people are originally the people of El. (See the section "The Names of Israel's God" in Chapter 3.)

The Judges narrative allows us to perceive Yahweh's cult emerging slowly in life-and-death competition with the cults of Baal and other local deities, but it also preserves an ancient tradition that Yahweh was also somehow associated with Edom (also called

Seir), a nation reputedly descended from Jacob's twin brother Esau (Gen. 36:1). According to the "Song of Deborah and Barak,"

> Yahweh, when you set out from Seir,
> as you trod the land of Edom,
> earth shook, the heavens quaked,
> the clouds dissolved into water.
> The mountains melted before Yahweh,
> before Yahweh, the God of Israel.
>
> Judg. 5:4–5

In this passage, perhaps one of the oldest texts in the Bible, the poet attributes to Yahweh the turbulent qualities of Hadad, a storm god widely known in Mesopotamia and other parts of the ancient Near East. Historically, scholars think that the concept of the biblical Deity developed, at least in part, through the assimilation of traits and functions of older Near Eastern divinities. Recognizing that Yahweh was once one among many competing gods, the author of Psalm 82 shows him standing before members of a heavenly council and condemning his rivals to death. Whereas they failed to protect the poor and defenseless, Yahweh was distinguished by his compassion and justice. Although the Book of Judges shows Yahweh fluctuating repeatedly between his pity for the Israelites and anger at their disloyalty, he ultimately proves to be the sole champion of a weak and vulnerable people.

condition in the book's second half. The transition from anecdotes in which judges bring Israel back to Yahweh to those reflecting a seemingly unstoppable downward spiral is the episode reporting Abimelech's attempt to make himself king at Shechem (Ch. 9). After this cautionary tale of bloody ambition, Israelite leadership seems ever more deeply flawed, with Jephthah, who follows Abimelech, committing human sacrifice and Samson, who never leads even a single clan to fight for Israel, almost totally absorbed in his own erotic pursuits. The DH editors save their worst example of social degradation for the important end position, concluding their review of premonarchic history with an extended tale of gang rape, murder, mutilation, and savage intertribal warfare.

Ehud The narrator begins his survey of prominent judges with **Ehud**, a left-handed Benjaminite who, acting alone, succeeds in murdering Eglon, the king of Moab. In a scene combining carnage with comedy, Ehud — claiming to bear a personal "message from God" for the king — deceives Eglon into granting him a private interview. Unexpectedly drawing his hidden dagger (presumably from his right side, where no one would expect to find it), Ehud plunges the blade into Eglon, who was so obese that the entire blade and hilt disappeared as "the fat closed over the blade." After Ehud escapes through a side window, the king's retainers speculate that their monarch, who has remained unusually quiet in his upper room, must be busy answering the call of nature. Safely returning to his tribe of Ephriam, Ehud then leads a decisive attack against Moab, which, without its military head, is easily defeated, giving Israel "rest for eighty years" (3:12–30).

Deborah and Barak   In the story of Deborah and Barak, a similar act of politically motivated murder is celebrated as an execution of divine judgment. Of all the judges, Deborah is the closest to a figure of conventional religious authority. She functions not only as a judge in the legal sense, regularly arbitrating disputes, but also as a "prophetess" (*isha n'viah* in Hebrew). When **Barak**, the general called upon to fight against Jabin, a local Canaanite prince, wants to know the most propitious time to attack, he must rely on Deborah to set the date, for only she is privy to Yahweh's plans (4:4–16).

Israel's God not only communicates through Deborah, he also employs another woman, **Jael**, who is married to a Kenite, to accomplish what Barak and other male soldiers cannot do. When **Sisera**, Jabin's army commander, flees from Barak and eludes capture, Jael lures him into her tent, where she hides and feeds him. While Sisera, having accepted the sacred protection of hospitality, sleeps, Jael drives a tent peg through the skull of her too-trusting guest. This act of homicidal treachery is hailed throughout Israel, proof that Yahweh could use the most unlikely instrument — a "mere" woman — to bring down his people's enemies. (Emphasizing the humiliation a male warrior would feel at being slain by a woman, the narrator later quotes Abimelech, who lay dying from wounds incurred when a woman standing atop a tower threw a millstone at his head. Abimelech orders his armor-bearer to stab him, "that no one may say of me, 'A woman killed him' " [9:52–54].)

Jael's heroic deed is related twice, first in prose (Judg. 4:17–22) and again in a long poem, the "song of Deborah and Barak," which not only praises Jael as "blessed . . . among women" but

also raises the overthrow of Jabin and Sisera to the level of a cosmic event:

> From high in heaven fought the stars,
> fought from their orbits against Sisera.
> Judg. 5:20

Gideon and Abimelech   One of the more attractive judges, the humble **Gideon** is presented in stark contrast to his son, Abimelech, who is the only leader who proudly aspires to kingship. Exemplifying one of the book's persistent themes — that Yahweh must work with deeply flawed human material — Gideon is depicted as peculiarly unsuited to become Yahweh's chosen deliverer — he comes from a family of devoted Baal worshipers. His given name, Jerubbaal, means "let Baal plead" or "Baal defend him," although the text gives a different interpretation of the name (6:32). When Yahweh's angel (or the God himself) suddenly appears to inform Gideon that "Yahweh is with you, valiant warrior," the devotee of Baal is skeptical: If Yahweh is really on their side, why has Israel been reduced to a state of utter poverty and famine by invading Midianite hordes, who have stripped the country bare, leaving the people nothing to live on? When the divine messenger insists that Gideon is nonetheless Yahweh's choice to rescue Israel from Midianite oppression, Gideon responds in the conventional manner of a prophet resisting his call, calling attention to his insignificance and inadequacy. Only after Yahweh miraculously sets an altar afire does Gideon acknowledge his divine master, erecting an altar to Israel's champion. At the Deity's direction, under cover of darkness he also tears down Baal's local altar, building a shrine to Yahweh on the site, much to the displeasure of his neighbors (6:11–32).

As Gideon, filled with Yahweh's spirit, prepares to make war on the Midianites, his God orders him to reduce the size of his Israelite army from a reported 22,000 to a small band of 300 men. The reason for this drastic cutback, Yahweh explains, is to make sure that the coming victory over Midian is publicly recognized as entirely God's work; otherwise, "Israel might claim the credit for themselves *at my expense*" (7:2, italics added).

Abimelech's Ruinous Experiment   Following Gideon's military successes, the people invite him to be their king, establishing a hereditary monarchy in which his sons would automatically succeed him — an offer he rejects on the grounds that in Israel only Yahweh "must be your lord" (8:22–24; cf. 1 Sam. 8:4–22). Gideon's refusal to assume permanent power because God alone is Israel's true ruler is not merely an act of heroic renunciation but also a paradigm for the Israelite theocracy. When Gideon's son Abimelech later accepts an offer of kingship at Shechem, the ancient Canaanite sanctuary where Joshua had assembled the tribes in a covenant-swearing ceremony, his behavior illustrates the potential evils of monarchy. Beginning his reign by slaughtering his seventy brothers, potential rivals to the throne, Abimelech is soon perceived as an object lesson in tyranny, a threat to Israel's traditional freedoms.

In a dramatic scene, Jotham, Gideon's only surviving legitimate son (Abimelech is the offspring of a slave girl), stands atop Mount Gerizim and declaims a long poem for the citizens of Shechem to hear. An allegory of kingship, Jotham's poem declares that his audience has selected the most unworthy candidate for a king, a "thorn bush" fit only to kindle a fire that will consume them all (9:7–15). As Jotham's poem had foreshadowed, after only three years of Abimelech's despotism, the men of Shechem revolt against him, setting off a fiery chain of events that ends with Shechem's destruction and Abimelech's death (9:22–57). From the narrator's perspective, this abortive experiment with kingship, in which thousands lost their lives, not only demonstrates the pitfalls of royal despotism but also anticipates the violent excesses of some later Israelite kings.

Jephthah and His Unnamed Daughter   Following the account of Abimelech's sorry reign, Judges shows Israel plunging further into a maelstrom of political instability and violence. The son of Gideon and a prostitute whom his father's family has disinherited, **Jephthah** is one of the most morally equivocal judges. Possessed by "the spirit of Yahweh," he vows that if Yahweh will give him victory over the Ammonites, he will sacrifice as a burnt offering the first person he meets after returning home from battle. Ironically, this person turns out to be his virgin daughter, who, "dancing to the sound of timbrels," has come to congratulate him on his triumph. After granting his child an interval to prepare herself, Jephthah, as the narrator laconically phrases it, "treated her as the vow that he had uttered bound him." The writer/editors do not condemn the human sacrifice, but cite the tale as an etiology explaining the ritual custom of Israelite women who annually lament the horrific fate of Jephthah's daughter (11:29–40).

Samson and Delilah   One of the most vividly remembered of Israel's folk heroes, **Samson** — famous for his brawn and his riddles — is strangely unlike any of the other judges whose exploits have been recorded. An angel twice foretells his birth to a childless couple who, as divinely instructed, dedicate the child as a Nazirite. As visible signs of their consecration to Yahweh, **Nazirites** were to abstain from wine and other alcoholic drinks, eat only ritually "clean" foods, and leave their hair uncut. A man of strong passions as well as superhuman physical strength, Samson hardly fits the Nazirite ascetic ideal. His battles with the Philistines are less the result of a divine calling than the often accidental byproduct of his amatory adventures. A seafaring people who then occupied the southwest coast of Canaan, the **Philistines** had already mastered the techniques of manufacturing iron weapons and horse-drawn war chariots, skills the Israelites apparently lacked. In the books of Judges and Samuel, they are the primary threat to Yahweh's people.

Unlike Gideon or Jephthah, Samson does not lead an army against the enemy but fights the Philistines single-handedly, typically for personal reasons involving his relationships with women. Samson's sexual affairs, whether with wife or harlot, repeatedly involve him in dangerous confrontations with the enemy (14:1–15:8; 16:1–3). The hero's most celebrated entanglement is with **Delilah**, whom the Philistines bribe to betray her hitherto invulnerable lover. Breaking his Nazirite vow by revealing the secret of his strength, Samson, shorn of his hair, is abandoned by Yahweh to be captured, blinded, and enslaved. Only when his hair begins to grow again does Yahweh's spirit empower Samson to exact a final revenge on his tormentors. In pulling down the temple of **Dagon**, a Philistine god, upon 3000 of his worshipers, the blinded hero surpasses his previous achievements: "Those he killed at his death outnumbered those he had killed in his life" (Judg. 16:30).

Some critics regard Samson, whose name in Hebrew, *Shimshon,* means "little sun," as a mythological figure whom a Hebrew writer transformed into an Israelite champion. Certainly, if Samson is a historic character, his fellow Israelites do not perceive him as Yahweh's chosen instrument against the Philistines (15:9–20). The Deuteronomistic editor, however, may have regarded him as an example of Yahweh's ability to use even the most unlikely human agents to accomplish his purpose. When Samson crushes thousands of Dagon worshipers, he proves himself, like Jael, an unexpectedly effective dispenser of vengeance on Israel's enemies.

The War Against Benjamin   The Deuteronomistic editors reserved the most barbarous narrative in Judges for the conclusion. Chapters 19–21 describe the rape-murder by the Benjaminites of a Levite priest's concubine, whose body the Levite cuts into eleven pieces and sends to eleven Israelite tribes, asking them to avenge the atrocity by declaring holy war on the Benjaminites. The tribe of **Benjamin** is thereafter almost totally exterminated. Having sworn never to marry their own daughters to any Benjaminite, the other tribes later conspire to get around their vow by encouraging the few surviving men of Benjamin to kidnap the women of **Shiloh**. In this way, the nearly extinct Benjaminites can recruit mates from fellow Israelites without the other tribes' breaking their oaths. Like the story of Abimelech, this episode may serve an antimonarchical purpose, because Israel's first king, Saul, was both a failure and a Benjaminite, the scion of a tainted group.

After describing the social and moral disorders afflicting early Israel, Judges' editor pens a final ambiguous comment: "In those days there was no king in Israel, and every man did as he pleased." Israel's premonarchic experience gave the people little to choose from: Charismatic leaders, no matter how temporarily successful, provided no lasting peace, and Abimelech's failed experiment in kingship boded ill for a future monarchy.

QUESTIONS FOR REVIEW

1. Explain Judges' cyclic view of Israel's premonarchic history. What function does the role of "judges"—military deliverers—play in this cycle? Why do the Israelite tribes repeatedly fall under the domination of neighboring kings and require rescuing from a series of oppressors?

2. How do the careers of individual judges, such as Ehud, Deborah, Barak, Gideon, and Jephthah, illustrate the Deuteronomistic theory? How does Samson differ from the usual kind of "judge"?

3. Explain the significance of women in the Judges narrative, including the tales of Deborah, Jael, and Delilah, as well as unnamed women, such as the defender of her city who crushed Abimelech's skull, Samson's mother, and the Levite concubine who was raped, killed, and dismembered.

QUESTION FOR DISCUSSION AND REFLECTION

What examples of different kinds of political-military leadership do such diverse figures as Deborah, Gideon, Abimelech, and Jephthah represent for Israel? After reading the stories about Abimelech and the tribe of Benjamin (from which Saul, Israel's first king, originated), what attitude toward the institution of monarchy do you think the author-editors of Judges wished to convey? What indications does the book give that Israel eventually will find a just and workable self-government?

TERMS AND CONCEPTS TO REMEMBER

Barak	Gideon
Benjamin	Jael
Dagon	Jephthah
Deborah	judge
Delilah	Nazirites
Ehud	Philistines

Samson   Sisera
Shiloh   syncretism

RECOMMENDED READING

Albright, William F. *Yahweh and the Gods of Canaan: A Historical Analysis of Two Contrasting Faiths.* Garden City, N.Y.: Doubleday/Anchor Books, 1969.

Boling, Robert G. *Judges.* Garden City, N.Y.: Doubleday, 1975.

Cross, Frank M. *Canaanite Myth and Hebrew Epic, Essays in the History of the Religion of Israel.* Cambridge, Mass.: Harvard University Press, 1973.

Fretheim, Terence E. *Deuteronomic History.* Nashville: Abingdon Press, 1983.

Olson, Dennis T. "The Book of Judges." In *The New Interpreter's Bible,* Vol. 2, pp. 723–888. Nashville: Abingdon Press, 1998. Detailed commentary places premonarchical Israel in Canaanite context.

Webb, Barry G. *The Book of Judges: An Integrated Reading.* Sheffield, England: JSOT Press, 1987.

1 Samuel

KEY TOPICS/THEMES

A remarkably vivid theologizing of history, 1 Samuel traces the origin and development of kingship in Israel, presenting the fulfillment of Yahweh's pledge to bring from Abraham a line of kings. Incorporating several different sources, including one favorable to the new institution of monarchy and another strongly opposing it, the first section records the career of Samuel (Chs. 1–12) and the second narrates the rise and tragic fall of Saul, Israel's first king (Chs. 13–31). Priest, prophet, and judge, Samuel functions as Yahweh's kingmaker and king-breaker, initially anointing Saul and, after this first choice proves unsatisfactory, later secretly anointing David, represented as the recipient of God's permanent favor. The book's second half relates Saul's psychological and political decline, to which the account of young David's ascent to power serves as an ironic counterpoint.

KEY QUESTIONS

How does Israel's military weakness trigger the establishment of the Davidic monarchy? How is Samuel a king-maker?

In Hebrew, which was originally written without vowels, the Book of Samuel was contained on a single scroll. When the book was translated into Greek, however, it required two scrolls; the Septuagint translators therefore divided the work into 1 and 2 Samuel. A coherent narrative unit, the two volumes present one overarching theme — the rise of David from obscure shepherd boy to king of "all Israel." As the figure of Moses dominates four books of the Torah, so that of David overshadows this literary account of Israel's political growth from a weak group of loosely confederated tribes to a powerful, united monarchy. David, in fact, is the pivotal character in the Deuteronomistic History: His appearance as Yahweh's divinely appointed ruler occupies the two central books. The first two, Joshua and Judges, act as a prologue to David's story, highlighting the chaotic conditions that prevailed "when there was no king in Israel," before David arrived to rescue the covenant people from their own disorganization. The last two books, 1 and 2 Kings, evaluate the reigns of David's successors, most of whom compare unfavorably to their forefather David, the one Yahweh favors. In vowing to maintain David's heirs on the royal throne forever (2 Sam. 7), Yahweh binds himself to David and his descendants as to no other Israelite constituency, guaranteeing that Davidic hopes are inextricably part of Israel's future history.

A CELEBRATION OF THE DAVIDIC LINE

Problems of Historicity   In recent years, a significant minority of historians has denied any reliability or historicity to the books of Joshua through Kings. Noting a number of inconsistencies and factual errors in the text, they dismiss the entire history as mere fiction, a work compiled late in the postexilic period to create an attractive past for the (then) politically impotent people of Judah. According to this theory, called *minimalist* because its advocates view the biblical story as having almost no historical value, David and his Israelite empire represent wishful thinking, a glamorous but mythical king and kingdom. While acknowledging that the Deuteronomistic author was more concerned with advancing a theological agenda than with dispassionately recording history, the majority of scholars believe that David, Solomon, and their successors were historical personages. Two recent archaeological discoveries, the Tel Dan stele and a stele of the Moabite king Mesha (both ninth century B.C.E.), refer to the "House [Dynasty] of David," providing extrabiblical confirmation that the Davidic line existed. These terse inscriptions, however, do nothing to support the biblical text's grandiose claims about David's political achievements or Solomon's fabled wealth and extensive diplomatic ventures. Archaeological excavations at Jerusalem have uncovered almost nothing from the tenth century B.C.E., when the Davidic kingdom supposedly was at its zenith.

The Nature of Theological Literature

Long before the Greek historian Herodotus compiled his account of the Persian War (c. 450 B.C.E.), as Baruch Halpern has observed, Israelite scribes created masterpieces of historical narrative, albeit highly theologized. (See Halpern, "Recommended Reading.") In parts of Judges, Samuel, and Kings, one finds passages that feature realistic characterization, psychological insight, and a sure grasp of historical cause and effect—particularly the interconnection between human ambition and social and military consequences—unmatched elsewhere in ancient Near Eastern literature.

Scholars have long recognized that the present books of Samuel represent several discrete stages of development, at different times incorporating sources that were originally separate documents. These sources include a narrative about the Ark of the Covenant, including its capture by the Philistines (1 Sam. 4:1–7:1), an account of Saul's abortive kingship (9:1–11:15), the story of David's spectacular early achievements (Chs. 16–31), and a long narrative about the various struggles of David's heirs to take over the throne, a document variously called the **Court History** or Succession Narrative (2 Sam. 9–20 and 1 Kings 1–2). Some critics have argued that much of Samuel was derived from the group that produced the J document, which forms the main narrative flow of the Pentateuch. Certainly, the final version contains poems of great antiquity, such as the Song of Han-

nah (1 Sam. 2:1–10), David's beautiful eulogy for Saul and Jonathan (2 Sam. 1:19–27), David's lament over Abner (2 Sam. 3:33 ff.), and the Hymn of David (2 Sam. 22). Apparently less thoroughly revised to conform to Deuteronomy's principles than Joshua, Judges, or Kings, the books of Samuel nonetheless include some passages interpolated by the Deuteronomistic editors (e.g., 1 Sam. 8, 12). In general, despite their tendency to idealize David and embellish his military and political career, many scholars regard the books of Samuel as marginally more reliable than the more thoroughly edited books of Joshua and Kings. Other historians underscore the inherent unreliability of all theologically oriented texts.

Conflicting Views of the Monarchy

Alert readers will notice that 1 Samuel features two strikingly different attitudes toward the monarchy, one positive and the other decidedly negative. In Chapter 8, the antimonarchical source represents Samuel as declaring that installing a king to reign over Israel is tantamount to rejecting Yahweh's theocratic rule. According to this passage, the establishment of a monarchy stems from the people's failure to trust in Israel's God to govern them either directly or through temporarily appointed deliverers, such as the judges. Samuel then warns the people of all the hardships—taxation, military conscription, tyranny—that await them if they insist on imitating other nations by having a king. Although cast in the form of prophecy, Samuel's warning actually represents Deuteronomistic hindsight, a looking back at the oppressive burden that the expensive splendors of David's royal dynasty imposed on Israel (see Deut. 17). A second version of Samuel's antimonarchical warning (1 Sam. 10:17–27) and a longer Deuteronomistic judgment (1 Sam. 12:1–25) make it clear that Yahweh only reluctantly consents to the people's demand for a king. As if coerced by popular pressure, Yahweh grudgingly permits Samuel to anoint Saul (Chs. 9 and 10), virtually assuring Saul's eventual failure. Only when Yahweh chooses freely does he select a king whom he will consistently support (1 Sam. 16:1–13).

In contrast to these negative views of the monarchy, some passages favorably portray Saul and his early accomplishments, such as the accounts of his anointing and his military victory over the Ammonites (1 Sam. 9:1–10:16; 11:1–15). When Saul has been eliminated and replaced by David, a generally promonarchical view prevails, implying that Yahweh is generally well served by the Davidic rulers (2 Sam. 7). After the negative verdict in 1 Samuel 12, no further criticism of the monarchy *as an institution* occurs in the Deuteronomistic History. Individual kings are condemned, but the legitimacy of the Davidic line itself is henceforth never questioned. Some scholars believe, in fact, that J's stories about sibling rivalry in Genesis were composed to provide ancestral precedents for problems afflicting the Davidic royal family (Box 5.4).

Observing Yahweh's Rule Besides the theme of divine election, the books of Samuel emphasize the absolute necessity of Israel's leaders adhering faithfully to Yahweh's commands. As commentators have pointed out, this theological motif is introduced at the opening of 1 Samuel, when **Hannah** offers her prayer of thanksgiving for Samuel's birth. Declaring that Yahweh exercises total control over human lives, awarding success to the humbly obedient and a catastrophic downfall to the arrogant, Hannah articulates the standard that will determine the fate of Israelite rulers:

> For Yahweh is an all-knowing God
> and his is the weighing of deeds.
> The bow of the mighty is broken
> but the feeble have girded themselves with
>   strength. . . .
> Yahweh makes poor and rich,
> he humbles and also exalts.
>
> 1 Sam. 2:3–4, 7

Supporting the weak and overthrowing the strong who grow proud or oppressive, Yahweh initiates unexpected reversals of fortune among Israel's leadership. In addition to exalting Samuel while removing Eli and his sons from priestly office at Shiloh, Yahweh brings about Saul's ruin even as he raises David from obscurity to unprecedented wealth and power. When David, in turn, grows overconfident and abuses his kingly prerogatives by treacherously arranging for the death of

Uriah, Yahweh punishes his favorite by creating for David the same kind of trouble that the king had inflicted on others (an ironic application of the *lex talionis* principle). Mirror images of their father—ambitious, lustful, opportunistic—David's sons Ammon and Absalom wreak havoc within the royal household. As if reenacting his father's undermining of Saul, Absalom captures the people's affections and temporarily drives David from power, causing him to experience what Saul must have felt when displaced by a younger rival. As Hannah had correctly observed, when dealing with Israel's God, even kings must expect their political ups and downs to correlate precisely with their degree of loyalty to Yahwistic principles.

SAMUEL, SAUL, AND THE PHILISTINE CRISIS

Although named for **Samuel**, the first major character to appear in the book, 1 Samuel is really David's story and that of the monarchy he founded. But there is no servile flattery such as is found in other Near Eastern dynastic histories. The Court History is justly admired for its clear-sighted candor in recording the human weaknesses and flaws of one who was already a national hero. On comparing Samuel's portrait of **David**, with his admixture of courage, ambition, calculation, and religious fervor, to the sanitized version in 1 Chronicles, Samuel's apparent objectivity is immediately obvious.

Despite the diversity of materials it uses, 1 Samuel is a skillfully constructed work of literature, tying together disparate sources with the same theme of divine election that motivates the action in Genesis and Exodus. As Yahweh suddenly, with no reasons given, calls selected individuals like Abraham, Jacob, Joseph, and Moses to perform special tasks, so he chooses Samuel from before birth to serve him. The stories of the principal characters, each of whom is divinely elected in turn, are intricately interwoven. When **Eli**, the well-meaning but ineffectual high priest who acts as Samuel's mentor, declines into impotence, God elevates Samuel to a position of moral leadership, ensuring that the cult rituals centered on the Ark of the Covenant will be properly maintained. As

Box 5.4 Were Tales in Genesis Devised to Support the Davidic Monarchy?

In attempting to date the various documents now incorporated into the Torah, scholars consider such questions as the author's purpose and original audience. Why and for whom specifically did he write? If a case can be made for a particular period or set of circumstances in Israel's history that fits the writer's presumed intent and recipients, this evidence can help pinpoint the probable time of composition. Although many elements in the Torah suggest that it assumed its final form after the Babylonian exile in the sixth century B.C.E., parts of the Genesis narra-

tive seem particularly relevant to the political situation of David and Solomon (tenth century B.C.E.). According to some proponents of this theory, many stories in Genesis function to justify or validate the actions and policies of David, Solomon, and their heirs. If this assumption is correct, some of the tales about Israel's ancestors, paralleling events in the reigns of Davidic rulers, may have been shaped to support the Davidic monarchy long before the Babylonians brought the dynasty to an end (587 B.C.E.).

STORY IN GENESIS	REPORT ABOUT DAVIDIC DYNASTY
1. God promises Abraham that "kings shall come from you" (Gen. 17:6).	1. David establishes a monarchy despite opposition from tribal leaders who insist that only Yahweh is Israel's king (cf. 1 Sam. 8:4–32).
2. Yahweh promises Abraham the region extending from "the river of Egypt to . . . the river Euphrates" (Gen. 15:18).	2. David extends Israel's borders to include the territory promised to Abraham (2 Sam. 8:3; cf. 1 Kings 4:21; 8:65).
3. One of the four rivers of Eden is the Gihon (Gen. 2:13).	3. David captures Jerusalem—a Canaanite stronghold—and centers his capital around the Gihon spring, a water source reminiscent of humanity's original paradise home.

Samuel replaces Eli, so he prepares **Saul**, who first appears in Chapter 8, to take over Israel's rulership. Saul no sooner ascends the throne (Ch. 13) than Samuel breaks with his protégé, becoming his chief critic (Ch. 15). David's appearance on the political stage (Chs. 16–17) introduces a new conflict, the jealous competition between King Saul and his predestined successor—a rivalry that ends with Saul's death (Ch. 31).

The Philistine Crisis   The first seven chapters, describing Samuel's career, also paint a bleak picture of Israel's political and religious situation, which is now even more desperate than that portrayed in Judges. Eli is feeble, and his sons are corrupt; the Philistines inflict a humiliating defeat on the Israelite armies and capture the Ark of the Covenant, the portable shrine on which Yahweh is

invisibly enthroned. Israel's loss of its most sacred possession is a terrible blow to national prestige, but its captors receive no benefits. The Philistines are afflicted with a strange plague of tumors, which they attribute to the Ark's malignant presence. Although a twenty-year peace ensues following the Ark's return to Israel, continued Philistine hostility denies the Hebrews any real security.

Samuel and Saul   Pressured by the Philistines and other aggressors, many Israelites may have doubted their nation's continued existence. Some may have recognized that the old tribal confederacy, which lacked central leadership and was riven by uncooperative individualism, was no match for a tightly organized enemy headed by a warrior-king. With Israel's future uncertain, pragmatic tribal leaders seem to have decided that national

Box 5.4 *(continued)*

4. Abraham pays a tithe to Melchizedek, the Canaanite king-priest of Salem (site of Jerusalem) (Gen. 14:18–24).

5. Genesis emphasizes the close kinship of Israel and its future neighboring states; Jacob's twin brother Esau "is Edom" (36:1); Ammon and Moab are descended from Abraham's nephew Lot (Gen. 19:36–38).

6. Yahweh declares that Esau (Edom) will "serve" Jacob (Israel) (Gen. 25:23).

7. Abraham prepares to sacrifice his son Isaac on Mount Moriah (Gen. 22), considered the future site of Jerusalem.

8. Throughout Genesis, God favors younger sons, preferring Abel to Cain, Jacob to Esau, Joseph to his older brothers, and Ephraim to Manasseh.

9. Judah, eponymous founder of David's tribe, has an affair with Tamar; after she tricks him into admitting his guilt, he is forgiven (Gen. 38).

4. David retains Zadok, high priest of Canaanite Jerusalem, as his high priest; Solomon uses forced labor (a form of taxation) to build Jerusalem Temple (1 Kings 5:13–17; 9:15).

5. David incorporates the states of Edom, Moab, and Ammon into his kingdom, making them part of the Israelite "family" (2 Sam. 8).

6. "All the Edomites became David's servants" (2 Sam. 8:14; cf. 1 Kings 11:14–17).

7. Solomon erects Yahweh's Temple on the traditional site of Isaac's "binding," the only place Israel's required sacrifices to Yahweh are permitted (cf. Deut. 12; 1 Kings 8).

8. God favors David over his older brothers; grants the succession to one of David's youngest sons, Solomon (1 Sam. 16:6–13; 1 Kings 1–2).

9. Judah's royal descendant, David, has an adulterous affair with Bathsheba; after confessing his guilt, he is forgiven (2 Sam. 11–12).

For a more complete discussion of this topic, see Gary A. Rendsburg, "Biblical Literature As Politics: The Case of Genesis." In Adele Berlin, ed., *Religion and Politics in the Ancient Near East*. Bethesda, Md.: University of Maryland Press, 1996, pp. 47–70.

survival required the political unity that only an able king could give. When the elders petition Samuel to appoint a king, however, no higher motive is assigned their request than a conformist desire to "be like the other nations" (1 Sam. 8:19).

Although the Deuteronomistic scribes edited the books of Samuel more lightly than Joshua or Judges, their ambivalence toward the monarchy is evident here. Samuel warns the people that a monarchy will exploit the people economically, including outright confiscation of their best property (1 Sam. 8:10–22). But when the people insist, Samuel privately anoints Saul (c. 1020 B.C.E.), an obscure member of the tribe of Benjamin (1 Sam. 9:14–10:8; cf. the second account of Saul's being chosen king in 1 Sam. 10:17–27).

Many scholars believe that the portrait of Saul that we now find in 1 Samuel is highly biased,

an unflattering revision of an older account of Saul's reign that his supporters composed. Regarding David's heirs as the nation's rightful rulers, pro-Davidic editors later transformed Saul into the neurotic, paranoid failure he had to be in order for David to supplant him. Samuel's original choice of Saul to lead the nation out of its social confusion and military weakness is logical. Tall, handsome, and brave, Saul belonged to a tribe so small and insignificant that his election does not arouse tribal jealousies. The incidents over which Samuel withdraws his support (in David's favor) illustrate, even after editing, how impossible was Saul's historical role. When the prophet-priest fails to appear to offer the sacrifices necessary before going into battle, and when the army is deserting in droves, Saul performs the ritual — only to be denounced as usurping priestly prerogatives (1 Sam. 13:8–15). (Both

David and Solomon later routinely assume priestly duties.) The decisive break occurs when Saul, perhaps feeling pity for a fellow ruler, spares the life of Agag, an **Amalekite** king who has been "put under the ban," designated as a sacrifice to Yahweh. Furious, Samuel proceeds to butcher Agag as an offering to God (1 Sam. 15:10–33). Withdrawing the support of Israel's religious institutions, Samuel not only repudiates Saul but also ensures his political demise. Depicted as suffering from epilepsy and extreme depression, Saul rapidly loses control of events, particularly when the Philistines launch a new attack.

THE RISE OF DAVID

At this critical moment, the narrative's real hero appears, a charismatic youth destined to replace Saul as king and to establish a dynasty that will endure for more than four centuries. The writers' use of multiple sources is apparent in the two different versions of David's introduction to Saul's court. In the first, David is presented as a "brave man and a fighter" who is also a musician, a harpist whom Saul employs to drive out the "evil spirits" with which Yahweh afflicts the king (1 Sam. 16:14–23). In the second, David is introduced as a stranger to Saul (1 Sam. 17:55–56), a mere "lad" who volunteers to fight single-handedly the Philistine champion **Goliath**. Otherwise unarmed, he fells Goliath with a stone from his slingshot (1 Sam. 17:4–54). As a leader who would transform Israel from a faltering confederacy into a powerful, if short-lived, Near Eastern empire, David is credited with legendary feats, some of which may have been accomplished by his associates. An appendix to 2 Samuel states that Goliath was slain by one of David's soldiers: "Elhanan son of Jair from Bethlehem killed Goliath of Gath" (2 Sam. 21:19).

The biblical narrators are concerned less with historical accuracy than with theological significance. As Yahweh's chosen one—Samuel secretly anoints him king even before he joins Saul's retinue (1 Sam. 16:1–13)—David acts as God's representative. When the writers portray him as an inexperienced shepherd boy who overcomes a heavily

armed giant, the purpose is to demonstrate that Yahweh can use weak human vessels to accomplish great deeds. David's speech to Goliath makes clear that defeating an enemy is Yahweh's work, for which no human being can take credit:

> You come against me with sword and spear and javelin, but I come to you in the name of Yahweh. . . . Today Yahweh will deliver you into my hand and I shall kill you . . . so that all the earth may know that there is a God in Israel, and . . . that it is not by sword or by spear that Yahweh gives the victory . . .
>
> 1 Sam. 17:45–47

That David basks in divine favor is also illustrated by the declaration of love that Saul's son **Jonathan** lavishes on the victorious youth. As the king's presumed heir, Jonathan should be David's chief rival, but instead he works to promote David's advancement, stripping off his armor and giving it to his friend—an act that foreshadows David's taking his place as Saul's successor (1 Sam. 18:1–5). Jonathan's sister **Michal** also becomes devoted to David, who, by marrying the king's daughter, further cements his ties to the royal family. If David's conquest of his children does not arouse Saul's suspicions, the song of Israelite women indiscreetly praising David's superiority to the king makes him consider the potential danger to his reign inherent in David's ambitions: "Saul has killed his thousands, and David his tens of thousands." The king determines to eliminate his rival by having him lead assaults on the Philistines (1 Sam. 18).

Blessed with an ability to command personal loyalty, David uses the partisanship of Jonathan and Michal, both of whom prefer to help him rather than their father, to circumvent Saul's attempts to murder him. When forced to flee Israel and take refuge among the Philistines, David even wins the friendship of their ruler, on whom he also practices his abundant powers of deception (1 Sam. 19–23). An outlaw and guerrilla fighter, David survives by his wits, eluding capture and twice refusing to kill Saul when he has the opportunity to do so. His restraint is well paid, for when the Philistines eliminate Saul and Jonathan at the Battle of **Gilboa**, the way is open for David to ascend the throne (1 Sam. 24–31).

2 Samuel

KEY TOPICS/THEMES

2 Samuel describes the long reign of King David, beginning with accounts of his brilliant military victories (Chs. 2–5), centralization of the national religion in his new capital (Ch. 6), and the inauguration of a royal covenant in which Yahweh swears to create a Davidic dynasty that will last forever. An abrupt reversal of his fortunes takes place, however, when David oversteps the ethical limits of kingly power by committing adultery with **Bathsheba**. David compounds his guilt by secretly ordering that Bathsheba's husband, **Uriah**, a Hittite mercenary who has faithfully served his king, be abandoned in the front ranks of battle, ensuring that the enemy will kill him (Chs. 11 and 12). Although Yahweh does not desert him, David's abuse of his position results in dire consequences—treachery and violence in his household (Chs. 13 and 14), and Absalom's rebellion that temporarily drives him from his throne (Chs. 15–20). An appendix of miscellaneous narratives and poetry closes the book (Chs. 21–24).

KEY QUESTIONS

Describe the Davidic Covenant. How do David's sins blight the latter part of his reign?

THE REIGN OF DAVID

Because 1 and 2 Samuel were originally a single volume, there is no true break in the narrative between the two books. 2 Samuel opens with David's receiving news of Saul's death, a scene that sets the tone of David's rise to power and reflects the hero's sometimes ambiguous character. When Saul and his sons—human obstacles to David's career—are eliminated without his having to lift a hand against them, David typically punishes the men responsible for advancing his cause, acquiring a public reputation for piously mourning fallen enemies. By executing the Amalekite who claims to have slain the former king, David not only absolves himself of any responsibility for Saul's death but also proclaims the life of Yahweh's anointed ruler to be sacrosanct—a policy indispensable for protecting his own anointed status (2 Sam. 1:1–16). Acknowledged king of **Judah**, his own tribe, David has yet to become ruler of the northern ten tribes, who accept Saul's son Ishbaal as their rightful monarch. After two Benjaminite chieftains assassinate Ishbaal, bringing his head to David, the Judean king explicitly refers to his treatment of the Amalekite messenger, sentencing his would-be benefactors to death (2 Sam. 4:1–12). Although he owes much of his success to **Joab**, commander of the army, David repeatedly condemns his general for dispatching the king's opponents (2 Sam. 3:22–39), particularly for Joab's removal of David's traitorous son **Absalom** (2 Sam. 18:9–19:9). David's exquisite laments over rivals whom others have swept from his path are justly famous, especially that for Saul and Jonathan, whose love for him had been "more wonderful than the love of a woman" (2 Sam. 1:26).

After Ishbaal's murder, David, who had reigned over Judah at **Hebron** for seven years, is acclaimed king of all twelve tribes (2 Sam. 5:1–5). Freed from pursuing intertribal warfare with the House of Saul, David undertakes military campaigns that eventually expand Israel's borders to the limits promised in the Abrahamic Covenant. One of his first exploits is to capture the Jebusite city of Jerusalem, which Joshua and his successors had been unable to conquer (Judg. 1:21). On the border between the territories of Judah and Benjamin, this ancient Canaanite sanctuary (Gen. 14:18–24) was an ideal administrative site. By bringing the Ark of the Covenant to Jerusalem, David makes his well-fortified capital the religious as well as the political center of the newly united nation (2 Sam. 6).

A shrewd exploiter of the military and executive abilities of loyal followers like Joab, Abishai, and Elhanan (2 Sam. 21:15–22), David quickly routs the Philistines, drives back the Ammonites and

Aramaeans, and reduces neighboring states like Edom, Moab, and Damascus to vassal dependents. At its greatest extent, David's kingdom stretches from the Euphrates River in the northeast to the frontiers of Egypt in the south. (The borders of the Davidic state thus correspond exactly to those Yahweh outlined to Abraham [Gen. 15:18], representing a culmination of the divine promises.) As the books of Samuel present it, a single man—whom Yahweh adopts as his son and whose political success is divinely ordained—rapidly transforms the fortunes of his nation, triggering a cultural revolution that affects almost every aspect of Israelite life. Commercial treaties with **Hiram of Tyre** and other trading peoples stimulate a flow of wealth and cosmopolitan influences into Israel such as it had never known before (Chs. 5 and 8). It is not surprising that in ages to come, when Israel had fallen far short of Davidic splendor, popular memories concerning this "lion of Judah" would shape the people's hopes for a new deliverer like David. Yahweh's Anointed (Messiah)—a term applied to all Davidic rulers—was to resemble David, beloved of God, a conquering hero, a political savior of his people. (See the section "The Messiah: First-Century Expectations" in Chapter 9.)

YAHWEH'S PROMISE TO DAVID AND HIS HEIRS

Davidic Covenant   Dwelling in a palace of cedar, David resolves to build a comparable house for Yahweh, at once honoring the God who had raised him to the pinnacle of earthly success and establishing the national cult under royal jurisdiction. At first, the court prophet **Nathan** agrees because Yahweh has so obviously favored David in his many enterprises. But—perhaps after consulting Israel's conservative elders—Nathan replies that the Deity, accustomed to dwelling in a tent (the wilderness tabernacle) will not be confined to a material shrine. Instead, Yahweh will build David a "house," an "everlasting" dynasty ensuring that heirs of David will remain on Israel's throne in perpetuity.

Yahweh's oath to establish David's royal line forever is *unconditional,* a striking contrast to the terms of the Mosaic Covenant, whose continued validity depends on the people's obedience (Box 5.5). Yahweh vows that although he may chastise Davidic heirs, he will never remove them from power as he had Saul (2 Sam. 7). The Deity's absolute promise to preserve the royal house, and by implication its capital city as well, eventually led to a popular belief in the impregnability of Jerusalem, an assumption later championed by Isaiah (Isa. 28:16; 29:5–8; 30:15; 36–37) and still later violently denounced by Jeremiah (Jer. 7 and 26). After the Babylonians deposed Zedekiah, the last Davidic king, in 587 B.C.E., the David–Zion Covenant was sometimes interpreted as applying to a future "son of David," the **Messiah**, who would restore his predecessor's kingdom. (See Chapter 9.)

David and Bathsheba   The refrain "Wherever David went, Yahweh gave him victory" (2 Sam. 8:7, 14, etc.) accompanies the recital of David's conquests like a leitmotiv. The theme changes abruptly, however, after Chapter 11, when David abuses his kingly authority by having an adulterous affair with the already married Bathsheba. This episode, which forms part of a source document known as the Court History or Succession Narrative (2 Sam. 9–20 and 1 Kings 1 and 2), reveals the fatal flaw that compromises David's relationship with Yahweh. Notable for its candor in depicting the moral errors and psychological weaknesses of a popular leader, the narrative shows David caught in the trap of his own schemes, for once unable to assign blame to others. After learning that Bathsheba is carrying his child, David, to cover his paternity, first tries to cajole Uriah into breaking his soldier's vow of celibacy. When Uriah, perhaps aware of the king's intentions, refuses to sleep with his wife, David contrives to send Uriah into the front lines of battle, where, according to the king's orders, he is betrayed and killed (2 Sam. 11:2–27). In any kingdom other than theocratic Israel, the matter would have ended there; the monarch would have satisfied his lust, and no one would have dared to protest. To the prophet Nathan, however, not even the king is above Yahweh's law. Appearing one day in court, he tells

Box 5.5 Kingship in the Ancient Near East and the Theology of the Davidic Covenant

According to ancient Mesopotamian records, the institution of kingship "descended from heaven" in the remote days before the Flood, permanently establishing the royal dynasties of Mesopotamian cities as extensions of the gods' cosmic domain. In Egypt, where the monarch held absolute power, living pharaohs were thought to be incarnations of the god Horus, a solar divinity who presided over the political and social order. After death, pharaohs were identified with Horus's father, Osiris, the powerful lord and judge of the afterlife. The great pyramids at Giza, dating from about 2500 B.C.E. and the only example of the ancient world's seven wonders to survive relatively intact, were monuments to deceased pharaohs' continuing importance, their triangular forms serving as giant stone ramps from which Pharaoh's soul ascended to the sun or stars. To an incalculable extent, Egyptian religious tradition functioned to validate Pharaoh's supreme power in Egyptian society, over which, alive or dead, he reigned as a god-king.

Although the kings of ancient Israel were never accorded divine status, the theology of kingship expressed in the biblical texts shows that rulers of the Davidic dynasty were believed to enjoy a special relationship with Yahweh, one qualitatively different from that of anyone else in the covenant community. The "royal" psalms, lyrics composed for recitation at ceremonies in which kings were consecrated and enthroned, emphasized the monarch's unique bond with God. On the occasion of his ascension to royal power, the king was reborn, begotten anew as Yahweh's son, allowing him to "proclaim Yahweh's decree; he [God] has told me, 'You are my son, today I have become your father'" (Ps. 2:7). As Yahweh tells David when swearing to establish his royal heirs forever, "I will be a father to him [the king] and he a son to me" (2 Sam. 7:14).

As God's anointed representative on earth, the Davidic king becomes the agent through whom God rules, extending the divine empire over nations that the Israelite army conquers and subjects to royal dominion. "Ask," Yahweh instructs the king, "and I will give you the nations for your heritage, the ends of the earth for your domain" (Ps. 2:8–9). According to Psalm 110, another example derived from the royal coronation liturgy, Yahweh tells the king that he

"will force all your enemies under the sway of your scepter in Zion [the hill upon which Solomon's Temple stood]" (Ps. 110:2). Assuming his role as divine Warrior, Yahweh will fight the king's battles on an unprecedented scale, permitting him to shatter opponents and give "the nations their just deserts, smashing their skulls, he heaps the wide world with corpses" (Ps. 110:5–6).

The special covenant that Yahweh makes exclusively with David and his descendants stands almost completely apart from the concept of the Mosaic Covenant, which involves the entire people of Israel, not merely one privileged family among them. Whereas the Mosaic Covenant is linked to the Exodus, in which God led the people from slavery to freedom, the Davidic covenant promotes a conventional Near Eastern concept of government in which a single man is given the power to oppress or exploit the general population. (Critics of the monarchy's potential for tyrannizing over a previously free society voice their objections to the institution in 1 Samuel 8:10–18.)

Whereas the Mosaic agreement between Yahweh and the people as a whole is conditional upon the people's obedience to his instruction and may be abrogated, the Davidic pact is presented as unconditional and eternal. Through the prophet Nathan, Yahweh unequivocally tells David: "Your house [royal dynasty] and your sovereignty will always stand secure before me and your throne be established forever." Although he reserves the right to punish disobedient kings, Yahweh swears that he will never abandon David's line as he rejected that of Saul (2 Sam. 7:9–16). Instead, Yahweh promises that David's subjects will henceforth enjoy uninterrupted peace, permanently free of the political instability and enemy attacks they suffered during the period of the judges.

As finally edited, the Davidic Covenant strikingly parallels the Genesis pact with Abraham, in which God makes similar unilateral promises — for land, fame, progeny (including a line of kings), blessings, divine presence, and a special relationship (cf. Gen. 12:1–3; 17:1–14). (Scholars believe that the present form of the Abrahamic Covenant, which so closely resembles the Davidic in both content and

(continued)

Box 5.5 *(continued)*

language, was probably composed long after the Israelite monarchy was established.)

The biblical texts reveal considerable tension between the conditional Mosaic pact and Yahweh's absolutely unconditional pledge to David's royal heirs in 2 Samuel 7 and 23:1–7 and in Psalm 89. Following historical developments such as the Davidic kingdom's division into two separate nations, Israel and Judah, in 922 B.C.E. and Babylon's termination of the Davidic monarchy in 587 B.C.E., postexilic Deuteronomistic editors composed revised versions of the Davidic pact to make it conform to the conditional terms of the Mosaic Covenant. Thus, in the current version of the Deuteronomistic History, Solomon is repeatedly reminded that the success of his reign depends upon his obedience to the Torah (1 Kings 2:4; 3:14–15; 6:12–14; 11:30–40; etc.). As the compilers of Deuteronomy had inserted into Moses' speeches a passage insisting that Israel's kings must dutifully uphold Torah principles (Deut. 17:14–20), so the prophet Jeremiah, whose teachings echo deuteronomic ideas, argued that because Judah's kings were guilty of covenant-breaking, Yahweh had abandoned them to Babylonian domination (Jer. 2:2–37; 5:1–25; 11:1–17; etc.). When Nebuchadnezzar, king of Babylon, brought the Davidic dynasty to a permanent end in 587 B.C.E., destroying at one blow Judah's capital, its Temple, and its reputedly "everlasting" line of kings, the Deuteronomists interpreted this national disaster as Yahweh's punishment for the community's faithlessness to the Moses–Sinai agreement. Even after Judah's exiles returned from Babylon following 538 B.C.E., the Judean state did not regain political autonomy, and the Davidic monarchy was never restored.

DH editors revised many passages in the books of Kings to reflect changing historical realities. But they permitted to remain Yahweh's unequivocal oath in 2 Samuel 7 and 23 to support Davidic kingship forever, perhaps because court theologians had already made it so widely known and because a significant portion of the postexilic population apparently expected an eventual reestablishment of the royal house.

The Hebrew Bible thus retains an unresolved conflict between the Mosaic and Davidic traditions. Whereas Jeremiah and the Deuteronomists agree that Judah's destruction resulted from the people's collective failure to adhere to Torah demands, a consequence inherent in the conditional nature of the Mosaic contract, other biblical writers saw the termination of Davidic kings, whose continuing existence Yahweh had unconditionally guaranteed, as the Deity's inexplicable failure to keep his word. In the case of the Davidic pact, it was not the people, but Yahweh who was the lawbreaker.

Meditating on the tragic contrast between Yahweh's saving acts in Israel's distant past and the people's present losses and sufferings, the author of Psalm 89 reviews the specifics of God's promises to David (Ps. 89:19–37), quoting Yahweh's ironclad vow to make the Davidic dynasty as perdurable as the heavens:

> His [David's] dynasty shall last for ever;
> I see his throne like the sun,
> enduring forever like the moon,
> that faithful witness in the sky.
> Ps. 89:36–37

As Jeremiah has prosecuted a covenant lawsuit against disobedient Judah, so the poet boldly accuses God of covenant-breaking:

> And yet you have rejected, disowned,
> and raged at your anointed;
> *you have repudiated the covenant with your servant*
> and flung his crown dishonored to the ground.
> Ps. 89:38–39, italics added

As if to remind Yahweh that he is distinguished from other gods by his "faithfulness" (Ps. 89), the psalmist asks God to recall that he swore his "oath to David on [his] faithfulness" (Ps. 89:49), basing his pledge on the bedrock of his divine justice.

In the absence of Davidic kings, leadership of the postexilic Judean community was largely transferred to priests. Utilizing the former close association of the monarchy and the priestly Temple cult (2 Sam. 6–7; Kings 5–9; Ps. 132), the priestly authors of 1 and 2 Chronicles rewrote the history of the Davidic monarchy, extensively reinterpreting David's role to portray him as the founder of priestly rituals and highlighting his establishment of the Ark of the Covenant in Jerusalem. Although the rebuilt Temple in Jerusalem was no longer a royal shrine as it had been in the days of Solomon, it remained the center of the state religion and provided a visible link with the monarchical past (Hag. 1–2; Zech. 3–4; 1 Chron. 13:15–17, 21–29; 2 Chron. 1–9, 24–28, 34–38).

Box 5.5 *(continued)*

The writers of Chronicles and other postexilic books, such as Ezra and Nehemiah, apparently accepted Yahweh's decision to abrogate his Davidic promises, emphasizing instead the rule of a priestly theocracy. As little Judah was oppressed by a series of Gentile empires—Persian, Greek, and Roman—some members of the covenant community began to reinterpret biblical passages about Davidic rulers in Isaiah (Chs. 7, 9, 11) and Psalms (2, 110, etc.) as prophetic of a future restoration of the royal line. In some cases, these references to ancient kings were applied to hopes for a future leader who would re-institute Davidic sovereignty as a political reality. Conceived as a conquering warrior like David before him, this imagined hero would be, as were all Davidic kings, Yahweh's Messiah (Hebrew, *mashiah,* or "Anointed One"). As Judah's political, social, and economic situation worsened over the years, some segments of Judean society apparently expected a messiah figure who would revitalize Yahweh's people and lead them to triumph over their enemies. Such expectations flourished during the period when the New Testament Gospels were written. (See Chapter 9.)

David of a rich man with many flocks who took the one lamb of a poor man and killed it. Indignant, David denounces the rich villain for his greed and lack of compassion. "You," Nathan answers, "are the man" (2 Sam. 12:1–15).

Perhaps in no other Near Eastern country would Nathan's head have remained on his shoulders after such an accusation. David, however, proves a model of submissive repentance, accepting Yahweh's verdict that the child born of his illicit union with Bathsheba must die. Yahweh's judgment extends far beyond the infant's death, precipitating a series of betrayals and rebellions that reduce David's royal household to a state of moral anarchy.

Having set the example of wrongdoing, David must now endure the consequences, which include incest and murder among his own children. After his firstborn son Amnon rapes his half-sister, **Tamar,** her full-brother Absalom avenges (his) honor by killing the rapist. The assault of brother against brother echoes that of Cain and Abel, as well as the recent fratricidal civil wars that divided the houses of Saul and David (2 Sam. 2–4). When Absalom, whose good looks and gift for attracting followers are a mocking image of the young David, rebels against his father, the aging king is forced to abandon his capital and seek refuge east of the Jordan River. Then Joab, once again coming to his master's rescue, eliminates Absalom. The ostentatious grief that David shows over his traitorous off-spring disgusts the army commander (Ch. 19). These disorders in the kingdom provide an opportunity for some Israelites, unhappy with the rule of a Judean king, to rebel. Although the revolt led by Sheba, a Benjaminite, is short-lived, it foreshadows the deep political discontent that will eventually strip the ten northern tribes from the Davidic monarchy (Ch. 20; see also 1 Kings 12–13).

Appendices   An anthology of supplementary documents that have not been chronologically integrated into the main narrative forms the conclusion of 2 Samuel. The appendices preserve six incidents, of which the most interesting for their theological views are the first and last additions. In the first (2 Sam. 21), a three-year famine, conveniently interpreted as a sign of divine anger against Saul's family, gives David an excuse to eliminate Saul's seven surviving sons, obvious rallying points for future rebellions, whom he delivers to their old enemies the Gibeonites for impalement.

The last supplement (2 Sam. 24) presents Yahweh inciting David to take a census of the people; the Deity then punishes this act by sending a pestilence that kills 70,000 Israelites. (Later biblical historians, apparently noting the moral illogic of such divine capriciousness, revise the story to make "Satan" the instigator of the census, a highly unpopular move because numbering the population was primarily for purposes of taxation and military conscription [see 1 Chron. 21].) On the advice of the prophet **Gad**, David buys a Jebusite threshing floor and erects upon it an altar to Yahweh. Perhaps because it is offered on the site of the future Jerusalem Temple, David's sacrifice halts the Angel of Death in his tracks, thus ending the epidemic. This final narration of David's actions is consistent with 2 Samuel's depiction of his paradoxical character: David is both the cause of his people's troubles and the instrument of its cure.

QUESTIONS FOR REVIEW

1. According to 1 Samuel, what was the national crisis that brought about the formation of the Israelite monarchy? How does the story of the Philistines' capture of the Ark of the Covenant illustrate Israel's dire circumstances?

2. Describe the two opposing views of kingship — positive and negative — in 1 Samuel's account of the monarchy's origin. Be sure to consider Samuel's warnings in Chapter 8. How does Hannah's prayer at the beginning of the book introduce themes involving Yahweh's control of the rise and fall of Israel's leaders? How does Saul's reversal of fortunes demonstrate the validity of Hannah's statements?

3. Describe David's multifaceted character and political career. When David succeeds at everything he undertakes, why do virtually all of his ardent supporters — including his former king, his beloved companion Jonathan, and his most competent general, Joab — end up dead? What qualities in David motivate him to commit the acts that bring about the domestic betrayals, political revolts, and personal losses that characterize his later reign?

4. Explain the terms of the Davidic Covenant (2 Sam. 7). In what ways does Yahweh's special pact with David and the Davidic dynasty (2 Sam. 7) reflect typical Near Eastern beliefs about divinely appointed kings? How did a Davidic ruler become Yahweh's "son"? How does the Davidic Covenant theology influence the concept of a future "anointed one" or Messiah?

QUESTION FOR DISCUSSION AND REFLECTION

Despite his many flaws, David is described as a "man after [Yahweh's] own heart," whom the Deity rewards by making him the agent for fulfilling the Abrahamic promises. In what specific ways does the *unconditional* vow made to David resemble that made to Abraham? How does it stand in tension with the *conditional* nature of the Mosaic Covenant?

TERMS AND CONCEPTS TO REMEMBER

Absalom	Hiram of Tyre
Amalekites	Joab
Bathsheba	Jonathan
Court History	Judah
David	Messiah
Eli	Michal
Gad	Nathan
Gilboa	Samuel
Goliath	Saul
Hannah	Tamar
Hebron	Uriah

RECOMMENDED READING

Brueggemann, Walter. *First and Second Samuel*. Interpretation. Louisville, Ky.: John Knox, 1990. An insightful commentary.

Cross, Frank M., ed. "The Ideologies of Kingship in the Era of the Empire: Conditional Covenant and Eternal Decree." In *Canaanite Myth and Hebrew Epic: Essays in the History of the Religion of Israel*. Cambridge, Mass.: Harvard University Press, 1973.

Dever, William G. *What Did the Biblical Writers Know and When Did They Know It?: What Archaeology Can Tell Us About the Reality of Ancient Israel*. Grand Rapids, Mich.: Eerdmans, 2001. Argues forcefully that the biblical narratives contain at least a nucleus of historical fact.

Friedman, John E. *The Hidden Book in the Bible*. San Francisco: HarperSanFrancisco, 1998. Argues that the Court History, on which much of 2 Samuel is based, was composed by the Yahwist (J) writer, who was also a major source of the Pentateuch.

Gordon, R. P. *1 and 2 Samuel*. Old Testament Guides. Sheffield, England: JSOT Press, 1984.

Gunn, David M., and Fewel, Dana N. *Narrative in the Hebrew Bible*. New York: Oxford University Press, 1993. Includes discussion of the Samuel narratives.

Halpern, Baruch. *The First Historians: The Hebrew Bible and History*. San Francisco: Harper & Row, 1988.

Hertzberg, H. W. *The Books of Samuel*. Translated by J. S. Bowden. Philadelphia: Westminster Press, 1964.

Hillers, Delbert R. *Covenant: The History of a Biblical Idea*. Baltimore: Johns Hopkins University Press, 1969.

McCarter, P. Kyle. *I Samuel*. Garden City, N.Y.: Doubleday, 1980.

———. *II Samuel*. Garden City, N.Y.: Doubleday, 1984.

Miscell, Peter D. *I Samuel: A Literary Reading*. Bloomington: Indiana University Press, 1986.

1 Kings

KEY TOPICS/THEMES

Opening with the death of David and the succession of Solomon, remembered for his wisdom, wealth, and enormous building projects (Chs. 1–10), 1 Kings presents a mixed judgment of Solomon's reign. The narrator attributes the breakup of the kingdom early in the reign of his heir Rehoboam to Solomon's cosmopolitan tolerance of foreign cults (Ch. 11). When Rehoboam foolishly refuses to change Solomon's oppressive policies, the northern ten tribes revolt against the Davidic monarchy. Led by Jeroboam I, the ten tribes establish an independent kingdom of Israel, with its first capital at Shechem (Chs. 12–14). Because the northern kings set up sanctuaries to rival the Jerusalem Temple, the Deuteronomistic account denounces them all for continuing the "sins of Jeroboam" (Chs. 15–16). The bitter contest between King Ahab and Elijah, archetypal prophet of the northern kingdom, concludes the book (Chs. 17–22).

KEY QUESTONS

What factors caused the division of Israel into two separate kingdoms? What single standard does the narrator apply to all rulers of Judah and Israel?

CENTRALIZING YAHWEH'S WORSHIP

Like the books of Samuel, 1 and 2 Kings were originally a single work that the Septuagint translators later divided into two parts. Together these volumes carry the history of Israel from the death of King David to the fall of Jerusalem and the Babylonian captivity (587 B.C.E.). As might be expected, the books are based on a number of older sources, including court archives and traditional material concerning the prophets Elijah and Elisha. The authors frequently refer to several dynastic histories that have since been lost: the Book of the Acts of Solomon (1 Kings 11:41), the Book of the Annals of the Kings of Israel (1 Kings 14:19), and the Book of the Annals of the Kings of Judah

(1 Kings 14:29). These sources were rigorously edited and reshaped to conform to the theological viewpoint of the Deuteronomistic historians, who produced the first version of Kings after Josiah's religious reforms late in the seventh century B.C.E. The first edition of the DH account may have been issued to help justify and support Josiah's policies, which the authors regard as the climactic fulfillment of the Mosaic Torah prescribed in the Book of Deuteronomy. After Babylon's dismantling of the Jewish state, a second edition was prepared for the exiled community in order to explain why Yahweh had permitted Jerusalem's fall and the end of the Davidic royal house.

Drawing material selectively from older court records to illustrate their historical theory, the writer-editors rigidly apply Deuteronomy's standard of obedience to all rulers of Judah and Israel. Authorial judgment focuses almost exclusively on the issue of centralizing Yahweh's worship "only in the place he himself will choose from among all your tribes, to set his name there and give it a home" (Deut. 12:5). Although the place is not specified in Deuteronomy's text, the redactors assume it to be Jerusalem and consequently condemn any ruler who tolerates sacrifices at the "high places," traditionally hilltop sites where Yahweh's rituals had been performed since the days of Abraham and Jacob. Because rulers of the northern kingdom set up rival shrines at Bethel and **Dan**, the Deuteronomistic writers denigrate them all, reserving their approval for a few of Judah's kings, primarily Hezekiah and Josiah, who consistently enforce centralization of the national cult at the Davidic capital.

THE REIGN OF SOLOMON

Given the vast importance that DH accords the Jerusalem **Temple**, it is not surprising that the books of Kings devote more space to describing the reign of Solomon, the Temple's builder, than to any other monarch (Chs. 1–11). 1 Kings opens with an account of King David's last days and the court intrigues, led by prophet Nathan and David's wife Bathsheba, to have her son, **Solomon**, rather than David's oldest son, **Adonijah**, succeed to the throne. (The story of Solomon's succession is probably based on the same Court History that underlies 2 Samuel 9–20.) Even on his deathbed, David behaves like a typical Near Eastern monarch, reminding Solomon that although he has promised to spare surviving enemies who had participated in Absalom's revolt, his successor is bound by no such vow. Taking his father's hint, Solomon begins his administration by murdering not only Adonijah but also David's loyal general Joab and numerous others who might threaten the security of his crown. In a special blessing, Yahweh then grants him "a heart to understand" how to govern (1 Kings 3:4–15), so that he soon earns international fame for the astuteness of his policies.

Israel's Prosperity   Although the final verdict on Solomon's long reign is decidely critical (Ch. 11), most of the narrative expresses strong admiration for his material accomplishments, particularly his wealth and extensive building program. Solomon's largest project is the royal palace, which includes a special mansion for his most important wife, the daughter of an unnamed pharaoh, with whom he concludes a political alliance. Covering 11,250 square feet, the palace is much larger than the Temple (2700 square feet), almost as if the sanctuary (on which the narrative focuses) were a religious extension of the royal power (cf. 1 Kings 6:2 and 7:2). Built to house the Ark of the Covenant, on which Yahweh's "glory" is enshrined, the Temple is a simple rectangular edifice that resembles the floor plan of other sanctuaries that archaeologists have recently excavated in Syria and **Phoenicia** (Figure 5.5). According to 1 Kings 8, Phoenician architects, designers, and artisans played a major role in constructing the Temple. Hiram, a Phoenician king who was one of Solomon's chief partners in a lucrative international trade, supplied both materials and skilled craftsmen. Despite his large income from commercial enterprises and increasingly heavy taxation of Israel's citizens, however, Solomon is eventually forced to cede twenty Galilean towns to Hiram to pay off his debts (9:10–14).

Dedication of the Temple   The first Israelite king to be raised in an urban palace rather than rural villages and pastures, Solomon assumes more of the trappings of royal privilege than his two predecessors. The extent to which royal power had increased since the days of King Saul is evident in Solomon's assumption of priestly duties in dedicating the Jerusalem Temple. Whereas Samuel had publicly withdrawn support from Saul when the king offered sacrifices, in the Temple ceremony Solomon, apparently without opposition, takes over priestly functions, not only consecrating the sanctuary but also making both animal and grain sacrifices (1 Sam. 13:8–15; 1 Kings 8:62–65). In the minds of many Israelites, particularly in the north, the Jerusalem Temple may have seemed too much like a dynastically controlled royal chapel (cf. 1 Kings 12).

In recounting the Temple's consecration, the narrator draws a fine distinction between the older Tabernacle theology and the later deuteronomic concept of Yahweh's connection with the Jerusalem sanctuary. In Exodus, Yahweh appears to take up residence in his tent-shrine, his "glory" encamped among the Israelites (Exod. 40:34–38). In contrast to Exodus's sense of divine immanence—reenforced in 1 Samuel when the young Samuel experiences Yahweh literally standing and speaking to him in the Tabernacle (1 Sam. 3:10)—the DH insists that a transcendent Yahweh places only his "name" in the Temple. Although both the Exodus writer and the Deuteronomistic historian employ the same symbol of divine presence—a "cloud" that envelops both Tabernacle and Temple as a sign of Yahweh's acceptance—the Deuteronomistic author makes clear that no earthly shrine can hold the Deity. The long dedicatory prayer ascribed to Solomon, a thoroughly Deuteronomistic composition, emphasizes that although Yahweh accepts the Temple, in reality "the heavens cannot contain [him]," much less the "house that [Solomon has] built" (1 Kings 8:27). At the very moment that sees the fulfillment of Genesis's promise of the divine presence—or at least Yahweh's "name"—abiding with Israel, the postexilic redactor inserts an ominous reminder that Yahweh's fu-

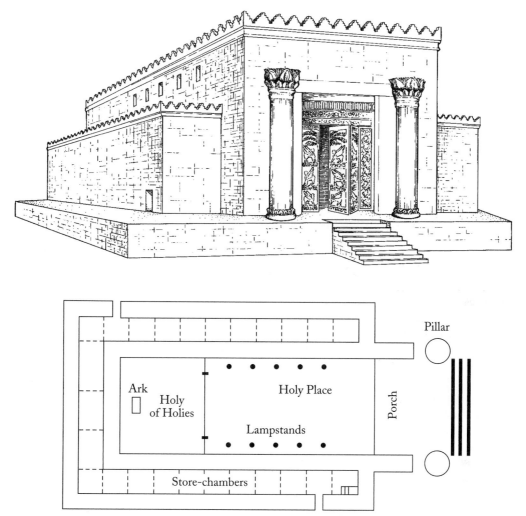

Figure 5.5 This reconstruction of Solomon's Temple shows both the exterior and the floor plan. The Davidic kings and their court theologians insisted that Jerusalem's royal sanctuary was the only place on earth at which Yahweh would accept sacrificial offerings, thus compelling Israelites to travel to the national capital to fulfill their Torah obligations.

ture support depends upon Israel's Torah observance. If Solomon's successors prove disloyal, Yahweh will bring to ruin the "house" he has just consecrated, a warning that had already been fulfilled at the time the book was edited (1 Kings 9:8–9; cf. 25:8–17).

After the generally positive evaluation of Solomon's accomplishments—his unprecedented opulence, fame, wisdom, and diplomatic prowess (Ch. 10), the narrator's final estimate of the king's significance seems almost incongruous. Chapter 11, which marks a change in attitude toward Solomon and severely critizes his taking of foreign wives (he is said to have married 700 princesses and appropriated 300 concubines), was probably interpolated by a postexilic redactor, which sought to find in Solomon's reign causes for the nation's subsequent misfortunes. From the redactor's perspective,

Solomon had compromised his Yahwistic faith by allowing his wives to worship their national gods, even building altars for these deities in the Temple precincts (Ch. 11). Although DH judges Solomon primarily from a religious standpoint, the king's economic policies probably played a more important role in the breakup of Israel that followed his death. Ignoring the old tribal allocations of Israelite territory, Solomon had divided the country into twelve administrative districts, each obligated to provide supplies for the royal court one month of every year. Even more unpopular was Solomon's practice of compelling Israelite citizens to work on his building projects, possibly using forced Israelite labor to construct the Temple (1 Kings 4:7–19; 5:13–18; cf. 9:15–22). In thus portraying the negative aspects of Solomon's administration, the DH implicitly evokes Samuel's impassioned warning about the grave disadvantages of establishing a monarchy (1 Sam. 8; cf. Deut. 17:14–20).

Out of respect for David, Solomon is allowed to die peacefully (922 B.C.E.), but his heirs will lose the largest part of the kingdom. Judah, however, the nucleus of the Davidic realm, is to remain under the rule of his successors "so that David may always have a [land] in [Yahweh's] presence" (1 Kings 11:12–13, 35–36), an assurance repeated when later Judean kings misbehave (1 Kings 15:3–4; 2 Kings 8:18–19). Scribes who produced the second edition of Kings during the Babylonian exile apparently agreed that Judah's Davidic kings, despite their faults, enjoyed an eternal commitment from Yahweh. When they added the tragic history of Josiah's heirs (2 Kings 23:26–25:30), the final editors did not delete the original writer's references to Yahweh's abiding by his promise to David (2 Sam. 7), perhaps because they regarded a restoration of the Davidic line as inevitable. (Figure 5.6 shows a map of the kingdom of David and Solomon.)

THE DIVIDED KINGDOMS

The Great Schism   Rehoboam (922–915 B.C.E.), Solomon's successor, foolishly refuses to lighten the heavy burden of taxes and forced labor that Solomon's building projects have placed on the people (1 Kings 12), and his rejection of the northern tribes' plea for a more humane administration sparks a widespread revolt against the House of David. The ten northern tribes withdraw from the monarchy and form their own kingdom, to be called **Israel**:

> What share have we in David?
> We have no inheritance in the son of Jesse!
> 1 Kings 12:16

Remaining loyal to the Davidic rulers, the southern tribes of Judah and Benjamin form the smaller and poorer kingdom of Judah with its capital at Jerusalem.

Hereafter, Kings will record the history of a divided kingdom, alternately describing reigns in the northern kingdom and then events in Judah (see Table 5.1). This jumping back and forth, coupled with a monotonous emphasis on obedience to the law, makes some of Kings rather turgid reading, although royal conflicts with certain prophets considerably enliven parts of the narrative.

The rebel leader **Jeroboam I,** the first king of northern Israel (c. 922–901 B.C.E.), sets up rival sanctuaries at Bethel and Dan, where he erects two golden calves, probably as pedestals for the invisibly enthroned Yahweh (1 Kings 12–13); indeed, most of the northern monarchs make some effort to follow the Mosaic faith. Whereas the southern nation of Judah, ruled by an unbroken succession of Davidic kings, maintains relative stability, the northern kingdom suffers repeated overthrows of its kings, none of whom is able to establish a dynasty as enduring as David's. Because the history is told from a disapproving southern (Judean) viewpoint, even **Omri** (876–869 B.C.E.), one of Israel's most effective rulers, is accorded only a few lines (1 Kings 16:23–24), although long after his dynasty had fallen the emperors of Assyria still referred to Israel as the "land of Omri."

Elijah and King Ahab (869–850 B.C.E.)   Considerably more space is allotted to the misdeeds of Omri's successor, King **Ahab** (1 Kings 17–22), who is married to the notorious **Jezebel,** daughter of the king of Tyre. Ahab's endorsement of Baal worship brings him into confrontation with the

Figure 5.6 Map of the kingdom of David and Solomon (c. 1000–922 B.C.E.). At its height, the Davidic kingdom incorporated the territories of several neighboring states, including Edom, Moab, and Ammon.

Table 5.1 Events and Rulers in the Divided Kingdom

DATE B.C.E.	MESOPOTAMIA AND EGYPT	ISRAEL	JUDAH	HEBREW PROPHETS
	Twenty-second Dynasty of Egypt (935–725) Pharaoh Shishak invades Palestine (c. 918)	Jeroboam I (922–901)	Rehoboam (922–915) Abijah (915–913) Asa (913–873)	
900		Nadab (901–900) Baasha (900–877) Elah (877–876) Zimri (876) Omri (876–869)	Jehoshaphat (873–849)	
	Shalmaneser III (859–825) of Assyria	Ahab (869–850)		Elijah (Israel)
850		Ahaziah (850–849)	Jehoram (849–842)	
	Battle of Qarqar (853) Hazael of Syria (842–806)	Jehoram (849–842) Jehu's Revolt (842) Jehu (842–815)	Ahaziah (842) Athaliah (842–837) Joash (837–800)	Elisha (Israel)
800		Jehoahaz (815–801) Jehoash (801–786)	Amaziah (800–783)	Amos (Israel)
		Jeroboam II (786–746)	Uzziah (Azariah) (783–742)	Hosea (Israel)
750	Tiglath-pileser of Assyri (745–727)	Zechariah (746–745) Shallum (745) Menahem (745–738)	Jotham (742–735)	
		Pekahiah (738–737)	Ahaz (735–715)	Isaiah (Judah)
	Shalmaneser V (726–722)	Pekah (737–732)		
	Twenty-fourth Egyptian Dynasty (725–709)	Hoshea (732–724)		Micah (Judah)
725		Fall of Israel (722/721)	Hezekiah (715–687)	
	Sargon II of Assyria (721–705) Twenty-fifth Egyptian Dynasty (716–663)			
700	Sennacherib (704–681) Assyrian invasion of Judah (701)			
	Esarhaddon of Assyria (681–669) Ashurbanipal (668–627)		Manasseh (687–642)	
650	Twenty-sixth Egyptian Dynasty (664–525)		Amon (642–640) Josiah (640–609) Deuteronomic reforms (621 and following)	Jeremiah Zephaniah Nahum

Table 5.1 *(continued)*

DATE B.C.E.	MESOPOTAMIA AND EGYPT	ISRAEL	JUDAH	HEBREW PROPHETS
	Fall of Nineveh (612)		Jehoahaz (609)	
	Pharaoh Necho (610–594)		Jehoiakim (609–598/597)	
600	Battle of Carchemish (605)		Jehoiachin (598/597)	
	Growth of Neo-Babylonian Empire under Nebuchadnezzar (605–562)		First Babylonian sack of Jerusalem (598/597)	Habakkuk
			Zedekiah (597–587)	Ezekiel
			Fall of Jerusalem (587)	Jeremiah taken to Egypt
			Babylonian captivity (587–538)	

Source: In general, this table follows the dates derived from W. F. Albright, *Bulletin of the American School of Oriental Research,* no. 100 (December 1945), and adopted by John Bright, *A History of Israel* (Philadelphia: Westminster Press, 1972), pp. 480–481.

most formidable prophet that Israel has yet produced, **Elijah** the Tishbite, who stages a contest between Yahweh and Baal on Mount **Carmel** near the Mediterranean coast (1 Kings 18). Despite their ritual antics, the Canaanite priests fail to arouse Baal to action, but Elijah's God sends fire from heaven, consuming the offered sacrifice. Triumphant, Elijah slaughters the priests of Baal and announces that Yahweh is ending the long drought that has afflicted Israel. (Figure 5.7 shows a map of the kingdoms of Israel and Judah during Elijah's time.)

Driven from his homeland by Jezebel's death threats, the solitary prophet—who believes that he is the only person still faithful to Yahweh—retreats to the desert origin of his faith, Horeb/Sinai. Hidden in the same rocky cleft that had once sheltered Moses, Elijah, too, encounters Yahweh—not in wind, earthquake, fire, or other spectacular phenomena, but in the "sound of a gentle breeze" (19:11–12). Yahweh then commissions Elijah to retrn to the political arena, anointing new leaders who will presumably carry out the divine will more effectively than Ahab: Hazael in Syria, Jehu in Israel, and Elisha in the prophetic realm (19:9–16).

Illustrating the need to replace Ahab, the narrative shifts to describe the king's unjust prosecution of **Naboth**, whose vineyards he covets. Following Jezebel's counsel, Ahab abuses provisions of the Mosaic Law by bribing witnesses falsely to accuse

Naboth of blasphemy, for which he is stoned and his property forfeited to the crown (Ch. 21). When Elijah denounces the king's sin, Ahab repents, causing Yahweh to delay his punishment, though shortly afterward the king is killed at the Battle of Ramoth-gilead (Ch. 22). Not only does Elijah survive his royal prosecutors, whose deaths he helps to hasten, but he soon receives the most spectacular validation of any Israelite prophet—a public ascent to heaven (2 Kings 2:1–12).

2 Kings

KEY TOPICS/THEMES

Although 2 Kings originally ended with a celebration of King Josiah's religious reforms, the book was revised to its present form to explain not only why Yahweh permitted the northern kingdom of Israel to suffer annihilation (721 B.C.E.) but also why he consigned Judah to the same fate (587 B.C.E.). By amassing detailed examples of Israelite and Judean rulers' covenant-breaking, the Deuteronomistic authors prepare readers for the final catastrophe. The opening narratives review events in the northern kingdom following Ahab's death, which plunges the nation into turmoil and weakness, conditions abetted by Elisha's prophetic backing of Jehu's fanatical Yahwism and slaughter

Figure 5.7 Map of
the kingdoms of Israel
and Judah in Elijah's
time (c. 860 B.C.E.)

The Kingdoms of Israel and Judah in
Elijah's Time (c. 860 B.C.E.)

Kingdom of Israel

Kingdom of Judah

of all Ahab's descendants (Chs. 1–10). The second part interweaves the reigns of Israelite and Judean monarchs with the rule of Queen Athaliah in Judah (c. 842–837 B.C.E.) briefly interrupting the Davidic line (Chs. 11–16). After succinctly describing the Assyrian conquest of Israel and the origin of the hated Samaritans (Ch. 17), the account focuses on the last days of Judah, giving qualified approval to the policies of Hezekiah (Chs. 18–20) and denouncing those of Manasseh, whose religious practices and detente with Assyria are blamed for Judah's collapse (Ch. 21). Josiah's hopeful reforms (Chs. 22–23) merely delay Yahweh's punishment of the nation for Manasseh's disloyalty. After Babylon has reduced Judah to the status of a vassal, Zedekiah, the last Davidic king, rashly rebels, inciting Nebuchadnezzar to destroy Jerusalem and raze Solomon's Temple (Chs. 24–25).

KEY QUESTIONS

According to the narrator, what caused the destruction of Israel and Judah? Why did Josiah's reforms not save the covenant people?

THE FALL OF ISRAEL

Elisha and Jehu   The history of Israelite and Judean rulers continues uninterrupted in 2 Kings. After reporting the death of Ahab's son Ahaziah in Chapter 1, the historian returns in Chapters 2–8 to the Elijah–Elisha prophetic cycle. When Elijah, the archetypal man of God, is carried to heaven in a fiery chariot and whirlwind, he leaves his prophetic cloak behind for his disciple **Elisha**, whose reported miracles are even more numerous and spectacular than those of his predecessor. In the course of his career, Elisha causes an iron ax head to float on water, a child to rise from the dead, jars of oil to fill magically, poisoned soup to become edible, twenty barley loaves to feed 100 men, and lepers to be cleansed; he also foretells droughts, famines, victories, and deaths.

The prophet's political influence is equally impressive. Through a messenger, Elisha secretly anoints **Jehu**, a former captain of Ahab's guard,

king of Israel. Jehu, supported by the army, plunges the nation into a bloodbath (2 Kings 9–10). Citing Elijah's curse on Ahab's house, Jehu massacres all of Ahab's surviving sons, grandsons, friends, priests, administrators, and political supporters, totally annihilating his dynasty. With **Jehonadab**, a Yahwist fanatic, Jehu then assembles all Baal worshipers in the great temple that Ahab had built in Samaria, the capital city, and after offering sacrifice to Baal, orders eighty trusted executioners to butcher everyone inside. The temple is demolished and its site turned into a public latrine.

For all his savage zeal, however, even Jehu does not entirely win the Deuteronomists' approval. In neglecting to remove Jeroboam's **golden calves** from Bethel and Dan, he did not serve Yahweh wholeheartedly (Figure 5.8). Nor was Jehu an effective king: His purges and massacres may have pleased some Yahwists, but he so depleted the nation's supply of trained and competent leaders that Israel rapidly lost territory on every side. When Jehu (842–815 B.C.E.) died after a reign of twenty-eight years (of which only the violent first year is described in Kings), he left Israel politically weak, without allies, and considerably smaller in size than it had been under Omri and Ahab (2 Kings 10:32–35).

Jehu's ultimate status is indicated on the Black Obelisk, a stone monument that pictures him — or his representative — groveling before his Assyrian overlord (Figure 5.9). A roughly contemporary inscription on the Moabite Stone records that after having been conquered by Omri, Moab broke free of Israel's "oppression," a national liberation achieved by the power of Chemosh, the Moabite god (Box 5.6).

A Queen Rules Judah   An indirect result of Jehu's massacre of Israelite and Judean royalty was the establishment of a queen on the Judean throne, her reign the only interruption of the Davidic line in its entire history. A daughter of Omri (or perhaps of Ahab and Jezebel), **Athaliah** (842–837 B.C.E.) was the wife of Jehoram, king of Judah. Their son was King Ahaziah. When Jehu murdered this king in 842 B.C.E., Athaliah seized control of Judah. Following Jehu's example, Queen Athaliah ordered

Figure 5.8 Hadad, Syrian god of storm, strides atop a bull in this basaltic stele. Grasping lightning bolts in each hand, Hadad invisibly rides an animal symbolizing power and terror. Because Canaanite artists commonly show El, father of the gods, also standing on a bull, many scholars believe that the notorious "golden calf" that Moses' brother Aaron manufactured and the two calf sculptures that Jeroboam set up in Israel were not intended as rivals to Yahweh, but only as pedestals on which the Deity could be invisibly enthroned (Exod. 32:1–35; 2 Kings 12:26–33).

the execution of all of Ahaziah's sons, rival heirs to the crown. Only one prince escaped when the chief priest, Jehoiada, secretly hid Ahaziah's infant son, Jehoash (Joash), in the Jerusalem Temple.

After Athaliah had reigned successfully for six years, the priest Jehoiada masterminded a palace revolt, in which Athaliah was murdered and the seven-year-old Jehoash placed on the throne. According to the DH, Jehoash's long reign (837–800 B.C.E.) was "pleasing" to Yahweh. Instructed by Jehoiada, Jehoash lavished Judah's resources on the Temple's care and upkeep (2 Kings 11–12).

Assyria and Judah   Although the northern kingdom enjoyed renewed prosperity under such kings as **Jeroboam II** (786–746 B.C.E.), revolution and violent changes of rulership continued to undermine Israelite strength. At the same time, a new threat appeared: After centuries of relative inactivity, **Assyria** was once again on the march, swallowing up kingdoms and peoples as it expanded. Assyria's territorial encroachments and increasing demands for tribute culminated in the siege of Samaria, which fell to **Sargon II** in 721 B.C.E. Because it was Assyria's policy to deport defeated populations to discourage future rebellions, the ten northern tribes were forcibly relocated elsewhere in the Assyrian empire, and new people were moved into Israelite territory.

Chapter 17 describes a plague of lions that afflicted the resettled foreigners until a priest of Yahweh was brought back from exile to teach them the proper ritual to pacify the god of the land. This passage is intended to explain how the northern Israelites came to be "lost tribes"; its biased account of the origin of the **Samaritans,** an ethnically mixed group that practiced a form of the Jewish religion, is of doubtful historical value. Despised by the "true" Jews of Judah, the Samaritans were uncharitably regarded as foreign corrupters of the faith — a hostility still current in New Testament

Figure 5.9 A witness to the Assyrian Empire's once irresistible might, the Black Obelisk of Shalmaneser III (859–825 B.C.E.) pictures representatives from five different regions — including King Jehu of Israel — bringing tribute to the Assyrian king. After Assyria destroyed the northern kingdom of Israel (721 B.C.E.), Judah maintained a precarious existence by stripping the Temple of its treasures to keep Assyrian armies at bay (2 Kings 18:13–16).

times, when Jesus probably shocked his Jewish audience by making a Samaritan the moral hero of a famous parable.

JUDAH ALONE

Assyria and Hezekiah Chapters 18–21 provide contrasting portraits of two very different Judean kings: **Hezekiah**, who receives praise for his adherence to the Mosaic Covenant, and his son **Manasseh**, whose fascination with foreign religions irrevocably angers Yahweh and dooms the nation. Hezekiah (715–687 B.C.E.) receives unstinting praise for abolishing the "high places," hilltop shrines where Yahweh was worshiped (possibly along with the Canaanite goddess Asherah), strongly enforcing the centralization of Yahweh's cult in Jerusalem. Besides smashing the poles and sacred pillars — symbols of the tree of life associated with Asherah — Hezekiah also destroyed the bronze serpent (called Nehushtan) that Moses had fashioned in the desert to cure people bitten by poisonous snakes (Num. 21:9). As a symbol of healing, the bronze image had become an object of veneration and hence a threat to Yahwist purity. No icon or relic, even one associated with God's spokesman Moses, could be permitted to deflect worship from Yahweh alone.

Although the Deuteronomistic scribes compare Hezekiah to David in adhering strictly to Yahwism and keeping Torah commands (2 Kings 18:3–8), the writers' attitude toward his reign as a whole is somewhat ambivalent. The text states that Yahweh made the king "successful in all he undertook" and notes with apparent approval Hezekiah's rebellion against Judah's Assyrian oppressors. At the same time, Hezekiah's "success" clearly is perilously close to failure: His refusal to pay Assyria tribute causes **Sennacherib** (704–681 B.C.E.) to invade Judah,

Box 5.6 The Moabite Stone

Discovered in 1868, this flat basaltic slab is important because the message with which it is inscribed demonstrates that Israel's neighbors had developed a theology of history virtually identical to that promulgated in the books of Joshua through 2 Kings. The Deuteronomistic historians interpreted Israel's political and military fortunes according to their degree of obedience to the Mosaic Torah (Deut. 28). Ascribing all national defeats to Yahweh's anger, the Deuteronomists believed that Yahweh used foreign armies to punish Israel's religious disloyalties. As the Moabite Stone reveals, the same theological view of events prevailed in **Moab**, Israel's close neighbor and traditional enemy. According to the inscription, Mesha, king of Moab (middle to late ninth century B.C.E.) attributed his country's invasion and occupation by Israelite troops to the wrath of **Chemosh**, the Moabite national god (Figure 5.10). Moab's successful rebellion and liberation from Israelite domination is regarded as the result of Chemosh's blessing of his people. Ironically, Moab's ability to break away from Israel was the result of a Yahwist revival led by Jehu, who usurped the Israelite throne, slaughtered all male members of the previous royal family, and conducted a bloody purge of Baal's adherents (cf. 2 Kings 3:4–27; 9:1–10:32). Jehu's fanatical policies irreparably weakened Israel, permitting formerly

subject nations like Moab to regain their independence. Israel's decline under Jehu is also reflected on an Assyrian monument, the Black Obelisk, which shows the Yahwist king groveling before the emperor **Shalmaneser III**, to whom he was forced to pay tribute (Figure 5.11).

Figure 5.10 *The enormously important Moabite Stone, found in 1868, records the victories of Mesha, king of Moab, over the northern state of Israel (ninth century* B.C.E.*). Grateful to Chemosh, the Moabite national god, for liberating him from the Israelite domination imposed by Omri and Ahab, Mesha articulates a Canaanite mirror image of the Deuteronomistic philosophy of history: "As for Omri, king of Israel, he humbled Moab many years, for Chemosh was angry at his land. And his son followed him and he also said, 'I will humble Moab.' In my time he spoke (thus), but I have triumphed over him and over his house, while Israel hath perished for ever!"*

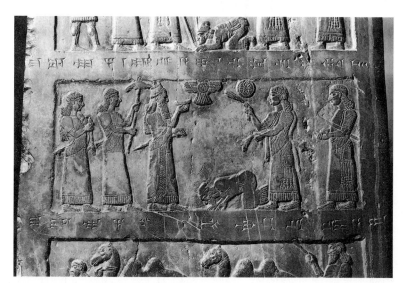

Figure 5.11 This panel of the Black Obelisk shows Jehu, king of Israel, groveling before the Assyrian emperor Shalmaneser III, to whom he pays tribute. The Deuteronomistic writers describe Jehu's revolt against Ahab's dynasty (842 B.C.E.) as a Yahwist-inspired movement (2 Kings 9:1–10:36). However, as a result of Jehu's butchery of Israel's former ruling class, the nation was fatally weakened and eventually destroyed. Ironically, the Black Obelisk identifies Jehu as "son of Omri," founder of the royal line that the Yahwist usurper exterminated.

capture most of its important cities, and levy a ruinously heavy fine on the nation. Hezekiah is forced to strip Yahweh's Temple of its decorations and treasure, paying Sennacherib enormous sums of silver and gold, and then to submit again to the Assyrian yoke. Although Isaiah's confidence that Jerusalem will not be conquered is vindicated by the event, Hezekiah ends his long reign impoverished and ruling over only a tiny scrap of his former domain.

Jerusalem's Deliverance Assyrian and biblical records concerning Sennacherib's invasion of Judah in 701 B.C.E. differ strikingly. Although some historians suggest that the two accounts may refer to two different invasions, most believe that the discrepancies result from fundamental differences between Assyrian and Israelite perspectives. According to Sennacherib's boast, his troops sealed Hezekiah within Jerusalem "like a bird in a cage," but he says nothing about why he failed to take the city. In 2 Kings and a parallel account in Isaiah 36–37, Jerusalem's survival is attributed to divine intervention: In a single night, Yahweh's Angel of Death strikes down 185,000 Assyrian soldiers, forcing Sennacherib to lift his siege and return to Nineveh. The biblical version has some confirmation from nonbiblical sources, including the Greek

historian Herodotus, but the exact cause of the Assyrian retreat and Jerusalem's deliverance is not clear. The holy city's unexpected escape from the Assyrian threat contributed to a popular idea that Jerusalem, site of Yahweh's Temple, would never fall into enemy hands—a view that the prophet Jeremiah would later vigorously attack (Jer. 7, 26).

Chapter 20 relates an incident that evidently took place before Sennacherib's invasion, when Hezekiah still possessed great wealth. Apparently trying to recruit Babylon as an ally against Assyria, Hezekiah foolishly takes the Babylonian ambassador on a tour of his richly furnished palace and overflowing treasury, displaying all of Judah's resources to the foreigner's gaze. Appalled at the king's action, Isaiah then prophesies that the country's entire treasure will be swept away to Babylon—a direct reference to Nebuchadnezzar's sacking of Jerusalem more than a century later. Probably added to the text during the exile, this passage depicts a morally ambivalent Hezekiah. When Isaiah informs him that the disaster still lies in the future, the king finds the news "reassuring" because he will enjoy "peace and security" during his own lifetime (2 Kings 20:12–19).

Manasseh's Reign The Deuteronomistic writers credit Hezekiah's son Manasseh with every Torah violation ever practiced by any king of Israel or Judah, including rampant Baalism, black magic, and human sacrifice. Promoting a syncretism abhorrent to Judah's prophets, Manasseh (687–642 B.C.E.) erects a "carved image of Asherah," perhaps conceived as a female consort to Yahweh, in the Jerusalem Temple. Accused of worse crimes than those perpetrated by the Canaanites whom Israel had driven from the land, Manasseh nonetheless reigned for almost half a century, longer than any other Davidic ruler.

Manasseh's Conversion   The Book of Chronicles, written more than two centuries after the Deuteronomistic History, adds a surprising conclusion to Manasseh's story, one not even hinted at in 2 Kings. According to 2 Chronicles, Manasseh was taken captive to Babylon, where he underwent a sudden conversion to Yahwism, repenting of his former misdeeds. Moved by his prayer, Yahweh permitted Manasseh's restoration to Judah's throne, after which the humbled and penitent king conducted a thoroughgoing religious reform anticipating that of **Josiah**. (The Chronicler cites the "Annals of Hozai" as the source of this remarkable tale [2 Chron. 33:11–20].) If the Deuteronomistic editors knew about a tradition in which Manasseh had been transformed into an ardent Yahwist reformer, they did not use it. In the Deuteronomistic scheme, there is no place for a repentant Manasseh: The sorcerer-king is singled out as the primary cause of Judah's demise, and his character is allowed no redeeming qualities (2 Kings 21:10–17; 23:26–27).

JOSIAH: THE DEUTERONOMISTIC HERO

King Josiah   With the ascension of Josiah, Manasseh's grandson, Judah entered a new era in the development of Yahwistic faith. Reviving the policies of his ancestor Hezekiah, Josiah (640–609 B.C.E.) fulfills both the letter and the spirit of Deuteronomy's commands—to honor one God and sacrifice to him at one sanctuary only. Although its legal core was probably composed in the northern kingdom several generations earlier, the Book of

Deuteronomy became Josiah's chief instrument in revitalizing Judah's national religion. Found during Temple repairs—renovations that probably involved removing Manasseh's Baalistic shrines and images—Deuteronomy brought the Mosaic tradition to general public notice, perhaps for the first time in Israel's history. The writer indicates that both king and people were unfamiliar with the laws and curses of the Mosaic legacy and notes that holding Passover ceremonies, so important in the Exodus account, was regarded as an innovation. No Passover celebration like Josiah's enactment of Deuteronomy's command had ever been observed "throughout the entire period of the kings of Israel and the kings of Judah" (2 Kings 23:21–23).

Taking advantage of Assyria's rapid decline in the late seventh century B.C.E., Josiah extends his reforms and political influence into the former northern kingdom, demolishing altars and desecrating tombs throughout the countryside. His renewal campaign is cut short, however, when Egypt's pharaoh **Necho** invades the area on his way to aid the last remnant of Assyrian power in northern Syria. Whereas Necho wanted a weakened Assyria to survive as a buffer state between Egypt and the newly revived empire of Babylon, Josiah may have hoped to rid Judah of all foreign occupation or, failing that, to support Babylon against Assyria. Attempting to intercept Necho's army, Josiah is killed at the Battle of Megiddo, thus bringing his deuteronomic reforms to a premature end and leaving Judah in the hands of weak or incompetent successors.

Theology and History   The Deuteronomistic theory of history equates Torah obedience with success and disloyalty with destruction. Yet, Manasseh, Judah's least faithful king, reigned longer than any other Davidic monarch and died peacefully in his palace bed. Conversely, Josiah, hailed as a ruler unprecedented in Yahwistic devotion, was cut down as a relatively young man while trying to defend his country—even though Yahweh's prophet Huldah had foretold that he would go to his grave "in peace" (cf. 2 Kings 22:20; 23:29–30). Despite the awkwardness of historical facts that would not fit into the deuteronomic framework, even the final edition of Israel's history adhered firmly to Deuteronomy's simple formula of retributive justice.

THE LAST DAYS OF JUDAH

In 612 B.C.E., Nineveh, Assyria's hated capital, falls to the combined forces of the Medes and Babylonians. Although Pharaoh Necho rushes into the power vacuum that Assyria's collapse created in the Near East, the Egyptians are soon defeated by Nebuchadnezzar, king of Babylon, at the Battle of **Carchemish** (605 B.C.E.). The tiny state of Judah must next submit to the Babylonian yoke; its last kings are merely tribute-paying vassals of **Nebuchadnezzar**, who is now master of the Near East.

Josiah's son **Jehoiakim** (609–598 B.C.E.), whom Nebuchadnezzar placed on Judah's throne, unwisely rebels but dies before the Babylonians can capture Jerusalem, leaving his son and successor, **Jehoiachin**, to suffer the consequences of the revolt. In 598/597 B.C.E., Jehoiachin and his family are taken as prisoners to Babylon, the Temple is stripped of its treasures, and 10,000 members of Judah's upper classes are deported to Mesopotamia (2 Kings 24). Nebuchadnezzar then appoints Jehoiachin's uncle **Zedekiah** (597–587 B.C.E.) king in his place.

When Zedekiah, too, rebels against Babylon, Nebuchadnezzar captures and destroys the holy city and its Temple. The Babylonians demolish the city walls, loot and burn surrounding villages, and carry off most of the remaining population, leaving only the poorest citizens behind. Nebuchadnezzar appoints Gedaliah governor of the ruined city, but even this token of survival is lost when Gedaliah is assassinated by fanatical Jewish nationalists. Fearing Babylonian retaliation, many of the peasant survivors flee to Egypt.

A NATIONAL CRISIS: QUESTIONING THE DEUTERONOMIC ASSUMPTIONS

The flight of Jerusalem's inhabitants to Egypt brings the story of Israel full cycle, back to conditions under which their pre-Mosaic ancestors had lived, strangers in a foreign land. Seeking to find moral sense in the national catastrophe, the Deuteronomistic historians blamed the victims: The covenant community deserved to suffer because it had broken faith with Yahweh. Apostate rulers like Manasseh had led the way, but the people themselves were so deeply ingrained with guilt that a righteous Deity could not refrain from punishing them. Prophetic witnesses to the disaster who were also influenced by the deuteronomic view of history, such as Jeremiah, similarly attributed Judah's demise to its failure to keep the Mosaic Torah.

Not all Bible writers agreed with this view, however, and some were tormented by what seemed to be Yahweh's failure to keep his word. The author of Psalm 44 contrasts ancestral traditions about God's saving acts in the remote past with the Deity's present abandonment of his people:

> You let us go to the slaughterhouse like sheep,
> you scatter us among the nations;
> you sell your people for next to nothing,
> and make no profit from the bargain.

Contrary to the deuteronomic thesis, the writer declares that his community had not violated its Torah obligations:

> All this happened to us though we had not forgotten you,
> though we had not been disloyal to your covenant;
> though our hearts had not turned away,
> though our steps had not left your path;
> yet you crushed us in the place where the jackals live,
> and threw the shadow of death over us.
>
> Ps. 44:17–19

It is, the psalmist reminds God, "for *his* sake we are being massacred daily," suffering precisely because they have put their trust in Yahweh as savior (Ps. 44:11–22, italics added).

Another psalmist directly charges Yahweh with violating his oath to David, in which he swore "I will not break my covenant, . . . I have sworn on my holiness, once for all, and cannot turn liar to David":

And yet you have rejected, disowned
and raged at your anointed;
you have repudiated the covenant with your
    servant
and flung his crown dishonored to the ground.
Ps. 89:38–39

Although the annihilation of the Davidic dynasty, never again restored to Judah's throne, brought into question the trustworthiness of the Deity's promises, the Jewish community in exile did not abandon Yahweh. Without land, kings, sacrifices, or temple, anonymous editors in Babylon—striving to understand their God's intentions—reworked ancient legal and prophetic traditions to produce the epic of Israel's creation and fall, Genesis through 2 Kings. Deuteronomistic writers found one single tangible hope: King Jehoiachin's release from prison (2 Kings 25:27–30), although this apparent harbinger of Davidic restoration was doomed to disappointment.

As presented in Genesis through 2 Kings, the totality of Israel's history is profoundly ironic. Israel's story begins with Abraham, a native of Ur in Mesopotamia, who receives Yahweh's promise that his descendants will possess land, multitudinous progeny, nationhood, and royal leaders. The long historical narrative ends with Abraham's last anointed descendant, King Jehoiachin, a deposed monarch without a country, the prisoner of a Mesopotamian ruler (cf. Gen. 11:28–12:3 and 2 Kings 25:27–30). (For a list of Babylonian kings and the Persian emperors who reigned over Yahweh's people after the exile, see Table 5.2. For a discussion of the postexilic community and the "disappearance of God," see Box 5.7.)

Despite this tragic loss, Israel's political failure was to become a new beginning. A few prophets in exile, such as the great poet known as Second Isaiah, proclaimed that Yahweh would lead a new exodus back to the Promised Land. More than a millennium after Abraham's journey from Mesopotamia to Canaan, a small group of his chastened descendants would retrace his steps to Jerusalem, bringing with them copies of their nation's history and the words of the prophets, which comprise the next section of the Hebrew Bible.

QUESTIONS FOR REVIEW

1. Define the theory of history given in the Book of Deuteronomy. How is this theory used to explain the rise and fall of Israel as presented in the books of Joshua through Kings? Why do scholars call this long narrative from the conquest of Canaan to the fall of Judah the Deuteronomistic History?

2. Describe the covenant-renewal ceremony in Joshua 24; how does this scene illustrate the deuteronomic requirement of total obedience to covenant laws? What choices are the Israelites—and readers—asked to make, and how do Israel's choices ultimately determine its historical fate?

3. In what ways did the Davidic Covenant theology influence the narrative in 1 and 2 Kings about David's royal descendants, such as Solomon, Hezekiah, Manasseh, and Josiah?

4. From the Deuteronomistic History's standpoint, what were the major events and achievements of Solomon's reign? Why did the Davidic empire split into two separate kingdoms after Solomon's death?

5. Why does the Deuteronomistic author approve of *no* ruler in the northern kingdom of Israel? When and how did the northern ten-tribe state come to an end?

6. In the story of Israel's developing religion, why is Josiah's reign considered so important? What were the nature of Josiah's religious reforms? What book, found during Temple repairs, influenced the direction of Josiah's policies? What did it prescribe?

QUESTIONS FOR DISCUSSION AND REFLECTION

1. The Deuteronomistic History (Joshua through 2 Kings) is a theologically oriented account of Israel's historical development as a nation, showing the fulfillment of Yahweh's ancient promises to Israel's ancestors for descendants, land, divine presence, and kings. According to the DH redactors, why did Yahweh ultimately strip Israel of all its promised blessings? Which Davidic ruler is particularly blamed for inciting Yahweh to abandon his people?

2. Considering that Josiah is credited with being the most faithful of all Davidic kings, why does Yahweh allow him to be killed by an Egyptian pharaoh? How do the contrasting reigns of Manasseh and Josiah fail to support the deuteronomic thesis that

Table 5.2 Neo-Babylonian and Persian Empires

DATE B.C.E.	EVENTS IN BABYLON OR PERSIA	EVENTS IN JUDAH
625	Nabopolassar of Babylon (626–605)	
600	Nebuchadnezzar creates New Babylonian Empire (605–562)	First captivity of Jerusalem (598/597)
		Ezekiel prophesies in Babylon
	Nebuchadnezzar conquers Judah (587)	Fall of Jerusalem and deportation of Jews (587)
	Amel-Marduk (562–560)	
	Neriglissar (560–556)	Exile
550	Nabonidus (556–539)	
	Cyrus (550–530) captures Babylon (539); founding of Persian Empire	Second Isaiah in Babylon
		Cyrus's edict freeing Jews (538)
		Jewish remnant returns to Judah
		Zerubbabel, governor of Judah
	Cambyses (530–522) extends Persian Empire to include Egypt	Haggai and Zechariah
	Darius I (522–486)	Temple rebuilt (520–515)
500		
	Persia invades Greece; defeated at Marathon (490)	Joel
	Xerxes I (486–465); second Persian invasion of Greece (480–479)	Malachi
	Artaxerxes I (465–424)	
450		
425	Xerxes II (423)	Nehemiah comes to Jerusalem (445)
	Darius II (423–404)	
400	Artaxerxes II (404–358)	Ezra's reforms; final (?) edition of Torah promulgated
350	Artaxerxes III (358–338)	
	Arses (338–336)	
	Darius III (336–331)	
	Alexander the Great of Macedonia (336–323); conquers Persia, Egypt, Mesopotamia, western India, etc.; begins Hellenistic period	

Box 5.7 Loss, Exile, and the Disappearance of God

With Babylon's destruction of the Judean state, national religious center, and Davidic monarchy, the nature of Israel's relationship with Yahweh changes decisively. As Jerusalem and Solomon's Temple went up in flames in 587 B.C.E., it looked as if all of Yahweh's promises to Israel's ancestors — for countless descendants, land, the divine presence, blessings, and covenant — had been voided. According to the prophet Ezekiel, the divine presence, which had accompanied the Israelites on their journey through the Sinai wilderness and their conquest of Canaan and which subsequently had been housed in the Temple, deserted Jerusalem even before Nebuchadnezzar's armies invaded the holy city. Illustrating Yahweh's break with the covenant community, Ezekiel reports a vision in which Yahweh's "glory [*kavod*]" rises from its customary position between the golden cherubs in the Temple's innermost sanctuary and flies out of Jerusalem via the east gate (Ezek. 10). Abandoning the place where he swore his name would "dwell forever," Yahweh leaves his people to deal with the crisis of his absence.

The theme of God's disappearance from the earthly scene is sounded as early as the last book of the Torah. Near the close of Deuteronomy, Yahweh informs Moses that at some time in the future, he will withdraw his presence: "I shall hide my face from them, and see what becomes of them" (Deut. 32:20). Following Jerusalem's fall, the permanent overthrow of the Davidic monarchy, and the Babylonian exile, Yahweh becomes progressively more hidden. Whereas God appears frequently during the formative stages of Israel's development — to Abraham, Jacob, Moses, Joshua, and crowds of Israelites at Sinai — in the biblical accounts of postexilic Israel, the Deity makes no more theophanies. Although a few prophets or sages experience visions of Yahweh's celestial throne (Job 1–2; Zeph. 3; Dan. 7), shortly after the exile Israelite prophecy ceases and God no longer visibly manifests himself or speaks directly to chosen individuals. In the words of the Psalms, God too often seems "asleep," strangely indifferent to his people's needs. The people's experience of Yahweh's great saving acts belong to the distant past, not to their present circumstances (Ps. 89).

When biblical writers resume their accounts of Israel's story after the exile, they depict a mundane era in which Yahweh no longer communicates through prophets or appears in fire and cloud to rescue his people. When the Jerusalem Temple is rebuilt and rededicated about 515 B.C.E., Yahweh does not descend in a radiant cloud to sanctify it as he had

covenant-keeping leads to success and covenant-breaking to disaster? What questions about divine justice does the national catastrophe of 587 B.C.E. raise? How would you resolve the apparent discrepancy between biblical theory and historical fact?

TERMS AND CONCEPTS TO REMEMBER

Adonijah	Chemosh	Israel	Nebuchadnezzar
Ahab	Dan	Jehoiachin	Necho
Assyria	Elijah	Jehoiakim	Omri
Athaliah	Elisha	Jehonadab	Phoenicia
Carchemish	golden calf	Jehoshaphat	Rehoboam
Carmel	Hezekiah	Jehu	Samaritans
		Jeroboam I	Sargon II
		Jeroboam II	Sennacherib
		Jezebel	Shalmaneser III
		Josiah	Solomon
		Manasseh	Temple
		Moab	Zedekiah
		Naboth	

Box 5.7 *(continued)*

when Solomon inaugurated the first Temple. Although Second Isaiah predicted a spectacular manifestation of divine power when the Judeans were released from Babylon, symbolized by a leveling of mountains and valleys to provide an unobstructed highway back to Jerusalem (Isa. 40), the historical reality was painfully different: an exhausting and dusty trek back to a bleak and ruined city. When the postexilic Book of Esther tells how the covenant community, scattered abroad in the Persian Empire, had to fight for its very existence, its narrator includes no story of miraculous plagues or other divine intervention to help the people. In Esther, the Judeans must defend themselves, and God is not even mentioned in the text.

As Mircea Eliade, a historian of religion, has pointed out, in cultures throughout the world, traditions about the gods' appearances almost invariably belong to the remote past, to a sacred era when the divine and human were more closely associated than they are in later history. The biblical theme of God's gradual disappearance from the world stage is thus consistent with developments in other global religions. The contrast between Israel's two exoduses — the first from Egypt and the second from Babylon — illustrates this change. When Yahweh delivers his people from Egyptian bondage, an event that was already a distant memory when the Yahwist author

first wrote of it, he publicly displays his fearful power through a series of miracles, restaging his primal victory over chaos by dividing the great sea. By contrast, the "second exodus," the people's return from Babylon, is accomplished through purely human agency. Instead of the Deity rescuing his people with "signs and wonders," Cyrus of Persia, following his general policy of supporting local cults in his empire, releases the Judean captives and sponsors the reconstruction of their Jerusalem shrine. Although the later biblical narratives, such as Ezra-Nehemiah, show normal historical processes replacing supernatural interventions, the covenant community retained its faith that Yahweh continued to control historical events, although now acting invisibly behind the scenes (see Chapter 7).

For individual members of the covenant group, Yahweh's refusal to manifest himself as he had to Abraham or Moses must have been problematic. Struggling to cope with the Deity's continuing silence, to find meaning in the prevalence of injustice and undeserved suffering, Yahweh's people are compelled to explore the universal human predicament of relating to an increasingly hidden God. (See Friedman in "Recommended Reading.")

RECOMMENDED READING

Cross, Frank M., ed. "The Themes of the Book of Kings and the Structure of the Deuteronomic History." In *Canaanite Myth and Hebrew Epic: Essays in the History and the Religion of Israel,* Chap. 10. Cambridge, Mass.: Harvard University Press, 1973.

Friedman, Richard Elliot. *The Hidden Face of God.* San Francisco: HarperSanFrancisco, 1995. Insightfully traces the phenomenon of God's progressive disappearance from the biblical text.

Gray, John. *1 and 2 Kings,* 2nd ed. Old Testament Library. Philadelphia: Westminster Press, 1970.

Long, Burke O. *1 Kings.* Grand Rapids, Mich.: Eerdmans, 1984.

Seow, Choon-Leong. "The First and Second Books of Kings." In *The New Interpreter's Bible,* Vol. 3, pp. 3–296. Nashville: Abingdon Press, 1999. Provides extensive commentary.

CHAPTER 6

The Prophets (Nevi'im) II
Collections Attributed to Individual Prophets

Key Topics/Themes

The second subunit of the Prophets (*Nevi'im*) contains anthologies of oracles (oral pronouncements believed to be divinely inspired) compiled in the names of fifteen different prophets. Although Israelite prophecy began before the time of King Saul (eleventh century B.C.E.), it was not until the mid-eighth century that disciples began the process of assembling oracles under the individual prophets' names and preserving them in written form. Spanning a period of more than three hundred years (roughly mid-eighth to late fifth centuries B.C.E.), the canonical prophetic books largely serve to reveal Yahweh's will during periods of social or political crisis, when first Assyria and then Babylon threatened to destroy the covenant community. The prophetic messages typically involve (1) warnings that foreign invasions and plagues are divine punishments for covenant-breaking and social injustice; (2) appeals to avoid national catastrophes by "returning" to Yahweh; and (3) visions of a distant future in which Yahweh reigns supreme from a splendidly restored Jerusalem. The

last prophets whose messages received canonical status were active a few generations after the return from the Babylonian exile, but editorial additions and revisions of virtually all the prophetic books continued well into the last centuries B.C.E.

KEY QUESTIONS

Describe the ethical and political issues to which Israel's prophets addressed their oracles. What series of historical events triggered the most intense periods of prophetic activity? At what audiences were the prophetic oracles mostly aimed?

Spokespersons for God

Whereas some postexilic biblical writers perceived Yahweh as absent, "hidden" (Ps. 89:46), or "asleep" (Ps. 44:23) during critical periods of Israel's history, the prophets (*nevi'im*) intensely felt his presence, which they communicated through **oracles**, pronouncements revealing the divine will or purpose. Israelite prophets, such as Nathan, Gad, Ahijah, Micaiah, Elijah, and Elisha, appeared prominently in the historical books of Samuel and Kings. But it was not until about 750 B.C.E. that a prophet's disciples began the practice of collecting and writing down their master's oracles under the individual prophet's name. Although emphasizing ethical and religious issues, the prophets also played leading roles in Israel's political affairs, intervening in dynastic disputes (1 Kings 1:11–53) or helping to elevate or overthrow kings (1 Sam. 8:10–10:27; 13:8–15; 15:10–35; 16:1–13; 1 Kings 11:26–39; 2 Kings 9:1–13). Some prophets were associated with religious shrines like Shiloh or Bethel, but most clustered at royal courts, where they offered counsel or criticism to kings like David, Solomon, Jehu, and Ahab. As a national influence, prophecy's rise and decline corresponded almost exactly to that of the Davidic monarchy. Flourishing from the tenth to the sixth centuries B.C.E., Hebrew prophecy almost disappeared shortly after the end of the Babylonian exile (c. fifth century B.C.E.). Its function of providing guidance during national emergencies was eventually taken over by priests, scribal interpreters of the Torah, and sages, professional teachers of wisdom (Box 6.1).

The Hebrew word for prophet, **navi (nabi)**, means "one who is called" or "one who announces." (The plural form is *nevi'im*.) Its Greek equivalent, *prophetes*, from which our English word is derived, means "a person speaking for God," one chosen to proclaim Yahweh's message, and includes both men and women.

To understand the nature and purpose of Israel's prophets, it is helpful to review what little is known about their historical development. In Deuteronomy 18 (which scholars believe was compiled in the seventh century B.C.E. when the *nevi'im* had already arisen in Israel), Moses is shown describing the prophetic office. The prophet is to function as a link between the people and Yahweh, who employs the prophet to convey Yahweh's "words" (oracles). The *navi* is specifically said to be Israel's means of ascertaining the divine will—in direct contrast to the Canaanite practice of seeking supernatural help by consulting sorcerers, soothsay-

ers, or spirit mediums who "call up the dead," religious figures to whom some Israelites apparently were attracted (Deut. 18:9–12). Yahweh sends Israel the *nevi'im*, whose messages have the force of divine commands. Anyone ignoring the prophetic word and attempting to communicate directly with the unseen world—a practice the Torah labels a Canaanite "abomination"—risked death by stoning or fire (Lev. 20:27; Exod. 22:18).

Among the earliest Hebrew prophets were those called "ecstatic"—individuals who, seemingly possessed by Yahweh's spirit, worked themselves into a religious frenzy, threw themselves writhing upon the ground, and uttered unintelligible sounds. As with the later Orphic and Dionysic cults in ancient Greece, such emotional seizures were induced through orgiastic music or dance (1 Sam. 10:5–6; 2 Kings 3:15). According to 1 Samuel 10, Saul was seized by Yahweh's spirit shortly after the prophet Samuel had anointed him king. Joining a prophetic band that played "harp, tambourine, flute, and lyre," Saul is thrown "into an ecstasy" and "changed into another man," temporarily losing his individual identity. A later account of the incident adds details associated with the primitive ecstatic experience: Saul stripped off his clothes, fell into a trance, and "lay there naked all that day and night" (1 Sam. 19:18–24).

Even in later Israel, prophets were noted for their bizarre, even grotesque, behavior. Isaiah, naked except for a loincloth, paraded through Jerusalem's streets to illustrate the city's imminent humiliation and ruin. Jeremiah wore a yoke first of wood and then of iron, symbolic of bearing the Babylonian oppression (Jer. 27). Ezekiel carried the prophets' symbolic acts to an even greater extreme, cooking his food over a fire of human excrement (Ezek. 4:12–15), refusing to mourn for his dead wife (Ezek. 24:15–27), and lying bound like a prisoner for 190 days on one side and then 40 days on the other (Ezek. 4:4–8). By dramatizing their messages through strange, even outrageous, conduct, the prophets publicly acted out their visions. Long before their oracles were written down, the *nevi'im* made prophecy *dramatic performance*—vivid displays of ecstatic passion that could not fail to attract onlookers' attention.

Box 6.1 Ancient Near Eastern Prophecy and Typical Prophetic Themes

As a global phenomenon recognized in many ancient cultures, prophecy functions to connect the human community with its gods, permitting worshipers to discern the divine will, particularly at times of social or political crisis. The prophet, inspired by his patron deity's spirit, serves as a link between the human and the divine, mediating a deity's intentions to reward, punish, or rescue his or her mortal subjects.

THE PROPHETIC TRADITION

In the ancient Near East, the activity of prophets commonly centered around a royal court or particular religious shrines, as it did in Israel and Judah. An inscription from Aram (Syria), one of Israel's close neighbors, reports that Zakkur, king of Hamath and Luash (c. 800 B.C.E.), appealed to his god Baal while enemy armies were besieging his city. Zakkur states that "I lifted up my hands to Baal . . . and Baal . . . answered me [and spoke] to me by means of visionaries . . . and Baal . . . [said] to me, 'Fear not, for I have made you king [and I will] stay with you and rescue you.'" As in the case of biblical prophets, the petitioned deity responds through "visionaries" who communicate his message, which is not unlike the divine reassurances given to some Davidic kings.

In Ammon, another small state bordering Israel, archaeologists found a plaster inscription (c. 700 B.C.E.) referring to Balaam, son of Beor, a "visionary of the gods," whose night visions evoked a group of numinous figures. This may allude to the same prophetic figure described in Numbers 22–24, where Balaam, son of Beor, "the man with far-seeing eyes, . . . who hears the word of God [and] . . . sees what Shaddai makes him see" is compelled by Yahweh to deliver a blessing upon Israel (Num. 24).

Using Balaam as an example of a foreign prophet under Yahweh's control, Torah editors apparently retrojected this figure from the late eighth century B.C.E. to the time of Moses, including his story as part of Israel's wilderness journey that traditionally took place centuries earlier.

Biblical texts use the same word, *navi,* for Phoenician prophets of Baal that they do for Israelite prophets. According to an Egyptian source, when a dignitary named Wen-Amun visited the Phoenician city of Byblos (after which the Bible is named) about 1090 B.C.E., the attendant of a Phoenician prince fell into ecstasy and prophesied, authenticating Wen-Amun's mission for Amun, a solar deity. Prophetic activity is also documented from the archives at such Mesopotamian cities as Uruk and Mari.

PROPHETIC THEMES

Israelite prophets, at least those whose oral pronouncements were included in the biblical canon, share several distinctive themes. Perhaps the most dominant is their vision of a righteous God who demands that his people worship him exclusively. Unlike the ancient world's other gods, Yahweh is "jealous," refusing to tolerate Israel's attentions to any rival deity. An ineffable being, Yahweh cannot be represented by any material image, so persons or nations who attempt to picture divinity in human or other form are inherently wrong, guilty of idolatry. Adamantly denying that idols — statues or other physical representations of divine beings — can be a legitimate focus of devotion, Israelite prophets categorically denounce them all.

The prophets also characteristically link Yahweh's exclusive worship with ethical behavior toward fellow Israelites. Amos, Hosea, and Isaiah of Jeru-

According to 1 Samuel 9, Israel's early prophets were called **seers**. The old term is appropriate, for Yahweh was believed to grant seers special insight into a given situation, permitting them to apprehend spiritual realities not accessible to others. Seers and prophets (the terms are *almost* interchangeable) traditionally received Yahweh's oracles

through dreams and visions (Num. 12:6). Some of the early prophets belonged to schools or brotherhoods called "sons of the prophets." Elijah and Elisha apparently were leaders of such guilds at Bethel, Jericho, and Gilgal (2 Kings 2:3–4; 4:38), though they were not permanently attached to a particular cultic center.

Box 6.1 *(continued)*

salem insist that Yahweh demands social justice: Israel's God is the champion of society's poor, powerless, and vulnerable. Whereas the preexilic prophets rarely cite Mosaic tradition to justify their understanding of Yahweh's ethical requirements, they repeatedly emphasize his divine nature—his *hesed* or "loving kindness"—as the basis for his bond to Israel, as well as the reason for extending *hesed* to one's neighbor.

GOD'S RESPONSE TO ISRAEL'S DISLOYALTY

Israelite prophets, so personally certain of Yahweh's power and presence, tended to express bafflement and outrage at the people's general indifference to their proclamation of "Yahweh alone." To prophetic eyes, Israel did not live up to its high calling; as a group, the Israelites demonstrably failed to renounce all other religious ties in favor of loving and obeying Yahweh wholeheartedly. As a result, prophets such as Amos, Micah, Jeremiah, and Ezekiel pronounced doom upon a disloyal community, declaring that because his chosen people ignored him and despised his teachings, Yahweh would reject them, turning them over to Assyria or Babylon, his instruments of punishment.

THE LASTING BOND BETWEEN YAHWEH AND ISRAEL

Whereas preexilic prophets emphasize Yahweh's impending punishment and rejection of Israel, those active during or after the Babylonian exile, such as Second Isaiah, offer the comfort of hope and restoration of divine favor. Presenting the return to Judah from Babylon as a new exodus, a new saving act by Israel's loving God, Second Isaiah is the first *navi* explicitly to portray Yahweh as the only real God, the sole Creator and Ruler of the universe. Although cosmic in stature, Second Isaiah's God is also caring and compassionate, manipulating historical events, such as Cyrus's overthrow of Babylon and release of Judean captives, to alleviate his people's suffering. (The promises of restoration found in Jeremiah 31 and parts of Ezekiel may also have been added to these collections during the postexilic period.)

AN IDEALIZED FUTURE

Whereas most civilizations of the ancient world saw human history moving in an endless cycle—the rise and fall of kingdoms replicating the eternal cycle of the seasons—Israel's prophets, along with some of its theologian-historians, saw history not as repeating itself mindlessly, but as moving forward toward a divinely ordained goal. Although biblical prophets are almost invariably concerned about announcing God's will in an immediate crisis, they also present brief glimpses of a future era when Yahweh will bring to full fruition his creative purpose, which human inadequacy has opposed. Thus, the various prophets who contributed to the composite Book of Isaiah envision a glorious period when formerly warlike nations will flock to Yahweh's Temple in Jerusalem, voluntarily transforming weapons of destruction into implements of construction. Then all peoples—as well as the animal kingdom—will be united in a universal peace. With such pictures of the divine purpose for humanity, the prophets, for all their repeated denunciations of human failure, also impart a message of ultimate hope.

A careful reading of prophetic literature distinguishes Israel's classical prophets from certain modern concepts of the role. The *nevi'im* were not primarily fortune-tellers or prognosticators of future history. Their function was to perceive and then announce Yahweh's will in an immediate circumstance—in terms comprehensible or at least relevant to their original audience. Rather than predicting events in a far-distant future, the *nevi'im* endeavored to illuminate Yahweh's intentions in the present. They strove to bring Yahweh's people back into harmony with the Mosaic Torah or, failing that, to specify the punishments for disobedience.

Box 6.2 The Language of the Prophets—Poetry

It was not until the eighteenth century C.E. that scholars began to recognize that approximately a third of the Bible is written in poetry. The Pentateuch and the Deuteronomistic History contain numerous short poems, ranging from Adam's rapturous verse about Eve's creation (Gen. 2:23), to Miriam's song at the great sea (Exod. 15:21), to Deborah's victory hymn (Judg. 5:1–31), to David's lament over Jonathan's death (2 Sam. 1:19–27). Whereas poems are scattered intermittently throughout the prose narratives in Genesis through 2 Kings, some Bible books are composed almost entirely in poetry, including not only Psalms, Proverbs, Lamentations, and Job, but also a large percentage of the prophetic collections. When delivering Yahweh's announcements to Israel, the prophets sometimes spoke in prose, but more often than not, they used that heightened, elevated style we class as poetry.

Unlike English poetry and the poetry of many Western cultures, Hebrew poetry is not distinguished primarily by rhyme or regular meter, although many poetic lines have a strongly rhythmic quality. Instead, the biblical poetic line is notable for its terseness, repetition of key words or phrases, vivid imagery, and, above all, various kinds of **parallelism**.

Biblical poets typically phrase their ideas so that one line parallels another, with similar thoughts expressed in similar word structures.

In *synonymous parallelism*, an idea articulated in the first line is repeated in slightly different words in the second, a device the psalmists use frequently:

> Praise Yahweh, all nations,
> extol him, all you peoples!
> Ps. 117:1

> Who else is God but Yahweh,
> who else a rock save our God?
> Ps. 18:31

> The heavens declare the glory of God,
> The vault of heaven proclaims his handiwork.
> Ps. 19:1

Conveying Yahweh's disappointment in Israel's ethical failures, Isaiah of Jerusalem uses synonymous parallelism in which the second line intensifies or expands upon the original statement:

> He [God] expected justice, but found bloodshed;
> integrity, but only a cry of distress.
> Isa. 5:7

The prophetic calling included women, the first of whom was Moses' sister Miriam (Exod. 15:20–21; Num. 12:2). In the period of the judges, Deborah was both a tribal leader and a prophet (Judg. 4:4). When priests discovered the lost manuscript of Deuteronomy during Josiah's reign, they brought the matter to Huldah, "a prophetess," for interpretation and advice (2 Kings 22:14). The prophetess Noadiah was one of Nehemiah's noted opponents in postexilic Jerusalem (Neh. 6:14; see also Isa. 8:2). Women participated in the prophetic dispensation well into New Testament times (Luke 2:36; Rev. 2:20).

The Hebrew Bible places the three **Major Prophets**—Isaiah, Jeremiah, and Ezekiel—first among the Latter ("writing") Prophets, a ranking that probably derives as much from their great length as from their enormous theological influence. The books of the twelve **Minor Prophets**—Hosea through Malachi—are minor only in length, not in religious significance. From the earliest, Amos, who prophesied during the eighth century B.C.E., to Jonah, a book written in the late sixth or early fifth century B.C.E., the twelve present a 300-year continuum of Yahweh's oracles to Israel. These Minor Prophets are arranged in roughly chronological order, although other factors, such as a book's size, also figured in their positioning. The following is an introductory survey of the Latter Prophets and a statement of the order in which the individual prophets appeared, if not that in which the books bearing their names were

Box 6.2 *(continued)*

In *antithetical parallelism,* the first statement expresses one idea and the second its opposite. Isaiah of Jerusalem contrasts the polar opposites of obedience and rebellion:

> If you are willing to obey,
> you shall eat the good things of the earth.
> But if you persist in rebellion,
> the sword will eat you instead.
>
> Isa. 1:19–20

Speaking of Judah's restoration from the Babylonian exile, Jeremiah underscores the difference between the people's feelings when they departed Jerusalem and when they return, contrasting their tears of desolation with the promise of God's future presence:

> They had left in tears,
> I will comfort them as I lead them back.
>
> Jer. 31:9

In addition to its distinctive qualities of conciseness and parallelism, Hebrew poetry employs similes (comparisons using "like" or "as") and metaphors (a figure of speech in which one object is implicitly likened to or "becomes" another). In Isaiah 5, the prophet creates a metaphor in which Israel is a vineyard that Yahweh has planted and carefully tended, but that disappointingly yields only "sour grapes." In this extended analogy, the misconduct of Israel's ruling class, especially its exploitation of the poor, causes the vineyard's divine owner to uproot its useless vines, reducing it to a weed patch. Evoking images of unproductive and abandoned vineyards, familiar to an agricultural society, Isaiah's poem demonstrates that Yahweh's judgment on Israel is as inevitable as a vintner's rejection of an infertile field.

Qualities that distinguish much prophetic poetry from other poetic genres in the Bible include the use of the vocative, directly addressing the hearer (or reader) in the second person "you," and the admonishing tone. Prophets typically offer considerable admonition—disapproving warnings about the results of bad conduct—as well as earnest counsel or encouragement for the hearer's ethical improvement, as in the first chapter of Isaiah cited above.

Utilizing vivid metaphors and other memorable figures of speech, the prophets typically make poetry the medium for conveying some of the inexpressible mystery of God's dealings with humankind. Whereas the Deuteronomistic writers appropriately used prose to present Yahweh's actions in human history, attempts to express the ineffable qualities of the divine nature and purpose invited the evocative power of poetry. (For further discussion of Hebrew poetry, see Chapter 7.)

---

written. (Box 6.2 examines the distinctively poetic language the prophets used to illumine the divine mysteries.)

The Three Great Crises

The Latter Prophets of Israel and Judah, like other contributors to biblical literature, appeared largely in response to urgent political or ethical crises that troubled their people. The final editors of the Hebrew Bible placed these prophetic collections immediately after the Deuteronomistic History because they effectively illustrate the reasons for Yahweh's rejecting his covenant people. As a group, the prophets bear witness to Israel's failure to heed Yahweh's warnings sent through his appointed messengers. Most of the Latter Prophets belong to one of three critical periods: (1) the Assyrian crisis, (2) the Babylonian threat, or (3) the postexilic readjustment.

THE ASSYRIAN CRISIS

The earliest of the "writing" prophets (those whose works were recorded in their names) were active during the second half of the eighth century B.C.E. A time of swift change and political upheaval, a revitalized Assyrian Empire then threatened the very existence of the two kingdoms of Israel and Judah. Amos and Hosea preached in the northern kingdom, warning of a terrible retribution for the people's faithlessness to the Mosaic Covenant ideals of social justice and loyalty to Yahweh. Within two decades after northern Israel's collapse before the Assyrian military juggernaut (722–721 B.C.E.), Judah seemed doomed to a similar fate. Like their two predecessors in the north, the Judeans Isaiah and Micah interpreted the historical situation as Yahweh's punishment for the covenant people's religious and social sins. (The two prophets, however, manifest strikingly different attitudes toward the Davidic monarchy and royal sanctuary in Jerusalem.)

THE BABYLONIAN THREAT

Another cluster of late seventh- and sixth-century prophets responded to a second period of international turmoil. In rapid succession, Assyria fell (612 B.C.E.), inspiring Nahum's rejoicing. Then Egypt's Pharaoh Necho attempted to fill the Near Eastern power vacuum (defeating and killing Judah's "good" King Josiah along the way), only to be defeated by Babylon's Nebuchadnezzar at the decisive Battle of Carchemish (605 B.C.E.). Judah, which had begun a profound religious reformation and political expansion under Josiah (c. 621 B.C.E.)—developments made possible by Assyria's growing weakness—quickly found itself subject to a new imperial master, the Neo-Babylonian Empire. Reduced again to tribute-paying vassal status, as it had been under Assyria, Judah plotted revolts against Nebuchadnezzar and looked to Egypt (a "frail reed") for military help.

During the Babylonian crisis, the prophets Habakkuk and Jeremiah interpreted political events as signs of Yahweh's will working through human activity. Using the form of a legal prosecution or "covenant lawsuit" against law-breaking Judah, Jeremiah urged political submission to Babylon, which unwittingly acted as Yahweh's punishing agent.

Deported to Babylonia (597 B.C.E.), Ezekiel similarly proclaimed that Yahweh had abandoned his dwelling place in Jerusalem's Temple because the people were promoting injustice and religious corruption. Ezekiel also produced visions of a new Jerusalem and splendidly rebuilt Temple where a restored "remnant" would one day properly worship their God. These glowing visions of a happier future helped encourage the Judean captives and provided a rallying point of hope that Yahweh had not utterly forgotten the covenant community.

THE POSTEXILIC READJUSTMENT

Toward the close of the Babylonian period, the unknown prophet called Second Isaiah announced not only that the captives' return to the Judean homeland was near but also that Yahweh planned a glorious triumph for his "servant" Israel. Declaring that Cyrus, emperor of Persia, was God's agent in overthrowing Babylon, Second Isaiah prepared his people for a postexilic readjustment to life in the Persian Empire. Second Isaiah's promises of divine favor, however, were not matched by the grim and impoverished realities of life in postexilic Jerusalem; the returned exiles experienced merely a brief renewal of prophetic encouragement. In about 520 B.C.E., the prophets Haggai and Zechariah renewed promises of a brighter future and incited the apathetic Judeans to finish rebuilding Yahweh's Temple. Still later, Joel, Malachi, and the anonymous poet known as Third Isaiah added their **eschatological** (referring to a doctrine of "last things") hopes to the prophetic writings. After the time of Ezra—priest, scribe, and transmitter of the Mosaic Law (c. 400 B.C.E.)—it was believed that traditional prophecy ceased. Late "prophetic" books like Daniel, for example, were not included among the canonical Prophets but were assigned to a later collection, the Writings.

Order of the Prophets' Appearances

THE EIGHTH CENTURY: THE ASSYRIAN CRISIS

Amos   A Judean called to prophesy in the northern kingdom, **Amos** reverses popular assumptions about the "Day of Yahweh." When Yahweh appears to judge the world, he will punish Israel along with other nations that foster social and economic injustice. Amos vigorously denounces the upper classes' luxurious living based on an unjust exploitation of the poor. Claiming that Israel had perverted religion into an empty ritual, Amos predicts political disaster and exile.

Hosea   Comparing Israel's disloyalty to Yahweh in its worship of Baal to the breaking of a marriage bond, **Hosea** renews Amos's theme of economic and social corruption and deserved national disaster. But Hosea also stresses Yahweh's *hesed* (loving devotion) and likens Yahweh's concern for Israel to a spouse's distress over a beloved but faithless mate.

Isaiah of Jerusalem   A prophet intimately associated with the Jerusalem sanctuary and Davidic royal family, **Isaiah** resembles the northern prophets in denouncing the ruling classes' acquisitive greed and callous disregard for the poor. Active during the Assyrian invasion of Judah, he counsels "isolationism," which reflects faith in a total reliance on Yahweh's power to save. He also predicts that a Davidic heir will establish universal peace and justice.

Micah   Unlike his contemporary Isaiah, **Micah** is a rural villager who unequivocally condemns the rich urban landowners who "skin" and "devour" the peasant farmers. Criticizing the Jerusalem kings who permit such practices, Micah declares that the city and Temple will be destroyed (Mic. 3:9–12).

THE SEVENTH CENTURY: THE DECLINE OF ASSYRIA AND THE RISE OF BABYLON

Zephaniah   Compiled during Josiah's reign (640–609 B.C.E.), the Book of **Zephaniah** opens with Yahweh's declared intention to sweep all life from the earth and continues with denunciations of Israel's neighbors, Moab and Ammon, and the oppressor, Assyria. But then, abruptly, Zephaniah switches course and asserts that Yahweh has changed his mind and "repealed his sentence" against Judah (Zeph. 3:14–18). The prophet's abrupt change in attitude may have been a reaction to Josiah's religious reforms.

Nahum   Shortly before Nineveh's fall (612 B.C.E.), **Nahum** gloats over Assyria's destruction.

Habakkuk   Faced with Babylon's imminent conquest of Judah, **Habakkuk** ponders Yahweh's fairness, concluding that the righteous person must live having faith in God's ultimate justice.

THE SIXTH CENTURY: THE BABYLONIAN EXILE AND THE PARTIAL RESTORATION OF JUDAH

Jeremiah   During the reigns of Judah's last kings (Josiah to Zedekiah, c. 626–587 B.C.E.), **Jeremiah** stresses that Yahweh employs Babylon as the divinely appointed instrument of punishment against covenant-breaking Judah. Declaring that only those submitting to Babylon (and Yahweh) can escape destruction, Jeremiah (or a later editor) envisions the future enactment of a covenant that will not be broken (Jer. 31:31). Unlike his predecessor Isaiah, who also advised Jerusalem's kings during foreign invasions, Jeremiah sees little merit in the Temple cult or the Davidic ruling family.

Obadiah   **Obadiah** condemns Edom for helping the Babylonians sack Jerusalem (587 B.C.E.).

Ezekiel   A priest and mystic exiled in Babylonia during Judah's last years (after 597 B.C.E.), **Ezekiel** declares that Yahweh is too holy to continue dwelling among an unjust and violent people. Envisioning Yahweh's "glory" abandoning Jerusalem to Babylon's power, Ezekiel also foresees a glorious rebuilt sanctuary and divinely protected new Jerusalem.

Second Isaiah   Living in Babylonia during Cyrus the Persian's rise to power (c. 550–539 B.C.E.), this anonymous poet, referred to as **Second Isaiah**, views Yahweh as the *only* God, the eternal foreordainer of human history who was then acting to restore Judah's faithful remnant to its homeland in

Palestine. The four Servant Songs depict the redemptive role of Yahweh's chosen agent, Israel.

Haggai   Under Zerubbabel, a Davidic descendant whom the Persians appointed governor of the tiny restored community of Judah, **Haggai** argues that Yahweh will cause the wealth of nations to flow into Jerusalem if the Judeans will obediently rebuild the Temple.

Zechariah   A contemporary of Haggai (c. 520 B.C.E.), **Zechariah** produces a series of mystic visions involving the rebuilt Temple, the high priest Joshua, the Davidic governor Zerubbabel, and Yahweh's messianic intentions for Israel. A later hand added Chapters 9–12.

THE LATE SIXTH OR FIFTH CENTURY: THE POSTEXILIC ADJUSTMENT

Third Isaiah   The third section of Isaiah (Chs. 55–66) includes oracles from almost the whole period of Israelite prophecy, including the work of a postexilic prophet, referred to as **Third Isaiah**, who is sharply critical of the restored community's religious failures.

Joel   Of uncertain date, Joel's book contains a series of apocalyptic visions that picture plagues and judgments signaling the Day of Yahweh. Calling for repentance, **Joel** foresees a climactic outpouring of the divine spirit upon all humanity.

Malachi   This anonymous prophet also predicts a coming judgment on the frightening day of Yahweh's visitation. Promising a "messenger" to purify the Temple cult, **Malachi** ends by announcing the future reappearance of Elijah.

Jonah   A moral fable contrasting **Jonah**'s narrow view of divine justice with Yahweh's universality and compassion, this humorous tale provides insight into the ethical value of prophecy going unfulfilled. It also seems implicitly critical of the whole concept of Israelite prophecy.

RECOMMENDED READING

Barton, John. "Prophecy (Postexilic Hebrew)." In D. N. Freedman, ed., *The Anchor Bible Dictionary*, Vol. 5, pp. 489–495. New York: Doubleday, 1992.

Blenkinsopp, Joseph. *A History of Prophecy in Israel*, rev. ed. Louisville, Ky.: Westminster/John Knox, 1996.

Clements, Ronald E. *Old Testament Prophecy: From Oracles to Canon.* Louisville, Ky.: Westminster/John Knox, 1996.

Heschel, Abraham J. *The Prophets.* New York: Harper & Row, 1963. A major work by a leading scholar.

Huffmon, H. B. "Prophecy (Ancient Near Eastern)." In D. N. Freedman, ed., *The Anchor Bible Dictionary*, Vol. 5, pp. 477–482. New York: Doubleday, 1992.

Koch, Klaus. *The Prophets.* Vol. 1, *The Assyrian Age.* Translated by M. Kohl. Philadelphia: Fortress Press, 1982.

———. *The Prophets.* Vol. 2, *The Babylonian and Persian Period.* Philadelphia: Fortress Press, 1984.

Miller, John W. *Meet the Prophets: A Beginner's Guide to the Books of the Biblical Prophets.* New York: Paulist Press, 1987.

Schmitt, John J. "Prophecy (Preexilic Hebrew)." In D. N. Freedman, ed., *The Anchor Bible Dictionary*, Vol. 5, pp. 482–489. New York: Doubleday, 1992.

von Rad, Gerhard. *Old Testament Theology.* Vol. 2, *The Theology of Israel's Prophetic Traditions.* Translated by M. G. Stalker. New York: Harper & Row, 1965.

Ward, James. *Thus Says the Lord. The Message of the Prophets.* Nashville: Abingdon Press, 1991.

Westermann, Claus. *Prophetic Oracles of Salvation.* Louisville, Ky.: Westminster/John Knox, 1991.

Amos

KEY TOPICS/THEMES

Beginning with a series of oracles condemning Israel's neighbors (1:3–2:3), Amos also threatens the northern kingdom with destruction (2:4–16), delivering three warnings of judgment (Chs. 3–6) followed by five visions of disaster (Chs. 7–9). An epilogue, promising restoration and peace, was added by a Judean editor (Amos 9:9–15).

KEY QUESTIONS

Why does Amos attack Israel's ruling class? What is the Day of Yahweh?

Although placed third among the Minor Prophets, Amos was the first biblical prophet to have his words recorded in book form and to introduce major themes that would thereafter become staples of Israelite prophecy. Active in about 750 B.C.E. during the reign of Jeroboam II, Amos was an older contemporary of Hosea and Isaiah of Jerusalem. A native of Judah from the small town of Tekoa, located about twelve miles south of Jerusalem, a shepherd and pruner of sycamore (fig) trees, Amos—as he insists—was not a professional prophet (7:14). Nonetheless, he answered Yahweh's call to proclaim a stern message of doom in the northern kingdom. His book shows considerable familiarity with northern customs, economic conditions, and religious practices, many of which Amos condemns vehemently.

YAHWEH'S DEMAND FOR ECONOMIC JUSTICE

Oracles of Doom   The first cluster of oracles, presented in an abrupt, austere style, consists of denunciations against Israel's various neighbors—Syria, Philistia, Tyre, Edom, and Moab—that the prophet excoriates for their inhumane treatment of conquered peoples. Then, unexpectedly switching targets, Amos suddenly attacks his Israelite audience, castigating its leaders for behaving no better than greedy foreign princes. His point is that Yahweh not only refuses to tolerate cruelty among the people whom he had rescued from Egypt but also requires higher standards of ethical conduct from Israel than from those who do not enjoy Yahweh's special guidance.

Foremost among Israel's crimes was its exploitation of the poor (Box 6.3). Although under Jeroboam the nation had grown rich and comfortable, the wealth had accumulated into too few hands, leaving many landless and needy. This unequal distribution of the nation's goods Amos condemned as abhorrent to Yahweh, who will punish the wealthy

> Because they have sold the virtuous man for silver
> and the poor man for a pair of sandals,

> because they trample on the heads of ordinary people
> and push the poor out of their path.
>
> Amos 2:6–7

Amos saw that behind the national prosperity and private luxury was a callous indifference to human rights, which was no less a sin than sacrificing to idols. He was the first prophet to argue that social justice is as vital to religion as worshiping one God alone (8:4–8).

Three Sermons   In the three sermons that follow (3–6), the prophet reminds Israel that Yahweh causes everything that happens, whether it be the fall of a city or the message of his prophets (3:3–8). He then predicts the destruction of Bethel's popular sanctuary and the ruin of the magnificent palaces and "houses of ivory" that the wealthy had built (3:13–15). Similarly, in Chapter 5, he foretells that the houses, fields, and vineyards that rich landowners have accumulated will never yield their benefits to those who cheat the poor and defenseless (5:7–12).

Nor is the ceremonial religion practiced by "respectable" citizens acceptable:

> I hate and despise your feasts,
> I take no pleasure in your solemn festivals.
> When you offer me holocausts,
> I reject your oblations. . . .
> Let me have no more of the din of your chanting,
> no more of your strumming on harps.
> But let justice flow like water,
> and integrity like an unfailing stream.
>
> Amos 5:21–24

Amos's insistence that ethical behavior is more important than ritual observances is typical of Israel's prophets, but he was the first to emphasize this important concept.

THE DAY OF YAHWEH: A NEW VISION

Visions of Judgment   Amos fostered another significant reversal in Israel's religious outlook. Until his time, the Day of Yahweh was thought to be a time of rejoicing, a future era when Yahweh would vanquish all Israel's enemies and cover his people

Box 6.3 Prophetic Warnings Against Economic Greed

As the God of justice and *hesed* (loving kindness or steadfast love), Yahweh demanded that his people form a just society that also manifested love of one's neighbor (Lev. 19:18). Although Canaan was pictured as a land of abundance, "flowing with milk and honey," not all Israelites benefited equally from the land's resources. The Torah accordingly made specific provisions for the poor, mandating that they were entitled to the same legal rights in court as the rich (Deut. 16:19)—a contrast to Mesopotamian law that applied different legal standards to nobles and peasants. The Torah also required that no interest be charged for loans made to the poor (Lev. 23:35–37) and that their debts be canceled every seventh year (Deut. 15:1–2). In addition, landowners were not to cut the wheat growing in the corners of their fields, leaving it for the poor to harvest, a stipulation that plays a major role in the Book of Ruth. (See Chapter 7.)

Despite these Torah statutes and the social customs they reflect, some of Israel's ruling class found ways to increase their wealth by exploiting the poor, a practice that the prophets denounce as hateful to Yahweh. Although commonly overlooked today, one of the major reasons the prophets give for Yahweh's anger against Israel is economic injustice, the painfully unequal distribution of material possessions in Israelite society. Eighth-century B.C.E. prophets, such as Amos, Micah, and Isaiah of Jerusalem, repeatedly point out that God is the champion of the poor and defenseless, and that he abhors the ruling classes' practice of gaining riches at the expense of the poor. Amos, the first prophet to have his oracles collected in written form, is also the first known to declare that Yahweh regards social justice as an indispensable aspect of faithfulness to him (Amos 8:4–8; cf. 2:6–7; 4:1–2; 6:4–6).

Particularly during times of drought, crop failure, and famine, the poor, who had little reserve to live on, were often forced to sell their farms and fields to wealthy landowners, a situation that Isaiah of Jerusalem indignantly denounces:

> Woe to those who add house to house
> and join field to field
> until everything belongs to them
> and they are the sole inhabitants of the land.
> Isa. 5:8

This practice of buying up others' property (ancestral land was regarded as Yahweh's heritage and was to be kept in the family) deeply offended Israel's God, who regarded such greedy acts as theft:

with glory. Blasting such complacent assumptions, Amos reversed popular expectations by proclaiming the Day of Yahweh to be a Day of Judgment, a period of darkness and grief for sinful Israel (5:18–20). This so distressed his hearers that Amaziah, the priest of Bethel, forbade the prophet to speak and expelled him from the sanctuary (7:10–17), which did not, however, prevent Amos from continuing his pronouncements of doom.

Israel, he said, was like a basket of summer fruit, ripe for destruction (8:1–4), and none would escape the day of wrath:

> Should they burrow their way down to Sheol,
> my hand will haul them out;
> should they scale the heavens,
> I will drag them down.
> Amos 9:2

Amos saw Yahweh as directing the fate of all nations, and not Israel alone. He had brought the Philistines from Crete just as he had brought Israel from Egypt; they and the Ethiopians were all the same to him (9:7–8). Assyria, then just beginning its imperial expansion, was also under Yahweh's jurisdiction and would be the chosen instrument to punish Israel. Amos thus anticipated the northern kingdom's fall to Assyria in 721 B.C.E., though he expressed this insight in terms of hyperbole and metaphor rather than by foretelling specific events and dates.

Epilogue So unrelieved was Amos's pessimism that a later hand added a brief epilogue predicting Israel's future restoration and prosperity (9:11–15). But his dire warnings and harsh judgments

Box 6.3 *(continued)*

You [privileged landowners] are the one who
destroy the vineyard [Israel]
and conceal what you have stolen from the poor.
By what right do you crush my people
and grind the faces of the poor?

                                              Isa. 3:15

And when legislators pass laws favoring the interests
of the rich over the have-nots, Yahweh is outraged:

Woe to the legislators of infamous laws,
to those who issue tyrannical decrees,
who refuse justice to the unfortunate
and cheat the poor among my people of their
rights,
who make widows their prey
and rob the orphan.
What will you do on the day of
punishment . . . ?

                                              Isa. 10:1–2

The "infamous laws" to which Isaiah refers may be
some that were eventually incorporated into the
Torah, particularly those that permitted destitute
persons to sell themselves and/or their families into
slavery in order to pay off debts (cf. Exod. 21:1–7,
22:2; Lev. 25:39; Deut. 15:16–17; 2 Kings 4:1). Although in some cases slave-owners were compelled
to free native-born Israelites after six years, the masters nonetheless exercised the legal right to control
their labor during that period.

Micah, a contemporary of Isaiah of Jerusalem,
accuses the wealthy, who "have the [political and
economic] strength" to do so, of conspiring not only
to confiscate debtors' property but also to enslave the
former owners:

Woe to those who plot evil,
who lie in bed planning mischief!
No sooner is it dawn than they do it
—their hands have the strength for it.
Seizing the fields that they covet,
they take over the houses as well,
owner and house they confiscate together,
taking both man and inheritance.

                                              Mic. 2:1–2

Picturing greedy leaders, "who should know what is
right," as cannibals, Micah shows them metaphorically devouring human flesh, tearing off their victims'
skin and crushing their bones (Mic. 3:1–3).

In the prophetic view, Israel was called to maintain high standards of social justice, which precluded
amassing possessions through the misfortunes of
others. Economic exploitation of the poor and vulnerable insulted the God who placed society's most
defenseless members under his special care.

---

nevertheless set the tone for many later prophets, among them Jeremiah, who resembles the
shepherd from Tekoa in delivering an unrelievedly
gloomy message.

RECOMMENDED READING

Auld, A. Graeme. *Amos.* Sheffield, England: JSOT
    Press, 1986.
Cathcart, K. J. "Day of Yahweh." In D. N. Freedman,
    ed., *The Anchor Bible Dictionary,* Vol. 2, pp. 84–85.
    New York: Doubleday, 1992.
Coote, Robert B. *Amos Among the Prophets: Composition
    and Theology.* Philadelphia: Fortress Press, 1981.
Gowan, Donald E. "The Book of Amos." In *The New
    Interpreter's Bible,* Vol. 7, pp. 339–431. Nashville:
    Abingdon Press, 1996.
King, Philip J. *Amos, Hosea, Micah—An Archaeological
    Commentary.* Philadelphia: Westminster Press, 1988.
Koch, Klaus. *The Prophets.* Vol. 1, *The Assyrian Age.*
    Translated by M. Kohl. Philadelphia: Fortress Press,
    1982.
Paul, Shalom M. *Amos: A Commentary on the Book of
    Amos.* Minneapolis: Fortress Press, 1991.
Willoughby, Bruce E. "Amos, Book of." In D. N. Freed-
    man, ed., *The Anchor Bible Dictionary,* Vol. 1,
    pp. 203–212. New York: Doubleday, 1992.

Hosea

KEY TOPICS/THEMES

Active during the last turbulent years of the northern kingdom, Hosea is the only native prophet of
Israel whose oracles have been preserved in book
form. Providing a unique view of late Israelite society and religion, Hosea uses the metaphor of an

unhappy marriage to illustrate Yahweh's relationship with Israel. Comparing his people to an unfaithful mate, the prophet urges a national return to Yahweh's loving embrace, a reaffirmation of the bond that alone can save Israel from disaster. The first part (Chs. 1–3) describes Hosea's marriage; the second (Chs. 4–13) enumerates Israel's crimes and punishments; and the third (Ch. 14) gives a brief epilogue promising future repentance and reconciliation.

KEY QUESTIONS

Why is Israel like an unfaithful wife? How does God's love accord with his justice?

Unlike Amos, the Judean shepherd who preceded him as a prophet in the northern kingdom, Hosea was a native son of Israel, the only Israelite prophet whose words have survived in a canonical book. Hosea also differs from his predecessor in tempering his announcements of Yahweh's punishments with expressions of grief at Israel's imminent sufferings and hope for his nation's future. Presenting a God who experiences mixed emotions—anger and wounded love—at his people's **apostasy**, Hosea began his career during the reign of **Jeroboam II** (c. 747 B.C.E.) and continued prophesying into the reign of Israel's last king, Hoshea (732–724 B.C.E). After the fall of the northern kingdom, his oracles were probably carried south to Judah, where Judean scribes wrote them down, adding references to the Davidic monarchy (1:7; 3:5). A copyist appended a postscript urging readers to take the prophet's message to heart (14:10).

YAHWEH'S DISLOYAL MATE

Hosea's Marriage   The social, religious, and moral decay that marked the last days of the northern kingdom is reflected not only in the prophet's message but also in his private life. The book's first section (Chs. 1–3) is intended to show that Hosea's domestic situation exactly paralleled his prophetic view of Yahweh's relationship to Israel: Both he and his God were loving husbands who had suffered betrayal by their wives. Israel, Yahweh's bride (whom he had redeemed from slavery in Egypt), had betrayed her divine protector by worshiping Baal, the Canaanite fertility god. To illustrate the nation's faithlessness, Hosea had been commanded: "Go, and marry a whore, and get children with a whore, for the country has become nothing but a whore by abandoning Yahweh" (1:2).

Hosea obediently married Gomer, who may have been a priestess of fertility in a Baalistic cult. The prophet fathered children by her, naming each one symbolically to reflect Yahweh's anger with Israel's religious infidelity. Hosea saw in Gomer's repeated adulteries a mirror image of Israel's "whoring" after Canaan's agricultural deities. It was to Baal the people looked to provide rain, bless their crops, and ensure general prosperity, having forgotten Yahweh's "marriage" covenant with them in the Sinai wilderness. Although for its sins Israel stands condemned to national death, the Deity will not permanently abandon his disloyal consort (Ch. 2). Yahweh's steadfast love eventually will reconcile him to his errant people, as Hosea is reunited with his faithless wife (Ch. 3).

Crimes and Punishments   Part 2 (Chs. 4–14) forms a somewhat random collection of poetic declarations against Israel's idolatries, foreign alliances, and exploitation of the poor. Hosea charges the corrupt priesthood with rejecting proper knowledge of its God (4:4–11). Priests, nobles, and kings are the nation's ruin (5:1–7); even the people's repentance is insincere and short-lived (6:1–6).

Hosea particularly laments the popularity of cultic rituals and sacrifices, which keep the people from recognizing how empty their religion is (8:11–13). What Yahweh desires is "love, not sacrifice; knowledge of God, not holocausts" (6:6). The prophet foresees that the Israelites will be scattered, with some returning to Egypt and others being carried to Assyria, where they will "eat food that is unclean" (9:3–6). Although he does not refer to these events, Hosea may have lived to experience the fulfillment of his oracles when Assyria devastated Samaria in 721 B.C.E. and deported many of the survivors.

Future Reconciliation   Despite their certain punishment, Hosea argues, Yahweh will remember his people. Chapter 11 contains one of the Bible's most moving expressions of divine love, which Hosea perceives as stronger than divine vengeance. Although the remaining chapters remind Israel of the reasons for its God's present wrath, they also assert that Yahweh waits to effect a reconciliation (12:9–11). Indeed, Israel's exile may lead to a "second honeymoon" with Yahweh, like the Mosaic sojourn in the Sinai desert (2:3, 16–17). The book concludes with a final call for Israel's return and a promise of future happiness (Ch. 14).

RECOMMENDED READING

Anderson, Francis I., and Freedman, David N. *Hosea.* Anchor Bible, Vol. 24. Garden City, N.Y.: Doubleday, 1980.

Brenner, Athalya, ed. *A Feminist Companion to the Latter Prophets.* Sheffield, England: Sheffield Press, 1995.

Mays, James L. *Hosea.* Philadelphia: Westminster Press, 1969.

Seow, C. L. "Hosea, Book of." In D. N. Freedman, ed., *The Anchor Bible Dictionary,* Vol. 3, pp. 291–297. New York: Doubleday, 1992.

Ward, James M. *Hosea: A Theological Commentary.* New York: Harper & Row, 1966.

Wolff, Hans W. *Confrontations with Prophets.* Philadelphia: Fortress Press, 1983.

Yee, Gale A. "The Book of Hosea." In *The New Interpreter's Bible,* Vol. 7, pp. 197–297. Nashville: Abingdon Press, 1996.

Isaiah

KEY TOPICS/THEMES

A diverse collection of Hebrew prophecy dating from the mid-eighth to the fifth centuries B.C.E., the Book of Isaiah is the work of at least three prophets responding to three different crises in Israel's history. In the first section (Chs. 1–39), the Assyrian Empire threatens to engulf tiny Judah, eliciting a series of poetic oracles from the historical Isaiah of Jerusalem (c. 742–701 B.C.E.), who advises Davidic kings to rely exclusively on Yahweh for deliverance. A prose narrative recounting the Assyrian failure to capture Jerusalem ends this section (Chs. 36–39). In the second main division

(Chs. 40–55), from which both the Assyrian threat and the figure of Isaiah are absent, an anonymous prophet speaks to Judean captives in Babylon, hailing Cyrus of Persia as Yahweh's Messiah, the divine agent of Israel's liberation from the Babylonian exile. The third part (Chs. 56–66) is a miscellaneous assemblage of prophetic oracles to an impoverished colony of exiles resettled in Judah, now under Persian rule. (The three parts are discussed separately.)

KEY QUESTIONS

How did Isaiah, counselor of Judean kings, respond to Assyria's aggression? How did the prophet make Jerusalem and Zion the center of his vision?

Israel's prophets appeared largely in response to specific sociopolitical crises that troubled the covenant community. The earliest of the "writing prophets"—those whose words were compiled in their names—were active during the second half of the eighth century B.C.E., when the Near Eastern political scene was undergoing rapid change. In the northern kingdom, Amos and Hosea had warned that Israel's economic exploitation of the poor and failure to worship Yahweh exclusively would result in dire consequences to the nation. Although Amos and Hosea did not directly invoke the agent of Israel's impending punishment—the military expansion of Assyria and its threat to both Israel and Judah—the brutal fact of Assyrian aggression provides the historical background for the prophets' negative view of Israel's future. In the southern kingdom of Judah, four eighth-century prophets—Isaiah, Micah, Zephaniah, and Nahum—explicitly address the Assyrian menace, viewing this revived Mesopotamian power as the instrument of divine wrath.

After centuries of relative weakness, during the reign of Tiglath-pileser (747–727 B.C.E.) a newly energized Assyria began a series of military conquests, rapidly bringing much of the Near East into subjugation. In addition to seizing the throne of Babylon, Tiglath-pileser also subdued Syria and Palestine, forcing small states such as Israel to pay enormous sums of tribute (2 Kings 15:19–20).

When Israel later revolted against Assyrian oppression, a later king, Shalmaneser V (reigned 726–772 B.C.E.) laid siege to Samaria, the Israelite capital. Shalmaneser's successor, Sargon II (reigned 721–705 B.C.E.) captured Samaria, destroying the city and deporting many of the former kingdom's inhabitants to Mesopotamia (2 Kings 17). Although Judah also paid heavy tribute to Assyria, it too eventually revolted under King **Hezekiah**, leading Sennacherib (ruled 704–681 B.C.E.) to lead a frightening assault on Jerusalem. The prophet Isaiah's advice to Hezekiah during the prolonged Assyrian threat to Judah's center of worship forms an important part of his message.

ISAIAH OF JERUSALEM

Preeminent among the prophetic books, Isaiah contains some of the most memorable passages in the Hebrew Bible, including visions of a future world peace in which all of creation, both human and animal, is subject to Yahweh's rule. Although traditionally regarded as the work of a single prophet, scholars believe that the Book of Isaiah is an anthology of prophetic literature that spans almost the entire era of Israelite prophecy, from the mid-eighth to the early fifth century B.C.E. Most scholars divide the book into three different parts, each representing a different historical period and a different author.

The first section of the book (Chs. 1–39) contains the oldest material, oracles by Isaiah of Jerusalem, the historical prophet for whom the entire collection is named. Isaiah was active between 742 and 701 B.C.E., a turbulent age that witnessed Assyria's destruction of Israel and threatened engulfment of Judah as well. Most of Isaiah's genuine sayings, embedded amid later prophetic and editorial additions, express advice to Davidic kings during the Assyrian threat and warnings of judgment against Judah for its sins. By contrast, in Chapters 40–55, the time of judgment is past and the prophet (who is never identified by name after Chapter 39) utters words of comfort and encouragement to a community exiled in Babylon and about to be released by Cyrus of Persia. The book's

abrupt change of setting from the Assyrian crisis to the Babylon captivity and from oracles of doom to oracles of hope, as well as differences in literary style, vocabulary, and theology, indicate a change of author, whom scholars dub Second Isaiah. The book's final ten chapters, encompassing a miscellany of oracles from almost the whole range of biblical prophecy, are thought to include passages from another anonymous prophet, Third Isaiah, who lived in Judah after the exiles' return from Babylon. (In this text, the messages of Second and Third Isaiah are considered separately below.)

According to the book's opening verse, Isaiah of Jerusalem served as prophet and counselor to three Judean kings, Jotham, Ahaz, and Hezekiah. Beginning in about 742 B.C.E., shortly after King **Uzziah's** death and the ascension of Jotham, Isaiah's career continued until at least 701 B.C.E. and perhaps as late as 687 B.C.E., a period of forty to forty-five years. In Chapter 6, which scholars think describes his call to prophecy, Isaiah recounts a mystical experience in the Jerusalem Temple that shaped both his concept of divine holiness and his sense of mission to the Judean people. Suddenly transported to God's throne room in heaven (which the earthly Temple symbolized), Isaiah experienced a vision of Yahweh presiding over the divine council and surrounded by myriads of **seraphim**, fiery creatures, each equipped with three sets of wings. Overwhelmed by the seraphim's praise of God's incomparable holiness and a corresponding awareness of his own imperfection, Isaiah feels his lips symbolically cleansed by a burning coal, and he volunteers to carry Yahweh's words to Judah. Drawing on the later experience of his fellow Judeans' stubborn refusal to heed his message, however, he presents his inability to persuade his hearers to change their ways as predestined (6:1–13).

Although editors did not arrange Isaiah's pronouncements either chronologically or topically, scholars have related various portions of the book to three principal crises of Isaiah's lifetime: the Syro-Ephraimite War (735–734 B.C.E.), Hezekiah's temptation to ally Judah with Egypt (c. 711 B.C.E.), and the Assyrian invasion of Judah (701 B.C.E.). In their present form, Chapters 1–39 contain both Isaiah's authentic sayings and material later added to expand and update his message. This section is commonly divided into six parts:

1. Prophetic denunciations against wrongdoing in Judah and Jerusalem, interspersed with visions of universal peace under a Davidic ruler (1–12)
2. Prophecies of judgment against foreign nations (13–23)
3. Eschatological visions of cosmic judgment and restoration (24–27), the Little Apocalypse, probably dating to the Persian period
4. Denunciations of Judah and Jerusalem (28–33), probably dating to the Assyrian invasion
5. Additional oracles of judgment and blessing (34–35), probably from the exilic period
6. Prose excerpts from 2 Kings showing Isaiah's interaction with Hezekiah (36–39)

A preface to the whole collection of oracles ascribed to First Isaiah, Chapter 1 provides a survey of his major prophetic themes. Like most Israelite prophets, Isaiah ranges between pronouncements of utter doom on one hand and proclamations of glorious future blessings on the other. For Isaiah, the opposite poles of destruction and salvation are not contradictory; they represent two different possible fates for the covenant community. If Judah's leaders persist in exploiting the poor and governing unjustly, they are doomed, but if they obey Yahweh by placing human welfare above profit they will prosper (1:17; cf. 3:13–15; 5:8–20; 10:1–4). The quality of Judah's future depends upon the ruling classes' willingness to show compassion and practice social justice.

> If you are willing to obey,
> you shall eat the good of the earth.
> But if you persist in rebellion,
> the sword will eat you instead. (1:19–20)

The nation's destiny is not fixed because, if the people change their behavior, Yahweh is willing to forgive, informing wrongdoers that though their "sins are like scarlet, they shall be as white as snow" (1:18).

As if to illustrate the universal benefits of transforming Judah into a just society, editors follow Yahweh's plea for compassion with one of Isaiah's most optimistic oracles — a vision of global peace with an exalted Jerusalem as the center of the new world order (2:1–4. As **Zion**, the Jerusalem hill on which Solomon's Temple stood, becomes the new holy mountian, Yahweh extends his "oracle" (and covenant?) to encompass all peoples. Now inscribed on the United Nations plaza in New York City, Isaiah's promise that all nations will convert their "swords" and other implements of war into "plowshares," instruments of peace, expresses a long-held and as yet unrealized idea in Western culture.

In considering the standard by which Isaiah judges the ruling classes' abuse of power, it is important to note that Isaiah never refers explicitly to the Mosaic Covenant. Instead of appealing to the Sinai/Horeb tradition, as Amos and Hosea commonly do, Isaiah emphasizes Yahweh's special relationship to the Davidic dynasty in Jerusalem, a concept with which his urban audience seems more familiar. This reliance on the Davidic royal line and the sanctity of the Davidic capital may explain why Isaiah regards every threat to Jerusalem and its anointed kings as an opportunity for the nation to demonstrate its absolute trust in Yahweh's sworn oath to preserve and protect David's heirs. The prophet repeatedly urges Judah's rulers to remain "quiet" in the face of military threats, avoiding foreign entanglements and relying exclusively on Yahweh's promise to David (cf. 2 Sam. 7).

The Syro-Ephraimite Crisis Isaiah's policy of trust is well illustrated by his prophetic advice during the Syro-Ephraimite War of the mid-730s B.C.E. As scholars reconstruct events, it appears that various Palestinian states, led by "Aram" (Syria) and "Ephraim" (Israel, so named for its most important tribe), formed a coalition to resist Assyrian expansion into the area. When the kings of Syria and Israel besieged Jerusalem to force King **Ahaz** of Judah (reigned c. 735–716 B.C.E.) to join their alliance, Isaiah counseled a passive reliance on Yahweh to keep his vow to David and deliver the holy city (Ch. 7).

Ignoring Isaiah's advice, Ahaz negotiated with Assyria, and thanks to Assyrian influence, the Syro-

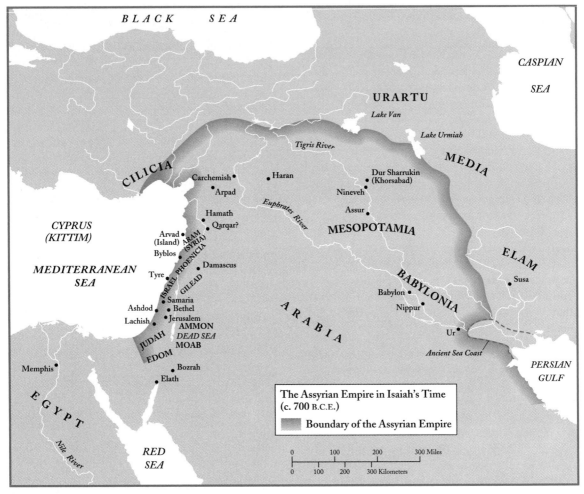

Figure 6.1 Map of the Assyrian Empire in Isaiah's time (c. 700 B.C.E.).

Ephraimite siege of Jerusalem was lifted. In saving his capital from the political coercion of neighboring Syrian and Israelite kings, however, Ahaz made it subservient to Assyria, so that Judah was reduced to the level of a vassal state in the Assyrian empire (Figure 6.1). Regarding Ahaz's compromise as a betrayal of Yahweh, Isaiah then announces that Assyria will soon become the "rod" of God's anger to punish Judah for the king's lack of faith (7:18–25; 10:5–6, 28–32). Should Assyria exceed its mandate to chastise his people, however, Yahweh will in turn destroy it (10:7–19).

As a pledge that Yahweh would rescue his people from the Syro-Ephraimite crisis, Isaiah stated that a young woman, perhaps Ahaz's wife, would conceive and bear a son, whose name, **Immanuel** ("God [El] is with us"), signified that Yahweh was present to protect his people (7:13–15). By the time the child is old enough to make wise decisions, Isaiah states, both Syria and Israel would have collapsed, ending their threat to Judah. Because both Damascus and Samaria, the respective capitals of these two neighboring states, were destroyed by Assyria within the next several years, Isaiah's confidence was vindicated by the event.

The heir born to Ahaz and his queen was Hezekiah, whose ascension to Judah's throne was perhaps the occasion for Isaiah's famous poem in Chapter 9, which provides the text for a joyful chorus in Handel's *Messiah:*

> For there is a child for us,
> a son given to us. . . .
> Wide in his dominion
> in a peace that has no end,
> for the throne of David
> and for his royal power . . .
> Isa. 9:7

Although Israel and other nearby states were crushed by Assyria, this coronation hymn for the new Davidic ruler predicts a flourishing Judah, secure because of God's pact with David (9:2–21). So forceful is Isaiah's Immanuel prophecy, with its optimism for Judah's divinely appointed monarchy, that — after the Davidic throne had been permanently overthrown — later generations viewed it as a messianic prediction. A term meaning "anointed" and applied to all Davidic kings, *Messiah* became identified with a future heir of David who would restore David's kingdom and vindicate Yahweh's people. In the New Testament, Jesus of Nazareth is portrayed as the royal figure whom Isaiah foretold, although this historical Jesus did not reestablish the Davidic monarchy or free the covenant community from its political oppressors. (See "The Messiah: First Century Expectations" in Chapter 9.)

Hezekiah's Alliance with Egypt The prophet's attention was drawn from a future peaceable kingdom to more immediate political concerns in 711 B.C.E., when the Assyrians attacked the city of **Ashdod**, which bordered on Judah's southwest frontier. This time Egypt attempted to form a defensive alliance of Canaanite states to protect its own boundaries. To dissuade King Hezekiah from involving Judah in this coalition, Isaiah, for three years, paraded naked through the streets of Jerusalem, graphically illustrating the public humiliations of defeat and slavery that would result from relying on Egypt instead of Yahweh to save them from the Assyrians (Ch. 20). Although Hezekiah did not then commit himself to Egypt — depending on this unreliable nation, Isaiah said, was equivalent to leaning on a broken reed that pierces the hand of one who grasps it (36:6) — a decade later Hezekiah did join Egypt in an anti-Assyrian treaty. Although this "unholy" alliance elicited some of Isaiah's harshest condemnations of Judah's king, courtiers, and other national leaders (Chs. 28–31), later editors inserted a passage into the collection asserting that even Egypt would "acknowledge Yahweh and worship him" (19:19–22). Perhaps most surprising, this interpolation states that Egypt and Assyria will join forces with Israel to form a trio of Near Eastern powers that, together, will be "blessed in the center of the world" (19:23–24).

Assyria's Assault on Jerusalem In 701 B.C.E., the Assyrians made their inevitably violent response to Hezekiah's move toward autonomy. Sweeping down from the north, **Sennacherib** (704–681 B.C.E.), one of Assyria's most formidable warrior-kings, cut off Judah's communication with Egypt and lay siege to Jerusalem — exactly as Isaiah had feared (29:1–4; see Chapter 5). Although Hezekiah at first followed Isaiah's advice not to surrender, the Assyrian capture and demolition of all forty-six fortified towns in Judah, which left Jerusalem a solitary oasis in a desert of total devastation, eventually forced the king to capitulate. The horrors of the Assyrian invasion are vividly depicted in artwork adorning Sennacherib's palace in Nineveh; one bas-relief shows Assyrian battalions attacking Lachish, one of Judah's largest walled cities, with Assyrian soldiers impaling captives on wooden stakes (Figure 5.1). Sennacherib spared Jerusalem, but Hezekiah was compelled to pay a staggeringly high price for his resistance — "three hundred talents [about eleven tons] of silver and thirty talents [one ton] of gold" (2 Kings 18:14–16), a huge payoff for Jerusalem's deliverance not mentioned in the edited version of 2 Kings that concludes the collection of First Isaiah's oracles (cf. Isa. 36–39; 2 Kings 18:13–20:19). His attempt at independence having failed, Hezekiah had to cede large parts of his kingdom to Assyria and resume his role as Assyrian vassal.

Figure 6.2 The cuneiform inscription on this hexagonal prism proclaims Sennacherib's military triumphs over Palestinian states and their Egyptian allies. Sennacherib, emperor of Assyria (704–681 B.C.E.), boasts that his armies overwhelmed Judah, his siege of Jerusalem trapping King Hezekiah (715–687 B.C.E.) "like a bird in a cage." Accounts of Sennacherib's invasion and Jerusalem's deliverance appear in 2 Kings 18:13–19:37 and Isaiah 36:1–37:38.

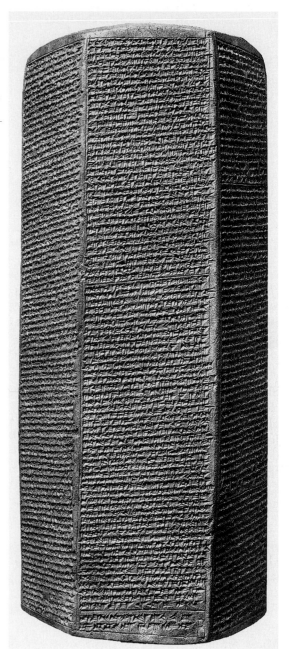

The apparent conflict between Sennacherib's archival report boasting that he had sealed Hezekiah in his capital "like a bird in a cage" (Figure 6.2) and the Isaiah-2 Kings claim that the Assyrian army withdrew from Jerusalem because Yahweh's angel slew 185,000 troops in a single night remains unresolved. Some scholars postulate that the two accounts refer to two different invaions, one in 701 B.C.E. and a second some time later. Whether there were one or two sieges of Jerusalem, for Isaiah the significant fact was that David's city escaped the destruction inflicted on all other Judean settlements, suggesting that Jerusalem, where Yahweh had placed his "name," enjoyed divine protection.

In addition to Isaiah's authentic proclamations, Chapters 1–39 also contain a variety of later interpolations. One section, known as Little Apocalypse (Chs. 24–27), probably dates from a period after the exile, when Judah was a small part of the Persian empire. Presenting visions of a future world judgment, this literary unit emphasizes Yahweh's universal reign. Although some passages apparently express new beliefs about life after death (25:7; 26:19–21), most scholars believe that these verses do not refer to an individual's posthumous fate, but, like Ezekiel's celebrated "valley of dry bones," symbolically portray the "resurrection" or rebirth of the covenant community from its political demise (cf. Ezek. 37). Allusions to Babylon's fall, such as the poem in Chapter 14, are also postexilic and were probably composed by members of a prophetic school that preserved and edited the work of Isaiah of Jerusalem.

Because they were delivered as assurances of hope to captive Judeans in Babylon, the oracles of Second Isaiah (Chs. 40–55) are discussed in the context of the Babylonian exile (see later).

RECOMMENDED READING

Childs, Brevard S. *Isaiah and the Assyrian Crisis.* Studies in Biblical Theology, no. 3. London: SCM Press, 1967.

Daves, Eryl W. *Prophecy and Ethics: Isaiah and the Ethical Tradition of Israel.* Sheffield, England: JSOT Press, 1981.

Hayes, John H., and Irvine, Stuart A. *Isaiah the Eighth-Century Prophet.* Nashville: Abingdon Press, 1987.

Millar, William R. "Isaiah, Book of (Chaps. 24–27)." In D. N. Freedman, ed., *The Anchor Bible Dictionary,* Vol. 3, pp. 488–490. New York: Doubleday, 1992. Discusses the apocalyptic passages incorporated into the Isaiah collection.

Seitz, Christopher R. "Isaiah, Book of (First Isaiah)." In D. N. Freedman, ed., *The Anchor Bible Dictionary,* Vol. 3, pp. 472–488. New York: Doubleday, 1992.

Tucker, Gene M. "The Book of Isaiah 1–39." In *The New Interpreter's Bible,* Vol. 6, pp. 27–305. Nashville: Abingdon Press, 2001.

Micah

KEY TOPICS/THEMES

Sharply critical of Jerusalem's ruling classes, including Davidic monarchs and priests, the rural prophet Micah prophesies doom upon Israel and Judah (Chs. 1–3). Expanded by later interpolations, Micah's oracles are edited to include predictions of Yahweh's future universal reign (Chs. 4–5), additional denunciations of social abuses, and hopes for restoration (Chs. 6–7).

KEY QUESTIONS

How does Micah's message differ from that of Isaiah? What oracles of peace do they share?

THE RURAL PROPHET

Micah, fourth and last of the eighth-century B.C.E. prophets, was a younger contemporary of Isaiah of Jerusalem. Active between 740 and 700 B.C.E., he directed his earliest prophecies against Israel's idolatries, predicting the fall of the northern kingdom (1:2–7). A native of Moresheth, a small town west of Jerusalem, Micah takes a country dweller's dim view of urban life and what he regarded as its inevitable corruption. He perceives the city as a source of sin that doomed both Samaria and Jerusalem (1:5). He denounces the tyranny of dishonest merchants and greedy landowners (2:1–5, 6–11; 3:1–4; 6:9–14), equating their guilt with that of Judah's corrupt princes, judges, priests, and false prophets (3:9–12; 7:1–4).

Unlike Isaiah, Micah espouses the cause of the village peasant and is sharply critical of the Davidic dynasty and Temple cult. He scornfully denies that the sanctuary's presence in Jerusalem will protect the holy city from harm and predicts that both city and Temple will be reduced to rubble (3:1–3, 9–12). Condemning the Jerusalem aristocracy and priesthood (6:1–2, 9–16), he also rebukes hired seers who offer false comfort and fear to tell the people unwelcome truths (3:5–8). Micah even rejects the belief that animal or any other sacrifice is required by Israel's Deity. In the book's most famous passage, he argues that Yahweh asks only for acts of justice and love and for humble communion with one's God (6:6–8). Here, the insight of the rural prophet wars with the prerogative of the city priest, for if Micah's words were to be taken literally, would Judah need either Levite or sanctuary?

Some scholars believe that Micah may have been one of Isaiah's disciples, which would account for a prediction of universal peace in almost exactly the same words as a passage in Isaiah (cf. Mic. 4:1–4 and Isa. 2:2–4). Other scholars suggest that the optimistic promises and visions of Judah's future glory (4:1–5:15; 7:8–20) were added by a later hand. According to the latter view, Micah originally condemned Judah for its violation of God's ethical demands, and an editor subsequently inserted references to Yahweh's unconditional promise to preserve the Davidic kingdom. The references to a faithful remnant returning to Judah after exile, at which time every citizen will sit under his or her vine and fig tree in peace and prosperity (2:12; 4:4–8), may have been interpolated into the text after Micah's time. The famous prophecy that Bethlehem one day will become the birthplace of a ruler whose "origin goes back to the distant past, to the days of old" (5:2) is viewed similarly as a later addition. Despite scholars' suspicion that Micah's original message underwent editorial modification, in its present form the book represents the typical prophetic paradox in which Yahweh is presented simultaneously as stern judge and merciful savior of his people.

Although his words must have been unpopular with the authorities, Micah's oracles were preserved on a scroll housed in the Temple, an institution whose destruction he had foretold (Jer. 26:16–18).

RECOMMENDED READING

Hillers, Delbert R. *Micah.* Philadelphia: Fortress Press, 1984.

Laberge, Léo. "Micah." In R. E. Brown et al., eds., *The New Jerome Biblical Commentary,* 2nd ed., pp. 249–254. Englewood Cliffs, N.J.: Prentice-Hall, 1990.

Mays, James L. *Micah.* Philadelphia: Westminster Press, 1976.

Simundson, Daniel J. "The Book of Micah." In *The New Interpreter's Bible,* Vol. 7, pp. 533–589. Nashville: Abingdon Press, 1996.

Wolff, Hans W. *Micah: A Commentary.* Minneapolis: Augsburg, 1990.

Zephaniah

KEY TOPICS/THEMES

Expanding on Amos's theme, the fearful day of Yahweh's coming judgment, Zephaniah predicts universal catastrophe, cursing Gentiles as well as unfaithful Jerusalemites (Chs. 1–3). The assurances of forgiveness and restoration (3:11–20) probably belong to a later compiler.

KEY QUESTIONS

Why does Yahweh resolve to destroy *all* life on earth? Why does God change his mind?

THE DAY OF YAHWEH

With Zephaniah, we return to the typical concerns of Israel's prophets: the condemnation of sin and declaration of Yahweh's impending wrath. Indeed, Zephaniah foresees a universal destruction in which all life forms—humans, beasts, birds, and fish—are to be exterminated (1:2–3). Yahweh will soon slaughter foreign kings, Judean royalty, greedy merchants, and skeptics alike who believe that "Yahweh has no power for good or for evil" (1:4–13). Like Amos, the prophet regards the Day of Yahweh as frighteningly near:

> A day of wrath, that day,
> a day of distress and agony,
> a day of ruin and devastation,
> a day of darkness and gloom,
> a day of clouds and blackness,
> a day of trumpet blast and battle cry. . . .
> I am going to bring such distress on men
> that they will grope like the blind . . .
> their blood will be scattered like dust,
> their corpses like dung.
>
> Zeph. 1:15–17

On the day of Yahweh's "jealousy," the earth will be consumed, and all its inhabitants will be destroyed (1:18). Zephaniah's dark vision contrasts sharply with Yahweh's vow, made immediately after the flood, that God would "never again" annihilate all earthly life (Gen. 8:21). The prophet seems unaware of this divine assurance.

Although we do not know what specific conditions fostered the prophet's pessimism, he wrote during the reign of King Josiah (640–609 B.C.E.) but before the discovery of the Book of Deuteronomy (621 B.C.E.) had stimulated Josiah's sweeping religious reforms. The Jerusalem whose sins Zephaniah denounces was thus a prereform city that may have been contaminated by the pro-Assyrian idolatries of Manasseh's administration. It seems, then, that Zephaniah was the first prophet to speak out after the long silence that Manasseh and his immediate successor, Amon, had imposed on the proponents of exclusive Yahwism.

After categorically asserting that Yahweh will spare no living thing, Zephaniah later concedes that a few humble people who keep the commandments "may perhaps find shelter" on the day of wrath (2:3). In fact, Chapter 2 implies the survival of a faithful remnant, for after Philistia, Moab, and

Ammon have been destroyed, Jewish survivors will confiscate their land (2:6–7, 9–10).

CURSES AND PROMISES

Chapter 3 attacks the "rebellious," "defiled," and "tyrannical" leaders of Jerusalem who have failed to learn justice from the object lessons to be found in the destruction of other cities. As a result, Yahweh will gather the nations to pour out his fury on Judah (3:8). After describing a bleak future for humanity, however, Zephaniah concludes by offering some rays of hope. In a series of terse oracles, he asserts that the Gentile states will come to worship Yahweh (3:9–10), that a humble remnant of Israel will seek refuge in Yahweh (3:11–13), and that Jewish exiles will be delivered from their oppressors (3:19–20).

It is tempting to suppose that the following uncharacteristically joyous passage was Zephaniah's response to King Josiah's reform movement:

> Shout for joy, daughter of Zion. . . .
> Yahweh has repealed your sentence;
> he has driven your enemies away.
> Yahweh, the king of Israel, is in your midst;
> you have no more evil to fear.
> Zeph. 3:14–15

If this surmise is true, perhaps Zephaniah believed that Josiah's cleansing of the Temple and his reinstituting the Passover and other Mosaic observances had restored Yahweh's presence to the Judean community. Josiah's military successes may also have indicated to the prophet that Yahweh had changed his mind about obliterating a nation stained with Manasseh's sins. In any case, the prophet's image of Yahweh dancing invisibly at Judah's festivals (3:18) represents a striking shift in his vision.

RECOMMENDED READING

Achtemeier, Elizabeth. *Nahum–Malachi: Interpretation.* Atlanta: Westminister/John Knox, 1986.

Bennett, Robert A. "The Book of Zephaniah." In *The New Interpreter's Bible*, Vol. 7, pp. 659–704. Nashville: Abingdon Press, 1996.

Szeles, M. E. *Habakkuk and Zephaniah: Wrath and Mercy.* Grand Rapids, Mich.: Eerdmans, 1987.

Nahum

KEY TOPIC/THEMES

The prophet rejoices over Nineveh's deserved fall.

KEY QUESTION

Why does God use Assyria as his "rod of punishment" and then destroy it?

Of Nahum's personal life or theological beliefs, we know nothing except that his message was unlike that of any other known Hebrew prophet. He neither decried his people's sins nor prophesied their retribution; instead, his entire book is composed of three poems rejoicing over the ruin of Nineveh, capital of the Assyrian Empire. His gloating, unmitigated by compassion, contrasts markedly with the merciful attitude found in Jonah.

THE FALL OF NINEVEH

Nahum probably wrote in about 612 B.C.E., either while the combined Medes and Babylonians were besieging Nineveh or shortly after the city's capture (Figure 6.3). In any case, the Medo-Babylonian coalition brought an end to Assyrian hegemony in the Near East, and the Jews were undoubtedly not alone in celebrating their enemy's downfall. Notoriously cruel, Assyria not only had deported whole populations from their homelands but also had routinely performed atrocities — mutilating and disfiguring captives, butchering women and children, and leading chained prisoners by metal hooks in their jaws.

Nahum sees Nineveh's collapse as evidence of Yahweh's vengeance on Assyrian inhumanity (1:2–3), for Yahweh is here perceived as the universal Sovereign. Although he had used Assyria as his "rod of correction" to punish Israel and Judah for their sins, Assyrian savagery had determined that it, too, must be humbled. Chapters 2 and 3 provide excellent examples of Hebrew poetry at its most vivid. Nahum's description of armed legions marching against Nineveh and plundering its treasures is harrowingly realistic (Ch. 2); his

Figure 6.3 Dominating the ancient Near East for two and a half centuries, the Assyrians effectively discouraged revolt by a policy of terror. This Assyrian bas-relief depicts the torturing and flaying alive of captives—defeated soldiers and civilian prisoners alike. When Nineveh, Assyria's capital, was about to fall to a coalition of Medes and Babylonians in 612 B.C.E., the prophet Nahum saw the event as Yahweh's punishment of a bloodthirsty nation (Nah. 3).

enumeration of Assyria's crimes is equally eloquent (Ch. 3).

Nahum interprets Nineveh's fate as part of Yahweh's long-range plan to improve the condition of his people. Released from Assyrian bondage, perhaps Israel but certainly Judah will enjoy an era of freedom and happiness (1:15; 2:2), "for never again shall the wicked come against you" (2:15, RSV). This optimism is unjustified, however, for only three years later, King Josiah is killed by Pharaoh Necho as Egyptian troops sweep across the Plain of Megiddo on their way to support remnants of the Assyrian army (2 Kings 23:29–35). Egypt then controlled Judah's affairs until about 605 B.C.E., when the Babylonians defeated Egyptian forces at the Battle of Carchemish and assumed jurisdiction over Palestine, reducing Judah once again to vassal status.

RECOMMENDED READING

Baker, David W. *Nahum, Habakkuk and Zephaniah.* Downers Grove, Ill.: Inter-Varsity Press, 1988.

Cathcart, Kevin J. "Nahum, Book of." In David H. Freedman, ed., *The Anchor Bible Dictionary*, Vol. 4, pp. 998–1000. New York: Doubleday, 1992.

Garcia-Treto, Francisco O. "The Book of Nahum." In *The New Interpreter's Bible*, Vol. 7, pp. 593–619. Nashville: Abingdon Press, 1996.

Habakkuk

KEY TOPICS/THEMES

Composed when Babylon was about to devastate Judah, Habakkuk contains a miniature theodicy, reflecting the prophet's effort to find a worthy purpose in Yahweh's permitting the destruction of his people by unbelieving foreigners.

KEY QUESTION

How does the prophet respond to Babylonian aggression?

THE BABYLONIAN THREAT

Yahweh's Justice Habakkuk is less a book of prophecy than a collection of philosophical meditations and a psalm describing Yahweh as a world conqueror. The first section (Chs. 1–2) is cast as a poetic dialogue between Yahweh and Habakkuk, who bitterly complains of his God's inaction in world affairs. Apparently written between about 600 and 587 B.C.E., when the Babylonian (Chaldean) armies threatened Judah, the first chapter asks why Yahweh remains silent while this "fierce and fiery" nation plunders and murders innocent people, including people much better than they.

The answer is that such Gentile oppressors are Yahweh's "instruments of justice" (1:12), chosen to carry out his will even though they do not recognize him as God. The implication is that Babylon's task is to punish Judah. Unlike Jeremiah or Ezekiel, however, Habakkuk does not argue that Judah's sins deserve so catastrophic a punishment. Indeed, he differs strikingly from the Deuteronomistic historians of the period in *not* asserting that the people's suffering is a result of their collective guilt.

In Chapter 2, Habakkuk declares that he will "stand on [his] watchtower" and await Yahweh's response, which is simply this: "The upright man will live by his faithfulness." That is, people must have faith that their God will eventually see justice done; this confidence in divine control of the outcome will sustain the righteous soul in its trials.

The balance of Habakkuk 2:5–20 is a veiled threat of vengeance on Babylon (or some other oppressor of the chosen people), whose punishment for abusing Yahweh's heritage is certain though it may not be swift. This section closes with a satire against idolatry, juxtaposed with the statement that "Yahweh is in his Holy Temple" and the nations should keep silent before him. Although this passage indicates that the Temple was still standing at the time of writing, it may come from a later hand than Habakkuk's and thus refer to the postexilic sanctuary.

Judge of the Earth The third chapter pictures Yahweh as angrily striding from the east amid storm clouds and lightning—a mighty warrior flashing his arrows, hurling his spear, and thundering along in horse-drawn chariots. This manifestation of divine strength is probably a response by a later writer to Habakkuk's original skepticism that Yahweh would bring justice to world affairs. In Chapter 3, the Deity clearly is willing and able to execute immediate vengeance on Israel's oppressors. This vision decisively answers Habakkuk's plaintive cry about "how long" Yahweh will tolerate wrongdoing (1:2). The militant psalm, which was probably sung in the second Temple, concludes with a quiet affirmation of trust in the Deity.

RECOMMENDED READING

Haak, Robert D. *Habakkuk: Translation and Commentary.* Leiden: E. J. Brill, 1992.

Hiebert, Theodore. "The Book of Habakkuk." In *The New Interpreter's Bible,* Vol. 7, pp. 623–655. Nashville: Abingdon Press, 1996.

Sweeney, Marvin A. "Habakkuk." In J. L. Mays, ed., *Harper's Bible Commentary,* pp. 739–741. San Francisco: Harper & Row, 1988.

Jeremiah

KEY TOPICS/THEMES

Proclaiming a message of submission to the Babylonian Empire, which he viewed as Yahweh's punitive instrument against Judah for its covenant-breaking, Jeremiah suffered rejection and condemnation as a traitor. The book containing his oracles of warning and doom, considerably revised and expanded by later disciples and postexilic editors, can be divided into four parts: (1) poetic oracles uttered during the reigns of Judah's last kings, particularly Jehoiakim and Zedekiah (Chs. 1–25), (2) biographical narratives interspersed with prophetic material, such as the promise of a "new covenant" (Chs. 26–45), (3) a collection of diatribes against pagan nations (Chs. 46–51), and (4) a brief historical appendix closely resembling 2 Kings 24–25 (Ch. 52).

KEY QUESTIONS

Why does Jeremiah advise Judean kings to submit to Babylon? What hope does he offer for the future?

THE LOSS OF MOSAIC PRINCIPLES

In its present form, the Book of Jeremiah is a bewildering collection of poetic prophecies and prose narratives, intermixed with introspective monologues, lamentations, messianic oracles, declarations of imminent disaster, and intimations of future hope. According to the opening verses, Jeremiah began his career during the reign of Josiah (c. 626 B.C.E.), perhaps inspired by the king's sweeping reforms and his attempt to bring national policy in line with the deuteronomic concept of the Mosaic Covenant. With Josiah's death in 609 and the rapid growth of Neo-Babylonian power that threatened to crush the tiny state of Judah, Jeremiah apparently became increasingly disillusioned with the policies of Josiah's Davidic successors. Although some dispute the claim, many scholars argue that Jeremiah perceived the deuteronomist reforms as superficial, a zealous cultivation of ritual masking deep social ills, especially a lack of social justice and economic equity. While supporting the Temple cult, the ruling classes did little to improve social conditions. "Wicked men among my people," Yahweh announces, "spread their nets" to catch the poor and powerless:

> Like a cage full of birds
> so are their houses full of loot;
> they have grown rich and powerful because of it,
> fat and sleek. . . .
> [T]hey have no respect for rights,
> for orphans' rights, to support them;
> they do not uphold the cause of the poor.
> And must I not punish them for such things
> — it is Yahweh who speaks —
> or from such a nation exact my vengeance?
>
> Jer. 5:266–29

In Jeremiah's view, Judah's failure to enforce Mosaic principles that protected impoverished laborers and their families, coupled with the government's implied mandate for the rich to use any means, including fraud and violence, to increase their wealth, compelled Yahweh to bring the entire system to an end. Rejecting a state that does not recognize the ethical implications of his worship, Yahweh feels no obligation to preserve a corrupt Davidic monarchy or Aaronic priesthood.

Chapter 36 gives a valuable insight into how at least part of the book took form. During the winter of 605–604 B.C.E., Jeremiah dictated to his secretary, **Baruch**, a scroll summarizing all the prophecies about Judah and Jerusalem that he had delivered during the previous twenty years. After Baruch read the scroll to an assembly in the Temple, word of it reached King **Jehoiakim**, who ordered it read in his presence.

As a royal scribe intoned excerpts from the scroll, Jehoiakim cut them from the manuscript, contemptuously burned them in an open brazier, and then ordered the arrest of Jeremiah and Baruch, who had already gone into hiding. Undeterred by the king's response, Jeremiah dictated a whole new scroll to Baruch, adding many similar prophecies. This second scroll may form the nucleus of our present Book of Jeremiah, for it probably contained large portions of Chapters 1–6 and 10–23, which are written mostly in the first person.

JEREMIAH'S UNPOPULAR MESSAGE

Oracles Against Judah   Acting under the conviction that Yahweh intended to crush Judah for abandoning his covenant, Jeremiah viewed Babylon as the Deity's chosen means of implementing his decision. Convinced that Judah's moral failures necessitated its punishment, Jeremiah issued pronouncements brimming with negative judgments and images of loss and suffering. Although he agonized over Judah's fate, Jeremiah believed that the punishment was deserved, because king and citizens alike abused the poor and powerless. Literally as well as metaphorically, exploitative nobles "filled the streets of Jerusalem with innocent blood."

If the introductory chronology is correct, Jeremiah delivered his unpopular message of doom for approximately forty years, causing him to be hated, shunned, and persecuted. Many of his fellow Judeans regarded his call to surrender to Babylonian domination as a shameful betrayal of his country (26:7–11; 32:1–5; 37:11–15; 38:14–28). Using the classic form of a covenant lawsuit—indictment and punishment—Jeremiah proclaimed Yahweh's verdict on the nation's collective guilt. In failing to uphold the Mosaic Covenant, Judah's ruling classes had committed a capital offense; unless they repented instantly, they would pay the penalty of death (7–8; 11:21–22; 26–28).

The prophet urged Judah's kings, particularly Jehoiakim and Zedekiah, to see that Babylon's supremacy was not merely a political reality against

Figure 6.4 The splendor of Nebuchadnezzar's Neo-Babylonian Empire is reflected in this museum reconstruction of the ceremonial Gate of Ishtar, Babylonian goddess of love, fertility, and war. While upper-class Jews were held captive in Babylon (587–538 B.C.E.), they probably witnessed the annual New Year's festival in honor of Marduk, creator of heaven and earth, which featured an elaborate parade that passed through these portals. Note that the figures decorating the enameled brick include a serpent with legs (a dragon), reminiscent of the Genesis serpent.

Figure 6.5 An artist's reconstruction of Babylon at the time of King Nebuchadnezzar (605–562 B.C.E.), founder of the Neo-Babylonian Empire and conqueror of Judah (587 B.C.E.), illustrates the city's massive fortifications. During their captivity in Babylon, Judah's former ruling classes reedited and/or produced much of the literature that now forms the Hebrew Bible. The towering ziggurat at the left, an artificial mountain crowned with a chapel to the Babylonian gods, is characteristic of Mesopotamian religious architecture; its predecessors at Ur and elsewhere may have inspired the "Tower of Babel" legend (Gen. 11).

which it would be disastrous to struggle. Burdened with a sense of the ruling class's guilt, Jeremiah struggled to make Judah's leaders realize that the newly reborn Babylonian Empire was Yahweh's judgment on his people for their faithlessness, idolatry, and social injustice (21; 22:1–9; 36; 37:16–21; 38:14–28). After Nebuchadnezzar had had thousands of Judah's religious and political leaders removed to Babylon (the first deportation in 598–597 B.C.E.), Jeremiah wrote to the exiles telling them not to expect an early return but to build houses, plant gardens, and settle down as comfortably as possible for a long captivity (Ch. 29) (Figures 6.4 and 6.5).

Jeremiah seems to have regretted the nature of his prophetic calling and to have suffered greatly at having to proclaim such a harsh view of Yahweh's intentions:

> Woe is me, my mother, for you have borne me
> to be
> a man of strife and of dissension for all the land.
> I neither lend nor borrow,
> yet all of them curse me.
>
> . . . .
>
> Yahweh, remember me, take care of me,
> and avenge me on my persecutors.
> Your anger is very slow; do not let me be snatched
> away.
> Realize that I suffer insult for your sake.
>
> Jer. 15:10, 15

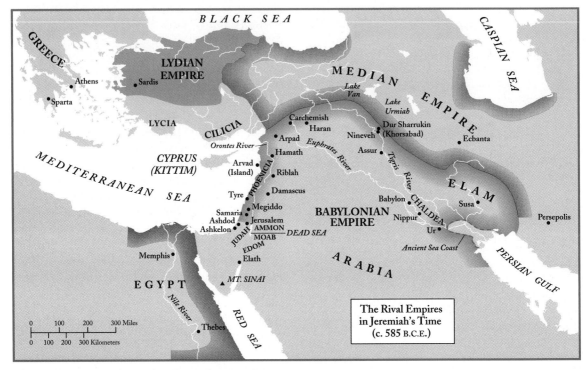

Figure 6.6 Map of the rival empires in Jeremiah's time (c. 585 B.C.E.).

Weary of rejection, he even tried to stop preaching to those who had no wish to hear it but found that the undelivered word burned "like a fire in [his] bones" and that he had to continue his work.

Biographical Narratives We know Jeremiah's inner life, his love for his people, and his unhappiness at being ostracized from them not only from several "confessions" (11:18–23; 12:1–5; 15:10–11, 15–20; 17:14–18; 18:18–23; 20:7–11) but also from the memoirs of Baruch, which are contained in Chapters 26–45. From these biographical sections, we learn that the prophet was born of a priestly family of Anathoth, a village three to four miles north of Jerusalem; that he was called to prophesy while still a boy; and that he witnessed rapid historical changes during his youth. Assyria's power was broken with Nineveh's fall in 612 B.C.E.; King Josiah's religious reforms and the accompanying territorial expansion were halted by the king's untimely death in 609 B.C.E. At the Battle of Car-

chemish in 605 B.C.E., the Babylonians, who there defeated Pharaoh Necho, became the dominant world power (Figure 6.6).

An "Unpatriotic" Prophet Although at one time Jeremiah probably supported Josiah's reforms, he seems to have become disillusioned when the people observed the correct sacrificial forms prescribed by Deuteronomy but did not otherwise change their behavior (3:6–10). Under King Jehoiakim, who tried to escape Babylon's control by allying Judah with Egypt, Jeremiah's bitter denunciation of such resistance as contrary to Yahweh's will was greeted with ridicule and charges of treason. After Nebuchadnezzar captured Jerusalem and deported many of its leading citizens (the first deportation, c. 597 B.C.E.), Jeremiah intensified his warnings. When the prophet Hananiah falsely promised deliverance from Babylon, Jeremiah contradicted him by walking the streets of Jerusalem wearing a wooden yoke, the symbol of coming slavery. After Hananiah angrily smashed the wooden yoke, Jeremiah returned wearing one of iron (Chs. 27–28).

During the Babylonians' final siege of Jerusalem, the prophet was accused of attempting desertion (Ch. 37) and was thrown into a muddy well to die (Ch. 38). This persecution was the Judean government's response to Jeremiah's "treason." The prophet advocated a radical — and "unpatriotic" — solution to the Babylonian threat: Jerusalem was to open its gates and surrender to the enemy. If the city capitulated, Jeremiah argued, it would not be burned, and its citizens would escape with their lives. In a secret interview with King **Zedekiah**, last of the Davidic monarchs, Jeremiah urged the king to act boldly, ignore his counselors' mistaken will to resist, and submit to Nebuchadnezzar, thereby sparing his people the horrors of slaughter and destruction after Jerusalem's inevitable fall. The prophet's recommendations were not based on political expedience, a policy of survival at all costs. Instead, he offered Zedekiah and the nation a religious challenge — to place their *trust* entirely in Yahweh's power to save. But Zedekiah, who was as weak and vacillating as his predecessor, Josiah, had been zealous and resolute, failed to accept Yahweh's offer of safety (38:14–28). As a result of the king's decision to heed his official advisers and not the prophet, Zedekiah saw his sons killed before his eyes and the holy city torched. He was then blinded, chained, and led into captivity (39:1–8).

To the Jerusalem leadership, Jeremiah's attitude toward Solomon's Temple was as offensive as his "defeatist" pacifism. Throughout the siege, he declared that those who believed that the sanctuary, center of sacrificial worship, could protect them were relying on an illusion (Chs. 7 and 26). Rather than depending on a mere building, which the corrupt had profaned, Judah must cleanse itself of crime and idolatry to regain Yahweh's favor and protection.

Shortly before Jerusalem fell, Jeremiah made a rare gesture of faith in the future. As his world was disintegrating around him, he bought a field in Anathoth to demonstrate his belief that land ownership in Judah would someday again be profitable

(Ch. 32). In 587 B.C.E., however, after a harrowing siege, Nebuchadnezzar took Jerusalem, demolishing its walls, palaces, and Temple.

Jeremiah in Egypt   Having learned of Jeremiah's policy of submission, the Babylonians offered to take him to Babylon along with other prominent Jews, but the prophet preferred to remain among the poor in the ruined city. After Gedaliah, Nebuchadnezzar's governor, was murdered, Jeremiah was forcibly carried into Egypt, where we last see him, aged but unmellowed, violently attacking the refugees in Egypt for worshiping the **Queen of Heaven** (perhaps envisioned as Yahweh's feminine consort) (Chs. 43–45). Though he was paid no more attention in exile than during his forty years of preaching in Jerusalem, legend suggests that the prophet was silenced only by martyrdom.

Promised New Covenant   Perhaps Jeremiah's greatest contribution to the survival of the Jewish religion was his perception that Judah's faith did not depend on outward signs of Yahweh's presence or protection. David's throne, the holy city, Solomon's Temple, and even the nation itself could vanish. When all the national religious symbols were destroyed, Yahweh would nonetheless maintain his relationship with those who believed in him. As the prophet's own communication with his God was not broken in the idolatrous land of Egypt, neither would the faithful in Babylon lose contact with Yahweh, who could be worshiped without a temple anywhere in the world.

Jeremiah's most famous prophecy foretold a time when the old covenant that Yahweh had made through Moses would be replaced by a new and better covenant:

> See, the days are coming — it is Yahweh who speaks — when I will make a new covenant with the House of Israel (and the House of Judah), but not a covenant like the one I made with their ancestors on the day I took them by the hand to bring them out of the land of Egypt. . . . No, this is the covenant I will make. . . . Deep within them I will plant my Law, writing it on their hearts. Then I will be their God and they shall be my people.
>
> Jer. 31:31–33

This new covenant inscribed on human hearts would not be a superficial or short-lived reform, but an everlasting bond between Yahweh and his people, because it would spring from the worshipers' deepest emotion, an inborn love for their divine partner (cf. Deut. 30:6).

RECOMMENDED READING

Bright, John. *Jeremiah*. Anchor Bible, Vol. 21. Garden City, N.Y.: Doubleday, 1965. A fine commentary.

Brueggemann, Walter. *A Commentary on Jeremiah*. Grand Rapids, Mich.: Eerdmans, 1998.

Carroll, Robert P. *Jeremiah*. Philadelphia: Westminster Press, 1986. Asserts that the book was written *after* the exile.

Holladay, William L. *Jeremiah: A Fresh Reading*. New York: Pilgrim Press, 1990. By a leading authority on the prophet.

Ludrom, Jack R. "Jeremiah, Book of." In D. N. Freedman, ed., *The Anchor Bible Dictionary*, Vol. 3, pp. 706–721. New York: Doubleday, 1992. Discusses the content and composition of the biblical book.

———. "Jeremiah (Prophet)." In D. N. Freedman, ed., *The Anchor Bible Dictionary*, Vol. 3, pp. 684–698. New York: Doubleday, 1992. Discusses the life and times of the prophet.

Miller, Patrick D. "The Book of Jeremiah." In *The New Interpreter's Bible*, Vol. 6, pp. 555–926. Nashville: Abingdon Press, 2001.

Obadiah

KEY TOPIC/THEME

The prophet blasts Edom for benefiting from Judah's destruction.

KEY QUESTION

What inspired animosity between the "brother" states of Israel/Judah and Edom?

ORACLES AGAINST EDOM

Shortest of the Hebrew Bible prophetic books, Obadiah is a single chapter of oracles against Israel's near neighbor **Edom**, probably delivered shortly after the Babylonians had destroyed Jerusalem in 587 B.C.E. Apparently, Edom had joined in the plundering of Judah, for which the writer

bitterly condemns Edom and predicts its imminent desolation. The **Edomites'** gloating over fallen Judah is seen as particularly heinous because, according to ancient traditions, they were descended from Esau, Jacob's (Israel's) twin brother. (See Gen. 25:19–27:45; 36:1–19.) Their unbrotherly conduct will be repaid in kind (v. 15), but Judah's exiles will return to occupy Mount Zion (vv. 19–21). Other Bible writers also cite Edom's ungenerous actions (Jer. 29:7–22; Ezek. 25:12–14; Ps. 137:7).

RECOMMENDED READING

Floyd, Michael H. "Obadiah." In J. L. Mays, ed., *Harper's Bible Commentary*, pp. 726–727. San Francisco: Harper & Row, 1988.

Pagán, Samuel. "The Book of Obadiah." In *The New Interpreter's Bible*, Vol. 7, pp. 435–459. Nashville: Abingdon Press, 1996.

Wolff, Hans W. *Obadiah and Jonah*. Minneapolis: Augsburg, 1986.

Ezekiel

KEY TOPICS/THEMES

A younger contemporary of Jeremiah, the priest-prophet Ezekiel was taken to Babylon during the first deportation of Judah's ruling classes in 597 B.C.E. Although tightly structured, with the oracles arranged in generally chronological order, Ezekiel's prophecies and mystical visions are filled with strange and grotesque images puzzling to modern readers. The first set of oracles (Chs. 1–24) describes the prophet's call (Chs. 1–3) and conveys messages of judgment and doom on Judah and the Jerusalem Temple, from which Ezekiel sees Yahweh's "glory" (*kavod*) depart, abandoning the holy city to Babylonian invaders (Chs. 8–11). Breaking with Mosaic principles that punished younger generations for their elders' misdeeds, Ezekiel emphasizes individual responsibility (Ch. 18). The second part records oracles of judgment against foreign nations such as Tyre (Ch. 28) and ends with news of Jerusalem's fall (Chs. 25–33). In turn, this provides a transition to the third section, oracles and visions of Israel's rebirth (Chs. 34–

39) and a future restoration of the Temple cult (Chs. 40–48).

KEY QUESTIONS

How do Ezekiel's visions of God's mobile throne-chariot and Yahweh's departure from Jerusalem relate to Babylon's destruction of Judah? What changes in Yahweh's relationship to the covenant community does Ezekiel introduce? What glorious future does he foresee?

The symbols that Ezekiel evokes to describe his visions are at once so bizarre and so compelling that in medieval times Jewish teachers commonly forbade anyone under thirty years of age to read the book. Whereas the prophet's strange images of Yahweh's celestial throne were once thought too likely to seduce young minds unready to venture into serious mysticism, today they often inspire wild speculation among untrained readers. One popular author, for example, maintains that in his picture of Yahweh's blazing chariot (1:4–28; 11:22–23) the prophet is describing alien spaceships and visitors from outer space. Even without this peculiarly technological slant, however, readers are sure to find Ezekiel's metaphors bewildering. No other prophetic book in the Hebrew Bible, with the possible exception of Zechariah, features such hallucinatory material. Even Daniel's animal symbolism is less perplexing.

EZEKIEL'S PROPHETIC WARNINGS

Visions and Symbols   The narrative begins in 593 B.C.E., during the fifth year of deposed King Jehoiachin's exile, when Ezekiel is living in a Jewish community on the "River Chebar," a large irrigation canal near the Euphrates River in Babylonia. In a trance, Ezekiel sees four winged animals "of human form" that closely resemble the colossal stone cherubs that guarded the gates of many Mesopotamian cities and that would have been familiar sights to the prophet and other exiles (Figure 6.7).

The accompanying image of wheels within wheels having eyes along their rims probably represents Ezekiel's attempt to picture Yahweh among

Figure 6.7 This stone cherub, over ten feet tall, once guarded the entrance to an Assyrian palace at Calah (Nimrud). A hybrid creature common in Mesopotamian art and mythology, the cherub commonly has a human face (symbolizing intelligence), the body of a bull or lion (representing strength), and the wings of an eagle (indicating its supernatural swiftness as the gods' emissary). Yahweh's cherub guards the tree of life (Gen. 3:24), and a pair of cherubim extend their wings over the Ark of the Covenant, figuratively sheltering God's throne (Exod. 37:6–9; Ps. 99:1). In Ezekiel's vision, cherubim with four faces draw Yahweh's heavenly chariot (Ezek. 1, 10). Such grotesque beasts are far removed from the chubby infants of popular lore.

his heavenly servants in other than strictly anthropomorphic terms. The prophet characteristically speaks of Yahweh's "glory" in the Jerusalem Temple rather than of the God himself. Certainly, images of fiery beings, a sapphire throne, and spiritual voices vividly express the awe and sense of mystery that Ezekiel feels during his communion with the divine (Chs. 1–2).

After eating a scroll (representing Yahweh's message to Judah) that tastes like honey, Ezekiel is appointed watchman over the House of Israel, earning his own salvation by warning others of the impending judgment (2:8–3:21). Those who heed the warning will be spared the holocaust; those who ignore it will suffer destruction. Ezekiel here sounds the note of free will and individual responsibility that recurs throughout the book.

Dramatizing His Message   In the first of many strange actions that Ezekiel performs to dramatize parts of his message, the prophet begins his ministry by being struck dumb and hence unable to communicate his warning (3:22–27). He cooks his food over human excrement to foreshadow how people trapped during Nebuchadnezzar's siege will be forced to eat "unclean food." When his wife dies, he neither weeps nor mourns; his actions are intended to illustrate that Yahweh will not mourn the loss of his polluted Temple (4:9–17; 24:15–27).

Ezekiel's public displays sometimes border on the abnormal. Tightly bound in ropes, he lies down on one side for 190 days to symbolize the duration—each day for a year—of the northern kingdom's exile. Then he lies on his other side for another 40 days to designate the length of Judah's captivity (4:1–8). Finally, he shaves off his beard and the hair on his head, burning a third of the hair, striking another third with a sword, and scattering the last third to the winds, retaining only a few stray hairs that he binds up in his robe. This demonstration is to inform the people that a third of them will die of pestilence and famine, a third will die by violence, and the remaining third will become captives in Babylon. The few hairs that he keeps represent those whom God will allow to escape (Ch. 5).

YAHWEH'S ABANDONMENT OF JERUSALEM

Chapters 8–11 form a unit concerning the profanation of the Temple and the departure of Yahweh's "glory" from Jerusalem. Stationed in Babylon, Ezekiel feels himself lifted by the hair and carried to Jerusalem, where he envisions the idolatry that pollutes the sanctuary. Women there weep for **Tammuz**, a young fertility deity similar to the Greek Adonis, while Judah's corrupt elders secretly burn incense to hideous reptilian deities. Yahweh sends an angelic scribe who strides through the city marking the foreheads of those who deplore the religious abominations committed in the Temple. Those unmarked, who have compromised their Yahwist faith with pagan rites, are to be slain by six divine executioners.

Ezekiel then sees the "glory of Yahweh" rise from its traditional seat between the gold cherubim in the Temple's innermost sanctuary and pass through the city gates to the east. This strange event is probably meant to show that Yahweh's *kavod* (a Hebrew term that can be translated as "glory" or "influence") has permanently abandoned the Temple and now roams the world, operating in new and unpredictable ways. Like Jeremiah, Ezekiel realized that Yahweh did not need a material shrine in which to house his presence, nor would he protect a sanctuary that had been contaminated. With Yahweh's departure from the Temple, he could be with his people anywhere, including idolatrous Babylon.

REVISION OF A TORAH PRINCIPLE

Individual Responsibility   Chapters 12–17 deal with a variety of themes, most of which involve the sins that have alienated God from Judah. Chapter 18, however, minutely examines the moral consequences of the national disaster for the individual Jews who have survived it. Here, Ezekiel declares that God will no longer judge and punish the people collectively; now that the nation is gone, each new generation has responsibility for its own fate. The sinner will still be punished, but not for the wrongdoing of others.

Ezekiel thus assumes the authority of a lawgiver, a latter-day Moses who corrects the old misconception of the second commandment in which Yahweh is represented as vowing to punish the father's sins in the sons even to the fourth generation (Exod. 20:5). Why, Ezekiel asks, cling mindlessly to the inherent injustice of the old system or persist in repeating the old proverb that when fathers eat sour grapes the sons' teeth are set on edge?

> As I live — this is the Lord Yahweh who speaks — there will no longer be any reason to repeat this proverb in Israel. See now: all life belongs to me; the father's life and the son's life, both alike belong to me. The man who has sinned, he is the one who shall die.
>
> Ezek. 18:3–4

Like Joshua, Ezekiel emphasizes the individual's freedom of choice — Yahweh and life or disobedience and death:

> House of Israel, in future I mean to judge each of you by what he does — it is the Lord Yahweh who speaks. Repent, renounce all your sins . . . and make yourselves a new heart and a new spirit! Why are you so anxious to die, House of Israel? I take no pleasure in the death of any one. . . . Repent and live!
>
> Ezek. 18:31–32

Oracle Against the King of Tyre Chapters 25–32 are devoted to denunciations and judgments against various foreign nations. Of particular interest is the oracle attacking the king of Tyre, a powerful Phoenician port city (Ezek. 28). This passage, like Isaiah 14, uses brilliant imagery to describe the downfall of a foreign king who opposes Yahweh's rule:

> You were once an exemplar of perfection,
> full of wisdom,
> perfect in beauty;
> you were in Eden, in the garden of God.
> . . . .
> Your heart has grown swollen with pride
> on account of your beauty.
> You have corrupted your wisdom
> owing to your splendor.
> I have thrown you to the ground.
>
> Ezek. 28:13, 17

It is possible that the prophet, a political prisoner who knew the value of symbolism, discreetly aimed his barbs at the Tyrian monarch rather than at Nebuchadnezzar, the real object of his attack.

EZEKIEL'S VISIONS OF THE FUTURE

Promises of Restoration and Defense Chapter 33, which is pivotal, briefly describes Jerusalem's fall and the miserable fate of those remaining amid the ruins. After this event, the prophet abandons his visions of judgment and concentrates on Israel's future restoration (Chs. 33–39), foreseeing that Yahweh will send a shepherd, a descendant of David, to guide Israel, with whom God will conclude a covenant of peace so that they will live in perfect security (Ch. 34; cf. 37:24–27). Yahweh declares that he will take vengeance on the nations who desolated Israel and Judah, not because he pities his people, but because he wants to vindicate his name, to convince them that he is supreme among gods. The phrase "then they will know that I am Yahweh" resounds throughout this section (Ch. 36; cf. 37:28).

Perhaps the most influential of Ezekiel's visions occurs in Chapter 37. Beholding a long valley littered with human bones, he hears a voice ask, "Son of man, can those bones live?" Miraculously, the fragmented skeletons reassemble themselves and are again clothed in flesh. Yahweh directs the winds to breathe life into them, and their **resurrection** is complete. Here, Ezekiel predicts the rebirth of Israel, which was symbolically dead; this image of rebirth eventually would become part of Israel's religious hope. It was not until the Book of Daniel was written four centuries later that a belief in the individual's resurrection was explicitly promulgated (Dan. 12:1–3).

Once the nation was restored to its homeland, however, what was to prevent its being devastated again by Gentile armies? To assure the people that Yahweh will protect Israel's future security, the prophet introduces the strange allegory of **Gog** and **Magog** (Chs. 38–39). In an eschatological vision, Ezekiel sees Jerusalem's would-be attackers destroyed by Yahweh's direct intervention, and Israel's slain enemies are so numerous that it takes seven months to bury their corpses.

This spectacular rescue is performed not only for the nation's sake but also for the additional vindication of Yahweh, whose stature in the eyes of other nations had been seriously reduced by the humiliating defeat of his people and destruction of his Temple. To restore his international prestige and reputation, Yahweh resolves to act resolutely in the future. Chapter 39 closes with his reaffirmation to return to Jerusalem all who are currently scattered among foreign countries so that the Gentiles will be forced to "know that I am Yahweh their God":

> When I bring them [Israel] back from the countries of their enemies, when I reveal my holiness in them for many nations to see, they will know that I am Yahweh their God. . . . I shall never hide my face from them again.
>
> Ezek. 39:27–29

Future Israel   The final section (Chs. 40–48), a kind of blueprint for the future Israelite theocracy, offers a concrete hope to the Jewish exiles in Babylon. Room by room and court by court, giving exact measurements and dimensions, Ezekiel describes the rebuilt Temple and then envisions Yahweh's return to his restored sanctuary:

> I saw the glory of the God of Israel approaching from the east. A sound came with it, like the sound of the ocean, and the earth shone with his glory. . . . The glory of Yahweh arrived at the Temple by the east gate. . . . I saw the glory of Yahweh fill the Temple.
>
> Ezek. 43:1–6

The prophet's visions have thus come full circle, from beholding Yahweh deserting the doomed sanctuary to beholding Yahweh's "glory" returning to a greater Temple.

The idealized new Temple was to be administered not by the Levites, but by descendants of the priest **Zadok**, whose name means "righteous." Levites may serve as attendants, but only Zadokites are to enjoy full priestly authority. After listing regulations and liturgical details of Temple worship, Ezekiel (or the disciples who compiled and edited his work) paints a final vision of a life-giving stream of water issuing from beneath the sanctuary, a fitting symbol of the spiritual cleansing that Yahweh will provide at his restored shrine.

In several ways, Ezekiel's message resembles that of Jeremiah. Both attribute the nation's political troubles to its many sins, especially social injustice and failure to worship Yahweh alone. Both predict that Yahweh will assuage his anger with a national catastrophe culminating in the destruction of Jerusalem and exile in Babylon. Both emphasize individual responsibility for one's life and foretell a return from the Babylonian captivity. A priest as well as a prophet, however, Ezekiel emphasizes the necessity of practicing Jewish rites, customs, holiday and dietary observances, and communal worship even in exile, realizing that the exiles' moral behavior *and* strict adherence to ceremonial requirements would ensure their national and religious survival. With this emphasis, Ezekiel became the spiritual progenitor of later **Judaism**.

RECOMMENDED READING

Ackroyd, Peter R. *Exile and Restoration: A Study of Hebrew Thought in the Sixth Century* B.C.E. Philadelphia: Westminster Press, 1968.

Boadt, Lawrence. "Ezekiel, Book of." In D. N. Freedman, ed., *The Anchor Bible Dictionary*, Vol. 2, pp. 711–722. New York: Doubleday, 1992.

Darr, Katheryn Pfisterer, "The Book of Ezekiel." In *The New Interpreter's Bible*, Vol. 6, pp. 1075–1607. Nashville: Abingdon Press, 2001. A thorough analysis of Ezekiel in its sociohistorical context.

Eichrodt, Walther. *Ezekiel*. Philadelphia: Westminster Press, 1970.

Greenberg, Moshe. *Ezekiel, 1–20*. Garden City, N.Y.: Doubleday, 1983.

Klein, Ralph W. *Ezekiel: The Prophet and His Message*. Columbia: University of South Carolina Press, 1988.

Raitt, Thomas M. *A Theology of Exile*. Philadelphia: Fortress Press, 1977.

Zimmerli, Walther. *Ezekiel*, 2 vols. Hermenica. Philadelphia: Fortress Press, 1979, 1983. A major form-critical study showing parallels between Ezekiel and laws in Leviticus 17–26.

"Second Isaiah"

KEY TOPICS/THEMES

In Isaiah 40–55, a new voice is heard, proclaiming to Judean exiles in Babylon that the time of punishment is past and that a new era is dawning, heralded by the conquests of Cyrus of Persia, who will defeat Babylon to become the Near East's new master. Presenting Cyrus as Yahweh's anointed king, the anonymous prophet known as "Second Isaiah" prepares his fellow exiles for a radically changed world in which their God will lead them in a new exodus to their homeland. The first prophet to declare explicitly that Yahweh is the only God, Second Isaiah states that the covenant people's historical role is henceforth that of Yahweh's servant, God's vehicle for bringing divine "light" to Gentile nations.

KEY QUESTIONS

How is the setting for Isaiah 40–55 different from that of Isaiah of Jerusalem? What message of comfort to Babylonian exiles does this prophet bring? Why can the exiles rely entirely on Yahweh?

One of the Hebrew Bible's greatest poets, the anonymous prophet known as Second Isaiah brought a message of hope and consolation to his fellow exiles during the last years of the Babylonian captivity (c. 540 B.C.E.). Announcing that Judah's time of punishment is fulfilled, Second Isaiah proclaims not ony that Yahweh has fully pardoned his people but also is granting them freedom, guiding them on a "new exodus" out of Babylon and back to the Promised Land.

To mark the transition from the oracles associated with Isaiah of Jerusalem (Chs. 1–39) to those of the unnamed poet who carried on Isaiah's prophetic tradition almost two centuries later (Chs. 40–55), postexilic editors inserted a long prose excerpt from 2 Kings. The interpolated passage ends with Isaiah warning King Hezekiah that all his wealth would one day be "carried off to Babylon" and that his descendants would serve as eunuchs "in the palace of the king of Babylon" (Isa. 39:5–7). From this point on, neither the name of Isaiah nor the Assyrian threat that preoccupied him is ever again mentioned. Henceforth all references to the Near Eastern political scene concern Assyria's successor, Babylon, which is already about to fall, and the rise of a new dominant power, that of the Medes and Persians.

Cyrus of Persia Urging the dispirited exiles to see these international developments as evidence of God's hand at work, Second Isaiah emphasizes

that Israel's God remains in full control of human history, directing political events to redeem his captive people. Yahweh's agent in delivering the exiles is **Cyrus the Great**, king of Persia, whose armies were then sweeping through the Near East. Although Cyrus does not "know" Yahweh, the Persian leader is nontheless God's instrument of change, winning a series of astonishing victories, beinning with his conquests of Media (549 B.C.E.) and Lydia (546 B.C.E.). Viewing Cyrus's triumphs as evidence of divine action, Second Isaiah declares that he is the "shepherd" who fulfills God's purpose of restoring the Judean community and rebuilding Jerusalem and the Temple, which the Babylonians had destroyed (44:28–45:6; cf. 41:1–9, 25–29; 48:12–16, 20–22). Unlike Isaiah of Jerusalem, the exilic prophet does not look to a Davidic heir to rehabilitate the covenant community; instead, he declares that Cyrus is Yahweh's "anointed," his "Messiah" (45:1).

Because he refers to Babylon's fall to Cyrus as imminent but not yet accomplished (Ch. 47), Second Isaiah's oracles were probably delivered shorting before 539 B.C.E., when Cyrus captured the city. A year after Cyrus took Babylon, the prophet's optimistic view of him as a liberator was vindicated by the Persian king's implementing a policy that encouraged all groups who had been deported to Babylon to return to their respective homelands. Although Second Isaiah regards Cyrus's liberation of exiles as if it were directed exclusively to the Judean community, the Persian emperor apparently pursued a general policy of repatriation and restoration of local shrines in the lands he conquered. Nor, in spite of the Judean prophet's pronouncements, did he ascribe his conquests to Yahweh. According to the Cyrus Cylinder, an artifact inscribed with an account of Babylon's capture, Cyrus officially attributed his success to Marduk, chief god of the Babylonian pantheon, who delivered his city to the Persians because Babylonian rulers had neglected Marduk's cult (Figure 6.8).

The Omnipotence of Judah's God Although he views a single group—Judean exiles—as occupying center stage of world history, Second Isaiah,

Figure 6.8 The Cyrus Cylinder, describing Cyrus the Great's capture of Babylon (539 B.C.E.), illustrates the radically different ways in which non-Israelites and biblical writers interpreted the same historical events. Second Isaiah views Cyrus, liberator of Jewish captives, as Yahweh's national deliverer, his "messiah" (Isa. 45:1–3). Whereas the author of 2 Chronicles shows Cyrus attributing his victories to Yahweh (2 Chron. 36:23), the Cylinder presents Cyrus ascribing them to the chief Babylonian god Marduk, who inspires the Persian conqueror to restore the Near Eastern gods' neglected altars. The editors who arranged the Hebrew Bible's contents regarded Cyrus's actions as so important that they made his order to rebuild the Jerusalem Temple the climactic final act in the Tanak canon, completing the creation sequence begun in Genesis 1:1.

more than any other prophet before him, makes categorial delarations about the uniqueness, universality, and eternity of the biblical God. Without beginning or ending, Yahweh alone is the creator and ruler of the cosmos; other gods do not exist: "they are nothing; . . . their images wind and emptiness" (41:29).

Even Marduk and his divine son, called "Bel" and "Nebo," supposedly responsible for Babylonian political supremacy, are nonentities, powerless before Judah's incomparable God:

> I am the first and the last;
> there is no other God besides me.
> Isa. 44:6

For Second Isaiah, God's will is irresistible, shaping human history in unforeseen ways to achieve his people's salvation. Because he is all-powerful and all-wise, Yahweh alone can predict the covenant community's restoration and guarantee its future reality:

> I am God unrivaled
> God who has no like.
> From the beginning I foretold the future,
> and predicted beforehand what is to be.
> Isa. 46:9–10; cf. 44:7–8

To the poet, Yahweh is both transcendent and immanent: From his heavenly perspective, mighty nations and empires are insignificant, no more than "a drop on a pail's rim" (40:15). Although he effortlessly commands the innumerable stars of heaven (representing the members of his celestial council), he also reaches out to earth, inspiring his frightened and exhausted people to trust in the restoration of Judah's fortunes and giving them "wings like eagles" for the return journey home (40:25–31).

In creating the covenant community anew, Yahweh extends to his people as a whole his promise to David, encompassing all the faithful in his "everlasting covenant" (55:3–5). Summoning the Judean exiles to a new role on the world stage,

the Davidic line (Chs. 1–8). The second half of the book contains increasingly obscure oracles from a later prophet, known as Second Zechariah (Chs. 9–14).

KEY QUESTION

How do the two distinct parts of this book illustrate the movement away from traditional prophecy to mystical eschatology?

Whereas Haggai's message was direct and straightforward, that of Zechariah, his fellow prophet of the postexilic period, is often ambiguous and obscure. The Book of Zechariah makes clear that Yahweh wishes to have the Temple rebuilt and that Zerubbabel is a likely candidate to restore Judah's political fortunes, but beyond that all certainty vanishes. Scholars divide the book into two parts. The first eight chapters are mostly by the "Historical Zechariah," who began prophesying in 520 B.C.E. Chapters 9–14, called the "Second Zechariah," seem to have been written by other seers, perhaps a Zecharian school of prophets, at various later dates.

HISTORICAL ZECHARIAH

Zechariah, who appears to have come from a priestly family, lived in a restored community in which want and insecurity had taken the place of the glorious future predicted by Second Isaiah. Although Zechariah stressed the necessity of rebuilding the Temple to attain Yahweh's favor and material blessings, he also addressed the community's underlying disillusionment in eight visions (Chs. 1–6), which, interpreted by an angelic figure, are generally aimed at calming the people's apprehensions about what Yahweh intends to do with them. Hopes that Zerubbabel would mount the throne of David are dashed when Darius, emperor of Persia, quells an incipient revolt and consolidates his power. After Zerubbabel disappears from history, Zechariah concentrates on the prospects of Joshua, the high priest, to whom he speaks about a "branch" or shoot from David's stock (3:8–10).

Particularly interesting is Zechariah's vision in Chapter 3 of Joshua standing before Yahweh's heavenly council. When Satan (the adversary) appears to accuse the high priest (who represents the Judean remnant), Yahweh's angel removes Joshua's dirty garments — symbolic of the community's sins — and reclothes him in splendid robes. This change of attire shows that Yahweh has forgiven his people's sins and that the period of national mourning is over; if the community henceforth keeps Yahweh's commandments, it will prosper. Zechariah's mystical experience thus provides hope that Yahweh is at last acting to improve the condition of his partly restored nation.

A RESTORATION OF DAVIDIC KINGS?

Similarly, the vision in 6:9–15 emphasizes Joshua's messianic role as "the branch," the person destined to rebuild the sanctuary, wear the royal insignia, and "sit on his throne as ruler" (6:13). Because this passage also refers to cooperation between a restored king and priest, scholars have suggested that the prophecy originally applied to the Davidic Zerubbabel who, with Joshua, was joint leader of the community. After Zerubbabel's aspirations came to nothing, however, scribes substituted Joshua's name for that of the former governor. Although plans for a renewed Davidic monarchy had become both futile and dangerous, it was still possible to envisage the high priest as Yahweh's anointed and spiritual leader of the Jewish state.

Chapters 7 and 8, respectively, survey the moral meaning of Israel's rise and fall as a nation and promise the people ultimate redemption through a Messiah who will create a new dispensation in which the whole earth will become a paradise. This section concludes with the prediction that not only will powerful nations come to Jerusalem to worship Yahweh, but ten foreigners will cling to a single Jew, begging him to teach them Yahweh's law. With its emphasis on Zion (or Jerusalem) as the religious center of the universe, this section echoes ideas first expressed in Isaiah 2, 9, and 11.

"SECOND ZECHARIAH"

The second half of Zechariah contains diverse oracles, some from as late as the Greek period in the fourth century B.C.E. These strange visions and predictions appear to be the work of several apocalyptic writers whose intended meanings are now nearly impossible to grasp, although the section (which resembles the apocalyptic passages in Isa. 24–27) was a favorite with early Christians, who found numerous messianic references in it.

Zechariah 9:9 declares that Jerusalem's king will come to the city "humble and riding on a donkey, on a colt, the foal of a donkey." The author of Matthew's Gospel, perhaps misunderstanding the poet's use of parallelism here, depicts Jesus as riding on two different animals at once (Matt. 21:1–7). Zechariah also mentions "thirty shekels of silver" (Zech. 11:13–14), the sum for which Judas betrays his Master. A particularly obscure oracle pictures Jerusalem as mourning "one whom they have pierced" (12:10), in a passage in which Yahweh also promises to make "the House of David like God" leading victorious armies. Equally cryptic is the allusion to striking a shepherd and scattering his sheep (13:7), which follows an apparent declaration that the gift of prophecy has been removed from Israel (13:2–6).

Chapter 14 is a full-fledged eschatological vision describing the end of history. In a climactic battle, Yahweh will gather all nations to Jerusalem. The enemy will plunder the city and slaughter nearly all its inhabitants. But at the last desperate moment, Yahweh will intervene, striding from the Mount of Olives—which will be sundered by titanic earthquakes—to fight for Israel.

After annihilating his enemies, Yahweh will transform the earth and its climate. Cold and frost will cease, streams will issue from Jerusalem, mountains will disappear, and all Palestine will become a plain (a highly desirable change for farmers and shepherds). Meanwhile, non-Jewish nations will suffer a plague that rots their eyes in the sockets and causes them to attack one another irrationally. The nations that survive this catastrophe will henceforth make pilgrimages to Jerusalem, then elevated above all other cities, to worship at Yahweh's Temple, and Yahweh "will be king of the whole world."

RECOMMENDED READING

Ackroyd, Peter R. *Exile and Restoration: A Study of Hebrew Thought in the Sixth Century* B.C.E. Philadelphia: Westminster Press, 1968.

Coggins, Richard J. *Haggai, Zechariah, Malachi.* Old Testament Guides. Sheffield, England: JSOT Press, 1987.

Ollenburger, Ben C. "The Book of Zechariah." In *The New Interpreter's Bible,* Vol. 7, pp. 735–840. Nashville: Abingdon Press, 1996.

Petersen, David L. "Zechariah." In J. L. Mays, ed., *Harper's Bible Commentary,* pp. 747–752. San Francisco: Harper & Row, 1988.

"Third Isaiah"

KEY TOPICS/THEMES

Isaiah 56–66 preserves a miscellaneous assemblage of prophetic oracles drawn from the entire era of Israelite prophecy. An anonymous prophet ("Third Isaiah") directs his message to an impoverished colony of exiles resettled in Judah, now under Persian rule.

KEY QUESTION

How would postexilic disappointments in the present stimulate visions of "new heavens and a new earth"?

DISAPPOINTMENTS IN THE RESTORED COMMUNITY

Parts of the third section of the Book of Isaiah appear to depict conditions in postexilic Judah when the returned exiles confronted an unsatisfying reality of poverty and political helplessness that was painfully different from the brilliant prospects that Second Isaiah had envisioned. At this juncture, a new member of the prophetic school descended from Isaiah of Jerusalem—known for want of a better title as "Third Isaiah"—added new messages to the prophetic collection, denouncing the restored community's lapses into idolatry, social injustice, religious apathy, and failure to keep the Sabbath properly.

The opening and closing parts of this section (56:1–8; 66:18–23) reveal a new dimension to Yahweh's worshiping community—the inclusion of foreigners who, the prophet declares, are to be integrated completely into Judah's religious life. These Gentile converts may have included the Jews' fellow victims of Babylonian oppression, as well as other former citizens of Mesopotamia.

Third Isaiah also injects an apocalyptic element, looking beyond the bleak present to "new heavens and a new earth" in which Judah's sins are forgotten and the land becomes an earthly paradise, enjoying peace, plenty, and longevity for all (65:17–25). This promise of a renewed creation, repeated in Isaiah 66:22–23 to include "all mankind," would become an important eschatological hope of early Christianity (2 Pet. 3:13; Rev. 21:1). The penultimate chapter of the last book of the Christian Bible describes the still-future fulfillment of Third Isaiah's vision (Rev. 21:1–4).

RECOMMENDED READING

Emmerson, Grace I. *Isaiah 56–66.* Old Testament Guides. Sheffield, England: Sheffield Academic Press, 1992.

Hanson, P. D. *Isaiah 40–66.* Louisville, Ky.: Westminster/John Knox, 1995.

Stuhlmueller, Carroll. "Deutero-Isaiah and Trito-Isaiah." In R. E. Brown et al., eds., *The New Jerome Biblical Commentary,* 2nd ed., pp. 329–348. Englewood Cliffs, N.J.: Prentice-Hall, 1990. Discusses the work of Second and Third Isaiah in the prophets' historical context.

Joel

KEY TOPICS/THEMES

After comparing a plague of locusts then devastating Judah (Ch. 1) to Yahweh's imminent day of wrath, Joel predicts an outpouring of the divine spirit on all humanity and proclaims judgment on foreign nations (Ch. 4).

KEY QUESTION

How does Joel balance threats of judgment with promises of future salvation?

The Book of Joel presents some of the most striking imagery found in the Hebrew Bible. Although it gives no conclusive evidence of the time it was written, the conditions it describes—locust invasions, drought, and crop failure—suggest that the prophet was active during the fifth century B.C.E., a period of severe economic hardship for the imperfectly restored community of Judah.

A PLAGUE OF LOCUSTS

The book consists of two parts. The first (1:1–2:27) vividly relates the devastation wrought by a plague of locusts, which Joel, following the prophetic-deuteronomic tradition, interprets as a sign that Yahweh is angry with his people. He urges the Judeans to repent (2:12–17), promising that Yahweh will then graciously end the plague (2:18–27). Chapter 2 either describes an invading army or likens the locusts to a foreign invasion. Which of the two is meant is unknown, but the crisis inspires Joel to declare that the Day of Yahweh, a gloomy time of judgment that Amos had previously announced (Amos 5:18–20), is at hand.

THE DAY OF YAHWEH

The second part of Joel (2:28–3:21) presents some difficulties because in the manuscript text, many passages seem to be out of order. For this reason, some modern editors, such as those of the Jerusalem Bible, have reconstructed the sequence of several verses to make better sense of Joel's message. The main theme, however, is clear: The locust or military invasion heralds Yahweh's imminent visitation of both Judah and the nations, an event of cosmic terror: "The sun will be turned to darkness, and the moon to blood, before the great and terrible day of the Lord comes" (2:31, RSV).

Although the Day of Yahweh will involve "portents in the heavens and on earth, blood and fire and columns of smoke" (2:30), it will also provide an opportunity to obtain individual salvation, for at that time "all who call on the name of Yahweh will be saved" (2:32). After repentance, Joel foresees the dawn of a new age. Not only will the land recover from its present desolation and prosper, but Yahweh will pour out his spirit upon all humanity so that dreams, visions, and prophecies will reopen channels of communication between the Deity and his creation (2:28–29).

A GLORIOUS FUTURE

In his climactic vision of the "End Time," Joel predicts that godless nations will be summoned to the Valley of Decision (3:14), where the ultimate war between Good and Evil (called Armageddon in Rev. 16:12–16) will take place. In a reversal of Isaiah's prophecy (Isa. 2:4), Joel sardonically urges the foreign warriors to

> Hammer your plowshares into swords,
> your sickles into spears.
>
> Joel 4:10

After the Gentile hosts suffer final defeat, Yahweh will send his people unprecedented blessings:

> When that day comes,
> the mountains will run with new wine,
> and the hills flow with milk,
> and all the river beds of Judah run with water.
>
> Joel 3:18

Joel specifically promises that Yahweh will never again publicly shame Judah, as he had done when it was conquered by Babylon (2:20). He foresees that Yahweh will always protect his holy city:

> But Judah will be inhabited for ever,
> Jerusalem from age to age . . .
> and Yahweh will make his home in Zion.
>
> Joel 3:19–21

Joel contains in miniature the pattern for Judgment Day and the New Age on which later biblical writers elaborated in such books as Daniel, 2 Esdras, and Revelation. The eschatological features that Joel foresees as occurring at the End of history include (1) a series of natural, political, and supernatural disasters—"signs" in heaven and earth—that portend the wrath to come, (2) a cosmic battle fought in both the material and spiritual realms, in which Yahweh and his people triumph over their enemies, (3) an outpouring of Holy Spirit on Yahweh's people, and (4) the divine presence among the faithful.

Understandably, Joel is frequently quoted by later Jewish and Christian writers. The pseudepigraphal Book of Enoch reflects Joel's ideas and imagery, as does the New Testament Book of Acts, which interprets the pentecostal miracle as the fulfillment of Joel 2:28–29 (see Acts 2:1–4, 7–21). The Synoptic Gospels cite Joel's references to astronomical phenomena as events heralding Jesus' Second Coming (see Mark 13:24–25; Luke 21:11, 25; Matt. 24:29).

RECOMMENDED READING

Achtemier, Elizabeth. "The Book of Joel." In *The New Interpreter's Bible*, Vol. 7, pp. 301–336. Nashville: Abingdon Press, 1996.

Prinsloo, William S. *The Theology of the Book of Joel.* New York: Walter de Gruyter, 1985.

Wolff, Hans W. *Joel and Amos.* Philadelphia: Fortress Press, 1977.

Malachi

KEY TOPICS/THEMES

Contrasting foreign nations that honor Yahweh with Judah's apathetic sacrificial cult, the prophet Malachi instructs a dispirited, disorganized audience of Judeans on how to please their God (Chs. 1 and 2) and predicts the future day of Yahweh, evoking the reappearance of Elijah and the coming of Yahweh's irresistible messenger of the covenant (Ch. 3).

KEY QUESTION

How does Malachi reinterpret the day of Yahweh to include traditions about Elijah's return?

In Protestant and Catholic bibles, Malachi appears as the last book of the Old Testament, an appropriate placement because the book concludes with a prediction that Yahweh will send a "messenger" who will prepare his people for the climactic event of history, the Day of Yahweh. The title of the book, *Malachi,* means "my messenger"; it may have been taken from the reference at 3:1 and may not be the name of a historical prophet. Although the text gives no information about the writer or time of composition, the book is customarily dated in the fifth century B.C.E., shortly before the time when traditional prophecy in Israel is thought to have ceased.

PLEASING YAHWEH

The first two chapters contribute little to Israel's prophetic legacy. Casting his message in question-and-answer form, the writer presents Yahweh's complaints that the people offend him by sacrificing defective animals at the Temple. The author's concern is exclusively with the physical aspects of worship; he has nothing to say about the moral implications. Even so, one can assume that he views the offering of an unblemished animal, as Mosaic law required, as the outward symbol of worshipers' wholehearted attempt to please God; to do less betrayed an imperfect commitment to Yahweh. Chapter 2 ends with a vigorous attack on divorce, which the prophet also regards as breaking faith with Yahweh. Some commentators see this passage as a reaction against the policies of Ezra and Nehemiah, who compelled Jewish men to divorce their non-Jewish wives (Ezra 10:3, 44; see also Neh. 13:23–29).

THE COMING MESSENGER

Malachi's prediction that the Temple will be inspected and cleansed by Yahweh's messenger, "the angel of the Covenant" (3:1), is thematically connected with the earlier denunciations of inferior sacrifices, but in Chapter 3 the prophet broadens his charge to include responsibilities to widows, orphans, strangers, and the poor. The author briefly returns to mundane functions, like tithing (3:6–12), but then asserts that Yahweh's justice will prevail only when the God himself intervenes to champion the righteous and punish the wicked. Although in this life the arrogant and ruthless often exploit the humble and faithful, justice will triumph when the Day of Yahweh arrives. It consequently behooves one to keep the commandments, even though one may temporarily suffer for it.

Finally, Malachi promises that before "that great and terrible day" arrives, Yahweh will send Elijah the prophet—who in 2 Kings 2:11–12 had been carried off alive to heaven—to reconcile the generations, fathers and children, lest Yahweh "strike the land with a curse" (3:24). The belief that Elijah would return to prepare the way for the Messiah or the kingdom of God and Day of Judgment played a significant part in later Jewish expectations. Even today, a place is set for Elijah, the long-awaited guest, at Passover observances. In the first century C.E., the Synoptic Gospels identify John the Baptist with Elijah's eschatological role (Mark 9:11–12; Matt. 17:9–13).

RECOMMENDED READING

Hanson, Paul D. "Malachai." In J. L. Mays, ed., *Harper's Bible Commentary*, pp. 753–756. San Francisco: Harper & Row, 1988.

Ogden, Graham S., and Deutsch, Richard R. *Joel and Malachi: A Promise of Hope, a Call to Obedience.* Grand Rapids, Mich.: Eerdmans, 1987.

Schuller, Eileen M. "The Book of Malachi." In *The New Interpreter's Bible*, Vol. 7, pp. 843–877. Nashville: Abingdon Press, 1996.

Jonah

KEY TOPICS/THEMES

A narrative about the vast difference between a God of infinite compassion and a prophet of painfully limited understanding, Jonah provides both a critique of some Israelite prophecy and an illustration of God's universality. Utilizing folklore, humor, and hyperbole to make his point, an unknown post-exilic author sets his fictional tale in the eighth century B.C.E., when Assyria dominated the ancient Near East.

KEY QUESTION

Is Jonah's story a critique of traditional Israelite prophecy?

A STRIKINGLY DIFFERENT PROPHETIC VISION

In both literary form and message, the Book of Jonah differs strikingly from other prophetic works in the Hebrew Bible. Rather than presenting a collection of poetic oracles that addresses an ethical issue or political emergency, Jonah is a prose narrative relating the misadventures of a prophet who fails utterly to understand the God who summons him to warn the citizens of Nineveh, capital of the hated Assyrian Empire, of impending divine judgment. Whereas most biblical books represent prophets who overcome their initial reluctance to accept God's call and then prophesy as commanded, Jonah portrays a cowardly and disobedient prophet who is consistenly resentful of God's use of him. When called to preach in Nineveh, Jonah—perhaps suspecting that Yahweh's kindness may lead him to spare that hated city—heads in the opposite direction. Aboard a foreign ship sailing for Tarshish (probably Spain) in the remote western Mediterranean, Jonah falls asleep during a raging storm that Yahweh has brought to halt his prophet's flight.

Although they are Gentiles who worship foreign gods, the sailors on Jonah's ship are portrayed as just and reasonable men, open to hearing the word of Israel's God. Casting lots, they learn that Jonah is the cause of the storm that threatens to drown them, but they are too humane to cast the Israelite jinx overboard. Only after begging Yahweh's forgiveness do they hurl Jonah into the sea, where God has arranged for a large fish (not a whale) to swallow him.

Chapter 2 consists largely of Jonah's desperate prayer from the belly of the sea creature. In this poetic passage, Jonah likens his predicament to being immersed in the original watery chaos that preceded creation and to burial in Sheol, abode of the hopeless dead (see Box 7.3). Yahweh then orders the fish to spew Jonah out, depositing him on shore.

The humor of the totally improbable dominates Chapter 3. After his "resurrection" from the fishy grave, Jonah again hears Yahweh's voice ordering him to go to Nineveh, described as so gigantic a metropolis that it takes three days to walk across it. Announcing his message as brutally as possible in a single sentence—"Only forty more days and Nineveh is going to be destroyed"—Jonah is unpleasantly surprised at the people's reaction. The entire Assyrian population, from the king downward, immediately repents; even the animals wear sackcloth, a garment of mourning and self-abasement, in the hope that Yahweh will relent and spare their city. Approving the Assyrians' response, Yahweh rewards their improved behavior by deciding not to obliterate them.

Furious at such divine softheartedness, Jonah disapprovingly paraphrases the Torah passages that identify Yahweh as "a God of tenderness and compassion, slow to anger, rich in graciousness, relenting from evil" (4:2–3; cf. Exod. 34:6–7; Num. 14:17–19). As Jonah implies, it is all very well for Israel's God to manifest *hesed* (steadfast love) to his own people, but quite another for him to bestow it on a Gentile nation that does not explicitly worship him. Feeling betrayed that Yahweh did not vindicate his preaching by executing a spectacular catastrophe, Jonah asks to die. Yahweh has but one question for him: "Are you right to be angry?" (4:5).

While the prophet sulks in solitude outside Nineveh's gates, Yahweh attempts to teach Jonah a much-needed lesson that might bring him closer to the divine perspective. First causing a leafy plant to grow, providing shade that will "soothe [Jonah's] ill-humor," Yahweh then sends a worm to kill the plant. Smoldering with resentment, the prophet again asks for death.

The book concludes with a conversation in which Jonah and his God discuss the implications of the plant's short life. How, Yahweh asks, can the prophet regret the death of a plant and not understand Yahweh's concern for the 120,000 humans living in Nineveh, people who "cannot tell their right hand from their left" (4:6–11)? The prophet who had learned that nowhere on land or sea could he escape Yahweh's reach is now also asked to contemplate the implications of Yahweh's universality. As Amos and Second Isaiah had recognized, Israel enjoys a special relationship with God but does not have exclusive claim to divine care—the same Deity who created Israel also directs the destinies of other nations (Amos 9:7; Isa. 42:4–6; 45:1–6, etc.). The author does not state whether Jonah was able to embrace this larger perspective, leaving the question for readers to ponder.

QUESTIONS FOR REVIEW

1. Define the nature and function of Israel's prophets. During what three crucial periods of Israel's ancient history did most of the prophets appear?

Were they typically more concerned with foretelling the far distant future or with declaring Yahweh's views on pressing ethical and social issues of their own day?

2. During the eighth century B.C.E., when the threat of Assyrian invasion loomed on the horizon, which prophets were active in the northern kingdom of Israel? What were their messages about economic and social justice? Which two prophets were active in Judah? Did Isaiah and Micah have the same opinion of the Davidic royal dynasty?

3. What was Judah's political situation during the decades that Isaiah counseled Jerusalem's kings? What "miraculous" event occurred during Hezekiah's reign in 701 B.C.E.?

4. Why do scholars believe that the Book of Isaiah represents the work of at least three different prophets from three different historical periods? Why does the Assyrian threat dominate the first part of Isaiah, whereas after Chapter 40 the rise of Cyrus and the Persian Empire becomes the most important political fact? Which passages in Isaiah 40–55 do you find most significant in establishing Judaism as a universal, monotheistic religion?

5. Habakkuk, Jeremiah, and Ezekiel prophesied during the Babylonian crisis. To what social abuses and failures of leadership does Jeremiah attribute the fall of Jerusalem? How does Ezekiel attempt to prepare his people for the future? Do you see any connection between Jeremiah's promise of a "new covenant" (Jer. 31:31) and Ezekiel's visions of a restored holy city and Temple?

6. Haggai and Zechariah were active after a Judean "remnant" had returned to Jerusalem from Babylon. What were their hopes about Zerubbabel's restoring Davidic rule in Judah? What role did the two prophets play in rebuilding Yahweh's Temple?

QUESTIONS FOR DISCUSSION AND REFLECTION

1. How does the prophets' characteristic concern for social justice, particularly their distrust of economic acquisitiveness, relate to their understanding of Yahweh's nature as a just God motivated by *hesed* (steadfast love or loving kindness)? Why is Yahweh consistently viewed as both the source of social justice and the champion of the poor?

2. Discuss the Book of Jonah as a critique of some aspects of Israelite prophecy. In what ways does the prophet fail to appreciate his God's character?

3. Using Amos, Hosea, Micah, Isaiah of Jerusalem, and Second Isaiah as examples, specify the contributions that each makes toward a composite portrait of Yahweh's nature and relationship to humanity. How do Amos's demand that Israel live up to a high standard of social and economic justice and Hosea's picture of God as a loving husband or father illustrate evolving concepts of Yahweh? How does Second Isaiah's vision of God as Lord of history and sole master of the universe promote the notion of universalism?

4. Historically, the phenomenon of Israelite prophecy rose with the establishment of the Davidic monarchy and rapidly declined after its termination in 587 B.C.E. How do you explain the relationship of these two institutions? Is it possible that, if prophecy appeared largely in response to national crisis, the monarchy itself constituted some kind of extended religious crisis for Israel? In answering, consider the tension between the concept of the Mosaic Covenant, which was made with the entire Israelite people, and the Davidic Covenant, which favored a single privileged family.

5. During their lifetimes, most of Israel's prophets were largely ignored or persecuted, partly because their messages, like that of Jeremiah, were not what people wanted to hear. If prophets similar to Amos or Jeremiah were to appear today, how do you think that most churches or synagogues would receive them? In terms of contemporary social, political, and economic problems, what do you think a modern Jeremiah would say that would alienate his audience?

6. According to Deuteronomy 18, how may one distinguish between a true prophet and an imposter? In what ways do prophets move people to detect the will of God in a difficult or even ethically ambiguous situation? What role does *hesed* play in responding to prophetic advice?

TERMS AND CONCEPTS TO REMEMBER

Ahaz	Ezekiel
Amos	Gog
apostasy	Habakkuk
Ashdod	Haggai
Baruch	Hezekiah
Cyrus the Great	Hosea
Deutero-Isaiah (Second Isaiah)	Immanuel
	Isaiah (of Jerusalem)
Edom, Edomites	Jehoiakim
eschatology	Jeremiah

Jeroboam II
Joel
Jonah
Judaism
Magog
Major Prophets
Malachi
Micah
Minor Prophets
Nahum
navi (nabi)
Obadiah
Oracle
parallelism
Queen of Heaven

resurrection
Second Isaiah
seer
Sennacherib
Seraphim
Tammuz
Third Isaiah
Uzziah (Azariah)
Zadok
Zechariah
Zedekiah
Zephaniah
Zerubbabel
Zion

RECOMMENDED READING

Ceresko, Anthony R. "Jonah." In R. E. Brown et al., eds., *The New Jerome Biblical Commentary*, 2nd ed., pp. 580–584. Englewood Cliffs, N.J.: Prentice-Hall, 1990.

Fretheim, Terence E. *The Message of Jonah*. Minneapolis: Augsburg, 1977.

Magonet, Jonathan. "Jonah, Book of." In D. N. Freedman, ed., *The Anchor Bible Dictionary*, Vol. 3, pp. 936–942. New York: Doubleday, 1992. A short introduction to issues raised in the book.

Trible, Phyllis. *Rhetorical Criticism: Context, Method, and the Book of Jonah*. Minneapolis: Fortress Press, 1994. Demonstrates the relationship between literary artistry and Jonah's theological message.

———. "The Book of Jonah." In *The New Interpreter's Bible*, Vol. 7, pp. 463–529. Nashville: Abingdon Press, 1996. A sensitive reading of this paradoxical view of Israelite prophecy.

CHAPTER 7

The Writings (Kethuvim)

Books of Poetry, Wisdom, Short Fiction, and Sacred History

Key Topics/Themes

The third major division of the Hebrew Bible and the last to be adopted into the canon, the Writings (*Kethuvim*) are as diverse in content as they are in literary form, ranging from devotional poetry (Psalms), to books of practical and speculative Wisdom (Proverbs, Job, and Ecclesiastes), to theological histories reinterpreting Israel's past (1 and 2 Chronicles). Although some books in the Writings, such as Psalms, contain preexilic material, most of the documents reflect the difficulties of the covenant community's postexilic readjustment, when Judah was subject to Persian domination.

KEY QUESTIONS

How do the Writings express Judea's postexilic function as a worshiping community led by priests and the theological crisis posed by Yahweh's apparent absence from the political scene? How do they address the mystery of God's failure to restore the Davidic dynasty, or to make Israel/Judah again a power among the nations? Why is the problem of

evil and undeserved suffering, examined in Job and Ecclesiastes, now more pressing than ever before?

After the Exile: A Reinterpretation of Judah's Religious Mission

After the Babylonian exile, nothing in the covenant community was ever again the same. Although successive waves of Judean exiles returned to Jerusalem following Cyrus's decree encouraging repatriation in 538 B.C.E., postexilic restoration was only partial. Despite the prophecies of Haggai and Zechariah (see Chapter 6), neither the Davidic dynasty nor the former state of Judah was restored. Known henceforth as the "province of Judea" (Ezra 5:8) and restricted to the territory surrounding Jerusalem, the Judean homeland was reduced to a small subunit of the Persian Empire. Except for a brief interval when the Maccabees (Hasmoneans) ruled (142–63 B.C.E.), the Judean people never again enjoyed political independence. Persian

Box 7.1 The Writings: Responses to Judah's Postexilic Experience

"Can these bones live?" When Yahweh asked this question of Ezekiel, who was then a captive in Babylon, the covenant people resembled desiccated skeletons scattered in a boneyard. The nation of Judah had perished in the flames rising from Jerusalem and Solomon's Temple. Further, as had happened to many other small states crushed by the Babylonian juggernaut, it looked as if Judah would vanish forever, buried in history's graveyard. Yahweh, however, regarded Judah's political death and interment—punishment for its faithlessness—as only a temporary state: "these bones [that were] the whole House of Israel" would live again. In Ezekiel's vision of his nation's future resurrection, the prophet witnesses Yahweh's miraculous reenactment of Adam's creation. Infusing Judah's apparently lifeless corpse with his spirit, Yahweh re-creates a people for his name (Ezek. 37:1–14).

The third principal division of the Hebrew Bible, the Writings (*Kethuvim*), provides the wide-ranging responses of postexilic authors to the radically changed circumstances of the covenant community. As Ezekiel had envisioned old bones infused with new life, so writers living after the exile labor both to revive Judah's old institutions, such as the Temple cult and priesthood, and to interpret anew Yahweh's

continuing purpose for Judah. Simultaneously preserving ancient traditions and infusing them with new meaning, the author of 1 and 2 Chronicles retold Israel's history from a priestly perspective in which the postexilic priesthood could, as community leaders, be viewed as the logical successors to the Davidic kings, the best of whom had devotedly supported the sanctuary cult. Opening his revised history with an extensive genealogy that links Adam, God's first human creation, with both Levite priests and Davidic kings, and concluding with Cyrus's resuscitation of the Judean state, the Chronicler emphasizes the continuity of his community's past and present.

The unknown author of Ruth fashions another re-creation of Israel's past by placing his gentle heroine back at the time of the Judges, even before the monarchy was established. At the same time that he celebrates an idealized past, picturing a far more peaceful environment than that depicted in the Book of Judges, Ruth's author tackles issues of exclusivity that had long troubled the covenant people. Perhaps deliberately protesting Nehemiah's law compelling all Israelite men to divorce their non-Israelite wives, the writer portrays Ruth, a Moabite woman—and presumably a worshiper of Chemosh—as entirely

administrators, following an imperial policy of promoting local religions in the Persian Empire, supported the reestablishment of Yahweh's cult at a rebuilt Jerusalem Temple, but the harsh reality of postexilic life seemed to mock Second Isaiah's visions of a glorious future. Only a tiny scrap of the land promised to Abraham's descendants was still theirs, and an increasingly large number of Yahweh's people lived far from their homeland in the Diaspora, the "scattering" of Jews abroad in **Gentile** (non-Jewish) nations.

THE POSTEXILIC COMMUNITY

Although Persia did not grant the province of Judea political autonomy nor allow Davidic heirs to reestablish the throne, it actively encouraged

Judea's religious function, mandating an official edition of the Mosaic Torah (Ezra 7) and at least partly subsidizing reconstruction of the Temple. Instead of being ruled by Davidic kings who strove to make their nation a political force in the Near East, the former Judah became a **theocracy**, a "God-ruled" society led by priests. The covenant community's historical transition from an independent kingdom aspiring to play a role in international politics to a people deprived of political influence and subservient to Persian authority also marks a change in the Judeans' understanding of their relationship with Yahweh. No longer governed by divinely appointed kings nor involved in the international political arena, Judea refocused its energies on its religious mission and priestly heritage.

Box 7.1 *(continued)*

sympathetic. Although the Torah had portrayed foreign women, whether Moabite or Midianite, as wanton temptresses who caused Israelite men to sin, and hence to deserve death (cf. Num. 31:1–20; Deut. 7:1–16; 20:17–18), the story of Ruth celebrates marriage between a foreign widow and her Yahwist husband, clearly implying that it fulfills the divine will.

In the Writings, poets and sages also explore the possible meanings of Israel's prolonged suffering and incomplete restoration, creating such masterpieces as Job and Ecclesiastes. Rejecting the simplistic deuteronomic thesis that equated prosperity with religious obedience, and misery with sin, the authors of these Wisdom books boldly question conventional biblical teachings, including traditional concepts of God. Representing a broad spectrum of literary categories, from lyric poetry and short fiction to lengthy historical narratives, the Writings bear eloquent testimony to the diverse ways in which Judah's postexilic thinkers creatively refocused and reinterpreted their religious legacy.

BOOKS OF THE WRITINGS

- Psalms (an anthology of deeply felt religious poetry)
- Proverbs (a compilation of wise sayings, and largely practical and conventional wisdom)
- Job (a philosophical exploration of Yahweh's ethical character and relationship to humanity)
- Ecclesiastes (a sage's quest for meaning and delight in paradox)
- Ruth (a short story about a Moabite woman's new life in Israel during the time of the Judges)
- Song of Songs (a collection of erotic love poems)
- Lamentations (an anguished complaint about Yahweh's destruction of his people)
- Esther (a short story about Jewish survival in a foreign empire)
- Ezra (a composite account of Ezra, the priest-scribe who brought the Torah from Babylon to re-create the covenant community in postexilic Jerusalem)
- Nehemiah (a narrative about rebuilding Jerusalem's fortifications under Persia's sponsorship)
- Daniel (an apocalypse, or revelation, that includes mystical visions of events leading to End time)
- [The last-written book in the Hebrew Bible canon, Daniel is discussed in its historical context in Chapter 8.]
- 1 and 2 Chronicles (a priestly revision of the Deuteronomistic History, emphasizing the Temple cult)

Many of the books included in the Writings illustrate the postexilic community's focus on priestly concerns, particularly Yahweh's formal worship at the rebuilt Temple. In editing this final section of the Tanak, postexilic editors placed the Psalms, a compendium of hymns and other songs performed at the Second Temple, at the head of the collection. The books of Chronicles, which reinterpret the role of Davidic kings to portay them as advocates of priestly Temple rituals, are given the climactic end position (Box 7.1). In this arrangement, both the Writings — and the Hebrew Bible as a whole — conclude with the proclamation of Cyrus, emperor of Persia, who invites Jews from throughout his empire to return to Jerusalem and support Yahweh's sanctuary (2 Chron. 36:22–23).

Between Psalms and Chronicles, which bracket the Writings, redactors assembled a richly diverse anthology of sacred literature that differs significantly from the other two parts of the Hebrew Bible. Although derived from many different sources, the material in the Torah is thematically bound together by Yahweh's series of promises to the patriarchs and the Sinai/Horeb agreement he made with their descendants. The theologically oriented narratives of Joshua through Kings (the Former Prophets) are unified by the author/editors' controlling intent to show Yahweh as Lord of History, expressing his will through Israel's rise and fall. Even the fifteen books of the Latter Prophets, for all their disparate responses to changing political and religious circumstances over a period of four centuries, form a comparatively coherent tradition.

In contrast, the Writings present a wide range of viewpoints expressing multifaceted religious, social, and psychological struggles of a covenant community living under foreign political control.

Whereas the long line of prophets began during the early monarchy and largely ended a few generations after Judah's return from exile, the Writings in their present form belong primarily to the postexilic era (approximately the fifth to the second centuries B.C.E.). Extremely varied in both literary form and theological content, the Writings include some unexpected selections from Hebrew literature, ranging from erotic lyrics in the Song of Solomon to a militaristic celebration of national survival in Esther, a volume that makes no direct reference to God. (As if to rectify this omission, however, the Greek edition of Esther in the Septuagint interpolates a series of prayers and other passages to demonstrate that the heroine was Torah-observant and obedient to the divine will; see Chapter 8.)

A BRIEF SURVEY OF THE WRITINGS

Placed first in the Writings, Psalms is a collection of devotional poetry that sets the tone for this part of the Tanak, which as a whole explores the complex nature of Israel's difficult postexilic partnership with Yahweh. The 150 individual lyrics compiled in this book run the entire gamut of religious feeling, from exulting praise of God to bitter complaints about his treatment of Israel. Although many were probably composed during the period of the Davidic monarchy and sung at the coronation of Davidic kings, others reflect the postexilic situation, expressing bewilderment and disappointment at Yahweh's apparent failure to honor his promises to David or to provide the national blessings enumerated in Genesis and Deuteronomy. Raising issues of divine justice that are addressed throughout the Writings, several psalm writers confront the painful disparity between the ancient promises and the bleak historical realities. Psalm 89 implies that Yahweh broke his word to David, to whom he had guaranteed an everlasting dynasty (Ps. 89:34–36). Babylon's overthrow of Davidic

line—never to be restored—appears to invalidate God's sworn oath (Ps. 89:38–39).

Yahweh's repudiation of the Davidic Covenant, which brought into question the trustworthiness of the Deity's promises, was not the only theological issue that troubled the postexilic Judean community. In striving to understand their God's intentions, devout Judeans confronted another paradox: The more faithful they were to Yahweh, worshiping him exclusively, the more they suffered from injustice and foreign oppression. As the poet in Psalm 44 observes, God's promise to protect those loyal to him—the major premise of Deuteronomy—was not fulfilled in Judah's actual historical experience. In contrast to ancient traditions about Yahweh's saving acts in the remote past, the postexilic God seems indifferent to the massacres and other violence inflicted on his people (Ps. 44:11–12). Rejecting the deuteronomic assumption that suffering results from sin, the psalmist insists that his community has kept its Torah obligations (Ps. 44:17–24). Although the covenant people survived their many afflictions, the disappointment of Yahweh's refusal to come to their aid as he had in Moses' day—as if he were now asleep or absent—perplexed many of the authors whose works appear in the Writings, particularly the Wisdom writers (see the discussions of Job and Ecclesiastes below).

Not vouchsafed an answer to the problem of Yahweh's increasing "hiddenness," the psalmists as a group focused on the covenant community's obligations as a worshiping community, emphasizing the importance of **liturgy**, a body of ceremonial rites performed in public worship. Liturgical concerns are similarly evident in the book of Chronicles, which are largely preoccupied with Temple rituals, enumerating the duties of singers, priests, Levites, and others in carrying out the sacrifices and other formal practices of Yahweh's cult. In editing the Hebrew Bible, Masoretic scribes gathered five short books—Ruth, Song of Solomon, Ecclesiastes, Lamentations, and Esther—together to form a small anthology within the Writings known as the *Megillot*. Sometimes called the Festival Scrolls, the **Megillot** was also designed to serve a liturgical purpose, with each one of the five docu-

Table 7.1 The Megillot and Associated Festivals

BOOK	FESTIVAL
Ruth	**Pentecost**—The harvest festival
Song of Songs	**Passover**—The annual holiday that commemorates the end of slavery for the Israelites in Egypt
Ecclesiastes	**Feast of Tabernacles** or **Feast of Booths**—The autumn agricultural feast of thanksgiving
Lamentations	**Fast of the Ninth of Av** (July–August)—Mourning for the destruction of the Jerusalem Temple by the Babylonians in 587 B.C.E. and the Romans in 70 C.E.
Esther	**Purim** or **Festival of Lots** (February–March)—The celebration of Jewish deliverance from Persian attack

ments read aloud at each of five principal festivals in the Jewish religious calendar (Table 7.1). Although the content of these five works is extremely diverse—Ruth is a pastoral love story; Esther a secular tale justifying Jewish military self-defense; Eccleaiastes a skeptical meditation on self-contradictory Wisdom and divine hiddenness; Lamentations a passionate complaint over Yahweh's abandonment of Jerusalem; and the Song of Solomon a celebration of sexual enjoyment—all were employed to serve the postexilic community's resolve to worship Yahweh alone.

The two historical narratives of Ezra and Nehemiah, which describe sociopolitical conditions in Judea under Persian domination, emphasize both a reorganization of postexilic society and the importance of teaching Torah requirements to a dejected population. Both books are concerned about preserving the covenant community as a worshiping body while subject to foreign control.

As the author of Nehemiah poignantly begged,

Our God, great and mighty God who must be feared . . . Count as no small thing this misery that has happened to us . . . from the time of the kings of Assyria to the present day. . . .
Here we are now, enslaved; here in the land you gave our fathers to enjoy its fruits and its good things, we are slaves. Its rich fruits swell the profit of the [Persian] kings whom for our sins you have set over us, who dispose as they please of our bodies and our cattle. Such the distress we endure!

Neh. 9:32, 36–37

Unlike any other book in either the Prophets (where it typically appears in Christian Old Testaments) or the Writings (where Jewish editors placed it), Daniel is an **apocalypse**, a "revelation" or "unveiling" of unseen realities in the spirit world and of future events. Composed during an episode of intense persecution during the mid-second century B.C.E., this apocalyptic work surveys the covenant people's history—cast in the form of prophecy—from the Babylonian exile to the Hellenistic era (see Chapter 8). The last-written book of the Hebrew Bible, Daniel also deals with issues of keeping Jewish identity and Torah obligations in the Diaspora, where pressures on Jews to conform to foreign culture were pervasive.

Whereas many books in the Writings are closely associated with Judean Temple observances and/or with maintaining Jewish worship in the Diaspora, other texts in this part of the Tanak—the Wisdom literature—embody a wide spectrum of responses to the covenant people's historical experience of both prosperity and extreme suffering. The compilation of largely conventional observations in Proverbs offers commonsense advice on the value of behaving prudently, serving God, and attaining a good life. In contrast, Job, a book of speculative Wisdom, radically departs from most biblical portraits of God, challenging conventional piety to reconcile the Deity's presumed goodness with the universal prevalence of injustice and undeserved pain. As a paradigm of the covenant community's tragic losses during and after the Babylonian exile,

Job raises ethical and theological issues that no one has yet satisfactorily resolved. (Two later Wisdom books, Ecclesiasticus and the Wisdom of Solomon, are discussed with the Apocrypha in Chapter 8.)

With a few exceptions, this text discusses the Writings in the canonical order of the Hebrew Bible, beginning with Psalms and ending with 1 and 2 Chronicles. For coherence, however, the Wisdom books, including Ecclesiastes, are covered together, with the simpler practical counsel of Proverbs discussed before Job's profound exploration of cosmic justice and the problem of evil. A special case, Daniel is examined in the context of the Maccabean Revolt and the apocalyptic movement (see Chapter 8).

Hebrew Poetry

Bible writers use the heightened language of poetry to achieve a broad spectrum of effects, from communication of the almost frenzied joy of a military victory (Judg. 5:2–31), to a meditation on the human condition (Ps. 90), to expressions of suicidal despair that invoke the return of chaos (Job 3:3–26). The third division of the Hebrew Bible encompasses a remarkable variety of poetic styles and subjects. In the Song of Solomon, two lovers ecstatically compare each other's bodies to luscious fruits, domestic and wild animals, and even topographical features, celebrating in almost grotesque imagery their own joy in sexual love. Employing a series of **similes**—comparisons using "as" or "like"—the speaker tells his beloved that

> Your hair is like a flock of goats,
>   frisking down the slopes of Gilead.
> Your teeth are like a flock of shorn ewes
>   as they come up from the washing.
> Each one has its twin,
>   not one unpaired with another.
> Song of Sol. 4:1–2

The poetic complaints in Lamentations also evoke strong emotions, but these are the feelings of pain and sorrow at the loss of homeland and sanctuary. Here, the poet uses a **metaphor**, an implied comparison that pictures Jerusalem as a captive woman, dirty and dressed in rags:

> Her filth clings to the hem of her clothes.
>   She had never thought of ending like this,
> sinking as low as this,
>   She has no one to comfort her.
> Lam. 1:9

Mixing prose passages with short poems, the Book of Ecclesiastes offers an emotionally detached contrast to Lamentations' passionate grief, citing traditional—and sometimes contradictory—examples of prudential wisdom in poetic couplets. Yet, the author, known as Koheleth, concludes his skeptical comments with a singularly haunting poem that compares the body of an aging man to a house deteriorating with age and disrepair. Creating a poetic **allegory**, in which one object or activity functions as a symbol of something else, Koheleth portrays a human body with its failing senses as an edifice ready to collapse:

> when the women grind no longer at the mill,
> because day is darkening at the windows
> and the street doors are shut; . . .
> Eccles. 12:3–4

Unable to chew, see, or hear, the aged man prepares for his "everlasting home," the grave.

Although the story of Job is introduced and concluded with brief prose narratives, most of the book (Chs. 3–42) is in poetry, the peculiar intensity of which closely fits the dramatic theme. In Job, a righteous person gradually discovers that conventional ideas about God do not square with the facts of observed life—both God's natural creation and human society are deeply flawed by random violence and unmerited suffering. Overwhelmed with grief, Job prays for a reversal of the creative process, asking for darkness and death instead of light and life. Composing what seems to be a bitter commentary on Genesis 1, the poet celebrates the three realms of total darkness: precreation chaos, the enclosing womb, and Sheol, the Underworld. All three have the advantage of non-existence, for to live is to feel pain:

> Why did I not die newborn,
>   not perish as I left the womb?

Why were there two knees to receive me,
    two breasts for me to suck?
Had there not been, I should now be lying in
    peace, wrapped in a restful slumber, . . .
Down there [in Sheol], bad men bustle no more,
    there the weary rest.
Prisoners, all left in peace, there no more the
    shouts of the jailer.
Down there, high and low are all one, and the
    slave is free of his master.

Job 3:11–12, 17–19

In the Book of Psalms, poetry is also the vehicle for exploring the enormous diversity of human religious experience, from a penitent's humble recognition of error and confidence in divine pardon (Ps. 51) to a poet's Job-like challenging of Yahweh to honor his broken promises (Ps. 89; cf. Ps. 44). As are many of the prophetic speeches, the poetry of Psalms is characterized by *synonymous parallelism,* the pairing or balancing of one line with another by structuring both in grammatically similar phrases. In the simplest examples of synonymous parallelism, the second lines express almost the same idea as the first, and in similar phrasing:

Praise Yahweh, all nations,
    extol him, all you peoples!

Ps. 117:1

In some of the many variations of synonymous parallelism, the second line offers a specific example to illustrate the general statement made in the first. In Psalm 106, the poet cites a famous instance in which the Israelites proved ungrateful to the God who had rescued them from Egypt:

They failed to appreciate your great love, they
    defiled the Most High at the Sea of Reeds.

Ps. 106:8

A set of two couplets from the same poem emphasizes related aspects of Israel's rescue by repeating the first statement in parallel but slightly different form:

One word from him dried up the Sea of Reeds,
he led them across the sea bed like dry land,
He saved them from the grasp of those who
    hated them
and rescued them from the clutches of the enemy.

Ps. 106:9–10

The following pair of lines links God's dual motives in saving Israel:

For the sake of his name he saved them,
    to demonstrate his power.

Ps. 106:8

In *antithetical parallelism,* one line makes a statement, and the next line expresses its opposite. Proverbs offers many examples of this form:

A wise son is his father's joy,
    a foolish son his mother's grief.

Prov. 10:1

The slack hand brings poverty,
    but the diligent hand brings wealth.

Prov. 10:4

The discreet man sees danger and takes shelter,
    the ignorant go forward and pay for it.

Prov. 22:3

Synthetic or *formal parallelism* is not, strictly speaking, parallelism at all. In this poetic form, the first line expresses a thought, the second adds a new idea, and the third completes the statement. David's lament over the fallen Saul and Jonathan illustrates this pattern:

O Jonathan, in your death I am stricken,
I am desolate for you, Jonathan my brother.
Very dear to me you were,
    your love to me more wonderful
than the love of a woman.

2 Sam. 1:26

(For a discussion of the prophets' use of poetic parallelism, see Box 6.2.)

In some poetic books, such as Proverbs, the author employs *personification,* the imparting of human attributes or personality to an idea or abstract concept, such as wisdom. Proverbs depicts divine Wisdom as a woman who roams city streets, imploring foolish young men to listen to her and avoid her opposite, Folly, whose ways lead to death (Prov. 8:1–11, cf. 1:20–33; 2:16–22; 5:3–23). In Proverbs 8, the poet personifies Lady Wisdom as God's firstborn, not only giving her cosmic stature but also making her the mediator between the human and divine realms. Speaking as God's honored companion at creation, she declares:

> The deep [primordial sea] was not, when I was
> born, there were no springs to gush with water.
> Before the mountains were settled,
> before the hills, I came to birth;
> before he made the earth, the countryside,
> or the first grains of the world's dust.
> When he fixed the heavens firm, I was there,
> when he drew a ring on the surface of the
> deep . . .
>
> Prov. 8:24–27

Existing before the created world, Lady Wisdom functions as a witness to the stages by which the cosmos developed, her balanced phrases offering firsthand testimony to God's creative activity.

Lady Wisdom's use of repetition, variation, and expansion of a central theme characterizes Hebrew poetry from its earliest war chants to its most sophisticated lyrics. With their rhythmic repetitiveness, concreteness, parallelism, and vivid images, biblical poets awaken the imagination and stir the feelings as do few other writers of ancient literature.

Psalms

KEY TOPICS/THEMES

An anthology of Hebrew devotional poetry, the Book of Psalms encompasses a broad range of religious responses to Israel's historical experience, particularly the prolonged theological crisis that followed Babylon's destruction of Judah in 587 B.C.E., with the attendant loss of kingship, land, and Temple. The collection of 150 poems, traditionally divided into five separate books, represents a variety of literary genres that are generally categorized by their form and/or content. The most common classifications include the hymn, or song of praise (e.g., Pss. 8, 19, 78, 100, 103, 104, 114, 117, and 150), psalms of thanksgiving (e.g., Pss. 18, 30, 40, 66, 116, and 118), laments, both individual and collective (e.g., Pss. 10, 22, 38, 42, 43, 44, 51, 58, 59, 69, and 74), royal psalms associated with Davidic kings (e.g., Pss. 2, 45, 51, 72, 89, and 110), enthronement psalms proclaiming Yahweh as king (e.g., Pss. 93 and 95–99), psalms of blessing or cursing (e.g., Pss. 109 and 137), and psalms of wisdom, instruction, or meditation (e.g., Pss. 1, 33–37, 49, 52, 73, 90, 112, 119, and 128).

KEY QUESTIONS

Describe the diverse range of religious expression found in the Psalms. In what ways are these Temple hymns and songs related to the Davidic monarchy?

A collection of 150 individual poems composed at different times over a span of perhaps six centuries, the Book of Psalms expresses virtually the full range of Israelite religious experience. Whereas some of the psalms were written to commemorate events during the Davidic dynasty, such as the coronation and enthronement of kings, others were written long after the Babylonian exile had brought a permanent end to the monarchy. The psalms are as diverse in religious feeling as they are in historical origin. Ranging from declarations of complete trust and confidence in divine protection (e.g., Pss. 23 and 91) to sorrowful complaints about God's apparent failure to shield his people from disaster (e.g., Pss. 44 and 89), the psalms explore both the heights and depths of Israel's special relationship with Yahweh.

The title comes from the Greek *psalmoi*, which refers to instrumental music and, by extension, the words accompanying the music. In translating the psalms, the editors of the Septuagint used *psalmoi* to render the Hebrew title *Tehillim*, which means "praises." Although each psalm has its own compositional history, as a collection the Psalms represent the lyrics performed — to the accompaniment of pipes, flutes, harps, and other musical instruments — at the second Temple as part of Yahweh's worship.

"DAVIDIC" AUTHORSHIP?

The tradition that David composed the Psalms probably owes much to David's popular reputation as a musician and poet (1 Sam. 16:23; Amos 6:5). Phrases, such as "by David," that are attached to particular psalms are interpolations by later editors and may mean only that the psalm thus denoted concerned one of David's royal successors. Besides ascribing many psalms to "David," editors attribute Psalm 72 to Solomon, Psalm 90 to Moses, and various others to Asaph and the sons of Korah. Many others are clearly post-Davidic, such as Psalm 72, which laments the destruction of the Jerusalem Temple, and Psalm 137, which describes conditions during the Babylonian exile. Of the 150 psalms, 116 have titles or superscriptions indicating authorship, setting, or directions to the Temple musicians. All these notations are thought to be late scribal additions to the texts.

Scholars believe that the present anthology of Psalms was put together by uniting several subcollections. These include Davidic psalms in which the name Yahweh predominates (Pss. 3–41), Davidic psalms in which *Elohim* is the preferred term for God (Pss. 51–72), two subcollections of psalms ascribed to the sons of Korah (Pss. 42–49 and Pss. 84–88), psalms attributed to Asaph (Pss. 83–93), psalms emphasizing Yahweh's kingship (Pss. 93–99), "songs of ascents" (Pss. 120–134), and two subsets of thanksgiving psalms using the imperative "hallelujah" (praise Yahweh) (Pss. 111–118 and 146–150).

Combining these subcollections, as well as other lyrics, into the present Book of Psalms, postexilic editors then divided this anthology of 150 poems into five separate books, perhaps to resemble the Torah's division into five books. Book 1 contains Psalms 1–41, some of which may be among the oldest in the collection; Book 2 includes Psalms 42–72; Book 3, Psalms 73–89; Book 4, Psalms 90–106; and Book 5, Psalms 107–150. Psalms 1 and 2 act as a general introduction to the collection; Psalm 150 is a **doxology**, an expression of praise to God that typically concludes a confession of faith, that rounds off the collection as a whole.

CATEGORIES OF PSALMS

Early in the twentieth century, Hermann Gunkel (1862–1932) pioneered modern techniques of analyzing the psalms critically, classifying them according to their literary form, presumed liturgical function, or topical content. Although scholars now recognize that many psalms combine several literary forms, mixing lament with praise and expressions of trust—and that some are too distinctively individual to be labeled at all—Gunkel's basic categorizations remain useful. In surveying the most common classifications of psalms, it should be remembered that these religious lyrics embody both private prayer and public worship, and that all were performed at the Jerusalem Temple as communal expressions of Israel's complex and ever-evolving relationship with God.

Hymns or Songs of Praise In composing songs of praise, the poet typically cites specific reasons for which God deserves Israel's worship: his creation of the world and his saving intervention in Israel's history. Psalm 8 honors God for establishing an orderly universe, fashioning humanity in his divine image, and placing the human being, who is "little less than a god," at the apex of his earthly hierarchy:

> You have crowned him [humanity] with glory
>   and splendor,
> made him lord over the work of your hands,
> set all things under his feet, . . .
>
> Ps. 8:5–6

Psalm 104, which seems to be a Hebrew poet's revision of a much older Egyptian hymn to the solar deity worshiped by Pharaoh Akhenaton, pays tribute to Yahweh's creative wisdom and might while incorporating typical Near Eastern motifs of earth originating amid a watery chaos:

> You stretch the heavens out like a tent,
> you build your palace on the water above; . . .
> You fixed the earth on its foundations,
> unshakable for ever and ever,
> you wrapped it with the deep [primal watery
>   abyss] as with a robe,
> the waters overtopping the mountains.
> At your reproof the waters took to flight,
> they fled at the sound of your thunder,
> cascading over the mountains, into the valleys,
> down to the reservoir you made for them;
> you imposed the limits they must never cross
>   again,
> or they would once more flood the land. . . .
> Glory for ever to Yahweh!
> May Yahweh find joy in what he creates. . . .
>
> Ps. 104:3, 5–9, 36

Like Genesis 1, Psalm 104 pictures Yahweh as effortlessly subduing the primal, chaotic waters. Other psalms, however, evoke ancient myths in which Yahweh had to fight primordial monsters of chaos, such as Rahab or Leviathan, at the time of creation:

> Yet, God, my king from the first,
> author of saving acts throughout the earth,
> by your power you split the sea in two,
> and smashed heads of monsters on the waters.
> You crushed Leviathan's heads,
> leaving him for wild animals to eat,
> you opened the spring, the torrent,
> you dried up inexhaustible rivers.
> Ps. 74:13–15; cf. Isa. 27:1; Job 3:8; 41:1–34

Echoing Baal's mythical battle against Yamm (the all-encompassing sea) or Marduk's brutal splitting in two of Tiamat, the primal ocean, Psalm 89 depicts Yahweh conquering Rahab, a personification of watery chaos:

> You control the pride of ocean,
> when its waves ride high, you calm them;
> you split Rahab in two like a carcass
> and scattered your enemies with your mighty arm.
> Ps. 89:9–10; cf. Job 9:13; 26:12–13

In addition to his acts of creative majesty, God is to be praised for his faithfulness in guiding and directing Israel's history. Psalm 78 surveys Yahweh's mighty deeds in rescuing Israel from Egypt, nurturing his people in the Sinai wilderness, and choosing David to shepherd the covenant community. In those ancient days, the poet recalls, Yahweh aroused himself from sleep to fight for Israel: "like a hero fighting-mad with wine, the Lord woke up to strike his enemies on the rump and put them to everlasting shame" (Ps. 78:65–66). Psalm 105 similarly reviews Israel's distant past, when Yahweh made his promises to Abraham and Jacob, brought plagues upon his people's Egyptian oppressors, and turned the Canaanites' territory over to Israelite tribes.

A subset of the psalms of praise, known as the "Songs of Zion," center on Jerusalem, the city made holy by God's invisibly dwelling in the Temple that stood on **Zion**, a prominent hill (Pss. 46, 48, 84, 87, and 122). Two of these psalms (46 and 48) seem to reflect a belief in Zion's invincibility, a confidence supposedly guaranteed by Yahweh's having placed his "name" there. (This view of Jerusalem's impregnability, however, is strongly rejected by Jeremiah, who declares that the sanctuary's presence could not protect the city from Babylon [Jer. 7, 26].)

Psalms of Thanksgiving Psalms of thanksgiving typically are prayers offered in gratitude for God's having saved or delivered the psalmist from danger (Pss. 18, 30, 40, 66, 116, and 118). They commonly begin with expressions of praise, describe the situation that formerly threatened or troubled the poet, gratefully acknowledge God as the source of deliverance, and, in some cases, exhort bystanders to share in the thanksgiving. In Psalm 30, the poet compares his former suffering to a descent into Sheol, the Underworld housing the dead:

> Yahweh, you have brought my soul up from
>   Sheol,
> of all those who go down to the Pit you have
>   revived me . . .
> Ps. 30:3

In his distress, the poet had reminded God that he would gain nothing by allowing his servant to die, for Sheol's eternally silent inhabitants can offer him no worship:

> I beg you to pity me,
> "What do you gain by my blood [death] if I go
>   down to the Pit?
> Can the dust praise you or proclaim your
>   faithfulness? . . ."
> Ps. 30:8–9

Now that Yahweh has rescued the poet from death, turning his "mourning into dancing," his worshiper can again join the living who "play [God's] music" at his Temple.

Laments Poems that emphasize sorrow, grief, mourning, or regret are classified as laments or complaints and feature both individual and communal supplications. Some individual laments, such as Psalm 55, are personal petitions that first praise God and then ask for rescue from the petitioner's enemies and vengeance upon them. Although many laments are concerned with forgiveness of personal sins (Pss. 38 and 51), some imply that God has been unaccountably slow to redress injustice (Pss. 10, 58, and 59).

Psalm 22, which opens with a plaintive cry— "My God, my God, why have you deserted me?"— represents a mixed genre combining lament with praise. Following graphic descriptions of the poet's suffering, the psalm introduces a petition begging for the Deity's help (22:1–21). Although the poem begins in bleak despair, following the petition (22:19–21), it changes abruptly to an exulting hymn of praise that culminates in a confident declaration of Yahweh's sovereignty (22:22–29). In the last two lines, the poet affirms that both he and his descendants will proclaim Yahweh to "generations still to come," ensuring a continuity of worship into the far-distant future (22:30–31). With its striking contrast between the poet's initial grief and his later resolve to praise Yahweh, this lament, moving from sorrow to joy, illustrates an important theme in the Psalms: Although Yahweh's people may endure almost unbearable pain, their God remains present with them, an everlasting source of spiritual renewal. Redemption, in fact, is found in the midst of suffering.

Several communal laments focus on the Babylonian conquest that stripped Israel of its essential identity and institutions, including land, kingship, and sanctuary. Gunkel observed that many of these collective laments follow a structural pattern, typically beginning with an *invocation* that addresses God. Psalm 74, a communal dirge lamenting the Temple's destruction, asks the Deity if this national calamity means that he has permanently severed his covenant ties:

> God, have you finally rejected us
> raging at the flock you used to pasture?
> Ps. 74:1

In the second part, the *complaint,* the psalm specifies the reasons for the lament. In Psalm 74, God is invited to inspect the pitiful ruin of his holy place:

> Pick your steps over these endless ruins:
> the enemy have sacked everything in the
> sanctuary.

> They roared where your assemblies used to take
> place, . . .
> Axes deep in the wood, hacking at the panels,
> they battered them down with mallet and hatchet;
> then, God, setting fire to your sanctuary,
> they profanely razed the house of your name to
> the ground.
> Ps. 74:3–4, 6–7

The poem next opposes the complaint with a *confession of trust,* asserting the poet's reliance on God. After citing Yahweh's mythic battle against Leviathan, recalling his primordial triumphs, Psalm 74 affirms God's continuing mastery of creation, manifest in earth's seasonal cycles:

> You are master of day and night,
> you instituted light and sun,
> you fixed the boundaries of the world,
> you created summer and winter.
> Ps. 74:16–17

This expression of confidence in the Deity's ability to act is followed by a *petition* in which God is asked to take action to remedy the problem. Urging Yahweh not to "forget" or "betray" his worshipers, the poet asks God to "remember" both the blasphemer who publicly despoiled his holy place and the covenant people who depend upon his vindication:

> Now, Yahweh, remember the enemy's blasphemy,
> how frenzied people dare to insult your
> name . . .
> Respect the covenant! We can bear no more—
> Ps. 74:18, 20

Although absent in two of the greatest communal laments, Psalms 44 and 74, some laments conclude with a statement of *thanksgiving* in which the lamenter promises to tell the community of faith what God has accomplished.

Psalm 44, which also manifests Gunkel's pattern, contrasts the mighty deeds Yahweh performed in the remote past—actions the current generation has only heard about—with the present misery that the people experience directly. This lament is particularly noteworthy in rejecting the traditional deuteronomic view that only disobedience will bring disaster on the covenant community. The psalmist flatly states that the people have remained faithful to their covenant vow and that they suffer simply because they keep Yahweh as their God. After describing the massacres and humiliations their enemies regularly inflict upon the community, the poet asserts that

> All this happened to us though we had not
>   forgotten you,
> though we had not been disloyal to your
>   covenant;
> though our hearts had not turned away,
> though our steps had not left your path;
> yet you crushed us . . .
> No, it is for your sake we are being massacred
>   daily,
> and counted as sheep for the slaughter.
>   Ps. 44:17–19, 22

These communal laments, including the second half of Psalm 89, which accuses God of breaking his sworn oath, collectively form a persistent theme illustrating God's strange inaction or apparent refusal to honor his ancient covenant promises. In preparing their final edition of Psalms, the redactors intermix these laments with royal psalms — songs focusing on the Davidic kings — and enthronement psalms, lyrics praising Yahweh as Israel's true and abiding ruler. This juxtaposition of negative and positive theological confessions effectively mirrors the ever-fluctuating sorrows and joys of a worshiping community that finds its God in both darkness and light.

Psalms of Blessing and Cursing   Another category — psalms of blessing and cursing — may appear somewhat shocking to modern sensibilities attuned to the concept that religion teaches the return of good for evil. Psalm 1, for example, arbitrarily divides all people into two classes — the righteous and the wicked — and promises doom for the latter; no shades of gray are acknowledged. In Psalm 109, the poet enthusiastically lists disasters with which the writer asks God to afflict persons who have offended him or her. These include the wish that one's enemies be condemned by a corrupt judge, punished for the sins of their ancestors, and tormented by the certainty that their orphaned children will be driven in poverty from their homes. Psalm 137, which begins in lyrical beauty ("By the streams of Babylon"), concludes in

vindictive fury, promising a blessing on the person who will seize Babylonian infants and dash out their brains against a rock. From these and other examples, it is obvious that some worshipers regarded retaliatory justice as more religiously fitting than mercy.

Royal Psalms   Classified by their content rather than literary form, royal psalms commemorate events and issues involving Davidic kings. Scattered throughout the entire collection, royal psalms vary widely in subject and mood, ranging from the celebration of a royal wedding (Ps. 45) or the coronation of a new ruler (Pss. 2, 72, and 110) to a review of God's original promises to David that culminates in a bitter complaint about the Deity's historical failure to honor his commitment to the Davidic dynasty (Ps. 89). Along with Psalm 1, Psalm 2 serves as a general introduction to the whole book, raising the issue of divinely ordained kingship. The psalm opens by describing a revolt against "Yahweh and his **Anointed**," directly associating the rule of God with political submission to his earthly representative, the king whose head is "anointed" or smeared with priestly oil at the time of his installation in office. Historically, the rebellious kings were probably princes of neighboring states, such as Edom or Moab, who attempted to break free of Israel's domination after the death of a Davidic ruler and before his successor could consolidate his position. Viewed as part of the collection as a whole, however, this psalm introduces a theme that runs throughout the book: Whereas Davidic monarchs may have been God's agents for governing his people, Yahweh himself is Israel's real king. An assertion that Yahweh rules the world, with or without Davidic kings and despite apparently unending human opposition, is perhaps the Psalm's most pervasive message.

In Psalm 110, Yahweh addresses the king as "my Lord," vowing to subdue his enemies and shatter all opposition:

> Yahweh has sworn an oath which he will never
>   retract,
> "You are a priest of the order of Melchizedek,
>   and for ever."
>   Ps. 110:4

This passage is unique in connecting the ruler with the mysterious figure of Melchizedek, the king-priest of Salem to whom Abraham paid tithes (Gen. 14:17–20). As many scholars have noted, the poet's attempt to present the king as both monarch and priest suggests that this particular psalm was composed not for a Davidic king, but for one of the Hasmoneans, non-Davidic Maccabean rulers who reigned in Judah from about 142 to 63 B.C.E. Although they were not descended from the Aaronic line of priests, the Hasmoneans appropriated the office of High Priest as well as that of king. They may have tried to legitimize their holding both offices by claiming descent from the king-priest Melchizedek. If these speculations are true, psalms that eventually became part of the canon were still being composed in the late second or early first century B.C.E.

The historical fact that Yahweh had not kept his oath to preserve David's descendants on Judah's throne "for ever" is forthrightly addressed in Psalm 89, which opens by celebrating God's creative majesty but then abruptly shifts gears to accuse the Deity of covenant-breaking. After quoting Yahweh's assertion that he gave his "servant David [his] sworn word" to establish a "dynasty to last forever," the psalmist carefully emphasizes the unconditional terms of the Davidic agreement (89:3–4, 19–37; cf. 2 Sam. 7). In verses 38–39, the poem shifts from the divine promise to the historical reality—Yahweh has "repudiated the covenant," doing the opposite of his vow in Psalm 2 by abandoning his anointed and allowing his enemies to triumph (89:38–45). Yahweh, qualitatively distinguished from all other gods by his "faithfulness" (89:49; cf. Ps. 82), seems to have betrayed his own nature.

Enthronement Psalms   Although the Davidic dynasty was overthrown in 587 B.C.E. and never restored, in at least some circles hope remained that Yahweh would someday remember his promise and appoint a descendant of David to lead his people. The explicit, unequivocal language of the Davidic Covenant assured some that in a future generation, God would at last "remember" his word. In the meantime, the covenant community was to recognize that Yahweh still reigned over the "nations," as well as Judah. The enthronement psalms, such as Psalms 93 and 95–99, extol Yahweh as king. "Far transcending all other gods," he is "Most High over the world" (97:9). His ceaseless reign is perceived not only in the mystery and beauty of nature (93:3–4; 96:6) but also in his "justice" and "truth" (96:13) and his strengthening presence among believers (97:10–12). Despite human rebellion and resistance to his reign, he continues as universal sovereign:

> From the depths of the earth to mountain top
> everything comes under his rule; . . .
>
> Ps. 95:4

Psalms of Wisdom and Instruction   Although the world at large may not perceive Yahweh's kingdom, several poets indicate the proper human response to divine rule. To some scholars, psalms that employ words typical of Israel's sages or teachers of wisdom, such as "instruction," "teaching," and the "fear of Yahweh," seem to comprise an identifiable category (Pss. 33–37, 49, 52, 73, 90, 112, 119, and 128). Some biblical wisdom, such as that contained in Proverbs, is characterized by the advice to pursue a virtuous life and follow the divine will by embracing good and rejecting evil. The first psalm, with its plea to avoid the wicked and "take pleasure in the law of Yahweh," echoes wisdom principles, as does Psalm 37, which urges readers not to envy the material success of the wicked, who will ultimately fail, but to emulate Yahweh's love and compassion, qualities that ensure divine approval. The poet states that despite having lived to old age, he has never seen "a virtuous man deserted, or his descendants forced to beg their bread" (37:25). Somewhat less optimistically, Psalm 34 states that even the virtuous endure "hardships in plenty," but that they are sustained by the divine presence (34:19–20).

THE RELIGIOUS POWER OF THE PSALMS

In the Torah and the prophetic books, God speaks to humanity through Moses or the prophets. In the Psalms, the covenant people speak to God, sometimes praising his past actions in delivering Israel and other times questioning the way in which he governs the cosmos. Even when fearing that Yahweh is absent or "asleep," the psalmists persist in an ongoing dialogue with their God, alternately voicing supreme confidence in his power to save, bewilderment at his present inaction, and confidence that he rules as universal king. Accepting both adversity and joy as inevitable components of their community's collective life, the psalmists affirm the redemptive value of the divine–human bond.

RECOMMENDED READING

Alter, Robert. *The Art of Biblical Poetry.* New York: Basic Books, 1985.

Anderson, Bernard W. *Out of the Depths: The Psalms Speak for Us Today.* Philadelphia: Westminster Press, 1974. A sensitive interpretation of the psalms' continuing relevance.

Berlin, Adele. *The Dynamics of Biblical Parallelism.* Bloomington: Indiana University Press, 1985. A helpful explanation of how parallelism functions in the biblical texts.

———. *Biblical Poetry Through Medieval Jewish Eyes.* Bloomington: Indiana University Press, 1991. An important work of critical interpretation.

———. "Parallelism." In D. N. Freedman, ed., *The Anchor Bible Dictionary,* Vol. 5, pp. 155–162. New York: Doubleday, 1992. A concise and useful introduction.

———. "Introduction to Hebrew Poetry." In *The New Interpreter's Bible,* Vol. 3, pp. 301–315. Nashville: Abingdon Press, 1994. A concise discussion of the characteristics of biblical poetry.

Gunkel, Hermann. *The Psalms: A Form-Critical Introduction.* Translated by T. M. Horner. Introduction by James Muilenberg. Philadelphia: Fortress Press, 1967. A standard work by the pioneer of the form-critical method.

Kugel, James A. *The Idea of Hebrew Poetry: Parallelism and Its History.* New Haven, Conn.: Yale University Press, 1981. A valuable historical-critical study.

McCann, J. Clinton, Jr. "The Book of Psalms." In *The New Interpreter's Bible,* Vol. 3, pp. 641–677. Nashville: Abingdon Press, 1994. Asserts that the five books of psalms are structured theologically, juxtaposing royal celebrations, complaints, and laments with songs exulting in God's cosmic reign.

Mowinckel, Sigmund. *The Psalms in Israel's Worship,* Vols. 1 and 2. Translated by D. R. Ap-Thomas. Nashville: Abingdon Press, 1962. Like Gunkel's, a fundamental study.

Sarna, Nahum M. *Songs of the Heart: An Introduction to the Book of Psalms.* New York: Schocken Books, 1993. Places the psalms in the context of the ancient Near East and relates them to later rabbinic interpretation.

Wilson, Gerald H. *The Editing of the Hebrew Psalter.* Chico, Calif.: Scholars Press, 1985. A seminal analysis of the psalms' literary and theological organization.

Wisdom Literature

In ancient Israel, people belonging to three callings or professions could speak with authority—the priest, the prophet, and the sage. According to Jeremiah (18:18), the priest's business was to instruct in covenant law (the Torah), the prophet's function was to convey Yahweh's "word," and the sage's office was to provide wise advice (see also Ezek. 7:26). The "wise," including both men and women, held positions of public respect and commonly served as counselors to kings (2 Sam. 14:21; 16:23; 20:14–22). Prophets were sometimes critical of the professional class of sages—as they were of priests—but the wisdom movement ultimately outlasted the prophetic line and produced some of the greatest books in the Bible.

The origins of Israel's wisdom tradition are unknown, but archaeological discoveries have revealed that long before Israel came into existence, thinkers in Egypt, Mesopotamia, Edom, and Phoenicia had produced astute guides to the "good life." Among Hebrew writers, however, wisdom material acquired a new tone and emphasis: "The fear of Yahweh is the beginning of knowledge" (Prov. 1:7). Although the writers of many proverbs—short, memorable sayings summarizing traditional insights about life—stressed observation and experience as a source of knowledge, they regarded wisdom as much a divine gift as the prophetic word (Prov. 2:6). Wisdom, rather than the Torah, was envisioned as Yahweh's first creation and, personified as a gracious divine woman, acted as a liaison between the Deity and humanity (Prov. 8). This theme of Wisdom as a creative spirit linking humanity with a primary attribute of the Creator is most fully developed in a late apocryphal work, the Wisdom of Solomon (7:22–9:18).

Renowned for his shrewd judgments, King Solomon stood at the head of Israel's wisdom tradition

(1 Kings 3:1–28, 4:29–34). Later ages, honoring Solomon's role in establishing a national institution of wise government counselors and other sages, attributed a large body of wisdom writings to him. These include the canonical books of Proverbs, Ecclesiastes, and Song of Solomon, the apocryphal Wisdom, and the pseudepigraphal poetry collections known as the Psalms and Odes of Solomon.

In Hebrew literature, wisdom was expressed in many different literary forms. Early types include riddles, fables, and proverbs (Judg. 9:18–15, 14:14; 1 Kings 4:32). In later times, anonymous sages produced far more complex and sophisticated works, such as the Book of Job, where subtle theological arguments are sustained through lengthy debates about divine justice and the meaning of human suffering. Works like Ecclesiastes contain an amalgam of the sage's personal reflections on life's futility and meditations on death, as well as paradoxic maxims, proverbs, and expressions of skeptical pessimism.

The author of only one wisdom book is known — Jesus ben Sirach, who compiled the observations, teachings, and experiences of a lifetime in Ecclesiasticus. This weighty volume, the longest of its kind in the Bible, reveals the existence of "wisdom schools" at which young people were educated by a recognized wisdom authority. One of the last-written books of the Apocrypha, the work entitled Wisdom of Solomon (written c. first century B.C.E.) is the only biblical work that specifically links the righteousness born of wisdom to hopes of personal immortality (Wisd. of Sol. 1:12–3:9; 5:4–24; etc.).

Besides these works, various psalms also contain wisdom motifs (e.g., Pss. 1, 8, 16, 17, 19, 34, 37, 49, 73, 92, 104, 112, 119, and 139), as do the prose tales of Joseph and Daniel, wise men loyal to their Israelite heritage, who rose to power in foreign nations (Gen. 39–41; Dan. 1–6). Both of these figures are depicted as recipients of a divine gift, the wisdom to interpret dreams that foreshadow the future. The greatest **wisdom literature**, however, is based on the authors' profound reflections on the significance of ordinary life, with its unequal distribution of good and evil fortune, its unexpected calamities, and the ambiguity of its ethical "message."

Because of its diversity in outlook, thought, and form, wisdom material defies easy classification. Its characteristic themes are strikingly different from those in the Torah and the Prophets. Wisdom books typically make no references to the covenant relationship that bound Israel to Yahweh. Neither Job nor Ecclesiastes even mentions the Mosaic Torah; but both agree that many religious assumptions, such as a divinely favored "right side's" winning in life's battles, are unjustified by human experience. The deuteronomic thesis that Yahweh directs human history, of which individual lives are a part, is also conspicuously absent.

Evaluating the ethical quality of human life from a variety of perspectives, the wisdom authors typically come to rather seditious conclusions. Their observations and analyses of experience tend to subvert some other biblical writers' interpretation of Israel's history. The prophetic tradition held that Yahweh observed all people's actions, inevitably punishing the bad and rewarding the good, an assumption shared by the Deuteronomistic historians, who interpreted Israel's growth and destruction as the consequence of keeping or breaking covenant laws. Among the Hebrew thinkers who vigorously disputed this simplistic view of life was the anonymous poet who wrote Job.

RECOMMENDED READING

Brueggemann, Walter A. *In Man We Trust: The Neglected Side of Biblical Faith.* Richmond, Va.: John Knox Press, 1972.

Bryce, Glendon E. *Israel and the Wisdom of Egypt.* Lewisburg, Pa.: Bucknell University Press, 1975. Analyzes the influence of Egyptian wisdom on the book of Proverbs.

Crenshaw, James L. *Studies in Ancient Israelite Wisdom.* New York: KTAV, 1976.

———. *A Whirlpool of Torment: Israelite Traditions of God as an Oppressive Presence.* Philadelphia: Fortress Press, 1984.

Fishbane, Michael. *Biblical Interpretation in Ancient Israel.* New York: Oxford University Press, 1985. A technical examination of ways in which later Bible writers reworked and revised older biblical traditions.

Grabbe, Lester L. *Priests, Prophets, Sages: A Socio-Historical Study of Religious Specialists in Ancient Israel.* Valley Forge, Pa.: Trinity Press International,

1995. Provides cross-cultural parallels to Israel's religious offices in the ancient Near East.

Humphreys, W. Lee. *The Tragic Vision and the Hebrew Tradition.* Philadelphia: Fortress Press, 1985.

Lambert, W. G. *Babylonian Wisdom Literature.* Oxford: Clarendon Press, 1960.

Murphy, Roland E. *Seven Books of Wisdom.* Milwaukee: Bruce, 1960.

———. *Wisdom Literature and Psalms.* Nashville, Tenn.: Abingdon Press, 1983.

Scott, R. B. Y. *The Way of Wisdom in the Old Testament.* New York: Macmillan, 1971.

Proverbs

KEY TOPICS/THEMES

Although ascribed to Solomon, traditional founder of Israel's wisdom schools, the Book of Proverbs contains practical advice drawn from diverse sources, ranging from ancient Egypt through many generations of Israelite thought. Besides "Solomonic" maxims (Chs. 10–22), the book's highlights include reflections on the value of wisdom (Chs. 1–6), personifications of wisdom and folly (Chs. 7–9), and a portrait of the "perfect wife" (Ch. 31).

KEY QUESTIONS

How does Proverbs define "wisdom"? What are the social and economic advantages of acquiring wisdom? Why is the figure of Wisdom depicted as Yahweh's first creation and his main channel of communication with humankind?

Whereas examples of speculative wisdom, such as Job and Ecclesiastes, deal with theological inquiries about the nature of God and the purpose of human life, the Book of Proverbs is devoted to advocating practical wisdom and guiding readers to find their proper place in the social and religious order. *Proverb* translates from the Hebrew term *mashal*, which means a "statement of truth" or "standard of appropriate behavior." The biblical proverbs typically are based on observation and experience rather than on divine revelation, and are commonly nonreligious in tone. Thus,

The rich man's wealth is his stronghold,
poverty is the poor man's undoing.
Prov. 10:15

is simply an observed fact of life: Riches give security, and poverty the opposite.

Like much wisdom literature, Proverbs is not distinctively Israelite; most of its admonitions could apply equally well in another society totally different from Israel's theocracy:

The generous man is his own benefactor,
a cruel man injures his own flesh.
Prov. 11:17

It is not surprising, then, that archaeologists have found close parallels to biblical proverbs in Mesopotamia and Egypt; indeed, a whole passage from the wisdom book of the Egyptian sage Amenemope has been taken over almost word for word in Proverbs 22:17–23:11 (Figure 7.1). Scholars now realize that proverbs and other wisdom writings were produced in many New Eastern cultures and that Israel's sages in some cases borrowed from older literary collections.

PROVERBS ATTRIBUTED TO SOLOMON

Because King Solomon, who was credited with more than 3000 proverbs (1 Kings 4:29–33), traditionally has been associated with the production of adages or wise sayings, the superscription ascribing Proverbs to Solomon (Prov. 1:1) may mean no more than that these proverbs are written in the "manner" of Solomon. Other writers, in fact, are specifically cited. Agur, son of Jakeb, is the author of Chapter 30; Lemuel, king of Massa, of Chapter 31; and various unnamed sages, of 24:23–24. Like the Psalms, Proverbs grew from many different sources over a span of centuries.

THE ROLE OF WISDOM

Value of Wisdom   What principally distinguishes some of Israel's proverbs from those of Edom, Babylonia, or Egypt is the theme that true wisdom promotes loyalty to Yahweh and sensitivity to the divine will. The wise person makes his or her behavior accord with divine law (3; 19:16); the wise person is the righteous person who harmonizes his or her conduct with Yahweh's will (16:1, 9; 19:21, 23). Proverbs also affirms the orthodox theme that in this world, the righteous are rewarded and the

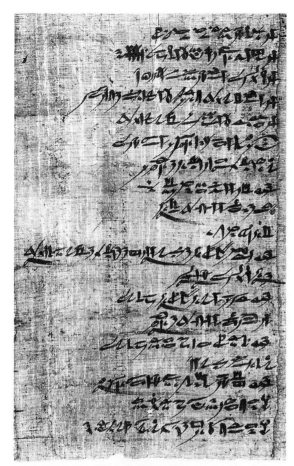

Figure 7.1 An ancient Egyptian papyrus recording the Wisdom of Amenemope (c. 1200 B.C.E.) contains sage advice that was later incorporated in the Book of Proverbs (Prov. 22:17–23:11). The wisdom movement permeated virtually the entire ancient Near East, creating an international legacy shared by Egypt, Mesopotamia, and Israel.

34.) Considerable proverbial wisdom is aimed at young people who wish to establish themselves at court and become the counselors of kings. Others offer advice on table manners and proper behavior in the company of rich and powerful persons whom one wishes to impress. The sages point out that achieving these ambitious goals requires self-discipline, reverence for Yahweh, and the special combination of humility and penetrating insight that enables the wise to perceive the cosmic order and attain their place in it.

Wisdom as Yahweh's Companion   The writer of Proverbs characteristically assumes the role of a father advising his son against bad company in general and seductive women in particular (Chs. 1–2). Folly (lack of wisdom) is likened to a harlot who corrupts youth, whereas Wisdom is personified as a noble woman who seeks to save young men from their own inexperience and bad judgment. In Chapter 1, Wisdom is pictured as calling from the streets and housetops, promising rich treasure to those not too ignorant to appreciate her. The theme of "Lady Wisdom's" supreme value climaxes in Chapter 8, in which she is presented as nothing less than Yahweh's associate in creation:

> Yahweh created me when his purpose first
>   unfolded,
>   before the oldest of his works.
> From everlasting I was firmly set,
>   from the beginning, before earth came
>   into being.
> .   .   .   .
> I was by his side, a master craftsman
>   [alternatively, "darling child"],
>   delighting him day after day,
>   ever at play in his presence,
> at play everywhere in his world,
>   delighting to be with the sons of men.
>   Prov. 8:22, 23, 30, 31

This passage, which shows Yahweh creating the world with Wisdom, a joyous feminine companion at his side, seems to have influenced such later Jewish thinkers as **Philo Judaeus**, who lived in Alexandria, Egypt, during the first century C.E. Philo's attempt to reconcile Greek philosophy with Hebrew revelation included his doctrine of the **Logos**, or **the Word**, by which God created the universe.

wicked punished (11:17–21; 21:21). Fearing Yahweh, observing the commandments, and behaving discreetly will ensure a long and prosperous life. Only the fool rejects that admonition and suffers accordingly.

Proverbs's emphasis on the pragmatic "getting ahead" in life endeared it to Israel's middle and upper classes. The directive to "study the ant, thou sluggard" (6:6–11, KJV) is one of several that attribute poverty to laziness. (See also Prov. 24:30–

(*Logos*, a masculine term in Greek, became more acceptable to Hebrew patriarchal thinking than *Sophia*, "Wisdom," which is feminine.) The Hymn to Logos with which John opens his Gospel is derived from Philo's (and ultimately Proverbs's) assumption that a divine mediator stands between God and the world.

The Perfect Wife   The book closes with a famous alphabetic poem on the perfect wife. Although promiscuous women and domineering wives receive considerable censure throughout Proverbs, the wife who works hard and selflessly to manage her husband's estate and increase his wealth is praised as beyond price (Ch. 31).

RECOMMENDED READING

Bryce, Glendon E. *Israel and the Wisdom of Egypt.* Lewisburg, Pa.: Bucknell University Press, 1975.

Camp, Claudia. *Wisdom and the Feminine in the Book of Proverbs.* Sheffield, England: Almond Press, 1985.

McKane, William. *Proverbs.* Philadelphia: Westminster Press, 1970.

Scott, R. B. Y. *Proverbs. Ecclesiastes.* Anchor Bible, Vol. 18. Garden City, N.Y.: Doubleday, 1965.

Van Leeuwen, Raymond C. "The Book of Proverbs." In *The New Interpreter's Bible*, Vol. 5, pp. 19–264. Nashville: Abingdon Press, 1997.

Whybray, R. N. *Wisdom in Proverbs: The Concept of Wisdom in Proverbs 1–9.* Studies in Biblical Theology, No. 45. London: SCM Press, 1965.

Job

KEY TOPICS/THEMES

A bold challenge to traditional views of God, the Book of Job dramatizes the plight of an innocent man whose tragic sufferings inspire him to question the ethical nature of a deity who permits evil and the unmerited pain of sentient creatures (Figure 7.2). The prose prologue (Chs. 1 and 2) features two scenes in Yahweh's heavenly court in which the Deity and humanity's adversary agree to test Job's loyalty. In the long poetic central section (Chs. 3–31), the author exposes the inadequacy of conventional religious explanations about divine–human relationships, expressly discrediting the

Figure 7.2 The cuneiform script on this clay tablet narrates a Sumerian variation of the Job story. Like the Book of Job, this text records the humiliating ordeals of a righteous man who nonetheless clings to his faith and is at last delivered from his undeserved sufferings. The problem of Evil, with its conflict between the concept of a good God and the fact of unmerited human pain, was a perplexing theme explored in Egyptian, Babylonian, and Israelite literature.

deuteronomic thesis that God is pledged to protect and reward the righteous, a position taken by Job's three friends who argue that suffering is an inevitable result of sin. After Elihu's interpolated discourse (Chs. 32–37), Yahweh delivers two speeches emphasizing cosmic wonders beyond human comprehension (Chs. 38–41). The prose epilogue recounts Job's restored fortunes (Job 42:7–17).

KEY QUESTIONS

Why does God allow "the satan" to tempt him to afflict innocent persons with undeserved suffering? According to Yahweh's speeches (Chs. 38–42), can a good and just God be found in the realm of physical nature?

ISSUES OF THE POSTEXILIC AGE

Although scholars do not agree on when Job was written, the general period of its composition can be inferred from the theological issues it confronts. The oldest extant reference to the title character was recorded during the Babylonian exile, when the prophet Ezekiel mentioned three ancient figures who were considered models of righteousness, Noah, Danel (not the biblical Daniel), and Job (Ezek. 14:14, 20). Although Ezekiel says nothing specific about Job, he may have had in mind a tradition about Job's patience under suffering, a motif emphasized in the folktale that opens the biblical book (cf. 1:22; 2:9–10). In its questioning of God's right to prosecute a person of exemplary goodness without just cause, however, the book is far more than an edifying study of the hero's fortitude and loyalty under severe testing. The Tanak's most fully developed **theodicy**—a literary attempt to reconcile beliefs about divine goodness with the prevalence of evil—Job seems to express the deepest concerns of the postexilic era, when old assumptions about rewards for faithfulness and penalties for wrongdoing had lost much of their former authority.

For Job's author, previous attempts to explain his community's suffering and the equity of God's judgments were insufficient. In dealing with the crisis of their nation's destruction, the Deuteronomistic redactors attributed both Israel's fall and Judah's collapse to their failure to obey Yahweh's commands. According to the deuteronomic theory of history, the covenant people were a collective entity, a corporate body that prospered or suffered together, not only for their own actions but also for those of their ancestors. Thus Judah was annihilated because Yahweh found the sins of one of its last kings unforgiveable (2 Kings 23:26–27; see

Chapter 5). While in exile, Ezekiel proposed a variation on the old principle of collective community responsibility: Henceforth, Yahweh would deal with his people in a new way, judging each new generation according to its individual merits, rather than making it pay for the past sins of its ancestors or the future errors of its descendants (Ezek. 18). Declaring that Yahweh took no "pleasure in the death of the wicked" but wished all to live, Ezekiel stated that God would look favorably upon new generations who turned from their parents' misdeeds to follow Torah commands.

While stating that God would, after the exile, judge each generation individually, Ezekiel nonetheless insisted on preserving the old deuteronomic formula that equated good conduct with divine blessings. Despite his innovations, Ezekiel's teaching clearly presupposes that Yahweh will favor the good and condemn only the wicked. Because it is unthinkable that Yahweh behaves unjustly, all individuals must deserve whatever evils befall them.

Some Wisdom writers advocated similar views. According to the Book of Proverbs, God's world manifests an intrinsic moral order in which all thoughts and actions bring predictable consequences. Proper "fear of the Lord" and diligent, prudent behavior will result in prosperity and honor, whereas disloyalty to Yahweh and evil deeds will ultimately bring failure and shame. Like the Deuteronomists, the authors of practical wisdom postulated a cosmic system of ethical cause and effect that equitably determined the degree of good or evil present in individual human lives. In times of peace and relative social stability, this philosophy seemed to work, and Israel's sages, who were presumably examples of the policies they preached, taught their students that Torah-keeping, honesty, and hard work almost invariably translated into economic success and public reputation.

After Babylon's destruction of Judah, however, when thousands of Torah-abiding people permanently lost family, health, land, and possessions, confidence that righteous behavior could ensure a good life was less easy to entertain. Observing widespread injustice that turned the deuteronomic thesis on its head—foreign overlords cruelly exploited even the most obedient of Yahweh's people — the anonymous author of Job could accept neither Deuteronomy's simplistic theories nor Ezekiel's implication that human misery always derives from sin. Combining traditional reverence for Yahweh with an acutely critical intelligence and demand for moral logic, Job's author protests comfortable but outmoded notions about the connection between good behavior and good fortune. Creatively expanding upon folklore about Job (Ezek. 14:14, 20) the writer, in some of the Hebrew Bible's greatest poetry, forcefully illustrates his conviction that old theological claims about the certainty of divine justice were woefully inadequate to explain the apparent random and arbitrary nature of human pain.

DIFFERENT NAMES OF GOD

Although most of the book is in poetry (Chs. 3:1–42:6), Job opens and closes with brief prose narratives. In the prose sections framing the central poetic drama, the Deity is Yahweh; in the poetic dialogues that comprise most of the book, however, the personal name of Israel's covenant patron is almost entirely absent (except for 12:9). Instead, Job frequently addresses God as *El* (or its variation, *Elohe*), or, less often, as *Shaddai,* an archaic title that occurs in Genesis but is otherwise rarely used in the Bible. (Exodus 6 states that before the time of Moses, Yahweh was known only as *El Shaddai.*) Not until the drama's final act, when Yahweh speaks to Job from a violent storm, does the poet invoke the Deity's personal name (Job 38–41).

THE PROSE PROLOGUE: YAHWEH AND THE DIVINE COUNCIL

An Innocent Victim   The prologue (Chs. 1–2) presents Job as a thoroughly admirable and godly person who in no way deserves the torments inflicted upon him. Described as "a sound and honest man who feared God and shunned evil" (Job 1:1, 1:8; cf. 2:3), he is a model of humanity created in God's image, one who enjoys a harmonious rela-tionship with his creator. So scrupulous is Job about not offending God that he offers sacrifices for his children in case they, even in thought, have sinned. No wonder Yahweh declares that "there is no one like [Job] on the earth" (1:8). Although Job's "friends" will vigorously dispute it, seeking to exonerate God by making Job guilty, Job's innocence is absolutely essential to the book's theological meaning. Commending Job's moral excellence, Yahweh himself regards the man as faultless (cf. 1:8, 2:3; cf. 42:7). The friends' attempt to uncover some secret flaw in Job's character or behavior — an effort in which many commentators have joined — is misguided, distracting attention from the real issue: the inadequacy of conventional ideas about God and the divine-human relationship.

Although Job's exemplary character differentiates him from most people, he is also a universal type, the person of goodwill found everywhere throughout history. For this reason the writer does not make him an Israelite but a native of Uz (a region south of Edom) who lived long before Israel's birth. Belonging to the patriarchal age, Job is not a member of the covenant community. As an archetypal figure who endeavors to please God in every aspect of his life, however, Job has an unwritten covenant with God, who, as proverbial wisdom later assumed, administers a just universe. When Job, still honoring his commitment to Yahweh, is suddenly plunged into extreme misery, readers are forced to confront the mystery of God's refusal to banish evil from his world.

Yahweh's Heavenly Court   Job's troubles begin in heaven, where Yahweh has called an assembly of divine beings — the *bene ha elohim* ("sons of the gods") — which includes "the satan," a member of Yahweh's council who serves as the Deity's prosecuting attorney. At this point in his historical evolution, *satan* is not a proper name (the Hebrew text uses the definite article for "the satan"), and he is not Yahweh's adversary, but his servant, a celestial functionary whose task is to seek out and expose any disloyalty in God's human subjects (Box 7.2). Ironically, it is Yahweh who initiates Job's ordeal by drawing the satan's attention to Job's perfect

Box 7.2 Evolution of the Satan Concept

Readers who think of Satan as a supernatural embodiment of Evil, a powerful rebel against God who reigns over an underworld of fire and brimstone, may be puzzled at the Hebrew Bible's portrayal of him as a regular member of Yahweh's heavenly council. In Job, he is included among the "sons of God," a celestial being whose role is limited to carrying out Yahweh's orders (Job 1–2). Despite the later popular mythology that transforms "the satan" into a God-defying "Prince of Darkness" responsible for all the world's ills, the Tanak grants him no independence of God.

Although commonly regarded as synonymous with the Hebrew figure of satan, the term **devil** occurs relatively infrequently in the New Testament and not at all in the Hebrew Bible. Derived from the Greek word *diablos*, *devil* means "accuser" or "slanderer." In Scripture, the Greek devil and Hebrew satan are not explicitly linked together in canonical writings until the author of Revelation so identifies them, equating "satan," "the devil," and the Genesis "serpent" who tempted Eve (Rev. 12:12). This correlation took place late in biblical history, however, appearing first in noncanonical works such as the Books of Adam and Eve (see Chapter 8).

"THE SATAN" AND THE HEBREW BIBLE

Although Revelation identifies the two figures, "the satan" of the Hebrew Bible is not precisely the same entity as the "devil" of the New Testament. The concepts expressed by these two different terms developed independently of each other. The word *satan* derives from a Hebrew root meaning "obstacle"; personified (given human qualities), it means "opposer" or "adversary." In the Tanak, "the satan" has an adversarial relationship with humanity, not with God, whose servant he remains.

According to historians of religion—scholars who analyze the historical evolution of religious ideas and beliefs—the concept of satan developed from the negative qualities once attributed to God. In this view, the satan figure is essentially the "dark side" or psychological "shadow" of Yahweh's ethically ambivalent character. By tracing in chronological order the biblical references to satan, it is evident that the violent and destructive traits formerly considered part of the divine nature were, over time, eventually ascribed

to "the satan." The tension between contrasting aspects of the biblical God—who is both Creator of light and life and a sometimes vindictive Destroyer—is thus partly resolved. God can be seen as all-good and all-loving, while the satan becomes responsible for the undesirable realities of existence.

At an early stage of this theological development, some biblical writers saw all things, good and evil alike, emanating from a single source—Yahweh. A form of monism—a belief that the universe contains only one divine principle—this view held that Yahweh alone caused both joy and sorrow, both prosperity and suffering (cf. Deut. 28). In the oldest literary strand of the Pentateuch, J shows Yahweh first creating life and then regretting it, annihilating most life forms on earth (Gen. 2, 6–8). At this point in Israel's religious thought, Yahweh is not only giver of life and pitiless executioner, he is also represented as tormentor and deceiver. After first selecting Saul to be Israel's first king, Yahweh then rejects him, driving Saul to madness by dispatching an "evil spirit" to torment him (1 Sam. 16:14–23). God also sends a "lying spirit" to lead King Ahab to his doom (1 Kings 22:18–28). Both of these texts show "evil" (defined from a human viewpoint and applied exclusively to disobedient persons) as one of the means Yahweh employs to effect his will. As late as the sixth century B.C.E., Second Isaiah depicts Yahweh as the originator of both light and darkness, good *and* evil (Isa. 45:7; see Chapter 3).

Taking another step in the development of the satan figure, some of Israel's thinkers placed the source of human trouble not in Yahweh alone but also among the *bene ha Elohim* (literally, "sons of the gods") who form Yahweh's heavenly court. These unnamed divine beings, which may include some of the ethically undeveloped deities that Yahweh denounces in Psalm 82, include "the satan," who has the job of "accusing" Yahweh's people and testing the loyalty of Yahweh's subjects (Zech. 3:1–9; Job 1–2). Although "the satan" is by this time viewed as separate from Yahweh himself, he remains completely under the Deity's control, doing nothing without God's express permission. He functions as God's obedient agent, an adjunct of the divine personality. As Yahweh's prosecuting attorney who tempts the divine Judge to

(continued)

Box 7.2 (continued)

punish the innocent, "the satan" also directly takes over God's previous role as destroyer, using the natural elements to kill Job's children and plunge the man of faith into despair. By contrast, in Zechariah's vision of the celestial throne room, Yahweh resists the adversary's attempt to persuade him to afflict his people; in this case, the Deity's compassion and mercy prevail. (It is important to remember that in each of the few Tanak passages in which "the satan" appears, he is always *humanity's* adversary, not God's.)

A clear example of "the satan's" assumption of the more sinister aspects of Yahweh's character occurs in the two accounts of King David's census. In the first version, which was probably written at the time of the monarchy, Yahweh puts it into David's head to sin by taking a census of Israel—always hated by the people because it was done for purposes of taxation and military conscription. David's census-taking angers God, who then punishes not the king who ordered it but the people at large, sending a plague that kills thousands of Israel's citizens (2 Sam. 24:1–25). In the second telling of this episode, written hundreds of years later, it is not Yahweh who inspires David's census, but "the satan"; Yahweh only punishes it (1 Chron. 21:1–30). The centuries that elapsed between the composition of these two parallel accounts had apparently witnessed a significant change in the covenant community's theological viewpoint. It was no longer possible to see Yahweh as both the *cause* of sin and the one who punished it. The contradictory actions that the author of Samuel had ascribed to God the Chronicler now separates, assigning the cause of David's guilt to "the satan."

After the Babylonian exile, when Judea was dominated by the Persian Empire, new religious ideas gradually infiltrated Jewish thinking. **Zoroastrianism**, the official Persian religion, viewed the universe as dualistic, ruled by two opposing supernatural forces of Good and Evil. The powers of Light were led by Ahura Mazda, while those of Darkness were directed by his opposite, Ahriman, the Zoroastrian devil. According to the religion's founder, the prophet Zoroaster, at the end of time a cosmic battle between Good and Evil would result in Ahriman's defeat and the triumph of Good. Until then, the two competing forces would struggle incessantly, generating the mixture of creative peace and destructive violence that characterizes human life.

With its hierarchies of angels and demons, systems of posthumous rewards and punishments, and concept of an all-good deity waging war against a wicked opponent, Zoroastrianism profoundly influenced later Judeo-Christian ideas about the nature of Satan, who eventually became not only the enemy of humankind but of God as well. Significantly, no biblical literature written before the Persian period gives names to individual angels or depicts "the satan" as an autonomous figure. Only in postexilic books like Tobit and Daniel are particular angels such as Michael, Gabriel, and Raphael, or demons, such as Asmodeus, given personal names. With the influx of Greek and other foreign ideas following Alexander's conquest of the Persian Empire, including Judea, in the fourth century B.C.E., views of an afterlife populated with angels and demons proliferated (see the discussions of Enoch and 2 Esdras in Chapter 8). By New Testament times, Persian, Greek, Syrian, and other originally non-Jewish ideas had been thoroughly assimilated by the covenant community and rigorously subordinated to the religion of Yahweh. After the first century C.E., however, Judaism rejected many of these Persian and Greek influences, denying many books that incorporated these concepts a place in the Tanak. The canonical Hebrew Bible grants "the satan" little space and scant respect.

For additional information about the historical development of "the satan," see Jeffrey B. Russell, "Hebrew Personification of Evil" and "The Devil in the New Testament." In *The Devil: Perceptions of Evil from Antiquity to Primitive Christianity,* pp. 174–220, 221–249. Ithaca, N.Y.: Cornell University Press, 1978. See also Elaine Pagels, *The Origin of Satan.* New York: Random House, 1995. Presenting a "social history of Satan," Pagels shows how religious sects, particularly the Essenes and some New Testament authors, associated their opponents with demonic influences.

devotion, as if to cite a conspicuous example of one whose virtue affirms God's wisdom in creating humanity (Job 1:6–8). Accepting his ruler's implied challenge, the satan suggests that Job would not remain loyal if deprived of children, property, and reputation. For reasons known only to himself, Yahweh accepts this challenge, withdrawing the protective "wall" with which he had previously shielded Job from misfortune.

Stripped of divine protection, Job immediately experiences the power of chaos—the sudden injection of violent change into his formerly stable environment. Predatory nomads sweep away his flocks and herds; the "fire of God" consumes his sheep and shepherds; a fierce wind demolishes the house where Job's children are feasting, killing them all. Robbed of everything he holds dear by chaotic forces of earth, air, and sky, Job still blesses Yahweh's name (1:1–2:21). As if tempting God to doubt further the integrity of his human creation, the satan next persuades Yahweh to infect his faithful worshiper with a painful and disfiguring disease, although God protests that such persecution is unjustified, stating that his cynical agent has "provoked [God] to ruin [Job]" for no good reason (2:3). In contrast to Yahweh, who yields to pressure from satan, Job rejects his wife's despairing plea to "curse God and die." Courageously, Job resolves to live, persisting in his quest to understand the nature of his drastically changed relationship with the Deity.

THE CENTRAL POETIC DRAMA

Job's Lament   In Chapter 3, the action shifts from the heavenly court to Job's dungheap, where, in a long monologue, he prays to have the process of creation reversed, asking for a return to the primeval darkness that shrouded all before God illuminated the cosmos (cf. Gen. 1:1–2). If light and life are mere vehicles for pain, it is better not to exist or, once born, to sink quickly into the oblivion of **Sheol**, the dark subterranean realm where the human dead remain in eternal nothingness (cf. Eccles. 9:5, 10; Box 7.3). Job's agony is intensified by God's silence, the total absence

of any communication that would give his pain ethical meaning. His evocation of **Leviathan**, the mythical dragon of chaos, the "fleeing serpent"—embodiment of darkness and disorder that Yahweh is portrayed as having subdued but not having eliminated during creation—expresses Job's direct experience of chaotic evil and anticipates the imagery in Yahweh's final speech at the end of the drama, when God depicts himself as the proud owner of this monster (cf. 3:8; 26:10–14; and 41:1–34) (Figure 7.3).

The Central Debate   After delivering his anti-creation hymn, Job is joined by three friends, **Eliphaz, Bildad,** and **Zophar,** exponents of the religious orthodoxy contained in Proverbs and the Deteronomistic writings. Throughout the book, the three do not move from their initial position—that Job's present misery must result from some vile but unknown sin. Championing long-accepted views of God, they argue, with increasing vehemence, that Job is guilty because God is just. An infallible sign of divine displeasure, Job's suffering confirms his error.

The book's central section is arranged in a series of debates between Job and his accusing friends: In three cycles of dialogue, each friend gives a speech, and Job, in turn, replies. In the last cycle, Job offers a final statement in which he reviews his life for any deed that might have offended God (Chs. 29–31). As the debates become more heated, Job's early patience gives way to a realization of two unorthodox truths: His humanity entitles him to innate moral rights, which God has violated; and if he is innocent and God is truly all-powerful, then the Deity must be responsible for the evil that he and all other people endure.

In Chapters 9 and 10, Job asks God to appear before him in human form so that their conflict may be settled in terms of legal justice. Even while demanding that God present evidence to prove Job's alleged wrongdoing, Job realizes that he has no chance to argue his cause before the Almighty. Anticipating Yahweh's climactic discourse, Job describes God's control of nature, the irresistible force that reduces all mortals to insignificance.

Box 7.3 Sheol—The Biblical Underworld

When Job asks, "once a man is dead can he come back to life?" (14:14), his rhetorical question about the possibility of an afterlife is answered in the negative; unlike trees that may revive after being cut down, the dead remain permanently dead (14:18–22). In contrast to the Egyptians, who went to great lengths to preserve their dead in the hope of future life, the ancient Israelites did not embrace a doctrine of posthumous immortality. The covenant people's relationship with Yahweh did not extend beyond the grave, an assumption that intensifies Job's need for divine justice in the present life. Instead of a future reward in heaven, Yahweh's worshipers anticipated only endless confinement in Sheol, a dark subterranean abyss that indiscriminately housed all the dead, good and evil alike.

Reminding God that only the living can serve or praise him, a psalmist begs for his life to be spared:

> For in death there is no remembrance of you,
> who can sing your praises in Sheol?
>
> Ps. 6:5; cf. Isa. 38:18–19

Another biblical poet suggest that keeping worshipers alive works to the advantage of a God who requires praise: "What do you gain by my blood if I go down to the Pit [another term for Sheol]? Can the dust praise you or proclaim your faithfulness?" (Ps. 30:9). A third psalmist reminds Yahweh that the dead, no matter how devout, can no longer bear testimony to his miraculous deeds:

> Are your marvels meant for the dead,
> can ghosts rise up to praise you?
> Who talks of your love in the grave, . . .
> Do they hear about your marvels in the dark,
> about your righteousness in the land of oblivion?
>
> Ps. 88:10–12

Death breaks the bond between God and humanity: "Those who go down to the Pit do not go on trusting your faithfulness" (Isa. 38:18). The most Job can hope for in Sheol is oblivion and respite from pain (Job 3:17–19).

The author of Eccleaiastes offers a similarly bleak view, urging the wise to savor the joys of this life because even the righteous can expect no posthumous blessings:

> The living know at least that they will die, the dead know nothing; no more reward for them, their memory has passed out of mind . . . nor will they ever again take part in what ever is done under the sun. . . . Whatever work you proposed to do, do it while you can; for there is neither achievement, nor planning, nor knowledge, nor wisdom in Sheol where you are going.
>
> Eccles. 9:5, 10

Postexilic leaders in Judea may have emphasized a negative view of the afterlife to discourage older folk beliefs about the dead, beliefs Israelites once probably shared with their Canaanite neighbors.

Furthermore, Job recognizes that the power that afflicts him as the same power that will judge him:

> Suppose I am in the right, what use is my
>   defense?
> For he whom I must sue is judge as well.
> If he deigned to answer my citation, could I be
>   sure that he would listen to my voice?
> He, who for one hair crushes me,
>   who, for no reason, wounds and wounds again,
> leaving me not a moment to draw breath,
>   with so much bitterness he fills me.
> Shall I try force? Look how strong he is!
>   Or go to court? But who will summon *him?*
>
> Job 9:15–19, italics added

Acknowledging God's power, Job can only conclude that, in practice, he makes no effort to distinguish between the innocent and the guilty:

> It is all one, and this I dare to say:
>   innocent and guilty, he [Yahweh] destroys
>   all alike.
> When a sudden deadly scourge descends,
>   he laughs at the plight of the innocent.
> When a country falls into a tyrant's hand,
>   it is he who blindfolds the judges.
>   Or if not he, who else?
>
> Job 9:22–24

With courage born of his realization that good people can be more compassionate and ethically

Box 7.3 (continued)

Many ancient societies assumed that the dead not only continued to exist in another dimension but also could communicate with the living, helping relatives or harming enemies. The biblical name *Sheol* is thought to derive from the verb *sha'al,* "to ask," perhaps a reference to the ancient and widespread practice of inquiring of the dead. A passage in Dueteronomy explicitly condemns anyone who "consults ghosts or spirits, or calls up the dead" (Deut. 18:10–11), showing that the custom was not unknown in the covenant community. An offense to Yahweh punishable by death (Lev. 19:31; 20:6, 27), consultation with diviners or fortunetellers is seen as tantamount to relying on rival sources of supernatural power. The Hebrew Bible's only example of *necromancy* (eliciting prophetic speech from the dead) is Saul's notorious visit to the medium of Endor, where a woman necromancer conjures up the spirit of the prophet Samuel, illustrating an old belief that ghosts of the departed could be summoned from Sheol to foretell the future (2 Sam. 28:3–25).

Although one psalmist declared that Yahweh could be present in both heaven *and* Sheol (Ps. 139:7–8), it was not until Daniel was written during the second century B.C.E. that a biblical author unambiguously promised the faithful a future life. (Other passages, such as the vision of "dry bones" coming back to life in Ezekiel 37, refer not to individuals but to Judah's restoration after its political "death" in Babylonian captivity.) For Daniel, postmortem existence takes the form of a resurrected body, in which the just will awake to "everlasting life," while the covenant-breakers will experience "shame and everlasting disgrace" (Dan. 12:1–3).

Perhaps the most optimistic vision of the afterlife, appearing in the late Old Testament period, occurs in the apocryphal Wisdom of Solomon (first century B.C.E.). The writer, deeply influenced by Greek ideas about the soul's intrinsic immortality taught by such philosophers as Pythagoras, Socrates, and Plato, rejected traditional biblical concepts about the soul's gloomy fate in Sheol, declaring that "God did make [humans] imperishable, he made [them] in the image of his own nature" (Wisd. of Sol. 2:23). Offering a solution to the problem of undeserved suffering, the author states that God's faithful servants, no matter how unjustly afflicted, will be compensated in the next world:

> But the souls of the virtuous are in the hands
>   of God,
> no torment shall ever touch them.
> In the eyes of the unwise, they did appear to die,
> their going looked like a disaster,
> their leaving us like annihilation;
> but they are at peace.
> If they experienced punishment as men see it,
> their hope was rich with immortality.
>   Wisd. of Sol. 3:1–4

responsible than the biblical God seems to be, Job suggests that God, who revels in exercising his omnipotence, also must learn what is means to be human, to experience the universe from the human perspective:

> I shall say to God, "Do not condemn me,
>   but tell me the reason for your assault.
> *Is it right* for you to injure me,
>   cheapening the work of your own hands
>   and abetting the schemes of the wicked?
> Have *you* got *human eyes,*
>   do *you see as mankind sees?*
> Is *your* life *mortal* like man's,
>   do your years pass as men's days pass?

> You, who inquire into my faults
>   and investigate my sins,
> *you know very well that I am innocent,*
>   and that no one can rescue me from your
>   hand."
>   Job 10:2–7, italics added

Reversing the traditional wisdom that asks us to look at things from the Deity's viewpoint, Job asks that God develop greater empathy for the human condition, experiencing his imperfect world as mortals must, without the divine prerogatives of omniscience, immortality, and immunity to pain.

In the final speech by one of Job's "false comforters," Bildad attacks the notion that any human

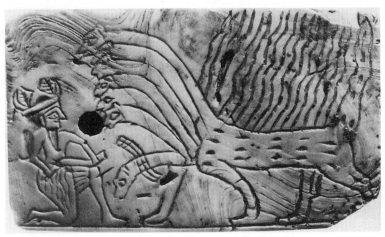

Figure 7.3 Mesopotamian god battling a seven-headed dragon. From the Sumerian Early dynastic period (c. 2800–2600 B.C.E.), the Sumerian god Ninurta, a divine warrior and son of Enlil, functions as a cosmic savior by defeating the primal monster of chaos. Biblical writers referenced Yahweh's struggles with Leviathan, another name for this primeval serpent (cf. Ps. 74:12–17; Job 3:8; 26:13; 41:1–34; Isa. 27:1). The mythical dragon rears his seven heads again in Revelation, where, identified with Satan and the devil, he is cast from heaven by the archangel Michael (Rev. 12:3, 9; 13:1; 17:3).

being can deserve God's favor, denigrating all mortals as mere "maggots" and "worms" (25:6; cf. similar views expressed by Eliphaz in 4:17–21; 15:14–16; and Zophar in 11:5–12). This attempt to justify human suffering by uniformly reducing humanity to moral baseness — an assumption to which Job also refers (9:2; 12:9; 14:4) — is sometimes used to support conventional beliefs about divine justice. The friends' emphasis on humankind's inborn depravity culminates historically in the later Christian doctrine of "original sin," which asserts that all humans inherit from Adam an inescapable tendency to sin, resulting in their blanket condemnation by a righteous Deity. Job's author, however, makes no reference to the Genesis story about the first couple's disobedience or its alleged consequences to humanity. When Yahweh later appears to Job, he categorically rejects the friends' arguments and makes no allusion to humankind's supposedly innate sinfulness (42:7).

Elihu's Interruption   Between Job's final challenge to God (Chs. 29–31) and God's appearance in the whirlwind that logically follows it (Chs. 38–41), redactors inserted a lengthy speech by **Elihu**, a character whom the text has not previously introduced. Perhaps scandalized by Job's unothodox theology, the writer of Elihu's discourse attacks Job for refusing to make things easy by simply confessing his sins (perhaps including self-righteousness) and thereby restoring the comfortable view of

God's perfect justice. Rehashing the three friends' arguments, Elihu adds little to the discussion, although he claims to resolve the problem that Job's case presents. Absurdly self-confident, Elihu presumes to speak "on God's behalf":

> I will range far afield for my arguments,
> to prove my Maker just.
> What I say to you contains no fallacies, I assure
>   you,
> you see before you an enlightened man.
>   Job 36:3–4

After six chapters of Elihu's empty rhetoric, readers may well feel that the opening question in Yahweh's first speech applies to him rather than to Job: "Who is this obscuring my designs with his empty-headed words?"

YAHWEH REVEALS HIS UNIVERSE

As Job foresaw in Chapter 9, when God at last appears, it is not in human form to explain why he subverts his assumed principles of justice by allowing the wicked to thrive and the good to suffer. Indeed, Yahweh appears in a superhuman display of power, celebrating his own strength and creative ingenuity and refusing to address any of Job's anguished questions. Speaking from the whirlwind as if to express the intractable, amoral energy of the natural world he has created, Yahweh emphasizes the enormous distance between divinity and humanity. In his first speech (38:1–39:30), he parades images of cosmic grandeur before Job's dazzled eyes. Sardonically, he demands that Job inform God about the miracle of creation, astronomical phenomena, and the curious habits of wildlife. He invites Job to share his creative pride in the world of animal violence, such as the fearless warhorse that delights in battle (39:19–25). In his final horrific example, Yahweh describes the eagle or vulture that "feed [their] young on blood," feasting on the bodies of the dying, oblivious to their pain (39:27–30).

Looking for the bread of understanding, Job is handed a scorpion, a catalogue of impersonal natural wonders, and a pitiless survey of predatory nature, "red in tooth and claw." When Yahweh asks if Job, now deluged with examples of the savage and inexplicable, is ready to give up, Job merely replies that he will speak no more. Is Job's retreat into silence before God's self-revelation an act of reverent submission or the numbness of moral shock?

Apparently unsatisfied with Job's wordless acquiescence, Yahweh then launches into a second long discourse in which he strikes at Job's deepest fear: that in the absence of a comprehensible divine ethic, humans will have to create — out of emptiness — their own meaning of life. When Yahweh asks, "Do you really want to put me in the wrong to put yourself in the right?" (40:8), Job's response must be no, for he has no wish to justify himself at the Diety's expense. He merely asks Yahweh to administer the cosmos according to ethical principles that will encourage good conduct in human life. As he had earlier observed, Yahweh's tolerance of the present system appears to support "the wicked," who commonly triumph over their moral betters.

Yahweh next invites Job to examine the divine regulation of human society, asking him if he can duplicate the divine thunder that (when it chooses) can obliterate the wicked (40:9–14). But Yahweh does not linger over his strangely inconsistent enforcement of justice in human affairs. Instead, he demands that Job consider the significance of two frightening monsters — Behemoth and Leviathan — that seem totally alien to human concerns. "The masterpiece of all God's work," **Behemoth** is

a creature so powerful, so grotesque, and so removed from any possible relation to normal human experience that God's admiration for the monster compels Job to realize the world is not a place designed primarily for human welfare. The universe Yahweh unveils is God-centered, a creation in which humans and dangerous beasts coexist, both the offspring of God. (This view contrasts markedly with that in Genesis 1:26–31, in which humanity, the pinnacle of creation, is divinely authorized to hold all other life forms in submission; cf. Ps. 8:5–8.)

Scholars formerly thought that Behemoth and Leviathan were, respectively, the hippopotamus and the crocodile, but since the discovery of Ugaritic texts referring to Baal's defeat of Lothan, the primeval sea dragon, it is known that Leviathan is a mythological beast symbolizing the chaos that existed before creation and which periodically reasserts itself, threatening to unravel the world order. The Canaanite Lothan and Hebrew Leviathan are variant forms of **Rahab**, another version of the chaotic dragon that Yahweh subdued when imposing order on the cosmos (Ps. 89:9–10). In Job, Yahweh describes Leviathan in mythic terms, as a dragon belching fire and smoke (41:18–21), at whose approach even "the ocean waves flee" (41:25). Yet, terrifying as it is, Yahweh delights in the brute:

> He has no equal on earth, being created
> without fear.
> He looks the haughtiest in the eye;
> of all the sons of pride he is the king.
> Job 41:33–34

Yahweh's allusion to Leviathan's supremacy among the "sons of pride" recalls his earlier declaration that he *can* subdue the "proud" and the "wicked" who oppress others (40:9–14), although he chooses to do so only intermittently. As he admires the monster of chaos, amoral energy that has not been assimilated into cosmic order, he apparently also incorporates arbitrary violence and unmerited suffering into his cosmic system.

Hearing Yahweh's acknowledgement of Leviathan's role in the world, Job withdraws his questions about divine justice (42:2–3). The universe is as it is, an unfolding process in which Light and Dark, Gentle and Savage, Good and Evil are intrinsic components. Leviathan, the dragon that periodically rears its head to shatter the peace of both nature and humanity, is perhaps a manifestation of the same mysterious, disruptive force that Yahweh had made part of the cosmic whole. Absolute sovereign, Yahweh is unlimited by merely human concepts of right and wrong, a monistic view that Second Isaiah also expresses:

> I am Yahweh unrivaled,
> I form the light and create the dark.
> I make good fortune and calamity,
> It is I, Yahweh, who do all this.
>
> Isa. 45:6, 7

In portraying his universe, Yahweh assigns no role to "the satan," either as an agent who tests the loyalty of humankind or as a theoretical source of cosmic evil and rebellion. For the author of Job, as well as Second Isaiah, Yahweh's unity and omnipotence leave no room for any competing supernatural entity.

After disclosing the divine paradox that encompasses polar opposites of light and dark, Yahweh asks Job to intercede for his three friends, because Eliphaz, Bildad, and Zophar have not spoken "truthfully about me as my servant Job has done" (42:7). Whereas the three friends had defended a traditional concept of God, Job had dared to point out the perplexing disparity between standard notions of divine justice and the facts of real life, where people do not always receive what they ethically deserve. After experiencing God directly in the whirlwind, Job abandons his attempt to find moral logic in divine governance of the world, for Yahweh has revealed himself far more concerned with the complex phenomena of the universe he has created than with resolving issues of good and evil that trouble humans.

After accepting Job's intercession for his friends, however, Yahweh restores all of Job's possessions twice over, again placing his worshiper in the secure and prosperous environment he had inhabited before God removed the "wall" that shielded Job from harm. Although Job is given ten more children, they are not the same children he had lost as a result of the controversy between Yahweh and his celestial prosecutor. Dispenser of both "good fortune" and "calamity," Yahweh administers a world in which — contrary to conventional wisdom — humans often find it agonizingly difficult to distinguish random chance from divine providence.

RECOMMENDED READING

Crenshaw, James L., ed. *Theodicy in the Old Testament.* Philadelphia: Fortress Press, 1983.

Dhorme, Edouard P. *A Commentary on the Book of Job.* Translated by H. Knight. London: Thomas Nelson, 1967. A reprint of a major study of Job, first published in 1926.

Gordis, Robert. *The Book of God and Man: A Study of Job.* Chicago: University of Chicago Press, 1965.

Habel, Norman C. *The Book of Job.* The Cambridge Bible Commentary. New York: Cambridge University Press, 1975. Offers NEB text and perceptive analysis.

Kallen, H. M. *The Book of Job as a Greek Tragedy.* New York: Moffat, Yard, 1918. A stimulating comparison of Job to the tragedies of Aeschylus and Euripides.

Levenson, Jon D. *Creation and the Persistence of Evil.* San Francisco: Harper & Row, 1988. A lucid study of divine omnipotence and the problem of evil.

MacKenzie, R. A. F., and Murphy, R. E. "Job." In R. E. Brown et al., eds., *The New Jerome Biblical Commentary,* 2nd ed., pp. 466–488. Englewood Cliffs, N.J.: Prentice-Hall, 1990. Offers a more conventional reading of the poem.

Mitchell, Stephen. *The Book of Job.* San Francisco: North Point Press, 1987. A fresh translation and insightful commentary.

Newson, Carol A. "The Book of Job." In *The New Interpreter's Bible,* Vol. 4, pp. 317–637. Nashville: Abingdon Press, 1996. Includes theological interpretation.

Penchansky, David. *The Betrayal of God: Ideological Conflict in Job.* Literary Currents in Biblical Interpretation. Louisville, Ky.: Westminster/John Knox Press, 1992.

Pope, Marvin H. *Job.* Anchor Bible, 5th ed. Garden City, N.Y.: Doubleday, 1978. A translation with many useful notes.

Sanders, Paul S., ed. *Twentieth-Century Interpretations of the Book of Job: A Collection of Critical Essays.* Englewood Cliffs, N.J.: Prentice-Hall, 1968. Offers a variety of viewpoints.

von Rad, Gerhard. *Wisdom in Israel.* Translated by J. D. Martin. Nashville, Tenn.: Abingdon Press, 1973. An excellent theological study.

Ecclesiastes

KEY TOPICS/THEMES

The Bible's finest example of skeptical wisdom, the Book of Ecclesiastes is ascribed to King Solomon but is actually the work of an anonymous Israelite sage who calls himself Koheleth (Qoheleth), one who presides over a circle of learners. Delighting in paradox, Koheleth denies the possibility of knowing anything for sure, except the inescapable facts of death and the ultimate futility of all human effort.

KEY QUESTIONS

Why does the author see all human endeavor as ultimately futile? What role does the concept of Sheol play in his thought?

If life is a tragedy to those who feel, as Horace Walpole once remarked in a letter of 1776, it is a comedy to those who think. Although both are works of speculative wisdom that unflinchingly acknowledge the world's moral anarchy, the books of Job and Ecclesiastes present radically different responses to cosmic injustice. Deeply committed to exploring the mystery of undeserved suffering, the author of Job invites readers to share Job's pain and to question God's purpose in permitting good to go unrewarded and evil to flourish. Whereas Job demands our emotional involvement in contemplating Yahweh's ultimate responsibility for cosmic violence and spiritual evil, the author of Ecclesiastes adopts an emotionally neutral position of coolly ironic detachment. An aloof observer of human folly, he derives a certain dry amusement from his ivory-tower perspective on the human predicament. He is puzzled by Yahweh's apparent unwillingness to enforce ethical principles, but he simply concludes that God chooses to operate with no coherent moral plan—at least not one that human beings can perceive (8:10–14, 16–17).

An element of Proverbs's practical wisdom also permeates the work. Having experienced much, the writer has found that there is "nothing new under the sun," nothing that has not been seen, said, or felt a thousand times before. He therefore advises his readers not to be taken in by the world's sham innovations. True wisdom lies in observing everything, knowing how little has genuine value, and refusing to become committed to the hopeless pursuits to which most people blindly devote their lives.

Although the superscription to the book attributes its authorship to **Koheleth** (Qoheleth), "son of David, king in Jerusalem"—presumably Solomon—most scholars regard this as merely a literary device that offers the writer an elevated position from which imaginatively to experience everything enjoyed by Israel's wealthiest and wisest monarch (1:12–2:12). The Solomon persona is soon dropped and is not referred to after the second chapter.

Koheleth means "one who presides over a congregation," a term the Septuagint translators rendered as "Ecclesiastes," from the Greek *ekklesia* (assembly). But Koheleth was not a preacher as some English translations call him; he was a professional sage living in Jerusalem who may have assembled a circle of student-disciples about him. Because the author seems familiar with various strands of Greek philosophy, including that of Heraclitus, Zeno the Stoic, and Epicurus, experts tend to place the book's composition sometime during the Hellenistic era, after the campaigns of Alexander of Macedonia had brought Greek culture to Palestine. In its present form, the book resembles a somewhat rambling essay studded with aphorisms, short poems, and meditations on the futility of existence. An epilogue (12:9–14) preserves some later editorial reactions to Koheleth's unorthodox teaching.

THE IMPOSSIBILITY OF FINDING MEANING IN LIFE

The Futility of Human Aspiration Most of Ecclesiastes' principal ideas are stated in the first two chapters. The remaining ten mainly illustrate and elaborate on the basic perception that the rewards of humanity's customary activities are either short-lived or nonexistent. The book opens with a description of the eternal cycle of nature, in which all things — sun, rivers, seas — are seen as moving in endless circles and eventually returning to their place of origin to begin the same cycle again. It is merely society's bad memory that causes people to imagine that anything new ever occurs. Individual observers simply are not around long enough to recognize that in the long view, all that is repeats itself without essential change.

Aware that knowledge is a burden because wisdom makes the illusion of happiness impossible, Koheleth nonetheless determines to sample the various pursuits that are commonly believed to provide fulfillment in life. He first tries pleasure, a deliberate savoring of "folly." Although he enjoys being able to "deny his eyes nothing they desired" and "refuse his heart no pleasure" (2:10), he finds the experiment in hedonism empty. He next tries "great" enterprises, such as elaborate building programs, but finds these endeavors equally unsatisfying. He then concentrates on amassing wealth but concludes that this, too, is meaningless. Koheleth acknowledges genuine satisfaction in hard work but cautions that all effort is ultimately "vanity" and a "chasing of the wind" (2:1–11).

The author offers several reasons for his negative view of human activity:

1. No matter what he achieves in life, he must ultimately die and leave everything to someone else, perhaps an unworthy heir who will waste it all.
2. Regardless of his successor's conduct, time itself will destroy whatever he builds or creates.
3. No matter how hard he labors or how wisely he plans, life can never compensate him for the toil and sacrifice expended to achieve his goals.
4. Death will inevitably frustrate all his intentions and hopes.

Sheol Lurking behind the author's pessimism is a conviction that death is the absolute end to life, that there is no conscious existence beyond the grave (Sheol) to which all will descend without reaping either rewards or punishments that the present world does not offer. He has no hope that the Deity will distinguish between human and animal lives, let alone between virtue and sin:

> Indeed, the fate of man and beast is identical; one dies, the other too, and both have the self-same breath; man has no advantage over the beast, for all is vanity. Both go to the same place [Sheol]; both originate from the dust; and to the dust both return. Who knows if the spirit of man mounts upward or if the spirit of the beast goes down to the earth?
>
> Eccles. 3:19–21

Because most Hebrew Bible writers assume that *all* the dead are indiscriminately housed in the grim Underworld of Sheol (see Box 7.3), the author's question here should be understood as purely rhetorical. Koheleth emphasizes the inequitable fact that the righteous worshiper fares no better after death than an animal. Indeed, it is better, the writer ironically continues, to be a "live dog" than a "dead lion." An expression of contempt, "dog" was a popular Israelite term for Gentiles; "lion" probably refers to the Davidic royal house, which the "king of beasts" symbolized. A person living ignorant of Torah is thus better off than a deceased king of the covenant people. For Koheleth, "the living know at least that they will die, the dead know nothing; no more reward for them, their memory has passed out of mind. Their loves, their hates, their jealousies, these all have perished, nor will they ever again take part in whatever is done under the sun" (9:5–6).

The dead in Sheol are eternally oblivious, without hope of future resurrection. Hence, Koheleth advises the living to live fully now (9:7–9), for "there is neither achievement, nor planning, nor knowledge, nor wisdom in Sheol where you are going" (9:10). Such counsel resembles that of the Epicurean philosophy, which held that humans are a chance collection of atoms that disintegrates at death. The consciousness or "soul" is as physical as the body and, like the body, perishes utterly. Like the Roman poet Horace, Koheleth advises the wise person to seize the day and wring from it whatever pleasures are possible.

The writer also entertains some ideas typical of Stoicism, a Greco-Roman philosophy that urged its adherents to bring their lives into harmony with the divine principles ruling the universe (see Chapter 9). Chapter 3, which begins with "there is a season for everything, a time for every occupation under heaven," seems to imply that a providence directs all things. Because the author is a Hebrew, he probably regarded Israel's God as the enforcer of the cosmic cycle of birth, growth, decline, and death. But Koheleth's God apparently is interested only in enforcing natural laws, not in giving meaning or order to human lives. Even the Stoic idea of a providentially managed universe is modified by Epicurean warnings that chance typically determines one's fate: "The race [of life] does not go to the swift, nor the battle to the strong; there is no bread for the wise, wealth for the intelligent, nor favor for the learned; all are subject to time and mischance" (9:11). It would be almost impossible to make a declaration more at variance with Israel's Prophets or the Deuteronomistic historians.

Paradoxes The author's love of paradox is a characteristic of the book that troubles some readers; he seldom makes a statement that he does not somewhere else contradict. Advising one to savor life and to drink wine with a joyful heart (9:7), he also states that it is better to frequent the house of mourning than the house of feasting (7:3). The day of death is better than the day of birth (7:1), but he would rather be a "living dog" than a "dead lion" (9:4). All people are "in the hand of God" (9:1) and should live righteously (8:10–13); but it is as much a mistake to behave too virtuously (7:16) as it is to be excessively wicked (7:17).

These paradoxic views are among the book's chief strengths, however, for the writer is not contradicting himself, but is asserting that life is too complex for absolute certainties. Just as there is a time to live and a time to die, there are occasions when radically different attitudes and behaviors are appropriate. Koheleth refuses to be confined to any single philosophical position. Whereas many Greek thinkers made logical consistency the test of truth, Ecclesiastes' author perceives the irrational

elements in life and refuses to omit observable variety in the interests of theoretical coherence. In a world where the Deity does not seem to act (and it is significant that Yahweh, the Lord of history, is mentioned by name nowhere in the work), illogic and absurdity must be acknowledged. Unlike Israel's prophets, who confidently proclaimed Yahweh's oracles, Koheleth declares that God has so obscured his purposes—and life's meaning—that "not even a sage can discover it, though he may *claim* to know" (8:17, emphasis added). The "work of God" is ultimately unknowable (11:5; cf. 3:9–11).

Postscripts The book closes with a poignant allegory in which human old age is compared to an aging, dilapidated edifice (12:1–8). Later writers added a series of brief postscripts. In the first, a disciple praises Koheleth for his wisdom and "attractive style," and adds a proverb extolling the value of wise teachers (12:9–11). A later editor, perhaps scandalized by the author's human-centered philosophy, warns the reader that writing and studying books is exhausting (12:12). It was perhaps a still later redactor who appended the final admonition to "fear God" and keep the commandments (12:14). The presence of this orthodox advice—inserted elsewhere into Koheleth's text as well (e.g., 5:6b)—could have been partly responsible for the eventual admission into the biblical canon of this deeply skeptical, religiously uncommitted book.

QUESTIONS FOR REVIEW

1. What diverse categories of literature appear in the third major division of the Hebrew Bible, the Writings? In what ways—subject matter, themes, and theological concerns—do these books commonly differ from the Torah, Deuteronomistic History, or Prophets?

2. Describe some major characteristics of Hebrew poetry, and provide some examples of parallelism, simile, metaphor, and personification. Which books of the Hebrew Bible are composed mainly in poetry? What effects can poetry achieve that prose usually cannot?

3. Describe the liturgical function of the Book of Psalms. What qualities or concerns typify the different categories of psalms, such as the hymn of praise, the lament or complaint, royal or enthronement psalms, and psalms of wisdom and instruction? How do the psalmists initiate a dialogue with God?

4. Describe some of the principal concerns of "practical" wisdom, such as the pragmatic advice and memorable aphorisms contained in the Book of Proverbs. How does conventional proverbial wisdom differ from the speculative or philosophic wisdom of Job and Ecclesiastes? In what ways do Wisdom writers challenge such assumptions as the belief that God reveals his nature and future plans through the prophets or that he directly manipulates historical events to reward the righteous and to punish wrongdoers?

5. Why does Yahweh call "the satan's" attention to Job? Who are the *bene ha elohim* (sons of God) gathered in the celestial court, and why does Yahweh permit one of them to initiate his affliction of Job? Who are Eliphaz, Bildad, and Zophar, and of what do they accuse Job? How do these three "friends" interpret Job's misfortunes according to Deuteronomistic principles? In Chapters 9–10 and 14, what does Job say about God's justice? What does Yahweh say to Job from the whirlwind?

6. Koheleth delights in collecting conventional sayings or proverbs that contradict each other. What examples of contradictory statements can you find in Ecclesiastes? Why does Koheleth state that humans cannot recognize any clear moral pattern or unmistakable sign of God's activity in the world? Why does he regard death as the enemy of human happiness? What were Koheleth's beliefs about humans' posthumous state in Sheol?

QUESTIONS FOR DISCUSSION AND REFLECTION

1. Whereas the first two parts of the Hebrew Bible, the Torah and Prophets, focus on presenting Yahweh's requirements — legal, ethical, and ritual — for the covenant community, the third division, the Writings, includes some of the community's varied responses to Yahweh's sometimes puzzling behavior. From your reading in Psalms, discuss the people's complaints about God's apparent absence or inattentiveness during critical periods of Israel's history. After the exile, why does Yahweh not intervene visibly

or publicly to rescue Israel, as he reportedly had done during the Exodus from Egypt? Why does Yahweh grow progressively more hidden during the later stages of Israel's history, at the very time when the covenant people were most fully united in Yahweh's worship?

2. A profound questioning of the conventional view of God, the Book of Job dramatizes the problem of Evil, particularly God's responsibility for undeserved suffering. The author uses none of the traditional explanations — sin inherited from Adam, a demonic rebellion against the Deity, or a future immortality to compensate for earthly pain — to excuse Yahweh's permitting humanity's torment. In keeping his integrity, why must Job refuse to put himself in the wrong? What revelation about his freedom from human concepts of Good and Evil does Yahweh make from the whirlwind?

3. The canonical Wisdom books — Proverbs, Job, and Ecclesiastes — present some strikingly different aspects of religious thought, including direct criticism of some traditional biblical ideas about the nature of God and the purpose (or lack thereof) of human life. Describe the different ways in which the authors of Job and Ecclesiastes respond to the mystery of natural violence, social injustice, and human suffering. Why do you think the Bible's editors include works that disagree with some fundamental religious assumptions of the Torah and the Prophets? Does the presence of these dissenting voices in the canon help to open a dialogue between contrasting views of God and his relationship with humanity? How does the inclusion of conflicting opinions in the Hebrew Bible encourage readers' religious growth and development?

4. Whereas the Torah and Prophets posit divine revelation — direct communication from the Deity — as the ultimate source of knowledge, many wisdom writers examine the nonhuman world of nature for Knowledge of God. From the observations of Koheleth and the speeches of Yahweh in Job 38–42, can an ethical God be found in the material workings of the cosmos? Explain your answer.

TERMS AND CONCEPTS TO REMEMBER

allegory	doxology
Anointed	Elihu
apocalypse	Eliphaz
Behemoth	Koheleth (Qoholeth)
Bildad	Leviathan

liturgy

Logos

Megillot

metaphor

Philo Judaeus

Rahab

Sheol

simile

wisdom literature

Word

Zion

Zophar

RECOMMENDED READING

Crenshaw, James L. *Ecclesiastes.* Philadelphia: Westminster Press, 1987.

Ellul, Jacques. *Reason for Being: A Meditation on Ecclesiastes.* Grand Rapids, Mich.: Eerdmans, 1991.

Gordis, Robert. *Koheleth: The Man and His World,* 3rd ed. New York: Jewish Theological Seminary of America Press, 1968. A translation with interpretative notes.

Scott, R. B. Y. *Proverbs and Ecclesiastes.* Anchor Bible, Vol. 18. Garden City, N.Y.: Doubleday, 1965.

Towner, W. Sibley. "The Book of Ecclesiastes." In *The New Interpreter's Bible,* Vol. 5, pp. 267–360. Nashville: Abingdon Press, 1997.

Wright, Addison G. "The Riddle of the Sphinx: The Structure of the Book of Qoheleth." In L. Crenshaw, ed., *Studies in Ancient Israelite Wisdom,* pp. 245–266. New York: KTAV, 1976.

———. "Ecclesiastes (Qoheleth)." In R. E. Brown et al., eds., *The New Jerome Biblical Commentary,* 2nd ed., pp. 489–495. Englewood Cliffs, N.J.: Prentice-Hall, 1990.

Festival Scrolls

The five books of the Festival Scrolls, or Megillot — Ruth, Song of Songs, Ecclesiastes, Lamentations, and Esther — are used, respectively, at the five principal festivals of the Jewish liturgical year (see Table 7.1). Their religious function is emphasized in late editions of the Masoretic text of the Hebrew Bible, where the five are placed together as a unit. In most English translations, however, they are scattered among the Prophets and the Writings, a practice that derives from the Septuagint but obscures the books' liturgical relationship. (Because it forms an integral part of Israel's wisdom tradition, Ecclesiastes is discussed along with Job and Proverbs.)

Although they differ greatly in style, tone, and theological content, the five scrolls collectively present a multifaceted view of human nature, ranging from the elegant cynicism of Ecclesiastes to the tender love story of Ruth. The Deity is seldom mentioned in these books, except in Lamentations; in Esther, he is not referred to at all. There are no legalistic absolutes here, such as we find in the Law, or certainties about Yahweh's will, such as we hear in the Prophets. Each book offers a different suggestion for handling life's problems; and each, despite the various crises and sorrows it depicts, affirms that life is good.

Ruth

KEY TOPICS/THEMES

A short story set in the time of Israel's judges, Ruth is the tale of a Moabite woman who became one of Yahweh's people and the great-grandmother of King David.

KEY QUESTION

Where is God in the lives of Ruth, Naomi, and Boaz?

A masterpiece of the storyteller's art, the Book of **Ruth** occupies a distinctive place in the Hebrew Bible. Unlike the books of Esther and Judith, which bear the names of Jewish national heroines, the titular character in Ruth is a foreigner, born and bred outside the covenant community. The Book of Ruth is one of only two canonical works named for a central character who is a non-Israelite; the other is the Book of Job. Ruth, a childless Moabite widow, and Job, an Edomite sage, also share the distinction of being Gentiles in whom Israel's God takes a special interest. Both Job and Ruth experience a fully realized divine–human relationship, albeit in strikingly different ways. Whereas Job relates to God by challenging him to reveal moral logic in human suffering, Ruth, who also suffers painful losses — her husband, family, and social identity — quietly builds a relationship with Yahweh through the people and events he brings into her life. In Job, God ultimately discloses himself through terrifying images of wild nature and cosmic violence; in Ruth,

Yahweh manifests the tender, caring aspects of the divine nature. Although Yahweh does not speak or intervene directly in Ruth, the characters' frequent references to him suggest his invisible presence, gently shaping human destinies.

GENTILES AS SYMPATHETIC FIGURES

Like the poet-sage who created Job, Ruth's unknown author takes the radical step of portraying Gentiles as sympathetic figures, worthy of both Yahweh's and the reader's respectful attention. In Deuteronomy and the Deuteronomistic History, Canaanites and other foreigners are categorically denied human value and condemned to mass extermination because their continued existence would tempt Israel to imitate their "abominable" religious practices. As a gentle protest against Israel's xenophobia, the writer depicts a Moabite heroine whose behavior is exemplary and whom Yahweh selects to fulfill his purpose in creating David's royal dynasty.

To appreciate the impact of a marriage between an Israelite male in good standing, **Boaz**, and a Moabite, it is illuminating to remember how harshly other Bible writers condemned intermarriage with foreigners. Viewing the practice as "treachery" to God and the Jewish state, Ezra, leader of the postexilic Judeans, forced all of his fellow countrymen to divorce their foreign wives, whether Egyptian, Canaanite, Ammonite, or Moabite (Ezra 9–10). Had Boaz lived in Ezra's Jerusalem, he would have been compelled to send Ruth away, along with any children they might have had.

Ruth's native land, Moab, and its close ally, Ammon, were traditionally regarded as Israel's enemies. According to Genesis, the Moabites and Ammonites were descended from Lot's incestuous union with his two daughters (Gen. 19:30–38). This tale of Moabite origins was intended to denigrate the entire nation. During the period of the Judges, the purported time of Ruth's story, a Moabite king named Eglon reportedly conquered and "enslaved" Israel (at least part of Benjamin's territory), tyrannizing over them for eighteen years

(Judg. 3:12–30). For some time, Moab was incorporated into David's empire. Later, it revolted against Israelite domination and regained its national independence (cf. 2 Sam. 8:2; 2 Kings 3; see also Box 5.6). The Book of Ruth, however, offers no hint of hostile relations between citizens of Moab and Israel—or between their respective gods, **Chemosh** and Yahweh. The author's purpose is to represent a Moabite woman as the peer of biblical heroines such as "Rachel and Leah who together built up the House of Israel" (Ruth 4:11).

DATE AND PLACEMENT IN THE CANON

In the Hebrew Bible, the Book of Ruth stands first in the Megillot, probably because it is set "in the days of the Judges" (1:1), chronologically the earliest period attributed to any of the five scrolls. In Jewish liturgy, Ruth was read at Pentecost, a harvest festival also called the Feast of Weeks, or Shavuoth. Following the Septuagint order, most English Bibles insert Ruth between Judges and 1 Samuel, a placement that puts the gentle figure of Ruth between the barbarous account of the Levite's murdered concubine (Judg. 19–20) and the story of Hannah's answered prayers to conceive a son, Samuel (1 Sam. 1–2). Although Ruth's story supposedly took place when warlike Judges led Israel (see Chapter 5), the setting at Bethlehem is remarkably peaceful, a serene landscape of farm laborers harvesting rich fields of grain. Unlike the Torah narratives, the Deuteronomistic History, or the books of Esther and Judith, Ruth is marked by the absence of great historical events, wars, or other violence. Focusing exclusively on the private lives of three ordinary people, Ruth shows God unobtrusively operating even in the most intimate of human relationships—friendship, love, and marriage.

Although the action takes place in the premonarchical period, Ruth is a difficult book for which to establish a date of origin. There is no scholarly agreement about when it was composed. Some critics think that it was written while Judean kings still reigned, as part of a literature celebrating Davidic ancestry; others assign it to the postexilic period, seeing in Ruth's story a counterargument to the prohibition against foreign wives enunciated in Ezra and Nehemiah. (The prophet Malachi's protest against divorce — separating from the bride of one's youth — is thought to reflect similar opposition to the Ezra–Nehemiah policies [Mal. 2].)

STRUCTURE AND CONTENT OF THE BOOK

Literary critics have noted that Ruth is artfully crafted, with a symmetrical structure in which the three sections of the book's first half (Chs. 1–2) parallel, in reverse order, three sections of the second half (Chs. 3–4). (See Trible in "Recommended Reading.") Most scholars believe that the narrative featuring Naomi, Ruth, and Boaz was orally composed and transmitted for many generations before being written down. Advanced largely through dialogue, the simple plot is skillfully developed. Because of a famine that afflicts Israel, the Judean Elimelech, his wife **Naomi**, and their two sons settle in Moab, which is located on Israel's southeastern border. After Elimelech dies, his two sons marry Moabite women, Orpah and Ruth, for whom Naomi develops a strong affection. Ten years later, the sons also die, leaving Naomi alone in a country typically regarded as enemy territory.

RUTH, NAOMI, AND BOAZ

When she hears that Israel's famine has ended and grain has become plentiful in Judah, Naomi determines to return to her home city of Bethlehem, advising her two widowed daughters-in-law to go back to their families and find new husbands. After expressing warm feelings for Naomi, Orpah returns to her people, but Ruth refuses to part from the Israelite woman she has come to love. In words that the King James translation has made a classic expression of devotion, Ruth declares, "Entreat me not to leave thee, or to return from following after thee: for whither thou goest, I will go: and where thou lodgest, I will lodge: thy people shall be my people, and thy God my God" (1:16). The intensity of Ruth's wish to identify herself completely with Naomi is matched in the Bible only by Jonathan's passionate attachment to young David. Jonathan "made a pact . . . to love him [David] as his own soul" (1 Sam. 18:1–5; cf. 2 Sam. 1:26).

Naomi and Ruth travel together to Bethlehem — future birthplace of King David — where, according to the Mosaic provision for the poor, Ruth gleans the fields of Boaz, a relation of Elimelech. Following Naomi's shrewd advice, Ruth makes a nocturnal visit to Boaz, who falls in love with her. In one of the fine psychological touches of this brief story, the middle-aged Boaz praises the young Moabite woman for having the perception to prefer him to a younger man. The kindly and wealthy landowner then makes sure that one of Elimelech's nearer kinsmen does not care to exercise his legal right to redeem — that is, to buy from Naomi — her dead husband's property, and with it Ruth's hand in marriage. Boaz thus is free to do so. By acquiring the dead man's estate and marrying Ruth, Boaz acts to perpetuate Elimelech's memory in Israel. Although Ruth is actually Elimelech's son's widow, in this legal arrangement she ranks as Elimelech's widow, so that a son later born to Ruth and Boaz will in effect belong to Naomi and Elimelech, ensuring the dead man an heir. Rejoicing that "a son has been born for Naomi," the women of Bethlehem name the child Obed. This child grows up to become the father of Jesse, the father of David, king of Israel.

Although Yahweh neither speaks nor appears in the narrative, the Book of Ruth illustrates that Yahweh actively assists both the living and the dead. His is the invisible presence that guides the lives of Naomi, Ruth, and Boaz. He is the life force that ensures that a man long dead will have a grandson to perpetuate his name and that an aged widow, Naomi, will again nurse her "own son" (4:13–16). That son, in turn, will become the grandfather of David, founder of Israel's God-appointed royal family. Yahweh's selection of a Moabite woman — one of the people of Chemosh — to carry out his purpose suggests that Gentiles, as well as Israelites, are part of the divine plan for humanity. Those who insist on ethnic exclusivity, such as Ezra, Nehemiah, and the

Deuteronomistic historian, do not necessarily express the attitude of Israel's universal God.

RECOMMENDED READING

Brenner, Athalya, ed. *A Feminist Companion to Ruth.* Sheffield, England: Sheffield Academic Press, 1993.

Campbell, Edward F. *Ruth.* Anchor Bible. Garden City, N.Y.: Doubleday, 1975.

Dare, Katherine P. *Far More Precious Than Jewels: Perspectives on Biblical Women.* Gender and the Bible Tradition Series. Louisville, Ky.: Westminster/John Knox Press, 1991. Examines traditional views on Ruth, Sarah, Hagar, and Esther.

Sasson, Jack M. *Ruth: A New Translation with a Philological Commentary and Formalist-Folklorist Interpretation,* 2nd ed., Sheffield, England: JSOT Press, 1989.

Trible, Phyllis. "Ruth, Book of." In D. N. Freedman, ed., *The Anchor Bible Dictionary,* Vol. 5, pp. 842–847. New York: Doubleday, 1992. A clear summary of current scholarship.

Song of Songs

KEY TOPIC/THEME

A cycle of erotic poems extolling sensual love, the Song of Songs presents a lyric drama of human passion.

KEY QUESTION

Why does the poet praise erotic love, calling it as strong as death?

A CELEBRATION OF SEXUAL PASSION

The only erotic poetry in the Bible, the Song of Songs defies easy classification or interpretation. Its frank celebration of sexual passion challenges interpreters to explain the book's presence in sacred Scripture. Puzzled or embarrassed by the poet's joyous reveling in physical sensuality, many commentators have labeled the work an allegory—a fictional narrative in which characters, objects, and actions symbolize some higher truth. To Jews, the Song became an allegory of Yahweh's love for Israel; to Christians, it became an expression of Christ's love for his "bride," the church. But to most modern scholars, this collection of love lyrics

is precisely what it appears to be, an affirmation of the human capacity for sexual pleasure.

That ancient commentators, both Jewish and Christian, regarded the book as functioning allegorically, however, suggests that the poem's eroticism may have a spiritual dimension. Perhaps implying the psychological affinity between sexual and spiritual ecstasy, in the final section the poet evokes cosmic images of death, the afterworld, and a "flame" (divine love) emanating from Yahweh. Equating the power of love with that of death, and sexual jealousy with the inexorability of Sheol, the subterranean abode of the dead, the author also invokes Yahweh, the "jealous God" who acts as Israel's lover (cf. Exod. 20:1–5; Hos. 2–3). Israel's God is a passionate Deity whose yearning for human reciprocity resembles "a flash of fire, a flame of Yahweh himself" (Song 8:6–7).

Like the books of Proverbs and Ecclesiastes, the Song of Songs traditionally is ascribed to Solomon (3:1), famous for both his wisdom and his 1000 wives and concubines. Although presumably an expert in the art of love, Solomon, nonetheless, is not thought to be the author. Some scholars believe that these erotic poems originated as hymns associated with a Near Eastern fertility goddess, such as Asherah, who was married to the god El (in Ugaritic lore) or Baal (in Canaanite tradition). If so, the Asherah–El–Baal cultic elements have entirely disappeared from the extant texts. Other scholars propose that these verses were intended to be sung at country weddings in ancient Israel.

Assuming that the Song of Songs echoes rustic marriage rites, editors of the Jerusalem Bible have edited the various lyrics to form a poetic drama in which individual lyrics are alternately sung by bride and groom. With choral responses interspersed throughout the work, it is easy to imagine the Jerusalem Bible version as a music drama or chorale of the kind performed at country weddings. More recent scholarship, however, tends to reject this view of the collection. Noting that references to marriage are almost entirely absent from the poems—the notable exception is an idealized description of Solomon's wedding procession (3:6–11)—most scholars now look for other ways to understand or classify them.

Of surviving ancient Near Eastern literature, the Song of Songs has the closest affinity with Egyptian love poetry, in which the female beloved is typically addressed as "sister" (4:8–10). Regardless of their literary precedents or original function, however, this cycle of love songs enthusiastically validates the universality of human desire, its tantalizing frustrations and joyous fulfillments. Whereas some poems lament the lover's absence, others rejoice in physical proximity with an extravagance of language unmatched elsewhere in the Bible. Intoxicated by emotion, the poet pours forth torrents of images that compare the human body—both male and female—to fruits, flowers, animals (both domestic and wild), and even topographical features. Containing numerous terms, including geographical place-names, that appear nowhere else in Scripture, the lyrics place the lovers in lush, scented environments where passion can flourish unrestrained. All of nature, rich in nourishment and sensation, provides metaphors for the lovers' intensely focused enjoyment of each others' bodies. As the pair create a private paradise in their sensuous absorption in each other, love overwhelms all thoughts of the mundane outside world. Only at the poem's conclusion is human love placed in a larger context that recognizes the existence of joy's limits: Death, the Underworld, and Yahweh. Even then, however, love is asserted to be as "strong as Death," and Yahweh, "a flash of fire," is himself both the source and paradigm of human love (8:6–7).

In a sense, this juxtaposition of Love and Death is the poet's response to the paradox posed in another book ascribed to Solomon, Ecclesiastes. Faced with the certainty of permanent extinction in Sheol, Koheleth had advised his readers to take refuge in finding satisfaction in work and life's other ordinary pleasures, including a joyful attention to "the woman you love" (Eccl. 9:9).

Writing in prose, a later commentator validated the poet's vision of love's surpassing value: If a rich man were to offer all of his wealth in exchange for love, "contempt is all he would purchase" (8:7). Both elusive and irresistible, human love is paradoxical: Desired by all, it cannot be commanded.

RECOMMENDED READING

Brenner, Athalya, ed. *A Feminist Companion to Song of Songs.* Sheffield, England: Sheffield Academic Press, 1993.

Murphy, Roland E. "Song of Songs, Book of." In D. N. Freedman, ed., *The Anchor Bible Dictionary,* Vol. 6, pp. 150–155. New York: Doubleday, 1992. Surveys the Song's history of interpretation.

Pope, Marvin H. *The Song of Songs.* Anchor Bible. Garden City, N.Y.: Doubleday, 1977.

Weems, Renita J. "The Song of Songs." In *The New Interpreter's Bible,* Vol. 5, pp. 363–434. Nashville: Abingdon Press, 1997.

Lamentations

KEY TOPICS/THEMES

Ascribed to Jeremiah, Lamentations is a collection of five poetic dirges and laments about the Babylonian destruction of Jerusalem. The lyrics explore the causes of evil and suffering and Yahweh's reasons for permitting the triumph of unbelieving nations.

KEY QUESTION

When God destroyed the covenant community, how do you think that he dealt with such extremes of emotion as Lamentations expresses?

DIRGES AND LAMENTS

Lamentations is the work that is chanted in sorrow when Jews gather each year to mourn the destruction of Jerusalem. According to tradition, the city fell to the Babylonians on August 9, 587 B.C.E., and again on the same day and month to the Romans in 70 C.E. The five poems composing this brief book express the people's collective grief for the loss of their holy city. While the prophetic books record public pronouncements of doom against the Judean capital, Lamentations embodies the private anguish of individuals who witnessed the fulfillment of Yahweh's harsh judgment.

Although a relatively late tradition assigns Lamentations to the prophet Jeremiah, its authorship is unknown. The book itself does not mention the writer, and many scholars believe that it is the work of two or three different poets. The oldest parts are thought to be Chapters 2 and 4, which were written shortly after Jerusalem's capture by Nebuchadnezzar. Chapters 1 and 3 appeared somewhat later in the sixth century B.C.E., and Chapter 5 at some point between 540 and 325 B.C.E. The first four poems are **acrostics**: Each has twenty-two verses, one for each of the twenty-two letters in the Hebrew alphabet, in which the first word of each verse begins with a different letter of the alphabet in sequential order. The last chapter also has twenty-two verses, but these are not arranged alphabetically.

From such artful wordplay, it is apparent that Lamentations is not a spontaneous outpouring of emotion, although the poets' feelings run deep and many passages are extremely moving. Chapters 2 and 4 seem to be the work of an eyewitness to the horror of the holy city's devastation:

My eyes wasted away with weeping,
    my entrails shuddered,
my liver spilled on the ground
    at the ruin of the daughter of my people,
as children, mere infants, fainted
    in the squares of the citadel.

They kept saying to their mothers,
    "Where is the bread?"
as they fainted like wounded men
    in the squares of the city,
as they poured out their souls
    on their mothers' breasts.

Lam. 2:11–12

The poet reports that some mothers ate the flesh of their infants during the famine caused by Nebuchadnezzar's siege. Formerly vigorous young men, wasted "thin as a stick," collapsed from hunger and died in the streets (4:7–10). Corpses became too numerous to bury.

The writers of Chapters 1, 2, and 4 agree that Jerusalem's fall was the direct result of its sins, particularly those of the priests and prophets who had falsely promised deliverance (4:13). The question now is, Has Yahweh forsaken his people permanently? Because they have suffered so greatly for their mistakes, will Yahweh at last show pity? Per-

haps because he lived to see Jerusalem's restoration, the writer of Chapter 3 is confident that Yahweh takes no pleasure in continuing to abuse his human creation (3:31–33). But the writer of Chapter 5, to whom Yahweh's future intentions remain a mystery, simply asks,

You cannot mean to forget us for ever?
You cannot mean to abandon us for good?

Lam. 5:20

RECOMMENDED READING

Gordis, Robert. *The Song of Songs and Lamentations,* rev. ed. New York: KTAV, 1974.

Hillers, Delbert R. *Lamentations.* Garden City, N.Y.: Doubleday, 1972.

O'Connor, Kathleen M. "The Book of Lamentations." In *The New Interpreter's Bible,* Vol. 6, pp. 1013–1077. Nashville: Abingdon Press, 2001.

Provan, Iain W. *Lamentations.* New Century Bible Commentary. Grand Rapids, Mich.: Eerdmans, 1991.

Westerman, Claus. *Lamentations: Issues and Interpretation.* Minneapolis: Fortress Press, 1994.

Esther

KEY TOPICS/THEMES

Depicting the plight of Jews scattered throughout the Persian Empire, Esther is a strongly nationalistic story in which a beautiful Jewish queen risks her life to help save her people from Haman's plot to annihilate them. This secular tale of heroic resistance to Gentile persecution celebrates the origin of the festival of Purim.

KEY QUESTION

In this fervently patriotic melodrama, why does the narrator never mention God?

Although the apocryphal Greek version of the tale of Esther reverts to the traditional view that Israel's God controls history and manipulates events to save his people, the Hebrew version of the story offers virtually no religious teaching. Though the covenant community is here threatened with genocide, the writer does not mention the Deity but implies that if Jews are to survive in a hostile

Figure 7.4 This bas-relief at Persepolis, the Greek-designed capital of the Persian Empire, shows an enthroned Darius I (522–486 B.C.E.), with his son and successor Xerxes I (486–465 B.C.E.) standing directly behind him. Both emperors launched ill-fated invasions of Greece, only to be routed by the Athenians and their allies at Marathon (490 B.C.E.) and Salamis (480 B.C.E.).

world, it will not be through divine intervention but by their own efforts. Set in the days when **Ahasuerus (Xerxes I)** ruled the Persian Empire (486–465 B.C.E.; Figure 7.4), the tale purports to explain how the joyous nationalistic feast of Purim came to be established. A long short story or novella, the Book of Esther lacks the sensitive characterization of the Book of Ruth but offers instead an exciting melodrama.

A PATRIOTIC FICTION

King Ahasuerus's Edict   When Ahasuerus divorces Queen **Vashti** for her refusal to exhibit herself before his male courtiers, **Mordecai**, who is both a supremely devout Jew and a loyal subject of the Persian emperor, maneuvers events so that his beautiful cousin **Esther**, whom he has adopted (Esther 2:7), becomes queen. In the meantime, Mordecai has discovered a conspiracy against the emperor's life but is able to send a warning in time so that the conspirators are discovered and executed. Although Mordecai's deed is recorded in the Persian court annals, Ahasuerus does not know that he owes his life to a Jewish subject.

Haman, whom the emperor has promoted to chief administrator at the court, becomes furious when Mordecai refuses to bow down before him and resolves not only to murder the Jew but also to liquidate his entire race. Telling Ahasuerus that an "unassimilated" people who obey their own customs rather than the emperor's laws are settled throughout the empire, Haman persuades Ahasuerus to issue an edict permitting their mass execution and confiscation of their property. Haman casts lots (*purim,* hence the name of the festival) to

determine the date of the massacre, which is to be the thirteenth day of the month of Adar (February–March).

Haman Outwitted   Having previously been commanded by Mordecai to keep her Jewishness a secret, Esther is now persuaded to appear unbidden before the emperor—even though intruding on the royal presence uninvited carries a penalty of death—and beg him to rescind his decree. As Haman erects a lofty gallows on which to hang Mordecai for disobeying the chief vizier, Ahasuerus learns from the court annals that Mordecai has saved his life, and Haman is duped into suggesting high honors for the emperor's rescuer. Esther then reveals Haman's evil machinations, which were intended to destroy her, a Jew, and Mordecai, to whom Ahasuerus owes his life. Dramatic justice is served when Haman is hanged on the gallows he had built for Mordecai.

The Feast of Purim   Unfortunately, the Jews living in the Persian Empire are still in danger, for the law of the Medes and Persians does not permit the theoretically infallible monarch to retract his orders. Ahasuerus does, however, issue a second edict instructing all Jews to fortify and defend themselves, which they do with spectacular success (Ch. 8). Chapter 9 recounts how the Jews slew all who would have murdered them, after which they hold a victory celebration, the feast of **Purim**. The irony is that their triumph falls on the very day that Haman had selected for their extermination.

Most scholars, Jewish as well as Christian, regard the Book of Esther as patriotic fiction rather than historical fact. Despite its authentic picture of

Persian court life and political intrigue during the fifth century B.C.E., the book contains several historical errors. Although we know much of Xerxes I, for example, there is no record that he was married to Vashti or that he had a Jewish queen named Esther. The Persian Empire was never (as the book insists) divided into 127 different provinces, nor did Xerxes order Jews in his territories to attack his Persian subjects. Mordecai, moreover, is said to have been deported to Persia from Babylon, which would make him at least 100 years old during Xerxes' reign, and the alluring Esther could not have been much younger.

There are, then, decidedly more fictional than historical elements in the story. The name Esther itself is a variation of "Ishtar," the Babylonian goddess of love and fertility. The name Mordecai derives from "Marduk," the leading Babylonian deity. Indeed, some interpreters have suggested that the book's Jewish author deliberately fictionalized an old Babylonian myth in which Marduk defeats his demonic enemies (Haman and his cohorts in this narrative). Certainly, the present book is a clear-cut example of the forces of Good triumphing over Evil as they did in the ancient myth.

At all events, Esther has found a vital place in the Jewish consciousness; to many pious Jews, it is the most significant book in the Megillot. The annual reading of the book at Purim does not merely commemorate the Jews' turning the tables on their enemies in ancient Persia; it is also a profound statement about the heroic resistance necessary, in the face of overwhelming anti-Semitic aggression, to ensure Jewish survival at any place and any time in the modern world.

QUESTIONS FOR REVIEW

1. Why were the five books of the Megillot placed together as a discrete unit of the Hebrew Bible? What common interests or themes connect such diverse works as Lamentations and the Song of Solomon? What place does a work of erotic poetry have in the Bible?

2. Why does the author of Ruth make his heroine a Moabite? Do you think that the writer is reacting against the ethnic exclusivism advocated by the Deuteronomistic historians and the books of Ezra and Nehemiah (discussed later in this section)? Compare and contrast the respective characters and situations of Ruth, Naomi, and Esther. How does Esther act to save her people?

QUESTIONS FOR DISCUSSION AND REFLECTION

1. How do such different books as Job, Ecclesiastes, and Ruth present an equally valid interpretation of God's interactions with humanity? In what important ways can people relate to God by criticizing — and perhaps rejecting — conventional religious ideas? How do people experience God through the quiet events of private relationships, as pictured in Ruth? Why do the Wisdom authors prefer rational observation and critical thought to the revelations and visions found in the Torah and Prophets?

2. In compiling the final edition of the Hebrew Bible, why did Jewish scribes include *both* divine revelations and writings that were skeptical of such revelations?

TERMS AND CONCEPTS TO REMEMBER

acrostic	Naomi
Ahasuerus (Xerxes I)	Passover
Boaz	Pentecost
Chemosh	Purim (Festival of Lots)
Esther	Ruth
Fast of the Ninth of Ab	Feast of Tabernacles
Haman	(Feast of Booths)
Mordecai	Vashti

RECOMMENDED READING

Berg, Sandra B. *The Book of Esther.* Chico, Calif.: Scholars Press, 1979.

Brenner, Athalya, ed. *A Feminist Companion to Esther, Judith and Susanna.* Sheffield, England: Sheffield Academic Press, 1995.

Crawford, Sidnie White. "The Book of Esther." In *The New Interpreter's Bible,* Vol. 3, pp. 855–941. Nashville: Abingdon Press, 2001.

Dumm, Demetrius. "Esther." In R. E. Brown et al., eds., *The New Jerome Biblical Commentary,* 2nd ed., pp. 576–579. Englewood Cliffs, N.J.: Prentice-Hall, 1990.

Fox, Michael. *Character and Ideology in the Book of Esther.* Columbia: University of South Carolina Press, 1991.

LaCocgne, André. *The Feminine Unconventional: Four Subversive Figures in Israel's Tradition.* Minneapolis: Fortress Press, 1990.

Moore, Carey A. *Esther.* Garden City, N.Y.: Doubleday, 1971.

Reinterpreting Israel's History for the Postexilic World

During their exile in Babylon, many Judean leaders had followed Jeremiah's advice, buying property and putting down roots in Mesopotamian soil (Jer. 29). When Cyrus, emperor of the new Persian Empire, captured Babylon (539 B.C.E.) and issued his famous decree permitting the exiles to return to their homeland, many displaced Judeans opted to remain in their adopted country. Those remaining included an intellectual leadership that, over many generations, produced extensive commentaries on the Torah, adapting Mosaic laws to new circumstances of Jewish life in the Diaspora ("scattering" of Jews abroad). Approximately 1100 years after the exile had begun, Mesopotamian Jewish scholars compiled the Babylonian **Talmud**, a vast compendium of oral tradition that eventually became the supreme guidebook of rabbinical Judaism. (See Chapter 9.)

Another group of Judeans had fled Jerusalem's ruins and taken refuge in Egypt, where they established permanent settlements. After Alexander of Macedonia conquered Egypt (c. 330 B.C.E.) and founded the great port city of Alexandria, a large colony of Jews flourished there. From the thriving Alexandrian community came the first translation of the Hebrew Bible into Greek, the Septuagint. Alexandrian Jews also produced a significant body of original literature, including the Wisdom of Solomon, which became part of Roman Catholic and Greek Orthodox Bibles.

The group most responsible for the creation of the Hebrew Bible, however, was a relatively small contingent of priests, scribes, and other influential leaders who returned from Babylon to Judah after 538 B.C.E. Perhaps inspired by the optimistic rhetoric of Second Isaiah, the first exiles to make the arduous trek back to Judah found conditions very different from those the prophet had envisioned. Instead of recovering paradise, they had to eke out a meager subsistence in an impoverished land that

Nebuchadnezzar's troops had thoroughly ravaged. Disappointed and dispirited, the former refugees were motivated to rebuild Yahweh's Temple only when the prophets Haggai and Zechariah promised that the "treasures of all the nations" would flow in to finance the project (Hag. 2:7).

ADJUSTING TO NEW POLITICAL REALITIES

Haggai and Zechariah also had fed the people's hopes that their new masters, the Persians, might allow a restoration of the Davidic monarchy. Because the Persian emperor had appointed **Zerubbabel**, a grandson of the deposed King Jehoiachin, as governor of Judah, the next step might be to recognize him as a legitimate king (1 Chron. 3:17–19). The Persians apparently refused to take that step, however, and Zerubbabel's unexplained disappearance from the scene left David's throne — in spite of Yahweh's sworn oath (2 Sam. 7; Ps. 89) — permanently vacant. The postexilic Judean community, forced to grapple with irreversible change, entered a new phase of history. Instead of being ruled by Yahweh's anointed kings, Judah, stripped of political or economic importance, would henceforth be led by anointed priests. As the covenant community had survived the transition from charismatic Judges to divinely ordained monarchs almost five centuries earlier, the covenant people of Judah now would prosper without Davidic leadership or even national autonomy. Reaffirming the Mosaic Law as their eternal heritage, Judean priests resolved to maintain their people's identity as a Torah-keeping group. Taking the lead from a new Joshua — the Aaronic High Priest who, with Zerubbabel, helped lead postexilic Judeans — the covenant people could, in effect, become a theocratic "nation of priests."

Ezra

KEY TOPICS/THEMES

The Book of Ezra pictures the difficult conditions that prevailed in the postexilic community of Judah, then a small part of the vast Persian Empire (Chs. 1–6; Figure 7.5). The Persian emperor authorizes Ezra, a priestly scribe returned from

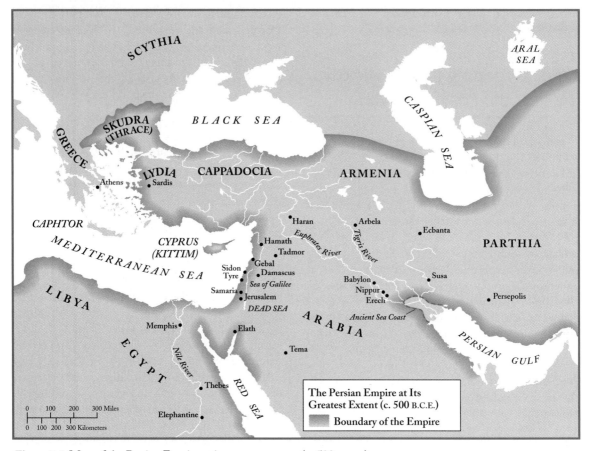

Figure 7.5 Map of the Persian Empire at its greatest extent (c. 500 B.C.E.).

Babylon, to reorganize the restored Judean community according to principles of the Mosaic Torah (Ch. 7). To prevent assimilation with the Gentile population, Ezra forbids intermarriage between Judeans and foreign women (Chs. 9 and 10).

KEY QUESTIONS

What role did Ezra play in reorganizing the postexilic community? What was his contribution to the development of the Mosaic Torah?

Although Ezra and Nehemiah probably formed a single book originally, the two histories present conflicting information about the sequence of events they record. Part of the confusion arises because we do not know who first returned to help rebuild Jerusalem—the priest-scribe **Ezra** or the Persian-appointed governor of Judah, **Nehemiah**. The Chronicler precisely dates his history by citing particular years of the Persian emperor **Artaxerxes**; but because two monarchs of this name ruled during the fifth century B.C.E., scholars are uncertain which one the writer meant. Although even experts do not agree on the basic order of events, it seems likely that Nehemiah came to Jerusalem first (c. 445 B.C.E.) and that Ezra appeared during the governor's second twelve-year term.

THE RETURN FROM EXILE

Ezra opens with Cyrus's proclamation endorsing the return of the Judeans from Babylon to Jerusalem to rebuild Yahweh's Temple (c. 538 B.C.E.), an edict consistent with the Persian ruler's policy of tolerating and even encouraging local religious cults throughout his empire. A long list of repatriated exiles follows in Chapter 2, while Chapter 3 describes the first sacrifices on a rebuilt altar "set up on its old site" and the laying of foundations for a second Temple. Poignantly, the tears of those old enough to remember the much larger dimensions of Solomon's Temple mingle with the joyous shouts of the younger generation as the priests lead the people in singing praises.

Chapters 4–6 record the Judean leader Zerubbabel's rejection of Samaritan aid in reconstructing the sanctuary. Consequently, Judah's slighted neighbors conspire to persuade the Persian emperor (then Xerxes I) that Jerusalem is a potentially rebellious city whose rebuilding should be stopped. The emperor agrees, and the Temple remains unfinished until two postexilic prophets, Haggai and Zechariah, convince Zerubbabel and **Joshua**, the high priest, to start work again. (For a discussion of the prophets Haggai and Zechariah, see Chapter 6.)

When a Persian official questions the legality of this project, the Judean elders appeal to the new Persian emperor, **Darius**, to investigate the court records for Cyrus's original authorization to erect a new Temple. Not only is Cyrus's edict found and enforced, but it obligates the Persians to supply money for rebuilding and procuring sacrifices (Figure 7.6). The second Temple is completed and dedicated in about 515 B.C.E., permitting a Passover celebration at Yahweh's sanctuary for the first time in more than seventy years.

EZRA'S MISSION

Chapter 7 introduces Ezra, a Babylonian scribe who had devoted himself to intense study and teaching of the Mosaic Law and who is represented as the first in a long line of distinguished rabbis who were decisive in forming and preserving Judaism. Emperor Artaxerxes commissions Ezra to travel to Jerusalem to supervise the Temple, to evaluate conditions in the Judean province according to Mosaic standards, and to appoint scribes and judges to administer civil and moral order for the whole Judean population (7:11–26). Chapter 8 lists the new returnees and the treasures

Figure 7.6 This silver figurine from the court of Artaxerxes I (465–424 B.C.E.) shows the kind of tunic, trousers, and hood that biblical figures such as Ezra, Nehemiah, and Haman may have worn, as officials associated with the Persian emperor's court. After Cyrus the Great defeated Babylon in 539 B.C.E. and encouraged former captives to restore the cults of their respective national gods, the Judeans returned to Palestine, rebuilt Yahweh's Temple, and enjoyed two centuries of Persia's remarkably tolerant rule.

of silver and gold that Ezra had been appointed to bring to the Temple.

Chapters 9 and 10 record Ezra's distress at the returned exiles' intermarrying with foreign women. He was raised in exclusively Judean circles in Babylon, where strict adherence to legal and ethnic exclusiveness was observed, so he determines to enforce his concept of the nation's duty. After begging his God to forgive the people for marrying

Figure 7.7 This bas-relief depicts a Persian satrap, or governor. The Persians divided their enormous empire into twenty administrative units called satrapies, each locally autonomous but ruled by the emperor's appointed governor. As the books of Ezra, Nehemiah, and Esther reveal, some upper-class Jews, including those from priestly families, rose to influential positions within the Persian administration. Because the Persians did not permit the restoration of the Davidic royal line, many priests assumed leadership roles in postexilic Judah.

those who follow pagan religions, Ezra calls on the people to reject these mixed alliances at a great assembly before the Temple. Weeping, the men agree to divorce their non-Judean wives, and Ezra arranges to see that the resolution is enforced. The book ends with a list of those guilty of unsanctified marriages.

The Book of Ezra gives a generally positive view of the Persian government's remarkable cooperation with and consideration of its Judean subjects, a view that accords with the picture of Jews dispersed amid the Persian state presented in the books of Esther and Tobit (Figure 7.7). Ezra himself, the priest and learned scribe who brings a copy of the Mosaic Law with him from Babylon to regulate and unify Judean life in the restored community, is a key figure in the further development of Judaism. Both the Pharisees and later rabbis could trace their roots to this zealous promoter of

Mosaic traditions, as could the writers of several apocryphal books, such as 1 and 2 Esdras (the Greek form of Ezra).

Nehemiah

KEY TOPICS/THEMES

Appointed governor of postexilic Judah by Emperor Artaxerxes, Nehemiah oversees the rebuilding and reorganization of Judah (Chs. 1–7). After promulgating a version of the Mosaic Torah compiled and edited during the Babylonian exile (perhaps the final form of today's Pentateuch), the priest Ezra institutes an atonement ceremony (Chs. 8–10). A report of Nehemiah's reforming zeal, enforcing Sabbath-keeping and the ban on foreign marriages, concludes the book (Ch. 13).

KEY QUESTION

What did Nehemiah and Ezra do to strengthen the postexilic covenant community?

THE RETURN TO JERUSALEM

Originally combined with Ezra, the Book of Nehemiah enlarges our picture of conditions in postexilic Judah and Jerusalem. The book opens with an account of Nehemiah's grief when, as an official cupbearer to the emperor at Susa, the Persian capital, Nehemiah learns of the miserable conditions in Jerusalem. Weeping over reports of the city's poverty and ruin, he persuades Emperor Artaxerxes to commission his return to Jerusalem to rebuild the city.

Nehemiah travels with an armed guard to Jerusalem, where he encounters local opposition to the refortification of the city. (Reconstructing the city's defensive walls would naturally increase its apparent independence, which the Judeans' enemies could interpret as subversive to Persian rule.) When Sanballat (the governor in Samaria), Tobiah the Ammonite, and Geshem the Arab first deride and then threaten to attack Nehemiah's workmen, Nehemiah arms his builders, who thereafter complete the city walls in record time. After Artaxerxes officially appoints Nehemiah governor, Nehemiah is able to maintain order and to institute significant economic and social reforms, such as canceling debts and freeing slaves.

PROCLAIMING THE TORAH

Promulgation of the Mosaic Law Perhaps the most significant incident recorded in the Book of Nehemiah is Ezra's extended public reading of the Mosaic Law (Ch. 8). Apparently, the resettled Judeans no longer understood the classical Hebrew in which the Torah was written, because Ezra, after declaiming aloud from the sacred scrolls, translated and "gave the sense"—that is, interpreted the Law's meaning—"so that the people understood what was read" (8:8). Scholars have debated exactly which form of the Torah Ezra presented to the people. Some scholars believe that it was the Pentateuch that we have now. During the Babylonian

captivity, schools of priests and scribes labored to compile, preserve, and interpret Israel's Mosaic legacy for their own day. (See Chapter 4.)

Whether the Torah that Ezra brought back to Jerusalem was the entire Pentateuch or merely a collection of legal material later integrated into it, his work thereafter became the basis and standard for the Judean community. The religious reforms that Ezra and Nehemiah impressed upon the national consciousness included revivals of such age-old festivals as the Feast of Tabernacles and a covenant-renewal ceremony (Ch. 9), the latter featuring additional public teaching of the Law and a long poetic recital of Israel's history, emphasizing its covenant obligations to Yahweh.

Nehemiah's Zeal Chapters 10–13 record the people's vow to abide by the covenant to support the Temple service, which involved numerous financial and other responsibilities. Marriages to foreign women are again forbidden, and strict observance of the Sabbath is enjoined. Chapters 11 and 12 report the repopulating of Jerusalem, Levitical genealogies, and the formal dedication of the new city wall. The final chapter concludes Nehemiah's memoir, recounting how he bustled about the city personally enforcing Sabbath keeping, persuading individuals to give up their foreign wives, and asking God to remember his good works "for [his] happiness."

Like Ezra, Nehemiah was a conscientious proponent of Judean exclusivism, tolerating neither Gentile customs nor non-Judean women in the holy city. While his rigid insistence on ceremonial and racial particularism may strike the modern reader as unsympathetic, these requirements were deemed necessary at a time when the Judeans were few in number and surrounded by enemies. Without such separatism, both national and religious identity might have been lost.

RECOMMENDED READING

Blenkinsopp, Joseph. *Ezra-Nehemiah: A Commentary.* Philadelphia: Westminster Press, 1988.

Eskenazi, Tamara C. *In an Age of Prose.* Atlanta: Scholars Press, 1988.

Fensham, F. Charles. *The Books of Ezra and Nehemiah.* Grand Rapids, Mich.: Eerdmans, 1982.

Klein, Ralph W. "The Books of Ezra and Nehemiah." In *The New Interpreter's Bible,* Vol. 3, pp. 663–851. Nashville: Abingdon Press, 1999.

Meyers, Jacob M. *Ezra, Nehemiah.* Garden City, N.Y.: Doubleday, 1965.

North, Robert. "The Chronicler: 1–2 Chronicles, Ezra, Nehemiah." In R. E. Brown et al., eds., *The New Jerome Biblical Commentary,* 2nd ed., pp. 362–398. Englewood Cliffs, N.J.: Prentice-Hall, 1990.

Williamson, H. G. M. *Ezra and Nehemiah.* Sheffield, England: JSOT Press, 1987.

Rewriting Israel's History: The Work of the Chronicler

Recognizing that Yahweh, Lord of history, had radically changed the direction of Israel's historical development, postexilic scribes undertook the necessary task of reinterpreting the nation's past. Whereas the first edition of the Deuteronomistic History had seen Israel's story culminating in Josiah's splendid reforms, the second edition, revised during the Babylonian exile, had presented it as culminating in Yahweh's destruction of the nation. Writing more than a century after the exiles' return, an anonymous priestly author known as the Chronicler again surveyed Israel's past, this time discovering national fulfillment in the restoration of Yahweh's worship at the rebuilt Jerusalem Temple. In the Chronicler's view, Israel's destiny was not necessarily to exercise political power on the world stage, but to promote Yahweh's cult with ethical and ritual purity—a view that historical events seemed to vindicate.

AUTHORSHIP

Because of their generally consistent priestly orientation, the four books of 1 and 2 Chronicles, Ezra, and Nehemiah are commonly assigned to the same redactor or editor. Many scholars, however, dispute the claim that the same person—the Chronicler—compiled all four, pointing to differences in attitude and theology that distinguish Ezra and Nehemiah from the two books of Chronicles. Although some commentators argue that the same

priestly scribe provided the final editing of the four volumes, preserving older material that differed from his viewpoint and adding commentary to impart thematic unity, most scholars now believe that the books of Ezra and Nehemiah, which underwent a series of complex revisions before reaching their present state, represent the work of an author different from the writer responsible for 1 and 2 Chronicles.

SOURCES AND THEMES

The books of 1 and 2 Chronicles are largely rewrites of Samuel and Kings, but with a significant change in emphasis. Instead of portraying David and Solomon as creators of a powerful—though short-lived—Israelite state, the Chronicler depicts them as priest-kings whose main concern was always the building, furnishing, and maintenance of the Jerusalem Temple. The stream of Israelite history thus flows not toward the goal of imperial success but toward the "proper liturgical service of Yahweh" at Jerusalem's rebuilt sanctuary—a religious mission that could be carried out regardless of Judah's political fortunes (2 Chron. 35:16; 36:22–23; Ezra 1:1–11; 5–7).

Samuel and Kings are the Chronicler's primary sources. He also borrows genealogical lists from the Pentateuch and passages from various psalms, as well as otherwise unknown documents, such as the "Annals of Samuel the seer, the Annals of Nathan the prophet, and the Annals of Gad the seer" (1 Chron. 29:29–30; see also references to Solomonic archives [2 Chron. 9:29] and those of Hezekiah [2 Chron. 32:32]). As for the historical reliability of the Chronicles material that did not appear in the Deuteronomistic History, scholars disagree about whether added—and extensive—passages about Hezekiah's reforms (2 Chron. 29–31) and Manasseh's repentance (2 Chron. 33) represent the author's use of authentic sources or his own creative imagination. As scholars have observed, the account of Manasseh's sins, deportation to Babylon, and promotion of religious reforms following his return to Jerusalem exactly parallel what happened to Judah. In the Chronicler's revisions, Manasseh comes to embody the covenant people's collective experience, that of a sinner redeemed by suffering and repentance.

The two parts of Chronicles originally were one volume, until the Septuagint editors divided the work into two scrolls entitled *Paralipomenon,* meaning "what was omitted" (that is, information not included in the books of Samuel and Kings). When translating the Latin Vulgate, Jerome called the work *Chronicon,* the Latin name from which the English title is derived. This closely approximates the Hebrew title, *Dibre Hayamim,* which means "annals" (literally, "the book of the acts of days"). As with Ezra and Nehemiah, the books of Chronicles show an overriding interest in genealogies (especially of priestly families), dates, Temple liturgy, and priestly functions.

1 Chronicles

KEY TOPICS/THEMES

First Chronicles retells the story of King David's career from a priestly viewpoint, emphasizing his association with the Ark of the Covenant, the Jerusalem cult, and the elaborate preparations for building the Temple. Portraying David as a monarch-priest, the account omits unflattering material from the older histories, such as David's adultery with Bathsheba and murder of Uriah (Chs. 10–29).

KEY QUESTION

How does the Chronicler reinterpret the Deuteronomistic portrayal of David?

First Chronicles opens with a genealogical survey of world history, beginning with Adam and culminating in lists of Judeans (particularly Levites) who returned from the Babylonian captivity (1:1–9:34). After a brief and negative judgment on the reign of King Saul—whose failure is set as a foil to his successor (9:35–10:14)—the remaining twenty chapters focus on King David's splendid accomplishments. In idealizing David, the Chronicler reminds his audience that past faithfulness to Yahweh's covenant brought Israel unprecedented blessings, thus recalling them to their present religious obligations.

In Chapters 11–29, David is depicted not as a military and administrative genius but as a devout religionist who establishes the elaborate Temple cult, contributes heavily to its support, and recruits whole retinues of artisans and musicians for its services. In the Chronicler's story, preparation for building the sanctuary becomes the main goal of David's kingship, as constructing, dedicating, and maintaining the sanctuary became the chief objective of Solomon's administration.

DAVID AS KING-PRIEST

With regard to the times of King David, the author's major alterations of his source material include the following:

1. Making Saul's death a judgment caused by his visit to the Witch of Endor (1 Chron. 10:13–14), an obvious betrayal of the Yahwist cult

2. Having David proclaimed king of all Israel at Hebron (1 Chron. 12:23–40), when historically only Judah first acknowledged him there

3. Interpolating a long prayer by David when he brings the Ark of the Covenant to Jerusalem (1 Chron. 16:7–36), thus clothing the monarch in priestly garb

4. Insisting that David contributed enormous sums of gold toward building the Temple as a good example to later Israelites (1 Chron. 22:14–16; 28:14–19)

5. Stating that David was responsible for assigning the Levites — cantors, gatekeepers, and bakers — their Temple duties (1 Chron. 23:2–27:34)

6. Asserting that David determined the plans, furnishings, and functions of the Temple and that Solomon merely carried them out (1 Chron. 28:1–31)

7. Deleting all references to David's misdeeds, including his adultery with Bathsheba and murder of Uriah

8. Attributing to David a final speech in which he urges generous financial support for the construction and upkeep of the Temple (1 Chron. 29:1–20)

9. Implying that David transferred the reins of power to Solomon while he was still alive and that Solomon ascended the throne without opposition (1 Chron. 29:22–28)

The Chronicler's primary intent here is not to provide fresh insights into David and Solomon (whose faults, recorded in 2 Samuel and 1 Kings, he omits), but to insist that the nation's principal mission is to worship Yahweh wholeheartedly and to demonstrate that the failure of later kings to honor the Jerusalem sanctuary led to the monarchy's collapse. By showing how royal apostasy and lack of zeal for Temple worship caused the nation's downfall, he hopes to rouse his audience from its apathy and revive participation in the Levitical services. And although his distortions of historical fact to make this point may be debatable, his thesis is nevertheless consistent with the rest of Israel's sacred history.

2 Chronicles

KEY TOPICS/THEMES

Continuing the priestly saga of preparation for and building of the Jerusalem Temple, 2 Chronicles depicts Solomon's reign as almost exclusively focused on the national cult and then recapitulates the narrative of Judah's Davidic rulers (derived largely from 1 and 2 Kings) through the reign of Josiah (Chs. 1–35). Adding a claim that Manasseh allegedly repented of his apostasy (Ch. 33), the book ends with Cyrus's decree restoring the exiled Jews to their homeland (Ch. 36).

KEY QUESTIONS

According to the Chronicler, what was the primary function of the Davidic kings? What is the climactic event in biblical history?

Second Chronicles opens with the glories of Solomon's reign and then surveys Judah's history from the time of his successor, Rehoboam, to the issuing of Cyrus's edict permitting the return of the Judeans to Jerusalem. Unlike the author of Kings, the Chronicler does not attempt to give a parallel history of the divided kingdom but concentrates almost entirely on Judah, referring to the northern kingdom only when it concerns Judah's affairs. As in the first book, the writer's interest revolves around the Temple.

THE ROYAL TEMPLE CULT

Solomon to Josiah   The first nine chapters recount the splendors of Solomon's legendary wealth and his building program, emphasizing the construction, dedication, and divine consecration of the Temple (Figure 7.8); nothing is said about Solomon's weaknesses or eventual corruption by his many foreign wives. He repeats the dramatic confrontation between Rehoboam and the rebellious northern tribes that withdraw from the monarch when the new king refuses to modify his harsh policies (Chs. 10–11).

Thereafter, the Chronicler rapidly scans the line of Judean rulers, pausing to elaborate on the reigns of four "good" kings—Asa, Jehoshaphat, Hezekiah, and Josiah—and to expand passages dealing with the prophets. He devotes much more space than the author of Kings to enumerating the reforms of Hezekiah, who is miraculously delivered from the Assyrian menace, and Josiah, whose reinstitution of the Passover feast became a standard for later observances (Chs. 28–32 and 34–35).

Manasseh's Sins and Repentance   Between these two approved monarchs came **Manasseh**, whose forty-five-year reign exceeded that of any other Judean king (Ch. 33). 2 Kings lists Manasseh's crimes, which include burning his son as a pagan sacrifice, but the text is silent on his alleged repentance. The Chronicler, however, states that while a captive of the Assyrians in Babylon, Manasseh sought Yahweh, who relented and restored him to his throne (though the Chronicler does not explain how this astonishing reversal occurred). Manasseh then personally conducted a religious reform, cleansing the Temple of the pagan cults he

Figure 7.8 The Hebrew inscription on this pottery fragment, which dates from the eighth or seventh century B.C.E., refers to the "gold of Ophir." According to the books of Kings and Chronicles, King Solomon imported vast quantities of this precious metal from Ophir, famous for the high quality of its gold. Although Egyptian documents also refer to Ophir, its location, perhaps somewhere in eastern Africa, is now unknown.

order of canonical books put 2 Chronicles in the climactic end position in the Hebrew Bible. Cyrus's decree promises restoration of Yahweh's religion in the Promised Land and thus forms a counterweight to the final scene at the end of the Torah, a poignant moment in which Moses looks across Jordan to the land he will not enter. Whereas the Torah closes with the pledges made through Abraham and Moses about to be fulfilled, the second division of the Hebrew Bible (Joshua through 2 Kings) recounts the tragic story of Israel's gain — and loss — of the promised homeland. To balance the Deuteronomistic vision, the Chronicler ends with another account promising Israel's repossession of its land. It is significant that the last words spoken in the Hebrew Scriptures are those of a Gentile conqueror who espouses the Judean cause — the same **Cyrus** whom Second Isaiah called Yahweh's "Messiah" (Isa. 45:1). The Persian king, to whom Yahweh "has given . . . all the kingdoms of the earth," calls to Jews scattered throughout the world to return to worship at the holy city: "Whoever there is among you of all his people, may his God be with him! Let him go up" (2 Chron. 36:23).

QUESTIONS FOR REVIEW

1. What historical figure made Judah's restoration possible? Under what political control did the covenant people live, between 538 and about 330 B.C.E.?

2. Describe Ezra's contribution to the development of Judaism. What role did he play in perpetuating the Mosaic tradition?

3. In what ways did Ezra and Nehemiah try to preserve the religious and ethnic identity of the postexilic community? Why were Israelite men forced to divorce their foreign wives? Would the author of Ruth have regarded all foreign women as inherently subversive of Yahwism?

4. Following the return from the Babylonian exile, what group replaced Davidic kings as leaders of the restored Judean community? Given Judah's changed circumstances and leadership, why do you think that the Chronicler prepared a revised edition of Israelite history?

5. How does the Chronicler's account of King David differ from that in the Deuteronomistic His-

had established there and rebuilding Yahweh's altar. The writer notes that the prayer that moved Yahweh to rescue the former "black magician" was preserved in the Annals of Hozai (33:20), which is not the same as the Prayer of Manasseh included in the Apocrypha.

Unexpectedly, portions of 2 Chronicles make somewhat more interesting reading than does the rather dry version of David's reign in the first book, where the author's concern for priestly ritual overwhelms the narrative. Although 2 Chronicles repeats much of 2 Kings, it adds some colorful details and ends with a hopeful promise of the people's liberation. As the last book in the Hebrew Bible canon, it apparently anticipates a future for Judaism in which the priest, not the king, will play the dominant role.

Although the events 2 Chronicles narrates take place before those recorded in Ezra and Nehemiah, the rabbinical editors who arranged the

tory? What episodes in David's personal life does he omit? In his revisionist account, what does the Chronicler depict as the main objective of David's reign?

6. In the Chronicler's view, what is the most important function of the postexilic Judean community?

QUESTIONS FOR DISCUSSION AND REFLECTION

1. After Ezra reintroduced the Torah to the postexilic Judean community, why did the institution of prophecy cease? Did publication of the Torah inhibit and replace the living prophetic voice? What role did the increase of priestly control and influence have on this process?

2. Most Jewish and Christian groups emphasize the teachings in the Torah and the Prophets and devote much less attention to the Writings. Although selected psalms are commonly read in most churches, the challenge of Israel's sages is often largely ignored. Why is this the case? Do you think most people find that obeying a set of legal decrees—such as the Ten Commandments—and seeing history as the Deuteronomistic historian(s) interpreted it offers a more clear-cut and easily acceptable view of religion?

TERMS AND CONCEPTS TO REMEMBER

Artaxerxes	Manasseh
Cyrus the Great	Nehemiah
Darius	Talmud
Ezra	Zerubbabel
Joshua	

RECOMMENDED READING

Ackroyd, Peter R. *The Chronicler in His Age.* JSOT Supplement Series, 101. Sheffield, England: JSOT Press, 1991.

Allen, Leslie C. "The First and Second Books of Chronicles." In *The New Interpreter's Bible,* Vol. 3, pp. 299–659. Nashville: Abingdon Press, 1999.

Klein, Ralph W. "Chronicles, Book of 1–2." In D. N. Freedman, ed., *The Anchor Bible Dictionary,* Vol. 1, pp. 992–1002. New York: Doubleday, 1992.

Meyers, Jacob M. *1 Chronicles.* Garden City, N.Y.: Doubleday, 1965.

———. *2 Chronicles.* Garden City, N.Y.: Doubleday, 1965.

Noth, Martin. *The Chronicler's History.* JSOT Supplement Series, 50. Sheffield, England: JSOT Press, 1987.

CHAPTER 8

Deuterocanonical, Apocalyptic, and Extracanonical Works

Key Topics/Themes

After Alexander the Great conquered the Persian Empire (late fourth century C.E.), the covenant community's subjugation to Greek rule sparked fierce dissension between Jews who willingly adopted Greek culture and those "pious ones" (*hasidim*) who resisted it, a struggle that culminated in Antiochus IV's attempt to abolish Judea's traditional forms of worship. While the apocryphal 1 and 2 Maccabees describe Antiochus's persecution and the Maccabee family's guerrilla warfare against it, the Book of Daniel translates this battle to preserve Israel's legacy into cosmic visions of End time, when Yahweh will overthrow all Gentile powers and establish his global rule. Written during the Hellenistic era (following 323 B.C.E.), when Greek culture was almost universally disseminated, the books of the Apocrypha, such as Tobit and Judith, commonly dealt with the problems of loyal Jews living in the Diaspora or under foreign domination in Judea. Although the Apocrypha are included in Catholic and Orthodox editions of the Old Testament, the Pseudepigrapha (documents

typically written under the name of some ancient biblical figure) did not achieve canonical status.

KEY QUESTIONS

How do books of the Apocrypha and Pseudepigrapha reflect the difficulties of Jewish life in the Diaspora? What social and political forces stimulated the production of apocalyptic works, such as Daniel and 2 Esdras? What contribution do the deuterocanonical and pseudepigraphal writings make to our understanding of Hellenistic Judaism, including developments in the wisdom tradition?

The Covenant People in the Hellenistic World

BOOKS OF THE "SECOND CANON"

As validated by ancient Jewish scholars, the Hebrew Bible (Tanak) closes with the books of Chronicles. Rabbis of the first centuries C.E. apparently decided not to recognize as authoritative

305

Table 8.1 Deuterocanonical (Apocryphal) Books

The Hebrew Bible (Tanak) omits fourteen books or parts of books that some Christian churches regard as part of the Old Testament. This table presents the canonical status—the acceptance or rejection—of the deuterocanonical (apocryphal) writings by various representative groups. A dash (—) indicates that the writing is not accepted. An empty circle (○) indicates that the book is not part of the canon but is given some religious value. A dark circle (●) indicates that the writing is included in the Bible but is not equal in authority to the Old and New Testaments. A dark square (■) means that the book is accepted as part of the Old Testament.

| | | | | EASTERN ORTHODOX | |
BOOK	JEWISH	PROTESTANT	ROMAN CATHOLIC	GREEK	RUSSIAN
1 Maccabees	—	○	■	■	●
2 Maccabees	—	○	■	■	●
Additions to Daniel	—	○	■	■	●
Tobit	—	○	■	■	●
Judith	—	○	■	■	●
Additions to Esther	—	○	■	■	●
Baruch	—	○	■	■	●
Letter of Jeremiah	—	○	■	■	●
Ecclesiasticus (ben Sirach)	—	○	■	■	●
Wisdom of Solomon	—	○	■	■	●
2 Esdras (4 Ezra)	—	○	○	■	●

For additional information on deuterocanonical and extracanonical works, see James H. Charlesworth, "Biblical Literature: Apocrypha and Pseudepigrapha," in Mircea Eliade, ed., *The Encyclopedia of Religion*, Vol. 2, pp. 173–183 (New York: Macmillan, 1987).

Scripture about fourteen books—including several additions to canonical Daniel and Esther—that had been included in the Septuagint or other Greek editions of the Tanak. The early Christian community, however, which used Greek translations of the Hebrew Bible, regarded these fourteen books as **deuterocanonical**—belonging to a later "second canon." In Catholic and Greek Orthodox Bibles, deuterocanonical works are interspersed among the Prophets and the Writings. Following the Protestant Reformation in the sixteenth and seventeenth centuries C.E., however, most Protestant editions of the Bible either omitted deuterocanonical books altogether or relegated them to a separate unit between the Old and New Testaments (Table 8.1). Taking the name assigned them by Jerome in the fourth century C.E., these "supplementary" books were called the **Apocrypha**. (See Chapter 1.)

Whether considered deuterocanonical or apocryphal, this group of books represents an indispensable record of evolving Jewish thought between the Old and New Testament periods. Like the canonical Writings, deuterocanonical works encompass a variety of literary categories, including Wisdom books, short stories, poetry, and historical narratives. As the canonical Writings reflect differing theological responses to the postexilic world when Judah was part of the Persian Empire, so the deuterocanonical books reflect responses to yet another challenge—the Hellenistic world.

ALEXANDER'S CONQUESTS AND THE HELLENISTIC WORLD

In the Writings, books such as Esther, Ezra, and Nehemiah give a generally favorable picture of Persian rule. Except when influenced by anti-Jewish advisers, such as Haman, Persian emperors tended to support Judean causes, particularly Yahweh's worship in the Judean homeland. While the Persian Empire lasted (539–330 B.C.E.), the Jewish

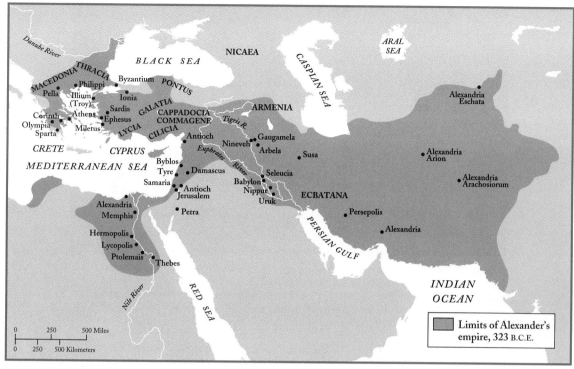

Figure 8.1 Map of the empire of Alexander the Great (323 B.C.E.).

people enjoyed two centuries of relative peace and stability, albeit with many social and economic humiliations resulting from foreign control (cf. Neh. 9:34–37). Conditions changed rapidly in the late fourth century B.C.E., however, when a new world conqueror burst onto the international scene. Blazing across the eastern Mediterranean region like a brilliant comet, Alexander the Great (356–323 B.C.E.) rapidly conquered the entire Persian Empire. Extending his dominion over parts of three continents — from Greece to Egypt to Afghanistan and western India — Alexander created the largest empire the world had yet known (Figure 8.1). Changing forever the way people lived, Alexander's conquests brought Greek language, art, literature, philosophy, and social customs to the millions of subjects inhabiting his vast domain. For the first time in history, a European power dominated — militarily, politically, and culturally — the older Near Eastern and Indian centers of civilization (Figure 8.2).

Before he could carry out his presumed goal of forging a single world government unified by Greek culture, however, Alexander died — at age thirty-two — of a sudden fever at Babylon. After Alexander's death, his empire slowly disintegrated, but large sections remained under the control of his successors, known collectively as the *diadochoi.* For biblical history, the two most important successors were **Ptolemy I,** who founded a dynasty that ruled Egypt for three centuries, and **Seleucus,** whose descendants ruled Syria, then a large territory stretching from Asia Minor (modern Turkey) to Mesopotamia (modern Iraq). The Ptolemaic dynasty, with its capital at **Alexandria,** controlled **Judea** until 199 B.C.E., when it was taken over by the Seleucid dynasty of Syria.

Although Alexander's successors did not achieve his vision of a permanently united world, they did preside over a new international culture known as **Hellenistic.** A mixture of the classical Greek (Hellenic) civilization with the older cultures of

Figure 8.2 This mosaic, in which Alexander of Macedonia (left) defeats the Persian emperor Darius III (right center) at the Battle of Issus (333 B.C.E.), pictures a decisive moment in later biblical history. Alexander's conquest of the older Near Eastern centers of power, including Egypt, Palestine, Mesopotamia, and Iran, introduced a new era in which Greek language, art, literature, science, and philosophy transformed the biblical world. By the time of Jesus, Judaism had been largely Hellenized — even in Palestine — and the New Testament was composed for a Greek-speaking audience molded by Greek ideas and culture.

the Near East, the Hellenistic synthesis produced a creative flowering of Greek and Oriental motifs in religion, philosophy, and the creative arts. Arbitrarily dated as beginning with Alexander's death in 323 B.C.E., the Hellenistic epoch chronologically overlaps the period of Roman expansion and the early Christian centuries. (See Chapter 9.)

JUDAISM AND HELLENISTIC ASSIMILATION

Israel's religion had originally developed in the geographically limited area of Canaan. After Alexander's conquests, however, Judeans were suddenly forced to cope with life in a much larger, more culturally complex environment. Throughout the Hellenistic kingdoms of Alexander's successors, people began to regard themselves as citizens not of a particular city-state (*polis*), but of the world (*cosmos*) as a whole. This *cosmopolitan* outlook helped break down barriers between different national traditions, allowing an integration of Greek with other ethnic customs, a process by which even many Jews became partly Hellenized.

The deuterocanonical books present several strikingly different reactions to the covenant people's encounter with Hellenism. For some authors, Hellenistic culture and the practice of an authentic Jewish religion peacefully coexisted. This view prevails in the Book of Tobit, which purports to be set in the days of Assyria and actually represents Jewish life during the Hellenistic **Diaspora**. The Book of Wisdom, attributed to King Solomon, similarly manifests an easy integration of Israelite tradition and Hellenistic philosophy. In sharp contrast, the books of **Maccabees** show faithful Jews heroically resisting a government-imposed policy of enforced Hellenization. Written in Greek, these two accounts vividly illustrate the life-and-death struggle between Torah loyalists and a Hellenistic king who tried to eradicate their religion. This extreme crisis — in which Jewish assimilation into the larger Hellenistic culture is seen as a threat to the covenant people's religious identity and purpose — is given a cosmic dimension in the canonical Book of Daniel. The only fully apocalyptic work in the Hebrew Bible, Daniel pictures

Box 8.1   Torah Loyalism, Martyrdom, and the Reward of Future Life

The persecutions of Antiochus IV mark the first time in biblical history that Jews died not for defending their country militarily against foreign invaders, but merely for practicing their faith. The Book of 2 Maccabees paints horrific pictures of faithful Jews paying for their integrity with torture, mutilation, and death. When Eleazar, a ninety-year-old Torah instructor, spits out the pig's flesh that Antiochus's soldiers had forced on him, he is viciously bludgeoned to death. Even worse were the agonies endured by seven young brothers who similarly refused to pass the king's test of religious conformity by eating what the Torah forbade. One by one, before their mother's eyes, they are scalped, their heads flayed, their tongues cut out, and their hands and feet lopped off; then, still conscious, they are thrust into huge pans and slowly fried alive (2 Macc. 7).

As martyrs who willingly died in a religious cause, the anonymous seven brothers not only served as models for other Jews forced to choose between life and Torah loyalty but also voiced a belief that their unspeakable sufferings would be compensated for in a future life. Expressing a conviction that God will resurrect the faithful dead—a view that enters the biblical record only with the Hellenistic Book of Daniel (Dan. 12:1–3)—the second brother places his martyrdom in the light of eternity: "The King of the world will raise us up, since it is for his laws that we die, to live again for ever" (2 Macc. 7:9). Appearing initially in the crisis ignited by enforced Hellenization, the concept that enduring a painful but holy death would lead to immortality ultimately exerted a pervasive influence on the early Christian community.

human history as a series of Gentile empires that repeatedly attempt to compromise the faith of their Jewish subjects. Because it concerns the same historical crisis that inspired the Maccabean revolt, Daniel is included here among discussions of the deuterocanonical works.

Traditionally, the deuterocanonical books are arranged with those attributed to Ezra (Esdras) first and the Maccabean histories last. In order not to interrupt the chronological flow of biblical history from the Persian into the Hellenistic periods, however, we will consider 1 and 2 Maccabees first. Depicting Antiochus's frontal attack on Judaism, these two narratives record a major shift in Israel's religious experience. For the first time, Judeans find themselves battling a foreign power not to defend their state militarily, but to defend their religion. Unlike previous Assyrian, Babylonian, and Persian conquerors, who permitted Judeans to worship Yahweh and keep the Torah, Antiochus deliberately set out to destroy Judaism. Determined to crush opposition to state-enforced assimilation, Antiochus made loyalist Jews suffer *for their faith*. Many Jews who refused to abandon their an-

cestral laws were imprisoned, tortured, and killed (Box 8.1). This "great tribulation," as the author of Daniel saw it, produced the first saints and martyrs, initial victims in what would become a long line of Jewish and Christian religious heroes who kept their integrity unto death. Antiochus's persecutions form the historical context of Daniel's eschatological visions, images of an ordeal so painful that it was thought to mark the climactic consummation of history.

After surveying the Maccabean conflict and the rise of apocalyptic literature, this text will examine both the canonical Book of Daniel and several other apocalyptic works produced between about the third century B.C.E. and the first century C.E. These visionary works include the deuterocanonical Book of 2 Esdras and the noncanonical books of 1 and 2 Enoch and the Sibylline Oracles, all of which represent eschatological concerns prominent both in some branches of Hellenistic Judaism and in early Christianity.

Following a review of some major apocalyptic writings, the text will discuss the other deuterocanonical books, beginning with Tobit, Judith, the

Additions to Esther, and Baruch, which offer imaginative portrayals of Jewish life in the Diaspora. Two important works of Hellenistic wisdom literature, Ecclesiasticus and the Wisdom of Solomon, complete our coverage of the Apocrypha or "second canon." This section concludes with a discussion of several other noncanonical books, including the Letter of Aristias, the Book of Jubilees, the Testaments of the Twelve Patriarchs, and the books of Adam and Eve. The books — canonical, deuterocanonical, and noncanonical—are discussed in the following order:

1. Books covering Antiochus's persecution and the rise of apocalyptic writing
   • 1 Maccabees (a historical account of the Jewish revolt against the oppression of the Seleucid king Antiochus IV)
   • 2 Maccabees (a vivid elaboration of the persecutions and tortures that Antiochus IV inflicted on Jewish martyrs)
   • Daniel (a canonical work—written during the persecutions of Antiochus IV—that combines quasi-historical narrative and apocalyptic visions of End time)
   • Additions to Daniel (prayers and anecdotes about Daniel added to the Septuagint edition)
2. Other (apocryphal and noncanonical) apocalyptic works
   • 2 Esdras (although deleted from the Roman Catholic canon by the Council of Trent in the sixteenth century C.E., an important book because it combines speculative Wisdom with eschatological visions; written about 100 C.E., after the Roman destruction of Jerusalem and the second Temple)
   • 1 Enoch (a noncanonical apocalypse composed of several different documents written during the Hellenistic period, some as early as the third century B.C.E.; the book's older parts, which identify some heavenly being as "the Watchers," may have influenced the author of Daniel)

   • 2 Enoch (another apocalyptic book ascribed to Enoch, written about the first century C.E., that includes visions of traveling through the ten levels of the spirit world)
   • The Sibylline Oracles (a collection of visionary utterances by various Hellenistic Jewish, Christian, and other writers compiled during the first few centuries C.E.)
3. Other deuterocanonical writings (books of the Apocrypha)
   • Tobit (a short story set at the time of the Assyrian Empire but reflecting Jewish life in the later Diaspora)
   • Judith (a fictional romance that highlights dangers threatening Diaspora Jews)
   • Additions to Esther (prayers and other pious sentiments added to a canonical book that does not mention God)
   • Baruch (a narrative about Jews living in foreign realms, ascribed to the prophet Jeremiah's secretary, Baruch)
   • Ecclesiasticus or Wisdom of Jesus ben Sirach (a compendium of proverbial wisdom and ethical advice to Jewish students, written by a Jerusalem sage c. 180 B.C.E.)
   • Wisdom of Solomon (a Wisdom book combining traditional Jewish and Hellenistic ideas, composed during the first century B.C.E.)
4. Other noncanonical writings (additional books of the Pseudepigrapha)
   • Letter of Aristeas (an account of how Hellenistic Jews living in Alexandria, Egypt, produced the first Greek translation of the Hebrew Bible, the Septuagint)
   • Book of Jubilees (a rewriting of Genesis and the first part of Exodus, emphasizing the eternal validity of the Torah)
   • Testaments of the Twelve Patriarchs (an elaborate rewriting of the Genesis passage in which Jacob [Israel] blesses his twelve sons)
   • Books of Adam and Eve (imaginative stories about the experiences of the original human couple after their expulsion from Eden)

1 Maccabees

KEY TOPICS/THEMES

A remarkably accurate history of the Jewish revolt against Seleucid oppression in the mid-second century B.C.E., 1 Maccabees recounts the persecution of Jews by Antiochus IV (Ch. 1), the uprising led by Mattathias and his sons (Ch. 2), and the guerrilla war led by Judas Maccabeus (Chs. 3–9), which after his death is carried on by his brothers Jonathan (Chs. 9–12) and Simon (Chs. 13–16) and Simon's son, John Hyrcanus I, the first priest-king of a new Maccabean (Hasmonean) dynasty.

KEY QUESTIONS

How did Antiochus IV's policies spark the Maccabbean Revolt? How did Judea achieve a temporary political independence?

The most accurate and valuable historical work in the Apocrypha, 1 Maccabees covers the tumultuous period from about 168 to 134 B.C.E., during which the Jews overthrew their Greek-Syrian overlords and established an independent state. Without this and the less trustworthy account in 2 Maccabees, we would have virtually nothing of Israel's history between Ezra's reforms (c. 400 B.C.E.) and the New Testament period. (Figure 8.3 shows a map of Palestine in the Maccabean period.)

Probably written in about 100 B.C.E., 1 Maccabees gives an apparent eyewitness description and remarkably unprejudiced account of the fight for religious freedom by **Judas Maccabeus** (for whom the book is named) and his brothers during the persecutions of the Seleucid tyrant **Antiochus IV**. Besides its objectivity, 1 Maccabees is notable for its plain, swiftly moving style and for its total lack of miracles, supernatural elements, and divine interventions. Like the canonical Book of Esther, it presents historical events as the result of purely human activity.

While his protagonists offer prayers and strictly observe the Mosaic Law, the author never attributes their military or political victories to God's direct help, though he does seem to indicate that faithful Jews who are willing to sacrifice their lives to oppose the heathen will achieve success. Because he never refers to divine providence or to the hope of immortality for the faithful dead, many scholars believe the unknown writer belonged to the Sadducee party, a religiously conservative group that developed during this period.

ANTIOCHUS'S PERSECUTION AND THE MACCABEAN REVOLT

The Great Persecution A brief preface recounts Alexander's conquest of Persia and his successor's division of the Macedonian Greek Empire. (Palestine was first awarded to the Ptolemies of Egypt and then conquered by the Seleucid Antiochus III; Table 8.2.) The book then focuses on Antiochus IV's misguided effort to impose religious unity on all his subjects by outlawing the Jewish religion. Antiochus burns copies of the Mosaic Law and forbids the offering of sacrifices to any but Hellenistic gods, the circumcision of infants, and the keeping of Sabbath or other holy days. To enforce his prohibitions, he erects a fortress citadel in Jerusalem and fills it with Seleucid soldiers. Finally, he builds an altar to Zeus in Yahweh's Temple and sacrifices pigs and other ceremonially unclean animals at the sanctuary.

Revolt of the Maccabees Fearful of the Seleucids' power, many Jews reluctantly compromise their faith and sacrifice to the state-imposed gods. Others, attracted by Greek culture and philosophy, more willingly support Antiochus's policies. A large number, however, refuse to abandon their ancestral faith; among these is the priest **Mattathias**, who with his five sons—John, Simon, Judas, Eleazar, and Jonathan—moves from Jerusalem back to their native village of Modein. When one of Antiochus's commissioners tries to bribe Mattathias into publicly obeying the royal edict, the old man kills both the commissioner and a fellow Jew who had sacrificed, then flees to the hill country with his sons (Ch. 2).

After Seleucid soldiers massacre 1000 Jews who piously refuse to defend themselves on the Sabbath, Mattathias and his followers prudently decide that

Figure 8.3 Map of
Palestine in the
Maccabean period
(c. 168–63 B.C.E.).

Palestine in the Maccabean Period
(C. 168-63 B.C.E.)

Kingdom of Alexander Jannaeus

Table 8.2 Hellenistic Successors of Alexander the Great (336–323 B.C.E.)

DATE B.C.E.	RULERS OVER PALESTINE		EVENTS IN JUDAH
	EGYPT (PTOLEMYS)	SYRIA (SELEUCIDS)	
323	Ptolemy I Lagi (323–285)		
		Seleucus I (312–280)	
300			
	Ptolemy II Philadelphus (285–246); Alexandrine Jews begin translation of the Torah and Prophets (Septuagint Bible)		
		Antiochus I (280–261)	
		Antiochus II (261–246)	Judah under Ptolemaic control
250			
	Ptolemy III Euergetes (246–221)	Seleucus II (246–226)	
		Seleucus III (226–223)	
		Antiochus III (223–187)	
	Ptolemy IV Philopator (221–203)		
200	Ptolemy V Epiphanes (203–181)	Seleucids capture Palestine (200–198/197)	Judah under Seleucid control
	Ptolemy VI Philometer (181–146)	Seleucus IV (187–175)	Persecution of Jews; desecration of the Temple (168 or 167)
		Antiochus IV Epiphanes (175–163)	
		Antiochus V (163–162)	Maccabean revolt under
150		Demetrius I (162–150)	Mattathias (d. 166) and Judas Maccabeus (d. 160); rededication of the Temple (165 or 164)
			Judah independent under Hasmoneans (142–63)

self-defense does not violate Sabbath rules. Fighting a guerrilla war against the occupation troops, Mattathias's group destroys many pagan altars and forcibly circumcises many Jewish boys. Near death, Mattathias appoints the most capable of his sons, Judas Maccabeus (in Greek, the "hammer") as his successor.

Judas Maccabeus Chapters 3–9 recount the incomparable service of Judas Maccabeus to the Hebrew nation. Against tremendous odds, he defeats the Seleucid armies in several decisive battles. Next he marches into Jerusalem, cleanses the ransacked Temple, and rebuilds its altar. He then institutes the joyous festival of rededication (**Hanukkah**)—according to tradition, three years after the day on which Antiochus had polluted the sanctuary. When Antiochus unexpectedly dies in 163 B.C.E.,

Judas concludes an armistice with the Seleucids, assuring his people religious freedom. After hostilities flare up three years later, Judas defeats the Seleucid general Nicanor, who had rashly threatened to burn the Temple.

Among the most significant of Judas's deeds is his treaty of friendship with Rome, the mighty new empire then rising in the West. The author of 1 Maccabees (who must have written before Rome took over Palestine in 63 B.C.E.) ironically regards Rome as the champion of peace and political integrity, the protector of smaller states that willingly place themselves within its sphere of influence.

Jonathan After Judas falls in battle, his brother Jonathan becomes leader of the Jews (160–142 B.C.E.). Sharing his predecessor's charismatic gifts, Jonathan rallies the people against further Seleucid

Figure 8.4 The coin on the right was struck during the time of John Hyrcanus II (67–40 B.C.E.), the Hasmonean ruler who invited the Roman occupation of Judea in 63 B.C.E. The bronze coin on the left features a menorah, the seven-branched lampstand kept in the Temple, and was issued during the brief reign of Antigonus (40–37 B.C.E.), last of the Hasmonean dynasty. Herod I, the Roman-appointed king of Judea, had Antigonus beheaded and ruthlessly eliminated all other Hasmonean claimants to the throne.

aggression, which is repelled. Alexander, the new claimant to the Seleucid throne, shrewdly concludes a peace settlement with Jonathan and in 152 B.C.E. appoints him high priest, by this time a political as well as religious office. This act establishes a line of **Hasmonean** (an ancestral name of the Maccabees) priest-kings that lasts until 40 B.C.E., when the Romans appoint Herod king of the Jews (Figure 8.4). During later political turmoil, however, Jonathan is lured into the Seleucid camp and treacherously slain (9:23–12:53).

Simon   The last of the Maccabean brothers, Simon now assumes military leadership and eventually the high priesthood as well. Although he marshals an army, he fights fewer battles than did his brothers; his forte seems to have been diplomacy, because he bribes Syrian troops to withdraw and thus ensures peace for about seven years. Taking advantage of this lull and of Seleucid internal strife, Simon builds numerous fortresses around the country and forms an alliance with the Syrian ruler, who confirms his appointment as high priest and simultaneously releases the Israelites from taxation and tribute. This act effectively ensures Jewish autonomy (142 B.C.E.) and marks a new independence for the Jewish state.

John Hyrcanus   In 134 B.C.E., however, the Seleucids again attack, and many Jews are imprisoned or killed. The aged Simon commissions two of his sons, Judas and John, who lead the Jewish army victoriously against the invaders. After Simon and his other sons, Mattathias and Judas, are murdered by Simon's traitorous son-in-law, John (surnamed "Hyrcanus") becomes Judah's priest-king (1 Macc. 16). This event is the last recorded in Old Testament history. (For a summary of Judean history in Roman times, see Chapter 9.)

Although the author of 1 Maccabees ignores the possibility of supernatural aid in the Jewish struggle for independence from Syria, his theme that faithfulness and courage under persecution can result in freedom is undeniably inspirational. The hectic period he describes, with its excesses on both sides, also provides the historical background for such canonical books as Esther, which similarly depicts the Jews fighting for their lives against pagan oppressors, and Daniel, which recounts the struggles between the Seleucids and Jews in eschatological terms (Dan. 11:21–12:13).

RECOMMENDED READING

Bickerman, Elias. *From Ezra to the Last of the Maccabees.* New York: Schocken Books, 1962. A brief introduction to the period.

Doran, Robert. "The Book of 1 Maccabbees." In *The New Interpreters Bible*, Vol. 4, pp. 1–178. Nashville: Abringdon Press, 1996. For historical background and intrepretive commentary.

Goldstein, Jonathan A. *1 Maccabees*. Garden City, N.Y.: Doubleday, 1976. Covers the Maccabean period thoroughly and includes a translation and interpretation of 1 Maccabees.

Hengel, Martin. *Judaism and Hellenism*, Vols. 1 and 2. London: SCM Press, 1974.

———. *Jews, Greeks, and Barbarians: Aspects of the Hellenization of Judaism in the Pre-Christian Period.* Philadelphia: Fortress Press, 1980.

Nickelsburg, George W. E. *Jewish Literature Between the Bible and the Mishnah.* Philadelphia: Fortress Press, 1981. A survey of both apocryphal and pseudepigraphal works in their historical context.

Stone, Michael. *Scriptures, Sects and Visions: A Profile of Judaism from Ezra to the Jewish Revolts.* Philadelphia: Fortress Press, 1980. A concise, clearly written discussion of ideas during the Hellenistic period.

2 Maccabees

KEY TOPICS/THEMES

An expanded revision of the first seven chapters of 1 Maccabees, 2 Maccabees is a theologically oriented interpretation of events, emphasizing tales of official corruption, persecution, and the integrity of martyred Torah loyalists (Chs. 1–15). The unknown author interpolates numerous innovative religious beliefs into the narrative (Chs. 6, 7, 10, 12, 15).

KEY QUESTION

What new beliefs about the afterlife inspire the martyrs of Antiochus's persecution?

A Greek work, probably written in Alexandria, Egypt, after 124 B.C.E., 2 Maccabees is not a continuation of the history of 1 Maccabees, but a revised version of events related in the first seven chapters of the earlier book. According to the compiler's preface (2:19–32), the book is an edited abridgement of a five-volume historical work (since lost) by "Jason of Cyrene," who is otherwise unknown. The period covered is approximately 176–161 B.C.E.

Whereas 1 Maccabees is a relatively straightforward, reliable, and human (perhaps Sadducean) account of the Jewish revolt against Antiochus IV's enforced Hellenization of Judah, the second book's credibility is undermined by its emphasis on exaggerated numbers, unlikely miracles, and supernatural apparitions. The writer of 2 Maccabees, who seems to have been a Pharisee, not only presents the successful rebellion as an act of God (11:13; 15:27) but injects considerable religious commentary into his narrative (5:17–20; 6:12–17; 8:36; 12:40), along with such typical Pharisaic doctrines as belief in a bodily resurrection (7:9; 14:46).

CORRUPTION, PERSECUTION, AND INTEGRITY

The book opens with two letters from Palestinian Jews to their fellow Jews in Egypt, urging them to observe Hanukkah, the festival of the Temple's rededication (1:1–2:18). After outlining his sources in a preface (2:19–32), the "abbreviator" traces the increasing corruption of the high priesthood in the persons of Jason and Menelaus (Chs. 3–4); Antiochus IV's campaign to unify his ethnically diverse subjects by imposing Hellenistic culture and religion on them; the Jews' consequent sufferings (Chs. 5–7); Judas Maccabeus's unexpectedly effective guerrilla resistance, which culminates in the purification of the Temple (Chs. 8–10); and Judas's further battles against such foes as Nicanor, chief general of Demetrius I, one of Antiochus's successors (Chs. 10–15).

Although some of its material is of doubtful authenticity, 2 Maccabees offers vivid descriptions of the greed, intrigue, and treachery of Jason and Menelaus (Chs. 4–5), who betray their people for personal gain. Equally memorable are the author's depictions of the tortures endured by Jews who refuse to compromise their faith. The nobility of the ninety-year-old Eleazar, a distinguished teacher who is bludgeoned to death, and the courage of seven brothers and their mother, all of whom are mutilated and burned alive by Antiochus, are classic examples of Jewish integrity (Chs. 6–7).

Also noteworthy is the author's theological philosophy of history, which attributes the Jewish people's martyrdom under Antiochus to their God's wish to discipline them. Intense suffering is here seen, paradoxically, as a sign of divine benevolence.

Whereas the Deity allows the Gentile nations to multiply their crimes and guilt — with the implication that the coming retribution will be all the more severe — Israel is punished *before* its "sins come to a head." That numerous disasters befall the Jews, in short, is evidence that their God has *not* deserted them (6:12–17).

The writer's other religious beliefs apparently include a future resurrection of the dead (7:9; 14:46), a belief in the efficacy of a prayer to release the dead from sin (12:43–45), the doctrine that the righteous dead can intervene on behalf of the living (15:12–16), and the concept that God created the world out of nothing (7:28). Such Pharisaic beliefs appear to have been increasingly prevalent in the time of Hellenistic Judaism. Certainly, such notions as prayers for souls in Purgatory and the intercessory prayers of saints later became important in Catholicism. Perhaps because it supported these doctrines, 2 Maccabees was condemned in Protestant circles.

QUESTIONS FOR REVIEW

1. Define the terms *deuterocanonical* and *noncanonical*. What is the relationship between deuterocanonical books and the Apocrypha? After reviewing the discussion of the biblical canon in Chapter 1, explain why Catholic and Greek Orthodox editions of the Bible include these books whereas many Protestant Bibles do not.

2. What political effects did the campaign of Alexander of Macedonia have on the biblical world? Which two kingdoms ruled by Alexander's successors sequentially controlled Judea?

3. Identify Antiochus IV, and describe his policies concerning the Jewish religion. What actions did Antiochus take against the Jerusalem Temple and the practice of the Jewish religion? What crisis did these policies provoke?

4. Summarize the main events in the books of Maccabees. Who were the Maccabees, and why did they lead a revolt against Antiochus? What political changes did they bring to the land of Judah by 142 B.C.E.? How are they related to the Hasmoneans?

QUESTION FOR DISCUSSION AND REFLECTION

How did the "great tribulation" of Antiochus's persecutions and the executions of martyrs loyal to Torah commands stimulate the rise of eschatological ideas, including new concepts of posthumous judgment and resurrection of the dead?

TERMS AND CONCEPTS TO REMEMBER

Alexandria	Hellenistic
Antiochus IV	Judas Maccabeus
Apocrypha	Judea
deuterocanonical	Maccabees
Diaspora	Mattathias
Hanukkah	Ptolemy I
Hasmonean	Seleucus

RECOMMENDED READING

Doran, Robert. "The Book of 2 Maccabees." In *The New Interpreter's Bible,* Vol. 4, pp. 179–299. Nashville: Abingdon Press, 1996.

Goldstein, Jonathan A. *2 Maccabees.* Garden City, N.Y.: Doubleday, 1979.

Apocalyptic Literature and the Book of Daniel

No form of biblical literature is more bewildering to the average reader than the apocalyptic, a term derived from the Greek *apokalypsis,* which means "an unveiling, an uncovering, a stripping naked of what is normally hidden." As a literary category, an **apocalypse** is a revelation of dimensions or events ordinarily closed to human view, such as the invisible realm of heaven or the future course of history. In the Hebrew Bible, only Daniel is a fully apocalyptic work, although there are apocalyptic elements in the visions of Yahweh's heavenly court, described by Isaiah (6:1–12), Zechariah (3:1–10), and a few other prophets. The "little apocalypse" of Isaiah 24–27 and the obscure predictions about Israel's future redemption and the final defeat of its enemies in Ezekiel (Chs. 30, 37–39) and Zechariah (Chs. 9–14) also illustrate apocalyptic concerns about the ultimate fate of God's people.

From the time the oldest parts of 1 Enoch were written in the late third century B.C.E. through the end of the first century C.E. when 2 Esdras (4 Ezra) and the New Testament Book of Revelation were composed, Jewish and Jewish-Christian authors produced a flood of **apocalyptic literature**. With the exception of Daniel, most of these visionary works were not included in the Hebrew Bible canon and are now classed among the Apocrypha or Pseudepigrapha, including 2 Esdras, 1 and 2 Enoch, 2 and 3 Baruch, and the Sibylline Oracles. (Pseudepigraphal books are discussed later in this chapter.) Much of the New Testament is permeated with apocalyptic thought, particularly the forecasts of Jesus' return (Mark 13, Matt. 24, and Luke 21), Paul's early letters (1 and 2 Thess. and 1 Cor.), and the epistles of Peter and Jude, the last of which quotes 1 Enoch as if it were Scripture.

ESCHATOLOGICAL CONCERNS

Apocalyptic literature typically is concerned with **eschatology**—speculations about "last things," such as the final consummation of history, the prophetic "Day of Yahweh" in which Israel's God judges the nations, rewards the righteous, and annihilates the wicked. Besides its "end-of-the-world" aspects, eschatology also concerns the ultimate fate of individual persons: death, posthumous judgment, heaven, hell, and resurrection. The belief that people will experience an afterlife, typically through **resurrection** of the body, is a by-product of the apocalyptic movement (Dan. 12:1–3).

The authors of the first two divisions of the Hebrew Bible, the Torah and the (Former) Prophets, showed little or no interest in eschatological matters, but the situation changed during the last three centuries B.C.E., when apocalyptic speculation reached its height. During the Hellenistic era, a general belief arose that Israelite prophecy had ceased after the time of Ezra (c. 400 B.C.E.). When Israel accepted the notion that prophets no longer spoke "in the name of Yahweh," writers who desired to communicate their understanding of the divine will commonly published their works under the name of some famous leader of the distant past. From about 250 B.C.E. to 100 C.E., numerous Jewish authors practiced the art of **pseudonymity**, attributing their writings to such revered figures as Enoch, Abraham, Moses, Daniel, or Ezra. Pseudonymity was a device that allowed apocalyptic writers, such as the author of Daniel, to review past history as if it were prophecy and then to predict the imminent outcome of the issue or crisis that had inspired the work. While such practices today might be regarded as dishonest or fraudulent, in the Hellenistic world both Jewish and Greco-Roman authors commonly wrote pseudonymously to honor an ancient luminary, presenting what they believed would be his views were he still alive. Some New Testament writers, with no thought of forgery, penned sermons or epistles in the name of apostles such as Peter or Paul. (See the discussions of Timothy and Titus in Chapter 12 and 2 Peter in Chapter 13.)

Recent studies of the sociological background of apocalyptic writings indicate that they commonly originate during times of crisis and tension, responding either to severe persecutions of the writer's religious community or to other forces that threaten the group's welfare, such as a widespread decline in religious enthusiasm or a growing consciousness of the disparity between the group's apocalyptic expectations and actual social or political realities. Thus, both Daniel and Revelation were composed to encourage their respective audiences to remain faithful before the threat of state persecution, foretelling their persecutors' certain doom and rekindling hopes of future blessedness following the present tribulation.

PROPHETIC AND WISDOM INFLUENCES

While differing significantly from both, apocalyptic literature seems to draw from a twofold source: Israel's prophetic and wisdom traditions. Like the prophets, apocalyptists exhort their audience to remain faithful to the ancestral religion. And like the wisdom writers, they explore the mysterious principles by which God rules the universe, seeking to learn the divine will as communicated through natural phenomena, human experience, and the arcane learning preserved in religious books. Thus,

Jesus ben Sirach, the head of a wisdom school in Jerusalem, observes that the professional sage

> . . . researches into the wisdom of all the
> Ancients,
> he occupies his time with the prophecies.
> He preserves the discourse of famous men,
> he is at home with the niceties of parables.
> He researches into the hidden sense of proverbs,
> he ponders the obscurities of parables.
> He enters the service of princes,
> he is seen in the presence of rulers.
> He travels in foreign countries,
> he has experienced human good and human
> evil. . . .
> He will grow upright in purpose and learning,
> he will ponder the Lord's hidden mysteries.
> Ecclus. 39:1–5, 10

Jesus ben Sirach's description of an educated **scribe** pondering cosmic secrets, ancient wisdom, and the cryptic language of sages may well apply to the class of persons who composed apocalyptic literature. The hero of the Book of Daniel, who combines Torah loyalty with arcane wisdom and divination, may also represent an idealized self-portrait of the apocalyptist. A devout Jew serving a foreign government, Daniel becomes one of several Jewish trainees whom King Nebuchadnezzar selects to be educated in a Babylonian wisdom school. Daniel is "trained in every kind of wisdom," taught "the language and literature of the Chaldaeans," and, most important for apocalyptic purposes, granted the divine "gift of interpreting every kind of vision and dream" (Dan. 1:3–4, 17–18). Although earlier biblical writers had warned against practicing the mantic arts—interpreting omens, portents, and dreams, and forecasting future events (Deut. 18:10–11; Jer. 14:14; etc.)— the author of Daniel implicitly identifies his central character with the professional class of Babylonian wise men, including the court "magicians and enchanters, sorcerers, and Chaldaeans [persons skilled in the art of divination]" (Dan. 2:1–4, 14–19). After successfully explaining Nebuchadnezzar's dream as a preview of future history, Daniel is made "head of all the sages of Babylon" (Dan. 2:24–49). A clue to the author's own identification as a sage versed in studying signs and

portents in order to discern God's will is given at the end of the book: "The learned [the wise] will shine as brightly as the vault of heaven, and those who have instructed many in virtue, as bright as stars for all eternity" (Dan. 12:3). This linking of sages with the stars recalls the astronomical section of 1 Enoch (Chs. 72–82), which combines observation of sun, moon, planets, and stars with eschatological predictions. And as Daniel notes, only "the learned will understand" the significance of eschatological developments (Dan. 12:10).

CHARACTERISTICS OF APOCALYPTIC WRITING

Although apocalyptists drew on Israel's prophetic and wisdom traditions, the literature they produced is distinguished from these older schools by several characteristics. Besides the practice of pseudonymity discussed previously, apocalypses are typified by a number of common threads.

Universality   In contrast to prophetic oracles, which focus almost exclusively on Israel and its immediate neighbors, apocalyptic visions are universal in scope. Although the writers' religious communities (Israel or the Church) are a central concern, their work encompasses the whole of human history and surveys events both in heaven and on earth. Apocalyptists view all spirit beings, as well as all nations and peoples, as swept together in a conflict of cosmic proportions.

Cosmic Dualism   The apocalyptic worldview borrows much of its cosmology from Greek philosophical ideas about parallel worlds of matter and spirit. Postulating a dualistic "three-story universe" composed of visible earth, Underworld (Sheol), and invisible heaven (see Figure 4.2), apocalyptists see human society as profoundly influenced by unseen forces, angels and demons, operating in a celestial realm. Events on earth, such as persecution of the righteous, reflect the machinations of these heavenly beings.

Chronologic Dualism   Besides dividing the universe into two opposing domains of physical matter and invisible spirit, apocalyptists regard all history as separated into two mutually exclusive periods of time, a current wicked era and a future age of perfection. Seeing the present world situation as too thoroughly evil to reform, apocalyptists expect a sudden and violent change in which God or his Messiah imposes divine rule by force. In the apocalyptic vision, there is no normal historical progression from one age to the next and no real continuity between them. Thus, the Book of Daniel depicts God's kingdom as abruptly interrupting the ordinary flow of time, shattering all worldly governments with the impact of a colossal meteorite (Dan. 2:31–45).

Ethical Dualism   In the apocalyptic view, there are only two kinds of human beings, just as there are only two epochs of world history and two dimensions of existence—material and spiritual. Apocalyptists see humanity as divided into two opposing camps of intrinsically different ethical quality. The vast majority of people walk in spiritual darkness and are doomed victims of God's wrath. Only a tiny minority—the religious group to which the writers belong and direct their message—remains faithful and receives salvation. Deeply conscious of human imperfection and despairing of humanity's ability to meet God's standards, apocalyptists take a consistently pessimistic view of society's future.

Predestination   Whereas most biblical writers emphasize that historical events are the consequences of our moral choices (e.g., Deut. 28–29, Josh. 24, Ezek. 18), apocalyptists view history as progressing in a straight line toward a predetermined end. Just as the rise and fall of worldly empires occurs according to God's plan (Dan. 2, 7–8), so will the end take place at a time God has already set. Human efforts, no matter how well intended, cannot avert the coming disaster or influence God to change his mind. The vast complexity of human experience means nothing in the context of the divinely prearranged schedule.

Exclusivism   Many apocalypses, including Daniel and Revelation, were composed to encourage the faithful to maintain their integrity and resist temptations to compromise with "worldly" values or customs. Apocalyptists typically equate religious fidelity with a total rejection of the ordinary goals, ambitions, social attachments, and other pursuits of unbelieving society. Regarding most people as condemned, apocalyptists commonly urge their audience to adopt a rigidly sectarian attitude, avoiding all association with unbelievers.

Limited Theology   Consistent with this strict division of history and people into divinely approved or disapproved units, apocalyptists usually show little sympathy for differing viewpoints or compassion for nonbelievers. All modes of life are either black or white, with no psychological or spiritual shades of gray in between. As a result of the authors' mindset, the apocalyptic picture of God is ethically limited. The Deity is almost invariably portrayed as an enthroned monarch, an omnipotent authority who brings history to a violent conclusion in order to demonstrate his sovereignty, confound his enemies, and preserve his few worshipers. The notion that God might regard all people as his children or that he might establish his kingdom by less catastrophic means does not appeal to the apocalyptic temperament or satisfy the apocalyptic yearning.

Belief in a Violent God   Assuming that the Deity achieves control over heaven and earth through a cataclysmic battle with a formidable opponent (the dragon of chaos, or, in the New Testament, Satan), apocalyptists imagine this transference of power by picturing God as a destroyer who exterminates much of his sentient creation. Using the Exodus story of the ten plagues that Yahweh inflicted on Egypt as their model, apocalyptists typically show God angrily punishing disobedient humanity with a devastating series of natural disasters, famines, and loathsome diseases. That the use of evil to defeat evil is ethically questionable does not seem to trouble the apocalyptic mentality.

Eschatological Preoccupations   Along with uncovering the mysteries of the invisible world, apocalyptists reveal the posthumous fate of people during

God's terrifying judgment. Because they were commonly written at a time when fidelity brought no earthly rewards but only the danger of imprisonment, torture, and death, apocalyptic works pioneered the way in popularizing new beliefs about compensatory blessings in the New Age. Apocalyptists were the first biblical writers to speculate about the nature of the afterlife, which they commonly pictured as resurrection of the body rather than as the survival of an immortal soul (Dan. 12:1–3). The apocalyptists' rejection of the old Hebrew belief that human souls were consigned to eternal oblivion in Sheol (the Underworld) and their insistence that God makes moral distinctions between virtuous and wicked lives marked a theological innovation that was adopted by several later Jewish groups, including the Pharisees, Essenes, and early Christians.

The Use of Symbols and Code Words   Perhaps because they are the work of sages immersed in arcane learning, almost all apocalypses contain deliberately obscure language that veils as well as expresses the author's meaning. In addition, most were written during periods of crisis and persecution, situations that encouraged apocalyptists to use terms and images that their original audiences could understand but that will bewilder outsiders. In Enoch, Daniel, Revelation, and other apocalypses, the authors employ symbols from a wide variety of sources, both pagan and biblical.

In its broadest sense, a **symbol** is a sign that represents something other than itself, typically an abstract quality or religious concept. Symbols take the form of persons, places, objects, or actions that suggest an association or connection with another dimension of meaning. Both Daniel and Revelation depict Gentile nations as animals because, to the authors, they resemble wild beasts in their savage and irrational behavior. Kings who demand worship are symbolized as idols, and paying homage to them is labeled idolatry. Using code words for a pagan opponent, such as the "little horn" to denote the persecutor Antiochus IV (Dan. 7:8, 24–27; 8:23–26; 11:21–39), a contemporary of Daniel's author, also shields the apocalyptist's seditious message.

Daniel

KEY TOPICS/THEMES

Written to encourage Jewish Torah loyalties during the persecutions of Antiochus IV (mid-second century B.C.E.), the Book of Daniel reviews past history as though it were prophecy, assuring readers that even when Israel is scattered and oppressed by Gentile powers, its God still controls all nations. A two-part drama of supernatural deliverance, the book portrays Daniel, one of Nebuchadnezzar's court magicians, and his three young friends as scrupulous Torah observers whom the Deity miraculously rescues from unjust punishments (Chs. 1–6). The second part (Chs. 7–12) consists of a series of apocalyptic visions surveying the rise and fall of Near Eastern empires, from Babylon to the Hellenistic states of Syria and Egypt, that dominated Palestine in the author's day. It ends by predicting the public vindication and physical resurrection of the wise, who remained faithful under persecution.

KEY QUESTIONS

How are Daniel and other Torah-observant Jewish exiles rewarded for their covenant loyalty? How does the author make past historical events appear as prophecies of the future?

The Book of Daniel purportedly was written during the Babylonian captivity in the sixth century B.C.E. when its author was successively a member of the Babylonian, Median, and Persian courts. But scrupulous examination of the text reveals that it was composed centuries later, between about 167 and 164 B.C.E., when the Jews were suffering intense persecution by the Macedonian-Syrian ruler Antiochus IV (Figure 8.5). It is chronologically the latest-written book in the canonical Hebrew Bible. This fact, together with its striking differences in form and style from the prophetic books, may explain why Tanak editors did not include it among the Prophets, but instead placed it among the Writings. Daniel is not a typically prophetic work, but seems a deliberately literary creation whose main character embodies

Figure 8.5 The notorious "little horn" of Daniel's vision (Dan. 7:8, 20–22, 24–26; 11:21–45), Antiochus IV Epiphanes (175–163 B.C.E.) was the Seleucid ruler of Hellenistic Syria who profaned the Jerusalem Temple by erecting a statue of Olympian Zeus there, an "abomination" that resounds through the books of Daniel and 1 Maccabees and resurfaces as a sign of End time in the Gospels of Mark and Matthew (Mark 13:14; Matt. 24:15–16). Shown in profile on this Greek coin, Antiochus IV tended to identify his rule with that of Zeus, king of the gods.

and reflects the long tradition of Israel's sacred literature.

DANIEL: A LITERARY FIGURE

Daniel himself is, like Joseph (see Gen. 39–41), a devout Israelite transported to a foreign nation of idol worshipers. Like Joseph, he remains faithful to his God under severe testing and is elevated by pagan rulers to positions of high honor. Like Joseph, too, he is basically a solitary figure, although an unusually shrewd one. Educated in the "wisdom of the **Chaldeans** [Babylonian practitioners of the mantic arts]," empowered to reveal the meaning of divinely inspired dreams and thereby to predict the future, supernaturally aided in his escapes from

danger, Daniel is not an ordinary person. It is difficult to regard him as merely a role model for Diaspora Jews struggling to maintain their religious integrity under adverse circumstances. Unlike the historical victims of Antiochus's persecutions described in 2 Maccabees, Daniel and his friends are supernaturally shielded from all harm.

If, however, Daniel were as outstanding a figure during the sixth century B.C.E. as the present book represents him, it is strange that he is never mentioned by his contemporaries or by later historians. Ezekiel, a prophet who lived in Babylon during the exile, thrice refers to an ancient sage named **Danel** who is associated with the patriarchs Noah and Job as a prototype of righteousness (Ezek. 14:4, 20; 20:3), but the Hebrew Bible nowhere speaks of a "Daniel" who lived with Ezekiel in captivity. Archaeological discoveries at Ugarit also have revealed the existence of a legendary King Danel who was a model of wisdom and rectitude. Thus, it is possible that over the centuries, the Israelites adopted this originally foreign character and reclothed him in Torah virtues until he eventually became the exemplar cited by Ezekiel. Later, a writer of the second century B.C.E., wishing to create a representative figure whose name and reputation for godliness would be well known but whose life and career were shrouded in mystery, chose "Daniel" as his hero.

Daniel divides naturally into two main sections. The first six chapters—which may have been written well before Antiochus's persecutions—recount Daniel's adventures under the successive reigns of Nebuchadnezzar, Belshazzar, "Darius the Mede," and Cyrus the Persian. The apocalyptic elements are subdued in this part, which concentrates on Daniel's strict allegiance to his God and the conflict into which it brings him with various Gentile authorities.

Like Esther and Mordecai, Daniel is a victim of court intrigue. Unlike the Jews in the Book of Esther, however, he scrupulously observes Hebrew dietary laws (which makes him stronger than those who dine on the "king's food") and publicly manifests his Torah loyalty by refusing to participate in the religious ceremonies of his Babylonian or Persian overlords. A thematically important event in the biographical portion of the book is Daniel's interpretation of Nebuchadnezzar's dreams, the contents of which prepare the reader for the apocalyptic visions in Chapters 7–12, which compose the second main section of the book.

INTERPRETING DREAMS AND RESISTING ASSIMILATION

Nebuchadnezzar's Dreams   According to Chapter 2, Nebuchadnezzar has dreamed of a huge statue with a head of gold, chest and arms of silver, belly and thighs of bronze, legs of iron, and feet of mixed iron and clay. Suddenly, a great stone uncut by human hands hurtles from heaven to smash the idol's clay feet; the colossus disintegrates, and the stone grows into a mountain that fills the entire earth. Daniel interprets the various metals composing this statue as symbolizing a series of kingdoms that rule his part of the world. Because the author lived long after the series of kings he describes, he is able to present past events as if they were fulfilled prophecy.

Nebuchadnezzar (Babylon) is the head of gold; and the nations that follow him — though Daniel does not specify them — are probably Media (silver), Persia (bronze), Macedonian Greece (iron), and the lesser Hellenistic kingdoms of Egypt and Syria (iron combined with clay to signify the weaker successors of Alexander's ironlike empire). The gigantic meteorite represents the kingdom of God that is destined to obliterate and replace all pagan governments and last forever (Dan. 2:44).

Chapter 3 tells of three faithful Hebrew youth — known by their Babylonian names as **Shadrach, Meshach**, and **Abednego** — who are thrown into a hot furnace for declining to worship Nebuchadnezzar's golden image. After they emerge unsinged, the Babylonian king is represented as enthusiastically praising the Jews' "Most High God" who so miraculously delivers his servants (3:24–30). Despite this reputed lip service, however, Nebuchadnezzar is given another lesson in that Deity's omnipotence.

In another dream, the king beholds an enormous tree sheltering all forms of bird and animal life but hears a heavenly authority order the tree cut down and given a "beast's heart" until all around acknowledge the sovereignty of the "Most High" (4:11–14). Called to explain the dream, Daniel, the "chief of magicians" (4:6), says that Nebuchadnezzar is the tree and that he is to be struck down — to lose his reason and kingship — "seven times" until he fully realizes that all power, political as well as celestial, comes from Daniel's God.

A short time later, while Nebuchadnezzar is touring his capital and boasting that he built it by his own power, he is afflicted with a form of insanity that drives him to flee society and live like a beast. When he finally extols the "Most High" as the universal king, his sanity is restored (4:25–34). This first-person narrative concludes with Nebuchadnezzar's prayerful recognition that Daniel's God humbles "those who walk in pride" (4:34).

There is no record, however, that Nebuchadnezzar, a successful conqueror and able administrator, ever suffered a seven-year fit of insanity or that he temporarily adopted the monotheistic beliefs of the Jews he held as prisoners and slaves. The modern reader's credulity may be strained by the notion that a polytheistic ruler in Babylon repeatedly and publicly praised the God whose Temple he had destroyed and whose nation he had defeated. But at the time these tales were first circulated, they may have provided a hope that whatever ungodly monarch then oppressed the Jews might still be taught humility before Yahweh.

The Fall of Babylon   In Chapter 5, **Belshazzar** is ostensibly Babylon's ruler, though historically he was merely acting governor or prince regent for his father, King Nabonidus. At the height of a riotous celebration — possibly the Babylonian New Year festival — handwriting mysteriously appears on the palace walls. Summoned to interpret the cryptic signs, Daniel declares that Belshazzar is doomed to have his kingdom stripped from him and given to "the Medes and the Persians" (5:25–31). That night, one "Darius the Mede" (unknown to history) takes the city. The author's blunder is puzzling because other biblical works, including Second Isaiah, Ezra, and Chronicles, make it clear that Cyrus of Persia captured Babylon (539 B.C.E.).

Chapter 6 states that Daniel underwent yet another test of his faith under the new "Median" administration. Like Ahasuerus in the Book of Esther, Darius is tricked by Daniel's rival courtiers into issuing an edict that for thirty days forbids anyone to pray except to the monarch. Loyal to his Torah obligations, Daniel is caught disobeying and is confined in a den of lions. When he leaves the den unharmed, the "Median ruler's" reaction to the miracle exceeds even that of Nebuchadnezzar. Darius not only concedes the supremacy of Daniel's God but orders that everyone in his far-flung empire learn to fear the Jewish Deity (6:26–28).

DANIEL'S VISIONS OF END TIME

Eschatological Visions   The strange visions and predictions of the second portion of Daniel, which is fully apocalyptic, make it the most controversial part of the Hebrew Bible, particularly among some fundamentalist groups. During the past few centuries, hundreds of sects have been founded on differing interpretations of Daniel's eschatology. Most experts agree, however, that Daniel's visions were intended primarily for the author's fellow Jews during the terrible days of Antiochus IV's attempt to eradicate the Jewish religion, perhaps just before the Maccabean revolt (c. 168–164 B.C.E.).

In this second section (Chs. 7–12), Daniel no longer interprets a Gentile ruler's dreams; instead he himself has four dreams or visions that survey Near Eastern history from the sixth to the second centuries B.C.E. from the perspective of a Babylonian or Persian captive. Writing in the mid-second century B.C.E., the author recasts his review of political history in the form of prophecy. He can thus describe past historical events as if they were visionary predictions of the future. Chapter 7 disguises the Babylonian, Median, Persian, and Macedonian empires as beasts: a lion with eagle's wings (Babylon), a bear with ribs in its mouth (Media), a winged leopard with four heads (Persia), and a ferocious ogre with iron teeth and ten horns (the Macedonian Greeks and their succes-

sors, the Ptolemies of Egypt and the Seleucids of Syria). The boastful "little horn" that also turns up is probably Antiochus, who intended to coerce the Jews into abandoning their traditional worship.

Daniel's parade of monsters is interrupted by a more traditional prophetic vision of the "Ancient of Days," who confers "glory and kingship" on "one like a Son of Man" (7:10–14). The identity of this unnamed heavenly figure has been hotly debated, with some commentators suggesting that he is a supernatural member of Yahweh's court, presumably the celestial "prince" **Michael**, who represents and does battle for Israel (10:13, 21). Although the author was probably referring to either an angel or to the faithful covenant community which Michael defended, later Christian writers interpreted the "Son of Man" concept as prophetic of the Messiah. In Mark's Gospel, "Son of Man" is Jesus' preferred way of designating himself (see Chapter 10). In Daniel, however, the writer apparently uses the figure to depict a supernaturally appointed, everlasting kingdom that will replace the bestial Gentile nations ruling in his own day. This section closes with more veiled remarks about the "little horn" (Antiochus IV) who makes war on the "saints" (devout Jews), tries to change the "law" (Temple observances), and attempts to abolish the Mosaic religion altogether. Again, it is certain that the persecutor will be overwhelmed by the coming kingdom.

The vision of Chapter 8 — supposedly given when Daniel was living at Susa, the Persian capital (Figure 8.6) — depicts a ram with two horns (the dual power of Medes and Persians) being gored by a he-goat sporting a great horn (Alexander of Macedonia), which, in turn, is broken and replaced by four smaller horns (the four divisions of Alexander's empire made after his death). From one of these lesser horns (the Seleucid dynasty of Syria) springs a prodigious horn (again Antiochus), which tramples the "Land of Splendor" (Judea), challenges the "armies of heaven," takes away the "perpetual sacrifice" (Antiochus forbade offerings at the Jerusalem Temple), and institutes an "abomination of desolation" (the Syrian king slaughtered a pig on the Temple altar and erected a statue of

Figure 8.6 These decorative bull heads were originally designed as the capitals of columns that supported massive wooden rafters in the imperial palace at Susa (Shushan), summer capital of the Persian Empire. Several biblical characters are associated with this city, including Daniel (Dan. 8:2), Nehemiah (Neh. 1:1), Esther, and Haman (Esther 1:2, 4).

Zeus in the inner court as part of his policy to force the Jews into accepting a Hellenistic way of life). The angel **Gabriel** makes most of this vision explicit to Daniel, except for the part concerning Antiochus, which for reasons of safety had to be kept vague. Following this angelic exegesis, Daniel falls ill for several days.

Chapter 9 features Daniel's most moving prayer, in which he confesses his people's sins and asks his God to deliver them from their enemies, for the first time in the book using the personal name Yahweh, God of the covenant and Lord of history (9:5–19). This prayer leads to the angel Gabriel's revisionist explanation of Jeremiah's prophecy that Jerusalem would lie desolate for "seventy years" after the Babylonian conquest and then be restored.

Why has the city been so consistently enslaved by foreign powers since then? Jeremiah, explains Gabriel, meant that "seventy weeks of years" (490 years?) were to pass before the consummation of all things. In the second century B.C.E., when this interpretation was written, the expected fulfillment was imminent.

Chapters 10–11 give a thicket of prophecies about battles between "the King of the South" (Ptolemies) and "the King of the North" (Seleucids) and the further machinations and fall of Antiochus. There seem to be allusions to the Maccabean wars here. Although at the time these passages were written, the Maccabees apparently had not yet recaptured the Temple and rededicated its altar, the author is confident that the Temple will be cleansed and priestly services resumed in the near future. He is less accurate in predicting Antiochus's punishment, however, because that fanatical king dies a natural death abroad, not in Palestine (11:21–45).

Resurrection   Undoubtedly regarding Antiochus's depredations as inaugurating the End time, the author of Daniel postulated a resurrection to compensate contemporary Jews who had died defending their faith against the Syrian persecutor. This explicit affirmation of a life after death (12:2–3) was to be the most enduring part of his message.

In Chapter 12, Gabriel tells Daniel that when history draws to its *predetermined* climax in the pagan nations' assault on the righteous, Michael (described as the prince or guardian spirit of Israel) will "stand up" for his people and decisively defeat their enemies. At that point, a resurrection of "many" just and unjust persons who had been "sleeping in the dust" will occur. Daniel—who as a literary character is placed during the Persian era—is told to sleep among his ancestors until he is raised for his "share" at the end of time (12:1–13).

Although a familiarity with the apocalyptic mode makes it evident that Daniel was not composed for people living in the early twenty-first century, the book's fundamental themes remain universally relevant. Its picture of the Deity firmly in control of earthly history, aiding the devout to survive adversity, and promising the ultimate triumph of life and faith over death and evil make Daniel an integral part of the biblical heritage.

RECOMMENDED READING

Charles, R. H. *Eschatology: The Doctrine of a Future Life in Israel*. New York: Schocken Books, 1963 (reprint).

Collins, John J. "Daniel, Book of." In D. N. Freedman, ed., *The Anchor Bible Dictionary*, Vol. 2, pp. 29–37. New York: Doubleday, 1992.

———, ed. *The Encyclopedia of Apocalypticism: Vol. I: The Origins of Apocalypticism in Judaism and Christianity*. New York: Continuum Publishing Group, 2000. A valuable scholarly resource.

Hanson, Paul D. *The Dawn of Apocalyptic: The Historical and Sociological Roots of Jewish Apocalyptic Sociology*, rev. ed. Philadelphia: Fortress Press, 1979.

———. *Old Testament Apocalyptic*. Nashville, Tenn.: Abingdon Press, 1987.

Hartman, Louis F., and De Lella, Alexander A. *The Book of Daniel*. Garden City, N.Y.: Doubleday, 1978.

Lacocque, André. *The Book of Daniel*. Atlanta: John Knox Press, 1978.

Mowinckel, Sigmund. *He That Cometh*. Nashville: Abingdon Press, 1956.

Porteous, Norman W. *Daniel*. Philadelphia: Westminster Press, 1965.

Russell, D. S. *The Method and Message of Jewish Apocalyptic: 200 B.C.–A.D. 100*. Philadelphia: Westminster Press, 1964.

———. *Apocalyptic, Ancient and Modern*. Philadelphia: Fortress Press, 1978.

———. *Daniel, An Active Volcano: Reflections on the Book of Daniel*. Louisville, Ky.: Westminster/John Knox Press, 1989.

Smith-Christopher, Daniel L. "The Book of Daniel." In *The New Interpreter's Bible*, Vol. 7, pp. 17–152. Nashville: Abingdon Press, 1996.

Additions to Daniel

KEY TOPICS/THEMES

A poetic prayer and two prosaic narratives were added to the Greek translation of Daniel: The Song of the Three Holy Children (Ch. 3), the tale of Susanna and the Elders (Ch. 13), and a primitive detective story, Bel and the Dragon (Ch. 14).

KEY QUESTION

What new roles do the Additions assign to Daniel?

THE SONG OF THE THREE HOLY CHILDREN

The Greek version of Daniel includes, among many briefer additions, three relatively long poetic and narrative units not found in the Hebrew canon. The first of these consists of psalms or hymns reputedly sung by Shadrach, Meshach, and Abednego while confined in a Babylonian furnace. Their songs are inserted into the Hebrew-Aramaic text of Daniel between verses 23 and 24 of Chapter 3 (forming vv. 3:24–90 in Catholic Bible editions).

The opening poem, the Prayer of Azariah (the Hebrew name of Abednego), is a lament confessing Israel's collective sins and beseeching its God for mercy, though the psalm strangely never alludes to Azariah's fiery ordeal. The references to Jewish suffering under "an unjust king, the worst in the whole world" (Song of Three Children 3:32), and to the suppression of Temple services (3:38–40) indicate that the poem may have been composed during the persecutions of Antiochus IV, perhaps about the same time the apocalyptic portions of Daniel 7–12 were written.

The choral psalm that the three young men sing in unison (3:52–90) is a vigorous hymn of praise extolling the "God of [their] ancestors" and inciting the natural elements—earth, air, sea, and sentient life—to praise the Deity. Some critics have suggested that this poem, which resembles the canonical Psalm 148 in thought and Psalm 136 in form, may be a popular hymn of thanksgiving for Maccabean victories. Experts are not agreed, however, on either the exact time of composition or the original language of these poems. Like other additions to Daniel, they may have been written in Hebrew, Aramaic, or Greek during the late second or early first century B.C.E.

SUSANNA

Because Daniel is still a "young boy" (Sus. 13:46) when the action takes place, this cleverly plotted short story is sometimes placed at the beginning of the book, although some modern Catholic translations such as the Jerusalem Bible include it as Chapter 13.

Figure 8.7 The difficulties that some early Christians experienced in Greco-Roman society are perhaps echoed in this third-century C.E. painting of an episode from the Additions to Daniel. Two elders, representing accepted religious authority, point accusingly at Susanna, whom they falsely charge with immorality. Daniel (left) observes the scene, about to pronounce on Susanna's innocence.

In Babylon during the captivity (587–539 B.C.E.), Susanna, a beautiful and virtuous young wife, rejects the lustful advances of two Jewish elders who are also judges. When they spitefully accuse her of adultery and she is condemned to death by their testimony, the "holy spirit" inspires Daniel to demand a more thorough investigation. Separating the elders, who then give contradictory evidence, he convicts them of bearing false witness, so that they suffer the fate they had planned for Susanna (Figure 8.7). Although commonly regarded as a suspenseful "detective story," Susanna's experience was probably recorded to criticize corrupt judges of the Jewish Diaspora who abused their legal authority.

BEL AND THE DRAGON

This third apocryphal addition, usually appended to Daniel as Chapter 14, is a prose account of three incidents in which Daniel demonstrates either his superior powers of deduction or the deceitful machinations of Gentile priests who attempt to ruin him. In the first incident, Daniel proves to "King Astyages" (Cyrus of Persia, who now rules at Babylon) that the great statue of **Bel** (the Babylonian god Marduk) does not eat the food left be-

fore it but that the offerings are consumed by lying priests and their families (Bel and Dragon 14:1–22). Disabused of his superstition, Cyrus orders the priests and their relatives slain and commissions Daniel to destroy Bel's idol and temple.

In the next episode, Daniel poisons a dragon, or large serpent, to show his credulous ruler that it is not a god, but a mortal reptile (14:23–27). When Babylonians who had revered the serpent learn that Daniel has killed it, they accuse the king of "turning Jewish" and persuade him to throw the iconoclastic foreigner into a lions' pit, where he remains for six days. During this period, an angel carries the prophet Habakkuk from Judah to Babylon so that he can feed Daniel, then immediately returns the prophet to Judah. When the king discovers on the seventh day that Daniel is still uneaten, he releases him, praises his God, and hurls his rivals into the pit, where they are promptly devoured (14:28–42).

As in the story of Susanna, the author here emphasizes that the biblical God will "not desert those who love him" (14:39). Indeed, like the canonical Daniel, the Additions consistently dramatize that the Jewish Deity watches over those who faithfully keep his commandments and reject the snares of idol-worshiping Gentiles.

RECOMMENDED READING

Moore, Carey A. *Daniel, Esther, and Jeremiah: The Additions.* Garden City, N.Y.: Doubleday, 1977.

Smith-Christopher, Daniel L. "The Additions to Daniel." In *The New Interpreter's Bible*, Vol. 7, pp. 153–194. Nashville: Abingdon Press, 1996.

Other Apocalyptic Works

As the sole fully apocalyptic work in the canonical Hebrew Bible, Daniel is unique. It is, however, only one book among a large body of similar apocalyptic writings that various segments of Jewish society produced during the Hellenistic and early Roman eras. Composed about the same time as the New Testament Book of Revelation, the Book of 2 Esdras commonly is included among the Apocrypha. (See both the New English Bible and the New Revised Standard Version.) Several other apocalyptic books, including 1 and 2 Enoch and the Sibylline Oracles, did not attain canonical or even apocryphal status, although the eschatological ideas they advocate were extremely influential in some Jewish and early Christian circles. Parts of 1 Enoch are echoed in Daniel's visions, and the book is directly quoted in the New Testament epistle of Jude.

2 Esdras (4 Ezra)

KEY TOPICS/THEMES

Attributed to the historical Ezra, a priestly scribe credited with assembling the final edition of the Mosaic Torah, 2 Esdras actually was written in about 100 C.E., thirty years after the Roman destruction of Jerusalem. Combining themes from wisdom and apocalyptic literature, the book includes a theodicy, a perceptive examination of the conflict between religious faith and the reality of Evil (Chs. 3–8); apocalyptic visions of future history and Israel's redemption (Chs. 9–13); and an account of Ezra's authorship of the Hebrew Bible and Apocrypha (Ch. 14). Composed about the same time as the New Testament Book of Revela-

tion, 2 Esdras was later framed by Christian additions (Chs. 1, 2, and 15).

KEY QUESTIONS

Why does the author use the apocalyptic mode in trying to understand God's purpose in allowing his people to suffer under Gentile oppressors? What hope for the future does he propose?

A composite work of Jewish and Christian origin, 2 Esdras is one of the latest books to find its way into the Apocrypha. Although Chapters 3–14, the central portion of the book, purport to have been written by the historical priest Ezra while he was a captive in Babylon in about 557 B.C.E., scholarly analysis of the text indicates that this section probably was composed in either Hebrew or Aramaic late in the first century C.E., after the Romans had destroyed Jerusalem and the Temple. Like the New Testament Book of Revelation, which it greatly resembles in theme and outlook, 2 Esdras reflects the tension existing between loyal Jews and Greco-Roman society.

After 2 Esdras had been translated into Greek, an anonymous Christian writer added Chapters 1 and 2 around 150 C.E. Perhaps a century later, another Christian, also writing in Greek, appended Chapters 15 and 16. But 2 Esdras did not appear in the Septuagint; it entered Christian Scripture via Old Latin translations and Jerome's Vulgate, although conflicting Ethiopic, Syriac, Greek, Arabic, Armenian, and other versions exist as well.

THE PROBLEM OF EVIL IN HUMAN HISTORY

Ezra's Theodicy   The first two chapters are mainly Christian apologetics implying that God has repudiated "natural" Israel as his chosen people and adopted instead a "spiritual" Israel, the Christian Church, as his own. Chapters 3–14 consist of seven apocalyptic visions, of which the first three are cast in the form of philosophical dialogues between Ezra and various angels. These angelic mentors counter Ezra's repeated questioning of his God's justice with attempts to defend the Deity's ways to humans. In general, Ezra's questions are more penetrating than the answers he receives.

If Babylon (read "Rome") was God's chosen instrument to punish Israel, Ezra asks, why are Babylon's citizens so much worse behaved than the Jewish people Babylon oppresses? Why has God allowed an enemy nation that mocks him to destroy those who have at least tried to worship him (3:25–32)? Would not God's lesson to both Jewish and pagan nations be less equivocal if he punished directly, "with his own hands," rather than through an ungodly intermediary like Babylon (Rome) (5:28–30)? Is it not better to remain unborn than to live and suffer without knowing why (4:12)? "To what end," Ezra asks, "has the capacity for understanding been given me? For I did not mean to ask about ways above [God's concealed purposes], but about those things which pass by us every day; why Israel . . . whom you loved [is] given up to godless tribes" (4:22–23). The angels' reply is that God will dispense justice in good time. The flourishing of wickedness is only temporary; it will be terminated according to a foreordained timetable (4:27–32), and the divine schedule is not humanity's concern.

Ezra is concerned about not only the earthly plight of his people but also the fate of their souls after death. Reluctantly agreeing that many act wrongly while only a few are righteous, he nonetheless disputes the justice of condemning sinners to everlasting torment without any further chance of repentance. Chapter 7, vividly picturing the blessings of salvation and the agonies of the damned, is the most complete picture of judgment and the afterlife in the Old Testament Apocrypha.

In addition, 2 Esdras gives us the Old Testament's first statements of *original sin*—the belief that all humanity has inherited Adam's sin and is therefore born deserving death (5:21–26; 7:46–48, 70–72). This doctrine of humanity's inherent propensity toward vice is also expounded by the Apostle Paul in Romans 5 and has since become dogma in many Christian denominations. Finally, the author also seems to express a belief in the existence of the human soul before birth (4:42).

Apocalyptic Visions In Chapter 9, the book changes from a Jobian theodicy to a more purely apocalyptic preview of the "last days." The fourth vision depicts a woman who mourns her dead son and who is suddenly transformed into a thriving city. Uriel explains that the woman is Jerusalem, her lost son the destroyed Temple, and the splendid city a future glorified Zion (Chs. 9–10). Chapters 11 and 12, with their portrait of a mighty eagle, are reminiscent of John's visions in Revelation. This proud eagle (Rome) that now dominates the earth is destined to disappear when a lion (the Messiah) appears to judge it for its persecution of the righteous (11:38–12:34). The sixth vision emphasizes the certainty of the Messiah's imminent appearance and his just destruction of the pagans who oppress Jerusalem (Ch. 13).

Ezra's Production of the Deuterocanonical Books
Ezra's preeminent importance to Jewish religion is emphasized in Chapter 14, where the "Most High" inspires him to write 94 sacred books. Of these books, 24 are canonical Scripture—the published Hebrew Bible—and the remaining 70 are reserved for the "wise" who alone can understand them. This passage indicates that the author credited Ezra with replacing the Hebrew Bible that the Babylonians had allegedly destroyed. The extrabiblical books are presumably the deuterocanonical books (Apocrypha) and other apocalyptic works, such as 2 Esdras itself.

Following his literary efforts, Ezra is transported to heaven to dwell with other holy men. In light of the Jewish traditions on which the author draws, Ezra is clearly seen as a heroic figure who embodies the virtues of priest, prophet, and lawgiver. A second Moses, he also incorporates the honors of Elijah and the antediluvian patriarch Enoch, both of whom had been similarly caught up to heaven.

The two final chapters, a Christian addition of the second century C.E., emphasize the Deity's coming vengeance on the wicked. Predicting a series of terrors and calamities (again reminiscent of Revelation), the book assures the reader that the ungodly nation (Rome), as well as all other empires that afflict the righteous, will fall and that the guilty will be consumed by fire (15–16).

QUESTIONS FOR REVIEW

1. As a literary type or genre, what is an *apocalypse?* List some apocalyptic works, both canonical and noncanonical. Why are apocalypses typically pseudonymous? How is the decline of prophecy in postexilic Judea related to the rise of apocalyptic ideas?

2. Define the term *eschatology.* In what ways does apocalyptic literature concern itself with eschatological matters, such as concepts of final judgment, resurrection, and the afterlife? In what ways do apocalyptic writers combine prophetic and wisdom traditions?

3. Apocalypses are commonly described as works of both hope and despair. Explain this apparent paradox. How does pessimism about the human condition lead to ideas about divine intervention in human history?

4. Discuss the possible connections between the historical failure of Israel's political aspirations and the rise of apocalyptic thought during the late Persian and Hellenistic period. How does the universality of apocalyptic concerns differ from the traditional prophetic focus on Israel's ethical, social, and political welfare?

5. By placing the figure of Daniel in the sixth century B.C.E., when Babylon was replaced by Persia as the dominant power in the Near East, how is Daniel's author—who lived during the reign of Antiochus IV—able to review past events as if they were prophecies of the future?

6. Enumerate the ten major characteristics of apocalyptic literature. What part does ethical and cosmic *dualism* play in apocalyptic thought? In what ways is the Book of Daniel apocalyptic? What new eschatological idea about a future life does it introduce?

7. When and under what circumstances do scholars believe that the Book of Daniel was composed? Describe the author's view of Gentile empires and Israel's suffering. What lessons for Jews living outside Judah do the stories of Daniel and the three Hebrew youths try to teach? Should Jews of the Diaspora retain their traditional customs, or should they follow the traditions of their host countries? Why is this issue important in Daniel?

QUESTION FOR DISCUSSION AND REFLECTION

Why did apocalyptic ideas become so popular among many Jews between about 200 B.C.E. and 200 C.E.? Compare and contrast the apocalypses of Daniel and 2 Esdras. Why are each of these books written in the name of a long-dead sage? Describe the differing political circumstances at the time of their respective compositions. What great national disaster does 2 Esdras lament? Which book—Daniel or 2 Esdras—deals more profoundly with the problem of Evil and the purpose of human suffering? Which shows the more highly developed eschatology?

TERMS AND CONCEPTS TO REMEMBER

Abednego	Gentile
apocalypse	Meshach
apocalyptic literature	Michael
Bel	pseudonymity
Belshazzar	resurrection
Chaldean	scribe
Danel	Shadrach
eschatology	Sheol
Gabriel	symbol

RECOMMENDED READING

de Lange, Nicholas. *Apocrypha: Jewish Literature of the Hellenistic Age.* New York: Viking Press, 1978.

Dentan, Robert C. *The Apocrypha: Bridge of the Testaments.* Greenwich, Conn.: Seabury Press, 1954.

Meyers, Jacob M. *1 and 2 Esdras.* Anchor Bible. Garden City, N.Y.: Doubleday, 1974.

Nickelsburg, George W. E. *Jewish Literature Between the Bible and the Mishnah.* Philadelphia: Fortress Press, 1981.

Pseudepigrapha

In addition to the deuterocanonical works, Hellenistic Jewish writers also produced a body of religious literature known collectively as the **Pseudepigrapha**, books that were not admitted to the canons of either the Hebrew or Greek editions of the Bible. Although designated as pseudonymous—ascribed by anonymous writers to luminaries of the past, such as Enoch, Noah, Moses, or

Isaiah — some books of the Pseudepigrapha, such as 3 and 4 Maccabees, make no claims of illustrious authorship.

Dating from about 200 B.C.E. to 200 C.E., these documents include a variety of literary types, ranging from apocalypses and sacred legends to interpretative retellings of canonical narratives, such as the Book of Jubilees. Like the Apocrypha, pseudepigraphal books appeared in Hebrew, Aramaic, and Greek. Because of limited space, only brief summaries of some representative works that may have influenced later Judeo-Christian thought are given here.

RECOMMENDED READING

Charles, R. H. *Apocrypha and Pseudepigrapha of the Old Testament,* Vol. 2. Oxford: Clarendon Press, 1913. Provides translations, with critical introductions and numerous annotations of the texts, of most of the pseudepigraphal books. Because this volume appeared long before discovery of the Dead Sea Scrolls, however, the reader must approach some of the author's conclusions with caution.

Charlesworth, James H., ed. *The Old Testament Pseudepigrapha.* Vol. 1, *Apocalyptic Literature and Testaments.* Garden City, N.Y.: Doubleday, 1983. A scholarly new edition of the Pseudepigrapha (including several documents not in Charles's collection), with new translations and historical-critical annotations on the text; a major work of scholarship.

———. *The Old Testament Pseudepigrapha.* Vol. 2, *Expansions of the "Old Testament" and Legends, Wisdom and Philosophical Literature, Prayers, Psalms and Odes, Fragments of Lost Judeo-Hellenistic Works.* Garden City, N.Y.: Doubleday, 1985. Includes annotated editions of Jubilees, Letter of Aristeas, and 3 and 4 Maccabees.

de Lange, Nicholas. *Apocrypha: Jewish Literature of the Hellenistic Age.* New York: Viking Press, 1978. Discusses several pseudepigraphal works.

Eissfeldt, Otto. *The Old Testament: An Introduction.* New York: Harper & Row, 1965. An English version of a standard German work that includes précis of the background and content of fourteen pseudepigraphal books.

Nickelsburg, George W. E. *Jewish Literature Between the Bible and the Mishnah.* Philadelphia: Fortress Press, 1981.

Rost, Leonhard. *Judaism Outside the Hebrew Canon: An Introduction to the Documents.* Nashville, Tenn.: Abingdon Press, 1976.

Russell, D. S. *The Old Testament Pseudepigrapha.* Philadelphia: Fortress Press, 1987. Examines the reinter-

pretation of patriarchal and prophetic figures in Hellenistic Judaism.

1 Enoch (Ethiopic Book of Enoch)

KEY TOPICS/THEMES

Perhaps the oldest surviving example of Jewish apocalyptic literature, 1 Enoch combines imaginative visions of the spirit world with images of End time (eschatology). Using a rich mythology involving cosmic conflict, fallen angels, and a tour of heaven, the apocalypse is editorially divided into five books: the Watchers (Chs. 1–36), the Similitudes (Parables) (Chs. 37–71), the Astronomical Writings (Chs. 72–82), the Dream Visions (Chs. 83–90), and the Epistle of Enoch (Chs. 91–107).

KEY QUESTIONS

Why is Enoch viewed as one familiar with heaven's secrets? How does this composite work reveal the mysteries of the unseen world?

Ascribed to **Enoch**, the antediluvian patriarch who was reputedly transported alive to heaven (Gen. 5:24), the Book of Enoch is a heterogeneous collection of the work of many unknown authors. Composed and compiled during the Hellenistic period, it is designated as Ethiopic because its text has been transmitted in that language.

The earliest materials in the compilation (found in 1 En. 6–11; 54–55:2; 60; 65–69; and 106–107) are believed to be fragments of a Book of Noah or Book of Lamech (mentioned in Bk. Jub. 10:13 and 21:10), which may date from the late third century B.C.E. The Ten Weeks Apocalypse (1 En. 91:12–17; 93), which apparently antedates the Book of Daniel, may have appeared about 170 B.C.E. Most of Enoch's other components may be assigned to the late second and first centuries B.C.E., with the "Similitudes" (Chs. 37–71) — with their messianic references to the "Son of Man" — probably dating from the first century C.E. or slightly earlier.

Emulating the Pentateuch, Psalms, Proverbs, and Ecclesiasticus, an editor-compiler arranged the

Enoch collection into five distinct parts. Its division into 108 chapters did not become standard until the nineteenth century. After a prefatory speech in which Enoch is depicted proclaiming the ultimate destinies of the wicked and righteous (Chs. 1–5), section 1 describes the fall of the Watchers (angels who mated with the daughters of humans to produce the giants; see Gen. 6:1–4); their punishment; and Enoch's metaphysical journeys though the earth and Underworld (Chs. 6–36).

Section 2 contains a series of parables concerning a variety of topics, including the Messiah, the rewards of the righteous, judgment by the **Son of Man**, the torments of the fallen angels, and similar eschatological matters (Chs. 37–71). Section 3 includes a primitive scientific treatise on astronomy—a discussion of the sun, moon, and planets and of human calendars based on them (Chs. 72–82). Section 4 presents a sequence of dream visions, notably of the (then) coming Flood, and an allegoric panorama of world history that designates Jews as tame animals and pagans as wild beasts. It begins with Adam as a white bull and culminates in the appearance of the Messiah as a lamb who becomes a "great animal" with black horns (Chs. 83–90).

Section 5 is a book of exhortation that includes Enoch's admonition for his children, an apocalypse in which world history is divided into periods of ten weeks of varying length, and pictures of blessings for the righteous and woes for the godless (Chs. 91–105). The book concludes with a fragment from the Book of Noah describing miracles occurring at the patriarch's birth and Enoch's last words of encouragement for the pious who await their God's day of reckoning (Chs. 106–198).

From even this cursory survey of its contents, it is apparent that the Book of Enoch—an anthology of history, astronomy, law, poetry, eschatological doctrines, and apocalyptic visions—provided a wealth of theological ideas, some of which were extremely influential on Hellenistic Judaism. After the disastrous wars with Rome (66–73 and 132–135 C.E.), however, which were apparently inspired in part by apocalypse-fed expectations, the Jews largely repudiated this kind of writing. By then,

Christians had taken up many of these speculations and eschatological hopes, adapting them to their own doctrinal needs.

Among the early Christians, then, Enoch was understandably popular, although after the fourth century C.E. its influence declined. In time, all complete manuscripts of this Hebrew-Aramaic work vanished. It was not until the end of the eighteenth century that an Ethiopic translation was found in Abyssinia. The first English version of the entire book appeared in 1821. In 1952, a number of Aramaic fragments of Enoch were found among the Dead Sea Scrolls, and some scholars believe that the book probably originated in the Qumran community.

RECOMMENDED READING

Charles, R. H. "Book of Enoch, with an Introduction." In *Apocrypha and Pseudepigrapha of the Old Testament,* Vol. 2, pp. 163–281. Oxford: Clarendon Press, 1913.

Charlesworth, James H., ed. *The Old Testament Pseudepigrapha.* Vol. 1, *Apocalyptic Literature and Testaments,* pp. 5–100. Garden City, N.Y.: Doubleday, 1983.

Knibb, Michael A., trans. *The Ethiopic Book of Enoch: A New Edition in the Light of the Aramaic Dead Sea Fragments.* Oxford: Clarendon Press, 1978.

Milik, Jozef T. *The Books of Enoch: Aramaic Fragments of Qumran Cave 4.* Oxford: Clarendon Press, 1976.

Nickelsburg, George W. E. *Jewish Literature Between the Bible and the Mishnah,* pp. 43–55, 145–160. Philadelphia: Fortress Press, 1981.

2 Enoch (Slavonic Book of Enoch)

KEY TOPICS/THEMES

An apocalyptic interpretation of the Enoch traditions, 2 Enoch describes a mystical journey through the ten levels of heaven (Chs. 1–21), a purview of human history (Chs. 22–38), an admonition based on Enoch's intimacy with the divine realm (Chs. 39–66), and a conclusion summarizing his supernatural experiences (Chs. 67 and 68).

KEY QUESTION

To what hidden realms does Enoch travel, and what mysteries does he reveal?

The Slavonic Book of Enoch (so called because it has survived only in a Slavonic translation) was originally written in Greek. Although the book's present form may represent a Christian edition from as late as the seventh century C.E., it undoubtedly arose from a Jewish original dating from perhaps the first century C.E. Injunctions to visit the Jerusalem Temple three times a year (51:4) and references to ongoing sacrificial procedures (59:1–2; 61:4; 62:1) indicate that at least these portions were written before 70 C.E. R. H. Charles suggests Alexandria, Egypt, as the likely place of composition. A first-person narrative of sixty-eight chapters, it describes Enoch's ascension to the tenth heaven, where he beholds the face of God and is taught all knowledge; his thirty-day return to earth to transmit this wisdom to his sons; and his permanent return to heaven.

The first section of the book (Chs. 1–21) offers a fascinating survey of the ten levels of the spirit world through which Enoch ascends. Although the concept may seem strange to modern theology, the author makes several of the levels places of darkness and torment. The "second heaven," for example, is a gloomy prison for rebellious angels (Ch. 7); the "third heaven" is divided into a sensuous Eden for the righteous and a flaming darkness for sinners (Chs. 8–10); the fifth level contains the giant angel who had provoked a revolt against God and whom Enoch persuades to beseech the Deity's pity (Ch. 18). Enthroned in the "tenth heaven" is God himself, a formidable image with a face burning "like iron made to glow in fire" (22:1). This section is an outstanding example of Hebrew mysticism and occult beliefs of the late Hellenistic period.

In the second part of the book (Chs. 22–38), the Deity instructs Enoch in the mysteries of creation and interprets human history from the time of Adam to the Flood. The third section (Chs. 39–66) shows Enoch imparting to his sons what he has learned and admonishing them to study his 366 books containing the divine wisdom. Typical of apocalyptic mentality is the author's insistence that all history, including that of individual lives, is predetermined (53:2–3). The last two chapters

record Enoch's final ascension and a summary of his extraordinary accomplishments (Chs. 67–68).

Although 2 Enoch may have appeared too late to influence Christian thought directly, its views of heaven and of the rewards and punishments of the afterlife remarkably parallel some New Testament beliefs. Certainly, its picture of the ten celestial stages strongly affected Dante's presentation of heaven in the *Divine Comedy*.

RECOMMENDED READING

Charles, R. H. "The Book of the Secrets of Enoch, with an Introduction." In *Apocrypha and Pseudepigrapha of the Old Testament*, Vol. 2, pp. 425–469. Oxford: Clarendon Press, 1913.

Charlesworth, James H., ed. *The Old Testament Pseudepigrapha*. Vol. 1, *Apocalyptic Literature and Testaments*, pp. 91–221. Garden City, N.Y.: Doubleday, 1983.

Sibylline Oracles

KEY TOPICS/THEMES

An adaptation of classical traditions about the Sibyl, this composite work is a miscellaneous collection of Hellenistic Jewish, Christian, and pagan oracles covering several centuries of Greco-Roman history.

KEY QUESTION

Why did Jews and Christians adopt the figure of a Greco-Roman prophet to voice their visions of God's eschatological plans?

The Sibyl, after whom this collection of prophecies is named, was a prophetess or series of prophetesses famous in classical Greece and Rome. Inspired by Apollo, the Sibyl foretold the fate of individuals and nations, although most such predictions were written down long after the events foretold had already occurred. During the second century B.C.E., this time-honored method of ascribing prophecies of more recent historical events to a figure of the remote past was taken up by Jewish writers who by this means could review past occurrences as if foretelling them and then go on to predict the immediate future. Such was the mode of apocalyptic writing that replaced Israel's classical prophecy, which was thought to have ended after Ezra's day.

Adopted by Jewish apocalyptists, the Sibyl became a daughter-in-law of Noah and thus associated with the very beginning of the present world system (Sib. Or. 3:826). In this new guise, she was moved to prophesy Israelite as well as Greek history and to denounce both idolatry and the Jews' political enemies. In all, fifteen books of oracles were collected in which pagan, Jewish, and Christian elements are combined, edited, and revised. Of the twelve books that survive (Books 1–8 and 11–14), the largest block of mainly Jewish writings occurs in Books 3–5; Books 6–8 and 13 are of Christian origin. These diverse materials were collected by a Christian editor in the sixth century c.e.

Especially noteworthy in Book 3, which contains a Jewish revision and expansion of earlier pagan material, is an eschatological passage foretelling the coming of a messiah at a time "when Rome shall rule over Egypt" (Sib. Or. 3:46–61) and predictions of disaster for foreign nations when the messianic kingdom arrives (3:573–812). Throughout Book 3, the author somewhat incongruously blends Gentile history with exhortations to unbelieving pagans and descriptions of eschatological catastrophes. References to the Egyptian monarch Ptolemy VII lead scholars to believe that the book was mostly written during his reign (145–116 b.c.e.). Allusions to later events—such as the second triumvirate (43 b.c.e.) and Cleopatra (c. 30 b.c.e.)—were probably added by a later editor.

Book 4, a series of cryptic utterances in which some historical events are cited as signs of imminent calamity, was written after the great eruption of Mount Vesuvius in 79 c.e. (4:130–136). The veiled reference to Nero's return from the dead at the head of an invading army (4:137–139; 8:140–155) expressed a belief popular in the late first century c.e. (See also the use of this legend in Rev. 17:8–9.)

Book 3 was written in Egypt; Book 4's place of origin is not known. Book 5, which includes a lament over the fall of Jerusalem (5:397–413), probably appeared in Egypt toward the close of the second century c.e. Some of the Christian books were probably written even later.

QUESTIONS FOR REVIEW

1. What are the Pseudepigrapha, and approximately when were they written?

2. According to Genesis, who was Enoch, and why is he associated with heavenly mysteries? Describe the contents of the Book of 1 Enoch, and specify some of its similarities to the canonical Book of Daniel. Define the respective roles of obedient and rebellious angels in this apocalypse.

3. How does the Book of 2 Enoch portray the different levels of heaven? What does the author of this document add to speculations about the nature of the spirit world?

4. What are the Sibylline Oracles? During what historical periods were they composed?

QUESTIONS FOR DISCUSSION AND REFLECTION

1. Drawing on the canonical Book of Daniel, the deuterocanonical Book of 2 Esdras, and the pseudepigraphal books of 1 and 2 Enoch and the Sibylline Oracles, discuss the evolution of ideas about the predestined flow of historical events and the nature of the afterlife, including speculations about the final consummation of human history and posthumous rewards for Torah observance and penalties for disobedience.

2. After reviewing this selection of apocalyptic and eschatological literature, discuss the reasons these works continue to intrigue the popular imagination. Why do ideas about the "end of the world" and future judgment in the afterlife appeal to so many people? What possible connections exist between the particular historical-social conditions that produced the apocalyptic movement and the influence it continues to exert on some religious groups today? What aspects of apocalyptic thought—such as its combination of pessimism and optimism, its universality, or its capacity for giving ultimate direction and meaning to humanity's historical experience—do you think help account for its long life and, in some quarters, continuing relevance?

TERMS AND CONCEPTS TO REMEMBER

Enoch   Son of Man
Pseudepigrapha

RECOMMENDED READING

Charles, R. H. "The Sibylline Books [3, 4, and 5 only], with an Introduction." In *Apocrypha and Pseudepigrapha of the Old Testament*, Vol. 2, pp. 377–406. Oxford: Clarendon Press, 1913.

Collins, J. J. *Sibylline Oracles*. In J. H. Charlesworth, ed., *The Old Testament Pseudepigrapha*, Vol. 1. Garden City, N.Y.: Doubleday, 1983. Includes the entire corpus, plus an introduction and notes.

Other Deuterocanonical Writings (Books of the Apocrypha)

In addition to the books of Maccabees and the apocalyptic 2 Esdras, the deuterocanon encompasses a wide range of literature. Although set in the Assyrian Empire, Tobit and Judith are fictional romances illustrating the ordeals and dangers of Jewish life in the Hellenistic Diaspora. Baruch and the Additions to Esther similarly emphasize the importance of adhering to Torah principles when living amid the temptations of a foreign culture. Two of Israel's finest works of practical and speculative wisdom, Ecclesiastes and the Wisdom of Solomon, demonstrate the creative synthesis of Greek thought with traditional Jewish values.

Tobit

KEY TOPICS/THEMES

A fictional narrative depicting the life of an exiled Israelite family (Tobit, Tobias, and Sarah) living in Nineveh, capital of the Assyrian Empire, during the seventh century B.C.E., Tobit demonstrates that God hears and answers the prayers of his landless and dispossessed faithful. Perhaps influenced by Zoroastrian mythology, the book contains the Bible's first account of an exorcism (Chs. 5–8).

KEY QUESTIONS

How does the story of Tobit and his family express Jewish life in the Diaspora? What role do angels and demons play?

LIFE IN THE DIASPORA

Although the Septuagint editors placed Tobit among the historical books, it is really a work of imaginative fiction. The action is set during the seventh century B.C.E. when many Jews from the northern kingdom were scattered throughout the Assyrian Empire. The central figure, Tobit, an aged and pious Jew of the Naphtali tribe, is an exile living in Nineveh, the Assyrian capital. Though remarkably true in its psychology of character and artistic handling of plot and theme, the book contains several historical and geographical errors. And while the customs, attitudes, and theological beliefs presented in the story suggest that it was written during the Hellenistic period, perhaps about 185–175 B.C.E., the author is unknown.

The book's purpose is to encourage Jewish exiles to maintain their religious integrity; the author insists that Israel's God hears their prayers and will eventually reward the faithful. This message is dramatized in a well-constructed plot consisting of three closely related narrative strands. The main plot concerns Tobit, an exemplary Jew who strictly observes all aspects of the law but who suffers the illnesses and privations of a latter-day Job. A subplot involves his kinswoman Sarah, a beautiful virgin whose seven husbands have all been killed on their wedding night by the jealous demon Asmodeus. A second subplot concerning Tobit's son Tobias, who travels to Media, exorcises the demon, and marries Sarah, effectively ties all the narratives together.

Tobit's story is joined to Sarah's when the Deity hears their simultaneous prayers for death (3:16–17). Tobit prays to die because, for piously burying slaughtered Israelites, he not only has been stripped of all his possessions but also has been blinded by bird droppings (2:9–3:6). Sarah, unhappy that a maid has accused her of murdering her seven husbands, similarly longs to end her life

(3:7–15). The earthly connection is provided when Tobias journeys to Ecbatana in Media to claim money that Tobit had entrusted to his kinsman Raguel, who is also Sarah's father.

The archangel Raphael, disguised as a man named Azariah, guides young Tobias to Ecbatana, provides the necessary instructions to exorcise Asmodeus (who flees to Egypt, where an angel binds him), and permits the union of Tobias and Sarah. Raguel, who had spent the wedding night digging a grave for his new son-in-law, is astounded by Tobias's survival. Upon Tobias's triumphant return to Nineveh with the money and a new wife, Raphael also cures Tobit's blindness with fish gall (11:10–15).

A treasure-house of second-century B.C.E. Jewish social customs and beliefs, this delightful tale deals with such matters as guardian angels (5:21; 12:12–13), priestly distinctions (1:6–7), dietary restrictions (1:10–12), personal prayers (3:2–15; 8:5–8), the importance of a decent burial (1:17–19; 2:3–8; 14:12), the power of demons and the use of fish entrails in exorcising them (3:8; 6:6–8; 8:1–3), the seven angels of the heavenly court (12:15), and the value of wise parental advice (4:3–19). Tobit's popular view of angels — guardian spirits who act as intercessors (12:12) — and demons seems to reflect the influence of Persian dualism (Zoroastrianism) with its doctrine of warring spirits of Good and Evil.

The last chapters — Tobit's thanksgiving psalm (Ch. 13) and an epilogue recounting his advice that Tobias and Sarah leave Nineveh to escape the city's impending destruction (Ch. 14) — may be later additions. The final section, in which Tobias prophesies Nineveh's fall and Jerusalem's restoration, contains the remarkable prediction that "all the nations of the world will be converted to the true worship of God" (14:6).

RECOMMENDED READING

Nowell, Irene. "Tobit." In R. E. Brown et al., eds., *The New Jerome Biblical Commentary*, 2nd ed., pp. 568–571. Englewood Cliffs, N.J.: Prentice-Hall, 1990.

———. "The Book of Tobit." In *The New Interpreter's Bible*, Vol. 3, pp. 973–1071. Nashville: Abingdon Press, 1999.

Judith

KEY TOPICS/THEMES

An anonymous historical romance, Judith resembles Esther in depicting the dangers and difficulties of Jews living in the Diaspora. Set during the Assyrian threat to Israel (Chs. 1–7), the book presents Judith's killing of Holofernes as an act of national heroism (Chs. 8–16).

KEY QUESTION

How did Judith become a national Jewish heroine?

Like Tobit, too, Judith is a historical romance written by an unknown author during the Hellenistic period and set in the distant past. The book begins with a glaring historical error — that Nebuchadnezzar (605–562 B.C.E.) reigned in Nineveh over the Assyrians, when in reality his father, the king of Babylon, had destroyed Nineveh in 612. This error may have been intentional, to show at the outset that the narrative was not meant to be factual history. The true political situation is probably that of the Syrian oppression of the Jews under Antiochus IV (175–164/163 B.C.E.). Nebuchadnezzar, then, represents Antiochus, the despot who tried to eradicate Israel's religion (1 Macc. 1:14–50; Dan. 3:3–15). The writer advises armed revolt, asserting that Israel's God will defend his people if they remain faithful to him (Jth. 13:11; 16:17).

A NATIONAL HEROINE

Judith was probably written around 150 B.C.E., about a decade after the Maccabees had successfully repulsed the Syrians. The heroine's name, the feminine form of "Judah," literally means "Jewess" and may be intended to symbolize the nation or to remind the reader of Judas, its Maccabean leader. Judith embodies the traditional biblical heroism of the solitary Israelite struggling against a pagan superpower, as David fought Goliath or as Jael felled Sisera (1 Sam. 17:20–54; Judg. 4:17–24; 5:25–30). Judith's triumph over Holofernes, the Assyrian commander, is her nation's victory over their collective enemies.

The book is divided into two parts. The first (Jth. 1–7) states that after conquering Media, Nebuchadnezzar sent Holofernes to punish countries that had not supported his campaign. After overrunning various other nations, the Assyrians laid siege to Bethulia, a fortified city that may represent Jerusalem, which Antiochus had sacked. When Bethulia is ready to submit, the ruler Uzziah decrees that Israel's Deity be given another five days to rescue the people.

In the second part (Jth. 8–15), Judith, a beautiful widow, berates the leaders who put their God to the test and volunteers to save the city herself. After offering a prayer, she perfumes herself, dresses in her gayest clothes and jewelry, and enters the Assyrian camp, pretending to defect because of her admiration of Holofernes. Flattered, the Assyrian commander invites the seductive woman into his tent, where, after plying him with wine, she takes his sword and decapitates him.

Stowing the head in her travel bag, Judith and her maid convey it to Jerusalem, where it is displayed on the city wall. Dispirited by their leader's death, the Assyrians withdraw, allowing the Jews to loot their camp. Judith dedicates her share of the booty to the Jerusalem Temple. In an epilogue, Judith hails her God for protecting his people (Jth. 16:17). After her death at an advanced age, she is honored by her compatriots as a national heroine.

Although Judith was written at a time when slaughtering an enemy could be regarded as an act of religious piety, it is more than a nationalistic war story. Its emphasis on the power of Israel's God to rescue an obedient people echoes a theme recurrent in biblical history: It is not "by sword or spear" that Israel carries the day, but only through the will of its God, who can save by the frail hand of a lone woman. (See also 1 Sam. 17:46–47.)

RECOMMENDED READING

Craven, Toni. "Judith." In R. E. Brown et al., eds., *The New Jerome Biblical Commentary*, pp. 572–575. Englewood Cliffs, N.J.: Prentice-Hall, 1990.

Moore, Carey A. *Judith*. Garden City, N.Y.: Doubleday, 1985

Wills, Lawrence M. "The Book of Judith." In *The New Interpreter's Bible*, Vol. 3, pp. 1073–1183. Nashville: Abingdon Press, 1999.

Additions to Esther

KEY TOPICS/THEMES

An unknown editor interpolated prayers and pious sentiments into the essentially secular Book of Esther, which originally did not even mention God (Chs. 10–16).

KEY QUESTION

What religious elements do the Additions inject into the secular story of Esther?

The Septuagint version of the Book of Esther contains six parts not found in the Hebrew original. Although a few scholars hold that the Additions existed first in Hebrew, most believe they were not composed and interpolated into the biblical text until 114 B.C.E. when Esther was translated into Greek. The Septuagint editors interspersed the Additions at various points in the story, weaving the Hebrew original and Greek expansions into a single whole; but when Jerome prepared the Latin Vulgate, he removed the Additions from the main body of the work and placed them at the end (Add. to Esther 10:3a–16:24).*

Modern translations that include the apocryphal excerpts handle the textual problem in various ways. The Jerusalem Bible restores the Additions to the canonical Hebrew narrative but prints them in italics to distinguish them from the Hebrew text. The New English Bible places them among the Apocrypha and, for coherence, translates the entire Greek version of Esther with the supplements fitted into their proper sequence.

A TORAH LOYALIST

The Additions apparently were intended to heighten the religious implications of Esther's story. Although the Hebrew version contains neither prayers nor references to Israel's God, the Additions emphasize the efficacy of prayer and the Deity's saving power (13:8–18; 14:3–19; 15:8). They even

---

*Chapter and verse numbers in the Additions follow Jerome's ordering of the Vulgate text.

preface the account with an apocalyptic dream of Mardochaeus (Mordecai) that places the Jews' deliverance from Persian attack in the con-text of Yahweh's ultimate victory over all worldly powers (11:2–12).

A devout practitioner of Torah Judaism and kosher dietary laws, the Esther of the Greek version refuses to eat Gentile food (14:17) and finds her marriage to a non-Jewish husband, Emperor Ahasuerus (Xerxes I), repellent (14:15). These added touches stress the strict observance of Jewish law and abhorrence of having to comply with the requirements of a pagan environment by a heroine who implores the Deity:

> As for ourselves, save us by your hand,
> and come to my help, for I am alone
> and have no one but you, Lord.
> You have knowledge of all things,
> and you know that I hate honors from the
>   godless,
> that I loathe the bed of the uncircumcised,
> of any foreigner whatever.
> You know I am under constraint,
> that I loathe the symbol of my high position
> bound round my brow when I appear at court;
> I loathe it as if it were a filthy rag
> and do not wear it on my days of leisure.
> Your handmaid has not eaten at Haman's table,
> nor taken pleasure in the royal banquets,
> nor drunk the wine of libations.
>   Add. to Esther 14:14–17

The Additions increase the suspense of Esther's unsolicited interview with the emperor by dramatizing the emotions it arouses (15:6–19). They also attempt to lend authenticity by reproducing the text of Artaxerxes' letter condemning Haman (who turns out to be a Macedonian spy), praising the king's Jewish subjects, and commanding them to defend themselves when attacked (16:1–24). Like the Hebrew original, the Additions present the Jewish characters operating in an atmosphere of intrigue and competition instigated by jealous pagans. But unlike the canonical tale, the Additions transform the violent episode of Jewish self-defense into a declaration of their God's omnipotence; for here, even Artaxerxes testifies to this Deity's control of events (16:4, 21).

RECOMMENDED READING

Moore, Carey A. *Daniel, Esther, and Jeremiah: The Additions.* Garden City, N.Y.: Doubleday, 1977.

Baruch

KEY TOPICS/THEMES

A composite work by at least three different writers, Baruch purports to be a prophetic document written by Jeremiah's secretary early in the Babylonian captivity. The book includes a prayer of the Judean exiles (Chs. 1–3), a hymn to Wisdom and religious poems (Chs. 3–5), and a letter of Jeremiah (Ch. 6).

KEY QUESTION

How does Baruch reinterpret Jeremiah's prophecy about the duration of the exile?

Baruch is the only book of the Apocrypha whose mode resembles the prophetic. Although it purports to have been written about 582 B.C.E. (Bar. 1:2) by the secretary and companion of the prophet Jeremiah (Jer. 36:4–10), scholars agree that it is a composite work to which at least three different writers anonymously contributed. The book's four parts have been dated from about 200 B.C.E. for the earliest additions to after 70 C.E. for the latest additions. Although set during the Babylonian exile, it more accurately reflects the problems of non-Palestinian Jews dispersed throughout the Hellenistic world.

COUNSEL FOR JEWISH EXILES

Exiles' Prayer   The first part (1:1–3:8) contains several confusing contradictions. It states, for example, that the "book of Baruch" was written in Babylon five years after the Babylonians had burned Solomon's Temple (1:2), yet it pictures the exiles asking the high priest and his assistants in Jerusalem to offer prayers in "the house of the Lord" (1:14). Equally confusing is the statement that Baruch read "this book" to an assembly of Judean exiles living in Babylon (1:1–4), when the book clearly relates events that occurred long after the public reading.

The rest of this prose section (1:15–3:8), which resembles parts of Daniel (see Dan. 9:4–19), depicts the exiled Judeans confessing the sins that caused their nation's downfall (1:15–2:10; 2:20–26) and beseeching divine mercy (2:11–19; 3:1–8). It also contains a prophecy that the scattered people will be restored to their homeland (2:27–35).

Hymn and Poems   The second part (3:9–4:4), apparently by a different author, is a didactic hymn praising Israel's God for revealing his wisdom in the Mosaic Law. The third section (4:5–5:9), echoing motifs in Second Isaiah and Lamentations, contains poems of hope and comfort, as well as of sorrow for Jerusalem's fall. The poet realizes that Israel's exile is a punishment for its violations of the law but foresees a joyous return to Palestine (5:1–9).

Letter of Jeremiah   Although the ancient manuscripts place this document after Lamentations, the Latin Vulgate and most English Bibles that include the Apocrypha attach it to Baruch, where it appears as Chapter 6. (The New English Bible prints it as a separate book following Baruch.) Purporting to be a letter from Jeremiah to Jews about to be deported to Babylon, the document is in fact a much later work, apparently modeled on the prophet's authentic sixth-century letter to Babylonian exiles (see Jer. 29). Estimates on the date of composition vary from 317 to about 100 B.C.E.

The writer's theme is the evil of idolatry, to which he devotes the most virulent and extensive attack in the Bible. Although the only foreign god specifically mentioned is Bel (Marduk) (6:4), scholars believe that he is really denouncing Hellenistic deities whom Jews scattered abroad might, for social and political reasons, be tempted to worship. "Babylon" would then be a symbol for areas outside Palestine where Jews had been dispersed.

The author extends Jeremiah's prediction that the exile would last seventy years (Jer. 25:12) to "seven generations" (Bar. 6:3), which, taking a biblical generation as forty years (Num. 32:13),

would mean that the Jews would remain exiled until the end of the fourth century B.C.E. The letter thus updates earlier biblical themes and applies them to contemporary situations in the Hellenistic Diaspora.

RECOMMENDED READING

Moore, Carey A. *Daniel, Esther, and Jeremiah: The Additions.* Garden City, N.Y.: Doubleday, 1977.

Saldarini, Anthony J. "The Book of Baruch." In *The New Interpreter's Bible,* Vol. 6, pp. 927–982. Nashville: Abingdon Press, 2001.

Ecclesiasticus (The Wisdom of Jesus, Son of Sirach)

KEY TOPICS/THEMES

A poetic compilation of proverbs, sage advice, and philosophical reflections, Ecclesiasticus was written early in the second century B.C.E. by Jesus (Joshua), son of Sirach, the head of a professional wisdom school in Jerusalem. Translated into Greek and published in 132 B.C.E. by Jesus' grandson, the book contains a lengthy collection of wise sayings and practical counsel (Chs. 1–42), including a famous speech by Wisdom herself (Ch. 24). The second part consists of hymns and a eulogy of famous Israelites (Chs. 42–51), ending with a biographical postscript.

KEY QUESTIONS

What does Sirach add to Israel's Wisdom tradition? How does he identify Lady Wisdom?

The longest Wisdom book in the Bible, Ecclesiasticus is also the only apocryphal writing whose author, original translator, and date are known. The writer identifies himself as Jesus ben (son of) Sirach (50:27), a professional teacher of wisdom who conducted a school or house of learning in Jerusalem (51:24). In a preface to the main work, ben Sirach's grandson reveals that he brought the book to Egypt, where he translated it from Hebrew into Greek at a date equivalent to 132 B.C.E.; his grandfather had composed it in Jerusalem about 180 B.C.E. The title, which means "church book," may reflect either its extensive use in church worship or the fact that though Jewish editors eventually denied it a place in the Hebrew Bible, the Christian church received it into the canon.

Written in the tradition of Proverbs, Ecclesiasticus is largely a collection of wise sayings, moral essays, hymns to wisdom, practical advice to the young and inexperienced, instructions in proper social and religious conduct, private meditations, and extended reflections on the human condition. Like other postexilic sages, ben Sirach perceives an ordered design in the universe and counsels others to conform their lives to it. A learned, respected, influential representative of upper-class Judaism, his tone is genial, pragmatic, and urbane. Writing more than a decade before the persecutions of Antiochus IV, he believes that life can be a positive experience if one only learns to conduct oneself with prudence, insight, and the right degree of shrewdness.

WISDOM AND THE GOOD LIFE

Completely a man of the present, ben Sirach rejects any belief in angels, demons, or life after death. Apocalyptic enthusiasms are not for him. "The son of man," he asserts, "is not immortal" (17:30). With his emphasis on the law, Temple service, good works, and denial of a resurrection or afterlife, ben Sirach seems to be a forerunner of the Sadducees. Like that intensely conservative, aristocratic party that largely controlled the priesthood and Temple in the first century c.e., he appears to regard the law as final and unchanging, an essentially static guidebook to both the moral and material good life.

Ecclesiasticus also resembles Proverbs and the Wisdom of Solomon in consisting mostly of poetry, chiefly couplets of parallel lines. The first forty-two chapters, containing many brief aphorisms interspersed with longer discourses, offer advice and admonitions on many diverse topics: the fear of God as the basis of wisdom (1:20; 32:14−33:3), humility (3:17−26), generosity to the poor (4:1−11; 7:32−40), prudent friendships (6:5−17; 12:8−19; 22:19−32), trust in God (2:1−23; 11:12−30), humanity's moral responsibilities (16:24−17:13), female spite (25:13−36), good wives (26:1−23), proper manners and control of drinking at banquets (31:12−32:17), honoring doctors and respecting scholars (38:1−15; 31:1−15), and the human predicament and fate of the wicked (40:1−11; 41:5−16).

Chapter 24:1−30 contains a splendid oration by Lady Wisdom, whom ben Sirach explicitly identifies with the Mosaic Law (19:20; 24:23):

> I came forth from the mouth of the Most High,
>   and I covered the earth like a mist . . .
> From eternity, in the beginning, he created me,
>   and for eternity I shall remain.
> I ministered before him in the holy tabernacle,
>   and thus was I established on Zion.
> In the beloved city he has given me rest,
>   and in Jerusalem I wield my authority.
>   Ecclus. 24:3, 9−11

Chapters 42:15−43:33 comprise a hymn praising the Deity's glory as revealed in physical nature, a poem that rivals Psalm 19 in beauty. This is followed by the best-known passage in the book—"let us now praise famous men"—a eulogy of twenty-nine biblical heroes, from Enoch to Nehemiah, and including Abraham, Joseph, Aaron (Israel's first high priest, who is given more space than the lawgiver Moses), David, Hezekiah, and Elijah. Ezra's name is conspicuously absent, presumably because this great interpreter of the law was regarded as the progenitor of a religious movement that culminated in Pharisaism, a development of which ben Sirach strongly disapproved.

The tribute to Israel's ancestors climaxes in the praise of Simon the high priest (c. 225−200 b.c.e.), whom ben Sirach lauds as personifying the best of his nation's traditions (50:1−24). As intercessor between the people and their God, Simon was privileged to enter the Temple's **Holy of Holies** annually on the Day of Atonement (see Lev. 16) and there pronounce the divine name Yahweh, which by Hellenistic times was considered too sacred to utter publicly. The book concludes with an epilogue containing ben Sirach's hymn of personal thanksgiving (51:1−12) and an autobiographical résumé of the rewards of pursuing wisdom (51:13−30).

Figure 8.8 Discovered at Masada, the hilltop fortress where the last important band of Jewish rebels held out against Roman armies (73 C.E.), this fragment of the Book of Ecclesiasticus (Wisdom of Jesus ben Sirach) is approximately 2000 years old.

The emphasis that ben Sirach places on the practical advantages of strict moral conduct, wealth, and worldly success and his view that Temple services are the most important part of Israel's worship well represent attitudes characteristic of latter Sadduceeism. His assumption that his God's intentions for humanity were completely and unchangingly revealed in the Mosaic code and Temple liturgy helps explain why the Sadducees as a party did not long survive the Roman destruction of Jerusalem and its sanctuary in 70 C.E. Ironically, a fragment of ben Sirach's work was found recently at Masada, site of the final zealot holdout against the Romans (Figure 8.8).

RECOMMENDED READING

Crenshaw, James L. "The Book of Sirach." In *The New Interpreter's Bible*, Vol. 5, pp. 601–867. Nashville: Abingdon Press, 1997.

Skehan, Patrick W., and Di Lella, Alexander A. *The Wisdom of Ben Sira.* Garden City, N.Y.: Doubleday, 1987.

Snaith, John G. *Ecclesiasticus: or The Wisdom of Jesus Son of Sirach.* Cambridge Bible Commentary on the New English Bible. London: Cambridge University Press, 1974.

The Wisdom of Solomon (Wisdom)

KEY TOPICS/THEMES

Although attributed to Solomon, this brilliant collection of poems, proverbs, and sage meditations was composed by an anonymous Hellenized Jew living in Alexandria, Egypt, during the last century B.C.E. A creative synthesis of Hebrew wisdom traditions with speculative Greek philosophy, the book surveys the nature of divine Wisdom and the rewards of virtue and immortality it imparts (Chs. 1–5), and describes the origin, character, and value of Wisdom (Chs. 6–9). The more prosaic second half surveys the role of Wisdom in Israel's sacred history (Chs. 10–19).

KEY QUESTIONS

What typically Greek ideas about the soul does the author integrate into the wisdom tradition? How has divine Wisdom directed human history?

Although the Wisdom of Solomon presents itself as King Solomon's address to the world's rulers

(1:1), it is really the work of an anonymous writer aimed at Jews living in exile, some of whom apparently were tempted to compromise or relinquish their religion under the allurements of Greek culture and philosophy or the pressure of Gentile discrimination. The author's familiarity with Greek terms and philosophic ideas (8:7, 19–20; 12:1) indicates that he lived during the Hellenistic period, perhaps about 100 B.C.E. He appears to have been a well-educated member of the Jewish community in **Alexandria**, Egypt, a populous and cosmopolitan city that then rivaled Athens as the world's leading intellectual center.

THE NATURE OF WISDOM

By demonstrating that Judaism's ethical and religious wisdom is superior to that of the Gentiles, the author hopes to encourage Jews to maintain their traditional allegiances. He endeavors also to show that his religion offers a view of world history and divine justice that will appeal to the moral and rational Gentile. A creative synthesis of Hebrew and Greek thought, the Wisdom of Solomon is theologically one of the most important books in the Apocrypha and a major contribution to biblical wisdom literature. The book can be divided into three parts: (1) the rewards of Wisdom (personified as God's Spirit) and the promise of immortality (Chs. 1–5), (2) the origin, character, and value of Wisdom (Chs. 6–9), and (3) the Wisdom of Israel's Deity operating in human history (Chs. 10–19).

Rewards of Wisdom   The first section contrasts the fate of the wicked—whose twisted reasoning is vividly rendered in 2:1–20—with that of the righteous. Although the ungodly may prosper on earth and oppress the good, the soul's survival after death (different from the bodily resurrection depicted in Dan. 12:2) guarantees that the Deity's justice ultimately will prevail. Asserting that "God created man for immortality" and "made him the image of his own eternal self" (2:23), the author assures his readers that "the souls of the just are in God's hand and torment shall not touch them" (3:1).

Foolish skeptics might believe that the just perish utterly, but their sufferings are merely a test to refine their worth. Even their deaths are a disguised blessing, for they are destined to judge nations and rule over the world (3:2–8; see also Rev. 2:26–27; 20:4). The ungodly, meanwhile, are punished not arbitrarily, but according to their own evil designs (3:10). This concept of an afterlife in which immortal souls are rewarded for their good deeds on earth is the author's response to the problem of undeserved suffering that had troubled writers of such other Wisdom books as Job. Here the Deity's justice toward his human creation is vindicated because he provides an eternity of bliss to compensate for temporary earthly pain.

Origin, Character, and Value of Wisdom   Comparable Greek ideas appear in the second section, which features "Solomon's" praise of Lady Wisdom, the bringer of immortality (6:1; 8:13). The speaker, who takes Wisdom as his "bride," implies that the soul exists in heaven prior to its incarnation or imprisonment in a physical body (8:19–20; 9:15). This belief in an immaterial, preexistent soul that escapes to the spirit realm at the body's dissolution is typical of Platonic and neo-Platonic thought.

Similarly representative of Greek ethical philosophy is the author's exposition of the four classical virtues, which became the four cardinal virtues of Christian morality:

> Or if it be virtue you love,
> why, virtues are the fruit of her labors,
> since it is she who teaches temperance
>   and prudence,
> justice and fortitude;
> nothing in life is more serviceable to men
> than these.
>
> Wisd. of Sol. 8:7

Wisdom in Sacred History   In the lengthy third part, the author presents an idealized survey of early humanity (Ch. 10) and of Israel's history, contrasting the Deity's judgments on the heathen with his saving care of the chosen people, to whom Wisdom lent strength and understanding. The moralistic discussion of Israel and Egypt (Chs. 11–19) is interrupted by a diatribe against idolatry (13:1–15:17) that is reminiscent of Second Isaiah's castigation of the Babylonian gods (Isa. 40, 46). The imaginative reinterpretation of Israel's past in the final chapters may have been intended to inspire hope among the Diaspora Jews that their God still intervened in human affairs on their behalf (16:7–8; 19:22).

The author attributes the presence of evil and death to the "Devil's spite" (2:23–24), an interpretation of the serpent's role in Genesis 3 that would culminate in the doctrine of inherited sin expounded by Paul (Rom. 5) and the writer of 2 Esdras 3:7. (For other passages that influenced New Testament writers, compare Wisd. of Sol. 1:7 with Col. 1:17; Wisd. of Sol. 3:7 with Matt. 13:42; Wisd. of Sol. 3:14 with Matt. 19:12; Wisd. of Sol. 5:16 with Rev. 2:10; Wisd. of Sol. 5:16–19 with Eph. 6:11–17; Wisd. of Sol. 6:3–4 with Rom. 13:1–12; and Wisd. of Sol. 14:22–31 with Rom. 1:18–32.)

Finally, the reference to divine Wisdom manifesting itself as God's "all-powerful Word" leaping "down from the heavens, from the royal throne" into the "heart of a doomed land" where "he touched the sky, yet trod the earth" (18:15, 16) anticipates the doctrine of the Word (Logos) developed by **Philo Judaeus**, a later Alexandrine Jewish scholar. Philo's Logos concept was then adopted and modified by the author of John's Gospel to explain the incarnation of the prehuman Jesus (John 1:1, 14). Such foreshadowing of ideas popular in Christianity may explain why the Wisdom of Solomon was recommended reading in many early churches and was included with New Testament writings in the Muratorian Canon.

QUESTIONS FOR REVIEW

1. What message do the books of Tobit and Judith have for Jews living under foreign rule? Identify Raphael and Holofernes.

2. The canonical Book of Esther does not mention God. How do the Additions to Esther make the book more conventionally religious?

3. Who was Baruch? According to the book ascribed to Baruch, what advice does Jeremiah give to Judeans exiled in Babylon? How does this advice apply to Jews living in the Diaspora?

4. To what general category do the books of Ecclesiasticus and Wisdom of Solomon belong? List some of their principal themes. When and where were they written, and for what presumed audience? What specific information do we have about the author, translator, and editor of Ecclesiasticus?

QUESTIONS FOR DISCUSSION AND REFLECTION

1. In what specific ways do such works as Tobit, Judith, and Baruch offer encouragement and counsel to members of the covenant community scattered among Gentile nations, far from Israel's Promised Land? What message do they have for communities of faith today?

2. Discuss the nature and function of divine Wisdom in Ecclesiasticus and the Wisdom of Solomon. What role does God's Wisdom play in human history? In what ways do these two books contribute to Israel's wisdom tradition? How does the concept of immortality promised in the Wisdom of Solomon add an important new dimension to the problem of undeserved suffering dramatized in older Wisdom books like Job?

TERMS AND CONCEPTS TO REMEMBER

Alexandria   Philo Judaeus
Holy of Holies

RECOMMENDED READING

Kolarcik, Michael. "The Book of Wisdom." In *The New Interpreter's Bible*, Vol. 5, pp. 435–600. Nashville: Abingdon Press, 1997.

Reese, James M. *Hellenistic Influence on the Book of Wisdom and Its Consequences*. Rome: Biblical Institute Press, 1970.

Winston, David. *The Wisdom of Solomon*. Garden City, N.Y.: Doubleday, 1979.

Wright, Addison G. "Wisdom." In R. E. Brown et al., eds., *The New Jerome Biblical Commentary*, 2nd ed., pp. 510–522. Englewood Cliffs, N.J.: Prentice-Hall, 1990.

Other Works of the Pseudepigrapha

Like most of the Apocrypha, books of the Pseudepigrapha deal with the challenge of preserving and adapting Israel's religious heritage in a rapidly changing world dominated by Greek culture and/or Roman political power. Whereas the Letter of Aristeas offers an imaginative account of the Hebrew Bible's first translation into Greek, the Book of Jubilees reinterprets Genesis and Exodus to validate later Jewish adaptations of Torah requirements. Both the Testaments of the Twelve Patriarchs and the Books of Adam and Eve revisit, respectively, Israel's and humanity's earliest ancestors to examine the virtues and flaws that can enhance or mar the divine-human relationship.

Letter of Aristeas

KEY TOPICS/THEMES

A fictionally embroidered account of the origin of the Septuagint, the first Greek translation of the Hebrew Bible, this document illustrates the increasing Hellenization of Judaism.

KEY QUESTION

How was a Greek edition of the Hebrew Bible produced in Alexandria?

This document ostensibly is a letter from Aristeas — a courtier of the Egyptian monarch Ptolemy II (285–246 B.C.E.) — to his brother Philocrates, containing an eyewitness account of the origin of the **Septuagint** Bible. A treatise rather than a letter, it relates how Ptolemy, when informed by the head of the Alexandria library that his collection lacks a copy of the Jewish Torah, sends Aristeas and Andreas to Jerusalem to obtain the original text.

The book describes negotiations with the high priest Eleazar, the selection of six leading scholars from each tribe of Israel, the reception of the seventy-two Jewish experts at the Ptolemaic court, their labors in translating the Hebrew text into Greek, and their production in seventy-two days of seventy-two identical translations, the reliability of which is affirmed by leaders of Alexandria's constituency. In popular usage, however, the number of translators was rounded off to seventy, a figure that gave the Septuagint its name.

Despite its wealth of concrete detail, scholars regard this story as more legend than historical fact. It is possible that in the mid-third century B.C.E., a librarian added a Greek transcription or translation of the Pentateuch to his official collection and that the reigning king may have sponsored the acquisition; but the royal honors that the author claims were showered on the Jewish translators are surely fictional.

Moreover, the Letter of Aristeas was not written by a contemporary of Ptolemy II, but about 150 years later. The author was probably an Alexandrian Jew familiar with the Egyptian court, who wrote to demonstrate the authority of the Septuagint and the superiority of Hebrew wisdom (manifested in the law) to Greek learning. Hence, the writer features extended dialogues between Torah-trained Jews and Greek philosophers, with the former triumphing in every dispute.

In this regard, the book well illustrates the tension between the Hebraic and Hellenic cultures that prevailed in the cosmopolitan setting of Hellenistic Alexandria. The fact that well-educated Jews found Greek ideas attractive made a Greek version of the Torah all the more necessary. Although an eventual fusion of Greek and Hebrew thought fertilized the growth of Hellenistic Judaism, later Palestinian rabbis rejected most of the synthesis.

RECOMMENDED READING

Charles, R. H. "The Letter of Aristeas, with an Introduction." In *Apocryphya and Pseudepigrapha of the Old Testament*, Vol. 2, pp. 83–122. Oxford: Clarendon Press, 1913.

Charlesworth, James H., ed. *The Old Testament Pseudepigrapha.* Vol. 2, *Expansions of the Old Testament and Other Legends, Wisdom, and Philosophical Literature.* Garden City, N.Y.: Doubleday, 1984.

Book of Jubilees

KEY TOPICS/THEMES

A Pharisaic expansion of Genesis and part of Exodus, Jubilees postulates the eternity of the Mosaic Torah, which predates the world's creation.

KEY QUESTION

How does Jubilees reinterpret the first books of the Torah?

The Book of Jubilees takes its name from the fact that the author divides world history into "Jubilees," or periods of forty-nine years, based on the **Jubilee** concept given in Leviticus 25. He further partitions each forty-nine-year epoch into seven weeks of years, all of which contain seven solar years of 364 days. This rigid compartmentalizing of the world's chronology is typical of the writer's priestly and legalistic approach.

Jubilees is also known as "Little Genesis" because it reproduces almost the entire narrative of the first Bible book, adding interpretative commentary and details from Jewish oral tradition along the way. In this expansion and elaboration of the canonical text, the author provides a virtual **midrash** characteristic of the late second century B.C.E. when Jubilees was written. (*Midrash* is a Hebrew term meaning an "explanation or scholarly interpretation of Scripture," typically produced by scribes and rabbinical Pharisees.)

As the Chronicler imbued Israel's monarchical history with a priestly slant, so the author of Jubilees retells the story of Genesis (and the first twelve chapters of Exodus) from a Pharisaic viewpoint, emphasizing the absolute supremacy of the Law, both canonical as preserved in the written Torah and oral as retained in the Pharisees' traditions. He therefore makes the patriarchs Abraham, Isaac, and Jacob fervent practitioners not only of the Mosaic legal system but also of the Pharisaic additions to that Law. His purpose is to show that the Law existed from the beginning, that it is thus the supreme moral value in the universe, and that its delivery to Moses on Mount Sinai was a complete and final manifestation of divine wisdom.

Jubilees presents an angel relating the whole story (Gen. 1 through Exod. 12) so that Moses can preserve it in the Pentateuch. As noted, however, Jubilees' version of Israel's prehistory includes many anachronistic elements. At age fourteen, Abraham is said to have rejected his father's idols and embraced a perfect monotheism (Bk. Jub. 11:16–18). After describing Abraham's death (23:1–8), the author interjects a long apocalyptic prophecy in which the angel tells Moses of the disasters to follow humanity's disobedience and Israel's future forsaking of the covenant. But after the chastened Israelites return to studying the Law and heeding its commands, their God will again restore them to long life and prosperity (23:13–32).

Such eschatological predictions give the author's theology a more flexible quality than his rather pedantic legalism might indicate. (See also Bk. Jub. 1:4–29 for a parallel eschatological prophecy.) At the same time, however, Jubilees strictly enjoins the reader to observe all distinctions between things clean and unclean, to avoid idolatry and other heathen contaminations, and to honor the Sabbath fully. The author insists, in addition, upon circumcision (Ch. 15); upon observation of all the ritual feast days; upon obligatory fruit, grain, and animal offerings; and upon regulations concerning women's sexual impurities (3:8; 15:31–32; 21; 22:16–20; 30:7–17; 50:6–13).

Some scholars have detected a resemblance between Jubilees' theology and that expressed in several documents recovered from the Qumran community. The presence of fragments from nine manuscripts of the original Hebrew version of the book found among the Dead Sea Scrolls confirms the link. Although written first in Hebrew, Jubilees survives most completely in an Ethiopic translation. Both it and Latin translations are taken from a Greek edition of the Hebrew original, which may be dated at about 100 B.C.E.

RECOMMENDED READING

Charles, R. H. "The Book of Jubilees, with an Introduction." In *Apocrypha and Pseudepigrapha of the Old Testament*, Vol. 2, pp. 1–82. Oxford: Clarendon Press, 1913. Includes the complete text, in English, with critical introduction and copious notes.

Charlesworth, James H., ed. *The Old Testament Pseudepigrapha.* Vol. 2, *Expansions of the Old Testament.* Garden City, N.Y.: Doubleday, 1984.

Davenport, Gene L. *The Eschatology of the Book of Jubilees.* Leiden, Netherlands: Brill, 1971.

Eissfeldt, Otto. *The Old Testament: An Introduction.* New York: Harper & Row, 1965.

Testaments of the Twelve Patriarchs

KEY TOPICS/THEMES

Each of Jacob's twelve sons, reputed founders of Israel's twelve tribes, gives ethical advice based on his life experiences.

KEY QUESTION

How does this book reinterpret Jacob's evaluation of his twelve sons (Gen. 49)?

This didactic work purports to be the last words or testaments of the twelve sons of Jacob to their descendants. Although modeled on the Blessing of Jacob to his twelve sons (Gen. 49), the Testaments of the Twelve Patriarchs does not for the most part contain prophecies about the individual tribes' future destiny. Rather, it consists mainly of exhortations by each patriarch, using his own particular character and moral behavior as a model either to shun or to emulate. With its many ethical precepts and wise sayings, the Testaments would seem a part of Israel's wisdom literature were it not that many passages embody visions or revelations of divine secrets, such as the nature of angels and the heavenly world.

The deathbed advice given by Jacob's twelve sons can be summarized as follows:

1. Reuben, citing his own case (see Gen. 35:22; 49:4), warns against "the seven spirits of deceit," which inspire lust and foster immorality.

2. Simon, referring to his murderous jealousy of Joseph, cautions against envy.

3. Levi, who has been privileged to visit the seventh heaven and receive direct divine appointment to the priesthood, urges respect for the Torah and for wisdom and states that he learned from the Book of Enoch that his progeny would corrupt the office until a messianic high priest appeared to establish the New Age.

4. Judah instructs his sons to avoid wine, women, and greed and to subordinate themselves to Levi's descendants. (The exaltation of the Levitical priesthood suggests that the Testaments have a priestly source.) He also notes that his tribe will produce a messianic king but that he will be secondary to the priestly Anointed One.

5. Isaachar promotes the values of a pious country-dweller.

6. Zebulun asks his sons to behave charitably.

7. Dan exhorts against wrath and lying.

8. Naphtali advises his progeny to conduct themselves with piety, purity, and kindliness, thus reflecting the harmony of the cosmos. But he also prophesies that Israel will rival Sodom in wickedness until, through Levi and Judah, their God ushers in the New Age.

9. Gad warns against hatred and urges brotherly love.

10. Asher exhorts his heirs to candor and honest dealings with their fellows.

11. Joseph delivers an elaborate oration on chastity.

12. Benjamin, who refuses any longer to be called "ravenous wolf" (Gen. 49:27), recommends uprightness in all things and cites Joseph as a model of godly conduct.

There is much scholarly debate about the origin of this work. Some experts believe that it is fundamentally a Jewish work with Christian interpolations; others believe that it is a Christian work incorporating an older Jewish text; still others maintain that it was composed by the Essenes or the Essene-like community of Qumran, which had many doctrinal similarities to Christianity.

Estimated dates for its various parts range from the second century B.C.E. to the second century C.E.

Biblical critics agree, however, that pseudepigraphal works like the Testaments contain many *haggadic* elements, a term that refers to the Hebrew **haggadah**—stories, legends, or explanatory narrations of the first centuries C.E. that supplement or expand the nonlegal sections of the Pentateuch. Typically, haggadic narratives are imaginative developments of a thought suggested by the Pentateuch, as are the sometimes fanciful additions to Genesis found in the Book of Jubilees and the Testaments. Such commentaries preserve a rich tradition of oral legends that have otherwise been lost.

RECOMMENDED READING

Charles, R. H. "The Testaments of the Twelve Patriarchs, with an Introduction." In *Apocrypha and Pseudepigrapha of the Old Testament,* Vol. 2, pp. 296–367. Oxford: Clarendon Press, 1913.

Charlesworth, James H., ed. *The Old Testament Pseudepigrapha.* Vol. 1, *Apocalyptic Literature and Testaments,* pp. 775–828. Garden City, N.Y.: Doubleday, 1983.

Eissfeldt, Otto. *The Old Testament: An Introduction,* pp. 631–636. New York: Harper & Row, 1965. Provides a good review of problems in determining the Jewish or Christian origin and date of the Testaments of the Twelve Patriarchs.

Nickelsburg, George W. E. *Jewish Literature Between the Bible and the Mishnah,* pp. 231–241. Philadelphia: Fortress Press, 1981.

Books of Adam and Eve

KEY TOPICS/THEMES

Imaginative interpretations of postbiblical traditions about the first human beings' Fall from grace, these two works present ideas later incorporated into basic Christian theology, identifying the Edenic serpent with the devil, a rebel angel.

KEY QUESTIONS

What reinterpretations of humanity's alienation from God do these books introduce? What new role does Satan play in humanity's alienation from God?

Jewish and early Christian writers delighted in producing fictional accounts of the first human pair. The haggadic narratives under consideration here, which derive from Hebrew sources but are in their present form Christian works, consist of two supplementary and sometimes contradictory tales: (1) the Life of Adam and Eve (*Vita Adae et Evae*), which survives in a Latin version translated from the Greek, and (2) a parallel Greek narrative that is misnamed the Apocalypse of Moses.

As the following summary will indicate, some elements of the Adam and Eve story are found only in the Life, others only in the Apocalypse, and still others in both. In R. H. Charles's standard edition of the Pseudepigrapha, however, passages from the Life and Apocalypse are interspersed to present a coherent narration. Analogous selections from a Slavonic translation of the Life also are included.

The Life opens with Adam and Eve already expelled from paradise. Unable to find nourishment, they attempt to assuage the Deity's wrath through prayer and penitence. But Eve, who punishes herself by immersing herself in the icy Tigris River, is again deceived by Satan into relinquishing her ascetic task, for which lapse Adam reproaches her (Chs. 1–11).

When Adam complains that Satan persecutes them without reason, the latter replies that Adam was the cause of his expulsion from heaven. According to Satan, after man was created "in God's image," the Deity commanded all the heavenly host to worship this human replica of the divine. Refusing to adore a younger and inferior creature, the devil and those who sided with him were permanently cast out of the celestial abode. By thus observing the biblical prohibition against idolatry and further pursuing the Mosaic Law of retaliation, the devil instigated Adam's deprivation of "joy and luxury" as he himself had been deprived for the man's sake (Chs. 12–17). Unmoved, Adam endures forty days' penance in the Jordan River.

The Life continues with the birth of Cain and **Abel**, the murder of Abel, and the birth of **Seth** and sixty additional children (Chs. 18–24). Adam then tells Seth of an earlier vision in which the Deity had described Adam's coming death (Chs. 25–

29). When Adam is dying, Seth and Eve try to obtain the healing oil from the "tree of mercy," but the archangel Michael orders them back from the gates of paradise and affirms the finality of Adam's death (Chs. 30–44; Apoc. M. 5–14). Eve then gives her version of the Fall (Apoc. M. 15–34), and Adam dies at age 930 (Life 45–48).

After Adam's soul is conveyed to paradise in the third heaven, angels accompany the Deity to earth, where he entombs Adam's body and the hitherto unburied corpse of Abel. Adam and all his progeny are promised a resurrection (Apoc. M. 35–42). Six days later, Eve also dies, praying to be buried in her husband's unknown tomb, after which Michael instructs Seth never to mourn on the Sabbath, which is a holy day symbolic of future life and the New Age (Life 49–51; Apoc. M. 52–53).

Although fanciful, the narrative is a sensitive re-creation by unknown Hellenistic Jews of what the original human couple's life was conceived to be like after the Fall. The Hebrew versions on which the later Christian edition is based may have been composed during the first century C.E., before the Roman destruction of Jerusalem.

QUESTIONS FOR REVIEW

1. Besides apocalypses, what kinds of literature do the Pseudepigrapha contain? During what period of history were they composed?

2. What tradition about the translation of the Septuagint Bible is found in the Letter of Aristeas? How much of this account do you think is reliable?

3. To what category of Jewish literature do the Book of Jubilees and the books of Adam and Eve belong? In what ways do they supplement the canonical accounts in Genesis and Exodus?

QUESTION FOR DISCUSSION AND REFLECTION

What do the books of the Pseudepigrapha contribute toward our knowledge of religious developments during the last few centuries B.C.E.? How do works such as the Book of Jubilees reinterpret older biblical traditions in Genesis and Exodus? How does the Letter of Aristeas show the covenant community coping with changing conditions in the Diaspora?

TERMS AND CONCEPTS TO REMEMBER

Abel   midrash
haggadah   Septuagint
Jubilee   Seth

RECOMMENDED READING

Charles, R. H. "The Books of Adam and Eve, with an Introduction." In *Apocrypha and Pseudepigrapha of the Old Testament*, Vol. 2, pp. 123–154. Oxford: Clarendon Press, 1913.

Charlesworth, James H., ed. *The Old Testament Pseudepigrapha*. Vol. 2, *Expansions of the "Old Testament" and Other Legends, Wisdom and Philosophical Literature, Prayers, Psalms, and Odes, Fragments of Lost Judeo-Hellenistic Works*, pp. 249–295. Garden City, N.Y.: Doubleday, 1984.

CHAPTER 9

Between the Two Testaments

Hellenistic Culture and the Growth of Multiple Judaisms

Key Topics/Themes

The international Greek culture which Alexander's conquests introduced throughout the eastern Mediterranean region forms the background for both the last-written books of the Hebrew Bible and the Apocrypha and for the emergence of Christianity, a Jewish messianic movement that originated in first-century C.E. Palestine. Although Jesus of Nazareth, executed by occupying Roman forces, taught entirely within the context of Palestinian Judaism, his followers quickly spread his message abroad in the Greco-Roman world, where Greek-speaking converts interpreted him in ways that paralleled some previously existing Greek concepts of divinity. The rich diversity of Hellenistic religion and philosophy, which combined Greek ideas with older Near Eastern traditions, produced the dynamic environment in which both mainstream Judaism and early Christianity originated.

KEY QUESTIONS

What major political events and cultural developments shaped the Greco-Roman world of the first century C.E.? Describe the religious and philosophical schools of the Hellenistic era. What different forms of Judaism existed in Jesus' day? How did early Christians revise traditional biblical views of Israel's Messiah?

Political Events

The Maccabean revolt (beginning c. 168 B.C.E.), supported by many of the **hasidim** ("pious ones," loyal to the Mosaic Torah), eventually resulted in the expulsion of the Syrian occupation forces. In 142 B.C.E., an independent Jewish state was established, ruled by a Maccabean dynasty known as the **Hasmoneans**. The sufferings of the hasidim, many of whom were commonly tortured and executed by Antiochus's decree, had significant consequences for some later writers of the Hebrew Bible, as well as for the early Christian community. Antiochus's desecration of the Jerusalem Temple, its rededication by Judas Maccabeus three years later, and the atrocities perpetrated on Torah loyalists, who became models of the faithful martyr—all helped ig-

Box 9.1 Alexander and the Establishment of the Ruler Cult

Besides the dissemination of Greek art, science, philosophy, language, and social organization throughout the known world, Alexander's legacy included a more problematic innovation—the Greco-Roman ruler cult. Regarded as godlike for his masterful leadership and achievement of absolute and undisputed power, in 331 B.C.E. Alexander is said to have received confirmation of his superhuman status from a priest of the god Ammon at Siwa in the Libyan desert. The priest reportedly hailed Alexander, who had just been crowned king of Egypt, as the son of Amon-Ra (the chief Egyptian deity, whom the Greeks identified with Zeus), a conventional form of address traditionally accorded Egypt's pharaohs. Because the oracle of Ammon enjoyed enormous prestige, however, many Greeks, including Alexander himself, seem to have taken the priest's words more literally, indicating the conqueror's divine nature and justifying the establishment of a cult in his honor.

Alexander's successors, particularly the Ptolemaic and Seleucid dynasties, also found it politically useful to elicit divine honors from their subjects. Many Hellenistic cities vied with one another in acknowledging the king as their divinely empowered benefactor, offering sacrifices and practicing other rites modeled on those granted the Olympian gods. Although many Greeks opposed treating human beings as if they were gods, the practice was widely accepted and eventually adopted by the Romans.

By the fourth century B.C.E., Romulus, the legendary founder of Rome, was given posthumous deification and identified with a minor Italian deity, Quirinus. After his assassination, the Roman Senate formally declared Julius Caesar (c. 100–44 B.C.E.) henceforth a god, an honor they also granted the emperor Augustus following his death in 14 C.E. Whereas Augustus and other "good" emperors did not accept divine honors during their lifetimes, a few, such as Gaius Caligula and Commodus, demanded to be worshiped while still alive, a requirement that sometimes brought Christians, who held that Christ alone combined the human and divine, into conflict with the state.

As Christian missionaries carried their proclamation of Jesus' death and resurrection to heavenly power from its original, monotheistic context in Judea into the Hellenistic world, they encountered a Greco-Roman audience long familiar with the concept of great persons being posthumously transformed into gods. In his *Metamorphoses of the Gods*, composed at about the turn of the Christian era, Ovid had vividly described the martyred Julius Caesar's soul ascending—like a blazing comet—to celestial glory. Jupiter (Zeus), Ovid states, guaranteed Caesar's entry into heaven "as a god," who will also "have his temples on earth."

Some emperors retained a wry sense of humor about receiving postmortem honors. When, on his deathbed, Vespasian was asked how he felt, he is said to have replied, "I fear I am becoming a god."

---

nite the fires of apocalyptic speculation among Hellenistic Jews. The authors of the Book of Daniel and several New Testament documents, including the Synoptic Gospels and Revelation, are deeply preoccupied with the imminent consummation of human history. (For a discussion of the Maccabean period, with its "great tribulation" for the people of God, review the sections covering the Books of Daniel and 1 and 2 Maccabees in Chapter 8.)

THE ROMAN OCCUPATION OF JUDEA

Weakened by endless wars with neighboring Hellenistic kingdoms, Syria and Palestine were absorbed into the Roman Empire in 63 B.C.E. Led by Pompey, the great military rival of Julius Caesar, Roman legions arrived in Palestine as ostensible peace-keepers, invited there to settle a dynastic dispute between two brothers contending for the Hasmonean throne. John Hyrcanus II appealed to Rome for help in ousting his younger sibling, Aristobulus II, who had made himself both high priest and king. After overthrowing Aristobulus, Pompey installed John Hyrcanus (63–40 B.C.E.) as high priest and ethnarch (provincial governor) over a Jewish state much reduced in size and prestige. The change in title from "king" to "ethnarch" is significant, because after 63 B.C.E., Jewish rulers were mere puppets of Rome, and the Holy Land was merely another province in the empire. (Box 9.1 traces the establishment of the ruler cult of the Roman Empire back to the time of Alexander the Great.)

HEROD "THE GREAT"

After the death of John Hyrcanus, the Roman Senate appointed **Herod**, son of a powerful Idumean (Edomite) governor, king of Judea, a territory he eventually extended to include much of Palestine (Figure 9.1). Although politically successful, Herod's long reign (40–4 B.C.E.) was unpopular with the Jews. Only half-Jewish himself, Herod tried to win his subjects' favor with an elaborate building program that transformed Jerusalem into one of the showplaces of the eastern Roman Empire. His most famous project, an extensive reconstruction of the Jerusalem Temple, was completed only a few years before the Roman armies destroyed it in 70 C.E. (Figures 9.2 and 9.3). An unstable mixture of shrewdness, suspicion, and savagery, King Herod ended his reign in paranoid homicide, executing three sons and his favorite wife, the Hasmonean Mariamne. His tyrannic behavior and violent reaction toward any person who might threaten his power forms the historical backdrop to Matthew's story of Herod's slaughtering the children of Bethlehem (Matt. 2:16–17).

On Herod's death, his kingdom was divided among his three surviving sons. **Herod Archelaus**, who received Judea, Idumea, and Samaria (4 B.C.E.– 6 C.E.), was a despot whom the emperor **Augustus** banished to Gaul, following which Archelaus's territory was administered by a Roman prefect or procurator who was directly responsible to the emperor (Figure 9.4). **Herod Antipas**, the second son, ruled Galilee and Perea (4 B.C.E.–39 C.E.), an area east of the Jordan River. An inept and unpopular leader, Antipas—whom Jesus styled "that fox"— ordered John the Baptist beheaded and, according to Luke's Gospel, gave Jesus a private hearing after his arrest (Luke 23:6–12). Whereas Antipas is the Herod mentioned most often in the New Testament, Herod's third son, **Herod Philip II**, was apparently the most able, reigning over the region northeast of Galilee (4 B.C.E.–34 C.E.) without notoriety.

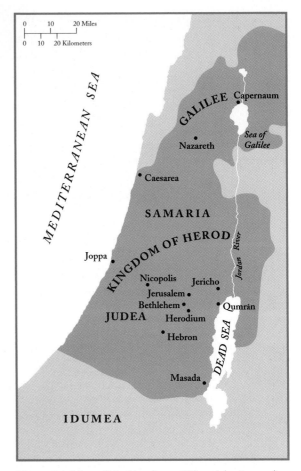

Figure 9.1 Map of the kingdom of Herod (c. 4 B.C.E.).

THE JEWISH WAR
AGAINST ROME (66–73 C.E.)

A grandson of Herod the Great and a favorite of the emperor Claudius, **Herod Agrippa I** (reigned 41–44 C.E.) briefly reunited Palestine but met an early death (Acts 12:20–23). His son, Herod Agrippa II, the last of the Herodian line to hold a kingdom, later was made ruler of Philip's former territory, as well as parts of Galilee and Perea. Notorious for a long-lived incestuous affair with his sister Bernice, Herod Agrippa II reportedly interrogated Paul when he was imprisoned at Caesarea (Acts 25:13–26:32). When tensions between Rome and its Jewish subjects culminated in the Jewish Revolt (60–73 C.E.), Agrippa remained

Figure 9.2 King Herod I's extensive renovations of the Jerusalem Temple, begun about 20 B.C.E., had been completed only a few years before the Romans destroyed it in 70 C.E. According to Josephus, the bejeweled curtain veiling the Sanctuary's innermost room, the Holy of Holies, depicted a panorama of heaven. Visible through the main entrance (shown here in a modern scale model), the curtain is said to have been "torn in two from top to bottom" at the moment of Jesus' death (Mark 15:38). In Mark's Gospel, this event corresponds to the heavens being "torn open" at the time of Jesus' baptism (Mark 1:10).

Figure 9.3 In this scale model of Jerusalem (first century C.E.), the simple flat-roofed tenements housing the general population contrast with the monumental public buildings that Herod I (40–4 B.C.E.) erected. The heavily fortified Temple area appears in the top left.

loyal to Rome. In ruthlessly suppressing the rebellion, Roman armies devastated the Judean countryside, slaughtering thousands of Jews. In 70 C.E. Jerusalem was besieged, captured, and demolished (Figure 9.5). At the command of General **Titus**, son of the emperor **Vespasian**, the Temple was razed, ending forever the daily sacrifices prescribed by the Mosaic Torah (Figures 9.6 and 9.7). As Jesus had forewarned, correctly assessing the political trends of his day, not a stone remained upon a stone of the sanctuary where Yahweh had placed his name (Mark 13). A last attempt to recover Jewish freedom in 132–135 C.E. was ruthlessly crushed by the emperor Hadrian, who built a shrine to Jupiter at the site where Herod's magnificent Temple had once stood. As a result of the two failed uprisings against the Roman occupation of Palestine, the Jewish people were dispersed throughout the empire. Almost 1900 years would pass before they again established an autonomous state on the land promised to Abraham's descendants. (Box 9.2 lists the Roman emperors during the period of early Christianity.)

The difficult relations caused by overlapping political jurisdictions in first-century Palestine are well illustrated in the Gospel accounts of Jesus'

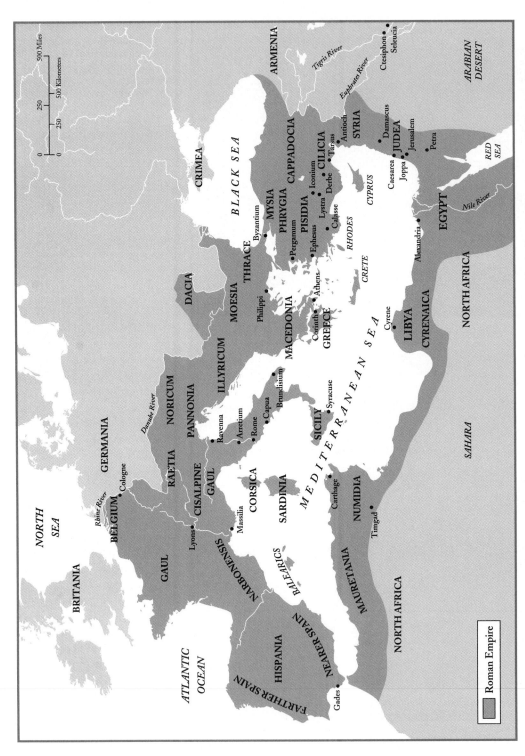

Figure 9.4 Map of the Roman Empire (c. 30 B.C.E.). By the reign of Augustus (30 B.C.E.–14 C.E.), the Roman Empire controlled most of the known world.

Figure 9.6 A shrewd and experienced soldier, Vespasian was dispatched by Nero to quell the Jewish revolt. After Nero's assassination (68 C.E.) and the year of political chaos that followed, the Roman legions declared Vespasian emperor (reigned 69–79 C.E.).

Figure 9.5 This silver shekel was coined about 67 C.E. during the Jewish revolt against Rome. Faith in the city that contains Yahweh's Temple is voiced in the inscription, "Jerusalem the holy."

trials, in which Jewish, Roman, and Herodian authorities compete in handling a delicate religio-political situation. The measure of religious liberty that the Romans accorded Jews was concentrated in the **Sanhedrin**, or Great Council, which was headed by the **Sadducees**. The council, a religious body, allegedly condemned Jesus for blasphemy, but it apparently lacked the legal right to execute him. **Pontius Pilate**, a representative of Rome, quizzed Jesus on his claim to be king of the Jews — a treasonous act against the emperor **Tiberius**. But, finding the accused to be a Galilean, Pilate sent him to Herod Antipas, the ruler of Galilee, who happened to be in Jerusalem at the time. It was Pilate, however, who gave the order to crucify Jesus on the grounds of sedition against Rome (Luke 22:66–23:25).

The historical period during which the canon of the Hebrew Bible was completed and the first books of the New Testament were composed is bracketed by two Jewish wars of independence.

Figure 9.7 The son of Vespasian who captured Jerusalem and ordered its Temple destroyed (70 C.E.), Titus ruled as emperor for only two years (79–81 C.E.). The best-known event of his brief reign was the eruption of Mount Vesuvius that buried Pompeii and Herculaneum (79 C.E.).

RECOMMENDED READING

Boardman, John; Griffin, Jasper; and Murray, Oswyn, eds. *The Oxford History of the Classical World.* New York: Oxford University Press, 1986. A collection of informative essays by leading historians and other scholars.

Boren, H. C. *The Ancient World: An Historical Perspective,* 2nd ed. Englewood Cliffs, N.J.: Prentice-Hall, 1986. A readable history surveying the world from ancient Sumer to the fall of Rome.

Cohen, Shaye J. D. *From the Maccabees to the Mishnah.* Philadelphia: Westminster Press, 1987. Surveys the period of Jewish history that gave rise to Judaism and Christianity.

Green, Peter. *Alexander to Actium: The Historical Evolution of the Hellenistic Age.* Berkeley: University of California Press, 1990. A scholarly examination of classical history from the time of Alexander's conquests to the establishment of the Roman Empire under Augustus.

Josephus, Flavius. *The Jewish War,* rev. ed. Translated by G. A. Williamson. Edited by E. M. Smallwood. New York: Penguin Books, 1981. The most important contemporary source for conditions in Palestine during the first century C.E.

Hellenistic Thought, Culture, and Religion

Hellenistic culture dominated the Western world, including that of Jews and Christians, from the time of Alexander through the reign of Marcus Aurelius in the late second century C.E., a span of 500 years. This period, during which the last books of the Hebrew Bible and the entire New Testament were written, also saw the production of a large body of noncanonical Jewish and Christian literature, most of which was significantly influenced by Greek thought. (See the discussions of Jewish and Christian Apocrypha and Pseudepigrapha, in Chapters 8 and 13.) The Greek passion for learning, intense intellectual curiosity, and confidence in the power of reason and logic to discover truth shaped educational standards throughout the Greco-Roman world. The Greek heritage not only offered a language with a huge vocabulary of scientific, religious, and philosophical terms but also

The first, in which the Maccabean patriots and other Torah loyalists revolted against Greek-Syrian oppression (168–142 B.C.E.), was successful, resulting in the formation of a free Jewish state. The second, in which Palestinian Jews rebelled against Rome—which had almost infinitely larger armies and other resources to draw on than had the Seleucid kings—ended in catastrophe, with the total annihilation of the Jewish political community (66–73 C.E.). The life of Jesus, as well as the writing of the oldest surviving Christian literature—the letters of Paul and the Gospel of Mark—are thus framed by two "great tribulations" for the biblical communities, cataclysmic historical events that shaped the outlook of several biblical writers.

Box 9.2 Roman Emperors of the New Testament Period

The imperial form of government, in which a single man ruled the entire Roman Empire, was established by Augustus a generation before the birth of Jesus and continued until the collapse of the western empire in 476 C.E. Emperors reigning during the rise of early Christianity, and some of the principal events that affected the Christian community, are given here.

THE JULIO-CLAUDIAN DYNASTY

Augustus (30 B.C.E.–14 C.E.): Establishment of *Pax Romana;* Jesus' birth (c. 6–4 B.C.E.); Jesus' youth in Nazareth, Galilee

Tiberius (14–37 C.E.): John the Baptist's revival campaign; Jesus' ministry in Galilee and Judea; the Crucifixion (c. 30 or 33 C.E.); the conversion of Paul

Gaius (Caligula) (37–41): Threatened installation of the emperor's statue in the Jerusalem Temple; Paul's early missionary journeys

Claudius (41–54): Expulsion of some Jews from Rome (c. 49)

Nero (54–68): Persecution of Christians in Rome; outbreak of the Jewish War; Vespasian's suppression of the Galilean revolt; executions of James (Jesus' kinsman), Peter, and Paul

THE YEAR OF THE FOUR EMPERORS AND THE FLAVIAN DYNASTY

Galba (68–69); Otho (69); Vitellius (69)

Vespasian (69–79): Destruction of Jerusalem (70) and Masada (73); Mark written

Titus (79–81)

Domitian (81–96): Luke-Acts' positive view of Rome; sporadic persecutions; Revelation's visions of Rome's fall; community of the Beloved Disciple's production of the Fourth Gospel

THE ADOPTIVE AND ANTONINE EMPERORS

Nerva (96–98)

Trajan (98–117): Letter of Pliny the Younger describing the persecution of Christians in Asia Minor

Hadrian (117–138): Second Jewish revolt, led by bar Kochba (132–135); Jews barred from Jerusalem

Antoninus Pius (138–161): Marcion's excommunication in Rome; composition of 2 Peter, the last canonical document written

Marcus Aurelius (161–180)

Commodus (180–192)

---

transmitted an incomparably rich legacy of art, architecture, literature, and speculative thought.

THE GREEK LOVE OF WISDOM

A Greek book that reflects the Hellenistic environment in which it originated, the New Testament also reveals its dual inheritance of Jewish biblical traditions and Greek philosophical concepts. A term meaning "love of wisdom," *philosophy* is an attempt to understand and interpret the nature of reality, including the purpose of human life. At first indistinguishable from primitive science, philosophy began at Miletus in the late seventh century B.C.E. when creative thinkers such as Thales began applying rational analysis to a body of ob-

servable facts. By the fifth century B.C.E., Athens emerged as the intellectual center of the Greek world, home to numerous schools of thought that used the tools of logic to discredit old superstitions and to construct new theories about the universe. Some philosophers, such as the Athenian **Socrates** (c. 469–399 B.C.E.), focused on ethical questions, particularly the mental disciplines by which one could discover and lead the "good life," a life worthy of responsible and intelligent human beings (Figure 9.8).

Greek Philosophy Combining brilliant originality with a delightful sense of humor, Socrates regarded human life as an ongoing quest for truth, a pilgrimage toward the unseen world of spirit

Figure 9.8 Condemned to death for challenging the religious assumptions of his fellow Athenians, Socrates' (c. 469–399 B.C.E.) life in some ways anticipated that of Jesus.

alike—demanding to learn how people could be so sure that their beliefs were valid.

While attracting a small circle of devoted followers, Socrates also irritated many of Athens' most influential citizens, some of whom viewed this "gadfly" and his stinging questions as a threat to conventional morality. Socrates eventually was tried, convicted, and executed for criticizing the ethical inadequacy of his opponents' policies and practices, the only thinker in Athens' long history to be put to death for expressing unpopular ideas.

Many readers find suggestive parallels between the respective careers of Socrates and Jesus, both of whom followed a divine calling, advocated cultivating spiritual values and eschewing the usual goals of a materialistic culture, and paid the supreme penalty for voicing ideas that leaders of their respective communities deemed subversive. Although both men were sages who taught that the ultimate realities were divine powers before whom all people's conduct would be judged posthumously, their cultural differences were perhaps greater than the roughly analogous patterns of their public ministries and martyrs' deaths.

Plato's Profound Influence   The historical situations for Jesus and Socrates are alike in one important respect, however: Neither Socrates nor Jesus left anything in writing. In both cases, their teachings were reconstructed by later writers whose accounts of their subjects' lives may owe as much to editorial interpretation as they do to biographical fact. Socrates' youthful disciple **Plato** (c. 427–347 B.C.E.) made his teacher the hero of a series of philosophical dialogues in which a saintly and impish Socrates always outargues and outwits his opponents (Figure 9.9). Because virtually all of Plato's compositions, which he continued to produce until his death at eighty years of age, feature Socrates as the chief speaker, separating Plato's ideas from those of his master is difficult. New Testament scholars face a similar problem in trying to distinguish Jesus' authentic sayings from the added commentary of the Gospel writers, who wrote between forty and sixty-five years after Jesus' death.

and eternal ideals, the ultimate goal of the human soul trapped in an earthly body. Questioning every belief that his fellow Athenians cherished as "obviously" true, Socrates good-naturedly cross-examined tradesmen, teachers, and politicians

Figure 9.9 Perhaps the most creative and influential thinker of all time, Plato (c. 427–347 B.C.E.) wrote a series of philosophical dialogues in which his mentor, Socrates, debates major ethical and cosmological questions. Plato's celebrated Theory of Ideas, which postulates the existence of a dualistic universe composed of parallel worlds of perishable matter and eternal spirit, underlies the New Testament worldview.

Although he was a philosopher and logician, Plato profoundly influenced the history of Western religion, particularly later beliefs about the immortality of the soul and the effects that decisions made in this life can have on posthumous rewards and punishments. Plato's dualistic view of reality also deeply affected subsequent religious thought. He posited the coexistence of two distinct worlds: one the familiar physical environment of matter and sense impressions and the other an invisible realm of perfect, eternal ideas. In this worldview, our bodies belong to the material sphere and are chained to the physical process of change, decay, and death. Our souls, however, originate in the unseen spirit world and after death return to it for posthumous judgment. Education involves recognizing the superiority of the soul to the body and cultivating those virtues that prepare the soul for its immortal destiny. Hence, the person who truly loves wisdom, the genuine philosopher, will seek the knowledge of eternal truths that make real goodness possible, helping others along the way to realize that ambitions for worldly power or riches are false idols. The wise seek the perfect justice of the unseen world and, with the pure spirits of divinity, find eternal life.

Over the centuries, Plato's ideas were modified and widely disseminated until, in one form or another, they became common knowledge during the Hellenistic era. Some New Testament writers, such as the author of Hebrews, used Platonic concepts to illustrate parallels and correspondences between the spiritual and physical worlds (Heb. 1:1–4, 9:1–14). This book's famous definition of faith is primarily a confession of belief in the reality of the invisible realm (Heb. 11:1–2).

Stoicism   Another Greek philosophy that became extremely popular among the educated classes during Roman times was **Stoicism**. Founded in Athens by Zeno (c. 336–263 B.C.E.), the Stoic school emphasizes the order and moral purpose of the universe. In the Stoic view, reason is the divine principle that gives coherence and meaning to our complex world. Identified as **Logos** (a Greek term for "word," or rational utterance that directs and shapes the universe), this cosmic intelligence unifies the world and makes it intelligible to the human intellect. Human souls are sparks of the divine Logos, which is symbolized by cosmic fire and sometimes associated with a supreme god. In the prologue of John's Gospel, the prehuman Jesus is identified with the Logos, the creative Word of God (John 1:1, 14).

Stoic teaching urges the individual to listen to the divine element within, to discipline both body and mind to attain a state of harmony with nature and the universe. Stoics must practice self-control, learning self-sufficiency and noble indifference to both pleasure and pain. The Stoic ideal is to endure either personal gain or loss with equal serenity, without any show of emotion. When the Apostle Paul discusses self-discipline or the ability to endure want or plenty, he echoes Stoic values that were commonplace in Greco-Roman society (Phil. 4:11–14).

Epicureanism   A strikingly different philosophical outlook appears in the teachings of Epicurus (c. 342–270 B.C.E.). Whereas the Stoics believed in the soul's immortality and a future world of rewards or penalties, **Epicureanism** asserts that everything is completely physical, including the soul, which after death dissolves into nothingness along with the body. The gods may exist, but they have no contact with or interest in humanity. Without a cosmic intelligence to guide them, people must create their own individual purposes in life. A major goal is the avoidance of pain, which means that the shrewd person will avoid public service or politics, where rivalry may destroy one's contentment. Cultivating a private life, the wise forgo merely sensual indulgences that weaken physically and mentally. Applying reason not to discover ultimate truth — which is unattainable — but to live well, the enlightened mind seeks intellectual pleasure because such enjoyments outlast those of the body.

Epicurus's emphasis on the material, perishable nature of both body and soul found support in the philosopher Democritus's atomic theory. Democritus (c. 460–370 B.C.E.) taught that all things are formed of tiny invisible particles called atoms. It is the nature of atoms to move and collide, temporarily forming objects, including sentient ones like animals and humans, and then to disintegrate and reform in other objects elsewhere. Wise or foolish, all persons are mere chance collections of atoms destined to dissolve without a trace. According to the Book of Acts, Paul debated both Epicurean and Stoic philosophers when he introduced Christianity to the Athenians in about 50 C.E. (Acts 17).

Greco-Roman Religion

THE TWELVE OLYMPIANS

In contrast to Jewish monotheism (belief in a single, all-powerful God), Greco-Roman religion was characterized by polytheism (belief in many gods). Although the Greeks and Romans accepted the existence of innumerable deities, the highest gods were only twelve in number. Because they dwelt on Mount Olympus, the loftiest peak in northern Greece, they were known as the Olympians. **Zeus**, whom the Romans called **Jupiter** or Jove, ruled as king of the Olympian gods, all of whom were part of a divine family consisting of Zeus's brothers, sisters, and children. The champion of justice, lawful order, and cosmic harmony, Zeus was a sky-god associated with both daylight and storm, a patriarchal deity who enforced his rule by obliterating opponents with his lightning bolt (Figure 9.10).

Wiser than the older generations of gods whom he had overthrown to assume universal sovereignty, Zeus willingly shared power with the other Olympians, each of whom had a distinctive function or sphere of influence. Zeus's hot-tempered brother Poseidon (the Roman Neptune) was lord of the sea and earthquakes, while his other brother **Hades** (Pluto), known as the "Zeus of the Underworld," presided over a subterranean realm that housed the dead. Representing a sinister aspect of divinity, Hades lent his name to the gloomy kingdom he ruled, a name that New Testament writers also used to designate the soul's posthumous abode (Rev. 20).

Zeus's sister-wife Hera (Juno) was queen of heaven and guardian of marriage and domesticity, his sister Demeter promoted the fertility of earth's soil that yielded life-sustaining grain, and his sister Hestia (Vesta) embodied the fixity and stability of the hearth and home. An important temple to Vesta stood near the Roman forum, where a sacred flame was kept burning, symbol of the eternal city's vital force.

Zeus's eldest child was Athene, goddess of wisdom, who — like a divine thought — had emerged

Figure 9.10 King of the Olympian gods, Zeus is both a personification of natural power and the divine enforcer of justice, lawful order, and cosmic harmony. Like Yahweh, who typically appears amid cloud, thunder, and lightning, Zeus is commonly depicted as a storm god wielding a lightning bolt. Unlike the biblical God, who is eternal, Zeus is the descendant of older generations of gods who ruled the universe before him. This larger-than-life bronze statue dates from the fifth century B.C.E.

fully formed from her father's head. Zeus also fathered Apollo, god of self-discipline, health, manly beauty, prophecy, and the creative arts; and Apollo's twin sister Artemis (Diana), virgin patron of wildlife and the hunt. Zeus's other Olympian children were Hermes (Mercury), messenger of the gods and guide of souls to the Underworld; Ares (Mars), god of war and aggression; Aphrodite, personification of feminine beauty and sexual allure; and Dionysus, god of wine and ecstasy. (When Zeus's son Dionysus ascended to Mount Olympus, Hestia was customarily demoted to keep the total number of resident Olympians at twelve.)

THE HYMN TO ZEUS

Although the Olympian religion has long since been supplanted by Christianity, nonetheless it was once capable of inspiring some worshipers with a deep sense of spiritual feeling. In his "Hymn to Zeus," the Stoic poet Cleanthes shows a profound reverence for the king of heaven, praising him in terms not unlike those found in the biblical psalms.

> O Zeus, most glorious of immortals,
> many-named, almighty and eternal,
> lord of nature who guides all things
> in accordance with law,
> it is fitting that all mortals
> should call upon you,
> *for we are your children.* . . .
> Obedient to your direction
> as it rolls around the earth,
> all the universe submits willingly to your rule.
> Your invincible hands hold nothing less
> than the eternal thunderbolt — two-edged,
>   flaming —
> whose stroke causes all nature to shudder. . . .
> Apart from you, lord, nothing is done on earth,
> in the sacred heights of heaven, or in the sea,
> except those things the wicked do in their folly.
> Indeed, you are able to make wrong things right
> and to create order out of chaos.
> In your sight even worthless things are worthy,
> for you have so fitted together
> all things good and evil
> that supreme Reason reigns forever over all.
>   Translated by Brad Nystrom; emphasis added

Cleanthes' reference to the fatherhood of God — "we are all your children" — expressed the Stoic belief in the universal brotherhood of all humanity. Another Stoic writer, Aratus, who voiced the same idea, is quoted in Acts 17, thus becoming part of Christian Scripture (Acts 17:28).

GODS OFFERING THEIR WORSHIPERS A PERSONAL RELATIONSHIP

By the time Augustus assumed imperial leadership of Rome in the first century B.C.E., the Olympian gods were still honored in the public sacrifices and rituals of the state-supported religion, but to many people, they seemed increasingly remote from ordinary human concerns. Only a few deities associated with the Olympian cult apparently offered a satisfying personal relationship with their worshipers. Two of the most accessible figures were Asclepius and Dionysus, both of whom were born mortal and underwent suffering and death before achieving immortality, experiences that allowed them to bridge the gulf between humanity and divinity.

Asclepius, the most humane and compassionate of Greek heroes, was the mortal son of Apollo and Coronis, daughter of a king in Thessaly (Figure 9.11). Inheriting from his divine father the gift of miraculous healing, Asclepius became the archetypal physician, devoting his abilities to curing the sick and maimed. When his skill became so great that he was able to raise the dead, however, Zeus killed him with a thunderbolt for disrupting the natural order. After attaining posthumous divinity, Asclepius, as the supreme patron of medicine, extended his benevolence throughout the Greco-Roman world. Professional healers, known as the Sons of Asclepius, officiated at hundreds of sanctuaries, such as Epidaurus in Greece, where patients flocked to be relieved of their afflictions. Reports of miraculous cures abounded, causing Asclepius to be hailed as the "savior" and friend of human beings.

People seeking divine help at Asclepius's many shrines commonly underwent treatment that combined faith healing with the practice of scientific medicine. To create a direct relationship with the god, patients usually began their cure by spending several nights sleeping at his temple, during which time Asclepius was said to appear in their dreams, asking questions about their health and giving advice. Attending physicians then prescribed a variety of therapies, ranging from changes in diet and exercise to surgical procedures. Grateful patients commemorated their restoration to health by dedicating inscriptions and plaster replicas of the body parts that the kindly god had healed. Although Asclepius demanded strict ethical behavior of those he helped, he was also acclaimed for welcoming the poor and disadvantaged to his sanctuaries.

Figure 9.11 The son of Apollo and a mortal woman, Asclepius rose from death to posthumous divinity. Known for his wisdom, compassion, and concern for human suffering, Asclepius, the world's first physician, was patron of the healing arts, worshiped throughout the Greco-Roman world. He was said to appear in the dreams of patients who slept overnight in his shrines, advising some about appropriate medical treatment and miraculously curing others.

DIONYSUS OF THEBES AND JESUS OF NAZARETH

Whereas Asclepius's compassionate nature and benevolent works anticipate aspects of Jesus' ministry, the myth of **Dionysus** foreshadows some later Christian theological interpretations of Jesus' cosmic role (Figure 9.12). Although Jesus is a historical figure and Dionysus purely mythological, Dionysus's story contains events and themes, such as his divine parentage, violent death, descent into the Underworld, and subsequent resurrection to immortal life in heaven, where he sits near his fa-

ther's throne, that Christians ultimately made part of Jesus' story (Box 9.3).

Like Asclepius, Heracles, Perseus, and other heroes of the Greco-Roman era, Dionysus has a divine father and human mother. The only Olympian born to a mortal woman, he is also the only major deity to endure rejection, suffering, and death before ascending to heaven to join his immortal parent. The son of Zeus and Semele, a princess of Thebes, Dionysus was known as the "twice-born." Motivated by jealousy of her husband's human mistress, Hera deceived Semele, then pregnant with Dionysus, into compelling Zeus to

Figure 9.12 This mosaic from the island of Delos shows Dionysus, god of wine, intoxication, and emotional freedom, riding a panther, symbol of the god's affinity with savage nature. As patron of Greek drama, he presided over both tragedy and comedy, representing the extremes of suffering and joy in human experience.

reveal himself in his true form. The resulting blaze of lightning incinerated Semele, but Zeus snatched the unborn child from her womb and placed it in his own body, from which the infant Dionysus had a second birth. In one version of the myth, Hera released the Titans, ancient gods whom Zeus had chained in Tartarus (the dark abyss below Hades), who attacked the young Dionysus, dismembered his body, and ate it (see the section "Dionysus and Orphism"). In another tradition, the risen Dionysus descended to the netherworld to retrieve his mother, Semele, and install her on the celestial Olympus. Having experienced an agonizing death and journey to Hades' realm, Dionysus, alone among Olympians, personally knew what it is to suffer and die.

Wine, the Beverage of Communion Between Gods and Humans As the inventor of wine making, Dionysus bestowed upon humanity a beverage that is a two-edged sword: It can liberate people from their cares, temporarily giving them the freedom of

a god, but its potentially negative aftereffects can also deliver a painful reminder of human limitations, the inability to assimilate a divine gift with impunity. Most authors of the Hebrew Bible similarly regard wine as a mixed blessing, overindulgence in which can bring misery but which, in general, represents God's benefaction, one that produces a "merry heart" (Ps. 104:15) and "gives joy to life" (Eccles. 10:19). Sacrificed to Yahweh in Israelite worship (Lev. 23:13; Num. 28:14), wine was also the drink to be served at the future messianic banquet celebrating God's ultimate dominion over the earth (Isa. 25:6).

Long before Jesus linked wine and bread as part of the Christian liturgy (Mark 14:22–25; Luke 22:17–20), the two tokens of divine favor were associated in the Dionysian tradition. In the *Bacchae* (worshipers of Bacchus, another name for Dionysus), the Athenian playwright Euripides (c. 485–406 B.C.E.) has the prophet Tiresias observe that Demeter and Dionysus, respectively, gave humanity two indispensable gifts: grain or bread to sus-

Box 9.3 Parallels Between Dionysus of Thebes and Jesus of Nazareth

Scholars of world religion and mythology detect numerous parallels between the stories of heroes and gods from widely different cultures and periods. Tales of mortal heroes who ultimately become gods characterize the ancient traditions of Egypt, Mesopotamia, India, Greece, and Rome, as well as the native cultures of Mesoamerica and North America. In comparing the common elements found in the world's heroic myths, scholars discern a number of repeated motifs that form a distinctive pattern. Although Jesus is a historical figure and Dionysus a mythic being, their received life stories reveal components of an archetypal pattern, including the hero's birth to a divine parent; his narrow escape from attempts to kill him as an infant; his "missing" formative years; his sudden appearance as a young adult manifesting miraculous gifts; his struggle with evil forces; his return to his place of origin, commonly resulting in rejection; his betrayal, suffering, and death; and his resurrection to divine status, followed by the establishment of a new cult honoring his name.

DIONYSUS	JESUS
Is son of Zeus, king of the Greek gods	Is Son of God (Mark 15:39)
Is son of Semele, a virgin princess of Thebes	Is son of Mary, a virgin of Nazareth (Luke 2)
Survives an attempt by Hera to kill him as an infant	Survives an attempt by King Herod to kill him as an infant (Matt. 2)
Performs miracles to inspire faith in his divinity	Performs healings and other miracles (Mark 1–2)
Battles supernatural evil in the form of the Titans	Resists Satan; exorcizes demons (Mark 1–3; Matt. 4; Luke 4)
Returns to his birthplace, where he is denied and rejected by family and former neighbors	Returns to his hometown, where he is rejected and threatened with death (Mark 6; Luke 4)
Invents wine; promotes his gift to humanity throughout the world	Transforms water into wine (John 2); makes wine the sacred beverage in communion (Mark 14)
Suffers wounding and death at the hands of the Titans	Suffers wounding and crucifixion at the hands of the Romans (Mark 15; John 19)
Descends into the Underworld	Descends into the Underworld (1 Pet. 3:19; 4:6)
Rises to divine immortality, joining his father Zeus on Olympus	Resurrected to glory; reigns in heaven at God's right hand (Phil. 2; Acts 7:55–57)
Evangelizes the world, establishing his universal cult	Directs his followers to evangelize the world (Matt. 28:19–20)
Punishes opponents who denied his divinity	Will return to effect judgment on nonbelievers (Matt. 24–25; Rev. 19–20)

tain life and wine to make life bearable. Tiresias urges his hearers to see in Dionysus's gift of wine a beverage that brings humans into communion with the divine:

> This new God [Dionysus] whom you dismiss,
> no words of mine can attain
> the greatness of his coming power in Greece.
> Young man,
> two are the forces most precious to mankind.
> The first is Demeter, the Goddess.

> She is the Earth — or any name you wish
>   to call her —
> and she sustains humanity with solid food.
> Next comes the son of the virgin, Dionysus,
> bringing the counterpart to bread, wine
> and the blessings of life's flowing juices.
> His blood, the blood of the grape,
> lightens the burden of our mortal misery.
> When, after their daily toils, men drink their fill,
> sleep comes to them, bringing release from all
>   their troubles.

There is no other cure for sorrow. Though himself
   a God,
it is his blood we pour out
   to offer thanks to the Gods. And through him,
we are blessed.

                              Translated by Michael Cacoyannis

Consumed in thanksgiving, and symbolic of the god's shed blood, wine bestows a blessing upon humanity.

Emblematic of divine generosity, bread and wine were tangible evidence of the gods' care for humankind. In this context, the Gospel tradition frames Jesus' public ministry with momentous feasts involving bread and/or wine. In John's Gospel, Jesus' first miraculous act is to change water into vintage wine at a Jewish wedding, a "sign" of his divinity that seems to mimic the wine-making magic of some Dionysian priests. In the Gospels of Mark, Matthew, and Luke (but, strangely, not in John), Jesus hosts a final Passover dinner with his friends at which he announces that the bread he disburses is his "body" and the wine he shares is his "blood" (Mark 14). The next day, Roman soldiers execute him; his wounding and crucifixion represent a form of *sparagmos,* the ritual tearing asunder of a male sacrificial victim, a fate reminiscent of Dionysus's at the hands of the Titans.

In interpreting the theological meaning of Jesus' life to a Greco-Roman audience, New Testament authors did not present their hero as a new version of Dionysus, but nonetheless they told his story in ways that strikingly parallel the Dionysian tradition (see Box 9.3). The Gospel accounts of Jesus' return to Nazareth, the Galilean town where he had grown up, strongly resemble the myth of Dionysus's return to Thebes, his birthplace. In both cases, family and former neighbors fail to recognize the hero's divinity — that he is God's son — and reject him, even threatening him with death (Mark 6:1–6; Luke 4:16–30). In Euripides' *Bacchae,* the unvalued god exacts a fearful revenge on those who are blind to his divine nature, whereas in the Gospel tradition, Jesus emphasizes forgiveness of those who reject and kill him (Luke 23:34). The author of Revelation, however, portrays the glorified Christ as behaving with Dionysian vindictiveness when he returns to punish nonbelievers (Rev. 19–20).

The Mystery Religions

Alongside the public state rituals honoring the principal Olympians, Greco-Roman society also fostered a number of "underground religions" that exerted a wide influence. Known as the **mysteries** (Greek, *mysteria*) because their adherents took oaths never to reveal their secrets, these cults initiated members into the sacred rites of gods who were thought to welcome human devotees, becoming their spiritual guardians and protectors. Because Greco-Roman deities did not demand exclusive devotion, people commonly were initiated into more than one mystery religion, simultaneously cultivating a mystic bond with such diverse gods as Dionysus, Demeter, Persephone, Isis, Osiris, and Mithras. Although scholars question the extent to which these esoteric cults anticipated Christian rites, in some cases participants shared a communal meal in which their god was invisibly present, perhaps allowing them to absorb the divine body into themselves and thus partake of the deity's immortality.

DIONYSUS AND ORPHISM

Although Dionysus was the most widely celebrated Greco-Roman example of the dying and rising god, other cults centered around such figures as Orpheus, a mortal poet and musician whose music delighted both gods and humans, exerting a power to calm even savage beasts. When Orpheus bravely descended into Hades' realm to rescue his deceased wife, Eurydice, he reputedly learned the mysteries of the next world. The poetry later written in Orpheus's name supposedly contained instructions for purifying the soul to attain a happy afterlife and magic formulae that deceased souls could recite to guarantee their safe journey through netherworld darkness. *Orphism,* based on a body of occult literature ascribed to Orpheus, may not have been a unified cult, but its arcane teachings significantly influenced many Greco-Roman ideas about the soul and its fate after death.

Orphic teachers promoted a distinctive version of Dionysus's story that emphasized both the wine god's triumph over death and his intimate connection with human nature. According to Orphic tradition, Dionysus originally was the son of Zeus and Persephone, a daughter of Demeter (goddess of the harvest and fertility) and queen of the Underworld. Because his son combined heavenly power with earth's secret wisdom, Zeus planned to enthrone Dionysus as king of the universe. After the Titans attacked and killed Dionysus, Zeus incinerated them with his lightning bolts. Orphic religion taught that the human race sprang from the Titans' ashes, which accounts for humanity's dual nature: Human beings are rebels against the gods, but they also contain elements of the divine, the flesh of Zeus's son, which the Titans had consumed. Although flawed by destructive impulses (the Titan heritage), humanity is partly redeemed by an inherent spark of divinity (Zeus's son, Dionysus).

Because they house a "god within," humans can be awakened to their divine potential. Through ritual purification and ethical behavior, initiates could, in the next world, eventually share their god's eternal life. The material body (Greek, *soma*), meanwhile, was the soul's prison (*sema*); death was merely the freeing of the soul to attain its ultimate home, the celestial realm.

In Orphic doctrine, the Underworld became a place of regeneration and eventual rebirth, commonly through the soul's reincarnation into new bodies until a state of spiritual purity and salvation was reached.

Because Orphism foreshadows some themes and symbols of Christianity, it is not surprising that early Christian artists commonly used the figure of Orpheus—or even Dionysus—to depict Christ.

MITHRAS AND MITHRAISM

Perhaps the most rigorously organized and politically effective mystery cult in the Roman Empire was that of **Mithras**, which became Rome's official state religion in the third century C.E. Although Mithras, whose name means "covenant," was originally a Persian god embodying the divine power of light, his mysteries did not appear in the Greco-Roman world until the first century C.E. Scholars believe that although *Mithraism* uses names taken from ancient Persian mythology, it developed as a new cult in the West under the influence of Hellenistic astrology. Pictorial carvings decorating the caves in which Mithraic rituals were performed show that Mithras was a solar deity who presided over the stars, planets, and other astronomical features of the celestial zodiac. He is born from a rock on December 25, then calculated as the winter solstice, the crucial turning point of the solar year when hours of daylight begin to lengthen. After his birthplace is visited by shepherds, Mithras goes forth to slay a bull (the zodiacal sign of Taurus), from whose blood and semen new life appears (Figure 9.13).

His sacred myth identifies Mithras with the invisible forces ruling the universe, his sacrifice of the cosmic bull a manifestation of his omnipotence. Although we do not know how Mithras's story relates to the rites practiced in the small underground chambers where men were initiated into his mysteries, the initiation ceremony represented a spiritual rebirth, making the worshiper a soldier of his god, committed to the principles of light and life that Mithras personified. Enormously popular among ordinary soldiers and merchants, Mithraism established sanctuaries in virtually every part of the Roman world, from Britain and Germany to Mesopotamia and Egypt.

Christianity's leading competitor during the first three centuries C.E., Mithraism featured some rituals paralleling those of the church, including baptism, communal meals, and oaths of celibacy. As Christians were figuratively washed in the "blood of the Lamb" (Rev. 7:14), Mithraic initiates were sprinkled and purified with the blood flowing from a sacrificed bull. Despite the fact that it apparently fulfilled its members' emotional and spiritual needs, Mithraism had a fatal flaw: Women could not be admitted to the god's service. When the Christian Church, which baptized women as well as men, overcame its chief rival, however, it retained one of Mithraism's most potent symbols, the natal day of its lord. Because the solstice appropriately signifies the birth of God's Son, "the light of the world" (as well as the rebirth of the Mithraic sun), the church eventually chose Mithras's birthday to celebrate as that of Jesus.

Figure 9.13 Mithras, a god of Persian origin adopted by Roman soldiers and merchants, is shown slaying a sacred bull. During the second and third centuries C.E., the cult of Mithras was Christianity's chief rival throughout the Roman Empire. Men (women were excluded) initiated into the god's mysteries received a cleaning baptism with the blood of a sacrificial animal and participated in a ritual meal.

THE MOTHER GODDESSES

Other mystery religions stress the importance of a female figure, a mother goddess who can offer help in this life and intervene for one in the next world. Demeter, who gave the world grain — the bread of life — and her daughter Persephone were worshiped at Eleusis and elsewhere in the eastern Mediterranean. Originally concerned with agricultural fertility and the cycle of the seasons, the Eleusinian Mysteries developed into a mystical celebration of death and rebirth.

Even more popular in Roman times was **Isis**, an Egyptian mother goddess (Figures 9.14 and 9.15). Representing motherly compassion allied with divine power, Isis was the center of a mystery cult that promised initiates personal help in resolving life's problems, as well as the assurance of a happy existence after death. As an embodiment of creative intelligence and cosmic wisdom, Isis was known as the goddess of "a thousand names," a deity whom the whole world honored in one form or another. Offering the individual worshiper far more comfort than the official state religions of Greece or Rome, the Isis cult found dedicated adherents throughout the Roman Empire.

In his novel *The Golden Ass,* the Roman author Apuleius (second century C.E.) reveals more about the mystical effects of initiation into a mystery cult than any other ancient writer, describing his visionary experience in which the goddess Isis became his personal savior. Like countless others before and after him, Apuleius seems to have undergone a religious awakening that transcended mundane reality and bound him to a beneficent and caring deity who redeemed him from his animal nature, unveiled heavenly secrets, and imparted new meaning to his life.

The myth of Isis involved her male consort **Osiris**, originally a mortal ruler of ancient Egypt. Like Dionysus, Osiris suffered death by being torn to pieces but was restored to new life as god of the Underworld. Osiris owed his postmortem existence to his sister-wife Isis, who had searched throughout the world to find and reassemble the pieces of his dismembered corpse. By Greco-Roman times, the cults of Isis and Osiris, king and judge of the dead, had developed mystical rituals that promised worshipers a posthumous union with the divine.

Figure 9.15 This Greco-Roman mural depicts an African priest of Isis directing a sacrifice to the goddess at her temple in Pompeii, Italy.

Figure 9.14 The most popular mother goddess in the Roman world, Isis, imported from Egypt, was the embodiment of wisdom and maternal concern who offered worshipers both material success and spiritual fulfillment in the afterlife. Her widespread cult anticipated the later veneration of the Virgin Mary.

QUESTIONS FOR REVIEW

1. Summarize the exploits of Alexander and the historical developments that caused the New Testament writers to use the Greek language and employ Greek concepts.

2. Define the term *philosophy,* and summarize Plato's teaching about the immortality of the soul and eternal spirit world.

3. How do the Stoics and Epicureans differ in their views of reality? How did ideas expressed in Cleanthes' *Hymn to Zeus* become part of the New Testament?

4. Identify the major Olympian gods and their principal attributes. In what ways does the Greek myth of Dionysus anticipate elements in Jesus' story? Name some parallels between the two "sons of God" who suffered, died, and attained posthumous immortality.

5. What were the "mystery religions"? What benefits did initiation into the cults of Dionysus, Demeter, Mithras, Isis, and Osiris confer on the worshiper? Enumerate some of the resemblances between some mystery cults, such as that of Mithras, and early Christianity.

QUESTIONS FOR DISCUSSION AND REFLECTION

1. Religion was an important part of life in the Greco-Roman world. How can we explain the parallels between some pre-Christian cults, such as those of Asclepius, Dionysus, and Mithras, and early

Christianity? Why do you suppose the idea of a hero with a divine father and mortal mother, one who underwent pain, death, and a descent into the Underworld, had such appeal to the Hellenistic imagination? Why did humans tend to regard their heroes and saviors as possessing the qualities of both god and man?

2. Discuss the practice of posthumously according divine honors to Greek and Roman rulers. With whom did the custom begin, and how do you think it may have prepared the way for people in the Roman Empire to accept the idea of a crucified Jewish prophet as the resurrected Son of God? Why was it perhaps easier in the Hellenistic world to accept supernatural interventions than it is today?

TERMS AND CONCEPTS TO REMEMBER

Asclepius	Logos
Augustus	Mithras
Dionysus	mysteries
Epicureanism	Osiris
Hades	Plato
hasidim	Pontius Pilate
Hasmoneans	Sadducees
Herod	Sanhedrin
Herod Agrippa I	Socrates
Herod Antipas	Stoicism
Herod Archelaus	Tiberius
Herod Philip II	Titus
Isis	Vespasian
Jupiter	Zeus

RECOMMENDED READING

Boring, M. Eugene; Berger, Klaus; and Colpe, Carsten, *Hellenistic Commentary to the New Testament.* Nashville: Abingdon Press, 1995. An invaluable resource that provides extensive parallels between ideas in the New Testament and concepts appearing in Hellenistic literature.

Burkert, Walter. *Ancient Mystery Cults.* Cambridge, Mass.: Harvard University Press, 1987.

Eusebius. *The History of the Church.* Translated by G. A. Williamson. Baltimore: Penguin Books, 1965. A valuable early history of Christian origins.

Fox, R. L. *Pagans and Christians.* New York: Knopf, 1987. A comprehensive and insightful investigation of Greco-Roman religious life from the second to the fourth centuries C.E.

Grant, F. C., ed. *Hellenistic Religions: The Age of Syncretism.* Indianapolis: Bobbs-Merrill, 1953. A collection of Greco-Roman religious writings.

Hengel, Martin. *Judaism and Hellenism,* Vols. 1 and 2. Philadelphia: Fortress Press, 1974. A thorough and detailed analysis of Hellenistic influences on Jewish thought during the period between the Old and New Testaments.

———. *Jews, Greeks, and Barbarians: Aspects of the Hellenism of Judaism in the Pre-Christian Period.* Philadelphia: Fortress Press, 1980.

Kee, H. C. *The New Testament in Context: Sources and Documents.* Englewood Cliffs, N.J.: Prentice-Hall, 1984. An important collection of Greco-Roman documents containing parallels to New Testament ideas and teachings.

Koester, Helmut. *Introduction to the New Testament.* Vol. 1, History, Culture, and Religion of the Hellenistic Age, 2nd ed. Philadelphia: Fortress Press, 1995. An informative and scholarly study.

Kramer, Ross S., ed. *Maenads, Martyrs, Matrons, Monastics: A Sourcebook on Women's Religion in the Greco-Roman World.* Minneapolis: Fortress Press, 1988.

Martin, Luther H. *Hellenistic Religions: An Introduction.* New York: Oxford University Press, 1987. A solid introduction to the principal Greco-Roman religious movements and cults.

Seltzer, Robert M., ed. *Religions of Antiquity,* 2nd ed. New York: Macmillan, 1989.

Tucan, Robert. *The Cults of the Roman Empire.* Translated by Antonia Nevill. Cambridge, Mass.: Blackwell, 1996. Provides a lucid survey of the major cults and mystery religions that rivaled early Christianity.

The Diverse World of First-Century Judaisms

Probably during the Maccabean period, Judaism fragmented into a variety of religious parties or denominations. In *Wars of the Jews* 2.8, an account of the revolt against Rome, **Flavius Josephus**, the first-century Jewish historian, describes the four major groups, two of which—the Pharisees and the Sadducees—the Gospel writers present as Jesus' leading opponents. In reviewing these four principal groups, however, it should be emphasized that most Jews of Jesus' day did not belong to such parties. Many of them probably admired the Pharisees' erudition and piety but followed no strict party line themselves. Classed as unteachable "sinners" by the orthodox, the people of the land worshiped as best they might (Mark 2:15), and it was to these generally poor and uneducated masses that Jesus directed his message.

THE PHARISEES

Although scholars have estimated that the **Pharisees** (from a word that apparently means "separatists") never had more than about 6000 members, their influence was nevertheless tremendous. According to Josephus (*Antiquities of the Jews* 13.10), so great was their authority that they were able to dictate public opinion on kings, priests, and nearly all religious matters. In New Testament times, they were Judaism's chief interpreters of Scripture, particularly of the Torah.

The Pharisees accepted as binding not only the Pentateuch, the Prophets, and the Writings (the three major divisions of the Hebrew Bible) but also the "oral law." This "tradition of the elders" (Mark 7:3), an extensive and growing body of legalistic interpretation that the rabbis had compiled over many generations, was later codified in the **Mishnah** (that which is learned by repetition). This record, compiled about 200 C.E. by Rabbi Judah ha-Nasi, is the first document of rabbinic Judaism. An informal term meaning "master" or "teacher" in Jesus' day, after the two Jewish wars against Rome, *rabbi* became a title designating scholars ordained or officially recognized as authoritative in their practice and exposition of Jewish law. In time, the Mishnah became the basis of further commentary, resulting in the **Gemara** (completion), which was added to the Mishnah to form the **Talmud** (teaching), an immense compendium of rabbinic scholarship containing about 2.5 million words. Two Talmuds developed, one in Palestine (also known as the Jerusalem Talmud) about 400 C.E. and one in Babylon about 550 C.E. The Babylonian Talmud, in thirty-six tractates or books, became the chief regulator of Jewish religious life.

Although many scholars believe that Pharisaism evolved into the rabbinic Judaism that eventually produced the Talmud—and hence modern Judaism—the rabbinic compilers never refer to themselves as Pharisees and seem to avoid the term. After the Temple's destruction, however, it was Pharasaic emphasis on reapplication of the Torah to the Jewish people's radically changed circumstances that helped make possible the survival of their religion and distinctive way of life.

Hillel and Shammai Two influential Pharisaic leaders whose teachings are remembered in the rabbinic commentaries were Hillel and Shammai, who lived into the first decades of the first century C.E. A famous anecdote illustrates the striking differences in temperament between these two eminent Pharisees. It was said that a **Gentile** persistently besought Shammai, known for his aloof personality and strict interpretation of the Law, to explain the essential meaning of the Law while the Gentile stood on one foot. Appalled that anyone could be simple enough to imagine that the profundities of the Mosaic revelation could be articulated in a single phrase, Shammai sent the Gentile packing. Undaunted, the Gentile then went to Hillel with the same question. Taking the man's inquiry as sincere, Hillel is said to have replied: "Do not do to your neighbor what is hateful to yourself. That is the entire Torah. All the rest is commentary." Although expressed negatively, Hillel's concise summary of the Law's human significance anticipates Jesus' expression of the golden rule (Matt. 7:12).

Despite his remembered disagreements with Pharisees on how the Law should be practiced, Jesus is known to have been on good terms with some of their number, dining at their homes and even benefiting from a friendly warning about a plot on his life (Luke 7:36–50; 13:31–32). Matthew's Gospel depicts Jesus as sharing the Pharisees' view that the Law is eternally binding (Matt. 5:17–19) and that it be interpreted correctly (Matt. 23:2–3). On numerous matters of belief, Jesus and the Pharisees see eye to eye (Mark 11:18–26). Unlike the Sadducees, they believe in a coming judgment day, resurrection of the dead, a future life of rewards and penalties based on deeds in this life, and the existence of angels, demons, and other inhabitants of the invisible world. By devotedly studying the Hebrew Bible and flexibly adapting its principles to the constantly changing situation in which Jews found themselves, the Pharisees depended on neither the possession of the Temple nor the Promised Land to perpetuate the Jewish faith. Some may have been too rigid in their application of the Torah's requirements, perhaps making the Law impossible for the poor or ignorant to keep (Matt. 23:6–23). As a group, however, they pursued a standard of religious commitment and personal righteousness that was virtually unique in the ancient world.

Gamaliel According to the Book of Acts, it was Rabbi **Gamaliel**, a leading first-century Pharisee, who protected the early Jesus movement from excessive repression by the Jerusalem authorities (Acts 5:34–42). Depicted in Acts as the apostle Paul's teacher and an advocate of religious tolerance, Gamaliel is rarely mentioned in the Mishnah, although the document observes that "when he died the glory of the Torah ended." Acts portrays Paul, even after his conversion to Christianity, as remaining proud of his Pharisaic background and appealing for support from his fellow Pharisees when he stood trial before the Jerusalem religious council (Acts 23:6–9; Phil. 3:4–7).

THE ACADEMY OF JAMNIA (YAVNEH)

After Rome's destruction of the Jewish state in 70 C.E., Roman authorities apparently wished to show their goodwill toward prominent Jews who had not advocated violent revolt against the empire. The leading force behind this Roman-endorsed movement to reorganize the postwar Jewish faith was Yohanan ben Zakkai (c. 1–80 C.E.), an eminent Pharisee. According to one tradition, during the Roman siege of Jerusalem, ben Zakkai—who favored a peaceful settlement with Rome—escaped from the city by feigning death and being carried in a coffin outside Jerusalem's walls for burial. Like the historian Josephus, who also went over to the Romans, ben Zakkai won the favor of Vespasian, the general (and later emperor) whom Nero had dispatched to quell the insurrection. Ben Zakkai received Vespasian's permission to travel to Jamnia

(also called Javneh, Jabneh, or Yavneh), a city west of Jerusalem on the Mediterranean coast that had not participated in the Jewish revolt.

At Jamnia, ben Zakkai gathered other Pharisaic teachers together and presided over an already-existing Jewish council there, the *Bet Din* (House of Judgment). During the years following 70 C.E., the pronouncements and interpretations of ben Zakkai and other sages of the **Academy of Jamnia** exercised tremendous influence over Judaism, which thus entered into a new stage of development known as formative Judaism. The Jamnia rabbis successfully confronted the challenge of enabling Judaism to survive without the Temple, an officiating priesthood, or even a homeland. It is said that when ben Zakkai visited the ruins of Jerusalem with another rabbi, his companion lamented the fact that with the Temple gone, their religion had no means of making the atonement sacrifices necessary to cleanse the people from sin. Ben Zakkai reportedly answered that henceforth "deeds of love"—humanitarian service—would replace the old system of animal sacrifice. He then quoted the Scripture in which God declares, "I require mercy, not sacrifice" (Hos. 6:6), a passage that Jesus is also said to have emphasized (Matt. 9:13).

After his retirement or death, ben Zakkai was succeeded by Gamaliel's grandson, Gamaliel the Younger (c. 30–100 C.E.). Along with debating the official contents of the Hebrew Bible, the Jamnia scholars also sought to define the essential requirements—and limits—of Judaism. According to a Talmudic tradition, the benediction against the *Minim* (heretics) was formulated during this period (c. 90 C.E.). Many scholars believe that this interdiction was aimed at the Christians, whose beliefs about Jesus' superiority to Moses, transmitter of God's Torah, increasingly separated them from Jamnia's views of acceptable Judaism. It seems probable that after 85 or 90 C.E. Jewish Christians were sporadically expelled from the **synagogues**, Jewish meeting places for study, prayer, and explication of the Scriptures. This expulsion caused a bitter division between the Christian and Jewish communities. The Gospel of John appears to reflect this exclusion of Jesus' followers (John 9:22, 34), as does the Gospel of Matthew, which vehemently denounces Pharisaic policies while simultaneously commending their general teachings (Matt. 23).

THE SADDUCEES

Because none of their writings survive, we know the Sadducees only through brief references in the New Testament and in secondary sources such as Josephus. Represented as among Jesus' chief opponents, the Sadducees were typically members of the Jewish upper class, wealthy landowning aristocrats who largely controlled the priesthood and the Temple. Their name (Greek *Saddoukaioi*, from the Hebrew *Zaddukim* or *tsaddiqim*) means "righteous ones" and may be descriptive, or it may reflect their claim to be the spiritual heirs of Zadok, the High Priest under David and Solomon (1 Kings 1:26). Because the prophet Ezekiel had stated that only the "sons of Zadok" could "approach Yahweh" in the Temple service (Ezek. 40:46), the Sadducees, the officiating priests at the Jerusalem sanctuary, emphasized their inherited right to this role. High Priests like **Caiaphas** (who condemned Jesus) were apparently always of their number. Along with their opponents the Pharisees, the Sadducees dominated the Great Council (Sanhedrin), Judaism's highest court of religious law.

Although the New Testament and Josephus give us an incomplete picture of the group, the Sadducees seem to have acted as the chief mediators between the Jewish people and the occupying Roman forces. As beneficiaries of the Roman-maintained political order, the Sadducees had the most to lose from civil disorder and typically opposed a Jewish nationalism that might attempt to overthrow the status quo. Their adoption of Hellenistic customs and their friendship with Rome made it possible for them to manipulate some Palestinian political affairs. The Sadducees' determination to preserve the uneasy accommodation with Rome is revealed in their eagerness to get rid of Jesus, whom they apparently regarded as a potential revolutionary and a threat to Judea's political security. Their view that rebellion against Rome would lead to total annihilation of the Jewish nation was vindicated during the Jewish revolt

(66–73 C.E.), when Roman troops decimated Jerusalem and Judea.

As conservative religiously as they were politically, the Sadducees practiced a literal reading of the Torah, rejecting the Pharisees' "oral law" and other interpretations of the biblical text. It is uncertain how much of the Prophets or Writings they accepted, but they did not share Pharisaic beliefs about a coming judgment, resurrection, angels, or demons (Mark 12:18; Acts 23:8). As a group, the Sadducees did not survive the first Christian century. Their close association with Rome; their refusal to accept developing ideas based on the Prophets, the Writings, and the Apocrypha; and their narrow concentration on Temple ritual—all spelled their doom. After the Temple's destruction (70 C.E.), the Sadducees disappeared from history. The Pharisees, emphasizing education and progressive reinterpretation of Scripture, became the leaders in formulating post-70s Judaism.

THE SAMARITANS

Named for the capital city, Samaria, of the ancient Northern Kingdom of Israel, the **Samaritans** were a distinctive Jewish group who occupied the territory lying between Judea and Galilee. Although 2 Kings 17 depicts Samaritans as the descendants of Mesopotamians whom Assyrian conquerors settled in the area during the late eighth century B.C.E.—and therefore not "authentic" Jews—this picture is historically inaccurate. By the time of the Roman occupation of Palestine, Jews in Judea regarded the Samaritans as an alien people who practiced a false version of the Jewish religion.

Whereas Jews worshiped at the Jerusalem Temple on Mount Zion, Samaritans viewed Mount Gerizim, near the ancient Israelite sanctuary of Shechem, as God's approved holy place (John 4:20). When the Hasmonean king John Hyrcanus invaded Samaria in 108 B.C.E., however, he destroyed the Samaritan temple erected on Mount Gerizim. For most observant Jews, the Samaritan branch of Hellenistic Judaism—which recognized the Mosaic Torah, but not the Prophets or other biblical writing, as binding Scripture—was little better than a Gentile cult.

By contrast, New Testament writers generally portray the Samaritans favorably, offering them none of the blistering denunciations they heap upon the Sadducees and Pharisees. The author of Luke-Acts not only shows Jesus conducting a brief ministry in Samaria (Luke 17:11–19) and making a Samaritan the hero of a famous parable (Luke 10:33–36) but also presents Samaria as the first step beyond Judea in the church's worldwide mission (Acts 1:8; 8:1–40). In John's Gospel, after Jesus holds a long discussion with a Samaritan woman about the differences between her people and the Jews of Jerusalem, she perceives that he is the Messiah and, acting as one of his first missionaries, persuades her fellow villagers to become Jesus' disciples (John 4). Some of Jesus' adversaries even label him a Samaritan (John 8:48)!

Although these Gospel anecdotes suggest that early Christianity found a more friendly reception among some Samaritans than among many adherents of mainstream Judaism, most Samaritans did not become Christians. Among the various Jewish parties cited in Josephus and the New Testament, the Samaritans are unique in being the only group — apart from what became rabbinical Judaism — that survives to the present day. A Samaritan community continues to practice its ancient rites at Mount Gerizim, near the modern city of Nablus.

THE ESSENES AND THE DEAD SEA SCROLLS

In 1947 began a series of sensational discoveries that have revolutionized scholars' understanding of Judaism's complexities during the early New Testament period. According to one version of the story, in that year a Bedouin shepherd boy, who had been idly throwing stones into the mouth of a cave near the Dead Sea, heard a sound like shattering pottery. When he climbed into the cave to investigate, he found pottery jars full of ancient manuscripts, now world famous as the **Dead Sea Scrolls**.

Before the young shepherd made his astonishing find, scholars had almost no Jewish literature dating from the centuries immediately before or during the formative period of Christianity. Books of the Hebrew Bible are considerably older than the time of Jesus, and the Mishnah was compiled almost two centuries after Jesus' death. With the unexpected discovery of the Dead Sea Scrolls, however, scholars now have an entire religious library that was composed or transcribed between the mid-second century B.C.E. and late first century C.E. This library not only encompasses the chronological period when Christianity first developed but also originated in a place near the Judean wilderness where John the Baptist held his revival campaign — the locale in which Jesus began his ministry.

Palestinian Roots of Early Christianity   Some scholars recently have proposed that the Dead Sea library represents not one but a variety of Jewish groups, a collective witness to the religious diversity and eschatological interests of first-century Judaisms. A large majority of scholars are convinced, however, that the scrolls were produced by the **Essenes**, an ascetic Jewish sect that flourished in Palestine from about 140 B.C.E. until 68 C.E., when it was destroyed or dispersed by Roman armies (Figure 9.16). First-century Jewish authors, such as **Philo Judaeus** of Alexandria and Josephus, had described some of the Essene beliefs and practices, but only after 1947 did their own extensive writings — found in eleven different caves — gradually become available. When some of the Dead Sea Scrolls were first published in English, a few scholars theorized that the Essene group practiced an early form of Christianity. More recently, some commentators have speculated that the "Teacher of Righteousness" — the sect's founder and early leader — was none other than Jesus of Nazareth or perhaps his brother (kinsman) **James**, who was known as "James the Righteous." Other scholars have claimed that Paul, who rejected Torah-keeping in favor of divine grace, was the "wicked priest" whom the scrolls condemn. One commentator has even assigned the "wicked priest" role to Jesus!

Despite a few extreme — and almost universally repudiated — claims, the scholarly consensus holds that the primary value of the scrolls in studying Christian origins is the evidence they provide for the Palestinian roots of earliest Christianity. Many ideas, terms, and phrases previously thought to

Figure 9.16 An apocalyptic sect that awaited Yahweh's call to battle the Romans, the Essenes maintained a monastic colony at Qumran near the northwest shores of the Dead Sea. After the Essenes had hidden their library—the Dead Sea Scrolls— in nearby caves, the Roman army destroyed Qumran (68 C.E.), the ruins of which have since been excavated.

have arisen in a non-Palestinian Hellenistic environment actually were present in Jesus' homeland during his lifetime. Documents outlining the Essenes' mode of worship, communal meals, purification rites involving immersion in water, and conviction that they alone formed a "New Covenant" community representing true Israel demonstrate abundant parallels to Christian teachings. Rather than prove that the Jesus movement developed out of Essene beliefs, however, the scrolls generally show that a marginal Jewish religious group anticipated a number of Christian practices. Some rituals, such as a shared meal of bread and wine or water baptism of initiates, are not unique to Christianity but are paralleled in earlier Essene rituals, just as Greco-Roman myths about a dying and rising savior deity foreshadow theological interpretations of Jesus' life and death.

Qumran Although many Essenes lived in cities, one particularly rigorous group settled in **Qumran**, located near the northwest corner of the Dead Sea. The Qumran group apparently pursued a monastic existence, renouncing marriage, holding all possessions in common, and unquestioningly obeying their priestly superiors. The Qumran community

may have been founded shortly after the Maccabean revolt when Hasmonean rulers assumed the office of High Priest, a practice the Essenes abhorred as an illegal usurpation that polluted the Temple. Withdrawn from the world in their isolated desert community, the Essenes patiently awaited the arrival of two **Messiahs**—a priestly Messiah descended from **Aaron**, Moses' brother and Israel's first High Priest, and a second "Messiah of Israel," a leader descended from King David. The only Jewish sect known to expect two such leaders, the Essenes may have influenced the author of the New Testament Book of Hebrews, which is unique in presenting the risen Christ as both a Davidic and a high priestly Messiah. Essene interest in **Melchizedek**, a mysterious king-priest mentioned briefly in the books of Genesis and Psalms, is similarly reflected in the Book of Hebrews's comparison of Christ to Melchizedek, the only canonical writing to do so. (See Chapter 13, "Hebrews.")

Contents of the Qumran Library The Dead Sea documents, which the Essenes may have hidden in caves shortly before the Roman armies razed Qumran, are enormously important for biblical

Figure 9.17 This Dead Sea Isaiah Scroll represents the oldest surviving example of a complete book of the Hebrew Bible. Found in a cave near the Essene monastery of Qumran, it is almost 1000 years older than the Masoretic Text.

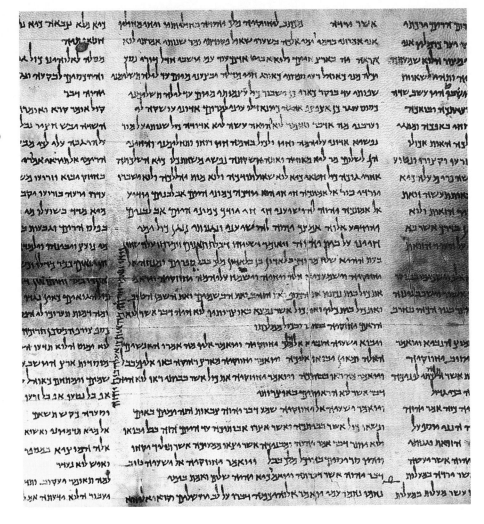

research. First, the manuscripts contain the oldest surviving copies of the Hebrew Bible, some fragments of which date back to the second century B.C.E. The complete scroll of Isaiah, which is perhaps 900 years older than any other previously known Isaiah manuscript, shows few variations from the Hebrew **Masoretic Text (MT)**, the medieval edition of the Hebrew Bible from which most translations are made (Figure 9.17). Other Qumran copies of Scripture differ significantly from the "standard" Masoretic edition. Extensive variations between some of the Qumran biblical texts and later copies of the Hebrew Bible suggest that by the first century C.E., Jewish scholars had not yet adopted a universally recognized version of their sacred writings.

Second, the Qumran scrolls include copies and fragments of apocryphal and pseudepigraphal works, such as Tobit, 1 Enoch, and the Book of Jubilees. Generally written later than the canonical books of the Hebrew Bible, Pseudepigrapha typically are ascribed to eminent figures of the distant past such as Enoch (mentioned in Gen. 5:21–24), who reputedly was carried up to heaven where he witnessed sacred mysteries and then returned to disclose esoteric knowledge to a select few. The presence of 1 Enoch (fragments were also found at the nearby fortress of Masada) interspersed among canonical books indicates that the Essenes may have accepted a larger canon than that eventually promulgated at Jamnia (Yavneh). Whether the Essenes regarded works like Enoch or the Book of Jubilees (a retelling of Genesis and part of Exodus) as part of the Bible is open to question, but numerous fragments of these and similar compositions among the Dead Sea Scrolls reveal that they were carefully preserved and studied. Like the Essenes, some New Testament writers apparently accepted the authority of Enoch, which is quoted verbatim in the Book of Jude. (See Chapter 13.)

Third, some of the most notable documents are Essene commentaries on canonical books, such as those on the prophets Habakkuk, Isaiah, Hosea, and Micah. The Habakkuk commentary is particularly illuminating because it shows that the Essenes used the same methods of interpreting biblical texts later employed by many New Testament writers. Gospel authors such as Matthew regard the Hebrew Bible as a repository of prophetic texts foretelling events fulfilled in his own day among his own community, an approach also adopted by the Habakkuk commentator, who interprets Habakkuk's words as predictions about recent Essene leaders and experiences. Both Essene and New Testament writers characteristically view their own group as God's only loyal worshipers and hence the culmination of the divine plan for humanity.

Finally, besides preserving the earliest extant copies of canonical and noncanonical biblical texts and commentaries typical of Christian **exegesis**, the scrolls include numerous compositions produced entirely by and for the Essene community. Although a minority of scholars argue that the Dead Sea collection represents a cross-section of Hellenistic Jewish beliefs, most still attribute its rule books and eschatological literature to Essene composition. Containing numerous works whose existence had not been previously suspected, this fourth group of scrolls includes the following:

1. A "Manual of Discipline" giving requirements and regulations for life in the Qumran monastery. Also called "The Community Rule," this document features a declaration that all humanity is divided into two mutually exclusive categories: (a) The "children of light" are guided by a "spirit of truth" and are ruled by the "Prince of Light"; (b) by contrast, the "children of falsehood" walk in darkness under an "Angel of Darkness." This truth–error and light–dark dichotomy also typifies the language of John's Gospel.

2. A compendium of messianic rules designating qualities of age, physical condition, ritual purity, and doctrinal orthodoxy for members of the community — especially relevant to Christians for its description of a solemn meal of bread and wine that strikingly resembles Gospel accounts of Jesus' Last Supper.

3. An extensive collection of Essene hymns that probably were sung during Qumran worship services. Because the Essenes rejected the Jerusalem Temple as contaminated by its (to them) illegitimate Sadducean priests, they attempted to duplicate certain rituals and ceremonies in their own settlement.

4. Liturgical fragments containing blessings for the obedient and curses for the wicked.

5. The "Zadokite Document" (a version of which had been discovered in a Cairo synagogue in the 1890s), which outlines the "New Covenant" made in the "land of Damascus" (presumably a code word for the Qumran establishment) under which the Essene group lived.

6. Passages of biblical interpretation on such topics as the Blessing of Jacob, the Admonition of Moses, a prayer attributed to the Babylonian king Nabonidus, an exposition of signs marking the last days, and an anthology of messianic predictions.

7. A scroll entitled the "War of the Sons of Light Against the Sons of Darkness," a surprisingly mundane battle plan for the cosmic war that would culminate in the defeat of the ungodly and the establishment of God's kingdom.

The New Testament is silent on the Essenes, their desert monastery, and their austere lives of pious scholarship. The absence of references to the Essenes may reflect the fact that by the time the Gospels were written the sect had ceased to exist as an identifiable group. Some historians, however, suggest that the Gospels' silence may reflect their authors' consciousness that Jesus and his first disciples may have been influenced by Essene teachings.

Although a few scholars argue that Jesus spent the "lost years" between ages twelve and thirty as a member of the Essene community, the suggestion has not been widely accepted. By contrast, **John the Baptist**—whom the Gospels paint as a desert ascetic condemning Jewish religious and political leadership and preaching a doctrine of repentance before an impending holocaust—seems to echo some of the Essenes' characteristic views. What relationship John might have had to the Essene movement, however, remains conjectural.

THE ZEALOTS

Known for their passionate commitment to Jewish religious and political freedom, the **Zealots** formed a party dedicated to evicting the Romans from Palestine. Opposition to the Roman occupation that began in 63 B.C.E. flared repeatedly during the first century C.E., climaxing in the Jewish War against Rome (66–73 C.E.). In 6 C.E. a Jewish patriot known as **Judas the Galilean** led an armed rebellion that fueled nationalistic hopes but that the Romans crushed easily. **Simon**, one of Jesus' disciples, is called a "zealot" (Luke 6:15; Acts 1:13), and in Acts, a parallel is drawn between Jesus' activity and that of Judas (Acts 5:37–39), causing some historians to suspect that Jesus may also have been involved in some form of rebellion against Rome. Most scholars, however, believe that Simon's designation as a "zealot" probably refers to his zeal or enthusiasm for the Law and that Jesus firmly refused to become involved in any political schemes (Mark 8:33; 10:38–39; Luke 24:21; Acts 1:6).

Although many Jews had fought against foreign oppression since the time of the Maccabees, the Zealots did not constitute an identifiable political party until shortly after the revolt against Rome began in 66 C.E. According to Josephus, the Zealots' blind nationalism forced the Palestinian Jews on a suicidal course. In his history of the Jewish War, Josephus argues that it was the Zealots' refusal to surrender, even after Jerusalem had been captured, and their occupation of the Temple precincts that compelled the Romans to destroy the sanctuary. According to Josephus, General Titus, and Roman commander-in-chief, had not originally intended to commit this desecration (Figure 9.18). This catastrophe and the later bar Kochba rebellion of 132–135 C.E. discredited both the Zealot party and its apocalyptic hope of divine intervention in achieving national liberation. Thanks to the Zealot failures, both armed revolution and end-of-the-world predictions were henceforth repudiated by mainstream Judaism.

The Messiah: First-Century Expectations

Given the vast diversity of first-century Judaisms, we should not expect to find general agreement among different Jewish groups about the nature and function of the Messiah. Many Jews seemingly did not make expectation of a coming Messiah a major part of their religious hope. The Sadducees apparently denied that there would be one, while the Essenes anticipated two separate figures who would, respectively, fill either a priestly or a political role. The Christian view that Jesus of Nazareth was the Messiah was not accepted by mainstream Judaism for a variety of reasons that will become clearer as we study the Gospels. (See Chapter 10.) Among other things, Jews could point to the fact that Jesus did not accomplish what Israel's prophets said the Messiah was commissioned to do: He did not deliver the covenant people from their Gentile enemies, reassemble those scattered in the Diaspora, restore the Davidic kingdom, or establish universal peace (cf. Isa. 9:6–7; 11:7–12:16, etc.). Instead of freeing Jews from their oppressors and thereby fulfilling God's ancient promises—for land, nationhood, kingship, and blessing—Jesus died a "shameful" death, defeated by the very political powers the Messiah was prophesied to overcome.

Figure 9.18 Detail from the Arch of Titus, which the Roman Senate erected in the Forum of Rome about 100 C.E. Created in honor of Titus's victories in the Jewish War, this frieze depicts Roman soldiers carrying off loot from the Jerusalem Temple, including the menorah — the seven-branched candelabrum formerly housed in the sanctuary.

Indeed, the Hebrew prophets did not foresee that Israel's savior would be executed as a common criminal by Gentiles (John 7:12, 27, 31, 40–44), making Jesus' crucifixion a "stumbling block" to scripturally literate Jews (1 Cor. 1:23). To many Jews, the manner of Jesus' death at Roman hands explicitly disqualified him from messianic status. According to Deuteronomy 21,

> When someone is convicted of a crime punishable by death and is executed, and you *hang him on a tree,* his corpse must not remain all night upon the tree; you shall bury him that same day, for *anyone hung on a tree is under God's curse.*
>
> Deut. 21:23, New Revised Standard Version; emphasis added

A literal reading of Deuteronomy indicates that when Jesus was officially condemned and hung on the cross — made from a tree — he was necessarily accursed. Confronted with such texts, Christians reinterpreted them creatively, as offering clues to the *meaning* of Jesus' execution. In Paul's letter to the Galatians, he skillfully turns a potential weakness into a strength, citing Deuteronomy and arguing that, through his crucifixion, Jesus voluntarily accepted the Law's curse. In his "accursed" suffering, Jesus bore the punishment deserved by others, sinners whom the Law had condemned (Gal. 3:13; see Chapter 12).

Although no canonical prophet specifically predicted that the Messiah would die as a criminal (or be resurrected thereafter), several biblical passages speak of an unidentified righteous man who suffers unjustly. The most famous of these occurs in Isaiah 53, which describes an anonymous "servant" whose pain and humiliation are borne for the sake of others. This concept of vicarious suffering — in which an innocent person willingly endures unmerited punishment as a substitute for those who are actually guilty—became an important factor in the Christian interpretation of Jesus' death. In the Hebrew Bible, however, none of these suffering servant texts is directly linked to prophecies about the Messiah.

In Mark's Gospel, which scholars believe was the earliest written, the author reveals his awareness of Jewish objections to Jesus as Messiah by emphasizing the unexpected or "hidden" quality of Jesus' messiahship. Mark also utilizes the notion of vicarious suffering, stating that Jesus generously gave his life "as a ransom for many" (Mark 10:45). Of all the Gospel authors, Matthew makes the most sustained effort to defend Christians' messianic claims, literally ransacking the Septuagint edition for passages, or even single words, that could provide scriptural support for the unusual kind of Messiah that Jesus proved to be (see Chapter 10).

Confronted with challenges that Jesus had not fulfilled many scriptural promises, the early Christian movement sometimes found ingenious ways of refuting criticism. According to a tradition contained in both Matthew and Luke, when Jesus resisted the devil's temptations by quoting from the Hebrew Bible, the devil retaliated in kind, citing verses from Psalm 91. This psalm, which states that the truly righteous person will enjoy God's certain favor, includes categorical assurances that Yahweh will protect his favored one from all physical harm.

> A thousand may fall at your side,
> ten thousand close at hand,
> but you it [misfortune] shall not touch; . . .
> For you the LORD [Yahweh] is a safe retreat;
> you have made the Most High your refuge.
> No disaster shall befall you,
> no calamity shall come upon your house.
> Ps. 91:7, 9–10

God unequivocally promises to deliver the one whose "love is set on me":

> I will lift him beyond danger, for he knows me by
> my name . . .
> I will rescue him and bring him to honor.
> I will satisfy him with long life
> to enjoy the fullness of my salvation.
> Ps. 91:14–16

Dying without "honor" or achievement of "long life," traditional signs of divine approval, Jesus appeared to many not to be the godly person whom the pslamist described. Convinced, however, that Jesus had suffered only temporary defeat and, through his resurrection, attained "the fullness of [God's] salvation," the Gospel authors indicated that it was inappropriate to apply the optimistic guarantees of Psalm 91 to Jesus' experience. If opponents cited such passages as evidence that Jesus (who was not rescued by divine intervention) could not have been God's chosen one, Christians had an effective defense: Quoting Scriptures that do not support their claims is the devil's work!

THE ROYAL COVENANT OF KING DAVID

Because the Gospels are a literary battleground in which the authors are continually fending off attacks on Jesus' messiahship, it is advisable to examine their sources—the Hebrew Bible—to trace the historical evolution of this concept. Derived from the Hebrew word *mashiah*, Messiah means "Anointed One" and refers to the ceremony in which priests anointed (poured oil on) the heads of persons singled out or commissioned by God for some special undertaking. In the Hebrew Bible, *mashiah* is most frequently applied to the kings of ancient Israel, particularly those descended from King David (Pss. 18:50; 89:20, 38, 51; 132:10, 17). Because of his outstanding success in establishing a powerful Israelite state, David was regarded as the prototype of the divinely favored ruler, and his kingdom a foreshadowing of the reign of God on earth. According to 2 Samuel 7, Yahweh concluded an "everlasting covenant" or treaty with David's "house" (dynasty). The covenant terms specified Yahweh's unconditional promise to maintain an unending line of Davidic kings on the throne of Israel. If some of David's royal descendants misbehaved, Yahweh would punish them, but he vowed never to remove them from the throne (2 Sam. 7:8–17; 23:1–5). Perhaps as a result of this "royal covenant theology," David's heirs ruled uninterrupted over the land of Judah for nearly 400 years (961–587 B.C.E.). (By contrast, the northern kingdom of Israel, separated from

Judah in 922 B.C.E., saw many changes of ruling families before its destruction by the Assyrians in 721 B.C.E.)

As described in Chapter 5, David's line of reigning kings came to an abrupt end in 587 B.C.E., when Nebuchadnezzar of Babylon destroyed Jerusalem and removed the last Davidic monarch, Zedekiah, from the throne. When a remnant of Judah's former leadership returned to Jerusalem from Babylon in 538 B.C.E., the Davidic monarchy was not restored. During the centuries that followed, the land of Judah was ruled by a succession of foreign powers—the empires of Persia, Macedonian Greece, Syria, and Rome.

Under Persia's administration of Judah, the first appointed governor was Zerubbabel, a descendant of the Davidic line. Zerubbabel apparently became, the focus of national hopes for a restoration of the Davidic kingdom and was hailed in messianic terms by the prophets Haggai and Zechariah (Hag. 2:20–23; Zech. 2:10; 6:12). Hopes for a renewed Davidic state failed to materialize, however, and the figure of Zerubbabel disappeared from history. Israel was never again to have a Davidic king, the "anointed of God."

During the long years of Persian rule, the Jewish people looked mainly to the spiritual leadership of their High Priest (who was also anointed with holy oil when installed in office [Lev. 4:3, 5]). The High Priest and his many priestly assistants administered the rebuilt Temple and provided a focus of communal religious identity. Without a king or political autonomy, Judah became increasingly a theocratic (God-ruled) community, guided by a priestly class that supervised the Temple sacrifices and interpreted the Mosaic Torah.

ISRAEL'S HOPES FOR A NEW DAVIDIC KING

Israel's collective memory of the Davidic Covenant, however, did not fade. Yahweh's sworn oath that his people would have a Davidic heir to rule them forever (2 Sam. 7; 23:1–5; Ps. 89:19–31) was reinforced by Israel's prophets who envisioned a future golden age when a man like David, "anointed of God," would rise to liberate Israel, defeat its enemies, and help bring God's kingdom to earth.

The prophet Isaiah of Jerusalem, a staunch supporter of the Davidic monarchy, had delivered unforgettable oracles (prophetic words) from Yahweh:

> For a boy has been born for us, a son given to us
>   to bear the symbol of dominion on his
>   shoulder;
> and he shall be called
>   in purpose wonderful, in battle
>   God-like,
>   Father for all time, Prince of peace.
> Great shall the dominion be and boundless the
>   peace
>   bestowed on David's throne and on his
>   kingdom,
>   to establish it and sustain it with justice and
>   righteousness from now and for evermore.
> The zeal of the LORD [Yahweh] of Hosts shall
>   do this.
>
> Isa. 9:6–7

Isaiah's further allusions to a righteous king "from the stock of Jesse [David's father]" (Isa. 11:1–9) and visions of a Davidic Jerusalem to which the Gentile nations would flock (Isa. 2:1–4) not only enhanced the prestige of the Davidic royal family but also associated it irrefutably with the coming earthwide reign of Yahweh.

All of Israel's Davidic kings were literally messiahs, "anointed ones." They ruled as Yahweh's "sons," adopted as such at the time of their consecration or coronation (Ps. 2:7). Because the prophets had conceived of the Messiah as a warrior-king like David, a hero whom Yahweh chose to act as his agent in establishing a dominion of universal peace, the messianic leader typically was regarded as primarily a political figure. His function was to demonstrate the omnipotence of Israel's God by setting up an earthly kingdom whose righteous government would compel the nations' respect for both Yahweh and his chosen people (Isa. 11; Dan. 2:44).

MESSIANIC CLAIMANTS BEFORE AND AFTER JESUS

Judea's troubled relationship with Rome inspired a series of prophets, revolutionaries, and other leaders who typically promised the Jewish people relief from Roman economic and social oppression.

Some rebel leaders reputedly claimed the title of Jewish king, the crime for which Pontius Pilate executed Jesus. Most of those aspiring to royal status did not claim to be a "*son* [descendant] of David" but merely to be "*like* David," a previously obscure youth who was raised from among the common people to become Israel's champion against a foreign military threat. It could be said of these popular national leaders what the psalmist's God said of David: "I have conferred the crown on a hero, and promoted one chosen from my people" (Ps. 89:19).

In his accounts of peasant uprisings against the Romans or their **Herodian** puppets, Josephus reported that several prominent rebels were also messianic pretenders (i.e., they assumed the function of Israel's *anointed kings*). Most of these popular kings appeared either during the turmoil following the death of Herod the Great (4 B.C.E.) or during the greater upheaval of the Jewish War against Rome (66–73 C.E.). After Herod's death, a rebel named Judas, son of a brigand or terrorist named Hezekiah, led Galilee in a revolt against Roman occupational forces. According to Josephus, this Judas was motivated by an ambition to achieve "royal rank" (*Antiquities of the Jews,* 17.271–272).

Another messianic pretender, Simon bar (son of) Giora, led the largest and most powerful force resisting the Roman reconquest of Jerusalem. Josephus states that after Titus's soldiers had captured and demolished the Temple, Simon, arrayed in royal robes, suddenly appeared among the ruins. If he hoped for a last-minute divine intervention to vindicate his kingly aspirations, he was disappointed: The Romans took him as a prisoner to Rome, where he was executed.

The most famous messianic claimant was Simon bar Kochba, who led the second Jewish revolt against Rome in 132–135 C.E. Akiba, a prominent rabbi, proclaimed that bar Kochba fulfilled the promise in Numbers 24:17 that "a star shall go forth from Jacob." Although Rabbi Akiba and other supporters called Simon "bar Kochba," which means "son of the star," his detractors derisively labeled the revolutionary "bar Koziba" (son of the lie). His attempt to liberate Judea and restore a theocratic state was doomed by Roman might, which again annihilated Jewish armies and brought a terrible end to Jewish political messianic hopes.

A REVISIONIST VIEW OF THE MESSIAH

As presented in the Gospels, Jesus of Nazareth takes a view of the Messiah's role and the kingdom of God that was disappointing or perplexing to many. Despite some modern commentators' attempts to associate him with the Zealot or revolutionary party, Jesus (as portrayed by the Evangelists) does not present himself as a military or political savior of Israel. As John's Gospel concludes, Jesus' "kingdom does not belong to this world" (John 18:36).

Many scholars believe that during his lifetime Jesus did not claim to be Israel's Messiah, but that after the experience of his resurrection—regarded as proof of divine vindication—his followers claimed the title for him. In recognizing Jesus as the Messiah, however, Jewish Christians were faced with a dilemma: They were convinced that he was David's predestined heir, the royal figure whom Isaiah and other prophets had foretold, but, as their detractors pointedly observed, he had "failed" in the essential messianic task of reestablishing David's kingdom. The writer of Luke-Acts expresses this tension between Christians' belief in Jesus' authentic messiahship and the seeming incompleteness of his earthly work. Repeatedly, the disciples voice their expectation that Jesus will finally make God's kingdom a reality (Luke 19:11) and that he will "establish once again the sovereignty of Israel" (Acts 1:6). Ordered not to speculate about when or how God's imperial domain will actually arrive, the disciples are instead assigned the task of carrying Jesus' message "to the ends of the earth" (Acts. 1:7–8).

With the fulfillment of biblical promises thus postponed to the indefinite future, Christians soon made an enormous leap of faith: The Messiah will make a second visit to earth to accomplish what was left unfinished at his first coming. Although the Hebrew Bible, the source of both Jewish and Christian messianic ideas, says nothing about the Messiah dividing his work into two separate installments — an initial earthly career that culminates ingloriously in a criminal's death and a second (long-delayed) reappearance as an all-powerful supernatural king — early Christianity readily embraced this belief in a two-part messianic sequence. In the oldest surviving Christian documents, Paul urges his Gentile converts to be prepared for Jesus' imminent return as world judge (1 Thess. 4–5; 1 Cor. 1:7–8; 7:29–31). Paul fully expects to witness Jesus descending in glory from heaven to gather up his loyal followers, who will be "caught up in clouds to meet the Lord in the air" (1 Thess. 4:16–17; cf. 1 Cor. 15:51–55).

For those living in the protracted interval between Jesus' ascension to heaven and his return to earth, New Testament writers emphasize the spiritual significance of Jesus' innovative messiahship. Instead of coming to earth to conquer political enemies and forcibly establish a theocratic monarchy, Jesus is seen as having appeared primarily to conquer less tangible but more formidable foes — human sin, evil, and death. After his sacrificial death, paying the ultimate penalty to redeem humankind, Jesus then ascends to the celestial throne room, standing at God's "right hand" (a position symbolic of his unity with God) (Acts 8:55–56; cf. Rev. 1:11–20, etc.). In thus being portrayed as God's co-regent, an immortal being of cosmic stature, the ascended Jesus becomes infinitely more powerful than a Davidic Messiah, ruling invisibly but eternally over human minds and hearts (Phil. 2:6–11). In Christian reinterpretation, traditional expectations of a renewed Davidic kingdom are transformed into the concept of a heavenly messianic reign, one in which believers — joined by sacrament and spirit — can participate.

The strongly apocalyptic nature of much (not all) New Testament Christianity serves to direct believers toward a culminating future, when the Deity's intentions will be accomplished "on earth, as in heaven," an omega point (ultimate goal) toward which all creation is now moving. The Christian concept of its Messiah is thus a paradox, a God-anointed king who is rejected and killed, but whose voluntary death is a triumph over forces of darkness and an unfailing source of hope for mortal humanity.

QUESTIONS FOR REVIEW

1. What rapidly expanding empire gobbled up the Hellenistic kingdoms of Syria and Egypt during the last centuries B.C.E.? How and when did Judea come under the rule of this new empire?

2. Who was King Herod, and for what great building project is he famous? Identify Herod Antipas and Herod Agrippa I.

3. Describe the two Jewish revolts against Rome (66–73 C.E. and 132–135 C.E.). What were the political consequences to the Jewish people?

4. Define *Hellenistic,* and describe some of the main characteristics of Hellenistic culture. Identify Socrates and Plato, and explain some of their influential ideas. Define Stoicism.

5. What were the "mystery religions"? What benefits did initiation into the cults of Dionysus, Mithras, Isis, or Osiris confer upon the worshiper?

6. Why do historians refer to "multiple Judaisms" when speaking of the period before 70 C.E., when the Romans destroyed the Jewish state? Describe the major groups and their distinctive beliefs, including Pharisees, Sadducees, Samaritans, Essenes, and Zealots.

7. Describe the importance of the Academy at Jamnia (Yavneh) for the development of modern rabbinical Judaism. What was the religious purpose of the Jamnia group?

8. Define the Dead Sea Scrolls. What kinds of documents do they include? When were they written, and when were they found? What is their probable connection to the Essenes?

9. Summarize the concept of the Messiah found in the Hebrew Bible. To what degree is the biblical Messiah a political figure related to the restoration of King David's royal dynasty? In what ways do New Testament writers modify the concept of the Davidic Messiah?

QUESTIONS FOR DISCUSSION AND REFLECTION

1. Discuss some of the beliefs that Pharisees, Essenes, and early Christians held in common. In what ways did their beliefs differ?

2. After the conquests of Alexander, Hellenistic art, philosophy, literature, and customs permeated the

entire Mediterranean world, causing many assimilated peoples to adopt the Greek way of life. Which aspects of Hellenistic culture seem to conflict with the biblical traditions? Why did the hasidim view many Greek ideas as threats to the purity of their ancestral religion?

3. Greek philosophy, particularly Plato's spiritual dualism and concept of the immortal soul, exercised great influence on later religious thought. Do you think that philosophy, with its emphasis on rational method and logical deduction, is inherently incompatible with the concept of a divinely revealed religion such as Judaism or Christianity? Can scientific reason (our Hellenic inheritance) and religious faith (the Hebraic legacy) complement each other? Does the current debate over evolution and creationism represent a continuing split between reason and revelation in the Western psyche? Explain.

4. Historians have discerned many parallels between some Hellenistic mystery cults of savior gods, such as Dionysus, and later Christian beliefs about Jesus of Nazareth. How do you explain the apparent similarities between the older cults and the Christian movement's deification of Jesus? How do common psychological needs shared by adherents of both old and newer religions account for parallels between them?

TERMS AND CONCEPTS TO REMEMBER

Aaron	Masoretic Text (MT)
Academy of Jamnia	Melchizedek
Caiaphas	Messiah
Dead Sea Scrolls	Mishnah
Essenes	Pharisees
exegesis	Philo Judaeus
Flavius Josephus	Qumran
Gamaliel	rabbi
Gemara	Samaritans
Gentile	scroll
Herodian	Simon
James	synagogue
John the Baptist	Talmud
Judas the Galilean	Zealots

RECOMMENDED READING

Charlesworth, James H., ed., *Jesus and the Dead Sea Scrolls.* New York: Doubleday, 1995. A collection of highly readable essays by expert scholars.

Cohen, Shaye J. D. *From the Maccabees to the Mishnah.* Philadelphia: Westminster Press, 1987. A readable survey of evolving Jewish religious ideas that gave birth to both rabbinic Judaism and Christianity.

Cross, Frank M. *Qumran and the History of the Biblical Text.* Cambridge, Mass.: Harvard University Press, 1975.

———. *The Ancient Library of Qumran,* 2nd ed. Grand Rapids, Mich.: Baker, 1980.

Evans, Craig A., and Porter, Stanley E., eds. *Dictionary of New Testament Background.* Downer's Grove, Ill.: InterVarsity Press, 2000. Offers scholarly coverage of major topics relating to study of the New Testament texts.

Finkelstein, Louis. *The Pharisees,* Vols. 1 and 2. Philadelphia: Jewish Publication Society of America, 1962. Provides reliable information.

Gaster, Theodor H. *The Dead Sea Scriptures in English Translation.* Garden City, N.Y.: Doubleday, 1976.

Hengel, Martin. *Judaism and Hellenism,* Vols. 1 and 2. Philadelphia: Fortress Press, 1974. A thorough and detailed analysis of Hellenistic influences on Jewish thought during the centuries preceding the birth of Christianity.

———. *Jews, Greeks, and Barbarians: Aspects of the Hellenism of Judaism in the Pre-Christian Period.* Philadelphia: Fortress Press, 1980.

Horsley, Richard A. "Messianic Movements in Judaism." In D. N. Freedman, ed., *Anchor Bible Dictionary,* Vol. 4, pp. 791–797. New York: Doubleday, 1992. An excellent introduction to political messianic claimants at the time of Jesus.

Horsley, Richard A., and Hanson, John S. *Bandits, Prophets, and Messiahs: Popular Movements at the Time of Jesus.* Minneapolis/Chicago/New York: Winston Press, 1985.

Josephus, Flavius. *Josephus: Complete Works.* Translated by W. Whiston. Grand Rapids, Mich.: Kregel, 1960. A dated translation, but one that contains the complete texts of *The Antiquities of the Jews* and *The Jewish War,* as well as the "Discourse on Hades."

———. *The Jewish War,* rev. ed. Translated by G. A. Williamson. Edited by E. M. Smallwood. New York: Penguin Books, 1981. The most important contemporary source for conditions in Palestine during the first century C.E.

Murphy, Frederick J. *The Religious World of Jesus: An Introduction to Second Temple Palestinian Judaism.* Nashville: Abingdon Press, 1991. A survey of pertinent cultural and religious groups at the time of Jesus.

Neusner, Jacob. *From Politics to Piety: The Emergence of Pharisaic Judaism.* Englewood Cliffs, N.J.: Prentice-Hall, 1973.

Newsome, James D. *Greeks, Romans, Jews: Currents of Culture and Belief in the New Testament World.* Philadelphia: Trinity Press International, 1992. A superbly researched compendium of historical documents relevant to Jewish religious thought and practice during the era of Christianity's inception.

Sanders, E. P. Judaism: *Practice and Belief 63 B.C.E. to 66 C.E.* Harrisburg, Pa.: Trinity Press International, 1992.

Sandmel, Samuel. *Judaism and Christian Beginnings.* New York: Oxford University Press, 1978.

Shanks, Hershel, ed. *Christianity and Rabbinic Judaism.* Washington, D.C.: Biblical Archaeological Society, 1992. A collection of scholarly essays profiling the parallel development of Christianity and formative Judaism.

———. *Understanding the Dead Sea Scrolls.* New York: Random House, 1992. A collection of popular essays from the Biblical Archaeology Review.

Stone, M. E. *Scriptures, Sects, and Visions: A Profile of Judaism from Ezra to the Jewish Revolts.* Philadelphia: Fortress Press, 1980. A readable introduction to the period.

Talmon, Shemaryahu, ed. *Jewish Civilization in the Hellenistic Period.* Philadelphia: Trinity Press International, 1991. A collection of scholarly essays about the fusion of Hebraic and Hellenistic culture that gave birth to rabbinic Judaism and Christianity.

Ulrich, Eugene, and VanderKam, James, eds. *The Community of the Renewed Covenant.* Chicago: University of Notre Dame Press, 1995. A collection of up-to-date scholarly essays on the Dead Sea Scrolls.

Vermes, Geza. *The Dead Sea Scroll in English.* New York: Penguin Books, 1997.

PART TWO

The New Testament
The Christian–Greek Scriptures

CHAPTER 10

The Books of the New Testament
The Gospels

Key Topics/Themes

A collection of twenty-seven Greek documents that early Christians appended to a Greek edition of the Hebrew Bible, the New Testament includes four Gospels, a church history, twenty-one letters, tracts, and sermons, and an apocalypse (a vision of End time). Three of the Gospels — narratives about Jesus' life and teachings — are so similar that they are known as the *Synoptics* (their parallel contents can be "seen together"). The literary relationship between Mark, Matthew, and Luke is known as the Synoptic Problem. By contrast, the Gospel of John not only presents a different order of events in Jesus' ministry, it also depicts Jesus' teachings in an entirely different way; instead of delivering vivid parables about the kingdom of God and offering brief pronouncements about Torah observance, John's Jesus speaks only in long metaphysical discourses about his divine nature.

KEY QUESTIONS

Why do scholars think that Mark was the first canonical Gospel written? In what sense are Mat-

thew and Luke probably expanded editions of Mark? What sources, written or oral, did the Gospel authors use? How does John differ from the Synoptic accounts?

Literary Categories in the New Testament

A Greek anthology of early Christian literature that the church added to the Septuagint edition of Israel's Scriptures, the New Testament roughly parallels the three-part organization of the Hebrew Bible. The four Gospels, which form the first unit of the New Testament, relate the actions and teachings of Jesus, just as the first section of the Hebrew Bible — the Torah — contains material traditionally ascribed to Moses. The second unit, the Book of Acts, is a narrative about the birth and growth of the Christian community, corresponding to the Deuteronomistic History (the Former Prophets) found in Joshua through 2 Kings. The thirteen letters commonly attributed to Paul are analogous to the fifteen prophetic books (the Latter Prophets) of the Tanak. The third section of the New Testament includes a miscellaneous assortment of books—Hebrews, the catholic (general) epistles, and Revelation—and roughly corresponds to the third main division of the Hebrew Bible, the Writings. (See Box 10.1 for an overview of the organization of the Hebrew and Christian-Greek Scriptures.)

The Gospels

A literary category invented by the early Christian community, the Gospels—a term derived from the Greek *evangelion,* meaning "good news"— are vehicles for transforming previously oral preaching about Jesus into the form of his biography. As scholars have learned, however, the **Gospel** authors—the **Evangelists**—do not pursue the same historical goals as modern biographers, who, ideally, attempt to compile an objective, complete, and factually accurate picture of their subject. The

Gospel writers are Christian believers presenting doctrinal confessions of faith in Jesus through biographical narratives (John 20:31).

Despite some important differences, the first three canonical Gospels—Matthew, Mark, and Luke—are strikingly similar. These three have so much material in common that one can arrange their contents in parallel columns and compare their three versions of the same saying or incident in Jesus' life at a single glance (Box 10.2 and Table 10.1). In general, Matthew, Mark, and Luke follow the same order of events in narrating Jesus' public ministry: All three begin with his baptism in the River Jordan, followed by descriptions of his tours through the villages of rural Galilee, where he heals the sick, teaches the crowds, and debates issues of Torah observance with opponents. In all three, Jesus makes only one trip to Jerusalem, where he spends the last week of his life, a momentous few days that the three describe in far greater detail than any other part of his career. Because they present Jesus' biography from essentially the same viewpoint, they are called the **Synoptic Gospels** (seeing the whole together).

Box 10.2 Some Parallels and Differences in the Four Gospels

In studying the Gospels, it is important to let each Gospel writer speak for himself. As scholars have recognized from careful analysis of the texts, each Evangelist arranges his story of Jesus primarily to convey a particular understanding of Jesus' theological significance. By analyzing both the similarities and differences in the four accounts, readers can learn much about an individual writer's characteristic concerns and intentions. Each Gospel author, for example, begins his narrative of Jesus' public ministry with a different episode, one that will express his distinctive themes. In Mark, Jesus' first acts are to drive out a demon (1:23–24) and cure Peter's mother-in-law of a fever (1:29–31), miraculous works that illustrate his power over evil, breaking the devil's hold on humanity and introducing God's kingdom (cf. Mark 1:14–15). In Matthew, Jesus' first public act is to deliver the Sermon on the Mount, demonstrating his authority as a teacher, upholding and reinterpreting the Mosaic Law (Matt. 5:1–7:29). In Luke, Jesus' first action is to preach at the Nazareth synagogue, applying Isaiah's prophecies to himself and outraging his hometown audience by emphasizing God's healing work among non-Jews (Luke 4:16–30), thus foreshadowing the later Christian mission to the Gentiles that the same writer describes in the sequel to his Gospel, the Book of Acts. In John, Jesus' initial task is to transform water into wine at a Jewish wedding in Cana, a joyout event in which his mother takes an active role (and that appears only in John's account [2:1–11]). For the author, the Cana celebration serves to foreshadow Jesus' final action, when,

on the cross, he drinks wine for the last time, the only other occasion in this Gospel at which his mother is also present (John 19:25–30). The beverage of Christian communion, wine also symbolizes the blood that gushes from Jesus' side (John 19:34–37; cf. John 6:53–56, where followers are instructed to consume Jesus' "blood").

Similarly, each Gospel writer utilizes Jesus' last words on the cross to emphasize his concept of Jesus' significance. From Mark's despairing wail, to Luke's accent on forgiveness, to John's serene affirmation of a completed purpose, Jesus' final utterances are made to summarize or illustrate the nature of his messianic role.

Although their narrative structure and content are so similar that many passages can be placed side-by-side for comparison, the three Synoptic Gospels also display significant variations in the way they portray Jesus and his teaching. The Fourth Gospel, that of John, is so different from the other three, in both content and theology, that it has few parallels with the Synoptic accounts. Table 10.1 lists a number of representative topics and episodes from all four Gospels to help readers compare the same incident or saying as the different authors present (or omit) it. Although the Gospels have only one miracle in common—Jesus' feeding of a large crowd with a few loaves and fish—they all provide roughly parallel descriptions of his arrest, trial, and crucifixion, only to part company again with disparate reports on the nature of Jesus' postresurrection appearances.

Table 10.1 Topic Comparison in the Four Gospels

Topic/Episode	Mark	Matthew	Luke	John
Jesus as eternal Word	—	—	—	1:1–14
Word made "flesh"	—	—	—	1:14
Jesus' genealogy	—	1:1–17	3:23–38	—
Birth story	—	1:18–2:23	1:5–2:40	—
John's baptizing work	1:9–11	3:21–24	3:1–21	1:6, 15, 19–28
Temptation by Satan	1:12–13	4:1–11	4:1–14	—
Teaching primarily or "only in parables"	4:1–24	13	8:4–18; 13:18–21	—

(continued)

Box 10.2 *(continued)*

Table 10.1 *(continued)*

TOPIC/EPISODE	MARK	MATTHEW	LUKE	JOHN
Teaching primarily in long, metaphysical discourses				
Conversation with Nicodemus	—	—	—	3:1–21
Conversation with a Samaritan woman	—	—	—	4:1–42
"I am" speeches				
Bread of Life	—	—	—	6:22–66
Good Shepherd	—	—	—	10:1–21
True vine	—	—	—	15:1–17
Farewell discourses (divine nature and return to the Father)	—	—	—	14–17
Exorcisms (casting out demons)	1:23–28; 5:1–20, etc.	8:28–34	8:26–39	—
Feeding multitudes	6:32–44; 8:1–10	14:13–21	9:10–17	6:1–13
Stilling the storm/walking on water	6:45–52	14:22–33	—	6:15–21
Resuscitation of the dead				
Daughter of Jairus	5:35–43	9:18–27	8–56	—
Widow's son	—	—	7:11–17	—
Lazarus	—	—	—	11:1–46
Jerusalem saints	—	27:52–53	—	—
Return to Nazareth	6:1–6	13:54–58	4:1–13	—
Assault on Temple	11:15–19	21:12–17	19:45–48	2:13–27
Prediction of Jerusalem's fall	13	24–25	21	—
Hearing before Jewish authorities	14:53–65	26:57–75	22:54–71	18:13–27
Hearing before Roman governor	15:1–20	27:1–31	23:1–25	18:28–19:16
Crucifixion	15:21–47	27:32–66	23:26–54	19:17–42
Empty tomb	16:1–8	28:1–8	24:1–9	20:1–3
Postresurrection appearances				
In Galilee	—	28:16–20	—	21
In Jerusalem	—	28:9–10	24:13–53	20:10–29

In contrast to the Synoptic Gospels stands the narrative "according to John." The general story is the same—a public ministry of miraculous acts and authoritative teaching followed by rejection and death in Jerusalem—but 90 percent of John's version is unique. Whereas the Synoptics show Jesus making only one final journey to Jerusalem, John depicts Jesus shuttling back and forth between Galilee and Jerusalem throughout his ministry. More important than the geographical and chronological differences, however, is the different way that Jesus speaks in John. In the Synoptics, Jesus teaches largely in **parables** (brief fictional narratives, typically comparing God's kingdom to some familiar object or action) or **aphorisms** (terse, quotable statements that often questioned conventional wisdom). John's Jesus, however, never uses parables of the Synoptic type; instead, he consistently offers long, philosophical discourses in which, not the kingdom, but his own divine nature and relationship to the Father are the principal subject. Because of substantial differences in both teaching form and the theologial content, John's portrayal of Jesus is difficult to reconcile with that in the Synoptics (see the discussion of "John's Gospel" below).

The Gospels and Modern Scholarship

If all four Gospels fully agreed on the sequence of events in Jesus' life and on the precise nature and manner of his teaching, scholars might find their work much easier. Comparative study of the Gospels, however, reveals inconsistencies and problems of historical plausibility that require careful attention. In reading the Gospels vertically (perusing each individually from top to bottom, beginning to end), most people will probably not notice many of the differences they contain. Almost everyone recognizes a few major discrepancies—that John places Jesus' assault on the Temple's moneychangers at the beginning of his ministry, whereas the Synoptics place it at the end—but few readers initially detect the significant differences in the way that Matthew, Mark, and Luke present some of the stories they share, such as Jesus' return to his hometown, Nazareth. When read horizontally, consecutively studying all three Synoptic versions of the Nazareth episode, however, it becomes clear that each Synoptic writer approaches this incident not as an objective reporter of factual events, but as an interpreter of its religious or thematic significance. In Mark, which scholars believe is the earliest version, the author emphasizes his former neighbors' failure to value Jesus, a lack of trust that renders him *unable* to perform the kind of miraculous works he had accomplished elsewhere among strangers (Mark 6:1–6). Matthew tells the story somewhat differently, avoiding any implication that Jesus may

have had limited powers and stating merely that Jesus "did not work many miracles there" (Matt. 13:54–58; see Box 10.11 for an analysis of specific differences between Mark and Matthew).

In the Third Gospel, Luke shifts the Nazareth episode from the middle to the beginning of Jesus' ministry, using it thematically to foreshadow both Jesus' later rejection in Jerusalem and the mission to the Gentiles that the same author describes in his sequel, the Book of Acts. In the Lucan account, Jesus outrages the local populace by highlighting stories about the prophets Elijah and Elisha performing miracles for non-Jews, an implied insult to Israel that triggers an attempt to kill him (elements of the Nazareth story found only in Luke) (Luke 4:16–30; see Box 10.13 for a discussion of Luke's distinctive handling of the Nazareth tradition).

In undertaking a systematic study of the Gospel, it is helpful to start by examining what the Gospel authors themselves say about how they approach the subject of Jesus' life and their specific purposes in writing. Luke is the only Gospel writer to offer an explicit statement about his authorial intentions and methodology. In a formal preface to his account, Luke makes clear that he did not personally know Jesus and that his work depends entirely on secondary sources, including oral traditions and previously existing Gospels:

> The author of Theophilus: Many writers have undertaken to draw up an account of the events that have happened among us, following the traditions handed down to us by the original eyewitnesses and servants of the Gospel. And so I in my turn, your Excellency, as one who has gone over the whole course of these events in detail, have decided to write a connected narrative for you, so as to give you authentic knowledge about the matters of which you have been informed.
>
> Luke 1:1–4

Although brief, Luke's introduction outlines the general procedures he followed in compiling a Gospel that built on the work of his predecessors. Acknowledging that "many writers" had already preceded him in documenting Christian origins—the "events" that had occurred "among us" (the Christian community)—Luke also makes clear that he stands some chronological distance from

Table 10.2 Major Events in New Testament History

Approximate Date	Event	Biblical Source
332 B.C.E.	Alexander the Great of Macedonia includes Palestine in his empire.	1 Macc. 1:1–5
323–197 B.C.E.	The Ptolemys of Egypt rule Palestine (Hellenistic period).	1 Macc. 1:6–10
197–142 B.C.E.	The Seleucid dynasty of Syria rules Palestine.	2 Macc. 4
167–164 B.C.E.	Antiochus IV attempts to force Hellenistic religion on the Jews and pollutes the Temple.	1 Macc. 1:10–67
164 B.C.E.	The Maccabean revolt is successful; the Temple is cleansed and rededicated.	1 Macc. 2–6; 2 Macc. 8–10; Dan 7:25, 8:14, 9:27, 12:7
142–63 B.C.E.	The Jews expel the Seleucids; Judea becomes an independent kingdom under the Hasmonean dynasty.	1 Macc.
63 B.C.E.	General Pompey makes Palestine part of the Roman Empire and partitions Judea.	
40–4 B.C.E.	Herod the Great rules as Roman-appointed king of Judea; he rebuilds the Temple.	
30 B.C.E–14 C.E.	Augustus Caesar rules as emperor of Rome.	
6–4 B.C.E.	Birth of Jesus.	Matt. 2; Luke 2
4 B.C.E.–39 C.E.	Herod Antipas rules as tetrarch of Galilee.	Luke 13:31–32; Mark 6:14–29
5–10 C.E.	Birth of Saul at Tarsus (the apostle Paul).	
14–37 C.E.	Tiberius Caesar rules as emperor of Rome.	Luke 3:1
26–36 C.E.	Pontius Pilate serves as procurator of Judea.	
27–29 C.E. (?)	The ministry of John the Baptist.	Mark 1:2–11, 6:17–29; John 1:19–36, 3:22–36
27–30 or 29–33 C.E. (?)	The ministry of Jesus.	Matt., Mark, Luke, John
30–33 C.E.	The crucifixion and resurrection of Jesus.	Matt., Mark, Luke, John
33–35 C.E.	The conversion of the apostle Paul.	Acts 9:1–19, 22:1–21, 26:1–23; Gal. 1:11–16
41–44 C.E.	Herod Agrippa I is king of Judea; he imprisons Peter and beheads James and possibly John as well (44 C.E.?)	Acts 12
41–54 C.E.	Claudius reigns as emperor of Rome; he banishes the Jews from Rome (49 C.E.?).	Acts 18:2
47–56 C.E.	Paul conducts missionary tours among the Gentiles.	
49 C.E.	Paul attends the first church council held in Jerusalem.	Acts 15; Gal. 2
50 C.E.	Paul writes 1 and 2 Thessalonians; the "Sayings" of Jesus are compiled (?).	

the developments he describes. Living perhaps two or three generations after the "original eyewitnesses" and other (later?) "servants of the Gospel," he must use the techniques of a researcher, investigating "in detail" the "whole course" of the Jesus movement. His goal is to create "connected narrative" (according to accepted Hellenistic literary standards) so that his readers can recieve "authentic knowledge" to take the place of the oral teachings on which they had formerly depended. (For a summary of major events in New Testament history, see Table 10.2.)

To understand Luke's intent in adding yet another Gospel to those already in existence, it is important to recognize that he was also the only Evangelist to compose an account of the early church, to follow a life of Jesus with a narrative about what Jesus' disciples accomplished after their

Table 10.2 (continued)

Approximate Date	Event	Biblical Source
54–62 c.e.	Paul writes a series of letters to various churches he had founded or visited.	1 Cor. (54–55 c.e.); 2 Cor. (55–56 c.e.); Gal. (56 c.e.); Rom. (56–57 c.e.); Col. (61 c.e.?); Philem. (61 c.e.); Phil. (62 c.e.)
54–68 c.e.	Nero reigns as emperor of Rome.	
60–62 or 63 c.e.	Paul under house arrest in Rome.	
62 c.e.	James, brother of Jesus, is martyred.	
64 c.e.	Rome is burned, and Christians are persecuted.	
66–70 c.e.	Gospel of Mark is written.	
66–73	**Jewish Revolt Against Rome; Destruction of Jerusalem and Temple**	
69–79 c.e.	Vespasian reigns as emperor of Rome.	
79–81 c.e.	Titus, conqueror of Jerusalem, is emperor.	
80–85 c.e.	Gospel of Matthew is written.	
80–90 c.e.	Gospel of Luke and Acts are written.	
80–100 c.e.	Letter of James is written.	
81–96 c.e.	Domitian is emperor; Christians in Asia Minor experience general hostility.	
85–90 c.e.	Book of Hebrews is written.	
90 c.e. (?)	Letter to the Ephesians is written; Paul's letters are collected (?).	
90–91 c.e.	Rabbis hold council at Jamnia; the third part of the Hebrew Bible — the Writings — is defined.	
90–100 c.e.	1 Clement is written; Gospel of John is composed.	
95–100 c.e.	Various Jewish and Christian apocalypses are composed: 2 Esdras, Revelation, and 3 Baruch.	
98–117 c.e.	Trajan reigns as emperor and persecutes the Christians.	
100–110 c.e.	Letters of 1, 2, and 3 John are written.	
100–140 c.e.	The Didache, Shepherd of Hermas, and Epistle of Ignatius are written; canonical New Testament books of 1 and 2 Timothy, Titus, 1 Peter, and Jude also appear.	
117–138 c.e.	Hadrian is emperor.	
132–135 c.e.	The Jews revolt against Rome for the last time.	
150 c.e. (?)	2 Peter is written.	

The Revolt against Rome marks the end of both the Jewish state and the original apostolic church.

Master's death. Aware that Christianity had undergone enormous changes during its first few decades — growing from an exclusively Palestinian Jewish movement to a largely Gentile faith in the Greco-Roman world — Luke felt the necessity of retelling Jesus' story in the light of its subsequent impact among non-Jews. Composing Luke-Acts as a literary unit, the author then portrays Jesus' ministry as anticipating the missionary activities of the later church, a literary agenda that helps to explain the way in which he revises the tradition of Jesus' return to Nazareth to make it a foreshadowing of the church's Gentile mission (see Chapter 12).

Although they do not include comparable statements of methodology, the other Gospels also draw on previously existing oral traditions and a variety of written documents (see "The Two-Document

Theory," on page 396). As we will discover in analyzing the individual Gospel accounts, the Evangelists not only tapped a large reservoir of traditions about Jesus but also carefully selected among this diverse material to create distinctive literary portraits of Jesus that expressed their individual community's understanding of Jesus' theological significance.

The Gospel of John contains several statements about authorial purpose and selective use of the Jesus tradition that are probably representative of the other Evangelists' accounts as well. Appended by a later editor, a note at the end of John's Gospel states (with some rhetorical exaggeration) that the author chose to utilize only a relatively small portion of materials available to him:

> There is much else that Jesus did [that is not included in the Gospel]. If it were all to be recorded in detail, I suppose that the whole world could not hold the books that would be written.
>
> John 21:25; cf. 20:30

As John's author makes clear, his standard for deciding what materials to include does not primarily involve goals of historical accuracy or biographical completeness. Acknowledging that there existed other information about Jesus that was "not recorded in this book," John adds that

> those [deeds of Jesus] here written have been recorded in order that you may hold the faith that Jesus is the Christ, the Son of God, and that through this faith you may possess life by his name.
>
> John 20:31

The author's purpose in writing is thus explicitly theological: to inspire life-giving faith in his readers. John's theological goals undoubtedly are shared by all the Gospel authors, who were convinced that Jesus was not an ordinary figure of history, but a person of supernatural abilities whose teachings and sacrificial death had the power to confer salvation and immortality on those who believed in him. For the Evangelists, it may have seemed irrelevant to try to present Jesus as a modern, post-Enlightenment biographer would do today, using strict criteria of historical accuracy and rational skepticism. In the early Christian view, it was far more important to portray Jesus as their faith re-

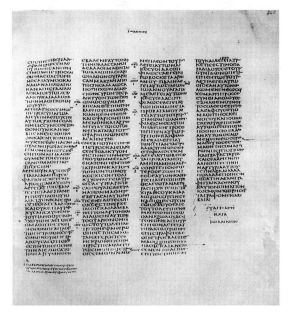

Figure 10.1 Christians pioneered the use of the **codex**, manuscript pages bound together like a modern book. This Greek text from the Gospel of John contrasts with older copies of New Testament books, which typically survive in only fragmentary form. After Constantine recognized Christianity as a legal religion in the early fourth century C.E., New Testament manuscripts increased in number and quality.

vealed him to be, God's instrument of humanity's redemption.

Because the Evangelists were committed believers in Jesus' divine Sonship and saw their writing tasks as more theological than historical, it is particularly difficult for scholars analyzing the Gospels to separate what may be authentic memories of Jesus' words and actions from later theological interpretation (and embellishment) of them. The challenge of distinguishing the historical Jesus from the Christ of faith is compounded by the fact that the Gospels tend to portray the living man in the light of his postresurrection splendor. This tendency is most pronounced in John, the Gospel that makes the most extensive claims for Jesus' divinity (Figure 10.1).

In a speech appearing only in John, the author emphasizes the role of the Paraclete (a term variously translated as "Advocate," "Helper," or "Comforter"), the divinely-sent Spirit that guides John's religious community after Jesus' departure. According to John, Jesus promised the disciples that after his death "the Holy Spirit will teach you everything, and will call to mind all that I have told you" (John 14:26). In other words, only after the Crucifixion and Jesus' ascension to heaven would his followers, in retrospect, be able to comprehend the meaning of his life and deeds. The author of John's Gospel therefore portrayed the earthly Jesus in radiant colors that reflected his community's understanding of Jesus' celestial "glory," presenting him with the attributes of the cosmic Christ. Although the extent to which John depicts the mortal Jesus as already manifesting divinity is unique to his Gospel — and accounts for many of his differences from the Synoptic writers — all of the Evangelists interpret Jesus in the light of their communities' postresurrection faith.

The Synoptic Problem

In contrast to John, the three Synoptic Gospels are so similar in content and narrative order that they appear to have a close literary relationship. One of the Synoptic writers must have used at least one of the others as a source. Scholarly attempts to unravel the literary dependence or connection among the three is known as the **Synoptic Problem**. For reasons described here, the overwhelming majority of scholars now believe that Mark was the first Gospel written and that Matthew and Luke, independently of each other, drew on Mark as their basic narrative source.

In analyzing the Synoptic accounts, scholars discovered a number of facts that point to Markan priority. All three Synoptics generally follow the same sequence of events, narrating Jesus' life in suggestively similar fashion. This shared narrative (and some teaching) material is known as the triple tradition. In addition, Matthew and Luke include a large quantity of teaching material that does not appear in Mark but that is remarkably comparable in form. This mysterious double tradition includes some of Jesus' best-known sayings, such as the Lord's Prayer, the golden rule, and the Beatitudes (blessings that Jesus pronounces on the poor, the meek, and the helpless). In many cases, there is almost verbatim agreement on the passages, absent from Mark, that Matthew and Luke share.

In scrutinizing the order of events in the Synoptic triple tradition, scholars also noticed that either Matthew or Luke may sometimes deviate from Mark's order, but almost never do they differ from Mark in the same place and in the same way. When Matthew departs from the Markan order, Luke does not; when Luke disagrees with Mark, Matthew does not. This pattern strongly suggests that Mark is the determining factor in the Synoptics' version of the principal events in Jesus' story, that his Gospel is the basis for other two.

Another factor indicating that Mark is the source for the other two Synoptic Gospels, rather than an abbreviation of them, is the relative amount of space each Evangelist devotes to narrating episodes that the three have in common. If Mark wished to produce a more concise account of Jesus' life by abridging Matthew and Luke, his version of events that all three share should be the shortest, a distillation of the other two. However, the opposite is true. In almost every case, Mark's version of a specific incident is longer than the parallel version in Matthew or Luke. Whereas Mark takes ten verses to narrate Jesus' cure of the woman afflicted with a chronic hemorrhage (Mark 5:25–34), Matthew tells the same story in only three verses (Matt. 9:20–23). Similarly, Matthew reports the raising of Jairus's daughter in seven verses (Matt. 9:18–19, 23–26), while Mark's version is almost twice as long (Mark 5:22–24, 35–43). In this and numerous other instances., Matthew appears to have abridged Mark rather than the other way around.

How, then, can we account for passages in Matthew and Luke that give an expanded account of events merely alluded to in Mark, such as Jesus' temptation in the wilderness? Mark mentions briefly that Jesus was tempted by the devil but provides no details (Mark 1:12–13). Matthew and Luke, however, offer elaborate dramatizations of Jesus' confronting the tempter, using almost identical dialogue (Matt. 4:1–11; Luke 4:1–13). Most

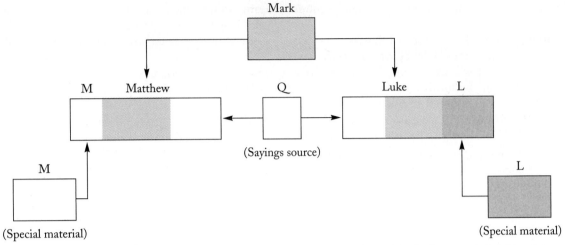

Figure 10.2 This drawing illustrates the two-document theory, an attempt to explain the literary relationship of the three Synoptic Gospels. Note that this theory takes Mark's Gospel as a major source for Matthew and Luke. In addition, both Matthew and Luke incorporate teaching material from Q (*Quelle,* a hypothetical collection of Jesus' sayings). Matthew also uses special material unique to his Gospel, here designated M; Luke similarly includes material found only in his account, here labeled L.

scholars agree that, although Matthew and Luke draw on Mark for a shared narrative sequence, they also incorporate other sources into their much larger Gospels.

THE TWO-DOCUMENT THEORY

Source criticism, the analysis of a document to discover and identify its written sources, has been particularly helpful in resolving the Synoptic Problem. After recognizing that Mark was the source for the chronologic framework in Matthew and Luke, source critics also identified a second major document to account for the extensive teaching material that does not appear in Mark but that Matthew and Luke have in common. According to the two-document theory, Matthew and Luke not only used Mark but also drew on a written collection of Jesus' sayings, including many of his parables. This hypothetical collection is known as the **Q** document (from *Quelle,* the German term for "source") (Figure 10.2).

FROM ORAL PREACHING TO WRITTEN GOSPEL

The Oral Period   In the view of most New Testament scholars, the two-document theory not only most satisfactorily resolves the Synoptic Problem but also allows us to trace several distinct stages of the Gospels' development over time (Box 10.3). The first stage was entirely oral, represented initially by Jesus' spoken teachings and then by his earliest followers' preachings about him. For approximately forty years—between the time of the Crucifixion (c. 30–33 C.E.) and the appearance of Mark (c. 66–70 C.E.)—the Christian *kerygma* (proclamation about Jesus) was almost entirely by word of mouth. Paul's letters were composed during this period (c. 50–62 C.E.), but Paul rarely mentions events in Jesus' life or quotes his teachings. (For exceptions, see Jesus' words of instruction at the Last Supper [1 Cor. 11:23–26] and the received tradition about the postresurrection appearances [1 Cor. 15:3–7].)

Box 10.3 From Oral *Kerygma* to Written Gospel: Hypothetical Stages in the Gospels' Historical Development

New Testament scholars employ a variety of critical methods to discover the processes by which originally oral traditions about Jesus gradually evolved into written form. Historical and literary analysis of the Gospels suggest that they developed over a relatively long period (c. 30–100 C.E.), undergoing several discrete stages of growth. The following list provides a hypothetical reconstruction of events and movements leading to the Gospels' creation.

DATE	EVENT OR DEVELOPMENT

I. Period of Exclusively Oral Traditions

30 C.E.	Oral preaching by Jesus in Galilee, Samaria, and Judea
30–33 C.E.	Crucifixion
30–50 C.E.	Oral preaching about Jesus by Aramaic-speaking disciples in Galilee, Samaria, Judea, and neighboring regions; formation of the first Christian community at Jerusalem, led by Peter, John, and James; formation of additional Aramaic-speaking communities throughout Palestine; development of a second major Christian center at Antioch in Syria
40–60 C.E.	Missionary tours of Paul and associates; establishment of new, larger Gentile, Greek-speaking churches in Asia Minor and Greece

II. Period of Earliest Written Documents

50–70 C.E.	Oldest surviving Christian documents (Paul's letters to Gentile congregations) composed; collection of Jesus' sayings, in Greek (the Q document), compiled; possible collection of Jesus' miraculous works, the Signs Gospel (later incorporated into the Gospel of John); possible first edition of the Gospel of Thomas (like Q, a Sayings Gospel)

III. Jewish Revolt Against Rome and the Appearance of the First Canonical Gospel

66 C.E.	Outbreak of Jewish War
66–70 C.E.	Mark's "wartime" Gospel composed, relating Jesus' suffering to that of his persecuted followers
70 C.E.	Roman destruction of Jerusalem, the Temple, and the original Christian center

IV. Production of New, Enlarged Editions of Mark

80–90 C.E.	Composition of Matthew and Luke, who use Mark and Q as their primary sources (plus their individual special sources, respectively M and L)

V. Production of New Gospels Promoting an Independent (Non-Synoptic) Tradition

90–100 C.E.	Composition of the Gospel of John, incorporating the older Signs Gospel; second edition of the Gospel of Thomas, incorporating the older Thomas sayings collection

The oral *kerygma* began in Judea, Galilee, and adjoining regions where Aramaic was spoken. When Christian missionaries carried their message into Greek-speaking territories, however, important changes had to be made. Not only were Jesus' sayings necessarily translated into *koinē* (common Greek), but they had to be explained, reinterpreted, and applied to urban conditions very different from those in rural Palestine where they originated. Busy merchants in the crowded Hellenistic marketplaces might require an explanation of Jesus' parables, initially designed for poor villagers and peasants in an agricultural economy, that perhaps challenged missionaries' ingenuity. Similarly, Christian preachers themselves eventually needed reinterpretations of some teachings. Jesus' homely parable of the laborer sowing seeds ultimately was transformed into an allegory illustrating Christians' diverse experience as preachers in the Hellenistic world, where they were sometimes welcomed, often rejected, and occasionally persecuted. (See Mark 4, with its elaborate application of the sower parable to conditions in the early church.)

As scholars have learned from studying the growth of oral traditions in different cultures around the globe, transmitting stories orally to new audiences inevitably produces variations in phrasing and emphasis as the speaker adapts the tale to different hearers and situations. Until a tradition is finally fixed in writing, it is characterized by extreme fluidity, changing with each fresh recitation. In the case of Jesus' sayings, which presumably were venerated even at the earliest stages of transmission, Christians probably made every effort to repeat them accurately. Even so, the Gospels contain a wide range of variation in what appear to have been the same sayings. To cite only one example among many, in Mark, Jesus states that "he who is not against us is for us," whereas in Matthew he says the opposite: "He who is not with me is against me, and he who does not gather with me scatters" (cf. Mark 9:40 and Matt. 12:30). To complicate the matter further, Luke preserves both forms of the saying (Luke 7:50; 11:23). The degree of variation in some traditions is so great that the meanings become mutually exclusive, as in the strikingly different versions of the wedding feast parable, which appears in two canonical Gospels, Matthew (22:2–13) and Luke (14:16–23), as well as the apocryphal **Gospel of Thomas** (64).

Divergent oral renditions of Jesus' sayings and parables multiplied in widely separated geographical areas, including important Christian centers at Jerusalem, Antioch in Syria, Ephesus in Asia Minor, and Corinth in Greece. Each center undoubtedly cultivated distinct traditions closely associated with the earliest missionaries, teachers, and prophets in their respective communities.

Given the multiplicity of variations that developed, it is difficult, if not impossible, to recover the original form of a given saying. Inheritors of a complex process of oral transmission, the Gospel writers compiled not necessarily what Jesus exactly said or did, but what the believing community collectively understood to be the tenor of his actions and sayings.

Form Criticism   Recognizing that originally Palestinian oral traditions about Jesus had been modified to accommodate a new, ethnically and religiously diverse Gentile audience, early twentieth-century German scholars began to emphasize the implications of such adaptations. The critical method that attempts to identify the oldest oral forms underlying the Gospels' written texts is called **form criticism** (see Chapter 1). Form critics discovered that the Gospels are made up of many individual units—brief narrative episodes, discrete conflict stories, pronouncements, parables, and sayings—that circulated orally and independently of one another before the Gospel authors assembled them in written form.

Mark's Gospel, for instance, seems to consist of a string of incidents, anecdotes, and sayings that are very loosely connected to one another. The individual units, such as the account of Jesus exorcizing demons or performing miraculous cures, are generally brief, self-contained narrative episodes that have clear-cut beginnings and endings and can stand alone. During the oral period, they were autonomous, existing free of a narrative framework. Jesus' pithy statements comparing God's kingdom to a mustard seed or a priceless pearl, for example, do not depend on the larger Gospel context to convey their message. Such detachable units are called **pericopes**. Derived from the Greek *peri* (about) and *koptein* (to cut), the term denotes the individual, orally transmitted building blocks from which the longer Gospel account is constructed.

The form critic searches for the *Sitz im Leben,* the probable "life-setting" or social circumstances from which stories about Jesus originated and were orally transmitted by the early church. The first Christians spoke about Jesus in many different situations and for many different purposes—preaching to fellow Jews, defending their beliefs to Greek or Roman officials, instructing new converts, settling disputes among themselves, and conducting worship services. By establishing the probable prewritten form of a particular saying or incident, the form critic enables us to see how the Gospel writers edited these previously free-floating units to express their respective views about Jesus.

THE Q (SOURCE) DOCUMENT

At an unknown date, Christians began to make brief compilations of Jesus' sayings, such as the cluster of kingdom parables underlying Mark 4 and Matthew 13. A much more comprehensive written collection of Jesus' teachings, the Q document, is thought to have been assembled between about 50 and 70 C.E. Because it does not survive as a separate document, scholars must reconstruct its contents from passages that Matthew and Luke have in common but that did not derive from Mark (Box 10.4).

These shared passages, totaling about 230 verses, contain some of Jesus' most celebrated teachings, including much of the material in Matthew's Sermon on the Mount (Matt. 5–7) and Luke's parallel Sermon on the Plain (Luke 6). An increasing number of scholars ascribe enormous importance to Q, for this Sayings Gospel, at least in its first edition, may preserve one of the earliest forms of Christianity. It appears to have been written, in Greek, by a community of itinerant preachers living in Galilee or western Syria who regarded Jesus as both prophet and wisdom teacher. Containing virtually no narrative, Q presents Jesus as one "greater than Solomon" (the traditional founder of Israel's wisdom school) who is the last in a long line of God's prophets and sages, a martyr rejected and killed by an unappreciative people. Q thus includes no theology interpreting Jesus' death as a saving act, focusing almost exclusively on the living man's moral exhortations, parables, and spiritual insights. Before being assimilated into Matthew and Luke, Q apparently was a Gospel in its own right, providing the first written witness to Jesus' primary teachings. (A scholarly reconstruction of Q appears in Miller's *The Complete Gospels;*

a detailed analysis of the text is available in Verbin et al.'s *Excavating Q.* See "Recommended Reading.")

Some scholars also posit the existence of another pre-Gospel narrative source, a primitive account of Jesus' miraculous deeds or "signs," that was later incorporated into the Gospel of John (see the section "John's Gospel" later in the chapter). Some also believe that at least parts of the Gospel of Thomas, the only noncanonical Gospel to survive intact, predated the composition of the canonical Gospels. Like the hypothetical Q, Thomas consists entirely of sayings, evidence that early Christians did create Gospels without either a Passion story or other narrative component (see Chapter 11).

REDACTION CRITICISM

In recent decades, scholars increasingly have focused on the role of the individual Gospel writer in editing, revising, and reshaping the oral and written traditions he inherited. A form of literary analysis, **redaction criticism** (from the German *Redaktions-geschite*) emphasizes the redactor's (author-editor's) importance in assembling, rearranging, and reinterpreting his sources. Matthew and Luke do not slavishly follow their primary sources—Mark and Q—but freely adapt them to express their individual theological viewpoints. The recognition that the Gospel writers were not mere compilers of older material but were active interpreters of it, creatively modifying traditions to make a theological point, deepens our understanding of differences in the three Synoptic accounts. By scrutinizing the way Matthew and Luke edit Mark's narrative and the changes they make in rendering the same saying or parable, scholars can discover their particular theological orientation. When either Matthew or Luke revises Mark or gives a different version of a shared saying, they invariably do it for theological reasons.

As readers become familiar with an Evangelist's distinctive views, they eventually will be able to explain why Matthew's rendition of the wedding feast parable, for example, differs from that of Luke or Thomas. In each case, the author edits a

Box 10.4 The Probable Contents of Q

Although we lack absolute proof that Q, a hypothetical collection of Jesus' sayings, ever existed, many scholars believe that it is possible to reconstruct its contents. By carefully isolating teaching material contained in both Luke and Matthew but absent from Mark, scholars have compiled a list of more than 200 verses they believe were originally part of Q. These passages include some of Jesus' most characteristic teachings, including the Beatitudes, his command to love one's enemies, his commissioning of the disciples, and his renunciation of material possessions.

Because Luke seems to have preserved Q's original order better than Matthew, Q sayings are customarily cited by Lukan chapter and verse. Although in many cases the two Gospel writers show an almost verbatim agreement on Q's wording, in places where they disagree scholars can typically reconstruct the original phrasing by taking the two Evangelists' editorializing tendencies into account. The saying about having a rafter lodged in one's eye (Luke 6:41–42/ Matt. 7:3–5), for example, reveals Luke and Matthew in total agreement. In the Beatitudes, however, Matthew appears to modify Jesus' original commendations of the literally poor and hungry, making them "poor in spirit" and hungry for "justice" or "righteousness," a characteristic Matthean term.

Because it contains little narrative and few references to Jesus' martyrdom, Q appears to have originated in a community that remembered Jesus primarily as a wisdom teacher and prophet whose death resembled those of Israel's earlier prophets. Mark, however, made Jesus' death of paramount importance, God's means of redeeming humanity. By combining Q's wisdom teachings with Mark's theology of the cross, Matthew and Luke demonstrated that the two ways of regarding Jesus' significance were not necessarily mutually exclusive.

The following summary of some representative Q material lists parallel verses in Luke and Matthew.

Q MATERIAL	LUKE	MATTHEW
The ministry of John the Baptist	3:7–9, 16–17	3:7–12
The testing of Jesus by Satan	4:1–9, 9–12, 5–8, 13	4:1–11
The Beatitudes	6:20–26	5:3, 4, 6, 11–12
The admonition to love one's enemies and abide by the golden rule	6:27–36	5:44, 39–42, 7:12; 5:46–47, 45, 48
The construction of houses on sand or rock	6:46–49	7:21, 24–27
The healing of a Roman officer's slave	7:1–10	7:28; 8:5–10, 13
Praise by Jesus for John the Baptist	7:24–28	11:7–11
The differences between Jesus and John	7:31–35	11:16–19
The commissioning of the disciples	10:2–12	9:37–38; 10:7–16
The Lord's Prayer	11:2–4	6:9–13
The sign of Jonah	11:16, 29–32	12:38–42
The rejection of God's wisdom	11:49–51	23:34–36
The avoidance of anxieties and reliance on God	12:22–31	6:25–33
The great feast	14:16–24	22:1–10
The rejection of family ties	14:26–27	10:37–39
The parable of invested money	19:12–26	25:14–30

For a complete reconstruction of Q's probable contents, see "The Sayings Gospel Q," pp. 249–300 in Robert J. Miller, ed., *The Complete Gospels*, 3rd ed. (San Francisco: HarperSanFrancisco, 1994).

particular parable to fit his religious perspective. At crucial moments in his narrative, such as Jesus' crucifixion, each Evangelist emphasizes his individual understanding of the event by ascribing different last words to Jesus. Whereas Mark and Matthew agree that the dying Jesus utters a single despairing cry, the other two Gospel authors present final statements that reflect a totally different mood and meaning, with Luke and John highlighting their hero's serene confidence and control of the situation (discussed later in the chapter). In their distinctive death scenes, the four authors ascribe to Jesus a climactic utterance consistent with the distinctive theological picture of Jesus depicted throughout their respective Gospels (see Box 10.20).

COMPOSITION OF THE CANONICAL GOSPELS

The author of Mark generally is credited with inventing the Gospel genre, reshaping previously fluid oral traditions about Jesus into the fixed written form of a popular Greek biography designed for a Hellenistic audience. Transforming the oral *kerygma* into a sequential narrative about Jesus' public career, Mark concluded with a long, remarkably detailed account of Jesus' arrest, trial, and execution. Because it emphasizes Jesus' suffering and death as the most important aspect of his biography, Mark's Gospel has been called a **Passion** narrative with a long introduction. Certainly, Mark's strong emphasis on the cross clearly distinguished its viewpoint from that of the Q community, which apparently did not give great theological weight to the manner of Jesus' demise. Even if Mark's author was aware of this Sayings Gospel, it is not surprising that he does not make use of it.

Gospel Authors   Other than an opening declaration to present Jesus' story as a gospel—"good news"—Mark's author says nothing explicit about his purpose in writing. Nor does he identify himself, his intended readers, his place of composition, or the date on which he writes. Mark's anonymity characterizes all four of the canonical Gospels, none of which gives the name of its author. The traditional Gospel titles—"The Gospel According to Mark," or "Matthew," or "Luke," or "John"—appear nowhere in the main texts and seem to be headings added late in the second century C.E., long after the Gospels themselves were written. Careful study of the Gospel texts does not confirm either the traditional authorship or the belief that the writers were eyewitnesses to the events they described. For convenience, we continue to refer to the authors by their traditional names, but it is a disappointing fact that scholarship as yet has found no way to identify the four Evangelists.

Matthew's Gospel   Incorporating about 90 percent of Mark into his narrative, the author of Matthew produced a new, enlarged edition of Mark that included extensive teaching material drawn from Q. In addition, the unknown author also used a source unique to his Gospel, which scholars designate as **M** (special Matthean material). Writing in about 80–85 C.E. to answer Jewish criticism of Christian claims about Jesus and to emphasize Jesus' adherence to the Mosaic Torah, Matthew portrays Jesus as a greater Moses who demands a "higher righteousness" than that practiced by the Pharisees. Into Mark's narrative outline, he inserts five clusters of sayings and parables—mostly borrowed from Q and M—arranging them as five separate speeches corresponding to the five books of the Torah.

Matthew frames Mark's narrative with accounts of Jesus' infancy and postresurrection appearances. Most distinctively, he represents Jesus' birth and ministry as fulfilling prophecies from the Hebrew Bible, which Matthew cites in Greek translation. He cites about 130 scriptural passages to refute Jewish arguments that Jesus had not lived up to prophetic expectations of the Messiah. So successful was his integration of Jesus' ethical teachings with Mark's older narrative that Matthew's Gospel—with its strong orientation toward the church—soon became the most popular, ranking first among the four.

Luke's Gospel   Between about 85–90 C.E., perhaps only five to ten years after the appearance of Matthew, Luke's Gospel, the most literate and formally correct of the Synoptic accounts, was written. Luke's narrative reproduces about half of Mark, along with generous portions of Q and the author's own special source, known as **L**, which forms about a third of his Gospel. The only Evangelist to provide a sequel to his version of Jesus' life, Luke also wrote the book of Acts, which continues the story of Christian origins, tracing the expansion of the new religion from Jerusalem, to Greece, to Rome. In Luke's two volume set, Jesus' career is presented as the turning point in Israel's history, the beginning of an innovative religious movement that brings salvation to Greeks as well as Jews. In Luke-Acts, Jesus is the model of service to others whose example is followed by many generations of disciples, including not only the apostles who founded the first church at Jerusalem but also an unlimited number of Gentiles who form a multiethnic, international community throughout the Roman Empire. According to Luke, the abiding presence of the Holy Spirit, which inspired Jesus' ministry, ensures that the Church functions as a successor and extension of Jesus himself, perpetuating his activity in the world (see Chapter 12).

The Griesbach Theory   Although most scholars think that the two-source theory most satisfactorily explains the literary relationship of the Synoptic Gospels, a small minority deny Markan priority. According to this view, Mark is a conflation (blending together) and abridgement of the other two Synoptics. Known as the Griesbach theory, after Johann Griesbach (1745–1812), who first published this solution to the Synoptic Problem, this hypothesis has been recently revived by several scholars, notably William Farmer. These dissenting scholars emphasize the fact that a few short passages in the triple tradition (material occurring in all three Synoptics) show Matthew and Luke agreeing *against* Mark. Proponents of the two-source theory, however, argue that such "minor agreements" merely suggest that both Mark and Q had some limited material in common, that in a few instances they overlapped. Other defenders of the theory suggest that the "minor agree-

ments" are the result of early scribal attempts to make the Synoptic texts more consistent, "harmonizing" the verbal differences (see Chapter 1). Despite some objections, most scholars think that the two-source hypothesis most adequately explains both the similarities and the differences in the Synoptic Gospels.

John's Gospel   Shortly before the end of the first century C.E., the fourth Gospel, ascribed to John, was composed, apparently both the last canonical Gospel written and the last to attain canonical status. (Numerous apocryphal Gospels also circulated in the early church, but only Thomas survives complete; the others exist only in fragments; see Chapter 11.) This document differs so extremely from the three Synoptic accounts that scholars regard it as a special case. John's narrative presents a radically different picture of Jesus' character and teaching. Instead of speaking in earthy images and parables drawn from the experience of his peasant listeners, John's Jesus delivers long, philosophical monologues about his closeness to the Father and his imminent ascension to heaven. Rather than focusing on the in-breaking kingdom of God and a reinterpretation of the Jewish Torah, the Johannine Jesus dwells primarily on his divinity and his significance to the believer as the "way," "truth," and "life." Whereas Mark, Matthew, and Luke show Jesus promulgating a modified form of traditional Judaism, John is less interested in preserving Jesus' own religion than he is in promoting a religion *about* Jesus, an approach in which the teacher, rather than his historical message, becomes the object of veneration. John's insistence on Jesus as a divinity walking the earth in human form — and the almost total absence of topics that characterized Jesus' Synoptic teachings — make scholars doubt the Fourth Gospel's historical value. Because both the Synoptics and John cannot be right about the form and content of Jesus' message — and John's version is outvoted three to one — scholars generally focus on the Synoptic accounts in their search for the historical Jesus, regarding John as essentially a theological meditation on Jesus' life.

Four Distinctive Portraits of Jesus

The fact that the early Christian community generally did not promote a single, uniform edition of Jesus' life or adopt one "offical" version free of seeming contradictions is significant. Instead of an "authorized" biography, the church accepted the four canonical Gospels, perhaps recognizing that different Christian groups scattered throughout the Roman Empire had already adopted one or more different Gospels as foundation documents of their particular communities. Although individual churches, such as Antioch, where Matthew was probably written, would not relinquish *their* Evangelist's work in favor of another, by the late second century C.E. many seem to have accepted two or three of the Synoptics. John, which some early church leaders condemned as a Gnostic fabrication, took longer to be accepted by the church at large. Its position as the Fourth Gospel may reflect its relatively late inclusion in the canon. (See Table 10.3.)

As Jesus elicited widely different responses during his lifetime, so he inspired the Evangelists to represent him in significantly different guises, ranging from the Galilean carpenter-prophet in Mark to the incarnate heavenly Word of God in John. This composite portrait, with all its attendant problems and unanswered questions, is the one deemed appropriate to reflect early Christianity's diverse community of faith.

QUESTIONS FOR REVIEW

1. What is the literal meaning of the word *gospel*, and what New Testament Greek word does it translate? Define *gospel* as a literary category. By definition, who and what must always be the subject of a *gospel?*

2. Define *Synoptic*, and describe the issue that scholars call "the Synoptic Problem." What is the hypothetical Q document? According to scholarly theory, approximately when was it written and what did it contain? In what two Gospels do its contents now appear?

3. Define the Griesbach hypothesis. According to the "two-source" hypothesis, which Gospel was written first? What relationship does this original Gospel have to the other two Synoptic Gospels? How does Q figure into the equation?

4. Describe several theoretical stages in the development of the four canonical Gospels. Begin with oral traditions—Christian oral preaching—about Jesus, and conclude with the composition of the fourth Gospel.

5. Define and describe the goals and functions of modern criticism, including form criticism and redaction criticism.

QUESTION FOR DISCUSSION AND REFLECTION

Scholars recognize that the Gospel authors are not historians or biographers in the modern sense. As you read the Gospel accounts carefully, consider whether the writers are interested primarily in preserving historical facts about Jesus or in explaining and interpreting his life in religious terms. Relate the Evangelists' theological concerns to redaction criticism.

TERMS AND CONCEPTS TO REMEMBER

aphorism	parable
codex	Passion
Evangelists	pericopes
form criticism	Q
Gospel	redaction criticism
Gospel of Thomas	source criticism
kerygma	Synoptic Gospels
L	Synoptic Problem
M	two-document theory

RECOMMENDED READING

Bultmann, Rudolf. *The History of the Synoptic Tradition.* Translated by J. Marsh. New York: Harper & Row, 1963. A masterful, if somewhat technical, study by the great German scholar.

Farmer, W. R. *The Synoptic Problem.* New York: Macmillan, 1964. Argues for the priority of Matthew.

Funk, Robert W., ed. *New Gospel Parallels.* Vol. 1, *The Synoptic Gospels;* Vol. 2, *John and the Other Gospels.* Philadelphia: Fortress Press, 1985. The most valuable scholarly tool for comparing the Gospel texts.

Funk, Robert W.; Hoover, Roy W.; and the Jesus Seminar. *The Five Gospels: The Search for the Authentic*

Table 10.3 Approximate Order of Composition of New Testament Books

APPROXIMATE DATE (C.E.)	TITLE OF BOOK	AUTHOR
50	1 Thessalonians	Paul
	2 Thessalonians (if by Paul)	
54–55	1 and 2 Corinthians	Paul
56	Galatians	Paul
56–57	Romans	Paul
61	Colossians (if by Paul)	Paul
61	Philippians	Paul
62	Philemon	Paul
66–70	Gospel of Mark	Anonymous
66–73	**Jewish Revolt Against Rome; Destruction of Jerusalem and Temple**	
80–85	Gospel of Matthew	Anonymous
85–90	Gospel of Luke and Acts	Anonymous
85–95	Hebrews, 1 Peter, Ephesians, James	Anonymous or Pseudonymous
90–95	Gospel of John	Anonymous
95	Revelation (the Apocalypse)	John of Patmos
95–100	Letters of John (1, 2, and 3 John)	The Elder
110–30	1 and 2 Timothy, Titus	Pseudonymous
130–50	Jude, 2 Peter	Pseudonymous

Words of Jesus. New York: Macmillan, 1993. The New Scholars Version of the Gospels, with Jesus' sayings printed in red, pink, gray, or black, depending on the scholars' view of their probable authenticity.

Green, Joe, ed. *Hearing the New Testament: Strategies for Interpretation.* Grand Rapids, Mich.: Eerdmans, 1995. Lists methodologies and goals of critical interpretations.

Hengel, Martin. *The Four Gospels and the One Gospel of Jesus Christ: An Investigation of the Collection and Origin of the Canonical Gospels.* Harrisburg, Pa.: Trinity Press International, 2000.

Kloppenborg, John S. *The Formation of Q: Trajectories in Ancient Wisdom Collections.* Studies in Antiquity and Christianity. Harrisburg, Pa.: Trinity Press International, 2000. A scholarly study of the presumed Q text that finds two layers of traditions, the first presenting Jesus as a wisdom teacher and the second, later addition picturing Jesus as an apocalyptic judge.

Koester, Helmut. *Introduction to the New Testament.* Vol. 2, *History and Literature of Early Christianity.* 2nd ed. New York: de Gruyter, 2000. Translated from the original German, this is a major and incisive study of New Testament origins.

Miller, Robert J., ed. *The Complete Gospels,* 3rd ed. San Francisco: HarperSanFrancisco, 1994. Contains the complete texts of all known canonical and noncanonical Gospels, including a reconstruction of Q.

Neirynck, Frans. "Synoptic Problem." In R. E. Brown et al., eds., *The New Jerome Biblical Commentary,* pp. 587–595. Englewood Cliffs, N.J.: Prentice-Hall, 1990. A detailed examination of the literary kinship of the Synoptics.

Robinson, J. M.; Hoffman, P.; and Kloppenborg, J. S., eds. *The Critical Edition of Q: A Synopsis Including the Gospels of Matthew and Luke, Mark and Thomas, with English, German and French Translation of Q and Thomas.* Louven, Germany: Peeters, publishers.

Streeter, B. H. *The Four Gospels.* London: Macmillan, 1924. A landmark scholarly study arguing that Mark is the earliest Gospel.

Tuckett, C. M. "Q (Gospel Source)." In D. H. Freedman, ed., *The Anchor Bible Dictionary,* Vol. 5, pp. 567–572. New York: Doubleday, 1992. "Synoptic Problem." In D. N. Freeman, ed., *The Anchor Bible Dictionary,* Vol. 6, pp. 263–270. New York: Doubleday, 1992. A lucid introduction to theories about the interdependence of Matthew, Mark, and Luke.

Verbin, John S.; Kloppenborg, John; and Kloppenborg, S. *Excavating Q: The History and Setting of the Sayings Gospel.* Minneapolis: Fortress Press, 2000. An authoritative study of the Q source.

Mark's Gospel

KEY TOPICS/THEMES

Considered the first Gospel written, Mark reflects the crisis affecting the Christian community between about 66 and 70 C.E. The church at Rome had just suffered Nero's devastating persecution, and Jerusalem, home of the first church, was about to be destroyed by Roman armies. Portraying Jesus as a "hidden Messiah" whose true identity is revealed only through his suffering and death, Mark presents his hero as universally misunderstood, rejected by his own people and condemned by the Romans, thus reminding his audience that Jesus' story anticipated their own harrowing experiences. Mark's Jesus is an apocalyptic preacher, healer, and exorcist whose Galilean campaign heralds the arrival of God's rule and imminent world judgment. The Gospel's five main divisions include a prelude to Jesus' public ministry (1:1–13), the Galilean campaign inaugurating God's kingdom (1:14–8:26), the journey from Caesarea Philippi to Jerusalem (8:27–10:52), the Jerusalem ministry (11:1–15:47), and a postlude in which women disciples discover the empty tomb (16:1–8).

KEY QUESTIONS

Why does Mark show all of Jesus' associates — including his family — as unable to value him? What part of Jesus' story does Mark give in greatest detail? Why?

Although he seems to have been the first author to transform oral traditions about Jesus into a biographical narrative, Mark was not the first Christian writer. About twenty years before Mark created his Gospel, Paul, Christianity's most successful missionary to the Gentiles, began composing a series of letters (c. 50–62 C.E.) in which he makes the risen Jesus his central focus. Except for the essential facts of Jesus' crucifixion and resurrection, however, Paul shows little interest in Jesus' earthly life or teachings. Paul's only extended quotation from Jesus is taken from a **tradition** passed on to him about Jesus' final meal with his disciples, the

Last Supper (1 Cor. 11:23–26). One or two written collections of Jesus' sayings — Q and perhaps an early edition of the **Gospel of Thomas** — were probably also circulating among some Christian communities when Mark wrote. But if Mark was aware of their existence, he chose not to use them. The Gospel of Mark, in fact, cites relatively few of Jesus' teachings, instead emphasizing Jesus' actions, particularly his miraculous healings and willingness to sacrifice himself for others.

MARK'S HISTORICAL SETTING

The earliest reference to Mark's Gospel comes from Papias, an early Christian writer who was bishop of Hierapolis in Asia Minor about 130–140 C.E. As quoted by Eusebius, Papias states that Mark had been the apostle **Peter**'s disciple in Rome and based his account on Peter's reminiscences of Jesus. Papias notes that Mark "had not heard the Lord or been one of his followers" so that his Gospel lacked "a systematic arrangement of the Lord's sayings" (Eusebius, *History,* 3.39). Although Papias is a relatively early witness to the Christian tradition, scholars caution that we have no means of verifying the historicity of his claims.

Mark's author offers few hints about where or for whom he wrote, except for his insistence that following Jesus demands a willingness to suffer for one's faith. Mark's near-equation of discipleship with suffering suggests that he directed his work to a group that was then undergoing severe testing and needed encouragement to remain steadfast. (See Mark 8:34–38; 10:38–40.) This theme of "carrying one's cross" may derive from the effects of Nero's persecution (c. 64–65 C.E.), when numerous Roman Christians were crucified or burned alive. Papias and Irenaeus, another early church leader, agree that Mark wrote shortly after Peter's martyrdom, which, according to tradition, occurred during Nero's attack on Rome's Christian community.

Although Rome is the traditional place of composition, most scholars now think that Mark wrote for an audience in Syria or Palestine. Critics favoring a Palestinian origin point to Mark's emphasis on the Jewish revolt (66–73 C.E.) and concurrent warnings to believers who were affected by the uprising (Mark 13). In Mark's view, the "tribulation" that climaxes in Jerusalem's destruction is the sign heralding Jesus' **Parousia**, his return in heavenly glory. The association of wars and national revolts with persecution of believers and Jesus' Second Coming gives an eschatological urgency to Mark's account.

Even though Papias and other second-century writers ascribe the Gospel to John Mark, a companion of Peter and Paul (Philem. 24; Col. 4:10; Acts 12:12–25; 14:36–40), the author does not identify himself in the text. The superscription — "The Gospel According to Mark" — is a later embellishment, for second-century churchmen tried to connect extant writings about Jesus with the apostles or their immediate disciples. The Gospel is anonymous; for convenience, we refer to the author as **Mark**.

MARK'S PUZZLING ATTITUDE TOWARD JESUS' CLOSE ASSOCIATES

Jesus' Family and Acquaintances   Strangely, Mark does not seem to have regarded Jesus' relatives — or any other ordinary source a modern biographer would consult — as worthy informants. One of the author's prevailing themes is his negative presentation of virtually everyone associated with the historical Jesus (Box 10.5). From "his [Jesus'] mother and brothers" (3:31) to his most intimate followers, Mark portrays all of Jesus' companions as oblivious to his real nature and/or as obstacles to his work. Mark's Gospel consistently renders all Jesus' Palestinian associates as incredibly obtuse, unable to grasp his teachings, and blind to his value.

The Markan picture of Jesus' family implies that they, too, failed to appreciate or support him. "When his relatives heard of this [his drawing large crowds around him], they set out to take charge of him, convinced he was out of his mind" (3:21, Jerusalem Bible). When "his mother and his brothers" send a message asking for him, apparently demanding that he cease making a public spectacle of himself, Mark has Jesus declare that "whoever does the will of God is my brother, my sister, my mother" — a startling repudiation of his blood ties — and an implication that in the Markan Jesus' view, his relatives were not doing the divine will (3:31–35). The force of this anti-family episode is intensified because Mark uses it to frame a controversy in which Jesus' opponents accuse him of expelling demons by the power of Beelzebub, another name for Satan. Jesus countercharges that those who oppose his work are defying **the Holy Spirit**, the invisible power of God at work in the world (3:22–30). At this point in the narrative, Mark shows Jesus' family attempting to interrupt his ministry, thus subtly associating them with his adversaries. (See also John 7:1–9.)

Mark also depicts Jesus' acquaintances in **Nazareth** as hostile to a local carpenter's unexpected career as prophet and healer, questioning his credentials as sage and teacher. "'Where does he get it from?'" his neighbors ask. "'What wisdom is this that has been given him?' and 'how does he work such miracles? Is not this the carpenter, the son of Mary, the brother of James and Joseph and Judas and Simon? And are not his sisters here with us?' So they [turned against] him" (6:2–3). In this incident of Jesus' revisiting his home turf, Mark argues that those who thought they knew Jesus best doubted not only his right to be a religious leader but also his legitimacy — note Mark's reference to "the son of Mary," a contrast to the biblical custom of identifying a son through his male parentage even if his father was dead. The Nazarenes' refusal to see any merit in him results in a troubling diminution of Jesus' power: "He *could work no miracle there* . . ." except for some routine healings (6:6, italics added). Mark thus seems to dismiss both family and hometown citizens as acceptable channels of biographical tradition: They all fail to trust, comprehend, or cooperate with his hero.

Mark's allusion to Jesus' "brothers" and "sisters" (see also Matt. 13:54–56) may disturb some readers. Because his Gospel does not include a tradition of Jesus' virginal conception or birth, the existence of siblings may not have been an issue with the Markan community (as it apparently was not for the Pauline churches; none of Paul's letters allude to a virgin birth). Matthew, however, explic-

Box 10.5 Mark's Leading Characters*

John the Baptist (1:4–9); executed (6:17–29)

Jesus introduced (1:9); final words (15:34)

Simon Peter and his brother Andrew (1:16–18); Peter's imperfect discipleship (8:27–33; 9:2–6; 14:26–31, 66–72)

James and John, the fishermen sons of Zebedee (1:19–20); wish to be first in the kingdom (10:35–45)

Levi (Matthew), a tax collector (2:13–17)

The Twelve (3:13–19).

Judas Iscariot, Jesus' betrayer (3:19; 14:17–21, 43–46)

Mary, Jesus' mother, and other family members (3:20–21, 31–35; 6:3)

The Gerasene demoniac (5:1–20)

Herod Antipas, ruler of Galilee (4 B.C.E.–39 C.E.) (6:17–29; 8:15)

The Syrophoenician (Canaanite) woman (7:14–30)

A rich young man (10:17–22)

The woman who anoints Jesus at Bethany (14:3–9)

The High Priest Caiaphas (14:53–64)

Pontius Pilate, procurator of Judea (26–36 C.E.) (15:1–15, 43–44)

Barabbas, the terrorist released in place of Jesus (15:6–15)

Simon of Cyrene, the man impressed to carry Jesus' cross (15:21)

Joseph of Arimathaea, the Sanhedrin member who buries Jesus (15:42–46)

Mary of Magdala (in Galilee) (15:40–41, 47; 16:1)

Mary, mother of James and Joseph (15:40, 47; 16:1)

*Characters are listed in general order of appearance, along with the chief quality or event that distinguishes them in Mark's narrative.

---

itly affirms that Jesus was virginally conceived (Matt. 1:18–25), and Luke strongly implies it (Luke 1:26–38). Some Protestant Christians believe that following Jesus' delivery, his mother may have borne other children in the ordinary way. According to Catholic doctrine, however, Mary remains perpetually virgin. Jesus' "brothers" (translating the Greek *adelphoi*) are to be understood as close male relatives, perhaps cousins or stepbrothers (sons of Mary's husband Joseph by a previous marriage).

The Disciples   Mark's opinion of the Galilean **disciples** whom Jesus calls to follow him (3:13–19) is distinctly unsympathetic, although these are the Twelve Apostles on whose testimony the Christian faith traditionally is founded. Almost without exception, Mark paints **the Twelve** as dull-witted, inept, unreliable, cowardly, and, in at least one case, treacherous. When Jesus stills a storm, the disciples are impressed but unaware of the act's significance (4:35–41). After his feeding of the multitudes, the disciples "had not understood the intent of the loaves" because "their minds were closed" (6:52). The harshness of Mark's judgment is better rendered in the phrase "their hearts were hardened" (as given in the Revised Standard Version). This is the same phrase used to describe the Egyptian pharaoh when he "hardened his heart" and refused to obey Yahweh's commands (Exod. 7:1–14; 10:1–27). Even after listening for months to Jesus' teaching, the disciples are such slow learners that they are still ignorant of "what [Jesus' reference to] 'rising from the dead' could mean" (9:9–10). Not only do they fail to grasp the concept of sharing in Jesus' glory (10:35–41), but even the simplest, most obvious parables also escape their comprehension (4:10–13). As Jesus asks, "You do not understand this parable? How then will you understand any parable?" (4:13).

Although he has "explained everything" (4:33–34; see also 8:31–32), and the disciples presumably have recognized him as the Messiah (8:27–32), they desert him after his arrest (14:30). Peter, who had earlier confessed Jesus to be the Messiah, three times denies knowing him (14:66–72). Virtually the only character in Mark shown as recognizing the significance of Jesus' death is an unnamed Roman soldier who perceives that "truly this man was a son of God!" (15:39).

Mark's antipathy toward the historical Jesus' closest associates and the original Jerusalem church is puzzling. Does this apparent hostility mean that the group for which Mark wrote wished to distance itself from the Jerusalem community, whose founders included Jesus' closest family members, Mary and James (Acts 1:14; 12:17; etc.)? Does Mark's negative attitude represent a power struggle between his branch of Gentile Christianity and the Jewish Christians who headed the original church? (See Box 12.3)

MARK'S BIPOLAR NARRATIVE STRUCTURE

Whatever the historicity of Mark's version of Jesus' career, it eventually exerted a tremendous influence on the greater Christian community, primarily through the enlarged and revised editions of Mark produced by Matthew and Luke. Because the two other Synoptic Gospels generally follow Mark's order of events in Jesus' life (Box 10.6), it is important to understand the significance of Mark's bipolar organization. Mark arranges his narrative around a geographical north–south polarity. The first half of his narrative takes place in **Galilee** and adjacent areas of northern Palestine, a largely rural area of peasant farmers where Jesus recruits his followers, performs numerous miracles, and — despite some opposition — enjoys considerable success. The second half (after Ch. 8) relates Jesus' fatal journey southward to Judea and Jerusalem, where he is rejected and killed. Besides dividing Jesus' career into two distinct geographical areas, Mark's Gospel presents two contrasting aspects of Jesus' story. In Galilee, Jesus is a figure of power, using his supernatural gifts to expel demons, heal the sick, control natural forces, and raise the dead.

Representing the Hellenistic concept of an awe-inspiring divine man (*theios aner*), the Galilean Jesus speaks and acts with tremendous authority, effortlessly refutes his detractors, and affirms or invalidates the Mosaic Torah at will. Before leaving **Caesarea Philippi**, however, Jesus makes the first of three Passion predictions, warning his uncomprehending disciples that he will go to Jerusalem only to suffer humiliation and death (8:30–38; 9:31–32; 10:33–34).

By using the Passion predictions as a device to link the indomitable miracle worker in Galilee with the helpless figure on the cross in Judea, Mark reconciles the two seemingly irreconcilable components in his portrait of Jesus. The powerful Son of God who astonishes vast crowds with his mighty works is also the vulnerable **Son of Man** who, in weakness and apparent defeat, sacrifices his life "as a ransom for many" (10:45) (Box 10.7). Thus, the author balances older Christian traditions of his hero's phenomenal deeds with a bleak picture of Jesus' sufferings, devoting the last six chapters to a detailed account of the Passion (Figure 10.3).

Mark's Gospel can be divided into five parts:

1. Prelude to Jesus' public ministry (1:1–13)
2. The Galilean ministry; inaugurating the kingdom (1:14–8:26)
3. The journey to Jerusalem (8:27–10:52)
4. The Jerusalem ministry (11:1–15:47)
5. Postlude: the empty tomb (16:1–8)

PRELUDE TO JESUS' PUBLIC MINISTRY

Like the writer of a classical epic, Mark plunges into the middle of the action, providing no background about his hero but introducing him with apocalyptic suddenness. The opening line, "here begins the gospel [good news] of Jesus Christ" (1:1), simultaneously announces his epic theme and echoes Genesis 1, alerting the reader that in Jesus, God has begun a new creative activity. Jesus is the **Christ** (Greek translation of the Hebrew *mashiah*) and the "Son of God," titles that Mark seldom uses in his narrative, because one of his purposes is to demonstrate that in his lifetime, the majority of people did not recognize Jesus' divine

Box 10.6 Mark's Order of Events in Jesus' Life

BEGINNING OF JESUS' MINISTRY (C. 27 or 29 C.E.)

Jesus is baptized by John at the Jordan River (1:9–11).

Jesus withdraws alone into the Judean desert (1:12–13).

Jesus begins preaching in Galilee (1:14–15).

Jesus recruits Peter, Andrew, James, and John to be his first disciples (1:16–20).

Jesus performs miraculous cures and exorcisms in Capernaum and throughout Galilee (1:21–3:12).

Jesus appoints twelve chief disciples from among his many followers; he explains the meaning of parables to this inner circle (3:13–34).

Jesus repeatedly crosses the Lake of Galilee, healing Jews on the western side and non-Jews on the eastern side (4:35–5:43).

Jesus returns to Nazareth, where his neighbors reject him (6:1–6).

Jesus sends the Twelve out on a mission to heal the sick and exorcise demons (6:7–13).

Herod Antipas beheads John the Baptist (6:14–29).

Jesus miraculously feeds a Jewish crowd of 5000 (6:30–44).

END OF JESUS' MINISTRY (C. 30 OR 33 C.E.)

Jesus debates Torah rules with the Pharisees, who increasingly oppose his teaching (7:1–23).

Jesus leaves Galilee and travels through non-Jewish territories in Phoenicia and the Decapolis (7:24–37).

Jesus miraculously feeds a second crowd, this time a group of Gentiles (8:1–10, 14–21).

Jesus cures a blind man, and, near the town of Caesarea Philippi, Peter's eyes are opened to Jesus' true identity as the Messiah; Jesus rebukes Peter for failing to understand that the Messiah must suffer and die (8:22–9:1).

Jesus is gloriously transfigured before Peter, James, and John (9:1–13).

Jesus travels with the Twelve through Galilee to Capernaum, instructing them privately (9:30–50).

Jesus travels south to Judea, teaching the crowds and debating with Pharisees (10:1–33).

On the road to Jerusalem, Jesus for the third time predicts his imminent suffering and death (the Passion predictions) (8:31–33; 9:30–32; 10:32–34).

Approaching Jerusalem via Jericho, Jesus performs his last public miracle, curing a blind man (10:46–52).

EVENTS OF THE LAST WEEK OF JESUS' LIFE

On Palm Sunday, Jesus arranges his public entry into Jerusalem; his followers hail him in terms of the Davidic kingdom (11:1–11).

After a night at the Jerusalem suburb of Bethany, Jesus returns to Jerusalem and drives the moneychangers out of the Temple (11:15–19).

Jesus debates the "chief priests," Sadducees, Pharisees, and other Jewish religious leaders in the Temple (11:27–12:40).

Seated on the Mount of Olives opposite Jerusalem, Jesus predicts the imminent destruction of the Temple (13:1–37).

Jesus' enemies conspire to kill him; Judas betrays Jesus (14:1–11).

Jesus holds a final Passover meal with the Twelve (14:12–31).

After the Last Supper, Jesus is arrested at Gethsemane on the Mount of Olives outside Jerusalem (14:32–52).

Jesus is tried on charges of blasphemy before the High Priest Caiaphas and the Sanhedrin (14:53–65).

After all of Jesus' followers have abandoned him, Peter denies ever having known him (14:66–72).

On Good Friday, Jewish leaders accuse Jesus before Pontius Pilate; Jesus is declared guilty of treason, flogged, and condemned to crucifixion (15:1–20).

A passerby, Simon of Cyrene, is impressed to carry Jesus' cross to Golgotha, where Jesus is crucified (15:21–39).

A group of Galilean women witness the Crucifixion; Joseph of Arimathaea provides a tomb for Jesus (15:40–47).

On Easter Sunday, Mary of Magdala and other women discover that Jesus' tomb is empty; a young man instructs them to look for Jesus in Galilee, but the women are too frightened to tell anyone of their experience (16:1–8).

Box 10.7 Mark's Identification of Jesus as "Son of God"

Although Mark's preferred designation of Jesus is "Son of Man," he also identifies Jesus as "Son of God" at strategic places in his narrative. In most editions of Mark, the first reference to Jesus' divine parentage occurs in the opening verse and is addressed directly to readers, who must be aware of Jesus' supernatural identity if Mark's way of telling his hero's story—an ironic contrast between who Jesus really is and whom people mistake him for—is to succeed. Because some early manuscripts omit the phrase "Son of God" in Mark 1:1, however, it is possible that the author originally intended readers to learn of Jesus' special relationship to the Father in the same manner that Jesus did, at his baptism, when a heavenly voice privately confides, "You are my beloved Son; in you I take delight" (Mark 1:11).

The "voice from heaven" paraphrases Psalm 2, a poem sung at the coronation of Israel's monarchs, a royal ceremony at which Yahweh is represented as adopting the newly consecrated king: "You are my son, . . . this day I become your father" (Ps. 2:7). Because Mark contains no reference to Jesus' virginal conception, many scholars think that he regards Jesus as becoming God's son by adoption, his baptism and visitation by the Holy Spirit the equivalent of Davidic kings' being anointed with holy oil.

In an ironic counterpoint to God's voice, Mark next uses the speech of a demon to reveal Jesus' hidden identity. When driven from a man he had possessed, the demon angrily declares: "*I* know who you are—the Holy One of God" (Mark 1:25). Whereas Mark's human characters fail to recognize Jesus' true nature until after his death, supernatural entities, including "unclean spirits," know and fear him. In a typically Markan paradox, human opponents accuse Jesus of being an agent of Beelzebub, "the prince of demons"—allegedly the source of his supernatural power—while the demons themselves testify that Jesus is "the Son of God" (Mark 3:11, 22–28). Mark draws further on the questionable testimony of evil spirits when describing the Gerasene demoniac: The satanic "Legion" boldly announces that Jesus is "son of the Most High God" (Mark 5:1–13).

By contrast, when Peter finally perceives that Jesus is "the Christ," he apparently does not also intuit Jesus' divinity, confining his witness to his leader's messianic (political) role. In Mark's narrative, Jesus' closest disciples lack the perceptiveness of Beelzebub's imps! (Compare Mark's account of Peter's "confession" with Matthew's version, in which the author has Peter employ a major christological title, "Son of the living God," absent in Mark [Matt. 16:13–16].) Even after Jesus is miraculously transfigured before their eyes and the celestial voice again affirms that he is God's son (Mark 9:8), the Galilean disciples remain oblivious.

At Jesus' trial before the Sanhedrin, Mark presents a darkly paradoxical glimpse of his hero's real identity. When the High Priest asks if his prisoner is indeed the "Son of the Blessed One" (a pious circumlocution for God), Jesus, for the first time in Mark's account, admits that he is—a confession of divinity that condemns him to death. Only when Jesus hangs lifeless on the cross does a human figure—a Roman centurion—belatedly speak of Jesus as "a son of God," a Hellenistic Gentile's recognition that Jesus had died a heroic death worthy of divine honor.

Sonship. No human being calls Jesus a "son of God" until almost the very end of Mark's Gospel. Significantly, at that point Jesus is already dead and the speaker is neither a Jew nor a disciple but a Roman centurion (15:39).

By citing as if from memory a blend of passages from Isaiah (40:3) and Malachi (3:1)—that a divinely appointed "herald" and a "voice crying aloud in the wilderness" are preparing a path for the Lord—Mark immediately places Jesus' story in the context of the Hebrew Bible. Mark identifies the "herald" with **John the Baptist**, a desert ascetic then conducting a religious campaign along the Jordan River, where John baptizes converts "in token of repentance, for the forgiveness of sins" (1:4). Jesus, implicitly included among the repentant, appears for **baptism**, perhaps as John's disciple. Mark has John predict a "mightier" successor, although he does not show the Baptist as explicitly identifying Jesus as that successor.

Empowered by the Holy Spirit at his baptism, Jesus resists **Satan**'s temptations in the desert

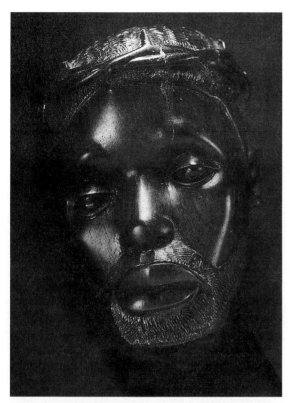

Figure 10.3 *Christ with the Crown of Thorns.* In this wooden carving of Jesus crowned with thorns, an anonymous twentieth-century African sculptor beautifully captures both the sorrow and the mystery of Mark's suffering Son of Man.

(1:12–13). In Mark's view, God's Son has arrived. Jesus' **exorcisms**—the casting out of demons who have possessed human beings—are an important Markan theme and are given proportionately greater space in Mark than in any other Gospel. (By contrast, John's Gospel does not contain a single reference to Jesus performing exorcisms.)

THE GALILEAN MINISTRY: INAUGURATING THE KINGDOM

Mark's Eschatological Urgency Mark launches Jesus' career with a startlingly eschatological message: "The time has come, the kingdom of God is upon you; repent and believe the Gospel" (1:15). Mark's sense of eschatological urgency permeates his entire Gospel, profoundly affecting his portrayal of Jesus' life and teaching. With the tradition that Jesus had prophesied the Temple's fall about to be fulfilled, Mark, writing in about 70 C.E., sees the *eschaton*—the end of history as we know it—about to take place (13:1–4, 7–8, 14–20, 24–27, 30, 35–37). He therefore paints Jesus as an eschatological figure whose words are reinterpreted as specific warnings to Mark's generation. In the crisis-oriented world Mark creates, the apocalyptic Son of Man who is about to appear in glory (13:24–31) is the same as the Son of Man who came forty years earlier to die on the cross (8:31, 38; 9:9–13, 31). The splendor of the One to come casts its radiance over Mark's portrait of the human Jesus (9:1–9).

Mark's style conveys his urgency: He uses the present tense throughout his Gospel and repeatedly connects the brief episodes, or pericopes, of his narrative with the transition word *immediately.* Jesus scarcely finishes conducting a healing or exorcism in one Galilean village before he "immediately" rushes off to the next town to perform another miracle. In Mark's breathless presentation, the world faces an unprecedented crisis. Jesus' activity proclaims that history has reached its climactic moment.

Mark represents Jesus as promising his original hearers that they will experience the *eschaton*—"the present generation will live to see it all" (13:30). The kingdom, God's active rule, is so close that some of Jesus' contemporaries "will not taste death before they have seen the kingdom of God already come to power" (9:1). The long-awaited figure of Elijah, the ancient prophet whose reappearance is to be an infallible sign of the last days (Mal. 4:5), has already materialized in the person of John the Baptist (9:12–13). Such passages indicate that Mark's community anticipated the imminent consummation of all things.

Mark as Apocalypse So pervasive is Mark's eschatology that some scholars regard the entire Gospel as a modified apocalypse, a revelation of unseen realities and a disclosure of events destined soon to climax in God's final intervention in human affairs. Mark's use of apocalyptic devices is particularly evident at the beginning and end of his Gospel. God speaks directly as a disembodied voice (a phenomenon Hellenistic Jews called the *bath qol*) at Jesus' baptism and again at the **Transfiguration**, an **epiphany** (manifestation of divine presence) in which the disciples see Jesus transformed into a luminous being seated beside the ancient figures of Moses and Elijah (1:11; 9:2–9). In this apocalyptic scene, Jesus appears with Moses and Elijah (who represent, respectively, the Torah and the prophets) to demonstrate his continuity with Israel's biblical tradition and his role as the one who embodies God's ultimate revelation to humanity.

Jesus as Son of Man   The author presents virtually all events during Jesus' final hours as revelatory of God's unfolding purpose. At the Last Supper, Jesus emphasizes that the eschatological "Son of Man is going the way appointed for him" and that he will "never again" drink wine with his disciples until he "drink[s] it new in the kingdom of God" (14:21, 25). At his trial before the **Sanhedrin**, the Jewish leaders' highest judicial council, Jesus reveals his true identity for the first time: He confesses that he *is* the Messiah and that the officiating High Priest "will see the Son of Man seated at the right hand of God and coming with the clouds of heaven" (14:62–63).

This disclosure—found only in Mark—associates Jesus' suffering and death with his ultimate revelation as the eschatological Son of Man. A designation that appears almost exclusively in the Gospels and then always on the lips of Jesus, "Son of Man" is Mark's favored expression to denote Jesus' three essential roles: an earthly figure who teaches with authority, a servant who embraces suffering, and a future eschatological judge (Box 10.8). Although many scholars question whether the historical Jesus ever used this title, many others regard it as Jesus' preferred means of self-identification. Still other scholars postulate that Jesus may have used the title *Son of Man* to designate another, future-coming figure who would vindicate Jesus' own ministry. The later church, because of its faith in Jesus' resurrection, inserted that title back into the account of Jesus' life, where it originally did not appear. In Mark's view, however, Jesus himself is clearly the eschatological Son of Man.

In Mark's modification of the Son of Man concept, he is both an apocalyptic ruler and a servant who must suffer and die before attaining the kind of heavenly glory that Daniel 7 and 1 Enoch attribute to him (cf. Mark 8:30–31; 10:45; 13:26–27; 14:62). It is as the Son of Man in his earthly role that Mark's Jesus claims the authority to exercise immense religious authority. As Son of Man, the Markan Jesus assumes the right to prescribe revolutionary changes in Jewish law and custom (2:10). Behaving as if he already reigns as world judge, Jesus forgives a paralytic's sins (2:1–12) and permits certain kinds of work on the Sabbath (3:1–5). The Torah-keeping Pharisees are outraged that the Galilean presumes to revoke Moses' inspired command to forbid all labor on God's day of rest (Exod. 20:8–10; Deut. 5:12–15). As Mark presents the case, it is Jesus' flexible attitude toward Sabbath observance that incites some Pharisees and supporters of Herod Antipas to hatch a murder plot against the Nazarene healer (Mark 3:5–6).

Conflict Stories   Mark devotes considerable space to recounting Jesus' controversies with four hostile groups:

1. Pharisees, who object to his apparently lax attitude toward the Mosaic Torah
2. Scribes, the preservers and copyists of the Torah, who resent what they see as unjustified claims to reinterpret the Mosaic tradition
3. Sadducees, the priestly aristocracy, who view him as disrupting their tenuous armistice with Rome
4. Herodians, who believe that he, like John the Baptist, threatens the rulership of Herod Antipas

Although these groups normally oppose one another, Mark pictures them as uniting to attack Jesus as subverting the security of the Jewish nation.

Throughout his Galilean campaign, Jesus is shown debating the Pharisees and scribes, who variously accuse him of blasphemy in daring to forgive sins (2:5), associating with "tax collectors and

Box 10.8 The Synoptic Gospels' Use of the Term *Son of Man*

The authors of the Synoptic Gospels use the expression *Son of Man* in three distinct ways, all of which they place on the lips of Jesus to denote three important aspects of his ministry. The three categories identify Jesus as the Son of Man who serves on earth, the Son of Man who must suffer and die, and the Son of Man who will be revealed in eschatological judgment. Representative examples of these three categories are given here.

THE EARTHLY SON OF MAN

Mark 2:10 (Matt. 9:6; Luke 5:24): Has authority to forgive sins.

Mark 2:27 (Matt. 12:8; Luke 6:5): Is Lord of the Sabbath.

Matthew 11:19 (Luke 7:34): Comes eating and drinking.

Matthew 8:20 (Luke 9:58): Has nowhere to lay his head.

Luke 19:20: Came to seek and save the lost.

THE SUFFERING SON OF MAN

Mark 8:31 (Luke 9:22): Must suffer.

Mark 9:12 (Matt. 17:12): Will suffer.

Mark 9:31 (Matt. 17:22; Luke 9:44): Is delivered into the hands of men.

Mark 10:33 (Matt. 20:18; Luke 18:31): Is delivered to the chief priests and is condemned to death.

Mark 10:45 (Matt. 20:28): Came to serve and give his life.

Mark 14:41 (Matt. 26:45): Is betrayed to sinners.

Matthew 12:40 (Luke 11:30): Will be three days in the earth.

THE ESCHATOLOGICAL SON OF MAN

Mark 8:38 (Matt. 16:27; Luke 9:26): Comes in glory of the Father and holy angels.

Mark 14:26 (Matt. 24:30; Luke 21:27): Will be seen coming with clouds and glory.

Mark 14:62 (Matt. 26:64; Luke 22:69): Will be seen sitting at the right hand of power.

Luke 12:40 (Matt. 24:44): Is coming at an unexpected hour.

Luke 17:26 (Matt. 24:27): As it was in the days of Noah, so in the days of the Son of Man.

Matthew 24:30: Then will appear the sign of the Son of Man.

Luke 17:30: So it will be on the day when the Son of Man is revealed.

For a fuller discussion of the Son of Man concept and its use by the Synoptic authors, see George Eldon Ladd, *A Theology of the New Testament* (Grand Rapids, Mich.: Eerdmans, 1974), pp. 145–158.

sinners" (2:15–17), violating Sabbath laws (2:23–28), using Satan's help in performing exorcisms (3:22–27), and profaning tradition by neglecting to wash ritually before a meal (7:1–8). Most of Mark's conflict stories end with Jesus issuing a pronouncement on some aspect of Torah observance: declaring all foods "clean" (7:14–23), making the Sabbath relevant to human needs (2:23–3:6), and revoking Moses' permission for men to divorce their wives (10:2–12). In each case, Jesus demonstrates authority to approve or invalidate both written and oral Torah.

Jesus and the Demons   Following his exorcisms at **Capernaum**, Jesus performs similar feats in Gentile territory, "the country of the Gerasenes." Driving a whole army of "unclean spirits" from a Gerasene madman, Jesus casts them into a herd of pigs—the religiously unclean animals becoming a fit home for spirits that drive people to commit unclean acts (5:1–20). The demons' name—"legion"—is an unflattering reference to the Roman legions (large military units) then occupying Palestine (and in Mark's day assaulting Jerusalem). In Mark's ironic vision, the demons recognize Jesus' identity, whereas human beings fail to do so.

Mark arranges his material to show that Jesus does not choose to work in isolation. At the outset of his campaign through Galilee, Jesus gathers followers who will form the nucleus of a new society, one presumably free from demonic influence. Recruiting a band of Galilean fishermen and peasants, Jesus selects two sets of brothers, Simon Peter (also called **Cephas**) and **Andrew**, and **James** and **John**—sons of **Zebedee**, also known as "**sons of thunder**" or *Boanerges*—to form his inner circle (1:16–20). Later he adds another eight disciples to complete the Twelve, a number probably representing the twelve tribes of Israel: **Philip**; **Bartholomew**; **Matthew**; **Thomas**; **James**, son of Alphaeus; **Thaddeus**; **Simon** the Canaanite; and **Judas** Iscariot (3:16–19; cf. the different list in Acts 1).

Jesus as Alleged Sorcerer In another incident involving demonic possession (3:22–30), Mark dramatizes a head-on collision between Jesus and opponents who see him as a tool of the devil. The clash occurs when "doctors of the Law" (teachers and interpreters of the Torah) from Jerusalem accuse Jesus of using black magic to perform exorcisms. Denying that evil can produce good, Jesus countercharges that persons who attribute good works to Satan "slander the Holy Spirit," the divine force manifested in Jesus' actions.

Matthew's version of the incident explicitly links Jesus' defeat of evil spirits with the arrival of the kingdom of God. The Matthean Jesus declares, "If it is by the Spirit of God that I drive out the devils, then be sure the kingdom of God has already come upon you" (Matt. 22–28). To both Evangelists, Jesus' successful attack on demonic control is a revelation that through his presence, God now rules. Willful refusal to accept Jesus' healings as evidence of divine power is to resist the Spirit, an obstinacy that prevents spiritual insight.

The Existence of Demons Mark, like other New Testament authors, reflects a common Hellenistic belief in the existence of unseen entities that influence human lives. Numerous Hellenistic documents record charms to ward off demons or free one from their control. In Judaism, works like the deuterocanonical Book of Tobit reveal a belief that demons could be driven out by the correct use of magical formulas (Tob. 6:1–8; 8:1–3). Josephus, who was Mark's contemporary, relates a story about Eleazar, who allegedly exorcised a demon in the presence of the emperor Vespasian (69–79 C.E.), drawing the malign spirit out through its victim's nose (*Antiquities*, 8.46–49).

Jesus the Healer Physical cures, as well as exorcisms, characterize Jesus' assault on Satan's realm. In Mark's portrayal, one of Jesus' most important functions is to bring relief to the afflicted. He drives a fever from Simon Peter's mother-in-law (1:29–31), cleanses a leper (1:40–42), enables a paralyzed man to walk (2:1–12), restores a man's withered hand (3:1–6), stops a woman's chronic hemorrhaging (5:25–34), and resuscitates the comatose daughter of **Jairus**, a synagogue official (5:21–24, 35–43).

THE JOURNEY TO JERUSALEM: JESUS' PREDESTINED SUFFERING

In Chapter 8, which forms the central pivot on which the entire Gospel turns, Mark ties together several themes that convey his essential vision of Jesus' ministry and what Jesus requires of those who would follow him. Beginning on a joyous note with his account of Jesus feeding a large crowd (8:1–10), this section continues through a crisis of misunderstanding between Jesus, Peter, and the other disciples (8:11–21, 27–33) and ends with Jesus' warning (to Mark's community) that he will disown unfaithful followers (8:38). The narrative movement from elation to gloom involves the disciples' failure to comprehend either the significance of Jesus' miracles or the purpose of his life and death.

Besides repeating the theme of the disciples' obtuseness, Chapter 8 also sounds Mark's concurrent themes of the hidden or unexpected quality of Jesus' messiahship—especially the necessity of his suffering—and the requirement that all believers must be prepared to embrace a comparably painful fate. In contrast to John's Gospel, in which Jesus' identity is publicly affirmed at the outset of his career, no one in Mark's Gospel even hints that Jesus is the Messiah until almost the close of the Galilean campaign when Peter — in a flash of insight — recognizes him as such (8:29). The Markan Jesus then swears the disciples to secrecy, as he had earlier ordered other witnesses of his deeds to keep silent (1:23–24, 34; 3:11–12; 5:7; 7:36; 8:30; see also 9:9). Jesus' reluctance to have news of his miracles spread abroad is known as the messianic secret, a term coined by the German scholar William Wrede (1901).

Most scholars believe that Mark's theme of the messianic secret represents the author's theological purpose. For Mark, people could not know Jesus' identity until *after* he had completed his mission. Jesus had to be unappreciated in order to be rejected and killed — to fulfill God's will that he "give up his life as a ransom for many" (10:45).

A conviction that Jesus must suffer an unjust death — an atonement offering for others — to confirm and complete his messiahship is the heart of Mark's **Christology** (concepts about the nature and function of Christ). Hence, Peter's confession at Caesarea Philippi that Jesus is the Christ (Messiah) is immediately followed by Jesus' first prediction that he will go to Jerusalem only to die (8:29–32). When Peter objects to this notion of a rejected and defeated Messiah, Jesus calls his chief disciple a "satan." Derived from a Hebrew term meaning "obstacle," the epithet *satan* labels Peter's attitude an obstacle or roadblock on Jesus' predestined path to the cross. Peter understands Jesus no better than do outsiders, regarding the Messiah as a God-empowered hero who conquers his enemies, not as a submissive victim of their brutality.

At the end of Chapter 8, Mark introduces a third idea: True disciples must expect to suffer as Jesus does. In two of the three Passion predictions, Jesus emphasizes that "Anyone who wishes to be a follower of mine must leave self behind; he must take up his cross, and come with me" (8:27–34; 10:32–45). Irony permeates the third instance when James and John, sons of Zebedee, presumptuously ask to rule with Jesus, occupying places of honor on his right and left. As Jesus explains that

reigning with him means imitating his sacrifice, Mark's readers are intended to remember that when Jesus reaches Jerusalem, the positions on his right and left will be taken by the two brigands crucified next to him (15:27).

THE JERUSALEM MINISTRY

If Mark was aware of Jesus' other visits to Jerusalem (narrated in John's Gospel), he dismisses them as unimportant compared with the visit made during Jesus' last week on earth. In Chapter 11, a crowd, probably of Galilean supporters, enthusiastically welcomes Jesus to Jerusalem, hailing him as restorer of "the coming kingdom of our father David" (11:9–10). For the first time, Jesus publicly accepts a messianic role, one that Roman guards at the city gate could interpret as a political claim to Jewish kingship and an act of treason to Rome (11:1–10). During his few days in the holy city, Jesus behaves in a manner that alienates both the Roman and Jewish administrations, arousing the hostility of almost every religious party and institution in official Judaism. His assault on the Temple (11:15–19) — overturning the moneychangers' tables and disrupting the sale of sacrificial animals — is seen as a dangerous attack on the Sadducean priesthood in charge of maintaining the Sanctuary, an act that probably seals his fate with the chief priests and Temple police.

As Jesus moves through the Temple courts (Figure 10.4), thronged with Passover pilgrims, Mark depicts him scoring success after success in a series of hostile confrontations. The Pharisees and Herod's party attempt to trap Jesus on the controversial issue of paying taxes to Rome, a snare he eludes by suggesting that Caesar's coins may be returned to their source, while God claims the rest.

The Sadducees also suffer defeat when they try to force Jesus into an untenable position they hope will illustrate the illogic of a belief in resurrection to future life. When asked to which husband a woman who has been widowed six times will be married when all the former spouses are raised, Jesus states that there will be no ethical problem because those resurrected are no longer confined to human sexual identities but are "like angels in

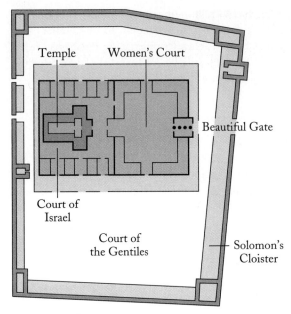

Temple   Women's Court

Beautiful Gate

Court of
Israel

Court of
the Gentiles

Solomon's
Cloister

Figure 10.4 This drawing shows the outline of Herod's Temple, Jerusalem. With its great courtyards and porticoes, the Temple covered many acres. The main sanctuary, however, was a simple rectangular building with an outer porch, a long inner room, and an innermost chamber known as the Holy of Holies. A heavily bejeweled curtain separated the two inner chambers.

heaven" (12:18–25). Citing the Torah, the only part of the Hebrew Bible that the Sadducees accept, he quotes Yahweh's words to Moses at the burning bush—that Yahweh is the God of Abraham, Isaac, and Jacob (Exod. 3:6). He argues that because Yahweh is "not God of the dead but of the living," the ancient patriarchs must still be alive from the Deity's perspective (Mark 12:26–27).

Attracted by this clever refutation of the Sadducees, a Torah expert asks Jesus to name the most important commandment. Agreeing that love of God (Deut. 6:4) and love of neighbor (Lev. 19:18) are paramount, the lawyer and Jesus exchange compliments. Although not a follower, the Jerusalem leader sees that love is the essence of Jesus' religion, a perception that Jesus says makes him "not far from the kingdom of God" (Mark 12:14)—a more favorable verdict than Jesus ever passes on the Twelve.

JESUS' PROPHECY OF THE TEMPLE'S FALL

In Chapter 13, Mark highlights the crisis that then deeply concerned his community—Rome's imminent destruction of the holy city and its Sanctuary, with all its implications for the original center of Christianity. The long speech predicting the Temple's doom appears to combine material from a variety of sources, particularly Jewish apocalyptic material. How much of the discourse on Jerusalem's destruction and the reappearance of the Son of Man originated with Jesus and how much represents interpretations by visionaries and prophets in Mark's church is unknown. Readers will notice that Mark incorporates two somewhat contradictory views of the *eschaton*. He states that a swarm of disasters and frightening astronomical phenomena will provide unmistakable "signs" that the End is near, just as the budding fig tree heralds the arrival of spring (13:8, 14–20, 24–31). Conversely, neither the Son nor his followers can know the time of Judgment Day, so one must keep constant watch because the End will occur without warning (13:32–37).

Mark's strong emphasis on political and social upheavals as portents of the End can be explained by the turbulent era in which he composed his Gospel. If, as historians believe, Mark wrote during the Jewish revolt, when battles and insurrections were daily occurrences, along with intense suffering by Palestinian Jews and Roman Christians, these events seemed to be a turning point in history, a crisis in which the Messiah's appearance was widely anticipated. In the 60s C.E., great earthquakes (13:8) shook the eastern Mediterranean, as well as central Italy, where Pompeii, Herculaneum, and Naples suffered heavy damage—precursors of Vesuvius's eruption in 79 C.E. Mark is particularly concerned that Christians are not misled by rumors of new messiahs or impostors claiming to be Jesus returned. Mark's anxiety about false prophets indicates that his community was familiar with predictions about Jesus' reappearance that were disproved when they failed to materialize (13:5–6, 21–23).

This painful tribulation, which threatens the people of God, will be ended when the Son of

Figure 10.5 A typical example of early Christian art in the catacombs of Rome, this wall painting shows communicants celebrating the Eucharist, or communal meal. The fish and the baskets recall Jesus' twin miracles of feeding 4000 and 5000 in Mark's Gospel.

Man returns with his angels to gather the faithful. Mark shows Jesus warning the disciples that all these horrors and wonders will occur in their lifetime, although no one knows the precise day or hour (13:24–32). Mark's eschatological urgency, which Matthew and Luke later mute in their respective versions of the apocalypse (cf. Matt. 24–25 and Luke 21), vividly conveys both the fears and hopes of Mark's Christian generation.

The Last Supper   Withdrawing with his disciples to an "upper room" in Jerusalem, Jesus presides over a **Passover** feast of unleavened bread, an observance that solemnly recalls the Israelites' last night in Egypt, where the Angel of Death "passed over" their homes to slay the Egyptian firstborn (Exod. 11:1–13:16). In a ritual at the close of their meal, Jesus gives the Passover a new significance, stating that the bread is his "body" and the wine his "blood of the [New] Covenant, shed for many" (Mark 14:22–25), a foreshadowing of his crucifixion. Mark's account of this Last Supper, the origin of the Christian celebration of the **Eucharist**, or Holy Communion, closely resembles Paul's earlier description of the ceremony (1 Cor. 11:23–26) (Figure 10.5).

Jesus' Passion   In describing Jesus' Passion—his final suffering and death—Mark's narrative irony reaches its height. Although the author emphasizes many grim details of Jesus' excruciatingly painful execution, he intends for his readers to see the enormous disparity between the *appearance* of Jesus' vulnerability to worldly power and the actual reality of his spiritual triumph. Jesus' enemies, who believe they are ridding Judea of a dangerous radical, are in fact making possible his saving death— all according to God's design.

Even so, Mark's hero is tested fully—treated with savage cruelty (14:65; 15:15–20), deserted by all his friends (14:50), and apparently abandoned by God (15:34). The agony begins in **Gethsemane**, a grove or vineyard on the **Mount of Olives** opposite Jerusalem to which Jesus and the disciples retreat after the Last Supper. In the Gethsemane episode (14:28–52), Mark places a dual emphasis on Jesus' fulfilling predictions in the Hebrew Bible (14:26–31, 39) and on his personal anguish. By juxtaposing these two elements, Mark demonstrates that while the Crucifixion will take place as God long ago planned (and revealed in Scripture), Jesus' part in the drama of salvation demands heroic effort. While the disciples mindlessly sleep,

Jesus faces the hard reality of his impending torture, experiencing "grief" and "horror and dismay." To Mark, his hero—emotionally ravaged and physically defenseless—provides the model for all believers whose loyalty is tested. Although Jesus prays that God will spare him the humiliation and pain he dreads, he forces his own will into harmony with God's. Mark reports that even during this cruel testing of the heavenly Father/Son of Man relationship, Jesus addresses the Deity as "*Abba*," an Aramaic term expressing a child's trusting intimacy with the parent (14:32–41).

Mark's skill as a storyteller—and interpreter of the events he narrates—is demonstrated in the artful way he organizes his account of Jesus' Passion. Peter's testing (14:37–38) and denial that he even knows Jesus (15:65–72) provide the frame for and ironic parallel to Jesus' trial before the Sanhedrin, the Jewish council headed by **Caiaphas**, the high priest. When Peter fulfills Jesus' prediction about denying him, the disciple's failure serves a double purpose: confirming Jesus' prophetic gifts and strengthening readers' confidence in Jesus' ability to fulfill other prophecies, including those of his resurrection (14:28) and reappearance as the glorified Son of Man (14:62).

Mark contrasts Peter's fearful denial with Jesus' courageous declaration to the Sanhedrin that he is indeed the Messiah and the appointed agent of God's future judgment (14:62). The only Gospel writer to show Jesus explicitly accepting a messianic identity at his trial, Mark may do so to highlight his theme that Jesus' messiahship is revealed primarily through humility and service, a denial of self that also effects humanity's salvation (10:45). Like the author of Hebrews, Mark sees Jesus' divine Sonship earned and perfected through suffering and death (Heb. 2:9–11; 5:7–10).

At daybreak on Friday, the "whole council held a consultation" (15:1)—perhaps implying that the night meeting had been illegal and therefore lacked authority to condemn Jesus—and sends the accused to **Pontius Pilate**, the Roman prefect or procurator who was in Jerusalem to maintain order during Passover week. Uninterested in the Sanhedrin's charge that Jesus is a blasphemer, Pilate focuses on Jesus' reputed political crime: claiming to be the Jewish king, a capital offense. After remarking that it is Pilate himself who has stated the claim, Jesus refuses to answer further questions. Because Mark re-creates almost the entire Passion story in the context of prophecies from the Hebrew Bible, it is difficult to know if Jesus' silence represents his actual behavior or the author's reliance on Isaiah 53, where Israel's suffering servant does not respond to his accusers (Isa. 53:7).

As Mark describes the proceedings, Pilate is extremely reluctant to condemn Jesus and does so only after the priestly hierarchy pressures him to do so. Whereas the Markan Pilate maneuvers to spare Jesus' life, the historical Pilate (procurator of Judea, 26–36 C.E.), whom Josephus describes, rarely hesitated to slaughter troublesome Jews (cf. *Antiquities*, 18.3.1–2; *The Jewish War*, 2.9.4). When a mob demands that not Jesus but a convicted terrorist named **Barabbas** be freed, Pilate is pictured as having no choice but to release Barabbas (the first person to benefit from Jesus' sacrifice) and order the Galilean's crucifixion.

Stripped, flogged, taunted, and crowned with thorns, Jesus apparently is unable to carry the crossbeam of his cross, so Roman soldiers impress a bystander, **Simon of Cyrene**, to carry it for him (15:16–21). Taken to Golgotha (Place of the Skull) outside Jerusalem, Jesus is crucified between two criminals (traditionally called "thieves" but probably brigands similar to those who formed the Zealot party in Mark's day). According to Pilate's order, his cross bears a statement of the political offense for which he is executed: aspiring to be the Jewish king—a cruelly ironic revelation of his true identity (15:22–32).

Although Mark's description of Jesus' undergoing a criminal's shameful death is almost unendurably harsh, his Passion story effectively conveys his dual purpose: creating a paradigm for Christians facing a similar fate and showing that out of human malice and blindness the divine goal is accomplished. The disparity between what witnesses to the Crucifixion think is happening and the saving work that God actually achieves through Jesus' death is expressed in Mark's report of Jesus' last words. Just before dying, Jesus cries out in Aramaic, *"Eli, Eli, lema sabachthani?"*: "My God, My God, why hast thou forsaken me?" (15:33). In placing this question — a direct quotation of Psalm 22:1 — on Jesus' lips, the author emphasizes that the bleak reality of Jesus' pain fulfills prophecy and that disciples who undergo similar martyrdoms can also expect to share in the glory of Jesus' resurrection.

Jesus' Burial   As in all four Gospels, **Mary of Magdala** provides the key human link connecting Jesus' death and burial and the subsequent discovery that his grave is empty (15:40–41, 47; 16:1). **Joseph of Arimathaea**, a mysterious figure introduced suddenly into the narrative, serves a single function: to transfer Jesus' body from Roman control to that of the dead man's disciples. An acquaintance of Pilate, a member of the Sanhedrin, and yet a covert supporter of Jesus' ministry, he bridges the two opposing worlds of Jesus' enemies and friends. Not only does Joseph obtain official permission to remove Jesus' body from the cross — otherwise it would routinely be consigned to an anonymous mass grave — but he also provides a secure place of entombment, a rock-hewn sepulcher that he seals by rolling a large flat stone across the entrance (15:42–47).

POSTLUDE: THE EMPTY TOMB

Because the Jewish Sabbath begins at sundown Friday, the day of Jesus' execution, the female disciples cannot prepare the corpse for interment until Sunday morning. Arriving at dawn, the women find the entrance stone already rolled back and the crypt empty except for the presence of a young man dressed in white.

Mark's description of the scene at the vacant tomb recalls themes recurring throughout his Gospel. Like the male disciples who could not understand Jesus' allusion to resurrection (9:9–10), the women are bewildered, unable to accept the youth's revelation that Jesus is "risen." Fleeing in terror, the women say "nothing to anybody" about what they have heard (16:8), leaving readers to wonder how spreading the "good news" of Jesus' resurrection ever began. The Gospel thus concludes with a frightened silence, eschewing any account of Jesus' postresurrection appearances (16:8).

Resurrection or Parousia?   Mark's belief in the nearness of Jesus' Parousia may explain why the risen Jesus does not manifest himself in the earliest Gospel. Some scholars think that Mark, convinced that the political and social chaos of the Jewish revolt will soon climax in Jesus' return, refers not to a resurrection phenomenon but to the Parousia. Forty years after the Crucifixion, Mark's community may believe that their wandering through the wilderness is almost over: They are about to follow Jesus across Jordan into "Galilee," his promised kingdom (16:6).

Conversely, Mark's climactic image of the empty tomb may express his wish to emphasize Jesus' *absence:* Jesus is present neither in the grave (that is, in death) nor yet as triumphal Son of Man. Mark's Jesus lives both in memories evoked by the Gospel story and in his enduring power over the lives of his followers.

Added Conclusions   Mark's inconclusiveness, his insistence on leaving his story open-ended, must have seemed as unsatisfactory to later Christian scribes as it does to many readers today. For perhaps that reason, Mark's Gospel has been heavily edited, with two different conclusions added at different times. All the oldest manuscripts of Mark end with the line stressing the women's terrified refusal to obey the young man's instruction to carry the resurrection message to Peter. In time, however, some editors appended postresurrection accounts to their copies of Mark, making his Gospel more consistent with Matthew and Luke (Mark 16:8b and 16:9–20).

QUESTIONS FOR REVIEW

1. According to tradition, who wrote the Gospel according to Mark? Why are modern scholars unable to verify that tradition? What themes in the Gospel suggest that it was composed after the Jewish revolt against Rome had already begun?

2. Outline and summarize the major events in Jesus' public career, from his baptism by John and Galilean ministry through his last week in Jerusalem. Specify the devices that Mark uses to connect the powerful miracle worker in Galilee with the seemingly powerless sacrificial victim in Jerusalem. Why does Mark devote so much space and detail to narrating the Passion story? Why does he have Jesus predict his own death three times?

3. Describe the three different categories Mark assigns the Son of Man concept. How is this concept related to earlier Jewish writings, such as the books of Ezekiel, Daniel, and 1 Enoch?

4. Define *parable*, and discuss Jesus' use of this literary form to illustrate his vision of God's kingdom. Why does Mark state that Jesus used parables to *prevent* people from understanding his message?

5. Explain a possible connection between the messianic secret concept and Mark's picture of the disciples as hopelessly inept and of Jesus' opponents as mistakenly seeing him as the devil's agent. What devices does the author employ to convey his view that Jesus *had to be misunderstood* for him to fulfill God's plan?

QUESTIONS FOR DISCUSSION AND REFLECTION

1. How does the historical context help account for Mark's portrait of Jesus as a suffering Messiah whose disciples must also expect to suffer? How would the wars, insurrections, and persecutions afflicting Mark's community have stimulated the author's sense of eschatological urgency?

2. Why does Mark paint so unflattering a picture of Jesus' Galilean family, neighbors, and disciples, all of whom fail to understand or support him? Is the author trying to disassociate Christianity from its Palestinian origins in favor of his Gentile church's understanding of Jesus' significance?

3. Discuss Mark's use of irony in his presentation of Jesus' story. List and discuss some incongruities between the spiritual reality that Jesus embodies and the way in which most people in the Markan narrative perceive him. In the literary world that Mark creates in his Gospel, how do appearance and reality conflict? How does Mark demonstrate that God achieves his purpose in Jesus even though political and religious authorities succeed in destroying him?

TERMS AND CONCEPTS TO REMEMBER

Andrew	Joseph of Arimathaea
baptism	Judas
Barabbas	Mark
Bartholomew	Mary of Magdala
Boanerges	Matthew
Caesarea Philippi	Mount of Olives
Caiaphas	Nazareth
Capernaum	Parousia
Cephas	Passover
Christ	Peter
Christology	Philip
disciples	Pontius Pilate
epiphany	Sanhedrin
Eucharist	Satan
exorcism	Simon
Galilee	Son of Man
Gethsemane	sons of thunder
Gospel of Thomas	Thaddeus
Holy Spirit, the	Thomas
Jairus	tradition
James	Transfiguration
John	the Twelve
John the Baptist	Zebedee

RECOMMENDED READING

Achtemeier, Paul J. "Gospel of Mark." In D. N. Freedman, ed., *The Anchor Bible Dictionary*, Vol. 4, pp. 541–557. New York: Doubleday, 1992. Applies the two-source hypothesis to Mark.

Bryan, Christopher. *A Preface to Mark: Notes on the Gospel in Its Literary and Cultural Setting*. New York: Oxford University Press, 1993. Links Mark with the oral tradition.

Funk, Robert W., and Hoover, Roy W. *The Five Gospels: The Search for the Authentic Words of Jesus*. A Polebridge Press Book. New York: Macmillan, 1993. A fresh, colloquial translation, with clear, scholarly annotations comparing Markan passages with parallels in Matthew, Luke, and Thomas.

Harrington, Daniel J. "The Gospel According to Mark." In R. E. Brown et al., eds. *The New Jerome Biblical Commentary*, pp. 596–629. Englewood Cliffs, N.J.: Prentice-Hall, 1990.

Kee, Howard C. *Community of the New Age: Studies in Mark's Gospel*. Philadelphia: Westminster Press, 1977. Reprint, Macon, Ga.: Mercer University Press, 1983. Examines the probable historical circumstances of Mark's community.

Kelber, W. H. *Mark's Story of Jesus*. Philadelphia: Fortress Press, 1979. A penetrating but succinct analysis of Mark's rendition of Jesus' life.

———. *The Oral and the Written Gospel: The Hermeneutics of Speaking and Writing in the Synoptic Tradition, Mark, Paul, and Q.* Philadelphia: Fortress Press, 1983. A major scholarly study of Mark's place in the Jesus tradition.

Ladd, George Eldon. *A Theology of the New Testament.* Grand Rapids, Mich.: Eerdmans, 1974.

Mann, C. S. *Mark: A New Translation, Interpretation, and Commentary.* Anchor Bible, Vol. 27. Garden City, N.Y.: Doubleday, 1986. Argues the Griesbach hypothesis that Mark is a conflation of Matthew and Luke.

Perkins, Pheme. "The Gospel of Mark." In *The New Interpreter's Bible,* Vol. 8, pp. 509–733. Nashville: Abingdon Press, 1995.

Schmidt, Daryl D. *The Gospel of Mark: The Scholars Bible I.* Sonoma, Calif.: Polebridge Press, 1991. A vivid translation with scholarly annotations.

Streeter, B. H. *The Four Gospels: A Study in Origins.* New York: Macmillan, 1924. A classic statement of the relationship of the Synoptic Gospels, arguing Mark's priority.

Matthew's Gospel

KEY TOPICS/THEMES

Most scholars believe that Matthew's Gospel is an expanded edition of Mark, which the author frames with accounts of Jesus' birth (Chs. 1 and 2) and postresurrection appearances (Ch. 28). Although retaining Mark's general sequence of events, Matthew adds five blocks of teaching material, emphasizing Jesus as the inaugurator of a new covenant (26:26–29) who definitively interprets the Mosaic Torah and, through fulfilling specific prophecies in the Hebrew Bible, proves his identity as Israel's Messiah. Writing a decade or two after the Roman destruction of Jerusalem, Matthew somewhat softens Mark's portrait of an apocalyptic Jesus, adding parables that imply a delay in the Parousia (Second Coming) (Chs. 24 and 25), an interval of indefinite length devoted to the missionary work of the church (*ekklesia*). Matthew's principal discourses include the Sermon on the Mount (Chs. 5–7), Instructions to the Twelve (Ch. 10), Parables of the Kingdom (Ch. 13), Instructions to the Church (Ch. 18), and Warnings of Final Judgment (Chs. 23–25).

KEY QUESTIONS

In what ways does Matthew edit Mark's Gospel to express his view of Jesus as an authoritative reinterpreter of the Torah? How does he modify expectations of the Second Coming?

MATTHEW'S GOSPEL: A LINK BETWEEN OLD AND NEW TESTAMENTS

If the Gospel of Mark was the first Gospel written, as most scholars believe, why does Matthew's account stand first in the New Testament canon? The original compilers of the Christian Scriptures probably assigned Matthew its premier position for several reasons. Besides offering a more extensive coverage of Jesus' teaching than any other Gospel, it was important to early Christian leaders because of the author's concern with the nature and function of the *ekklesia* (church), a term that appears only in Matthew's Gospel (Chs. 10 and 18) (Box 10.9; for a list of new characters introduced in Matthew, see Box 10.10). As both an instructional tool and a rudimentary guidebook to administering the Christian community, Matthew was supremely useful.

Placing Matthew at the opening of the New Testament is also thematically appropriate because it forms a strong connecting link with the Hebrew Bible. Matthew starts his account with a genealogy to associate Jesus with the most prominent heroes of ancient Israel. Beginning with Abraham, progenitor of the Hebrew people, Matthew lists as Jesus' ancestors celebrated kings like David, Solomon, and Josiah. The manner in which Matthew presents his record of Jesus' ancestors is typical of his use of the Hebrew Bible. His purpose is not only to establish Jesus' messianic credentials — by right of descent from Abraham and David — but also to present Jesus' birth at the climax of Israelite history. He therefore arranges Jesus' family tree in three distinct segments, each representing a particular phase of the biblical story. From the time of Abraham, bearer of the covenant promises for land, nationhood, and universal blessing (Gen. 12:1–3; 22:18), to that of David, bearer of the

Box 10.9 Representative Examples of Material Found Only in Matthew

A "Table of Descent [genealogy]" listing Jesus' ancestors (1:1–17)

Matthew's distinctive version of Jesus' miraculous conception and birth at Bethlehem (1:18–2:23)

Some parables, sayings, and miracles unique to Matthew:

- The dumb demoniac (9:32–34)
- Wheat and darnel [weeds] (13:24–30)
- Buried treasure (13:44)
- The pearl of "special value" (13:45)
- Catching fish in a net (13:47–50)
- A learner with treasures old and new (13:51–52)
- Earthly rulers collecting taxes (17:25–26)
- Finding a coin in a fish's mouth to pay the Temple tax (17:27)

- The unforgiving debtor (18:23–35)
- Paying equal wages to all vineyard laborers (20:1–16)
- The two sons and obedience (21:28–32)
- The improperly dressed wedding guest (22:11–14)
- The wise and foolish virgins (25:1–13)
- The judgment separating sheep from goats (25:31–46)
- Judas and the chief priests (27:3–10)
- The dream of Pilate's wife (27:19)
- The resurrection of saints (27:52–53)
- The Easter morning earthquake (28:2)
- The chief priests' conspiracy to deny Jesus' resurrection (28:11–15)

Box 10.10 New Characters Introduced in Matthew

Joseph, husband of Mary (1:16, 18–25; 2:13–14, 19–23)

Herod the Great, Roman-appointed king of Judea, 40–4 B.C.E. (2:1–8, 16–19)

The Magi, astrologers or "wise men" from the east (2:1–12)

Satan, the devil (as a speaking character) (4:1–11)

Two blind men (9:27–31)

A dumb demoniac (9:32–34)

A revised list of the Twelve (10:1–4)

The mother of James and John, sons of Zebedee (20:20–21)

covenant promise of an everlasting line of kings (2 Sam. 7:16), is fourteen generations. From the time of David, whose prosperous kingdom is the high point of Israel's history, to the Babylonian exile, the lowest ebb of Israelite fortunes, is another fourteen generations. From the time of Babylonian captivity to the appearance of Jesus, who inherits all the promises made to Abraham and David, is also fourteen generations (Matt. 1:17). As fourteen generations intervened between Yahweh's vow to Abraham and the establishment of David's throne, so an equal span of time elapsed between the Babylonian overthrow of the Davidic line and the appearance of David's ultimate heir, the Messiah. Although the neatness of Matthew's numerical scheme conveys the author's sense of Jesus' crucial importance to the covenant people — and his view of the mathematically precise way in which God arranges Israel's history — closer examination of the genealogy raises some difficulties.

First, Matthew actually lists thirteen, not fourteen, generations between the Babylonian destruction of Jerusalem and Jesus' birth. Second, one of Matthew's sources for the period between David and the exile, 1 Chronicles 3:10–12, reveals the names of several Davidic kings (at least three generations) that he omitted from the list, presumably to fit his desired sequence of fourteen. Finally, at the end of his genealogy, Matthew unexpectedly states that the line of royal descent directly connects not with Jesus, but with Joseph, who the writer believes was not Jesus' biological father. Somewhat paradoxically, Matthew concludes his list by noting that Jesus' paternal grandfather is "Jacob [father] of Joseph, the husband of Mary, who gave birth to Jesus called Messiah" (Matt. 1:16). The Evangelist may assume that Joseph is Jesus' legal and social parent, and thus can transmit his Davidic legacy to a nonrelative, perhaps through adoption, even if he did not transmit it genetically.

Writing independently of Matthew, Luke compiled a strikingly different genealogy, which further clouds the issue of Jesus' Davidic ancestry (Luke 3:25–38). Using many names not on Matthew's list, Luke states that people "thought" that Jesus was Joseph's son and that his paternal grandfather was Heli (not Jacob, as Matthew has it). Almost since the two Gospel genealogies were first published, Christians have sought to resolve their apparent disagreement, but although ingenious solutions have been proposed, none yet has been universally accepted. Whatever its historical credibility, the family tree with which Matthew begins his Gospel (and hence the New Testament itself) proclaims Jesus as the culminating figure in a long biblical tradition. As several scholars have observed, Matthew may have devised his genealogical pattern of fourteen for its messianic significance. Because Hebrew, like Greek and many other ancient languages, uses letters to signify numbers, each letter of the alphabet has a numerical value. In Hebrew, the three consonants making up David's name (DWD) total fourteen, which can function as the symbolic number of David's promised heir.

Although biblical genealogists uniformly recorded only the male line, linking fathers to sons, Matthew included four female ancestors of Je-

sus—Tamar (1:3), Rahab (1:5), Ruth (1:5), and Bathsheba, "the wife of Uriah," who later became David's queen and the mother of King Solomon (1:6). Matthew's reasons for departing from biblical tradition are unclear, but scholars have found at least two factors that thematically bind these women together and that may have influenced the Evanelist's decision to make them part of Jesus' heritage. Besides the fact that all four were Gentiles (Ruth was a Moabite, Tamar and Rahab Canaanites, and Bathsheba a Hittite), all four were also involved in irregular sexual activity. While Tamar posed as a prostitute to beguile her father-in-law into impregnating her (Gen. 38), Rahab actually plied the trade of a "harlot" in Canaanite Jericho (Josh. 2; 6). A young widow, Ruth seduced Boaz into marrying her (Ruth 1–4), and Bathesheba committed adultery with David, becoming his wife only after the king had arranged to have her husband Uriah slain in battle (2 Sam. 11–12; 1 Kings 1–2).

Matthew states that, when Joseph discovered that his future bride, Mary, was already expecting a child, he planned to divorce her secretly to spare her public dishonor. He accepts Mary as his wife only after he dreams of an angel informing him that she had "conceived this child" by the "Holy Spirit" (1:18–25). Although he connects Jesus with Abraham and David explicitly through Joseph, he also specifies that Mary is the sole human parent (1:16). As Matthew arranged Jesus' forebears in groups of fourteen to express divine providence at work, so he underscores the presence of ancestresses (and their male partners) with questionable pasts to illustrate God's unexpected use of flawed humanity to accomplish his purpose.

Matthew's wish to connect Jesus with the Hebrew Bible goes far beyond genealogical concerns. More than any other Gospel writer, he presents Jesus' life in the context of biblical Law and prophecy. Throughout the entire Gospel, Matthew underscores Jesus' fulfillment of ancient prophecies, repeatedly emphasizing the continuity between Jesus and the promises made to Israel, particularly to the royal dynasty of David. To demonstrate that Jesus' entire career, from conception to resurrection, was predicted centuries earlier by biblical writers from

Moses to Malachi, Matthew quotes from, paraphrases, or alludes to the Hebrew Bible at least 60 times. (Some scholars have detected 140 or more allusions to the Hebrew Scriptures.) Nearly a dozen times, Matthew employs a literary formula that drives home the connection between prophecy and specific events in Jesus' life: "All this happened in order to fulfill what the Lord declared through the prophet . . . ," Matthew writes, then citing a biblical passage to support his contention (1:22–23; 2:15; 2:23; see Table 10.4).

Matthew takes great pains to show that Jesus both taught and observed the principles of the Mosaic Torah (5:17–20), which he presents as still binding on his church. Regarded as the "most Jewish" of the Evangelists, the author is well versed in the methods of interpreting a biblical text practiced in the Judaism of his day. Like the Essenes of Qumran, Matthew interprets the Hebrew Bible as applying exclusively to his group of believers, whom he regards as the true Israel. He also typically presents Jesus' teaching as a kind of midrash on the Torah. A detailed exposition of the underlying meaning of a scriptural passage, a **midrash** includes an interpretation of the Scripture's legal rules for daily life (called **halakah**) and an explanation of nonlegal material (called **haggadah**). At various points in his Gospel, Matthew shows Jesus providing halakic interpretations of the Torah (see 5:17–48), particularly on such legal matters as Sabbath-keeping and divorce (12:1–21; 19:3–12).

Although an early tradition assigns the Gospel of Matthew to Jesus' apostle of that name, the book itself makes no such claim. The assumption that the author is the "publican" or tax collector mentioned in Matthew 9:9–13 (and called "Levi" in Mark 2:14) dates from the second century c.e. and cannot be verified. According to Papias (c. 140 c.e.), whom Eusebius quotes in his *History of the Church*, "Matthew compiled the Sayings [*logia*] in the Aramaic language, and everyone translated them as well as he could" (*History* 3.39.16).

As many commentators have observed, the Sayings, or *logia*, are not the same as the "words" [*logoi*] of Jesus, nor are they the same as the Gospel of Matthew we have today. Papias may refer simply to

an early Christian, perhaps named Matthew, who assembled a list of messianic prophecies in the Hebrew Bible, a collection that the creator of our present Gospel may have used. The main difficulty in accepting Matthew's authorship is that the writer relies heavily on Mark as a source. Scholars believe it extremely unlikely that one of the original Twelve would depend on the work of Mark, who was not an eyewitness to the events he describes. Like all the Gospels, Matthew was originally composed in Greek and circulated anonymously.

A Greek-speaking Jewish Christian, Matthew (we use the traditional author's name to avoid confusion) may refer to himself or a "school" of early Christian interpreters of the Hebrew Scriptures when he states, "When, therefore, a teacher of the law [a scribe] has become a learner [disciple] in the kingdom of Heaven, he is like a householder who can produce from his store both the new and the old" (Matt. 13:52–53). The author effectively combines "the new" (Christian teaching) with "the old" (Torah Judaism), providing a continuity between the two testaments.

The oldest reference to Matthew's Gospel appears in the letters of Ignatius, who was bishop of Antioch in Syria about 110–115 c.e. The Gospel text itself implies that it was written after the destruction of Jerusalem (which is apparently referred to in 22:7) and after the split between Church and synagogue, which occurred about 85–90 c.e. (9:35; 10:17; 12:9; 13:54). Hence, most scholars believe that it was composed in Antioch, a major Jewish-Christian center, in the late 80s or early 90s c.e.

MATTHEW'S STRUCTURE AND THEMES

Sources   Analysis of Matthew's text suggests that he used at least four different sources. Besides incorporating about 90 percent of Mark into his account, Matthew apparently used the Q document as well. A hypothetical collection of Jesus' sayings compiled between about 50 and 70 c.e., Q contained numerous kingdom parables, instructions to the disciples, and prophecies of the Second Coming (Parousia) that are present in both Matthew and Luke but absent from Mark.

Besides Mark and Q, Matthew had a source peculiar to his Gospel, known as M (Matthean). M includes sayings and parables, such as the stories about the vineyard laborers (20:1–16) and many of the kingdom pronouncements in Chapter 13 (13:24–30, 44–45, 47–52). Finally, Matthew used his special versions of Jesus' ancestral background and infancy, as well as his distinctive account of the postresurrection appearances (28:8–20).

Organization Matthew adheres to Mark's north–south polarity, presenting Jesus as making only one journey southward from Galilee to Jerusalem. Closely reproducing Mark's order of events, which forms the narrative framework of his Gospel, he inserts five large sections of teaching material into the Markan sequence and brackets it with his unique accounts of Jesus' birth and resurrection. This discussion focuses on Matthew's distinctive contribution to Jesus' story, particularly the five speeches the author ascribes to his hero (Chs. 5–7, 10, 13, 18, and 23–25).

Matthew's Editing of Mark While preserving most of his Markan source, Matthew edits it to convey his theological views. He thus modifies or omits Markan elements that do not reflect the Torah-respecting practices of the Matthean church, deleting Mark's assertion that Jesus declared all foods "clean" (cf. Mark 7:18–23 and Matt. 15:15–20) and changing the absolute prohibition against divorce to permit it in cases of "unchastity" (cf. Mark 10:11–12 and Matt. 5:31–32). (For more examples of Matthew's editing of Markan material, see Box 10.11.)

Matthew also edits Mark to emphasize the miraculous and supernatural character of Jesus' mission (Figure 10.6). In recounting Jesus' unfriendly reception in Nazareth, Matthew changes Mark's observation that Jesus "could work no miracle there" (Mark 6:5) to the declaration that "he did not work many miracles there," eliminating the implication that the human Jesus had any limit to his powers (13:58). He similarly omits Mark's definition of John's baptism as a rite performed "for the forgiveness of sins" (3:2, 6, 11; Mark 1:4), transferring the exact phrase to his account of the

Last Supper (26:26–28). Matthew may have effected this change to ensure that readers understood that "forgiveness of sin" comes not from John's baptism, but from Jesus' redemptive death.

Matthew's edition of the Passion narrative also intensifies the supernatural element. In Gethsemane, the Matthean Jesus reminds his persecutors that he has the power to call up thousands of angels to help him (26:53), a claim absent from Mark. Matthew's Christ allows himself to be arrested only to fulfill Scripture (26:54).

Matthew also revises Mark's crucifixion account, inserting several miracles to stress the event's cosmic significance. To Mark's plague of darkness and the rending of the Temple curtain, Matthew adds that an earthquake occurred, violent enough to open graves and permit suddenly resurrected "saints" (holy persons) to rise and walk the streets of Jerusalem (27:50–53). (This mysterious raising of saints is not mentioned elsewhere in the New Testament but probably appears here to express Matthew's conviction that Jesus' death makes possible the resurrection of the faithful.) Matthew introduces yet another earthquake into his description of the first Easter morning, stating that the women disciples arrive at Jesus' tomb in time to see a divine being descend and roll away the stone blocking the tomb entrance. Mark's linen-clad youth becomes an angel before whom the Roman guards quake in terror (28:1–4). What Mark's account may only imply, Matthew's typically makes explicit, ensuring that the reader will not miss the hand of God in these happenings. Nor does Matthew leave the Galilean women wondering and frightened at the empty sepulcher. Instead of being too terrified to report what they have seen, in Matthew's version the women joyously rush away to inform the disciples (28:8; Mark 16:8). In this retelling, the women set the right example by immediately proclaiming the good news of Jesus' triumph over death (28:19).

THE INFANCY NARRATIVE

Except for Matthew and Luke, no New Testament writers refer even briefly to the circumstances surrounding Jesus' birth. Nor do Matthew and Luke

Table 10.4 Representative Examples of Matthew's Use of the Septuagint (Greek) Edition of the Hebrew Bible to Identify Jesus as the Promised Messiah

MATTHEW (CITING GREEK VERSION)	HEBREW BIBLE SOURCE
"All this happened in order to fulfill what the Lord declared through the prophet. . . ." (Matt. 1:22)	
1. "The Virgin will conceive and bear a son, and he shall be called Emmanuel." (Matt. 1:22)	1. A young woman is with child, and she will bear a son and will call him Immanuel. (Isa. 7:14)
2. "Bethlehem in the land of Judah, you are far from least in the eyes of the rulers of Judah; for out of you shall come a leader to be the shepherd of my people Israel." (Matt. 2:5–6)	2. But you, Bethlehem in Ephrathah, small as you are to be among Judah's clans, out of you shall come forth a governor for Israel, one whose roots are far back in the past, in days gone by. (Mic. 5:2)
3. So Joseph . . . went away . . . to Egypt, and there he stayed till Herod's death. This was to fulfill what the Lord had declared through the prophet: "I called my son out of Egypt." (Matt. 2:15)	3. When Israel was a boy, I loved him; I called my son out of Egypt. (Hos. 11:1)
4. Herod . . . gave orders for the massacre of all children in Bethlehem and its neighborhood, of the age of two years or less. . . . So the words spoken through Jeremiah the prophet were fulfilled: "A voice was heard in Rama, wailing and loud laments; it was Rachael weeping for her children, and refusing all consolation, because they were no more." (Matt. 2:16–18)	4. Hark, lamentation is heard in Ramah, and bitter weeping, Rachel weeping for her sons. She refuses to be comforted: they are no more. (Jer. 31:15)
5. "He shall be called a Nazarene." (Matt. 2:23) [*This statement does not appear in the Hebrew Bible; it may be a misreading of Isaiah 11:1.*]	5. Then a shoot shall grow from the stock of Jesse, and a branch [Hebrew, *nezer*] shall spring from his roots. (Isa. 11:1)
6. When he heard that John had been arrested, Jesus withdrew to Galilee; and leaving Nazareth he went and settled at Capernaum on the Sea of Galilee, in the district of Zebulun and Naphtali. This was to fulfill the passage in the prophet Isaiah which tells of "the land of Zebulun, the land of Naphtali, the Way of the Sea, the land beyond Jordan, heathen Galilee," and says: The people that lived in darkness saw a great light: light dawned on the dwellers in the land of death's dark shadow (Matt. 4:12–16)	6. For, while the first invader has dealt lightly with the land of Zebulun and the land of Naphtali, the second has dealt heavily with Galilee of the Nations on the road beyond Jordan to the sea. The people who walked in darkness have seen a great light: light has dawned upon them, dwellers in a land as dark as death. (Isa. 9:1–2)
7. And he drove the spirits out with a word and healed all who were sick, to fulfill the prophecy of Isaiah: "He took away our illnesses and lifted our diseases from us." (Matt. 8:16–17)	7. Yet on himself he bore our sufferings, our torments he endured, while we counted him smitten by God, struck down by disease and misery. (Isa. 53:4)
8. Jesus . . . gave strict injunctions that they were not to make him known. This was to fulfill Isaiah's prophecy: Here is my servant, whom I have chosen, my beloved on whom my favour rests; I will put my spirit upon him, and he will proclaim judgment among the nations.	8. Here is my servant, whom I uphold, my chosen one in whom I delight, I have bestowed my spirit upon him, and he will make justice shine on the nations. He will not call out or lift his voice high, Or make himself heard in the open street. He will not break a bruised reed, or snuff out a smouldering wick;

(continued)

Table 10.4 (continued)

MATTHEW (CITING GREEK VERSION)	HEBREW BIBLE SOURCE
"All this happened in order to fulfill what the Lord declared through the prophet. . . ." (Matt. 1:22)	

He will not strive, he will not shout,
    nor will his voice be heard in the streets.
He will not snap off the broken reed,
    nor snuff out the smouldering wick,
until he leads justice on to victory.
In him the nations shall place their hope.
                    (Matt. 12:16–21)

he will make justice shine on every race,
    never faltering, never breaking down,
he will plant justice on earth,
    while coasts and islands wait for his teaching.
                    (Isa. 42:1–4)

9. In all his teaching to the crowds Jesus spoke in parables; in fact he never spoke to them without a parable. This was to fulfill the prophecy of Isaiah:

    I will open my mouth in parables;
    I will utter things kept secret since the world
        was made.   (Matt. 13:34–35)

9. Mark my teaching, O my people,
    listen to the words I am to speak.
I will tell you a story with a meaning,
    I will expound the riddle of things past,
things that we have heard and know,
    and our fathers have repeated to us.
                    (Ps. 78:2—*not* in Isaiah)

10. Jesus instructs his disciples to bring him a donkey and her foal. "If any speaks to you, say 'Our Master needs them'; and he will let you take them at once." This was to fulfill the prophecy which says, "Tell the daughter of Zion, 'Here is your king, who comes to you riding on an ass, riding on the foal of a beast of burden.'" (Matt. 21:2–5)

    [*Matthew shows Jesus mounted on two beasts — the donkey and her foal. See Luke 19:29–36, where a single mount is mentioned.*]

10. Rejoice, rejoice, daughter of Zion,
    shout aloud, daughter of Jerusalem;
for see, your king is coming to you,
    his cause won, his victory gained,
humble and mounted on an ass,
    on a foal, the young of a she-ass.
                    (Zech. 9:9)

11. [*Judas returns the bribe — "thirty silver pieces" — given him to betray Jesus.*]

    . . . and in this way fulfillment was given to the saying of the prophet Jeremiah: "They took the thirty silver pieces, the price set on a man's head (for that was his price among the Israelites) and gave the money for the potter's field, so the Lord directed me."

11. [*Matthew is wrong in citing Jeremiah as the source of this passage, which, in the form he quotes it, does not appear in the Hebrew Bible. It is Zechariah who reports being paid "thirty shekels of silver," which he then donates to the Temple treasury.*]

So they weighed out as my wages thirty shekels of silver. Then the Lord said to me, "Throw it into the treasury"— this is the lordly price [the standard price of a slave] at which I was valued by them. So I took the thirty shekels of silver and threw them into the treasury in the house of the Lord.

[*Jeremiah does record investing in a field near Jerusalem (Jer. 32:6–15) and refers to visiting a potter's house (Jer. 18:1–3), but neither he nor Zechariah provides support for Matthew's claim of prophetic fulfillment.*]

Box 10.11 Examples of Matthew's Editing of Markan Material*

JESUS' BAPTISM

Mark: It happened at this time that Jesus came from Nazareth in Galilee

and was baptized in the Jordan by John. At the moment when he came up out of the water, he saw the heavens torn open and the Spirit, like a dove, descending upon him. And a voice spoke from heaven: "Thou art my Son, my Beloved; on thee my favour rests." (Mark 1:9–11)

Matthew: Then Jesus arrived at the Jordan from Galilee, and came to John to be baptized by him. **John tried to dissuade him, "Do you come to me?" he said. "I need rather to be baptized by you." Jesus replied, "Let it be so for the present; we do well to conform in this way with all that God requires." John then allowed him to come.** After baptism Jesus came up out of the water at once, and at that moment heaven opened; he saw the Spirit of God descending like a dove to alight upon him; and a voice from heaven was heard saying, **"This is my Son,** my Beloved, on whom my favour rests." (Matt. 3:13–17)

In comparing the two accounts of Jesus' baptism, the reader will note that Matthew inserts a speech by John into the Markan narrative. Recognizing Jesus as "mightier" than himself, John is reluctant to baptize him. By giving John this speech, Matthew is able to stress Jesus' superiority to the Baptist. Matthew also changes the nature of Jesus' experience of the "Spirit" after his baptism. In Mark, the heavenly voice is addressed directly to Jesus and apparently represents Jesus' own private mystical experience of divine Sonship at the event. Matthew changes the "thou art," intended for Jesus' ears, to "this is," making the divine voice a public declaration heard by the crowds.

JESUS' HEALINGS

Mark: That evening after sunset they brought to him all who were ill or possessed by devils; and the whole town was there, gathered at the door. He healed many who suffered from various diseases, and drove out many devils.

He would not let the devils speak, because they knew who he was. (Mark 1:32–34)

Matthew: When evening fell, they brought to him many who were possessed by devils;

and **he drove the spirits out with a word and healed all who were sick.**

to fulfill the prophecy of Isaiah: "He took away our illnesses and lifted our diseases from us." (Matt. 8:16–17)

In reproducing Mark's story, Matthew edits it in several ways that are characteristic of his particular concerns as an author. First, he condenses Mark's narrative, omitting various details to focus on a single aspect of Jesus' miraculous power, in this case the exorcising of "devils." Second, he emphasizes the totality or comprehensiveness of Jesus' power, changing Mark's "he healed many" to "healed all." Finally, most characteristically, he adds to the account a quotation from the Hebrew Bible, citing Isaiah's poem about the suffering servant (Isa. 53:4), to demonstrate that Jesus' activities fulfilled ancient prophecy.

---

* Matthew's chief editorial changes are printed in boldface type.   *(continued)*

Box 10.11 *(continued)*

JESUS' RECEPTION BY HIS NEIGHBORS IN HIS HOMETOWN OF NAZARETH

Mark: He left that place and went to his home town accompanied by his disciples. When the Sabbath came he began to teach in the synagogue; and the large congregation who heard him were amazed and said,
"Where does he get it from?", and, "What wisdom is this that has been given him?", and, "How does he work such miracles? Is not this the carpenter, the son of Mary, the brother of James and Joseph and Judas and Simon? And are not his sisters here with us?"
So they [turned against] him. Jesus said to them, "A prophet will always be held in honour except in his home town, and among his kinsmen and family." He could work no miracle there, except that he put his hands on a few sick people and healed them; and he was taken aback by their want of faith. (Mark 6:1–6)

Matthew: Jesus left that place, and came to his home town, where he taught the people in their synagogue.

In amazement they asked,

"Where does he get this wisdom from, and these miraculous powers? **Is he not the carpenter's son? Is not his mother called Mary,** his brothers James, Joseph, Simon, and Judas? And are not all his sisters here with us? Where then has he got all this from?" So they [turned against] him, and this led him to say, "A prophet will always be held in honour, except in his home town, and in his own family." And **he did not work many miracles there: such was their want of faith.** (Matt. 13:54–58)

In editing Mark's account of Jesus' unsatisfactory reunion with his former neighbors in Nazareth, Matthew reproduces most of his source but makes some significant changes and deletions. He omits Mark's reference to the Sabbath, as well as Mark's brief list of Jesus' "few" deeds there and Jesus' apparent surprise at his fellow townsmen's refusal to respond to his healing efforts. Matthew also substitutes the

phrase "the carpenter's son" for Mark's "the son of Mary," with its implication of Jesus' illegitimacy. In both accounts, the Nazareans' familiarity with Jesus' background and family (naming four "brothers" and referring to two or more "sisters") is enough to make them skeptical of Jesus' claims to special wisdom or authority.

JESUS' STILLING OF A STORM

Mark: [Immediately after miraculously feeding the multitudes who had gathered to hear him preach, Jesus sends the disciples by boat across the sea of Galilee to Bethsaida.] After taking leave of them [the crowds], he went up the hill to pray. It was now late and the boat was already well out on the water, while he was alone on the land. Somewhere between three and six in the morning, seeing them laboring at the oars against a head wind, he came toward them, walking on the lake. He was going to pass by them; but when they saw him walking on the lake, they thought it was a ghost and cried out; for they all saw him and were terrified.

Matthew: As soon as they had finished, he made the disciples embark and cross to the other side [of the Sea of Galilee] ahead of him, while he dismissed the crowd; then he went up the hill by himself to pray. It had grown late, and he was there alone. The boat was already some distance from the shore, battling a head wind and a rough sea. Between three and six in the morning he came towards them, walking across the lake. When the disciples saw him walking on the lake they were so shaken that they cried out in terror: "It is a ghost!" But at once Jesus spoke to them: "Take heart! It is I; do not be afraid."

(continued)

allude to Jesus' virginal conception in the main body of their Gospels. In both cases, the infancy narratives are self-contained units that act as detachable prefaces to the central account of Jesus' public ministry.

Matthew constructs his narrative (1:18–2:23) with phrases and incidents taken from the Hebrew Bible. Jesus is born in Bethlehem to fulfill Micah 5:2 and to a virgin to fulfill the Greek version of Isaiah 7:14 (Figures 10.7 and 10.8). Whereas Matthew's Greek source uses the term *parthenos* (virgin), the Hebrew text of Isaiah merely states that a "young woman (*'almah*)" will give birth. Foreshadowing that the child will be worshiped by many non-Jews, Matthew describes the nativity visit of foreign astrologers, "wise men" from Persia or Babylonia who apparently had concluded from a horoscope of Judah that its king was then due to appear. Roused by the news, King Herod—the Roman-appointed ruler of Judea—attempts to eliminate a potential rival by ordering the slaughter of all Bethlehem children under the age of two (2:1–18). Herod's "massacre of the innocents" is intended to parallel a similar tradition about Moses' infancy, when the child was threatened by Pharaoh's murderous schemes (Exod. 1:8–2:25). It is also cited as fulfillment of a prophecy in Jeremiah.

The holy family's flight into Egypt to escape Herod's wrath is similarly explained as a fulfillment of Hosea 11:1 ("out of Egypt I called my son"). Because Hosea refers not to the Messiah's infancy, but to Israel's Exodus under Moses and is clearly cited out of context, many scholars doubt the historicity of the entire Herod episode. Some critics have questioned whether Matthew, in his eagerness to find or create analogies between Moses and Jesus, the dominant figures of the old and new covenants, has not invented some aspects of the infancy story. The only other New Testament account of Jesus' birth (Luke 2) does not mention either Herod's plot or the Egyptian journey, nor does Josephus or any other contemporary source refer to Herod's alleged murder of Jewish infants.

In fairness to Matthew's use of Hebrew Bible proof texts to validate Jesus as the expected Messiah, it should be noted that biblical **exegesis**—

Figure 10.6 *Christ with the Sick Around Him, Receiving Little Children,* by Rembrandt (1606–1669). In this painting, healing light radiates from the central figure of Jesus and creates a protective circle of illumination around those whom he cures.

analysis and interpretation of the text—was in first-century Palestine a very different discipline from what it is today. Modern scholars respect the integrity of a text, endeavoring to discover its primary meaning by placing it in its original social and historical setting. In Matthew's time, however, every word, sometimes even every letter, of Scripture was regarded as having an inspired meaning. In this view, a passage's original context did not matter if a single word or phrase seemed applicable to the interpreter's theological purpose.

THE BEGINNING OF JESUS' PROCLAMATION

Matthew starts his account of Jesus' adult life (3:1–4:25) at exactly the same point as Mark (1:1–13), giving no information about Jesus' life during the

thirty years (Luke 3:1, 23) that separate his birth from his baptism. Note that Matthew revises Mark's baptism narrative to emphasize Jesus' superiority to John by omitting the reference to baptismal "forgiveness" and adding a brief dialogue in which the Baptist admits Jesus' greater authority (3:13–17).

Mark (1:12–13) alludes to Satan's tempting Jesus in the desert, uninhabited wastes where demons were popularly believed to roam, but Matthew expands the scene to include a dramatic dialogue between the Messiah and his Adversary (4:1–11). As Matthew and Luke present the incident, apparently drawn from Q, it functions to clarify the nature of Jesus' messiahship. Satan prefaces his first two temptations with the phrase "if you are the Son of God," an attempt to capitalize

Figure 10.7 *Virgin and Child.* In this conception of Mary and the infant Jesus, the artist pictures the Madonna as an archetypal image of abundance and fertility, giving her a crown to depict her queenly status and surrounding her with flowers to suggest her association with natural fecundity. This twentieth-century rendition of the Virgin by F. Botero of Uruguay effectively demonstrates her thematic connection with nurturing goddesses of pre-Christian antiquity.

on any doubts that the human Jesus may have entertained about his origins or his future legitimacy as God's agent. In the second temptation, Satan quotes from Psalm 91, a poem in which the Deity vows unconditionally to shield from harm his Chosen One. By placing this passage in the devil's mouth, Matthew may wish to refute Jews who quoted this passage as evidence that God's true Messiah would not have died a shameful criminal's death as did Jesus. The third attempt to subvert Jesus' understanding of his role is Satan's offer to make Jesus master of all the world's kingdoms — if he would but "do homage" to the evil one. The lure of political power — perhaps the popular concept of a Davidic Messiah as conquering hero — Jesus also rejects. To rule as Alexander and Augustus — or King David — had ruled would inevitably entail

bloodshed, a use of the devil's methods that honors not God but Satan.

FIRST MAJOR DISCOURSE: THE SERMON ON THE MOUNT

After showing his hero rejecting some of the functions then commonly associated with the Messiah, Matthew demonstrates how radically different Jesus' concept of his messiahship is from the popular expectation of a warrior-king who delivers Israel from its pagan oppressors. The celebrated Sermon on the Mount, which Matthew constructs from widely scattered sayings and the Q material (cf. Luke's version, the Sermon on the Plain, in Luke 6:17–7:1), represents Jesus' view of the kingdom as the arts of peace, service, and endurance in doing

Figure 10.8 *Virgin and Child.* This wooden sculpture from Africa shows the infant Jesus being nursed by Mary, a rendition illustrating the archetypal image of mother and child, nurturer and bearer of new life, as well as an image of black holiness.

good. Delivering his catalogue of ethical instructions like a greater Moses, Jesus introduces a radical concept of "higher righteousness" that must surpass and transcend the older values of the Mosaic Torah.

The sermon opens with the **Beatitudes** (blessings or happinesses), assertions that some kinds of people — the sorrowful, the peacemakers, the hungry, the persecuted — uniquely enjoy divine favor. Jesus' statements significantly challenge assumptions typical of some biblical thought. Deuteronomy and Proverbs had argued that material prosperity and earthly success were signs of God's approval, whereas poverty and suffering were evidence of divine punishment. In the Beatitudes, Jesus reverses these traditional views, affirming that

Israel's God takes the part of those suffering grief or loss. The poor and powerless persons lauded here are exactly those to whom Jesus will direct his ministry.

Matthew's Torah-Abiding Community   Although Matthew presents Jesus as a staunch upholder of the Mosaic Torah, he is aware that other churches — primarily those established by Paul, who declared Christianity's independence of the law covenant (discussed in Chapter 12) — do not share this conviction. Conceding that such nonobservant believers are still part of "the kingdom of Heaven" (a term Matthew sometimes applies to the church), the author nonetheless regards them as ranking below Torah loyalists:

> If any man therefore sets aside even the least of the Law's demands, and teaches others to do the same, he will have the lowest place in the kingdom of Heaven, whereas anyone who keeps the Law, and teaches others so, will stand high in the kingdom of Heaven.
>
> Matt. 5:19

The Antitheses   For Matthew's Jewish Christian community, Jesus' teachings did not replace the Mosaic Law, they intensified it. Rather than serving as a refutation of Jewish tradition, Jesus' Torah pronouncements illustrate how his disciples should observe it, emphasizing the essential core of ethical meaning that lies behind each commandment. Immediately after his declaration of the Law's unchanging validity, Matthew introduces a set of Jesus's sayings, known as the **antitheses**, that are found only in his Gospel. Employing a rhetorical formula, Jesus makes an initial statement (the thesis), which he then follows with an apparently opposing idea (the antithesis). In this series, he appears to contrast biblical tradition with his own authoritative opinion; as scholars have pointed out, however, he does not contradict Torah rules, but rather interprets them to reveal the human motivation that often causes them to be broken:

> You have learned that our forefathers were told, "Do not commit murder: anyone who commits murder must be brought to judgment." But what I tell you is this: Anyone who nurses anger

against his brother must be brought to judgment. If he abuses his brother, he must answer for it to the court; if he sneers at him he will have to answer for it in the fires of hell [Gehenna].

Matt. 5:21–22

Anger, the emotion triggering murderous rage, must be rooted out, for if it leads to overt behavior, it will be punished by both human courts and divine judgment.

In another antithesis, Jesus looks beyond the literal application of a Torah command to seek a more effective way to obey the principle it embodies:

You have learned that they [the biblical Israelites] were told, "Eye for eye, tooth for tooth." But what I tell you is this: Do not set yourself against the man who wrongs you. If someone slaps you on the right cheek, turn and offer him your left. If a man wants to sue you for your shirt, let him have your coat as well. If a man in authority makes you go one mile, go with him two.

Matt. 5:38–41

The *lex talionis,* or law of retaliation, that Jesus quotes before giving his three examples of recommended behavior is central to the Mosaic concept of justice and appears in three different Torah books (Exod. 21:23–25; Lev. 24:19–20; Deut. 19:21). Although it may seem harsh by today's standards, in ancient society the *lex talionis* served to limit excessive revenge: Simply receiving an injury did not entitle one to kill the offending party. In the world inhabited by the (generally poor and powerless) members of Jesus' audience (the "you" whom he addresses), however, retaliatory actions of any kind against those who exploited them automatically led to severe reprisals, including torture and death. Recognizing that the law's intent was to curb violence, Jesus goes beyond its literal application to demand that his listeners give up their traditional right to retaliate in kind. Is Jesus, then, urging people to submit passively to those who wrong them?

Some commentators believe that Jesus' main objective was probably to discover and apply the essential precepts contained in the Mosaic tradition. Matthew's version of the "golden rule" most succinctly expresses this view: His Jesus states that treating others as one would like to be treated by them encapsulates the essential biblical message, succinctly embodying "the Law and the prophets" (7:12; cf. Luke 6:31). Similarly, after reciting the Torah injunctions to love God and neighbor wholeheartedly, Jesus states, "Everything in the Law and the prophets hangs on these two commandments" (22:34–40; cf. Mark 12:28–34).

In Matthew's final antithesis, Jesus expands on this fundamental perception, contrasting the command to love one's neighbor (Lev. 19:18) with the aparently common assumption that it is permissible to hate an enemy (5:43–48). Again, he demands a "higher righteousness" that will imitate God's own character, revealed in the daily operation of physical nature, where he lavishes his gifts equally on both deserving and undeserving people:

But what I tell you is this: Love your enemies and pray for your persecutors; only so you can be children of your heavenly Father, who makes his sun rise on good and bad alike, and sends the rain on the honest and the dishonest. If you love only those who love you, what reward can you expect? . . . There must be no limit to your goodness, as your heavenly Father's goodness knows no bounds.

Matt. 5:44–48

"Boundless" in loving generosity, the Father provides the supreme model for Jesus' disciples to emulate, refashioning them in his image. In seeking first the kingdom of God's "justice" (6:33), they personally "pass no judgment" on others, for judgmental attitudes blind people to their own defects (7:1–5). Instead, disciples must focus on the infinite graciousness of the Father, who endlessly "gives good things to those who ask him" (7:9–11).

Jesus' Authority The sermon ends with Jesus' parable about the advantages of building one's life firmly on the rock of his teachings (7:24–27), after which, Matthew reports, the crowds "were astounded" because "unlike their own teachers he taught with a note of [his personal] authority" (7:28). Matthew's phrase "when Jesus had finished this discourse," or a variation thereof, marks the conclusion of the four other blocks of teaching material in his Gospel (11:1; 13:53; 19:1; 26:1).

SECOND MAJOR DISCOURSE: INSTRUCTIONS TO THE TWELVE

In his second major collection of ethical teaching, Matthew presents Jesus' instructions to the twelve chief disciples (listed by name in 10:2–4). Matthew insists that the Twelve are sent exclusively to the "lost sheep of the house of Israel" and forbidden to preach to Gentiles or Samaritans (10:5–6), an injunction found only in this gospel. (By contrast, both Luke and John show Jesus leading his disciples on a brief Samaritan campaign [Luke 9:52–56; John 4:3–42]. Matthew himself ends the Gospel with a command to convert people of all nations [28:19–20].) The Twelve are to preach the kingdom's imminent appearance, the same apocalyptic message that the author attributes to both the Baptist (3:2) and Jesus at the outset of his career (4:17). While healing the sick, cleansing lepers, and raising the dead—thus replicating Jesus' spectacular miracles—the disciples are to expect hostility and persecution. This extended warning (10:16–26) seems to apply to conditions that existed in the author's generation, not in the time of Jesus' Galilean ministry. Matthew's apparent practice of combining Jesus' remembered words with commentary relating them to later experiences of the Christian community is typical of all the Gospel writers.

A strong eschatological tone pervades the entire discourse. Followers are to be loyal at the time of testing because destruction in Gehenna awaits the unfaithful. The New Testament name for a geographical location, the "Valley of the Son of Hinnom," **Gehenna** is commonly rendered as "hell" in English translations, although it is uncertain that the later Christian notion of a metaphysical place of punishment accurately expresses the original meaning of Gehenna. A site of human sacrifice in ancient Israel (Jer. 7:32; 1 Kings 11:7; etc.), the Valley of Hinnom later housed a garbage dump that was kept permanently burning, a literal place of annihilation for "both soul and body" (Matt. 10:28; 18:8; 25:30, 46; etc.) (Box 10.12).

Equally arresting is the statement that before the Twelve have completed their circuit of Palestine, "the Son of Man will have come" (10:23).

Writing more than half a century after the events he describes, Matthew surprisingly retains a prophecy that was not fulfilled, at least in historical fact. The author's inclusion of this apocalyptic prediction indicates that he may not have accepted it literally. Matthew may have regarded the "Son of Man" as already spiritually present in the missionary activity of the church. If so, this suggests that many of Matthew's other references to "the end of the age" and Jesus' Parousia (Chs. 24 and 25) also are to be viewed metaphorically.

THIRD MAJOR DISCOURSE: PARABLES OF THE KINGDOM

Matthew brackets Jesus' third discourse with his version of Jesus' alienation from his family (12:46–50; cf. Mark 3:31–35) and Jesus' rejection by the citizens of Nazareth (13:54–58; Mark 6:1–6). The author divides Jesus' parable teachings into two distinct episodes: the first public, the second private (13:10–23). Although only the Twelve are initiated into the secrets of God's rule, Matthew softens Mark's explanation of Jesus' reasons for speaking in parables. Instead of using figures of speech to *prevent* understanding (Mark 4:11–12), Matthew says that Jesus speaks metaphorically because most people have the wrong attitude and unconsciously shut their mental eyes and ears (13:11–15; Isa. 6:9–10). Notice that Matthew's version of the parable lesson explicitly states that the Twelve *do* understand and appreciate Jesus' teaching (13:16–17, 51–52), thus banishing Mark's image of the disciples' chronic stupidity.

FOURTH MAJOR DISCOURSE: INSTRUCTIONS TO THE CHURCH

In Chapter 18, Matthew assembles disparate sayings of Jesus and applies them to the Christian community of the writer's generation. Taken together, Chapters 10 and 18 form a rudimentary instruction manual for the early church. The author skillfully combines numerous small literary units to achieve his intended effect. A brief glimpse of the disciples' squabbling for power (18:1–2) introduces opposing images of a powerless child and a

Box 10.12 Some Biblical Concepts of Hell and the Afterlife

The term that many English-language Bibles translate as "hell" is Gehenna (*gē hinnōm*) (Matt. 5:22, 29–30; 10:28; 23:15, 33), which originally referred not to a place of posthumous torment, but to a specific geographical location, a ravine near Jerusalem. A valley bordering Israel's capital city on the southwest, Gehenna was named for the "sons of Hinnom [*gē ben(e) hinnōm*]," the biblical designation of an ancient Canaanite group that occupied the site before King David captured it about 1000 B.C.E. Gehenna had an evil reputation as the place where humans were sacrificed and burned as offerings to false gods, a practice that Israelite prophets vehemently condemned (Jer. 7:31; 19:11; 32:35; cf. 2 Kings 23:10; 2 Chron. 28:3; 33:5).

In time, perhaps influenced by Persian ideas about afterlife punishments in fire, some Jewish writers made Hinnom's valley (Gehenna) the symbol of God's eschatological judgment, where the wicked would suffer after death (1 Enoch 26:4; 27:2–3). A potent image of alienation from God, the earthly Gehenna eventually was associated with mythical concepts of an Underworld "lake of fire," the future abode of unrepentant sinners (2 Esd. 7:36; Rev. 20).

SHEOL AND HADES

The concept of eternal punishment does not occur in the Hebrew Bible, which uses the term **Sheol** to designate a bleak subterranean region where the dead, good and bad alike, subsist only as impotent shadows. When Hellenistic Jewish scribes rendered the Bible into Greek, they used the word *Hades* to translate Sheol, bringing a whole new mythological association to the idea of posthumous existence. In ancient Greek myth, Hades, named after the gloomy deity who ruled over it, was originally similar to the Hebrew Sheol, a dark underground realm in which all the dead, regardless of individual merit, were indiscriminately housed (see Homer's *Odyssey*, Book 11). By the Hellenistic period, however, Hades had become compartmentalized into separate regions. These included Elysium, a paradise for the virtuous, and Tartarus, a place of punishment for the wicked. Influenced by philosophers such as Pythagoras and Plato and the Orphic mystery religions, Greek religious thought eventually posited a direct connection between people's behavior in this life and their destiny in the next. Good actions earned them bliss, whereas injustices brought fearful penalties.

HELL

Popular concepts of Hell derive from a variety of sources extending back in time to the earliest Mesopotamian and Egyptian speculations about the terrors of the next world. Although absent from the Hebrew Bible and most of the New Testament, a few scattered references to the concept (primarily involving Gehenna or a fiery lake) appear in the Synoptic Gospels and the Book of Revelation, as well as some noncanonical Jewish and Christian books, such as 1 and 2 Enoch and the Apocalypse of Peter. In general, pre-Christian mythologies and other extrabiblical sources supply most of the frightening imagery for such celebrated literary works as Dante's *Inferno* and Milton's *Paradise Lost*, as well as the "hellfire" sermons of many Puritan divines and their modern successors. The word itself, not found in the Bible, commemorates *Hel*, the fierce Norse goddess who reigned over the netherworld.

---

drowning man (18:2–7), which are quickly followed by pictures of self-blinding and the flames of Gehenna (18:8–9). The variety of literary forms gathered together here makes the author's prescription for an ideal Christian community intensely vivid. The writer's devices include hyperbole (exaggeration for rhetorical effect), parable (the lost sheep and the unforgiving debtor [18:12–14, 23–35]), advice on supervising troublesome people (18:15–17), prophetic promises (18:10, 18–20), and direct commands (18:22). In Matthew's view of the church, service, humility, and endless forgiveness are the measure of leadership. Practicing the spirit of Torah mercy, the church is the earthly expression of divine rule (18:23–35), a visible manifestation of the kingdom.

Matthew gives the individual "congregation" the right to exclude or ostracize disobedient members (18:15–17). In later centuries, this power of *excommunication* was to become a formidable weapon in controlling both belief and behavior. The same authority accorded Peter in Jesus' famous "keys of the kingdom" speech (16:16–20) is also given to individual congregation leaders (18:18).

FIFTH MAJOR DISCOURSE: WARNINGS OF FINAL JUDGMENT

This fifth and final block of teaching material summarizes the Matthean Jesus' adverse judgment on Jerusalem, particularly its Temple and religious hierarchy (Chs. 23–25). It opens with a blistering denunciation of the scribes and Pharisees — professional transmitters and interpreters of the law — upon whom Jesus is pictured as heaping "seven woes," perhaps corresponding to the curses on a disobedient Israel listed in Deuteronomy 28. According to Matthew, Jesus blames the Pharisees and their associates for every guilty act — every drop of innocent blood poured out — in Israel's entire history. He condemns the religious leadership to suffer for their generation's collective wrongdoing, as well as that of their distant ancestors.

Matthew implies that the Roman devastation of Jerusalem in 70 C.E., an event that occurred during the author's lifetime, is tangible proof of God's wrath on Israel (23:35–36). Matthew intensifies this theme in his version of Jesus' trial before Pilate (Ch. 27); the author depicts a Jerusalem crowd demanding the Messiah's crucifixion, hysterically inviting the Deity to avenge Jesus' blood upon them and their children (27:25). Matthew edits Mark's Passion narrative by adding that Pilate, symbol of imperial Rome, washed his hands of responsibility for Jesus' death — even while ordering Jesus' execution (27:24). All four Gospel writers shift the blame from the Roman government to the Jewish leadership, but only Matthew extends responsibility to the Jews' as-yet-unborn descendants.

Many commentators find an ethical paradox in Matthew's vindictive attitude toward his fellow Jews who did not accept Jesus as the national Messiah. Earlier in his Gospel, Matthew presents Jesus as reinterpreting the *lex talionis* (5:38–40), stressing instead the necessity of practicing infinite forgiveness (6:12, 14–16; 18:21–35) and exercising mercy (5:7). In dealing with his church's opponents, however, Matthew judges without compassion, apparently regarding Jewish rejection of his Messiah as falling beyond the tolerable limits of charity. The author reverts to a literalist view of retaliation that Jesus himself rejected. Historically, the consequences of New Testament writers attributing collective guilt to the Jewish people have helped fuel the waves of anti-Semitism that repeatedly swept through the Western world (see Farmer in "Recommended Reading").

To place Matthew's negative verdict on the first-century Jewish establishment in historical perspective, we must remember that he condemns only the Jerusalem leadership, not Judaism itself. Despite his dislike of Pharisaic customs, the author agrees with Pharisaic teaching. He reminds his readers to "pay attention to their words" and "do what they tell you," for they occupy "the seat of Moses" and their teachings are authoritative (23:1–3).

THE FALL OF JERUSALEM AND THE PAROUSIA

Signs of the Times The second part of Jesus' fifth discourse is based largely on Mark 13, the prediction of Jerusalem's impending destruction. Whereas Mark states that the disciples asked only about when the Temple would fall (Mark 13:1–4), Matthew expands the disciples' question to include an inquiry about Jesus' Second Coming (the Parousia) and the "end of the age," the final consummation of human history (24:1–3). Jesus' reply is a good illustration of how first-century Jewish eschatology was incorporated into the Christian tradition.

Matthew's presentation of the "signal" or "signs" leading to Jesus' return are a complex mixture of first-century historical events, such as the Jewish wars, and prophetic images from the Hebrew Bible, particularly Daniel, Joel, Zechariah, and the pseudepigraphal 1 Enoch. All three Synoptic writers link the Jewish revolt against Rome (66–73 c.e.) with supernatural portents of End time and Jesus' reappearance. Mark, the first to make this association of events, seems to have written at a time when the revolt had already begun (note the "battles" and "wars" in 13:7–8) and Jerusalem was about to fall. These cataclysmic events he called "the birth pangs of the new age." Both Matthew and Luke follow Mark's lead and connect these political upheavals with persecution of believers, perhaps allusions to Nero's cruel assault on Roman Christians (c. 64–65 c.e.). The Synoptic authors concur that attacks on the church, then a tiny minority of the Greco-Roman population, are of critical importance. The sufferings of the Christian community will bring God's vengeance on all humanity.

Jesus' cryptic reference to an "abomination of desolation" (24:15) echoes passages in Daniel that alluded to Antiochus's profanation of the Jerusalem Temple (Dan. 9:21; 11:31; 12:11). In Matthew and Mark, it may refer to the Zealot party's violent occupation of the Temple in 67–68 c.e. and their pollution of its sacred precincts with the blood of their victims, which may have included some Christians. Matthew's caution —"let the reader understand" (24:16)— suggests that the passage is not from Jesus' oral teaching, but from a written source. In his version of the Parousia prediction, Luke omits the mysterious "abomination" reference and substitutes an allusion to Roman armies besieging Jerusalem instead (Luke 21:20–24). To Matthew, the Temple's pollution is a warning for believers to flee Judea because it introduces a time of distress so severe that if not "cut short, no living thing could survive" (24:21–22)— unmistakable allusions to the Roman troops' destructive assault on Jerusalem, home of the apostolic church. Matthew may refer to extrabiblical traditions about a group of Judean Christians who fled the besieged holy city to seek refuge in Pella, east of Jordan.

Both Mark and Matthew are aware that in the white heat of apocalyptic expectation, there were many false reports of the Messiah's return (Mark 13:21–23; Matt. 24:23–27). Some Christians must have experienced crushing disappointment when their prophets' "inspired" predictions of Jesus' reappearance failed to materialize. Thus, both Evangelists caution that even "the Son" does not know the exact date of the Parousia (Mark 13:32; Matt. 24:36). Matthew adds that when the Son does return, his coming will be unmistakable in its universality, "like lightning from the east, flashing as far as the west" (24:27).

Matthew preserves the "double-vision" nature of the Parousia found in Mark. Jesus' supernatural coming will be preceded by unmistakable "signs" that it is near (24:21–22, 29–35); at the same time, he will come without warning and when least expected (24:42–44). Although contradictory, both concepts apparently existed concurrently in the early church, which was deeply influenced by eschatological thinking.

Although the author of Revelation connects End time with cosmic catastrophe, other New Testament writers (perhaps aware of the repeated failure of attempts to calculate the date of the Parousia) stress that the Son's return is essentially unheralded (1 Thess. 5:1–5; 2 Pet. 3:10).

Matthew probably wrote about two decades after Mark's Gospel was composed, but he retains the Markan tradition that persons who knew Jesus would live to see his predictions come true (24:34; Mark 13:30). To Matthew, the Roman annihilation of the Jewish state, which coincided with the emergence of the Christian church as an entity distinct from Judaism, may essentially have fulfilled Jesus' words, or at least an important part of his prophecy. From the writer's perspective, the "New Age" had already dawned with God's alleged abandonment of Israel and the church's new and decisive role in future human history (28:19–20).

Parables of Jesus' Return   Chapters 24 and 25 contain three parables and a prophetic vision of Jesus' unannounced Parousia. Whatever their original meaning to Jesus, in Matthew they serve to illustrate believers' obligation to await faithfully and patiently their absent Lord's return. The first parable contrasts two servants, one of whom abuses his fellow employees until the master suddenly reappears to execute him (24:45–51)— a clear warning to church members to treat others honorably. The parable about a delayed bridegroom similarly contrasts two kinds of believers, those who are alert and prepared for the wedding event and those who are not. Note that the "bridegroom" is "late in coming," a hint that Christians must reconcile themselves to a delay in the Parousia (25:1–13).

The parable of the talents, in which a master's servants invest huge sums of money for him, emphasizes the growth and productivity of the church during its Lord's prolonged absence (25:14–30). Once again, the servants—the master's church—are unexpectedly called to account, in this case to demonstrate that they have significantly increased the value of the treasure entrusted to them.

The fourth and final judgment parable concerns not only the church but also "the nations." The term *nations* refers primarily to Gentiles living outside of the Mosaic Law, but it may be intended to include all humanity. In the parable about separating worthy "sheep" and unworthy "goats," all are judged exclusively on their behavior toward Jesus' "little ones," Matthew's favored term for Christian disciples (25:31–46).

Matthew's eschatological vision makes charitable acts, rather than "correct" religious doctrines, the standard for distinguishing good people from bad. In such passages, Matthew reflects the ancient Israelite prophets who regarded service to the poor and unfortunate as acts of worship to God. The Book of James, which defines true religion as essentially humanitarian service to others (James 1:27), espouses a similar view.

THE PASSION STORY AND RESURRECTION

Although Matthew's account of Jesus' last two days (Thursday and Friday of Holy Week) generally follows Mark's narrative sequence, he adds details from his own distinctive source. Perhaps drawing from oral traditions in his community, he states that the chief priests paid Judas Iscariot thirty pieces of silver for betraying Jesus (26:14–16). He also links Judas's treachery to the fulfillment of a passage in Jeremiah, although the relevant text actually appears in Zechariah (26:14–15, 20–25, 47–50; 27:3–10; Jer. 32:6–13; Zech. 11:12–13).

The theme of a warning dream, used frequently in the infancy narrative, reappears when Pilate's wife, frightened by a dream about Jesus, urges her husband to "have nothing to do with that innocent man" (27:19).

Besides adding his mysterious reference to the sudden resurrection of "God's saints," a phenomenon associated with the Final Judgment (27:50–53), Matthew also states that not only Mark's centurion but also his men confess Jesus' divinity (27:54). This editorial change may express Matthew's view that the Roman soldiers' belief foreshadows that of the future Gentile church.

Roman Guards at the Tomb Matthew's principal addition to Mark's account of Jesus' burial is the posting of Roman soldiers to guard the tomb, an effort to prevent Jesus' disciples from stealing the body and then claiming that he had been raised from the dead (27:62–66). Matthew also reports a Jewish conspiracy to undermine belief in Jesus' resurrection; Jerusalem priests bribe the guards to say that the disciples had removed and hidden Jesus' corpse (28:11–15).

Matthew implies that Jews of his day used the soldiers' false testimony to refute Christian preaching about the Resurrection. However, his counterargument that Roman soldiers had admitted falling asleep while on duty is not convincing. Severe punishment, including torture and execution, awaited any Roman soldier found thus derelict. A rumor about the possible theft of Jesus' body undoubtedly circulated, but probably not for the reasons that Matthew gives.

Postresurrection Appearances In Mark's Gospel, Jesus promises that after his crucifixion he will reappear in Galilee (14:28; 16:7), a tradition that Matthew also follows in his extremely brief account of the Resurrection. When the eleven disciples encounter the risen Jesus at a prearranged mountain site, Matthew observes that some disciples had doubts about seeing him, as if mistrusting the evidence of their own senses. The author seems to imply that absolute proof of an event so contrary to ordinary human experience is impossible (28:16–17).

The concluding command to recruit followers from "all nations" further emphasizes Matthew's theme that the church has much work to do before Jesus returns. It suggests that the author's tiny community has only begun what was to become a vast undertaking—a labor extending into the far-distant future.

In composing a new version of Jesus' life, Matthew accomplishes several purposes. Citing ancient biblical prophecies, he argues that Jesus of Nazareth is the expected Messiah foretold in the Hebrew Bible. Into Mark's narrative about Jesus' mighty deeds, he incorporates five large blocks of teaching material, emphasizing Jesus' authority to reinterpret the Torah for the Christian community (Chs. 5–7) and to direct its future behavior (Chs. 10 and 18). While retaining Mark's apocalyptic themes, he significantly modifies them to stress the church's global task during the interval between Jesus' resurrection and Parousia. A guidebook providing instruction and discipline for the community of faith, Matthew's Gospel became the church's premier source of wise counsel to encourage and discipline all believers.

QUESTIONS FOR REVIEW

1. According to the two-source theory, in what ways is Matthew's Gospel a revised and expanded edition of Mark? What five blocks of Jesus' teaching does Matthew add to Mark's narrative? Summarize nativity and resurrection accounts with which the author frames his story.

2. How does Matthew use the Greek version of the Hebrew Bible (the Septuagint) to demonstrate Jesus' messiahship? List some of Matthew's major themes, including his attitude toward keeping the Mosaic Law.

3. Define *parable,* and give several examples from Mark 4 or Matthew 13. To what images or natural processes does Jesus compare the kingdom of God? What specific commands or principles in Matthew's Sermon on the Mount (Matt. 5–7) illustrate the nature of God's reign?

4. What does Matthew add to Mark's story of Jesus that tends to deemphasize early Christians' eschatological expectations? Compare Mark 13 with Matthew 24–25.

QUESTION FOR DISCUSSION AND REFLECTION

How do you explain the disjunction between Matthew's presentation of Jesus as rejecting the biblical law of retaliation and his portrayal of Jesus' severe condemnation of the Jewish leadership? Compare Matthew 5:38–44 with Matthew 23:1–39. Note also Matthew 5:22, in which Jesus forbids angry and abusive language. How do you think that Matthew would explain the apparent contradiction?

TERMS AND CONCEPTS TO REMEMBER

antitheses	haggadah
Beatitudes	halakah
exegesis	midrash
Gehenna	Sheol

RECOMMENDED READING

Andersen, J. C. *Matthew's Narrative Web.* Sheffield, England: Sheffield Academic Press, 1994.

Boring, M. Eugene. "The Gospel of Matthew." In *The New Interpreter's Bible,* Vol. 8, pp. 89–505. Nashville: Abingdon Press, 1995. Extensive scholarly commentary on the origin, purpose, and text of Matthew.

Brown, R. E. *The Birth of the Messiah: A Commentary on the Infancy Narratives in Matthew and Luke.* New York: Doubleday, 1977. A thorough analysis of traditions surrounding Jesus' birth.

———. *The Death of the Messiah,* Vols. 1 and 2. New York: Anchor-Doubleday, 1994. An exhaustive analysis by a leading biblical scholar of the Gospel accounts of Jesus' arrest, trial, and execution.

Edwards, R. A. *Matthew's Story of Jesus.* Philadelphia: Fortress Press, 1985. An introductory study.

Farmer, W. B. *Jesus and the Gospel: Tradition, Scripture, and Canon.* Philadelphia: Fortress Press, 1982. An argument for the primacy of Matthew's Gospel.

———, ed. *Anti-Judaism and the Gospels.* Harrisburg, Pa.: Trinity Press International, 1999. A compendium of scholarly essays on the Gospels' role in fostering anti-Jewish sentiment.

Gundry, R. H. *Matthew: A Commentary on His Literary and Theological Art.* Grand Rapids, Mich.: Eerdmans, 1982. A thorough scholarly analysis and exposition.

Kingsbury, J. D. *Matthew: Structure, Christology, Kingdom.* Philadelphia: Fortress Press, 1975.

———. *Matthew as Story.* Philadelphia: Fortress Press, 1986. A more advanced analysis of the Gospel.

Meier, John P. *The Vision of Matthew: Christ, Church and Morality in the First Gospel.* Theological Inquiries. New York: Paulist Press, 1979.

———. "Matthew, Gospel of." In D. N. Freedman, ed., *The Anchor Bible Dictionary,* Vol. 4, pp. 622–641. New York: Doubleday, 1992. A lucid survey of current scholarship on the origin and purpose of Matthew's Gospel.

Overman, J. A. *Matthew's Gospel and Formative Judaism: The Social World of the Matthean Community.* Minneapolis: Fortress Press, 1991. A solid sociological approach.

Stendahl, Krister. *The School of St. Matthew and Its Use of the Old Testament.* Philadelphia: Fortress Press, 1968.

Wink, Walater. *The Powers That Be: Theology for a New Millennium.* New York: Galilee/Doubleday, 1998. Includes a chapter, "Jesus' Third Way" (between the extremes of violence and passivity), that perceptively interprets Matthew's Sermon on the Mount.

Luke's Gospel

KEY TOPICS/THEMES

The first part of a two-volume work (Luke-Acts), Luke's Gospel presents Jesus' career not only as history's most crucial event but also as the opening stage of an indefinitely extended historical process that continues in the life of the church (Acts 1–28). Writing for a Greco-Roman audience, Luke emphasizes that Jesus and his disciples, working under the Holy Spirit, are innocent of any crime against Rome and that their religion is a universal faith intended for all people. The parables unique to Luke's Gospel depict the unexpected ways in which God's inbreaking kingdom overturns the normal social order and reverses conventional beliefs. After a formal preface and extended nativity account (Chs. 1 and 2), Luke generally follows Mark's order narrating the Galilean ministry (Chs. 3–9). He then inserts a large body of teaching material, the "greater interpolation" (9:51–18:14), supposedly given on the journey to Jerusalem, returning to Mark for his narration of the Jerusalem ministry and Passion story (18:31–

23:56). Luke's final chapter reports postresurrection appearances in or near Jerusalem (Ch. 24).

KEY QUESTIONS

What distinctive ideas and themes does Luke add to his account of Jesus' life? How is Jesus portrayed as a model of service for the early church?

LUKE'S HISTORICAL VISION

The author of Luke-Acts is unique among New Testament writers, manifesting a breadth of historical vision comparable to that shown in the sweeping narrative of Israel's history from the conquest of Palestine to the first destruction of the Jewish state (the Hebrew Bible books of Joshua through 2 Kings). Consciously working within the tradition of Hellenistic historians, who labored not only to preserve facts but also to interpret their moral significance, Luke ambitiously seeks to trace the course of a new religious movement from its inception in a Bethlehem stable to its (hoped-for) status as a legitimate faith of the Roman Empire (Figure 10.9). Thus, Luke's two-volume work places Jesus' career precisely at the center of history, his life forming the connecting link between Israel's biblical past and the future age of a multinational Gentile church. Luke views John the Baptist, whose birth story he interweaves with that of Jesus, as both the last of Israel's prophets and the forerunner of the Messiah: "Until John, it was the Law and the prophets; since then there is the good news of the kingdom of God, and everyone forces his way in" (16:16).

By making Jesus' life the central act of a three-part drama that begins with Israel and continues with the Christian church, Luke offers a philosophy of history that is important to Christianity's later understanding of its mission. Instead of an apocalyptic End, Jesus' ministry represents a new beginning that establishes a heightened awareness of God's intentions for humanity. Luke thus ties Jesus' resurrection to the disciples' job of evangelizing the world (24:44–53; Acts 1:1–8). He creatively modifies early Christianity's initial emphasis

Figure 10.9 This bust shows Octavius, grandnephew of Julius Caesar, as a thoughtful youth. After defeating his chief rival, Marc Antony, at the Battle of Actium (31 B.C.E.), Octavius became the sole ruler of the Roman Empire (30 B.C.E.–14 C.E.), accepting the title Augustus. Absolute monarch of the largest empire the world had yet known, Augustus established the *Pax Romana*—the Roman peace that brought lasting order and stability to the entire Mediterranean world.

but by expressing Paul's resolve to concentrate on ministering to the Gentiles (28:27–28).

THE AUTHOR AND HIS SOURCES

The most important early reference to the author of Luke-Acts confirms that, like Mark, he was not an eyewitness to the events he describes. In the Muratorian list of New Testament books (compiled about the fourth century C.E.), a note identifies the author as **Luke**, "the beloved" physician who accompanied Paul on some of the Apostle's missionary tours. It also states that he did not know Jesus. A few years earlier, Irenaeus, a bishop of Lyons in Gaul (France), also referred to the author as a companion of Paul, presumably the same Luke named in several Pauline letters (Col. 4:14; Philem. 24; 2 Tim. 4:11).

Although some scholars accept the author's traditional identification as Paul's travel companion, a great many do not, pointing out that the writer seems unaware of Paul's letters and never refers to his writing. Although Paul dominates the second half of Acts, Luke only twice refers to him as an apostle, a title for which the historical Paul vigorously fought. Even though the author's identity is not conclusively settled, for convenience we refer to him as Luke. Because of his interest in the Gentile mission and his fluency in the Greek language (he has the largest vocabulary and most polished style of any Evangelist), the writer may have been a Gentile, the only non-Jewish writer of the Bible.

According to most scholars, Luke-Acts was written after 70 C.E., when Titus demolished Jerusalem (Figures 10.10 and 10.11). Luke reveals detailed knowledge of the Roman siege (21:20–24), referring specifically to the Roman method of encircling a town, a military technique used in the assault on Jerusalem: "Your enemies will set up siege-works against you; they will encircle you and hem you in at every point; they will bring you to the ground, you and your children within your walls, and not leave you one stone standing on another" (19:43–44). Luke-Acts apparently was composed at some point after the Jewish wars of 66–73 C.E. and before about 90–95 C.E., when Paul's letters were first collected and published.

on eschatological expectations to focus on the future work of the church. Acts thus portrays the disciples entering a new historical epoch, the age of the church, and thereby extends the new faith's operations indefinitely into the future. Acts concludes not by drawing attention to the Parousia,

Figure 10.10 A victory monument commemorating Rome's success in crushing the Jewish revolt (66–73 C.E.), the Arch of Titus still stands in the Roman Forum. After his father, Vespasian, became emperor (69 C.E.), Titus laid siege to Jerusalem, capturing and destroying the city and its Temple in August 70 C.E. Titus's campaign ended not only 1000 years of Jewish Temple sacrifices but also the hegemony of the apostolic church centered there.

Figure 10.11 This bas-relief inside the Arch of Titus shows Roman soldiers and captives transporting treasures looted from Herod's Temple in 70 C.E., including the menorah, a seven-branched lampstand that formerly illuminated the sanctuary.

Many scholars place the Gospel and its sequel in the mid-to-late 80s and favor Ephesus, a Hellenistic city in Asia Minor with a relatively large Christian population, as the place of composition.

Preface Luke is the only Gospel author to introduce his work with a formal statement of purpose. In this preface (1:1–4), he briefly refers to the methods used in compiling his Gospel and addresses it to Theophilus, the same person to whom he dedicates the Book of Acts (1:1; Acts 1:1). Mentioned nowhere else in the New Testament, **Theophilus**, whose name means "lover of God," may have been a Greek or Roman official, perhaps a well-to-do patron who underwrote the expenses of publishing Luke's work.

Luke states that he wishes to write "a connected narrative," supplying readers with "accurate knowledge." Luke's use of the term translated as "connected narrative" or "coherent account" may not refer to an attempt to create a chronologically accurate biography, for Luke generally follows Mark's order of events. Luke's use of the phrase probably voices his intention to arrange his subject's life in a proper literary form acceptable to a Greek-speaking Gentile audience.

Use of Sources As a Christian living two or three generations after Jesus' time, Luke must rely on other persons' information, including orally transmitted recollections about Jesus and traditional Christian preaching. Besides using memories of "eyewitnesses" and later missionary accounts, the author depends on his own research skills — the labor he expends going "over the whole course of these events in detail" (1:1–4).

Luke is aware that "many" others before him produced Gospels (1:1). His resolve to create yet another suggests that he was not satisfied with his predecessors' efforts. As Matthew did, he chooses Mark as his primary source, incorporating about 45–50 percent of the older work into his narrative. Editing Mark more extensively than did Matthew, he omits several large units of Markan material (such as Mark 6:45–8:26 and 9:41–10:12), perhaps to make room for his own special additions. Adapting Mark to his creative purpose, Luke often rearranges the sequence of individual incidents to emphasize his particular themes. Whereas Mark placed Jesus' rejection at Nazareth midway through the Galilean campaign, Luke sets it at the beginning (4:16–30). Adding to Mark's account a claim that the residents of Nazareth attempted to kill Jesus, he uses the incident to foreshadow his hero's later death in Jerusalem (Box 10.13).

In addition, Luke frames Mark's central account of Jesus' adult career with his own unique stories of Jesus' infancy (Chs. 1 and 2) and resurrection (Ch. 24). Luke further modifies the earlier Gospel by adding two large sections of teaching material. The first section inserted into the Markan framework — called the "lesser interpolation" (6:20–8:3) — includes Luke's version of the Sermon on the Mount, which the author transfers to level ground. Known as the Sermon on the Plain (6:20–49), this collection of Jesus' sayings apparently is drawn from the same source that Matthew used, the hypothetical Q document. Instead of assembling Q material into long speeches as Matthew does, however, Luke scatters these sayings throughout his Gospel.

Luke's second major insertion into the Markan narrative, the "greater interpolation," is nearly ten chapters long (9:51–18:14). A miscellaneous compilation of Jesus' parables and pronouncements, this material supposedly represents Jesus' teaching on the road from Galilee to Jerusalem. It is composed almost exclusively of Q material and Luke's special source, which scholars call **L** (Lukan). After this interpolation section, during which all narrative action stops, Luke returns to Mark's account at 18:15 and then reproduces an edited version of the Passion story.

Like the other Synoptic writers, Luke presents Jesus' life in terms of images and themes from the Hebrew Bible, which thus constitutes another of the author's sources. In Luke's presentation, some of Jesus' miracles, such as his resuscitating a widow's dead son, are told in such a way that they closely resemble similar miracles in the Tanak. Jesus' deeds clearly echo those of the prophets Elijah and Elisha (1 Kings 17–19; 2 Kings 1–6). Luke introduces the Elijah–Elisha theme early in the Gospel (4:23–28), indicating that for him

Box 10.13 Luke's Editing and Restructuring of Mark

Because we have one of Luke's principal written sources, the Gospel of Mark, it is possible to learn something of Luke's authorial intentions by examining the way in which he characteristically revises the material he inherited. Although Luke is generally faithful to Mark, which constitutes about 35 percent of his narrative, he makes a number of significant changes in the Markan text. He omits large sections of Mark's account (Mark 6:45–8:26 and 9:41–10:12), possibly to avoid repetitions, such as Mark's second version of the multiplication of loaves and fishes. Luke also typically deletes Markan passages that might reflect unfavorably on Jesus' family or disciples. Consistent with his exaltation of Mary in the birth stories (Ch. 2), he omits Mark's story of Jesus' "mother and brothers" trying to interfere in his ministry (Mark 3:21, 33–34) and rewrites the Markan Jesus' statement about not being respected by his "family and kinsmen" (cf. Mark 6:4 and Luke 4:22, 24). Similarly, Luke excises Mark 8:22–26, an incident symbolic of the disciples' slowness to see or understand Jesus' identity, as well as Markan passages equating Peter with "Satan" (Mark 8:33) or dramatizing the disciples' ineptitude or cowardice (Mark 14:27, 40–41, 51–52).

In one of his most significant changes to the Markan sequence of events, Luke places Jesus' rejection in Nazareth at the outset of his ministry, rather than midway through it as do Mark (6:1–6) and Matthew (13:53–58). Luke also thoroughly rewrites the Nazareth episode, transforming it into a paradigm of his entire two-volume work. Previewing the church's mission to Gentile nations later described in Acts, Luke has Jesus antagonize his hometown congregation by implying that God transfers his favor from the covenant people to non-Jews (Luke 4:25–29).

Another distinctive feature of Luke's Gospel anticipates the narrative thrust in Acts: the journey motif. Whereas Mark only briefly refers to Jesus' journey from Galilee to Jerusalem (Mark 10:17, 32–33), Luke repeatedly emphasizes the importance of Jesus' movements, devoting a full ten chapters to the trek (Luke 9:51–19:28). This restructuring of Mark's account prepares readers to see parallels to Paul's missionary travels in Acts, highlighting the continuity between Jesus' activities and those of his later followers. As Jesus resolves to go to Jerusalem (Luke 9:51),

so Paul similarly decides to travel to Rome (Acts 19:21), the city where a martyr's death, like that of Jesus, awaits him.

Luke's view of the centrality of Jerusalem also significantly shapes his narrative structure. It is the place where his Gospel account begins (Luke 1:8–22), the setting of Jesus' first public appearance (2:43, 46), the goal of Jesus' life journey (9:51), the only site appropriate for Jesus the prophet to die (13:33, a statement unique to Luke), and the location of *all* of Jesus' postresurrection appearances (24:1–53). Whereas Mark explicitly states that the risen Jesus will appear in Galilee (Mark 14:28; 16:7), Luke not only locates Jesus' resurrection and ascension to heaven in or near Jerusalem (Luke 24; Acts 1) but also makes it the center where Christianity first develops. As scholars have noted, in the Gospel, everything progresses toward Jerusalem, where the early church is born. Beginning with the second half of Acts, however, everything moves *away* from Jerusalem—culminating in Paul's arrival in Rome, the imperial capital where the new faith finds its natural audience.

Because Luke presents Jesus' story as a prophetic model for the activities of the early church, the author introduces themes and incidents into the Gospel that later characterize Acts' picture of the church's relationship with Rome. The author emphasizes specific parallels between Jesus' dual trials—before the Sanhedrin and before a Roman governor—and similar trials in Acts, where Paul is hailed before both priestly and Roman courts (cf. Luke 22:66–23:25; Acts 22:25–23:19). Thus, Luke is the only Gospel writer to include in his Passion story an episode in which Jesus appears before Herod Antipas (Luke 23:6–12)—an incident that parallels and foreshadows Paul's similar hearing before another member of the Herodian dynasty, Herod Agrippa II (Acts 25:13–26:32). As the Roman magistrates before whom Paul appears declare him guiltless of any crime against the government (Acts 25:25; 26:30–32), so Pilate exonerates Jesus from the political charge of sedition (Luke 23:13–15, 22). Luke even changes Mark's report of the centurion's speech at the cross: Instead of perceiving Jesus' divine Sonship, the Roman soldier now simply states that Jesus was

(continued)

Box 10.13 *(continued)*

legally "innocent" (cf. Mark 15:39; Matt. 27:54; Luke 23:47).

Finally, Luke modifies Mark's narrative to express his theological view of Jesus. Besides deleting Mark's crucial statement about Jesus' dying sacrificially as a "ransom for many" (Mark 10:45) and emphasizing instead his example of service that will be a pattern for disciples later in Acts (Luke 22:27), Luke also eliminates Markan passages that show Jesus as too humanly vulnerable. In the Gethsemane scene, Luke severely edits the Markan description of Jesus' des-

perate anguish, totally eliminating his prayer to be spared the cup of suffering (cf. Mark 14:32–42 and Luke 22:39–46). The famous verses that describe Jesus as "sweating blood" do not appear in some of the oldest and best Lukan manuscripts; later scribes may have inserted them to make Luke's account consistent with the other two Synoptics. The Lukan Jesus thus utters no final cry of abandonment, but instead serenely commits his spirit to God (cf. Mark 15:33–37; Luke 23:46–47).

---

these ancient men of God were prototypes of the Messiah.

Special Lukan Material   Although he shares material from Mark, Q, and the Hebrew Bible with Matthew, Luke gives his "connected narrative" a special quality by including many of Jesus' words that occur only in his Gospel (the L source). Only in Luke do we find such celebrated parables as those of the prodigal son (15:11–32), the lost coin (15:8–10), the persistent widow, the good Samaritan (10:29–32), and Lazarus and the rich man (16:19–31). These and other parables embody consistent themes, typically stressing life's unexpected reversals and/or God's gracious forgiveness of wrongdoers.

Despite the inclusion of some of Jesus' "hard sayings" about the rigors of discipleship, Luke's special material tends to picture a gentle and loving Jesus, the Good Shepherd who tenderly cares for his flock (the community of believers) (Figure 10.12). Luke has been accused of "sentimentalizing" Jesus' message; however, the author's concern for oppressed people — the poor, the socially outcast, and women — is genuine and lends his Gospel a distinctively humane and gracious ambience (Boxes 10.14 and 10.15).

SOME TYPICAL LUKAN THEMES

A number of Luke's themes appear in both the Gospel and the Book of Acts, such as his emphasis on prayer, forgiveness, compassion, interest in the poor, concern for women, the active role of the Holy Spirit, God's direction of human history, the universality of Jesus' messiahship, and the new religion's positive relationship with the Greco-Roman world.

The Holy Spirit   Both of Luke's books argue that Jesus' career and the growth of Christianity are not historical accidents, but are the direct result of God's will, which is expressed through the Holy Spirit. Luke uses the term *Holy Spirit* — an invisible force from God that guides human thought and action — a total of fourteen times, more than Mark and Matthew together. It is by the Spirit that Jesus is conceived and by which he is anointed after baptism. The Holy Spirit leads him into the wilderness (4:1) and empowers his ministry in Galilee (4:14). The spirit is conferred through prayer (11:13), and at death the Lukan Jesus commits his "spirit" to God (23:46).

The Holy Spirit reappears with overwhelming power in Acts 2 when, like a "strong driving wind," it rushes upon the 120 disciples gathered in Jerusalem to observe **Pentecost**. Possession by the Holy Spirit confirms God's acceptance of Gentiles into the church (Acts 11:15–18). To Luke it is the Spirit that is responsible for the rapid expansion of believers throughout the Roman Empire. Like Paul, Luke sees the Christian community as charismatic, Spirit-led and Spirit-blessed.

Prayer   Another of Luke's principal interests is Jesus' and the disciples' use of prayer. Luke's in-

Figure 10.12 Early Christian artists commonly pictured Jesus in the guise of earlier Greco-Roman gods or heroes, particularly Apollo, Dionysus, or Orpheus, all of whom were associated with music, inspiration, and flocks and shepherds. In this mosaic at Ravenna, Christ appears as the Good Shepherd.

fancy narrative is full of prayers and hymns of praise by virtually all the adult participants. In his account of John's baptizing campaign, the Holy Spirit descends upon Jesus not at his baptism as in Mark, but afterward while Jesus is at prayer (3:21). Similarly, Jesus chooses the disciples after prayer (6:12) and prays before he asks them who he is (9:18). The Transfiguration occurs "while he is praying" (9:29). Jesus' instructions on prayer are also more extensive than in other Gospels (11:1–13; 18:1–14). The Lukan emphasis on prayer carries over into Acts, in which the heroes of the early church are frequently shown praying (Acts 1:14, 24–26; 8:15; 10:1–16).

Jesus' Concern for Women From the beginning of his account, Luke makes it clear that women play an indispensable part in fulfilling the divine plan. Elizabeth, Zechariah's wife, is chosen to produce and raise Israel's final prophet, the one who prepares the way for Jesus. Her cousin Mary responds affirmatively to the Holy Spirit, conceiving and nurturing the world-savior. During his adult ministry, Jesus accepts many female disciples, praising those who, like **Mary**, the sister of **Martha**, abandon domestic chores to take their places among the male followers — a privilege Jesus declares "will not be taken from [them]"

(10:38–42). Galilean women not only follow Jesus on the path to Jerusalem but also financially support him and his male companions (8:2–3). As in Mark, it is these Galilean women who provide the human link between Jesus' death and resurrection, witnessing the Crucifixion and receiving first the news that he is risen (23:49; 23:55–24:11).

Jesus' Affinity with the Unrespectable Closely linked to Jesus' concern for women, who were largely powerless in both Jewish and Greco-Roman society, is his affinity for many similarly vulnerable people on the margins of society. "A friend of tax-gatherers and sinners" (7:34), the Lukan Jesus openly accepts social outcasts, including "immoral" women, such as an apparently notorious woman who crashes a Pharisee's dinner party and seats herself next to Jesus, bathing his feet with her tears, much to his host's indignation (7:37–50). Luke alone preserves one of Jesus' most provocative stories, in which the central character is an ungrateful son who consorts with prostitutes and sinks to groveling with swine — but who is unconditionally loved by his father (15:11–32). In Luke, Jesus not only conducts a brief ministry in **Samaria** (traditionally viewed as a center of religious impurity [9:52–56]) but also makes a **Samaritan** the embodiment of neighborly love (10:30–37).

Box 10.14 Representative Examples of Material Found Only in Luke

A formal preface and statement of purpose (1:1–4)

A narrative about the parents of John the Baptist (1:5–25, 57–80)

Luke's distinctive story of Jesus' conception and birth (1:26–56; 2:1–40)

Jesus' childhood visit to the Jerusalem Temple (2:41–52)

A distinctive Lukan genealogy (3:23–38)

The Scripture reading in the Nazareth synagogue and subsequent attempt to kill Jesus (4:16–30)

Details on the Roman siege of Jerusalem (19:43–44; 21:21–24)

Jesus' hearing before Herod Antipas (23:6–12)

The sympathetic criminal (23:39–43)

Jesus' postresurrection appearances on the road to Emmaus (24:13–35)

Some parables, sayings, and miracles unique to Luke:

A miraculous catch of fish (5:1–11)

Raising the son of a Nain widow (7:11–17)

Two forgiven debtors (7:41–43)

Satan falling like lightning from heaven (10:18)

The good Samaritan (10:29–37)

The friend asking for help at night (11:5–10)

The rich and foolish materialist (12:13–21)

Remaining alert for the Master's return (12:36–38)

The unproductive fig tree (13:6–9)

Healing a crippled woman on the Sabbath (13:10–17)

Curing a man with dropsy (14:1–6)

A distinctive version of the kingdom banquet (14:12–24)

Counting the costs of going to war (14:31–33)

Parable of the lost coin (15:8–10)

The prodigal (spendthrift) son (15:11–32)

The dishonest manager (16:1–13)

Lazarus and the rich man (16:19–31)

Healing ten lepers (17:11–19)

The unjust judge (18:1–8)

The Pharisee and the tax collector (18:9–14)

Restoring the ear of a slave (22:47–53)

Box 10.15 New Characters Introduced in Luke

Elizabeth and the priest Zechariah, parents of the Baptist (1:5–25, 39–79)

Gabriel, the angel who announces Jesus' virginal conception (1:26–38)

Augustus, emperor of Rome (2:1–2)

Simeon, who foretells Jesus' messiahship (2:25–35)

Anna, an aged prophetess (2:36–38)

The widow of Nain (7:11–16)

The unidentified sinful woman whom Jesus forgives (7:36–50)

The sisters Mary and Martha (10:38–39)

Zacchaeus, the wealthy tax collector (19:1–10)

Herod Antipas, as one of Jesus' judges (22:7–12; also 9:7–9)

Cleopas and another unidentified disciple (24:13–35)

Additional minor characters, including a crippled woman (13:10–17), a man with dropsy (14:1–4), and ten lepers (17:11–19).

Accused of being "a glutton and a drinker," Jesus personally welcomes "tax-gatherers and other bad characters" to dine with him, refusing to distinguish between deserving and undeserving guests (7:29–34; 15:1–2). In Luke's version of the great banquet, the host's doors are thrown open indiscriminately to "the poor, the crippled, the lame, and the blind," people incapable of reciprocating hospitality (14:12–24). To Luke, it is not the "poor in spirit" who gain divine blessing, but simply "the poor," the economically deprived for whom productive citizens typically show little sympathy (cf. 6:20–21 and 6:24–25).

Christianity as a Universal Faith   The author designs Luke-Acts to show that, through Jesus and his successors, God directs human history to achieve humanity's redemption. Luke's theory of salvation history has a universalist aspect: From its inception, Christianity is a religion intended for "all nations," especially those peoples who have hitherto lived without Israel's Law and prophets. As **Simeon** prophesies over the infant Jesus, the child is destined to become "a revelation to the heathen [Gentiles]" (2:32). Luke's emphasis on Jesus' universality also appears in his genealogy, which, like that of Matthew, traces Jesus' descent through Joseph (Luke 3:23). Unlike Matthew, however, who lists Jesus' ancestors back to Abraham, "father of the Jews," Luke takes Jesus' family tree all the way back to the first human, Adam, whom he calls "son of God" (Luke 3:23–38). By linking Jesus with Adam, the one created in God's "image" and "likeness," Luke presents Jesus as savior of the whole human race. Whereas Matthew stresses Jesus' heritage as Jewish Messiah, Luke shows him as the heir of Adam, from whom all of humanity is descended. In Acts, therefore, the risen Christ's final words commission his followers to bear witness about him from Jerusalem "to the ends of the earth" (Acts 1:8), conveying his message to all of Adam's children.

Christianity as a Lawful Religion   Besides presenting Christianity as a universal faith, Luke works to show that it is a peaceful and lawful religion. In reporting Jesus' trial before the Roman magistrate and Paul's similar hearings before various other Roman officials, Luke is careful to mention that in each case the accused is innocent of any real crime. Although Pilate condemns Jesus for claiming to be "king of the Jews," an act of sedition against Rome, in Luke's Gospel, Pilate also affirms Jesus' innocence, explicitly stating that he finds the prisoner "guilty of no capital offence" (23:22). In Acts, Luke creates parallels to Jesus' trial in which the apostles and others are similarly declared innocent of subversion. Convinced that Christianity is destined to spread throughout the empire, Luke wishes to demonstrate that it is no threat to the peace and stability of the Roman government.

Jesus as Savior   Finally, Luke portrays Jesus in a guise that his Greek and Roman readers will understand. Matthew had labored to prove from the Hebrew Bible that Jesus was the Davidic Messiah. In his account of Jesus' infancy, Luke also sounds the theme of prophetic fulfillment. But he is aware as well that his Gentile audience is not primarily interested in a Jewish Messiah, a figure traditionally associated with Jewish nationalism. Although Mark and Matthew declared their hero "Son of God," Luke further universalizes Jesus' appeal by declaring him "Savior" (1:69; 2:11; Acts 3:13–15). He is the only Synoptic writer to do so. Luke's term (Greek, *soter*) was used widely in the Greco-Roman world and was applied to gods, demigods, and human rulers alike. Hellenistic people commonly worshiped savior deities in numerous mystery cults and hailed emperors by the title "god and savior" for the material benefits that they conferred upon the public. For Luke, Jesus is the "Savior" of repentant humanity, one who delivers believers from the consequences of wrongdoing, as the judges of ancient Israel "saved" or delivered their people from military oppressors. (The NEB translators therefore use the English term *deliverer* for *soter* in Luke [1:24, 69; 2:11].)

INFANCY NARRATIVES IN LUKE

Only the Gospel of Luke tells of the aged priest **Zechariah** and his barren wife **Elizabeth**, who become the parents of John the Baptist, precursor of Jesus (1:5–25, 39–45, 57–80). To Luke, John the Baptist is the culmination of Israel's purpose—to prepare the way for the Christ: "Until John, it was the Law and the prophets, since then there is the good news of the kingdom" (16:16). Jesus' birth begins a new stage in God's plan for human salvation.

Luke opens his Christmas story with the angel **Gabriel**'s announcement to **Mary** that she will bear a son conceived by the Holy Spirit (1:26–28). In Latin translation, Gabriel's salutation to Mary becomes the *Ave Maria,* one of Christendom's most celebrated prayers. Mary's praise of the Deity's graciousness—the *Magnificat* (1:46–53)—is typical of the formal set pieces, apparently drawn from liturgies in Luke's worshiping community, that the author incorporates into his Gospel. This prayer is modeled on **Hannah**'s song in 2 Samuel (2:1–10), in which a previously childless wife rejoices in conceiving a son.

Luke's depiction of Jesus' birth in a stable in the Davidic city of **Bethlehem** (2:1–40) differs from Matthew's account (Matt. 2:13–23) in several respects. Luke tells of humble Judean shepherds visiting the infant, rather than of foreign astrologers, as in Matthew. Luke also omits any reference to Herod's attempt to kill the child or a flight to Egypt. Jesus' presentation at the Jerusalem Temple a month after his circumcision is the occasion for Simeon's prophecy that the babe will be a "light" and "revelation" benefiting "all the nations"—the Nunc Dimittis hymn (2:29–32)—which expresses Luke's theme that Christianity is intended as "good news" to "all people" (2:10, Revised Standard Version), Gentiles as well as Jews.

Luke includes the only tradition about Jesus' boyhood contained in the New Testament, an anecdote about the twelve-year-old boy's visit to the Temple in Jerusalem, where he impresses some learned scribes with the acuteness of his questions (2:41–52). The statement that Jesus "advanced in wisdom and in favor with God and men" (2:52) almost exactly reproduces the Hebrew Bible description of young Samuel (1 Sam. 2:26) and is probably a conventional observation rather than a historically precise evaluation of Jesus' youthful character.

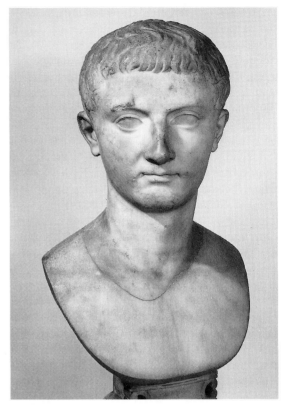

Figure 10.13 This bust shows the emperor Tiberius (14–37 C.E.). According to Luke, Jesus was "about thirty years old" when he began his Galilean campaign during the fifteenth year of Tiberius's reign (c. 27–29 C.E.) (Luke 3:1, 23).

THE GALILEAN MINISTRY

While reproducing much of Mark's account, Luke modifies it to articulate his distinctive themes. By placing Jesus' rejection in Nazareth at the outset of the Galilean campaign (rather than after Jesus' ministry is well under way, as Matt. 13:54–58 and Mark 6:1–6 do), Luke anticipates the final rejection in Jerusalem (Figure 10.13). He also introduces specifically Lukan motifs by having Jesus read from Isaiah (61:1–2 and 58:6), announcing the kind of Messiah the author takes him to be—a Spirit-empowered bringer of health and joy to society's "broken victims," particularly the poor, the imprisoned, and the physically afflicted. Luke's references to Elijah and Elisha performing miracles among non-Jewish peoples also foreshadow Christianity's later mission to the Gentiles.

Luke's Sermon on the Plain   Luke also changes Mark's sequence of events by placing Jesus' call to the Twelve after the Nazareth episode (6:12–19). This transposition serves to introduce Jesus' first public discourse, the Sermon on the Plain (6:20–49). The Sermon opens a long section, the "lesser interpolation," in which Luke interweaves material shared with Matthew (presumably from Q) with material that appears only in his own Gospel (6:20–8:3).

In comparing Matthew's Sermon on the Mount with Luke's version, it is notable that the Lukan Beatitudes are shorter, simpler, and directed at the hearer-reader—"you!" Whereas Matthew spiritualizes their meaning, blessing "those who hunger and thirst to see right prevail," Luke gives a bluntly material version: "how blest are you who now go hungry, your hunger shall be satisfied" (6:21). Luke's "poor" are the financially destitute, the powerless to whom God gives his kingdom. In a passage unique to his gospel, Luke concludes the Beatitudes with "woes" ("alas for you") in which the "rich" and "well-fed" are cursed with future loss and hunger. Persons who benefit unduly from the present world order will see a total reversal of their fortunes (6:24–26).

To Luke, Jesus is the model of compassionate service whom Christians are to imitate. When Jesus raises a widow's son from the dead (7:11–17), the miracle (found only in this Gospel) expresses the twin Lukan themes of God's special love for the poor and deprived and Christ's role as Lord of the Resurrection.

In emphasizing the importance of the women, Luke commonly uses Jesus' interaction with women to reveal his concept of Jesus' character, stressing his hero's combination of authoritative strength and tenderness. After restoring the widow of Nain's son, Jesus reveals compassion for a different kind of vulnerable woman, a prostitute. All four Gospels contain some version of this incident, in which a woman anoints Jesus' feet. Luke uses it in a special way to show Jesus accepting an act of devoted love from an anonymous woman whom others consider unfit because of her "immoral life" (7:36–50; cf. Mark 14:3–9; Matt. 26:6–13; John 12:1–8).

Luke alone relates the parables of the persistent widow (18:2–5) and the woman's lost coin (15:8–9), and describes the female disciples who help support Jesus and his male followers "out of their own resources" (8:1–3). Mary Magdalene (from the Galilean suburb of Magdala), from whom Jesus drove seven devils, and Joanna, whose husband is a steward to Herod Antipas, are present at the Crucifixion and are also among the women who find Jesus' tomb empty (23:55–24:12). The sisters Mary and Martha, whose differing personalities allow Jesus to teach a lesson in spiritual values (10:38–42), number among his closest friends.

JESUS' TEACHING ON THE JOURNEY TO JERUSALEM

The "Greater Interpolation"   Luke begins this long section (9:51–18:14), known as the "greater interpolation," with the declaration that Jesus "set his face resolutely towards Jerusalem," signaling Jesus' resolve to confront the Jerusalem authorities who will reject and condemn him. Although ostensibly the record of a journey from Galilee to Judea, this part of the Gospel is largely a miscellaneous collection of brief anecdotes, sayings, and parables. Here the author intermixes Q material with his individual source (L), including most of the parables unique to his Gospel.

Jesus' brief tour through Samaria and his sending forth of seventy-two disciples to evangelize the countryside (10:1–16) anticipate the later Christian mission to Samaria described in Acts 8. In Jewish terminology, the number seventy or seventy-two represents the sum total of non-Jewish nations. As the Twelve sent to proselytize Israel symbolize the traditional twelve Israelite tribes (9:1–6), so the activities of the seventy-two foreshadow Christian expansion among Gentiles in the Roman Empire.

The Parable of the Good Samaritan   The context in which Luke sets the parable of the good Samaritan is significant. In 10:25–28, a Torah expert defines the essence of the Mosaic Law in the twin commandments to love God (Deut. 6:5) and neighbor (Lev. 19:18). Jesus confirms that in loving thus a person "will live." This episode provides a good example of the way in which Luke adapts Markan material to his theological purpose. Whereas Mark places this dialogue with the Torah instructor in the Jerusalem Temple, Luke transfers it to an unidentified site on the road to Jerusalem and uses it to introduce his parable of the kindly Samaritan. The author creates a transition to the parable by having the instructor ask Jesus to explain what the Torah means by "neighbor."

In typical rabbinic fashion, Jesus does not define the concept, but instead tells a story in which the questioner must find his own meaning in a specific human situation. Analyzing the tale (10:29–35), most students will find that it not only follows Luke's customary theme of the unexpected but also contains some distinctively subversive themes.

In making a Samaritan the moral hero of this tale, Jesus asks his listeners to find nobility in a class of people whom observant Jews must despise as apostates and pariahs. Note that the priest and Levite who fail to help the robbers' victim do so in observance of Torah rules. If the victim were dead and they touched his corpse, they would automatically become ritually unclean and disqualified from performing their Temple duties. Jesus' directive to behave as the Samaritan does stresses a typical Lukan reversal: The person his audience regarded as an unclean foreigner and heretic becomes the model to emulate. Ignoring both religious and racial barriers, the Samaritan recognizes the injured Jew as his neighbor, thereby fulfilling the Torah commands that the legal expert had cited.

Parables About Wealth and Poverty The parables of the rich fool (12:13–21) and Lazarus and the rich man (16:19–31) illustrate Luke's dim view of a life spent acquiring great wealth. The Lukan Jesus urges his disciples to sell their possessions, give to the poor, and thus earn "heavenly treasures" (12:22–34; 14:12–14). Luke consistently emphasizes that helping the deformed and unattractive, society's rejects and have-nots, must be the Christian's primary concern in attaining Jesus' ultimate approval (14:15–24). One version of the author's ideal social order is the commune that the disciples establish following Pentecost, an economic arrangement in which the well-to-do sell their goods, share the proceeds, and hold "everything in common" (Acts 2:42–47).

Jesus' Association with Outcasts The Synoptic authors agree that Jesus sought the company of "tax-gatherers and sinners," a catch-all phrase referring to the great mass of people in ancient Palestine who were socially and religiously unacceptable because they did not or could not keep the Torah's requirements. This "unrespectable" group stood in contrast to the Sadducees, the Pharisees, the scribes, and others who conscientiously observed all Torah regulations in their daily lives. In the Synoptic tradition, Jesus ignores the principle of contamination by association. He eats, drinks, and otherwise intimately mixes with a wide variety of persons commonly viewed as both morally and ritually "unclean." At one moment, we find him dining at the homes of socially honored Pharisees (7:36–50) and the next enjoying the hospitality of social outcasts like Simon the leper (Matt. 26:6–13) and Zacchaeus the tax collector (19:1–10). Jesus' habitual associations lead some of his contemporaries to regard him as a pleasure-loving drunkard (7:34). According to Luke, Jesus answers such criticism by creating parables that express God's unfailing concern for people whom the "righteous" dismiss as worthless.

The Prodigal Son The parable of the prodigal son might better be called the story of the forgiving father, because the climax of the narrative focuses on the parent's attitude toward his two very different sons (15:11–32). The younger son violates the most basic standards of Judaism, squandering his inheritance and reducing himself to the level of an animal groveling in a Gentile's pigpen. Vivid exaggerations characterize Jesus' parables, and he here paints a picture of a youth who is totally insensitive to his religious heritage and as "undeserving" as a human can be. Even his decision to return to his father's estate springs from an unworthy desire to eat better food.

Yet, the parable's focus is not on the ungrateful son, but on the father's love for both his children, the obedient older son and the prodigal son. Acknowledging his elder son's superior claim to his favor, the father attempts to explain the unlimited quality of his affection. The father's nature is to love unconditionally, making no distinction between the deserving and undeserving. The parable illustrates the character of the divine Parent, who "is kind to the ungrateful and wicked," whom Luke describes in his Sermon on the Plain (6:35–36). At the parable's conclusion, the elder brother's response is left open: Will he overcome his natural resentment to join the celebration?

THE JERUSALEM MINISTRY: JESUS' CONFLICT WITH ROME

Although returning to Mark's narrative in 18:15 for his account of the Jerusalem ministry, Luke significantly modifies his source to soften the older Gospel's intense apocalypticism and to emphasize his major theme that Jesus is innocent of plotting treason against Rome. Luke's account retains elements of primitive Christian apocalypticism, including admonitions to be constantly alert and prepared for the *eschaton*, but he also distances the End, placing it at some unknown time in the remote future.

In Luke's Gospel, we find Jesus' sayings about the imminence of the kingdom intermixed with exclusively Lukan material about the kingdom already being a reality present in Jesus' miraculous deeds and teaching. When the Pharisees accuse Jesus of exorcising demons by the power of "Beelzebub [Satan]," he answers, "If it is by the finger of God that I drive out the devils, then be sure the kingdom of God has already come upon you" (11:20). Jesus thus challenges onlookers to see in his successful fight against Evil the inbreaking reign of God. A similar concept of the kingdom appears in Jesus' answer to some Pharisees who ask when God's dominion will begin: "You cannot tell by observation when the kingdom of God comes. There will be no saying, 'Look, here it is!' or 'there it is!'; for in fact the kingdom of God is among you [or in your midst]" (17:20–21).

Predictions of Jerusalem's Fall Luke retains Mark's eschatological prediction of Jerusalem's destruction (Mark 13) but edits it extensively to show that a period of indefinite length intervenes between the city's fall and the actual Parousia (Ch. 21). The author is aware that many of Jesus' followers expected his ministry to culminate in God's government being established visibly on earth. He reports that "because [Jesus] was so close to Jerusalem . . . they thought the reign [or kingdom] of God might dawn at any moment" (19:11), an expectation that persisted in the early church (Acts 1:6–7). Luke counters this belief with a parable explaining that their Master must go away "on a long journey" before he returns as "king" (19:12–27). (Matthew uses this parable of the talents [Matt. 25:14–30] for the same purpose of explaining the delayed Parousia.)

Luke separates historical events preceding Jerusalem's destruction from cosmic events that signal Jesus' return. After the Romans demolish the city and raze the Temple, an indefinitely extended period of secular history will intervene. Luke's Jesus states that "Jerusalem will be trampled down by foreigners until their day has run its course" (21:24). This reference to an epoch of Gentile domination occurs only in Luke and replaces the apocalyptic "sign" of the "abomination of desolation" that appears at this point in Mark's apocalyptic prophecy (Mark 13:14; Matt. 24:15). The fact that Luke follows his Gospel with an account of the church — the Book of Acts — indicates that he foresees a long earthly history for his community. Luke's emphasis on the church's long-range commission to witness about Jesus "to the ends of the earth" (Acts 1:8) expresses his belief that Christians have much unfinished business to take care of before the End.

It is also possible that Luke regards the astronomical phenomena — "portents . . . in sun, moon, and stars" — that immediately precede Jesus' reappearance (21:25–28) as essentially metaphoric. In Acts, Peter is shown declaring that such celestial wonders, prophesied in the Hebrew Bible's Book of Joel, were historically fulfilled in the spiritual activities of the early church (Acts 2:16–24). In presenting the Holy Spirit's visitation in images associated with Jesus' Parousia, Luke anticipates the doctrine of realized eschatology in John's Gospel.

Jesus as Servant   Although Luke's account of Jesus' last days roughly parallels that of Mark (14:1–16:8), Luke introduces several variations to express his particular theological views and to demonstrate that Jesus is innocent of any sedition against Rome (22:1–23:56). Mark had stated that Jesus' death was sacrificial: His life is given "as a ransom for many" (Mark 10:45). In the Lukan equivalent of this passage (placed in the setting of the Last Supper), Jesus merely says that he comes to serve (cf. Mark 10:42–45 and Luke 22:24–27). Luke's theology does not interpret Jesus' crucifixion as a mystical atonement for human sin. Instead, Jesus appears "like a servant," providing an example for others to imitate, the first in a line of Christian models that includes Peter, Stephen, Paul, and their companions in the Book of Acts.

Luke's version of the Last Supper also expresses his theological intent. In the Lukan ceremony, the wine cup is passed first and then the unleavened bread. The author may present this different order in the ritual because he wants to avoid giving Jesus' statement about drinking wine again in the kingdom the apocalyptic meaning that Mark gives it. Luke also omits the words interpreting the wine as Jesus' blood, avoiding any suggestion that Jesus sheds his blood to ransom humanity from sin or that he gives his blood to establish a new covenant. In Luke, Jesus' only interpretative comment relates the bread to his "body" (22:17–20). The author also inverts Mark's order by having Jesus announce Judas's betrayal after the ritual meal, implying that the traitor was present and participated in the communion ceremony.

LUKE'S PASSION STORY

Luke's Passion story emphasizes a theme that will also dominate Acts: Jesus, like his followers after him, does nothing illegal or threatening to the peace and stability of Roman rule. (See Figure 10.14 for a map of Palestine during the ministry of Jesus.) In Luke, the Sanhedrin can produce

Figure 10.14 The political divisions of Palestine during the ministry of Jesus (c. 30 C.E.). Note that Rome directly administered Judea and Samaria through its procurator Pontius Pilate; Herod Antipas ruled Galilee (Jesus' home district) and Peraea; another son of Herod the Great, Philip, ruled an area to the northeast. The Decapolis was a league of ten Greek-speaking cities on the east side of the Jordan River.

no witnesses and no conviction on charges of blasphemy. Its members bring Jesus to Pilate strictly on political terms: The accused "subverts" the Jewish nation, opposes paying taxes to Rome, and claims to be the Messiah, a "king," and therefore a traitor to Caesar. In his account of the trial before Pilate, Luke repeatedly has the Roman governor pronounce Jesus innocent. The episode in which Pilate sends Jesus to **Herod Antipas** (23:6–12), a tradition found only in Luke, serves to reinforce the author's picture of an innocent Jesus. Pilate twice declares that the prisoner "has done nothing to deserve death" (23:15) and is legally "guilty of [no] capital offense" (23:22). The Roman procurator, whom other contemporary historians depict as a ruthless tyrant contemptuous of Jewish public opinion, is here only a weak pawn manipulated by a group of his Jewish subjects.

The same theme reappears in the crucifixion scene, where one of Jesus' fellow victims remarks that "this man [Jesus] has done nothing wrong" (23:41). Whereas in Mark and Matthew the Roman soldier confesses that Jesus is divine, in Luke it is his political innocence that the centurion affirms: "Beyond all doubt, . . . this man was innocent" (23:47).

Other typically Lukan themes are sounded in Jesus' "last words" on the cross. Only in Luke do we find Jesus' prayer that his executioners be forgiven because they do not understand the meaning of their actions (23:24). Because the author regards both Jews and Romans as acting in "ignorance" (see Acts 2:17), Jesus' request illustrates the principle of all-encompassing love that freely pardons enemies (6:27–38) and ends the cycle of retaliation that perpetuates evil in this world. Jesus' final words are to the Father whose Spirit he had received following baptism (3:21; 4:1, 14) and to whom

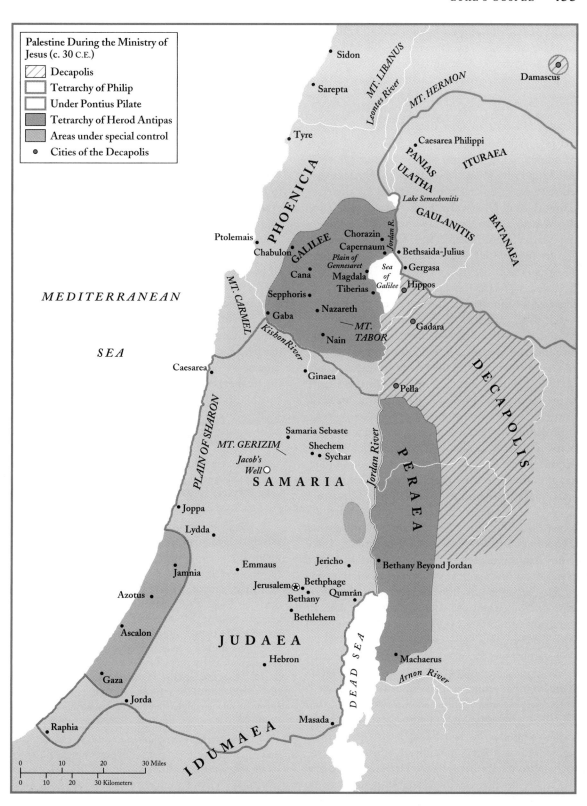

Palestine During the Ministry of Jesus (c. 30 C.E.)

Decapolis
Tetrarchy of Philip
Under Pontius Pilate
Tetrarchy of Herod Antipas
Areas under special control
• Cities of the Decapolis

in death he commits his own spirit (23:46–47). Rather than being a sacrifice for sin, the Lukan Jesus is an example of compassion and forgiveness for all who receive the Spirit to emulate.

POSTRESURRECTION APPEARANCES

Because early editions of Mark contain no resurrection accounts, it is not surprising that Matthew and Luke, who follow Mark through the discovery of the empty sepulcher, differ widely in their reports of Jesus' postresurrection appearances. Consistent with his emphasis on Jerusalem, Luke omits the Markan tradition that Jesus would reappear in Galilee (Mark 16:7; Matt. 28:7, 16–20) and places all experiences of the risen Jesus in or near Jerusalem. The first posthumous appearance, on the road to Emmaus, suggests Luke's understanding of the risen Jesus' relationship to followers left behind on earth. The two disciples, Cleopas and an unnamed companion, who encounter Jesus do not recognize him until they share a meal together. Only in breaking bread—symbolic of the Christian communion ritual—is Jesus' living presence discerned.

Luke's second postresurrection appearance takes place inside Jerusalem, reinforcing themes expressed in the Emmaus incident. After having appeared to Peter—an event that Luke does not describe but that was an early church tradition (see 1 Cor. 15:1–5)—Jesus materializes in the midst of a large group, including the Eleven. Reporting that this apparition was sudden and stunning, Luke states that the resurrected figure displayed familiar physical qualities, perhaps to demonstrate the continuity between the human Jesus and the risen Christ. Thus, the Lukan Jesus bears the marks of crucifixion and shares ordinary food (communion) with his disciples (24:33–43).

Linking the Emmaus and Jerusalem events, Luke emphasizes that the resurrected Jesus offers teaching that connects his ministry and death with the Hebrew Bible. By showing the risen Christ interpreting biblical texts (24:13–32), the author expresses his belief that Jesus continues to guide the Christian community, inspiring fresh insights into the meaning of the Hebrew Scriptures. To Luke, neither the Bible nor Jesus' life can be clearly understood except in the light radiated through Christ's resurrection.

Luke ends his Gospel with Jesus' promise to send the disciples his "Father's gift," the Holy Spirit that enables the church to appreciate Jesus' significance and hear his continuing voice. That living voice instructs them to remain in Jerusalem, awaiting "power from above" (24:44–53; fulfilled in Acts 2).

Emphasizing God's compassion and willingness to forgive all, the Lukan Jesus provides a powerful example for his followers to imitate in service, charity, and good works. An ethical model for Jews and Gentiles alike, Jesus establishes a Spirit-led movement that provides a means of salvation for all people. The earlier belief that the Son of Man would return "soon" after his resurrection from the dead is replaced with Luke's concept of the disciples' role in carrying on Jesus' work "to the ends of the earth," a commission that extends the time of the End indefinitely into the future. In the meantime, a law-abiding and peaceful church will convey its message of a savior for all nations throughout the Roman Empire—and beyond.

QUESTIONS FOR REVIEW

1. Describe some of Luke's major themes and concerns. How do parables that appear only in Luke's Gospel, such as Lazarus and the rich man and the prodigal son, illustrate typically Lukan ideas?

2. Describe the roles that women play in Luke's account. Which women, absent in Mark and Matthew, appear in Luke's version of Jesus' ministry? What qualities of Jesus does their presence elicit?

3. Evaluate the evidence for and against the tradition that Luke, Paul's traveling companion, wrote the Gospel bearing his name. Because the author was aware that "many" other accounts of Jesus' life and work had already been composed, why did he—who was not an eyewitness to the events he describes—decide to write a new Gospel? Does the fact that the writer added the Book of Acts as a sequel to his Gospel narrative suggest something about his purpose?

4. Show some of the specific ways that Luke's version of Jesus' arrest, trial, and execution reflects an awareness of the political realities with which the Christian community had to deal. How does Luke

take pains to show that Jesus is innocent of sedition against Rome?

QUESTIONS FOR DISCUSSION AND REFLECTION

1. Much of the material that appears only in Luke's Gospel highlights Jesus' concern for women, the poor, and the socially outcast. The parables unique to his account—such as the prodigal son, the good Samaritan, and Lazarus and the rich man—stress unexpected reversals of society's accepted norms. What view of Jesus' character and teaching do you think Luke wishes to promote?

2. Luke consistently shows Jesus gravitating toward economically and politically powerless persons, including women, social outcasts, and the poor. Do you think that the Lukan Jesus' example of concern for socially marginal and "unrespectable" people—such as prostitutes, notorious sinners, and tax collectors who collaborated with Rome—is sufficiently recognized or honored by today's political and religious leaders? Can someone be a Christian and *not* follow Jesus' example of siding with the poor and oppressed? Explain your answer.

TERMS AND CONCEPTS TO REMEMBER

Bethlehem	Luke
Elizabeth	Mary
Gabriel	Samaria
Hannah	Samaritan
Herod Antipas	Theophilus
L	Zechariah

RECOMMENDED READING

Conzelmann, Hans. *Theology of St. Luke.* Translated by G. Buswell. New York: Harper & Row, 1960. An influential and incisive analysis of Luke's theological purposes.

Danker, F. W. *Luke.* Philadelphia: Fortress Press, 1976. A good general introduction.

Edwards, O. C., Jr. *Luke's Story of Jesus.* Philadelphia: Fortress Press, 1981.

Fitzmyer, J. A., ed. *The Gospel According to Luke.* Vols. 1 and 2 of the Anchor Bible. Garden City, N.Y.: Doubleday, 1981, 1985.

Johnson, Luke Timothy. "Luke-Acts, Book of." In D. N. Freedman, ed., *The Anchor Bible Dictionary,* Vol. 4, pp. 403–420. New York: Doubleday, 1992. A lucid summary of current scholarly studies of Luke's two-volume work.

Karris, Robert J. "The Gospel According to Luke." In R. E. Brown et al., eds., *The New Jerome Biblical Commentary,* 2nd ed., pp. 675–721. Englewood Cliffs, N.J.: Prentice-Hall, 1990. Provides detailed commentary on Lukan account.

Leaney, A. R. C. *A Commentary on the Gospel According to St. Luke,* 2nd ed. Harper's New Testament Commentary. London: Black, 1966.

Powell, M. A. *What Are They Sayng About Luke?* New York: Paulist Press, 1989. A good place to begin a study of current scholarship on Luke's Gospel.

Schüssler Fiorenza, Elizabeth. *In Memory of Her: A Feminist Theological Reconstruction of Christian Origins.* New York: Crossroads Press, 1983. An important contribution to understanding women's roles in the formation of early Christianity.

Talbert, C. H. *Luke-Acts: New Perspectives from the Society of Biblical Literature Seminar.* New York: Crossroads Press, 1984.

———. *Reading Luke: A Literary and Theological Commentary on the Third Gospel.* New York: Crossroads Press, 1986.

John's Gospel

KEY TOPICS/THEMES

In John's Gospel, the order of events and the portrayal of Jesus and his teaching are strikingly different from those in the Synoptic accounts. Whereas the Synoptics depict Jesus as an eschatological healer-exorcist whose teachings deal primarily with Torah reinterpretation, John describes Jesus as an embodiment of heavenly Wisdom who performs no exorcisms and whose message centers on his own divine nature. In John, Jesus is the human form of God's celestial Word, the cosmic expression of divine Wisdom by which God created the universe. As the Word incarnate (made flesh), Jesus reveals otherwise unknowable truths about God's being and purpose. To John, Jesus' crucifixion is not a humiliating ordeal (as Mark characterizes it), but a glorification that frees Jesus to return to heaven. Although John's Gospel alludes briefly to Jesus' future return, it contains no prophecies of the Second Coming comparable to those found in the Synoptics. Instead, of emphasizing the Parousia, it argues that the risen Christ is eternally present in the invisible form of a surrogate—the Paraclete, or Holy Spirit, which continues to inspire and direct the believing community. The Gospel is commonly

Box 10.16 The Johannine Community: A Distinctive Group Within Early Christianity

Most scholars believe that the Gospel of John, as well as the Epistles of 1, 2, and 3 John, originated in a somewhat marginal Christian community distinguished by a uniquely high Christology. The Gospel's final chapter, apparently an epilogue added by a later editor, ascribes the Gospel to a disciple whom Jesus loved (21:24), one who had been present at the Last Supper and the Crucifixion (13; 19:25–27). Close study of the Gospel and Epistles suggests that a variety of Jewish or other Palestinian groups, including former disciples of John the Baptist, Samaritans, Essenes, and proto-Gnostics, influenced different stages of the community's development and hence of the Gospel's composition. Several eminent New Testament scholars, notably Raymond E. Brown in *The Community of the Beloved Disciple* and J. L. Martyn in *History and Theology in the Fourth Gospel,* have employed sociohistorical methods to reconstruct the evolution of the eclectic group that produced the Johannine literature (see "Recommended Reading").

Although scholars do not agree on the Johannine group's precise stages of development—no one knows when or where it originated or why it produced an interpretation of Jesus so different from the Synoptic model—most accept some general inferences about the community. Like most early Christian believers, members of what would become the Johannine community were Jews with connections to local synagogues. They probably differed from their compatriots only in their belief that Jesus of Nazareth was the promised Davidic Messiah, a God-sent prophet in the tradition of Elijah and Elisha (a relatively low Christology). The galvanizing force behind this group may have been one of Jesus' followers who later became known as the beloved disciple.

At some point relatively early in its growth, some members introduced ideas typical of the Qumran teachings, with their dualistic concepts of cosmic opposites: Light-Dark, Good-Evil, Truth-Lie, Spirit-Flesh, and children of God (the believers' sect) versus spawn of the devil (the believers' religious critics). As the community promoted an increasingly exalted view of Jesus, identifying him with the heavenly Wisdom by which the universe was created, its burgeoning claims for Jesus' divinity brought it into open conflict with some synagogue leaders, who probably saw Johannine Christology as a threat to Jewish monotheism. Conflict with orthodox Judaism may have been exacerbated as Samaritans—whom Jews regarded as heretics—also

(continued)

---

divided into a prologue (1:1–51); a Book of Signs recounting seven miraculous deeds (2:1–11:57); the Book of Glory, a reinterpretation of the Passion (12:1–20:31); and an epilogue (21:1–25).

KEY QUESTIONS

How does John's presentation of Jesus' nature and teaching differ from that in the Synoptics? What does John want us to believe about Jesus' function and continuing presence among his disciples?

A DIFFERENT GOSPEL

The Gospel of John is so different from the Synoptics that most scholars conclude that it is fundamentally not a portrait of the historical Jesus, but a profound meditation on his theological significance. The community that produced this Gospel held a uniquely high view of Jesus' divinity, ascribing to him a heavenly preexistence before his coming to earth and equating him with an eternal attribute of God, the divine Wisdom used to create the universe. A mystical reflection upon Jesus' cosmic meaning and a tribute to his divinity, the Fourth Gospel presents Jesus' earthly life almost exclusively in terms of his postresurrection glory. According to the author, it represents an understanding of Jesus' career that the **Paraclete** (Holy Spirit) later bestowed on a small "brotherhood" originally founded by a "disciple whom Jesus loved."

The author clearly states his purpose: to inspire faith in Jesus' divinity. He describes Jesus' mira-

Box 10.16 (continued)

influenced the community, their presence reflected in the Gospel's stories of Samaritan conversions (John 4) and Jewish accusations that Jesus was a Samaritan (8:48).

Incorporating the Signs Gospel, a narrative of Jesus' public miracles, the first edition of John's Gospel probably appeared in the 90s C.E., shortly after Johannine Christians were expelled from the synagogue (John 9). By that time, Johannine Christology had acquired elements that anticipated later Gnostic doctrines, including a belief that Jesus was God's Eternal Word who descended from heaven to reveal divine knowledge (1:1–4, 14; 17:3), reascended to his celestial place of origin, and caused followers to be "born from above." Under the guidance of the beloved disciple, the community also emphasized the continuing reality of Jesus' postascension presence, the Paraclete, which illuminated their understanding of Jesus' divine nature.

After their insistence on Jesus' near-equality to God had alienated them from the synagogue, further speculation on Jesus as pure spiritual Being apparently produced a decisive split within the community membership, a division reflected in the Epistles of 1 and 2 John. Perhaps about 100–110 C.E., the anonymous writer of 1 John berated a segment of his group that had withdrawn from the Johannine community, accusing them of capitulating to the world and being anti-Christs. He states that the secessionists deny

that Jesus has come "in the flesh" (in genuinely human form), suggesting that the author's opponents were proto-Gnostic Christians who viewed Christ as entirely spirit. A Johannine editor, not the Gospel's original author, may have appended Chapter 21 to the Gospel during this period. The appendix insists that the Being who descended from heaven was also physically human (the risen Jesus eats breakfast with his followers) and that the beloved disciple lends his authority to the editor's group because that disciple is the Gospel's principal source.

After their bitter parting, the two Johannine groups moved in different directions. The secessionists, who took John's Gospel with them, seem to have evolved into full Gnosticism, accounting for the historical fact that the Fourth Gospel was widely used in Gnostic circles. The first commentary written on John's Gospel was by a Gnostic scholar, Heracleon, who lived near the end of the second century C.E.

The other Johannine group, which had produced the Epistles denouncing an extreme Gnostic interpretation of Jesus, eventually merged with the proto-orthodox church, bringing their Gospel and its revolutionary view of Jesus' relationship to the Father with them. Accepted only slowly by the international church, John's Gospel became the work that ultimately defined Christian belief in Jesus' dual nature, paving the way for the post–New Testament dogma of the Trinity.

---

cles—which he calls "signs"—"in order that you may hold faith that Jesus is the Christ, the Son of God, and that through this faith you may possess life by his name" (20:31). This declaration follows the Gospel's climactic scene—a postresurrection appearance in which the reality of Jesus' living presence conquers the doubts of his most skeptical disciple, Thomas. Confronted with a sudden materialization of the risen Jesus, Thomas recognizes him as "My Lord and my God!"—a confession of faith that the reader is intended to echo.

THE AUTHORSHIP OF JOHN

Since the late second century C.E., the Gospel has been attributed to the Apostle John, son of Zebedee and brother of James. According to one

tradition, John eventually settled in Ephesus, where he lived to an exceptionally old age, writing his Gospel, three letters, and the Book of Revelation. These five works are known collectively as the "Johannine literature."

The tradition ascribing authorship to the son of Zebedee is relatively late. Before about 180 C.E., church writers do not mention the Gospel's existence. After that date, opinion on its origin is divided, with some church leaders accepting it as John's composition and others doubting its authenticity. Some even suggested that it is the work of Cerinthus, a Gnostic teacher (Box 10.16).

Most contemporary scholars doubt that the Apostle John wrote the document that bears his name. The Gospel itself does not mention the author's identity, stating instead that it is based on the testimony of an anonymous disciple "whom Jesus loved" (21:20–24). Some traditions identify this **"beloved disciple"** with John (whose name does not appear in the text), but scholars can find no evidence to substantiate this claim. Jesus predicted that John would suffer a death similar to his (Mark 10:39), whereas the Gospel implies that its author, unlike Peter, James, and John, did not die a martyr's death (21:20–22). Some historians suggest that Herod Agrippa may have executed the Apostle John along with his brother James, about 41–43 C.E. (Acts 12:1–3).

A few critics propose that another John, prominent in the church at Ephesus about 100 C.E., is the author. Except that he was called "John the Elder" (*presbyter*), we know nothing that would connect him with the Johannine writings. Lacking definite confirmation of traditional authorship, scholars regard the work as anonymous. For convenience, we refer to the author as John.

The Beloved Disciple Although the Gospel text does not identify its author, editorial notes added to the final chapter associate him with the unnamed beloved disciple, suggesting that at the very least, this disciple's teachings are the Gospel's primary source (21:23–24). Whether this anonymous personage was a historical character, he is certainly an idealized figure, achieving an intimacy and emotional rapport with Jesus unmatched by Peter or the other disciples. In the Gospel, he does not appear (at least not as the one "Jesus loved") until the final night of Jesus' life, when we find him at the Last Supper, lying against his friend's chest (13:23). (The Twelve dined in the Greco-Roman fashion, reclining two-by-two on benches set around the table.)

Designed to represent the Johannine community's special knowledge of Christ, the beloved disciple is invariably presented in competition with Peter, who may represent the larger apostolic church from which the disciple's exclusive group is somewhat distanced. At the Last Supper, the beloved disciple is Peter's intermediary, transmitting to Jesus Peter's question about Judas's betrayal (13:21–29). Acquainted with the high priest, he has access to Pilate's court, thus gaining Peter's ad-

mittance to the hearing, where Peter denies knowing Jesus (18:15–18). The only male disciple at the cross, he receives Jesus' charge to care for Mary, becoming her "son" and hence Jesus' "brother" as well (19:26–27).

Outrunning Peter to the empty tomb on Easter morning, he arrives there first and is the first to believe that Jesus is risen (20:2–10). In a boat fishing with Peter on the Sea of Galilee, the disciple is the first to recognize the resurrected Jesus standing on the shore, identifying him to Peter (21:4–7). Peter, future "pillar" of the Jerusalem church, is commissioned to "feed" (spiritually nourish) Jesus' "sheep" (future followers), but Jesus has a special prophecy for the beloved disciple's future: He may live until the Master returns (21:20–22). (This reference to the Second Coming is virtually unique in John's Gospel.)

Editorial comments appended to the Gospel, apparently after the favored disciple's death, indicate how the Johannine church interpreted Jesus' prophecy. The editor notes that although Jesus' remark had circulated among "the brotherhood" (the community in which the Gospel originated), the saying did not mean that the "disciple would not die." It meant only that Jesus' intentions for his favorite did not involve Peter (21:21–23). The editor's comments hint at the differences between the Johannine and most apostolic Christian communities, which, during the first century C.E., were generally independent of one another. The disciple's "brotherhood" would produce a Gospel promoting Jesus' theological meaning in ways that paralleled the Petrine churches' teachings but that revealed, they believed, Jesus' "glory" (1:14) more fully than other Gospel accounts.

Place of Composition and Date Despite the use of Hellenistic terms and ideas in John's Gospel, recent studies indicate that this book is deeply rooted in Palestinian tradition. It shows a greater familiarity with Palestinian geography than the Synoptics and reveals close connections with first-century Palestinian Judaism, particularly concepts prevailing in the Essene community at Qumran. Study of the Dead Sea Scrolls from Qumran reveals many parallels between Essene ideas and those in John's

Gospel and letters. Like the Essene authors, John typically contrasts pairs of abstract terms, such as light (symbolizing Truth and Goodness) and darkness (symbolizing Deceit and Evil), to distinguish between his group and the rest of the world. He sees the universe as a duality, an arena of polar opposites in which the Devil (synonymous with "liar") and his "spirit of error" oppose Jesus' "spirit of truth" (8:44; 14:17; 15:26; 1 John 4:6). As the "light of the world," Jesus comes to illuminate humanity's mental and spiritual darkness. The Gospel's use of such terminology does not necessarily imply borrowing from Essene sources but suggests that the author's thought may have developed in a Palestinian religious environment.

Many scholars favor a Palestinian or Syrian location for the Gospel's place of composition, but others accept the traditional site of Ephesus. A wealthy, populous seaport and capital of the Roman province of Asia (the western part of modern Turkey), Ephesus was a crossroads for Greek and Near Eastern religious ideas and home to many Jews and early Christians. A center for Paul's missionary work, it was also the base of a John-the-Baptist sect (Acts 19:1–7). If the Gospel originated in a territory where the Baptist was viewed as Jesus' superior, it would explain the writer's severe limitation of John's role in the messianic drama, denying that he represents Elijah and reducing his function to a mere "voice" bearing witness to Jesus (1:6–9, 19–28).

Some critics once believed that John's Gospel was composed late in the second century (when Christian authors first mention it), but tiny manuscript fragments of John discovered in the Egyptian desert have been dated at about 125 and 150 C.E., making them the oldest surviving copy of a New Testament book. Allowing time for the Gospel to have circulated abroad as far as Egypt, the work could not have originated much later than about 100 C.E. The Gospel's references to believers being expelled from Jewish synagogues (9:22, 34–35)—a process that began about 85 or 90 C.E.—suggest that the decisive break between church and synagogue was already in effect when the Gospel was written. Hence, the Gospel is usually dated between about 90 and 100 C.E.

DIFFERENCES IN JOHN'S PORTRAIT OF JESUS

Although John's Gospel contains a few close verbal parallels to Mark's (e.g., John 6:7 and Mark 6:37; John 12:3, 5 and Mark 14:3, 5), indicating that the author was familiar with the Synoptic tradition, he takes such a novel approach that most scholars conclude that the Fourth Gospel does not depend on the earlier accounts. Concentrating on Jesus as a heavenly revealer of ultimate truth, John presents his hero not as a vulnerable man of sorrows but as a divine being who projects his heavenly radiance even while walking the earth.

The following list presents a dozen of the principal differences between John and the Synoptic accounts, along with brief suggestions about the author's possible reasons for omitting so many characteristic Synoptic themes (Box 10.17).

1. John has no birth story or reference to Jesus' virginal conception, perhaps because he sees Christ as the eternal **Logos** (Word) who "became flesh" (1:1, 14) as the man Jesus of Nazareth. John's doctrine of the **Incarnation** (the spiritual Logos becoming physically human) makes the manner of Jesus' human conception irrelevant.

2. John includes no record of Jesus' baptism by John, emphasizing Jesus' independence of and superiority to the Baptist.

3. John reports no period of contemplation in the Judean wilderness or temptation by Satan. His Jesus possesses a vital unity with the Father that makes worldly temptation impossible.

4. John never mentions Jesus' exorcisms, preferring to show Jesus overcoming Evil through his personal revelation of divine truth rather than through the casting out of demons (which plays so large a role in Mark's and Matthew's report of his ministry).

5. Although he reports some friction between Jesus and his brothers (7:1–6), John does not reproduce the Markan tradition that Jesus' family thought he was mentally unbalanced or that his neighbors at Nazareth viewed him as nothing extraordinary (Mark 3:20–21, 31–35; 6:1–6). In

Box 10.17 Representative Examples of Material Found Only in John

Doctrine of the Logos: Jesus preexisting in heaven, where he was God's mediator in creating the universe, before coming to earth (1:1–18)

Miracle at Cana: Jesus changing water into wine (the first "sign") (2:1–12)

Doctrine of spiritual rebirth: conversation with Nicodemus (3:1–21; see also 7:50–52; 19:39)

Jesus as the water of eternal life: conversation with the Samaritan woman (4:1–42)

Jesus healing the invalid at Jerusalem's Sheep Pool (5:1–47)

The "I am" sayings: Jesus speaking as divine Wisdom revealed from above, equating himself with objects or concepts of great symbolic value, such as "the bread of life" (6:22–66), "the good shepherd" (10:1–21), "the resurrection and the life" (11:25), "the way," "the truth" (14:6), and "the true vine" (15:1–17)

Jesus, light of the world, existing before Abraham (8:12–59)

Cure of the man born blind: debate between church and synagogue (9:1–41)

The resurrection of Lazarus (the seventh "sign") (11:1–12:11)

A different tradition of the Last Supper: washing the disciples' feet (13:1–20) and delivering the farewell discourses; promise of the Paraclete, the Spirit that will empower the disciples and interpret the meaning of Jesus' life (13:31–17:26)

Resurrection appearances, in or near Jerusalem, to Mary Magdalene and the disciples, including Thomas (20:1–29)

Resurrection appearances, in Galilee, to Peter and to the beloved disciple (21:1–23)

John, Jesus meets considerable opposition, but he is always too commanding and powerful a figure to be ignored or devalued.

6. John presents Jesus' teaching in a form radically different from that of the Synoptics. Both Mark and Matthew state that Jesus "never" taught without using parables (Mark 4:34; Matt. 13:34), but John does not record a single parable of the Synoptic type (involving homely images of agricultural or domestic life). Instead of brief anecdotes and vivid comparisons, the Johannine Jesus delivers long philosophical speeches in which Jesus' own nature is typically the subject of discussion. In John, he speaks both publicly and privately in this manner, in Galilee and in Jerusalem.

7. John includes none of Jesus' reinterpretations of the Mosaic Law, the main topic of Jesus' Synoptic discourses. Instead of the many ethical directives about divorcing, keeping the Sabbath, ending the law of retaliation, and forgiving enemies that we find in Mark, Matthew, and Luke, John records only one "new commandment"—to

love. In both the Gospel and the letters, this is Jesus' single explicit directive; in the Johannine community, mutual love among "friends" is the sole distinguishing mark of true discipleship (13:34–35, 15:9–17).

8. Conspicuously absent from John's Gospel is any prediction of Jerusalem's fall, a concern that dominated the Synopticists' imagination (Mark 13; Matt. 24–25; Luke 21).

9. John also deviates from the Synoptic tradition by minimizing expectations of Jesus' Second Coming, offering no prophecies of an imminent return comparable to those in Mark and Matthew. John's Gospel refers to the tradition of Jesus' eventual return only twice. At the Last Supper, Jesus promises that he will "come again," specifically to transport his followers to their heavenly abode (perhaps at the time of their deaths) (14:1–3). In John 21 (an epilogue to the Gospel thought to have been added by an editor), the narrator indicates that some in the Johannine community looked forward to Jesus' reappearance (21:21–23).

Nowhere in John's Gospel, however, are there Synoptic-style predictions of social upheavals or cosmic portents that would signal the nearness of the Parousia. Instead, John promotes the view that Jesus is already present among believers in the form of the Paraclete, the Holy Spirit that serves as Christians' Helper, Comforter, or Advocate (14:25–26; 16:7–15). To John, Jesus' first coming means that believers have life *now* (5:21–26; 11:25–27) and that divine judgment is a current reality, not merely a future event (3:18; cf. 9:39; 12:31). Scholars find in John a **realized eschatology**, a belief that events usually associated with the *eschaton* (world's End), such as divine judgment and the awarding of eternal life, are even now realized or fulfilled by Jesus' spiritual presence among believers. For John, the earthly career of Jesus, followed by the infusion of his Spirit into the disciples (20:22–23), has already accomplished God's purpose in sending the Messiah. We do not know how the Johannine community may have envisioned Jesus' return, but for them, in his hour of "glory" (crucifixion), he had essentially finished his work (19:30). As John's doctrine of the Incarnation makes the concept of a virgin birth theoretically unnecessary, so his view of the Paraclete effectively mutes expectations of an imminent Second Coming.

10. Although he represents the sacramental bread and wine as life-giving symbols, John does not preserve a communion ritual or the institution of a new covenant between Jesus and his followers at the Last Supper. Stating that the meal took place a day before Passover, John substitutes Jesus' act of humble service — washing the disciples' feet — for the Eucharist (13:1–16).

11. As his Jesus cannot be tempted, so John's Christ undergoes no agony before his arrest in the Garden of Gethsemane. Unfailingly poised and confident, Jesus experiences his painful death as a glorification, his raising on the cross symbolizing his imminent ascension to heaven. Instead of uttering a cry of despair, as portrayed in Mark, in John, Jesus dies with a declaration that he has "accomplished" his life's purpose (19:30).

12. Finally, it must be emphasized that John's many differences from the Synoptics do not simply result from the author's attempting to "fill in" the gaps in his predecessors' Gospels. By carefully examining John's account, readers discover that he does not write to supplement earlier narratives about Jesus; rather, both his omissions and inclusions are determined almost exclusively by the writer's special theological convictions (20:30–31; 21:25). From his opening hymn praising the eternal Word to Jesus' promised reascension to heaven, every part of the Gospel is calculated to illustrate Jesus' splendor as God's fullest revelation of his own ineffable Being.

DIFFERENCES IN CHRONOLOGY AND ORDER OF EVENTS

Although John's essential story resembles the Synoptic version of Jesus' life — a public ministry featuring healing and other miracles followed by official rejection, arrest, crucifixion, and resurrection — the fourth Gospel presents important differences in the characters, chronology, and order of events (Box 10.18). Significant ways in which John's narrative sequence differs from the Synoptic order include the following:

1. The Synoptics show Jesus working mainly in Galilee and coming south to Judea only during his last days. By contrast, John has Jesus traveling back and forth between Galilee and Jerusalem throughout the duration of his ministry.

2. The Synoptics place Jesus' assault on the Temple at the end of his career, making it the incident that consolidates official hostility toward him; John sets it at the beginning (2:13–21).

3. The Synoptics agree that Jesus began his mission after John the Baptist's imprisonment, but John states that their missions overlapped (3:23–4:3).

4. The earlier Gospels mention only one Passover and imply that Jesus' career lasted only about a year; John refers to three Passovers (2:13; 6:4;

Box 10.18 Characters Introduced in John or Given New Emphasis

Andrew, Peter's brother, as a speaking character (1:40–42, 44; 6:8–9; 12:20–22)

Philip, one of the Twelve (1:43–49; 6:5–7; 12:20–22; 14:8–11)

Nathanael, one of the Twelve (1:45–51)

Mary, as a participator in Jesus' ministry (2:1–5), at the cross (19:25–27)

Nicodemus, a leading Pharisee (3:1–12; 7:50–52; 19:39)

A Samaritan woman (4:7–42)

A paralyzed man cured in Jerusalem (5:1–15)

Jesus' unbelieving "brothers" (7:2–10)

The woman taken in adultery (8:3–11; an appendix to John in NEB)

A man born blind (9:1–38)

Lazarus, brother of Mary and Martha (11:1–44; 12:1–11)

An unidentified disciple whom "Jesus loved" (13:23–26; 18:15–16; 19:26–27; 20:2–10; 21:7, 20–24)

Annas, father-in-law of Caiaphas, the High Priest (18:12–14, 19–24)

11:55), thus giving the ministry a duration of three to nearly four years.

5. Unlike the Synoptics, which present the Last Supper as a Passover celebration, John states that Jesus' final meal with the disciples occurred the evening before Passover and that the Crucifixion took place on Nisan 14, the day of preparation when paschal lambs were being sacrificed (13:1, 29; 18:28; 19:14). Many historians believe that John's chronology is the more accurate; it is improbable that Jesus' arrest, trial, and execution took place on Nisan 15, the most sacred time of the Passover observance.

JOHN'S PURPOSE AND METHOD

Relation to Gnostic Ideas   John's stated intent is to elicit belief in his community's distinctively high Christology (17:3–5; 20:30–31), but other purposes can also be inferred from studying the text. Although he emphasizes Jesus' supernatural character, John stops short of the position that viewed Christ as pure spirit. A widespread and extremely diverse movement in early Christianity, **Gnosticism** argued that believers gain salvation through a special knowledge (*gnosis*) revealed through a spiri-

tual savior, presumably Jesus. Gnostic thinkers are dualists, viewing the world as composed of two mutually exclusive realms. The invisible world of spirit is pure and good, whereas the physical world is inherently evil, the inferior creation of a lesser god, whom some Gnostics identify with Yahweh. The divine redeemer who descends from heaven to bring saving knowledge to a spiritual elite belongs entirely to the spirit realm. Hence, some Christian Gnostics argued that Jesus only *seemed* to be human. Docetists (a name taken from the Greek verb "to seem") concluded that Christ was wholly spiritual, uncontaminated by a material body. At the Crucifixion, he ascended to heaven, leaving behind another's corpse on the cross.

Although his Gospel contains Gnostic elements, John avoids Gnosticism's extremism by insisting on Jesus' physical humanity (1:14). Even after resurrection, Jesus displays fleshly wounds and consumes ordinary food (Chs. 20–21). To show that Jesus was a mortal person who truly died, John eliminates from his Passion story the tradition that Simon of Cyrene carried Jesus' cross (lest the reader think that Simon might have been substituted for Jesus at the Crucifixion). John also introduces an incident in which a Roman soldier pierces Jesus' side, confirming physical death (19:34–35).

Despite including details to modify Gnostic beliefs, John also contains statements expressing classic Gnostic ideas. Knowing the divine Beings—Father and Son—is equated with "eternal life" (17:3). The assertion that the "spirit alone gives life; the flesh is of no avail" (6:63) and the unique emphasis on spiritual rebirth (Ch. 3) strikingly parallel Gnostic concepts.

Role of the Paraclete   Another of the author's implied goals is to picture Jesus as revealed through the Paraclete. A term found only in John's Gospel, the Paraclete is the Holy Spirit that Jesus bestows on his followers after his death. Variously translated as "Advocate," "Helper," "Comforter," or "Spirit of Truth," the Paraclete functions as a substitute for Jesus' own presence, his surrogate among the disciples. In John's view, the Paraclete inspires his community to continue Jesus' miraculous works of healing; it answers their prayers for power and knowledge; it provides defenses against their opponents' hostility. And, most important for the presentation of Jesus' life and teachings, it enables the "brotherhood" to explain and interpret Jesus' full theological significance (14:12–26).

One of the Paraclete's main purposes is to unveil Jesus' true likeness, to portray the spiritual reality hidden during his human incarnation. Thus, John represents Jesus as saying that "he [the Paraclete] will glorify me," revealing Jesus' cosmic splendor to the author's privileged group (16:12–15). John's community thus creates a portrait of Jesus that not only preserves traditions about his historical ministry but also uses the insights into his character and nature that the Paraclete discloses to them. In John's Gospel, the author's task is not to record external facts about his subject's earthly biography, but to fashion a picture of Jesus that duplicates what the Paraclete reveals. Because the Paraclete's function is to define Jesus' glory—both its heavenly origin and its continuing presence on earth—John's account must meet the formidable challenge of portraying the "true" Jesus, allowing his celestial radiance to shine through the man of flesh and history. (Compare John's purpose with Luke's similar implication that Jesus' real story can

be told only in terms of his postresurrection divinity [Luke 24:25–27, 44–53].)

John's portrait of Jesus is thus painted with supernal colors chosen by the Paraclete. His subject's self-revealing speeches—long metaphysical discourses, so different from the short, vivid pronouncements in Mark and Luke—appear to have a similar origin. Most scholars find it virtually impossible to detect the voice of the historical Jesus in the Johannine speeches; rather than being attempts to reconstruct Jesus' remembered words, they are confessions of faith in his divine nature and cosmic stature. As they stand in the Gospel, they are largely the author's creation—tributes to Jesus' unique role in human redemption.

JESUS AS DIVINE WISDOM

In the prologue (1:1–18), John identifies the human Jesus with the Logos (Word). A philosophical term since the time of Heraclitus (born before 500 B.C.E.), in John's day Logos was a concept that Stoic philosophers used to denote the principle of cosmic reason, the intelligent force that orders and sustains the universe, making it accessible and intelligible to the human mind. Greek philosophy also saw the Logos as a creative power that had formed the cosmos (world order) out of the original chaos (dark void). In the Hebrew biblical tradition, a similar concept developed. According to Proverbs (8:22–31), Yahweh had **Wisdom**, personified as a gracious young woman, as his companion when he created the world. She not only was Yahweh's intimate helper in the creative process but also served as God's channel of communication with humanity. In later manifestations of this biblical idea, Wisdom became both the agent or means of creation and the revealer of the divine mind (Ecclus. 24; Wisd. of Sol. 6:12–9:18).

These parallel Greek and Hebrew ideas converge in the writings of **Philo Judaeus**, a Jewish scholar who lived in Alexandria during the first century C.E. A pious Jew profoundly influenced by Greek thought, Philo attempted to reconcile Hellenistic logic with the revelation contained in the

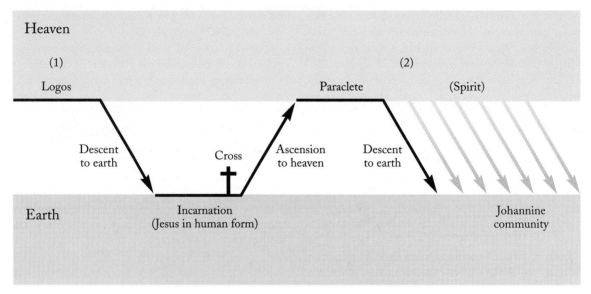

Figure 10.15 This diagram shows John's concept of the Incarnation (the Word made flesh). Note that Jesus' ascension to heaven (return to his place of spiritual origin) is followed by a descent of the Paraclete, Jesus' Spirit — an invisible surrogate that inspires the Johannine brotherhood. Whereas Jesus' human presence on earth was brief, John implies that the Paraclete abides permanently with the believing community.

Hebrew Bible. Philo used the Tanak concept of Wisdom as the creative intermediary between the transcendent Creator and the material creation. But he employed the Greek term *Logos* to designate its role and function. (Philo may have preferred *Logos* because it is masculine in Greek, whereas *Wisdom* [*Sophia*] is feminine.) Philo's interpretation can be illustrated by an allegoric reading of Genesis 1, in which God's first act is to speak — create the Word (Logos) — by which power heaven and earth come into being.

Echoing the Genesis creation account and Philo's interpretation of it, John identifies Jesus, in his prehuman existence, with the divine Logos that formed the universe (1:1–5, 9–14). The heavenly Logos then "became flesh" (1:14) to walk the earth as Jesus of Nazareth, the embodiment of God's creative Wisdom (Figure 10.15). With this statement of the Incarnation (the spiritual Logos becoming the man Jesus), John asserts his hero's innate superiority to all other divine messengers, whether angels or prophets, including John the

Baptist. Jesus not only speaks the Word of God; he *is* that Word and reveals the divine nature fully.

THE BOOK OF SIGNS: MIRACLES REVEALING DIVINITY

John organizes his account of Jesus' public ministry around seven miracles or "signs," among which he inserts long discourses and dialogues, including several "I am" sayings (2:1–11:57). (For a summary of the signs, see Box 10.19.)

THE MIRACLE AT CANA

The first Johannine sign occurs at the Galilean town of Cana (not mentioned in the Synoptics), where Jesus, attending a wedding with his disciples and his mother, changes water into wine. Although the transformation of water into wine has no parallel in any other Gospel, the miracle — reminiscent of festivals honoring Dionysus, the Greco-Roman god of wine — is consistent with

Box 10.19 The Signs Gospel

Many scholars believe that the author of John's Gospel used an earlier narrative of Jesus' miraculous deeds known as the Signs Gospel. The author's hypothetical source contained accounts of the following miracles (listed here in the Johannine order):

1. Turning water into wine at Cana (in Galilee, 2:1–11)

2. Healing an official's son (in Galilee, 2:12a; 4:46b–54)

3. Healing a crippled man (in Jerusalem, 5:2–9)

4. Feeding 5000 people (in Galilee, 6:1–15)

5. Walking on water (in Galilee, 6:16–25)

6. Restoring sight to a blind man (in Jerusalem, 9:1–8)

7. Raising Lazarus from the dead (near Jerusalem, 11:1–45)

Some scholars also think that the disciples' huge catch of fish (21:1–14) was originally a Galilean miracle that the Gospel's final editor incorporated into his appended account of Jesus' postresurrection appearances.

Synoptic traditions that depict Jesus' propensity toward eating and drinking with all kinds of people (Luke 7:33–35, etc.). John's narrative of the Cana event similarly highlights Jesus' paradoxical combination of ethical leadership with almost outrageous behavior, acting in a way that seems to invite excess. When informed that the host's supply of wine has run out, indicating that the wedding guests are probably already intoxicated, Jesus adds to the party's merriment by providing an additional 180 gallons of a vintage superior to that which the guests have already consumed. In John's view, Jesus' offering the means for celebrants to continue imbibing "good wine" reveals "his glory" and causes the disciples to "believe in him" (2:11), as if confirming his qualifications to host the promised Messianic banquet. Presented as Jesus initial "sign" that God is present in his actions, this joyous celebration of life, symbolized not only by the marriage ceremony but also by the shared enjoyment of a divinely bestowed beverage, foreshadows a more solemn celebration described at the end of John's narrative—that of Jesus' "glorious" death on the cross. Using the images of water and wine—and the blood these liquids symbolize—the author thematically links the beginning of Jesus' ministry at Cana with its culmination at Golgotha, where a Roman soldier thrusts his spear into Jesus' body,

releasing a flow of "blood and water" (19:34). Underscoring the connection between these two framing incidents, John has Jesus' mother present at both Cana and the Crucifixion, the only two occasions on which she appears in his Gospel (cf. 2:1–11; 19:25–27).

ASSAULT ON THE TEMPLE

Reversing the Synoptic order, John shows Jesus driving moneychangers from the Temple during a Passover at the outset of his ministry. For John, the episode's significance is Jesus' superiority to the Jerusalem sanctuary. The Temple is no longer sacred because the Holy Spirit now dwells in Jesus' person rather than the shrine King Herod constructed. Jesus' physical body may be destroyed, but unlike the Herodian edifice, he will rise again as proof that God's Spirit imbues him (2:13–25).

Jesus' conversation with **Nicodemus**, a Pharisee and member of the Sanhedrin, typifies John's method of presenting Jesus' teaching (3:1–21). In most of the Johannine dialogues, Jesus uses a figure of speech that someone misinterprets, causing Jesus to explain his metaphoric language in a long monologue that typically culminates in a meditation on his nature and unique relationship with the Father. Nicodemus takes Jesus' reference to

Figure 10.16 This Ravenna mosaic shows Jesus conversing with a Samaritan woman drawing water from Jacob's well (John 4). Both Luke and John emphasize Jesus' characteristic concern for women.

spiritual rebirth literally, triggering a metaphysical discourse on Jesus' heavenly origin and role as "Light of the world."

John shares with Luke a tradition about Jesus' special concern for women and outsiders. These interests coincide in Chapter 4, in which Jesus scandalizes his male disciples by holding a public conversation with a Samaritan woman of questionable reputation (Figure 10.16). Note that Jesus selects this person—foreign, "immoral," heretical, female—to serve as his first non-Jewish prophet. Through her, "many Samaritans" become believers. Similar themes appear in the anecdote concerning a woman about to be stoned for adultery. Although absent from many New Testament manuscripts and relegated to an appendix in the New English Bible, this episode (7:1–11) well illustrates Jesus' compassion for the powerless and oppressed.

The second miraculous sign occurs when Jesus, again in Cana, cures the dying son of a Roman centurion (4:46–54), the second non-Jew to whom he brings comfort. The third sign occurs when Jesus heals a chronic invalid (5:2–9) at the sheepgate pool in Jerusalem, the significance of which appears in the discourse that follows (5:19–47).

Here Jesus describes the Son's intimacy with the Father, who has committed powers of judgment and forgiveness to him.

The fourth sign is Jesus' feeding of the 5000, the only miracle that appears in all four Gospels (6:1–12; Mark 6:30–44; Matt. 14:13–21; Luke 9:10–17). In John, this event symbolizes Jesus' providing the world with spiritual nourishment (6:25–59), although, as usual in this Gospel, Jesus' listeners misunderstand his intent. This time they forcibly attempt to make him king (6:15), not realizing that his kingdom "does not belong to this world" (18:36). A fifth sign, Jesus' walking on water, quickly follows, demonstrating the Son's power over nature (6:16–21).

Jesus and Yahweh: The "I Am" Sayings   This section contains the first of Jesus' "I am" pronouncements. Scholars believe that these discourses are modeled not on recollections of his actual words, but on Wisdom's speeches in the Hebrew Bible. Hebrew writers typically picture Wisdom speaking in the first person, using the phrase "I am" and then defining her activities as God's agent. John casts many of Jesus' discourses in exactly the same form, beginning with a declaration "I am" and then equating himself with a term of great religious significance. Compare some of Wisdom's utterances with those of the Johannine Jesus:

> The Lord created me the beginning of his works,
> before all else that he made, long ago.
> Alone I was fashioned in times long past,
> at the beginning, long before earth itself.
> Prov. 8:22–23

Identifying Wisdom with God's verbal command to create light (Gen. 1:3), the author of Ecclesiasticus represents her as saying,

> I am the word which was spoken by the
>   Most High; . . .
> Before time began he created me,
> and I shall remain for ever. . . .
> Ecclus. 24:3, 9

Sent by God to live among his people, Israel, Wisdom invites all to seek her favor:

> Come to me, you who desire me,
> and eat your fill of my fruit; . . .
> Whoever feeds on me will be hungry for more,
> and whoever drinks from me will thirst for more.
> Ecclus. 24:19, 21–22

The Johannine Jesus echoes Wisdom's promise even while fulfilling it:

> Everyone who drinks this water [of Jacob's well] will be thirsty again, but whoever drinks the water that I shall give him will never suffer thirst any more. The water that I shall give him will be an inner spring always welling up for eternal life.
> John 4:13–15

Besides associating Jesus with the principle of eternal Wisdom, John's "I am" speeches also express an important aspect of his Christology. They echo Yahweh's declaration to Moses (Exod. 3:14), in which God reveals his sacred personal name. In the Hebrew Bible, only Yahweh speaks of himself (the "I Am") in this manner. Hence, Jesus' reiterated "I am . . . the bread of life" (6:35), "the good shepherd" (10:11), "the resurrection and the life" (11:25), or "the way," "the truth," and

"the life" (14:6) stress his unity with god, the eternal "I am."

John attributes much of "the Jews'" hostility toward his hero to their reaction against Jesus' apparent claim to divinity. When Jesus refers publicly to his prehuman existence, declaring that "before Abraham was born, I am," his outraged audience in the Temple attempts to stone him for blasphemy (8:56–59). Many scholars doubt that Jesus really made such assertions. According to this view, the attempted stoning represents Jewish leaders' response to the preaching of John's community, which made extraordinarily high claims about Jesus' divine status. Like Matthew, John regards all fellow Jews who do not accept his beliefs about Jesus as enemies, a sectarian view that historically has fostered anti-Semitism.

John's Double Vision   John's presentation of the sixth sign — restoring sight to a man born blind (9:1–41) — illustrates what some scholars refer to as the author's double vision or two-level drama. Careful analysis of this long passage suggests that the Evangelist is combining traditions about the miracles of the historical Jesus with healing activities of his own time and community. The two elements — Jesus and his later disciples — can be equated because the same Paraclete operates through both parties. Because Jesus had promised that his followers would accomplish "greater things" than the human Jesus had (14:12), the author's group could perceive their Master's continuing presence in their own ministry. In John's imaginative conflation of history, the human Jesus of the past and the believers of the present perform the same Spirit-empowered work.

In the episode of the man born blind, John skillfully combines historical past and present to tell his story. Jesus' miracle is followed by a series of debates and confrontations among the cured man, his parents, and officials of the synagogue. The Jewish officials' interrogation of the man reproduces circumstances prevailing not in Jesus' day but in the writer's own time, when Torah authorities cross-examined Jews suspected of regarding Jesus as the Messiah. This passage also refers to the expulsion of Jesus' followers from the synagogue (9:23, 34), a situation that did not develop until well after Jerusalem's fall in 70 C.E.

The conversation with Nicodemus (Ch. 3) offers a similar blending of Jesus' past actions with the Johannine community's ongoing ministry. Jesus' pretended astonishment that one of Israel's most eminent teachers does not understand the Spirit that motivates Jesus' followers reflects the late first-century debate between the Jewish authorities and the author's group. Using the first-person plural "we" to signify the whole believing community, John affirms that his community experiences the Spirit's power, while "you" (the disbelieving opponents) refuse to credit the Johannine testimony (3:9–11). The reader will also observe that in this dialogue Jesus speaks as if he has already returned to heaven (3:13), again expressing a belief held by the author's community.

The Raising of Lazarus The seventh and most spectacular sign—raising **Lazarus** from the dead (11:1–44)—demonstrates another Johannine conviction: that Jesus is the source of everlasting life. Concluding the Book of Signs, this episode connects the story of Jesus' ministry with his imminent Passion and resurrection. As John presents it, Jesus' ability to raise a man who has been dead for four days is the act that consolidates priestly opposition to him and leads directly to his death (11:45–53).

Although no other canonical Gospel mentions the climactic Lazarus event, John may draw on a primitive resuscitation narrative that appears in an Egyptian edition of Mark. Discovered in 1958, this fragment, called "Secret Mark," is quoted in a letter by Clement of Alexandria (c. 200 C.E.). Secret Mark describes Jesus' resurrecting a rich youth whom he then initiates into the "mystery of the kingdom of God." According to Clement, the excerpt would appear in canonical Mark between 10:34 and 10:35. Although present editions of the Synoptics are silent about the episode, Secret Mark indicates that a version of John's resuscitation story was once part of the Synoptic tradition (see Box 11.1 for the full text of "Secret Mark").

Whatever the historical foundation of the Lazarus incident, John uses it to illustrate his theme of realized eschatology—that in Jesus' activity and presence events normally relegated to the End of time are now taking place. In a climactic "I am" speech, Jesus declares, "I am the resurrection and I am life. If a man has faith in me, even though he die, he shall come to life; and no one who is alive and has faith shall ever die" (11:25).

Faced with overwhelming evidence of Jesus' eschatological powers, the Jerusalem opposition resolves to eliminate him. The priests fear that if the Jewish people accept his messiahship (making him "king of the Jews"), their response will incite the Romans to destroy their state. (This passage refers to the Roman destruction of Jerusalem in 70 C.E.) The remark attributed to Caiaphas, the High Priest—that "it is more to your interest that one man should die for the people, than that the whole nation should be destroyed" (11:50)—is deeply ironic in unwittingly expressing the Christian belief that Jesus' death benefits others.

THE BOOK OF GLORY

In the second part of his Gospel, John pictures Jesus' final days in a way that transforms the Messiah's betrayal and suffering into a glorious triumph. After a joyous entry into Jerusalem, Jesus foretells his death in terms resembling Mark's description of the agony in Gethsemane (Figure 10.17), but reinterpreted to stress the Crucifixion's saving purpose: "Now my soul is in turmoil, and what am I to say? Father, save me from this hour [cf. Mark 14:32–36]. No, it was for this that I came to this hour. Father, glorify thy name" (12:27–28). When a celestial voice affirms that God is glorified in Christ's actions, Jesus interprets his "lifting up" (crucifixion) as God's predestined means of drawing all people to him, a process of human salvation that cannot occur without his death (12:28–33).

Jesus' Farewell Speeches Chapters 13–17 contain Jesus' farewell discourses delivered at the Last Supper. John's account differs significantly from

Figure 10.17 *The Crucifixion* by Matthias Grunewald (c. 1470–1528). Painted on wood, this small version of Jesus' tortured death heightens the sense of the sufferer's physical pain and grief. Although his emphasis on Jesus' agony reflects Mark's account, Grunewald follows John's Gospel in showing Jesus' mother and the beloved disciple (as well as another Mary) present at the cross.

the Synoptic tradition, omitting all references to the communal bread and wine or a new covenant and presenting instead Jesus' washing his disciples' feet (13:3–17). John links this act of humble service to Jesus' foreknowledge of his imminent return to the Father and his "new commandment"—to love others in the way he has loved his own (13:1, 3, 34–35). In contrast to the many ethical directives found in the Synoptics, the Johannine tradition preserves only this single command (see also 15:11–14).

A Johannine composition, the farewell speeches (13:31–17:26) emphasize Jesus' unity with the Fa-

ther and the work of the Paraclete, or "Spirit of Truth" (14:16–17). An invisible counterpart of Jesus, the Paraclete enables his disciples to understand the true significance of Jesus' teaching (16:1–15). By implication, the Paraclete also empowers the author to create a Gospel that fully portrays Jesus' glory.

In John's view, Jesus imparts the promised Paraclete (advocate, or spirit) at his resurrection, merely by breathing on the disciples and saying, "Receive the Holy Spirit" (20:21–23). The risen Lord's action recalls the creation scene in Genesis 2 when Yahweh breathes into Adam's nostrils "the breath of life," making him an animate being. As his Gospel begins with the Word creating the universe (1:1–5), so it closes with the Word breathing the pure spirit of life into his renewed human creation.

As he fixes the date of the Last Supper on the day before Passover (the slaying of the Passover lambs at that time suggests the symbolization of Jesus as God's sacrificial lamb), so John presents a version of Jesus' Passion that differs significantly from that in the Synoptics.

John's portrayal of Jesus' behavior in Gethsemane is typical of his distinctive approach, which emphasizes Jesus' divinity in a way that contrasts markedly with the Synoptic tradition. In Mark, Jesus begs God to spare him a painful and public humiliation, hurling himself full-length on the ground in an agony of anticipated suffering (Mark 14:32–36). The Johannine Jesus, however, shows neither fear nor dread, remaining fully in control of the situation. When soldiers and the Temple police ask if he is the one they are looking for, he replies "I am he," a revelation of divine identity that causes the soldiers to recoil and fall to the ground (18:4–8). Instead of lying stretched out in prayer, as in Mark, John's Jesus remains standing, while his tormentors are thrown down. The last of Jesus' "I am" statements, this declaration echoes John's earlier association of Jesus and Yahweh (8:58; cf. Exod. 3:8–16), a claim to divinity that triggers an attempt to stone the apparent blasphemer. Those plotting Jesus' downfall only *seem* to be in charge. As Jesus had stated earlier, he alone makes the decision to give up his life (10:17–18). Pilate, the representative of Roman imperial power, is specifically informed that his role as dispenser of life or death is only illusory (19:9–10).

John's depiction of Jesus' trial also disagrees with the Synoptic account. Instead of appearing before the entire Sanhedrin (Mark 14), Jesus is examined secretly at the residence of **Annas**, father-in-law of the High Priest Caiaphas. Many historians believe that John's account of an impromptu session in Annas' private quarters is more plausible than the Synoptic version of a full-scale (but probably illegal) Sanhedrin trial.

Although John parallels the Synoptics in citing prophetic fulfillments in the crucifixion scene (18:9, 32; 19:24, 29), he is the only Evangelist to include the incident of the Roman soldier's spear thrust into Jesus' side. The blood and water pouring from Jesus express the typical Johannine themes that Christ is the source of salvation, his blood the sacramental wine, and the water a symbol of baptism and truth. (Box 10.20 summarizes key similarities and differences among the Evangelists regarding Jesus' last words.)

Postresurrection Appearances John's resurrection account also reveals his distinctive concerns. Only John includes the race between Peter and the beloved disciple (the only male follower present at the crucifixion) to confirm Mary Magdalene's report of the empty sepulcher (Ch. 20). Only he reports Thomas's skepticism and subsequent confession of Jesus' divinity. To John, Jesus' resurrection is the final victorious "sign" toward which all his earlier miracles pointed.

Most scholars believe that Chapter 21, which presents traditions about Jesus' posthumous appearances in Galilee, is the work of an editor, who may have prepared the Gospel manuscript for publication. This epilogue reiterates the theme of differences between Peter, who represents the apostolic Church, and the beloved disciple, who represents the author's community, noting Jesus' distinctive messages to each. The Gospel ends with the editor's musing over the vast oral tradition surrounding Jesus. If his entire career were to be recorded in detail, the "whole world" could not contain "the vast number of books that would be produced" (21:25).

More than any other single book in the New Testament, John's Gospel lays the foundations for later theological interpretations of Christ's nature and function. In post–New Testament times, theologians came to interpret such Johannine statements as "the Father and I are one" as equating Christ and God. This high Christology viewed Jesus as the Second Person in the **Trinity** (a term that does not appear in canonical Scripture), coequal, consubstantial, and coeternal with the Father. Although the Johannine writings do not articulate so formal a dogma, historically John's

Box 10.20 Jesus' Last Words: A Summary of the Evangelists' Beliefs About Him

Jesus' final utterances, compiled from the four different Gospel accounts of his crucifixion, are traditionally known as the "seven last words on the cross." Whereas Mark and Matthew agree that Jesus is almost entirely silent during his agony, crying out only once—in Aramaic—to ask why God has deserted him, Luke and John ascribe several short speeches to their dying hero, showing him in full control of his final hours. The particular statements that each Evangelist has Jesus voice represent that author's individual understanding of Jesus' nature and the meaning of his death.

MARK (15:34)

Eli, Eli, lema sabachthani?

(My God, my God, why have you forsaken me?)

MATTHEW (27:46)

Eli, Eli, lema sabachthani?

(My God, my God, why have you forsaken me?)

LUKE (23:34, 43, 46)

Father, forgive them [Roman executioners]; they do not know what they are doing.

Truly I tell you: today you [the sympathetic felon next to him] will be with me in Paradise.

Father, into your hands I commit my spirit.

JOHN (19:26–27, 28, 30)

Mother, there is your son . . . There is your mother. [placing Mary (the church) in the future care of the beloved disciple (the Johannine community)]

I am thirsty [to fulfill scripture].

It is accomplished!

Writing to a vulnerable group then undergoing hardship and suffering, Mark devotes much of his Gospel to a bleak description of Jesus' Passion, emphasizing that if God permitted his son to endure pain and humiliation, the disciples may expect no better fate. Jesus' cry of despair anticipates his persecuted followers' sense of similarly being abandoned by God. Although Matthew modifies the Passion story to underscore its fulfillment of biblical prophecy, he retains Mark's stress on Jesus' solitary and extreme anguish.

Luke, who presents Jesus as a model of self-sacrificing service to others, thoroughly edits the Passion narrative to highlight Jesus' innocence of any crime against Rome and to illustrate the themes of forgiveness and spirituality that color his portrait of Jesus. Unlike Mark's account, in which Jesus appears almost numb with shock at his brutal treatment, Luke's Jesus is neither silent nor despairing: He speaks repeatedly and confidently, as if he were already enthroned as eschatological judge. He pardons his Roman tormentors, absolving them of responsibility for his execution, and comforts the felon crucified next to him, granting him a posthumous reward in Paradise. Because Luke presents Jesus as led by the Holy Spirit throughout his earthly ministry, it is thematically appropriate for him to show, at the end, Jesus calmly relinquishing his own spirit to God.

Consistent with his picture of Jesus as fully aware of his divine nature, including his prehuman existence in heaven, John paints a Jesus absolutely untroubled by doubt or dejection. Acting out the purpose for which he descended to earth, John's Jesus remains in complete charge of his destiny, allowing soldiers to capture him only to fulfill the divine will (John 18:4–9). The Johannine Jesus thus undergoes no agony in Gethsemane or despair on the cross. In contrast to Mark's picture of lonely abandonment, John shows Jesus accompanied by his mother and his favorite disciple, whose future lives together he arranges. When he says he thirsts, it is not because he experiences ordinary human suffering, but only to fulfill prophecy. His moment of death is simultaneously his "hour of glory," when he can announce that he has accomplished all the Father sent him to do. In his serene omniscience, the Johannine Jesus seems altogether a different being from Mark's disconsolate Son of Man.

portrait of Jesus' divinity influenced Christendom's eventual understanding of its Master.

QUESTIONS FOR REVIEW

1. List some of the principal differences between the Gospel of John and the three Synoptic Gospels. Compare the order of events in Mark with those in John, specifying differences in chronology.

2. What role does the beloved disciple play in John's account? How does he compete with Peter?

3. Contrast the nature of Jesus' teaching in the Synoptics — his use of parables, aphorisms, and reinterpretations of Torah — with the teachings of the Johannine Jesus, which emphasize Jesus' divine preexistence and unique relationship to the Father. List as many differences as you can between John's portrait and the Synoptic picture of Jesus.

4. Define John's concept of realized eschatology and his view that Jesus' death is glorious, a *return* to his previous heavenly abode. How does the Paraclete substitute for the earthly Jesus?

5. In presenting Jesus as a spiritual redeemer descended from heaven, John reflects or parallels some Gnostic ideas. In what specific ways does John's Gospel resemble — or differ from — Gnostic teachings?

QUESTIONS FOR DISCUSSION AND REFLECTION

1. More than any other single New Testament book, the Gospel of John has influenced subsequent Christian thought about Jesus' divinity. What specific Johannine teachings do you think most contributed to the conception of the Trinity — the doctrine that defines the Christian God as embodying the triune Being: Father, Son, and Holy Spirit? In discussing the idea that the heavenly Being (Logos) who became the human Jesus had no beginning but dwelt from eternity with the Father, interpret such diverse Johannine statements as "he who has seen me has seen the Father" and "the Father is greater than I am."

2. The idea that Jesus is divine — to be identified with the God of the Hebrew Bible — is perhaps the chief source of division between monotheistic Jews and orthodox Christians. Is Jesus' "full divinity" a major preoccupation of the Synoptic writers? How

does John's claim of Jesus' virtual godhood work to separate today's Jews and Christians?

TERMS AND CONCEPTS TO REMEMBER

Annas	Nicodemus
beloved disciple	Paraclete
Gnosticism	Philo Judaeus
Incarnation	realized eschatology
Lazarus	Trinity
Logos	Wisdom

RECOMMENDED READING

Brodie, Thomas L. *The Quest for the Origin of John's Gospel: A Source-Oriented Approach.* New York: Oxford University Press, 1993. Argues that John composed his Gospel by theologically transforming the Synoptic accounts.

Brown, R. E. *The Gospel According to John.* Vols. 29 and 29a of the Anchor Bible. Garden City, N.Y.: Doubleday, 1966 and 1970. Provides the most complete historical and theological background and the most thorough commentary on John's Gospel.

———. *The Community of the Beloved Disciple.* New York: Paulist Press, 1979. A readable and insightful study of the Christian group that produced the Gospel and the Letters of John.

———. *The Epistles of John.* Vol. 30 of the Anchor Bible. Garden City, N.Y.: Doubleday, 1982. A thoroughly annotated edition.

Bultmann, Rudolf. *The Gospel of John.* Translated by G. R. Beasley-Murray. Philadelphia: Westminster Press, 1971. An insightful and influential interpretation.

Culpepper, R. A. *Anatomy of the Fourth Gospel: A Study in Literary Design.* Philadelphia: Fortress Press, 1983.

Dodd, C. H. *Historical Tradition in the Fourth Gospel.* Cambridge: Cambridge University Press, 1963.

———. *The Interpretation of the Fourth Gospel.* Cambridge: Cambridge University Press, 1965.

Fortna, R. T. *The Fourth Gospel and Its Predecessor: From Narrative Source to Present Gospel.* Philadelphia: Fortress Press, 1988. The definitive analysis of the hypothetical Signs source underlying John's Gospel.

Kysar, Robert. *John, the Maverick Gospel.* Atlanta: John Knox Press, 1976. An influential study of the fourth Gospel.

———. "John, Epistles of." In D. N. Freedman, ed., *The Anchor Bible Dictionary,* Vol. 3, pp. 900–912. New York: Doubleday, 1992. Relates circumstances of the Gospel's composition to later epistles.

———. "John, the Gospel of." In D. N. Freedman, ed., *The Anchor Bible Dictionary,* Vol. 3, pp. 912–931.

New York: Doubleday, 1992. A thoughtful review of Johannine literature and scholarship.

Martyn, J. L. *History and Theology in the Fourth Gospel,* 2nd ed. Nashville: Abingdon Press, 1979. A brilliant interpretation of John's method of composition that focuses on John 9.

Miller, Robert J., ed. *The Complete Gospels,* 2nd ed. San Francisco: HarperSanFrancisco, 1994.

Olson, A. M., ed. *Myth, Symbol and Reality.* Notre Dame, Ind.: University of Notre Dame Press, 1981. Includes essays on the Logos.

Perkins, Pheme. "The Gospel According to John." In R. E. Brown et al., eds., *The New Jerome Biblical Commentary,* 2nd ed., pp. 942–985. Englewood Cliffs, N.J.: Prentice-Hall, 1990. An insightful commentary on the Gospel.

———. "The Johannine Epistles." In R. E. Brown et al., eds., *The New Jerome Biblical Commentary,* 2nd ed., pp. 986–995. Englewood Cliffs, N.J.: Prentice-Hall, 1990.

Schnackenburg, Rudolf. *The Gospel According to John,* Vols. 1–3. Various translators. New York: Seabury Press, 1980, and Crossroads Press, 1982. Challenging but insightful analysis.

Smith, D. Moody. *The Theology of John.* Cambridge: Cambridge University Press, 1994. A solid introduction to major themes in John's Gospel.

Additional Portraits of Jesus
Noncanonical Gospels and the Quest for the Historical Jesus

Key Topics/Themes

Besides the four canonical Gospels, early Christians produced numerous other Gospels, each with a distinctive perspective on Jesus' teachings and theological significance. Exhibiting great diversity, the noncanonical Gospels, such as those ascribed to Thomas, Peter, Mark, and James, reflect the wide range of viewpoints about Jesus that prevailed in the early churches. Because both canonical and noncanonical accounts present Jesus' life almost exclusively in theological terms, scholars face a formidable challenge in trying to distinguish the Jesus of history from the church's later interpretations of him. In their ongoing quest to recover the historical Jesus, scholars generally agree on the criteria used to evaluate the probable authenticity of Jesus' sayings and deeds, but they reach strikingly different conclusions about his essential teachings and self-identity, particularly on the issue of his eschatology.

KEY QUESTIONS

How does the Gospel of Thomas portray Jesus? What views of Jesus do Secret Mark, the Gos-

pel of Peter, and the Infancy Gospel of James convey? What methodologies have scholars devised to screen the various words and actions attributed to Jesus? How are contemporary scholars divided about the degree to which the historical Jesus shared the apocalyptic concerns of his own day?

The diverse portraits of Jesus found in the four canonical Gospels, ranging from Mark's account of a suffering Messiah who apparently dies feeling abandoned by God to John's vision of a triumphant divine man whose execution is really an "hour of glory," did not exhaust the early Christian community's ways of portraying Jesus. During the first centuries C.E., Christian writers produced a host of other Gospels, each of which presents a distinctive vision of Jesus' theological significance. As Luke noted in the preface to his Gospel, even in his day "many writers" had already "undertaken to draw up an account" of Jesus' life (Luke 1:1–4). Except for Mark, all these earlier narratives have been lost. Many scholars believe, however, that some of the Gospels not admitted to the canon may contain traditions about Jesus as old as those preserved in John and the Synoptics.

Contrasting Portrayals of Jesus

Surviving mostly in isolated fragments or in brief summaries and quotations by Christian writers of the first four centuries C.E., the noncanonical Gospels display a wide range of ideas about Jesus. Many were composed at a time when the new faith was still fluid, in the process of defining what would eventually become its primary doctrines and before a central church authority had acquired sufficient power to regulate effectively beliefs and practices throughout the Roman Empire. Although it is common to think of early Christianity as harmonious and united, the existence of diverse Gospels and numerous other writings from the end of the first century C.E. on demonstrates that many Christians held beliefs that diverged considerably from those that eventually emerged as official **orthodoxy** (correct teaching).

Before examining a representative selection of noncanonical Gospels, we should note that some Christian churches used selectively edited versions of the present New Testament Gospels. Several groups of Jewish Christians employed Gospels based on one or more of the Synoptic accounts, revising them to express their distinctive views of Jesus. One group, the Ebionites, had congregations scattered throughout the eastern Roman Empire from the second to the fourth centuries C.E. Deriving their name from a Hebrew word meaning "the poor," the Ebionites apparently saw themselves as the "poor" to whom Jesus had promised the kingdom (Matt. 5:3; Luke 6:20); they also may have regarded themselves as spiritual descendants of the disciples who had established the original Christian commune in Jerusalem and for whom Paul had agreed to take up a collection (cf. Gal. 1:10; Rom. 15:26; Acts 4:32–36; 11:29). Like many other Jewish Christians, the Ebionites continued to observe the Mosaic Law and to advocate the absolute oneness of Israel's God (Deut. 6:4). While accepting Jesus as a sacrifice for sin, they regarded him as

fully human, a righteous prophet but not a divinity. According to the church historian Eusebius, who tended to minimize the importance of early Jewish Christianity, one branch of the Ebionites believed that Jesus was "the child of a normal union between a man and Mary," while another accepted his virginal conception but denied his "preexistence as God the Word" (*Eccl. Hist.* 3.27; 5.8; 6.17). The Gospel of the Ebionites, which survives only in brief quotations by orthodox church leaders, appears to have been a synthesis or harmonization of Matthew, Mark, and Luke.

Another group of Jewish Christians reportedly used an Aramaic edition of Matthew's account, the Gospel of the Nazoreans, from which the first two chapters, relating Jesus' virginal conception and miraculous birth, had been deleted. An excerpt from the Gospel of the Nazoreans, quoted by Origin, a Christian scholar of the early third century C.E., gives insight into how this Jewish Christian group edited Matthew's account. The Nazorean text revises Matthew's version of Jesus' encounter with a rich young man (Matt. 19:16–30) to emphasize a traditionally Jewish concern for compassion and responsibility toward the poor:

> The second rich man said to him, "Teacher, what good do I have to do to live?"
> He said to him, "Mister, follow the Law and the Prophets."
> He answered, "I've done that."
> He said to him, "Go sell everything you own and give it away to the poor and then come follow me."

But the rich man didn't want to hear this and began to scratch his head. And the Lord said to him, "How can you say that you follow the Law and the Prophets? In the Law it says: 'Love your neighbor as yourself.' Look around you: many of your brothers and sisters, sons and daughters of Abraham, are living in filth and dying of hunger. Your house is full of good things and not a thing of yours manages to get out to them." Turning to his disciple Simon, who was siting with him, he said, "Simon, son of Jonah, it's easier for a camel to squeeze through a needle's eye than for a wealthy person to get into heaven's domain."

G. Naz. 6–8

At the opposite end of the theological spectrum, a Roman Christian, Marcion (c. 140 C.E.), wished to free Christianity entirely from its Jewish associations and to advance a distinctively Gnostic Christology. Marcion argued that Israel's God was an ethically inferior deity who had created a degenerate physical world and that Jesus, originating from the superior true God, did not belong to the material realm at all. In liberating mortals from the chains of earthly existence, Jesus was pure spirit, human in appearance only, who revealed divine knowledge (gnosis) to those whose minds were capable of rising above the mundane (see Chapter 1). Because Paul seems to reject the Israelite Torah, which contains the Bible's defining portrait of Yahweh, Marcion made Paul's letters the nucleus of a new Christian Scripture, to which he added a version of Luke from which he had removed (to him) offensive references to the morally unacceptable biblical God, as well as other allusions to Jewish Scripture. Widely influential among many Christians, Marcion's Gnosticism was later denounced as the church's first major **heresy**, an opinion or doctrine contrary to official church teaching. Although it is possible to view Marcion as presumptuous for reshaping Luke to express his understanding of Jesus, we must remember that both Luke and Matthew took exactly the same approach to Mark, freely revising and adding to the earlier Gospel in order to advance their own theological viewpoints (see Chapter 10).

Perhaps to help counteract the strong current of diversity that flowed through the early churches, about thirty years after Marcion, a Christian scholar named Tatian compiled a single Gospel for the congregations of Syria. Tatian drew primarily on the four Gospels that eventually became canonical, but he also utilized some material from a lost work called the History of Joseph the Carpenter and a "Hebrew Gospel." Called the *Diatesseron*, Tatian's selective harmonizing of the Gospels may have eliminated some of the problems of repetition, contradiction, and theological dissimilarity that characterize the four disparate accounts now included in the New Testament. Although Tatian's harmonization was popular in Syria, the international church did not adopt it, and by the late

fourth century, even the Syrian Christians had replaced it with the four canonical Gospels.

The Gospel of Thomas

In 1945, an Egyptian farmer named Mohammed Ali made what is perhaps the most important New Testament archaeological find of the modern era. While Ali and his brother were digging for fertilizer near the village of Nag Hammadi, they unearthed an ancient pottery jar. Breaking it open, they found inside thirteen leather-bound codices — papyrus books — containing more than fifty individual documents. As scholars who later studied and translated the manuscripts learned, their contents are extraordinarily varied, ranging from excerpts from Plato's *Republic* to dozens of noncanonical texts, mostly of Gnostic origin, such as the Gospel of Truth, the Gospel of the Egyptians, the Apocryphon of John, the Acts of Peter and the Twelve Apostles, and the Apocalypse of Peter. Of greatest significance, however, was the complete manuscript of the Gospel of Thomas, a work previously known only from a few Greek fragments.

Like the other documents from Nag Hammadi, the Gospel of Thomas had been translated from its original Greek into **Coptic**, a form of the Egyptian language (written in Greek letters) used by early Christians in Egypt. Although the Coptic manuscript of Thomas was copied about 350 C.E., older fragments of the Gospel in Greek, found in Egypt almost fifty years before, have been dated to about 200 C.E. Scholarly estimates for the Gospel's date of composition range from about 50 C.E. to the mid-second century C.E.; a growing number of scholars now believe that an early version of Thomas may have been compiled before 100 C.E., perhaps about the same time as the Synoptic Gospels.

Unlike the canonical Gospels, the Gospel of Thomas contains no narrative of Jesus' miracles or other deeds; it consists solely of 114 sayings. According to the opening statement, "These are the secret sayings that the living Jesus spoke and Didymos Judas Thomas recorded." Although this Gospel does not even mention Jesus' death or resurrection, the "living" speaker in Thomas is the risen Jesus, who transmits spiritual enlightenment to his disciples. The sayings are "secret" because their true meaning is evident only to those who can understand them correctly, a life-giving "interpretation" that saves spiritually aware persons from "tasting death" (G. Thom. 1; cf. sayings 18, 19, 85, and 111). (John's Gospel, which shares several themes with the Gospel of Thomas, makes similar connections between knowing Jesus' message and achieving immortality: "In very truth I tell you, if anyone obeys my teachings he shall never know what it is to die" [John 8:51–52]; similarly, Jesus tells Lazarus's sister Martha that "no one who is alive and has faith will ever die" [John 11:25–26; cf. 17:3].)

THE OSTENSIBLE AUTHOR

The "Didymos Judas Thomas" credited with compiling Jesus' words is commonly identified with the Thomas who appears prominently in John's Gospel. Since both "Didymos" (a Greek term) and "Thomas" (an Aramaic word) mean "twin," it seems significant that John's Thomas is repeatedly identified as "the Twin" (John 11:16; 20:24; 21:4). Best known as "doubting Thomas" (John 20:24–29), this figure is also named in each list of the twelve chief disciples (Mark 3:18; Luke 6:15; Acts 1:13). Some commentators have suggested, however, that the reputed author of the Gospel of Thomas may have had an even closer relationship to Jesus than that of disciple. According to the noncanonical Acts of Thomas, "Judas Thomas" is the same Judas (Jude) whom Mark names as one of Jesus' "brothers" (Mark 6:3), and thus the twin of Jesus himself! Although the New Testament writings consistently indicate that members of Jesus' family did not become followers until after the Resurrection, the tradition that Thomas was Jesus' twin brother places him in a unique position to convey otherwise unavailable knowledge about Jesus.

The Gospel of Thomas reserves its highest praise, however, for another of Jesus' "brothers," James. When the disciples ask Jesus who their leader will be after Jesus' departure, he replies that wherever the disciples are they must consult "James the Just, for whose sake heaven and earth came into being" (G. Thom. 12). Called "the just [righteous]" in early Jewish Christian circles for his strict observance of the Mosaic Law, James was also known as a "pillar" of the Jerusalem church, a leader to whom Peter deferred and from whom even the independent Paul reportedly took advice (Gal. 2:1–20; Acts 15:1–29; 21:17–26). Many scholars believe that Thomas's emphasis on James, representative of a Jewish Christianity that rapidly lost influence after Jerusalem's destruction in 70 c.e., is another indication of the Gospel's early date of composition (mid-to-late first century).

THOMAS'S DIVERSE CONTENTS

In browsing through Thomas, readers will find approximately 79 statements (out of the 114 into which scholars have divided the text) that resemble passages in the Synoptics, as well as some imagery and themes that otherwise appear only in John. Some of Jesus' sayings, particularly those that parallel statements in the Synoptics, are remarkably clear and terse:

> No prophet is welcome on his home turf.
> G. Thom. 31; cf. Mark 6:4; Matt. 13:13:57; Luke 4:24; John 4:44 (all Thomas quotations are taken from the Scholars Version (SV), published in *The Five Gospels;* see "Recommended Reading")

> One who seeks will find, and for [one who knocks] it will be opened.
> G. Thom. 94; cf. Matt. 7:7–8; Luke 11:9–10

> If you have money, don't lend it at interest. Rather, give [it] to someone from whom you won't get it back.
> G. Thom. 95; cf. Matt. 5:42; Luke 6:34–35

Other sayings, however, particularly those for which there is no real parallel in the canonical accounts, are difficult to decipher, their meaning typically obscure or enigmatic. When the disciples ask Jesus how their "end" will come, Jesus replies:

> Have you found the beginning, then, that you are looking for the end? You see, the end will be where the beginning is. Congratulations to the one who stands at the beginning; that one will know the end and will not taste death.
> G. Thom. 18

The disciples also pose a variation of Matthew's question about the Second Coming (cf. Matt. 24:3), inquiring when Jesus will "appear" so that they can "see" him. But Jesus' reply, unlike that in Matthew, is thoroughly nonapocalyptic, turning attention from himself to the disciples' own future development:

> Jesus said, "When you strip without being ashamed, and you take your clothes and put them under your feet like little children and trample them, then [you] will see the son of the living one and you will not be afraid.
>
> G. Thom. 37

Assuming that Thomas 37 is a brief allegory expressing Gnostic ideas, most commentators regard "clothes" as symbolizing the physical body, which is stripped away at death to liberate the soul, returning the disciples to a spiritual purity ("like little children") and allowing them to be spiritually reunited with Jesus.

Although it is also commonly given a Gnostic interpretation, some critics have recently suggested that Jesus' statement in Thomas 18 about the "beginning" and "end" is actually directing the disciples' attention toward the world's origin and purpose, as described in Genesis 1–2. According to Stevan Davies, Jesus' many allusions to the "light" and the "beginning" suggest that God's first creation, the "light" of Genesis 1:3, still permeates both the created world and the souls of human beings. Fashioned in God's "image" and "likeness" (Gen. 1:27; 5:1–3) and containing elements of the divine light within, people who discover this inner divinity are then able to perceive the universe as it was when God first created it. Guided by and into the divine light that illuminates the immediacy of God's presence and rule, people awakened to this realization of the divine-human bond transcend both sexual gender and worldly delusions:

> Jesus said, "Images are visible to people, but the light within them is hidden in the image of the Father's light. He will be disclosed, but his image is hidden by his light."
>
> G. Thom. 83; cf. G. Thom. 22

After reaching a new state of spiritual growth in which the divine image, "the light within," is re-vealed, the initiated then can see what others, still "drunk" on the material, sensory world, cannot. Like Jesus, they now observe the kingdom of God "spread out upon the earth":

> It [the Father's kingdom] will not come by watching for it [in apocalyptic expectation]. It will not be said, "Look here!" or "Look there!" Rather the Father's imperial rule is spread out upon the earth, and people don't see it.
>
> G. Thom. 113

As Thomas's next-to-last saying, this declaration of the kingdom's presence balances a similar statement placed near the Gospel's beginning:

> Jesus said, "If your leaders say to you, 'Look, the (Father's) imperial rule is in the sky,' then the birds of the sky will precede you. If they say to you, 'It is in the sea,' then the fish will precede you. Rather, the (Father's) imperial rule is within you and it is outside you."
>
> G. Thom. 3; cf. Luke 17:20–21

Both a divine spark "within" and a power "outside," emanating from creation's eternal light, God's rule is universal, encompassing both internal and external states of being. Jesus continues:

> When you know yourselves [the inner divine image], then you will be known, and you will understand that you are children of the living Father. But if you do not know yourselves, then you live in poverty, and you are the poverty [lacking awareness of both inner spirit and divine omnipresence].
>
> G. Thom. 3

One of the principal differences between Thomas and the canonical Gospels is the relative absence in Thomas of a developed Christology. In Thomas, Jesus is not a savior, a human sacrifice given in atonement for sin, or even the Jewish Messiah. Only a few passages allude to Jesus' role as revelator of heavenly wisdom; in one rare statement, however, he appears to associate himself with the source of divine light:

> I am the light that is over all things. I am all: from me all came forth, and to me all attained. Split a piece of wood; I am there. Lift up the stone, and you will find me there.
>
> G. Thom. 77; cf. John 8:12; 10:7

The first statement parallels a declaration of the Johannine Jesus: "I am the light of the world" (John 8:12); the second resembles another distinctively Johannine concept, adapted from the Jewish wisdom tradition, that Jesus is God's agent of creation and channel of divine light (John 1:1–5). The third, which has no parallel in the canonical tradition, implies that the truths which Jesus represents can be discovered through common actions and objects, mundane avenues to higher realities.

INDEPENDENCE OF THE CANONICAL GOSPELS

For many scholars, one of the most valuable aspects of Thomas's Gospel is that many of its parables seem to represent earlier forms of Jesus' teachings than many of those in the Synoptics. Of Thomas's fourteen parables, eleven have clear parallels in Mark, Matthew, or Luke, but they tend to be shorter, simpler, and less extensively edited by their compilers than the canonical versions. The author of Thomas does not fit the parables into a narrative context, apply them to Jesus' biography, or generally give them allegorical interpretations as the Synoptic writers do. Whereas Thomas simply recounts the parable of the sower, without commentary (Thom. 9), Mark interprets it allegorically, comparing the sowing of seed to the church's later preaching (Mark 4).

Although scholars largely agree that the Gospel of Thomas preserves some forms of Jesus' teachings that are as old as, if not older than, those in the canonical Gospels, it is not known how much, if any, material unique to this Gospel stems from the historical Jesus. In addition to its value in the comparative study of the canonical Gospels, Thomas demonstrates that some groups of early Christians regarded Jesus' teachings, as opposed to his actions, as the most important part of his legacy. Emphasizing Jesus' wisdom, Thomas shows that it was possible to create a Gospel without including a narrative and without even alluding to Jesus' exorcisms, miraculous cures, confrontations with Roman authorities, trial, crucifixion, death, or ascent from the grave. A sayings collection very similar in form to what scholars imagine the hypothetical Q to have been, Thomas also shows that some followers could revere Jesus exclusively for his liberating insights and his perceptions of elusive spiritual realities, without also presenting him as a human sacrifice or an incarnate divinity. In Thomas, Jesus' redemptive work is accomplished through his teaching rather than his death, a factor that probably helps to explain why the emerging orthodox church did not preserve this Gospel.

Secret Mark

The tradition that Jesus reserved "secret" teachings for his innermost circle of disciples — information denied the general public who heard him speak exclusively in parables — is firmly embedded in the Synoptic Gospels. According to Mark, after telling the parable of the seed sower to a Galilean crowd, when "alone with the Twelve" Jesus privately conveyed to them knowledge revealed only to a favored few insiders. "To you," he informs the disciples, "the secret of the kingdom of God has been given, but to those who are outside everything comes by way of [typically incomprehensible] parables" (Mark 4:10–11, 33–34; cf. Matt. 13:10–13; Luke 8:9–10). That Jesus disclosed "secrets" or "mysteries" to specially privileged intimates was typical of philosophers and other teachers in the ancient world. Plato allegedly remarked that his dialogues were composed only to lure qualified members of the general public into pursuing the study of philosophy; the real core of his teachings was oral and reserved for initiates who were intellectually prepared to understand the more profound aspects of philosophy. It was also reported that Alexander of Macedonia quarreled with his mentor, Aristotle (a former student of Plato), when Aristotle published information that Alexander thought should be disclosed only to the philosopher's closest disciples.

Curiosity about what Jesus may have divulged secretly to his disciples probably led to considerable speculation in many Christian circles. According to Clement, a church leader in Alexandria about 200 C.E., a special edition of Mark used with

Box 11.1 Secret Mark: A Source for John's Account of the Raising of Lazarus?

The Secret Gospel of Mark consists of a fragment that Clement of Alexandria (c. 180–200 C.E.) copied into a letter concerning a "secret" edition of canonical Mark used by some Christians in Egypt. Clement's excerpt was preserved in a manuscript transcribed during the eighteenth century and discovered by the New Testament scholar Morton Smith in 1958. Because Jesus' raising of Lazarus—a man who had been dead for four days and hence in a state of rapid decomposition—is the most spectacular miracle attributed to him, it seems inexplicable that the Synoptic writers never mention it. The existence of Secret Mark, however, shows that this story of Jesus' resurrecting a man whom "he loved" was once part of the Synoptic tradition, at least in Egypt. The fact that the earliest fragments of John's Gospel were found in Egypt (and the tradition, recorded by Eusebius, that Mark was the first to bring Christianity to that country) may suggest some otherwise unknown connection between the Secret Mark account and John 11.

Whether the author of John was familiar with Secret Mark or knew of the oral tradition behind it, it seems likely that he borrowed the names of Lazarus's sisters, Mary and Martha, from the same oral or written tradition found in Luke (10:38–41), whose Gospel does not mention that they had a brother. The name Lazarus (the beggar who died and went to the paradise of **Abraham's bosom**)—the only character given a name in one of Jesus' parables—also occurs in Luke (16:19–26).

THE SECRET GOSPEL OF MARK

*Fragment 1: To be located between
Mark 10:34 and 10:35.*

¹And they come into Bethany, and this woman was there whose brother had died. ²She knelt down in front of Jesus and says to him, "Son of David, have mercy on me." ³But the disciples rebuked her. ⁴And Jesus got angry and went with her into the garden where the tomb was. ⁵Just then a loud voice was heard from inside the tomb. ⁶Then Jesus went up and rolled the stone away from the entrance to the tomb. ⁷He went right in where the young man was, stuck out his hand, grabbed him by the hand, and raised him up. ⁸The young man looked at Jesus, loved him, and began to beg him to be with him. ⁹Then they left the tomb and went into the young man's house. (Incidentally, he was rich.) ¹⁰Six days later Jesus gave him an order; ¹¹and when evening had come, the young man went to him, dressed only in a linen cloth. ¹²He spent that night with him, because Jesus taught him the mystery of God's domain. ¹³From there [Jesus] got up and returned to the other side of the Jordan.

Fragment 2: To be located between 10:46a ("Then they came to Jericho") and 10:46b ("As he was leaving Jericho . . .")

¹The sister of the young man whom Jesus loved was there, along with his mother and Salome, ²but Jesus refused to see them.

1:7a This *young man* seems to play a rather important role in Mark. Most notably, his reappearance in the empty tomb announcing to the women Jesus' resurrection suggests that this story of his own resurrection serves to foreshadow Jesus'.

1:7b The action is comparable to that found in Mark 5:41; 9:27.

1:7c *Grabbed him by the hand* could be linked with what follows in v. 8, rather than with what precedes: "Grabbing him by the hand, the young man . . ."

1:10 *gave him an order:* The meaning of the Greek is obscure; it may imply that Jesus gave the young man instructions.

1:11 *dressed only in a linen cloth:* The text reads literally: "a linen cloth having been draped over the naked body." The Markan "young man" appears so dressed also in Mark 14:15. The significance of the linen cloth worn over a naked body is a longstanding riddle in Markan scholarship. It may be some sort of early Christian baptismal garb. Hippolytus, *Apostolic Tradition* 21.11, specifies that in the ceremony of baptism both the catechuman and the presbyter are to stand in the water naked.

2:1a The *young man* is the same one as in the first fragment.

From Robert J. Miller, ed., *The Complete Gospels,* 2nd ed. (San Francisco: HarperSanFrancisco, 1994) p. 411.

some Alexandrian congregations showed Jesus engaged in such esoteric teaching. Known as the Secret Gospel of Mark, this account is quoted in one of Clement's letters (see Box 11.1 for the complete text). The existence of Secret Mark was not even suspected until 1958, when Morton Smith discovered it in a collection of ancient manuscripts. Although some scholars initially regarded Smith's discovery as inauthentic, and perhaps even a forgery, many now regard it as a genuine fragment of an otherwise unknown Gospel associated with canonical Mark. According to a passage of Secret Mark that Clement said appeared between verses 10:34 and 10:35 of our canonical Mark, Jesus resuscitates a rich young man who had recently died (perhaps the same wealthy youth to whom Jesus' "heart [had] warmed" a few verses earlier in the same chapter [Mark 10:20–22]). Upon rising from the tomb, "the young man looked at Jesus, loved him, and began to beg to be with him" (Secret Mark vs. 8). Six days later, Jesus summons the young man, "dressed only in a linen cloth," to "[spend] the night with him," during which Jesus "taught him the mystery of God's domain" (the same phrase translated as "the secret of the kingdom of God" in canonical Mark 4:11). A similar nocturnal ritual, perhaps involving a special intimacy with Jesus, as well as baptism, may explain the presence in canonical Mark of a "young man with nothing on but a linen cloth." When Jesus is arrested at Gethsemane, this youth escapes from the soldiers by "[slipping] out of the linen cloth and [running] away naked," an incident that appears only in Mark's Gospel (14:51–52).

Some scholars have suggested that the oral tradition underlying Secret Mark was also known to the author of John's Gospel, who adapted it for his narrative about Jesus' resuscitation of Lazarus, a spectacular miracle, unique to John, that the Synoptic authors apparently ignore (John 11). Like the unidentified young man in Secret Mark, John's Lazarus has two sisters; unnamed in Secret Mark, they are called Mary and Martha in John. (The sisters' names also appear in Luke [10:38–42], but the tradition that they had a brother raised after four days in his tomb is, strangely, not mentioned.) John's portrayal of a disciple whom Jesus particu-

larly loved may also derive in part from stories about Jesus' bonding with a young man, such as that related in Secret Mark. Of even greater significance to scholars, Secret Mark demonstrates that a primitive version of the Johannine story of Lazarus was once part of the Synoptic tradition.

The Gospel of Peter

Like Secret Mark, the Gospel of Peter is a narrative work that offers a brief glimpse into mysteries that the canonical authors merely allude to—in this case, the moment of Jesus' actual rising from his tomb. Although longer than Secret Mark, the Gospel (incorrectly) ascribed to Peter, Jesus' chief disciple, is only partially preserved, beginning and ending in mid-sentence. Found in 1886, the extant portion is a Passion account, dramatically narrating Jesus' trial, crucifixion, burial, and resurrection. Because of the manuscript's fragmentary state, we do not know if the original Gospel also included a report on Jesus' public ministry and miracles; the narrative ends abruptly with Peter fishing at the Sea of Galilee, apparently about to witness an appearance of the risen Lord.

The Gospel of Peter resembles Matthew's Gospel in many respects, including the story of Pilate's posting Roman soldiers to guard Jesus' grave, but it contains even more spectacularly supernatural, even bizarre, phenomena. Late Saturday night, while Pilate's guards watch in awe, the predawn heavens part, and two celestial beings descend to earth in a blaze of light and cause the massive stone that sealed the tomb entrance to roll away. The transformed Jesus is then shown emerging from the sepulcher, supported on each side by the two towering celestial beings, whose heads reach the sky. Standing even taller than his angelic companions, Jesus' head "reached beyond the skies." When a heavenly voice, reminiscent of that at the Transfiguration, asks if Christ has brought his message to the subterranean realm of the dead, a cross, the fourth figure in Jesus' triumphal procession, testifies that he has. The tradition of a speaking cross, an inanimate object suddenly given life

Box 11.2 The Gospel of Peter

[Following the Crucifixion, a Roman guard is stationed at Jesus' tomb.]

When the scholars and the Pharisees and the priests had gathered together, and when they heard that all the people were moaning and beating their breasts, and saying "If his death has produced these overwhelming signs, he must have been entirely innocent!", they became frightened and went to Pilate and begged him, "Give us soldiers so that [we] may guard his tomb for three [days], in case his disciples come and steal his body and the people assume that he is risen from the dead and do us harm." So Pilate gave them the centurion Petronius with soldiers to guard the tomb. And elders and scholars went with them to the tomb. And all who were there [with] the centurion and the soldiers helped roll a large stone against the entrance to the tomb. And they put seven seals on it. Then they pitched a tent there and kept watch.

Early, at first light on the sabbath, a crowd came from Jerusalem and the surrounding countryside to see the sealed tomb. But during the night before the Lord's day dawned, while the soldiers were on guard, two by two during each watch, a loud noise came from the sky, and they saw the skies open up and two

men come down from there in a burst of light and approach the tomb. The stone that had been pushed against the entrance began to roll by itself and moved away to one side; then the tomb opened up and both young men went inside.

Now when these soldiers saw this, they roused the centurion from his sleep, along with the elders. (Remember, they were also there keeping watch.) While they were explaining what they had seen, again they see three men leaving the tomb, two supporting the third, and a cross was following them. The heads of the two reached up to the sky, while the head of the third, whom they led by the hand, reached beyond the skies. And they heard a voice from the skies that said, "Have you preached to those who sleep?" And an answer was heard from the cross: "Yes!"

These men then consulted with one another about going and reporting these things to Pilate. While they were still thinking about it, again the skies appeared to open and some sort of human being came down and entered the tomb. When those in the centurion's company saw this, they rushed out into the night to Pilate, having left the tomb which they were supposed to be guarding. . . .

---

to vocalize the Christian *kerygma,* is unique to this account.

Although scholars agree that the historical Peter had nothing to do with the Gospel attributed to him, they are sharply divided about the document's importance to the Jesus tradition. Whereas a majority see it as a secondary document, derived primarily from Matthew and other canonical sources, others, such as John D. Crossan, argue that in its earliest edition the Gospel of Peter may represent the first Passion story on which the canonical accounts, at least in part, are based. In the extant version, the Gospel exhibits several Gnostic touches. Jesus' silence during the Crucifixion intimates that (as pure spirit) he does not feel physical pain. Also, instead of shouting that God has for-

saken him (as in Mark and Matthew), he complains that his "Power" has deserted him (perhaps indicating the departure of the supernatural being that had previously dwelt within him). Jesus's death, moreover, is expressed euphemistically, for he is described as "taken up," implying a divine rescue or escape to the spirit world (Gosp. Pet. 2:1; 5:5).

The cross's testimony that Jesus devoted the interval between his (assumed) death and visible resurrection to preaching in the netherworld also suggests that this Gospel's author saw Jesus' spiritual existence, in this life and the next, as a continuum. (The two canonical letters ascribed to Peter also refer to Jesus' postmortem activities in the Underworld [1 Pet. 3:19; 4:6; cf. 2 Pet. 2:4].) (An excerpt from the Gospel of Peter appears in Box 11.2)

Gospels About Jesus' Infancy and Childhood

Early Christians not only composed Gospels that recounted some mystical revelations of the risen Jesus (Gospel of Thomas), secret teachings given to favored initiates (Secret Mark), and the dazzling splendor of his resurrection (Gospel of Peter); they also explored the mystery of Jesus' early life. If Jesus was the Son of God, possessing supernatural knowledge and power, what was he like as a child? Although Matthew and Luke provide infancy narratives, and Luke briefly mentions an incident when the twelve-year-old Jesus visited the Jerusalem Temple, no canonical author preserves any information about the period between Jesus' birth and his baptism by John, when he was "about thirty years old" (Luke 3:23).

THE INFANCY GOSPEL OF THOMAS

During the second century, curiosity about Jesus' boyhood prompted several narratives that attempted to fill in the "missing years" of Jesus' youth. The Infancy Gospel of Thomas, dating from about 150 C.E., is ascribed to the apostle Thomas. Unrelated to the Gospel of Thomas, the first edition of which was probably written much earlier, this account of incidents from Jesus' childhood uncritically incorporates popular legends and speculations about the Messiah's youthful character and behavior. Opening with anecdotes about the five-year-old Jesus performing mischievous tricks in his home village, the Gospel closes with a retelling of Luke's story about Jesus, at age twelve, visiting the Temple in Jerusalem. It says nothing, however, about Jesus' young manhood, leaving blank the eighteen years that pass before the adult Jesus comes to John for baptism.

Modern readers are likely to be perplexed by this Infancy Gospel's portrait of Jesus, who as a mere child possesses godlike powers that he at first seems too inexperienced or undisciplined to use wisely. Acutely aware that he merits respect and deference from everyone, the young Jesus is easily angered by even casual slights and, repeatedly, employs his superhuman abilities to punish the offenders. When a playmate disrupts pools of water that Jesus had formed in a stream, he furiously curses the child, withering him into a state of premature aging. When another boy, running through the village, accidently bumps into Jesus, Jesus strikes him dead. After the dead boy's parents demand that Joseph teach his son to bless people rather than to curse them, and Joseph privately warns Jesus about the negative effects of his conduct, Jesus causes those who criticized him to go blind (Chs. 3–5).

Jesus' neighbors in Nazareth are appalled at the child's antics, for he is, literally, a holy terror. As they indignantly ask Joseph, "What kind of child do you have who does such things?" (3:3). "Grief-stricken," Joseph privately tells Mary not to let Jesus out of the house "because anyone who angers him dies" (14:3).

As Jesus grows somewhat older, however, the beneficial aspects of his powers begin to outweigh the destructive. After his public shaming of Zaccheus, "all those who had fallen under his curse" are healed, and Jesus begins a series of miraculous cures and resuscitations. When a playmate dies after falling off a roof and Jesus is held responsible, he revives the boy to testify to his innocence (9:1–3). He also heals a young woodcutter whose misplaced axe blow had nearly severed his foot (10:1–2) and saves his brother James from death by a poisonous snake bite (16:1–2). In the last two reported miracles, Jesus resuscitates a dead child (17:1–2) and a deceased workman (18:1–2). Witnessing these deeds, the villagers now recognize Jesus' special status: "This is a heavenly child, for he saved many souls from death, and can save them all his life" (18:2).

In the Infancy Gospel's first episode, Jesus had "profaned" the Sabbath by shaping twelve sparrows from clay, technically violating the commandment to refrain from all work on the day of rest. When Joseph confronts him, Jesus claps his hands and, instantly, the twelve clay birds fly away, removing the evidence of his misdemeanor. In the Gospel's final incident, set in the Temple, Jesus' precocity has deepened into a wisdom that foreshadows the man he will become. Seated in the sanctuary, amid the "elders and teachers of the people," Jesus (as in Luke) amazes them with his ability to solve "the chief problems of the Law and the parables of the prophets" (19:1–5). As the narrator concludes, Jesus "*grew* in wisdom . . . and grace" (emphasis added), perhaps suggesting that even God's son—future Judge of all humanity—underwent a learning process characteristic of the human condition.

THE INFANCY GOSPEL OF JAMES

Also called the Book of James or Protoevangelium of James, this Gospel supplies background information on Jesus' parents and family, covering events that occurred up to and including his birth. Based partly on the infancy accounts in Matthew and Luke and partly on oral tradition, this prologue to Jesus' life story may include a few historical facts among its purely legendary components. The work states that its author is James, who in this Gospel is identified as Jesus' older stepbrother, the son of Joseph by a former marriage. The story focuses on the personal history of Mary, Jesus' future mother, who is born to a previously childless couple—Joachim, a wealthy herdsman, and his wife, Anna (Anne). At age three, Mary is taken to the Jerusalem Temple, where she is raised by priests until her sexual maturation makes her ritually impure and disqualifies her from dwelling in the sanctuary. The priests then consign the twelve-year-old Mary to the care of Joseph, a widower with children, who functions as her guardian and strictly respects her virginity.

The genealogies in Matthew and Luke both trace Jesus' Davidic ancestry through his presumed father, Joseph. By contrast, the Infancy Gospel of James states that Mary, too, descended from David. Thus, her virgin-born son inherits his messianic heritage directly from her. Written during the mid-second century C.E. when veneration of Mary and curiosity about her origins were growing trends in many Christian circles, this Gospel provides not only the names of Mary's parents

and the manner of her extraordinary birth and upbringing but also a doctrine of her perpetual virginity.

Divided into three approximately equal parts, the Infancy Gospel of James is largely a prose hymn of praise to Mary the Virgin, regarded as the most divinely favored of all women. The first section recounts the divine intervention that resulted in Mary's miraculous birth to Joachim and Anna and the immaculate purity of her Temple childhood; the second part explores the perplexities that Mary and Joseph faced in their unusual life together. Although the narrator emphasizes that Joseph is only Mary's devoted protector, not her husband, their relationship becomes particularly complicated after an angel visits Mary, announcing that she will bear a child conceived by the Holy Spirit. When Joseph returns home after a long absence at work to find that Mary is six months pregnant, he agonizes over his apparent failure to protect her virginity. Composing a lively conversation between the almost equally bewildered—and celibate—pair, the author creates a scene that combines sensitivity to the plight of a human couple caught up in forces beyond their control and the inescapable humor inherent in their strange predicament.

Interspersing elements from the canonical infancy stories with his own special material, the narrator devotes the final third of his Gospel to an account of Jesus' birth at Bethlehem, closing with Herod's murderous attempts to eliminate a future rival. As if to guarantee the historicity of his account, the writer then reveals that he is none other than James (whom Paul calls "the Lord's brother"), the son of Joseph by his deceased wife. This final section contains a scene in which two midwives examine Mary after she has given birth to Jesus, discovering, to their astonishment, that she is still physically a virgin.

Traditional lore about Mary incorporated into the Infancy Gospel of James probably contributed significantly to the unique position that Jesus' mother eventually held in both the Greek Orthodox and Roman Catholic Churches. Its immense popularity in the church is reflected in the Gospel's survival in over 130 Greek manuscripts. Although never officially admitted to the New Testament canon, in some Christian groups the book has exerted as much influence in shaping orthodox belief as have the canonical Gospels.

Multiple Interpretations of Jesus

The proliferation of Gospels during the first centuries C.E. (of which we have sampled only a few) suggests that the early church did not quickly or unanimously settle on a single view of Jesus. As we have seen, Gospel portraits of Christ varied widely, from Mark's anguished servant and eschatological prophet, to John's serene incarnation of eternal Wisdom, to Secret Mark's confider of divine mysteries, to Thomas's revelator of mystical spirituality. Scholars believe that the contrasting depictions of Jesus in different Gospels represent their respective authors' attempts to promote a distinctive understanding of Jesus' theological significance. Either directly or implicitly, each writer claims that his version of Jesus is the correct one—and that his portrayal is therefore authoritative. Many scholars also see in the conflicting portraits of Jesus a reflection of power struggles between the different groups that produced them. From this perspective, the Gospels are literary battlefields on which the authors attack theological opponents. To cite only two examples, Matthew denounces fellow Jews (in diatribes against "scribes and Pharisees") who do not accept Jesus as Messiah and simultaneously criticizes fellow Christians who do not follow Jesus in obeying the Torah requirements (see Chapter 10); and John battles not only "the Jews" who have expelled members of his community from the synagogue but also incipient Gnostics who reject Jesus' physical humanity. Given these ongoing conflicts, it was necessary to ask, Who possesses genuine knowledge of Jesus, and who has the authority to interpret him? The Christian community's prolonged struggle to answer this question, and hence to achieve a unified understanding of Jesus' nature and role in humanity's sal-

vation, continued well into the fifth century (see Chapter 14). With the support of later Roman emperors, the church eventually succeeded in establishing a doctrinal orthodoxy that resulted in the dismissal of most of the noncanonical Gospels as heretical, thus consigning them to oblivion. However, by canonizing four disparate Gospel portraits of Jesus, the Christian community also ensured that questions about which might represent the "real" Jesus would remain an issue.

QUESTIONS FOR REVIEW

1. Describe some early Christian Gospels, such as the Gospel of Thomas, Secret Mark, and the Gospel of Peter, that were not included in the New Testament canon. Why do you think that these and other Gospels were not officially approved? In what ways do they differ from the canonical accounts of Jesus' life?

2. What value as a resource for recovering some sayings of the historical Jesus may the Gospel of Thomas have?

3. What distinctive elements appear in the Secret Mark and the Gospel of Peter?

4. Describe the character and actions of the young Jesus in the Infancy Gospel of Thomas. How does Jesus appear to mature in the handling of his divine powers as he grows older?

QUESTIONS FOR DISCUSSION AND REFLECTION

1. What do you think we can learn from the use of traditions about Jesus in the early church? How diverse in their teaching about Jesus were some of these Christian communities?

2. Do you think that the New Testament canon is irrevocably closed? What are the possibilities that existing noncanonical writings—or even books not yet written—will eventually be added to the church's approved list? Describe the effect on Christian doctrine if such works as the Gospel of Thomas, Secret Mark, or the Gospel of Peter were officially approved to be read in church as examples of legitimate Christian thought and experience.

TERMS AND CONCEPTS TO REMEMBER

Abraham's bosom	Infancy Gospel of James
Coptic	Infancy Gospel of Thomas
Gospel of Peter	orthodoxy
Gospel of Thomas	Secret Mark
heresy	

RECOMMENDED READING

Cameron, Ron, ed. *The Other Gospels: Non-Canonical Gospel Texts.* Philadelphia: Westminster Press, 1982. Scholarly translations of several early Christian Gospels, including those attributed to Peter, James, and Mark.

Crossan, John D. *The Cross That Spoke: The Origins of the Passion Narrative.* San Francisco: Harper & Row, 1988. Analyzes the Gospel of Peter as source for the canonical Gospels.

Davies, Stevan. "The Christology and Protology of the Gospel of Thomas." *Journal of Biblical Literature* III (4) (1992): 663–682.

Ehrman, Bart D. *The New Testament and Other Early Christian Writings: A Reader.* New York: Oxford University Press, 1998. Anthologizes both canonical and noncanonical writings composed by the mid-second century C.E.

Eusebius. *The History of the Church from Christ to Constantine.* Translated with an introduction by G. A. Williamson. Baltimore: Penguin Books, 1965. Read with caution, provides excellent atmospheric background for the early church and fascinating traditions about the apostles and second-century church leaders.

Funk, Robert W.; Houver, Roy W.; and the Jesus Seminar. *The Five Gospels: The Search for the Authentic Words of Jesus.* New York: Macmillan, 1993. Features colloquial translations and extensive notes on each Gospel.

Josephus, Flavius. *The Jewish War.* Translated by G. A. Williamson; revised by E. M. Smallwood. Baltimore: Penguin Books, 1981. An eyewitness account of political events in Palestine that provided the background for the birth and growth of Christianity, including the Jewish Revolt against Rome (66–73 C.E.), its causes and aftermath, and a few references to Jesus and the martyrdom of his "brother" James.

Koestler, Helmut. *Ancient Christian Gospels: Their History and Development.* Philadelphia: Trinity Press International, 1990. Provides technical analysis of all extant Gospels and fragments.

Miller, Robert J., ed. *The Complete Gospels,* 3rd ed. Annotated Scholars Version. San Francisco: HarperSanFrancisco, 1994. Includes complete texts of the Gospel of Thomas, Infancy Gospel of Thomas, Infancy Gospel of James, Gospel of Peter, Secret Gospel of Mark, and numerous fragmentary works.

Pagels, Elaine. *The Gnostic Gospels.* New York: Random House, 1979. Argues that the church suppressed Gnostic Christianity on political grounds.

Patterson, Stephen J., and Robinson, James M. *The Fifth Gospel: The Gospel of Thomas Comes of Age.* Philadelphia: Trinity Press International, 2000. Features a new translation and extensive commentary on Thomas's meaning to modern scholarship.

Robinson, James M., ed. *The Nag Hammadi Library,* rev. ed. San Francisco: Harper & Row, 1988. Includes fresh translations of all the documents discovered in 1945.

Schneemelcher, Wilhelm, ed. *New Testament Apocrypha,* rev. ed. Vol. 1, *Gospels and Related Writings,* Philadelphia: Westminster Press, 1990; Vol. 2, *Writings Relating to the Apostles.* Philadelphia: Westminster, 1992.

The Continuing Quest for the Historical Jesus

After reading the four canonical narratives of Jesus' ministry—not to mention the many noncanonical accounts, such as Secret Mark, the Gospel of Peter, and the Gospel of Thomas—students may wonder who the "real" Jesus of Nazareth was. Almost from the moment that an oral gospel of the risen Jesus was first proclaimed among Palestinian Jews about 30 C.E., believers have tried to "capture" the man and his message, typically interpreting them from a biblical and/or Greco-Roman perspective.

The first person to commit his views on Jesus to writing—years before the earliest canonical Gospel appeared—was a Hellenistic Jew named Paul, a man brought into the Christian fold by his vision of the postresurrection Jesus. Although Paul may have known little about the living Jesus (and his letters rarely refer to Jesus' teaching), he was convinced that he knew the "real" Jesus intimately, the cosmic Christ whose sacrificial death removed the barrier of the Mosaic Law that separated Jews and Gentiles and thus opened the way for Gentiles to become "justified" before God through their faith in Jesus' redemptive power (see Chapter 12). Although it was a minority opinion at the time he wrote (c. 50–62 C.E.), Paul's concept of Jesus' supreme importance for humanity's salvation has influenced virtually every interpretation of Jesus' life since. Even John's uniquely "high" Christology, which portrays Jesus as the eternal Word, an incarnation of divine Wisdom, may represent a natural development of themes and ideas initially explored in Paul's letters.

Showing little interest in Jesus' earthly career, except for his death, Pauline Christology emphasizes Jesus' posthumous divinity, his exaltation in heaven and superiority to all others (Phil. 2:9–11). According to Colossians (written either by Paul or by a disciple pursuing the implications of his thought), Jesus is "the image of the invisible God," in whom "the complete being of the Godhead dwells embodied" (Col. 1:15–20; 2:9–10). In both Colossians and the prologue to John's Gospel, Jesus' existence predates that of the universe, of which he is the source. As both the agent and the ultimate goal of creation, he so fully reveals God's purpose that John represents him as saying that "anyone who has seen me has seen the Father" (John 14:9).

As the worship of Jesus gradually replaced the older Greco-Roman religions throughout the Mediterranean region, the church placed ever greater emphasis on Jesus' divine nature and unity with the Father. Assembling in Asia Minor at the town of Nicaea in 325 c.e., church leaders rejected the idea that Jesus was ever entirely human or that there had been a time when he did not exist, declaring that he was not merely Son of God, but God himself, the Second Person in the Trinity. Although fierce debates over the issue of Jesus' precise relationship to the Father and the Holy Spirit continued to divide Christians long after the conference at Nicaea, a formal statement of orthodox Christian doctrine, the Nicene Creed, eventually emerged. Regularly recited by hundreds of millions of believers throughout Christendom as a definitive declaration of faith, the creed's repeated insistence on Jesus' absolute equality with God reflects the intense doctrinal controversy in which it historically originated.

We believe in one Lord, Jesus Christ,
the only Son of God,

eternally begotten of the Father,
God from God, Light from Light,
true God from true God,
begotten, not made,
of one Being with the Father.
Through him all things were made.
For us and for our salvation
he came down from heaven;
by the power of the Holy Spirit
he became incarnate from the virgin Mary, and
    was made man. *(emphasis added)*

As many commentators have observed, the Nicene Creed's intense focus on Jesus' godhood leaves a vacuum at the center: It says nothing about what Jesus himself believed or what he taught others.

Although they wrote more than two centuries before the council at Nicaea, the Gospel authors were almost equally concerned about Jesus' theological function — the role he played not only during his earthly life but also after his resurrection and ascension to heaven, where he now stands at God's right hand. Regarding Jesus as qualitatively different from every other human being, the Evangelists emphasize his supernatural status, commonly shaping their narratives and reports of Jesus' teaching to illustrate his unique nature. Although most scholars believe that the Synoptic Gospels, as well as the Gospel of Thomas, incorporate many authentic traditions about Jesus' words and deeds, they face the challenge of separating reliable history from theological overlay.

In searching for the historical Jesus, it is important to distinguish scholarly goals from those of theology. Whereas theologians are concerned with Jesus' cosmic meaning, a dimension of spirit informed by faith, historians can examine only the material world, evaluating evidence to judge its plausibility in terms of ordinary human experience; the spiritual and supernatural lie beyond the reach of scientific inquiry. Gospel reports of events that by definition occur outside life's normal historical processes — such as Jesus' miraculous ability to control a storm, walk on water, or rise from the dead — cannot be investigated in themselves, but only as a phenomenon of belief among early Christians. Historians have no means of "proving" that the Resurrection did (or did not) occur; they can merely study the reported behavior of believers who were convinced that it did happen. Scientific analysis cannot deal with Jesus conceived as divinity, but must approach the living man only as a legitimate object of historical research, leaving to theologians the task of interpreting the paradox of Jesus as both completely human and fully divine.

Aware that Gospel authors are more theologians than biographers interested in factual reporting, students often ask if it is possible to find the authentic man amid the sometimes conflicting sayings and deeds that the Evangelists attribute to their hero. Are there any "unbiased" historical sources that give us reliable information about the human Jesus?

Early Historical References to Jesus

Unfortunately, non-Christian writers tell us almost nothing about the Nazarene except that he existed, was crucified under Pilate, and inspired a new religious movement in the Roman Empire. The earliest writer to mention Jesus is Tacitus, a Roman senator and historian of the first century c.e., who seems to have based his report largely on second-hand evidence. His single allusion to Jesus is tantalizingly brief, stating merely that Jesus "had been executed in Tiberius's reign by the governor of Judaea, Pontius Pilate" (*Annals* 15.44). Tacitus's statements about Jesus and his followers are incidental to the historian's main purpose — illustrating the cruelty and corruption of Nero, who tried to blame the Christians for a great fire that consumed much of Rome about 64 c.e.:

Nero had self-acknowledged Christians arrested. Then, on their information, large numbers of others were condemned — not so much for incendiarism as for their anti-social tendencies. Their deaths were made farcical. Dressed in wild animals' skins, they were torn to pieces by dogs, or crucified, or made into torches to be ignited after dark as substitutes for daylight. . . . Despite

their guilt as Christians, and the ruthless punishment it deserved, the victims were pitied. For it was felt that they were being sacrificed to one man's brutality rather than to the national interest.
Annals 15.44

Nero's persecution, which was apparently confined to the imperial capital, represents the Roman government's first official recognition of the new faith. That even an enlightened author such as Tacitus could regard Christians as so "notoriously depraved" that they deserved the death penalty indicates the extent to which Rome's ruling classes misunderstood the Jesus movement. Given first-century officialdom's ignorance of early Christian beliefs, it is likely that few educated non-Christians were in a position to know the facts of Jesus' life and teachings.

Suetonius, a Roman historian writing in the early second century c.e., records that even before Nero, the emperor **Claudius** (reigned 41–54 c.e.) had expelled the Jews from Rome because of trouble arising from "Chrestus" (probably a variant spelling of Tacitus's "Christus" [the Greek *Christos*, or Christ]) (*Twelve Caesars* 25). The alleged "constant rioting" that Claudius punished about 49 c.e. may have resulted from conflicts between Roman Jews and Jewish Christian missionaries who brought their innovative religion from Palestine. (The author of Acts refers to Claudius's expulsion of Jews, including Priscilla and Aquila, who met Paul in Corinth about 50 c.e. [Acts 18:2].)

Flavius Josephus, the first-century Jewish historian who interpreted his people's customs for a Greco-Roman audience, twice mentions Jesus. With its later Christian interpolations deleted, Josephus's comments originally may have run as follows:

Now there was about this time [the administration of Pontius Pilate (26–36 c.e.)], Jesus, a wise man, . . . a doer of wonderful works, a teacher of such men as receive the truth with pleasure. He drew over to him . . . many of the Jews, . . . and when Pilate, . . . had condemned him to the cross, those that loved him at the first . . . [believed] that he appeared to them alive again the third day. . . . [A]nd the tribe of

Christians, so named from him, are not extinct at this day.

Antiquities 18.3.3

Josephus's second reference deplores the illegal execution of James, "the brother of Jesus, who was called Christ" (*Antiquities* 20.9.1). Although from a later date, allusions to Jesus in the Talmud, which condemns him for practicing sorcery and "for leading Israel astray," similarly attest to Jesus' historicity.

Pliny the Younger, who governed the Roman province of **Bithynia** (north-central Turkey) from about 111 to 115 C.E., wrote to the emperor **Trajan** for advice about dealing with Christians who refused to participate in "emperor worship," a public ritual then popularly regarded as much an expression of patriotism as of religious commitment. Pliny's letter notes that Christians gathered to "partake of a meal [probably the Eucharist or Holy Communion]" and to sing "a hymn to Christ, as if to a god" (*Letters* 97), adding that cities, villages, and even the rural districts had been "thoroughly infected" by the "seditious" cult.

Whereas the Greco-Roman authors' cursory allusions to Jesus tend to confirm his martyrdom under Pilate and posthumous influence, they offer almost no information with which to construct a biography. Virtually everything we can learn about Jesus derives from the New Testament and a few other Christian documents, such as the Gospel of Thomas. Because no nonbeliever has left behind a comprehensive account of Jesus' life to use as a check against what the Evangelists claimed about him, we are forced to rely almost entirely on the testimony of Christian partisans.

The Modern Search for the Historical Jesus

It was not until the eighteenth century Age of Enlightenment that European scholars began to analyze the Gospels critically, consciously distinguishing between the Jesus of history and the church's doctrines, about him. Isolating Jesus' authentic

voice in passages about a dawning "kingdom of God," scholars began to place the historical figure in the context of first-century Jewish eschatology. This approach, which saw Jesus as a product of his Palestinian religious environment, culminated in Albert Schweitzer's monumental study, *Quest of the Historical Jesus,* first published in 1906.

In Schweitzer's view, Jesus is convinced that he is God's chosen instrument to announce the impending consummation of history. Burning with eschatological zeal, he demands that followers abandon all earthly ties and work with him to hasten the arrival of God's kingdom, which will overturn the present satanic world order and usher in the New Age. Jesus' driving goal is to establish the prophetic conditions that will lead to a supernaturally inspired chain of events culminating in his cosmic reign as the Son of Man. When Jesus' early expectations do not materialize (Matt. 10:22–23), he marches to Jerusalem, confident that he can compel the kingdom's appearance through his voluntary death, the final "tribulation" leading to God's direct imposition of his sovereignty. The anticipated divine intervention does not occur, however, and Jesus is crushed by the system he defies.

Schweitzer's reading of Jesus as a devoted but misguided apocalyptist made Christianity's core figure seem irrelevant to the modern worldview. No matter how sincere, a prophet whose eschatological predictions had been disproved by the world's stubborn failure to end had little to say to twentieth-century thinkers accustomed to scientific rationalism. As a result of this uncongenial historical Jesus, scholars for several decades after Schweitzer concentrated almost exclusively on the Gospels, employing form criticism and similar techniques to disentangle Palestinian traditions of the Jesus movement from later Hellenistic strands. The Jesus of history, apparently linked to an outmoded and unacceptable eschatology, was ignored while theologians focused on the postresurrection Christ of faith.

Rudolf Bultmann (1884–1976) is perhaps the single most influential New Testament scholar since Schweitzer. In his *Jesus and the Word* (1934) and *Jesus Christ and Mythology* (1958), Bultmann provided an exhaustive analysis of the different literary forms contained in the Synoptic Gospels, arguing that in most cases the material indicates an origin, not in the life of Jesus, but in the life of the early church. Bultmann also argued that the Gospels largely present Jesus in terms of Hellenistic mythology, portraying him as a supernatural figure who descends from heaven to reveal divine Wisdom. According to Bultmann, one can make Jesus' essentially timeless message relevant to modern believers only by interpreting the Gospels' mythic language in terms of twentieth-century ethical philosophy. Although it is both impossible and undesirable to recover the finite historical personality of Jesus himself, the universal concepts for which Jesus stands can still summon people to make conscious decision of ethical commitment. For Bultmann, the human Jesus espoused a form of Judaism, while Christianity is essentially a Hellenistic creation, thus rendering the historical Jesus of only marginal significance to faith in the risen Christ.

Scholarly Portrayals of Jesus

The international scholarly community remains deeply divided on the issue of the historical Jesus' actions and teachings. Particularly during the past two decades, the majority of scholars seem to have split into two opposing camps. One group argues, as had Schweitzer, that Jesus was an apocalyptist preaching the imminent arrival of God's eschatological kingdom; his historical role and teachings are therefore best understood in terms of first-century Jewish eschatology. By contrast, another group, including members of the Jesus Seminar and its associates, contends that Jesus was essentially a Jewish Wisdom teacher whose followers, misunderstanding his figurative language, later misinterpreted him apocalyptically. Although these two groups have reached extremely different conclusions, they generally agree on the scholarly methodologies to be used in attempting to recover Jesus' historical identity.

Some Criteria for Testing the Authenticity of Jesus' Words and Deeds

ORALITY

The first challenge facing scholars is to distinguish between the historical Jesus' actual sayings and those attributed to him in the written sources. Recognizing that Jesus' original teaching was entirely oral and that it was transmitted only by word of mouth for several decades before being written down, scholars have devised a test that respects the implications of this orality. To be remembered and quoted repeatedly, Jesus' words must have been both memorable and relatively brief. Statements likely to qualify as genuine will be vivid and attention-getting.

Examples of concise, highly quotable sayings include Jesus' declaration that "the Sabbath was made for the sake of man and not man for the Sabbath: therefore the Son of Man is sovereign even over the Sabbath" (Mark 2:27–28; cf. Matt. 12:1–8; Luke 6:1–5). Equally terse are the advice to pay Caesar [the government] his due but to give God what belongs to God (found in both Mark 12:17 and Thom. 100) and the wry observation that prophets are honored everywhere except on their home turf and/or among their relations (Mark 6:4; Matt. 13:15; John 4:44; Thom. 33).

FORM

The distinctive literary form in which Jesus casts his sayings also offers a clue to their probable historicity. In both the Synoptic Gospels and Thomas, Jesus' most characteristic forms of speech are aphorisms and parables that draw on familiar religious, domestic, and agricultural practices in rural Palestine. Jesus' frequent use of **aphorisms**—terse, snappy pronouncements that typically overturned conventional wisdom—forced people to think about the world in new ways. "It is not what goes into a person that defiles," he said, "but what comes out" (Mark 7:15, Scholars Version)—an almost scatological criticism of biblical dietary laws. Although they resemble proverbs in form, Jesus' aphorisms are typically nonproverbial in rejecting commonsensical assumptions, such as his declaration "It's easier for a camel to squeeze through a needle's eye than for a wealthy person to get into God's domain" (Mark 10:25, SV). Such statements would not only elicit a double-take among Jesus' peasant listeners, most of whom probably envied the rich, but also would reverse traditional assurances that wealth is a divine blessing (Prov. 6:6– 11; 10:15; 24:30–34; Job 42:12; Deut. 28:1–14).

Utilizing such rhetorical devices as hyperbole, humor, surprise, and paradox, Jesus' genuine aphorisms tend to shock with their audacity or to provoke with their reversal of social norms. Such aphorisms include the recommendation to take a "plank" out of one's eye (Matt. 7:3–5; Luke 6:41–42; Thom. 26), to be sly as a snake and simple as a dove (Matt. 10:16; Thom. 39), and to rob a strong man (Mark 3:27; Matt. 12:29; Luke 11:21–22; Thom. 35).

Using the homeliest of images, Jesus' authentic parables compare God's "domain" or kingdom to familiar settings and actions of everyday peasant life, typically stressing quiet processes of growth or almost imperceptible change. Unlike the well-known apocalyptic vision in Daniel, in which the kingdom literally crashes into the earth, violently shattering and replacing other nations (Dan. 2:44), Jesus' metaphors commonly emphasize a slow or hidden development. God's impending rule is thus likened to the sowing of seeds (Mark 4:3–8; Matt. 13:3–8; Luke 8:5–8a; Thom. 9), the sprouting of a mustard plant (Mark 4:30–32; Matt. 13:31–32; Luke 13:18–19; Thom. 20), and a woman baking bread, in which leaven gradually transforms the dough (Matt 13:33; Luke 13:20–21; Thom. 96).

DISSIMILARITY

The criterion of dissimilarity holds that a saying is likely to be authentic if it differs significantly from *both* first-century Jewish attitudes or practices and those of the later Hellenistic church. Jesus' use of the Aramaic word *Abba* (an informal term for "fa-

ther") (Mark 14:36; Luke 11:2) differs from the church's more formal way of addressing the Deity (Matt. 6:9) and probably represents Jesus' personal style. Luke's Gospel preserves some of Jesus' most distinctive teaching, containing numerous parables that defy conventional thought and overturn ordinary expectations. These include provocative stories involving an irresponsible and ungrateful son (Luke 15:11–32), a despised Samaritan who is a moral hero (Luke 16:1–8a), a lazy and unjust judge (Luke 18:1–8), and a righteous Pharisee who is outclassed by a sinful tax collector (Luke 18:9–14a).

The obvious weakness in the dissimilarity criterion is that many of Jesus' characteristic teachings, including his emphasis on love, were shared by other Palestinian teachers of his day (Mark 12:28–34). In fact, historians find Judean parallels to virtually all of Jesus' ethical pronouncements. Many scholars now believe that Jesus is best understood when seen operating in his first-century Palestinian-Jewish milieu. Recent studies have shown that Jesus has much in common with the Essenes and Pharisees, in both the content and the parabolic style of his teachings (see Chilton in "Recommended Reading").

MULTIPLE ATTESTATION

With this standard for determining reliable material, scholars consider the variety of different sources in which a particular statement or teaching occurs. If a saying appears in Mark, the Q document, and the Gospel of Thomas—all of which are presumed to be independent of one another—it is likely to be genuine. Jesus' emphasis on the kingdom of God appears to be confirmed by its frequent appearance in all three of these sources. (The specific form or interpretation of an individual kingdom pericope, however, is open to question. Each Christian writer or editor tends to modify individual sayings when incorporating them into a written text.) The criterion of multiple attestation also affirms several other traditions, including Jesus' interest in women, the poor, and social outcasts such as lepers, tax collectors, prostitutes, and other "sinners." The tradition that Jesus performed healings, emphasized Wisdom precepts, and challenged both religious and political authority structures is also multiply attested.

Examples of material found in different sources, such as Mark, Q, and/or Thomas, include the parable of the dinner party (Matt. 22:1–14; Luke 14:16–24; Thom. 64); the perplexing command to hate one's relatives (Matt. 10:37; Luke 14:26; Thom. 55 and 101); asking, seeking, and finding (Matt. 7:7–8; Luke 11:9–10; Thom. 2 and 94); new wine and old wineskins (Mark 2:22; Luke 5:37–38; Thom. 47); and blessing the hungry (Matt. 5:6; Luke 6:21a; Thom. 69).

COHERENCE

This standard allows the scholar to regard material as potentially authentic if it resembles material already established by the criteria of orality, distinctiveness, and multiple attestation. If a saying or action is consistent with themes and concepts generally recognized as genuine, it, too, may be accepted.

THE EMBARRASSMENT FACTOR

Some scholars believe that a tradition about Jesus that the early church apparently found awkward or problematic—such as the reputed irregularity of Jesus' birth, his baptism by John for "remission of sins," his proclivity for associating with notorious sinners, and (above all) his shameful execution by a Roman governor—is likely to be authentic. Traditions that church apologists found embarrassing or difficult to explain caused too much general discomfort for believers to have added them as accretions to Jesus' story. This criterion of discomfort is particularly helpful in evaluating the plausibility of Jesus' actions, including his inability to win over most of his contemporaries and his controversial behavior in the Temple.

Potentially embarrassing traditions about Jesus include his baptism by John (Mark 1), his family's belief that he behaved irrationally (Mark 3:21, 31–35), his inability to heal those who do not trust him (Mark 6:5), his alleged reputation as a drunkard and a glutton who cultivated bad company (Matt. 11:16–19; Luke 7:31–35), his refusal to be called good (Mark 10:18, changed in Matt. 19:16–17), and the brutal fact of his crucifixion as a threat to the Roman government. (For a partial list of sayings that many scholars believe form an authentic core of Jesus' teachings, see Box 11.3.)

Although generally agreeing on the techniques by which Jesus' sayings and deeds can be tested for historical plausibility, today's scholars have arrived at enormously disparate views of who Jesus really was. The process that began with the earliest Gospel writers' efforts to portray Jesus according to their differing visions of his significance continues unabated today. Whereas the Evangelists' main goal was to interpret Jesus theologically for the authors' believing community (cf. John 20:31), contemporary historians attempt a more objective approach. Even so, as many scholars have rightly cautioned, pure objectivity is rarely achieved; the picture that one tries to paint of Jesus typically says more about the painter than it does about the subject. Almost all efforts to reconstruct Jesus' personal character and motivation tend to be projections of qualities that the individual researcher consciously or unconsciously accepts as valuable. Students and scholars alike generally assume that Jesus, when found, will be relevant to contemporary needs and expectations. Most persons still reject the possibility that Jesus was too limited by his exclusively religious preoccupations as a first-century Jew to have anything meaningful to say to our largely secular and technological society.

A Nonapocalyptic Wisdom Teacher

In the late 1980s, a group of leading North American New Testament scholars formed the Jesus Seminar. Its purpose was to screen all the Gospels and other documents composed during the first three centuries of Christianity for reliable data about the historical Jesus. Over the next decade, the Seminar participants met regularly as a group, collectively analyzing each and every word and action ascribed to Jesus, in both canonical

Box 11.3 The Authentic Voice of Jesus

These are a few of the approximately one hundred sayings that meet the Jesus Seminar's criteria for genuineness (all quotations are from the Scholars Version). Many scholars also regard some of Jesus' eschatological pronouncements as authentic.

Love your enemies . . . God causes the sun to rise on both the bad and the good, and sends rain on both the just and the unjust. Tell me, if you love those who love you, why should you be commended for that? Even the [tax] collectors do that. (Matt. 5:44–46)

Congratulations, you poor! God's domain belongs to you.

Congratulations, you hungry! You will have a feast.

Congratulations, you who weep now! You will laugh. (Luke 6:20–21)

When someone strikes you on the cheek, offer the other as well. When someone takes away your coat, don't prevent that person from taking your shirt along with it . . . Give to everyone who begs from you. (Luke 6:29–30)

Forgive, and you'll be forgiven. (Luke 6:37b)

Foxes have dens, and birds of the sky have nests; but the son of Adam has nowhere to rest his head. (Luke 9:58)

You won't be able to observe the coming of God's imperial rule. People are not going to be able to say, "Look, here it is!" or "Over there!" On the contrary, God's imperial rule is right here in your presence. (Luke 1720–21)

Every government divided against itself is devastated, and a house divided against a house falls. If Satan is divided against himself — since you claim that I drive out demons in Beelzebub's name — how will his domain endure? If I drive out demons in Beelzebub's name, in whose name do your own people drive (them) out? In that case, they will be your judges. But if by God's finger I drive out demons, then for you God's imperial rule has arrived. (Luke 11:17–20)

What does Heaven's imperial rule remind me of? It is like leaven which a woman took and concealed in fifty pounds of flour until it was all leavened. (Luke 12:20–21)

To what should we compare God's imperial rule, or what parable should we use for it? Consider the mustard seed: When it is sown on the ground, though it is the smallest of all the seeds on the earth, yet when it is sown, it comes up, and becomes the biggest of all garden plants, and produces branches, so that the birds of the sky can nest in its shade. (Mark 4:30–32)

Heaven's imperial rule is like treasure hidden in a field: when someone finds it, that person covers it up again, and out of sheer joy goes and sells every last possession and buys that field. Again, Heaven's imperial rule is like some trader looking for beautiful pearls. When that merchant finds one priceless pearl, he sells everything he owns and buys it. (Matt. 13:44–45)

That's why I tell you: don't fret about life — what you're going to eat — or about your body — what you're going to wear. Remember, there is more to living than food and clothing. Think about the crows: they don't plant or harvest, they don't have storerooms or barns. Yet God feeds them. You're worth a lot more than the birds! . . . Think about how the lilies grow: they don't slave and they never spin. You let me tell you, even Solomon at the height of his glory was never decked out like one of these. If God dresses up the grass in the field, which is here today and tomorrow is tossed into an oven, it is surely more likely (God cares for) you, you who don't take anything for granted. (Luke 12:22–28)

So I tell you, ask — it'll be given to you; seek — you'll find; knock — it'll be opened for you. Rest assured: everyone who asks receives; everyone who seeks finds; and for the one who knocks it is opened. (Luke 11:9–10)

No man can be a slave to two masters. No doubt that slave will either hate one and love the other, or be devoted to one and disdain the other. You can't be enslaved to both God and a bank account. (Matt. 6:24; Luke 16:13)

There was a rich man whose fields produced a bumper crop. "What do I do now?" he asked himself, "since I don't have any place to store my crops. I know," he said, "I'll tear down my barns and build larger ones so I can store all my grain and my goods. Then I'll say to myself, "You have plenty put away for years to come. Take it easy, eat, drink, enjoy yourself." But God said to him, "You fool! This very night your life will be demanded back from you. All this stuff you've collected — whose will it be now?" (Luke 12:16–20)

Figure 11.1 Head of Christ. This mosaic portrait of Jesus (artist unknown) is composed of hundreds of tiny fragments of stone or tile arranged to create the lineaments of a human face. The result is not a realistic picture of an individual, but a highly stylized representation of a type of humanity. The stern and grimly determined face shown here embodies Mark's image of a Messiah predestined to endure rejection and suffering. As the artist assembled many different pieces of material to achieve this stereotype, so today's scholars work to assemble a coherent picture of the historical Jesus from thousands of literary fragments embedded in both canonical and noncanonical sources.

and non-canonical sources (Figure 11.1). Unique among scholarly bodies, members of the Seminar, after extensive deliberations, voted on the authenticity of each ascribed saying and deed, thus achieving an unprecedented consensus.

THE WORK OF THE JESUS SEMINAR

Applying the standard scholarly criteria of orality, dissimilarity, awkwardness, and multiple attestation, the Jesus Seminar worked to isolate the true voice of Jesus from the redactional speeches that the Gospel authors had injected into their theologically oriented accounts. Looking for a core of Jesus' most distinctive teachings—those that differed from both typically Jewish and typically Christian assumptions—the Seminar found them primarily in Jesus' aphorisms and parables. After years of sifting through the evidence, Seminar members concluded that only about 20 percent of the words that the Gospel writers attribute to Jesus probably originated with him.

Because Jesus' most characteristic speech forms—the parable and the aphorism—contain little apocalyptic material, the Seminar scholars became increasingly skeptical that Jesus was a prophet of eschatological doom. Among many other passages regarded as inauthentic, the scholars almost unanimously dismissed the long apocalyptic prophecies about Jesus' Second Coming (Mark 13; Matt. 24; Luke 21) as largely the composition of the Evangelists. The lengthy Johannine meditations on Jesus' divine nature were similarly judged to reflect the Christology of the author's own community, not the speech of the historical Jesus. Neither the Synoptic's eschatological predictions nor John's metaphysical discourses correlated with Jesus' known forms of speech, which were characterized by brevity and images from daily life.

Results of the Jesus Seminar's work were published in two large volumes, *The Five Gospels: The Search for the Authentic Words of Jesus* (1993) and *The Acts of Jesus: What Did Jesus Really Do?* (1998). Extensively annotated, these works are valuable study aids, providing detailed arguments for accepting or rejecting the authenticity of each saying in the Gospels. While somewhat reticent about endorsing many of the Evangelists' versions of Jesus' words, the Seminar members generally agree that Jesus was known during his lifetime as both a healer and an exorcist, as well as a teacher of unconventional wisdom. Printing in red or pink the actions and statements of Jesus judged likely to be historical, these books create a portrait of Jesus as a compassionate sage deeply concerned with social justice—particularly for the poor and downtrodden—and with each person's intimate relationship with God.

Scholars advocating a nonapocalyptic Jesus believe that they have stripped away the Synoptic Gospel's eschatological overlay and the Johannine Gospel's high Christology to reveal a more unified and focused character portrait than is possible if one uncritically accepts *all* the claims the Evangelists make about their subject. In the view of some readers, regarding Jesus as primarily a sage and healer seems more historically credible than John's omniscient figure who descends from heaven and serenely embraces his cross as the necessary means

of reclaiming his preexistent divinity. For some critics, discovering Jesus as a wisdom teacher, even a kind of Hellenistic-Jewish-Cynic philosopher, removes the embarrassment of regarding him as an apocalyptist whose promise to return (within his disciples' lifetimes) as the eschatological Son of Man was not kept.

An Apocalyptic Jesus

Other scholars doubt that rescuing a historical figure from his eschatological misconceptions is a reputable criterion for scholarship. Many scholars point out that, if Jesus did not advocate an eschatological viewpoint, it is extremely difficult, if not impossible, to fit him into his historical environment. There is general scholarly agreement that Jesus' immediate predecessor, John the Baptist, warned Judah of an impending divine visitation and that Jesus' most influential interpreter, the apostle Paul, eagerly anticipated Jesus' imminent return as eschatological judge (see Chapter 12). With Jesus' career closely bracketed by two such proponents of the approaching *eschaton,* advocates of a noneschatological Jesus face a formidable challenge in explaining the continuity (or lack of it) in the sequence from John to Jesus to Paul.

Because of widespread public interest in searching for the historical Jesus, in recent years a veritable flood of new books on the subject has occurred. Scholars who opt for a noneschatological Jesus who did *not* expect the world to end in his own day include Marcus Borg, whose *Jesus: A New Vision* sensitively explores Jesus' ethical teachings and his concept of the divine-human relationship. Borg's *Jesus at 2000* offers a concise, lucidly written examination of current Jesus scholarship. John Dominic Crossan's monumental work *The Historical Jesus* and *Jesus: A Revolutionary Biography,* a briefer summation of his research, present Jesus as a champion of social justice whom Roman tyranny crushed. Robert Funk, founder and convener of the Jesus Seminar, has succinctly compiled Jesus' most characteristic teachings in *The Gospel of Jesus,* which encompasses the entire ministry in a brief eighty-seven pages.

Although the issue of whether the historical Jesus was primarily a wisdom teacher or an apocalyptist (or a mixture of both) is likely to remain unresolved for the foreseeable future, many studies of Jesus published at the turn of the twenty-first century argue strongly that he was a proponent of Jewish eschatology. In *Jesus of Nazareth, King of the Jews,* Paula Fredriksen marshals impressive evidence to place Jesus firmly in his Jewish context as an apocalyptic preacher. In Fredriksen's reading, Jesus is a Torah-observant Palestinian Jew who shared John the Baptist's sense of impending eschatological crisis and preached that the kingdom of God would arrive during his final Passover week in Jerusalem, a seditious message for which Pilate executed him. Bart D. Ehrman subtitles his book *Apocalyptic Prophet of the New Millennium;* like Fredriksen he seems to regard Mark's portrayal of Jesus as an eschatological preacher who expected the Son of Man's imminent appearance as generally reliable. Similarly, in *Jesus of Nazareth: Millenarian Prophet,* Dale C. Allison emphasizes Jesus' apocalyptic expectation that God would set up the long-awaited kingdom during Jesus' lifetime. These scholars, as well as many others, believe that the Synoptic tradition provides conclusive evidence that Jesus was motivated by the same kind of apocalyptic hope that inspired both the Baptist and Paul. However, as Schweitzer devastatingly pointed out a century ago, all three were wrong; the kingdom did not come.

In addition to the books already mentioned, students pursuing the issue of Jesus' historical identity will find several other works helpful, including *The Historical Figure of Jesus* by E. P. Sanders and *The Historical Jesus: A Comprehensive Guide* by Gerd Theissen and Annette Merz, the latter a comprehensive review of contemporary Jesus research. John P. Meier's *A Marginal Jew: Rethinking the Historical Jesus,* of which three out of a projected four volumes have been published, exhaustively investigates the sociocultural world in which Jesus grew up, as well as his distinctive kingdom teachings. Another useful aid is *The Jesus Movement: A Social History of Its First Century* by Ekkhard W. Stegemann and Wolfgang Stegemann, which also examines in detail the social, economic, and political environment in which Jesus and his early followers lived (see "Recommended Reading").

It is said that each new generation re-creates the great figures of the past according to its own values and aspirations. For this reason, scholars urge us to avoid retrojecting our present ideals on a Jesus who lived at a time and in a place qualitatively different from our own, making him appear too congenial to twenty-first-century tastes. However, scholarly portraits of a Jesus who was deluded and doomed by his eschatological obsessions may not satisfy most New Testament readers. Among other considerations, the man embodied in the Gospels seems far too profound and insightful to attempt forcing an egocentric and literalist eschatology into historical fulfillment. In the Jesus-as-apocalyptist view, he is entirely the product of his own time. But the opposing theory of a noneschatological Jesus, a benign wisdom teacher committed to helping the oppressed, creates a Jesus who is suspiciously compatible with the modern temperament.

To scholars who see Jesus as having promoted a realized eschatology, Jesus' challenge to discern that God's kingdom reigns now—if people can get over their spiritual blindness and recognize its transcendent power—is intellectually attractive. Perpetuating the Johannine doctrine of cultivating eternal life in the present, this view has the advantage of presenting a Jesus who transcends his ancient Palestinian milieu to speak directly to contemporary experience. Most scholars, however, advise us to beware of discovering a Jesus who appears too acceptable by today's standards. No matter how much Jesus may have differed from his peers, the historical person was a first-century rural Jew and, in many ways, would undoubtedly seem disturbingly alien to twenty-first-century sensibilities.

Some General Agreements About the Historical Jesus

Although scholars have not reached a consensus about Jesus' primary teachings, many do agree on the general outline of his life. The Gospel traditions contain numerous data about Jesus that are relatively "theology-free," particularly biographical

Figure 11.2 *The Holy Family.* The unknown years of Jesus' boyhood are given a Japanese setting in this twentieth-century painting on silk. Shouldering his share of the family's work, the young Jesus carries wood to help Joseph, his carpenter father, while Mary, his mother, is busy at her spinning wheel. The themes of productive labor, mutual assistance, and familial harmony dominate the domestic scene in Nazareth, providing a contrast to the adult Jesus' later rejection of family ties and obligations (Mark 3).

information that is not cited as a fulfillment of biblical prophecy or a promulgation of christological doctrine. We may accept the tradition, then, that Jesus was born late in the reign of Herod the Great (between 6 and 4 B.C.E.); that he was raised in Nazareth (which is not mentioned in the Hebrew Bible); that he was the presumed son of Joseph, a carpenter, and his wife, Mary; and that he had brothers (or close relatives) named James (a future leader of the Jerusalem church), Joseph, Simon, and Judas (Jude), and an unknown number of sisters (or stepsisters) (Mark 6; Matt. 13:55). If Jesus and his putative father were carpenters (or some other kind of artisan), it probably means that the family had lost its hereditary land, which reduced them to a social status below that of Galilee's landowning peasants. (For two contemporary portrayals of the holy family, see Figures 11.2 and 11.3.)

When "about thirty years old" (Luke 3:1), Jesus came to John the Baptist for baptism in the River Jordan (c. 27 or 29 C.E., depending on how one calculates Luke's "fifteenth year of the emperor Tiberius"). Mark's report that John baptized Jesus "in token of repentance for the forgiveness of sins" (Mark 1:4) is not an event that the early church would have invented. Because official doctrine held that Jesus was "sinless" and superior to the Baptist, Mark's baptismal story could not have emerged unless there was a firm tradition that Jesus had indeed submitted to John's ministrations. Some scholars think it likely that Jesus was, for an indefinite period, a disciple of the Baptist and did not begin his

Figure 11.3 The Holy Family. In depicting Jesus, Mary, and Joseph as indigenous Americans, the twentieth-century painter Fr. John B. Giuliani emphasizes both the archetypal sacredness of the family and the tradition of spirituality attained by pre-Columbian peoples of North America.

own ministry until after Herod Antipas had arrested and beheaded the prophet. Although it is impossible to confirm this theory, apparently Jesus held the Baptist in the highest regard, perhaps regarding him as a mentor.

Following his baptism and perhaps an interlude of solitary meditation, Jesus began proclaiming a distinctive variation on the Baptist's message — the kingdom of God is near (or perhaps already present). In Jesus' proclamation, God's burgeoning rule reversed ordinary social values and encompassed people who were typically devalued by "respectable" society. The Synoptic tradition consistently shows Jesus as an active friend of the poor and outcast, going out of his way to share meals with known "sinners" and other disreputable people. Jesus' penchant for unsavory associations — along with his reputation as "a glutton and a drinker" — passes the credibility test because no believer would invent such tales (Matt. 10:18–19; Luke 15:1–3; 7:33–8:3). Some commentators have even suggested that Jesus' parable of the prodigal son — which features a young man who squanders his inheritance in riotous living, much to the dismay of his disapproving brother — may hint at a situation in Jesus' own life before he underwent John's

cleansing baptism. Although anything said about Jesus before his association with the Baptist is necessarily conjectural, the twin traditions of his public repentance and his unfailing sympathy for social pariahs suggest that he knew this class of people well (and may once have been counted among them). His family's objections to Jesus' suddenly embarking on a controversial ministry and his neighbors' doubts about his new-found prophetic claims (Mark 3:20–21, 31–35; 6:1–6) also suggest that Jesus' early life was qualitatively different from his later career. The antifamily sentiments Jesus repeatedly expressed — including the "hard sayings" about hating father and mother and leaving "the dead to bury their dead" — emphasizes a sharp break with his former connections and way of life.

Whereas Jesus' Nazarene acquaintances had defined (and thereby limited) him in terms of his occupation and blood ties — he was merely "Mary's son," "the carpenter" — Jesus seems to have attained a radically new identity: He called God *Abba* (father). This divine-Parent/human-child relationship appears to underlie some of his most distinctive pronouncements, such as his injunction to be as giving and gracious to other mortals as God is to all his children, regardless of their merits (Matt.

Figure 11.4 *Christ Separating Sheep from Goats.* This early sixth-century Ravenna mosaic illustrates Matthew's parable of eschatological judgment (Matt. 25:31–46). At his Parousia (Second Coming), an enthroned Jesus, flanked by two angels, divides all humanity into two mutually exclusive groups. The sheep are gathered in the favored position at Jesus' right hand, whereas the goats, at Jesus' left, are condemned to outer darkness for their failure to help others.

5:44–48). The paradoxical command to "Love your enemies!" is practicable because God perceives human "enemies" as potential allies and friends.

Jesus' invitation to share in the divine relationship seems to have been remarkably inclusive: He breaks bread with Pharisees, lepers, tax collectors, slaves, women, and children (who, in the Greco-Roman world, were at the bottom of the social hierarchy). While raising their spirits, he also shows concern for their bodies: *All* the traditions agree that Jesus was a healer. How Jesus accomplished his healings and exorcisms is not known, but the people he helped were convinced that he had changed them for the better, not least by validating their intrinsic worth and accepting some of them

among his disciples. Issuing witty, provocative statements that challenged widely accepted values and attitudes, baiting religious authorities, and imparting a sense of physical and spiritual health to persons desperately in need of curative attention, Jesus, whether he wished to or not, could not help attracting followers. (For two artistic interpretations of Jesus' role as shepherd of humanity, see Figures 11.4 and 11.5.)

Pursuing an itinerant life of deliberately chosen poverty and wandering randomly through Galilee from village to village, Jesus inevitably drew around him a mixed group of Galilean fishermen, farmers, women, and other ordinary working people. In parables and other figures of speech, he illustrated

Figure 11.5 *The Good Shepherd.* In this early Christian painting of Christ on the ceiling of a crypt in the catacombs of St. Priscilla in Rome, the artist pictures Jesus in a pose that would be familiar to a Greco-Roman audience. Like earlier renditions of Apollo, the Greek god of prophecy, intellect, music, and shepherds, the youthful Jesus carries a lamb on his shoulders to demonstrate his concern for his human flock.

the desirability of living in God's kingdom — or perceiving the reality of divine rule, despite the oppression of secular authority, in the worlds of nature and human society. Although the Synoptic writers imply that the Galilean campaign lasted about a year, John's Gospel may be right in stating that it extended over at least three years and included several visits to Jerusalem.

While attracting throngs of mostly powerless admirers, Jesus also aroused powerful enemies. His apparent habit of relying on his own authority to pronounce on religious observances, such as Sabbath keeping — so different from the rabbinic tradition of citing the honored view of one's predecessors — irritated some and outraged others. Whereas many disciples were probably delighted with Jesus' authoritative dismissal of some purity laws and criticism of the Temple's priestly administration, some influential Sadducean officials in Jerusalem were undoubtedly suspicious of his motives. The priestly leadership may have regarded him as a blasphemer and a potential threat to the

delicate balance between Roman rule and Jewish welfare.

Jesus' healings, his preaching about God's kingdom, and his drawing of large, unruly crowds may have inspired some persons who particularly hated Roman occupation of the Holy Land to speculate that he was Israel's Messiah — the promised deliverer who would rid them of Gentile domination. John's report that a crowd wanted to proclaim him "[a Davidic] king" (John 6:15) and Luke's observation that as Jesus approached Jerusalem to celebrate Passover there his disciples "thought the reign of God might dawn at any moment" (Luke 19:11) may echo actual historical conditions. Although most scholars do not think that Jesus presented himself as Israel's Messiah, some of his followers may have viewed him as the one prophesied to restore David's monarchy (Box 11.4). If such claims were being circulated on Jesus' behalf, it would explain Pilate's action in executing Jesus on the charge of treason, pretending to be "king of the Jews." To the Roman procurator, Jesus was merely

Box 11.4 Developing Views of Jesus as the "Son of God"

Individual New Testament writers preserve different stages of a Christian concept that apparently developed over time — the conviction that Jesus was the "Son of God." Historically, Jesus' divine Sonship has been interpreted in various ways. To understand the Christian authors' evolving views, we must start where they did, with the Hebrew Bible.

1. *The Davidic kings as God's adopted sons.* According to the covenant made with David's royal dynasty, the kings of Israel — Yahweh's anointed ones or "messiahs" — enjoyed a special relationship with their God, comparable to that of a son with his father. Speaking of David's heirs, Yahweh promises, "I will be his father, and he shall be my son . . . My love will never be withdrawn" (2 Sam. 7:14–15). Psalm 2, sung at the enthroning of one of David's descendants, expresses a similar view of the filial bond between king and God. Yahweh tells his "anointed" ruler (Messiah): "You are my son . . . this day [the date of his crowning] I become your father" (Ps. 2:7). Thus, the Davidic king's coronation was simultaneously the time of his becoming God's "son" by adoption.

2. *Son by resurrection.* The oldest recorded Christian interpretation of Jesus' Sonship — Paul's letter to the Romans (mid-50s C.E.) — states that Jesus "was declared Son of God by a mighty act in that he rose from the dead" (Rom. 1:3). In this passage, Paul follows Israel's ancient tradition that David's ultimate heir — the Messiah — would also in some sense become God's Son. As Paul expresses the concept, Jesus receives Sonship at his resurrection, the Deity's miraculous confirmation of his messianic worthiness. The author of Acts preserves a similar view, representing Peter shortly after the Resurrection as saying that by exalting Jesus to his "right hand," "God has made this Jesus . . . both Lord and Messiah" (Acts 2:36). The oldest layer of preserved tradition suggests that the first Christians saw Jesus, like Israel's anointed kings, becoming God's Son by adoption, a

reward conferred at his resurrection and ascension to heaven.

3. *Jesus' own witness.* The early church's identification of Jesus as a divine Son was undoubtedly stimulated by Jesus' practice of addressing God as *Abba,* an Aramaic term children used to express intimacy with their male parent (Mark 14:36; Luke 11:2). The use of *Abba* suggests Jesus' sense of personal closeness to the Deity. Paul attests to his church's continued evocation of the word (Rom. 8:15; Gal. 4:6).

4. *Jesus' adoption at baptism.* If Mark's Gospel (mid-60s C.E.) were our only Gospel, we might conclude that Jesus was designated God's Son at his baptism (Mark 1:11), apparently through adoption and anointing by the Holy Spirit. In Mark, the demons recognize Jesus' relationship to God (3:11–12), but no human being acknowledges it until he has proven his faithfulness unto death (15:39). Jesus' final act of filial devotion affirms his divine Sonship (an idea also expressed in Hebrews [2:20; 5:7–9]).

5. *Sonship at conception.* Adding infancy narratives to their accounts of Jesus' life, Matthew and Luke (mid-80s C.E.) push the beginning of Jesus' Sonship back in time, to the moment of his conception (Matt. 1:10; Luke 2:26–35). Matthew and Luke interpret Yahweh's promise to become as a father to the Davidic "son" (2 Sam. 7; Ps. 2) as meaning more than mere adoption; they see the Heavenly Voice at Jesus' baptism as simply confirming the biological fact of divine parentage.

6. *The son as creative Word.* Eschewing traditions of Jesus' virginal conception, John's Gospel, the last one written (mid-90s C.E.), declares that Jesus existed as God's Son long before he came to earth, even before the universe came into being (John 1:1–18). A variation of the concept appearing in Colossians (1:15–20; 2:9–10), John's doctrine of Jesus' eternal deity and Sonship ultimately became the Christian standard of belief.

another messianic (royal) claimant, such as those who led popular uprisings after Herod the Great's death (see Chapter 9).

Jesus' crucifixion under Pilate, which Tacitus and other non-Christian historians confirm, was

not the kind of death — public, shameful, and associated with slaves and criminals — believers would fabricate for their leader. In the considered opinion of many Jews, the fact that Jesus was crucified meant that he could not have been the

Messiah: No passage in the Hebrew Bible even hinted that the Messiah would die, let alone be executed as a felon by Gentile agents. (Proof texts that Christians later cited, such as the suffering servant poem in Isaiah 53 or Psalm 22, to explain Jesus' death are not specifically messianic prophecies.) Paul candidly describes the awkward fact of Jesus "nailed to the cross" as a "scandal"—a "stumbling block to Jews" and "sheer folly" to the Greeks (1 Cor. 1:23, 18). The humiliating fact of Jesus' crucifixion—so contrary to scriptural expectations—was probably the chief obstacle that kept most Jews from taking Christian preaching about him seriously. Some scholars believe that the first narrative about Jesus' miracles (and perhaps including his Passion)—the hypothetical Signs Gospel presumably later incorporated into John's Gospel—was composed to demonstrate that Jesus was Israel's Anointed One and that he was killed only because people refused to believe in his wondrous deeds (see Chapter 10).

Jesus' Teachings About the Kingdom

God as Universal King   Jesus' attempts to convey his vision of God's kingdom inspired some of his most celebrated parables and figures of speech. The English phrase "kingdom of God" translates the Greek expression *basileia tou theou. Basileia* refers primarily to the act or process of ruling, a quality or privilege that distinguishes a king or other ruler. To have *basileia* is to possess control, power, freedom, and independence. The biblical God, whose infinite kingship Second Isaiah and the psalmists celebrate, has these attributes in abundance. Psalm 145 proclaims Yahweh's universal sovereignty:

> All thy creatures praise thee, Lord [Yahweh],
>   and thy servants bless thee.
> They talk of the glory of thy kingdom
>   and tell of thy might,
> they proclaim to their fellows how mighty are
>   thy deeds,
>   how glorious the majesty of thy kingdom.

> Thy kingdom is an everlasting kingdom, and thy dominion stands for all generations.
>   Ps. 145:11–12

Israel's God is thus the supreme possessor of *basileia*, a concept that must be kept in mind when considering Jesus' possible intentions as he combines his kingdom teaching with assertions of his own autonomy and dominion.

Although he is never shown defining what he means by the term, in the Gospels Jesus is pictured using *basileia tou theou* in four major ways: (1) to express the kingdom's preeminence, (2) to defend his personal authority to represent the kingdom and interpret the divine will, (3) to imply the nature of his self-awareness—the views he holds about his relationship with God and the meaning of kingship—and (4) to proclaim the kingdom's radical demand for total commitment. Because it dominates his message throughout the Synoptic Gospels, we will concentrate on the first category, emphasizing those sayings that scholars believe are most likely to stem from the historical Jesus.

In the Sermon on the Mount, Matthew presents Jesus as giving top priority to seeking the kingdom. The disciple who puts God's kingdom and his "justice [righteousness]" "before everything else" will also receive all that ordinary life requires (Matt. 6:33). Matthew and the other Synoptic writers then present such a variety of conflicting, even contradictory references to the kingdom that it is difficult to harmonize these disparate statements into a coherent view of what is meant. In different pericopes, the Synoptic Jesus speaks as if the kingdom were (1) a prophesied future event, (2) an unexpected occurrence, (3) a hidden power that grows slowly, (4) a present reality, and (5) physically present but unnoticed.

The Kingdom as Future Event   The Synoptic writers typically emphasize the eschatological nature of the kingdom, presenting Jesus' message as a continuation of John the Baptist's warning of imminent divine judgment (cf. Matt. 3:3 and 4:17). In the Synoptic view, the kingdom is so close that people who first hear it proclaimed will live to see "the kingdom of God already come in power" (Mark 9:1; Matt. 16:28; Luke 9:27). All three

Synoptic authors link Jesus' death with the kingdom's nearness. At the Last Supper, Jesus tells the disciples that he will never again drink "from the fruit of the vine until the day when I drink it new in the kingdom of God" (Mark 14:25; Matt. 26:19; Luke 22:16, 18).

The Kingdom as an Unexpected Event In their apocalyptic predictions that link Jerusalem's fall and Jesus' return in glory, the Synoptic Gospels also implicitly associate the Parousia with the kingdom's arrival (cf. Mark 13, Matt. 24, and Luke 21). These passages anticipating the *eschaton* are inherently paradoxical: While asserting that spectacular portents will herald the End, they also emphasize the suddenness and unexpectedness of divine intervention. Thus, the kingdom appears stealthily, "like a thief in the night," its abrupt materialization a striking contrast to the parables that stress its quiet growth (Mark 13:33; Matt. 24:42; 25:13; Luke 12:40, 21:36). These and other texts that relate the kingdom to the Second Coming incorporate traditional themes of Hellenistic-Jewish eschatology, including world judgment and resurrection. In this context, the kingdom's appearance signifies the End of history as we know it and the inception of a radical "New Age." As noted previously, scholars continue to debate the extent to which the Synoptic writers' eschatological expectations accurately mirror Jesus' historical views of the kingdom.

The Kingdom as a Hidden Power That Grows Slowly Many of the best-known parables depict the kingdom as a hidden power that grows slowly until it achieves greatness. In contrast to the apocalyptic tradition — in which God's kingdom bursts suddenly and catastrophically into human affairs (Dan. 2:44) — Jesus' kingdom parables typically reject destruction imagery in favor of similes depicting serene germination. Jesus compares the kingdom to a tiny mustard seed that develops "underground," gradually maturing into a "tree" that shelters wildlife (Mark 4:30–32; Matt. 13:31–32; Luke 13:18–19; Gos. Thom. 20). That the mustard plant actually is a *weed* perhaps adds an ironic dimension to Jesus' simple analogy.

The parable of "leaven" that causes bread dough to rise and expand also suggests the kingdom's slow and quiet maturation (Matt. 13:33; Luke 13:20–21; Gos. Thom. 96). The parables comparing the kingdom to seeking what is lost or unexpectedly finding an invaluable object — a pearl, a buried treasure, or a lost coin — highlight a gradual and *private* process on the part of individuals. In parables of this kind, a solitary figure — a widow, a lone merchant, a shepherd — takes time to focus on the process of discovery, a quiet personal search that ends in rejoicing (Matt. 13:44; 18:12–13; Luke 15:4–6; Gos. Thom. 107). Employing images of life as it is daily lived, Jesus' parables of planting, growing, and recognizing unforeseen treasures have little affinity with apocalyptic violence.

The Kingdom as a Present Reality Jesus' metaphors of seeking and finding harmonize with pronouncements in which he declares the kingdom a present reality. In Luke 11:20, he tells opponents, "But if it is by the finger of God that I drive out the devils, then be sure that the kingdom has already come upon you" (see also Matt. 12:28). Expelling demons is here equated with psychological healing and spiritual power, an expression of God's invisible dominion. Jesus' response to the Baptist's disciples, who inquire if he is really the Messiah, similarly implies that Jesus' present activity is a realization of the kingdom. When John's disciples behold the blind restored to sight, the deaf restored to hearing, and the dead raised to life, we know that God now reigns (Matt. 11:2–6; Luke 7:22–23). When the seventy-two disciples return from a successful campaign of exorcisms, Luke has Jesus declare that he now sees Satan fall "like lightning" from heaven (Luke 10:18). The spiritual healings performed by Jesus and his followers are a defeat of Evil and a manifestation of divine sovereignty.

The Kingdom as Physically Present Yet Unnoticed Luke preserves Jesus' most explicit statement about the kingdom's already being present: "You can not tell by observation when the kingdom of God comes. There will be no saying, 'Look, here it is!'

or 'there it is!'; for in fact the kingdom of God is among you" (or "right there in your presence") (Luke 17:20). With this startling declaration, Jesus informs the Pharisees that in his person and healing activity, they can witness the kingdom in operation. Divine rule, Jesus adds, is as immediately obvious and universal as sheet lightning that flashes over the entire sky (Luke 17:22–24). The same perception of the kingdom's paradoxically elusive yet pervasive presence is also found in the Gospel of Thomas: "It will not come by watching for it. It will not be said, 'Look, here!' or 'Look, there!' Rather, [the Father's] imperial rule is spread out upon the earth, and people don't see it" (Gos. Thom. 113). As Jesus implies in calling the disciples' attention to the beauty of the flowers growing in a field or the fall of a sparrow, God rules the world unnoticed by unperceptive or unappreciative humans.

Luke's assertion that the kingdom rules everywhere, even among Jesus' opponents, has another parallel in the apocryphal Gospel of Thomas, which may preserve some of Jesus' authentic sayings. Here Jesus is represented as stating that

> the Kingdom is inside you, and it is outside of you. When you come to know yourselves, then you will become known, and you will realize that it is you who are the sons of the living Father. But if you do not know yourselves, you dwell in poverty and it is you who are that poverty.
>
> Gos. Thom. 3

Whereas the Lukan saying depicts the kingdom appearing through Jesus' presence, that in Thomas seems to equate it with a state of heightened spiritual awareness. Knowing the true "self" (the divine "image" within each person) means awakening to one's kinship with God. Remaining ignorant of the "god within" is "poverty." Despite alleged Gnostic elements in the Thomas saying, this concept of an indwelling divine spirit—perhaps similar to what Paul called the "mystery" of "Christ in [the believer]" (Col. 1:27)—may represent an integral part of Jesus' kingdom concept.

Scholars who champion a noneschatological Jesus believe that the historical Galilean did not preach about a future eschatological kingdom of God, violently imposed by divine intervention. Instead, he taught that God's rule is presently active in creation but difficult for most people to perceive. According to this view, Jesus had a highly subtle sense of time, a vision of divine immanence in which God's eternal presence operates unseen, drawing and guiding into his dominion those who respond to his will. Entering God's domain means discerning and embracing the simultaneity of present and future, which combine into a profound sense of the unbroken continuity of divine rule.

Many other scholars object that if Jesus' concept of seeking the kingdom meant a persistent quest for recognizing God's "finger" at work in the overfamiliar world, how can one account for an apocalyptically oriented John the Baptist, an eschatologically driven Paul, and an early church that anticipated Christ's Second Coming at any moment? (1 Thess. 4:15–17; Mark 13.) Would it not be more reasonable to assume that Jesus was an eschatological prophet similar to his predecessors, many Jewish contemporaries, and successors? One possible defense of a noneschatological view of Jesus is that the Gospel traditions make it clear that even his closest followers did not understand him. Misconstruing his complex and subtle vision of divine sovereignty, more pedestrian followers simply applied their inherited eschatological ideas to the one they accepted as Lord. Indeed, if Jesus had *not* taught that the kingdom reigns now in those doing the divine will, how did his apocalyptist followers conceive of such sayings as those expressed in Luke 11:20 and 17:20–21 and Gospel of Thomas 3 and 113? Because these sayings run counter to the trend of later eschatologically oriented Christianity, they pass the test of distinctiveness and may possibly represent Jesus' actual views. Still other scholars observe that like many first-century Jews, Jesus may have promoted a double vision of the kingdom: God rules now through the work of his servants, but full implementation of divine sovereignty lies in the future.

WISDOM AND THE KINGDOM OF GOD

In contrast to Mark and Matthew, who apparently were inspired by the apocalyptic disaster that befell Judea in 70 C.E., the authors of John and Thomas show that it was possible to follow a Jesus who was fundamentally an exponent of divine Wisdom rather than a purveyor of eschatological judgment. The Johannine writer rarely mentions the kingdom as an integral part of Jesus' teaching, but he may convey a significant historical truth when he makes the nature of Jesus' personal kingship the crucial issue on which Pilate's execution of Jesus hinges (John 18:33–19:22). During the confrontation with Pilate, the Johannine Jesus states that his kingdom is not of this world — that it is not political — but he fails to define either his government or his own kingly role (John 18:36).

John nonetheless gives his readers a relatively clear idea of what Jesus' kingdom involves. From the outset of his Gospel, the author identifies Jesus with the eternal Word, the expression of immortal Wisdom by and through which God created the universe (John 1:1–18; Prov. 8:22–36). In his person, Jesus reveals and shares with others the vital Wisdom by which God rules and communicates his will. As noted previously, John firmly links Jesus with Israel's **wisdom literature**, the teachings of which associate the wise person with God's *basileia*— heavenly kingship.

The deuterocanonical Wisdom of Solomon expresses the affinity between Wisdom and divine kingship that may have influenced John's view of Jesus:

> For she [Wisdom] ranges [the earth] in search of those who are worthy of her. . . . The true beginning of wisdom is the desire to learn, and a concern for learning means the keeping of her laws; to keep her laws is a warrant of immortality; and immortality brings a man near to God. Thus the desire of wisdom leads to kingly stature [a *basileia*].
>
> Wisd. of Sol. 6:16–20

In this passage, learning and keeping God's wise laws, the principles by which he orders the cosmos, lead to eternal life and make the obedient possessor of Wisdom a king.

Wisdom also reveals the kingdom of God:

> She [Wisdom] guided him [Jacob, the embodiment of Israel] on straight paths; she showed him the *basileia tou theou* [literally, the kingdom or sovereignty of God].
>
> Wisd. of Sol. 10:10

In Israel's wisdom writings, Wisdom (Sophia, a personification of God's primary attribute) imparts knowledge, divine favor, and immortal life (Prov. 2:1–10; Job 28:12–23; Ecclus. 24; Wisd. of Sol. 8:4, 13). She discloses secrets of the unseen world to those who seek her, satisfying their intellectual and spiritual thirst (Wisd. of Sol. 7:17–29). The references to Jesus' unveiling the "secret" or "mystery of the kingdom of God" in Mark (4:11) and Secret Mark (2:10) may preserve a parallel to the Johannine tradition that Jesus' teaching focuses not on the eschatological, but on Wisdom's revelation of previously hidden cosmic truths.

According to this view of Jesus' kingdom message, Jesus teaches that followers must come under God's rule by imitating and participating in the divine *basileia*. As noted previously, *basileia* implies kingly autonomy, freedom, and self-determination — living one's life as the master of one's situation. The Johannine Jesus tells his followers that he has already "conquered the world" (John 16:33). The self-confidence or "authority" with which Jesus habitually teaches may derive from his profound sense of possessing the celestial Wisdom that sets people free (Matt. 7:28–29; Mark 1:22; John 8:22). At liberty to proclaim his personal views on the Torah, he inevitably antagonizes many rival teachers of the Law. As a sage through whom Wisdom speaks, he is also free to recognize his own kingship — the *basileia* that Wisdom imparts (Wisd. 6:17–20; 10:10). If Jesus publicly equated his wisdom teaching with kingship, the connection may have inspired Pilate's suspicion. As governor for Rome, Pilate could tolerate no Jew claiming to be a king of any kind.

The Johannine Jesus informs his disciples that he fully reveals the Father, the supreme reality with whom he — and they — enjoy a life-giving unity (John 17:1–8, 20–23). Spiritual union with the Deity confers a power upon Jesus' disciples that will enable them to accomplish greater deeds than he could (John 14:10–14). The arrival of the Paraclete, or Spirit of Truth, endows believers with additional heaven-sent Wisdom and allows them to continue imitating Jesus' example of kingly rulership. Indeed, the Paraclete manifests the same power of *basileia* that characterizes Jesus (John 16:7–15). Initiated into the mystery of divinity and empowered by the Spirit, the Johannine disciple possesses a kingdom authority resembling that of Jesus himself (John 14:12–21).

Scholars in large part agree that the historical Jesus taught about God's kingdom (whatever his precise meaning for the phrase), but most question the belief that he taught about himself. Although he seems to have perceived the world and his mission from the vantage point of one who holds a peculiarly close relationship to God, he is not believed to have called himself Christ, Son of God, or the Holy One of Israel. All these honorific titles, scholars believe, were bestowed upon him posthumously by a community that—in retrospect—recognized him as Israel's Messiah and as God's chief agent, the means by which the Deity reconciles humanity to himself. In telling Jesus' story so that readers could understand his true significance, it was natural for the Gospel writers to apply titles such as *Christ* and *Son of God* to the historical figure. In the Evangelists' view, they could not write the truth about who Jesus was unless they presented him in the light of his resurrection and glorification. The Galilean prophet and teacher who had challenged the world's norms in the name of a radical egalitarianism for all God's children was—by his continuing life in the believing community—vindicated as divine, the Wisdom and love of God made flesh.

QUESTIONS FOR REVIEW

1. Define the problem confronting scholars in their quest to find the historical Jesus. In what ways do the four Gospel writers' theological portraits of Jesus make it difficult to determine exactly what the man Jesus said and did? Besides the Gospels, which were written by believers in Jesus' unique divinity, what other first-century sources do we have that might help illuminate his life?

2. When did the modern quest to discover the "real" Jesus begin, and what are its goals? Describe the picture of an "apocalyptic" Jesus that Albert Schweitzer drew in his famous *Quest of the Historical Jesus*. What different conclusions about Jesus' teachings have some later scholars drawn? Describe the work of the Jesus Seminar.

3. Summarize some of the criteria scholars use to screen for authenticity the Gospel sayings ascribed to Jesus, including the tests of orality, distinctiveness, dissimilarity, and awkwardness (the "embarrassment" factor). What standards can we use to distinguish between what Jesus himself taught and what the believing community may have attributed to him later?

4. Describe several areas in which some scholars generally agree about the historical Jesus. Review Jesus' teaching about the "kingdom of God" as it appears in the Synoptic Gospels.

QUESTIONS FOR DISCUSSION AND REFLECTION

1. How can we reconstruct a coherent picture of Jesus and his teaching using the source materials currently available? What sources do you regard as most trustworthy, as most likely to represent Jesus as he might have been rather than as he appeared to the believing community that worshiped him?

2. Teachings about the kingdom or rule of God are central to Jesus' message. After analyzing the different kinds of kingdom sayings found in the Gospels, do you find a consistent pattern of meaning in some or all of the sayings? How are readers likely to project their own values onto the recorded sayings and accept or stress only those that accord with their own preconceptions?

3. Do we possess any sure means of finding out what Jesus actually thought about himself and his purpose? In reading the four Gospels, do you detect any clues that reliably indicate the nature of Jesus' own self-awareness? Explain your answer.

4. Contrast the Synoptic portrait of Jesus as an apocalyptic exorcist and preacher with John's portrayal of him as a revealer of heavenly Wisdom. How would you distinguish Mark's idea of Jesus' kingdom from John's concept of Jesus' kingship?

5. The communities that produced the Synoptic Gospels clearly had very different traditions about Jesus from those treasured in the group that created John's Gospel. How do you account for such divergent views about Jesus' nature and teaching in two roughly contemporaneous Christian communities? In what ways do these divergent traditions about Jesus' teaching make it difficult to define the term *kingdom* as Jesus uses it?

TERMS AND CONCEPTS TO REMEMBER

basileia tou theou
(kingdom of God)
criteria for testing
Jesus' authentic sayings
Jesus as apocalyptist

realized eschatology
relationship of
divine Wisdom
and *basileia*
Schweitzer, Albert

RECOMMENDED READING

Allison, Dale C. *Jesus of Nazareth: Millenarian Prophet.* Minneapolis: Fortress Press, 1998. Provides cogent arguments supporting an apocalyptic view of Jesus' teaching.

Borg, Marcus J. *Jesus: A New Vision.* San Francisco: Harper & Row, 1988. A scholarly and perceptive study showing that the historical Jesus' message was not primarily eschatological.

———. *Jesus at 2000.* San Francisco: HarperSanFrancisco, 1996. A collection of scholarly papers debating Jesus' historical, religious, and cultural significance on the two thousandth anniversary of his birth.

Bultmann, Rudolf. *History of the Synoptic Tradition,* rev. ed. Translated by John Marsh. San Francisco: Harper & Row, 1961. A major achievement in New Testament scholarship; shows how the Evangelists reinterpreted Jesus mythically.

Chilton, Bruce. *Rabbi Jesus: An Intimate Biography.* New York: Doubleday, 2000. Places Jesus' life and teachings within their first-century Jewish context.

Chilton, Bruce, and Evans, Craig A., eds. *Studying the Historical Jesus: Evaluations of the State of Current Research.* Kinderhook, N.Y.: Brill, 1994. A collection of valuable essays by major New Testament scholars.

Crossan, John Dominic. *The Historical Jesus: The Life of a Mediterranean Peasant.* San Francisco: Harper SanFrancisco, 1991. A distinctive scholarly interpretation of Jesus as a sage advocating radical social egalitarianism.

———. *Jesus: A Revolutionary Biography.* San Francisco: HarperSanFrancisco, 1994. A distillation of Crossan's earlier book for the general reader.

Ehrman, Bart D. *Jesus: Apocalyptic Prophet of the New Millennium.* New York: Oxford University Press, 1999. Stresses Jesus' eschatological expectation of God's kingdom.

Fredriksen, Paula. *Jesus of Nazareth, King of the Jews: A Jewish Life and the Emergence of Christianity.* New York: Knopf, 1999. Places Jesus firmly in the context of apocalyptic Judaism.

Funk, Robert W., and the Jesus Seminar. *The Acts of Jesus: What Did Jesus Really Do?* San Francisco: HarperSanFrancisco, 1998. A radical evaluation of Jesus' historical actions that portrays Jesus as a healer, exorcist, and wisdom teacher who associated with social outcasts.

———. *The Gospel of Jesus According to the Jesus Seminar.* Santa Rosa, Calif.: Polebridge Press, 1999. Portrays Jesus using only sayings and actions judged historically reliable.

Funk, Robert W.; Hoover, Roy W.; and the Jesus Seminar. *The Five Gospels: The Search for the Authentic Words of Jesus.* A Polebridge Press Book. New York: Macmillan, 1993. Features a highly colloquial translation of the canonical Gospels and Thomas, with Jesus' authentic words printed in red or pink, doubtful sayings in gray, and speeches ascribed to him by tradition or Gospel authors in black.

Jacobson, Arland D. *The First Gospel: An Introduction to Q.* Sonoma, Calif.: Polebridge Press, 1992. A study and tentative reconstruction of material in the hypothetical sayings source.

Johnson, Luke T. *The Real Jesus: The Misguided Quest for the Historical Jesus and the Truth of the Traditional Gospels.* San Francisco: HarperSanFrancisco, 1995. Challenges the Jesus Seminar's methodology without providing a persuasive alternative.

Josephus, Flavius. *Josephus: Complete Works.* Translated by W. Whiston. Grand Rapids, Mich.: Kregel, 1960. A dated translation but containing the complete texts of *The Antiquities of the Jews* and *The Jewish War,* as well as brief references to Jesus, John the Baptist, and Jesus' brother James.

———. *The Jewish War,* rev. ed. Translated by G. A. Williamson. Edited by E. M. Smallwood. New York: Penguin Books, 1981. A modern translation of Josephus's eyewitness account of the Jewish revolt and its consequences.

Kloppenborg, John S. *The Formation of Q: Trajectories in Ancient Wisdom Collections.* Philadelphia: Trinity Press International, 2000.

Kloppenborg, John S.; Meyer, Marvin W.; Patterson, Stephen J.; and Steinhauser, Michael G. *Q Thomas Reader.* Sonoma, Calif.: Polebridge Press, 1990.

Koester, Helmut. *Ancient Christian Gospels: Their History and Development.* Philadelphia: Trinity Press International, 1990. A thorough and detailed study of the Gospels' literary evolution; for more advanced students.

Mack, Burton I. "The Kingdom Sayings in Mark." *Forum* 3(1) (1987): 3–47. Argues that Jesus' kingdom teachings were not eschatological.

Meier, John P. *A Marginal Jew: Rethinking the Historical Jesus,* Vols. 1 and 2. New York: Doubleday, 1991 (vol. 1), 1994 (vol. 2). The first two volumes of a projected four-part biography by an eminent New Testament scholar, the most comprehensive study to date.

Meyer, Ben. "Jesus Christ." In D. N. Freedman, ed., *The Anchor Bible Dictionary,* pp. 773–796. New York: Doubleday, 1992. Provides a good introductory review of contemporary scholarship on Jesus' life and teachings.

Miller, Robert J. *The Complete Gospels: Annotated Scholars Version*, 2nd ed. San Francisco: HarperSanFrancisco, 1994. Includes all known Gospels, including fragments, produced during the first three Christian centuries.

Patterson, Stephen J. and Robinson, James M. *The Fifth Gospel: The Gospel of Thomas Comes of Age*. Philadelphia: Trinity Press International, 2000. Includes a new translation and interpretative commentary.

Robinson, James M., ed. *The Nag Hammadi Library*, 3rd ed. San Francisco: Harper & Row, 1988. Contains English translations of Christian documents found at Nag Hammadi.

Robinson, John A. T. *Jesus and His Coming*. Philadelphia: Westminster Press, 1979. Argues that Jesus was not an apocayptist and that beliefs about his Second Coming developed from a misunderstanding of his teachings.

Sanders, E. P. *Jesus and Judaism*. Philadelphia: Fortress Press, 1985. A scholarly and highly readable evaluation of the Gospel traditions about Jesus and his message, particularly about the kingdom and its original meaning in the context of Palestinian Judaisms.

———. *The Historical Figure of Jesus*. New York: Viking Press, 1994. A readable work of solid scholarship.

Schweitzer, Albert. *The Quest of the Historical Jesus: A Critical Study of Its Progress from Reimarus to Wrede*. New York: Macmillan, 1961 (1906). Raises issues that still influence scholars' search for the real figure of history.

Sheehan, Thomas. *The First Coming: How the Kingdom of God Became Christianity*. New York: Random House, 1986. A perceptive scholar's careful account of historical and theological developments that transformed the Jesus of history into the Christ of faith.

Stegemann, Ekkhard W., and Stegemann, Wolfgang. *The Jesus Movement: A Social History of Its First Century*. Minneapolis: Fortress Press, 1999. A detailed survey first-century Mediterranean society in general and Palestinian Judaism in particular.

Stein, Robert H. *Jesus the Messiah*. Downers Grove, Ill.: InterVarsity Press, 1996.

Tatum, W. Barnes. *In Quest of Jesus*, rev. ed.: Nashville: Abingdon Press, 1999. An enlarged edition offering an excellent introduction to scholarly investigations of the historical Jesus.

Theissen, Gerd, and Merz, Annette. *The Historical Jesus: A Comprehensive Guide*. Minneapolis: Fortress Press, 1998. A detailed review of contemporary Jesus scholarship.

Van Voorst, Robert E. *Jesus Outside the New Testament: An Introduction to the Ancient Evidence*. Grand Rapids, Mich.: Eerdmans, 2000. Examines all known ancient noncnonical references to Jesus.

Verbin, John S., and Kloppenburg, John S. *Excavating Q: The History and Setting of the Sayings Gospel*. Minneapolis: Fortress Press, 2000. Examines the origins and contents of hypothetical collection of Jesus; sayings.

Witherington, Ben, III. *The Jesus Quest: The Third Search for the Jew of Nazareth*. Downers Grove, Ill.: InterVarsity Press, 1995. A conventional defense of traditional religious views of Jesus.

Wright, N. T. *The Original Jesus*. Grand Rapids, Mich.: Eerdmans, 1996. A conventional evaluation of the historical Jesus.

Aids for Comparing Gospel Texts

Aland, Kurt, ed. *Synopsis of the Four Gospels*. English ed. New York: United Bible Societies, 1985. A helpful presentation of parallels among the four canonical Gospels.

Crossan, John D., ed. *Sayings Parallels: A Workbook for the Jesus Tradition*. Philadelphia: Fortress Press, 1986. A comprehensive collection of Jesus' sayings arranged to include texts for all four canonical Gospels plus those from apocryphal sources, including the Gospel of Thomas and the Apocryphon of James.

Funk, R, W. *New Gospel Parallels*. Vols. 1 and 2, *Foundations and Facets*. Philadelphia: Fortress Press, 1985. A major achievement in New Testament scholarship. Volume 1 provides parallels to the three Synoptic Gospels; Volume 2 assembles parallels to the Gospels of John, Thomas, and Peter, the Infancy Gospel of Thomas, the Protoevangelium of James, the Acts of Pilate, and various manuscript fragments.

CHAPTER 12

A Christian History and the Pauline Letters

Key Topics/Themes

Like the second major division of the Hebrew Bible (the Prophets) on which it is partially modeled, the second part of the New Testament consists of two subunits: a theologically oriented historical narrative (the Book of Acts) and a collection of documents containing authoritative messages for the believing community (the letters of Paul). Whereas the four Gospel accounts of Jesus' life and teachings take place entirely in a Palestinian Jewish environment, this second section focuses on the larger Greco-Roman world, describing the process by which an originally Jewish messianic movement was transformed into an international faith composed mainly of Gentiles. After emphasizing the Jewish roots of Christianity, with its center at a Jerusalem commune, Acts then narrates "the new way's" numerical growth and geographical expansion into the northeastern Roman Empire, a missionary effort spearheaded by Paul. The only New Testament figure who is both a literary character (dominating the second half of Acts) and an au-

thor of canonical texts, Paul preached a revolutionary doctrine: faith in Christ had replaced obedience to the Mosaic Torah as the means of humanity's salvation. Writing to newly established urban churches in Greece, Italy, and Asia Minor, Paul insisted that all people — regardless of ethnic background — who trusted in Christ's saving power were "children of Abraham" and heirs to the divine promises. So pervasive was Paul's influence on Western Christianity that after his death, additional letters were written in his name and were eventually included in the canon.

KEY QUESTIONS

How did a Jewish messianic movement develop into a Gentile religion? What sequences of events and ideas effected this transformation? How is it that Paul, who did not know the historical Jesus, became his chief interpreter? Why did Paul's innovative "gospel" of salvation by faith appeal more to Gentiles than to Jews?

The Book of Acts: A Story of Christian Beginnings

KEY TOPICS/THEMES

In the Book of Acts, Luke continues his two-part narrative of Christian origins, depicting characters who, like Jesus, are models of Christian behavior and service. This theologically shaped account of the early church emphasized many of the same themes that dominated Luke's Gospel. First, God's ancient promises to Israel through Abraham and Moses are fulfilled in the life and work of Jesus and his successors, who constitute a Spirit-blessed community, the true Israel. Second, emphasizing that "the new way [Christianity]" is a universal means of salvation encompassing all nations, Jewish and Gentile alike, Luke then shows biblical promises being fulfilled when the Jewish disciples are empowered by the Holy Spirit at Pentecost (2:1–47). Third, the author illustrates divine promises were extended to non-Jewish peoples, beginning with campaigns in Samaria and Syria (8:1–12:25). The climactic events of this first section are the conversions of Paul, a Pharisee (Ch. 9), and Cornelius, a Roman soldier, the first Gentile anointed by the Holy Spirit (Chs. 10–11).

In the second part of Acts (Chs. 13–28), Luke focuses almost exclusively on the travels of Paul, who leads a successful mission to Gentiles in Asia Minor and then carries the new religion into Europe, arriving in Rome about 60 C.E. Arguing that Christianity is a natural extension of Judaism that offers no threat to the Roman state, Luke designs his narrative to demonstrate that the church's task is to create an international and ethnically diverse community, a work that extends indefinitely into the future (28:28).

KEY QUESTIONS

How does Acts show Jesus' disciples, motivated by the same Spirit that had inspired Jesus, carrying his work into the Greco-Roman world? What is Paul's contribution to the international mission?

A continuation of Luke's Gospel, the Book of Acts is an idealized story of Christian beginnings. Addressing his second volume to the same (otherwise unknown) Theophilus, the author creates a step-by-step account of early Christianity's progression from a Jewish apocalyptic movement to a largely Gentile faith destined to hold an honorable place in the Greco-Roman world. A spirited defense of "the new way" (9:2), Acts presents Christianity as a legitimate religion that does not threaten the Roman government, dramatically staging a series of courtroom scenes in which Roman magistrates and governors find Christians innocent of any illegal activity. At the same time, Luke structures his story to demonstrate that the new faith's rapid transition from a Jewish to a mostly Gentile phenomenon directly fulfills God's will. The book's linear progression — from Jerusalem, where Palestinian disciples and members of Jesus' family lead the church, to Rome, where Paul, an advocate of Hellenistic Christianity, vows to focus exclusively on converting Gentiles — illustrates the author's controlling purpose: Through the proclamation of the risen Lord, God opens the way for "all peoples" to join his flock (10:35–48). (See Box 12.1.)

In composing his story, the author (whom we call Luke) is highly selective in his use of the oral "traditions" and "eyewitness" reports on which Acts presumably is based (cf. Luke 1:1–4). Although he lists the names of the original eleven apostles (1:13), Luke tells us almost nothing about most of them. Instead, he concentrates on only a few figures, using them to represent crucial stages in early Christianity's swift transition from a Jewish to a Gentile movement. The apostle Peter, representing Palestinian Jewish Christianity and the original Jerusalem church, presides over the first half of Acts (Chs. 1–12). Paul, exemplifying Hellenistic Christianity's mission to the Gentiles, dominates the second half (Chs. 13–28). Except for brief references to James and John, the sons of Zebedee (3:1–4:22; 12:1–3; cf. Gal. 2:6–10), Luke rarely mentions Jesus' Galilean disciples or their activities. Whatever anecdotes about other apostles the author may have heard, he does not include them in his narrative; nor does he explain how some major churches, such as that of Rome were founded. More significant, although Paul is Luke's heroic exemplar of true Christianity, the author does not

Box 12.1 Major Milestones in the Book of Acts

According to Acts's version of Christian origins, the new faith began at a particular moment in time—at the Jewish Feast of Pentecost, in Jerusalem, when the Holy Spirit descended upon a gathering of Jesus' Galilean disciples (Acts 2). In Luke's theologically oriented account, the Jesus movement—called "the new way" (9:2)—is directed by the same Spirit that had anointed Jesus at his baptism and represents a momentous new development in God's relationship with all humanity. Expanding rapidly from its original geographical center in Jerusalem into the surrounding countryside of Judea and Samaria, early Christianity symbolically reaches "the ends of the earth" when Paul, by then a Roman prisoner, reaches the imperial capital in Rome (cf 1:8).

In Luke's carefully structured presentation, Christianity's growth in adherents and geographical expansion are marked by significant milestones, crucial events at which it enters into a new stage of development. Each step along the evolutionary path from a Palestinian Jewish sect to a largely Gentile faith preached throughout the Greco-Roman world is indicated by a representative episode, headlining the author's "good news" bulletins.

1. The Christian church is born in Jerusalem—the Holy Spirit anoints 120 disciples at Pentecost, followed by mass conversions to the new Jesus movement (2:1–47).

2. Peter performs the first miraculous cure "in Jesus' name" (3:1–10), continuing Jesus' work

3. Stephen, a "Hellenist" Jew, becomes the first Christian martyr (6:8–7:60); a zealous Torah observer named Saul (Paul) approves Stephen's execution (7:59; 8:1–3).

4. Another Hellenist, Philip, makes the first non-Jewish converts—a sorcerer and a eunuch (8:4–40).

5. Saul (Paul) of Tarsus, while fiercely persecuting "the way," is suddenly converted by a vision of the risen Jesus on the road to Damascus (9:1–30; cf. 22:6–11; 26:12–19).

6. Peter converts the Roman centurion Cornelius, who becomes the first non-Jew to receive the Holy Spirit (10:1–42). This event foreshadows the transition to eventual Gentile dominance of the church.

7. Believers in Jesus are first called "Christians" in Antioch, Syria, which becomes the second major center of Christianity (11:19–26).

8. James, the son of Zebedee and brother of John, becomes the first member of the Twelve to suffer martyrdom (12:1–3); he is beheaded by Herod Agrippa I, who is promptly "eaten up with worms" (c. 44 C.E.) (12:21–23).

9. Paul, following Barnabas, makes his first missionary journey from Antioch to Asia Minor (modern Turkey) (13:1–14:28), carrying Pauline Christianity to the Greek-speaking world.

10. The first church council, held at Jerusalem to discuss whether Gentile converts must observe Mosaic Law, decides in favor of admitting uncircumcised males, opening "the way" to all nationalities (15:1–35) and freeing converts from Torah observance:

11. Carrying the faith from western Asia to Europe, Paul makes his first missionary tour of Greece, founding churches at Philippi, Thessalonica, and Corinth (16:9–18:23).

12. An angry Jerusalem mob attacks Paul for allegedly desecrating the Temple; he is arrested by a Roman officer (21:15–22:29). After two years in a Caesarea prison, Paul appears before Governor Festus and Herod Agrippa II (25:6–32), fulfilling the risen Jesus' prediction that Paul will testify "before kings" (9:15).

13. Exercising his right as a Roman citizen, Paul is sent to Rome for trial; he survives a near-fatal shipwreck near Crete (27:9–44). Under house arrest in Rome, Paul gives up on trying to convert his fellow Jews and vows to focus exclusively on recruiting Gentiles (28:16–30).

actually portray Paul as he reveals himself in his letters, omitting controversial Pauline ideas and even contradicting some of Paul's own versions of events.

In looking at maps depicting Paul's journeys (see Figures 12.2, 12.3, and 12.6), it is immediately obvious that Luke is interested in only one trajectory of Christianity's geographical expansion—that which resulted in the founding of Pauline churches in Asia Minor and Greece and in Paul's preaching in Rome. Focusing exclusively on the northeastern Mediterranean region, Luke says nothing about other large areas where churches were concurrently being established, such as those in Egypt, Cyrene, and other locations in North Africa. According to tradition, the author of Mark's Gospel founded a church in Alexandria (Eusebius, *History* 2.16), where the noncanonical Secret Mark was also produced. Although we cannot be sure why Luke ignores the southern Mediterranean churches, his silence may result from a strong preference for Pauline Christianity, a branch of the faith that historically came to dominate the Western church.

In reading Acts, we must remember that Luke's account of early Christianity is as theologically oriented as his Gospel. Luke believes that the apostles and missionaries who brought "the new way" to Greece and Rome were led by the same Holy Spirit that inspired Jesus. Continuing Jesus's ministry in the world, the disciples perform similar miracles—exorcisms, healings, and resuscitations of the dead—thereby demonstrating divine gifts virtually identical to those of Jesus. For Luke, the church preserves and maintains the same ethical and spiritual qualities that distinguished Jesus' career, making the "acts of the apostles" a true sequel to the Gospel story.

The Divine Plan of Humanity's Salvation

The incidents from early Christianity that Luke chose to include in Acts are arranged to express the author's overarching theme: the Spirit-directed growth of the church and its expansion westward from Palestine to Italy. In general, the narrative advances chronologically, showing the religion's incremental expansion into new geographical areas. Luke's organizing principle is stated in Acts 1:8, in which the risen Jesus gives the disciples his final command: They are to "bear witness" to him "in Jerusalem, and all over Judea and Samaria, and away to the ends of the earth."

Acts thus begins in Jerusalem (Chs. 1–7), records a mission to Samaria (Ch. 8), gives a detailed account of Paul's three missionary journeys throughout Asia Minor and Greece, and concludes with Paul's arrival in Rome, heart of the Roman Empire, and perhaps representing "the ends of the earth" (Chs. 13–28).

LUKE'S MAJOR THEME: GOD'S SPIRIT OPERATING IN HUMAN HISTORY

In tracing Christianity's course from its Palestinian roots to Gentile soil, Luke illustrates the manner in which God has kept his biblical promises to Israel. Jesus and his Jewish followers are the fulfillment of Israel's prophetic goals, a demonstration of God's faithfulness that will reassure Theophilus and other Gentiles who join their ranks. At the end of his Gospel and the beginning of Acts, Luke takes pains to remind readers of Israel's hopes for a Davidic king. The disciples approaching Jerusalem wonder if the kingdom is at last about to materialize (Luke 19:11), a question they reformulate to Jesus immediately before his ascension to heaven. "Lord, is this the time when you are to establish once again the sovereignty of Israel?" (Acts 1:6). Jesus' answer—that they must remain in Jerusalem to "receive power" from above and then evangelize the earth—implies a positive response to their question. In Luke's view, God indeed reestablishes his rule over true citizens of Israel, the Jewish disciples of Jesus who represent the covenant people.

Luke further highlights the theme of Israel's restoration when the Eleven elect a replacement for Judas Iscariot (who had committed suicide), thus re-creating a leadership of Twelve, symbolic of Israel's twelve tribes (1:23–26). Once this continuity between Israel and the Christian community has been affirmed, however, Luke never again refers to the replacement (Matthias) or to any of the Twelve except for Peter and (briefly) John. (James, John's brother, is mentioned only to record his beheading by Herod Agrippa I [12:2].)

At **Pentecost**, when the Lukan Peter states that God's eschatological promise of Israel's Spirit-anointing is fulfilled (2:14–36), 3000 Jews join the Galilean disciples (2:37–41). Throughout both his Gospel and Acts, Luke is careful to distinguish the Jewish people, many of whom accept Jesus as the national Messiah, from the small group of their priestly leaders who had advocated Jesus' execution. Not only had the Jews as a whole — including their "rulers"— acted in ignorance of Jesus' identity, but it was also God's foreordained will that the Messiah *had* to suffer — no human action could have prevented it (3:17–24).

Peter's second Jerusalem speech emphasizes the Lukan theme that Jews remain the "heirs of the prophets" and "within the covenant" that God made with Abraham. Hence, God sent his "servant" and offered his "blessing" to them first, keeping the oath he had sworn to Israel's patriarchs and prophets (3:25–26). As Luke presents his history of salvation, Jerusalem and its Temple — where Pharisees and Jewish Christians worship side by side — are the nucleus of God's redemptive acts for all humanity.

Even when traveling in Gentile territories, the Lukan Paul consistently offers his message first to members of the local synagogues, before proselytizing Syrians or Greeks. Although Paul repeatedly threatens to devote himself entirely to recruiting Gentile believers, he continues to minister to fellow Jews. At the end of Acts, however, Paul cites a portentous verse from Isaiah 6 about God's people being deaf and blind to his prophetic word. (This is the same passage that Mark had used to explain why Jesus spoke in parables — to *prevent* his hearers from understanding him [cf. Mark 4:10–12; Acts 28:23–27].) When an exasperated Paul declares that henceforth he will concentrate all his efforts on "the Gentiles" because "the Gentiles will listen" (28:28), he expresses an unforseen twist of history. By the time Luke wrote the sequel to his Gospel, Christianity, originally a Jewish phenomenon, had become a faith dominated by Gentiles. In this paradoxical event, Luke saw God's will accomplished: the gathering of every ethnic and national group into a universal worshiping community.

LUKE'S USE OF SPEECHES

Like other historians of his day, Luke acribes long, elaborate speeches to his leading characters, such as Peter, Stephen, James, and Paul. But whoever the speaker, most of the speeches sound much alike in both style and thought. This similarity among Acts' many discourses, as well as the fact that they seem to reflect attitudes prevalent in the author's time rather than those of the historical figures he describes, suggests to most scholars that they are largely Luke's own compositions. In the absence of exact transcriptions of apostolic speeches, many of which were delivered amid noisy and unruly crowds, Luke apparently follows the standard practice of Greco-Roman authors by supplementing what was remembered with material of his own creation. Ancient historians and biographers like Thucydides, Livy, Tacitus, and Plutarch commonly enlivened their narratives with speeches put in the mouths of historical characters. The classical writer composed such discourses based on his conception of the speaker's character and major concerns at the time the speech was given. He was not expected to reproduce a particular speech exactly as it was delivered. Thucydides explains the historian's method clearly and briefly:

> I have found it difficult to remember the precise words used in the speeches which I listened to myself and my various informants have experienced the same difficulty; so my method has been, while keeping as closely as possible to the general sense of the words that were actually used, to make the speaker say what, in my opinion, was called for by each occasion.
>
> *The Peloponnesian War* I.22

In short, while attempting to reproduce the "general sense" of what people said, Thucydides created their speeches according to his understanding of what "was called for by the occasion." Although we cannot know the extent to which Luke's speeches reflect ideas expressed in generations before his time, they serve the important purpose of illustrating character and preserving aspects of early apostolic teaching.

Organization   Luke arranges his narrative in ten major sections:

1. Prologue and account of Jesus' ascension (1:1–11)
2. Founding of the Jerusalem church (1:12–2:47)
3. Work of Peter and the apostles (3:1–5:42)
4. Persecutions of the "Hellenist" Jewish Christians and the first missions (6:1–8:40)
5. Preparation for the Gentile mission: the conversions of Paul and Cornelius (9:1–12:25)
6. First missionary journey of Barnabas and Paul: the Jerusalem conference (13:1–15:35)
7. Paul's second missionary journey: evangelizing Greece (16:1–18:21)
8. Paul's third missionary journey: revisiting Asia Minor and Greece (18:22–20:38)
9. Paul's arrest in Jerusalem and imprisonment in Caesarea (21:1–26:32)
10. Paul's journey to Rome and his preaching to Roman Jews (27:1–28:31)

PROLOGUE AND ASCENSION

Luke is the only New Testament writer to state that Jesus' postresurrection appearances spanned a period of forty days and to describe his visible **ascension** to heaven, indicating that he would return in a similar manner (1:9–11). He is also the only author to report that **Matthias** was chosen to replace **Judas Iscariot** (1:12–26), apparently to maintain an apostolic membership of twelve, symbolizing the complete tribes of Israel. This passage also defines Luke's understanding of an **apostle**, a person who had physically accompanied Jesus during his entire ministry and witnessed his resurrection (1:21–22). Because Paul had not personally known Jesus, Luke almost never calls him an apostle, although in his letters Paul passionately fights to make others acknowledge his right to that title (see Gal. 1).

FOUNDING THE JERUSALEM CHURCH: THE ROLE OF THE HOLY SPIRIT

The first two chapters emphasize the divine power that transforms the **Jerusalem church** from a group of about 120 persons (1:15) to several thousand worshipers, including some priests (2:41; 4:4; 5:14–16; 6:1, 7). Symbolically rendered as wind and flame, the Holy Spirit inspires the disciples to speak in foreign tongues — representing the multinational nature of Christianity. In a long speech, Peter interprets this ecstatic phenomenon, known as **glossolalia**, as the fulfillment of Joel's prediction that in the last days "everyone" would prophesy (2:1–24; see Joel 2:28–32). See Figure 12.1.

The Lukan Peter says that the Spirit-giving event is linked to "portents in the sky" and other astronomical displays foretold in Joel's prophecy. Interestingly, Luke represents Peter as equating the disciples' religious ectasy with Joel's vision of cosmic upheaval, such as the sun's being darkened and the moon's turning to blood. (This interpretation of the astronomical "portents" as purely metaphorical suggests that the author's references to identical pheonmena in Luke 21:25–28 may also be seen as figurative language rather than as forecasts of literal events in future history.) Luke's main point, however, is that God has anointed his church, giving it the power to preach in every known tongue, the many languages of Pentecost representing the universality of the Christian mission.

Peter's declaration that by resurrecting Jesus, God has made him "both Lord and Messiah" may preserve important aspects of early Christian teaching. It does not reflect Luke's view that Jesus was Messiah during his lifetime. But it may transmit a primitive Jewish-Christian belief that Jesus — the "man singled out by God" — became confirmed as Messiah only upon his ascent to heaven (2:22).

Luke's picture of the original Jerusalem community repeats a theme prominent in his Gospel. He reports that believers sold their possessions, distributing the money to establish a community without rich or poor. Holding "everything" "in common" (2:43–45; 4:32–35), the Jerusalem church meets Jesus' challenge to sacrifice material goods to attain true discipleship (Luke 18:18–30).

THE WORK OF PETER AND THE APOSTLES

In the next section (3:1–5:42), Luke presents a series of dramatic confrontations between the apostles and the Jerusalem authorities. He attributes much of the church's trouble to the Sadducee party, whose priests control the Temple (4:1–6; 5:17–18). By contrast, many Pharisees tend to tolerate or even champion some Christian activities (5:34–40; 23:6–9). During Peter's second hearing before the Sanhedrin, the Pharisee **Gamaliel**, a famous first-century rabbinical scholar, is represented as protecting the infant church.

PERSECUTION OF THE HELLENISTS

In the following section (6:1–8:40), Sadducean hostility focuses on **Stephen**, a leading **Hellenist**, or Greek-speaking Jew of the Diaspora. The episode culminates in Stephen's impassioned "witness" to the Jews who stone him for blasphemy (6:8–7:60). The execution of this first Christian **martyr** and the persecution that follows have the unintended effect of promoting the church's growth. Scattered throughout Judea and Samaria, Hellenist Christians carry the "new Way" to new populations, making such diverse converts as **Simon** the magician (8:9–13) and an Ethiopian eunuch, treasurer of Queen Kandake (Candace) (8:26–40).

CONVERSIONS OF PAUL AND CORNELIUS

Luke represents the progress of Christianity from its origin as a Palestinian Jewish sect to its (hoped-for) status as a world religion in two additional conversion stories of monumental importance. In the first, **Saul of Tarsus**—a Pharisaic persecutor of the church—is converted by a dazzling revelation of the risen Jesus (9:1–19). Henceforth known by his Roman name, **Paul** is seen as God's principal instrument of transforming Christianity into a largely Gentile religion (9:15). More than any other individual, Paul is responsible for the future universality of the Christian church.

Luke devotes the next two chapters (Chs. 10–11) to the second landmark conversion, that of **Cornelius**, the Roman **centurion**, and his household. Although Peter generally represents the conservative Jewish position in the Jerusalem community, the author here shows him as the agent who first opens the church's door to Gentiles. Peter first receives a vision implying that all foods, as well as the non-Jewish people who eat them, are now

Figure 12.1 *The Descent of the Holy Spirit at Pentecost* by El Greco (1541–1614). Depicting the Holy Spirit as a radiant dove and as tongues of flame playing above the disciples' heads, El Greco portrays the miraculous anointing of Jesus' followers at Pentecost. The event parallels Luke's version of Jesus' receiving the Holy Spirit after his baptism.

"clean" and acceptable to God (10:9–16). Following the vision, a delegation brings Peter to Cornelius's house, where Peter, directed by the Holy Spirit, baptizes the entire family (10:1–8, 17–48). Underscoring his view that the Spirit's presence validates a religious decision, Luke shows Cornelius and his entire household speaking in tongues exactly as the Jewish Christians had at Pentecost. Peter then interprets the incident's religious meaning: "God has no favorites, but . . . in every nation . . . the God-fearing [person who] does what is right is acceptable to him" (10:34). Luke also represents Peter as persuading the "circumcision party" (Jewish Christians who strictly observe the Mosaic Torah) in Judea that "God has granted life-giving repentance to the Gentiles also" (11:18). When Gentiles flock to the church at **Antioch**, the Jerusalem Apostles dispatch **Barnabas**, a Greek-speaking Jewish Christian from Cyprus, to report on the situation. Impressed by the converts' zeal, Barnabas imports Paul, who had returned to Tarsus, to help instruct them (11:19–30).

Having demonstrated the fulfillment of Jesus' command to preach "all over Judea and Samaria" (1:8), Acts concludes its first half with an account of Herod Agrippa's persecution of the Jerusalem community. After executing James, "the brother of John," he imprisons Peter, who is promptly delivered by "an angel" (12:1–19). Decisive evidence of divine displeasure at Herod's arrogance is manifested when the king, after accepting divine honors, suddenly dies of a hideous disease, thus ending his reign (41–44 c.e.) over a briefly reunited Jewish kingdom (12:20–23).

FIRST MISSIONARY JOURNEY OF BARNABAS AND PAUL

Acts' remaining sixteen chapters are largely devoted to the international missionary travels of Paul and his fellow workers. The first part of this section shows Barnabas and Paul successfully evangelizing among the "God-fearing" Gentiles who attend synagogues in various Hellenistic cities of Asia Minor (modern Turkey) (Figure 12.2), although local Jewish leaders typically are depicted as violently opposing their efforts (13:1–14:28). Their tour is interrupted, however, when dissen-

Figure 12.2 Paul's first missionary journey. According to Acts, Paul made three major tours through the northeastern Mediterranean region. Although the account in Acts may oversimplify Paul's complex travel itineraries, it correctly shows him focusing his efforts on major urban centers in Asia Minor (modern Turkey).

sion breaks out between Gentile and Jewish Christians over adherence to the Mosaic Torah. Among other requirements, the Judaizing element insists that Gentile converts be circumcised and observe Jewish dietary laws.

The Jerusalem Conference According to Acts 15, the first recorded church council takes place at Jerusalem, where the apostles and "elders" gather to consider whether a believer must first become a Jew in order to be a Christian. Christian Pharisees demand that the entire Torah be kept, but Peter reportedly opposes this (15:10) and, citing his own key role in bringing uncircumcised Gentiles into the church (15:7–11), thereby silences the Judaizers.

Box 12.2 Circumcision, the Consumption of Blood, and the Inclusion of Gentiles

According to Acts 15; the first church conference was held in Jerusalem to decide what parts of the Mosaic Law Gentile converts had to obey to become members of the Christian community, which was then primarily Jewish. In Luke's account, Paul's argument that Gentile males did not need to become circumcised prevailed, with Peter and James, leaders of the Jerusalem church, agreeing. In order to enjoy full fellowship with Jewish Christians, however, it was stipulated that all converts had to observe four provisions of the Torah, which were addressed to both Israelites and foreign residents (15:19–21). Besides abstaining from sexual misconduct (such as various forms of incest listed in Lev. 18), Gentile Christians were also required to obey specified Mosaic dietary prohibitions, such as not consuming blood or eating animals that had not be properly drained of blood (a kosher process described in Lev. 17). In addition, converts were not to consume the flesh of animals sacrificed to alien gods. Whereas Acts shows Paul accepting these restrictions, in his own version of the meeting, he yielded to no Torah demands (Gal: 1–2).

Although both Acts and Paul's letters agree that circumcision is not to be required of Gentile males, many Jewish Christians in Palestine and elsewhere probably thought that they had good scriptural reasons to insist on the requirement. According to the Book of Exodus, any foreigner or alien resident — whether enslaved or free — who wished to participate in the Passover feast had first to be circumcised (Exod.12:43–45, 48–49). Because Exodus specifically states that "the same law shall apply to both the native born and to the alien who is living with you," Jewish Christians, believing that God's law is universal and unchanging, could argue that persons desiring to partake of the Lord's supper (communion), which derived from Jesus' final Passover meal (Mark 14:12–26; Matt. 26:17–30; Luke 22:14–38), must be circumcised in order to qualify for full participation. After all, God's decree that circumcision is the distinguishing mark of membership in the covenant community predates the giving of the Mosaic Law and is the physical expression of Yahweh's original promises to Abraham (Gen. 17).

This dispute between Torah-keeping Christians who advocated **circumcision** and their opponents who denied its necessity bitterly divided the early church. As a church historian writing many years after the issue had been settled in favor of uncircumcised Gentiles, Luke does not attempt to reproduce the hostilities that then prevailed. His purpose is to create a paradigm or model for dealing peacefully with such internal controversies (Box 12.2).

In describing the Jerusalem conference, held about 49 C.E., Luke presents an ideal of orderly procedure in which delegates from Antioch and Christian Pharisees agree unanimously on a compromise solution. After Peter advises against laying the Torah "yoke" upon converts, Barnabas and Paul plead their case for the Gentiles' freedom from Torah rules.

According to Luke, the deciding voice is that of **James** (Jesus' "brother" or kinsman), the person who later succeeds Peter as head of the Jerusalem church. Although Paul's letters paint James as a strongly conservative advocate of circumcision (see Gal. 2), the Lukan James is a "moderate" who imposes only limited Torah mandates. James' dietary restrictions are based on rules from Leviticus, in which both Jews and foreign residents are forbidden to eat meat that has not been drained of blood (15:13–21; Lev. 17–18).

The author completes his example of model church procedures by illustrating the manner in which James's recommendation is carried out. Themes of unity and cooperation dominate Luke's account: The "whole church" agrees to send "unanimously" elected delegates back to Antioch with a letter containing the Jerusalem church's directive. Characteristically, Luke notes that the decision of this precedent-setting conference is also "the decision of the Holy Spirit" (15:22–29). To the author, the church's deliberations reflect the divine will.

Paul's Independence of the Apostolic Church
Luke's picture of Paul's cooperative relationship with the apostolic leadership in Jerusalem differs significantly from the account in Paul's letters. According to Luke, shortly after his conversion Paul went to Jerusalem, where he "tried to join the body of disciples there" but was rebuffed. After Barnabas took this zealous convert under his wing, however, Luke implies that Paul became an accepted member of Jerusalem's Christian community (9:26–30). In his own version of events, Paul categorically denies that he had early contact with the Jerusalem church or that his teaching about Jesus owed anything to his apostolic predecessors. After describing his private "revelation" of the risen Jesus, Paul states: "without consulting any human being, without going up to Jerusalem to see those who were apostles before me, I went off at once to Arabia, and afterwards returned to Damascus" (Gal. 1:17). Three years later, Paul notes, he did make a trip to Jerusalem "to get to know Cephas [Peter]," but he did not confer "with any other of the apostles, except James, the Lord's brother" (Gal. 1:18–19) (Box 12.3). When Paul immediately adds: "What I write is plain truth; before God I am not lying" (Gal. 1:20), he clearly rejects any suggestion that he was ever under the influence or jurisdiction of the Jerusalem leadership.

Given Luke's policy of depicting Paul as an obedient churchman, willingly subject to apostolic decrees, it is not surprising that Acts' picture of the Jerusalem conference contrasts markedly with Paul's eyewitness report (Gal. 2:1–10). Whereas Acts shows the Gentile–Torah issue peacefully and unanimously settled, Paul declared that "not for one moment" did he compromise his position that Gentile Christians should live absolutely free of Torah "bondage." According to Galatians, Paul accepted no restrictions, whereas Acts states that he unhesitatingly agreed to James's four Torah prohibitions. In addition, Paul reveals an attitude toward eating meat sacrificed to Greco-Roman gods that differs from that ascribed to him in Acts (1 Cor. 8:8; 10:27).

Some historians believe that the apostolic decree involving dietary matters may have been is-sued at a later Jerusalem conference, one that Paul did not attend. In this view, Luke has combined the results of two separate meetings and reported them as a single event. Later in Acts, the author seems aware that Paul did not know about the Jerusalem church's decision regarding Torah-prohibited meats. During Paul's final Jerusalem visit, James is shown speaking about the dietary restrictions as if they were news to Paul (21:25).

PAUL'S SECOND MISSIONARY JOURNEY: EVANGELIZING GREECE

Shortly after the Jerusalem conference, Paul and Barnabas separate. Acts attributes the parting to a quarrel over John Mark's alleged unreliability, but in Galatians Paul states that he and Barnabas differed over the question of Torah observance, Barnabas having been "carried away" by the "circumcision party" (Gal. 2:13). As a result, Paul and Silas alone visit the newly founded churches of **Syria** and Asia Minor until a vision directs Paul into **Macedonia** (15:40–16:10) (Figure 12.3), where Luke shows him following his usual pattern of preaching in local synagogues and then being abused by Jewish leaders (16:11–17:15).

Driven from the Macedonian cities of **Philippi**, **Thessalonica**, and Beroea, Paul finds unusual tolerance in **Athens**, the center of Greek philosophy, where he is invited to speak before an intellectually curious group at the **Areopagus** (highest council) (17:16–34) (Figure 12.4). After making few converts among the sophisticated Athenians, Paul enjoys greater success in **Corinth**, a prosperous Greek seaport, where he founds a thriving church. Paul's letters to the Corinthians (discussed later in this chapter) contain some of his most vivid writing.

PAUL'S THIRD MISSIONARY JOURNEY: REVISITING ASIA MINOR AND GREECE

A third missionary tour, in which Paul revisits the churches of Greece and Asia (Chs. 18–21), culminates in **Ephesus, a cosmopolitan port in what is now western Turkey** (Figure 12.5). Luke frames Paul's adventures in Ephesus with intimations of

Box 12.3 Jesus' Family and the Jerusalem Church

In describing Jesus' return to Nazareth, Mark lists four of Jesus' "brothers" (or close kinsmen) by name: James, Joseph, Judas, and Simon, as well as at least two unidentified "sisters" (6:3). Mark's report that Jesus' "mother and his brothers" attempted to interfere with his ministry (3:21, 31–35) is consistent with the New Testament tradition that none of Jesus' family followed him until after his resurrection. Paul cites James as one of the prominent individuals to whom Jesus made a postresurrection appearance (1 Cor. 15:7), which was undoubtedly the experience that made James a disciple. (Acts 1:14 states that Mary, Jesus' mother, and "his brothers" assembled with the Twelve in Jerusalem shortly after the ascension; they presumably were also present at the community's Spirit-anointing at Pentecost.)

When Paul made his postconversion visit to Jerusalem (probably about 35 C.E.), he found that "James the Lord's brother" was already an acknowledged leader of the Jerusalem church (Gal. 1:18–19). At the time of Paul's second Jerusalem visit (c. 49 C.E.), James was recognized as one of three "reputed pillars of our society" (along with the apostles Cephas [Peter] and John) (Gal. 2:6–10). After Peter and John had left Jerusalem, James assumed undisputed leadership of the church (Acts 15:13–21; 21:18–26).

The author of Acts does not record the executions of any of his leading missionary characters, including Peter and Paul (who were probably martyred in Rome under Nero). But the Jewish historian Josephus reports that James, "the brother of Jesus, who was called Christ," was illegally brought to trial by some Sadducees and stoned to death (c. 62 C.E.; Josephus, *Antiquities* 20.9.1).

In *The History of the Church*, Eusebius reports that James, who "was called Christ's brother," was the first bishop (overseer) of Jerusalem and known to his fellow Jewish Christians as James the Righteous. He also records a version of James's death different from that given in Josephus. Quoting Clement, a late first-century writer, Eusebius states that James was hurled down from "the parapet [Temple walls?] and beaten to death with a fuller's club" (*History* 2.1, 23; 3.5, 11; 4.5, 22; 7.19).

According to another (unverifiable) tradition preserved in Eusebius, even after James's death, Jesus' relatives continued to play influential roles in the Jerusalem church. Shortly after the Romans destroyed Jerusalem (c. 70 C.E.), Eusebius says, "apostles and disciples of the Lord who were still alive" gathered together from different parts of the country, along with "kinsmen of the Lord, for most of them were still living." Their purpose was to appoint a successor to James who would preside over Christians in postwar Jerusalem. As Luke represents Christians voting unanimously twenty years earlier at the first Jerusalem council (Acts 15), so Eusebius states that Jesus' disciples and family members, forty years after his death, voted "unanimously" for Jesus' cousin, Symeon, to "occupy the throne" of the Jerusalem church. (Because Eusebius does not ordinarily refer to a bishop's "throne," the Jerusalem congregation may have accorded royal or Davidic status to Jesus' heirs.) Eusebius adds that Symeon was a son of Clopas (John 19:25), who was supposedly a brother of Joseph, Jesus' putative father (*History* 3.11).

According to Eusebius's source, an early church historian named Hegesippus, Symeon remained head of the Jerusalem church until persecutions under the emperor Trajan (98–117 C.E.), when, at age 120, he was tortured and crucified for being both a Davidic descendant and a Christian. Symeon was then succeeded by another Jewish Christian, Justus; Eusebius does not mention whether he, Jerusalem's third bishop, was also a member of Jesus' family (*History* 3.32, 35).

To his testimony about members of Jesus' family taking leadership roles in the early church, Eusebius adds an anecdote about the grandsons of Jude (Judas)—"the brother, humanly speaking, of the Savior." Again citing Hegesippus as his source, Eusebius states that the emperor Domitian (81–96 C.E.), ordered a search made for royal descendants of David who might push messianic claims to restore the Jewish throne. According to Hegesippus's account, when Jude's grandsons were brought before Domitian, the emperor dismissed them contemptuously when he found that they were poor peasants with work-worn, callused hands. After this close call with Roman authority (they were more fortunate than Symeon in Trajan's reign), the two apparently took a more active part in the Christian community, becoming church leaders (*History* 3.19–20). The lingering influence of James and Jude in the Christian tradition is evident in the two New Testament books ascribed to them.

Figure 12.3 Paul's second missionary journey. As Acts depicts it, this journey brought Christianity to Europe, with new cells of Christians established in Philippi, Thessalonica, and Corinth. Note that Antioch in Syria is Paul's missionary headquarters.

the apostle's final journey — to Rome (Figure 12.6). As Luke had pictured Jesus turning his face resolutely toward Jerusalem and the servant's death that awaited him there (Luke 9:51), so the author shows Paul determined to complete his last tour and head for the imperial capital (19:21–22). After summoning Ephesian church leaders to Miletus, an ancient Greek city on the Aegean, Paul delivers a farewell speech, predicting his imminent imprisonment and possible martyrdom (20:17–38).

The remainder of Acts is largely concerned with Paul's legal difficulties with the Roman government. Reinforcing his theme that Christianity offers no threat to Roman security, the author takes pains to demonstrate that Paul is charged with sedition only because "envious" Jews stir up trouble against him. Roman officials repeatedly testify that he is guilty of no punishable action. When some Corinthian Jews charge him with defaming God, the Roman proconsul **Gallio** throws the case out of court (18:12–17). Similarly, when the Greek

Figure 12.4 Perhaps the world's most famous ruins, the Parthenon originally housed an ivory and gold statue of Athene Parthenos (Athene the Virgin). This gleaming marble temple to the goddess of wisdom and victory dominated the skyline of Athens when Paul visited the city in the late 40s C.E. and still does today, twenty-five centuries after it was built.

Figure 12.5 The ruins of a magnificent city open to the sky mark the site of Ephesus, a Greco-Roman seaport in Asia Minor (western Turkey). This view looks across an amphitheater toward the Arcadian Way. A major base of Paul's missionary activity (Acts 19), Ephesus later became an important Christian center, as reflected in later traditions that the Apostle John took Jesus' mother there, whence she ascended bodily to heaven.

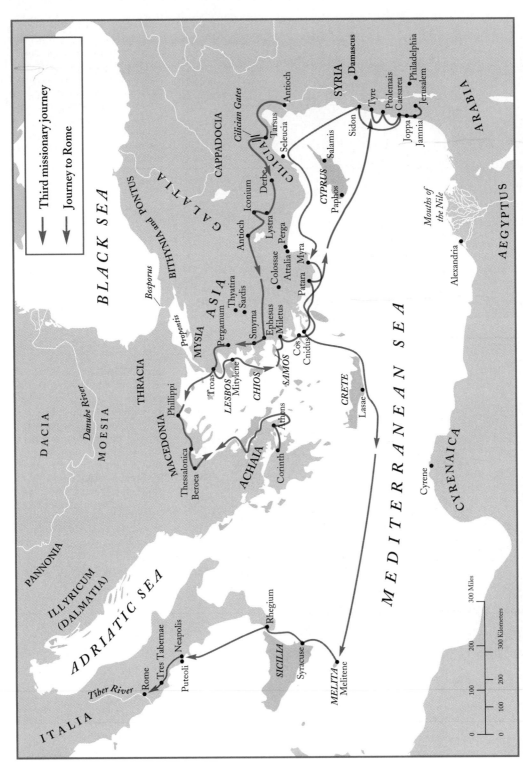

Figure 12.6 Paul's third missionary journey. According to Acts, this journey ended with his arrest in Jerusalem and two-year imprisonment in Caesarea. The bottom line shows the route of Paul's sea voyage to Rome, where he was taken to be tried in the imperial courts.

THE BOOK OF ACTS: A STORY OF CHRISTIAN BEGINNINGS

Figure 12.7 This cult statue of Diana of Ephesus, where the world's largest temple was erected in the goddess's honor, emphasizes her function as giver of fertility. Although the Romans identified Diana with Artemis, the Greek virgin goddess of wild creatures and the hunt, the Ephesian Diana bears a greater resemblance to older Near Eastern fertility deities such as Ishtar and Astarte. Acts records a confrontation between Paul and the silversmiths of Ephesus, whose livelihood making silver figurines of Diana was threatened by the apostle's monotheistic gospel (Acts 19:23–41).

silversmiths of Ephesus, who fashion images of the goddess Artemis **(Diana)** for sale to tourists, try to force Paul to stop his anti-idolatry campaign, local authorities argue that they have no legal cause to do so (19:23–41) (Figure 12.7).

PAUL'S ARREST IN JERUSALEM AND IMPRISONMENT IN CAESAREA

On Paul's return to Jerusalem, Jewish resistance reaches a climax as certain "Jews from the province of Asia" (21:27) accuse him of blasphemy and of profaning the Temple. When a mob attacks him, Roman soldiers intervene and conduct him to the Sanhedrin. Disclosing that he is a Pharisee, Paul succeeds in dividing the Council so that scribes of his party call for his release while the Sadducees and others denounce him (21:27–23:10). The divine plan operating through Paul's suffering is now revealed: He must proclaim the Christian witness in Rome as he has in Jerusalem (23:11).

After being taken into protective custody by Lysias, a Roman army commander, Paul is imprisoned for two years at **Caesarea** under Governor **Antonius Felix**, who apparently has no plans to release his troublesome prisoner without receiving the customary bribe. Under Felix's successor, **Porcius Festus**, Paul exercises his birthright as a Roman citizen and "appeals to Caesar," demanding to be tried in the emperor's own court (25:1–21). The detailed narration of Paul's defense before Festus, King **Herod Agrippa II**, and his sister Bernice (25:8–26:32) is intended to demonstrate his innocence of any religious or political crimes. Paul's long defense (26:1–29) is a vivid summary of his career as depicted in Acts, including a third account of his "heavenly" vision of the risen Jesus. Luke's main purpose in this courtroom scene is to establish Christianity's potentially friendly relationship to the **Roman Empire**. Echoing Pilate's opinion of Jesus, Governor Festus admits that Paul is guilty of "nothing that deserves death or imprisonment." Agrippa drives home the point: Paul could have been set free if "he had not appealed to the Emperor" (26:30–32). In Luke's introduction of the Christian church to his Greco-Roman audience, the author makes clear that missionaries like Paul are prosecuted in Roman courts only through officials' misunderstanding or the malice of false accusers.

PAUL'S JOURNEY TO ROME AND HIS PREACHING TO ROMAN JEWS

Luke begins his final section—Paul's sea journey to Rome—with an exciting description of a shipwreck (27:1–28:31). This segment of the narrative is told in the first person, one of several "we" passages appearing in the latter part of Acts. Scholars are unsure whether this represents an eyewitness report or is merely a literary device to heighten the immediacy of the account.

The author concludes his survey of the early church with Paul's arrival in Rome, where, although under house arrest, he is free to preach "quite openly and without hindrance" (28:31). This final statement is probably a reminder to Roman authorities that Paul established a kind of legal precedent. Awaiting trial, and with full knowledge of his captors, Christianity's greatest missionary continued to evangelize the Roman population.

Although Acts ends abruptly without telling us of Paul's subsequent fate, Luke has accomplished his stated purpose of tracing Christianity's expansion from Jerusalem to "the ends of the earth" (1:8), a goal metaphorically achieved by Paul's witness in Rome, heart of the pagan empire. His hero's last words emphasize another major Lukan theme: Paul (and his successors) will henceforth direct the gospel primarily to non-Jews, for "the Gentiles will listen" (28:28). In Acts' final speech, Luke shows Paul quoting from Isaiah 6, the same passage about Jewish refusal to heed the prophet's oracles that Mark had cited to explain why Jesus' people failed to accept his teaching (Mark 4:10–13). Luke does not use this Markan interpretation in his Gospel account of Jesus' parables, but instead places it at the end of his church history to express his view that Christianity's future belongs to the Gentiles.

QUESTIONS FOR REVIEW

1. A sequel to Luke's Gospel, the Book of Acts continues the story of Christian origins. Which of the same themes that appear in the Gospel are also found in Acts? Compare the account of Jesus' trial before Pilate with that of Paul before Pilate's successors, Felix and Festus.

2. How does Luke organize his account of Christianity's birth and growth to demonstrate fulfillment of Jesus' commission in Acts 1:8? Describe the major milestones in Luke's history of the "new way" from Pentecost through the conversion of Cornelius, the first church council in Jerusalem, Paul's missionary journeys, and Paul's arrival in Rome.

3. In what ways does the Jerusalem community described in Acts 2 put into operation the social and economic principles enunciated in Luke's Gospel? How does the early church "equalize" wealth and poverty?

4. Cite two or three examples from the Book of Acts in which the author attempts to minimize controversies within the church in order to present the early Christian movement as an ideally harmonious, Spirit-directed community led by people of exemplary faith.

QUESTION FOR DISCUSSION AND REFLECTION

By adding a history of primitive Christianity to his Gospel narrative, how does Luke deemphasize apocalyptic hopes of Jesus' early return? What does Paul's preaching in Rome forecast for the church's future relationship with the Roman Empire?

TERMS AND CONCEPTS TO REMEMBER

Antioch	Herod Agrippa II
Antonius Felix	Holy Spirit
apostle	James
Areopagus	Jerusalem church
ascension	Judas Iscariot
Athens	Macedonia
Barnabas	martyr
Caesarea	Matthias
centurion	Paul
circumcision	Pentecost
Corinth	Philippi
Cornelius	Porcius Festus
Diana (of the Ephesians)	Roman Empire
Ephesus	Saul of Tarsus
Gallio	Simon
Gamaliel	Stephen
glossolalia	Syria
Hellenists	Thessalonica

RECOMMENDED READING

Arlandson, James M. *Women, Class, and Society in Early Christianity: Models from Luke-Acts.* Peabody, Mass.: Hendrickson, 1997. Applies social theory to the role of women in ancient society and the church.

Cadbury, H. J. "Acts of the Apostles." In *The Interpreter's Dictionary of the Bible,* Vol. 1, pp. 28–42. Nashville: Abingdon Press, 1962. A general introduction.

Conzelmann, Hans. *The Theology of St. Luke.* Translated by G. Buswell. New York: Harper & Row, 1961. A scholarly and influential work.

Dibelius, Martin. *Studies in the Acts of the Apostles.* Translated by M. Ling. Edited by H. Greeven. New York: Scribner, 1956. A standard reference.

Dillon, Richard J. "Acts of the Apostles." In R. E. Brown et al., eds., *The New Jerome Biblical Commentary,* pp. 722–767. Englewood Cliffs, N.J.: Prentice-Hall, 1990. A thorough introductory study.

Dunn, J. D. G. *Unity and Diversity in the New Testament.* Philadelphia: Westminster Press, 1977. A stimulating analysis of the several different forms of early Christianity; covers the conflicts between the Palestinian-Jewish Christians and the Hellenistic Gentile church.

Haenchen, Ernst. *The Acts of the Apostles: A Commentary.* Philadelphia: Westminster Press, 1971. An excellent study.

Hanson, R. P. C. *The Acts.* New York: Oxford University Press, 1967.

Hengel, Martin. *Acts and the History of Earliest Christianity.* Philadelphia: Fortress Press, 1980.

Juel, Donald. *Luke-Acts: The Promise of History.* Atlanta: John Knox Press, 1984.

Keck, L. E., and Martyn, J. L., eds. *Studies in Luke-Acts.* Nashville: Abingdon Press, 1980 (1966). An important collection of scholarly essays on recent approaches to Luke's writings.

Lohse, Eduard. *The First Christians: Their Beginnings, Writings, and Beliefs.* Philadelphia: Fortress Press, 1983.

Malherbe, A. J. *Social Aspects of Early Christianity,* 2nd ed. Philadelphia: Fortress Press, 1983.

Markus, R. A. *Christianity in the Roman World.* New York: Scribner, 1974. Traces the growth of Christianity from outlawed sect to state religion of imperial Rome.

Powell, M. A. *What Are They Saying About Acts?* New York: Paulist Press, 1991. A helpful survey of current scholarship on Acts.

Schüssler Fiorenza, Elizabeth. *In Memory of Her: A Feminist Reconstruction of Christian Origins.* New York: Crossroads Press, 1983.

Talbert, C. H. *Acts.* Atlanta: John Knox Press, 1984.

———. *Luke-Acts: New Perspectives from the SBL Seminar.* New York: Crossroads Press, 1984.

Theissen, Gerd. *The Sociology of Early Palestinian Christianity.* Philadelphia: Fortress Press, 1978.

Tiede, D. L. *Prophecy and History in Luke-Acts.* Philadelphia: Fortress Press, 1980.

Wilken, R. L. *The Christians as the Romans Saw Them.* New Haven, Conn: Yale University Press, 1984. A careful analysis of the social, religious, and political conflicts between early Christians and their Roman critics.

Paul and the Gentile Mission

Paul, former Pharisee and persecutor of the church who later pioneered Christianity's mission to the Gentiles, dominates the second half of Acts. To an incalculable extent, he also dominates the later history of Christian thought. His letters, which form a crucial part of the New Testament, represent the new religion's first — and in important ways most lasting — attempt to interpret the meaning of Jesus' sacrificial death and its significance for human salvation. Paul's startling view is that Jesus' crucifixion introduced a radically different relationship between God and all humanity — Gentiles and Jews. Paul's declaration that faith in Christ superseded Torah obedience as the means

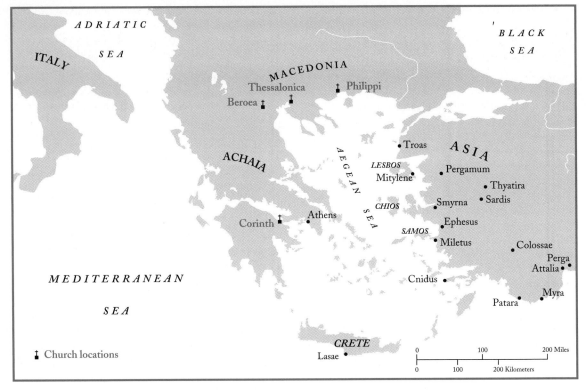

Figure 12.8 Paul's churches. Paul established largely Gentile churches in the northeastern Mediterranean region at Philippi, Thessalonica, Beroea, and Corinth. Paul's teaching was also influential in the Asia Minor city of Ephesus, where he lived for at least two years. The sites of some other prominent Christian centers are also given.

of reconciliation to God transformed Christianity from a Jewish sect into a new world religion. In his letters to the Romans and Galatians, Paul outlined a theology of redemption through faith that has become central to Christianity's self-understanding. Later theologians as diverse as the Roman church father Augustine (354–430 C.E.) and Martin Luther (1483–1546), the German monk who sparked the Protestant Reformation, derived many of their doctrines from Paul's letters.

Many historians have remarked that there is perhaps more of Paul than Jesus in official Christianity. Even Mark, the earliest story of Jesus' life, bears the imprint of Pauline ideas in its bias toward Gentile believers, its account of the Last Supper, and its theology of the cross. Some commentators accuse Paul, who did not know the historical Jesus, of largely ignoring Christ's original proclamation—God's active rule in individual human lives—in favor of promulgating a mystery cult about Jesus. Certainly, Paul almost never cites Jesus' kingdom teaching and instead emphasizes his own personal experience of the risen Christ, which he interprets in cosmic and mystical terms.

In contrast to Jesus, who apparently wrote nothing, Paul speaks directly to us through his letters, permitting us to compare what he says about himself with what later writers, such as Luke, say about him. Paul's position in the canon is unique: He is the only historical personage who is both a major character in a New Testament book and the author of New Testament books himself. Church tradition ascribes no fewer than thirteen canonical letters to Paul, in total length nearly one-third of the New Testament. Most scholars regard only seven as genuinely Pauline, but the presence of other works attributed to him shows in what high esteem he was held. His ideas and personality so captured the imagination of later Christian authors that they paid tribute to the great apostle by writing in his name and perpetuating his teachings. (Figure 12.8 hints at the extent of Paul's influence even in his own time.)

SEEKING THE HISTORICAL PAUL

As a Christian thinker, Paul never forgets his Jewishness. Although he fights to free Christianity from the "bondage" of Torah observance, Paul consistently stresses the unbroken continuity between Judaism and the new religion. For him, as for Matthew, Christianity is revealed through Jesus' ministry but shaped and largely defined by the Hebrew Bible. Throughout his letters, Paul quotes selected parts of the Hebrew Scriptures to support the validity of his particular gospel. Despite Paul's ambivalent attitude toward the Mosaic Torah, much of the Hebrew biblical tradition retains its teaching authority for him.

Our most reliable source of Paul's biography is his letters, in which he repeatedly stresses his Jewish heritage. Describing himself as a circumcised "Hebrew born and bred" from the Israelite tribe of Benjamin (Phil. 3:5–6), Paul states that as a "practicing Jew" he outstripped his Jewish contemporaries in strict observance of "the traditions of [his] ancestors" (Gal. 1:13–14). A member of the **Pharisee** sect, he obeyed the Torah completely. "In legal rectitude"—keeping the Torah commandments—Paul judges himself "faultless" (Phil. 3:6).

Before his call to follow Jesus, Paul demonstrated his loyalty to Pharisaic Judaism by persecuting those who believed that Jesus was the Jewish Messiah. Whatever the nature of Paul's supernatural encounter with the risen Christ (Acts 9:1–9; 22:3–11; 16:12–19), it radically changed his attitude toward Christianity without modifying his essential personality. According to Acts and his own testimony, he displayed the same quality of religious zeal before Jesus appeared to him as he does afterward. Paul's experience seems less a conversion from one religion to another (he always stresses the connection between Judaism and the new faith) than a redirection of his abundant energies. (Box 12.4 describes a possible sequence of events in Paul's life.)

THE HISTORICAL RELIABILITY OF ACTS

Acts supplies much information about Paul not contained in his letters, but most scholars urge great caution about accepting Acts' data at face value. A great deal of the material in the letters is difficult to reconcile with Acts' narrative sequence. Where discrepancies occur, scholars prefer Paul's firsthand version of events. The author of Acts investigated various sources to compile his account of Christianity's beginnings (Luke 1:1–4), but he appears to have worked with inadequate documentation in recording Paul's career. As noted previously, the author either is unaware of or deliberately ignores Paul's voluminous correspondence, his insistent claims to apostleship, and his distinctive teaching. Acts says virtually nothing about Paul's essential gospel—that people are saved not by obedience to Torah commands, but by faith in Christ. A growing number of scholars believe that the writer of Acts set out to tame or domesticate Paul, minimizing his fierce independence and picturing him as a dutiful son of the institutional church. In his letters, Paul passionately defends his autonomy and recognizes no superior churchly authority.

Acts provides biographical details that Paul never mentions, such as his birth in **Tarsus**, capital city of Cilicia (now included in southeastern Turkey) and the belief that Paul's family possessed Roman citizenship. These and similar traditions—such as Paul's originally being named Saul, his studying at the feet of Rabbi Gamaliel (the leading Pharisee scholar of his day), and his supporting himself by tent making—are never referred to in the Pauline letters, so we have no way of verifying

Box 12.4 A Tentative Sequence of Events in Paul's Life

Except for a few incidents, such as Paul's visit to Corinth when Gallio was proconsul in Achaea (Greece) (c. 51–53 c.e.), scholars do not agree on the dates of major events in Paul's life. From references in Paul's letters and a cautious use of material in Acts, however, it is possible to reconstruct a general outline of Paul's biography.

1. Paul is born a Hellenistic Jew (in Tarsus, first decade c.e.?). He is educated as a Pharisee (Phil. 3:5–6; 2 Cor. 11:22).

2. [Jesus is crucified (c. 30 c.e.?).]

3. Paul harasses members of the early Jesus movement (1 Cor. 15:9; Gal. 1:13–14).

4. Paul encounters the risen Jesus (c. 32–34 c.e.) (1 Cor. 15:9–10; Gal. 1:10–12, 16).

5. After his revelation, Paul travels to "Arabia" and then returns to Damascus (without visiting Jerusalem) (Gal. 1:16–17).

6. "After three years," he visits Jerusalem to meet Peter (Cephas) and James "the Lord's brother" (Gal. 1:18–19).

7. He than travels to "Syria and Cilicia [southeast Turkey]," presumably as a missionary to Gentiles (and steering clear of Jewish churches) (Gal. 1:22).

8. "Fourteen years later," with Titus and Barnabas, Paul makes a second visit to Jerusalem (c. 49 c.e.), presumably to confer with Peter, John, James, and representatives from Antioch about admitting Gentiles as equal members of the church (Gal. 2:1–10; cf. Acts 15).

9. After the Jerusalem consultation, Paul returns to Antioch, where he opposes Peter over the issue of dining with Gentiles (Gal. 2:11–14).

10. Traveling from Antioch to Greece, Paul establishes the first Christian congregations of Europe (Philippi, Thessalonica, and Corinth); he remains in Corinth for eighteen months (c. 49–51 c.e.), and writes letter to the Thessalonians (c. 50 c.e.). (See Acts 18:11–12.)

11. Paul visits Ephesus (c. 52–55 c.e.); he writes 1 Corinthians (c. 54–55 c.e.).

12. Paul makes a (second?) tour of Macedonia and Greece (Acts 19:1, 10, 22); he writes various parts of 2 Corinthians (and Galatians?).

13. Paul makes a third and final visit to Corinth; he writes Romans and plans to revisit Jerusalem and then to stop by Rome en route to Spain (Rom. 15:23–29).

14. Paul makes a third visit to Jerusalem, where he is arrested and then imprisoned at Caesarea under Antonius Felix (procurator of Judea, c. 52–59 c.e.) and Felix's successor, Porcius Festus.

15. Under armed guard, Paul is transported to Rome, where he remains under house arrest for two years (c. 60–62 c.e.) (Acts 27–28).

16. Paul is executed in Rome under Nero (c. 62–64 c.e.).

their historical accuracy. (Box 12.5 summarizes some differences between Acts and Paul's letters.)

PAUL'S EXPERIENCE OF THE RISEN JESUS

In both Acts and Paul's letters, Paul's life can be divided into two contrasting parts. In his early career, he was a devout Pharisee who "savagely" persecuted the first Christians. In his later years, he was a Christian missionary who successfully implanted the new religion in non-Jewish territories and established the first churches of Europe. The event that changed Paul from a persecutor of Christians into an indomitable Christian evangelist was, in his words, "a revelation [*apokalypsis*] of Jesus Christ" (Gal. 1:12). Acts depicts the "revelation" as a blinding vision of the risen Messiah on the road to **Damascus**. The author stresses the importance of the event by narrating it fully three times (Acts 9:1–9; 22:3–11; 26:12–19). Paul's briefer allusions to the experience speak simply of being called by God's "grace" (Gal. 1:15) to an "abnormal birth" and of witnessing a postresurrection appearance of Jesus (1 Cor. 15:8–9). Paul does not state what form the apparition took, but he does imply that he maintained an ongoing communica-

Box 12.5 Some Differences Between Acts and Paul's Letters

ACTS	PAUL'S LETTERS
Is named Saul and raised in Tarsus	Is not mentioned (but was born to tribe of Benjamin, whose first king was Saul [Phil. 3:5])
Studies under Rabbi Gamaliel	Is not mentioned
Belongs to the Pharisee party	Is confirmed in Philippians 3:6
Persecutes Christians	Is mentioned several times
Experiences a vision of Jesus on the road to Damascus	Receives a "revelation" of Jesus (Gal. 1:12, 16)
Following his call, goes immediately to Damascus, where he preaches in synagogues	Goes to "Arabia" for an unspecified period (Gal. 1:17)
Is initially shunned by Jerusalem disciples but is later introduced to apostles (9:26–30)	Does not go to Jerusalem until three years after his return from "Arabia" and meets only Peter and James (Gal. 1:17–20)
Receives the Holy Spirit after **Ananias** baptizes and lays hands upon him	Asserts he owes his apostolic gospel and commission to no one; never refers to baptism (Gal. 1:11–12, 16–17)
Attends an apostolic conference in his third Jerusalem visit	Attends the conference in his second Jerusalem visit (Gal. 2:1–10)
Agrees to impose Torah dietary restrictions on Gentile converts	Refuses to accept any legal restrictions (Gal. 2:5)
Agrees to forbid eating meat sacrificed to idols	Regards eating such meat as undefiling (1 Cor. 8; 10:27; Rom. 14:13–15:6)

tion with divine beings, experiencing a number of mystical visions (2 Cor. 12:1–10).

Paul's physical stamina — even today duplicating his travel itinerary would exhaust most people — is matched by the strength of his feelings. Paul's letters reveal their author's emotional intensity, ranging from paternal tenderness to biting sarcasm. In one letter, he insults his readers' intelligence and suggests that some of their advisers castrate themselves (Gal. 3:1; 5:12). In other letters, he reacts to criticism with threats, wild boasting, and wounding anger (2 Cor. 10–13). In still others, he expresses profound affection and gentle tact (1 Cor. 13; Phil. 1:3–9; 2:1–4; 4:2–3) (Figure 12.9).

Paul's conviction that Jesus had privately revealed to him the one true Gospel (Gal. 1–2) isolated the apostle from many fellow believers. Acts and the letters agree that Paul quarreled with many of his intimate companions (Acts 15:37–39; Gal.

2:11–14), as well as with entire groups (Gal.; 2 Cor. 10–13). This sense of a unique vision, one not shared by most other Christians, may have shaped Paul's admitted preference for preaching in territories where no Christian had preceded him. The more distant his missionary field from competing evangelizers, the better it suited him. Paul's desire to impress his individual gospel upon new converts may have influenced his ambition to work in areas as far removed from established churches as possible (Rom. 15:20–23).

PAUL'S LETTERS

The Genuine Letters New Testament historians generally agree that Paul became a Christian in the mid-30s C.E. and that he traveled extensively as a missionary during the 40s and 50s C.E., arriving in Rome about the year 60 (Figure 12.10). Scholarly

Figure 12.9 *The Apostle Paul* by Rembrandt (1606–1669). Rembrandt's somber portrait shows Paul in a deeply reflective mood and stresses the apostle's consciousness of the enormous burden he bears — the task of communicating his unique vision of Christ to the Gentiles. In his letters, Paul expresses a wide variety of emotions — joy, anger, bitter sarcasm — but Rembrandt captures here the sense of melancholy and isolation that typically characterize this great missionary.

agreement disappears, however, in attempting to date Paul's letters or even to establish the exact order in which he wrote them.

The majority of scholars accept seven letters as authentically Pauline. Virtually all scholars regard Romans, 1 and 2 Corinthians, Galatians, Philippians, 1 Thessalonians, and Philemon as Paul's own writing. Some also accept 2 Thessalonians and Colossians. But the majority doubt that Ephesians is genuine and are certain that three — Titus and 1 and 2 Timothy — were composed by a Pauline disciple after the apostle's death. Almost no reputable scholar believes that Hebrews, which is a sermon rather than a letter, is a Pauline composition (Box 12.6).

Order of Composition   Although scholars debate the exact order in which Paul composed his letters, they generally agree that 1 Thessalonians was written first (c. 50 C.E.) and is thus the oldest Christian writing in existence. If Paul also wrote 2 Thessalonians, it also dates from about 50 C.E. 1 and 2 Corinthians usually are placed in the mid-50s, and the more theologically mature letters, such as Romans and Philippians, are dated later. Four letters — Colossians, Philemon, Philippians, and possibly Ephesians — reputedly were composed while Paul was imprisoned and are known as the "captivity letters." Unfortunately, Paul does not reveal in the letters where he was jailed, so we do not know whether he wrote them from Ephesus, Caesarea,

Figure 12.10 *St. Paul in Prison* by Rembrandt (1606–1669). In his murky cell, Paul composes letters to inspire faith and hope in the membership of his tiny, scattered churches. Notice that the light from the cell's barred window seems to emanate from Paul himself, surrounding his head like a halo and glowing from the pages of the manuscripts he holds.

or Rome, all cities in which he presumably suffered imprisonment. The canonical letters (others have been lost) were probably all written during a relatively brief span of time, the decade between about 50 and 60 C.E.

Paul's Use of the Letter Form   Paul is aware that his letters are persuasive documents. He consciously uses letters as substitutes for his own presence, making them an effective means of influencing people and events from a distance. Although he gives directions on a wide variety of matters, his primary objective is to correct his recipients' beliefs and to discipline their behavior. His letters are also potent weapons for combatting opposition to his teaching.

Writing to the Corinthians, Paul states that his critics contrast his "weighty and powerful" letters with his unimpressive physical appearance and ineffectiveness as a speaker (2 Cor. 10:9–11). The apostle may exaggerate his defects for rhetorical effect, but he is right about his letters. From the time they were first written until now, they have exerted enormous influence on Christian thought and conduct.

Paul writes letters so effectively that he makes this literary category the standard medium of communication for many later Christian writers. The large majority of New Testament authors imitate Paul by conveying their ideas in letter form. Twenty-one of the twenty-seven canonical books are (at least theoretically) letters. Even the writer of

Box 12.6 Paul's Letters: Authentic, Disputed, and Pseudonymous

Paul's genuine letters, composed between about 50 and 62 C.E., form the oldest surviving Christian literature. In the decades after Paul's death, his influence became so great that different Christian groups apparently competed for the role of authoritative interpreter of his teaching. Following the Hellenistic-Jewish practice of **pseudonymity** (writing in the name of an honored religious authority of the past, such as Moses or one of the apostles), some Christian authors composed letters in Paul's name, using their understanding of the Pauline heritage to address problems of their own day. Whereas Paul's genuine letters invariably deal with specific problems besetting individual congregations (and presume a relatively informal church structure), pseudonymous letters such as 1 and 2 Timothy and Titus (the **pastoral epistles**) typically deal with such issues as maintaining the doctrinal purity of apostolic traditions and presume a much more structured church administration.

LETTERS BY PAUL	LETTERS PROBABLY NOT BY PAUL	LETTERS DEFINITELY NOT BY PAUL
1 Thessalonians	2 Thessalonians	Ephesians
1 and 2 Corinthians	Colossians	1 and 2 Timothy
Galatians		Titus
Romans		Hebrews (Even in early Christianity, most churchmen did not believe that Hebrews was by Paul.)
Philemon		
Philippians		

Revelation uses this form to transmit Jesus' message to the seven churches of Asia Minor (Rev. 2–3).

Hellenistic Letters   In general, Paul follows the accepted Hellenistic literary form in his correspondence, modifying it somewhat to express his peculiarly Christian interests. Much Greco-Roman correspondence, both personal and business, has survived from early Christian times, allowing us to compare Paul's letters with those of other Hellenistic writers.

The Hellenistic letter writer typically begins with a prescript, identifying the writer and the reader, and a greeting, wishing good fortune to the reader and commonly invoking the blessing of a god. Paul varies this formula by mentioning the Christian allegiance of the writer and recipients, substituting "grace" and "peace" for the customary greetings, and frequently including an associate's name in the salutation. He also elaborates on the Hellenistic custom by giving praise, thanks, or prayers for the welfare of his recipients.

Paul also modifies his letters' prescripts according to his attitude toward the church he is addressing. Paul's letter to his trusted friends at Philippi opens with an effusive outpouring of affection and praise for the Philippians (Phil. 1:1–11). By contrast, when he writes to the churches in Galatia, he is furious with the recipients and includes no warm or approving salutation (Gal. 1:1–5).

After stating the letter's principal message, the Hellenistic writer closes with additional greetings, typically including greetings from other people and sometimes adding a request that the recipient(s) convey the sender's respects to mutual acquaintances. Paul often expands this custom to include a summary statement of faith and a benediction, as well as a list of fellow Christians to be greeted (Rom. 16; 1 Cor. 16:10–21; Col. 4:7–18).

The Role of Dictation   As was customary in Greco-Roman correspondence, Paul apparently dictated all his letters to a secretary or scribe, occasionally adding a signature or a few other words in his own hand. In antiquity, secretaries ordinarily did not record the precise words of those dictating, but paraphrased the gist of what was said (Rom. 16:21–22; Gal. 6:11; Col. 4:18; Philem. 19; 2 Thess. 3:17), a practice that helps explain the spontaneous quality of Pauline letters.

Circumstances of Writing   Most of Paul's letters were composed under the pressure of meeting an emergency in a given church. With the exception of Romans, which is addressed to a congregation that he had not yet visited, every Pauline letter is directed to a particular group, and most of the groups are personally known by the writer. In virtually every case, the recipients are experiencing some form of crisis, either of belief or behavior, which the author tries to resolve.

Paul's main concern is always pastoral; he deals with individual problems caused by church members' teaching or conduct. In counseling these small groups of infant Christians, Paul typically invokes theological arguments or examples to reinforce his advice. Because Paul's presentation of theological issues is secondary to his counseling, the letters do not represent a complete or systematic statement of Pauline belief. In addition, the reader will find Paul's thought changing and developing from one letter to another.

PAUL'S MAJOR ASSUMPTIONS AND CONCERNS

Pauline thought is commonly subtle and complex, making it difficult even for scholars to achieve a consensus about the apostle's views on many important topics. In studying Paul's letters, it helps to keep in mind several of their author's basic beliefs about his relationship to God, Christ, and the spirit world. Based partly on the experience of divine intervention in his personal life, Paul's assumptions about God's intentions for humanity and the imminent End of history significantly shaped his theological views and motivated his behavior.

Mysticism and Eschatology   Understanding Paul's writings means recognizing his sense of the spiritual power that inspired his apostolic career. As noted previously, Paul bases his authority as a

Christian leader and the validity of his distinctive gospel on an *apokalypsis,* a private revelation of the postresurrection Jesus (Gal. 1:11–12, 15–17). This encounter with Christ, which he insists he received as a direct heavenly communication, and not from any apostolic predecessor, informs Paul that the glorified Jesus now exists in two separate but related dimensions: the macrocosm (great world) of God's spiritual domain and the microcosm (little world) of human consciousness. This **dualism,** characteristic of apocalyptic thought (see Chapter 13), expresses Paul's conviction that Christ possesses both an objective and a subjective reality. Christ is at once a cosmic figure who will soon return to judge the world and a being who mysteriously dwells within the individual believer. The tension between the transcendent and the immanent Christ, one who is simultaneously universal and yet intimately experienced by the faithful, appears in almost every letter Paul wrote.

Paul's mysticism — his powerful sense of union with an unseen spiritual reality — is an important component of his worldview. In 2 Corinthians, he writes of being "caught up as far as the third heaven," "into paradise," where he "heard words so secret that human lips may not repeat them" (2 Cor. 12:1–4). These "visions and revelations granted by the Lord," which undoubtedly played their part in sustaining Paul through the many dangers and hardships he endured, may not have occurred as often as he would have liked. He adds that to prevent him "from being unduly elated by the magnificence of such revelations," he was given "a sharp physical pain," perhaps to remind him that even sporadic experiences of the infinite could not allow him to escape his finite humanity (2 Cor. 12:7–8).

Paul may have been familiar with the Book of 1 Enoch, which describes **Enoch's** vision of God's heavenly throne — or at least traditions surrounding it — for he clearly shares its aspiration for mystical oneness with the divine. Paul also shares Enoch's apocalyptic viewpoint. His conviction that the Messiah's appearance has inaugurated the End of time permeates his thought and underlies much of his ethical teaching. Paul's advice on marriage, divorce, slavery, celibacy, and human behavior in general is largely shaped by his expectation of an imminent Final Judgment. In his oldest surviving letter, he states that he expects to witness the Parousia: "We who are left alive until the Lord comes . . . [will be] caught up in the clouds to meet the Lord in the air" (1 Thess. 4:15–17).

In 1 Corinthians, his expectation to live until the End is equally certain; hence, he advises his correspondents that "the time we live in will not last long. While it lasts, married men should be as if they had no wives; . . . buyers must not count on keeping what they buy, nor those who use the world's wealth. . . . For the whole frame of this world is passing away" (1 Cor. 7:29–31). Eagerly anticipating the *eschaton*, he also tells the Corinthians, "Listen! I will unfold a mystery: we shall not all die, but we shall all be changed in a flash, in the twinkling of an eye, at the last trumpet-call. For the trumpet will sound, and the dead will rise immortal, and we shall be changed" (1 Cor. 15:51–52).

Like many Jewish apocalyptists of the first century, Paul sees human history as divided into two qualitatively different ages, or periods of time. The present evil age will soon be replaced by a New Age, a new creation, in which God will reign completely (Gal. 6:14; 1 Cor. 15; 20–28; 2 Cor. 5:17). Because the Messiah's arrival denotes the final consummation of history, Paul regards his generation as the last. His letters thus burn with special urgency because he believes that his day marks the crucial transition period between the two ages. Those about to be judged, especially members of his infant churches, must therefore prepare for the impending visitation, pursuing lives of unblemished virtue.

The Centrality and Preeminence of Jesus Absolutely central to Paul's thought is his conviction that in Jesus, God accomplishes the world's salvation. Although Paul shows almost no interest in Jesus' earthly ministry or teachings (if he knew them in any detail), he sees the heavenly Christ in three roles: (1) as God's revealed Wisdom (1 Cor. 1–4), (2) as the divine Lord through whom God rules (Phil. 2:11; Rom.10:9; 1 Cor. 15:24–28), and (3) as the means by whom God's Spirit dwells in believers (Rom. 8; 14:17). The operation of the Spirit, God's active force denoting his presence and effecting his will in the world, characterizes all of Paul's churches.

Christ and Humanity In contrasting Christ with the symbol of earthly humanity, **Adam** (in Genesis, God's first human creation), Paul emphasizes the vast change Jesus' activity has effected for the human race. Prior to Jesus' coming, humans existed in Adam's perishable image, victims of sin and death (Rom. 5:12–21). By contrast, believers now "in Christ" (living under his power) will also share in the glorified Christ's life-giving nature: "As in Adam all men die, so in Christ all will be brought to life" (1 Cor. 15:21–24, 45–49).

The Faithful as Christ's Body Using a corporate image to identify the believing community as the earthly manifestation of the exalted Christ, Paul states that the faithful collectively are Christ's "body" (1 Cor. 10:16–18; 12:12–30; Rom. 12). As a people defined and influenced by the Spirit, the church functions in union with Christ so fully that it reveals his visible form.

Christ as Liberator from Sin, Torah, and Death In Paul's view, all human beings are negatively influenced by sin's power and hence alienated from the perfect God (Rom. 7). Sin's invariable consequence is death, a condition of the defective humanity we share with Adam (Rom. 5:12–21). By defining both the nature and the punishment of sin, the Torah increased its power, revealing the universality of sin and condemning all sinners — the entire human race (Rom. 1–3).

Christ's total obedience to the Father and his selfless death on the cross, taking unto himself the Torah's penalty for sin, liberates those persons accepting him (living fully under his power) from sin, death, and the Torah's curses (Gal. 3–5; Rom. 3–7). For Paul, "freedom in Christ" means deliverance from the old order of sin and punishment, including the Torah's power to condemn.

Christ's Universal Sufficiency To Paul, Jesus' sacrificial death and God's act in exalting Christ as the agent by whom God rules and imparts his Spirit constitute a total change in the relationship between God and humanity. Christ is the final and complete means of canceling the powers of sin and destruction. Because Christ is now all-sufficient in reconciling human beings to God, neither "angelic powers" nor the Torah any longer play a decisive role in achieving human salvation.

Justification by Faith   Historically, one of Paul's most influential concepts was his understanding of the moral logic by which a perfectly righteous God can accept or "justify" human beings whose unrighteous behavior makes them veritable "slaves" to sin. Does God, who sits as Judge over the universe, compromise his ethical standards by granting salvation to sinful humans? Paul's personal experience of divine mercy, expressed through an *apokalypsis* (revelation) of Jesus, convinces him that in Christ he has been justified or "made right" before God. This conviction — that faith in Christ delivers him from sin more effectively than had obedience to the Mosaic Law — places Paul on a collision course with his native Judaism, as well as with many Jewish Christians who saw no reason to abandon their Mosaic heritage. For Jewish Christians of the first century C.E. (probably including Jesus' "brother" James), to accept Jesus as Israel's Messiah (Christ) was to follow the same Torah obligations that Jesus had.

For observant Jews, the Law provided a God-given — and fully adequate — means of atoning for sin and maintaining a right relationship with the Deity. Mosaic Law prescribes detailed rituals by which genuinely repentant sinners can express their desire to make peace with God. (As many scholars have noted, Torah statutes involving "sin offerings" and other sacrifices to effect forgiveness presuppose that petitioners have already experienced appropriate sorrow and remorse for their errors.) Both personal contrition and sacrificial rites were part of the biblical arrangement for restoring harmony between Israel's God and his worshipers.

Although Paul claims that, "by the law's standard of righteousness [he had been] without fault" (Phil. 3:6), at some point after his encounter with the risen Jesus he came to believe that the Mosaic Covenant was no longer the means by which God reconciled sinful humanity to himself. In two of his most theologically important letters, Galatians and Romans, Paul argues that the Law serves only to expose the universal reality of human sin, which it justly condemns. By his sacrificial death on the cross, however, Jesus paid for *everyone* the Law's penalty for human sin, effectively canceling the Law's authority. Through spiritual union with Christ, who is now God's sole instrument of human redemption, believers share in the benefits of Jesus' self-sacrifice and freely receive the divine favor that grants them eternal life. For Paul, the Law can no longer confer forgiveness, a function that in God's new arrangement belongs exclusively to Christ. In Paul's view, it is God's *grace* — his undeserved kindness and mercy — that opens the way to salvation for Jews and Gentiles alike, graciously assigning them the capacity to accept and believe in Jesus. Believers are thus justified before God only through their faith — complete trust — in Jesus' power to save those with whom he is spiritually united. (For further discussion of Paul's ideas about faith in Christ replacing works of Torah, see "Galatians" and "Romans" later in this chapter.)

During the sixteenth century C.E., European Christians were bitterly divided over the interpretation of Paul's doctrine of justification by faith. Martin Luther, the Protestant reformer, held that it is through faith alone that believers are saved, whereas the Catholic Church maintained that salvation also came through deeds, particularly observance of such sacraments as baptism, confession, and absolution. It was not until the close of the twentieth century that Catholics and Protestants reached an accord on Paul's teaching. In 1999, on the 482nd anniversary of Luther's posting his protests against church practices on the door of Castle Church in Wittenberg, Germany — an act that sparked the Protestant Reformation — leaders of the Catholic and Lutheran churches signed a historic agreement stating that faith is essential to salvation. According to this joint Catholic-Lutheran declaration, "By grace alone, in faith in Christ's saving work and not because of any merit on our part, we are adopted by God and receive the Holy Spirit, who renews our hearts while equipping and calling us to good works."

ORDER OF PAUL'S LETTERS

In the New Testament canon, Paul's letters are listed roughly according to their length. Letters to churches, such as Romans, appear first, and those to individuals, such as Philemon, appear last. In this text, we discuss the letters in the general order of their composition, beginning with 1 Thessalonians and concluding with later works like Romans, Philippians, and Philemon.

A sensitivity to Paul's eschatological hope and his mystical experience of Christ may make it easier for readers to appreciate Paul's ideas. Despite the difficulty of understanding some passages (2 Pet. 3:15–16), the rewards of entering the brillian world of Pauline thought are well worth the effort.

RECOMMENDED READING

Beker, J. C. *Paul the Apostle: The Triumph of God in Life and Thought.* Philadelphia: Fortress Press, 1980.

Betz, Hans D. "Paul." In D. N. Freedman, ed., *The Anchor Bible Dictionary,* Vol. 5, pp. 186–201. New York: Doubleday, 1992. Surveys Paul's life and theological views.

Cousar, Charles B. *The Letters of Paul.* Nashville: Abingdon Press, 1996. Places the letters in their historical and theological context.

Engberg-Pedersen, Troels. *Paul and the Stories.* Louisville, Ky.: Westminster/John Knox Press, 2000. An important attempt to place Pauline thought in a stoic context.

Fitzmyer, Joseph. *Paul and His Theology,* 2nd ed. Englewood Cliffs, N.J.: Prentice-Hall, 1989. A brief but careful introduction to Paul's central teachings.

———. "Paul." In R. E. Brown, et al., eds., *The New Jerome Biblical Commentary,* 2nd ed. pp. 1329–1337. Englewood Cliffs, N.J.: Prentice-Hall, 1990. A helpful survey of Paul's contribution to Christian thought by an eminent Roman Catholic scholar.

Holmberg, B. *Paul and Power.* Philadelphia: Fortress Press, 1980. An incisive study of the social forces at work in the Pauline communities and of Paul's difficult relationships with other apostolic leaders.

Jewett, Robert. *A Chronology of Paul's Life.* Philadelphia: Fortress Press, 1979. Evaluates earlier systems of dating events in Paul's career and provides a new chronology.

Keck, Leander E., and Furnish, Victor P. *The Pauline Letters.* Nashville: Abingdon Press, 1984. A good place to begin studying Paul's thought.

Murphy-O'Connor, Jerome. *Paul: A Critical Life.* New York: Clarendon, 1996. Explores psychological motivation for Paul's persecution of Christians, his Pharisaic background, and his missionary tours.

Neyrey, Jerome H. *Paul, in Other Words: A Cultural Reading of His Letters.* Louisville, Ky.: Westminster Press/John Knox Press, 1990. Analyzes Paul's writings to discover the underlying cultural and social assumptions on which Paul based his worldview and theology.

Roetzel, Calvin. *The Letters of Paul: Conversations in Context,* 3rd ed. Atlanta: John Knox Press, 1991. Provides excellent introductions to each Pauline letter.

Sanders, E. P. *Paul, the Law, and the Jewish People.* Philadelphia: Fortress Press, 1983. An excellent exploration of Paul's Jewish heritage.

Segal, Alan F. *Paul the Convert: The Apostolate and Apostasy of Saul the Pharisee.* New Haven, Conn., and London: Yale University Press, 1990. Examines Paul's views of the Christ event in the light of his Jewish heritage.

Soards, Marion L. *The Apostle Paul: An Introduction to His Writings and Teaching.* Mahwah, N.J.: Paulist Press, 1987. A clearly written introduction to Paul's thought, emphasizing his eschatology.

Theissen, Gerd. *The Social Setting of Pauline Christianity.* Philadelphia: Fortress Press, 1982. A study of the social dynamics operating in the church at Corinth; one of the most illuminating studies of primitive Christianity yet published.

1 Thessalonians

KEY TOPICS/THEMES

1 Thessalonians is Paul's earliest surviving letter, and thus the oldest Christian document in existence. Written from Corinth about 50 C.E. to a church that Paul, with his companions **Timothy** and **Silas** (Silvanus), had recently founded, it is remarkable chiefly for its eschatology, particularly the urgent expectation of Christ's Parousia (5:1–11) and the resurrection of the dead (4:13–18).

KEY QUESTIONS

What great event did Paul expect to happen in his lifetime? How would it affect believers?

1 Thessalonians preserves our earliest glimpse of how Pauline Christianity was established in Gentile territory. Capital of the Roman province of Macedonia, Thessalonica (now called Thessa-

loniki) was a bustling port city located on the Via Egnatia, the major highway linking Rome with the East. According to the Book of Acts, Paul spent only three weeks there, preaching mainly in the local synagogue to generally unreceptive Jews, who soon drove him out of town (17:1–18:5).

Paul's letter to the newly founded Thessalonian congregation, however, gives a different picture, making no reference to a synagogue ministry and implying that his converts were largely Gentile (1:9). Probably written in Corinth about 50 C.E., a scant twenty years after the Crucifixion, 1 Thessalonians is remarkable in showing how quickly essential Christian ideas had developed and how thoroughly apocalyptic Paul's message was. Referring to the Parousia in no fewer than six different passages, at least once in each of the letter's five brief chapters, Paul makes the imminence of Jesus' return his central message (1:10; 2:19; 3:13; 4:13–18; 5:1–11).

The Thessalonians, he says, have become a shining example to other Greek churches because they have "turned from idols to be servants of the true and living God, . . . to wait expectantly for his Son from heaven, whom he raised from the dead, Jesus our deliverer from the retribution to come" (1:10). This passage may, in fact, epitomize the principal themes of Paul's oral gospel, the *kerygma* he preached in urban marketplaces, shops, and homes. In general content, it resembles the more elaborate proclamation that Luke placed on Paul's lips when he spoke to the Athenians (Acts 17:22–31). Urging the Greeks to forsake lifeless idols for the "living God" of Judaism, Paul presents Jesus' resurrection from the dead as introducing history's climactic moment: his soon-to-occur descent from heaven to rescue his followers from the catastrophe of divine judgment.

For Paul, the implications of the impending apocalypse are clear: The Thessalonians must reform their typically lenient Gentile attitudes toward sexual activity. They have already made progress in living "to please God," but they can do better, abstaining from "fornication," becoming "holy," living "quietly," and showing love to all (4:1–12).

Although the Thessalonians do not exhibit the kind of opposition Paul describes in letters to the Corinthians and Galatians, he devotes considerable space to self-justification, emphasizing how nurturing, altruistic, and hard-working he was when in their company (2:1–12). In particular, he stresses the fact that he remained financially independent of the people he taught, working "night and day" to be self-supporting (2:9). The passage concluding Chapter 2, in which he suddenly departs from praising his healthy relationship with the Thessalonians to castigate his fellow Jews, referring to the "retribution" inflicted on them, may have been inserted by a later copyist after Rome's destruction of Jerusalem in 70 C.E. (2:13–16).

THE PAROUSIA AND THE RESURRECTION

After the long introductory section (1:1–4:12), Paul arrives at his principal reason for sending the letter—a clarification of his teaching about End time (4:13–5:11). Christians must cling firmly to their newfound faith and live ethically correct lives because Jesus will soon return to judge them. Apparently, some Thessalonians believed that the **Parousia** would occur so swiftly that all persons converted to Christ would live to see his Second Coming. That belief was shaken when some believers died before Jesus had reappeared. What would become of them? Had the dead missed their opportunity to join Christ in ruling over the world?

Paul explains that the recently dead are not lost, but will share in the glory of Christ's return. Revealing his conviction that he would personally witness the Parousia, Paul states that "we who are left alive until the Lord comes" will have no advantage over the faithful dead. Using the traditional language of Jewish apocalyptic writing, Paul writes that when the trumpet call of Final Judgment sounds, the Christian dead will rise first. Simultaneously, Christians who are still alive—Paul and his fellow believers—will be lifted from earth into the air to join the resurrected saints on their journey to heaven. In both life and death, then, the believer remains with Jesus (4:13–18). (Compare 1 Thessalonians with Paul's more elaborate discussion of the resurrection in 1 Corinthians 15.)

THE FUTILITY OF CALCULATING "DATES AND TIMES"

Although he eagerly expects Jesus' reappearance "soon," Paul has no patience with those who try to predict the exact date of the Parousia. He discourages speculation and notes that calculating "dates and times" is futile because the world's final day will come as quietly as a thief at midnight. Stressing the unexpectedness of the Parousia, Paul declares that it will occur while men proclaim "peace and security" (a common political theme in Roman times as well as the present). Disaster will strike the nations suddenly, as labor pains strike a woman without warning (5:1–3).

In the Hebrew Bible, the "Day of the Lord" was the time of Yahweh's intervention into human history, his visitation of earth to judge all nations and to impose his universal rule (Amos 5:18; Joel 2:14–15). In Paul's apocalyptic vision, Jesus serves as the divinely appointed agent of *eschaton*. As the eschatological Judge, Jesus serves a double function: He brings punishment to the disobedient ("the terrors of judgment") but vindication and deliverance to the faithful. Paul's cosmic Jesus is paradoxical: He dies to save believers from the negative judgment that his return imposes on unregenerate humanity. Returning to his main theme, Paul concludes that "we, awake [living] or asleep [dead]" live in permanent association with Christ (5:4–11).

ROLE OF THE SPIRIT

In anticipation of Jesus' speedy return, Paul reminds the Thessalonians that the Holy Spirit's visible activity among them is also evidence of the world's impending transformation. As noted in Acts, the Spirit motivating a believer to prophesy, heal, or speak in tongues was taken as evidence of the Deity's presence. Thus, Paul tells his readers not to "stifle inspiration" or otherwise discourage believers from prophesying. Christian prophets, inspired by the Spirit, play a major role in Pauline churches, but Paul is aware that enthusiastic visionaries can cause trouble. Believers are to distinguish between "good" and "bad" inspirations,

avoiding the latter, but they are not to inhibit charismatic behavior. Besides providing evidence that the End is near, the Spirit's presence also validates the Christian message (Joel 2:28–32; Acts 2:1–21; 1 Cor. 2:9–16; 12–14).

(A disputed letter, 2 Thessalonians, is discussed later in the chapter.)

RECOMMENDED READING

Beker, J. C. *Paul's Apocalyptic Gospel: The Coming Triumph of God.* Philadelphia: Fortress Press, 1982.

Collins, R. F. "The First Letter to Thessalonians." In *The New Jerome Biblical Commentary,* pp. 772–779. Englewood Cliffs, N.J.: Prentice-Hall, 1990.

Keck, L. E., and Furnish, V. P. *The Pauline Letters.* Nashville: Abingdon Press, 1984.

Krentz, Edgar M. "Thessalonians, First and Second Epistles to the." In D. N. Freedman, ed., *The Anchor Bible Dictionary,* Vol. 6, pp. 515–523, New York: Doubleday, 1992.

Marshall, I. H. *1 and 2 Thessalonians.* Grand Rapids, Mich.: Eerdmans, 1983.

Orr, W. F., and Walther, J. A., eds. *1 and 2 Corinthians and 1 and 2 Thessalonians.* Vol. 32 of the Anchor Bible. Garden City, N.Y.: Doubleday, 1976.

Reese, J. M. *1 and 2 Thessalonians.* Wilmington, Del.: Michael Glazier, 1979.

1 Corinthians

KEY TOPICS/THEMES

Paul's letters to Corinth urge the recipients to overcome their serious divisions, abandon competitive behavior, and strive for unity of belief and purpose. The most important topics include differences between human and divinely revealed wisdom (1:10–3:23), Christian ethics and responsibilities (5:1–11:1), proper conduct at Communion (11:17–34), appreciation for gifts of the Spirit (Chs. 12–14), and resurrection of the dead (Ch. 15).

KEY QUESTIONS

Why does Paul urge the Corinthians to achieve unity? What essential beliefs does he describe?

Paul's letters to the congregation in **Corinth**, a wealthy port city noted for its licentiousness and cult of the love goddess Aphrodite (Venus), mirror the problems of an infant church divided by doctrinal disputes, rival leaderships, and sexual immorality. His most extensive correspondence to any one group, the Corinthian letters are particularly valuable for their references to Paul's personal life, their portrait of a first-century Christian community, their theological content, and their memorable passages on love (1 Cor. 13) and a future life (1 Cor. 15; 2 Cor. 4:7–5:10).

PROMOTING CHRISTIAN UNITY

Causes of Division   Paul's first objective is to halt the rivalries that divide the Corinthians. Without imposing a dogmatic conformity, he asks his readers to work together cooperatively for their mutual benefit (1:8–10). Like all early Christian congregations, the one at Corinth met in a private house large enough to accommodate the entire group. Although membership was small, numbering perhaps 50 or 100 persons, it was broken into several opposing cliques. Some members placed undue importance on the particular leader who had converted or baptized them—Paul, **Cephas** (Peter), or **Apollos**, an Alexandrine Jew whose eloquence had impressed many—and competed with one another over the prestige of their respective mentors.

A more serious cause of division may have sprung from the members' unequal social and educational backgrounds, particularly because the Corinthians included both slaves and slave-owners. Even among free citizens, some individuals apparently believed that they were demonstrably superior to their neighbors (Figure 12.11). Close examination of Chapter 1 reveals that Paul's attack on false "wisdom" is really an attempt to discourage human competitiveness. In Paul's view, all believers are fundamentally equal: "For through faith you are all [children] of God in union with Christ Jesus. . . . There is no such thing as Jew and Greek, slave and freeman, male and female; for you are all one person in Christ Jesus" (Gal. 3:26, 28). When Paul reminds the Corinthians that he taught his message as simply as possible, he does so to show that the new faith is essentially in-

Figure 12.11 In this portrait uncovered at Pompeii (buried by the eruption of Mount Vesuvius in 79 C.E.), Terentius Neo and his wife proudly display the pen and wax tablets that advertise their literary skills. Similar young Roman couples of the professional classes undoubtedly were among the members of Paul's newly founded churches in Corinth and other Greco-Roman cities.

compatible with individual pride or competitiveness. (Paul's relative lack of success debating Athenian philosophers just before coming to Corinth [Acts 17] may have influenced his decision to preach henceforth without any intellectual pretensions [1:23; 2:1].)

Wisdom: Human and Divine   Paul's argument (1:17–2:5) is sometimes misused to justify an antiintellectual approach to religion, in which reason and faith are treated as if they were mutually exclusive. The apostle's attack on "wisdom" is not directed against human reason or logic, however. It is aimed at individual Corinthians who boast of special insights that supposedly give them a deeper understanding than that granted their fellow Christians. This elitism led some persons to cultivate a false sense of superiority that devalued less educated believers, fragmenting the congregation into groups of the "wise" and "foolish."

Paul reminds the Corinthians that humans did not come to know God through reason by itself, but that God revealed his saving purpose through Christ as a free gift (1:21). Because all are equally undeserving recipients of the divine benefits, no believer has the right to boast (1:21–31).

The apostle, however, does teach a previously hidden wisdom to persons mature enough to appreciate it. This wisdom is God's revelation through the Spirit that now dwells in the Christian community. The hitherto unknown "mind" of God — the ultimate reality that philosophers make the object of their search — is unveiled through Christ (2:6–16). The divine mystery, although inaccessible to rational inquiry, is finally made clear in the weakness and obedient suffering of Christ, the means by which God reconciles humanity to himself.

Having dealt with factionalism, Paul turns to the problem of sexual misconduct, another source of disunity among the Corinthians, urging the excommunication of a man who had scandalized the community by living openly with his stepmother (5:1–8). This consigning to the outside world ("Satan") any Christian who is a slanderer, drunkard, idolator, or otherwise conspicuous sinner (5:9–13) was later to prove a formidable weapon, for the excommunicated person, deprived of both religious and social rights, became a pariah. Paul's theological justification for this practice is that the Christian's body is "a shrine of the indwelling Holy Spirit" (6:19) that must not be profaned by sinful acts such as intercourse with prostitutes. Finally, in Chapter 6, Paul orders the Corinthians to stop bringing lawsuits against fellow believers, stating that it is better to suffer a wrong than to expose other Christians to public criticism by airing their disputes in pagan courts (6:1–8).

ANSWERING QUESTIONS FROM THE CONGREGATION

Beginning in Chapter 7, Paul answers additional ethical and theological questions about which the Corinthians had written him. His dim view of marriage and unequivocal preference for a single

life of sexual abstinence can be understood in the light of his eschatology. Anticipating the return of Christ and the End of the world (7:26, 29–31), he believes that it is best to devote oneself wholeheartedly to the Lord's work (7:1–40). To a second problem — concerning whether a believer may lawfully eat food sold after it had been sacrificed on a pagan altar — Paul's solution is that the Christian, although technically free to act as he or she judges best, should do nothing that will trouble another believer's conscience (8:1–11:1).

REGULATING BEHAVIOR IN CHURCH

Chapters 11–14 contain Paul's advice regulating behavior in church. The issues he addresses include the particpation of women, conduct during reenactments of the Last Supper, and the handling of charismatic "gifts," such as the Spirit-given ability to prophesy, heal, or speak in tongues.

The Importance of Women in the Church   In recent decades, Pauline regulations about women's roles in the church have been attacked as culture-bound and chauvinistic. Because we know so little of very early Christian practices, it is difficult to establish to what degree women originally shared in church leadership (Box 12.7). Jesus numbered many women among his most loyal disciples, and Paul refers to several women as his "fellow workers" (Phil. 4:3). In the last chapter of Romans, in which Paul lists the missionary Prisca (Priscilla) ahead of her husband, Aquila, the apostle asks the recipients to support **Phoebe**, a presiding officer in the Cenchreae church, in discharging her administrative duties (Rom. 16:1–6).

In Corinthians, however, Paul seems to impose certain restrictions on women's participation in church services. His insistence that women cover their heads with veils (11:3–16) is open to a variety of interpretations. Is it the writer's concession to the existing Jewish and Greco-Roman custom of secluding women, an attempt to avoid offending patriarchal prejudices? If women unveil their physical attractiveness, does this distract male onlookers or even sexually tempt angels, such as those who "lusted" for mortal women before the Flood

Box 12.7 The Roles of Women in the Early Church

Few issues provoke more controversy, even today, than that involving the roles of women in the Christian church, particularly the question of women's assuming positions of leadership. Historically, the church's dominant view is the one expressed in 1 Timothy, a passage in which the writer categorically relegates women to perpetual passivity, silence, and submission:

> A woman must be a learner, listening quietly and with due submission. I do not permit a woman to be a teacher, nor must woman domineer over man; she should be quiet. (1 Tim. 2:11–12)

The author's scriptural justification for denying all women a teaching role derives from his singular interpretation of the second of two different stories about humanity's creation narrated in Genesis. Whereas the first version states that "male and female" came into being simultaneously, both in the divine "image" (Gen. 1:26–27), the second, which the writer selects to support his argument, awards Adam (the first male) priority in time and importance. In the writer's view, Eve (the first female) is implicitly inferior to Adam because she was formed "afterwards" (1 Tim. 2:13; cf. Gen. 2:18–25). However, 1 Timothy's most damaging charge against Eve (and hence, all her daughters) is her alleged susceptibility to deceit: "It was not Adam who[m] [the serpent] deceived; it was the woman, who, yielding to deception, fell into sin" (1 Tim. 3:14; cf. Gen. 3). In a stroke, the ultimate responsibility for humanity's disobedience of and alienation from God is thus placed on Eve, whose credulity and irresponsibility manifestly exclude her entire sex from positions of trust in the Christian community. Yet, as the writer concedes, nature accords women one clear means of redemption: They can be "saved through motherhood"—bearing children.

The insulting estimate of women's innate character found in 1 Timothy is but one reason almost all scholars do not think that Paul wrote it. In Paul's genuine letters, he emphasizes the spiritual equality of all believers: For those baptized "into union" with Christ, "There is no such thing as Jew and Greek, . . . male and female, for you are all one person in Christ Jesus" (Gal. 3:28). Besides recognizing women such as Prisca (Priscilla), Euodia, and Syntyche as his co-workers, the historical Paul also refers to a Roman woman, Junia (Junias), as

"eminent among the apostles" (Rom. 16:7). How, then, does one of Paul's authentic letters, 1 Corinthians, contain a diatribe against women similar to that in 1 Timothy 2? Scholars have long believed that this passage forbidding women to speak in church (1 Cor. 14:34–35), which clearly interrupts the focus on the function of prophesying, was inserted into manuscripts of 1 Corinthians by scribes who wanted to harmonize Paul's authentic writings with the restrictions on women later imposed by the author of 1 Timothy. Many scholars do not think that this view of women was part of Paul's original message.

If Jesus included numerous women among his disciples—some of whom were the first to bring the "good news" of his resurrection—and Paul endorsed women such as Phoebe as congregational leaders (Rom. 16:1–2ff.), how did the Christian community eventually come to reject women's leadership in favor of exclusively male domination? Recently, several scholars have suggested that the gradual shrinking of women's roles in the church may have been related to a historic change in the kinds of places in which believers assembled. In Paul's day, relatively small groups of Christians assembled in private houses—no separate church buildings then existed. Because only comparatively well-to-do homeowners had dwellings large enough to accommodate even a few dozen people, the host and/or hostess probably took a leading role in presiding over gatherings in their home. If a congregation assembled at the house of a wealthy widow—one no longer under a husband's control—it is likely that she participated actively in worship services, praying, prophesying, and teaching others (1 Cor. 11:5; cf. the story of Lydia, who offered her house to Paul, in Acts 16:13–15).

As congregations grew, attracting larger numbers of qualified men, however, the prominence of women householders who hosted Christian meetings gradually declined. The gradual shift from gathering in private accommodations, traditionally run by women, to assembling in larger edifices in the public sphere, where men dominated, had an inevitable effect on the composition of church leadership. This change in meeting place from the domestic to the public arena was reinforced by two other concurrent trends. By the second and third centuries C.E., the Christian community was no longer living in the fervent apocalyptic hope that had characterized its be-

(continued)

Box 12.7 *(continued)*

ginnings. As expectations that God would soon bring history to an end diminished, Jesus' kingdom ethic—in which "the first would be last, and the last first"—also had less impact. Early believers, eagerly awaiting the Parousia, could form a subculture in which the kingdom values prevailed, incorporating the least and "last" of society's members—including women—into full community participation (Gal. 3:28). But after belief in an imminent divine kingdom waned and the church accepted an indefinitely delayed Parousia, the Christian community increasingly adapted itself to the customs and assumptions of the larger Greco-Roman world. The adaptation seems to have included almost wholesale acceptance of Roman society's view of male-female relationships, a view that the author of 1 Timothy uncritically endorses. In the Roman social structure, men achieved status—and positions of public honor—by exercising power over other men, whether economic, political, social, or military. While men universally controlled all public activities and institutions, women, regarded as physically weaker and less capable, were confined to the domestic realm.

Given Roman society's universal approval of masculine dominance, if a free man were to join a Christian congregation supervised by a woman, he would be publicly shamed, forfeiting his claim to honor. In the light of Roman mores, it is not surprising that the church, desiring as many converts as possible, chose to model its leadership structure in a way that Roman males would find acceptable. As many feminist critics have pointed out, however, Western society has experienced such radical changes since the Enlightenment that the Christian community is now free to construct more inclusive models of leadership, creating an organization that does not depend on the social and sexual assumptions of antiquity.

For further reading, see Ross Kraemer, *Her Share of the Blessings: Women's Religions among Pagans, Jews, and Christians in the Greco-Roman World.* New York: Oxford University Press, 1992; and Elizabeth Schüssler Fiorenza, *In Memory of Her: A Feminist Theological Reconstruction of Christian Origins.* New York: Crossroad, 1983.

(Gen. 6:1–4)? Conversely, is the veil a symbol of women's religious authority, to be worn when prophesying before the congregation?

Paul's argument for relegating women to a subordinate position in church strikes many readers as labored and illogical. (Some scholars think that this passage [11:2–16] is the interpolation of a later editor, added to make Corinthians agree with the non-Pauline instruction in 1 Tim. 2:8–15.) Paul grants women an active role, praying and prophesying during worship, but at the same time he argues that the female is a secondary creation, made from man, who was created directly by God. The apostle uses the second version of human origins (Gen. 2) to support the sexual hierarchy, but he could as easily have cited the first creation account in which male and female are created simultaneously, both in the "image of God" (Gen. 1:27). Given Paul's revelation that Christian equality transcends all distinctions among believers, including those of sex, class, and nationality (Gal. 3:28),

many commentators see the writer's choice in a Genesis precedent as decidedly arbitrary.

The Communion Meal (the Last Supper, or Eucharist)

Christianity's most solemn ritual, the reenactment of Jesus' last meal with his disciples, represents the mystic communion between the Lord and his followers. Meeting in private homes to commemorate the event, the Corinthians had turned the service into a riotous drinking party. Instead of a celebration of Christian unity, it had become another source of division. Wealthy participants came early and consumed all the delicacies of the communion meal before the working poor arrived, thus leaving their social inferiors hungry and humiliated (11:17–22).

Paul contrasts this inconsiderate behavior with the tradition coming directly from Jesus himself. Recording Jesus' sacramental distribution of bread and wine, he stresses that the ceremony is to be decorously repeated in memory of Christs' death until he returns. This allusion to the nearness of Jesus' reappearance reminds the Corinthians of the seriousness with which they must observe the **Last Supper** cememony (11:23–34).

Gifts of the Spirit Led by the Holy Spirit, the early Christian community was composed of many persons gifted with supernatural abilities. Some had the gift of prophecy; others were apostles, teachers, healers, miracle workers, or speakers in tongues. In Corinth, these individual gifts, and the rivalries among those possessing them, were yet another cause of division. Reminding them that one individual spirit grants all these different abilities, Paul employs a favorite metaphor in which he compares the church to the human body, with its many different functioning parts. Each Christian gift is to be used to benefit the whole body, the church.

The Hymn to Love (Agapē) In his most celebrated burst of inspiration, Paul interrupts his advice on the use of spiritual gifts to show the Corinthians "the best way of all" (13:1–13). Listing the most highly honored charismatic gifts — prophecy, knowledge, power, and self-sacrifice — Paul states that "without love" these gifts are meaningless. His description of love (in Greek, *agapē*, meaning "selfless giving") stresses its human application: Love is patient, kind, forgiving; it keeps no record of offenses. Its capacity for loyal devotion is infinite: "there is no limit to its faith, its hope, and its endurance." Love once given is never withdrawn. Whereas other spiritual gifts are only partial reflections of the divine reality and will be rendered obsolete in the perfect world to come, the supreme trio of Christian virtues — faith, hope, and love — endures forever.

Speaking in Tongues (Glossolalia) Although he gives love top priority, Paul also acknowledges the value of other spiritual gifts, especially prophecy, which involves rational communication. "Ecstatic utterance" — **speaking in tongues**, or *glossolalia* — may be emotionally satisfying to the speaker, but it does not "build up" the congregation as do teaching and prophecy. Although he does not prohibit

ecstatic utterance (Paul states that he is better at it than any Corinthian), the apostle ranks it as the least useful spiritual gift (14:1–40).

THE ESCHATOLOGICAL HOPE: RESURRECTION OF THE DEAD

Paul's last major topic — his eschatological vision of the **resurrection** (15:1–57) — is theologically the most important. Apparently, some Corinthians challenged Paul's teaching about the afterlife. One group may have questioned the necessity of a future bodily resurrection because members believed that at baptism (and upon receiving the Spirit) they had already achieved eternal life. Others may have denied Paul's concept of resurrection because they shared the Greek philosophical view that a future existence is purely spiritual. According to Socrates, Plato, and numerous mystery religions, death occurs when the immortal soul escapes from the perishable body. The **soul** does not need a body when it enters the invisible spirit realm. To believers in the soul's inherent immortality, Paul's Hebrew belief in the physical body's resurrection was grotesque and irrelevant.

The Historical Reality of Jesus' Resurrection
To demonstrate that bodily resurrection is a reality, Paul calls on the Corinthians to remember that Jesus rose from the dead. Preserving our earliest tradition of Jesus' postresurrection appearances, Paul notes that the risen Lord appeared to as many as 500 believers at once, as well as to Paul (15:3–8; Box 12.8). Paul uses his opponents' denial against them and argues that if there is no resurrection then Christ was not raised and Christians hope in vain. He trusts not in the Greek concept of innate human immortality, but in the Judeo-Christian faith in God's ability to raise the faithful dead. Without Christ's resurrection, Paul states, there is no afterlife, and of all people Christians are the most pitiable (15:12–19).

Paul now invokes two archetypal figures to illustrate the means by which human death and its opposite, eternal life, entered the world. Citing the Genesis creation account, Paul declares that the "first man," Adam (God's first earthly son),

Box 12.8 Resurrection Traditions in Paul and the Gospels

The oldest surviving account of Jesus' postresurrection appearances occurs in Paul's first letter to the Corinthians, which contains a tradition "handed on" to Paul from earlier Christians. None of the Gospels' resurrection narratives, written fifteen to forty years after the date of Paul's letter, refers to Jesus' manifestations to his kinsman James or to the "over 500 brothers" who simultaneously beheld him (cf. 1 Cor: 15:3–8.)

PAUL (C. 54 C.E.)	MARK (C. 66–70 C.E.)	MATTHEW (C:85 C.E.)	LUKE (C. 85 C.E.)	JOHN (C. 90–100 C.E.)
Jesus appears to Cephas (Peter) to "the Twelve" to "over 500" to James (Jesus' "brother") to "all the Apostles" to Paul (as an *apokalypsis*, or "revelation," Gal. 1:15–16	No postresurrection account in original text (Two accounts were added later: Mark 16:8b and 16:9–19, in which Jesus appears first to Mary Magdalene, and then to the Eleven.)	No parallels Jesus appears to "the eleven disciples" (minus Judas Iscariot) in Galilee"	Reference to "Simon [Peter]" to "the Eleven" (in Jerusalem) Jesus appears to "Cleopas"and an unnamed disciple on the road to Emmaus (near Jerusalem)	No parallels Jesus appears to Mary Magdalene (in Jerusalem) to "the disciples," particularly Thomas (in Jerusalem) to "the sons of Zebedee," Simon Peter, and the "beloved disciple" (in Galilee)

brought death to the human race, but Christ (Adam's "heavenly" counterpart, a new creation) brings life. The coming resurrection (and perhaps salvation as well) is universal: "as in Adam all men die, so in Christ all will be brought to life." The first product of the resurrection harvest, Christ will return to raise the obedient dead and defeat all enemies, including death itself. Christ subjects the entire universe to his rule but himself remains subordinate to God, so that God is "all in all" (15:20–28). Noting that Corinthians practice baptism of their dead (posthumously initiating them into the church), Paul argues that this ritual presupposes the resurrection's reality (15:29).

Paul next responds to the skeptics' demands to know what possible form bodily resurrection might take. Although he admits that "flesh and blood can never possess the [immaterial] kingdom of God," Paul retains his Hebraic conviction that human beings cannot exist without some kind of body. First, he uses analogies from the natural world, demonstrating that life grows from buried seeds and that existence takes different forms. As heavenly bodies surpass earthly objects in beauty, so the resurrected body will outshine the physical body: "Sown [dead and buried] . . . as a perishable thing [it] is raised imperishable." Paul describes here a supernatural transformation of the human essence, a process that creates a paradox, a contradiction in terms—a material body that is also spirit (15:35–44).

Paul gives his exposition immediacy by unveiling a divine mystery: When the last trumpet sounds, he and other living Christians will be instantly transformed and clothed with an imperishable, immortal existence. In the universal restoration, death itself will perish, consumed in Christ's life-giving victory (15:51–57).

Closing Remarks Returning abruptly from his cosmic vision of human destiny to take up earthly affairs again, Paul reminds the Corinthians of their previous agreement to help the Jerusalem church. They are to contribute money every Sunday, an obligation Paul had assumed when visiting the Jerusalem leadership (Gal. 2). The letter ends with Paul's invocation of Jesus' speedy return—"Marana tha" (Come, O Lord)—an Aramaic prayer dating from the first generation of Palestinian Christians.

2 Corinthians

KEY TOPICS/THEMES

A composite work consisting of several letters or letter fragments, 2 Corinthians shows Paul defending his apostolic authority (Chs. 10–13); the first nine chapters, apparently written after Chapters 10–13, describe Paul's reconciliation with the church at Corinth.

KEY QUESTIONS

Why did many Christians doubt Paul's claim to apostleship? How did Paul persuade the Corinthians to accept his authority?

Whereas 1 Corinthians is a unified document, 2 Corinthians seems to be a compendium of several letters or letter fragments written at different times and reflecting radically different situations in the Corinthian church. Even casual readers will note the contrast between the harsh, sarcastic tone of Chapters 10–13 and the generally friendlier, more conciliatory tone of the earlier chapters. Many scholars believe that Chapters 10–13 represent the "painful letter" alluded to in 2 Corinthians 2:3–4, making this part necessarily older than Chapters 1–9. Some authorities find as many as six or more remnants of different letters in 2 Corinthians, but for this discussion we concentrate on the work's two main divisions (Chs. 10–13 and 1–9), taking them in the order in which scholars believe they were composed.

APOSTOLIC ATTACKS ON PAUL'S AUTHORITY

Behind the writing of 2 Corinthians lies a dramatic conflict between Paul and the church he had founded. After he had dispatched 1 Corinthians, several events took place that strained his relationship with the church almost to the breaking point. New opponents, whom Paul satirizes as "superlative apostles" (11:5), infiltrated the congregation and rapidly gained positions of influence. Paul then made a brief, "painful" visit to Corinth, only to suffer public humiliation (2:1–5; 7:12). His visit a failure, he returned to Ephesus, where he wrote the Corinthians a severe reprimand, part of which is preserved in Chapters 10–13. Having carried the severe letter to Corinth, his associate **Titus** then rejoins Paul in Macedonia, bringing the good news that the Corinthians are sorry for their behavior and now support the apostle (7:5–7). Paul subsequently writes a joyful letter of reconciliation, included in Chapters 1–9. Although this reconstruction of events is conjectural, it accounts for the sequence of alienation, hostility, and reconciliation found in this composite document.

THE SEVERE LETTER: PAUL'S DEFENSE OF HIS APOSTOLIC AUTHORITY

In the last three chapters of 2 Corinthians, Paul writes a passionate, almost brutal defense of his apostolic authority. A masterpiece of savage irony, Chapters 10–13 show Paul boasting "as a fool," using every device of rhetoric to demolish his opponents' pretensions to superiority. We do not know the identity of these opponents, except that they were Jewish Christians whom Paul accuses of proclaiming "another Jesus" and imparting a "spirit" different from that introduced by *his* "gospel." The label "superlative apostles" suggests that these critics enjoyed considerable prestige, perhaps as representatives from the Jerusalem church. They may have been emissaries from James, "the Lord's brother," similar to those who drove a wedge between Peter and Paul in Antioch. In both cases, Paul describes their "gospel" as differing from his (Gal. 2:11–15).

Although Paul's bitter sarcasm may offend some readers, we must realize that this unattractive quality represents the reverse side of his intense emotional commitment to the Corinthians' welfare. Behind the writer's "bragging" and threats (10:2–6; 11:16–21; 13:3, 10) lies the sting of unrequited affection. The nature of love that Paul had so confidently defined in his earlier letter (1 Cor. 13) is now profoundly tested.

It is not certain that the "superlative apostles" (11:5) who question his teaching are the same as the "sham apostles" (11:13) whom Paul accuses of being Satan's agents (11:12–15). Whoever they were, these opponents apparently base their authority at least partly on supernatural visions and revelations. Paul responds by telling of his own mystical experience in "the third heaven" (in some extrabiblical beliefs, the spiritual Eden), where he learned secrets too holy to reveal to the uninitiated (12:1–13).

THE LETTER OF RECONCILIATION

Recognizing True Apostolic Leadership   After Titus left to carry the disciplinary letter from Ephesus to Corinth, Paul began a journey to Macedonia. When Titus caught up with Paul, he brought the welcome news that the Corinthians had disavowed their divisive leaders and now gave Paul their full support, acknowledging him as a genuine apostle who had treated them honorably.

Despite the reconciliation, the Corinthian church is still troubled by Paul's rivals, whom he denounces as mere "hawkers" (salespersons) of God's word (2:17). Although he is more controlled than in Chapters 10–13, his exasperation is evident when he asks if he must begin all over again proving his apostolic credentials (3:1). Placing the responsibility for recognizing true apostolic leadership squarely on the Corinthians, the writer reminds them that *they* are his living letters of recommendation. Echoing Jeremiah 31:31, Paul contrasts the Mosaic Covenant—inscribed on stone tablets—with the new covenant written on human hearts. Inhabited by the Holy Spirit, the Christian reflects God's image more splendidly than Moses (3:2–28).

Nurturing a Spiritual Body   In this section (4:16–5:10), Paul further develops the concept of a "spiritual body" that he had outlined in 1 Corinthians 15. In his earlier letter, Paul wrote that the believer will become instantly transformed—receive an incorruptible "spiritual body"—at Christ's return. He said nothing about the Christian's state of being or consciousness during the interim period between death and the future resurrection. In 2 Corinthians, Paul seems to imply that believers are already developing a spiritual body that will clothe them at the moment of death.

Paul appears to state that God has prepared for each Christian an eternal form, a "heavenly habitation," that endows the bearer with immortality. Yearning to avoid human death, he envisions receiving that heavenly form now, putting it on like a garment over the physical body, "so that our mortal part may be absorbed into life immortal." The presence of the Spirit, he concludes, is visible evidence that God intends this process of spiritual metamorphosis to take place during the present lifetime (5:1–5). United with Christ, the believer thus becomes a new creation (5:11–17).

The spiritual renewal is God's plan for reconciling humanity to himself. As Christ's ambassador, Paul advances the work of reconciliation; his sufferings are an act of love for them (5:18–6:13). Imploring the Corinthians to return his affection, Paul ends his defense of the apostolic purpose with a not-altogether-convincing expression of confidence in their loyalty (7:2–16).

Chapters 8 and 9, which concern Paul's collection for the Jerusalem poor, seem redundant and may have originated as separate missives before an editor combined them. Citing the generosity of Macedonia's churches, Paul reminds the Corinthians that "God loves a cheerful giver" (2 Cor. 9:7).

RECOMMENDED READING

Betz, H. D. "Corinthians, Second Epistle to the." In D. N. Freedman, ed., *The Anchor Bible Dictionary*, Vol. 1, pp. 1148–1154. New York: Doubleday, 1992.

Betz, H. D., and Mitchel, M. M. "Corinthians, First Epistle to the." In D. N. Freedman, ed., *The Anchor Bible Dictionary*, Vol. 1, pp. 1139–1148. New York: Doubleday, 1992.

Bruce, F. F. *1 and 2 Corinthians*. Grand Rapids, Mich.: Eerdmans, 1978.

Furnish, V. P. *Second Corinthians*. Anchor Bible Commentary, Vol. 32A. Garden City, N.Y.: Doubleday, 1984.

Goulder, Michael J. *Early Christian Conflict in Corinth: Paul and the Followers of Peter*. Peabody, Mass.: Hendrickson, 2000. Argues that the chief source of division in Corinth resulted from in-fighting between disciples of Peter and Paul.

Hays, Richard B. *Interpretation: First Corinthians*. Louisville, Ky.: Westminster/John Knox Press, 1997. Examines Paul's theological response to socioeconomic problems at Corinth.

Hooker, M. D. "Authority on Her Head: An Examination of 1 Cor. 11:10." *New Testament Studies* 10 (1963): 410–416.

Hurd, J. C. *The Origin of 1 Corinthians*. Macon, Ga.: Mercer University Press, 1983.

Meeks, Wayne. *The First Urban Christians: The Social World of the Apostle Paul*. New Haven, Conn.: Yale University Press, 1983. An insightful investigation into the cultural environment and socioeconomic background of the earliest Christians.

Murphy-O'Connor, Jerome. *St. Paul's Corinth: Text and Archaeology*. Wilmington, Del.: Michael Glazier, 1983. An archaeologist's illumination of the Corinthian life and customs in Paul's day.

Schmithals, Walter. *Gnosticism in Corinth: An Investigation of the Letters to the Corinthians*. Translated by J. Steely. Nashville: Abingdon Press, 1971.

Schütz, J. H., ed. *The Social Setting of Pauline Christianity*. Philadelphia: Fortress Press, 1982.

Soards, Marian L. *The Apostle Paul: An Introduction to His Writings and Teaching*. New York: Paulist Press, 1987.

Soards, Marian L.; Sampley, Paul; and Wright, N. T., eds. *Romans–First Corinthians*. The New Interpreters Bible, Vol. 10. Nashville: Abingdon Press, 2000. Includes critial analysis of Pauline letters.

Talbert, C. H. *Reading Corinthians: A Literary and Theological Commentary on 1 and 2 Corinthians*. New York: Crossroads Press, 1987.

Theissen, Gerd. *The Social Setting of Pauline Christianity: Essays on Corinth*. Edited, translated, and with an introduction by J. H. Schütz. Philadelphia: Fortress Press, 1982.

Galatians

KEY TOPICS/THEMES

Like the letters to Corinth, this letter to the Galatian churches reflects Paul's ongoing struggle with opponents who challenged his apostolic authority and his "gospel" that believers must live free of the Mosaic Law. An angry declaration of Christianity's independence of Judaism, Galatians vigorously defends Paul's doctrine of salvation through faith. The letter also proclaims Paul's independence of Jerusalem's Christian leadership.

KEY QUESTIONS

What is Paul's relationship to the Jerusalem church? Why does he reject Torah obedience as the source of salvation?

AN ANGRY LETTER TO THE GALATIANS

A brief but extremely important letter, Galatians outlines Paul's most distinctive and innovative doctrine: Obedience to Torah commandments cannot justify a person before God. Only trust (faith) in God's gracious willingness to redeem humanity through Christ can win one divine approval and obtain a believer's salvation.

This uniquely Pauline gospel revolutionized the development of Christianity. By sweeping away all Torah requirements, including circumcision and dietary restrictions, Paul opened the church wide to Gentile converts. Uncircumcised former adherents of Greco-Roman religions were now granted full equality with Jewish Christians. Although the process was only beginning in Paul's day, the influx of Gentiles would soon overwhelm the originally Jewish church, making it an international community with members belonging to every known ethnic group. This swift transformation could not have been possible without Paul's radical insistence on the abandonment of all Mosaic observances, which for centuries had separated Jew from Gentile.

The Recipients The identity of the Galatian churches Paul addresses is uncertain (Figure 12.12). In Paul's time, two different geographical areas could be designated **"Galatia."** The first was a territory in north-central Asia Minor (now Turkey) inhabited by descendants of Celtic tribes that had invaded the region during the third to first centuries B.C.E. Brief references to Galatia in Acts

Figure 12.12 Potential locations of Paul's Galatian churches. The identity of Paul's Galatians is uncertain. The letter may have been directed to churches in the north-central plateau region of Asia Minor (near present-day Ankara, Turkey) or to churches in the southern coastal area of east-central Asia Minor (also in modern Turkey). Many scholars believe that the Galatians were Christians living in Iconium, Lystra, Derbe, and other nearby cities that Paul had visited on his first missionary journey.

(16:6; 18:23) suggest that Paul traveled there, but this is not certain.

The other possibility, which many historians support, is that Paul was writing to Christians in the Roman province of Galatia. The southern portion of this province included the cities of Iconium, **Lystra**, and Derbe, places where the apostle had established churches (Acts 14). If the "southern Galatia" theory is correct, it helps explain the presence of Judaizers (persons advocating circumcision for all converts), because the Roman province was much closer to Jewish-Christian centers at Antioch and Jerusalem than was the northern, Celtic territory.

The Identity of Paul's Opponents Some commentators identify Paul's opponents as emissaries of the Jerusalem church, such as those sent by James to inspect the congregation at Antioch (2:12). It is unlikely, however, that Jewish Christians from Jerusalem would be unaware that requiring circumcision also meant keeping the entire Torah (5:2–3). Paul's opponents appear to combine aspects of a Greco-Roman cult that involved honoring cosmic spirits and observing religious festival days (4:9–10), with selected Torah requirements (6:12–14). This **syncretism** (mixing together elements of two or more different religions to create a new belief) suggests that the opponents are Galatian Gentiles. In Paul's view, their attempt to infuse Jewish and pagan components into Christianity misses the point of the Christ event.

Purpose and Contents Writing from Corinth or Ephesus in about 56 c.e., Paul has a twofold purpose: (1) to prove that he is a true apostle, possessing rights equal to those of the Jerusalem "pillars" (Chs. 1 and 2), and (2) to demonstrate the validity of his gospel that Christian faith replaces works of law, including circumcision. The letter can be divided into five parts:

1. A biographical defense of Paul's autonomy and his relationship with the Jerusalem leadership (1:1–2:14)
2. Paul's unique gospel: justification through faith (2:15–3:29)
3. The adoption of Christians as heirs of Abraham and children of God (4:1–31)
4. The consequences and the obligations of Christian freedom from Mosaic Law (5:1–6:10)
5. The final summary of Paul's argument (6:11–18)

Largely dispensing with his usual greetings and thanksgiving, Paul opens the letter with a vigorous defense of his personal autonomy. His apostolic rank derives not from ordination or "human appointment," but directly from the Deity (1:1–5). Similarly, his message does not depend on information learned from earlier Christians but is a direct "revelation [*apokalypsis*] of Jesus Christ" (1:12). Because he regards his gospel of faith as a divine communication, Paul sees no need to consult other church leaders about the correctness of his policies (1:15–17).

PAUL'S FREEDOM FROM INSTITUTIONAL AUTHORITY

In contrast to Acts, in Galatians Paul presents himself as essentially independent of the mother church at Jerusalem. Nonetheless, he apparently recognizes the desirability of having his work among the Gentiles endorsed by the Palestinian Christian leadership. His visit with the Jerusalem "pillars"—Peter (Cephas), John, and James—is probably the same conference described in Acts 15. According to Paul, the pillars agree to recognize the legitimacy of his Gentile mission. Imposing no Torah restrictions on Gentile converts, the Jerusalem trio ask only that Paul's churches contribute financially to the mother church, a charitable project Paul gladly undertakes (2:10; see 2 Cor. 8–9; Rom. 15).

After the Jerusalem conference, Paul meets Peter again at Antioch, a meeting that shows how far the Jewish-Gentile issue is from being resolved. Paul charges that Jesus' premier disciple is still ambivalent about associating with uncircumcised believers. When James sends emissaries to see if Antiochean Christians are properly observing Mosaic dietary laws, Peter stops sharing in communal meals with Gentiles, perhaps because he fears James's disapproval. Although Paul publicly denounces Peter's action as hypocrisy, claiming that Peter privately does not keep Torah regulations, we cannot be sure of Peter's motives. He may have wished not to offend more conservative Jewish believers and behaved as he did out of respect for others' consciences, a policy Paul himself advocates (1 Cor. 8:1–13) (Figure 12.13).

PAUL'S GOSPEL OF JUSTIFICATION BY FAITH

Paul's strangely negative attitude toward the Mosaic Law puzzles many Jewish scholars. Why does a Pharisee trained to regard the Torah as God's revelation of ultimate Wisdom so vehemently reject this divine guide to righteous living? Is it because of a personal consciousness that (for him) the law no longer has power to justify his existence before God? In both Galatians and Romans, Paul closely examines his own psychological state, attempting to show how the experience of Christ achieves for him what the law failed to do—assurance of God's love and acceptance.

Replacing Law with Faith In Paul's understanding of the Crucifixion, Jesus' voluntary death pays the Torah's penalty for all lawbreakers (3:13–14).

Figure 12.13 Because early church traditions assert that both Peter and Paul were executed in Rome during Nero's reign, their images are commonly paired, as in this fourth-century Roman lime relief depicting the two apostles. However, Paul's letter to the Galatians indicates that their historical relationship was not so close (Gal. 2:11–13).

Thus, Paul can say that "through the law I died to law." He escaped the punishments of the Torah through a mystical identification with the sacrificial Messiah. Vicariously experiencing Jesus' crucifixion, Paul now shares in Christ's new life, which enables him to receive God's grace as never before (2:17–21).

Paul also appeals to the Galatians' experience of Christ, reminding them that they received the Spirit only when they accepted his gospel, not when they obeyed the Law (3:1–5). In addition, he provides what people versed in the rabbinic tradition expect in an argument over doctrine—a precedent from the Hebrew Bible. Paul argues that his formula—"faith equals righteousness"—is explicitly present in the Genesis story of Abraham. It is Abraham's "faith" in God's call, Paul notes, that "was counted to him as righteousness" (citing Gen. 15:6). Therefore, he reasons, people who exercise faith today are Abraham's spiritual children, heirs to the promise that God will "bless," or justify, pagan nations through faith (3:6–10). Faith, not obedience to law, is the key to divine approval.

In support of his appeal to biblical authority, Paul finds only one additional relevant text, Habak-

kuk 2:4: "He shall gain life who is justified through faith." Paul interprets the Habakkuk text as prophetic of the messianic era and contrasts its emphasis on faith with the Law's stress on actions (3:11–12). The faith Habakkuk promised comes to the lawless Gentiles because Christ, suffering a criminal's execution, accepted the Law's "curse" on unlawful people and allowed them to become reconciled to God (3:13–14).

The Role of the Mosaic Torah in Human Salvation   If, as Paul repeatedly asserts, the Torah cannot really help anyone, why was it given? Paul's answer is that the Mosaic Torah is a temporary device intended to teach humans that they are unavoidably lawbreakers, sinners whose most conscientious efforts cannot earn divine favor. Using an analogy from Roman society, Paul compares the Law to a tutor—a man appointed to guide and protect youths until they attain legal adulthood. Like a tutor imposing discipline, the Law makes its adherents aware of their moral inadequacy and their need for a power beyond themselves to achieve righteousness. That power is Christ. Having served its purpose of preparing Abraham's children for Christ, the Torah is now obsolete and irrelevant (3:19–25).

The Equality of All Believers Paul abolishes the Law's power to condemn and separate Jew from Gentile and asserts the absolute equality of all believers, regardless of their nationality, social class, or sex. Among God's children "there is no such thing as Jew and Greek, slave and freeman, male and female," because all are "one person in Christ Jesus" (3:26–28).

All Believers as Heirs of Abraham Because Jesus purchased Christians' freedom from slavery to the Torah's yoke, all are now God's adopted heirs. As such, they are entitled to claim the Deity as *Abba* ("father" or "daddy") and to receive the Abrahamic promises. Paul stresses the contrast between the church and Judaism by interpreting the Genesis story of Abraham's two wives as an allegory, a narrative in which the characters symbolize some higher truth. **Hagar,** Abraham's Egyptian slave girl, is earthly Jerusalem, controlled by Rome. Sarah, the patriarch's free wife, symbolizes the "heavenly Jerusalem," the spiritual church whose members are also free (4:21–31).

Responsibilities of Freedom What does freedom from Torah regulations mean? Aware that some Galatians used their liberty as an excuse to indulge any desire or appetite (a practice called **antinomianism**), Paul interprets his doctrine as freedom to practice neighborly love without external restrictions. Quoting lists of vices and virtues typical of Stoic ethical teaching, the apostle notes that the Spirit will enable believers to transcend their natural selfishness and to act generously (5:13–26).

Paul's exasperation with the Galatians' failure to understand that Jesus' death and resurrection are God's complete and all-sufficient means of human salvation inspires his most brutal insult. With savage irony, he suggests that persons who insist on circumcision finish the job by emasculating themselves (5:7–12). Paul's remark may refer to an infamous practice among male adherents of the goddess Cybele, some of whom mutilated themselves

in a religious frenzy. This oblique allusion to a pagan cult also implies that Paul's opponents were Galatian syncretists.

In closing his letter, Paul seizes the pen from his secretary to write a final appeal to the Galatians in his own hand. Accusing his opponents of practicing circumcision only to escape persecution, presumably from Torah-abiding Jews, Paul summarizes his position: Torah obedience is meaningless because it implies that God's revelation through Jesus is not sufficient. Contrary to his opponents' limited view, Paul asserts that Jesus alone makes possible the new creation that unites humanity with its Creator. Note that Paul's closing words are as abrupt and self-directed as his opening complaint (1:6): "In future let no one make trouble for me" (6:11–17).

RECOMMENDED READING

Barclay, J. M. G. *Obeying the Truth: Paul's Ethics in Galatians.* Minneapolis: Fortress Press, 1991.
Betz, H. D. *Galatians.* Hermeneia. Philadelphia: Fortress Press, 1979. A scholarly analysis.
Cousar, C. B. *Galatians.* Interpretation. Atlanta: John Knox Press, 1982.
Ebeling, Gerhard. *The Truth of the Gospel: An Exposition of Galatians.* Philadelphia: Fortress Press, 1985.
Koperski, Vernonica. *What Are They Saying About Paul and the Law?* Mahwah, N.J: Paulist Press, 2001. Essays on current interpretations of Paul's view on the Torah.
Martyn, J. Louis. *Galatians.* Anchor Bible Series. New York: Doubleday, 1997. A new translation and commentary.

Romans

KEY TOPICS/THEMES

In Romans, Paul offers the most comprehensive statement of his views on God's plan for humanity's salvation. Probably written from Corinth about 56–57 C.E., this letter surveys the predicament of humanity, alienated from God and enslaved to imperfection, and argues that Jews and Gentiles suffer equally from the results of Adam's original disobedience and its punishment, death (Chs. 1–3). The Torah, although "holy" and "just,"

serves merely to increase awareness of human inadequacy by condemning the universal failure to
keep its standards. Only God's undeserved love,
expressed through Christ and accepted in faith,
can ethically justify humanity and reconcile it to
the Creator (Chs. 4–8). The Jewish lack of faith in
Jesus as the divinely appointed agent of redemption is only temporary, a historical necessity that
allows believing Gentiles also to become God's
people (Chs. 9–11).

KEY QUESTIONS

Why does Paul think that all people, both Jew and
Gentile, are condemned? How does trust in Jesus'
power to save reconcile humanity to God?

PAUL'S GOSPEL OF FREEDOM FROM
TORAH AND JUSTIFICATION BY FAITH

A Comprehensive Theology   Whereas Galatians
was dictated in the white heat of exasperation, Romans is a more calmly reasoned presentation of
Paul's doctrine of salvation through faith. In this
letter, written about 56–57 C.E. when he had not
yet visited Rome but hoped to make the imperial
capital his departure point for a pioneering mission
to Spain, Paul offers the most comprehensive and
systematic expression of his theology. Here the author thoughtfully explores an issue central to all
world religions: how to bridge the gap between
God and humankind, to reconcile imperfect, sinful
humanity to a pure and righteous Deity. As a Jew,
Paul is painfully aware of the immense disparity
between mortals and the immaculate holiness of
the Supreme Being, whose justice cannot tolerate human wrongdoing. Paul's gospel, or "good
news," is that these seemingly irreconcilable differences between God and humanity are overcome in
Christ, the Son who closes the gulf between perfect Father and imperfect children. In Paul's view,
God himself takes the initiative by re-creating a
deeply flawed humanity in his own transcendent
image.

Form and Organization   In form, Romans resembles a theological essay or sermon rather than
an ordinary letter, lacking the kind of specific

problem-solving advice that characterizes most
Pauline correspondence. Some commentators regard Romans as a circular letter, a document intended to explain Paul's teachings to various Christian groups who may at that time have held
distorted views of the apostle's position on controversial subjects. Most scholars view Chapter 16,
which contains greetings to twenty-six different
persons — more than the writer is likely to have
known personally in a city he had never visited —
as a separate missive. This section originally may
have been a letter of recommendation for Phoebe,
who was a deacon of the church at Cenchreae, the
port of Corinth.

The longest and most complex of Paul's letters,
Romans can be divided into nine thematically related parts:

1. Introduction (1:1–15)
2. Statement of theme (1:16–17) and exploration of the human predicament: God's
   wrath directed at all humanity because all
   people are guilty of deliberate error (1:18–
   3:31)
3. Abraham as the model of faith (4:1–25)
4. Faith in Christ ensuring deliverance from
   sin and death (5:1–7:25)
5. Renewed life in the Spirit (8:1–39)
6. The causes and results of Israel's disbelief
   (9:1–11:36)
7. Behavior in the church and the world (12:1–
   15:13)
8. Paul's future plans and greetings (15:14–33)
9. Appendix: letter recommending Phoebe
   (16:1–27)

HUMANITY'S NEED FOR REDEMPTION

Human Error   After an introductory greeting
that affirms his apostolic authority (1:1–15), Paul
boldly surveys the human predicament (1:18–
3:20), a sorry condition in which all people, Jews
and Gentiles, are incapable of justifying their existence before God. He announces his main theme
by citing Habakkuk 2:4, the same verse proclaiming salvation "through faith" that he had earlier
quoted to the Galatians (1:17; Gal. 3:11).

Echoing passages from the Wisdom of Solomon (see Chapter 8), Paul argues that the Gentiles' error is based on worshiping created objects — images of the Greco-Roman gods — rather than the Creator. His comments on male and female homosexuality, common in Hellenistic society, assume a deliberate turning from "natural" to "unnatural" behavior (1:26–28). Although this passage has been used frequently to condemn same-sex relationships, many medical researchers now believe that homosexual orientation is either genetically determined or formed at such an early stage of development that it is not a matter of moral choice. (Paul's views on human sexuality in general are largely shaped by his eschatological assumptions [1 Cor. 7].)

Paul adds that Jews, despite possessing the Law and covenant promises, fare no better than idolatrous Gentiles in achieving justification before God. The Torah, Paul asserts, cannot effect a right relationship between God and the lawkeeper; it serves only to make one conscious of sin (2:17–3:31).

ABRAHAM AS THE MODEL OF ONE "JUSTIFIED" BY FAITH

Paul realizes that if his doctrine is to convince Jewish Christians it must find support in the Hebrew Bible. He therefore argues that God's plan of rescuing sinners through faith began with Abraham, foremost ancestor of the Jewish people. As in Galatians, he cites Genesis 15:6: Abraham's faith in God "was counted to him as righteousness." For Paul, the fact that God pronounced Abraham "righteous" while the patriarch was still uncircumcised has enormous implications for the uncircumcised Gentiles, providing a prophetic model of God's plan to save all peoples through faith. In achieving justification by placing his trust in God, Abraham is not only the father of his Jewish descendants but also "the father of all who have faith when uncircumcised, so that righteousness is 'counted' to them" (4:3–11). Therefore, Gentiles who imitate Abraham's example — trusting that God will do what he has promised — are also heirs of the divine promises given in Genesis. Without

compromising his impartiality, God succeeds in justifying both Jew and Gentile, encompassing previously distinct groups in an act of redemptive grace. As Abraham proved his faith by obediently responding to God's voice, so must the faithful now respond to God's new summons through Christ (4:15–25). "Justified through faith" in Jesus' sacrificial death, a demonstration of divine love, believers are now reconciled to God (5:1–11).

In using Abraham's example to support this thesis that people are "justified by faith quite apart from success in keeping the law" (3:28; cf. 4:1–25), Paul selects only one verse (Gen. 15:6) from the thirteen chapters that Genesis devotes to Abraham's story. Another New Testament letter — traditionally written by James, Jesus' Torah-keeping "brother" — cites a different part of the Genesis narrative to argue that it was not Abraham's faith in itself but his faith expressed *in action* that pleased God. Insisting that "faith divorced from deeds is barren," the author of James interprets Abraham's significance as that of a person who demonstrates his faith through his deeds, such as (almost) offering his son Isaac as a human sacrifice. Only by translating his trust into action, James declares, did Abraham prove "the integrity of his faith." Tellingly, James then cites the same Genesis verse that Paul had evoked to illustrate the sufficiency of faith alone, but, by placing Genesis 15:6 in the broader context of Abraham's works, James interprets the passage quite differently (James 2:14–26). Although most commentators believe that James is merely correcting a later misinterpretation of Paul's doctrine of faith, and not contradicting it, his conclusion that people are "justified by deeds and not by faith in itself" (2:25) does not precisely accord with the Pauline equation of faith and righteousness (see Chapter 13).

FAITH IN CHRIST ENSURING DELIVERANCE FROM SIN AND DEATH

The Roles of Adam and Christ   At the outset of his letter (1:5), Paul declares that he tried to bring the whole world to a state of obedient faith. In Chapter 5, he outlines a theory of history in which God uses these two qualities — obedience

Box 12.9 Paul's Views on the Origin of Sin and Death

In Romans 5, Paul attributes the existence of sin and death to the first man's deliberate disobedience of a divine command, that which prohibited Adam and Eve from eating the fruit of the tree of knowledge (Rom. 5:12–23; cf. Gen. 3). According to orthodox interpretations of Paul's thought, particularly Augustine's doctrine of original sin, the first couple's error resulted in a death sentence not only for them but also for their descendants, all of whom are born under divine condemnation. In scrutinizing Genesis 3, however, readers will notice that most of the terms commonly used to describe the tale of Adam's and Eve's alienation from Yahweh are entirely absent. The Genesis narrator makes no reference to sin, evil, rebellion, disobedience, punishment, damnation, or a fall from grace — all are interpretative terms supplied by later theologians. The narrator, moreover, does not present the talking serpent who persuades Eve to taste the forbidden fruit as "bad," but only as "subtle" or "shrewd." Interestingly, after Genesis 3, no writer in the canonical Hebrew Bible (Tanak) ever again refers to this Genesis episode or accords it any theological significance.

It was not until shortly before Paul's day that Hellenistic Jewish writers began to reinterpret the events related in Genesis 3. During the first century B.C.E., a Hellenistic Jew in Alexandria, Egypt, composed the Wisdom of Solomon, a book that integrated Greek philosophy with the Hebraic biblical tradition. (Excluded from the Tanak, the Wisdom of Solomon was part of the Septuagint Apocrypha and is included in Catholic and Orthodox editions of the Old Testament.) According to this source, the devil was responsible for introducing death into human experience: "God created man for immortality, and made him the image of his own eternal self; it was the devil's spite that brought death into the world" (Wisd. of Sol. 2:23–24). Other extrabiblical traditions that it was the devil, speaking through the serpent, who tempted Eve to sin were eventually incorporated into the noncanonical Life of Adam and Eve, a Hellenistic work that imaginatively dramatizes Satan's role in corrupting the first humans (see Chapter 8). Whether directly influenced by this work or by the oral traditions underlying it, Paul evidently adopts the book's Hellenistic view that Adam and Eve are the sources of sin and death (Rom. 5:12–21; 2 Cor.11:3; cf 1 Tim. 2:4).

---

and faith — to achieve human salvation. God's intervention into human affairs became necessary when the first human, Adam (whose name means "humankind"), disobeyed the Creator. Through this act, Adam alienated not only himself but all his descendants from their Maker (Box 12.9). Like other Jewish teachers of the first century C.E., Paul interprets the Genesis story of Adam's disobedience as a tragic **Fall** from grace, a cosmic disaster that introduces sin and death into the world. (Paul's word for "sin" — *hamartia* — is a Greek archery term that means "missing the mark" or "falling short of a desired goal." Aristotle used the same term to denote the "fatal flaw" of the tragic hero in Greek drama. *Hamartia* commonly refers to an error of judgment rather than an act of inborn human wickedness.) In Paul's moral scheme, the entire human race fails to hit the target of reunion with God, thus condemning itself to death — permanent separation from the Source of life.

Obedience to the Torah cannot *save* because the Law merely defines errors and assigns legal penalties. It is God himself who overcomes the hopelessness of the human predicament. He does this by sending his Son, whose perfect obedience and sacrificial death provide a saving counterweight to Adam's sin. As all Adam's children share his mortal punishment, so all will share the reward of Christ's resurrection to life. It is the believer's faith in the saving power of Christ that makes him or her "righteous," enabling the just Deity to accept persons trustfully responding to his call (5:12–21).

Some later theologians used Romans 5 to formulate a doctrine of **original sin**, which states that all human beings inherit an unavoidable tendency to do wrong and are innately corrupt. From Augustine to Calvin, such theologians had a deeply pessimistic view of human nature, in some cases regarding the majority of people as inherently depraved and justly damned.

Paul, however, stresses the joyful aspects of God's reconciliation to humanity. It is the Deity who initiates the process, and God's "grace"—his gracious will to love and to give life—far exceeds the measure of human failings. So powerful is God's determination to redeem humankind, Paul implies, he may ultimately save all people:

> It follows, then, that as the issue of one misdeed was the condemnation for all [people], so the issue of one just act is acquittal and life for all [people]. For as through the disobedience of the one man [Adam] the many were made sinners, so through the obedience of the one man [Christ] the many will be made righteous.
>
> Rom. 5:18–19; see Paul's similar
> declaration in 1 Cor. 15:21–23

This passage, in which Paul optimistically seems to envision a universally redeemed humanity, must be balanced against his more negative evaluation of human sinfulness in Romans 8. In this chapter, he contrasts two different ways of life that produce opposite results. Those who submit to their "lower nature" make themselves God's enemies and earn "death"; those united with Christ, however, live on a higher plane, "the level of the spirit," which produces "life and peace" (Rom. 8:5–13).

A Distortion of Paul's Teaching on Freedom

In Chapter 6, Paul seems to be refuting misconceptions of his doctrine on Christian freedom. As in Galatia, some persons were apparently acting as if liberty from the Law entitled them to behave irresponsibly. In some cases, they concluded that "sinning" was good because it allowed God's grace more opportunity to show itself. Paul reminds such dissidents that sin is a cruel tyrant who pays wages of death. By contrast, Christ treats his servants generously, bestowing the gift of everlasting life (6:1–23).

THE LAW'S HOLINESS AND HUMAN PERVERSITY

Paul makes one final attempt to place the Torah in the context of salvation history and to account for its failure to produce human righteousness. In Galatians, Paul describes the Law harshly, referring to it as slavery, bondage, and death. Writing more temperately in Romans, he judges the Law "holy and just and good" (7:12). If so, why does it not serve to justify its practitioners?

In this case, Paul answers that the fault lies not in the Torah but in human nature. The Torah is "spiritual," but human beings are "unspiritual" and enslaved by sin. Throughout this long passage (7:7–25), Paul uses the first person, as if he were analyzing his own nature and then projecting his self-admitted defects onto the rest of humanity. His "I," however, should probably read "we"—for he means to describe human nature collectively. Laws not only define crimes, he asserts, but create an awareness of lawbreaking that does not exist in their absence. Thus, the Torah makes sin come alive in the human consciousness (7:7–11).

Speaking as if sin were an animate force inside himself, Paul articulates the classic statement of ethical frustration—the opposition between the "good" he wishes to do and the "wrong" he actually performs. As he confronts the huge gap between his conscious will and his imperfect actions, Paul can only conclude that it is not the real "he" who produces the moral failure, but the "sin that lodges in me" (7:14–20).

With his higher reason delighting in the Torah but his lower nature fighting against it, he finds that he incurs the Law's punishment—death. He bursts with the desire to attain God's approval but always "misses the mark." In agony over his fate, he seeks some power to rescue him from an unsatisfying existence that ends only in death (7:21–25). Paul may be accused of attributing his personal sense of moral imperfection to everyone else, but his despairing self-examination illustrates why he believes that the Law is unable to deliver one from the lethal attributes of imperfect human nature (8:3).

Renewed Life in the Spirit   God rescues humanity through Christ. By sharing our imperfect nature and dying "as a sacrifice for sin," Christ transfers the Torah's penalties to himself, condemning it, and not the human nature in which sin exists (8:3–4). Because Christ's Spirit now dwells within the believer, sin no longer exerts its former control, and new life can flourish in the Christian's body. Thus, Christians escape their imperfection, having put it to death with Christ on the cross (8:5–17).

Paul uses mystical language to describe not only human nature but also the physical cosmos itself struggling to shake off the chains of mortality. During this period of cosmic renewal, the whole universe wails as if in childbirth. Believers now hope for a saving rebirth, but the reality is still ahead. Then they will be fully reshaped in the Son's image, the pattern of a new humanity reconciled to God (8:18–30):

> For I am convinced that there is nothing in death or life, in the realm of spirits or super-human powers, in the world as it is or the world as it shall be, in the forces of the universe, in heights or depths — nothing in all creation that can separate us from the love of God in Christ Jesus our Lord.
> Rom. 8:38–39

Israel's Disbelief   In Chapters 9–11, Paul discusses Israel's continuing role as God's chosen people, even though most have not accepted Jesus as the national Messiah. Paul suggests that his fellow Jews misunderstand God's purpose in Christ because they seek salvation through Torah obedience, allegedly depending on their own efforts to earn divine approval. True "children of Abraham," however, recognize the necessity of placing faith in Christ. Jews withhold their faith, but the Gentiles benefit from this refusal. In a famous analogy, Paul compares Gentile believers to branches from a wild olive tree that have been grafted onto the cultivated olive trunk, which is Israel. Paul also assumes that Israel's unbelief is only temporary. After the Gentiles have been attached to the main trunk, then the natural branches will be regrafted onto God's olive tree and "the whole of Israel will be saved" (11:16–27).

Behavior in the Church and the World   Paul's ethical instruction (Chs. 12–15) is closely tied to his sense of apocalyptic urgency. Because the New Age is about to dawn (13:11), believers must behave prudently in both public and private life. The apostle's policy toward the Roman government, composed before his imprisonment and prosecution, is strongly positive, advocating civil obedience and cooperation. Echoing the Stoic view that the state exists to maintain public order and punish wrongdoing, Paul argues that the Roman Empire is a "divine institution"—an opinion that contrasts with his earlier view that the present world is ruled by demonic forces (2 Cor. 4:4).

Although he emphasizes the Christian's duty to pay taxes and submit to legally constituted authority, Paul does not consider the ethical problem of a citizen's duty to resist illegal or unethical acts by the state. As Luke does in Acts, Paul advises accommodation with the empire, probably because he believes that the existing system would not endure long. (Compare Paul's similar acceptance of the state-supported institution of human slavery in Philemon, discussed later in this chapter.)

When Paul implied that voluntary cooperation with Rome might benefit Christians, he could not know that he soon would be among the first victims of a government persecution. Following the emperor **Nero's** execution of many Roman believers (c. 64–65 C.E.), some New Testament authors came to regard the state as Satan's earthly instrument to annihilate God's people. After Rome destroyed Jerusalem (along with the original church there) in 70 C.E., the empire became the new Babylon in the eyes of many Christians. The author of Revelation pictures Rome as a beast and predicts its fall as a cause for universal rejoicing (Rev. 17–19). At the time Paul wrote, however, the adversarial relationship between church and state was still in the future.

RECOMMENDED READING

Achtemeier, Paul J. *Romans.* Atlanta: John Knox Press, 1985.

Cranfield, C. E. B. *A Critical and Exegetical Commentary on the Epistle to the Romans.* International Critical Commentary. 2 Vols. Edinburgh: T. & T. Clark, 1975, 1979. A standard work incorporating the history of Pauline interpretation.

Donfried, Karl P., ed. *The Romans Debate.* 2nd ed. Peabody, Mass.: Hendrikson, 1991. A collection of essays by prominent scholars investigating the purpose of Paul's letter to Rome.

Fitzmyer, Joseph A. *Romans.* The Anchor Bible, Vol. 33. New York: Doubleday, 1993. A new translation with extensive commentary.

Kasemann, Ernst. *Commentary on Romans.* Grand Rapids, Mich.: Eerdmans, 1980. An intensely scholarly study for more serious readers.

Sanders, E. P. *Paul and Palestinian Judaism.* Philadelphia: Fortress Press, 1978. An important scholarly study of Paul's relationship to rabbinic Judaism.

———. *Paul, the Law and the Jewish People.* Philadelphia: Fortress Press, 1983.

Soards, M. L.; Sampley, J. P.; and Wright, N. T., eds. *Romans–First Corinthians. The New Interpreters Bible,* Vol. 10. Nashville: Abingdon Press, 2000. Provides extensive commentary.

Philippians

KEY TOPICS/THEMES

Paul's letter to the church at Philippi, the first church established in Europe, contains important biographical information about the author (3:4–8) and his imprisonment (either at Rome or Ephesus) (1:12–26). An unusually warm and friendly missive, it includes Paul's quotation of an early Christian hymn that depicts Jesus as the opposite of Adam—a humbly obedient son whose denial of self leads to his heavenly exaltation (2:5–11).

KEY QUESTIONS

How does Paul view his imprisonment? How does he use Jesus' example as a model of Christian humility?

A LETTER FROM PRISON

This letter expresses Paul's special affection for the church at **Philippi**, the first in Europe, which he and his associate Timothy had founded (Acts 16:11–40) (Figure 12.14). Paul's unusual intimacy with the Philippians is reflected in the warmth of his greetings (1:1–11) and by the fact that they were the only group from whom he would accept financial support (4:15–16).

Place of Origin According to an early church tradition, Philippians is one of four canonical letters—including Philemon, Colossians, and Ephesians—that Paul wrote while imprisoned at Rome. Scholarly analysis of the four works, however, has raised serious questions about the time and place of their composition, as well as the authorship of two of them. Whereas scholars accept Philippians and Philemon as genuine Pauline documents, a majority challenge Paul's authorship of Colossians, and nearly all doubt that he wrote Ephesians (discussed later in this chapter).

If Philippians was not written during Paul's house arrest in Rome (Acts 28), it may have originated in a prison at Ephesus. The letter implies that Paul's friends made four journeys between Philippi and Paul's place of imprisonment and that a fifth trip was planned (2:25–26). Because the distance between Philippi and Rome seems too great for such frequent trips, some historians propose that he wrote the letter in Ephesus, which is only about ten days' travel time from Philippi. Still other scholars suggest that Caesarea, where Paul spent two years in prison, was the place of origin (Acts 23–25).

Whereas numerous scholars retain the traditional view that Paul wrote Philippians at Rome, an increasing number believe the canonical work is a composite document, made up of several letter fragments written at different times (Figure 12.15). According to this theory, the note thanking the Philippians for their financial help (4:10–20 or 23) was composed first, followed by a letter warning the church about potential troublemakers (partially preserved in 1:1–3:1a and 4:2–9). A third letter

Figure 12.14 Little remains of the Greco-Roman city of Philippi, where Paul established the first Christian church in Europe. This crumbling wall gives scant indication of the massive Roman structures that once occupied the site.

bitterly attacks advocates of circumcisions (3:1b–4:1). The letter may be a unity, however, for Paul's letters typically leap from topic to topic, reflecting the author's quick changes of mood as he addresses different issues.

THE SIGNIFICANCE OF PAUL'S IMPRISONMENT

Paul gives a surprisingly mellow response to his prison experience, courageously stressing its positive results. His case, he believes, allows other believers the opportunity to witness publicly for Christ. Interestingly, not all of Paul's fellow Christians support him; some use his incarceration as a means of stirring up new troubles for the prisoner. The writer does not identify those Christians whose personal jealousies complicate his already difficult situation, but some commentators suggest they are the "advocates of circumcision" denounced in Chapter 3. In Acts' narration of Paul's arrest and imprisonment in Caesarea, the Jerusalem church leadership is conspicuously absent from his defense. Perhaps those who shared James's adherence to Torah obligations were to some degree re-

lieved to see Paul and his heretical views under legal restraint.

THE HYMN TO CHRIST

Chapter 2 contains the letter's most important theological concept. Urging the Philippians to avoid rivalry and cultivate humility, Paul cites Jesus' behavior as the model to emulate and quotes or paraphrases a liturgical hymn about Christ's "emptying" of himself, surrendering completely to God's will. The rhythmic and poetic qualities of this passage, as well as the absence of typically Pauline ideas and vocabulary, indicate that it is a pre-Pauline composition. The first stanza reads:

> Who though he was in the form of God,
> Did not count equality with God
> A thing to be grasped.
> But emptied himself,
> Taking the form of a servant,
> Being born in the likeness of men.
> And being found in human form
> He humbled himself
> And became obedient unto death.
> Phil. 2:6–8, RSV

Figure 12.15 Potential sites where Paul wrote his "prison letters." Paul may have written these letters in Rome (in the far west on this map), in Ephesus (on the coast of present-day Turkey), or in Caesarea (in the far eastern Mediterranean). Note that Ephesus is much closer to Philippi than either of the other two cities.

The hymn's second stanza (2:9–11) describes how God rewards Jesus' selfless obedience by granting him universal lordship, which elevation glorifies "God, the Father."

Although this famous passage is commonly believed to demonstrate Jesus' heavenly preexistence and Incarnation, its depiction of Jesus' relation to the Father is ambiguously rendered. In view of Paul's explicit subordination of Jesus to God in 1 Corinthians 15:24–28, modern commentators are cautious about interpreting the hymn as a statement of Jesus' preexistent divine nature.

A growing number of scholars believe that Paul employs the hymn in order to contrast implicitly two "sons" of God—Adam (Luke 3:38) and Jesus. (The Adam–Christ contrast figures prominently in 1 Corinthians 15:21–23, 45–49, and Romans

5:12–19.) Paul's use of the term *form* (Greek, *morphe*) may refer to the divine image that both Adam and Jesus reflect (Gen. 1:27–28). But, whereas Adam tried to seize God-like status (Gen. 3:5), Jesus takes the form of a slave. Instead of rebelling against the Creator, he is submissively obedient unto death.

Finally, Adam's disobedience brings shame and death, but Jesus' total obedience brings glory and exaltation. Jesus' self-emptying earns him the fullness of God's reward, the bestowal of the "name above all names," before whom all creation bows. Consistent with his usual method of using theology to drive home behavioral advice, Paul implicitly compares the reward given Jesus' humility with that in store for humbly obedient Christians. Now shining like "stars in a dark world," they will inherit a future life similar to that which Jesus now enjoys (2:14–18).

The references to Timothy and **Epaphroditus**, two of his favorite companions, suggest Paul's capacity for friendship. Timothy, whose name appears as courtesy coauthor of this letter (1:1), is half-Jewish and half-Greek, a dependable supporter of Paul's radical policy toward recruiting Gentiles. In the apostle's absence, Paul trusts him to act as he would (2:19–24).

Epaphroditus, who had brought Paul the Philippians' monetary gifts, apparently touched Paul with the depth of his personal devotion. Epaphroditus's dangerous illness, which delayed his return to Philippi, may have resulted from having risked his life to help the prisoner. Paul implies his gratitude when urging the Philippians to give his friend an appreciative welcome home (2:25–3:1a).

Chapter 3, which may belong to a separate letter, contains flashes of Paul's old fire as he attacks Judaizers who insist on circumcising Gentile converts. Denouncing the practice as "mutilation," he contemptuously dismisses his opponents as "dogs"—the common Jewish tag for the uncircumcised. Paul provides valuable autobiographical information when he cites his ethnic qualifications—superior to those of his enemies—to evaluate the advantages of being a Jew. Despite his exemplary credentials—and his former perfection in keeping Torah regulations—he discounts his Jewish heritage as "garbage." All human advantages are worthless when compared to the new life God gives in Christ (3:1–11).

RECOMMENDED READING

Byrne, Brendan. "The Letter to the Philippians." In R. E. Brown et al., *The New Jerome Biblical Commentary*, 2nd ed., pp. 791–797. Englewood Cliffs, N.J.: Prentice-Hall, 1990.

Martin, R. P. *Carmen Christi: Philippians 2:5–11 in Recent Interpretation and in the Setting of Early Christian Worship*, rev. ed. Grand Rapids, Mich.: Eerdmans, 1983.

———. *Philippians*. New Century Bible Commentary. Grand Rapids, Mich.: Eerdmans, 1983.

Stendahl, K., ed. and trans. *Romans, Galatians, and Philippians*. Anchor Bible, Vol. 33. Garden City, N.Y.: Doubleday, 1978. A recent translation with editorial commentary.

Philemon

KEY TOPICS/THEMES

In his only surviving private letter, Paul urges his recipients to treat the runaway slave Onesimus as a brother in Christ.

KEY QUESTION

Why did early Christians accept the institution of slavery?

Although Paul's shortest letter, Philemon deals with an important subject—the problem of human slavery among Christians. From prison, Paul writes to **Philemon**, a citizen of Colossae, to plead for the runaway slave **Onesimus**, who had apparently stolen money from his master's household. Onesimus's flight brought him from Colossae to Rome (or Ephesus, if that is where Paul's captivity letters originated), where the slave was converted to Christianity, perhaps by Paul himself.

Perhaps compelled by Roman law, Paul decides to send the slave back to his owner. Maintaining a fine balance between exercising his apostolic authority and appealing to the voluntary equality cultivated among all Christians, Paul asks Philemon to receive Onesimus kindly, treating him "no longer as a slave, but . . . as a dear brother" (v. 15). Paul also gives his guarantee that he will reimburse Philemon for any debt he may have incurred (or, perhaps, money he may have stolen) (vv. 18–20). Besides appealing to Philemon's compassion, Paul hints broadly that returning Onesimus deprives him of a major comfort: "I should have liked to keep him with me to look after me as you would wish, here in prison for the Gospel. But I would rather do nothing without your consent, so that your kindness may be a matter not of compulsion, but of your own free will" (vv. 13–14).

THE QUESTION OF SLAVERY

Readers may be disappointed that Paul does not denounce human slavery as incompatible with Christian belief in God's equal love for all humanity. Instead, he merely accepts its existence as a social fact, nowhere ordering believers to free the human beings they owned as chattel. Paul's attitude is consistent with both the biblical tradition and the practices of Greco-Roman society.

The Hebrew Bible regulates slavery, distinguishing between Gentile slaves captured in battle and Hebrew slaves who sold themselves or their children to pay off debts. In Exodus, the law decrees that after six years' servitude, a male Hebrew slave is to be set free. Any children born to him and one of his master's female slaves, however, are to remain the master's property. If at the end of six years' time, the freed man wishes to remain with his wife and family, he must submit to a mutilation of the ear (the organ of obedience) and remain a slave for life (Exod. 21:2–6; see also Chapter 4 in this text).

Following the Torah and the institutions of society at large, the New Testament writers neither condemn slavery nor predict its abolition. At the same time, the persistence of slavery was strangely inconsistent with the principles of freedom and a human being's innate worth advocated in Paul's letters and the Gospels. In United States history, both proslavery and antislavery parties used the New Testament to support their conflicting views. Slavery's proponents argued that biblical writers, including Paul, implicitly accepted the institution as a "natural" condition. Those against slavery extrapolated from Paul's doctrine of freedom and Christian equality (Gal. 3:28) a corresponding social and legal freedom for all people.

QUESTIONS FOR REVIEW

1. Find the passages in 1 Thessalonians and 1 Corinthians indicating that Paul believed the End to be very near. If Paul was wrong about the occurrence of the Parousia during his lifetime, to what extent should his mistaken view affect a reader's confidence in Paul's teachings?

2. Paul regards the Messiah's death and resurrection as immediately inaugurating a new era of divine judgment and eschatological hope. In what ways do Paul's beliefs about the imminent resurrection of the dead (1 Thess. 4–5 and 1 Cor. 15) relate to his view of Christ as the "last Adam" (Rom. 5:12–19; 1 Cor. 15:45–49)?

3. What are the sources of Paul's difficulties with the church at Corinth? Why does Paul boast "as a fool" in 2 Corinthians 10–13 and cite his mystical vision of heaven as part of his apostolic credentials?

4. Describe the reasons scholars believe that 2 Corinthians is a composite document.

5. Both Galatians and Romans deal with Christianity's relationship to Torah Judaism. Define and explain Paul's gospel of justification by faith.

QUESTIONS FOR DISCUSSION AND REFLECTION

1. In both Galatians and Romans, Paul cites excerpts from Genesis 15 and Habakkuk 2 to prove that God always intended faith to be the means by which humanity was to be "justified" or "made righteous." Compare Paul's interpretation of Abraham's example with that given by James (2:14–26). How do these two writers differ on the issue of faith versus "works"?

2. Although the hymn Paul quotes in Philippians 2 is commonly interpreted as describing Jesus' prehuman existence, many commentators believe that it contains instead an implied contrast between the disobedience of Adam (who was God's human image) and the obedience of Christ (who reflects the divine image perfectly). Discuss the arguments for and against these differing interpretations.

3. Identify Philemon and Onesimus and their connection to Paul. Why do you think Paul does not condemn human slavery as an evil institution?

4. Although slavery has long been judged a social evil, the subordination of women is still widely practiced in many churches, partly because of Paul's apparent views on the subject. If Paul was wrong on such issues as slavery, uncritical submission to Roman authority, and the nearness of the Parousia, how should we now regard his teachings on the roles of women, celibacy, homosexuality, and the state as a divinely empowered institution? If they had followed Paul's advice in Romans 13, could the leaders of the American Revolution have framed the Declaration of Independence or broken free of British control?

TERMS AND CONCEPTS TO REMEMBER

Adam	*apokalypsis*
Ananias	Apollos
antinomianism	Cephas (Peter)

Corinth
Damascus
dualism
Enoch
Epaphroditus
Fall, the
Galatia
Hagar
Last Supper
Lystra
Nero
Onesimus
original sin
Parousia

pastoral epistles
Pharisee
Philemon
Philippi
Phoebe
pseudonymity
resurrection
Silas
soul
speaking in tongues
syncretism
Tarsus
Timothy
Titus

RECOMMENDED READING

Barth, M., ed. and trans. *Colossians and Philemon.* Vol. 34a of the Anchor Bible. Garden City, N.Y.: Doubleday, 1974. A scholarly translation and analysis.

Knox, John. *Philemon Among the Letters of Paul,* rev. ed. New York: Abingdon Press, 1959. Develops Edgar Goodspeed's theory that about 90 C.E. a Paulinist— perhaps the former slave Onesimus, who may then have been bishop of Ephesus—collected Paul's letters and circulated them among the entire church.

The Disputed Pauline Letters

Paul's continuing influence on the church was so great that for years after his death, various Pauline disciples composed letters honoring his name and spirit. Some documents written in his name, such as those purportedly addressed to Timothy and Titus, are universally rejected by modern scholars. The authorship of others, such as 2 Thessalonians and Colossians, is still vigorously disputed, with sizable minorities defending the documents' authenticity. A large majority of scholars, however, doubt that Paul wrote Ephesians.

2 Thessalonians

KEY TOPICS/THEMES

Although repeating themes from 1 Thessalonians, 2 Thessalonians reinterprets Paul's original eschatology, asserting that a number of traditional apocalyptic "signs" must precede the eschaton.

KEY QUESTIONS

Why do many scholars doubt Paul's authorship of 2 Thessalonians? What traditional apocalyptic ideas does the letter promote?

AUTHORSHIP AND PURPOSE

Many scholars question Paul's authorship of 2 Thessalonians. If Paul composed it, why does he repeat—almost verbatim—so much of what he had just written to the same recipients? More seriously, why does the author present an eschatology so different from that given in the first letter? In 1 Thessalonians, the Parousia will occur stealthily, "like a thief in the night." In 2 Thessalonians, a number of apocalyptic "signs" will first advertise its arrival. The interposing of these mysterious events between the writer's time and that of the Parousia has the effect of projecting the *eschaton* further into the future—a contrast to 1 Thessalonians, in which the End is extremely close.

Scholars defending Pauline authorship advance several theories to explain the writer's apparent change of attitude toward the Parousia. In the first letter, Paul emphasizes the tension between the shortness of time the world has left and the necessity of believers' vigilance and ethical purity as they await Christ's return. In the second missive, Paul writes to correct the Thessalonians' misconceptions or abuses of his earlier emphasis on the nearness of End time.

If Paul, in fact, wrote this document, his purpose is twofold: (1) to stop his recipients from assuming that the "Day of the Lord" had already arrived (2:2) and (2) to insist that believers who lazily awaited the End must work to support themselves (3:11–12). The false notion that the Parousia had already occurred may have arisen partly from a misunderstanding of 1 Thessalonians, with its several references to the imminence of Christ's return (1 Thess. 1:10; 2:19; 4:15–5:11). Now counseling his readers not to "lose their heads," the author outlines specific events or "signs" that must occur before the day arrives (2:3–12). Although still maintaining that the Parousia is near (1:6– 10), he insists that it cannot come "before the final rebellion against God, when wickedness will be revealed in human form, the [person] doomed to perdition" (2:3). This unidentified "enemy" will attack all religion, claim to be a god himself, and even take "his seat in the Temple of God" (2:4).

TRADITIONAL (NON-PAULINE?) SIGNS OF THE END

Paul rarely predicts specific events in the course of future history, particularly in the vague and cryptic style of 2 Thessalonians. Whoever the author, his statement that the mysterious enemy's identity will not be disclosed until the appointed time expresses a typically apocalyptic belief. All future history is predestined, and nothing can happen before its divinely prearranged hour. The present is linked to the coming revelation, however, because evil forces are already at work, secretly gathering strength until the unnamed "Restrainer" disappears, allowing the wicked personage to emerge in power.

In this passage, the writer paints a characteristically apocalyptic worldview, a moral dualism in which the opposing powers of Good and Evil have their respective agents at work on earth. The enemy figure is Satan's agent; his opposite is Christ. As Jesus is God's representative working in human history, so the wicked rebel is the Devil's tool. Operating on a cosmic scale, the conflict will culminate in Christ's victory over the demonic enemy, who has deceived the mass of humanity into believing the "Lie." An evil parody of the Messiah, the anonymous Satanic dupe functions as an **anti-Christ** (2:3–12).

The author's language is specific enough to arouse speculation about the identities of the enigmatic "wicked man" and the "Restrainer" who at the time of writing kept the anti-Christ in check. It is also vague enough to preclude connecting any known historical figures—in the first century C.E. or any period since—with these apocalyptic roles. In typical apocalyptic fashion, the figures are mythic archetypes that belong to a realm beyond the reach of historical inquiry.

After his bedazzling preview of future history, the writer makes sure that the Thessalonians do not neglect the practical affairs of their present lives. Notice that this section (3:6–16) firmly reanchors the church to its earthly obligations. The

author cites Paul's example of hard work and directs his readers to avoid persons who sponge off others. When he asserts that people who do not work will not eat, the writer suggests that at least some Thessalonians lived in a Christian commune similar to that in Jerusalem (Acts 2), where leaders could control the food supply.

2 Thessalonians contains a warning that forged letters were already circulating in Paul's name (2:1–3) and ends by insisting that Paul verified his genuine letters with his own signature (3:17–18). Scholars doubting Pauline authorship view the pseudonymous writer as protesting overmuch, but the apostle appends similar comments to undisputed letters (1 Cor. 16:21–24; Gal. 6:11).

Colossians

KEY TOPICS/THEMES

In Colossians, which may be the work of a Pauline disciple, the author emphasizes Jesus' identity with the cosmic power and wisdom by and for which the universe was created. The divine secret is revealed as Christ's Spirit dwelling in the believer.

KEY QUESTION

How does Colossians depict the cosmic supremacy of Christ?

AUTHORSHIP AND PURPOSE

If Paul is the author of Colossians, as a large minority of scholars believe, he had not yet visited the town of Colossae when he wrote this theologically significant letter. A small town in the Roman province of Asia, **Colossae** was located about 100 miles southeast of Ephesus, the provincial capital. **Epaphras**, one of Paul's missionary associates, had apparently founded the church a short time prior to Paul's writing (1:7).

If genuine, Colossians was probably composed at about the same time as Philemon, to which it is closely related. In both letters, Paul (or a disciple) writes from prison, including his friend Timothy in the salutation (1:1) and adding greetings from many of the same persons cited in the earlier missive (4:9–18), including Onesimus, Epaphras, Mark, and Luke.

The author, whom we call Paul for convenience, writes to reaffirm the validity of what Epaphras had preached and to refute a false "philosophy" that threatened to distort the proper understanding of Christ's uniqueness. Some members of the Colossian church were apparently involved in a cult that blended pagan and marginal Jewish speculations about angels and "elemental spirits of the universe," to which they accorded some form of worship (2:8, 18). The writer denounces these "hollow and delusive" notions that failed to recognize Christ's preeminence. Christ is not only supreme but also the only channel to spiritual reality; lesser spirit beings are merely his "captives," reduced to servant status by his triumphant death and heavenly ascension.

The letter advances two important Christological concepts: (1) Christ is supreme because God's power now manifested in him is the same power that created the entire universe, including those invisible entities that the false teachers mistakenly worship, and (2) when they realize Christ's supremacy and experience his indwelling Spirit, the Colossians are initiated into his mystery cult, voluntarily harmonizing their lives with the cosmic unity he embodies.

CHRIST: THE SOURCE OF COSMIC UNITY

In the opinion of some analysts, both the complex nature of the false teachings, which may represent a form of Gnosticism, and the **Christology** of Colossians seem too "advanced" for the letter to have originated in Paul's day. Other critics point out that if the letter was written late in Paul's career to meet a situation significantly different from others he had encountered, it could well have stimulated the apostle to produce a more fully developed expression of his views about Christ's nature and function.

The Use of Wisdom Language   As in Philippians 2, the author appears to quote an older Christian hymn to illustrate his vision of the exalted Jesus' cosmic role:

> He is the image of the invisible God, the first-
>   born of all creation;
> for in him all things were created, in heaven and
>   on earth, visible and invisible, whether thrones
>   or dominions or principalities or authorities
> all things were created through him and for him.
> . . . .
> For in him all the fullness of God was pleased to
>   dwell,
> and through him to reconcile to himself all things,
>   whether on earth or in heaven,
> making peace by the blood of his cross.
>   Col. 1:15–16, 19–20, RSV

Like the prologue to John's Gospel, this beautiful poem is modeled on biblical and Hellenistic Jewish concepts of divine Wisdom (Prov. 8:22–31; Ecclus. 24:1–22; see also the discussion of John's use of the Logos [Word], in Chapter 10). Hellenistic Jews had created a rich lore of speculative thought in which God's chief attribute, his infinite Wisdom, is the source of all creation and the means by which he communicates his purpose to humanity. Many historians believe that early Christian thinkers adopted these ready-made wisdom traditions and applied them to Jesus.

Recognizing the Colossian hymn's use of wisdom language, many scholars view it as a declaration that the same divine presence and power that created the universe now operates in the glorified Christ. The personified Wisdom whom God employed as his agent in fashioning the cosmos is now fully revealed in Christ, the agent through whom God redeems his human creation.

The phrase "image [*eikon*] of the invisible God" (1:15) may correspond to the phrase "form [*morphes*] of God" used in Philippians 2:6. In both cases, the term echoes the words of Genesis, in which God creates the first human beings in his own "image" and "likeness" (Gen. 1:26–27; 5:1). The author believes that Christians reconciled to God also come to bear the divine "image" (3:10). Rather than asserting the Johannine view that the prehuman Jesus was literally present at creation, the hymn may affirm that he is the ultimate goal toward which God's world trends.

Whatever christological origins he promotes, the writer's main purpose is to demonstrate Christ's present superiority to all rival cosmic beings. The "thrones, sovereignties, authorities and powers" mentioned (1:6) probably represent the Jewish hierarchy of angels. Christ's perfect obedience, vindicating God's image in humanity, and his ascension to heaven have rendered these lesser beings irrelevant and powerless. By his triumph, Christ leads them captive as a Roman emperor leads a public procession of conquered enemies (2:9–15).

Union with the Divine Image Moving from Christ's supremacy to his own role in the divine plan, Paul states that his task is to deliver God's message of reconciliation. He is the agent chosen to reveal the divine "secret hidden for long ages"— the glorified Christ dwelling in the believer, spiritually reuniting the Christian with God. Christians thus form Christ's visible body, here identified with the church (1:21–2:8).

The Mystical Initiation into Christ Employing the rather obscure language of Greek mystery religions (discussed in Chapter 9), Paul compares the Christian's baptism to a vicarious experience of Christ's death and resurrection (2:12, 20; 3:1). It is also the Christian equivalent of circumcision, the ritual sign that identifies one as belonging to God's people, and the rite of initiation into Christ's "body" (2:12–14). Raised to new life, initiated believers are liberated from religious obligations sponsored by those "lesser" spirits who transmitted the Torah revelation to Moses.

Paul reminds the Colossians that they need not be intimidated by self-styled authorities who mortify the body and piously forbid partaking of certain food and drink, for Christ's death put an end to such legal discriminations. No longer is there "Greek and Jew, circumcised and uncircumcised, barbarian, Scythians, slave and freeman; but Christ is all, and is in all" (2:20–3:11). Like persons initiated into Greco-Roman mystery cults, Christians now enjoy a union of social and religious equality.

Characteristically, Paul moves from doctrinal matters to ethical exhortations: Christians are to live godly lives and to meet all domestic and social obligations. The list of vices (3:5–9) and virtues (3:12–25) is typical of other Hellenistic teachers of ethics, but the writer adds a distinctively Christian note: Believers conduct themselves well because they are being re-created in Christ's nature and "image" (3:10).

RECOMMENDED READING

Barth, Markus, ed. and trans. *Colossians and Philemon.* Anchor Bible, Vol. 34A. Garden City, N.Y.: Doubleday, 1974. A scholarly translation and analysis.

Horgan, Maurya P. "The Letter to the Colossians." In R. E. Brown et al., eds., *The New Jerome Biblical Commentary,* 2nd ed., pp. 876–882. Englewood Cliffs, N.J.: Prentice-Hall, 1990. Concludes that the letter is by a later Pauline disciple.

Lohse, Eduard. *Colossians and Philemon.* Hermeneia. Philadelphia: Fortress Press, 1971. A scholarly analysis, concluding that Colossians is by a Pauline disciple.

O'Brien, P. T. *Colossians, Philemon.* Word Biblical Commentary, 44. Waco, Tex.: Word Books, 1982. Defends Pauline authorship of Colossians; includes the author's translation.

Schweizer, Eduard. *The Letter to the Colossians: A Commentary.* Minneapolis: Augsburg, 1982. Less technical than works by Lohse and O'Brien; suggests that Timothy played a role in writing Colossians.

Ephesians

KEY TOPICS/THEMES

Scholars believe that Ephesians is a tribute to Pauline thought penned by a later disciple who modifies and updates Paul's ideas to address concerns of his own day. The writer argues that the unity of Christ and the cosmos must be reflected in the unity of the church, whose members engage in spiritual warfare with supernatural Evil.

KEY QUESTIONS

How does the believing community unite the human and the divine? What are the unseen powers that Christians must oppose?

ARGUMENTS FOR NON-PAULINE AUTHORSHIP

Many scholars question Paul's authorship of Colossians, but an overwhelming majority doubt that he composed the document we call Ephesians.

Although it closely resembles Colossians (the style and theology of which also seem untypical of Paul), Ephesians differs from the undisputed Pauline letters in (1) vocabulary (containing over ninety words not found elsewhere in Paul's writings), (2) literary style (written in extremely long, convoluted sentences, in contrast to Paul's typically direct, forceful statements; its quietly devotional tone and smoothly organized sequence of thoughts also differ from the apostle's usual welter of ideas and impassioned language), and (3) theology (the absence of such typically Pauline doctrines as justification by faith and the nearness of Christ's return).

Despite its similarity to Colossians (75 of Ephesians's 155 verses parallel phrases in Colossians), it presents a different view of the sacred "secret" or "mystery" revealed in Christ. In Colossians, God's long-kept secret is Christ's mystical union with his followers (Col. 1:27), but in Ephesians it is the union of Jew and Gentile in one church (Eph. 3:6).

More than any other disputed letter (except those to Timothy and Titus), Ephesians seems to reflect a time in church history significantly later than Paul's day. References to "Apostles and prophets" as the church's foundation imply that these figures belong to the past, not the author's generation (2:20; 3:5). The Gentiles' equality in Christian fellowship is no longer a controversial issue but an accomplished fact; this strongly suggests that the letter originated after the church membership had become non-Jewish (2:11–22). Judaizing interlopers no longer question Paul's stand on circumcision, again indicating that the work was composed after Jerusalem's destruction had largely eliminated the Jewish influence of the mother church.

When Paul uses the term *church* (*ekklesia*), he always refers to an individual congregation (Gal. 1:2; 1 Cor. 11:16; 16:19; etc.). By contrast, Ephesians's author speaks of the church collectively, a universal institution encompassing all communities of faith. This view of the church as a worldwide entity also points to a time after the apostolic period.

The accumulated evidence convinces most scholars that Ephesians is a **deutero-Pauline** document, a secondary work composed in Paul's name

by an admirer thoroughly steeped in the apostle's thought and general theology. The close parallels to Colossians, as well as phrases taken from Romans, Philemon, and other letters, indicate that unlike the author of Acts, this unknown writer was familiar with the Pauline correspondence. Some scholars propose that Ephesians was written as a kind of "cover letter," or essay, to accompany an early collection of Paul's letters.

The phrase "in Ephesus" (1:1), identifying the recipients, does not appear in any of the oldest manuscript copies. That fact, plus the lack of any specific issue or problem being addressed, reinforces the theory that Ephesians was intended to circulate among several churches in Asia Minor. It probably functioned to provide an updated summary of Paul's ideas, tailored to fit the changing needs of a largely Gentile and cosmopolitan church.

GOD'S PLAN OF SALVATION THROUGH THE UNITED BODY OF CHRIST

Probably written between 90 and 100 C.E., Ephesians is more a sophisticated theological meditation than a real letter. Its principal theme is that the unity of the universe through Christ (Chs. 1–3) must be reflected in the unity of the church, which is the earthly manifestation of the divine oneness (Chs. 4–6). God has now revealed his "hidden purpose": to bring "all in heaven and earth . . . into a unity with Christ" (1:10). Although the human race had become alienated from God, God's redemptive act in Jesus' death and resurrection has reconciled the believing world to him. The Deity's age-old secret plan is now clear: "The Gentiles are joint heirs with the Jews, part of the same body, sharers in the promise made in Christ Jesus" (3:6).

In the second part of his letter (Chs. 4–6), the author explores four areas in which the Spirit imparts unity. The first area is the church, where all believers "at last attain to the unity inherent in our faith" (4:4–16), for there is "one body and one Spirit . . . one Lord, one faith, one baptism, one God" (4:5–6). The second area is the pagan world (4:17–5:20), whose ignorance and "foul desires"

Figure 12.16 The Book of Ephesians's famous description of a Christian's spiritual defenses against Evil is based on the armor and other military equipment used by Roman soldiers depicted in this bas-relief (Eph. 6:13–17).

the Christian abandons to be "made new in mind and spirit," thus acquiring a "new nature of God's creating" (4:21–24). In the third area, the Spirit permeates family life so that husbands, wives, children, and slaves show mutual love and forbearance (5:21–6:9).

Heavenly Armor In Ephesians' most famous passage, the Pauline analogy of Christians armed like Roman soldiers is vividly elaborated (Figure 12.16). In 1 Thessalonians (5:8), Paul urges believers to imitate armed sentries who stay awake on guard duty, for Christians must remain similarly alert for Christ's sudden reappearance. Ephesians discards the eschatological context of Paul's metaphor, however, and instead presents an ongoing battle between Good and Evil with no end in sight. In the genuine Pauline letters, the apostle foresees Evil demolished at Christ's Second Com-

ing. The Ephesian writer, by contrast, paints a picture of cosmic conflict reminiscent of Zoroastrianism — the Persian religion in which the world is viewed as a battlefield between invisible forces of light and dark, Good and Evil.

In Zoroastrian terms, the Ephesian Paul describes two levels of "cosmic power" — the earthly rulers of the present dark age and the invisible forces of evil in heaven (6:10–12). Like Mark, the author apparently sense the reality of an evil so powerful that mere human wickedness cannot explain it. (For an insightful interpretation of the "powers" as social attitudes and practices that resist God's Spirit, see Wink in "Recommended Reading.") Instead of desparing, however, he rejoices that God provides ammunition with which to successfully defeat even supernatural evil. According to the author, each article of God's armor is a Christian virtue; cultivated together, qualities like truth and faith offer full protection from even the devil's worst attacks (6:13–19).

Rich in spiritual insight, Ephesians s a creative summary of some major Pauline concepts. Even if not by Paul, it is nevertheless a significant celebration of Christian ideals, an achievement worthy of the great apostle himself.

QUESTIONS FOR REVIEW

1. Why do scholars believe that 2 Thessalonians, Colossians, and Ephesians represent the work of later Pauline disciples rather than that of the apostle himself? What subtle differences in style, theology, and outlook do you find in these disputed letters?

2. Summarize Paul's major contributions to Christian thought, including his beliefs about the *eschaton,* his teachings about the nature and function of Christ (Christology), and his doctrine of justification by faith.

QUESTION FOR DISCUSSION AND REFLECTION

1. Identify and interpret Ephesians's metaphor of Christian armor. How does the attitude in Ephesians toward Christians' continuing battle against supernatural evil differ from Paul's view of the imminent End of the present evil age?

TERMS AND CONCEPTS TO REMEMBER

anti-Christ   deutero-Pauline
Christology   Epaphras
Colossae

RECOMMENDED READING

Barth, Markus, ed. and trans. *Ephesians.* Vols. 34 and 34a of the Anchor Bible. Garden City, N.Y.: Doubleday, 1974. An extensive commentary defending Pauline authorship.

Bruce, F. F. *The Epistles to the Colossians, to Philemon, and the Ephesians.* New International Commentary on the New Testament. Grand Rapids, Mich.: Eerdmans, 1984.

Furnish, V. P. "Ephesians, Epistle to the." In D. N. Freedman, ed., *The Anchor Bible Dictionary,* Vol. 2, pp. 535–542. New York: Doubleday, 1992.

Goodspeed, E. J. *The Meaning of Ephesians.* Chicago: University of Chicago Press, 1933. An older but perceptive study arguing that Ephesians was written as a cover letter for the first collected edition of Paul's correspondence.

Mitton, C. L. *Ephesians.* New Century Bible. Grand Rapids, Mich.: Eerdmans, 1981. A brief study of Ephesians as a work produced by one of Paul's disciples.

Taylor, W. F., and Reumann, J. H. P. *Ephesians, Colossians.* Augsburg Commentary on the New Testament. Minneapolis: Augsburg, 1985.

Wink, Walter. *The Powers That Be: Theology for a New Millennium.* New York: Galilee Doubleday, 1998. Interprets traditional biblical imagery about supernatural forces—angels and demons—as social/cultural assumptions and practices that inhibit God's rule in human society.

The Pastoral Letters

The three letters addressed to Paul's young missionary companions, Timothy and Titus, are known as the pastoral epistles (from *pastor,* the "shepherd" of a flock). The Pauline authorship of 1 and 2 Timothy and Titus, however, has been under critical attack since the eighteenth century. Besides the fact that they do not appear in early lists of Paul's letters, the pastoral epistles (or pastorals) seem to reflect conditions that prevailed long after Paul's day. Their views of ecclesiastical offices, "bishops," "elders," and "deacons," mirror the more tightly organized church of the second century C.E.,

in which such offices had far more specialized functions than in Paul's time.

Lacking Paul's characteristic ideas about faith and the Spirit, the pastorals are also un-Pauline in their flat style and different vocabulary (containing 306 words not found in Paul's undisputed letters). Scholars believe that a single Pauline disciple—who possessed little of his mentor's fire or originality—wrote all three, between about 100 and 140 C.E.

1 Timothy

KEY TOPICS/THEMES

Writing to Timothy as representing a new generation of Christians, an anonymous disciple (known as the pastor) warns his readers against false teachings and recommends the standards necessary for ensuring proper order and discipline within the church.

KEY QUESTION

How does the writer wish the church to model itself on the hierarchial arrangement of Greco-Roman society?

The first two pastorals are addressed to Timothy, the son of a Jewish mother and Greek father (Acts 16:1). However, if scholars are correct in concluding that the pastorals are not by Paul but by an early to mid-second century Christian writer deeply influenced by Pauline thought, it becomes clear that "Timothy" is not the historical evangelist, but a literary character intended to symbolize orthodox (correct) leadership in the postapostolic church. Such pastors struggled to keep alive Paul's "wholesome doctrine" at a time when "subversive teachings [heresies] inspired by devils" threatened to disrupt Christian unity (4:2).

ESTABLISHING ORTHODOXY AND INSTITUTIONAL ORDER

Erroneous Doctrines   The writer's primary purpose is to combat "erroneous doctrines" (1:3) then circulating among the church membership. As

Christianity spread among diverse Gentile groups, some converts apparently brought ideas from older Greco-Roman religions and philosophies, which they applied to Christian traditions. Because the pastor does not offer a rational criticism of his opponents' errors, we do not know the exact nature of the beliefs attacked. Some commentators suggest that the false teachers practiced an early form of **Gnosticism**, a cult of secret "knowledge" mentioned in 6:20, but the letter reveals too little about the **heresies** taught to identify them as Gnostic.

The author describes such deviation from the true faith as involving "interminable myths," "genealogies," and fruitless "speculations" (1:3–4). Its practitioners may have included Jewish legalists, self-appointed "teachers of the moral Law" (1:7–11), and ascetics or "puritans" who forbade marriage and abstained from certain foods that, in the pastor's opinion, God intended everyone to eat (4:1–3). Timothy (and the pastorship he represents) must correct this misguided austerity by transmitting the correct Pauline teachings (4:11), thereby saving himself as well as those who obey him (4:16).

Qualifications for Church Offices

The pastor's second concern is to outline the qualifications for aspirants to church offices (3:1–13). Church officers must demonstrate all the virtues typical of Hellenistic ethical philosophy: They are to be "above reproach" in public reputation, sober, courteous, hospitable, in control of their families, and good teachers (3:2–23). It is remarkable that the pastor's list of qualifications does not include either intellectual ability or possession of the Spirit. Instead of the spiritual gifts that prevailed in Paul's churches, the pastor's congregation seems content with typically middle-class respectability.

The pastor regards the institution of the church—rather than the Spirit of Christ dwelling in the believer—as "the pillar and bulwark of the truth" (3:15). By the time this letter was composed, a tightly organized structure administered by a thoroughly conventional male leadership had replaced the dynamic and charismatic fellowship of the genuinely Pauline congregations.

Ranking the Church Membership

In 1 Timothy, the church membership mirrors the social order of the larger Greco-Roman society out of which its members came. Bishops (overseers), deacons (assistants), and elders (seasoned congregants) govern a mixed group composed of different social classes, including heads of households, masters, slaves, wives, widows, and children—all of whom are ordered to submit to their respective superiors. Rather than the spontaneous equality Paul had advocated, in which slaves and masters, men and women, were urged to escape social categorization and stratification in Christian fellowship, the pastoral church adopted the rigid class system of the outside world.

Women's Roles

Whereas Paul recognizes women as prophets and speakers (1 Cor. 11:5), the pastor does not permit a woman to teach because the first woman, Eve, was weak-minded and tempted her husband to sin (2:8–15). The detailed instructions on women's dress and conduct probably applies to public worship and parallels the restricted position assigned women in some Hellenistic circles. Because it reflects then-current social customs, many commentators observe that the pastor's advice is not a timeless prescription for women's roles in the Christian community.

As Christians are to pray for government rulers (2:1–3), so slaves are to obey their masters (6:1–2). Yet, the rich and powerful are reminded to share their wealth (6:17–19). Those ambitious to acquire riches are told that a passion for money is the cause of much evil, a source of grief and lost faith (6:9–10).

In closing, the pastor instructs Timothy, the prototype of the wise church supervisor, to safeguard the apostolic heritage and to avoid "so-called knowledge" disseminated by (Gnostic?) heretics (6:20–21). Anyone who disagrees with the pastor's interpretation of the Pauline legacy is "a pompous ignoramus" (6:3).

2 Timothy

KEY TOPICS/THEMES

In a style more closely resembling that of Paul than the other pastoral Epistles, 2 Timothy counsels against various false teachings.

KEY QUESTION

What standards of correct teaching does the author advocate?

2 Timothy more closely resembles Paul's genuine letters than either 1 Timothy or Titus. Although similarly concerned with refuting false teachings, its tone is more intimate and personal. Several passages in which the author depicts himself as abandoned by former associates and languishing alone in prison except for the companionship of "Luke" (1:15; 4:9–11, 16) are especially poignant. Although these and other flashes of Paul's characteristic vigor and emotional fluctuations (4:6–8, 17–18) have led some critics to speculate that the work contains fragments of otherwise lost Pauline letters, such proposals have not won general acceptance.

The part of 2 Timothy with the best claim to Pauline authorship is the section that ends the letter (4:6–22), in which the writer emulates the fluctuations between lofty thoughts and mundane practicalities so typical of the apostle. In the first part, he compares himself to a runner winning the athlete's coveted prize—not the Greek competitor's laurel crown, but a "garland of righteousness" justifying him on Judgment Day (6:6–8). Switching abruptly to practical matters, the author then asks the recipient to remember to bring his books when he visits. In another quick change of subject, he complains that during his court hearing, nobody appeared in his defense and that the testimony of one "Alexander the coppersmith" seriously damaged his case. Then, in a seemingly contradictory about-face, the writer states that he has (metaphorically) escaped the "lion's jaws" and expects to be kept safe until the Parousia (6:13–18).

Although such rapid shifts from gloom to optimism characterize Paul's authentic letters, most scholars believe that the entire document is the pastor's work. The more vivid passages are simply the writer's most successful homage to the apostle's memory.

In describing the false teaching within the church that he identifies as signs of the last days, the pastor reveals that he is using Paul to predict conditions that characterize the writer's own time. During the world's final days (3:1), hypocrites insinuate their way into Christians' homes, corrupting the occupants. These predators typically prey on women because, in the pastor's insulting opinion, even when eager to learn, women lack the ability to understand true doctrine (3:6–8). Instead of the false teachers' being punished at the Second Coming, the pastor implies that the mere passage of time will expose their errors (3:9).

As in 1 Timothy, the pastor does not refute the heretics with logical argument, but merely calls them names and lists their vices (3:1–6, 13; 4:3–4), duplicating the catalogues of misbehavior common in Hellenistic philosophical schools. Whereas the church is the stronghold of faith in 1 Timothy, in 2 Timothy the Hebrew Bible is the standard of religious orthodoxy (correct teaching) confounding error and directing the believer to salvation. Scripture also provides the mental discipline necessary to equip the believer for right action (3:15–17).

Concluding with his memorable picture of the apostle courageously facing martyrdom, the pastor graciously includes all of the faithful in Christ's promised deliverance. Not only Paul but all who trust in Jesus' imminent return will win the victor's crown at the Parousia (6:6–8).

Titus

KEY TOPICS/THEMES

The letter to Titus, who represents the postapostolic church leadership, urges him to preserve the Pauline traditions and sets forth the requirements and duties of elders and bishops.

KEY QUESTION

What specific social and family values does the pastor advocate?

Although it is the shortest of the pastorals, Titus has the longest salutation, a fulsome recapitulation of Paul's credentials and the recipient's significance (1:1–4). This highly formal introduction would be inappropriate in a personal letter from Paul to his younger friend, but it is understandable as the pastor's way of officially transmitting Paul's authoritative instruction to a postapostolic successor.

The historical Titus, a Greek youth whom Paul refused to have circumcised (Gal. 2), accompanied the apostle on his missionary tours of Greece, acting as Paul's emissary to reconcile the rebellious Corinthians (Gal. 2:1, 3, 10; 2 Cor. 8:6, 16–23). Like the "Timothy" of the other pastorals, however, "Titus" is a symbolic figure, representing a late postapostolic generation interested in preserving Pauline traditions. Hence, "Titus" functions as a mediator to a later age who can establish the requirements and some of the duties of church leaders who will adhere to Pauline orthodoxy.

REVISING THE PAULINE LEGACY

Qualifications for Church Officers   The writer states that he left "Titus" in Crete, an island center of Greek civilization, to install church assistants (elders) in every town (1:5). Such persons must be socially respectable married men who keep their children under strict parental control (1:6). Whereas Paul had preferred Christians to remain single (1 Cor. 7), the pastor insists that church leaders be married! Besides possessing these domestic credentials, bishops (church supervisors) must also have a reputation for devotion, self-control, and hospitality (1:7–8). Again, the writer says nothing about the leaders' mental or charismatic gifts so highly valued in the Pauline churches (2 Cor. 11–14).

One of the bishop's main functions is to guard the received religion, adhering to established beliefs and correcting dissenters (1:7–9). Titus is the only book in the New Testament that uses the term *heretic* (3:10), which at the time of writing (early to mid-second century) probably meant a person who held opinions of which the elders disapproved. Such dissenters are to be warned twice and then ignored (excluded from the church?) if they fail to change their ways (3:10–11).

The author reminds his readers that because they are Christians in a nonbelieving world, they must live exemplary lives of obedience and submission to government authorities (3:1). Men and women, old and young, slaves and masters — all are to behave in a way that publicly reflects well on their religion (2:1–10). Christians must maintain an ethically pure community while awaiting Christ's return (2:13–14).

In a moving passage, the author contrasts the negative personality traits that many believers had before their conversion with the grace and hope for eternal life that they now enjoy (3:3–8). In counsel similar to that in the letter of James, he urges believers to show their faith in admirable and useful deeds and to refrain from "foolish speculations, genealogies, quarrels, and controversies over the Law" (3:9–10).

The Pastor's Contribution   Although the pastor's style is generally weak and colorless compared to Paul's (except for some passages in 2 Timothy), he successfully promotes Paul's continuing authority in the church. His insistence that Paul's teaching (as he understood it) be followed and that church leaders actively employ apostolic ideas to refute false teachers helped ensure that the international Christian community would build its future on a (modified) Pauline foundation.

Although the pastor values continuity and tradition, he does not seem to show an equal regard for encouraging the individual revelations and ecstatic experiences that characterized the Pauline churches. (Regarding the "laying on of hands" as the correct means of conferring authority [2 Tim. 1:16], he would probably not welcome another like Paul who insisted that his private experience of Jesus — not ordination by his predecessors — validated his calling.) Using Scripture, inherited doctrines, and the institutional church as guarantors of orthodoxy, the pastor sees the Christian revelation as already complete, a static legacy from the past. He ignores Paul's injunction not to "stifle inspiration" or prophetic speech (1 Thess. 5:19–20); his intense conservatism allows little room for future enlightenment.

QUESTIONS FOR REVIEW

1. List the reasons that the large majority of New Testament scholars think that the pastoral epistles were composed after Paul's time by later Christian writers deeply influenced by Pauline thought. What ideas are missing from the pastorals that characterize Paul's genuine letters?

2. After reviewing the works addressed to Timothy and Titus, explain what you think motivated the author to write them. What ideas or principles is he writing to advocate?

QUESTIONS FOR DISCUSSION AND REFLECTION

1. All three pastorals have a similar purpose — to combat heresy and affirm the author's orthodox understanding of apostolic teachings. In what specific ways do the pastorals reflect church conditions that are different from those obtaining in Paul's day?

2. Discuss the pastor's views about women, children, and slaves. How does his prescription for internal church order reflect the hierarchical organization of the contemporary Greco-Roman society? What similarities and differences do you see between the character and behavior of Jesus and the pastor's list of qualifications for church leaders? Would the historical Jesus, an unmarried itinerant prophet, have met the pastor's standards to qualify for church leadership?

3. The pastoral epistles reveal the extent to which a dynamic and charismatic fellowship of Christians has developed into a tightly organized church structure. In your opinion, is this a positive or a negative development? Explain your answer.

TERMS AND CONCEPTS TO REMEMBER

Gnosticism   heresy

RECOMMENDED READING

Dibelius, Martin, and Conzelmann, Hans. *The Pastoral Epistles.* Hermeneia Commentary. Philadelphia: Fortress Press, 1972. Conzelmann's updating of Dibelius's famous commentary, first published in German in 1913.

Hanson, A. T. *The Pastoral Epistles.* New Century Bible. Grand Rapids, Mich.: Eerdmans, 1982. A brief but helpful treatment.

MacDonald, D. R. *The Legend and the Apostle.* Philadelphia: Westminster Press, 1983.

Quinn, J. D., ed. and trans. *1 and 2 Timothy and Titus.* Vol. 35 of the Anchor Bible. Garden City, N.Y.: Doubleday, 1976. A recent translation with commentary.

———. "Timothy and Titus, Epistles to." In D. N. Freedman, ed., *The Anchor Bible Dictionary,* Vol. 6, pp. 560–571. New York: Doubleday, 1992.

CHAPTER 13

General Epistles and Some Visions of End Time

Key Topics/Themes

The third unit of the New Testament contains a variety of letters, tracts, and sermons addressed to early Christian congregations scattered throughout the Roman Empire and an apocalypse (revelation) addressed to seven churches in Asia Minor. Declaring that God's revelation through Jesus is final and complete, Hebrews is the only canonical work to portray Jesus as both God's Messiah (Christ) and eternal High Priest. The catholic (general) letters are ascribed to Peter, James, John, and Jude, leaders associated with the original Jewish Christian church in Jerusalem. 1 John advocates standards of belief and behavior that define the true disciple, particularly a correct understanding of Jesus' Incarnation; James equates "true religion" with charitable acts; 1 Peter sets examples of ethical conduct required for baptized believers, while 2 Peter reaffirms the eschatological doctrine of the Second Coming. Revelation similarly emphasizes the world's imminent transformation, symbolically portraying Rome's persecution of the faithful as culminating in the ultimate cosmic battle between Good and Evil and the establishment of "new heavens and a new earth."

Several other Christian documents were once considered canonical in some churches: The Didache (Teaching) of the Twelve Apostles preserves an important glimpse into forms of early Christian worship; 1 Clement offers instructions on church organization and legitimate leadership; the Epistle of Barnabas presents a method of interpreting the Hebrew Bible as prophetic of Christ; and the Apocalypse of Peter portrays the fiery horrors awaiting sinners in the afterlife.

KEY QUESTIONS

What specific issues about belief and behavior in early Christianity do Hebrews and the catholic epistles address? How do the visions in Revelation serve to encourage hope in humanity's future? Why does the Apocalypse of Peter offer such terrifying views of the afterlife?

Hebrews and the Catholic ("General") Epistles

Paul's extensive use of the letter form influenced many later New Testament writers. Besides authors like the pastor, who wrote in Paul's name, other early Christians imitated the apostle by composing "letters" to instruct and encourage the faithful. Unlike Paul's genuine correspondence, these later documents commonly are not addressed to individual congregations but are directed to the Christian community as a whole. This group of eight disparate writings, headed by the Book of Hebrews, forms a discrete unit between the collection of letters traditionally ascribed to Paul and the Book of Revelation.

Because of their general nature, seven of these writings are known collectively as the **catholic epistles** (referring to the fact that they were intended for the church at large). The seven—James; 1 and 2 Peter; 1, 2, and 3 John; and Jude—are called **epistles** because most of them are formal communications intended for public reading in many different churches. In this respect, they differ from genuine letters like those of Paul, which were composed for specific recipients known to the author and which are much less formal.

Even the term *epistle* does not adequately describe the diverse literary forms encompassed in these works. Of the three missives ascribed to John, for example, the first is actually a sermon or tract, the second a warning letter to a specific group, and the third a private note.

Besides their dubious categorization as epistles, another significant factor links these seven writings. All are attributed to prominent leaders of the original Jerusalem church. Six are ascribed to the three Jerusalem "pillars"—Peter, James, and John (Gal. 2). The seventh, Jude, is purportedly by James's brother.

The practice of creating new works under the identity of a well-known but deceased person is called **pseudonymity**. In our discussion of the Pseudepigrapha (see Chapter 8), we noted that from about 200 B.C.E. to 200 C.E., many Jewish writers composed books attributed to famous leaders of the past, including Moses, Enoch, Isaiah, Solomon, Ezra, and Daniel. These pseudepigraphal works should be thought of *not* as forgeries, but as attempts to perpetuate the teachings of great sages and prophets, updating them to address problems faced by later generations.

Early Christians followed the Jewish lead, producing numerous documents attributed to the apostles and their associates, including Peter, John, James, Barnabas, and Paul (see Chapter 12 and examples given below). As mentioned in our discussion of the pastorals, some of these pseudonymous writings were eventually included in the New Testament.

Hebrews

KEY TOPICS/THEMES

The work of an accomplished stylist who combines allegorical interpretation of the Hebrew Bible with elements of Greek philosophy, Hebrews argues that Jesus was both a kingly and priestly Messiah. The final and complete revelation of God's purpose, Christ now serves in heaven as an eternal High Priest and mediator for humanity.

KEY QUESTIONS

What is the author's theory of correspondences and what are his arguments for Jesus' total supremacy. How is Jesus both king and priest?

AUTHORSHIP AND DATE OF HEBREWS

An old tradition that Paul wrote Hebrews, which was disputed even in the early church, is now generally discredited. Besides differing in vocabulary and style, the book does not reflect Paul's characteristic thoughts on faith, justification, reconciliation, or union with Christ. Although various attempts have been made to show that Barnabas, **Priscilla** (mentioned in Rom. 16:3; 1 Cor. 16:19; 2 Tim. 4:19), or the eloquent Apollos of Alexandria was the author, most scholars now conclude that the work is anonymous.

The last section of Hebrews (13:18–25), with its salutations and first-person references to Timothy, may originally have been part of another document, which a later editor added to make Hebrews seem more like a letter. Despite this epistolary ending, however, Hebrews reads more like an oratorical treatise or sermon than a letter. Mixing theological analysis with exhortation, the work does not follow the rules prescribed by any particular literary form.

Because the text itself does not contain the phrase "to the Hebrews" or otherwise identify its recipients, scholars are also unsure of its intended destination. The final "greetings to you from our Italian friends" (13:24) suggests that it originated in Italy, perhaps in Rome, but some scholars have argued persuasively that it was written in Alexandria or Palestine. The date of composition is equally problematic, with estimates ranging from about 65 to 100 C.E.

A DUALISTIC VIEW AND METHODS OF INTERPRETATION

The Book of Hebrews was written by an anonymous Christian scholar who was equally well acquainted with Greek versions of the Hebrew Bible and with Greek philosophical concepts. The work challenges the reader as does no other New Testament book except Revelation. With the warning that he offers "much that is difficult to explain" (5:11), the writer presents a dualistic view of the universe in which earthly events and human institutions are seen as reflections of invisible heavenly realities. Employing a popular form of Platonic thought, the writer assumes the existence of two parallel worlds: the eternal and perfect realm of spirit above, and the inferior constantly changing world below. Alone among New Testament authors, he attempts to show how Christ's sacrificial death links the two opposing realms of perishable matter and eternal spirit. He is the only biblical writer to present Jesus as a heavenly priest who serves as an everlasting mediator between God and humanity.

Like **Philo Judaeus**, the Hellenistic Jewish scholar of Alexandria, the author of Hebrews uses a highly sophisticated method of biblical interpretation. In both Hebrews and Philo's work, the Hebrew Bible is not merely a record of Israel's history; it is an allegory in which earthly events symbolize heavenly realities.

Like all New Testament writers, however, the author of Hebrews makes subtle theological interpretation not an end in itself, but only a means of reinforcing his attempt to influence readers' ethical behavior. The theological argument—that Christ is the final and complete revelation of God's will—serves to remind believers that they must hold fast to their faith or risk destruction. Thus, the recipients are exhorted to remember their former loyalty during persecution and avoid the common pitfalls of apathy or indifference (10:32–34).

After an introduction (1:1–4), Hebrews is arranged in three main sections:

1. Christ, the image of God, superior to all other human or heavenly beings (1:5–4:16)
2. The Torah's priestly regulations—including sanctuary, covenant, and sacrifice—foreshadowing Jesus' role as a priest like Melchizedek (5:1–10:39)
3. The need for believers to act on faith in unseen realities, emulating biblical figures of old (11:1–13:16)

CHRIST'S SUPERIORITY TO ALL OTHER BEINGS

Hebrews' principal theme is the supremacy and absolute finality of the divine revelation through Jesus Christ. As the perfect "image of God," Christ is superior to all biblical sages, prophets, and angels, and to the priesthood of the Mosaic Torah (4:44–7:28). Hebrews is the only canonical book to argue that Jesus was not only a Davidic Messiah-king but an eternal High Priest as well.

CHRIST AS A KING-PRIEST

To demonstrate that Jesus is greater than the Levitical priests who administered the Mosaic tabernacle (and by implication the Jerusalem Temple), the author cites the Torah story of Abraham and

Melchizedek (Gen. 14:17–20) and a reference to Israel's kings as "like Melchizedek" (Ps. 110:4). According to Genesis, Abraham, returning from a successful war, paid **Melchizedek**, the mysterious king of Salem and priest of "God Most High" (El Elyon), a tenth of his victor's spoils. Because the account mentions neither Melchizedek's ancestors nor descendants, the author concludes that his priesthood is without beginning or end. As king of righteousness and peace and an "eternal priest," Melchizedek is the prototype of Christ. Superior to Abraham, who paid him tithes, he is also superior to Abraham's levitical descendants, the Jewish priests. Sinless, deathless, and confirmed by divine oath, Christ's priesthood endures forever (7:3, 21–28).

In the author's view, Christ's high priesthood supersedes that of the Levites, as do his Temple sanctuary, covenant, and sacrifice (8:1–10:39). Employing a form of Platonic **dualism**—an eternal world of spirit paralleling our perishable world of matter—Hebrews envisions Israel's earthly ceremonies of sacrifice and worship as reflections, or copies, of invisible heavenly realities (8:5) (Figure 13.1). The author then provides an allegorical interpretation of priestly rituals on the **Day of Atonement (Yom Kippur).**

In the visible Israelite tabernacle (or Temple), the High Priest enters the innermost Holy of Holies once a year on the Day of Atonement to make a sin offering for the people (Lev. 16)—an imperfect offering that must be renewed annually. Christ, however, has entered the spiritual reality—the heavenly Temple—once and for all time with the sacrifice of his life, thus canceling the need for any further sacrifices in the earthly sanctuary.

Christianity is thus the only true religion, the fulfillment of Judaism, which was but a shadow of the final revelation. Christ's sacrifice is superior to Israel's atonement offerings not only because it is sinless, perfect, and nonrepeatable but also because it inaugurates a new covenant (9:15). Like the Mosaic Law, Christ's covenant is ratified by blood—that poured out at his crucifixion, for the author subscribes to the old priestly view that without blood no forgiveness of sin takes place (9:22). Whereas the old law demands endlessly repeated animal sacrifices, the new law has but one—Christ's—which is permanently effective.

Those benefiting from Christ's everlasting sacrifice can hope, like him, to enter the heavenly sanctuary, their sins forgiven and their salvation ensured (10:5–19). Meanwhile, Christians should loyally adhere to the true religion because the **Day of Judgment** is near. If they willfully sin after having known the truth, they are condemned because Christ cannot die for them a second time (10:20–31). Although this rigorous view apparently was common in early Christianity, no other New Testament author so categorically denies erring believers a second chance at salvation. (See also Heb. 6:4–9).

FAITH IN UNSEEN REALITIES

In Chapter 11, one of the most famous passages in the Bible, the writer reaches the climax of his presentation—a soaring discourse on **faith.** The writer proposes that believers accept God's ultimate revelation in the Son through faith, which "gives substance to our hopes and makes us certain of realities we do not see" (11:1). Unlike Paul, who always associates faith with trust in Christ, the author of Hebrews defines the concept in classically Platonic terms—perception of an unseen universe transcending the material world (11:1–3). It is the invisible cosmos—the celestial realm where Christ sits at God's right hand—upon which the eyes of faith are fixed. After presenting a brilliant survey of Hebrew Bible figures who lived by faith—from Abel, the first martyr, to the countless men and women who suffered death to attain the spiritual kingdom above—the author urges his readers to run a similar race for eternal life (11:2–12:2). Like the biblical characters who had only a glimpse of what was to come, the Christian, who has the reality, must stand firm, enduring suffering as a necessary discipline (12:3–13).

In a memorable image, the author reminds his readers that the ancient Israelites saw the Torah introduced with awesome phenomena: fire, thunder, and earthquake. Christians now witness an even more holy covenant, which is promulgated not on earthly Mount Sinai, but "before Mount

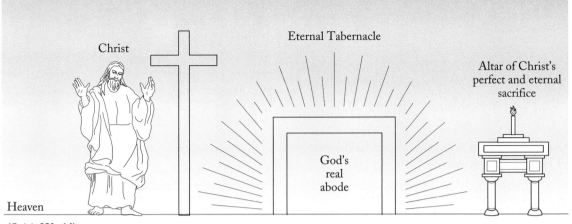

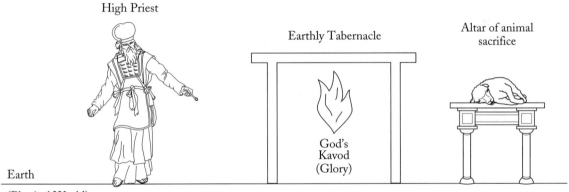

Figure 13.1 The Book of Hebrews expounds a theory of correspondences, the belief that reality exists in two separate but parallel dimensions — the spirit world (heaven) and the physical world (earth). Material objects and customs on earth are temporary replicas, or shadows, of eternal realities in heaven. The author's notion that Jesus' "perfect" sacrifice has rendered Jewish worship obsolete is clearly partisan and a claim that many scholars find highly unacceptable.

Zion and the city of the living God, heavenly Jerusalem." The Exodus imagery inspires a last warning: If the Israelites who disobeyed that law were punished by death, how much more severe will be the punishment of those who fail to keep the faith in the new dispensation (12:1–29).

RECOMMENDED READING

Attridge, Harold W. *The Epistle to the Hebrews.* Philadelphia: Fortress Press, 1989. An authoritative analysis of the book's origin and theology.

Bourke, Myles M. "The Epistle to the Hebrews." In R. E. Brown et al., eds., *The New Jerome Biblical Commentary*, 2nd ed., pp. 920–941. Englewood Cliffs, N.J.: Prentice-Hall, 1990. A helpful introduction.

Buchanan, G. W., ed. and trans. *Hebrews.* Vol. 36 of the Anchor Bible. Garden City, N.Y.: Doubleday, 1972. Provides the editor's translation and commentary.

Fuller, R. H. "The Letter to the Hebrews, James, Jude, Revelation, 1 and 2 Peter." In G. Krodel, ed., *Proclamation Commentaries*. Philadelphia: Fortress Press, 1977.

Kasemann, E. *The Wandering People of God: An Investigation of the Letter to the Hebrews.* Minneapolis: Augsburg, 1984.

James

KEY TOPICS/THEMES

A Jewish-Christian anthology of ethical instruction, James defines both religion and faith in terms of humanitarian action.

KEY QUESTIONS

How does James illustrate his views on the nature of religion and faith? In what ways do these ideas differ from those of Paul?

Although relatively late church traditions ascribe this epistle to **James**, whom Paul called "the Lord's brother" (Gal. 1:19), most scholars question this claim. The work reveals no personal knowledge of either Nazareth or Jesus, to whose life or gospel the author never refers. According to Flavius Josephus, James was martyred by command of the High Priest **Ananias II** (*Antiquities* 20.9.1), in about 60–62 C.E. Scholars regard it as an anonymous compilation of early Christian ethical advice made between about 80 and 100 C.E. Accepted only reluctantly by the Western and Syrian churches—perhaps because of the writer's attack on the Pauline doctrine of faith—it was one of the last New Testament books to attain canonical status.

James is addressed to the "Twelve Tribes dispersed throughout the world" (1:1), which probably refers not to the Israelites of the Diaspora, but to Christians scattered throughout the eastern Mediterranean region. Lacking salutations, greetings, or a complementary closing, the work resembles a sermon more than a letter. A collection of ethical precepts and proverbial counsel, it strongly resembles Hebrew wisdom books. Its tone is impersonal and didactic; its advice is extremely general. Without a discernible controlling theme, James presents practical exhortation on a series of miscellaneous topics ranging from gossip to the misuse of wealth.

A RELIGION OF PRACTICAL EFFORT

Although this book lacks a unifying theme, one principle that lends some coherence to the work is James's conception of religion, which he defines as typically Jewish good works (1:26–27), charitable practices that will save the soul and cancel a multitude of sins (5:19–20). The religion God approves is eminently practical: helping "orphans and widows" and keeping "oneself untarnished by the world" (1:27). In James's two-part definition, the "orphans and widows" are Judaism's classic examples of the poor and defenseless who need God's special care (Figure 13.2), and "the world" represents a society that repudiates God. Thoroughly Jewish in its emphasis on merciful deeds, James's "true religion" cannot be formulated into doctrines, creeds, or rituals (cf. Matt. 25:31–46).

Addressing a problem that plagues virtually every human institution, whether religious or secular, James denounces all social snobbery, especially intimidation of the poor, whose cause God himself defends. Interestingly, the author does not quote from Jesus' sayings about care for the destitute but from the Torah (Lev. 19:18).

Criticizing Paul's Doctrine of Faith The book's most celebrated passage—a denunciation of those who claim to have faith but do nothing to help others—is also its most controversial (2:14–26). Many interpreters see James as attacking Paul's doctrine of salvation through faith (the apostle's rejection of "works" of Torah obedience in favor of trust in God's saving purpose in Christ). Like Paul, James cites the Genesis example of Abraham to prove his point, but he gives it a strikingly different interpretation. James asserts that it was Abraham's action—his willingness to sacrifice his son Isaac—that justified him in God's eyes. The writer's conclusion is distinctly un-Pauline: "A man is justified by deeds and not by faith in itself" (2:24). With its implication that one earns divine approval through hard work and service to others, this conclusion apparently contradicts Paul's assertion that people are saved through a trusting acceptance of God's grace. (See Gal. and Rom. 1–8.)

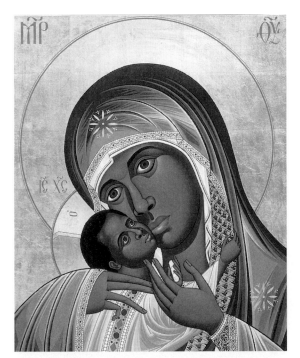

Figure 13.2 *Mother of the Streets.* In painting this (homeless) black Madonna and Christ child, the artist Robert Lentz invites viewers to remember that the Judeo-Christian tradition emphasizes God's unceasing concern for the poor and powerless of society. In the Epistle of James, "true religion" is defined as displaying generosity toward persons who lack adequate food, clothing, shelter, or medical care.

James's conclusion that faith without actions is as dead as a corpse without breath (2:26) seems to repudiate Paul's distinctive teaching. Some commentators point out, however, that James may have intended only to correct a common misuse of Pauline doctrine. Paul himself was a model of "good works," laboring mightily for others' welfare and condemning selfish indolence. Nonetheless, Martin Luther rejected James's argument, describing the work as "strawlike" for its failure to recognize the primacy of divine grace.

Attack on the Rich In another memorable passage (4:13–5:4), James provides the New Testament's most severe criticism of the rich. He denounces Christian merchants and landowners who use their wealth and power to exploit their economic inferiors. Without conscience or compassion, employers have defrauded their workers, delaying payment of wages on which the laboring poor depend to live. Such injustice outrages the Creator, who views the luxury-loving exploiters as overfed animals ripe for slaughter.

Reminding his audience that the Lord will return (5:7), presumably to judge those who economically murder the defenseless (5:6), James ends his sermon on a positive note for any who have strayed from the right path. Sinners and others who are "sick," perhaps spiritually as well as physically, can hope for recovery. God's healing grace operates through congregational prayer for the afflicted. A good person's prayer has the power to rescue a sinner from death and to erase countless sins (5:13–20).

RECOMMENDED READING

Chester, Andrew, and Martin, Ralph. *The Theology of the Letters of James, Peter, and Jude.* Cambridge: Cambridge University Press, 1994.

Dibelius, Martin, and Greeven, Heinrich. *A Commentary on the Epistle of James.* Hermeneia Commentary. Translated by M. A. Williams. Philadelphia: Fortress Press, 1976. An excellent study.

Laws, Sophie. *A Commentary on the Epistle of James.* Harper's New Testament Commentary. San Francisco: Harper & Row, 1980.

Leahy, Thomas W. "The Epistle of James." In R. E. Brown et al., eds., *The New Jerome Biblical Commentary,* 2nd ed., pp. 909–916. Englewood Cliffs, N.J.: Prentice-Hall, 1990.

1 Peter

KEY TOPICS/THEMES

Often compared to a baptismal sermon, 1 Peter reminds Christians of their unique privileges and ethical responsibilities.

KEY QUESTIONS

What are the privileges and obligations of Christian life? How should believers cope with the secular state?

AUTHORSHIP, DATE, AND STRUCTURE

Scholars are divided on the authorship of 1 Peter. Traditionalists maintain that it is the work of the Apostle **Peter**, who reputedly composed it in Rome during Nero's persecution of Christians (64–65 C.E.). If true, it is surprising that the epistle is addressed to churches in Asia Minor (1:1), because official persecution was then confined to the imperial capital. The epistle's closing remarks note that it was written "through Sylvanus [Silas]" (5:12), which, among those who champion Petrine authorship, supposedly accounts for the work's excellent Greek.

Most scholars believe that 1 Peter is pseudonymous and was produced during postapostolic times. Its references to "fiery ordeals" (4:12–13) lead most experts to date it either during the time of **Domitian** (c. 95 C.E.) or **Trajan** (c. 112 C.E.). Because the situation it reflects closely parallels that described in the correspondence between Trajan and Pliny the Younger, governor of **Bithynia**, the latter date is commonly preferred (Pliny, Letters 97) (Figure 13.3).

The greetings from "her who dwells in Babylon" (5:13) provide the key to the work's place of origin, for "her" refers to the church, and "Babylon" (the Hebrew prophets' archetypal example of the ungodly nation) was a Christian code word for Rome. (See Rev. 14:8; 18:2.) The author's purpose is to encourage believers to retain their integrity (as Christians like Peter did in Nero's time) and to promote Christian ethics. He urges the faithful to live so blamelessly that outsiders can never accuse them of anything illegal or immoral. If one suffers persecution, it should be only "as a Christian" (4:14–16).

The first letter of Peter is commonly described as a baptismal sermon, because it presents readers with a vivid survey of both the privileges and dangers involved in adopting the Christian way of life. The letter can be divided into three sections:

1. The privileges and values of the Christian calling (1:3–20:10)
2. The obligations and responsibilities of Christian life (2:11–4:11)

Figure 13.3 Under Trajan (reigned 98–117 C.E.) the Roman Empire reached its greatest geographical extent, stretching from Britain in the northwest to Mesopotamia (Iraq) in the east. Pliny the Younger's letters to Trajan about the proper method of handling Christians reveal that the emperor opposed anonymous accusations and ordered that accused persons who demonstrated their loyalty to the state by making traditional sacrifices should not be prosecuted.

3. The ethical meaning of suffering as a Christian (4:12–5:11)

THE REWARDS AND DANGERS OF CHRISTIAN LIFE

Addressing an audience that had not known Jesus, Peter emphasizes the rarity and inestimable value of the faith transmitted to them. They must regard their present trials and difficulties as opportunities to display the depth of their commitment and the quality of their love (1:3–7). Christians, including Gentiles, are the new "chosen race"—"a royal priesthood, a dedicated nation, and a people claimed by God for his own" (2:9–10).

OBLIGATIONS AND RESPONSIBILITIES
OF CHRISTIAN LIFE

The second section of 1 Peter focuses on the responsibilities and moral conduct of God's people (2:11–4:11). Many commentators have noted that these passages contain numerous Pauline ideas, particularly on matters of Christian behavior and obedience to the Roman state. Echoing Romans 13, the author advises peaceful submission to government authorities (3:13–15), just as servants should submit to their masters (2:18) and wives to their husbands (3:1–2). Those who suffer unjustly from the burdens of this hierarchy must bear it as Jesus bore his sufferings (1:19–25; 3:13–18; 4:1–5).

This section includes two brief but fascinating allusions to Jesus' descent into the Underworld (Hades), presumably during the interval between his death and resurrection (3:18–20; 4:6). This material inspired the medieval tradition that Jesus entered hell and rescued the souls of those who died before the way to heaven was open.

ETHICAL MEANING
OF CHRISTIANS' SUFFERING

The third part of 1 Peter (4:12–5:11) examines the ethical meaning of suffering "as a Christian." Persons embracing the new faith should not be surprised by their "fiery ordeal" because as followers of Christ they must expect to share his sufferings (4:12–16). Judgment has come, and it begins "with God's own household"—the church. If the righteous are but narrowly saved, what will happen to the wicked (4:17–19)? Elders must shepherd the flock with loving care; younger people must submit humbly to their rule (5:1–7); and all must remain alert because the devil prowls the earth "like a roaring lion" seeking to devour the unwary. The faithful who resist him will share in Christ's reward.

RECOMMENDED READING

Best, Ernest. *1 Peter.* London: Oliphants, 1971.

Brown, R. E.; Donfried, K.; and Reumann, J.; eds. *Peter in the New Testament: A Collaborative Assessment by Protestant and Roman Catholic Scholars.* Minneapolis: Augsburg, 1973. A recommended study of Peter's role in the New Testament tradition and literature.

Dalton, William J. "The First Epistle of Peter." In R. E. Brown et al., eds., *The New Jerome Biblical Commentary,* 2nd ed., pp. 903–908. Englewood Cliffs, N.J.: Prentice-Hall, 1990.

Elliott, J. H. *A Home for the Homeless: A Sociological Exegesis of 1 Peter, Its Situation and Strategy.* Philadelphia: Fortress Press, 1981. A sociological analysis of historical conditions underlying the message and meaning of 1 Peter.

Kelly, J. N. D. *A Commentary on the Epistles of Peter and Jude.* New York: Harper & Row, 1969. A good introductory study.

Reicke, Bo. *The Epistles of James, Peter, and Jude.* Anchor Bible, Vol. 37. Garden City, N.Y.: Doubleday, 1964.

Jude

KEY TOPICS/THEMES

Defending orthodoxy, Jude warns of impending judgment on false teachers.

KEY QUESTION

Why does Jude quote from the noncanonical 1 Enoch as if it were Scripture?

Although the author identifies himself as **Jude** (Judas), "servant of Jesus Christ and brother of James"—and presumably also a kinsman of Jesus (see Mark 6:3; Matt. 13:55)—the text implies that the time of the apostles is long past and that their predictions are now coming true (v. 17). Scholars generally agree that Jude is a pseudonymous work composed about 125 C.E., perhaps in Rome.

A WARNING AGAINST FALSE TEACHERS

Placed last among the general epistles, Jude is less a letter than a tract castigating an unidentified group of heretics. Its primary intent is to persuade the (also unidentified) recipients to join the writer in defending orthodox Christian traditions (v. 3). In literary style, Jude represents a kind of rhetoric known as invective—an argument characterized by verbal abuse and insult. Rather than specify his opponents' doctrinal errors or logically refute their arguments, the author merely calls them names, denouncing them as "brute beasts" (v. 10), "enemies of religion" who have wormed their way into the church to pervert it with their "licentiousness" (v. 4). A "blot on [Christian] love feasts" (v. 12), they are doomed to suffer divine wrath as did Cain, Balaam, Korah, and other villains of the Hebrew Bible. Because the author does not try to correct their errors rationally, but merely fires off bitter accusations along with threats of doom, Jude has been called the least creative book in the New Testament.

Besides its vituperation, Jude is notable for citing several nonbiblical sources along with well-known passages from the Hebrew Bible. In verses 14–15, the author directly quotes the pseudepigraphal books of Enoch and alludes to or paraphrases them elsewhere as well (cf. 1 En. 18:12; 1:1–9; 5:4; 27:2; 60:8; 93:2). From copies of Enoch preserved among the Dead Sea Scrolls, we know that the Essenes studied the work. Jude's use of the text to support his contentions proves that some early Christian groups also regarded Enoch as authoritative.

In addition, Jude's reference to a postbiblical legend about the archangel **Michael**'s contending with the devil for Moses' body (v. 9) may be taken from the incompletely preserved Assumption of Moses, another pseudepigraphal work. To balance its largely vindictive tone, the epistle closes with a remarkably lyrical **doxology** (vv. 24–25).

RECOMMENDED READING

Reicke, Bo. *The Epistles of James, Peter, and Jude.* Anchor Bible, Vol. 37. Garden City, N.Y.: Doubleday, 1964.

2 Peter

KEY TOPICS/THEMES

Incorporating most of Jude into his second chapter, a second-century Christian writing in Peter's name attacks false teachers and urges a return to the apocalyptic hope of apostolic times. Explaining the delayed Parousia as God's means of allowing more people to repent, the author outlines the "three worlds" of apocalyptic history.

KEY QUESTION

How does the author account for the long delay in the Parousia?

MEETING THE CHALLENGE OF THE DELAYED PAROUSIA

Only a few reputable New Testament scholars defend the Petrine authorship of 2 Peter, which is believed to have been written by an anonymous churchman in Rome about 140–150 C.E. The book's late date is confirmed by (1) the fact that it incorporates most of Jude (2:2–17), itself a second-century work; (2) its references to Paul's letters as "Scripture" (3:16), a status they did not attain until the mid-second century; and (3) its concern with the delayed Parousia (Ch. 3), which would not have been a problem for believers until after the apostolic generation. In addition, many leaders of the early church doubted 2 Peter's authorship, resulting in the epistle's absence from most lists of "approved" books well into the fourth century. Not only was 2 Peter one of the last works to gain entrance into the New Testament, but scholars believe that it was the last (eventually canonized) book written.

The author assumes Peter's identity for the purpose of representing the epistle's contents as embodying true apostolic doctrine. He takes pains to present himself in apostolic terms, mentioning his presence at the Transfiguration (1:17–18), Jesus' prediction of his death (1:14), his authorship of 1 Peter (3:1), and his association with Paul (3:15). Having thus established his credentials, he rails against the "false teachers" who pervert the apostolic traditions, upon whom judgment will fall as it did upon rebellious angels whom God chained in Tartarus (2:4), upon the corrupt world of Noah's day, and upon Sodom and Gomorrah (2:5–6).

The Delayed Parousia   In Chapter 3, the author reveals that his primary goal is to reinstate the early Christian apocalyptic hope of the **Parousia** (Second Coming). Skeptics may point out that the "fathers" (apostles) who promised Christ's early return have all died and yet the world continues on exactly as before, but they forget that the world has already been destroyed once in Noah's Flood (3:3–6). Similarly, the present world will be consumed by fire (3:7). In predicting a cosmic holocaust, the author apparently borrows the Stoic philosophers' theory that the cosmos undergoes cycles of destruction and renewal. Employing Stoic images and vocabulary, 2 Peter foretells a universal conflagration in which heaven will be swept away in a roaring fire and the earth will disintegrate, exposing all its secrets (3:10).

Citing either Revelation's vision (21:1–3) or the Isaiah passages upon which it is based (Isa. 65:17; 66:22), the author states that a third world will replace the previous two destroyed, respectively, by water and fire. "New heavens and a new earth" will host true justice (3:13), the apocalyptic kingdom of God.

2 Peter's Theodicy   The author is aware that some Christians who doubt the Parousia may do so because God, despite the arrival, death, and ascension to heaven of the Messiah, has not acted to conquer Evil and deliver the faithful. God's seeming delay, however, has a saving purpose. Withholding judgment, the Deity allows time for more people to repent and be spared the final catastrophe (3:9, 15). Although exercising his kindly patience in the realm of human time, God himself dwells in eternity where "a thousand years is like one day." From his vantage point, the Parousia is not delayed; his apparent slowness to act is only a manifestation of his will to save all people (3:8–9).

Because the universe is destined to perish in flames (an extreme view that even Revelation does not advocate), the author urges believers to shield themselves with good works, which will serve to "hasten" the End (3:11–12). While awaiting the fulfillment of the Lord's design, they must study the Scriptures (including Paul's letters), which the ignorant ruinously misinterpret (3:14–16). Some critics suggest that if 2 Peter originated in Rome, this reference to Paul's work as possessing scriptural authority may reflect a mid-second-century controversy in which Marcion and other Roman Gnostics claimed that Paul's writings supported their doctrines.

RECOMMENDED READING

Bauckham, Richard J. "Peter, Letters of 2 Peter." In B. M. Metzger and M. D. Coogan, eds., *The Oxford Companion to the Bible,* pp. 586–588. New York: Oxford University Press, 1993.
Neyrey, Jerome H. "The Second Epistle of Peter." In R. E. Brown et al., eds., *The New Jerome Biblical Commentary,* 2nd ed., pp. 1017–1022. Englewood Cliffs, N.J.: Prentice-Hall, 1990.

1 John

KEY TOPICS/THEMES

An important tract directed against secessionists from the Johannine community, 1 John establishes a set of criteria by which to distinguish true belief from error.

KEY QUESTION

What standards does the writer propose for testing the validity of beliefs about Jesus?

LETTERS FROM THE JOHANNINE COMMUNITY

The three letters traditionally ascribed to the Apostle John give us some important insights into the Johannine community that produced and used the Fourth Gospel as its standard of belief. The author of 2 and 3 John identifies himself as "the Elder" (*presbyteros*) (2 John v. 1; 3 John v. 1); the writer of 1 John does not mention his office or function in the church.

Most scholars believe that the same person wrote all three documents but that he is not to be identified with either the Apostle John or the author of the Gospel. Although some critics link him with the editor who added Chapter 21 to the Gospel, most commentators view the letter writer as a separate party, albeit an influential member of the Johannine "brotherhood" (John 21:23). The majority of scholars date the letters to about 100–110 C.E., a decade or two after the Gospel's composition.

Rather than a letter, 1 John is a sermon or tract against former members who have recently withdrawn from the Johannine community. The author calls them "anti-Christs" who have deserted his church to rejoin the outside world (2:18–19), where they spread false ideas about the nature of Christ and Christian behavior.

Revealing a more conventional view about End time than the Gospel writer, the Elder opines that the "anti-Christ's" activity proves that the "last hour" has arrived (2:18; see also John 21:22–23). (In the Johannine church, the Gospel's "realized eschatology" may have existed side by side with more traditional ideas about the Parousia.) Like most early Christian churches, the Elder's community relied on prophetic inspiration, an ongoing communication with the Holy Spirit that continued the process of interpreting Jesus' message and meaning (John 15:26–27; 16:12–14). Problems arose when Christian prophets contradicted one another, as the anti-Christ secessionists were then doing. How was the believer to determine which among many opposing "inspirations" was truly from God?

Writing to a charismatic group long before a central church authority existed to enforce orthodoxy, the Elder is the first Christian writer to propose standards by which believers can distinguish "the spirit of error" from "the spirit of truth" (4:1–6). He echoes the Apostle Paul, who experienced similar difficulties (1 Thess. 5:19–21), when he asks Christians to "test the spirits" critically (4:1) to evaluate the reliability of their message.

STANDARDS FOR BELIEF AND BEHAVIOR

Because the Elder sets up his particular tests to refute the secessionists' errors, we can infer something about their teaching from the nature of his proposals. Basically, he offers two areas of testing—doctrinal and behavioral. His document is accordingly divided into two parts, the first beginning with his affirmation of the community's pristine teaching: "Here is the message we heard from him and pass on to you: that God is light" (1:5). The light from God illuminates the doctrinal truth about Jesus. In his prologue (1:1–7), which strikingly resembles the Gospel's Hymn to the Logos, the Elder claims that his group possesses a direct, sensory experience of Jesus' humanity. The Word was visible and physical; he could be seen and touched. Yet, those who abandoned the community apparently deny Christ's full humanity, causing the Elder to impose a christological test of the true faith: Jesus (the man) and Christ (the heavenly being) were one person, "in the flesh." Those who deny this "light" now walk in "darkness."

Many scholars suggest that the Elder's opponents were Gnostics or Docetists, who insisted that "the Christ" was a divine Revealer from heaven who temporarily occupied the body of Jesus, separating from the Galilean at death and reascending to the spirit realm. The Johannine community insists that Jesus and the Christ are the same being and that he truly suffered and died.

Next to the **Incarnation** test, the Elder places a requirement expressing his community's cardinal rule. He begins the second part of his discourse with a declaration that parallels his first criterion: "For the message you have heard from the beginning is this: that we should love one another" (3:11). Like Cain, who murdered his brother, the secessionists fail to show love for the former associates whom they have abandoned. In his most quoted statement, the author declares that people who do not love cannot know God because "God is love" (4:8–9). Emphasizing the unity between divine and human love, the Elder reminds us that to love God is also to cherish God's human creation (4:19–21).

Implying that the secessionists not only fail to love but also neglect Christian ethics, the author insists that loving God necessitates keeping his commandments (5:5). This means living as Jesus did, serving others' welfare (2:6). The author refers to "the old command" that his group has always possessed, apparently the single commandment that John's Gospel ascribes to Jesus—the instruction to love (John 13:34–35; 15:12, 17). The Elder can cite no other ethical injunction from his group's tradition.

2 John

KEY TOPICS/THEMES

This letter is a warning against false teachings of the secessionists.

KEY QUESTION

What single rule for Christian behavior does the author cite?

A letter of only thirteen verses, 2 John is from the Elder to another church in the Johannine community. As in 1 John, the writer's purpose is to warn of the "**anti-Christ,**" the deceiver who falsely teaches that Jesus Christ did not live as a material human being (v. 7). He urges his recipients not to welcome such renegade Christians into the believers' homes or otherwise encourage them (vv. 10–11). As before, the author can counter the secessionists' attacks by citing only one cardinal rule, the love that is their community's sole guide (vv. 5–6).

3 John

KEY TOPICS/THEMES

This letter is an appeal to show hospitality to an itinerant Johannine teacher.

KEY QUESTION

How should believers treat each other?

In 3 John, a private note to his friend Gaius, the Elder asks his recipient to extend hospitality to some Johannine missionaries led by Demetrius (otherwise unknown). The writer asks Gaius to receive these travelers kindly, honoring their church's tradition of supporting those who labor to spread their version of "the truth" (v. 8).

By contrast, one Diotrephes, a rival leader, offends the Elder by not only denying his emissaries of hospitality but also expelling from the congregation any persons who attempt to aid them. We do not know if the spiteful charges Diotrephes brings against the Elder relate to the secessionists' false teaching denounced in 1 John. Although Diotrephes may not be one of the "anti-Christ" faction, his malice and lack of charity suggests that he does not practice the Johannine community's essential commandment.

Some scholars have noted that the Elder's disapproval of Diotrephes may stem from the latter's acting with undue authority. Whereas the Johannine community seems to have existed with little ecclesiastical structure, Diotrephes behaves as if he has the power, in effect, to excommunicate a member of the Elder's group. In exercising this prerogative, Diotrephes anticipates the actions of monarchical bishops in the hierarchically organized church of later centuries.

Other Early Christian Letters and Tracts

Early Christian writers produced many documents besides those now included in the New Testament, including several that once hovered on the fringes of the canon. Such works as the Didache (Teaching of the Twelve Apostles), 1 Clement, and the Epistle of Barnabas were once widely read in many Christian churches and their titles appear in early lists of books their compilers apparently regarded as canonical (see Chapter 1). Some of these texts, particularly 1 Clement and the Didache, are actually older than a number of books eventually admitted to the canon, including the pastorals, the Johannine epistles, Jude, and 2 Peter. Along with the New Testament literature, these texts provide fascinating glimpses into the rich diversity of late first- and second-century Christianity. (Another noncanical work, the Apocalypse of Peter, is discussed at the end of this chapter.)

The Didache (Teaching) of the Twelve Apostles

One of our most valuable sources for the form of worship practiced in early Christian churches, the **Didache** (Teaching) of the Twelve Apostles was probably compiled about 100 C.E., before most of the catholic epistles were written. Although known to early Christian leaders, such as Clement of Alexandria and the church historian Eusebius, the Didache was thought to have been lost until a copy was discovered in Constantinople in 1873 C.E. A two-part volume, the Didache's first section outlines the "Two Ways of Life and Death," while the second includes a primitive manual of church ritual and discipline, including instructions for performing baptism, saying prayers, and celebrating the **Eucharist** (partaking of the bread and wine commemorating Jesus' final meal with his disciples). Although some scholars believe that the Didache may have originated in Egypt, scholarly opinion now favors Syria—perhaps the city of Antioch—as the place of composition. In his introduction, the author cites typically Matthean versions of Jesus' teachings; since Matthew's Gospel was probably written in Antioch, it seems likely that the Didache also derives from the same general locale.

Opening with a survey of the opposing behaviors that lead either to "Life" or to "Death," the Didache borrows from a previously existing treatise on the "Two Ways" that was apparently well known in the early church (a slightly different version also appears in the Epistle of Barnabas; discussed later). Devoting only one of the six brief chapters in this section to misdeeds that are spiritually fatal, the author takes four chapters to emphasize the life-giving benefits of following Jesus' injunctions to love not only God and neighbor but enemies as well. As some scholars have observed, this rephrasing of passages from Matthew's Sermon on the Mount may reflect the oral traditions behind the written Gospel rather than a direct knowledge of the document itself, another indication of the Didache's early date.

In interpreting Jesus' teachings about behaving generously, the writer translates them into simple, direct commands. Loving others means refraining from wrong actions, such as lying, stealing, or killing; it also demands positive action, such as giving freely to the poor and sharing possessions with fellow believers. After dealing briefly with the "Ways of Death"—which include turning away from God, oppressing the needy, supporting only the rich, and committing infanticide—the writer concludes with a strikingly pragmatic bit of advice: Those who can obey Jesus' words entirely will be "perfect," but if full compliance is beyond them, they should simply "do as much as [they] can."

For historians of Christianity, particularly of its **liturgy** (the customary rites observed in public worship), the second part of the Didache is of particular interest. In this section (Chs. 7–16), the author prescribes the correct procedures for church rituals and practices, ranging from the proper way to perform baptism or hold communion to practical ways of dealing with traveling "apostles and prophets," differentiating genuine servants of Christ from others who exploit the faithful. According to this very early form of the Christian liturgy, baptisms should occur in cold "running water" (a river or stream) or in "warm" water (indoor pools?). If such are not available, however, the person performing the rite should sprinkle water three times on the convert's head, reciting the Matthean formula "in the name of the Father, and the Son, and the Holy Spirit" (Matt. 28:19–20) (Figure 13.4). As in Matthew's community, Christians are to fast, but they are to go without food on Wednesdays and Fridays to distinguish them from Jews (here called "hypocrites," as in Matt. 23), who observe the biblical rule on Mondays and Thursdays. Christians are also to recite the Lord's Prayer (reproduced here in a version almost identical to that in Matthew) three times daily.

The Didache's regulations for the Eucharist differ slightly from those reported in the Gospel tradition. Whereas in Mark Jesus first breaks bread and then passes the cup of wine, in the Didache the wine is offered before the bread. Interestingly, by the time the Didache was written, an elaborate series of prayers and set responses from the congregation had already been established for the Eu-

Figure 13.4 This early Christian baptistery (pool for performing baptisms) belongs to St. John's Basilica in Ephesus, traditionally the city where John, son of Zebedee, spent his last years and where he allegedly wrote the Gospel and letters bearing his name (a view disputed by most scholars). According to the author of the Didache (late first century C.E.), cold river water was the preferred medium for baptisms, but "warm" indoor pools, or even sprinkling, could also be used in the ritual by which new members were initiated into the church.

charist ceremony. Both praise of God and petitions for the welfare of the church are included.

Chapters 11–15 contain instructions on how churches are to deal with itinerant teachers, prophets, and "apostles," who, if they are true servants of the faithful, are to be welcomed as if they were Jesus himself. True prophets will accept a congregation's hospitality for no more than two days before moving on; if they decide to stay per-

manently to strengthen the church with sound teaching and spiritual guidance, they are to be treated like the priests of ancient Israel, receiving a portion of the group's income. False prophets can be distinguished by their indolence or greed; no one who asks for money or refuses to work will be tolerated.

The Didache concludes with an eschatological warning in which the author urges Christians to be prepared at all times for Jesus' return, which will occur unexpectedly. Echoing the apocalyptic scenario given in 2 Thessalonians, the writer outlines the sequence of events that will take place at history's End: Deceivers will mislead the church, leading to "lawlessness" and attempts to change Christian love to "hate," after which an anti-Christ will seize control of the world. Believers will be subjected to a "fiery" test of faith (perhaps government persecution), which "multitudes" will fail. Then, in rapid order, the eschatological climax will be achieved: The heavens will open, the final trumpet will sound, the righteous dead will rise from their graves, and the "whole world" will behold Christ appearing in clouds of glory.

1 Clement

The pastoral epistles' concern for a solidly organized church that could withstand the assaults of false teachers or other troublemakers is further developed in a letter known as 1 Clement (2 Clement, a later work, is not by the same author). Although this letter "from the Church of God at Rome" to the "Church of God at Corinth" does not claim Pauline authorship, it is written to a congregation that Paul had founded and to which he had directed some of his most memorable correspondence (referred to in 1 Clement, Chs. 47 and 49). Citing Paul as "the greatest of all examples of endurance" and alluding to his martyrdom in Rome, the letter's place or origin, 1 Clement implicitly appropriates the apostle's valuable legacy (Ch. 5). Composed in about 95 or 96 C.E., forty years after 1 and 2 Corinthians were written, 1 Clement addresses issues of church leadership—

particularly the means by which leaders possess legitimate authority—with which the pastorals had also wrestled.

Although the writer does not give his name, an early church tradition identifies him as **Clement**, the third overseer (bishop) of Rome (after Peter and his immediate successor, Linus). In the light of later church history, the fact that a representative of the Roman church takes it upon himself to intervene in the affairs of a church in faraway Greece is significant. The author (assumed to be Clement) does not hesitate to reprimand the Corinthians for allowing their presbyters (elders) to be overthrown and replaced by new leaders, an "unacceptable" innovation that is the occasion for his letter. For Clement, the Corinthians' unauthorized change in leadership violates an important principle—the orderly transmission of church authority—that would eventually emerge in the later second century C.E. as an official policy of apostolic succession.

According to Clement, there must be a direct line of succession from Jesus and his original apostles to current church supervisors if those leaders are to be seen as truly legitimate. This principle is most cogently expressed in Chapters 42–44, where Clement lays out his concept of a church leadership that ultimately stems from God himself. After "Christ received his commission from God," the apostles received theirs from Christ; in turn, the apostles then conferred authority upon selected converts who were worthy to lead congregations. Originating with God and Christ, this human chain of leadership appointments continues from generation to generation, extending indefinitely into the future. Because this succession is divinely authorized, those who resist it—as the Corinthians did by ousting their former overseers—are actually opposing God. Submission to properly authorized leaders is thus required of all Christians (Chs. 45–46).

Urging the Corinthians to remember Paul's famous discourse on love (1 Cor. 13), Clement orders them to restore their former leaders, avoiding preference for any others. Although he gives no information about why the Corinthians had rejected the former presbyters and set up new supervisors,

Clement asks any potential opponents to remove themselves from the fray, if necessary going into voluntary exile to end dissension and restore peace to the congregation. By showing nobility and "compassion," those who withdraw will "earn a great name for [themselves] in Christ" (Chs. 54–59). Praising the virtues of humility, patience, and submission to duly constituted authority, Clement ends his letter by appealing for the Corinthians' cooperation, which will bring the church "peace and joy."

The Epistle of Barnabas

Another indirect claim on the Pauline heritage, the Epistle of Barnabas is attributed to Paul's mentor and traveling companion. An influential work in parts of the early Christian community, Barnabas was included in the Codex Sinaiticus, a fourth-century text of the New Testament. According to Acts, **Barnabas** was a Greek-speaking Levite from Cyprus who introduced Paul, a fellow Diaspora Jew, to the newly formed church at Jerusalem (Acts 4:36–37; 9:27), after which the two made a missionary tour together in Asia Minor (Acts 11:19–30). In Acts' version of events (which many scholars dispute), Barnabas was instrumental in opening the church to Gentile converts and supported Paul's position on admitting uncircumcised Gentiles to full membership (Acts 15). The two missionaries parted company, not over this crucial issue, but merely over allowing John Mark (Barnabas's cousin; cf. Col. 4:10) to accompany them on a second journey (Acts 15:36–41). According to Paul's own account, however, they quarreled because Barnabas sided with the more conservative Peter and James in a dispute about Jewish Christians in Antioch continuing to share meals with Gentiles (Gal. 2:11–14).

The historical Barnabas's position on Gentiles' observing Jewish dietary laws is important in considering the epistle ascribed to him because this noncanonical work portrays a Barnabas who virulently attacks Jewish customs, including the prohibition on "impure" foods and the entire system of ritual sacrifice. Composed in the second century c.e., this pseudonymous document is more a treatise than a letter. While the first part (Chs. 1–17) is a radical reinterpretation of the Hebrew Bible, arguing that the Jewish Scriptures can be understood only as a series of complex prophecies and foreshadowings of Christ, the shorter second part (Ch. 18–20) contains a version of the "Two Ways" (here called the opposite paths of "Light" and "Darkness"), a previously existing discourse on spiritual life and death that had earlier been included in the Didache.

In his survey of the biblical tradition, the author insists that the Jews misunderstand their own Scriptures, taking Torah commands about sacrifice, fasting, and other practices at face value when they should be interpreted symbolically as previews of Christian ethics. According to the writer (whom we call Barnabas for convenience), the divine promises made to Israel for land, a covenant relationship, and kingship are actually metaphors for the coming of Christ, pledges fulfilled in Jesus' incarnation, crucifixion, and heavenly reign. Everything that Jews take literally, including Mosaic laws about dietary restrictions and animal sacrifice, is meant to be seen as an allegory of the Christ event. Denying Judaism any intrinsic religious value, the author views the Hebrew Bible as entirely a Christian book.

Barnabas's version of the "Two Ways" leading to life or death may be an adaptation of an older Jewish document, perhaps incorporating ideas about the opposing forces of God's "Light" and Satan's "Darkness" that were common in Essene writings.

Barnabas ends his epistle by stating that he has taken considerable pains to work out his ingenious methods of scriptural interpretation, putting his "best efforts" into the project for his recipients' benefit. Approaching Scripture to discern its hidden symbols of truth, he says, will help safeguard his audience on the coming Day of Judgment.

QUESTIONS FOR REVIEW

1. Describe the practice of pseudonymity among Jewish and early Christian circles. Why are pseudonymous works to be regarded not as deceptions or forgeries, but as tributes to the persons in whose name and memory they are written?

2. Define the term *catholic epistle*, and describe the general nature of these seven documents. According to tradition, to what specific group of authors are these works attributed? Why do most scholars conclude that all seven are pseudonymous?

3. Identify and explain the major themes in Hebrews. How does the author's belief in a dualistic universe — an unseen spirit world that parallels the visible cosmos — affect his teaching about Jesus as an eternal High Priest officiating in heaven?

4. Almost every book in this unit of the New Testament — Hebrews and the catholic epistles — contains a theme or concept not found in any other canonical document. For example, only Hebrews presents Jesus as a celestial priest foreshadowed by Melchizedek; it is also unique in being the only New Testament work to define faith (Heb. 11:1).

Indicate which of the catholic epistles contains the following definitions or statements:
a. A definition of religion
b. A belief that Jesus descended into Hades (the Underworld) and preached to spirits imprisoned there
c. A definition of God's essential nature
d. A set of standards by which to determine the truth of a religious teaching
e. An argument that actions are more important than faith
f. A concept that human history is divided into three separate eras, or "worlds"
g. A defense of the primitive apocalyptic hope involving Jesus' Second Coming (the Parousia)
h. Citations from the noncanonical books of the Pseudepigrapha, including the Book of Enoch
i. The New Testament's most severe denunciation of the rich

QUESTIONS FOR DISCUSSION AND REFLECTION

1. Discuss the contributions of such diverse books as Hebrews, James, and 1 John to Christian doctrine. Why were these books, although attributed to figures from the first generation of Christians, among the last to be accepted as part of the New Testament?

2. From your readings in the catholic epistles, 1 Clement, and the Didache, what seem to be the principal concerns of Christian writers during the last decades of the first century C.E. and the first part of the second century C.E. In what ways is the Christian community striving to define itself and preserve its message in a sometimes hostile world?

TERMS AND CONCEPTS TO REMEMBER

Ananias II	epistle
anti-Christ	Eucharist
Barnabas (reputed	faith
author of the epistle	Incarnation
of Barnabas)	James
Bithynia	Jude
catholic epistles	liturgy
Clement of Rome	Melchizedek
Day of Atonement	Michael
(Yom Kippur)	Parousia
Day of Judgment	Peter
Didache, the	Philo Judaeus
Domitian	Priscilla
doxology	pseudonymity
dualism	Trajan

RECOMMENDED READING

The Johannine Letters

Brown, R. E. *The Community of the Beloved Disciple.* New York: Paulist Press, 1979. An extraordinarily insightful analysis of the Johannine group that produced the Gospel and letters of John.

———. *The Epistles of John.* Anchor Bible, Vol. 30. Garden City, N.Y.: Doubleday, 1982. A scholarly translation and commentary on the letters of John.

———. *The Churches the Apostles Left Behind.* New York: Paulist Press, 1984. A wonderfully concise study of several different Christian communities at the end of the first century C.E.

Culpepper, R. A. *1 John, 2 John, 3 John.* Knox Preaching Guides. Atlanta: John Knox Press, 1985.

Perkins, Pheme. "The Johannine Epistles." In R. E. Brown et al., eds., *The New Jerome Biblical Commentary,* 2nd ed., pp. 986–995. Englewood Cliffs, N.J.: Prentice-Hall, 1990.

von Wahlde, Urban C. *The Johannine Commandments: 1 John and the Struggle for the Johannine Tradition.* New York: Paulist Press, 1990. For advanced study.

The Didache, 1 Clement, and the Epistle of Barnabas

Niederwimmer, Kurt. *The Didache: A Commentary.* Minneapolis: Fortress Press, 1998. Examines the Didache for insights into the life of a first-century Christian community.

Staniforth, Maxwell, and Louth, Andrew, eds. *Early Christian Writings: The Apostolic Fathers,* rev. ed. New York: Penguin Books, 1987. Includes translations of the Didache, Barnabas, and 1 Clement.

Visions of End Time

Revelation

KEY TOPICS/THEMES

Revelation affirms Christianity's original hope for an immediate transformation of the world and assures the faithful that God's prearranged plan, including the destruction of Evil and the advent of Christ's universal reign, is about to be accomplished. The book presents an *apokalypsis* (unveiling) of unseen realities, both in heaven as it is now and on earth as it will be in the future. Placing government oppression and Christian suffering in a cosmic perspective, Revelation conveys its message of hope for believers in the cryptic language of metaphor and symbol.

KEY QUESTIONS

How did John's mystical visions serve to encourage and strengthen the churches to which he wrote? What is the ultimate goal of world history?

CONTINUING THE ESCHATOLOGICAL HOPE

Although Revelation was not the last New Testament book written, its position at the end of the canon is thematically appropriate. The first Christians believed that their generation would witness the end of the present wicked age and the beginning of God's direct rule over the earth. Revelation expresses that apocalyptic hope more powerfully than any other Christian writing. Anticipating a "new heaven and a new earth" (21:1), it envisions the glorious completion of God's creative work begun in the first book of the Bible. In this sense, it provides the **omega** (the final letter of the Greek alphabet) to the **alpha** (the first letter) of Genesis.

Revelation's climactic placement is also fitting because it reintroduces Jesus as a major character. Its picture of an all-powerful heavenly Jesus provides a counterweight to the Gospels' portrait of the human Jesus' earthly career. In Revelation, Jesus is no longer Mark's suffering servant or John's embodiment of divine Wisdom. Revelation's Jesus is the Messiah of popular expectation, a conquering warrior-king who slays his enemies and proves beyond all doubt his right to universal rule. In striking contrast to the Gospel portraits, the Jesus of Revelation comes not to forgive sinners and instruct them in a higher righteousness, but to inflict a wrathful punishment upon his opponents (19:11–21).

Revelation's depiction of Jesus' character and function, qualitatively different from that presented in the Gospels, derives partly from the author's rigorously apocalyptic view of human history. Like the authors of Jude and 2 Peter, the writer of Revelation perceives a sharp contrast between the present world, which he regards as hopelessly corrupt, and God's planned future world, a realm of ideal purity. In the author's opinion, the righteous new order can be realized only through God's direct intervention in human affairs, an event that requires Jesus to act as God's Judge and Destroyer of the world as we know it. Revelation's emphasis on violence and destruction, with its correspondingly harsher picture of Jesus' cosmic role, has led many commentators to question the book's theological or ethical validity. Many churches did not accept it as part of the biblical canon until after the fourth century C.E., and Martin Luther frankly doubted the authenticity of its Christology.

THE APOCALYPTIC TRADITION

Although the Gospels and Paul's letters contain strongly apocalyptic passages, Revelation is the only New Testament document composed entirely in the form of a literary **apocalypse**. Combining visions of the unseen world with previews of future history—all rendered in highly symbolic language—it belongs to a tradition that began with Enoch and Daniel in the early second century B.C.E. and continued well into the second century C.E. The apocryphal book of 2 Esdras, which was probably composed at almost the same time, is cast in the same visionary form and uses some of the same cryptic images. Revelation is unique in the New Testament, but it can best be understood by studying it in the context of the literary tradition to which it belongs. (See Chapter 8.) Although deliberately mystifying, the powerful **symbols** it employs—the **dragon, serpent, beast, and Celestial Woman**—represent the conventional vocabulary of apocalyptic discourse.

ORIGINS AND STRUCTURE OF REVELATION

Authorship and Date Although one tradition states that Revelation is the work of John the Apostle, son of Zebedee, and that he is the same person who wrote John's Gospel, this assertion was questioned even in the early church. The author identifies himself only as "John," God's "servant" (1:1, 4, 9; 22:8), does not claim apostolic authority, never mentions having known the historical Jesus, and portrays Jesus' character as radically different from that shown in the Gospels. To him, the apostles belong to an earlier generation and have already become the twelve "cornerstones" of the heavenly Temple (21:14).

Eusebius suggests that another John, known as "the Elder," who lived at Ephesus about 100 C.E., may have been the author. A few critics accept this view, although the majority believe that we can know little about the writer except for his name and his assertion that he had been exiled to **Patmos**, a tiny Aegean island off the western coast of Asia Minor (western Turkey). From the contents of his work, scholars can infer something of John's background. He is intimately familiar with internal conditions in the seven churches addressed (Chs. 2 and 3), even though he seems to belong to none of them. To some commentators, this indicates that

Figure 13.5 *Christ over New York City*. In this painting on a steel door, an unknown Ukrainian-American artist projects the image of a cosmic Christ above the skyscrapers of Manhattan. Depicting two dimensions of reality, the painter contrasts New York's towers of cold steel and concrete — monuments to modern commerce and banking — with his vision of Jesus' unseen presence. Encompassing the largely unaware inhabitants of American secular society in his spiritual embrace, Christ extends his arms in a gesture that is both protective and beseeching. In his apocalyptic visions, John of Patmos exhibited a similar, if somewhat less compassionate, view of Christ's relation to the Roman Empire.

John of Patmos was an itinerant Christian prophet who traveled among widely scattered churches. Although he held no congregational office, his recognized stature as a mystic and visionary gave him considerable influence in the communities to which he directed his apocalypse (Figure 13.5).

Because he writes Greek as if it were a second language, phrasing idiosyncratically in a Semitic style, most scholars believe that John was a native of Palestine, or at least had spent much time there. A few critics suggest that he had some connection with the Johannine community, because, like the author of John's Gospel, he refers to Christ as Logos (Word), Lamb, Witness, Shepherd, Judge, and Temple. Both Revelation and the Gospel express a duality of spirit and matter, Good and Evil, God and the devil. Both regard Christ as present in the church's liturgy and view his death as a saving victory. Important differences range from the quality of the Greek — excellent in the Gospel and awkward in the apocalypse — to the writers'

respective theologies. Whereas the Gospel presents God's love as his primary motive in dealing with humanity (John 3:15–16), Revelation mentions divine love only once. The Johannine Jesus' preeminent command to love is pervasively absent from Revelation.

Writing about 180 C.E., the churchman Irenaeus stated that Revelation was composed late in the reign of **Domitian**, who was emperor from 81 to 96 C.E. Internal references to government hostilities toward Christians (1:9; 2:10, 13; 6:9–11; 14:12; 16:6; 21:4), policies then associated with Domitian's administration, support Irenaeus's assessment. Most scholars date the work about 95 or 96 C.E.

The Emperor Cult Domitian was the son of Vespasian and the younger brother of Titus, the general who had successfully crushed the Jewish revolt against Rome and destroyed the Jerusalem Temple. After Titus's brief reign (79–81 C.E.), Domitian

Figure 13.6 Son of Vespasian and younger brother of Titus, Domitian (reigned 81–96 C.E.) was a generally unpopular emperor whose reign ended with his assassination. According to some sources, he enjoyed being addressed as "Lord and God" and may have encouraged the cult of emperor worship, particularly in the province of Asia, which may have triggered sporadic persecution of Christians there for their "unpatriotic" refusal to honor the emperor.

inherited the imperial throne, accepting divine honors offered him and allowing himself to be worshiped as a god in various parts of the empire (Figure 13.6). We have no real evidence that Domitian personally enforced a universal observance of the emperor cult, but in some areas — especially in Asia Minor — governors and other local officials demanded public participation in the cult as evidence of citizens' loyalty and patriotism. During this period, persecution for Christians' refusal to honor the national leader seems to have been local and sporadic. Despite the lack of a concentrated official assault on the faith, however, John clearly feels a growing tension between church and state, a sense of impending conflict that makes him regard Rome as a new Babylon, destroyer of God's people.

Purpose and Organization Viewing the outside world as an increasingly hostile threat to his community, John writes to encourage believers to maintain a strict separation between themselves and Greco-Roman society. He defines his group in a rigidly sectarian way: a tiny point of light almost swallowed up by a dark world dominated by idolatry, oppression, and the soulless pursuit of wealth. Whether facing active persecution or the threat of social assimilation, the faithful must resist all compromise. To make the Christians' fight for integrity as graphic as possible, John describes the situation from a cosmic perspective — a conflict between invisible spirit forces of Good and Evil that contend for human allegiance.

Despite its vast complexities, Revelation can be outlined as follows:

1. Prologue: the author's self-identification and authority (1:1–20)
2. Jesus' letters to the seven churches of Asia Minor (2:1–3:22)
3. Visions from heaven: breaking seven seals on a scroll; seven trumpets (4:1–11:19)
4. Signs in heaven: visions of the woman, the dragon, the beast, the lamb, and the seven plagues (12:1–16:21)
5. Visions of the "great whore" and the fall of Babylon (Rome) (17:1–18:24)
6. Visions of the *eschaton:* the warrior Messiah, the imprisonment of the beast and Satan, judgment of the dead, and the final defeat of Evil (19:1–20:15)
7. Visions of the "new heaven and a new earth"; descent of the heavenly Jerusalem to earth (21:1–22:5)
8. Epilogue: authenticity of the author's prophetic visions and the nearness of their fulfillment (22:6–21)

From this outline, we observe that John begins his work in the real world of exile and suffering (1:1–10), then takes his readers on a graphic tour of the spirit world — including a vivid dramatization of the imminent fall of satanic governments and the triumph of Christ. He returns at the end to earth and gives final instructions to his contemporary audience (22:6–21). The book's structure thus resembles an immense circle starting and ending in physical reality but encompassing a panorama of the unseen regions of heaven and the future.

THE AUTHOR'S USE OF IMAGES FROM THE HEBREW BIBLE

A consciously literary artist, John borrows many of his characteristic symbols and themes from the Hebrew Bible, particularly from apocalyptic sections in Daniel, Ezekiel, Joel, and Zechariah. Although he almost never directly quotes a biblical text, he paraphrases the Hebrew Bible in almost every line. Scholars have counted approximately 500 such allusions. (The Jerusalem Bible helps the reader recognize John's biblical paraphrases by printing them in italics.)

John employs striking images largely to convey his vision of the unseen forces affecting his churches' experience in the world. The more powerful, even grotesque, his symbols are, the more they serve to alert readers to the spiritual realities operating behind the familiar modes of everyday existence. In describing persons whose teaching he opposes, for example, John gives them larger-than-life stature by identifying them with notorious figures from Hebrew Bible times. Thus, a Christian prophetess in **Thyatira** is "Jezebel" (2:20–21) because she regards meat sacrificed at pagan rituals as acceptable food. (Note that Paul shares "Jezebel's" attitude in 1 Cor. 8:1–13; 10:25–33.) A proponent of this policy in **Pergamum** is "Balaam," a latter-day Canaanite tempter (2:14–16). In his first portrait of a heavenly being (1:12–16), John paints a male deity with snow-white hair, flaming eyes, incandescent brass feet, and a sharp sword protruding from his mouth. These images derive chiefly from Daniel (Chs. 7 and 10). To universalize this figure more completely, John adds astronomical symbols. Like a Greek mythological hero transformed into a stellar constellation, the divinity is pictured as holding seven stars in his hand and shining with the radiance of the sun.

The next verses (1:17–19) reveal the figure's identity. As the "first and the last" who has died but attained immortality, he is the crucified and risen Christ. The author's purpose in combining biblical with nonbiblical imagery is now clear: In strength and splendor, the glorified Christ surpasses rival Greco-Roman gods like Mithras, Apollo, Helios, Amon Ra, or other solar deities worshiped throughout the Roman Empire.

John further explains his symbols in 1:20. There, Christ identifies the stars as angels and the lampstands nearby as the seven churches of John's home territory (Figure 13.7). The identification reassures the author that his earthly congregations do not exist solely on a material plane, but are part of a larger visible-invisible duality in which angelic

Figure 13.7 The seven churches in Asia Minor (western Turkey) addressed in Revelation 1–3. These sites include Ephesus, one of the major seaports of the Roman Empire, and Sardis, once capital of the older Lydian Empire (sixth century B.C.E.). John pictures the heavenly Christ dictating letters to seven angels who act as invisible guardians of the individual churches. With this image, John reminds his audience that the tiny groups of Christians scattered throughout the Roman Empire do not stand alone. Although seemingly weak and insignificant, they are part of God's mighty empire of the spirit and are destined to triumph over their earthly oppressors.

spirits protect Christian gatherings. In his unveiling of spiritual realities, John implies that the seven churches are as precious as the golden candelabrum that once stood in the Jerusalem sanctuary. Like the eternal stars above, they shed Christ's light on a benighted world.

JESUS' LETTERS TO SEVEN CHURCHES

Having validated his prophetic authority through the divine source of his prophecy, John now surveys conditions in the seven light-bearing churches of Asia Minor. Like his contemporary fellow apocalyptist, the author of 2 Esdras (14:22–38), John presents himself as a secretary recording the dictation of a divine voice. (Mohammed later employed this device when dictating the Qur'an [Koran], the Scriptures of Islam.)

After reading Jesus' messages to Ephesus (2:1–7), **Smyrna** (2:8–11), Pergamum (2:12–17), Thyatira (2:18–29), **Sardis** (3:1–6), **Philadelphia** (3:7–13), and **Laodicea** (3:14–22), students will have a good idea of John's method. The situation in each city is rendered in images that suggest the religious issues prevailing there. Thus, Pergamum is labeled the site of Satan's throne (2:13), probably because it was the first center of the emperor cult. The author regards any worldly ruler who claims divine honors as Satan's agent and hence an anti-Christ.

VISIONS FROM HEAVEN

John's visions of heaven resemble those in the books of Enoch, Daniel, and 2 Esdras. Entering the spirit realm through an open "door," John is caught up to God's throne, where—in cinematic style—he views pictures of events about to occur (4:1–2). In this long section (4:1–11:19), John's purpose is not merely to predict future happenings but to remove the material veil that shrouds heavenly truths and to allow his readers to see that God retains full control of the universe.

The two series of visions that involve seven seals and seven trumpets serve to reassure Christians that their deliverance is near and that their enemies are predestined to suffer God's wrath. (The number *seven* corresponds to the seven days of the creative week [Gen. 1] and probably represents the completeness of divine action.) In the ancient world, paper documents were wrapped around a stick, forming a scroll, which was then sealed with hot wax. After the soft wax was imprinted with the writer's personal signet, the scroll could not be opened without breaking the seal, ensuring the privacy of its contents until it reached the intended recipient. In John's vision, the Lamb (Christ) opens each of the seven seals in sequence, disclosing either a predetermined future event or a further revelation of God's will. Opening the first four seals unleashes four horses and riders—the famous Four Horsemen of the Apocalypse—representing earthly disasters, including military conquest, war, famine, and death (6:1–8). Breaking the fifth seal discloses Christian martyrs who cry out for vengeance (6:9–11). Opening the sixth brings seismic and astronomical phenomena (6:12–17), painting the End in livid colors of cosmic dissolution. During a quiet interval, a symbolic 144,000 Israelites and a "vast throng" (probably of Gentiles) are designated to worship at the celestial throne (7:1–17). The breaking of the seventh seal introduces the vision of seven trumpets, in which additional plagues afflict the earth (8:7–11:19).

SIGNS IN HEAVEN

Chapter 12 opens with a series of unnumbered visions dramatizing the cosmic battle between the lamb and the dragon. In this section (12:1–16:21),

John parallels unseen events in heaven with their experienced consequences on earth. The spiritual conflict (12:1–12) finds its earthly counterpart in the climactic battle of **Armageddon** (16:12–16).

The Woman   This section's first astronomical sign is rendered as a woman dressed in the sun, moon, and stars, a figure resembling Hellenistic portraits of the Egyptian goddess Isis. Despite its nonbiblical features, however, John probably means the figure to symbolize Israel, historically the parent of Christ. Arrayed in "twelve stars" suggesting the traditional twelve tribes, the woman gives birth to the Messiah. The author of 2 Esdras similarly represents Jerusalem, the mother of all believers, as a persecuted woman (2 Esd. 9:38–10:54). Like most of John's symbols, this figure is capable of multiple interpretations, including the Roman Catholic view that it denotes the Virgin.

The Dragon   The seven-headed dragon—a composite of apocalyptic beasts—is identified as **Satan**, the "serpent of old" (12:9; Gen. 3:1, 14–15). Revelation's dragon image harkens back to ancient prebiblical Mesopotamian myths of creation. In the *Enuma Elish*, Marduk—the Mesopotamian creator-god, vanquishes Tiamat, the primordial dragon of chaos, and fashions the cosmos out of her dismembered body. In John's vision, the archangel **Michael**—the traditional spirit prince of Israel (Dan. 11:1)—defeats the chaotic reptile, permitting the birth of a new cosmic order. Expelled from heaven, as were the opponents of Marduk, the dragon then wars against representatives of God's earthly kingdom—the church (12:5–9). By thus updating one of the world's oldest conflict myths, John simultaneously explains Roman society's sudden hostility toward his community and reassures the faithful that the One who overthrew the dragon will soon rescue them.

The Roman Beast   Most scholars believe that the beast with "ten horns and seven heads" symbolizes Rome, the earthly focus of the dragon's power (13:8). The two-horned beast may represent the Roman priesthood that helps promote emperor worship (13:11–17). The occult "number of the beast" (666)—signifying a man's name—is a mys-

Figure 13.8 This ancient coin shows a portrait bust of Nero (reigned 54–68 C.E.). According to the Roman historian Tacitus, Nero was the first emperor to persecute Christians. Nero's violence toward believers made him seem to some the image of bestial attacks on God's people. In depicting the "beast" who demands his subjects' worship, John of Patmos may have had Nero — and other worldly rulers who imitated the emperor's methods — in mind.

Figure 13.9 This bust of Julia, daughter of the emperor Titus, shows the elaborate hairstyles popular among aristocratic women of the late first century. Julia's contemporary, the author of Revelation, denounces Rome in the symbol of a vain and luxurious woman (Rev. 17).

tery no scholar has been able to solve. Among apocalyptic groups, the trend has been to identify the beast with a contemporary figure whom the group fears or distrusts, commonly some prominent leader of the period. In John's day, all numbers, whether in Hebrew, Aramaic, or Greek, were represented by letters of the alphabet. Because each letter in a person's name was also a number, it was possible to assign individual names a numerical value. Noting that in Aramaic "Nero Caesar" corresponds to 666, some scholars think that John intended **Nero**, the first emperor to persecute Christians, as the archetypal beast or anti-Christ (Figure 13.8). Although a popular first-century rumor speculated that Nero (reigned 54–68 C.E.) had not really committed suicide but would reappear at the head of a foreign army, most scholars do not accept the Neronian hypothesis. Even if we do not possess the key to unlock John's riddle, we must remember that the purpose of apocalyptic writing is not necessarily to predict specific persons and events, but to create images of Good and Evil so powerful that they compel the reader to view human history on the author's cosmic terms.

VISIONS OF THE GREAT WHORE

In asking readers to perceive the universe as God sees it, John challenges them to respond emotionally and intuitively as well as intellectually to his symbols. Thus, he pictures Rome not as a mighty empire ruling almost the entire known world, but as a corrupt whore bedecked with jewels and gold (17:1–18:24) (Figure 13.9). (Note that the wealth and precious stones, soon to be stripped from the harlot, will reappear to adorn the lamb's virgin bride, the heavenly Jerusalem [21:10–21].) The whore is the dragon's city — Rome — a new "Babylon" doomed to fall before God's sovereignty (18:1–24).

VISIONS OF THE *ESCHATON*

John's last series of conflict visions (19:11–21:8) features the lamb's ultimate triumph over the dragon. An angel hurls the dragon into the abyss, the primordial void—the great "deep" of Genesis—that existed before God shaped the cosmos into its present order (20:1–3). With the dragon imprisoned, Christ's reign begins. Known as the **millennium** because it lasts 1000 years, it ends paradoxically with the dragon's release to wage yet another war on the faithful. The only New Testament writer to present a 1000-year prelude to God's kingdom, John states that during the millennium, the martyrs who resisted the beast's influence are resurrected to rule with Christ (20:4–6).

The dragon's attack on God's people (based on Ezekiel's prophetic drama involving the mythical Gog of Magog [Ezek. 38–39]), climaxes with fire from heaven destroying the attackers. A resurrection of the dead ensues. Released from the control of death and Hades (the Underworld), they are judged according to their deeds (20:7–13).

John's eschatology includes a place of punishment represented by a lake of fire, an image drawn from popular Jewish belief (see Josephus's "Discourse to the Greeks Concerning Hades," in "Recommended Reading"). Defined as "the second death" (20:15), it receives a number of symbolic figures, including death, Hades, the beast, the false prophet, and persons or human qualities not listed in God's book of life (19:20; 20:14–15). Although John uses his picture of eternal torment to encourage loyalty to Christ, his concept of hell incites many commentators to question the author's understanding of divine love, a quality almost entirely absent from Revelation's portrait of the Deity.

Unlike myths of some world religions, John's cosmic vision does not transcend the polar opposites of Good and Evil to achieve a universal harmony. In his vision, Evil—the subversive force of disorder troubling God's universe—is not transformed but simply annihilated. Whereas Yahweh astonished Job with his tolerance of Leviathan (another aspect of the chaotic dragon [Job 41–42; see also Chapter 7]), Revelation's God violently eliminates his opposition. John's solution ultimately compounds the problem of Evil, for his God not only fails to redirect chaotic energy to a higher Good but also eternally perpetuates the pain of sentient creatures (14:9–11; 19:20; 20:14–15; cf. 2 Esd. 7:36–38). In some respects, it is difficult to distinguish between the natures of Revelation's Deity and his adversary, the devil. As John presents them, God and Satan use similar methods—violence, destructiveness, and the wholesale infliction of pain and suffering. Although John's God represents the Good, it is not recognizable as such until after the final conflict when the Deity at last expresses his beneficence (Rev. 21:1–4).

VISIONS OF THE NEW HEAVEN AND THE NEW EARTH

Borrowing again from ancient myth in which epics of conflict are commonly ended in a union of supernatural entities, John pictures a sacred marriage (*hieros gamos*) of the Lamb with the holy city that descends from heaven to earth. In this final vision, human beings do not rise to heaven, but instead God comes to dwell with humanity, at last fulfilling the promise of Yahweh's sporadic visits to Eden (Gen. 3). The "new heaven and a new earth" from which all pain and sorrow are excluded (21:1) includes a glorified capital, constructed of gems and precious metals like those stripped from imperial Rome. The new Eden provides **trees of life** that restore humanity to full health, completing the renewal of God's creation.

Whereas the prophet Daniel had been instructed to seal his vision until End time (Dan. 12:4), John is told not to do so because "the hour of fulfillment is near" (22:10). The writer apparently expected an immediate vindication of his eschatological hopes. Cursing anyone who tampers with his manuscript, the author ends his cosmic vision by passionately invoking Jesus' speedy return.

The Apocalypse of Peter

With its images of a warring dragon, celestial women, lake of fire, and great city descending from heaven, Revelation has such a strong impact on readers' imaginations that many people think of the book as unique. As noted earlier in this chapter, however, Revelation is only one of many similar apocalyptic works that Hellenistic Jewish and early Christian writers produced between about 300 B.C.E. and 200 C.E. To place Revelation in historical perspective, it is helpful to review some other books representing the apocalyptic genre to which Revelation belongs. (See Chapter 8 for discussions of 1 Enoch, a composite work written in several stages by different authors from about 300 B.C.E. to the first century C.E. and 2 Esdras [4 Ezra], a Jewish apocalypse composed about the same time as Revelation [c. 100 C.E.].) The Apocalypse of Peter, a Christian work dating from the second century C.E., is discussed below.

These three apocalyptic books are noteworthy not only because they employ the same kinds of imagery used in Revelation but also because their portrayals of the spirit world and the fate of souls after death have been extraordinarily influential on Christian thought. Almost two millennia after they were written, the eschatology they present continues to shape popular beliefs about divine judgment, heaven, and hell. The persistence of these eschatological speculations about postmortem existence—particularly the Apocalypse of Peter's detailed descriptions of fiery torments afflicting the damned—results, at least in part, from their views of the afterlife being later incorporated into masterpieces of Western literature, such as Dante's *Divine Comedy* and Milton's *Paradise Lost*. In contemporary Western culture, any student who has figuratively descended into Dante's Inferno or visited "the darkness visible" of Milton's hell has encountered ideas that were vividly articulated by the authors of 1 Enoch and the Apocalypse of Peter. (Traditions embodied in the Apocalypse of Peter were known to Dante through a late-fourth-century work, the Apocalypse of Paul, which incorporated concepts expressed in the earlier apocalyptic work.)

In tracing the chronological evolution of eschatological ideas expressed in both canonical and noncanonical apocalypses, readers will find a major shift in emphasis over time. The earliest apocalyptic visions, such as the previews of world history contained in 1 Enoch and the Book of Daniel (the only apocalypse admitted to the Hebrew Bible

canon), tend to be cosmic in scope, presenting the rise and fall of political empires and the ultimate triumph of God's kingdom (cf. 1 Enoch 91:12–17; 93:1–10; Dan. 2; 7–11). Focusing on God-ordained changes in the macrocosm (the great world), Daniel says little about the microcosm (the smaller world of individual humans). Almost as an afterthought, Daniel's visions conclude with the Hebrew Bible's first explicit prophecy of an afterlife for both righteous and wicked persons: "Of those who lie sleeping in the dust of the earth many will awake, some to everlasting life, some to shame and everlasting disgrace" (Dan. 12:3). Other than this terse allusion to physical resurrection of the dead, Daniel (c. 165 B.C.E.) says nothing about the nature of their future lives. By the close of the first century C.E., however, when Revelation and 2 Esdras were written, ideas about personal eschatology (the posthumous fate of individuals) receive greater attention. Destinies of good and evil persons are now sharply distinguished, with the former enjoying heavenly bliss and the latter condemned to eternal pain. By the time the Apocalypse of Peter was composed, in the second century C.E., typical apocalyptic concerns about the future of the cosmos had been subordinated to microcosmic preoccupations with the unspeakable agonies awaiting those who have offended God.

The historical transition from apocalypses devoted to global eschatology to those emphasizing personal eschatology may reflect a concurrent change in the church's evolving beliefs about Jesus' Second Coming. As the Christian church gradually accepted the idea that Christ's Parousia would be indefinitely delayed, its attention inevitably moved from expectations of the world's End and universal judgment to contemplation of the posthumous judgment of individual souls.

THE APOCALYPSE OF PETER AND THE SHIFT FROM COSMIC TO PERSONAL ESCHATOLOGY

Although it was ultimately excluded from the New Testament, the pseudonymous Apocalypse of Peter once stood on the margins of accepted Christian Scripture. The Muratorian Canon (late second to early fourth century C.E.), a list of books that the author regarded as canonical, does not include such works as Hebrews, James, 1 and 2 Peter, and 3 John. But it does mention the apocalypse ascribed to Peter, an originally Greek work that survives complete only in an Ethiopic translation discovered in the late nineteenth century. Despite the popularity this work formerly enjoyed—and its usefulness in converting people who hoped to escape the terrors of eternal punishment it describes—the church, probably because of its pseudonymity, rejected it, along with numerous other writings, such as the Gospel of Peter, also incorrectly assigned to Jesus' preeminent disciple. (The present New Testament, however, does contain two Petrine documents that most scholars believe are also pseudonymous).

The Apocalypse of Peter opens with a familiar Gospel scene: On the Mount of Olives, Jesus' disciples ask about the "signs" of his Parousia and "the end of the world" (cf. Mark 13; Matt. 24). After first reiterating Jesus' warnings about false messiahs and future persecutions, the author soon switches to his main interest: the eschatological consequences of Jesus' return and the judgment of individual souls. The writer's point of departure is a phrase from Matthew's parable in which the Son of Man returns to divide all humanity into two classes, "sheep" and "goats." Judged adversely, the goats are dispatched to "the eternal fire that is ready for the devil and his angels" (Matt. 25:41). In the Synoptic Gospels, Jesus makes several references to Gehenna and "eternal punishment" (see Box 10.12), but the Evangelists do not explore the implications of these allusions to posthumous suffering—an oversight that the author of the Apocalypse enthusiastically addresses.

Quickly moving from the Parousia to visions of the next world, the writer devotes the main part of his work to surveying the tortures endured by various kinds of sinners, in general following a principle of retributive justice in which the punishment supposedly fits the crime. It is difficult to be certain whether Jesus actually takes Peter on a tour of hell, as the spirit of the poet Virgil later guides Dante through the Inferno, or whether Christ simply describes the different sinners' torments so graphically that Peter can virtually "see" them. In

any case, the fate of those who have displeased God is to feel maximum pain with no hope of release, to suffer the highest pitch of agony imaginable for all eternity.

As many commentators have recognized, the Apocalypse of Peter focuses largely on sexual sins, punishing erotic behaviors with "cataracts of fire." Women who beautified themselves with cosmetics to seduce men hang by their hair (regarded as the chief feminine attraction) in a dark fiery pit. Expectant mothers who aborted their babies are submerged in pools of flaming excrement, while the spirits of their dead children stand nearby, piercing their mothers' eyes with lightning bolts. Men who enjoyed sex outside of marriage are strung up by their genitals over glowing coals. Souls who "doubted" God's "righteousness" are tortured with "red hot irons" that bore into their eyes, while other sinners, their bodies aflame, are devoured by immortal worms. Slaves who dared to disobey their masters gnaw on their own tongues (the organ of impudence) while immersed in fire. When souls try to repent of their misdeeds and cry to God for mercy, the angel Tatirokos suddenly appears to increase their suffering, angrily declaring that the "time for repentance" has passed—the Deity has made no provision to redeem souls in hell.

Endeavoring to account for the vindictive, sadistic tone of the Apocalypse of Peter, some interpreters have suggested that it reflects some Christians' negative response to Roman persecutions of their faith during the second century C.E. Widespread persecution of Christians in Gaul (France) during the late second century C.E. involved brutal interrogations, mutilations, and other tortures. To some Christians, the Roman practice of burning martyrs alive invited divine retaliation, in which the persecutors would suffer the same kinds of torture, with the difference that their pain would not end at death. Tertullian, a Christian theologian of the late second and early third centuries C.E., looked forward to an eschatological reversal in which familiar figures from Roman society would soon be writhing in hellish agony, providing an entertaining spectacle for the souls of their former victims. Anticipating the day of judgment, Tertullian states that he will not know whether to "laugh" or "applaud" at the sight of Roman administrators who had ordered Christians burnt at the stake now "melting in flames fiercer than those they had kindled for brave Christians." He delights at the prospect of "philosophers and their students" (promoters of rival beliefs) burning together, while tragic actors who had enraptured audiences in Roman theaters will bellow their lines in genuine anguish (see Fox and Turner in "Recommended Reading"). Offering better entertainment than any of Rome's circuses or athletic events, Tertullian's fantasy makes beholding the suffering of the damned one of the major rewards of the faithful. (It should also be remembered that in the only Gospel parable about the afterlife Lazarus's paradise is in full view of the rich man's fiery torments [Luke 16:19–31]; 2 Esdras portrays a similar juxtaposition of joy and suffering [2 Esd. 7:36–38].)

QUESTIONS FOR REVIEW

1. Define the term *apocalypse,* and explain how the Book of Revelation unveils realities of the unseen spirit world and previews future events.

2. Connect John's apocalyptic visions with conditions prevailing in his own time. What events taking place during the late first century C.E. would cause Christians to despair of the present evil world and hope for divine intervention in the near future?

3. Describe some of the main symbols John uses to convey his understanding of the spiritual reality behind earthly appearances. Define the general meanings represented by the lamb, the dragon, the heavenly woman, the whore, and the marriage of the lamb and the heavenly city.

4. What portrayal of divine justice in the afterlife does the Apocalypse of Peter offer?

QUESTIONS FOR DISCUSSION AND REFLECTION

1. Revelation repeatedly shows God's kingdom triumphing only to be engaged again in further cosmic battles with Evil, until the symbol and source of Evil — the chaotic dragon — is finally exterminated by fire. Is the Book of Revelation meaningful only as a reference to a "once-and-for-all" *cosmic event* (e.g.,

the end of the world)? Discuss how John's visions can apply to recurring historical phenomena (e.g., the decline and fall of government structures, the decay and collapse of social order, or the end of a culture or civilization). How can futuristic scenarios help people reevaluate their perception of present changes and their significance?

2. Martin Luther thought that Revelation did not truly reveal the nature of God or Christ. Discuss the ethical strengths and religious limitations of John's view of the Deity and the divine purpose.

3. Do you think that Revelation's frequently repeated battles between Good and Evil indicate a continuing cycle in which divine rule (the kingdom) alternates with wicked influences on humanity — a cycle in which each nation and individual particpates until the final judgment? Cite specific passages to support your answer.

4. Apocalyptic works such as 1 Enoch, Revelation, 2 Esdras, and the Apocalypse of Peter contain horrific visions of the afterlife in which condemned souls suffer unending torment in hell. How do you reconcile Christianity's belief in infinitely loving God with a doctrine of eternal punishment for sinners? If suffering on earth can be a learning porcess that brings insight and wisdom, what ethical purpose does the pain of the damned serve? Would a sane human father condemn a disobedient child to unendurable torment — without hope of release? Why do many religions ascribe this practice to God? In what ways do officially endorsed fears about the afterlife tend to support religious authorities and institutions?

5. Although their suggestions were later condemned by the church, some early Christian leaders, such as Origin, believed that God's unlimited love would eventually result in the redemption of all human souls. If God desires the salvation of all souls, how do you think he would accomplish this objective? How would Origin's doctrine of universal salvation work to enhance human appreciation of divine glory?

TERMS AND CONCEPTS TO REMEMBER

abyss, the	apocalyptic dualism
alpha	apocalyptic literature
apocalypse (literary form)	*apokalypsis*
	Armageddon
Apocalypse of Peter and personal escatology	astronomical images
	authorship of Revelation
	beast, the

RECOMMENDED READING

Revelation

Aune, David. *Prophecy in Early Christianity and the Ancient Mediterranean World*. Grand Rapids, Mich.: Eerdmans, 1983. Places Christian apocalyptism in historical perspective.

Batto, Bernard F. *Slaying the Dragon: Mythmaking in the Biblical Tradition*. Louisville, Ky.: Westminster Press/ John Knox Press, 1992. Devoted mainly to the Hebrew Bible; also shows how New Testament writers used archetypal myths to express their understanding of Christ and the cosmic battle between God and the primordial dragon of chaos.

Collins, A. Y. *The Apocalypse*. Wilmington, Del.: Glazier, 1979.

———. *Crisis and Catharsis: The Power of the Apocalypse*. Philadelphia: Westminster Press, 1984. A carefully researched, clearly written, and rational analysis of the sociopolitical and theological forces affecting the composition of John's visions.

———. *Early Christian Apocalypticism: Genre and Social Setting*. Semeia 36. Decatur, Ga.: Scholars Press, 1986.

———. "The Apocalypse (Revelation)." In R. E. Brown et al., eds., *The New Jerome Biblical Commentary*, 2nd ed., pp. 996–1016. Englewood Cliffs, N.J.: Prentice-Hall, 1990. A close reading of the text that places John's visions in their original Greco-Roman social and historical context.

Collins, J. J., ed. *The Encyclopedia of Apocalypticism: Volume I: The Origins of Apocalypticism in Judaism and Christianity*. New York: Continuum, 2002. A collection of scholarly essays, including eschatology in Jesus, Paul, Revelation, and the Apocalypse of Peter.

Hanson, P. D. *The Dawn of Apocalyptic: The Historical and Sociological Roots of Jewish Apocalyptic Eschatology*. Philadelphia: Fortress Press, 1979.

Josephus, Flavius. "Josephus' Discourse to the Greeks Concerning Hades." In *Josephus: Complete Works*. Translated by William Whiston. Grand Rapids, Mich.: Kregel Publications, 1960. Presents first-century Jewish views of the afterlife similar to those postulated in the Synoptic Gospels and Revelation.

Perkins, Pheme. *The Book of Revelation*. Collegeville, Minn.: Liturgical Press, 1983. A brief and readable introduction for undergraduate students.

Russell, D. S. *The Method and Message of Jewish Apocalyptic: 200 b.c.–a.d. 100*. Philadelphia: Westminster Press, 1964. A useful review of apocalyptic literature of the Greco-Roman period.

Schüssler Fiorenza, Elizabeth. *The Book of Revelation: Justice and Judgment*. Philadelphia: Fortress Press, 1985.

Stone, M. E. *Scriptures, Sects, and Visions: A Profile of Judaism from Ezra to the Jewish Revolts*. Philadelphia: Fortress Press, 1980.

The Apocalypse of Peter

Bernstein, Alan E. *The Formation of Hell: Death and Retribution in the Ancient and Early Christian Worlds*. Ithaca, N.Y.: Cornell University Press, 1993. A comprehensive study of evolving ideas about the afterlife and the influence of Greco-Roman beliefs on Christian eschatology.

Ehrman, Bart D., ed. *The New Testament and Other Early Christian Writings: A Reader*. New York: Oxford University Press, 1998. Includes the complete text of the Apocalypse of Peter.

Fox, Robin Lane. *Pagans and Christians*. New York: Knopf, 1987. Includes discussion of Christian eschatology, the legal basis of Roman persecutions, and the cult of martyrdom.

Turner, Alice. *The History of Hell*. New York: Harcourt Brace, 1993. Discusses the social and legal environment of Rome in the second century c.e. that provides a context for Christian ideas about hell.

CHAPTER 14

Interpreting the Judeo-Christian Bible in a Changed World

Key Topics/Themes

A paradigm of the divine-human relationship, the Bible continues to exert enormous influence in a world radically different from the ancient Near Eastern and Greco-Roman cultures in which its documents originated. Contemporary readers, whether or not they consciously accept these developments, inevitably interpret biblical texts in the light of historical events and movements that have shaped Western culture of the twenty-first century, ranging from the rise of Islam and the Protestant Reformation to revolutionary scientific discoveries and the proliferation of religious diversity.

KEY QUESTIONS

What happened to Christianity when it was transformed from a persecuted faith to the state religion of Rome? Describe the historical events, including the rise of Islam, the Protestant Reformation, and the discoveries of contemporary sci-

ence, that affect our understanding of the Judeo-Christian Bible.

The "great tribulation" that marked Rome's destruction of the Jewish state (70 C.E.)—along with the original center of Palestinian Christianity—offers a chaotic background to the formation of the Judeo-Christian Bible. The loss of homeland, Temple, and priesthood was a terrible blow to Palestinian Jews and also a shock to infant Christianity, which lost its mother church and center of apostolic teaching. Jerusalem's devastation evoked a series of religious responses that influenced not only modern Judaism and Gentile Christianity but also the form and content of their Scriptures.

Of the twenty-seven New Testament documents, only Paul's letters, Q (a collection of Jesus' sayings), and the Gospel of Mark existed at that time. Most of the Christian-Greek Scriptures were yet to be written, and it would be centuries before the church agreed upon their exact contents. Although the Hebrew Bible was complete, the precise number of books to be included had not yet been agreed on.

The Evolution of the Hebrew Bible and the Christian-Greek Scriptures

Throughout the wars, trials, and persecutions of the calamitous late first century C.E., the Hebrew Bible remained the primary authority for both Judaism and the fledgling church. Led by Rabbi Yohanan ben Zakkai, a small group of rabbinical scholars assembled at Jamnia (Yavneh) on the Palestinian coast to provide essential leadership in coping with the post–70 C.E. crisis, particularly in shaping the final contours of the Hebrew Bible. As noted in Chapter 9, the rabbis at Jamnia did not formally close the biblical canon, but they seem to have applied several criteria that excluded numerous books used by Jewish congregations outside Palestine. Accepting the thesis that inspired prophecy had ceased shortly after the time of Ezra (c. 400 B.C.E.), the Jamnia scholars apparently rejected books clearly composed after that period, such as Ecclesiasticus or 1 Maccabees. Only Daniel, of all the apocalypses, was accepted, because its author plausibly claimed to write during the sixth century B.C.E. Books that contradicted the Torah or that were not originally written in Hebrew, such as the Wisdom of Solomon, were also excluded. Whether some books that eventually achieved canonical status were appropriate—such as Ezekiel (which radically modified some Torah principles), Esther (which did not mention God), Ecclesiastes (which encouraged skepticism), and the Song of Songs (which celebrated erotic love)—was hotly debated. In the end, the official Palestinian edition of the Hebrew Bible included these controversial documents but rejected many more that had found a place in Greek editions of the Scriptures. The Christian community, however, which adopted the Septuagint as its preferred version of the Bible, generally recognized the deuterocanonical status of these disputed books—commonly known as the Apocrypha—

and later included them in Latin editions of the Old Testament.

Today's Hebrew and Christian Bibles differ not only in the number of accepted books but also in the order of their contents. Rabbinical scholars place the books of Chronicles at the end of the canon, thus giving a climactic position to Cyrus the Great's order to repatriate Jewish exiles and rebuild the Jerusalem Temple (2 Chron. 36:22–23). This promise of national and cultic restoration, presented as Yahweh's intervention in Judah's history, may have voiced Jewish hopes that their God would again restore his people as he had done after the Babylonian captivity (587–538 B.C.E.).

By contrast, Christian editions of the Hebrew Bible follow the Septuagint order and place Chronicles, despite its late date, among the Former Prophets and conclude the Old Testament with the twelve Minor Prophets. Christian editions of the Bible thus make Malachi's prediction that "Elijah the prophet" will return to earth just before Yahweh's eschatological Day of Judgment (Mal. 3:22–24) the ultimate Old Testament message. (The Synoptic Gospel writers relate Malachi's prophecy to Christian origins, identifying John the Baptist, seen as Jesus' forerunner, as the predestined Elijah [Mark 6:14–15; Matt. 11:10–14; Luke 7:27–28].) The church's rearrangement of the Hebrew Bible expressed its christological interests, an assumption that the Jewish Scriptures serve largely to foretell and elucidate the Christ event.

When added to Greek translations of the Hebrew Bible canon, the twenty-seven New Testament books—all of which extensively quote from or allude to Israel's Scriptures—promulgate a christological fulfillment of Tanak covenant promises. In the Christian reinterpretation, virtually the entire Hebrew Bible becomes prophetic of Christ, giving startlingly innovative meanings to familiar scriptural passages. Jesus of Nazareth becomes Eve's "seed" (Gen. 3:15), his death and resurrection are foreshadowed in the Abraham–Isaac drama (Gen. 22), and his universal rulership is anticipated by the reigns of Davidic kings (2 Sam. 7; Pss. 2, 110; Isa. 7, 11; etc.).

Jesus is also the commanding figure who binds together the diverse collection of narratives, letters, sermons, and apocalyptic visions that form the New Testament. The order in which the canonical books are arranged reinforces his dominance: The New Testament opens with Matthew's genealogy, proclaiming "Jesus Christ, son of David, son of Abraham," at the outset as the embodiment of Israel's prophetic hopes. Matthew and the other Gospels provide theological interpretations of Jesus' Jewish messiahship, and Acts and Paul's letters offer profound meditations on Jesus' meaning to the world at large. The pseudo-Pauline letters, Hebrews, and the general epistles further explore Jesus' continuing significance to the community developing in his name, typically distinguishing between correct and incorrect views about his being and nature.

The New Testament closes with John's dazzling revelation of the postresurrection Jesus as a cosmic divinity, empowered at last to establish the longed-for universal kingdom. As the first Gospel's opening verse roots Jesus in Israel's historical past, the "son" or heir of David and Abraham, so the last New Testament book concludes with a Christian mystic's passionate evocation of Jesus' return to finish the task he had begun on earth, echoing Malachi's fervent call for the reappearance of God's agent. Because Christianity emerged historically as an apocalyptic movement within first-century Judaism, it is fitting that its canonical text closes with the apocalyptic conviction that Christ is "coming soon," preserving as a final word the assurance of Jesus' imminent Parousia (Second Coming) (Rev. 22:17–21).

Before the end of the first century C.E., some Christians were keenly aware that expectations for a speedy Parousia had failed to materialize. Neither Christ nor the kingdom had rescued the church from Rome's intermittent persecutions. In 1 Clement, an epistle included in some editions of the New Testament, Clement, bishop of Rome, states:

> Let that Scripture be far from us which says: "Wretched are the double-minded, those who doubt in their soul and say, 'We have heard these things [predictions of the End] even in our fathers' times, and see, we have grown old and none of this has happened.'"
>
> 1 Clem. 23:3–5; c. 96 C.E.

A generation or more after Clement, in a work attributed to the apostle Peter, the problem of the "delayed Parousia" was again raised. Skeptics complained that Jesus' promised coming had proved to be a nonevent; everything "continues exactly as it has always been since the world began" (2 Pet. 3:1–10). The writer responded to this criticism of an unconfirmed doctrine by asserting that a delayed world judgment allowed time and opportunity for sinners to repent and was thus an act of divine mercy.

Nonetheless, Jesus' failure to return undoubtedly provoked a crisis of belief among many second-century Christians. Yet, the church not only survived its initial disappointments, but prospered. Despite dashed hopes that the Parousia would follow any number of seemingly "final" events — the Jewish revolt, the destruction of Jerusalem, the deaths of the last apostles, or the first- and second-century Roman persecutions, the believing community continued to grow in stature, wealth, and influence. By the fourth century, it had become the state religion of the Roman Empire.

Constantine the Great

Following his victory at the Milvian Bridge over Maxentius, his rival for the imperial throne (312 C.E.), the emperor Constantine effected one of the most unexpected reversals in human history. Having reputedly experienced a vision in which Jesus was revealed as the divine power that enabled him to defeat his enemies, Constantine began a slow process of conversion to the Christian faith. The emperor's ultimate championing of the Christian community had immense repercussions throughout the empire, altering forever the relationship of church and state (Figure 14.1).

Shortly before Constantine began his long reign (306–337 C.E.), his predecessor, Diocletian (284–305 C.E.), had initiated the most thorough and devastating persecution that Christians had yet endured, which ended only with Diocletian's abdication and death. When Constantine issued his celebrated decree of religious toleration, the Edict of

Figure 14.1 Only the head and other fragments of a colossal statue of Constantine (reigned 306–337 C.E.) remain, but they reflect the enormous power wielded by this remarkable general and administrator. Seeking the support of a unified church, Constantine summoned and presided over the Council of Nicaea (325 C.E.), which, amid intense theological controversy, formulated the Trinitarian creed affirming that the Son is coequal, consubstantial, and coeternal with the Father.

Milan (313 C.E.), and subsequently began restoring confiscated church property, consulting Christian leaders about official affairs, and appointing bishops to high public office, it was as if a miraculous deliverance of the faithful had occurred — as if a new Cyrus had arrived to rescue God's chosen ones (Figure 14.2). To many who benefited from Constantine's policy it seemed that Revelation's seventh angel had sounded his trumpet: "the sovereignty of the world has passed to our Lord and his Christ" (Rev. 11:15).

In a more modest metaphor, the churchman **Eusebius**, who later became Constantine's biogra-

pher, compared the emperor's enthusiastic support of the church to the dawn of a brilliant new day, opening up glorious possibilities for the Christian religion. With the exception of Julian (361–363 C.E.), who was known as the Apostate for trying to revive pagan cults, all of Constantine's successors were nominally Christians. For the last century and a half of its existence, the empire that had crucified Jesus was ruled by emperors who professed to be his servants.

The Church and the Secular World

Rome's belated emergence as a putatively Christian empire that supported and protected the church was sometimes viewed as a historical fulfillment of apocalyptic expectations, with Christ now ruling through his imperial representatives on earth. In fact, historical developments during the fourth and fifth centuries C.E. bore out Luke's nonapocalyptic vision of a church expanding in cooperation with the imperial power more than Revelation's picture of violent conflict between church and state resolved only when God intervened to destroy the latter. Officially muting sporadic revivals of apocalyptic fervor, the church espoused the Gospel of John's doctrine of realized eschatology — with Jesus invisibly present among the believing community — as theologically desirable.

In part, the church preserved eschatological principles by adapting and applying them to individual lives. Christianity originally borrowed most of its eschatological beliefs from Jewish sources, which emphasized the external and material triumph of Yahweh's sovereignty over Gentile nations. This general eschatology — the terrifying Day of Yahweh, cosmic battles between Good and Evil, divine judgment and the supernatural imposition of God's kingdom — was replaced by personal eschatology. Jewish eschatological literature, such as 2 Baruch, the Testament of Abraham, the books of Enoch, and 2 Esdras, had stressed Yah-

Figure 14.2 The Arch of Constantine, standing near the Roman Forum and Flavian Amphitheater (Colosseum), commemorates the political and military achievements of Rome's first Christian emperor. After defeating his rival Maxentius at the Battle of Milvian Bridge (312 C.E.), Constantine (reigned 306–337 C.E.) issued the famous Edict of Milan, legitimizing the Christian church and ending centuries of intermittent persecution.

weh's (or the coming Messiah's) universal rule, violently imposed, but they had also provided graphic images of the consequences of apocalyptic events on individual humans.

After the two disastrous Jewish wars against Rome (66–73 C.E. and 132–135 C.E.) that may have been partly fueled by apocalyptic hopes, rabbinic Judaism rejected such visionary speculations as typically misleading. However, the church embraced their eschatological revelations of heaven, hell, and the afterlife. In later Roman Christianity, eschatological ideas retained their emotional impact on a personal, individual level. All believers were faced with inevitable death and the attendant dangers and terrors of the next world. Jewish and Christian apocalyptic writers had painted memorable scenes of the fates awaiting the righteous and the wicked. Anticipation of the world's End might fade, but to the believer, postmortem judgment involving permanent assignment to celestial joy or eternal torment seemed certain. The church defined and regulated these eschatological concerns. While normative Judaism abandoned virtually all its eschatological literature, with its ethically problematic views of divine justice, the Christian community effectively transferred its in-

herited doctrines of "last things" to the human microcosm, postponing its hopes for the Parousia to an unknowable time in the indefinite future.

Whereas John of Patmos had eagerly anticipated Rome's fall, many Christian leaders who lived through the Roman Empire's disintegration regarded it as an unmitigated catastrophe for society, including the church. Writing of Alaric the Goth's invasion of Rome in 410 C.E., Jerome — the scholar who created the Vulgate Bible — lamented the "great city's" humiliation.

Judaism and Christianity, originator and inheritor of the world's first ethical monotheism, endured the Roman Empire's slow collapse as they had survived the earlier destruction of Jerusalem, the crisis under Domitian that inspired the writing of Revelation, and far more intense attacks on the Judeo-Christian communities under later emperors. The church replaced the state's crumbling authority with its own spiritual leadership. Along with descendants of the people who had created them, the Hebrew and Christian Scriptures survived the empire's demise, providing a continuity with Israel's ancient prophets and early Christian visionaries and a fixed standard of belief in a rapidly changing world.

Shocks and Readjustments

Today, as Christianity enters its third millennium, it faces a world enormously different from the Palestinian-Jewish and Greco-Roman environments in which it began. Among its many other challenges, the believing community must interpret ancient biblical ideas to a world that has been thoroughly transformed by a series of historical and cultural developments that were not anticipated in biblical times. A brief review of some representative events that have radically altered the world since Jesus' day—changes whose effects have persisted into the present—suggests some of the formidable difficulties that believers must deal with if they are to convey the biblical message successfully into the future.

THE RISE OF ISLAM

Of the many shocks that have jarred Christianity's self-image since the collapse of the western Roman Empire, one of the greatest was the birth and rapid expansion of a new world religion—Islam, meaning "submission" (to the will of one God, Allah). Islam originated in Arabia during the seventh century C.E. but quickly swept through the Near East, western Asia, and North Africa. During its first century, Islam not only came to dominate vast areas that had previously been Christian, including Syria, Palestine, Egypt, and the entire southern Mediterranean basin, but also penetrated into southwestern Europe. It was only at the Battle of Tours (732 C.E.), a mere 100 miles from Paris, that the advance of Islamic armies into Europe was finally checked. With rare exceptions, such as in Spain, Christendom has been unable to regain territories and populations lost to the rival faith 1300 years ago. Small, isolated pockets of Christians have survived in the Islamic world, but they represent only a tiny presence compared to the Muslim majority.

Muhammad (c. 570–632 C.E.), the Arab prophet who founded Islam, was familiar with the oral teachings of both Judaism and Christianity, some of which he incorporated into the Qur'an, the sacred Scripture of Islam. For Muhammad, Islam represented a return to the true faith, stemming ultimately from the patriarch Abraham, that Jews and Christians had failed to preserve. A crucial aspect of Islamic reform was an emphasis on the unity of God, the absolute singleness of being expressed in the Torah—"the LORD is our God, one LORD" (Deut. 6:4). In the Islamic view, Christians had distorted the concept of monotheism by elevating the man Jesus to equality with God. For Muhammad and his followers, the Christian doctrine of **the Trinity**, with its mystical notion of triune Deity, was illogical and unacceptable. Some historians have recently suggested that many former Christians in the Mediterranean region who voluntarily converted to Islam may have done so partly because they welcomed its clear and uncompromising vision of divine unity.

THE SPLIT BETWEEN THE WESTERN AND EASTERN CHURCH

With its capital at Constantinople, the city founded by the emperor **Constantine I**, the eastern half of the Roman Empire, the Byzantine, survived the collapse of the western Roman Empire by almost 1000 years. Although Islamic invaders had reduced Byzantine territory to a mere sliver of its former size, the bishop of Constantinople remained a major power in Christendom. In 1054 C.E., however, an extended dispute over papal authority culminated in the Great Schism, a rupture that permanently divided the international Christian community, with representatives of Rome and Constantinople excommunicating each other. This decisive split within Christendom resulted in two competing branches of the faith: the Roman Catholic Church in the west and the Greek-speaking Orthodox Church in the east. (After 1965, the two churches became partly reconciled.) In 1453 C.E., when the Ottoman Turks captured Constantinople, swallowing up the last remnants of the Byzantine Empire, the Orthodox Church, although henceforth politically powerless and subjected to Islamic rule, managed to preserve its identity.

THE PROTESTANT REFORMATION

Separated from its eastern counterpart and threatened by repeated Islamic invasions, the Catholic Church experienced an internal crisis during the sixteenth century that has further divided Christendom. Sparked by Martin Luther's criticism of abuses within the church, the Protestant Reformation spread throughout northern Europe and England, separating Catholic and Protestant Christians into frequently hostile groups and inciting a series of destructive religious wars. Debates between Catholic and Protestant leaders over matters of belief and ritual brought the New Testament writings into renewed prominence. Luther claimed that "only Scripture"—not custom or tradition—formed the valid basis of Christian teaching. As a result, the Bible was quickly translated into a variety of modern European languages and, thanks to the invention of the printing press, widely distributed among believers in rapidly proliferating new denominations (see Chapter 1). In most Protestant circles, biblical texts were thought to provide the sole means of defining Christian doctrine and practice. By contrast, Roman Catholicism continues to place the authority of Scripture within the broader context of the church, emphasizing unwritten tradition, the sacraments, and a concept of progressive revelation through church councils, along with the biblical texts.

Exploration and the Scientific Revolution

Only decades before Luther inaugurated the Reformation by nailing his famous theses on the door at a Wittenberg church in 1517 C.E., new geographical discoveries showed Europeans that our planet is much larger and more culturally diverse than previously suspected, containing not only the newfound continents of North and South America, but also hitherto unknown civilizations, such as those of the Aztecs in Mexico and the Inca in Peru. Little more than a century later, the even more revolutionary astronomical discoveries of Galileo (1564–1642), building on the work of Copernicus (1473–1543), offered visible proof that the earth was not, as had been generally assumed, the center of the universe. Because the earth was regarded as the stage on which God and Satan battled for human souls—an essential axiom of the religious worldview—church leaders had long defended the theories of Ptolemy, a Greek astronomer of Alexandria (second century C.E.), who held that the moon, sun, and planets revolved around an unmoving earth. This *geocentric* view, which also provides the cosmic structure described by Dante and Milton, seemed, in the opinion of most church leaders, to accord well with biblical cosmology. Although the Catholic Church officially condemned Galileo's research claiming that the sun is the center of the solar system, and—after threatening him with the tortures of the Inquisition—imprisoned the astronomer for life, the evidence for a *heliocentric* system soon became overwhelming. Over time, religious authorities gradually accepted the humbling fact that, far from being the fixed center of existence, the earth is merely a tiny speck orbiting a medium-sized star in the arm of a spiral galaxy that is but one of hundreds of billions of similar galaxies scattered irregularly over immense distances of space.

The dawning realization of the earth's insignificant cosmic rank necessarily called into question the cosmology assumed by many biblical authors. Instead of the traditional three-story universe inherited from antiquity (heaven, earth, and hell), modern astronomy revealed an unimaginably vast cosmos in which terrestrial notions of "up" or "down" are meaningless. As a rocky globe suspended in empty space, one of nine planets and innumerable asteroids orbiting the sun, the earth's astronomical placement makes conventional ideas about directions such as north or south irrelevant. Whereas the ancients believed that one could rise vertically to heaven, as Luke pictures Jesus doing in Acts 1 and as Paul predicts for his followers in 1 Thessalonians 4, or descend into a cosmic sub-basement, as the Petrine writings indicate that Jesus did, earth's everchanging position as it wheels through a cosmic void makes these traditional religious claims literally impossible. Recognizing the importance of metaphor in these passages, however, some commentators interpret them symbolically. Attempting to reconcile science and faith, a few theologians point to speculations in modern physics that postulate the existence of parallel universes, dimensions of reality presently inaccessible to scientific investigation. As many Buddhists have long supposed, ultimate reality may encompass an infinite number of dimensions, of which our visible cosmos is but one. Because science has only begun to unravel the complexity of even the physical universe, some thinkers suggest that future discoveries may eventually unveil planes of existence that the ancients called heaven (a spiritual state of being). Although science is still far from offering theoretical proof that nonmaterial dimensions actually exist, let alone validating religious visions of an unseen spirit realm, some believers are optimistic that the more we learn about the universe the closer we will come to encountering what Einstein called "the mind of God."

Perhaps even more disturbing to conventional beliefs than Galileo's dethronement of the earth from the cosmic center are the advances made in geology and biology during the last two centuries. Before geologists acquired the techniques to decipher the stratigraphical record of the earth's history, Christian leaders used biblical texts to calculate our planet's age, confidently adding together all the human generations listed in the Hebrew Bible to establish the exact date on which the universe came into existence. One of the most famous computations was that made by James Ussher (1581–1656), an Irish archbishop and scholar who, assuming that Genesis referred to six twenty-four-hour days of creation, determined that God fashioned the first human pair, Adam and Eve, in 4004 B.C.E. (Ussher would have preferred an even 4000 B.C.E., but he was aware of a four-year miscalculation in fixing the date of Jesus' birth, which occurred before King Herod's death in 4 B.C.E., as computed by modern calendars.) Widely accepted and printed in the marginal notes of many Bibles, Ussher's chronology, with some slight modifica-

tions, is still used by some denominations which insist on a literal reading of Genesis.

Traditional assumptions about both the relative youth of the earth and of the human race were forcibly dispelled during the eighteenth and nineteenth centuries as geologists such as James Hutton (1726–1797), Charles Lyell (1797–1875), and Louis Agassiz (1807–1873) systematically gathered evidence illuminating the earth's past. Whereas Western scholars had commonly supposed that the earth's present features, including all river valleys and mountains, had been formed only a few thousand years ago in the Genesis Flood, Hutton and his colleagues demonstrated that the planet's topography was not shaped by a catastrophic deluge but by a long, slow process involving the same geological forces of deposition and erosion that we observe operating today. (With the mid-twentieth-century discoveries of radiocarbon and potassium-argon methods in dating rock layers, it became possible to show that the earth is at least 4.5 billion years old, a span lengthy enough to account for virtually every known formation at the present geologic rate.) At the same time that geologists began recognizing the earth's great age, the naturalist Charles Darwin (1800–1882) proposed his theory of biological evolution through natural selection in *The Origin of Species* (1859), a work that revolutionized our view of life's beginnings. For some believers, the implication of Darwin's theory — that all forms of earthly life, including humans, had evolved slowly over the long epochs of geologic time — was blasphemous. For many others, however, the revolutionary theory simply illuminated the *means* by which creation had been accomplished and provided a more accurate understanding of the Creator's design.

As many theologians have observed, if evolution was God's tool in creating humanity, old ideas about some biblical passages, such as Paul's contrast between the "first man [Adam]" and Christ (Rom. 5; 1 Cor. 15), will need to be reassessed. Whereas Augustine and other interpreters of Paul's thought formulated a doctrine of "original sin," stating that by disobedience humanity "fell" from a state of original perfection, anthropologists studying human prehistory instead uncover abundant evidence of ancient humanoids from which modern humankind gradually developed. Will the traditional doctrine of original sin — the idea that humans are born innately "depraved," prone to violence and other sins — have to be reinterpreted as simply the consequence of our biological heritage, that the human frame incorporates animal traits inherited from distant pre-human ancestors? Following the lead of Teilhard de Chardin, the Jesuit scientist who tried to reconcile the concept of evolution with Christian teaching, will twenty-first-century theologians devise new ways to interpret human origins and the Genesis narrative of humanity's alienation from God? (See works on "Science and Judeo-Christian Beliefs" in "Recommended Reading.")

At the dawn of a new millennium, different religious groups have responded in strikingly different ways to science's revolutionary claims. Perhaps feeling threatened by discoveries that would seem to overthrow cherished ideals and throw some biblical traditions into doubt, fundamentalist groups categorically reject any data that conflict with a presupposition that every scriptural statement — as interpreted by leaders of church or synagogue — is literally factual. The majority of believers who are not fundamentalists, however, wonder how long a systematic denial of scientific discoveries about the universe can endure without shattering from its own rigidity. Rather than fearing new disclosures about the nature of the world we inhabit — and their ramifications for the future — many believers accept expanding ideas about the cosmos and its life forms as further revelations of divine power and wisdom.

In studying the Bible, most readers find it difficult to escape viewing its diverse texts — written between about 3100 and 1900 years ago — in the light of contemporary Western culture, particularly its scientific rationalism and religious diversity. Today three main divisions of Judaism and thousands of Christian denominations, each claiming the Bible as its doctrinal authority, compete for believers' allegiance. Some people regret the Judeo-Christian world's lack of unity, but those who carefully study the Bible's historical development possess an important clue to the present religious pluralism. Although some individual groups offer their members a promise of religious "truth," absolute certainty in the midst of the world's perplexities, readers familiar with both the Hebrew Bible and the New Testament know that they contain a wide range of theological viewpoints and that this diversity embodies a religious strength that helps to account for the Bible's enduring appeal. The Tanak encompasses works (such as the Torah) that testify to God's redemptive acts in history, from the creation of life to the salvation of Israel; it also includes books (for example, the Book of Job) in which the traditional concept of God is questioned and reevaluated or in which the Deity's strange reluctance to give human life an unequivocal meaning is examined (as in Ecclesiastes). Aware that different biblical authors living in different historical epochs and circumstances had vastly different goals and experiences of the divine-human relationship, readers encounter a tremendous variation in biblical thought. As 2 Peter observes, Paul's letters contain passages that are difficult to understand and open to more than one interpretation — a principle that applies equally well to the rest of the biblical canon. The multiplicity of contemporary religious groups results not from the breakup of a theoretically monolithic biblical religion but from the rich variety of ideas articulated in both Jewish and Christian canonical literature.

In today's world, with its extreme fragmentation of both religious and secular institutions, the Bible's theological diversity offers a distinct advantage. Because this collection of documents — spanning 1100 years of human interaction with the divine — does not conform to a single doctrinaire vision, it welcomes all kinds of pilgrims seeking to tap its spiritual resources. Each biblical composition reflects an individual writer's intensely personal response to God's impact on human life and history, allowing an enormous variety of readers with equally varied emotional and intellectual needs to find some form of enlightenment or validation in the biblical texts. Whether exulting in the glory of Creation (Gen. 1), sharing Moses' conversations with God (cf. Exod. 3–4; 32; Num. 14), lamenting the Deity's silence in the face of his people's distress (Ps. 44; 89; Eccl.), or glimpsing God through ethical insights (Matt. 5–7), readers can experience almost innumerable examples of humanity's mysterious encounters with the divine.

RECOMMENDED READING

Rome and Christian History

Brown, R. E. *The Churches the Apostles Left Behind.* New York: Paulist Press, 1984. A concise but extremely important analysis of the theological diversity present in early Christian communities.

Dunn, J. D. G. *Unity and Diversity in the New Testament.* Philadelphia: Westminster Press, 1977. A thoughtful study of the variety of belief found among different canonical authors; highly recommended.

Eusebius. *The History of the Church.* Translated by G. A. Williamson. Baltimore: Penguin Books, 1965. Our principal source for the study of the growth and development of early Christianity.

Fox, R. L. *Pagans and Christians.* New York: Knopf, 1986. A comprehensive study of the historical processes that resulted in Constantine's conversion and the religious transformation of the Roman Empire.

Gonzalez, J. L. *The Story of Christianity.* Vol. 1, *The Early Church to the Dawn of the Reformation.* San Francisco: Harper & Row, 1984.

MacMullen, Ramsay. *Christianizing the Roman Empire, A.D. 100–400.* New Haven, Conn.: Yale University Press, 1984. A historical investigation of the social, political, and religious conditions under which the Roman people were converted.

Meeks, W. A. *The Moral World of the First Christians.* Philadelphia: Westminster Press, 1986. Explores the pagan and Jewish ethical context in which Christianity developed.

Robinson, J. M., and Koester, Helmut. *Trajectories Through Early Christianity.* Philadelphia: Fortress Press, 1971.

Wilken, R. L. *The Christians as the Romans Saw Them.* New Haven, Conn.: Yale University Press, 1984. A careful analysis of the social, educational, religious, and political conflicts between early Christians and their Roman critics.

Science and Judeo-Christian Beliefs

Edwards, Denis. *The God of Evolution: A Trinitarian Theology.* Mahwah, N.J.: Paulist Press, 1999. A relatively conventional search for order and design in the physical universe.

Griffin, David Ray. *Religion and Scientific Naturalism: Overcoming the Conflict.* (SUNY Series in Constructive Postmodern Thought). Ithaca, N.Y.: State University of New York Press, 2000. Highly recommended for its informed and honest critique of both religious dogmatism and scientific materialism.

Haught, John F. *God after Darwin: A Theology of Evolution.* Boulder, Col.: Westview Press, 1999. Candidly faces the ethical and theological implications of the amoral natural forces revealed in evolution.

Korsmeyer, Jerry D. *Evolution and Eden: Balancing Original Sin and Contemporary Science.* Mahwah, N.J.: Paulist Press, 1998. Explores the theological ramifications of Christian doctrine and evolutionary theory.

Miller, Kenneth. *Finding Darwin's God: A Scientist's Search for Common Ground Between God and Evolution.* New York: Cliff Street Books, 1999.

Polkinghorne, John, and Welker, Michael, eds. *The End of the World and the Ends of God: Science and Theology on Eschatology.* (Theology for the Twenty-First Century). Harrisburg, Penn.: Trinity Press International, 2000. A collection of essays discussing such topics as the mass extinctions that occurred in earth's geologic past and their implications for the meaning of biblical eschatology.

Ruse, Michael. *Can a Darwinian Be a Christian? The Relationship between Science and Religion.* New York: Cambridge University Press, 2000. Examines the basic tenets of Christianity in the light of evolutionary theory.

Teilhard de Chardin, Pierre. *The Phenomenon of Man.* San Francisco: HarperCollins, 1980. A landmark study by a Jesuit palaeontologist who saw evolution ultimately culminating in a cosmic "omega point," the Christ.

QUESTIONS FOR REVIEW

1. Discuss the differences in attitude toward Rome expressed in Romans 13 (and 1 Peter) on the one hand and in Revelation on the other. What changing historical conditions can help account for the shift from the positive attitude of Paul to the negative judgment of John of Patmos?

2. List and explain some historical developments, beginning with Constantine's imperial patronage of the church, that played a significant role in the evolution of Christianity. What impact did the rise of Islam have on Christendom?

QUESTIONS FOR DISCUSSION AND REFLECTION

1. After the ascension of Constantine to the imperial throne, Christianity's position in the Roman Empire changed dramatically. Describe and explain the church's role during the later empire. How did many leading Christians react to the barbarian invasions that eventually destroyed the Roman world?

2. What role did the Bible play in formulating later church creeds and doctrines? In what ways did the Protestant Reformation during the sixteenth and seventeenth centuries increase the influence of the biblical texts?

3. Given the enormous changes that have occurred since Christianity began, what adaptations to new realities do you think will ensure the religion's survival for another 2000 years? Which of the basic concepts expressed in the Hebrew Bible and the New Testament do you think will continue to guide human behavior in the future? What biblical ideas are still applicable to the human condition?

TERMS AND CONCEPTS TO REMEMBER

Constantine I
Diocletian
Edict of Milan
Eusebius
Great Schism, the
Islam
Jamnia, Academy of
Jesus' enduring role
Martin Luther
    and the Reformation
Muhammad
post-Reformation
    proliferation of
    denomination, the
Rome and the church
scientific discoveries
Trinity, the
unity of God, the

Glossary of Major Biblical Characters, Terms, and Concepts

The following glossary identifies or defines a representative selection of major characters, concepts, places, and terms found in the canonical Hebrew Bible and New Testament. For a more comprehensive treatment of individual terms, the reader is directed to David Noel Freedman, ed., *The Anchor Bible Dictionary,* Vols. 1–6 (New York: Doubleday, 1992), an indispensable resource. For useful one-volume references, consult Paul Achtemeier, ed., *Harper's Bible Dictionary* (San Francisco: Harper & Row, 2nd ed., 1996); David Noel Freedman, ed., *Eerdman's Dictionary of the Bible* (Grand Rapids, Mich.: Wm. B. Eerdmans Publishing Company, 2000; Raymond Brown, Joseph Fitzmyer, and Roland Murphy, *The New Jerome Biblical Commentary,* 2nd ed. (Englewood Cliffs, N.J.: Prentice-Hall, 1990); and B. M. Metzger and M. D. Coogan, eds., *The Oxford Companion to the Bible* (New York: Oxford University Press, 1993).

Aaron   The older brother of Moses and first head of the Israelite priesthood, Aaron was the son of Amram the Levite and his aunt Jochebed (Exod. 6:20). Because Moses reputedly had a speech defect, Aaron served as his spokesman before the Pharaoh (Exod. 4:14). According to the priestly source in the Pentateuch, which stresses Aaron's special role, Moses anointed him and his four sons as founders of Israel's priesthood (Num. 3:1–3), consecrating them to administer the Tabernacle (see Lev. 8 and Exod. 29). Although he led in the worship of the golden calf (Exod. 32:1–6), Aaron remained in divine favor. His son Eleazar succeeded him as High Priest of Israel.

Aaronites   Priestly descendants of Aaron's line (1 Chron. 12:27; Ps. 115:10). In the New Testament, Zechariah and Elisabeth, the parents of John the Baptist, were both Aaronites (Luke 1).

Abednego   In the Book of Daniel, the Babylonian name given to Azariah, one of the three Hebrew youths whom Nebuchadnezzar cast into a fiery furnace (Dan. 1–3).

Abel   The second son of Adam and Eve (Gen. 4:2) and brother of Cain, who murdered Abel when his animal sacrifice was accepted by Yahweh whereas Cain's grain offering was rejected. This story of the first murder (Gen. 4:3–10) occurs in the J portion of the Pentateuch and is referred to in the New Testament by Jesus (Matt. 23:35) and the author of Hebrews (Heb. 11:4). In Hebrew, the name *Abel* means "breath" or "vanity."

Abigail   Wife of Nabal the fool, a wealthy shepherd who denied young David a share of his property. By wisely making a peace offering to David's guerrilla band, Abigail saved her husband's life. After Nabal's death, she married David (1 Sam. 25) and bore him a son, Chileab (2 Sam. 3:3).

Abimelech   (1) In Genesis, a king of Gerar at whose court Abraham presented his wife Sarah as his sister (Gen. 20:1–18). The ruler and patriarch later made a covenant with each other (Gen. 21:22–34).

(2) A Philistine king at Gerar to whom Isaac passed off his wife Rebekah as his sister and with whom he, too, later established a covenant (Gen. 26:1–33). (3) In Judges, the son of Gideon who slew his seventy brothers and made himself king at Shechem until he was killed during a siege (Judg. 9).

Abraham   In Genesis 12–24, Abraham (at first called *Abram,* meaning "exalted father") is the supreme example of obedience to Yahweh and the founder of the Hebrew nation. By divine order, he leaves his adopted home in Haran, in northern Mesopotamia, and travels to Canaan (Palestine), which land is promised to his descendants who are to become a mighty nation (Israel). Yahweh later demands that he sacrifice his only son by his wife Sarah. Because of Abraham's willingness to surrender Isaac, Yahweh reaffirms the Abrahamic Covenant, by which the patriarch's descendants are to become as numerous as "the sands of the sea" and a source of blessing to all nations. According to Genesis, the twelve tribes of Israel are descended from Abraham's grandson Jacob. The Age of Abraham, a period of mass nomadic movement in the ancient Near East, may have occurred during the nineteenth or eighteenth century B.C.E.

Abraham's bosom   In Luke's parable of the afterlife, the posthumous paradise to which the beggar Lazarus is assigned (Luke 16:19–31). Luke's contemporary, the historian Josephus, describes a similar postmortem abode for the righteous in his "Discourse on Hades."

Absalom   In 2 Samuel, the son of David and Maacah (2 Sam. 3:3). Noted for his physical beauty and fiery temperament, Absalom killed his half-brother Amnon to avenge the rape of his sister Tamar, fled to Geshur in Aram, but was reconciled with his father three years later. He later rebelled against David and drove him from Jerusalem but was defeated and killed by the loyalist Joab (2 Sam. 13–14).

acrostic   In Hebrew poetry, a series of lines or verses of which the first word begins with consecutive letters of the alphabet. Examples of this alphabetic sequence are found in Lamentations 1–4 and Psalm 119.

Adam   In Genesis, the name *Adam* literally means "ruddy," from the Hebrew for "red"; it possibly derives from an Akkadian word meaning "creature." In the older creation account (Gen. 2:4–4:26), Adam is simply "the man [earthling]," which is not rendered as a proper name until the Septuagint version (c. 250 B.C.E.). New Testament writers typically use Adam as a symbol of all humanity (as in 1 Cor. 15:21–49 and Rom. 5:12–21). *See* Fall, the.

Adonai   The Hebrew word for "Lord," a title of honor and majesty applied to the Israelite Deity, particularly during the late postexilic period, as a substitute for the personal name *Yahweh,* which was considered too sacred to pronounce.

Adonijah   The son of David who tried unsuccessfully to succeed his father on Israel's throne and whom Solomon put to death (1 Kings 1:9–2:25).

Ahab   Son of Omri and king of Israel from about 869–850 B.C.E. Although Ahab practiced the Yahwist religion, he allowed his wife Jezebel, daughter of a Phoenician ruler, to encourage the Baal cult, which brought the condemnation of the prophet Elijah (1 Kings 17–22). A contemporary of Judah's King Jehoshaphat, Ahab was killed while defending Israel against Assyria's Shalmaneser III.

Ahasuerus (Xerxes I)   Son of Darius Hystaspes and Atossa, daughter of Cyrus the Great, the Ahasuerus of the Book of Esther is usually identified with Xerxes I (486–465 B.C.E.), who led the second Persian invasion of Greece and was defeated at the Battle of Salamis (480 B.C.E.). There is no record that he ever had a Jewish queen named Esther.

Ahaz   King of Judah (c. 735–716 B.C.E.) and father of Hezekiah, who succeeded him. Although Ahaz reigned during the ministries of Isaiah and Micah, he compromised the Yahwist religion to curry favor with Assyria, whose vassal Judah became (2 Kings 16).

'Ai   "The ruin" in Hebrew, 'Ai was a city reputedly destroyed by Joshua's conquest of Canaan (Josh. 7:2–5; 8:1–29). But archaeology has demonstrated that it had already been abandoned in the thirteenth century B.C.E. when the Israelites entered Palestine.

Akhenaton   Egyptian pharaoh (1364–1347 B.C.E.) who radically altered the state religion, introducing a monotheistic cult of the solar deity Aton and outraging the conservative priests of the Theban state god Amun. Abandoning his original name, Amenhotep IV, Akhenaton founded a new capital, Akhetaton (now known as Tell el-Amarna); archaeologists call his reign the Amarna period.

Akkad (Accad)   The narrow plain of Babylonia lying north of Sumer, locale of the Akkad dynasty, founders of the first real empire in world history (c. 2360–2180 B.C.E.). In Akkad, named for its capital city, were many of the great cities of antiquity, some of which are mentioned in Genesis 10.

Akkadian (Accadian)   (1) The period during which the early Semitic dynasty established by Sargon I dominated Mesopotamia (twenty-fourth–twenty-second centuries B.C.E.). (2) The Akkadian language, written in cuneiform script but sharing many features with Hebrew, Arabic, and Aramaic, was a Semitic tongue used in Mesopotamia from about the twenty-eighth to the first centuries B.C.E.

Alexander the Great   One of the most brilliant leaders and military conquerors of the classical world. Son of King Philip of Macedonia, Alexander was born at Pella in Macedonia in 356 B.C.E. and died in Babylon in 323 B.C.E. During his relatively brief career, he conquered most of the known world, created an empire that extended from Greece to India, propagated Greek culture throughout the Near East, and instituted a period of cosmopolitanism termed Hellenistic. His influence on Palestine is recounted in 1 Maccabees 1.

Alexandria   A major port city and cultural center founded by Alexander the Great on the Egyptian coast. The home of a large Jewish colony during the Hellenistic period, Alexandria nourished a fusion of Hebraic and Hellenic (Greek) ideas, one result of which was the Greek Septuagint translation of the Hebrew Bible.

allegory   A literary narrative in which persons, places, and events are given a symbolic meaning. Some Hellenistic-Jewish scholars of Alexandria tended to interpret the Hebrew Bible allegorically, as Paul does the story of Abraham, Sarah, and Hagar (Gal. 4:21–31).

alpha   The first letter of the Greek alphabet, presented as a symbol of creation (Genesis). *See* omega.

Amalekites   According to Genesis 36:12, these nomadic tribes were descendants of Esau who occupied the desert south and southeast of Canaan. Persistent enemies of ancient Israel, the Amalekites attacked Moses' group (Deut. 25:17–19), were defeated by Joshua at Rephidim (Exod. 17), and conquered by Gideon (Judg. 6:33; 7:12) but were still troublesome in Saul and David's time (1 Sam. 15; 30:18).

Amarna Age   A title assigned to the reign of Pharaoh Amenhotep IV (Akhenaton), whose new capital had been built at Amarna, Egypt.

Amen   A term derived from a Hebrew work whose root suggests "so be it." Typically used as a confirmation (1 Kings 1:36), it implies agreement, as at the conclusion of a prayer (Matt. 6:13; 1 Cor. 14:16). In Revelation 3:14, "the Amen" is a synonym for Jesus Christ, who affirms the divine purpose.

Ammon   A tribal state located northeast of the Dead Sea, one of Israel's traditional enemies. *See* Ammonites.

Ammonites   A Semitic group supposedly descended from Abraham's nephew Lot (Gen. 19:38). Chronic enemies of Israel (1 Sam. 11; 1 Kings 11), they occupied the eastern margin of the Transjordan plateau to harass the Israelites.

Amorites   A Semitic people (called "Westerners" or "highlanders") who moved into the ancient Near East about 2000 B.C.E. and founded the states of Mari and Babylon, of which Hammurabi is the best-known Amorite ruler. The term was also applied to a tribe living in Canaan before the Israelite conquest (Num. 13:29; 21:26; Judg. 1).

Amos   A shepherd and "dresser of sycamore [fig] trees" from the Judean village of Tekoa who denounced the religious and social practices of the northern kingdom (Israel) during the reign of Jeroboam II (c. 786–746 B.C.E.), Amos was the first biblical prophet whose words were collected and preserved in a book.

amphictyony   A confederation of tribes or cities (typically of six or twelve members) organized around a particular deity's shrine. The term is commonly applied to the league of Israelite tribes during the period of the judges (c. 1200–1000 B.C.E.).

Ananias II   The High Priest who presided over the full council (Sanhedrin) before which Paul was brought by Claudius Lycias for creating a "riot" in the Jerusalem Temple (Acts 22:22–23:22).

Anath   A Canaanite agricultural goddess, sister-consort of the fertility god Baal.

Andrew   A disciple of John the Baptist (John 1:35–40) who, according to John's Gospel, became the first of Jesus' followers and brought his brother Peter to Jesus (John 1:41–42). Mark gives another version of this calling (Mark 1:16–18; see also John 6:5; 12:22).

angel   From a Greek word meaning "messenger"; angels were commonly conceived in biblical times as emissaries from the deity who employed them to communicate his will to humanity. The oldest known rendition of angels in art occurs on the stele of Urnammu, a Sumerian king, but many scholars suggest that Israel's belief in angelology derives from Persian sources. Angels named in canonical Scripture include Michael and Gabriel, although apocryphal and pseudepigraphal literature lists others. Angels are particularly important in the birth stories of Jesus (Luke 1–2; Matt. 1).

Annas   A former high priest before whom Jesus was brought for trial (John 18:13), Annas was father-in-law of Caiaphas, then the currently reigning High Priest (see also Luke 3:2 and Acts 4:6).

Annunciation   The name given to the angel Gabriel's declaration to Mary of Nazareth that she was to bear a son, Jesus, who would inherit David's throne (Luke 1:28–32).

anointed   The literal meaning of the Hebrew word *mashiah,* a term applied to Davidic kings who were consecrated in office by the ritual smearing (anointing) of their heads with holy oil. *See* messiah.

anthropomorphism   Attributing human characteristics to something not human; particularly, ascribing human shape and form to a deity.

anti-Christ   The ultimate enemy of Jesus Christ who, according to Christian apocalyptic traditions, will manifest himself at the End of time to corrupt many of the faithful, only to be vanquished when Christ appears. The term is used only in 2 and 3 John but is clearly referred to in 2 Thessalonians (2:1–12) and Revelation 13.

antinomianism   Literally meaning "opponents of law," the name applies to specific early Christian groups that argued that faith in Christ absolves the believer from obeying the moral law, a libertarian attitude attacked by Paul (Gal. 5:13–6:10) and the author of 1 and 2 John. *See* heresy.

Antioch   Two Hellenistic cities famous in Maccabean and New Testament times bore this name. (1) In Syria, Antioch was the capital of the Macedonian Seleucid kings and, under Roman rule, the capital of a province of the same name. According to Acts, the first Gentile Christian church was founded in Antioch (Acts 11:20, 21), where followers of "the way" were first called Christians (Acts 11:26). Paul began all three of his missionary journeys from here. (2) Pisidian Antioch, a major city in Galatia (in Asia Minor), was also the site of an important early church, this one founded by Paul and Barnabas (Acts 13:14–50).

Antiochus   The name of several Syrian monarchs who inherited power from Seleucus I, a general and successor of Alexander the Great. The most famous were Antiochus III, who gained control of Palestine from Egypt in 198/197 B.C.E., and Antiochus IV (*Epiphanes,* or "God Manifest") (175–163 B.C.E.), whose persecution of the Jews led to the Maccabean revolt.

antitheses   A technical term describing six of Jesus' sayings in Matthew's Sermon on the Mount, a rhetorical structure in which Jesus cites a biblical law, "you have learned that they were told" (the thesis), and then contrasts it with his interpretation, "but what I tell you is this" (the antithesis). (Matt. 5:21–48).

Antonius Felix   The Roman procurator or governor of Judea before whom Paul was tried at Caesarea about 60 C.E. (Acts 23:23–24:27).

Anu   A sky god of Uruk, head of the older generation of Mesopotamian gods, and the Babylonian version of the Sumerian deity An, whose name means "heaven." Regarded as father of the gods, Anu was worshiped from ancient times through the Hellenistic period.

aphorism   A brief, pithy saying that challenges or overturns conventional wisdom. Jesus was believed to have favored aphorisms in speech.

'Apiru   Egyptian version of the term *Habiru. See* Habiru.

apocalypse   From the Greek *apokalypsis,* meaning to "uncover" or "reveal," the term refers to a special kind of prophetic literature that purports to foretell the future in terms of symbols and mystical visions and deals primarily with eschatological events.

Apocalypse of Peter   One of many significant extracanonical works. Existing only in an Ethiopian translation, it describes in excruciating detail the suffering of souls condemned to hell by Jesus at his Second Coming.

apocalyptic literature   A branch of prophetic writing that flourished in Judaism from about 200 B.C.E. to 140 C.E. and greatly influenced Christianity. Works such as Daniel, Enoch, 2 and 3 Baruch, 2 Esdras, and the Christian Book of Revelation are distinguished by cryptic language, symbolic imagery, and the expectation of an imminent cosmic catastrophe in which the forces of Good ultimately defeat the powers of Evil, resulting in the establishment of a messianic rule and consequent transformation of the universe. Jesus' prophecies of his return (Mark 13; Luke 21; Matt. 24) are a form of apocalyptic discourse.

Apocrypha   From the Greek, meaning "hidden" books, Apocrypha refers to noncanonical or deuterocanonical literature, especially the fourteen books included in the Greek Septuagint and later editions of the Vulgate but not in the Masoretic Text of the Hebrew Bible. It also applies to a body of Christian works that typically parallel or spuriously "supplement" the New Testament canon.

apodictic law   Law cast in the form of unconditional demands, such as the "thou shalt nots" in the Decalogue (Exod. 20). *See also* policy law.

apokalypsis   English transliteration of a Greek term meaning "a revelation, an unveiling of what is hidden." Paul uses the term to describe the divine source of his unique teaching (Gal. 1:12).

Apollos   A Hellenistic Jew of Alexandria, Egypt, noted for his eloquence, who first was a follower of John the Baptist, then embraced Christianity (Acts 18:24–28), and inadvertently became a rival of Paul at Corinth (1 Cor. 1:12; 3:4–6, 22–23; 4:6).

apostasy   From a Greek term meaning "to revolt," apostasy is the act of abandoning or rejecting a previously held religious faith. An apostate is one who has defected from or ceased to practice his or her religion.

apostle   A person sent forth or commissioned as a messenger, such as (but not restricted to) the Twelve whom Jesus selected to follow him. According to Acts 1, in the early Jerusalem church, an apostle was defined as one who had accompanied Jesus during his earthly ministry and had seen the resurrected Lord. Lists of the original Twelve differ from account to account (Matt. 10:2–5; Mark 3:16–19; Luke 6:13–16; Acts 1:13–14).

apothegm   A term in biblical criticism referring to brief sayings or instructive proverbs found in the Gospels. *See also* pericope.

apotheosis   In the Greco-Roman context, the elevation of a hero to divine stature, such as the posthumous deification's of Alexander or Julius Caesar.

Aqabah, Gulf of   A northern arm of the Red Sea, part of the Jordan rift, which separates the Sinai peninsula from Midian and Arabia.

Aquila   A prominent early Christian expelled from Rome with his wife, Priscilla, by Claudius's edict (49 C.E.), Aquila is often associated with Paul (Acts 18; Rom. 16:3–5; 1 Cor. 16:19).

Aram   According to Genesis 10:22, Aram was the son of Shem (a son of Noah) and progenitor of the Arameans, whom the Hebrew Bible identifies with the Syrians (Gen. 24).

Aramaic   The language of the Arameans (Syrians), Aramaic was a west-Semitic tongue used in parts of Mesopotamia from about 1000 B.C.E. The official language of the Persian Empire after about 500 B.C.E., it was spoken by the Jews after the Babylonian exile. Parts of the Hebrew Bible were composed in Aramaic, and a Galilean dialect of Aramaic was probably the language spoken by Jesus.

archetype   The primal form or original pattern from which all other things of a like nature are descended. The term refers to characters, ideas, or actions that represent the supreme and/or essential examples of a universal type, as Moses is the archetypal model of prophet and lawgiver.

Areopagus   The civic court in Athens and the location of an important legal council of the Athenian democracy where, according to Acts 17, Paul introduced Christianity to some Athenian intellectuals.

Ark   The rectangular houseboat that Noah built to contain his family and pairs of all animals during the Flood (Gen. 6:14–16).

Ark of the Covenant   The portable wooden chest, supposedly dating from Mosaic times (Exod. 25:10–22), that contained sacred artifacts of Israel's religion, such as Aaron's staff and the two stone tablets representing the Decalogue. Sometimes carried into Battle (Josh. 6:4–11; 1 Sam. 4), the Ark of the Covenant was eventually brought to Jerusalem and kept in the innermost sanctuary of Solomon's Temple. Its fate after the Temple's destruction is unknown.

Armageddon   A Greek transliteration of the Hebrew *Har Megiddon,* or "Mountain of Megiddo," a famous battlefield in the Plain of Jezreel in ancient Israel (Judg. 5:19; 2 Kings 9:27; 23:29). In Revelation 16:16, it is the symbolic site of the ultimate war between Good and Evil.

Artaxerxes   King of Persia (465–423 B.C.E.), son of Xerxes I. According to Nehemiah 2, Artaxerxes commissioned Nehemiah, his Jewish cupbearer, to go to Jerusalem and rebuild the city's walls. Scholars are not agreed on whether Ezra returned to Jerusalem during the reign of Artaxerxes I or Artaxerxes II.

Asa   The third king of Judah (c. 913–873 B.C.E.) whose long reign was marked by various religious reforms. The authors of Kings and Chronicles judge him a "good" ruler (1 Kings 15:8–24; 2 Chron. 14:1–16:14).

Ascension   The resurrected Jesus' ascent to heaven (Acts 1:6–11).

Asclepius The Greek god of medicine, he was the son of a mortal woman, Coronis, and Apollo, god of prophecy, health, purification, and the creative arts. As the archetypal physician whose skill could even raise the dead, he was posthumously deified and allegedly effected miraculous cures at shrines throughout the Greco-Roman world.

Ashdod One of the five major cities of the Philistines (Josh. 13:3), where the captured Ark of the Covenant was placed in Dagon's temple (1 Sam. 5:1–8).

Asher Reputed founder of an Israelite tribe that occupied a strip of Palestinian coast between Carmel and Phoenicia (Josh. 17:10–11; 19:24–31; Judg. 1:31–32; 5:17).

Asherah Hebrew name for the Canaanite goddess Asherat, "Lady of the Sea," a consort of El, Canaan's chief deity, whom the apostate Israelites worshiped at various times (see 1 Kings 11:5; 16:33; 18:19; etc.).

Ashkelon One of the five leading Philistine cities (Josh. 13:3; 2 Sam. 1:20).

Ashurbanipal IV Assyrian emperor (c. 668–627 B.C.E.), grandson of Sennacherib, son and successor of Esarhaddon; called Asnapper in Ezra 4:10.

Assur (Asshur) (1) Chief deity of the Assyrians, king of their gods, and personification of war. (2) Assyria's first capital, located on the west bank of the Tigris River, site of an earlier Sumerian city. (3) The name of the country from which the Assyrians took their name.

Assyria (1) A large territory centered along the upper Tigris River in Mesopotamia, including the major cities of Assur, Calah, and Nineveh. (2) The empire that dominated the Near East from the eleventh to the seventh centuries B.C.E. and whose leaders destroyed Israel in 721 B.C.E. and besieged Jerusalem in 701 B.C.E. It was destroyed by a coalition of Babylonians and Medes in 612 B.C.E.

Assyrians The "people of Assur," the chief god of Assyria, the Assyrians controlled the Fertile Crescent from about 1100 to 612 B.C.E. Israelite prophets such as Isaiah of Jerusalem regarded them as Yahweh's instruments of punishment for Israel's disobedience.

Athaliah Queen of Judah (842–837 B.C.E.), she was the daughter of Omri (or of Ahab and Jezebel). After Jehu murdered her husband Jehoram, king of Judah, she assumed the throne, the only woman to do so in the entire history of Israel and Judah.

Athanasius A leading Christian theologian (c. 295–373 C.E.) who participated in the Council of Nicaea (325 C.E.) and was later bishop of Alexandria, Egypt. His Easter Letter (367 C.E.) is the earliest document to list the books of the New Testament in their present content and canonical order.

Athens Greece's leading city-state and cultural capital in the fifth century B.C.E. and its leading intellectual center during Hellenistic and Roman times. According to Acts 17, the apostle Paul introduced Christianity in Athens.

Aton (Aten) Egyptian sun god whom Akhenaton proclaimed the sole deity to be worshiped, he was represented by a solar disk from which beams of life-giving light emanated.

Atrahasis A name meaning "extra-wise," an epithet commonly applied to Utnapishtim, the Mesopotamian hero who was the only man who, with his household, survived the global deluge.

Augustus The first emperor of Rome (30 B.C.E.–14 C.E.), Augustus Caesar brought peace to the Roman Empire after centuries of civil war. According to Luke 2:1, his decree ordering a census of "the whole world" brought Mary and Joseph to register in their ancestral hometown, Bethlehem, where Jesus was born.

Azazel The unidentified place or demon to which the scapegoat was sent on the Day of Atonement (Lev. 16:8, 10, 26).

Baal A Canaanite-Phoenician term meaning "lord" or "master," the name applied to Canaan's most popular fertility god. Worshiped as the power that caused germination and growth of farm crops, Baal was a serious rival to Yahweh after the Israelites settled in Palestine and became dependent on agriculture (Judg. 2:11–14). He is pictured as a god of storm and rainfall in a contest with the Yahwist Elijah on Mount Carmel (1 Kings 18:20–46).

Babel A term meaning "the gate of God," Babel became synonymous with the confusion of languages that typified cosmopolitan Babylon (Gen. 11:4–9). The Tower of Babel ("House of the Terrace-platform of Heaven and Earth") was a ziggurat. *See* ziggurat.

Babylon An ancient city on the middle Euphrates that was capital of both the Old and Neo-Babylonian empires. Under Nebuchadnezzar II (605–562 B.C.E.), who joined forces with the Medes to defeat Egypt at the Battle of Carchemish (605 B.C.E.) and create the second Babylonian Empire, Babylon destroyed Jerusalem and its Temple (587 B.C.E.). Babylon fell to the

Persians in 539 B.C.E. Alexander the Great's plans to rebuild the old sanctuaries ended with his death in 323 B.C.E., and the city never regained its former glory. As the archetypal enemy of God's people, Babylon became the symbol of Satan's worldly power (Rev. 14:8; 18:2).

Babylonian exile   The period between 587 and 538 B.C.E. during which Judah's upper classes were held captive in Babylon. An earlier deportation of Jewish leaders in 597 B.C.E. included the prophet Ezekiel. After Cyrus of Persia conquered Babylon in 539, Jews who wished to do so were encouraged to return to their Palestinian homeland.

Balaam   A Bedouin prophet or fortune-teller from Pethor on the Euphrates River whom Balak, king of Moab, hired to curse the Israelites when they attempted to cross Moab on their way to Canaan. Yahweh caused the hired soothsayer to turn his curse into a blessing on Israel (Num. 22–24), although another tradition blames Balaam for corrupting the Israelites (Num. 31:8, 15–17).

ban   The practice of dedicating all conquered enemies and their property to the victors' god, a policy of holy war that required the mass slaughter of all defeated peoples. According to Deuteronomy, the Israelites were commanded to place all Canaanites under the ban.

baptism   A religious ceremony first associated with John the Baptist (Mark 1:4; 11:30; Luke 7:29) and performed on converts in the infant Christian community (Acts 2:38–41; 19:3–5). Baptism may have derived from ritual cleansings with water practiced by the Essenes, from some Pharisees' use of it as a conversion alternative to circumcision, or from initiation rites into Hellenistic mystery religions. In Christianity, it is the ceremony of initiation into the church, performed either by total immersion in water or by pouring water on the head.

Barabbas   A condemned murderer and possibly a revolutionary whom the Roman procurator Pontius Pilate released instead of Jesus (Mark 15:6–15; Matt. 27:15–18; Luke 23:16–25; John 18:39–49).

Barak   An early Israelite judge (military commander), apparently subordinate to the judge Deborah, who fought against the Canaanites oppressing Israel. He failed to capture his chief opponent, Sisera, who was killed by Jael, a woman (Judges 4–5).

Barnabas   A prominent leader of the early church in Jerusalem, associate and traveling companion of the apostle Paul (Acts 9:26–30; 11:22–30; 13:1–3; 13:44–52; 14:1–15:4; 15:22–40; Col. 4:10; 1 Cor. 9:6; Gal. 2:1–13). The noncanonical Epistle of Barnabus is ascribed to him.

Barsabbas   The Christian leader of the Jerusalem church who was considered but not chosen to replace Judas among the Twelve (Acts 1:23–26).

Bartholomew   One of the twelve apostles mentioned in all three Synoptics as well as in the list in Acts (Matt. 10:3; Mark 3:18; Luke 6:14; Acts 1:13), Bartholomew is sometimes identified with the Nathanael of John's Gospel (John 1:45–51 and 21:2).

Baruch   Secretary and friend of Jeremiah, Baruch (blessed) recorded the prophet's message, which probably became the nucleus of the Jeremiah scroll (Jer. 36; 32:9–14; 43:6). The apocryphal Book of Baruch was attributed to him, as were the apocalypses of 2 and 3 Baruch in the Pseudepigrapha.

Bathsheba   Wife of Uriah, a Hittite soldier working in King David's service, Bathsheba's adultery with David and his murder of her husband evoked the denunciation of the prophet Nathan (2 Sam. 11:1–4; 12:1–23). Mother of Solomon, she conspired to place her son on Israel's throne (1 Kings 1:15–17).

Beatitudes   The list of blessings or happinesses with which Jesus begins the Sermon on the Mount (Matt. 5:3–12). Luke gives a variation of these pronouncements (Luke 6:20–23).

Beersheba   An ancient well in southern Palestine identified with the Genesis patriarchs (Gen. 21:22–34; 26:23–25, 32–33; 46:1); later a traditional location of the extreme southern border of the Israelite kingdom (Judg. 20:1; 2 Sam. 24:2; 1 Kings 4:25; etc.).

Behemoth   A mysterious beast probably derived from Mesopotamian mythology but sometimes identified with the hippopotamus (Job 40:15–24). *See also* Leviathan.

Bel   The Babylonian-Assyrian version of Baal, a common name for Marduk, chief god of Babylon (Isa. 46:1–4), sometimes called Merodach by the Jews (Jer. 50:2).

Belial   An adjective meaning "not profitable" or "wicked" but used in the Hebrew Bible as a proper name to denote an evil character, as "son of" or "daughter of" (Deut. 13:13; Judg. 19:22; 1 Sam. 10:27). In 2 Corinthians 6:15, Paul uses the term as if it were synonymous with the devil.

beloved disciple   The unnamed "disciple whom Jesus loved" (John 13:23) whom the author of John's

Gospel depicts as enjoying a more intimate relationship with Jesus than Peter or any other follower (John 13:21–29; 19:26–27; 20:2–10; 21:20–24). Although tradition identifies this disciple with the apostle John, neither the Gospels nor scholars can verify the assumption.

Belshazzar   In Daniel, the last king of Babylon, son of Nebuchadnezzar (Dan. 5:1–31), though archaeological discoveries indicate that he was neither, but merely prince regent for his father, Nabonidus.

Beltshazzar   A name meaning "protect the king's life," given to Daniel by his Babylonian masters (Dan. 1:7; 2:26; 4:8, 9).

Benjamin   The twelfth and last son of Jacob, second son of the patriarch's favorite wife, Rachel, and thus full brother of Joseph and half-brother of Jacob's other ten sons. Benjamin figures prominently in Joseph's saga (Gen. 42–44) and is regarded as the founder of the tribe of Benjamin, which, under the Israelite monarchy, occupied territory adjacent to that of Judah (Josh. 18:11–28; Judg. 1:8, 21). When the ten northern tribes seceded from the Davidic monarchy, Benjamin remained with the southern kingdom of Judah (1 Kings 12:21; Ezra 4:1).

Bethany   An impoverished suburb of Jerusalem, home of Jesus' friends Mary, Martha, and Lazarus (John 11:1–44).

Bethel   An ancient site, meaning "house of God," associated with the patriarchs Abraham (Gen. 12:8) and Jacob (Gen. 28:11–13, 22). Under the divided kingdom, Jeroboam I built a shrine at Bethel, near Judah's northern boundary (1 Kings 12:32). Amos denounced a prophet at the royal sanctuary there (Amos 7:10–17).

Bethlehem   A village about five miles south of Jerusalem, birthplace of David (1 Sam. 17:12) and the place where Samuel secretly anointed him king of Israel (1 Sam. 16:1–2; 20:6). According to Micah 5:2, it was to be the Messiah's birthplace, an idea that influenced the Gospel writers' accounts of Jesus' nativity (Matt. 2:5–6; Luke 2; John 7:42).

Beth-peor   An unidentified site east of the Jordan River in Moab, near which the Israelites camped before crossing Jordan and where Moses was buried (Deut. 3:29; 4:46; 34:6).

Bethsaida   A village on the north shore of the Sea of Galilee, the home of Peter, Andrew, and Philip (John 1:44; 12:21). In New Testament times, it consisted of an older Jewish section and a newer town, the capital of Philip the Tetrarch (see also Luke 10:13; Matt. 11:21).

Bildad   One of Job's three friends who dispute with him the meaning of his afflictions (Job 2:11; 8; 18; etc.).

Bithynia   In New Testament times, a Roman province in northern Asia Minor (modern Turkey) along the Black Sea coast and the location of several early Christian communities (Acts 16:7; 1 Pet. 1:1).

blasphemy   Speech defaming the Deity, a capital offense in Hebrew Bible times (1 Kings 21:9–13) and the charge the Sanhedrin levels against Jesus (Matt. 9:3; 26:65; John 10:36).

Boanerges   "Sons of thunder," an epithet Jesus applies to James and John (Mark 3:17; Luke 9:52–56).

Boaz   A wealthy landowner of Bethlehem (Ruth 2:1) who married the Moabite Ruth and became an ancestor of David (Ruth 4:22).

Book of the Covenant   The collection of statutes and commandments appearing in Exodus between the giving of the Decalogue and the ratification of the Sinai covenant (Exod. 20:18–23:33), it contains some of the oldest legal material in the Hebrew Bible. This compilation takes its title from Exod. 24:7, where Moses reads from the "book of the covenant."

Booths, Feast of   In ancient Israel, an autumn agricultural festival of thanksgiving during which the celebrants erected booths or shelters reminiscent of the wilderness encampments used during Israel's journey from Egypt to Canaan (Exod. 34:22); also known as the Feast of Tabernacles or Sukkoth (Lev. 23:39–44; Neh. 8:13–18).

Caesar   A hereditary name by which the Roman emperors commemorated Gaius Julius Caesar, great-uncle of Augustus (Octavian), the first emperor (Luke 2:1; 3:1; Mark 12:14; Acts 11:28; 25:11).

Caesarea   An important Roman city that Herod the Great built on the Palestinian coast about sixty-four miles northwest of Jerusalem and named in honor of Caesar Augustus. Caesarea was Pontius Pilate's administrative capital and later a Christian center (Acts 8:40; 10:1, 24; 18:22; 21:8). Paul was imprisoned there for two years (Acts 23:23–35; 24–26).

Caesarea Philippi   An inland city north of the Sea of Galilee built by Philip, son of Herod the Great (4 B.C.E.–34 C.E.), and named for the emperor Tiberius; the site of Peter's "confession" that Jesus was the Messiah (Mark 8:27; Matt. 16:13).

Caiaphas Joseph Caiaphas, high priest of Jerusalem during the reign of the emperor Tiberius (Matt. 26:3, 57–66; John 9:49; 18:13–28; Acts 4:6). Son-in-law to his immediate predecessor, Annas, he was appointed to the office by the procurator Valerius Gratus and presided over Jesus' trial before the Sanhedrin.

Cain According to the J source of Genesis, the first son of Adam and Eve, who slew his brother Abel, thus becoming the archetypal murderer and fugitive (Gen. 4). The "mark of Cain" is not a curse, but a sign that Yahweh protected him from his enemies.

Calah An ancient city on the Tigris, one of the early capitals of Assyria (Gen. 10:11–12).

Caleb Along with Joshua, one of the two spies sent to reconnoiter Canaan who brought back a favorable report of Israel's chances (Num. 13:14). For his trust in Yahweh, Caleb was allowed to enter Canaan, while all others of his generation died in the wilderness (Num. 13:30; 14:38).

Calvary The site outside Jerusalem's walls, exact location unknown, where Jesus was crucified (Luke 23:33). Calvary derives from the Latin word *calvaria,* a translation of the Greek *kranion,* meaning "skull"; Golgotha comes from the Aramaic for "skull" (Matt. 27:33; John 19:17).

Cana A town in Galilee where Jesus turned water into wine at a wedding feast (John 2:1–11) and healed a nobleman's son (John 4:46–54).

Canaan The Tanak name for the land of Palestine west of the Jordan River, from Egypt in the south to Syria in the north (Gen. 10:19). According to Hebrew tradition, Canaan was the territory promised to Abraham's descendants (Gen. 15:7–21; 17:1–8) and infiltrated by the Israelite tribes during the thirteenth and twelfth centuries B.C.E. (Num. 21; Josh. 1–24; Judg. 1–2).

canon A term derived from the Greek *kanon,* which may be related to the Semitic *qaneh,* a "reed," perhaps used as a measuring rod. In modern usage, a canon is a standard of measure by which a religious community judges certain writings to be authoritative, usually of divine origin. The Hebrew Bible alone is the canon of Judaism, whereas Christianity accepts both it (sometimes including the Apocrypha) and the Greek New Testament. The canon is thus an official list of books considered genuine, worthy to be used in teaching and liturgy, and hence binding in doctrine and morals. The adjective *extracanonical* refers to books not included in the official canon or list.

Capernaum The "village of Nahum," a small port on the northwest shore of the Sea of Galilee that Jesus used as headquarters for his Galilean ministry and where he performed many "mighty works" (Matt. 9:1, 9–11; Mark 1:21–29; 2:3–11; Luke 7; John 4:46–54).

Carchemish An important Hittite site in northern Syria that overlooked the main crossing of the Euphrates on the trade route from Assyria to the Mediterranean. In 605 B.C.E., Nebuchadnezzar II defeated the Egyptian forces of Pharaoh Necho II here (2 Chron. 35:20; Jer. 46:2), thus ending Egypt's last significant attempt to reassert its hegemony in the Near East and establishing Babylon as the dominant power.

Carmel The name (meaning "garden" or "orchard") of a hilly range along the western border of Asher (Josh. 19:26), extending from the hill country of Samaria to the Mediterranean where Mount Carmel projects into the sea. Sacred to Baal because of its lush vegetation, Carmel was the site of Elijah's contest with the Canaanite priests (1 Kings 18).

case law Law expressed in conditional terms: If such an act is committed, then such must be the punishment. This legal form characterizes ancient Near Eastern legal forms, including those found in Mosaic Law. *See also* legal procedures.

catholic epistles A term referring to seven short New Testament documents, most of which were addressed to no specific person or church and therefore were intended for catholic ("universal") use.

centurion A low-ranking officer in the Roman army in charge of a "century," or division of 100 men. A centurion named Cornelius became the first Gentile convert to Christianity (Acts 10).

Cephas A name meaning "stone" that Jesus bestowed upon Simon Peter (John 1:42).

Chaldea A Mesopotamian territory occupied by Semitic Arameans who founded the Neo-Babylonian Empire under Nabopolassar and his son Nebuchadnezzar, first in a brief line of Chaldean rulers (2 Kings 24:2; 25:4–13; Jer. 37:5–12). The Chaldeans were famous for their mastery of astronomy and astrology.

chaos The Greek term designating the original void or abyss that predated the world's creation; in the ancient Near East, it was typically portrayed as a vast dark waste of boundless sea out of which the cosmos was created.

Chedorlaomer   King of Elam, a country east of Babylonia on the Persian Gulf (Gen. 14).

Chemosh   The national god of Moab to whom children were sacrificed as burnt offerings (Num. 21:29; Jer. 48:7, 13, 46). King Solomon erected an altar to Chemosh (1 Kings 11:7) that was not dismantled until Josiah's reforms more than three centuries later (2 Kings 23:13). Like the Israelites, the Moabites ("people of Chemosh") attributed their country's defeats and failures to their deity's anger.

cherub, cherubim (pl.)   Mythological creatures — part bird, part human, part other animal — that were placed in pairs at each side of the mercy seat of the Tabernacle, and later in the innermost sanctuary of Solomon's Temple, to protect the sacred relics in the Ark of the Covenant (Exod. 25:18–22). Their images were also embroidered on the veil of the Temple (2 Chron. 3:14) and sculpted on a frieze around the Temple walls and on the bases of the "Molten sea" (1 Kings 6:23; 7:29; 1 Chron. 28:18; Heb. 9:5). Such winged creatures, with a lion's or ox's body, eagle's wings, and human face, were common in ancient Near Eastern art and have been found in Byblos, Nineveh, and elsewhere. Originally the guardians of divine beings, they were later identified with the angels of Yahweh's heavenly court.

Christ   From the Greek *Christos,* a translation of the Hebrew *Messiah,* meaning "anointed one," the term derives from the ancient practice of anointing kings at their coronation. The Messiah or Christ was to be a kingly descendant of David.

Christology   The theological discipline that deals with the nature of Jesus Christ, particularly his divinity, relation to the divine Father, and role in human redemption.

church   A term translating the Greek *ekklesia,* meaning "assembly of ones called out"; in New Testament usage, the community of believers in Jesus Christ. Individual churches or congregations make up the international church, which is conceived as the visible part of Christ's spiritual body (Matt. 16:18; 18:17; Eph. 5:27; 1 Tim. 3:15; 1 Cor. 12:12–27; Col. 1:18).

circumcision   An ancient Semitic operation in which the foreskin of eight-day-old males is removed as a ceremony of initiation into the religion and community of Israel. Circumcision is represented as beginning with Abraham (Gen. 17:10–14) or Moses (Exod. 4:24–46; see also Lev. 1:59; 2:21; 12:3). The question of whether to circumcise Gentile converts to the early Christian Church was an important source of dissension (Acts 15; Gal. 2).

Claudius   Fourth Roman emperor (41–54 c.e.), who expelled the Jews from Rome (Acts 11:28; 18:2).

Clement of Alexandria   A church leader (c. 190–200 c.e.) known for his scholarship, he wrote a letter preserving the text of Secret Mark.

Clement of Rome   A Roman bishop thought to have written (c. 95 c.e.) the letter of 1 Clement.

Code of Hammurabi   The compilation of Sumero-Babylonian laws inscribed on the basaltic Stele of Hammurabi (1728–1686 b.c.e.), founder of the first Babylonian Empire. A number of Hammurabi's statutes anticipate those of the biblical Torah.

codex   A manuscript book of an ancient biblical text, first used by Christians to replace the unwieldy scrolls on which the Scriptures were first recorded.

Codex Sinaiticus   An ancient Greek edition of the New Testament, which contains several books that supplement the central canon.

Colossae   An ancient Phrygian city situated on the south bank of the Lycus River in central Asia Minor, important for its position on the trade route between Ephesus and Mesopotamia (Col. 1:1–2; 4:13).

conquest of Canaan   The gradual occupation of Palestine during the thirteenth and twelfth centuries b.c.e. by previously nomadic Israelites, an idealized account of which is given in Joshua 1–24.

Constantine   Roman emperor (306–337 c.e.) who was converted to Christianity and whose rule began a period of state support for the early church. Constantine issued the Edict of Milan in 313 c.e., mandating general tolerance of Christianity. He also presided over the Council of Nicaea in 325 c.e., establishing a precedent for imperial leadership of the church.

Coptic   A term relating to the church or liturgical language of the Copts, a group reputedly descended from the ancient Egyptians who preserved an early form of Christianity. Using Greek letters to record the Egyptian language, Coptic editors produced the Nag Hammadi library (found in 1945), which includes, among other Christian documents, the only complete manuscript of the Gospel of Thomas.

Corinth   A cosmopolitan center of trade and commerce in ancient Greece, destroyed by the Romans in 146 b.c.e. but later rebuilt. Home of a large population of Hellenistic Jews, Corinth was later a Christian center established by the apostle Paul and his associates (Acts 18:24; 19:1; 1 and 2 Cor.).

Cornelius   A Roman centurion associated with the Jewish synagogue in Caesarea who became the first Gentile convert to Christianity (Acts 10 – 11).

cosmos   The Greek term for the ordered universe, a system characterized by structure, stability, and harmony.

Court History   Also called the *Succession Narrative,* it is the account of David's reign and Solomon's succession to Israel's throne, the narrative underlying 2 Samuel 9 – 24 and 1 Kings 1 – 2.

covenant   In Hebrew Bible terms: (1) an agreement or compact between individuals, such as Abraham and Abimelech (Gen. 21:27) or David and Jonathan (1 Sam. 18:3); (2) a promise Yahweh makes to certain people, such as Noah (Gen. 9:13) and Abraham (Gen. 15:18 – 21; 17:4 – 14); (3) a legal bond Yahweh forms with a chosen group, such as Israel, and the demands he makes in return. The Mosaic or Sinatic Covenant is that from which the Old "Testament" (a synonym for "covenant" or "contract") takes its name (Exod. 20 – 24; 34; Deut. 29; Josh. 24). In Christian terminology, Jesus introduced a "new covenant" at the Last Supper (Mark 14:22 – 25; Matt. 26:26 – 29, etc.) that Christians believe superseded the Mosaic Covenant and embraced believers of all nations (1 Cor. 11:25).

Covenant Code   A name given to the collection of ancient Hebrew laws found in Exodus 20:23 – 23:33, often called the Book of the Covenant (Exod. 24:7).

cult   The formalized religious practices of a people, particularly its system of veneration, public rites, and liturgies.

cult legend   The oral tradition explaining or validating the sacredness of a particular place or shrine, such as the Genesis stories about Jacob's mystical experiences at Bethel or Peniel.

cuneiform   A wedge-shaped writing that originated in ancient Sumer about 3000 B.C.E. and spread throughout Mesopotamia.

Cyrus the Great   Founder of the Persian Empire and conqueror of Babylon (539 B.C.E.) who liberated the Jews from captivity and decreed their return to Jerusalem to rebuild the Temple (2 Chron. 36:22 – 23; Ezra 1:1 – 8). Second Isaiah calls him Yahweh's "shepherd" (Isa. 44:28) and his "Anointed" or "Messiah" (Isa. 45:1).

D   *See* Deuteronomist.

Dagon   An ancient Canaanite agricultural deity worshiped by the Philistines at Ashdod and Gaza (1 Sam. 5:1 – 7) and whose Gaza temple reputedly was destroyed by Samson (Judg. 16:23 – 30).

Damascus   The capital of Syria and terminus of ancient caravan routes in the Fertile Crescent. Damascus was supposedly founded by Uz, grandson of Noah's son Shem (Gen. 5:32; 6:10; 10:23) and was visited by Abraham (Gen. 11:31; 12:4; 14:14). Paul's conversion to Christianity occurred near Damascus (Acts 9).

Dan   (1) Son of Jacob and Rachel's servant, Bilhah (Gen. 30:1 – 6). (2) One of the twelve tribes of Israel, which first occupied a small territory between Judah and Ephraim (Josh. 19:40 – 48) but later migrated north to an area close to the Jordan's source (Josh. 19:47; Judg. 1:34; 18). (3) A Danite city formerly known as Laish, where Jeroboam I later established a cult center (1 Kings 12:26 – 30). As the phrase "from Dan to Beersheba" (Judg. 20:1; 2 Sam. 24:2; 1 Kings 4:25; etc.) indicates, the city of Dan was regarded as the extreme northern boundary of Israel.

Danel   An ancient king whose name (Danel) appears in the *Ras Shamrah* epics and who was incorporated into the same tradition as Noah and Job (Ezek. 14:14; 28:3). He is not the same as the character in the Book of Daniel, who is referred to in no other canonical Hebrew Bible work.

Darius   The name of several Persian rulers mentioned in the Hebrew Bible. (1) Darius I (522 – 486 B.C.E.), son of Hystaspes, was the emperor whose forces invaded Greece and were defeated at Marathon (490 B.C.E.). He continued Cyrus the Great's favorable treatment of the Jews (Ezra 5 – 6). (2) Darius "the Mede" (Dan. 5:31; 9:1), alleged to have condemned Daniel to the lion's den (Dan. 6:7 – 26), is unknown to history.

Dathan   A Reubenite who rebelled with Korah against Moses and Aaron in the Sinai desert (Num. 16:1 – 35; 26:7 – 11).

David   Son of Jesse (Ruth 4:18 – 22), successor to Saul, and second king of the united twelve-tribe monarchy (1000 – 961 B.C.E.), David expanded Israel's boundaries to their greatest extent, founded a new administrative and religious capital at Jerusalem, and created a prosperous though short-lived Palestinian Empire. His story is told in 1 Samuel 16 through 1 Kings 2; the Chronicler gives an often unreliable, idealized version of his cultic activities (1 Chron. 2, 3, 10–29). So great was David's effectiveness and popularity, especially in retrospect, that he became the prototype of the Messiah figure, who was prophesied to be his descendant (Isa. 9:5–7; 11:1–16; Jer. 23:5; 30:9; Ezek. 34:23–31; etc.).

Day of Atonement (Yom Kippur)   A solemn, annual Jewish observance in which Israel's high priest offered blood sacrifices ("sin offerings") to effect a reconciliation between the Deity and his people (Lev. 16). The banishment of a "scapegoat" to which the priest had symbolically transferred the people's collective guilt climaxed the atonement rites (Lev. 16). The Day of Atonement marked the once-yearly entrance of the priest into the Temple's Holy of Holies. The author of Hebrews argues that these ceremonies foreshadowed the sacrificial death of Jesus and his ascension to the heavenly sanctuary (Heb. 9).

Deacon   Literally, a "servant," a term applied to one of the lower orders of the Christian ministry — in the early church, probably to the bishop's assistant.

Dead Sea   Known in biblical times as "the salt sea" (Gen. 14:3; Num. 34:3; Josh. 3:16; 12:3), the "sea of the plain [Arabah]" (Josh. 3:16; 12:3), and "the east sea" (Ezek. 47:18; Joel 2:20), this lake, forty-six miles long, was given its present name by Greeks in the second century B.C.E. Occupying a basin into which the Jordan River empties, and located in a geological fault zone that extends from Syria to the Gulf of Aqabah and thence into East Africa, it lies 1290 feet below sea level and has a depth of approximately 1200 feet, making it the lowest body of water in the world. With a saline content five times that of the ocean, it supports no fish or other forms of life.

Dead Sea Scrolls   Biblical and other religious manuscripts dating from the second century B.C.E. to the first century C.E., found in caves near Qumran on the northwest shore of the Dead Sea.

Deborah   A judge and prophetess who, with Barak, helped bring about Israel's victories over the Canaanite forces of Sisera (Judg. 4–5).

Decalogue   *See* Ten Commandments.

Delilah   A woman from Sorek whom the Philistines bribed to discover and betray the secret of Samson's strength (Judg. 16). Her name means "coquette" or "flirtatious."

demythologizing   The process of transforming ancient traditions about the gods and their activities into ostensibly historical narratives, such as the Bible writers' adaptations of Mesopotamian myths of creation and the Flood to create the Genesis creation and deluge accounts. In the process of demythologization, beliefs about the gods' heavenly council were changed to conform to later Israelite monotheism, with the older deities reduced to subordinate members of Yahweh's divine court (Job 1–2).

Deuterocanon   The fourteen books or parts of books found in the Greek Septuagint and later editions of the Latin Vulgate — such as Tobit, 1 and 2 Maccabees, and the Wisdom of Solomon — but not included in the Hebrew Bible or most Protestant Old Testaments that Roman Catholics and some others regard as forming a second or later canon. After the Council of Trent, the books of 1 and 2 Esdras and the Prayer of Manasseh were deleted from the deuterocanonical list. When Protestant editions of the Bible include these works, they are typically classed as Apocrypha.

Deutero-Isaiah   Also known as Second Isaiah, the name assigned to the anonymous prophet responsible for Chapters 40–55 of the Book of Isaiah and to the work itself.

Deuteronomic Reformation   The label that biblical scholars apply to King Josiah's reforms of the Jewish religion following 621 B.C.E. The name derives from the assumption that the law book found during Josiah's repairs of the Temple was a form of the Book of Deuteronomy (probably Deut. 12–26) and that the work's insistence on the centralization of Israel's cult at a single (undesignated) sanctuary inspired Josiah's sweeping destruction of all rival shrines (2 Kings 22–23).

Deuteronomist   The unknown writer who compiled and edited the present form of the Book of Deuteronomy. Some scholars believe that he added the introductory material (Deut. 1–11) and appendixes (Deut. 27–34) to the older deuteronomic code (Deut. 12–26).

Deuteronomistic History (DH)   The Book of Deuteronomy and the books of the Former Prophets (Joshua, Judges, Samuel, Kings) as compiled and revised from older sources by an anonymous author or editorial school deeply influenced by Deuteronomy's historical philosophy. The first edition was probably compiled late in Josiah's reign (c. 610 B.C.E.), and a second edition followed Jerusalem's destruction in 587 B.C.E. It was further edited during the Babylonian exile.

deutero-Pauline   New Testament books attributed to Paul but probably not written by him (e.g., Ephesians and the Pastorals).

devil   The English word commonly used to translate two Greek words with different meanings: (1) *diabolos*, "the accuser" (John 8:44); (2) *daimonion*, one of many evil spirits inhabiting the world, which were thought to cause disease, madness, and other afflictions (see Matt. 10:25; Mark 3:22; Luke 8; 11:14–16; etc.). In Revelation 12:9, the devil is identified with the Hebrew Satan and the serpent of Genesis.

Diana (of the Ephesians)   The Near Eastern form of the Greek goddess Artemis (whom the Romans identified with Diana) worshiped in Ephesus, which in Paul's time was the capital of the Roman province of Asia (Acts 19).

Diaspora   Literally, a "scattering," the term refers to the distribution of Jews outside their Palestinian homeland, such as the many Jewish communities established throughout the Greco-Roman world.

Didache   A two-part extracanonical work, also called the Teaching of the Twelve Apostles, that contains a manual of primitive church discipline that may date to apostolic times.

Dinah   The only daughter of Jacob, by his wife Leah, she was raped by Shechem, who wished to marry her. Insulted by the Canaanite prince's method of courting their sister, Dinah's brothers first deceived Shechem into having himself and his male kin circumcised, and then, while the Canaanites were in a vulnerable state, slaughtered his entire family, an act of treachery that Jacob protested (Gen. 34).

Dionysus   Ancient Greek god of wine, ecstasy, and emotional freedom, he was the son of Zeus and a mortal woman, Semele. Representing the natural cycle of life, death, and rebirth, he is killed, descends into the Underworld (Hades), and is resurrected to immortal life among the Olympian gods.

disciple   From the Greek word meaning "learner," the term is applied in the New Testament to followers of particular religious figures, such as Moses (John 9:28), John the Baptist (Luke 11:1; John 1:35), the Pharisees (Mark 2:18), or Jesus. Although it applies especially to the Twelve (Matt. 20:17), it also designates others who associated with Jesus (Matt. 14:26). Paul made numerous disciples "for Christ" (Acts 20:1, 7; 21:16).

divine council   The heavenly assembly of gods, a concept common throughout the ancient Near East.

In Israelite tradition, Yahweh presides as king of the council, surrounded by lesser divine beings who serve as his emissaries (Ps. 82; Job 1–2; Zech. 3).

documentary hypothesis   A scholarly theory associated with Julius Wellhausen that argues that the Pentateuch is not the work of one author but the result of many generations of anonymous writers, revisers, and editors (redactors) who produced the four main literary strands or components found in these five books: J (the Yahwist); E (the Elohist); D (the Deuteronomist); and P (the Priestly component).

Domitian   Roman emperor (81–96 C.E.), younger son of Vespasian, who ascended the throne following the death of his brother Titus. The Book of Revelation was written late in his reign.

doublet   A literary term denoting two or more versions, from different sources, of the same material (cf. Gen. 12:10–20; 20:1–18; 26:6–11; Exod. 3:1–20; 6:2–13; 20; Deut. 5; etc.).

doxology   In a religious writing or service, the formal concluding expression of praise or formula ritually ascribing glory to God.

dragon   A symbolic reptile derived from ancient Near Eastern mythology, related to the serpent in Eden (Gen. 3) and identified with the devil and Satan (Rev. 12). *See* Leviathan.

dualism   A philosophic or religious system that posits the existence of two parallel worlds, one of physical matter and the other of invisible spirit. Moral dualism views the universe as divided between powers of Good and Evil, Light and Dark, which contend for human allegiance.

E   *See* Elohist.

Ea   Babylonian god of wisdom, fresh water, and incantations (counterpart of the Sumerian Enki), he was a benefactor to humanity. In the Gilgamesh epic Ea warned Utnapishtim of Enlil's plans to drown the world in a flood and gave the man directions to build an ark and stock it with birds and animals.

Ebedmelech   The Ethiopian (Cushite) eunuch who rescued Jeremiah from the cistern where the prophet's enemies had left him to die (Jer. 38:1–13; 39:15–18).

Ebla   A large ancient Canaanite city (located in modern Syria), Ebla contained an extensive library of clay tablets inscribed in Mesopotamian cuneiform. Compiled during the late third millennium B.C.E., Ebla's archives predate the oldest biblical documents by 1000 years.

Eber The legendary ancestor of various Hebrew, Arab, and Aramean tribes (Gen. 10:24–30; 11:15; 1 Chron. 1:18); listed in the New Testament as an ancestor of Jesus (Luke 3:35).

Eden The gardenlike first home of humanity (Gen. 2:8); an earthly paradise from which the first couple was expelled (Gen. 3:24). See also Ezekiel 28:13, where the "king of Tyre" enjoyed an "Eden," possibly a lush forested region (Ezek. 31:18; 36:25; Isa. 51:3; Joel 2:3).

Edom In Hebrew Bible times, a region or country extending southward from the Dead Sea to the Gulf of Aqabah, bordered on the north by Moab, on the northwest by Judah, on the east and southeast by the Sinai desert (Num. 20:14–21; 2 Kings 3:20; etc.). It was also called "Seir" (Gen. 32:3; Num. 24:18; Judg. 5:4), identified with Esau (Gen. 36:1), and thought to be Yahweh's original homeland (Deut. 33:2; Judg. 5:4–5; Hab. 3:3). Famous for its wisdom tradition (Obad. 8; Jer. 49:7), Edom is the setting for the Job story and may have contributed the central ideas of that philosophical work.

Edomites According to Genesis, descendants of Jacob's twin brother, Esau, "who is Edom" (Gen. 36:1); a Semitic people who occupied the territory southeast of Judah and were among Israel's bitterest enemies (Judg. 11; 2 Kings 8:20–22; Ps. 137:7; Amos 1–2; 9; Ezek. 25:12–14; 35:1–15). The Edomites later infiltrated southern Judea, which in Hellenistic times was called Idumea (Mark 3:8).

Egypt Ancient nation centered along the Nile River southwest of Palestine, visited by Abraham (Gen. 12:10–20) and settled in by his Israelite descendants (Gen. 41–50) for a reputed 430 years (Exod. 12:40). Moses, raised at the Egyptian court, led the enslaved Israelites from Egypt in about 1280–1250 B.C.E. (Exod. 1–15). Many of Israel's classical prophets advised against turning to Egypt for political or military help (Isa. 30:1–7; 31:1; 36; Jer. 46; Hos. 7:11), although King Solomon had once made an alliance with the pharaohs (1 Kings 9:16–18, 24). Egyptian attempts to restore its hegemony in Palestine were finally ended at the Battle of Carchemish (605 B.C.E.), when Nebuchadnezzar of Babylon defeated Pharaoh Necho's troops.

Ehud The left-handed judge (military leader) from the tribe of Benjamin who murdered the obese Moabite king, Eglon, at Jericho and then led an Israelite army to rout the Moabite invaders (Judg. 3).

El, Elohim (pl.) A Semitic term for a divine being. In Canaanite religion, El was the high god, father of lesser deities. In the Hebrew Bible, El, when used as a name for the Israelite Deity, typically occurs as part of a phrase, such as El Shaddai (God of the Mountain), El Bethel (God of the House of God), or El Elyon (God Most High). In its plural form, the Hebrew generic term for deity applied to both their national God (Gen. 1:1; 2:5; etc.) and foreign deities (Exod. 15:2, 11).

Elam An ancient civilized center across the Persian Gulf from Sumer (now in Iran), supposedly founded by Elam, son of Shem (Gen. 10:22). Chedorlaomer, king of Elam, headed several Babylonian states (Gen. 14:1–11). Elamites later helped Assyria invade Judah (Isa. 11:11; 22:6).

Eleazar (1) The third son of Aaron, a chief of the Levites, who succeeded his father as High Priest (Exod. 6:23; Num. 3:2, 32; 20:25–29; Josh. 14:1). (2) In 2 Maccabees, the aged "teacher of the Law" who was bludgeoned to death for refusing to eat pig's flesh (2 Macc. 6:18–31).

Eli In 1 Samuel 2:22–4:18, an ineffectual judge and priest at Shiloh under whose jurisdiction young Samuel served (1 Sam. 3:1).

Elihu A young man who condemns Job's alleged self-righteousness (Job 32–37).

Elijah Literally, "Yahweh is my God"; a fiercely Yahwist prophet from the northern kingdom whose anti-Baalism and attacks on Ahab's dynasty had a tremendous impact on Israel's political course during the ninth century B.C.E. and who shaped his nation's prophetic traditions for centuries thereafter (1 Kings 17–19; 21; 2 Kings 1–2). Reportedly carried to heaven in a fiery chariot (2 Kings 2:1–13), he was expected to reappear shortly before the Day of Yahweh arrived (Mal. 4:5–6). Although some Christian writers identified John the Baptist with Elijah (Luke 1:17; Mark 9:12–13), some contemporaries viewed Jesus as Elijah returned (Mark 9:28; 16:14). Along with Moses, Elijah appears in Jesus' Transfiguration (Mark 9:4; Matt. 17:3; Luke 9:30).

Eliphaz The most moderate and restrained of Job's critics (Job 4, 8, 15, 22–24, etc.).

Elizabeth A Levite, wife of the priest Zechariah, and mother of John the Baptist (Luke 1).

Elisha   A ninth-century c.e. prophet in the northern kingdom, successor to Elijah (1 Kings 19:15–21; 2 Kings 2:1–15). Like his predecessor, Elisha was a clairvoyant who worked numerous miracles, including the resuscitation of a dead child (2 Kings 4:18–37; 6:32–7:2; 8:7–13; 13:14–19). So great was his prestige that he not only brought an end to the Omri–Ahab–Jezebel dynasty in Israel by having the upstart Jehu anointed king (2 Kings 9:1–13) but also made Hazael king of Syria (2 Kings 8:7–15).

Elohim   *See* El.

Elohist   The scholarly term designating the anonymous author or compiler responsible for the E document or tradition in the Pentateuch. The name arose from his characteristic use of *Elohim* to denote the Hebrew Deity.

El Shaddai   Although commonly translated "God Almighty," this term probably means "God of the Mountain," referring to the Mesopotamian cosmic "mountain" inhabited by divine beings. One of the patriarchal names for the Mesopotamian tribal god, it is identified with Yahweh in the Mosaic revelation (Exod. 6:3). Except for a few occurrences in Job (5:17; 8:5; etc.), Isaiah (13:6), and Ezekiel (10:5), it appears chiefly in the Pentateuch (Gen. 17:1; 28:3; 35:11; 43:14; 48:3; Exod. 6:3; etc.). *Shaddai* alone appears in Ruth (1:20–21) and Job (13:3; 20:15–20; 31:2; 40:2; etc.).

Emmaus   A village (site unknown) near Jerusalem, along the road to which the resurrected Jesus appeared to several disciples (Luke 24:13–32).

Endor   Literally, "fountain of habitation"; a small town southeast of Nazareth, remembered for its medium whom King Saul solicited (1 Sam. 28:7–25).

Enoch   A son of Cain (Gen. 4:17, J's account) or of Jared (Gen. 5:18, P's version) and father of Methuselah (Gen. 5:21). P's statement that "God took him" (Gen. 5:24)—apparently to heaven and without death—strongly influenced later Hebrew notions of immortality and gave rise to a whole body of pseudepigraphal literature in which Enoch is a model of divine wisdom.

Enuma Elish   The Babylonian creation epic that takes its name from the opening phrase (in Akkadian), "when above."

Epaphras   An early Christian of Colossae who reported on the Colossian church to the imprisoned Paul (Col. 1:7; 4:12; Philem. 23).

Epaphroditus   A Macedonian Christian from Philippi who assisted Paul in prison (Phil. 2:25–27).

Ephesus   A wealthy Hellenistic city, later capital of the Roman province of Asia, site of the famous temple of Artemis (Diana) (Acts 19–20). Ephesus is frequently mentioned in various Pauline and deutero-Pauline letters (1 Cor. 16:19; 2 Cor. 12:14; 13:1; 1 Tim. 3:1; 2 Tim. 4:12; etc.). The author of Revelation (Rev. 2:1–7) judged the church there favorably. Later Christian traditions made it the site of the Virgin's assumption to heaven and the final ministry of the apostle John.

Ephod   An apronlike garment worn by the high priest Aaron and his successors (Exod. 28).

Ephraim   (1) Son of Joseph and Asenath (daughter of the priest Potipherah) and adopted by Jacob (Gen. 48:1–20). (2) The Israelite territory occupied by the tribe of Ephraim, bordered on the south by Dan and Benjamin, on the west by the Mediterranean, on the north by Manasseh, and on the east by the Jordan Rift Valley. Shechem (Josh. 21:20) was its most important city and served as an early capital of the northern kingdom (1 Kings 12:1). (3) The half-tribe of Ephraim, along with Manasseh, was one of the twelve tribes. After the ten northern tribes seceded (922 b.c.e.) from the Davidic union, Ephraim became dominant in Israel and was commonly used as a synonym for the whole ten-tribe nation.

Epicureanism   A Greco-Roman philosophy founded by Epicurus that advocated avoiding pain and pursuing intellectual rather than sensual pleasure. Epicurus taught that the universe is entirely physical, including the human soul, which perishes at death.

epiphany   An appearance or manifestation, particularly of a divine being; typically sudden and accompanied by dramatic natural effects (Exod. 3, 6, 19, 24; Isa. 6; Job 38–42; etc.).

epistle   A formal letter intended for a wide public audience rather than for a specific group or individual.

Epistle of Barnabas   Ascribed to Barnabas, Paul's senior fellow missionary to the Gentiles, this apocryphal second-century document emphasizes the differences between Judaism and Christianity. It once stood on the fringes of the New Testament canon.

eponym   The person from whom a people or group is reputed to have taken its name (Gen. 36:1).

Erech (Uruk)   An ancient Sumerian city, home of the legendary King Gilgamesh.

Esarhaddon   Son of the Assyrian emperor Sennacherib, Esarhaddon ruled from about 680 to 669 B.C.E., despoiled Tyre and Sidon, colonized Samaria, and reputedly took Manasseh, king of Judah, captive to Babylon (2 Kings 19:37; Isa. 37:38; 2 Chron. 33:11; Ezra 4:2).

Esau   Firstborn son of Isaac and Rebekah, twin brother of Jacob (Gen. 25:25–34), Esau gave up his birthright to his cleverer sibling (Gen. 27–28), thus becoming the prototype of the person who is insensitive to his heritage (Heb. 12:16). He was thought of as the progenitor of the Edomites, traditional enemies of Jacob's descendants (Israel) (Gen. 36).

eschatology   From the Greek, meaning a "study of last things," eschatology is a doctrine or theological concept about the ultimate destiny of humanity and the universe. Having both a personal and a general application, it can refer to (1) beliefs about the individual soul following death, including divine judgment, heaven, hell, and resurrection; or (2) larger concerns about the fate of the cosmos, such as events leading to the Day of Yahweh, the final battle between supernatural Good and Evil, judgment of the nations, and the establishment of the Deity's universal sovereignty. In Christian terms, it involves the Parousia (return of Christ), the chaining of Satan, introduction of the millennium, and so on. Apocalyptic works like Daniel, Revelation, 2 Esdras, and the books of Enoch typically stress eschatological matters.

Essenes   According to Josephus, one of the three major sects of first-century C.E. Judaism. Semi-ascetic in nature, the Essenes were spiritual descendants of the hasidim (meaning "pious") who had resisted Antiochus IV's attempts to destroy the Jewish religion. Their apocalyptic convictions and certain of their rituals akin to baptism have suggested to some scholars that they were an influence on such representative pre-Christian figures as John the Baptist. They are commonly identified with the Qumran community, which produced the Dead Sea Scrolls.

Esther   Heroine of the canonical book bearing her name, cousin and adopted daughter of Mordecai (Esther 2:15), queen of Persia under Xerxes (Esther 1:1–2:18), Esther became a national heroine by delivering her people from a mass slaughter planned by Haman (Esther 2:19–4:17). The Book of Esther commemorates the Feast of Purim (Esther 9:17–10:3).

Ethiopia   An area of northeast Africa (Abyssinia), which the Hebrews called Cush or Kush, supposedly settled by a son of Ham (Gen. 10:6–8). Classical writers mention a line of Ethiopian queens named Candace, one of whom is cited in Acts 8:27.

etiology   Literally, a statement of causes or origins; in literary terms, a narrative created to explain the origin or meaning of a social practice, topographical feature, ritual, or other factor that arouses the storyteller's interest.

Eucharist   From the Greek work for "gratitude" or "thanksgiving," Eucharist is a name for the Christian ceremony of consecrated bread and wine that Jesus initiated at the Last Supper (Mark 14:22–25; Matt. 26:26–29; etc.).

Euphrates River   The longest river of southwest Asia; one of the four streams of Eden (Gen. 2:14), the Euphrates was the extreme northeastern border of Israel's kingdom at its height (2 Sam. 8:3; 10:16; 1 Kings 4:24).

Eusebius   A Christian scholar (c. 260–339 C.E.) famous for his *History of the Church* (through about 323 C.E.) and forty other works, including a biography of Constantine, the first Christian emperor, whom Eusebius served as chief theological adviser. Born in Palestine, where he spent most of his life, Eusebius was also bishop of Caeserea and a major participant at the Council of Nicaea.

Evangelist   From the Greek *evangelion*, "good news"; the writer of a Gospel.

Eve   The first woman, wife of Adam, who derived her name from the Hebrew verb "to live" because she was "the mother of all those who live" (Gen. 3:30). Paul's interpretation of her role in the fall of humanity is given in 2 Corinthians 11:3. (See also 1 Tim. 2:11–15.)

Evil-merodach   Son and successor of Nebuchadnezzar who reputedly treated well Judah's captive monarch Jehoiachin (2 Kings 25:27–30; Jer. 52:31–34). The name means "man of Marduk."

exegesis   A literary term denoting close analysis and interpretation of a text to discover the original author's exact intent and meaning. Once this has been established, later interpretations may also be considered.

exile   Period during which the Jews were captive in Babylon (587–538 B.C.E.).

Exodus   A Greek term meaning "a going out" or "departure." In the Hebrew Bible, it refers to the escape of Israelite slaves from Egypt under Moses' leadership (c. 1280–1250 B.C.E.), an event the Hebrews regarded as Yahweh's crucial saving act in their history (Exod. 15; 20:1–2; Deut. 5:6; Josh. 24:1–13; Ps. 105:26–39; Amos 2:10; etc.).

exorcism   The act or practice of expelling a demon or evil spirit from a person or place (Tob. 8:1–3; Mark 1:23–27, 32–34; 5:1–20; Matt. 8:28–34; Acts 19:13–19; etc.).

expiation   In religious terms, the act of making atonement for sin, usually by offering a sacrifice to appease divine wrath (Lev. 16).

Ezekiel   A major prophet of the sixth century B.C.E., exiled to Babylon, who was distinguished by his strange visions and priestly concerns. The name means "God strengthens."

Ezra (Esdras)   A postexilic Jewish priest who returned to Jerusalem from Babylon during the reign of the Persian Emperor Artaxerxes (Ezra 7:1) to promulgate the Mosaic Torah and supervise a reformation of the Jewish religion (Neh. 8–10; Ezra 7–10). His influence on later Judaism was so great that he was conceived as the re-creator of the Hebrew Bible and author of several pseudohistorical and apocalyptic works (1 Esd. 8–9; 2 Esd. 14).

faith   In biblical terms, the quality of trust, reliance on, and fidelity to God. Both the New Testament and the Greek translation of the Hebrew Bible use two terms (*pistis, pisteuein*) to express the concept, which reaches its fullest development in Paul's doctrine of salvation through trust in the saving power of Christ (Rom. 10:17; Gal. 3:5–29, 5:6, etc.).

Fall, the   In some Christian theologies, a term that denotes humanity's loss of innocence and divine favor through Adam's sin of disobedience (Gen. 3). According to some interpretations of Pauline thought (Rom. 5:12–21; 1 Cor. 15:45–49), the primal human sin resulted in the transmission of death and a proclivity toward depravity and evil to the entire human race. As a medieval rhyme expressed it, "In Adam's fall, we sinned all." Despite the emphasis given the Fall by some theologians, such as Augustine, the Yahwist's account of Adam's behavior is never mentioned again in the Hebrew Bible.

Fast of the Ninth Av   A solemn observance mourning the two destructions of the Jerusalem Temple, the first by the Babylonians (587 B.C.E.) and the second by the Romans (70 C.E.), both in the month of Av (August). The dirges in the Book of Lamentations are read to commemorate the sanctuary's dual fall.

Feast of Dedication   An eight-day Jewish celebration (now known as Hanukkah) instituted in 165 B.C.E. by Judas Maccabeus and held annually on the twenty-fifth day of Kislev (November-December) to commemorate the cleansing and rededication of the Jerusalem Temple, which Antiochus IV had polluted. Referred to in John 10:22–38, it is also known as the Festival of Lights.

Feast of Tabernacles   Also called the Festival of Booths, it was a joyous annual celebration of the autumn harvest (late September–early October). Commemorating the Mosaic period when Israel dwelt in tents or huts (booths) in the wilderness, it expressed the people's gratitude to Yahweh for supplying them with grain and wine (Exod. 23:16; 34:22; Lev. 23:39–43; Deut. 16:13–15). *See* Succoth.

Fertile Crescent   The name by which James H. Breasted designated the arch or semicircle of fertile territory stretching from the Persian Gulf on the northeast to Egypt on the southwest and including Mesopotamia, Syria, and Palestine.

Festus, Porcius   The procurator of Judea whom Nero appointed to succeed Felix and through whom Paul appealed to be tried by Caesar's court in Rome (Acts 24:27–26:32).

firmament   The Hebrew Bible term for the vault or arch of the sky that separated the earthly oceans from the heavenly ocean of rain-giving clouds and in which Elohim placed the sun, moon, and stars (Gen. 1:6–8, 16–20; 7:11; 2 Sam. 22:8; 2 Kings 7:2; Pss. 24:2; 78:23; 104:2, 5; Job 26:11; 27:18).

Flavius Josephus   *See* Josephus, Flavius.

Flood, the   The global deluge of Noah's day (Gen. 6:5–8:22), based on ancient Mesopotamian flood stories akin to that found in the *Epic of Gilgamesh* and later used as a prototype of world judgment and destruction (Matt. 24:36–41; Luke 17:26–30; 2 Pet. 2:5; 3:5–7).

form criticism   An English rendition of the German *Formsgeschichte,* a method of biblical criticism that attempts to isolate, classify, and analyze individual units or characteristic forms contained in a literary text and to identify the probable preliterary form of these units before their incorporation into the written text. Form criticism also attempts to discover the setting in life (*Sitz-im-Leben*) of each unit — that is, the historical, social, religious, and cultural environment from which it developed — and to trace or reconstruct the process by which various traditions evolved from their original oral state to their final literary form.

fundamentalism   A largely North American Protestant movement, beginning about the turn of the twentieth century, that affirmed the literal factuality of all biblical statements and rejected post-Enlightenment questioning of biblical infallibility.

Gabriel   In the Hebrew angelic hierarchy, one of the seven archangels whose duty it was to convey the Deity's messages. Gabriel explained Daniel's visions to him (Dan. 8:15–26; 9:20–27) and, in the New Testament, announced the births of John the Baptist and Jesus (Luke 1:5–17; 26–38). The name may mean "person of God" or "God has shown himself mighty."

Gad   (1) Firstborn son of Jacob and Zilpah (Gen. 30:1–11; 35:26), Gad was the eponymous ancestor of the Israelite tribe of Gad (Num. 2:14) whose territory was located northeast of the Dead Sea, east of the Jordan River (Num. 32; Deut. 3:16–20). Gad joined the revolt against Rehoboam and was part of the ten-tribe northern kingdom. (2) A prophet at David's court (1 Sam. 22:5; 2 Sam. 24; 1 Chron. 21; 2 Chron. 29:25, 29).

Gadara   A Hellenistic city belonging to the Decapolis (ten-member league of Greek cities in Palestine), where Jesus exorcised a demoniac (Mark 5:1–20; Matt. 8:28–34; Luke 8:26–39).

Galatia   A region in the interior of Asia Minor (Turkey) settled by Gauls; in New Testament times, a Roman province visited by Paul and his associates (Acts 16:6; 18:23; 1 Cor. 16:1; Gal. 1:2; 1 Pet. 1:1).

Galilee   From the Hebrew term *Galil ha-goyim*, meaning "circle of Gentiles," the name given northern Palestine lying west of the Jordan, an area originally assigned to the tribes of Ashur, Zebulun, and Naphtali, who failed to evict the Canaanites living there (Josh. 19; Judg. 1, 4, 5). The region where Jesus grew up (Matt. 2:23; Luke 2), Galilee was then under Roman control but administered by the tetrarch Herod Antipas (4 B.C.E.–39 C.E.) (Luke 23:5–7).

Galilee, Sea of   The major body of fresh water in northern Palestine and source of livelihood to many Galilean fishermen, such as Peter, Andrew, and John (Matt. 4:18–22). The towns and fields along its shores were the site of many of Jesus' public discourses and miracles (Mark 6:30–52, etc.) and of a resurrection appearance as well (John 21:1–14).

Gallio   A proconsul of Achaia (the Roman province of Greece) who dismissed charges brought against Paul by Corinthian Jews (Acts 18:12–17), Gallio was a brother of Seneca, the Stoic philosopher.

Gamaliel   A leading Pharisee, scholar, member of the Sanhedrin (Acts 5:34), reputed teacher of Paul (Acts 22:3), and exponent of the liberal wing of the Pharisaic party developed by his grandfather Hillel, Gamaliel persuasively argued for a policy of toleration toward the new religion preached by Peter and other apostles (Acts 5:38–40).

Gath   Of the Philistines' five major cities, the one nearest to Hebrew territory (Josh. 13:3; 1 Sam. 17; 27; etc.).

Gaza   The southernmost of the Philistines' five principal cities (Josh. 13:3) where Samson destroyed the temple of Dagon (Judg. 16). During the Israelite monarchy, Gaza marked the southernmost boundary of Judah (1 Kings 4:24).

Gehenna   New Testament name for the "Valley of the Son [or Children] of Hinnom" that bordered Jerusalem on the south and west and was the site of human sacrifices to Molech and other pagan gods (Jer. 7:32; Lev. 18:21; 1 Kings 11:7; 2 Chron. 28:3; 33:6). Later used as a dump in which to burn garbage, it became a symbol of punishment in the afterlife and is cited as such by Jesus (Matt. 5:22; 10:28–29; 18:8; 25:30, 46; etc.).

Gemara   The second part of the Talmud; an extensive commentary, in Aramaic, on the Hebrew Mishnah.

Gentile   Someone who is not a Jew, an uncircumcised person, one belonging to "the nations" (Ps. 9:17; Isa. 2:2; Zeph. 2:1; Hag. 2:7; Matt. 1:11; 12:21; Luke 21:24; etc.).

Gethsemane   The site of a garden or orchard on the Mount of Olives where Jesus took his disciples after the Last Supper; the place where he was arrested (Matt. 26:36–56; Mark 14:32–52; Luke 22:39–53; John 18:1–14).

Gibeah   A small hill town in the territory of Benjamin, prominent in the eleventh century B.C.E. because it was the home of Saul (1 Sam. 10:26) and the first capital of the united monarchy (1 Sam. 13–14; 2 Sam. 21:6).

Gibeon   A city of the Hivites (Horites) (Josh. 9:17; 11:19), whose people deceived Joshua into making a treaty of protection with them (Josh. 9–10), Gibeon became an Israelite cult center (2 Sam. 21:1–9; 1 Kings 3:4–5; 1 Chron. 16:39–40; 2 Chron. 1:3, 13; etc.).

Gideon   Also called *Jerubbaal* (let Baal plead), a military judge who delivered Israel from the Midianites (Judg. 6 – 8). Although Gideon refused to accept a crown (Judg. 8:22 – 32), his son Abimelech reigned for three years at Shechem (Judg. 9).

Gilboa   A prominent hill on the west side of the Jordan Valley, site of the battle in which the Philistine armies defeated King Saul and killed three of his sons, including Jonathan, thus clearing the way for David to mount Israel's throne (1 Sam. 31; 2 Sam. 1).

Gilead   A rugged highland in central Transjordan located between the Yarmuk and Arnon rivers (Josh. 13; Jer. 8:22; 46:11).

Gilgal   The name of several Israelite towns, including one located southeast of Jericho where Joshua erected twelve stones symbolic of Israel's twelve tribes (Josh. 4:1 – 9, 20); the site of the confirmation of Saul's kingship (1 Sam. 11:15; 13:4 – 15); and a cultic center in southwest Samaria associated with a school of prophets, particularly Elijah and Elisha (2 Kings 2:1 – 4; 4:38).

Gilgamesh   Legendary king of Uruk, hero of the Sumero-Babylonian *Epic of Gilgamesh,* fragments of which date from shortly after 3000 B.C.E., describing his adventures battling Evil and searching for immortality. The Babylonian version incorporates a story of the Flood narrated by Gilgamesh's ancestor Utnapishtim.

glossolalia   A religious phenomenon in which a person is inspired to speak in a language not his own. In Acts 2, this emotional "speaking in (foreign) tongues" symbolizes the multinational nature of the early Christian movement.

Gnosticism   A movement in early Christianity which taught that salvation was gained through special knowledge (*gnosis*) revealed through a spiritual savior (presumably Jesus) and was the property of an elite few who had been initiated into its mysteries. Gnosticism became a major heresy in the primitive church, though little is now known about its precise tenets.

Gog   The term Ezekiel uses to depict a future leader of Israel's enemies (Ezek. 38) whose attack on the Jerusalem sanctuary will precipitate Yahweh's intervention and the ultimate destruction of the wicked (Rev. 20:8).

golden calf   (1) An image that the apostate Israelites fashioned out of gold jewelry and other treasures taken from Egypt and that, under Aaron's direction, they worshiped as their deliverer from slavery (Exod. 32:1 – 6; Deut. 9:16). (2) Two calf images that

Jeroboam I set up at Bethel and Dan as rivals to the Jerusalem sanctuary were probably not revered as idols in themselves but as visible pedestals of the invisibly enthroned Yahweh (1 Kings 12:29).

Goliath   The Philistine giant from Gath whom the young David defeated with a slingshot (1 Sam. 17; 2 Sam. 21:19).

Goshen   An area in northeastern Egypt where Jacob and his clan settled to escape a Near Eastern famine (Gen. 46:28 – 34; 47:5 – 12).

Gospel   (1) The Christian message — literally, "good news." (2) The name applied to the literary form of the religious biographies of Jesus, especially Matthew, Mark, Luke, and John.

Gospel of Peter   An early noncanonical Gospel ascribed incorrectly to Peter. This Gospel, which may date from as early as the first century C.E., is the only Gospel that depicts Jesus' actual rising from the tomb during the Resurrection.

Gospel of Thomas   A Gnostic collection of approximately 114 sayings attributed to Jesus and allegedly the work of his disciple Didymus Judas Thomas. Although found in Egypt in 1945 as part of a thirteen-volume work containing forty-nine Coptic-language books dating from the fourth and fifth centuries C.E., it may have been written as early as the last part of the first century C.E.

Habakkuk   A prophet of the late seventh or early sixth century B.C.E., perhaps a Levitical temple musician (Hab. 1:1; 3:1, 19), and presumed author of the book bearing his name.

Habiru   An ancient Near Eastern term designating people or clans who were outside the urban social and legal structure. The Habiru appear to have been nomads who raided the settled populations during the Amarna period (fourteenth century B.C.E.) in Palestine. The biblical Hebrews may have been related to this group.

Hades   The Greek term for the Underworld, abode of the dead, named for Zeus's brother Hades, god of the nether regions. In the Septuagint Bible, it is used to translate *Sheol,* the Hebrew word for the gloomy subterranean place where all the dead, good and evil alike, were eternally housed (Gen. 42:38; 1 Sam. 2:6; Job 7:9; Ps. 6:5; Prov. 27:20; Eccles. 9:10; Isa. 38:18; etc.). In the New Testament, *Hades* is also the usual term for the Underworld, although *Gehenna* (often translated "hell") is cited as the place of punishment

(Matt. 5:22, 29, 30; 16:18; Mark 9:43, 45, 47; Luke 12:5; Acts 2:31; Rev. 1:18, 20:14; etc.).

Hagar   In Genesis 16, Sarah's Egyptian handmaiden, who bears Abraham's first son, Ishmael. In Genesis 21, the jealous Sarah persuades Abraham to drive Hagar and Ishmael into the wilderness, whence an angel rescues them.

haggadah   Jewish narrative writings dating from the early centuries C.E. that illustrate and interpret the nonlegal portions of the Torah (law).

Haggai   A postexilic prophet who, with his contemporary Zechariah, urged the restored community of Jerusalem to rebuild the Temple (520 B.C.E.).

Hagiographa   A Greek term, meaning "sacred writings," that applies to the third major division of the Hebrew Bible (the Kethuvim), encompassing books of poetry, wisdom, late historical texts (Chronicles-Ezra), and the apocalypse of Daniel.

halakah   A collection of Jewish interpretations and applications of the Mosaic Law dating from the early centuries C.E.; a part of the legal sections of the Talmud.

Ham   According to Genesis, a son of Noah (Gen. 5:32; 6:10; 7:13; 9:18, 22) and the father of Canaan (Gen. 9:22), Ham was considered the progenitor of various nations in Phoenicia, Africa, and West Arabia (1 Chron. 8). "The land of Ham" is usually taken to be Egypt (Pss. 78:51; 105:23; etc.).

Haman   An official at Ahasuerus's (Xerxes') court who attempted to engineer the mass extermination of the Jews (Esther 3, 7).

Hammurabi   Sixth king of Babylon's First Dynasty (1728–1686 B.C.E.) and founder of the first Amorite Empire in Mesopotamia. Hammurabi is best remembered for his law code, inscribed on an eight-foot stone monument in Akkadian cuneiform, whose legal forms resemble those of Hebraic covenant law. *See* Code of Hammurabi.

Hannah   Wife of Elkanah and mother of Samuel (1 Sam. 1). Hannah's lyric prayer (1 Sam. 2:1–10) anticipates the Magnificat of Mary (Luke 1:42–45).

Hanukkah   *See* Feast of Dedication.

Haran   An ancient trade center in northwestern Mesopotamia, about sixty miles above the confluence of the Belikh and Euphrates rivers, Haran was the site of an important moon cult and of Abraham's call to follow Yahweh (Gen. 11:28–12:5, 24). The last refuge of the Assyrians, it was destroyed by the Medes about 606 B.C.E. (Zeph. 2:13–15; Nah. 3:1–3).

hasidim   Devout Jews who refused to forsake their religion during the persecutions of the Syrian monarch Antiochus Epiphanes (second century B.C.E.).

Hasmoneans   The Jewish royal dynasty founded by the Maccabees and named for Hasmon, an ancestor of Mattathias. The Roman conquest of Palestine in 63 B.C.E. brought Hasmonean rulership and Jewish independence to an end.

Hazael   An Aramean official of Damascus who murdered his king, Ben-hadad II, at the prophet Elisha's instigation (2 Kings 8:7–15; see also 1 Kings 19:15–18), usurped the Syrian kingship, and despoiled parts of Israel and Judah (Amos 1:3; 2 Kings 12; 2 Chron. 22). The name means "God sees."

Hebrew   (1) A member or descendant of one of a group of northwestern Semitic peoples, including the Israelites, Edomites, Moabites and Ammonites. According to Genesis 10:21–31 and 11:15, the Hebrews were descended from Eber, great-grandson of Shem (1 Chron. 1:18; Luke 3:35), and apparently belonged to an Aramean (ancient Syrian) branch of Semites who had originally migrated from Arabia. The Israelites' Aramean ancestry is referred to in the famous creed of Deuteronomy 26:5 (see also Gen. 25:20; 28:5). (2) The Semitic language spoken by the Israelites.

Hebron   An ancient city nineteen miles southwest of Jerusalem (Num. 13:22), located near the sacred oaks of Mamre associated with Abraham (Gen. 13:18; 18; 35:27), and one of the oldest continuously inhabited sites in Palestine.

Heilsgeschichte   A term from German biblical scholarship, usually translated as "sacred history" or "salvation history," which refers to the fact that Hebrew Bible writers told Israel's story not as an objective series of events, but as a confession of faith that their God was operating through the history of his chosen people, directing events in order to save them, or at least those faithful to their covenant relationship.

Hel   In Germanic and Icelandic myth, the goddess of the Underworld who ruled over the subterranean abode of the dead. She is the daughter of Loki, the Norse trickster god, and Angrboda, a giantess. She lends her name to the Christian concept of a posthumous place of torment. *See* Gehenna.

Hellenism   The influence and adoption of Greek thought, language, values, and culture that began with Alexander the Great's conquest of the eastern

Mediterranean world and intensified under his Hellenistic successors and various Roman emperors.

Hellenists   Jews living outside Palestine who adopted the Greek language and, to varying degrees, Greek customs and ideas (Acts 6:1; 9:29).

henotheism   The worship of a single god with a belief that other gods exist. Psalm 82 appears to represent a henotheistic stage of Israelite religion, as do such passages as the victory song in Exodus 15.

heresy   Holding or teaching a religious opinion contrary to church dogma. Applied to Christianity by its detractors (Acts 24:14), the term was not generally used in its modern sense during New Testament times except in the pastoral epistles (1 Tim. 1:3; 2; Titus 3:10).

hermeneutics   Study of the methodology of applying the principles and rules of interpreting a biblical text; especially, applying the results of such analysis to a contemporary situation, as one might apply the message of Hosea to modern problems of monogamy and religious faith.

Herod   The name of seven Palestinian rulers.

1. Herod I (the Great), the Idumean Roman-appointed king of Judea (40–4 B.C.E.), was ruling when Jesus was born (Matt. 2:1). An able administrator who completely reconstructed the Jerusalem Temple, he was notorious for reputed cruelty and was almost universally hated by the Jews.
2. Herod Antipas, son of Herod I, tetrarch of Galilee (Luke 3:1) and Perea (4 B.C.E.–39 C.E.), is frequently mentioned in the New Testament. Jesus, who called him "that fox" (Luke 13:31–32) and regarded him as a malign influence (Mark 8:15), was tried before him (Luke 9:7, 9; 23:7–15). Antipas was also responsible for executing John the Baptist (Matt. 14:1–12).
3. Herod Archelaus, ethnarch of Judea, Samaria, so misruled his territory that he was recalled to Rome, an event to which Jesus apparently refers in Luke 19:12–27. Archelaus's evil reputation caused Joseph and Mary to avoid Judea and settle in Nazareth (Matt. 2:22–23).
4. Herod, a son of Herod the Great and half-brother to Herod Antipas (Matt. 14:3; Mark 6:17).
5. Herod Philip II, son of Herod the Great and half-brother of Herod Antipas, ruled portions of northeastern Palestine and rebuilt the city of Caesarea Philippi near Mount Hermon (Luke 3:1).
6. Herod Agrippa I, son of Aristobulus and grandson of Herod the Great, ingratiated himself at the imperial court in Rome and, under Claudius, was made king over most of Palestine (41–44 C.E.). A persecutor of Christians, he reportedly died a horrible death immediately after accepting divine honors (Acts 12:1–23).
7. Herod Agrippa II, son of Herod Agrippa I and great-grandson of Herod the Great, was the first king of Chalcis (50 C.E.) and then of the territory formerly ruled by Philip the Tetrarch, as well as of the adjoining area east of Galilee and the upper Jordan. This was the Herod, together with his sister Bernice, before whom Paul appeared at Caesarea (Acts 25:13–26:32).

Herodians   The name applied to members of an influential political movement in first-century C.E. Judaism who supported Herod's dynasty, particularly that of Herod Antipas. Opposing messianic hopes (Mark 3:6), they conspired with the Pharisees to implicate Jesus in disloyalty to Rome (Mark 12:13; Matt. 22:16).

Herodias   Granddaughter of Herod the Great, daughter of Aristobulus, and half-sister of Herod Agrippa I, Herodias was criticized by John the Baptist for having deserted her first husband for her second, Herod Antipas, who divorced his wife to marry her. In revenge, she demanded the head of John the Baptist (Mark 6:17–29; Matt. 14:1–12; Luke 2:19–20).

Hexateuch   A term meaning "six scrolls" that scholars use to denote the first six books of the Hebrew Bible — the Torah plus the conquest narrative in Joshua — which some experts believe once formed a continuous account (J).

Hezekiah   Son of Ahaz and fourteenth king of Judah (c. 715–686 B.C.E.), Hezekiah ruled during the Assyrian crisis when Sargon II and then Sennacherib overran Palestine. His reign was notable for the prophetic careers of Isaiah and Micah and for sweeping religious reforms, which included purging the Jerusalem Temple of non-Yahwistic elements (2 Kings 18–20; Isa. 22:15–25, 36–39; 2 Chron. 29–32).

hierocracy   A form of government controlled and administered by religious authorities, the term characterizes Jerusalem and Judah followed the return from exile and the rebuilding of the Temple in the late sixth century B.C.E. and after.

hieroglyphic   The ancient Egyptian system of writing in pictorial script.

higher criticism   The branch of biblical scholarship that attempts to analyze biblical writings for the purpose of determining their origins, their literary history, and their authors' purpose and meaning. Unlike lower criticism, which confines itself to studying the written texts to discover (if possible) the authentic words of the original writers or their redactors, higher criticism endeavors to isolate and interpret the religious, political, and historical forces that produced a given book and caused it in many cases to be revised and reedited by later hands. *See* textual criticism.

Hinnom, Valley of   A topographical depression lying south and west of Jerusalem; also called "the Valley of the [Children] of Hinnom" (Jer. 7:32; 2 Chron. 28:3; 2 Kings 23:10, etc.). *See also* Gehenna (a corruption of *Ge-Hinnom*).

Hiram   (1) The name of a series of rulers of Tyre, an ancient Phoenician seaport, with whom David and Solomon engaged in trade and commerce (2 Sam. 5:11; 1 Kings 5:1; 9:11; 1 Chron. 14:1; 2 Chron. 3; Ezek. 26–28). (2) A half-Tyrian, half-Israelite architect and craftsman whom King Hiram sent from Tyre to cast the bronze or copper fixtures and decorations of Solomon's Temple (1 Kings 7:13–51; 2 Chron. 2:13–14; 4:16).

historical criticism   Analyzing a written work by taking into consideration its time and place of composition in order to comprehend the events, dates, personages, and other factual elements mentioned in or influencing the text.

Hittites   Mentioned forty-seven times in the Hebrew Bible either by this name or as descendants of Heth (a grandson of Ham, son of Noah), the Hittites were among the most powerful people in the ancient Near East. A non-Semitic Indo-European group, they formed an older kingdom (c. 1700–1400 B.C.E.) contemporaneous with the Hebrew patriarchal period (Gen. 23), as well as a later "new kingdom" (c. 1400–1200 B.C.E.). Archaeologists have found remains of their cities in Asia Minor (central Anatolia), northern Mesopotamia, Syria, and Palestine, where the Pentateuch and Joshua list them among the nations occupying Canaan (Gen. 15:20; Exod. 3:8; Deut. 7:1; 20:17; Josh. 3:10, 11:3; 24:11).

The Hebrews from Abraham to Solomon had various commercial and political relations with the Hittites (Gen. 23:1–18; 26:34; Josh. 1:4; Judg. 3:5–6; 2 Sam. 11:2–27; 1 Kings 9:20–22; 11:1; 2 Kings 7:6; 2 Chron. 1:17; 8:7–9; Ezek. 16:3, 45). About 1200 B.C.E., however, the Hittite kingdom in Asia Minor fell to an invading Aegean people, probably Thracians and Phrygians. The Hittites centered near Carchemish in northern Syria were defeated by Sargon II in 717 B.C.E. and absorbed into the Assyrian Empire.

Holiness Code   The name given to the body of laws and regulations set forth in Leviticus 17–26 derives from the code's emphasis on holiness (separateness, religious purity) of behavior, which was to distinguish Israel and set its people apart from the rest of the world.

Holy of Holies   In Hebrew, a superlative referring to the Most Holy Place, the innermost room of the Tabernacle and Temple, where Yahweh was believed to be invisibly present.

Holy Spirit, the   The presence of God active in human life, a concept most explicitly set forth in John 14:16–26 and in the Pentecost miracle depicted in Acts 2. The Hebrew Bible speaks of "the spirit of God" (based on the Hebrew word for "wind" or "breath") as the force that created the universe (Gen. 1:2; Job 26:13; Ps. 104:29–30) and that inspires humans to prophesy and otherwise carry out the divine will (Exod. 31:3; Judg. 3:10; 1 Sam. 16:13–14; Isa. 61:1–3; Joel 2:28–30). In post–New Testament times, the Holy Spirit was declared to be the Third Person in the Trinity (Matt. 28:19–20).

Horeb, Mount   The name that the E and D traditions use for the mountain in the Sinai desert at which Moses received Yahweh's law (Exod. 17:6; 33:6; Deut. 1:2, 6, 19; 4:10, 15; also Ps. 106:19). Called Sinai in the J and P sources, its exact location is unknown. According to 1 Kings 19:1–21, Elijah fled there to renew his prophetic inspiration.

Hosea   An eighth-century prophet active in the northern kingdom from before the death of Jeroboam II (c. 746 B.C.E.) until shortly before its fall to Assyria in 721 B.C.E.; the source of the Book of Hosea, first in the printed list of Minor Prophets.

Hoshea (Hosea)   Last king of Israel (732–724 B.C.E.).

Huldah   A woman prophet associated with King Josiah's royal court in Jerusalem who pronounced on the authenticity of a "book of law" thought to be an early form of Deuteronomy. In the biblical record, she is the first person to decide on the authority of a scriptural document and thus stands at the head of the canonizing process (2 Kings 22; 2 Chron. 34).

Hyksos The Egyptian name (perhaps meaning "rulers of foreign lands") for a racially mixed but largely Semitic group that infiltrated and overran Egypt about 1720–1570 B.C.E., establishing the Fifteenth and Sixteenth Dynasties; themselves expelled by the Theban kings Kamose and Ahmose I, who founded the native Egyptian Eighteenth Dynasty. Some scholars believe that the Hebrews entered Egypt during the friendly rule of the Semitic Hyksos and were enslaved when the native Egyptians returned to power.

Hyrcanus Name of John I, son of Simon Maccabeus, Hasmonean king and high priest of Judah (134–104 B.C.E.). John II (63–40 B.C.E.), a high priest and puppet ruler installed by Rome, was succeeded by Herod the Great.

Idumea The name, meaning "pertaining to Edom," that the Greeks and Romans applied to the country of Edom, Judah's southern neighbor; the home of Herod the Great (Mark 3:8; 1 Macc. 4:29; 5:65).

immanence The divine quality denoting God's presence in the material world, including human society and history.

Immanuel The name (meaning "God is with us") that Isaiah gave to a child whose birth he predicted as a sign to King Ahaz during the Syro-Ephraimite War (late eighth century B.C.E.). Although not presented as a messianic prophecy, it was nevertheless interpreted as such (Mic. 5:3; Matt. 1:22–23).

Incarnation The Christian doctrine asserting that the prehuman Son of God became flesh, the man Jesus of Nazareth, to reveal the divine will to humanity—a doctrine based largely on the Logos hymn that opens the fourth Gospel (John 1:1–18, especially 1:14; see also Col. 1:15–20; 2:9–15; Phil. 2:5–11; Heb. 1:1–4; 2:14–18).

Infancy Gospel of Thomas A noncanonical gospel that dates from the mid-second century C.E. and is ascribed to the apostle Thomas. This work provides a fictional account of Jesus' youth.

Isaac Son of Abraham and Sarah (Gen. 21:1–7), child of the covenant promise by which Abraham's descendants would bring a blessing to all the earth's families (Gen. 17:15–22; 18:1–15) but whom Yahweh commanded to be sacrificed to him (Gen. 18:1–18). Reprieved by an angel, Isaac marries Rebekah (Gen. 24:1–67), who bears him twin sons, Esau and Jacob (Gen. 25:19–26), the latter of whom tricks his dying father into bestowing the firstborn's birthright on him (Gen. 27:1–45). Paul interprets the near-sacrifice of Isaac as an allegory of Christ (Gal. 4:21–31).

Isaiah An eighth-century prophet and counselor of Judean kings, Isaiah of Jerusalem was active during the reigns of Uzziah, Jothan, Ahaz, and Hezekiah (collectively, 783–687 B.C.E.) (Isa. 1:1; 6:1; 7:1–12; 38:1–6). Oracles attributed to this historical figure are found in Isaiah 1–39, particularly in Chapters 1–11, 20, 22, and 28–31. (Chs. 24–27, 33–35, and 36–39 are thought to be by other hands.) Second Isaiah, who lived during the Babylonian exile (587–538 B.C.E.), contributed Chapters 40–55. Third Isaiah, whose work is found in Chapters 56–66, lived during the postexilic period. A complete text of Isaiah, possibly dating from the second century B.C.E., was found among the Dead Sea Scrolls.

Ishmael The son of Abraham and Sarah's Egyptian handmaiden Hagar (Gen. 16), Ishmael and his mother were exiled to the desert, where an angel rescued them (Gen. 21). Cited as the eponymous ancestor of twelve princes (Gen. 25:12–16), he is also regarded as the progenitor of the Arabs and a forefather of Mohammed, founder of Islam. In Galatians 4:21–31, Ishmael, son of a slave woman, is compared to the Jerusalem of Paul's day.

Ishmaelites The name the J sources apply to caravan merchants trading with Egypt (Gen. 37:25–28; 39:1) but whom the E document calls Midianites (Gen. 37:28, 36). Although the twelve tribes of Ishmael were a populous nation (Gen. 17:20), the biblical record seldom refers to them.

Ishtar Goddess of love and war in the Assyrian and Babylonian religions; prototype of later fertility and erotic deities such as Ashtoreth, Aphrodite, and Venus (Jer. 44).

Isis Ancient Egyptian goddess, wife of Osiris and mother of Horus, who was worshiped from prehistoric to Roman times. As a beneficent mother who protected her devotees, Isis was pictured in Egyptian art as a madonna with child, an iconography that influenced later Christian portraits of Mary and the baby Jesus.

Israel (1) The name given Jacob by an angel in Transjordan (Gen. 32:28, J source) and by Yahweh at Bethel (Gen. 35:10, P source). Although interpreted as "he has been strong against God" (Gen. 32:28), it probably means "may God show his strength" or "may God rule." (2) The Israelite nation descended from the twelve sons of Jacob (Israel); the covenant people chosen at Sinai. (3) The northern kingdom as opposed to the southern state of Judah during the period of the divided monarchies (922–721 B.C.E.).

Issachar Son of Jacob and Leah (Gen. 30:14–18), the eponymous progenitor of the inland tribe bearing his name (Gen. 49:14–15; Josh. 19:17–23; Deut. 33:18–19; Num. 1:29; 26:25; 1 Chron. 7:2).

itinerary An ancient literary genre dealing with geographical locations and features that mark the stages of a journey narrative. Accounts of the patriarchs' wanderings in Genesis and the Israelites' prolonged trek through the Sinai wilderness in Exodus-Numbers include itineraries.

J *See* Yahwist.

Jabal According to Genesis 4:20, a son of Lamech and Adah whom the J source regards as the progenitor of itinerant tent dwellers and keepers of livestock.

Jabesh-gilead A city built in the rugged country east of the Jordan River, destroyed by Israelites who resented the town's failure to send representatives to a tribal assembly at Mizpah (Judg. 21:8–14). Men from this city rescued the decapitated body of Saul from the Philistines (1 Sam. 11; 31:12; 1 Chron. 10:11–12), for which courageous feat David rewarded them (2 Sam. 2:5–7).

Jachin and Boaz Names that Hiram, a half-Phoenician craftsman, gave to the twin pillars of copper decorating the entrance to Solomon's Temple (1 Kings 7:13–22; 2 Chron. 3:17). Their exact appearance, religious function and significance, and the meaning of their names are conjectural.

Jacob The younger of twin sons born to Isaac and Rebekah (Gen. 25:21–26), Jacob is famous for his shrewdness, opportunism, and craftiness. He stole his brother Esau's birthright and Isaac's blessing (Gen. 25:29–34; 27:1–29), acquired great wealth in stock breeding (Gen. 29–30), and absconded with his father-in-law's household gods (Gen. 31:1–21) but later concluded a covenant with him (Gen. 31:22–25). Jacob was also the recipient of several divine visitations: the dream vision of a ladder to heaven at Bethel (Gen. 28) and wrestling with a divine being at Jabbok, Transjordan, after which his name was changed to Israel (Gen. 32:24–32; 33:4), a revelation renewed at Bethel (Gen. 35:1–15).

Father of twelve sons, eponymous ancestors of Israel's twelve tribes (Gen. 46:1–27), Jacob suffered in old age largely because of the temporary loss of his favorite children, Joseph (Gen. 37:2–36) and Benjamin (Gen. 43:1–14), and other filial problems reflected in his deathbed blessings (Gen. 49:1–28). In accordance with his wishes, he was buried in a cave near Mamre, which his grandfather Abraham had purchased from a Hittite (Gen. 49:29–33; 50:7–13).

Jael Wife of Heber the Kenite (member of a nomadic tribe of metal workers), who offered hospitality to Sisera, the Canaanite general, and then murdered him, thus becoming a national heroine in Israel (Judg. 4:11–22; 5:24–31).

Jairus The head of a synagogue in Galilee who asked Jesus to heal his dying child, for which act of faith he was rewarded with the girl's miraculous cure (Luke 8:41–42, 49–56; Mark 5:35–43; Matt. 9:18–20, 23–26).

James

1. Son of Zebedee, brother of John, and one of the Twelve Apostles (Mark 1:19–20; 3:17; Matt. 4:21–22; 10:2; Luke 5:10; 6:14). A Galilean fisherman, he left his trade to follow Jesus and, with John and Peter, became a member of his inner circle. He was among the three disciples present at the Transfiguration (Mark 9:2–10; Matt. 17:1–9; Luke 9:28–36) and was at Jesus' side during the last hours before his arrest (Mark 14:32–42; Matt. 26:36–45). James and John used their intimacy to request a favored place in the messianic kingdom, thus arousing the other apostles' indignation (Mark 10:35–45). James was beheaded when Herod Agrippa I persecuted the Jerusalem church (41–44 C.E.) (Acts 12:2).

2. James, son of Alphaeus and Mary (Acts 1:13; Mark 16:1), one of the Twelve (Matt. 10:3–4), called "the less" or "the younger" (Mark 15:40).

3. James, the eldest of Jesus' three "brothers" (or close male relatives) named in the Gospels (Mark 6:3; Matt. 13:55), first opposed Jesus' work (Matt. 12:46–50; Mark 3:31–35; Luke 8:19–21; John 7:3–5) but was apparently converted by one of Jesus' postresurrection appearances (1 Cor. 15:7) and became a leader in the Jerusalem church (Acts 15:13–34; 21:18–26). According to legend, a Nazirite and

upholder of the Mosaic Law, he was known as James "the righteous." James apparently clashed with Paul over the latter's policy of absolving Gentile converts from circumcision and other legalistic requirements (Gal. 1:18–2:12). The reputed author of the New Testament Epistle of James, he was martyred at Jerusalem in the early 60s C.E.

Jamnia   Coastal village in Palestine. *See* Jamnia, Academy of.

Jamnia, Academy of   An assembly of eminent Palestinian rabbis and Pharisees held about 90 C.E. in the coastal village of Jamnia (Yavneh) to define and guide Judaism following the Roman destruction of Jerusalem and its Temple. According to tradition, a leading Pharisee named Yohanan ben Zakkai had escaped from the besieged city by simulating death and being carried out in a coffin by his disciples. Yohanan, who had argued that saving human lives was more important than success in the national rebellion against Rome, was given Roman support to set up an academy to study Jewish law. Under his direction, the Pharisees not only preserved the Torah traditions but also apparently formulated what was to become the official biblical canon of Palestinian Judaism. Out of the deliberations at Jamnia came the authoritative list of books in the Writings, the third major division of the Hebrew Bible.

Japheth   According to Genesis 5:32, 6:10, 9:18, and 10:1, one of Noah's three sons, the eponymous ancestor of various Indo-European nations, especially Aegean Sea peoples, including the Greeks (Ionians) and Philistines (Gen. 10:1–5).

Jashar, Book of   Apparently a collection of Hebrew poetry (since lost), quoted in Joshua 10:12–13, 2 Samuel 1:18, and 1 Kings 8:53 (Septuagint version only).

Javan   According to Genesis 10:4–5, the fourth son of Japheth and progenitor of the Ionian Greeks and other coastal and island peoples of the northeastern Mediterranean (1 Chron. 1:5, 7).

JE   The designation scholars give the hypothetical document uniting J's (the Yahwist's) account of Israel's beginnings with E's (the Elohist's) parallel narrative. After the northern kingdom of Israel fell to Assyria in 721 B.C.E., refugees may have brought the E document south to Jerusalem, where it was combined with the older J to produce JE, thus preserving E's north-

ern tribal stories about the national ancestors and Exodus.

Jebus   The city held by Jebusites, an ancient Canaanite tribe (Gen. 10:16; Josh. 11:3; 1 Chron. 1:14; Ezek. 16:3), which later became Jerusalem, it may have been the same town called Urusalim (city of peace) in the Amarna letters and called Salem, city of Melchizedek, in Genesis 14:18–20 (see also Josh. 18:16, 28; Judg. 19:10; 1 Chron. 11:14). David captured the city and made it his capital (2 Sam. 5:7–9; 6–10; 1 Chron. 11:4–9), placed the Ark of the Covenant there (2 Sam. 6:4–5), and purchased from a Jebusite an ancient stone threshing floor (2 Sam. 24:16–24; 1 Chron. 21:15–28) that became the site of Solomon's Temple (1 Kings 6:1–8:66).

Jeduthun   The representative leader or eponymous founder of a guild of Temple singers and musicians (1 Chron. 25:1, 3, 6; 16:40–42) who provided music for services at the Jerusalem sanctuary. This group officiated during the reigns of Solomon (1 Chron. 5:12–13), Hezekiah (2 Chron. 29:14), and Josiah, whose magnificent revival of the Passover liturgies they helped celebrate (2 Chron. 35:15–16). Jeduthun's name appears in the superscriptions of Psalms 39, 62, and 77 and among the list of exiles returned to Jerusalem from Babylon (Neh. 11:17).

Jehoiachin   King of Judah (598/597 B.C.E.), son and successor of Jehoiakim. After inheriting the throne at age eight and reigning for only three months and ten days, he was taken captive to Babylon (2 Kings 24:10–12; 2 Chron. 36:9–10), where he remained the rest of his life. Babylonian records indicate that he was at first accorded favored status but later imprisoned until Nebuchadnezzar's successor, Evilmerodach (Amel-Marduk), released him (562 B.C.E.) and honored him above other captive kings (2 Kings 25:27–30; Jer. 52:31–34).

Jehoiakim   Second son of Josiah, Jehoiakim was made king of Judah about 609 B.C.E., when Pharaoh Necho of Egypt placed him on the throne, deposing his brother Jehoahaz, who had reigned only three months (2 Kings 23:34; 2 Chron. 36:4). Another brother, Zedekiah, replaced Jehoiakim's heir, Jehoiachin, to become Judah's last Davidic monarch. The Deuteronomistic historians, the Chronicler, and the prophet Jeremiah all denounced his religious apostasy and misguided attempts to combat Babylonian domination with Egyptian alliances (2 Kings 23:36–24:6; 2 Chron. 36:5–8; Jer. 25–26; 36).

Ignoring Jeremiah's advice (Jer. 36:1–26), Jehoiakim died or was assassinated before paying the consequences of his rebellion against Babylon (2 Kings 24:6). The Chronicler states that he was chained and carried off to Babylon (2 Chron. 36:6–7), but this was the fate of his son and heir, Jehoiachin (2 Kings 24:12–16; 2 Chron. 36:10).

Jehonadab   Son of Rechab the Kenite (1 Chron. 2:55), he assisted Jehu in massacring King Ahab's family and slaughtering Baal worshipers in Israel (2 Kings 10:14–27). According to Jeremiah 35:1–19, he was a nomadic ascetic who condemned drinking wine, planting vineyards, cultivating fields, or building cities. His support of Jehu's fanatical Yahwism may have been in part a revolt against Ahab's urban culture.

Jehoram   (1) A son of Ahab and king of Israel (849–842 B.C.E.) who enlisted King Jehoshaphat's help in quelling Moab's rebellion against paying Israel tribute (2 Kings 3:1–27). Jehu later murdered him (2 Kings 8:25–29; 9:22–26). (2) Son of Jehoshaphat and king of Judah (839–842 B.C.E.), he married Ahab's daughter Athaliah and fostered the religion of Baal in Judah (2 Kings 8:16–24; 2 Chron. 21:1–20). His reign was marked by wars with the Arabs and Philistines and by the loss of Judah's control of Edom. The name means "Yahweh is exalted."

Jehoshaphat   Son of Asa and king of Judah (873–849 B.C.E.), his name means "Yahweh judges." Although the Deuteronomistic historians give him short shrift (1 Kings 15:24; 22:41–51), the Chronicler emphasizes the general success of his twenty-four-year reign (2 Chron. 17:1–21:1), which was marked by important religious reforms, effective wars against Edom, Moab, and Ammon (2 Chron. 20:1–30), and the achievement of relative political security and prosperity for his people.

Jehovah   An English rendering of the divine name created by adding the vowels of *Elohim* and *Adonai* to the four consonants (YHWH) of the Tetragrammaton, the term entered the language via a Roman Catholic Latin translation about 1518 C.E., though the name *Yahweh* is considered a more accurate rendition of the Hebrew original.

Jehu   A son of Jehoshaphat (not the king of Judah) whom the prophet Elisha had anointed king of Israel in 842 B.C.E. (2 Kings 9:1–3), fulfilling an earlier command of Elijah (1 Kings 19:16–17). Thus commissioned by Israel's prophetic guild, Jehu proceeded to slaughter Ahab's family and all connected with it (2 Kings 9:14–10:27), including King Jehoram, King Ahaziah of Judah and his forty-two sons, Queen Jezebel, Ahab's seventy sons, and numerous other Israelites who worshiped Baal. Jehu's long reign (842–815 B.C.E.) saw Israel's territory shrink to a fraction of what it had been under Omri and Ahab (2 Kings 10:32–33). Although he murdered in Yahweh's name, his actions were condemned by the prophet Hosea (Hos. 1:3–5). Nor was he a wholehearted Yahwist (2 Kings 10:31), though his name means "Yahweh is He."

Jephthah   The son of Gilead and a harlot, Jephthah was driven as a youth from the area of Gilead by his legitimate brothers (Judg. 11:1–3) but was recalled by Gilead's elders when the Ammonites attacked Israel. An effective military leader, he defeated the Ammonites and was judge (general) in Israel for six years (Judg. 12:7). Best known for vowing to make a burnt offering of the first person he met after the battle if Yahweh would grant him victory, he presumably immolated his own daughter, who had come to congratulate him on his success (Judg. 11:29–40; see 2 Kings 3:27). The author of Hebrews praises him for his faith (Heb. 11:32).

Jeremiah   One of Israel's greatest prophets, Jeremiah warned Jerusalem and its kings of their misdeeds and of coming doom by the Babylonians for approximately forty years (c. 627–587 B.C.E.) (Jer. 1:1–3). Beginning in the thirteenth year of Josiah's reign (640–609 B.C.E.), he also prophesied during the reigns of Jehoiakim (609–598 B.C.E.), Jehoiachin (598/597 B.C.E.), and Zedekiah (597–587 B.C.E.), continuing after Jerusalem's fall (587 B.C.E.) and during a forced exile in Egypt (Jer. 40–44).

Although persecuted by both government officials and his compatriots for his unpopular (and seemingly treasonous) message that Yahweh had forsaken Judah and determined its annihilation, Jeremiah persisted in attacking official policy and denouncing those who trusted in the Temple (Jer. 1:11; 15; 21–22; 25–28; 36–38). After Jerusalem's fall, he was treated well by the Babylonians (Jer. 39–40), but his fellow survivors forcibly transported him to Egypt (Jer. 42–44). His message is known for its promise of a new covenant and a restoration of Judah (Jer. 30–33).

Jericho   One of the world's oldest cities, Jericho's ruins lie near an oasis on the west side of the south Jordan River Valley. Partly excavated by archaeologists, its earliest occupation dates to about 7800 B.C.E. Although according to Joshua 2 and 5:13 – 6:26 its fortified walls crumbled when the Israelites marched around the city, radiocarbon dating indicates that the site was already abandoned at the time of the conquest (thirteenth century B.C.E.). Jericho was partly rebuilt by Hiel of Bethel during Ahab's reign (869 – 850 B.C.E.) (1 Kings 16:34), but no evidence of this occupation remains. It was extensively rebuilt during Herod's day (40 – 4 B.C.E.) and is mentioned several times in the New Testament (Matt. 20:29; Mark 10:46; Luke 10:30; 18:35; 19:1; Heb. 11:30).

Jeroboam I An Ephraimite who led the ten northern tribes' secession from the Davidic monarchy and became the first ruler of the northern kingdom (1 Kings 11:26 – 12:33). Jeroboam I reigned from approximately 922 – 901 B.C.E. His first capital was Shechem, site of the old tribal confederacy (Josh. 24), but he later moved his administration to Tirzah, his former home and an ancient Canaanite royal sanctuary (1 Kings 12:24 – 25). The Deuteronomistic historians condemned Jereboam I for establishing rival Yahwist shrines at Bethel and Dan to compete with the Yahwist Temple at Jerusalem, and they condemned him for tolerating the worship of such foreign deities as Chemosh, Ashtoreth, and the Ammonite Milcom (1 Kings 11:33; 12:26 – 13:34).

Jeroboam II A descendant of Jehu, son of King Jehonash, and ruler of Israel (786 – 746 B.C.E.) whose long reign brought relative peace and material prosperity to the northern kingdom, Jeroboam II won major victories over Ben-hadad, king of Syria, and extended Israel's territory so that it included almost all the territory over which David and Solomon had ruled, except Judah. The Deuteronomistic account of his reign (2 Kings 14:23 – 29) gives no indication of its importance. The prophets Amos and Hosea, who were active during the time of Jeroboam II, denounced the country's economic oppression of the poor as well as its widespread materialism.

Jerome Eminent Christian scholar and teacher (347 – 419/420 C.E.) known for his translation of the Bible into Latin. *See* Vulgate Bible.

Jerusalem An ancient Palestinian holy city, sometimes identified with the Salem of Genesis 14:17 – 20 but more often with Jebus, a city of the Jebusite tribe (Josh. 18:28; Judg. 19:10), Jerusalem became King David's capital after he had captured it from the Jebusites (2 Sam. 5:6 – 10; 2 Chron. 4:5). Solomon centralized the worship of Yahweh on a hill called Zion there (1 Kings 5 – 7; 2 Chron. 2 – 4), and Jerusalem

remained the capital of Judah after the secession of the northern tribes (922 B.C.E.). The city suffered three major destructions: in 587 B.C.E. when the Babylonians razed Solomon's Temple; in 70 C.E. when the Romans destroyed the city and its Herodian Temple; and in 135 C.E. when the Romans decimated the city for the last time.

Jerusalem church According to Luke-Acts, the original center of Christianity from which the "new Way" spread outward to "the ends of the earth" (Acts 1 – 15). Inspired by the Spirit at Pentecost, the Jerusalem believers formed a commune led by three "pillars" — Peter (Cephas), John, and James, Jesus' kinsman (Acts 2 – 3; Gal. 1:18 – 2:10).

Jesse The son of Obed and grandson of Ruth and Boaz (Ruth 4:17, 22), Jesse was a Judean shepherd and father of seven or eight sons, including David (1 Sam 16:10 – 11; 17:12; 1 Chron. 2:12 – 17), who became king of Israel. He is mentioned in the messianic prophecies of Isaiah 11:1, 10, and in Matthew's and Luke's genealogies of Jesus (Matt. 1:5 – 6; Luke 3:32; *see also* Rom. 15:12).

Jesus The English form of a Latin name derived from the Greek *Iesous,* which translated the Hebrew *Jeshua,* a late version of *Jehoshua* or *Joshua,* meaning "Yahweh is salvation." The name was borne by several biblical figures, including Joshua, leader of the conquest of Canaan; an ancestor of Jesus Christ (Luke 3:29); and a Jewish Christian, also called Justus (Col. 4:11). It appears several times in the Apocrypha, notably as the name of the author of Ecclesiasticus, Jesus ben Sirach.

Jesus Christ The name and title given the firstborn son of Mary and Joseph (the child's legal father), the one whom Christians regard as the Spirit-begotten Son of God and Savior of the world. According to Matthew 1:21 and Luke 1:31, he received the name *Jesus* because he was to "save his people from their sins." The term *Christ* is not a proper name, but the English version of the Greek *Christos,* a translation of the Aramaic *Meshiha* and the Hebrew *Mashiah* (Messiah, the Anointed One). Although we know almost nothing about the historical Jesus, the New Testament presents a thorough documentation of what the early Christian community believed about the historical Christ.

Jesus Seminar A group of about 100 leading New Testament scholars in North America who are attempting to reconstruct Jesus' actual teachings in Scripture. Among their contribution to biblical scholarship is their work *The Five Gospels: The Search for the Authentic Words of Jesus* (1993) and *The Acts of Jesus: What Did Jesus Really Do?*

Jethro A shepherd and priest of the Kenites, a Midianite tribe of coppersmiths, with whom Moses took refuge during his flight from Egypt and whose daughter Zipporah he married (Exod. 2:15–22; 18:1–12). Moses apparently identified Jethro's god, Yahweh, with El Shaddai, god of Israel's ancestors (Exod. 3; 6; 18).

Jew Originally a member of the tribe or kingdom of Judah (2 Kings 16:6; 25:25), the term later included any Hebrew who returned from Babylonian captivity and finally encompassed all members of the covenant community scattered throughout the world (Esther 2:5; Matt. 2:2). Some New Testament writers refer to "the Jews" as any Israelites opposing Christianity (John 1:19; 5:16, 18:20; Acts 14:19; 16:20; 1 Cor. 1:23; Rev. 2:9).

Jezebel Daughter of King Ethbaal of Tyre and wife of King Ahab, Jezebel promulgated Baal worship in Israel and persecuted Yahweh's prophets (1 Kings 16:29–33; 18:4, 19; 19:1–3). After she perverted the Mosaic Law to confiscate Naboth's vineyard (1 Kings 21:1–16), Elijah predicted her shameful death (1 Kings 21:24–26), a prophecy fulfilled when Jehu threw her body to the dogs to eat during his bloody purge of Ahab's dynasty (2 Kings 9:30–37). In Revelation 2:20, she is a symbol of false religion.

Jezreel (1) A fertile valley, known as the Plain of Esdraelon, extending southeast across Palestine from north of Mount Carmel to the Jordan River. (2) A fortified city and the site of Naboth's vineyard (1 Kings 21:1–24) and of Jehu's murders of King Joram, of the Queen-mother Jezebel (2 Kings 9:24, 30–37), and of all Ahab's heirs (2 Kings 10:1–11).

Joab A son of Zeruiah, half-sister of David (2 Sam. 2:18), Joab was the cruelly efficient commander-in-chief of David's armies who managed the capture of Jerusalem (2 Sam. 5:8; 1 Chron. 11:6–8) and successful wars against the Syrians, Ammonites, and Edomites (2 Sam. 12:26–31; 1 Kings 11:15–17). He murdered Abner, general of the northern tribes under Saul's heir, Ishbaal (2 Sam. 2:18–23; 3:22–30); arranged Uriah's death so that David could marry Bathsheba (2 Sam. 11:6–21); reconciled David and Absalom (2 Sam. 14:28–33) but later murdered David's rebellious son (2 Sam. 18:9–17); and supported the wrong contender for David's throne (1 Kings 1:5–33), for which he was executed

early in Solomon's reign (1 Kings 2:28–34), supposedly on David's deathbed advice (1 Kings 2:5–6).

Joanna Wife of Chuza, an administrator in Herod Antipas's Jerusalem household, who became a follower of Jesus (Luke 8:3) and was among the women who discovered his empty tomb (Luke 23:55–24:11).

Joash (Jehoash) The name of several Hebrew Bible figures. (1) Judge Gideon's father (Judg. 6:11, 31–32). (2) A son of King Ahab (1 Kings 22:26–27; 2 Chron. 18:25–26). (3) The eighth king of Judah (c. 837–800 B.C.E.), a son of Ahaziah, who reduced Baal worship and repaired the Temple but later had to forfeit some of its treasures to pay Hazael, king of Aram, who besieged Jerusalem. Joash's reign, including the machinations of his grandmother, the Queen-regent Athaliah, is recorded in 2 Kings 11–12 and 13:10–13 and 2 Chronicles 22:11–24:27. (4) The twelfth king of Israel, third of the Jehu dynasty, who recovered some of the Israelite territory that his predecessors had lost to Syria, defeated King Amaziah of Judah, and transported some of the Temple's treasures from Jerusalem to Samaria (2 Kings 13:1–25; 14:8–16; 2 Chron. 25:18–19).

Job The name apparently dates from the second millennium B.C.E. and may mean "one who comes back to God," a penitent. It may derive from the Hebrew *ayab*, "to be hostile," denoting one whom God makes his enemy. The central character of the wisdom book bearing his name, Job is linked with Noah and Danel as a person of exemplary righteousness (Ezek. 14:14, 20). All three of Ezekiel's heroes were non-Israelite; Job was probably an Edomite.

Joel Although numerous biblical figures bore this name (meaning "Yahweh is God"), the best known is the son of Pethuel (Joel 1:1), a prophet of postexilic Judah (perhaps c. 350 B.C.E.).

John the Apostle A son of Zebedee and brother of the apostle James, John was a Galilean fisherman whom Jesus called to be among his twelve most intimate followers (Mark 1:19–20; Matt. 4:21–22). Jesus called James and John *Boanerges* (sons of thunder), possibly because of their impetuous temperaments (Mark 3:17; 9:38; Luke 9:52–56). Always among the first four in the Gospel lists of the Twelve (Mark 3:14–17; Matt. 10:2; Luke 6:3–14), John was present at the Transfiguration (Matt. 17:1; Mark 9:2; Luke 9:28) and at Gethsemane (Matt. 26:37; Mark 14:33). Tradition identifies him with the "beloved disciple" (John 13:23; 21:20) and as the author of the Gospel of John, a premise that most scholars believe is impossible to prove. Along with Peter and James, he was one of the triple "pillars" of the Jerusalem church (Acts 1:13; 3:1–4:22; 8:14–17; Gal. 2:9). He may have been martyred under Herod Agrippa, although a late second-century tradition states that he lived to old age in Ephesus.

John the Baptist The son of Zechariah, a priest, and Elisabeth (Luke 1:5–24, 56–80), John was an ascetic who preached the imminence of judgment and baptized converts in the Jordan River as a symbol of their repentance from sin (Matt. 3:1–12; Mark 1:2–8; Luke 3:1–18). The Gospel writers viewed him as an Elijah figure and forerunner of the Messiah (Luke 1:17; Matt. 11:12–14; John 1:15, 9–34; 3:22–36) who baptized Jesus but also recognized his superiority (Matt. 3:13–17; Mark 1:9–11; Luke 3:21–22). When imprisoned by Herod Antipas, he inquired whether Jesus were the expected "one who is to come." Jesus' answer was equivocal, but he praised John's work as fulfilling prophecy (Matt. 11:2–19; Luke 7:24–35). At his step-daughter Salome's request, Herod had John beheaded (Matt. 14:6–12; Mark 6:17–29). Some of John's disciples later became Christians (John 1:37; Acts 18:25).

John of Patmos The author of Revelation, exiled to the Aegean island of Patmos where he experienced visions of heaven and End time (Rev. 1:1, 4, 9; 22:8). He is not to be confused with the apostle John, son of Zebedee and brother of James.

Jonah A son of Amittai, a Zebulunite from Gath-hepher whom Yahweh sent as prophet to warn Nineveh of its impending doom (Jon. 1:1–16). The "sign of Jonah," who was reputedly delivered from death inside a sea monster (Jon. 1:17–2:10), is cited in the Synoptics as prophetic of Jesus' death and resurrection (Matt. 12:40; 16:4; Luke 11:29–30).

Jonathan Son and heir of King Saul (1 Sam. 13:16; 14:49; 1 Chron. 8:33) and famous for his unselfish devotion to young David (1 Sam. 18:1–5; 19:1–7; 20:1–21:1; 23:15–18). Along with his father, Jonathan was killed by the Philistines at the Battle of Gilboa (1 Sam. 31:1; 2 Sam. 1:16), a loss David lamented in one of his most moving psalms (2 Sam. 1:17–27).

Joppa An important harbor of ancient Palestine, located on the Mediterranean coast about thirty-five miles northwest of Jerusalem and now a suburb of Tel Aviv (1 Macc. 10:76; 12:33–34; 13:11; 14:5, 34; 2 Macc. 12:3–4). It was in Joppa that Peter raised Tabitha (Acts 9:43) and experienced his vision welcoming Gentiles into the church (Acts 10:1–48).

Jordan River The main river of Palestine, which occupies a deep north-south rift valley connecting the Sea of Galilee with the Dead Sea (a distance of about sixty-five miles) and forms the boundary between east and west Palestine. The Jordan is mentioned in the narratives concerning Lot, Abraham, and Jacob (Gen. 13:10; 14:12–16; 32:10) but is best known as the last barrier Israel crossed before entering Canaan — an event marked by a miraculous stopping of the river's flow (Josh. 3:1–5:1) — and as the site of John the Baptist's activity (Matt. 3:5; Mark 1:5; Luke 3:3), including the baptism of Jesus (Matt. 3:13–17; Mark 1:9–11; Luke 3:21–22). Naaman was cured of leprosy by bathing in the Jordan (2 Kings 5:10–14).

Joseph

1. The son of Jacob and Rachel, who aroused his ten brothers' jealousy, was sold into slavery and taken to Egypt where, aided by his ability to interpret dreams, he rose to power second only to that of Pharaoh himself. His story is told in Genesis 30:22–24 and Genesis 37–50. The name *Joseph* is used to represent the combined tribes of Ephraim and Manasseh (Josh. 16:1–4) and the northern kingdom (Ps. 80).

2. The husband of Mary and legal father of Jesus, a descendant of the Bethlehemite David (Matt. 1:20) but who lived in Nazareth (Luke 2:4) where he was a carpenter (Matt. 13:55). Little is known of him except for his piety (Luke 2:21–24, 41–42) and his wish to protect his betrothed wife from scandal (Luke 2:1–5). Because he does not appear among Jesus' family members during his (supposed) son's public ministry, it is assumed that he died before Jesus began his preaching career (Matt. 1:18–2:23; 13:55–56).

3. Joseph of Arimathaea, a wealthy member of the Sanhedrin and, according to John 19:38, a secret follower of Jesus who claimed Jesus' crucified body from Pilate for burial in his private garden tomb (Matt. 27:57–60; Mark 15:42–46; Luke 23:50–53; John 19:38–42).

Josephus, Flavius An important Jewish historian (c. 37–100 C.E.) whose two major works —*Antiquities of the Jews* and *The Jewish Wars* (covering the revolt against Rome, 66–73 C.E.)— provide valuable background material for first-century Judaism and the early Christian period.

Joshua The son of Nun, an Ephraimite, Joshua (meaning "Yahweh is salvation") was Moses' military assistant (Exod. 17:8–13), in charge of the Tabernacle (Exod. 33:11), one of the two spies optimistic about Israel's prospects of conquering Canaan (Num. 13:1–16; 14:6–9), and chosen to succeed Moses (Num. 27:18–23; Deut. 3:28; 31:23; 34:9). He led the Israelites across the Jordan (Josh. 3), captured Jericho (Josh. 6) and 'Ai (Josh. 7–8), warred against the Canaanite kings (Josh. 10–12), allotted the land to various tribes (Josh. 13:1–22:8), and made a covenant with Yahweh and the people (Josh. 24).

Josiah   Son of Amon (642–640 B.C.E.), Josiah (meaning "Yahweh heals") became king of Judah after his father's murder. The outstanding event of his reign (640–609 B.C.E.) was the discovery of a Book of the Law (probably an early edition of Deuteronomy) and the subsequent religious reform it inspired (following 621 B.C.E.). Josiah purged Judah and part of Israel's old territory of their rural shrines and "high places," centering all worship at the Jerusalem Temple (2 Kings 23:27). He was killed at Megiddo attempting to intercept Pharaoh Necho's army on its way to support the collapsing Assyrian Empire (609 B.C.E.) (2 Kings 22:1–23:30; 2 Chron. 34:1–35:27).

Jotham   (1) The youngest son of Jerubbaal (Gideon) (Judg. 9:5), who denounced his brother Abimelech to the people of Shechem for the latter's murder of Jerubbaal's seventy sons (Judg. 9:7–21). (2) Son of Uzziah, who was king of Judah as regent for his father (c. 750–742 B.C.E.) and later in his own right (742–735 B.C.E.) (2 Kings 15:32–38; 2 Chron. 27:1–9). The name means "Yahweh is perfect."

Jubilee   Derived from the Hebrew word for "ram's horn" or "trumpet," the term refers to the sabbatical year described in Leviticus 25:8–24 to be kept every half-century and proclaimed by a trumpet blast on the Day of Atonement. During a Jubilee year, all debts were to be canceled and private property returned to its rightful owners.

Judah   (1) The fourth son of Jacob and Leah (Gen. 29:35) who, according to the J account, received his father's most powerful blessing (Gen. 49:8) and became the progenitor of the tribe of Judah, which along with that of Ephraim was the most important in Israel's history. David was of this populous tribe, which loyally supported his dynasty (2 Sam. 2:4; 1 Kings 12:20). (2) The kingdom of Judah, the southern kingdom of the divided monarchy, was composed chiefly of the tribes of Judah and Benjamin, which supported the Davidic dynasty when the northern ten tribes seceded from the union (922 B.C.E.). It was destroyed by the Babylonians in 587 B.C.E.

Judaism   The name applied to the religion of the people of Judah (the Jews) after the northern kingdom of Israel fell (721 B.C.E.) and particularly after the Babylonian exile (587–538 B.C.E.).

Judas   A late form of the name *Judah*, popular after the time of Judas (the Jew) Maccabeus and borne by several New Testament figures: (1) the brother (or son) of James, one of the twelve apostles (Luke 6:16), who is sometimes identified with the Thaddeus of Matthew 10:3 or the Judas of John 14:22; (2) the "brother" or kinsman of Jesus (Mark 6:3; Matt. 13:55); (3) Judas Iscariot (Judas the man of Kerioth), son of Simon Iscariot (John 6:71; 13:26), the apostle who betrayed Jesus to the priests and Romans for thirty pieces of silver (Mark 3:19; 14:10; Luke 6:16; Matt. 26:14–16, 47; John 18:3) but later returned the blood money and committed suicide (Matt. 27:3–5; Acts 1:18–20). The Gospel writers little understood Judas's motives, attributing them to simple greed or to the influence of Satan (Luke 22:3; John 6:71; 12:1–8; 13:11, 27–29).

Judas Maccabeus   The third of five sons of the Judean priest Mattathias, leader of a successful uprising (c. 167–160 B.C.E.) against the Syrian king Antiochus IV. The epithet *Maccabeus* is believed to mean "the hammer," referring to Judas's effectiveness in striking blows for Jewish freedom. His story is told in 1 Maccabees. *See* Maccabees.

Judas the Galilean   A Jewish revolutionary who led a revolt against Rome when Quirinius was governing Syria (6 or 7 C.E.) (Acts 5:27).

Jude   An Anglicized form of the name Judah or Judas; one of Jesus' "brothers" (or a close male relative) (Mark 6:3; Matt. 13:55), perhaps a son born to Joseph before his marriage to Mary. Jude is less prominent in the early Christian community than his brother James (Jude 1:1) and is considered, according to tradition, the author of the Epistle of Jude, though most scholars doubt this claim.

Judea   The Greco-Roman designation for territory comprising the old kingdom of Judah, the name first occurs in Ezra 5:8, a reference to the "province of Judaea." In the time of Jesus, Judea was the southernmost of the three divisions of the Roman province of western Palestine, the other two of which were Samaria and Galilee (Neh. 2:7; Luke 1:39; John 3:22, 11:7; Acts 1:1; Gal. 1:22).

judge   (1) In the Book of Judges, charismatic (spirit-filled) men and women who led Israelite tribes or clans mainly by the force of their character; in the period before the monarchy, these leaders rallied some Israelites to fight against oppressors from neighboring Canaanite regions, such as the Moabites or Philistines. There were twelve officially designated as such: Othniel of Judah, Ehud, Shamgar, Deborah, Gideon, Tola, Jair, Jephthah, Ibzan, Elon, Abdon, and Samson, though Eli and Samuel were also spoken of as judges (1 Sam. 4:18; 7:15). (2) In the Hebrew Bible, a civil magistrate (Exod. 21:22; Deut. 16:18), administrator of a judiciary system traditionally organized by Moses (Exod. 18:13–26; Deut. 1:15–17; 16:18–20; 17:2–13; 19:15–20). Under the monarchy, the king became the supreme civil judge (2 Sam. 15:2; 1 Kings 3:9, 28; 7:7).

Judgment, Day of A theological concept deriving from the ancient Hebrew belief that the Day of Yahweh would see Israel's triumph and the destruction of its enemies, a confidence the prophet Amos shattered by proclaiming that it would mean calamity for Israel as for all who broke Yahweh's laws (Amos 5:18–20). This view prevails in Zephaniah 1:1–2; 3 and Malachi 3:1–6; 4:1–6. Isaiah also refers to "that day" of coming retribution (Isa. 11:10–16; 13:9, 13), while it is given an apocalyptic setting in Daniel 7:9–14, an idea developed in several apocryphal and pseudepigraphal books as well as in the New Testament (Matt. 25; Rev. 20).

Jupiter Latin name of the chief Roman deity, counterpart of the Greek Zeus, king of the Olympian gods for whom some ignorant men of Lycaonia mistook Paul's companion Barnabas (Acts 14:12–18).

Kadesh The central campsite of the Israelites during their wanderings through the Sinai wilderness (Num. 13:26–33; 20:1–11; 32:8; Deut. 1:19–25).

Kavod Hebrew term for Yahweh's "glory" that was believed to be invisibly present in the Jerusalem Temple.

Kenite hypothesis A theory arguing that Yahweh was originally the tribal god of the Kenite clan from which Moses and his Hebrew followers borrowed and adapted their religion (Exod. 18:1–12).

Kenites A Midianite clan of nomadic coppersmiths and metalworkers to which Jethro, Moses' father-in-law, belonged (Exod. 18:1–12; Num. 10:29–32; Judg. 1:16; 4:11; 1 Sam. 15:6).

kerygma A Greek term meaning "proclamation," it refers to the act of publicly preaching the Christian message.

Kethuvim (Ketubim or **Kethubim)** The Hebrew term designating the Writings, the third division of the Hebrew Bible: Psalms, Job, Proverbs, Song of Songs, Ecclesiastes, Esther, Ruth, Lamentations, Daniel, Ezra, Nehemiah, and 1 and 2 Chronicles.

Kittim Originally a Hebrew Bible name for the Island of Cyprus and its inhabitants (Gen. 10:4), thought to be descendants of Noah's grandson Javan, it was later applied to Macedonian Greeks (1 Macc. 1:1) and others (Dan. 11:30).

KJV Abbreviation for the King James Version of the Bible, published in 1611.

Koheleth (Qoheleth) The title—meaning "the president" or "the preacher" of an assembly or church (*qahal*)—that the otherwise anonymous author of Ecclesiastes (the Greek equivalent of the term) gives himself (Eccles. 1:1; 12:9–10).

koinē The "common" or popular form of Greek spoken by Alexander's soldiers and transmitted as an international language throughout the Greco-Roman world. The Septuagint and New Testament are written in *koinē*.

Korah The son of Izhar, who rebelled against Moses' leadership during the Sinai wanderings (Num. 16–17).

L Abbreviation for special Lukan material, the scholarly term designating passages that appear only in the Gospel of Luke.

Laban A descendant of Nahor, brother of Rebekah (Gen. 24:29; 25:20), father of Leah and Rachel, and thus father-in-law of Jacob. An Aramean living in Haran, Laban was noted for his duplicity and greed (Gen. 24:29–31:55).

Lachish A major fortified city in Judah about thirty miles southwest of Jerusalem and twenty miles from the Mediterranean coast (2 Kings 14:19; 2 Chron. 11:5–12; 14:6; 32:9; Jer. 34:7).

Lamech According to J, the son of Methuselah and father of Tubal and Jubal (Gen. 4:1–24); according to P, the son of Methuselah and father of Noah (Gen. 5:25–31). His boastful song of vengeance is given in Genesis 4:23–24.

Laodicea A commercial city on the Lycus River in Asia Minor and one of the seven churches of Asia (Col. 4:15–16; Rev. 3:14–22).

Last Supper The ritual meal that Jesus held with his closest disciples the night before his death. Here he introduced the new covenant and shared the bread and wine that symbolized his body and blood about to be sacrificed on behalf of humanity (Mark 14:22–25; Matt. 26:26–29; Luke 22:14–20). Paul first calls the Christian "love feast" (*agapē*) or Communion by this name in 1 Corinthians 11:20, where he describes the ceremony of the Eucharist (1 Cor. 11:23–26). John's version of the event (John 13:1–35) differs strikingly from that in the Synoptics.

Latter Prophets Also known as the "writing prophets," the term refers to the books of Isaiah, Jeremiah, Ezekiel, and the twelve Minor Prophets.

Law The Torah (meaning "teaching," "instruction") or Pentateuch, the first five books of the Bible containing the legal material traditionally ascribed to Moses.

Lazarus (1) The brother of Mary and Martha, a resident of Bethany whom Jesus restored to life (John 11:1–12:10). (2) The beggar in Jesus' parable of rewards and punishments in the afterlife (Luke 16:20–25).

Leah Laban's older daughter, whom he married to Jacob by trickery after the latter had worked seven years for her younger sister, Rachel (Gen. 29:16–30:21; 31:14). Although Jacob disliked Leah, she bore him six sons and a daughter: Reuben, Simeon, Levi, Judah, Issachar, Zebulun, and Dinah (Ruth 4:11).

legal procedures Also known as 'case law' or 'casuistic law,' this refers to legal decrees phrased in a qualifying manner, typically in the form: "if this happens, then that must be done." This formulation contrasts with the absolute demands of apodictic or policy law. *See also* case law.

legend A term denoting unverifiable stories or narrative cycles about celebrated people or places of the past. Legends grow as the popular oral literature of a people. Their purpose is not to provide historical accuracy, but to entertain and to illustrate cherished beliefs, expectations, and moral principles. Scholars consider much of the material associated with the stories of the patriarchs, Moses, and prophets as legendary.

Levi The third son of Jacob and Leah (Gen. 29:34; 35:23), Levi earned his father's disapproval for his violence in slaughtering tribal neighbors (Gen. 34:30; 49:5–7). He was the eponymous ancestor of the tribe of Levi to which Moses, Aaron, and Miriam belonged (Exod. 6:16; Num. 3:1–39).

Leviathan A mythical sea monster, the ancient Near Eastern dragon of chaos and symbol of Evil that Yahweh defeated in creating the universe (Ps. 74:14;

Dan. 7:2; Isa. 27:1; Job 41:1–34; see also Rev. 11:7; 12:3; 13:1–8).

Levites The Israelite tribe descended from Levi, son of Jacob (Num. 3; 1 Chron. 5:27–6:81) that was given priestly duties in lieu of land holdings when Israel conquered Canaan (Deut. 18:1–8). According to P, only descendants of Aaron were to be priests (Exod. 28:1; Num. 18:7); the Levites were regarded as their assistants and servants (Num. 18:2–7; 20–32). They served as priests of secondary rank and as Temple functionaries during the postexilic period, which was dominated by a priestly hierarchy (1 Chron. 24–26). Other stories involving Levites appear in Judges 19–21 and Luke 10:32.

lex talionis The law of strict retaliation, the principle of retributive justice expressed in the Torah command to exact "eye for eye, life for life" (Exod. 21:23–25; Lev. 24:19–20; Deut. 19:21) and rejected by Jesus (Matt. 5:38–39).

literary criticism A form of literary analysis that attempts to isolate and define literary types, the sources behind them, the stages of composition from oral to written form with their characteristic rhetorical features, and the stages and degree of redaction (editing) of a text.

liturgy A body of rites, including both actions and spoken formulas, used in public worship, such as the ceremony of the Eucharist (Holy Communion). The Didache (c. 100 C.E.) describes some of the church's earliest liturgical practices, including baptism and Communion.

Logos A Greek term meaning both "word" and "reason," used by Greek philosophers to denote the rational principle that creates and informs the universe. Amplified by Philo Judaeus of Alexandria, Egypt, to represent the mediator between God and his material creation, as Wisdom had been in Proverbs 8:22–31, the term found its most famous expression in the prologue to the Fourth Gospel to denote the prehuman Jesus —"the Word became flesh and dwelt among us" (John 1:14).

Lot Nephew of Abraham, with whom he migrated from Ur to Haran and finally to Canaan (Gen. 11:31; 12:5). Lot separated from his uncle, who rescued him from kidnappers (Gen. 13:1–14:16). Lot later entertained angels come to destroy Sodom (Gen. 19:1–29), who directed his escape from the doomed city. He reputedly fathered the nations of Moab and Ammon by incest with his two daughters (Gen. 19:30–38). Jesus referred to Lot's experience in Sodom (Luke 17:28–30), as did the author of 2 Peter 2:6–8.

Lucifer   A term meaning "light bearer" and referring to the planet Venus when it is the morning star, the English name Lucifer translates the Hebrew word for "shining one" (Isa. 14:12). An epithet applied to the king of Babylon, it was later mistakenly taken as a name for Satan before his expulsion from heaven.

Luke   A physician and traveling companion of Paul (Col. 4:14; Philem. 24; 2 Tim. 4:11) to whom a late second-century tradition ascribes the Gospel of Luke and Book of Acts.

LXX   A common abbreviation for the Septuagint, the Greek translation of the Hebrew Bible made in Alexandria, Egypt, during the last three centuries B.C.E.

Lycaonia   A district in Asia Minor added to the Roman Empire around 25 B.C.E., where Paul endured persecution (Acts 13:50; 14:6–19).

Lycia   A small province in southwestern Asia Minor, bordering the Mediterranean, which Paul visited on his missionary travels (Acts 21:1; 27:5–7).

Lydia   A once powerful kingdom of western Asia Minor with its capital at Sardis, Lydia (Lud) is mentioned in Jeremiah 46:9 and Ezekiel 30:5.

Lystra   A city in the Roman province of Galatia where Paul and Barnabas performed such successful healings that they were identified as Zeus and Hermes (Jupiter and Mercury) (Acts 14:6–19; 16:1; 18:23).

M   Abbreviation for special Matthean material, the scholarly term designating passages found only in the Gospel of Matthew.

Maat   Ancient Egyptian goddess of truth and justice.

Maccabees   A name bestowed on the family that won religious and political independence for the Jews from their Greek-Syrian oppressors. Judas, called Maccabeus (meaning "the hammer"), son of the aged priest Mattathias, led his brothers and other faithful Jews against the armies of Antiochus IV (Epiphanes) (175–163 B.C.E.). The dynasty his brothers established was called Hasmonean (after an ancestor named Hashmon) and ruled Judea until 63 B.C.E., when the Romans occupied Palestine.

Macedonia   The large mountainous district in northern Greece ruled by Philip of Macedon (359–336 B.C.E.), whose son Alexander the Great (356–323 B.C.E.) extended the Macedonian Empire over the entire ancient Near East as far as western In-

dia, incorporating all of the earlier Persian Empire. Conquered by Rome (168 B.C.E.) and annexed as a province (146 B.C.E.), Macedonia was the first part of Europe to be Christianized (Acts 16:10–17:9; 18:5; 19:29; 20:1–3).

Magdala   A town on the northwest shore of the Sea of Galilee and home of Mary Magdalene (of Magdala) (Matt. 15:39).

Magnificat   Mary's beautiful hymn of praise, recorded in Luke 1:46–55.

Magog   *See* Gog.

Malachi   The title of the last book of the Minor Prophets, the word means "my messenger" (Mal. 3:1) and may have been affixed by an editor (Mal. 1:1) who mistook it for a proper name.

Mamre   A plain near what later became the city of Hebron in southern Palestine, where Abraham temporarily settled under its ancient oaks (Gen. 13:18) and where angels on the way to Sodom visited him (Gen. 18). From a Hittite, Abraham bought a cave near Mamre in which his wife Sarah (Gen. 23:17, 19) and then he himself (Gen. 50:13) were buried.

Manasseh

1. The elder son of Joseph and the Egyptian Asenath, daughter of a high priest at On, who received a lesser blessing from the dying Jacob than his full brother Ephraim (Gen. 48:1–20), reflecting the tribe of Ephraim's greater importance in the later history of Israel.

2. One of Israel's twelve tribes, divided into two sections and occupying land east and west of the Jordan River (Josh. 17:1–18).

3. A son of Hezekiah and Hephzibah who was king of Judah longer than any other Davidic monarch (c. 687–642 B.C.E.). Despite the Deuteronomistic condemnation of him as the most evil ruler of Judah for his encouragement of Baalism, astrology, and human sacrifice, he proved an effective king, maintaining his country's relative independence during troubled times (2 Kings 21:1–18; 2 Chron. 33:1–20). The historicity of his supposed deportation to and return from Babylon has been questioned. In 2 Kings 23:26–27, Judah's final destruction is attributed to Manasseh's wickedness.

manna   The food miraculously supplied the Israelites during their wanderings in the Sinai wilderness (Exod. 16:1–36). Described in Numbers 11:7–9 and commonly referred to as "bread" from heaven (Deut. 8:3; Nah. 9:20; Ps. 78:24; John 6:31–35; Heb. 9:4; Rev. 2:17), its appearances ceased when Israel entered Canaan (Josh. 5:12).

Manoah   A pious member of the tribe of Dan and father of Samson, Israel's Herculean judge (Judg. 13:2–25; 14:2–10; 16:31).

Marcion   A Gnostic Christian (second century C.E.) who attempted to establish a Christian Scripture distinct from the Hebrew Bible, which he rejected. Marcion's canon included only Paul's letters and an edited version of Luke's Gospel. Although the church at Rome expelled him (c. 140 C.E.), he remained an influential leader for many years.

Marduk   Patron god of Babylon, hero of the Babylonian creation epic, *Enuma Elish,* in which he defeats the monster Tiamat and creates the cosmos from her bifurcated corpse.

Mari   An ancient Near Eastern city located on the Middle Euphrates River near the boundary of modern Syria and Iraq. Destroyed by Hammurabi of Babylon (c. 1738–1686 B.C.E.), Mari's royal palace has yielded thousands of clay tablets that preserve a rich array of information about the Mari period (c. 1750–1697 B.C.E.).

Mark (John Mark)   Son of Mary, a Jerusalem Jew who accompanied Barnabas (his cousin) and Paul on an early missionary journey (Acts 12:12–25; 13:5, 13; 15:37). For reasons unstated, he left them at Perga (Acts 13:13), which so angered Paul that he refused to allow Mark to join a later preaching campaign (Acts 15:38), though he and the apostle were later reconciled (Col. 4:10; Philem. 24). Some identify Mark with the youth who ran away naked at the time of Jesus' arrest (Mark 14:51–52). An early tradition ascribes authorship of the Gospel of Mark to him, as Papias and Eusebius (*Ecclesiastical Histories* 3.39.15) testify.

Martha   The sister of Mary and Lazarus of Bethany (Luke 10:38–42; John 11:1–12:2), whose home Jesus frequently visited.

martyr   A "witness" for Christ who prefers to die rather than relinquish his faith. Stephen, at whose stoning Saul of Tarsus assisted, is known as the first Christian martyr (Acts 22:20; Rev. 2:13; 17:6).

Mary   From the Latin and Greek *Maria,* from the Hebrew *Miryam* (Miriam), a name borne by six women in the New Testament.

1. Mary the virgin, wife of Joseph and mother of Jesus, who, the angel Gabriel informed her, was conceived by the Holy Spirit (Matt. 1:18–25; Luke 1:26–56; 2:21). From her home in Nazareth, Mary traveled to Bethlehem, where her first son was born (Luke 2:1–18), and thence into Egypt to escape Herod's persecution (Matt. 2:1–18), returning to Nazareth in Galilee after Herod's death (4 B.C.E.) (Matt. 2:19–23). She had one sister (John 18:25), probably Salome, wife of Zebedee, mother of James and John (Matt. 27:56), and was also related to Elisabeth, mother of John the Baptist (Luke 1:36). Gabriel's annunciation of the Messiah's birth occurs in Luke 1:26–36; the Magnificat, in Luke 1:46–55.

   Mary visited Jerusalem annually for the Passover (Luke 2:41) and reprimanded the twelve-year-old Jesus for lingering behind at the Temple (Luke 2:46–50). She may have been among family members convinced that Jesus' early preaching showed mental instability (Mark 3:21) and apparently humored his requests during the wedding celebration at Cana (John 2:1–12). Although Jesus showed his mother little deference during his ministry (Mark 3:31–35; Luke 11:27–28; John 2:4), on the cross he entrusted her care to his "beloved disciple" (John 19:25–27). Mary last appears in the upper room praying with the disciples just before Pentecost (Acts 1:13–14).

2. Mary Magdalene, a woman from Magdala, from whom Jesus cast out seven demons (Luke 8:1–2) and who became his follower. A common tradition asserts that she had been a prostitute whom Jesus had rescued from her former life (Mark 16:9; Luke 7:37–50), but this is by no means certain. She was present at the Crucifixion (Mark 15:40; Matt. 15:47), visited Jesus' tomb early Sunday morning (Matt. 28:1; Mark 16:1; Luke 24:10; John 20:1), and was one of the first to see the risen Jesus (Matt. 28:9; Mark 16:9; John 20:11–18), although the male disciples refused to believe her (Luke 24:9–11).

3. Mary, sister of Lazarus and Martha, whose home at Bethany Jesus frequented (Luke 10:38–42; John 11:1–12:8).

4. Mary, wife of Cleophas, mother of James the Less and Joseph (Joses), was a witness of Jesus'

crucifixion, burial, and resurrection (Matt. 27:56–61; 28:1; Mark 15:40, 47; 16:1; Luke 24:10; John 19:25).

5. Mary, sister of Barnabas and mother of John Mark, provided her Jerusalem home as a meeting place for the disciples (Acts 12:12; Col. 4:10).

6. An otherwise anonymous Mary mentioned in Romans 16:6.

Masada   A stronghold built by Herod the Great on a fortified plateau 800 feet above the Dead Sea, Masada was captured by Zealots during the revolt against Rome (66 c.e.). When the attacking Romans finally entered Masada (73 c.e.), they found only seven women and children alive, 953 others having died in a suicide pact.

masoretes   From a Hebrew term meaning "tradition," the name given to medieval Jewish scholars who copied, annotated, and added vowels to the text of the Hebrew Bible.

Masoretic Text (MT)   The standard text of the Hebrew Bible as given final form by the Masoretes in the seventh through ninth centuries c.e.

Mattathias   A Jewish priest who, with his sons John, Simon, Judas, Eleazar, and Jonathan, led a revolt against the oppressions of Antiochus IV (c. 168–167 b.c.e.) (1 Macc. 2:1–70).

Matthew   A Jewish tax collector working for Rome whom Jesus called to be one of the twelve apostles (Matt. 9:9; 10:3; Mark 2:13–17; 3:18; Luke 5:27–32; 6:15; Acts 1:13), Matthew (also called Levi) is the traditional author of the Gospel of Matthew, an attribution contested by most scholars.

Matthias   The early Christian elected to replace Judas among the Twelve (Acts 1:23–26). The name means "gift of Yahweh."

Medes   An ancient Ayrian (Iranian) Indo-European people occupying mountainous country south of the Caspian Sea who established a kingdom that by 600 b.c.e. extended from near the Persian Gulf to the Black Sea. In 612 b.c.e., they joined the Neo-Babylonians and Scythians to destroy Nineveh and terminate the Assyrian Empire. They were subdued by Cyrus the Great (549 b.c.e.), whose dominion was commonly known as the Medo-Persian Empire (Nah. 2:3–3:19; Esther 1:19; Dan. 5:28). The "law of the Medes and Persians" was traditionally immutable (Esther 1:19; Dan. 6:8, 15) and once given could not be rescinded, a factor that plays an important part in the Book of Esther (Esther 8:7–12).

Megiddo   An old Palestinian city overlooking the Valley of Jezreel (Plain of Esdraelon), the site of numerous decisive battles in biblical history (Josh. 12:21; 2 Kings 9:27; 23:29–30; 2 Chron. 35:20–24; Zech. 12:11) and symbolic location of the climactic War of Armageddon (Rev. 16:16).

megillot   A Hebrew word meaning "scrolls"; the five Hebrew Bible books — Song of Songs, Ruth, Lamentations, Ecclesiastes, and Esther — each of which was read publicly at one of Israel's annual religious festivals.

Melchizedek   The king-priest of Canaanite Salem (probably the site of Jerusalem) to whom Abraham paid a tenth of his spoils of war (Gen. 14:17–20); cited by the author of Hebrews as foreshadowing Jesus Christ (Ps. 110:4; Heb. 5:6–10; 7:1–25).

Mercury   Roman name for Hermes, Greek god of persuasion, business, trade, and messenger of Zeus, for whom Paul was mistaken in Lystra (Acts 14:12).

Merneptah   Egyptian pharaoh, son and successor of Rameses II, who reigned in about 1224–1211 b.c.e. His stele commemorating the defeat of several Canaanite nations includes the earliest known reference to Israel, which Merneptah claimed that he had totally eradicated.

Merodach   A Hebrew form of the Akkadian Marduk (also called Bel), the chief Babylonian god, ridiculed by Second Isaiah (Isa. 46:1–4) and Jeremiah (Jer. 51:44–45).

Meshach   The Babylonian name of Mishael, one of Daniel's three Hebrew companions whom Nebuchadnezzar unsuccessfully tried to incinerate in a furnace (Dan. 1–3).

Mesopotamia   The territory between the Euphrates and Tigris rivers at the head of the Persian Gulf (modern Iraq); cradle of the Sumerian, Akkadian, Assyrian, and Neo-Babylonian civilizations (Gen. 24:10; Judg. 3:8–10; 1 Chron. 19:6; Acts 2:9; 7:2).

messiah   A Hebrew term meaning "anointed one," designating a king or priest of ancient Israel who had been consecrated by having his head smeared with holy oil, marking him as set apart for a special role. King David is the model of Yahweh's anointed ruler; all his descendants who ruled over Judah were Yahweh's messiahs (2 Sam. 7:1–29; Ps. 89:3–45). After the end of the Davidic monarchy (587 b.c.e.), various Hebrew prophets applied the promises made to the Davidic dynasty to a future heir who would eventually restore the kingdom of David (Pss. 2, 110; Dan. 9:25–26). Christians believe that Jesus of Nazareth was the promised Messiah (Christ) as expressed in Peter's "confession" (Matt. 16:13–20; Mark 8:27–30; Luke 9:18–22; etc.).

metaphor   A figure of speech in which one object is used to describe the quality of another, an implied comparison of one thing to another, inferring that the first has a hitherto unrecognized likeness to the second. Biblical poets, for example, call Yahweh a "shepherd" because he guides and protects Israel, his "flock," and a "rock" because he is solid and reliable (cf. Ps. 23:1; Deut. 32:4).

Methuselah   According to Genesis 5:21–27, an antediluvian patriarch descended from Seth and Enoch who attained an age of 969 years. He appears as Methushael in Genesis 4:18 and in Luke's genealogical list (Luke 3:37).

Micah   A Judean prophet of the late eighth century B.C.E. and younger contemporary of Isaiah of Jerusalem (Isa. 2:2–4; Mic. 4:1–3). A rural figure who denounced the evils of urban life (Mic. 1:5) and predicted Jerusalem's fall (Mic. 3:12; cited in Jer. 26:18–19), his oracles form most of the present Book of Micah in the Minor Prophets. His name means "Who is like Yahweh?"

Micaiah   An eighth-century B.C.E. prophet who predicted Ahab's defeat and death at the Battle of Ramoth-gilead (1 Kings 22:8–28; 2 Chron. 18:6–27).

Michael   The angel whom the Book of Daniel represents as being the spirit prince, guardian, and protector of Israel (Dan. 10:13, 21; 12:1). Jude 9 depicts him as an archangel fighting with Satan for Moses' body. In Revelation 12:7, he leads the war against the dragon (Satan) and casts him from heaven. His name means "Who is like God?"

Michal   A daughter of Saul (1 Sam. 14:49) who was offered to David as his wife for his exploits against the Philistines (1 Sam. 18:20–27). Michal helped David escape Saul's wrath (1 Sam. 19:11–17), only to be rejected when she criticized his dancing naked before the Ark (2 Sam. 6:14–23).

Midian   An ancient tribal territory, the exact location and extent of which is unknown, that lay in the northwestern Arabian desert, east of the Gulf of Aqabah, opposite the Sinai Peninsula, and south of Moab. According to Exodus, Moses is in Midian when he first encounters Yahweh. *See* Midianites.

Midianites   A nomadic or seminomadic group of shepherds and traders that played a significant role in Israel's early history. According to Genesis 25:1–6,

they were descended from Abraham and his wife Keturah and thus closely associated with Israel's forebears. In Exodus, Moses takes refuge with the Midianite priest Jethro (or Ruel), whose daughter he marries (Exod. 2:15–3:1; 18:1–15). Although the Moses tradition presents them in a favorable light, later biblical writers portray them negatively as encroaching upon Israel's territory (Judg. 1:16; 4:1; 6–8; cf. Num. 22; 25:6–18, where an Israelite is executed for following Moses' example by taking a Midianite wife).

midrash   From a Hebrew work meaning "to search out," midrash refers to a commentary on or interpretation of Scripture. Collections of such haggadic or halakic expositions of the significance of the biblical text are called midrashim.

millennium   A 1000-year epoch, particularly the period of Christ's universal reign (Rev. 20:1–8) during which Satan will be chained and the dead resurrected.

Minor Prophets   Twelve prophetic books short enough to be recorded together on a single scroll: Hosea, Joel, Amos, Obadiah, Jonah, Micah, Nahum, Habakkuk, Zephaniah, Haggai, Zechariah, and Malachi.

Miriam   The daughter of Amram and Jochebed, older sister of Aaron and Moses, who brought her mother to nurse the infant Moses after he was found and adopted by Pharaoh's daughter (Exod. 2:4–8; Num. 26:59; 1 Chron. 6:3). Miriam led the victory celebration after the crossing of the Sea of Reeds (Exod. 15:20–21). Although later stricken with leprosy for criticizing Moses, she was cured and readmitted to Yahweh's favor after her brother interceded for her (Num. 12:2–15).

Mishnah   From the Hebrew verb "to repeat," a collection of Pharisaic oral interpretations (halakah) of the Torah compiled and edited by Rabbi Judah ha-Nasi about 200 C.E.

Mithras   A young Persian god, born from a rock on December 25, who slew the bull of heaven and introduced a salvation cult that swept through the Roman Empire. A serious rival to early Christianity, Mithraism was limited by its acceptance of only male worshipers.

Mizpah   The name of several Israelite sites, the most important of which was located in the territory of Benjamin (Josh. 18:26) near the border of Judah and Israel, perhaps a cult site (Judg. 20:1–11) on Samuel's prophetic circuit (1 Sam. 7:5–16; 10:17–24) and the temporary center of Jews remaining in Palestine after Nebuchadnezzar's deportations (2 Kings 25:23; Jer. 40–41).

Mizraim According to Genesis 10:6, a son of Noah's son Ham and the progenitor of the Hamitic nations of Lower Egypt, North Africa, and Canaan. It is also the Hebrew name of Egypt.

Moab An ancient neighbor-state of Israel located in the Jordan highlands east of the Dead Sea and north of Edom. Supposedly descended from Lot's incestuous union with his daughter (Gen. 19:30–38), the Moabites were Israel's traditional enemies (Num. 22:3; 24:17; Judg. 3:12–20; 11:15; 2 Kings 1:1; 3:4–27) and frequently denounced by the prophets (Isa. 15:16; 25:10; Jer. 9:26; 25:26; 48; Ezek. 28:8–11; Amos 2:12; Zech. 2:8–11; Ps. 60:8). Yet, both David and Jesus were descended from Ruth, a Moabite (Ruth 4:13–22; Luke 3:31–32). In extreme emergencies, the national god Chemosh was sometimes worshiped with human sacrifice (2 Kings 3:27; 13:20).

Molech (Moloch) The national god of Ammon whose worship characteristically involved human sacrifice, an act specifically forbidden the Hebrews (Lev. 18:21; 20:2; Amos 5:26) but allegedly introduced by King Manasseh (2 Kings 21:6; 2 Chron. 33), rooted out by Josiah (2 Kings 23:10), and denounced by the prophets Jeremiah (Jer. 7:29–34; 19:1–13) and Ezekiel (Ezek. 16:20–21; 20:26, 31).

money In early biblical times, before coins were first minted, value in business transactions was determined by weighing quantities of precious metals. In the early period, the term *shekel* refers not to a coin, but to a certain weight of silver. The use of coinage was first introduced into Palestine during the Persian era when the daric or dram, named for Darius I (521–486 B.C.E.), appeared. After Alexander's conquest of Persia, Greek coinage became the standard. The silver drachma (Luke 15:8), a coin of small value, was equivalent to the Roman denarius. The lepton was a small copper coin (Luke 12:59; 21:2), the least valuable in circulation, and one of the denominations coined by the Jews for use in the Temple. This was the "widow's mite" (Mark 12:42). The talent (Matt. 18:24) was not a coin but money of account; it was divided into smaller units — 60 minas or 6000 drachmas — and was worth at least $2000. The denarius (Matt. 18:28), the basic unit in the New Testament, was a silver coin, the day's wage of a rural laborer (Matt. 20:2).

monolatry The worship of one god while conceding the existence of others.

monotheism Belief in the existence of one god, a major theme of Second Isaiah (Isa. 40–46).

Mordecai His name derived from Marduk or Merodach (the chief Babylonian deity), Mordecai was the cousin and foster father of Esther, who according to the book bearing her name, was the Jew married to Ahasuerus, emperor of Persia. Representing the typically devout but politically ambitious Jew living in the Diaspora, Mordecai saved his sovereign's life (Esther 2:21–23) and outwitted Haman, who attempted to exterminate him and all Jews throughout the Persian domain (Esther 3:6–15), a plot he employed his beautiful cousin to foil so that, by his astuteness, he became second in power to the emperor (Esther 8–10).

Mosaic Covenant An agreement between God and the nation of Israel that was mediated by Moses. According to the terms of this pact, Israel swore to keep all of the laws enumerated in the Torah. Failure to do so would result in suffering all the curses contained in Leviticus and Deuteronomy.

Moses The great Hebrew lawgiver, religious reformer, founder of the Israelite nation, and central figure of the Pentateuch was the son of Amram (a Levite) and Jochebed and brother to Aaron and Miriam (Exod. 2:1–4). Adopted by Pharaoh's daughter and raised at the Egyptian royal court (Exod. 2:5–10; Acts 7:22), he fled Egypt after killing an Egyptian bully and settled in Midian among the Kenites, where he married Jethro's daughter Zipporah (Exod. 2:11–22).

After an encounter with Yahweh at the burning bush (Exod. 3:1–4:17), he returned to Egypt (Exod. 4:18–31), interceded with Pharaoh during the ten plagues (Exod. 5–11), led the Israelites across the Reed Sea (Exod. 14–15) to Sinai where he mediated the law covenant between Yahweh and Israel (Exod. 19–31), pled for his people (Exod. 33–34; Num. 14), directed their migration through the Sinai wilderness (Num. 11–14; 20–25), appointed Joshua as his successor (Num. 27:18–23), and died in Moab (Deut. 34:1–7; Acts 7:20–44). He is also credited with building the Tabernacle (Exod. 35–40), organizing Israel (Exod. 18:13–26), restating Israel's law code shortly before his death (Deut. 1–31), and composing several hymns (Deut. 32–33; Ps. 90).

Although Moses' name became synonymous with the covenant concept and Israel's traditions (Pss. 77:20; 103:7; 105:26; 106:23; Isa. 63:12; Mic. 6:4; Matt. 17:3; Luke 16:29; John 1:17; 3:14; 5:46; 7:19; 9:29; Acts 3:22; 21:21), modern scholars have concluded that much of the material in the Pentateuch dates from post-Mosaic times. (*See* documentary hypothesis.) Moses also figured prominently in Paul's theology (Rom. 5:14; 10:5; 1 Cor. 10:2; 2 Cor. 3:7; 3:15) and that of the author of Hebrews (Heb. 3:2; 7:14; 9:19; 11:23). Jude preserves an old tradition, probably derived from the pseudepigraphal Assumption of Moses, that the devil disputed the angel Michael for Moses' body (Jude 9; Rev. 15:3).

Muratorian Canon   A fragmentary document listing books of the New Testament regarded as canonical by the anonymous author. Although written in Latin during the eighth century C.E., the fragment is a translation of a much older Greek work. The Greek original was traditionally dated to the late second century C.E., but some recent scholars argue that it was compiled during the fourth century.

mystery   Derived from a Greek word meaning "to initiate" or "to shut the eyes or mouth," probably referring to the secrets of Hellenistic "mystery religions," the term is used variously in the New Testament. Jesus speaks at least once of the "mystery" of the kingdom (Matt. 13:11; Mark 4:11; Luke 8:10), but Paul employs the term frequently as if the profounder aspects of Christianity were a religious secret into which the Spirit-directed believer becomes initiated (Rom. 11:5; 16:25; 1 Cor. 2:7; 4:1; 13:2; 14:2; 15:51; Col. 1:26; 2:2; 4:3; 2 Thess. 2:7; 1 Tim. 3:9; 3:16; see also Rev. 1:20; 10:7; 17:5–7).

myth   From the Greek *mythos* (story), the term denotes a narrative expressing a profound psychological or religious truth that cannot be verified by historical inquiry or other scientific means. When scholars speak of the "myth of Eden," for example, it is not to denigrate the tale's significance, but to emphasize the Eden story's archetypal expression of humanity's sense of alienation from its Creator. Myths typically feature stories about divine beings and national heroes who represent natural or psychological forces that deeply influence humans but that they cannot control. The psychologist Carl Jung interpreted myth as humanity's inherited concept of primeval events that persists in the unconscious mind and finds expression through repeated reenactments in ritual worship and other cultic practices. Israel's covenant-renewal ceremonies and retellings of Yahweh's saving acts during the Exodus are examples of such cultic myths.

mythology   A system or cycle of myths, such as those featuring the deities of ancient Greece or Rome. Once the embodiment of living religious beliefs, Greco-Roman and other mythologies are now seen as archetypal symbols that give symbolic meaning to universal human experiences. Mythologies are thus "falsehoods" only in the narrowest literal sense. They are probably akin to dreams in revealing persistent images and attitudes derived from the human unconscious.

Naaman   The Syrian commander-in-chief of Benhadad, king of Damascus and an enemy of Israel, whom the prophet Elisha bathes in the Jordan River to cure his leprosy (2 Kings 5:1–27).

Nabal   An epithet meaning "fool," the name applied to the rich shepherd, husband of Abigail, who refused to feed David's band of outlaw guerrillas (1 Sam. 25:2–42).

Nabonidus   Son of Nabu-balatsuikbi, father of Belshazzar, and last ruler of the Neo-Babylonian Empire (556–539 B.C.E.).

Nabopolassar   The name means "son of a nobody." Nabopolassar founded the Neo-Babylonian Empire by revolting against Assyria, a move that enabled King Josiah of Israel to carry out his religious reforms without Assyrian interference and to regain much of the old territory of the northern kingdom. Allied with the Medes, Nabopolassar destroyed Nineveh (612 B.C.E.) and was succeeded by his son Nebuchadnezzar II (Nah. 3:1–3; Zeph. 2:12–14; Jer. 46). *See also* Josiah.

Naboth   A landowner in the city of Jezreel whose vineyard King Ahab coveted, Naboth was illegally executed through Queen Jezebel's machinations (1 Kings 21:1–16). This crime, denounced by the prophet Elijah, became the focal point of resistance to Ahab's royal dynasty and culminated in its extermination by Jehu (1 Kings 21:17–29; 2 Kings 9:1–10:11).

Nahor   According to Genesis 11:27–30, the son of Terah, brother of Abraham and Haran. By Milcah (and a concubine) Nahor fathered twelve sons, eponymous ancestors of the north-Semitic Aramean tribes (Gen. 21:33; 24:24; 29:5–6).

Nahum   A prophet from Elkosh (Nah. 1:1) who delivered poems rejoicing in Nineveh's fall and the destruction of the Assyrian Empire (612 B.C.E.).

Naomi   Wife of Elimelech of Bethlehem (Ruth 1:2) and mother-in-law to Ruth, whose marriage she arranged to her Jewish kinsman Boaz (Ruth 3–4). Her name means "my pleasantness."

Naphtali   (1) According to Genesis 30:7–8, Naphtali was the son of Jacob and Rachel's handmaid Bilhah and compared to a wild hind in his father's blessing (Gen. 49:21); the eponymous ancestor of one of the northern tribes of Israel (1 Chron. 7:13; Exod. 1:4; Num. 1:15, 42; 26:50). (2) The tribe of Naphtali was assigned territory north of Megiddo along the upper Jordan and western shores of the Sea of Galilee (Josh. 19:32–39; Judg. 1:33). It supported King David (1 Chron. 12:34–40) but became part of the northern kingdom after 922 B.C.E. (1 Kings 15:20) and was dispersed by the Assyrians in 722–721 B.C.E. (2 Kings 15:29).

Naram-Sin Akkadian military leader and a grandson of Sargon I, Naram-Sin (c. 2260–2223 B.C.E.) campaigned throughout Mesopotamia and Iran, conquering numerous cities including Ebla, with its extensive cuneiform library.

narrative A literary composition that tells a story, arranging the characters and events in a sequential order. Most of the Bible's first eleven books are theologically oriented narratives constructed to illustrate the origin, nature, and consequences of Israel's covenant relationship with Yahweh (Gen.–2 Kings).

Nathan (1) A son of David (2 Sam. 5:14; Zech. 12:12; Luke 3:31). (2) A prophet and political counselor at David's court who enunciated the concept of an everlasting Davidic dynasty (2 Sam. 7), denounced the king for his adultery with Bathsheba (2 Sam. 12:1–23), revealed Adonijah's plan to seize power (1 Kings 1:5–8), helped Solomon succeed to David's throne (1 Kings 1:8–45), and is credited with writing a history of David's and Solomon's reigns (1 Chron. 29:29; 2 Chron. 9:29).

national epic The long prose narrative extending from the call of Abraham in Genesis 12 to Judah's fall to Babylon in 2 Kings 24–25; it includes the narrative portions of the Torah and of the Deuteronomistic History, the first eleven books of the Bible.

navi (nabi) The Hebrew word for "prophet," a spokesperson for Yahweh who delivered his God's judgments on contemporary society and expressed his intentions toward the world (Deut. 13:1–5; 18:9–22; Amos 3:7; etc.).

Nazarenes A name applied to early Christians (Acts 24:5).

Nazareth A town in Lower Galilee above the Plain of Esdraelon (Megiddo) where Jesus spent his youth and began his ministry (Matt. 2:23; Luke 1:26; 4:16; John 1:46).

Nazirites From the Hebrew *nazar* (to dedicate), referring to a group in ancient Israel that rigorously observed ascetic principles, including refusing to drink wine, cut their hair, come in contact with the dead, or eat religiously "unclean" food (Num. 6:1–21). Samson, despite his ill-fated love affairs, belonged to this sect (Judg. 13–16).

Nebuchadnezzar (1) A Fourth Dynasty king of the Old Babylonian Empire (twelfth century B.C.E.). (2) Son of Nabopolassar and the most powerful ruler of the Neo-Babylonian Empire (605–562 B.C.E.), Nebuchadnezzar II defeated Pharaoh Necho at the Battle of Carchemish (605 B.C.E.) (2 Kings 24:1–7; Jer. 46:2) and brought much of the Near East under his control. He attacked Judah and deported many of its upper classes in 598–597 B.C.E., besieged and destroyed Jerusalem in 587 B.C.E., and took much of its population captive to Babylon (2 Kings 24:10–25; 25:11–21; 2 Chron. 26:6–21; Jer. 39:1–10; 52:1–30). The portrait of him in Daniel is probably not historical (Dan. 2:1–13; 3:1–7; 4:4–37).

Nebuzaradan Commander of the Babylonian guard under Nebuchadnezzar who was sent to oversee the destruction of Jerusalem (587 B.C.E.) and the deportation to Babylon of Judah's population (2 Kings 25:8–20).

Necho Pharaoh Necho II, son of Psammetichus I (Psamtik), second king of the Twenty-Sixth Egyptian Dynasty (610–594 B.C.E.), defeated and killed King Josiah of Judah at Megiddo (609 B.C.E.), thus ending Josiah's religious reforms and Judah's political renaissance (2 Kings 23:29–35; 2 Chron. 35:20–24; 36:4). His plans to reassert Egyptian hegemony in the Near East were permanently thwarted when Nebuchadnezzar of Babylon defeated Egyptian forces at Carchemish (605 B.C.E.) (2 Kings 24:7; Jer. 46).

Negeb, The The largely desert territory south of Beersheba in Judah (Deut. 1:42–46; Josh. 10:40; 15:21–32; 19:1–9; Judg. 6:3; 1 Sam. 27:5–10; etc.).

Nehemiah A Jewish court official (cupbearer) living at the Persian capital in Susa who persuaded the emperor Artaxerxes I (465–423 B.C.E.) to commission him to go to Judea and rebuild Jerusalem's walls (Neh. 1:1–2:20). Although he encountered resistance from Judah's jealous neighbors, Nehemiah finished the rebuilding in record time (Neh. 3:33–6:19) and, with the priest Ezra, effected numerous social and religious reforms among the returned exiles (Neh. 8:1–9:3; 11:1–3; 12:27–13:3).

nephesh In biblical Hebrew, the term for "living being" or "animate creature" that applies to both humans and animals. A physical body infused with God's *ruah* ("breath" or "spirit"), the first human is created a *nephesh* (Gen. 2:7), a mortal unity of clay and spirit. In Greek translations of the Hebrew Bible, *nephesh* was commonly rendered as *psyche,* the Greek term for "soul" that had connotations of immortality absent in the Hebrew word.

Nergal-sharezer   A high Babylonian official present at the capture of Jerusalem who, at King Nebuchadnezzar's orders, helped protect the prophet Jeremiah (Jer. 39:1–14). He later became king of Babylon (560–556 B.C.E.) after murdering Amel-Marduk (the Evil-merodach of 2 Kings 25:27).

Nero   Nero Claudius Caesar Augustus Germanicus, emperor of Rome (54–68 C.E.), the Caesar by whom Paul wished to be tried in Acts 25:11 and under whose persecution Paul was probably beheaded (64–65 C.E.). A first-century superstition held that Nero, slain during a palace revolt, would return at the head of an army. Regarded by some Christians as the anti-Christ, Nero's reappearance is apparently suggested in Revelation 13:4–18.

Nethinim   A group of Temple servants who performed such menial tasks as carrying wood and water (Ezra 7:7, 24; 8:20; Neh. 3:26–31; 10:28–31).

Nevi'im (Prophets)   The Hebrew term designating the second major division of the tripartite Hebrew Bible (Tanak), the Prophets.

New Year Festival (*Rosh Hashanah*)   Also called the Feast of Trumpets (Lev. 23:23–25), this was a time when work ceased and the Israelites assembled together (Num. 29:1–6). Before the exile (587–538 B.C.E.), the Jews observed the festival in the autumn, but afterward they adopted the Babylonian celebration held in the spring, the first day of the month of Nisan (March-April). With a new emphasis on atonement, it became the first of Ten Days of Penitence, a solemn introduction to the Day of Atonement (*Yom Kippur*) (Lev. 16). Ezekiel urged the keeping of both New Years (Ezek. 40–48).

Nicanor   (1) A general of Antiochus IV whom the Maccabees defeated (1 Macc. 3:38; 7:26–32). (2) A deacon in the Jerusalem church (Acts 6:1, 5).

Nicodemus   A leading Pharisee and member of the Sanhedrin (John 3:1; 7:50; 19:39) who discussed spiritual rebirth with Jesus (John 3:1–21), visited him by night and defended him against other Pharisees (John 7:45–52), and, with Joseph of Arimathaea, helped entomb his body (John 19:38–42).

Nimrod   According to J, the great-grandson of Noah, grandson of Ham, son of Cush, and a legendary hunter and founder of cities in Mesopotamia (Gen. 9:19; 10:8–12). Several ruined sites in Iraq preserve his name.

Nineveh   The last capital of the Assyrian Empire, located on the east bank of the Tigris River, and supposedly founded by Nimrod (Gen. 10:11), Nineveh was one of the greatest cities in the ancient Near East (Jon. 1:2; 3:2–4; 4:11). Several Judean kings, including Hezekiah, sent tribute there (2 Kings 18:13–16). Its destruction was foretold by the prophets (2 Kings 19:5–37; Zeph. 2:13) and celebrated by Nahum (Nah. 1–3). Assyria's last major ruler, Ashurbanipal (668–627 B.C.E.), was an antiquarian who collected thousands of literary works on clay tablets — including the *Epic of Gilgamesh* and the *Enuma Elish*— for the royal library at Nineveh. After a three-month siege, the city was destroyed in 612 B.C.E. by a coalition of Medes, Babylonians, and Scythians. Jesus ironically refers to the "men of Nineveh" as more spiritually receptive than his contemporaries (Matt. 12:41).

Noah   The son of Lamech (Gen. 5:28–30), father of Ham, Shem, and Japheth (Gen. 4:32), whom Yahweh chose to build a wooden houseboat containing pairs of all living creatures to survive the Flood (Gen. 6:13–8:19) and with whom Yahweh made an "everlasting" covenant (Gen. 8:20–9:17). In another story (Gen. 5:29; 9:18–27), Noah is the first vinegrower and a victim of excessive drinking. Infrequently mentioned elsewhere in the Hebrew Bible (Isa. 54:9; Ezek. 14:14), he and the Flood are often cited in the New Testament as examples of divine judgment (Matt. 24:37–39; Luke 17:26–28; Heb. 11:7; 1 Pet. 3:20; 2 Pet. 2:5; 3:5–6).

Obadiah   (1) One of Ahab's stewards, who hid 100 Yahwist prophets in caves during Jezebel's persecutions and who arranged the meeting between Ahab and Elijah (1 Kings 18:3–16) that resulted in a contest between Yahweh and Baal on Mount Carmel (1 Kings 18:17–46). (2) Traditionally recognized as author of the Book of Obadiah, about whom nothing is known. His book is fourth and shortest among the Minor Prophets.

Obed   Son of Ruth and Boaz, and father of Jesse, father of David (Ruth 4:17–22; 1 Chron. 2:12; 11:47).

Obed-edom   (1) A citizen of Gath in whose house David placed the Ark of the Covenant before taking it to Jerusalem (2 Sam. 6:10–12; 1 Chron. 13:13–14). (2) The founder of a group of singers at the second Temple (1 Chron. 15:21; 16:5).

Olives, Mount of (Olivet) A mile-long limestone ridge with several distinct summits paralleling the eastern section of Jerusalem, from which it is separated by the narrow Kidron Valley. Here David fled during Absalom's rebellion (2 Sam. 15:30–32), and according to Zechariah 14:3–5, here Yahweh will stand at the final eschatological battle, when the mountain will be torn asunder from east to west. From its summit, with its panoramic view of Jerusalem, Jesus delivered his apocalyptic judgment on the city that had rejected him (Matt. 24–25). He often retreated to its shady groves in the evening (John 7:53; 8:1), including the night before his death (Matt. 26:30–56; Mark 14:26; Luke 22:39; see also Matt. 21:1; Mark 11:1; Luke 19:29; Acts 1:12).

omega The last letter in the Greek alphabet, used with alpha (the first letter) as a symbol of the eternity of God (Rev. 1:8; 21:6) and Jesus (Rev. 1:17; 22:13), probably echoing Isaiah's description of Yahweh as "the first and the last" (Isa. 44:6; 48:12).

Omri Sixth ruler of the northern kingdom (876–869 B.C.E.) and founder of a dynasty that included his son Ahab (869–850 B.C.E.), his grandson Ahaziah (850–849 B.C.E.), and a younger son Jehoram (849–842 B.C.E.), whose important military, political, and economic successes are minimized by the Deuteronomistic historians (2 Kings 16:23–28). Omri's leadership raised Israel to a power and prestige considerably above that of Judah. Even a century after his death and the extinction of his dynasty, Assyrian records referred to Israel as the "land of the House of Omri."

Onesimus The runaway slave of Philemon of Colossae whom Paul converted to Christianity and reconciled to his master (Philem. 8–21; Col. 4:7–9).

Ophel The southern end of Jerusalem's eastern or Temple hill, the site of David's city (2 Chron. 27:3; 33:14; Neh. 3:26–27; 11:31).

oracle (1) A divine message or utterance (Rom. 3:2; Heb. 5:12; 1 Pet. 4:11) or the person through whom it is conveyed (Acts 7:38). (2) An authoritative communication, such as that from a wise person (Prov. 31:1; 2 Sam. 16:23). (3) The inner sanctum of the Jerusalem Temple (1 Kings 6:5–6; 7:49; 8:6–8; Ps. 28:2). (4) The supposedly inspired words of a priest or priestess at such shrines as Delphi in ancient Greece and Cumae in Italy.

oral tradition Material passed from generation to generation by word of mouth before finding written form. Scholars believe that much of Israel's early history, customs, and beliefs about its origins, such as the stories about the patriarchs and Moses in the Pentateuch, were so transmitted before J first committed them to writing.

original sin The theological concept declaring that the entire human race has inherited from the first man (Adam) a tendency to sin. Some theologians, such as Augustine and Calvin, argued that humanity is born totally corrupt and justly condemned to damnation, a fate escaped only through accepting Jesus' sacrifice for sin. The doctrine is partly based on an extremist interpretation of Romans 5:12.

orthodoxy Literally "correct opinion," holding beliefs or doctrines established by a religious or political authority.

Osiris Ancient Egyptian god of fertility and also of the underworld.

P *See* Priestly document.

Palestine A strip of land bordering the eastern Mediterranean Sea, lying south of Syria, north of the Sinai peninsula, and west of the Arabian desert. During the patriarchal period, it was known as Canaan (Gen. 12:6–7; 15:18–21). Named for the Philistines, it was first called Palestine by the Greek historian Herodotus about 450 B.C.E.

Pamphylia A small area (after 74 C.E., a Roman province) along the southern coast of Asia Minor where Paul broke with Barnabas and John Mark (Acts 13:13; 14:24–25; 15:38; 27:5).

pantheon The accepted list or roster of a people's chief gods, such as the Olympian family of gods worshiped in classical Greece. It is also the name of a famous temple in Rome, the house of "all the gods."

parable From the Greek *parabole* (a placing beside, a comparison), a short fictional narrative that compares something familiar to an unexpected spiritual value. Using a commonplace object or event to illustrate a religious principle was Jesus' typical method of teaching in the Synoptic Gospels (Matt. 13:3–53; 22:1; 24:32; Mark 4:2–3; 13:28; Luke 8:4–18; 13:18–21; 21:29). Yet, a recurrent tradition held that Jesus used parables to prevent most of his hearers from understanding his message (Mark 4:10–12; Matt. 13:10–15; Luke 8:9–10). Famous Hebrew Bible parables or fables include Nathan's (2 Sam. 12:1–14), Isaiah's (Isa. 5:1–7), Jotham's (Judg. 9:7–21), Jehoash's (2

Kings 14:8–10), and Ezekiel's (Ezek. 17:22–24; 24:1–14), the last two of which are allegories.

Paraclete　A Greek term (meaning "an advocate" or "intercessor summoned to aid") that the Gospel of John uses to denote the Holy Spirit, Paraclete is variously translated "Comforter," "Helper," "Advocate," or "Spirit of Truth" (John 7:39; 14:12, 16–18; 15:26; 16:7; see also 1 John 2:1).

paradise　Literally, a "park" or walled garden, paradise is the name applied to Eden (Gen. 2:8–17) and in post–Hebrew Bible times to the abode of the righteous dead, of which the lower part housed souls awaiting the resurrection and the higher was the permanent home of the just. It is possible that Jesus referred to the lower paradise in his words to the thief on the cross (Luke 23:43). Paul's reference to being "caught up" into paradise may refer to the third of the seven heavens postulated in later Jewish eschatology (as in the books of Enoch) (2 Cor. 12:2–5). John's vision of the tree of life in "the garden of God" (Rev. 2:7; 22:1–3) depicts an earthly paradise.

parallelism　A structural feature typical of Hebrew poetry, consisting of the repetition of similar or antithetical thoughts in similar phrasing: "The wicked will not stand firm when Judgment comes nor sinners when the virtuous assemble" (Ps. 1:5).

Parousia　A Greek term (meaning "being by" or "being near") used to denote the Second Coming or appearance of Christ, commonly regarded as his return to judge the world, punish the wicked, and redeem the saved. It is a major concept in apocalyptic Christianity (Mark 13; Matt. 24–25; Luke 21; 1 and 2 Thess.; 2 Pet. 2–3; Rev.); but see also John 14:25–29; which emphasizes Jesus' continued spiritual presence rather than an eschatological apparition.

Passion　The term commonly used to denote Jesus' suffering and death (Acts 1:3).

Passover　An annual Jewish observance commemorating Israel's last night of bondage in Egypt when the Angel of Death "passed over" Israelite homes marked with the blood of a sacrificial lamb to destroy the firstborn of every Egyptian household (Exod. 12:1–51). Beginning the seven-day Feast of Unleavened Bread, it is a ritual meal eaten on Nisan 14 (March-April) that traditionally includes roast lamb, unleavened bread, and bitter herbs (Exod. 12:15–20; 13:3–10; Lev. 23:5; Num. 9:5; 28:16; Deut. 16:1). The Passover was scrupulously observed by Israel's great leaders, including Joshua (Josh. 5:10), Hezekiah (2 Chron. 30:1), Josiah (2 Kings 23:21–23; 2 Chron. 35:1–18), and the returned exiles (Ezra 6:19), as well as by Jesus and his disciples (Matt. 26:2, 17–29; Mark 14:1–16; Luke 22:1–13; John 13:1; 18:39). According to the Synoptics, Jesus' Last Supper with the Twelve was a Passover celebration (Matt. 26; Mark 14; Luke 22) and the model for Christian Communion (the Eucharist) (1 Cor. 11:17–27).

pastoral epistles　The name applied to the New Testament books of 1 and 2 Timothy and Titus, presumably written by the apostle Paul to two of his fellow ministers (pastors), but which modern scholars believe were composed by an anonymous disciple of Pauline thought living near the mid-second century C.E.

Patmos　A small Aegean island off the coast of western Asia Minor (Turkey) where John, author of Revelation, was exiled by the emperor Domitian about 95 C.E. (Rev. 1:9).

patriarch　The male head (father) of an ancient family line, a venerable tribal founder or leader; especially (1) the early ancestors of humanity listed in Genesis 4–5, known as the "antediluvian patriarchs"; (2) prominent "fathers" living after the Flood to the time of Abraham (Gen. 11); (3) the immediate progenitors of the Israelites: Abraham, Isaac, and Jacob (Gen. 12–50; Exod. 3:6; 6:2–8). Acts 7:8–9 includes Jacob's twelve sons among the patriarchs.

Paul　The most influential apostle and missionary of the mid-first-century C.E. church and author of seven to nine New Testament letters. Saul of Tarsus (Paul's original name) was born in the capital of the Asia Minor province of Cilicia (Acts 9:11; 21:39; 22:3) into a family of Pharisees (Acts 23:6) of the tribe of Benjamin (Phil. 3:5) and had both Roman and Taurean citizenship (Acts 22:28). Suddenly converted to Christianity after persecuting early Christians (Acts 7:55–8:3; 9:1–30; 22:1–21; 26:1–23; 1 Cor. 9:1; 15:8; Gal. 1:11–24; Eph. 3:3; Phil. 3:12), he undertook at least three international missionary tours, presenting defenses of the new faith before Jewish and Gentile authorities (Acts 13:1–28:31). His emphasis on the insufficiency of the Mosaic Law for salvation (Gal. 3–5; Rom. 4–11) and the superiority of faith to law (Rom. 4–11) and his insistence that Gentiles be admitted to the church without observing Jewish legal restrictions (Gal. 2, 5; Rom. 7–8) were decisive in determining the future development of the new religion. He was probably martyred in Rome about 64–65 C.E.

Pella　A Gentile city in Palestine east of the Jordan River, to which tradition says that Jesus' family and other Jewish Christians fled during the Jewish revolt against Rome (66–70 C.E.). Before this time, Jerusalem had been the center of the Palestinian Jewish-Christian church. References in Acts and Paul's letters indicate that Palestinian Christian teachings differed significantly from those Paul stressed in the churches of Gentile Christianity. No writings from the Palestinian Christians survive, so the fate of the Pella community is not known.

Pentateuch From a Greek word meaning "five scrolls," the term denotes the first five books of the Hebrew Bible, the Torah.

Pentecost (1) Also known as the Feast of Weeks (Exod. 34:22; Deut. 16:10), the Feast of Harvest (Exod. 23:16), and the Day of the First Fruits (Num. 28:26), Pentecost was a one-day celebration held fifty days after Passover at the juncture of May and June. (2) The occasion of the outpouring of Holy Spirit on early Christians assembled in Jerusalem (Acts 2:1–41), regarded as the spiritual baptism of the church.

Peniel A site on the Jabbok River in Jordan where Jacob wrestled with El (God) and thereby won a blessing (Gen. 33:22–33).

Peor A mountain in Moab on which King Balak commanded the prophet Balaam to build seven altars (Num. 23:28–30), Peor may also have been the place where Israel sinned by worshiping Baal (Num. 25:1–18; Josh. 22:17).

Peraea (Perea) A name the historian Flavius Josephus gave the area that the Hebrew Bible called the land "beyond" or "across" (east of) the Jordan River (Gen. 50:10; Num. 22:1; Matt. 4:14; 19:1; John 10:40). Both John the Baptist and Jesus retreated to this rugged territory (John 1:28; 10:40–42; 11:3).

Pergamum A major Hellenistic city in western Asia Minor (modern Bergama in west Anatolian Turkey), site of a magnificent temple of Zeus, which some commentators believe is referred to as "Satan's Throne" in Revelation 2:13, Pergamum is one of the seven churches that the author John of Patmos addresses (Rev. 1:11; 2:12–17).

pericope A term used in form criticism to describe a literary unit (a saying, anecdote, parable, or brief narrative) that forms a complete entity in itself and is attached to its context by later editorial commentary. Many of Jesus' pronouncements probably circulated independently as pericopes before they were incorporated into the written Gospel records.

Persepolis A capital of the Persian Empire established by Darius I (522–486 B.C.E.) and burned by Alexander the Great (330 B.C.E.) (2 Macc. 9:2).

Persia A large Asian territory southeast of Elam inhabited by Indo-European (Ayrian, hence "Iran") peoples, Persia became a world power under Cyrus the Great, who united Media and Persia (549 B.C.E.); conquered Lydia (546 B.C.E.) and Babylon (539 B.C.E.), including its former dominion, Palestine; then permitted the formerly captive Jews to return to their homeland (2 Chron. 36:20–22; Ezra 1). Under the emperor Darius I (522–486 B.C.E.), the Jerusalem Temple was rebuilt (Ezra 3–6). A son of Darius, Xerxes I (486–465 B.C.E.) was probably the Ahasuerus of the Book of Esther (Esther 1:2; 2:1; 3:1; 8:1). Artaxerxes I (465–423 B.C.E.) decreed the return of two other exile groups under Ezra and Nehemiah.

pesher A Hebrew word denoting an analysis or interpretation of Scripture, it is applied to the commentaries (*persherim*) found among the Dead Sea Scrolls.

Peshitta A version of the Hebrew Bible translated for Christian churches in Syria during the fifth century C.E.

Peter The most prominent of Jesus' twelve chief disciples, Peter was also known as Simon (probably his surname), Simeon (Symeon), and Cephas (the Aramaic equivalent of *petros,* meaning "the rock" or "stone") (John 1:40–42). The son of Jonas or John (Matt. 16:17; John 1:42; 21:15–17), brother of the apostle Andrew, and a native of Bethsaida, a fishing village on the Sea of Galilee (John 1:44), he was called by Jesus to be "a fisher of men" (Matt. 4:18–20; Mark 1:16–18; Luke 5:1–11). The first to recognize Jesus as the Messiah (Matt. 16:13–20; Mark 8:27–30; Luke 9:18–22), Peter later denied him three times (Matt. 26:69–75; Mark 14:66–72; Luke 22:54–62; John 18:15–18).

Commanded to "feed [the resurrected Jesus'] sheep" (John 21:15–19), Peter became a leader of the Jerusalem church (Acts 1:15–26; 2:14–42; 15:6–12) and miracle worker (Acts 3:1–10) and was instrumental in bringing the first Gentiles into the church (Acts 10–11), although Paul regarded him as a conservative obstacle to this movement (Gal. 2:11–14). He appeared before the Sanhedrin (Acts 4:1–12) and was miraculously rescued from at least one imprisonment (Acts 5:17–42; 12:1–19). A married man (Matt. 8:14; Mark 1:30; Luke 4:8; 1 Cor. 9:5), Peter was to be the "rock" on which Jesus' church was built (Matt. 16:16–20). Although some scholars regard him as the source of 1 Peter, virtually all experts deny Petrine authorship to the second epistle bearing his name. He was martyred under Nero in about 64–65 C.E.

pharaoh The title of Egypt's king, commonly used in place of a ruler's proper name in the Hebrew

Bible. Thus, the pharaohs who confiscated Abraham's wife (Gen. 12:14–20), rewarded Joseph (Gen. 41:37–57), enslaved the Israelites (Exod. 1:8–22), and opposed Moses (Exod. 5:1–6:1; 6:27–15:19) are all anonymous, although many scholars believe that the pharaoh of the Exodus was Rameses II (c. 1290–1224 B.C.E.). Solomon later made Egyptian pharaohs his allies (1 Kings 3:1; 7:8). Pharaoh Shishak (Sheshonk I) sacked the Jerusalem Temple during King Rehoboam's time (c. 922–915 B.C.E.) (1 Kings 14:25–28; 2 Chron. 12:2–9). Pharaoh Necho killed King Josiah at Megiddo but was later defeated by Nebuchadnezzar at Carchemish (2 Kings 23:29–34; 24:7; 2 Chron. 35:20–36:4).

Pharisees   A leading religious movement or sect in Judaism during the last two centuries B.C.E. and the two first centuries C.E., the Pharisees were probably descendants of the hasidim who opposed Antiochus IV's attempts to destroy the Mosaic faith. Their name may derive from the Hebrew *parush* (separated) because their rigorous observance of the law bred a separatist view toward common life. Although the New Testament typically presents them as Jesus' opponents, their views on resurrection and the afterlife anticipated Christian teachings. The "seven woes" against the Pharisees appear in Matthew 23:13–32. Paul was a Pharisee (Acts 23:6; 26:5; Phil. 3:5).

Philadelphia   A city in Lydia (modern Turkey) about twenty-eight miles from Sardis, one of the seven churches in Revelation 3:7–13.

Philemon   A citizen of Colossae whose runaway slave, Onesimus, Paul converted to Christianity (Philem. 5, 10, 16, 19).

Philip   (1) King of Macedonia (359–336 B.C.E.), father of Alexander the Great (1 Macc. 1:1; 6:2). (2) One of the Twelve, a man of Bethsaida in Galilee (Matt. 10:3; Mark 3:18; Luke 6:14; John 1:43–49; 12:21–22; 14:8–9; Acts 1:12–14). (3) An evangelist of the Jerusalem church who was an administrator (Acts 6:1–6) and preacher (Acts 8:4–8), the convertor of Simon the sorcerer (Acts 8:9–13) and of an Ethiopian eunuch (Acts 8:26–39). Paul visited Philip at Caesarea (Acts 21:8–15). (4) A son of Herod the Great and Palestinian tetrarch (4 B.C.E.–34 C.E.) (Luke 3:1).

Philippi   A city of eastern Macedonia, the first European center to receive the Christian message (Acts 16:10–40), Philippi became the apostle Paul's favorite church (Acts 20:6; Phil. 4:16; 2 Cor. 11:9) and the one to which his letter to the Philippians is addressed.

Philistines   A people from Aegean Sea islands (called Caphtor in Amos 9:7) who settled along the southern coast of Palestine during the twelfth century B.C.E. to become the Israelites' chief rivals during the period of the judges and early monarchy (c. 1200–1000 B.C.E.) (Josh. 13:2–4; Judg. 1:18–19; 13:1–16:31; 1 Sam. 4:2–7:14; 13:1–14:46; 17:1–54; 2 Sam. 5:17–25; 8:1–2; 21:15–18; see also Jer. 47:1–7; Zeph. 2:4–7).

Philo Judaeus   The most influential philosopher of Hellenistic Judaism, Philo was a Greek-educated Jew living in Alexandria, Egypt (c. 20 B.C.E.–50 C.E.), who promoted a method of interpreting the Hebrew Bible allegorically (which may have influenced Paul in such passages as 1 Cor. 10:4 and Gal. 4:24, as well as the authors of the fourth Gospel and Hebrews). His doctrine of the Logos (the divine creative Word) shaped the prologue to the Gospel of John.

Phinehas   Grandson of Aaron, son of Eleazar, Israel's third high priest (Num. 10:8–10; 25:6–13; Josh. 22:13, 30–32; 24:33).

Phoebe   A servant or deaconess of the church at Cenchrae, a port of Corinth, whose good works Paul commends in Romans 16:1–2.

Phoenicia   A narrow coastal territory along the northeast Mediterranean, lying between the Lebanon range on the east and the sea on the west. It included the ports of Tyre and Sidon. Notable Hebrew Bible Phoenicians are Ethbaal, king of Tyre (1 Kings 16:21); his daughter Jezebel, wife of Ahab (1 Kings 18:19); Hiram, king of Tyre (2 Sam. 5:11; 1 Kings 5:1–12; 2 Chron. 2:3–16); and Hiram, the architect-decorator of Solomon's Temple (1 Kings 7:13–47; 2 Chron. 2:13). Jesus visited the area, where he healed the daughter of a Syro-Phoenician woman (Matt. 15:21; Mark 7:24, 31; Acts 15:3; 21:2–7).

phylacteries   One of the two small leather pouches containing copies of four scriptural passages (Exod. 13:1–10, 11–16; Deut. 6:4–9; 11:13–21), worn on the left arm and forehead by Jewish men during weekday prayers (Exod. 13:9, 16; Deut. 6:8; 11:18; Matt. 23:5).

Plato   Greek philosopher (427–347 B.C.E.) who postulated the existence of a dualistic universe consisting of an invisible spiritual realm containing ideal forms of everything that exists and an inferior material realm composed of imperfect replicas of those forms. Plato's view of the immortal human soul and its posthumous destiny greatly influenced virtually all subsequent Western thought, including that of official Christianity.

policy law   Also known as apodictic or absolute law, this term refers to laws stated unconditionally, such as the Ten Commandments of the Decalogue. *See also* apodictic law.

Polycarp   A bishop of Smyrna who was reputed to have been a disciple of John and who was martyred in 155 C.E. Letters to and from Polycarp are considered important noncanonical works.

polytheism   Belief in more than one god, the most common form of religion in the ancient world.

Pompey   A leading Roman general and rival of Julius Caesar, with whom he established a temporary political alliance known as the First Triumvirate, Pompey (106–49 B.C.E.) conquered much of the eastern Mediterranean region for Rome, including Syria and Judea (63 B.C.E.).

Pontius Pilate   The Roman prefect (also called a procurator) of Judea (26–36 C.E.) who presided at Jesus' trial for sedition against Rome and sentenced him to be crucified (Luke 3:1; 13:1; 23:1–25; Matt. 27:1–26; Mark 15:1–15; John 18:28–19:22; Acts 3:13; 13:28; 1 Tim. 6:13).

Potiphar   The head of Pharaoh's bodyguards who placed Joseph in charge of his household but later threw him in prison when the Hebrew slave was accused of seducing Potiphar's wife (Gen. 37:36; 39:1).

priestly document   The priestly composition, referred to as P. This is the final written addition to the Pentateuch, consisting largely of genealogical, statistical, and legal material compiled during and after the Babylonian exile (c. 550–450 B.C.E.). Major blocks of P occur in Exodus 25–31 and 35–40, Leviticus 1–27, and Numbers 1–10. P incorporated the earlier J and E sources and provided an editorial framework for the entire Torah. Some recent scholars believe that P is responsible for most of the Pentateuch.

Priscilla (Prisca)   The wife of Aquila and a leading member of the early church (Acts 18:18; Rom. 16:3; 2 Tim. 4:19).

proconsul   A Roman governor or administrator of a province or territory, such as Gallio, proconsul of Achaia, before whom Paul appeared (Acts 18:12).

procurator   The Roman title of the governor of a region before it became an administrative province. During the reigns of Augustus and Tiberius, Judea was governed by a prefect, the most famous of whom was Pontius Pilate. The office was upgraded to the level of procurator under Claudius.

prophet   One who preaches or proclaims the word or will of his or her Deity (Amos 3:7–8; Deut. 18:9–22). A true prophet in Israel was regarded as divinely inspired. Prophets, both male and female, abounded in the early church. *See navi.*

Prophets *(Nevi'im)*   The second major division of the Hebrew Bible, including Joshua through 2 Kings, Isaiah, Jeremiah, Ezekiel, and the twelve Minor Prophets.

Protoevangelium of James   Also called the Book of James, a noncanonical gospel, supposedly written by James (pictured as Jesus' older step-brother), that provides an account of Jesus' parents and family. Although this work is not part of the New Testament canon, it has been influential in church history because of its portrait of Mary, Jesus' mother.

proverb   A brief saying that memorably expresses a familiar or useful bit of folk wisdom, usually of a practical or prudential nature.

Providence   A quasi-religious concept in which God is viewed as the force sustaining and guiding human destiny. It assumes that events occur as part of a divine plan or purpose working for the ultimate triumph of Good.

psalm   A sacred song or poem used in praise or worship of the Deity, particularly those in the Book of Psalms.

Pseudepigrapha   (1) Literally, books falsely ascribed to eminent biblical figures of the past, such as Enoch, Noah, Moses, or Isaiah. (2) A collection of religious books outside the Hebrew Bible canon or Apocrypha that were composed in Hebrew, Aramaic, and Greek from about 200 B.C.E. to 200 C.E.

pseudonymity   A literary practice, common among Jewish writers of the last two centuries B.C.E. and the first two centuries C.E., of writing or publishing a book in the name of a famous religious figure of the past. Thus, an anonymous author of about 168 B.C.E. ascribed his work to Daniel, who supposedly lived during the 500s B.C.E. The Pastorals, 2 Peter, James, and Jude are thought to be pseudonymous books written in the mid-second century C.E. but attributed to eminent disciples connected with the first-century Jerusalem church.

psyche   The Greek word for "soul," which such philosophers as Pythagoras, Socrates, and Plato taught was the invisible center of rational consciousness and personality that survived bodily death to experience rewards or penalties in the afterlife. Although biblical concepts of the soul do not presume its inherent immortality, the Greek philosophic position deeply influenced later Christian teachings on the subject.

Ptolemy   (1) Ptolemy I (323–285 B.C.E.) was a Macedonian general who assumed rulership of Egypt after the death of Alexander the Great. The Ptolemaic dynasty controlled Egypt and its dominions until 31 B.C.E., when the Romans came to power. (2) Ptolemy II (285–246 B.C.E.) supposedly authorized the translation of the Hebrew Bible into Greek (the Septuagint).

publican   In the New Testament, petty tax collectors for Rome, despised by the Jews from whom they typically extorted money (Matt. 9:10–13; 18:17; 21:31). Jesus dined with these "sinners" (Matt. 9:9–13) and called one, Levi (Matthew), to apostleship (Matt. 9:9–13; Luke 5:27–31). He also painted a publican as more virtuous than a Pharisee (Luke 18:9–14).

Purim   A Jewish nationalistic festival held on the fourteenth and fifteenth days of Adar (February-March) and based on events in the Book of Esther.

Q   An abbreviation for *Quelle,* the German term for "source," a hypothetical document that many scholars believe contained a collection of Jesus' sayings (*logia*). The theory of its existence was formed to explain material common to both Matthew and Luke but absent from Mark's Gospel. It is assumed that Matthew and Luke drew on a single source (Q), assembled in about 50–70 C.E., for this shared material.

Queen of Heaven   A Semitic goddess of love and fertility worshiped in various forms throughout the ancient Near East. Known as Ishtar to the Babylonians, she was denounced by Jeremiah but worshiped by Jewish refugees in Egypt after the fall of Jerusalem (Jer. 7:18; 44:17–19, 25).

Qumran   Ruins of an Essene monastic community located near the northwest corner of the Dead Sea, near which the Essene library (Dead Sea Scrolls) were hidden in caves. The Romans destroyed it in 68 C.E.

rabbi   A Jewish title (meaning "master" or "teacher") given to scholars learned in the Torah. Jesus was frequently addressed by this title (Matt. 23:8; 26:25, 49; Mark 8:5; 10:51; 11:21; 14:45; John 1:38, 49; 3:2; 4:31; 6:25; 9:2; 11:8; 20:16), as was John the Baptist (John 3:26), although Jesus supposedly forbade his followers to be so called (Matt. 23:7–8).

Rachel   Daughter of Laban, second and favorite wife of Jacob, mother of Joseph and Benjamin (Gen. 29:6–30; 30:1–24; 35:16–19). When Rachel fled her father's house with Jacob, she stole Laban's household gods (Gen. 31:32–35). Jeremiah prophesied that Rachel (Israel) would "weep for her children," which the author of Matthew's Gospel regarded as fulfilled when Herod slaughtered the children of Bethlehem (Jer. 31:15; Matt. 2:18; see also Ruth 4:11).

Rahab   (1) A prostitute of Jericho, possibly a priestess in a Canaanite fertility cult, who hid Israelite spies and was spared her city's destruction (Josh. 2:1–24; 6:25; Ps. 87:4; Heb. 11:31). (2) A mythological sea monster, the dragon of chaos, whom Yahweh subdued before his creation of the universe (Ps. 89:10); also a symbol of Egypt (Ps. 87:4; Isa. 30:7).

Rameses (Raamses)   One of the two "store cities" that the enslaved Israelites built for Pharaoh (probably Rameses II) (Exod. 1:11; 12:37; Num. 33:3–5).

Rameses II   Ruler of Egypt (c. 1290–1224 B.C.E.) who many scholars think was the pharaoh of the Exodus.

Ramoth-Gilead   A town in Gilead, east of Jordan near the Syrian border, that was a city of refuge (Deut. 4:43; Josh. 20:8) and a Levitical center (Josh. 21:38; 1 Chron. 6:80) for the tribe of Gad. Ahab of Israel (869–850 B.C.E.) was killed trying to recapture it from Aram (Syria) (1 Kings 22:1–38; 2 Chron. 18:1–34), and the usurper Jehu was anointed there (2 Kings 9:1–21).

Ras Shamra   *See* Ugarit.

realized eschatology   A belief that events usually associated with the *eschaton* (world End) are even now realized or fulfilled by Jesus' spiritual presence among believers (John 5:24–25; 11:25–26).

Rebekah (Rebecca)   The daughter of Milcah and Bethuel, son of Abraham's brother Nahor (Gen. 24:15, 47), and sister of Laban (Gen. 25:20), whom Abraham's representative found at Haran and brought back to Canaan as a bride for Isaac (Gen. 24). Of Esau and Jacob, the twin sons she bore Isaac, she preferred Jacob and helped him trick her dying husband into giving him the paternal blessing (Gen. 25:21–28; 27:5–30; see also Rom. 9:10).

Rechab   The father of Jehonadab (Jonadab), who assisted Jehu in exterminating Ahab's entire household and associates (2 Kings 10:1–28). The Rechabites were a group of ascetics who abstained from wine, settled dwellings, and other aspects of what they considered urban corruption.

redaction criticism   A method of analyzing written texts that tries to define the purpose and literary procedures of editors (redactors) who compile and edit older documents, transforming shorter works into longer ones, as did the redactor who collected and ordered the words of the prophets into their present biblical form.

redactor   Editor. *See* redaction criticism.

Rehoboam   A son of Solomon and Naamah (an Ammonite princess), the last ruler of the united kingdom (922–915 B.C.E.), whose harsh policies resulted in the ten northern tribes' deserting the Davidic monarchy in Judah and forming the independent northern kingdom of Israel (922 B.C.E.) (1 Kings 11:43; 12:1–24; 14:21–31; 2 Chron. 9:31–12:16) and in Pharaoh Shishak's (Sheshonk I) despoiling the Jerusalem Temple (1 Kings 14:25–28).

rephaim   The Hebrew Bible's term for the shades of the dead, which, like the souls in Homer's portrayal of Hades (*Odyssey* XI), had a grim, joyless posthumous quasi-existence in the depths of Sheol (Ps. 88:10). The term is also applied to the pre-Israelite inhabitants of Transjordan (Gen. 14:5; Deut. 2:10–11) and to Philistine giants (2 Sam. 21:16, 18, 20; 1 Chron. 20:4, 6, 8). The connection between these diverse usages of *rephaim* is unknown.

resurrection   The returning of the dead to life, a late Hebrew Bible belief (Isa. 26:19; Dan. 12:2–3, 13) that first became prevalent in Judaism during the time of the Maccabees (after 168 B.C.E.) and became a part of the Pharisees' doctrine. Like the prophets Elijah and Elisha (1 Kings 17:17–24; 2 Kings 4:18–37), Jesus performed several resuscitations: of the widow of Nain's son (Luke 7:11–17), the daughter of Jairus (Mark 5:21–43), and Lazarus (John 11:1–44). Unlike these personages, however, Jesus ascended to heaven after his own resurrection (Acts 1:7–8). Paul gives the fullest discussion of the resurrection in the New Testament (1 Thess. 4; 1 Cor. 15), although he leaves many questions unanswered (see also Matt. 25:31–46 and Rev. 20:13).

Reuben   (1) The son of Jacob and Leah, eldest of his father's twelve sons (Gen. 29:32; Num. 26:5), Reuben slept with his father's concubine (Gen. 35:22), which cost him a paternal blessing (Gen. 49:3–4), but he defended Joseph against his brothers (Gen. 37:21–30). (2) The northern Israelite tribe supposedly descended from Reuben (Num. 32:1–38)

that along with Gad settled in the highlands east of the Jordan River.

rhetorical criticism   A method of textual analysis that studies not only the form and structure of a given literary work but the distinctive style of the author.

Roman Empire   The international, interracial government centered in Rome, Italy, that conquered and administered the entire Mediterranean region from Gaul (France and southern Germany) in the northwest to Egypt in the southeast and ruled the Jews of Palestine from 63 B.C.E. until Hadrian's destruction of Jerusalem during the second Jewish revolt (132–135 C.E.).

Rosetta Stone   A granite block bearing the same message inscribed in both Greek and ancient Egyptian hieroglyphics, a bilingual inscription that enabled scholars to decipher the language of the pharaohs. Discovered in 1799 and translated by the French linguist Champollion, it records a proclamation by Ptolemy V (c. 203–181 B.C.E.).

ruah   In biblical Hebrew, a word meaning "wind," "breath," or "spirit" (Gen. 1:2). It can be interpreted as the mysterious power or presence of God operating in nature and human society, implementing the divine will and inspiring individuals or communities to carry out the divine purpose.

Ruel   In J's account, a priest of Midian and the father-in-law of Moses, whom E calls Jethro (Exod. 2:15–22). *See* Jethro.

Ruth   A widow from Moab who married Boaz of Bethlehem and became an ancestor of King David (Ruth 4:17).

Saba (Sheba)   A Semitic kingdom in western Arabia noted for its merchants and luxury trade but best known for the visit of one of its queens to Solomon's court (1 Kings 10:1–13; 2 Chron. 9:1–12; 2 Matt. 12:42; Luke 11:31).

Sabbath   The seventh day of the Jewish week, sacred to Yahweh and dedicated to rest and worship. Enjoined upon Israel as a sign of Yahweh's covenant (Exod. 20:8–11; 23:12; 31:12–17; Lev. 23:3; 24:1–9; Deut. 5:12–15) and a memorial of Yahweh's repose after six days of creation, the Sabbath was strictly observed by leaders of the returned exiles (Neh. 13:15–22; Isa. 56:2–6; Ezek. 46:1–7). Jesus was frequently criticized for his liberal attitude toward the Sabbath, which he contended was made for humanity's benefit (Matt. 12:1–12; Mark 2:23–28; Luke 6:1–9; John 5:18).

Sabbatical Year   According to the Torah, every seventh year was to be a Sabbath among years, a time when fields were left fallow, native-born slaves freed, and outstanding debts canceled (Exod. 21:2–6; 23: 10–13; Lev. 25:1–19; Deut. 15:1–6).

sacrifice   In ancient religion, something precious — usually an unblemished animal, fruit, or grain — offered to a god and thereby made sacred. The Mosaic Law required the regular ritual slaughter of sacrificial animals and birds (Lev. 1:1–7:38; 16:1–17:14; Deut. 15:19–23; etc.).

Sadducees   An ultraconservative Jewish sect of the first century B.C.E. and first century C.E. composed largely of wealthy and politically influential landowners. Unlike the Pharisees, the Sadducees recognized only the Torah as binding and rejected the Prophets and Writings, denying both resurrection and a judgement in the afterlife. An aristocracy controlling the priesthood and Temple, they cooperated with Roman rule of Palestine, a collusion that made them unpopular with the common people (Matt. 3:7; 16:1; 22:23; Mark 12:18; Luke 20:27; Acts 4:1; 5:17; 23:6).

saints   Holy ones, persons of exceptional virtue and sanctity, believers outstandingly faithful despite persecution (Dan. 7:18–21; 8:13; Matt. 27:52; Acts 9:13; 26:10; Rom. 8:27; 1 Cor. 6:2; 1 Thess. 3:13; 2 Thess. 1:10; Heb. 13:24; Rev. 5:8; 13:7–10; 17:6; 20:9).

Salem   The Canaanite settlement ruled by the king–priest Melchizedek (Gen. 14:18), later identified with Jerusalem (Ps. 76:2).

Salome   (1) Daughter of Herodias and Herod (son of Herod the Great) and niece of Herod Antipas, before whom she danced to secure the head of John the Baptist (Matt. 14:3–11; Mark 6:17–28). Anonymous in the New Testament, her name is given by Flavius Josephus (*Antiquities* 18.5.4). (2) A woman present at Jesus' crucifixion (Matt. 27:56; Mark 15:40) and at the empty tomb (Mark 16:1).

Samaria   Capital of the northern kingdom (Israel), Samaria was founded by Omri (c. 876–869 B.C.E.) (1 Kings 16:24–25) and included a temple and altar of Baal (1 Kings 16:32). The Assyrians destroyed it in 721 B.C.E. (2 Kings 17), a fate the prophets warned awaited Jerusalem (Isa. 8:4; 10:9–11; Mic. 1:1–7).

Samaritans   Inhabitants of the city or territory of Samaria, the central region of Palestine lying west of the Jordan River. According to a probably biased southern account in 2 Kings 17, the Samaritans were regarded by orthodox Jews as descendants of foreigners who had intermarried with survivors of the northern kingdom's fall to Assyria (721 B.C.E.). Separated from the rest of Judaism after about 400 B.C.E., they had a Bible consisting of their own edition of the Pentateuch (Torah) and a temple on Mount Gerizim, which was later destroyed by John Hyrcanus (128 B.C.E.) (Matt. 10:5; Luke 9:52; John 4:20–21). Jesus discussed correct worship with a woman at Jacob's well in Samaria (John 4:5–42) and made a "good Samaritan" the hero of a famous parable (Luke 10:29–37).

Samson   Son of Manoah of the tribe of Dan, Samson was a Nazirite judge of Israel famous for his supernatural strength, abortive love affair with Delilah, and spectacular destruction of the Philistine temple of Dagon (Judg. 13–16).

Samuel   The son of Hannah and Elkanah, an Ephraimite (1 Sam. 1:1–2), Samuel was Israel's last judge (1 Sam. 7:15; Acts 13:20), a prophet and seer (1 Sam. 9:9) who also performed priestly functions (1 Sam. 2:18, 27, 35; 7:9–12). Trained by the High Priest Eli at Shiloh (1 Sam. 2:11–21; 3:1–10), he became the single greatest influence in Israel's transition from the tribal confederacy to monarchy under Saul, whom he anointed king (1 Sam. 8:1–10:27) but later rejected in favor of David (1 Sam. 13:8–15; 15:10–35).

sanctuary   A holy place dedicated to the worship of a god and believed to confer personal security to those who took refuge in it. Solomon's Temple on Mount Zion in Jerusalem was such a sacred edifice, although Jeremiah denounced those who trusted in its power to save a disobedient people from punishment (Jer. 7; 26).

Sanhedrin   The supreme judicial council of the Jews from about the third century B.C.E. until the Romans destroyed Jerusalem in 70 C.E., its deliberations were led by the High Priest (2 Chron. 19:5–11). Jesus was tried before the Sanhedrin and condemned on charges of blasphemy (Matt. 26:59; Mark 14:55; 15:1; Luke 22:66; John 11:47). Stephen was stoned as a result of its verdict (Acts 6:12–15). Peter, John, and other disciples were hailed before its court (Acts 4:5–21; 5:17–41), and Paul was charged there with violating the Mosaic Torah (Acts 22).

Sarah   The wife and half-sister of Abraham (Gen. 11:29; 16:1; 20:12), Sarah traveled with him from Ur to Haran and ultimately to Canaan and after a long period of barrenness bore him a single son, Isaac (Gen. 18:9–15; 21:1–21). She died in Hebron (Gen. 23:2) and was buried at Machpelah in Canaan (Gen. 23:19; see also Rom. 4:9; Heb. 11:11; 1 Pet. 3:6).

Sardis   Capital of the kingdom of Lydia (modern Turkey), captured by Cyrus the Great (546 B.C.E.); later part of the Roman province of Asia and the site of a cult of Cybele, a pagan fertility goddess (Rev. 3:1–6).

Sargon I   The Semitic founder of a Mesopotamian Empire incorporating ancient Sumer and Akkad and stretching from Elam to the Mediterranean (about 2360 B.C.E.).

Sargon II   Successor of Shalmaneser V and king of Assyria (722–705 B.C.E.) who completed his predecessor's three-year siege of Samaria and captured the city, bringing the northern kingdom (Israel) to an end in 721 B.C.E. (Isa. 20:1; 2 Kings 17).

Satan   In the Hebrew Bible, "the satan" appears as a prosecutor in the heavenly court among "the sons of God" (Job 1–2; Zech. 3:1–3) and only later as a tempter (1 Chron. 21:1; cf. 2 Sam. 24:1). Although the Hebrew Bible says virtually nothing about Satan's origin, the pseudepigraphal writings contain much legendary material about his fall from heaven and the establishment of a hierarchy of demons and devils. By the time the New Testament was written, he was believed to head a kingdom of Evil and to seek the corruption of all people, including the Messiah (Matt. 4:1–11; Luke 4:1–13). Satan (the "Opposer" or "Adversary") is also "the Evil One" (Matt. 6:13; 13:19; Eph. 6:16; 1 John 2:13; 5:18–19), "the Devil" (Matt. 4:1; 13:39; 25:41; John 8:44; Eph. 4:27), and the primordial serpent who tempted Eve (Rev. 12:9).

Saul   Son of Kish, a Benjaminite, and the first king of Israel (c. 1020–1000 B.C.E.), Saul was anointed by Samuel to meet the Philistine crisis, which demanded a strong centralized leadership (1 Sam. 9:1–10:27). He defeated the Ammonites (1 Sam. 11:1–11) and Philistines at Geba and Michmash but rapidly lost support after antagonizing Samuel (1 Sam. 13:8–15) and refusing to kill the Amalekite king (1 Sam. 15:7–35). He was also upstaged by David, of whom he became intensely jealous (1 Sam. 18:6–24:23). Saul and his son Jonathan were killed by the Philistines at the Battle of Gilboa (1 Sam. 31) and commemorated by one of David's most beautiful psalms (2 Sam. 1:17–27).

Saul of Tarsus   According to Acts, the name by which the apostle Paul was known before his conversion on the road to Damascus. *See* Paul.

Savior   One who saves from danger or destruction, a term applied to Yahweh in the Hebrew Bible (Ps. 106:21; Isa. 43:1–13; 63:7–9; Hos. 13:4) and to Jesus in the New Testament (Luke 2:11; John 4:42; Acts 5:31; 13:23; Phil. 3:20; 1 Tim. 4:10; 2 Tim. 1:10; 1 John 4:14).

scapegoat   According to Leviticus 16, a sacrificial goat on whose head Israel's high priest placed the people's collective sins on the Day of Atonement, after which the goat was sent out into the desert to Azazel (possibly a demon). The term has come to signify anyone who bears the blame for others (see Isa. 53).

scribes   Professional copyists who recorded commercial, royal, and religious texts and served as clerks, secretaries, and archivists at Israel's royal court and Temple (2 Kings 12:10; 19:2; Ezra 4:8; 2 Chron. 34:8; Jer. 36:18). After the Jews' return from exile, professional teachers or "wise men" preserved and interpreted the Mosaic Torah (Ezra 7:6; Neh. 7:73–8:18). In the New Testament, scribes are often linked with Pharisees as Jesus' opponents (Matt. 7:29; 23:2, 13; Luke 11:44) who conspired to kill him (Mark 14:43; 15:1; Luke 22:2; 23:10), although some became his followers (Matt.8:19; *see also* Acts 6:12; 23:9; 1 Cor. 1:20).

scroll   A roll of papyrus, leather, or parchment such as those on which the Hebrew Bible and New Testament were written. The rolls were made of sheets about nine to eleven inches high and five or six inches wide, sewed together to make a strip up to twenty-five or thirty feet long, which was wound around a stick and unrolled when read (Isa. 34:4; Rev. 6:14; Jer. 36).

Scythians   A fierce nomadic people from north and east of the Black Sea who swept southward toward Egypt and Judah in about 626 B.C.E. Jeremiah prophesied that Judah would be devastated (Jer. 4:5–31; 5:15–17; 6:1–8, 22–26), and Zephaniah saw the invasion as a sign that the Day of Yahweh had arrived (Zeph. 1:7–8, 14–18); but the Scythians were bribed by Pharaoh Psammetichus I (664–610 B.C.E.) and returned north by the coastal route without attacking Palestine.

Sea of Reeds   A body of water or swampland bordering the Red Sea that the Israelites miraculously crossed during their flight from Egypt (Exod. 14:5–15:21). The origin of the name is uncertain because there are no reeds in the Red Sea, which is more than 7200 feet deep.

Second Isaiah   *See* Isaiah.

Second Temple period   The span of Judean history from the rebuilding of the Jerusalem Temple in 515 B.C.E. to the Temple's destruction by the Romans in 70 C.E., a period in which Judea was consecutively occupied by Persians, Greeks, and Romans.

Secret Mark   One of several noncanonical gospels. This gospel may provide a link between the Synoptic Gospels and the fourth Gospel's account of Lazarus' resuscitation.

seer   A clairvoyant or diviner who experiences ecstatic visions (1 Sam. 9:9–11); forerunner of the prophets.

Seir   A mountain range running through Edom almost to the Gulf of Aqabah through which the Israelites passed during their desert wanderings (Deut. 2:1; 33:2). Seir was regarded as the home of the Esau tribes, rivals of Israel (Gen. 36:8, 20–21; Josh. 24:4) and was also an early name for Edom (Gen. 32:3; 35:20–21, 30; Num. 14:18).

Seleucids   The Macedonian Greek dynasty founded by Alexander's general Seleucus (ruled 312–280 B.C.E.), centered in Syria with Antioch as its capital. After defeating the Ptolemies of Egypt, it controlled Palestine from 198 to 165 B.C.E., after which the Maccabean revolt defeated the forces of Antiochus IV and eventually drove the Syrians from Judea (142 B.C.E.) (1 and 2 Macc.).

Seleucus   *See* Seleucids.

Semites   According to Genesis 10:21–31, peoples descended from Noah's son Shem, whose progeny included Elam, Asshur, Arpacshad (Hebrews and Arabs), Lud (Lydians), and Aram (Syrians) (Gen. 10:22). In modern usage, the term applies to linguistic rather than to racial groups, such as those who employ one of a common family of inflectional languages, including Akkadian, Aramaic, Hebrew, and Arabic.

Sennacherib   Son of Sargon II and king of Assyria (704–681 B.C.E.). In 701 B.C.E., Sennacherib devastated Tyre and besieged Jerusalem, after which he levied heavy tribute upon King Hezekiah of Judah (2 Kings 18). A clay prism recording Sennacherib's version of the Judean campaign tallies well with 2 Kings 18:14–16 but strikingly diverges from the story of 185,000 Assyrian soldiers slain by Yahweh's angel in a single night (2 Kings 19:10–35; Isa. 37:9–36).

Septuagint (LXX)   A Greek translation of the Hebrew Bible traditionally attributed to seventy or seventy-two Palestinian scholars during the reign of Ptolemy II (285–246 B.C.E.), the Septuagint was actually the work of several generations of Alexandrine translators, begun about 250 B.C.E. and not complete until the first century C.E. The later additions to the Septuagint were deleted from the standard Hebrew Bible (Masoretic Text) but included in the Christian Scriptures as the Apocrypha.

seraphim   Heavenly beings, usually depicted with six wings (Isa. 6), who attended the throne of God; perhaps derived from Assyrian or Egyptian mythology.

serpent   A common symbol in Near Eastern fertility cults, a snake was the original tempter of humanity (Gen. 3–4) and a symbol of Assyria, Babylon (Isa. 27:1), and the Israelite tribe of Dan (Gen. 49:17). A bronze image of a snake that was used to heal the Israelites during a plague of snakes in the wilderness (Num. 21:4–9) was later destroyed by King Hezekiah (2 Kings 18:4). Revelation 12:9 identifies the serpent with the devil and Satan (the primordial dragon).

Seth   The third son of Adam and Eve (Gen. 4:25–26; 5:2–8), cited as the first man to invoke Yahweh's sacred name.

Shadrach   The name the leading eunuch of Babylon gave the Hebrew boy Hananiah (Dan. 1:7; 2:49). Along with Abednego and Meshach, he survived incarceration in a fiery furnace (Dan. 3:1–30).

Shalmaneser   The name of five Assyrian kings, two of whom appear in the Hebrew Bible. (1) Shalmaneser III (859–824 B.C.E.), one of Assyria's most effective rulers, defeated a coalition of Syrian and Palestinian states led by Ben-hadad (Hadadezer) of Damascus and King Ahab of Israel, a defense league that disintegrated largely because of Elijah's and Elisha's interference in Israelite and Syrian politics (2 Kings 8:7–15, 9–10). Shalmaneser's Black Obelisk shows either Jehu, who overthrew Ahab's dynasty, or one of his representatives groveling at the Assyrian king's feet and paying him tribute. (2) Shalmaneser V (726–722 B.C.E.), successor to Tiglath-pileser, extorted tribute from Hoshea, last ruler of the northern kingdom (732–724 B.C.E.). When Hoshea later refused payment, Shalmaneser captured him and laid siege to Israel's capital, Samaria, for three years but died before taking the city (2 Kings 17:3–5; 18:9).

Shamash   Babylonian sun god associated with justice and prophecy, the Akkadian counterpart of the Sumerian Utu.

Shaphan   Scribal secretary of state for King Josiah (640–609 B.C.E.), to whom Hilkiah the priest entrusted the "lost" Book of the Law (probably Deuteronomy) found during repairs on the Jerusalem Temple. After reading it to Josiah, Shaphan was sent to ask the prophetess Huldah what Yahweh wished done with the book. He may have been instrumental in the subsequent religious reforms (2 Kings 22:3–20).

Sharon, Plain of   The most fertile part of the coastal plain of Palestine, stretching about fifty miles north to the headland of Mount Carmel, belonged to the northern kingdom after 922 B.C.E. Its desirable fields became an image of the messianic bounty (Isa. 35:2).

Sheba, Queen of   *See* Saba.

Shechem   (1) The son of Hamor the Hivite from whom Jacob bought land in Canaan and who later raped and wished to marry Jacob's daughter Dinah (Gen. 33:18–20; 34:1–31). Despite Hamor's friendly wish to ally his clan with Jacob's, Simon and Levi led Jacob's sons in a murderous attack on Shechem's clan to avenge their sister's dishonor. (2) An ancient Canaanite city located about forty-one miles north of Jerusalem in the hill country later allocated to the tribe of Ephraim, Shechem was the first site in Canaan that Abraham visited (Gen. 12:6) and the first place where the Hebrews came in touch with Canaanite culture (Gen. 33:18–20; 34:1–31). Here Joshua held a covenant-renewal ceremony uniting the Israelite tribes under Yahweh and, according to some scholars, including native tribes friendly to the Israelites. Abimelech attempted to make himself king here (Judg. 9), and here Rehoboam came to be crowned (1 Kings 12), only to be divested of his northern territories by Jeroboam I, who made Shechem his capital. Although the Deuteronomists mention its religious importance (Deut. 11:26–32; 17:1–26; Josh. 8:30–37), Shechem fell into obscurity until the mid-fourth century B.C.E. when the Samaritans built a temple on Mount Gerizim. The city was destroyed by John Hyrcanus in the late second century B.C.E. but rebuilt as Flavia Neapolis.

Shem   Noah's oldest son, brother of Ham and Japheth, the eponymous ancestor of the Semites, including the Arameans, Hebrews, Akkadians, and Arabs (Gen. 5:32; 9:21–27; 10:1).

Shema   Judaism's supreme declaration of monotheistic faith, expressed in the words of Deuteronomy 6:4–9 beginning "Listen [Hebrew *shema,* "hear"], Israel, Yahweh our God is the one Yahweh." It also includes Deuteronomy 11:13–21 and Numbers 14:37–41 (cf. Mark 12:29–34).

Sheol   According to the Hebrew Bible, the subterranean region to which the "shades" of all the dead descended, a place of intense gloom, hopelessness, and virtual unconsciousness for its inhabitants. The term was translated *Hades* in the Greek Septuagint and in later Hellenistic times was regarded as an abode of the dead awaiting resurrection (Gen. 42:38; 1 Sam. 2:6; Job 7:9; 14:13–14; 26:6; Pss. 6:5; 16:10; 55:15; 139:8; Prov. 27:20; Eccles. 9:10; Isa. 14:15; 28:15; 38:10, 18; Hos. 13:14; Jon. 2:2; cf. references to Hades in Matt. 16:18; Luke 10:15; Acts 2:31; Rev. 1:18; 20:15). It is *not* the same theological concept as hell or Gehenna (Matt. 10:28; 23:33; Mark 9:43; Luke 12:5).

Shepherd of Hermas   One of several extracanonical works contained in the Codex Sinaiticus. This mystical, apocalyptic work incorporates documents that may date from the first century C.E.

shewbread   The term the King James Version uses for the twelve loaves of consecrated unleavened bread placed in the Holy Place of the Tabernacle and Temple (Exod. 25:30; Lev. 24:5–9; 1 Sam. 21:2–6).

shibboleth   The password Jephthah used to determine whether fugitives from a battle between the Ephraimites and his own Gileadites were his people or the enemy's. The Ephraimites pronounced *sh* as *s* (Judg. 12:4–6). In contemporary usage, the term refers to the slogans or distinctive values of a party or class.

Shiloh   A prominent town and religious center that the Israelites established in the highlands of Ephraim, where Joshua assigned the tribes of Israel their territorial allotments (Josh. 18). Apparently a headquarters for the tribal confederacy during the time of the judges (Josh. 21:2; 22:9; Judg. 21:15–24; 1 Sam. 2; 12–17; 3:30), the Ark of the Covenant was kept there until the Philistine war, when it was taken to a camp at Ebenezer, where the Philistines captured it (1 Sam. 4). Returned, it was not again placed in Shiloh (1 Sam. 6:21–7:2), possibly because the Philistines had devastated the site. Jeremiah predicted that Yahweh would deal with Jerusalem as he had with Shiloh (Jer. 7:12–15; 26:6–9).

Shinar, Plain of   An alluvial lowland between the Tigris and Euphrates rivers at the head of the Persian Gulf. Settled by Sumerians about 4000 B.C.E., it was later known as Babylonia after the principal city in the area (Gen. 11:2; 14:1, 9). This region is the traditional homeland of Abraham, ancestor of the Israelites (Gen. 11:31; see also Isa. 11:11; Zech. 5:11; Dan. 1:2).

Shishak   An Egyptian pharaoh (Sheshonk or Sheshonq I) (935–914 B.C.E.), founder of the Twenty-Second Dynasty, who during Solomon's reign gave asylum to the rebellious Jeroboam (1 Kings 11:40) but later invaded Judah and stripped the Temple of many of its treasures (1 Kings 14:25–28; 2 Chron. 12:2–9).

Shittim   Site of the Israelites' encampment in Moab, opposite Jericho, prior to their crossing the Jordan River into Canaan (Num. 24–36).

shrine   A sacred place or altar at which a god is worshiped, usually with ritual sacrifices. The discovery of Deuteronomy (621 B.C.E.), which prohibited sacrifice at any but a designated central sanctuary (assumed to be the Jerusalem Temple), inspired Josiah's sweeping destruction of all rival shrines in Judah and Samaria (2 Kings 22–23; 2 Chron. 34–35).

Shunammite   The "Shulamite" bride who is praised in the Song of Solomon 6:13; the origin and meaning of the name are uncertain.

Sibylline Oracles   A collection of futuristic visions written in imitation of Greco-Roman prophecies attributed to Apollo's oracle, the Sibyl.

Sidon   A wealthy Phoenician port city (Gen. 10:15, 19; 1 Chron. 1:13) that suffered repeated destructions during the Assyrian, Babylonian, and Persian periods (Jer. 25:22; 27:3; Ezek. 27:8; 28:21–23) but was rebuilt and visited by Jesus and Paul during Roman times (Mark 7:24–31; Acts 27:3). *Siddonians* is a common biblical term for Phoenicians.

Silas   The Semitic, perhaps Aramean, name of an early Christian prophet (Acts 15:32), otherwise called Silvanus, who accompanied Barnabas and Paul to Antioch with decrees from the Jerusalem council (Acts 15:1–35) and who joined Paul on his second missionary journey (Acts 16–18; 1 Thess. 1:1; 2 Thess. 1:1). He may have been the author of 1 Peter (1 Pet. 5:12).

Simeon   (1) The second son of Jacob and Leah (Gen. 29:33) who helped avenge his sister's rape upon the people of Shechem (Gen. 34). The tribal group named after him, the Simeonites, was probably absorbed by Judah and is seldom mentioned in the Hebrew Bible (Deut. 27:12). (2) Another name for Simon Peter (Acts 15:14; 2 Pet. 1:1). (3) The devout

old man who recognized the infant Jesus as the promised Messiah (Luke 2:22–34).

simile   A comparison, usually to illustrate an unexpected resemblance between a familiar object and novel idea. Jesus' parables about the kingdom of God are typically cast as similes (Matt. 13:31–5, 44–50; Mark 4:26–32; Luke 13:18–19).

Simon   The name of several New Testament figures. (1) Simon Peter (Matt. 4:18; 10:2). (2) One of the twelve apostles, Simon the Canaanite (Matt. 10:4; Mark 3:18), a nationalist Zealot (Luke 6:15; Acts 1:13). (3) One of Jesus' "brothers" (Matt. 13:55; Mark 6:3). (4) A leper whom Jesus cured (Mark 14:3–9). (5) Simon of Cyrene, the man from North Africa who was forced to carry Jesus' cross (Mark 15:21). (6) A Pharisee who entertained Jesus in his home (Luke 7:36–50). (7) Simon Iscariot, father of Judas the traitor (John 6:71; 13:26). (8) A leather tanner of Joppa with whom Peter stayed (Acts 9:43; 10).

Simon Magus   A Samaritan sorcerer (magus) who tried to buy the power of the Holy Spirit from Peter (Acts 8:9–24); thought by some to be the forerunner of the Faust figure. The sale of church office is known as *simony*.

Sin   An Akkadian deity known to the Sumerians as Nanna, the moon god.

Sin, Wilderness of   A desert plain on the Sinai peninsula through which the Israelites passed on their way to Mount Sinai (Exod. 16:1; 17:1; Num. 33:11–12).

Sinai   (1) A peninsula at whose southern apex the Gulf of Aqabah joins the Gulf of Suez at the head of the Red Sea. Its 150-mile inverted base borders the Mediterranean, forming the boundary between Egypt and Palestine. (2) According to the J and P accounts, Mount Sinai, the sacred mountain in the wilderness where Moses experienced Yahweh's call (Exod. 3, 6) and to which he led the Israelites from Egypt for Yahweh's revelation of the Torah (Exod. 19–24, 34:4). This site, which has never been positively identified, is called Horeb by E and D (Exod. 3:1; 17:6; Deut. 1:6; 4:10).

Sisera   The Canaanite leader whose forces Deborah and Barak defeated and whom Jael, wife of Heber the Kenite, murdered in her tent (Judg. 4–5).

Sitz-im-Leben   German term used in form criticism to denote the social and cultural environment out of which a particular biblical unit grew and developed.

Smyrna   An Aegean port city of western Asia Minor (Turkey), site of an early Christian church that the author of Revelation praises for its poverty and faithfulness (Rev. 1:11; 2:8–10).

Socrates   Athenian philosopher (c. 469–399 B.C.E.) and mentor of Plato, he taught that life's purpose was to seek the good and prepare the soul for immortality in the afterlife. After being executed for questioning conventional ideas about the gods, he became the subject of his disciples' memoirs, including very different accounts by Plato and Xenophon.

Sodom   Along with Gomorrah, Admah, Zebolim, and Zoar (Gen. 13:10–12; 14:2; Deut. 29:23), one of the "five cities of the plain" (near the south shore of the Dead Sea) destroyed by a great cataclysm attributed to Yahweh (Gen. 19:1–29). Abraham, who had been royally welcomed by Sodom's king (Gen. 14:13–24), pleaded for it to be spared (Gen. 18:16–32). Contrary to legend, its sins were regarded as violence and inhospitality to strangers rather than homosexuality. Later Bible writers cite it as a symbol of divine judgment upon wickedness (Isa. 3:9; Lam. 4:6; Matt. 10:15; 2 Pet. 2:6; Jude 7; Rev. 11:8).

Solomon   Son of David and Bathsheba and Israel's third king (c. 961–922 B.C.E.) (2 Sam. 12:24–25), who inherited the throne through David's fondness and the intrigues of his mother and the prophet Nathan (1 Kings 1:9–2:25). He became famous for his wisdom (1 Kings 3:5–28); allied himself with Hiram of Tyre (1 Kings 5); built and dedicated Yahweh's Temple in Jerusalem (1 Kings 6, 8); built a huge palace for himself (1 Kings 7:1–12); received Yahweh's renewal of the Davidic Covenant (1 Kings 9:1–9); was visited by the Queen of Sheba (1 Kings 10:1–13); worshiped other gods than Yahweh, presumably because of his foreign wives' influence (1 Kings 11:1–40); and died leaving his people financially exhausted and politically discontented (1 Kings 11:41–12:25). An idealized account of his reign is given in 2 Chronicles 1–9.

Solomon's Porch   A magnificent covered colonnade built along the east side of Herod's Temple in Jerusalem in which Jesus walked (John 10:23); the site of several apostolic miracles (Acts 3:11; 5:12).

Son of Man

1. A Hebrew Bible phrase used to denote a human being (Pss. 8:4; 80:17; 144:3; 146:3; Isa. 56:2; Jer. 51:43), including a plural usage (Pss. 31:19; 33:13; Prov. 8:4; Eccles. 3:18–19; 8:11; 9:12). The phrase is characteristic of the Book of Ezekiel, where it is commonly used to indicate the prophet himself (Ezek. 2:1).

2. In Daniel 7:12–14, "one like a son of man" refers to Israel itself or to a divinely appointed future ruler of Israel, although this figure is not given specific messianic significance.

3. In some pseudepigraphal writings, particularly the Similitudes of the Book of Enoch, he who serves as Yahweh's agent in the coming Day of Judgment is variously called "the Elect One," "the Anointed One," and "the Son of Man."

4. In the Gospels, the phrase is always spoken by Jesus and in most cases applied to himself (Matt. 8:20; 9:6; 11:19; 12:8; 16:27–28; 19:28; 24:30; 28:31; Mark 2:28; 8:38; 9:31; 10:45; 13:26; Luke 12:8–10; 18:8; 21:27; 22:22; John 3:14). Outside the Gospels, it is used only once (Acts 7:56), although the author of Revelation echoes Daniel 7:13 (Rev. 14:14).

sons of thunder   An epithet (*Boanerges*) applied to the apostles James and John (Mark 3:17), possibly because of their impulsive temperaments (Luke 9:52–56).

Sopherim   The name applied to Jewish scribes, from the time of Ezra and after, who copied and transmitted the manuscripts of the Hebrew Bible.

soul   In Hebrew, *nephesh* (breath), applied to both humans and animals as living beings (Gen. 1:20; 2:7; 2:19; 9:4; Exod. 1:5; 1 Chron. 5:21). It was translated *psyche* in the Greek Septuagint, the same term used (commonly for "life" rather than the immortal personality) in the New Testament (Matt. 10:28; 16:26; Acts 2:27; 3:23; Phil. 1:27; Rev. 20:4).

source criticism   Analysis of a biblical document to discover the sources, written or oral, that the author(s) incorporated into it. Close study of the Pentateuch has led scholars to conclude that at least four main literary units—J, E, D, and P—were blended in its composition.

speaking in tongues   An ecstatic phenomenon of the early church (Acts 2:1–45), presented at first as a miraculous and intelligible speaking and understanding of foreign languages by those who did not know these tongues (Acts 2:5–12) but later criticized by Paul as an inferior spiritual gift (1 Cor. 12–14).

stele (stela)   An upright slab or pillar inscribed with a commemorative message, such as those bearing the law Code of Hammurabi (early seventeenth century B.C.E.) or that of King Mesha of Moab (c. 835 B.C.E.), who commemorated his victory over Israel following Jehu's revolution.

Stephen   A Hellenistic Jew of Jerusalem who was stoned for his Christian heresy (Acts 6:8–60), thus becoming the first martyr of the early church. The name means "royal" or "crown."

Stoicism   A Greek philosophy that became popular among the upper classes in Roman times, Stoicism emphasized duty, endurance, self-control, and service to the gods, the family, and the state. Its adherents believed in the soul's immortality, rewards, and punishments after death, and in a divine force (providence) that directs human destiny. Paul encountered Stoics when preaching in Athens (Acts 17:18–34), and Stoic ideas appear in Ecclesiastes, the Wisdom of Solomon, Proverbs, John 4:23 and 5:30, James 1:10, and 1 Peter 2:17.

Succession Narrative   The account of David's rise to kingship and his succession by Solomon that underlies the narrative in 2 Samuel 9–24 and 1 Kings 1–2. *See* Court History.

Succoth (Sukkoth)   A Hebrew Bible term meaning "booths." (1) A town east of the Jordan River in the area allotted to Gad (Josh. 13:27), where Jacob had erected booths (Gen. 33:17). (2) An Egyptian site in the Nile delta given as the first Israelite camp during the Exodus (Exod. 12:37; 13:20). *See* Feast of Tabernacles.

Sumer   The land at the head of the Persian Gulf between the Tigris and Euphrates rivers, site of the oldest high civilization in the ancient Near East, and traditional homeland of Abraham and his ancestors. Its cities include Erech (Uruk), Ur (Gen. 10:10; 11:10–27; 15:7), and Calah (Nimrud). Whereas Sumer occupied southernmost Mesopotamia, Akkad lay to the north (Gen. 10:11–12); the two regions together were later known as Babylonia.

symbol   From the Greek *symbolon*, a "token" or "sign," and *symballein*, to "throw together" or "compare." In its broadest usage, it means anything that stands for something else, as the star of David signifies Judaism and the cross represents Christianity. The use of symbols characterizes prophetic and apocalyptic writing. In Daniel, for example, wild beasts symbolize pagan nations; in Ezekiel, Yahweh's presence is symbolized by his radiant "glory."

synagogue   In Judaism, a gathering of no fewer than ten adult males assembled for worship, scriptural instruction, and administration of local Jewish affairs. Synagogues probably began forming during the Babylonian exile when the Jerusalem Temple no longer existed. Organization of such religious centers throughout the Diaspora played an important role in the faith's transmission and survival. The synagogue liturgy included lessons from the Torah, the Prophets, the Shema, Psalms, and eighteen prayers.

syncretism   The blending of different religions, a term Bible scholars typically apply to the mingling of Canaanite rites and customs (Baalism) with the Israelites' Mosaic faith. Although a practice repeatedly denounced by the prophets (Judg. 2:13; 3:7; 6:31; 8:33; 1 Kings 16:31; 18:26; 2 Kings 10:18; Jer. 2:8; 7:9; 19:5; 23:13; Hos. 2:8), Judaism borrowed many of its characteristic forms, psalms, concepts, and religious rituals from earlier Canaanite models.

Synoptic Gospels   The first three Gospels, so named because they share a large quantity of material in common, allowing their texts to be viewed together "with one eye."

Synoptic Problem   The scholarly term for the question of relationship — the nature of the literary interdependence — of the first three Gospels: Matthew, Mark, and Luke. Most scholars believe that Matthew and Luke are expanded editions of Mark.

Syria   (1) The territory extending from the upper Euphrates River to northern Palestine. (2) The kingdom of Aram, with its capital at Damascus (Isa. 7:8). As the creed in Deuteronomy 26:5 states, the Israelites regarded themselves as descended from Arameans (Syrians). Isaiah 7 refers to the Syro-Ephraimite coalition against Assyria.

Syro-Phoenician   The name applied to a woman living near the Phoenician cities of Tyre and Sidon whose daughter Jesus healed (Mark 7:24–30; Matt. 15:21–28).

Tabernacle   The portable tent-shrine, elaborately decorated, that housed the Ark of the Covenant (Exod. 25–31, 35–40; Num. 7–9) from the Exodus to the building of Solomon's Temple (1 Kings 6–8); used in both the Hebrew Bible and the New Testament as a symbol of God's presence with humanity (Num. 9:5; Deut. 31:15; Pss. 15:1; 43:3; 61:4; 132:7; Isa. 4:6; 33:20; Hos. 12:9; Acts 7:46; Heb. 8:2; 9:11; 2 Pet. 1:14; Rev. 21:3).

Tables (Tablets) of the Law   The stone slabs on which the Ten Commandments were inscribed (Exod. 24:12; 32:15–20).

Tabor   A prominent limestone hill in Galilee (Deut. 33:19; Josh. 19–22; Judg. 4:6; 5:15–21; Ps. 89:12–13; Jer. 46:18).

Talmud   A huge collection of Jewish religious traditions consisting of two parts: (1) the Mishnah (written editions of ancient oral interpretations of the Torah), published in Palestine by Judah ha-Nasi (died c. 220 C.E.) and his disciples; (2) the Gemara, extensive commentaries on the Mishnah. The Palestinian version of the Talmud, which is incomplete, was produced in about 450 C.E.; the Babylonian Talmud, nearly four times as long, was finished in about 500 C.E. Both Talmuds contain Mishnah and Gemara.

Tamar   (1) The wife of Er, son of Judah (Gen. 38:6), who, when widowed, posed as a prostitute to trick her father-in-law into begetting children (the twins Pharez and Zerah) by her (Gen. 38:6–30). (2) Absalom's sister who was raped by her half-brother Amnon, whom Absalom later killed (2 Sam. 13:1–32; 1 Chron. 3:9).

Tammuz   An ancient Near Eastern fertility god, a counterpart to the Semitic-Greek Adonis, at whose mythic death women ritually wept (Jer. 22:18; Amos 8:10; Ezek. 8:14).

Tanak   A comparatively modern name for the Hebrew Bible, an acronym consisting of three consonants that represent the three major divisions of the Bible; the Torah (law), the Nevi'im (Prophets), and the Kethivim (Writings).

Targum   Interpretative translations of the Hebrew Bible into Aramaic, such as that made by Ezra after the Jews' return from the Babylonian exile (Neh. 8:1–18). The practice may have begun in the postexilic synagogues, where Hebrew passages were read aloud and then translated into Aramaic with interpretative comments added.

Tarshish   (1) A son of Javan (Greece, Aegean peoples) (Gen. 10:4; 1 Chron. 1:7). (2) A Hebrew Bible term used to designate ships and ports, particularly the Phoenician variety (1 Kings 10:22; 22:48; Jon. 1:3; 2 Chron. 20:36).

Tarsus   Capital of the Roman province of Cilicia (southeastern Turkey) and birthplace of Paul (Saul) (Acts 9:11; 11:25; 21:39; 22:3); a thriving commercial center in New Testament times.

tell (tel)   Flat-topped artificial mounds consisting of the ruins of ancient cities that dot the landscape of Mesopotamia, Syria, and Palestine.

Temple, the

1. The imposing structure built by King Solomon (using Phoenician architects and craftsmen) on Mount Zion in Jerusalem to house the Ark of the Covenant in its innermost room (the Holy of Holies) (1 Kings 5:15–9:25). Later recognized as the only authorized center for sacrifice and worship of Yahweh, it was destroyed by Nebuchadnezzar's troops in 587 B.C.E. (2 Kings 25:8–17; 2 Chron. 36:18–19).

2. The Second Temple, rebuilt by Jews returned from the Babylonian exile under Governor Zerubbabel, was dedicated in about 515 B.C.E. (Ezra 1:1–11; 3:1–13; 4:24–6:22; Hag. 1–2; Zech. 1:1–8:13).

3. Herod's splendid Temple replaced the inferior edifice of Zerubbabel's time and took nearly a half-century to complete (John 2:20).

   Jesus, who visited the Temple as a child (Luke 2:22–38, 41–50) and often taught there (Matt. 21:23–24:1; Luke 20:1; John 7:14–52; 10:22–39), cleansed it of its moneychangers (Matt. 21:12–17; Mark 11:15–19; Luke 19:45–46; John 2:13–22), and prophesied its destruction (Matt. 24:1–2; Mark 13:1–4; Luke 21:5–7), which was fulfilled when the Romans sacked Jerusalem in 70 C.E. Until that event, the apostles continued to preach and worship there (Acts 3:1–26; 5:42; 21:26–22:29).

Ten Commandments (Decalogue)   The set of ten religious and moral laws that Yahweh inscribed on stone tablets and gave Moses (Exod. 20:1–17; repeated in Deut. 5:6–21). Some scholars believe that a ritual Decalogue is contained in Exodus 34:1–16 and 22:29b–30; 23:12, 15–19 (see also Exod. 31:18–32:16).

Tent of Meeting   *See* Tabernacle.

Terah   A son of Nahor, father of Abraham, a younger Nahor, and Haran (Gen. 11:26; 1 Chron. 1:26–27), Terah migrated from the Sumerian city of Ur to Haran in northwest Mesopotamia (Gen. 11:27–32).

teraphim   Household gods, probably in the form of human figurines, perhaps representing a family's guardian spirit or ancestors and thought to confer good luck on their possessor. When secretly absconding with her husband Jacob, Rachel stole and hid her father's teraphim (Gen. 31:30–35). Even as late as the monarchy, owning such domestic idols was not necessarily viewed as conflicting with Yahweh's worship (Judg. 17:4–13; Hos. 3:4), although Samuel likened their use to idolatry (1 Sam. 15:23) and King

Josiah outlawed them (2 Kings 23:24). They may have been used in fortune-telling.

testament   From the Latin for "covenant," this is the term used for the two main divisions of the Bible — the Old Testament (canonical Hebrew Scriptures) and the New Testament (Christian-Greek Scriptures).

Tetragrammaton   The four consonants (YHWH) comprising the sacred name Yahweh, the God of Israel. Although the name appears nearly 7000 times in the canonical Hebrew Bible, some modern Bible translations continue the Jewish practice of inaccurately rendering it as "the Lord."

Tetrateuch   A critical term for the first four books of the Bible. Genesis through Numbers are composed primarily of J, E, and P material, with little or no discernible contribution from the Deuteronomist (D), who is responsible for Deuteronomy, the fifth book of the Torah.

textual criticism   Comparison and analysis of ancient manuscripts to discover copyists' errors and, if possible, to reconstruct the true or original form of the document; also known as *lower criticism.*

Thaddeus   One of the most obscure of Jesus' apostles, he is listed among the Twelve in Matthew 10:3 and Mark 3:18 but not in Luke 7:16 or Acts. 1:13.

theocracy   A state or society thought to be ruled by God, typically through the intermediary of priests, divinely appointed kings, or other religious leaders.

theodicy   From a Greek term combining "god" and "justice," theodicy denotes a rational attempt to understand how an all-good, all-powerful God can permit the existence of Evil and undeserved suffering. Job, Habakkuk, and 2 Esdras contain notable theodicies.

Theodosius I   Roman emperor (reigned 379–395 C.E.) who championed orthodox Christianity, persecuted heretics, and, probably under the influence of Ambrose, Bishop of Milan, ordered all Greco-Roman temples closed (391 C.E.), in effect making Christianity the state religion of Rome.

theology   The study and interpretation of concepts about God's nature, will, attributes, and relationship with humanity; from the Greek *theos* (god) and *logos* (reason).

theophany   From the Greek, meaning an appearance of a god to a person, as when El wrestled with Jacob (Gen. 32:26–32), Yahweh appeared to Moses (Exod. 3:1–4:17; 6:2–13) and the elders of Israel (Exod. 24:9–11), or the resurrected Jesus revealed himself to Thomas (John 20:24–29) and Paul (Acts 9:3–9).

Theophilus   The otherwise unknown man to whom the Gospel of Luke and Book of Acts are addressed. He may have been a Roman official who became a Christian.

Thessalonica   A major Macedonian city (modern Salonika) where Paul and Silas converted "some" Jews, "many" Greeks and "God-fearers," and numerous "rich women," to Christianity (Acts 17:1–9). Paul later revisited the city (1 Cor. 16:5) and wrote two of his earliest surviving letters to its congregation (1 and 2 Thess.)

Third Isaiah   *See* Isaiah.

Thomas   One of the Twelve Apostles (Matt. 10:3; Mark 3:18; Luke 6:15; Acts 1:13), seldom mentioned in the Synoptics but relatively prominent in the fourth Gospel, where he is called *Didymus* (twin) (John 11:16; 20:24; 21:2). Unable to believe the other disciples' report of Jesus' resurrection, Thomas is suddenly confronted with the risen Jesus and pronounces the strongest confession of faith in the Gospel (John 20:24–29).

Thummim   *See* Urim and Thummim.

Thyatira   A city of ancient Lydia in Asia Minor (modern Turkey), original home of Lydia, Paul's first European convert (Acts 16:14) and one of the seven churches of Asia in Revelation 2:18–29.

Tiberias   A city on the western shore of the Sea of Galilee founded by Herod Antipas and named for Emperor Tiberius; a well-known spa in Jesus' day.

Tiberius (Tiberius Claudius Nero)   Stepson of Augustus and second emperor of Rome (14–37 C.E.). According to Luke 3:1, Jesus came to John for baptism in the fifteenth year of Tiberius' reign. Except for Luke 2:1, he is the Caesar referred to in the Gospels (Matt. 22:17; Mark 12:14; Luke 20:22; John 19:12).

Tiglath-pileser III   Emperor of Assyria (745–727 B.C.E.), the biblical "Pul" (2 Kings 15:19) who captured Damascus in 732 B.C.E. and coerced tribute from kings Menahem of Israel and Ahaz of Judah (2 Kings 16:7–18; 2 Chron. 28:20–25). Ahaz's stripping of the Jerusalem Temple and sponsoring of pagan cults were probably done to placate Assyria's king.

Tigris River According to Genesis 2:14 (where it is called the Hiddekel), the Tigris was the third of four rivers that watered Eden (see Dan. 10:4). Approximately 1146 miles long, it forms the eastern boundary of Mesopotamia (the land between the Tigris and Euphrates). On its banks rose the ancient cities of Nineveh, Asshur, and Calah (Gen. 10:11), centers of the Assyrian Empire.

Timothy Younger friend and fellow missionary of Paul, who called him "beloved son" (1 Cor. 4:17; 1 Tim. 1:2–28; 2 Tim. 1:2), Timothy was the son of a Greek father and devout Jewish mother (Acts 16:1; 2 Tim. 1:5). To please the Jews, Paul circumcised Timothy before taking him on his second evangelical tour (Acts 16:1–4; 20:1–4). Paul later sent him to Macedonia (1 Thess. 3:6) and thence to Corinth to quiet the dissension there (Acts 19:22; 1 Cor. 4:17; 16:11), which he failed to do (2 Cor. 7:6, 13–14; 8:6, 16, 23; 12:18). The picture of Timothy in the pastoral Epistles seems irreconcilable with what is known of him from Acts and Paul's genuine letters.

Tirzah A Canaanite city that Joshua captured (Josh. 12:24), later the home of King Jeroboam (1 Kings 14:17), and the northern kingdom's capital during the reigns of Baasha (c. 900–877 B.C.E.), Elah (877–876 B.C.E.), Zimri (seven days, c. 876 B.C.E.), and Omri (c. 876–869 B.C.E.), who took it by siege and ruled there for six years until he transferred the capital to Samaria (1 Kings 15:33–16:28).

Tishbite A term used to describe the prophet Elijah (1 Kings 17:1; 21:17; 2 Kings 1:3, 8; 9:36). Its origin and meaning are uncertain.

tithe Paying a tenth of one's income in money, crops, or animals to support a government (1 Sam. 8:15–17) or religion (Lev. 27:30–33; Num. 18:24–28; Deut. 12:17–19; 14:22–29; Neh. 10:36–38). In Israel, the high priest, Levites, and Temple upkeep were supported by required levies. Abraham is reported to have paid Melchizedek tithes (Gen. 14:20; see also Heb. 7:2–6). Jesus regarded tithing as an obligation of his people (Luke 11:42; 12:13–21; 18:12).

Titus A Greek whom Paul converted and who became a companion on his missionary journeys (2 Cor. 8:23; Gal. 2:1–3; Titus 1:4), Titus effected a reconciliation between Paul and the Corinthians (2 Cor. 7:5–7; 8:16–24; 12:18). A post-Pauline writer makes him the type of the Christian pastor (Titus 1–3).

Titus, Flavius Sabinius Vespasianus Son and successor of Vespasian and emperor of Rome (79–81 C.E.), he directed the siege of Jerusalem, which culminated in the destruction of the city and Herodian Temple in 70 C.E. His carrying of the Temple treasures to Rome is commemorated in the triumphal Arch of Titus that still stands in the Roman Forum.

Tobiah A partly Jewish Ammonite who occupied a storeroom in the rebuilt Temple area after the exile and whom Nehemiah threw out of his lodgings (Neh. 13:6–9), Tobiah allied himself with Sanballat the Samaritan in opposing Nehemiah's reconstruction of Jerusalem's walls (Neh. 2:10; 4:3, 7; 6:1–19).

Torah A Hebrew term usually translated "law," "instruction," or "teaching," it refers primarily to the Pentateuch, the first five books of the Hebrew Bible, and in a general sense to all the canonical writings, which are traditionally regarded as a direct oracle or revelation from Yahweh.

tradition (1) Collections of stories and interpretations transmitted orally from generation to generation and embodying the religious history and beliefs of a people or community. Traditions of the patriarchs were eventually included in the J and E sagas and finally incorporated into the first book of the Torah. (2) Oral explanations, interpretations, and applications of the written Torah (1 Chron. 4:22; Mark 7:5, 9; Matt. 15:2; Gal. 1:15), many of which were eventually compiled in the Mishnah. (3) Recollections and interpretations concerning Jesus that circulated orally through various early Christian churches and some of which were included in the Gospel narratives (1 Cor. 15:1–8; 2 Thess. 2:15).

tradition criticism Analysis of the origin and development of specific biblical themes—such as the Exodus motif in the Hebrew Bible and the eschatology of the kingdom of God in the New Testament—as presented by different biblical writers. In some cases, tradition criticism emphasizes the early and oral stages of development.

Trajan (Marcus Ulpius Nerva Trajanus) Emperor of Rome (98–117 C.E.) who was born in Spain in about 53 C.E., became a successful military leader, and brought the Roman Empire to its greatest extent, annexing Dacia, Armenia, Mesopotamia, Assyria, and Arabia. Probably following the policies of Vespasian (69–79 C.E.), he conducted a persecution of Christians, although he wrote to Pliny the Younger, governor of Bithynia, that they were not to be sought out or denounced anonymously.

transcendence The quality of God expressing the Deity's inherent limitlessness and transcending of all physical and cosmic boundaries.

Transfiguration A supernatural happening that Jesus' three closest disciples — Peter, James, and John — experienced when, alone with him on an isolated mountaintop, they saw Jesus transformed into a being of light accompanied by Elijah (symbolizing the Hebrew prophetic tradition) and Moses (symbolizing the Torah) (Matt. 17:1–13; Mark 9:2–13; Luke 9:28–36). A heavenly voice identified Jesus as his "beloved son," thus revealing Jesus as the culmination of and superior to the Law and prophets.

Transjordan The rugged plateau area east of the Jordan River, a region Joshua assigned to the tribes of Reuben, Gad, and half of Manasseh (Josh. 13) but which they failed to wrest from other Semites living there.

tree of life An ancient Mesopotamian symbol of rejuvenation or immortality (as in the *Epic of Gilgamesh*), the J (Yahwist) author places it in the Garden of Eden, humanity's original home, where its fruit would confer everlasting life on the eater (Gen. 2:9; 3:22–24). Yahweh's express motive for expelling the first human couple from Eden was to prevent their rivaling him further by eating from the tree of life (Gen. 3:22–24). It is often referred to in apocalyptic literature (En. 24:4; 25:4–6; Asmp. M. [Life of Adam and Eve] 19:2; 22:3; 28:2–4; XII P.: Levi 18:11), where it is usually reserved for the righteous to eat after the Day of Judgment (2 Esd. 8:52; cf. Rev. 2:7 and 22:2, 24).

Trinity A post–New Testament doctrine that posits God existing as three divine persons in One: Father, Son, and Holy Spirit. After generations of ecclesiastical debate on the subject had seriously divided the church, Constantine, the first Christian emperor of Rome but then unbaptized, called a council of church leaders in Nicea to settle the issue (325 C.E.). The council decreed the orthodoxy of the trinitarian formula, so that the mystery of trinity in unity henceforth became central to the Christian faith (Matt. 28:19–20; 2 Cor. 13:14; Gal. 1:1–5).

Trumpets, Feast of The Hebrew month began with a new moon. On the first day of the seventh (sabbatical) month, a festival, assembly, and sacrifice were to be held (Lev. 13:23–25; Num. 29:1–7).

Tubal-cain According to J, the son of Lamech and Zillah and the ancestor of all metalworkers in bronze and iron (Gen. 4:19–26). He may have been regarded as the eponymous progenitor of the Kenites.

Twelve, Book of the The twelve books of the Minor Prophets — Hosea to Malachi — originally compiled on a single scroll.

Twelve, the The twelve apostles whom Jesus specifically chose to follow him. Different names appear on different New Testament lists of the Twelve (Matt. 10:1–5; Mark 3:16–19; Luke 6:12–16; Acts 1:13–14).

Twelve Tribes of Israel In ancient Israel, tribes were confederations of clans, which in turn were composed of families related by blood, adoption, or long association, all forming a corporate community with a distinct social, religious, or ethnic identity. Traditionally believed to have descended from the twelve sons of Jacob (Israel) (Gen. 49:2–28; a parallel list, Moses' Blessing, mentions only eleven, omitting Simeon; Deut. 33:6–25), the tribes were Reuben, Simeon, Levi, Judah, Issachar, Zebulun (born of Jacob's wife Leah), Joseph (later divided into the tribes of Ephraim and Manasseh) and Benjamin (both born to Jacob's favorite wife, Rachel), Gad and Asher (by the slave girl Zilpah), and Dan and Naphtali (by another concubine, Bilhah).

The apportionment of tribal territories in Palestine is described in Joshua 13–19. Ezekiel foresaw an idealized tribal state in Israel (Ezek. 48), and the author of Revelation multiplied the traditional twelve tribes by 12,000 to symbolize the number of Jews redeemed in Christ (Rev. 7:4–8). (See also Matt. 19:28; Luke 22:30; and James 1:1, where the twelve tribes represent "spiritual Israel," the Christian community.) The so-called ten lost tribes were those of the northern kingdom assimilated into the Assyrian Empire after 721 B.C.E. (2 Kings 17).

Tychicus A loyal helper and companion of Paul who accompanied him through the Roman province of Asia on his third missionary journey (Acts 20:4), Tychicus delivered Paul's letters to the Colossians (Col. 4:7–9) and Ephesians (Eph. 6:21).

Tyre An ancient Phoenician seaport famous for its commerce and wealth, Tyre was originally built on a small offshore island about twenty-five miles south of Sidon. King Solomon made an alliance with its ruler, Hiram, whose architects and craftsmen he used in constructing the Jerusalem Temple (1 Kings 5:15–32; 7:13–51). Its power and luxury were later denounced by the prophets (Isa. 23; Ezek. 26–28; Amos 1:9–10; Zech. 9:3–4). Alexander the Great sacked the city in 332 B.C.E., although it had been rebuilt by Jesus' day (Mark 7:24–31; Luke 3:8).

Ugarit   Ancient Canaanite city (Arabic Ras Shamra) in modern Syria where cuneiform archives were found that preserve prebiblical religious texts and myths about El and Baal, some of which anticipate traditions later associated with Yahweh.

under the thigh   A euphemistic expression for the grasping of another's male organs during the conclusion of a vow, oath, or covenant (Gen. 24:2, 9; 47:29; see also Judg. 8:30).

Ur   One of the world's oldest cities, in Sumer, Ur was the ancestral homeland (Gen. 11:28–31) from which Abraham and his family migrated to Haran, although some scholars have suggested a northern location for the Abrahamic Ur. Archaeologically, the Sumerian Ur is notable for its well-preserved ziggurat and "royal cemetery," whose tombs have yielded a number of beautifully crafted artwork, furniture, jewelry, and other sophisticated artifacts (mid-third millennium B.C.E.).

Uriah   (1) A Hittite practicer of Yahwism and soldier of David whose wife, Bathsheba, the Israelite king seduced and wished to marry. David ordered him exposed in the front lines of battle so that he was inevitably killed, a crime the prophet Nathan denounced to the king's face (2 Sam. 11–12). (2) A priest whom King Ahaz of Judah (c. 735–716 B.C.E.) commissioned to remodel the Temple area and construct an altar modeled on that which Ahaz had seen in Assyrian-dominated Damascus (2 Kings 16:10–16). (3) A Judean prophet who predicted the Babylonian destruction of Jerusalem, fled to Egypt to escape King Jehoiakim's wrath, but was murdered. His body was returned to Judah, where it was buried in a common grave (Jer. 26:20–23).

Urim and Thummim   Undescribed objects (whose names may mean "oracle" and "truth") that were used by Israel's priests in casting lots to determine Yahweh's will on a specific matter. They could apparently indicate only yes or no responses (Exod. 28:29–30; Num. 27:21; 1 Sam. 28:6; Ezra 2:63; Neh. 7:65).

Uruk   One of Mesopotamia's oldest cities, it was the capital of Gilgamesh.

Utnapishtim   The Babylonian Noah, the only man (with his wife and servants) to survive the flood. The gods later granted him immortality in a remote island paradise. His story is told in the epic of Gilgamesh.

Uz   Job's unidentified homeland, which various scholars have suggested to be Edom, Arabia, or a location east of the Jordan River.

Uzziah (Azariah)   Son of Amaziah, king of Judah (783–742 B.C.E.), and a contemporary of King Jeroboam II of Israel (786–746 B.C.E.) (2 Kings 14:22; 15:1–7; 2 Chron. 26:1–23), Uzziah fortified Jerusalem; defeated the Philistines, Ammonites, and Arabs; and greatly extended Judah's political jurisdiction. Both the Deuteronomist and the Chronicler rate him as "pleasing" Yahweh, although the latter attributes the king's leprosy to his usurping priestly functions in the Temple.

Vashti   The empress of Persia (unknown to history) who refused to exhibit herself to the male friends of her husband, Ahasuerus (Xerxes I), and whom Esther replaced as queen (Esther 1:9–2:18).

veil   The elaborately decorated curtain separating the Holy Place from the Most Holy Place in the Tabernacle and Jerusalem Temple (Exod. 26:31–37), which was reputedly rent in two at Jesus' crucifixion (Matt. 27:51; Heb. 6:19; 9–10).

Vespasian   The emperor of Rome (69–79 C.E.) who led Roman legions into Judea during the Jewish revolt (66–70 C.E.), the siege of Jerusalem passing to his son Titus when Vespasian became emperor.

Vulgate Bible   Jerome's Latin translation of the Bible (late fourth century C.E.), eventually including the Apocrypha, which became the official version of Roman Catholicism.

Wisdom   A personification of the divine attribute of creative intelligence, pictured in the form of a gracious woman (Yahweh's daughter) who mediates between God and humanity (Prov. 1:20–33; 8:1–31; 9:1–6; Ecclus. 24; etc.). This Hebrew concept of Wisdom merges with the Greek philosophic doctrine of the heavenly Logos in John's Gospel (John 1:1–18) and Colossians (1–2).

wisdom literature   Biblical works dealing primarily with practical and ethical behavior and ultimate religious questions, such as the problem of Evil. The books include Proverbs, Job, Ecclesiastes, Ecclesiasticus, and the Wisdom of Solomon. Habakkuk, 2 Esdras, and the New Testament Book of James also have characteristics of wisdom writing.

woes, the seven messianic   The series of seven condemnations of scribes and Pharisees attributed to Jesus when he was rejected by official Judaism (Matt. 23:13–32).

word, the   (1) The "word" or "oracle" of Yahweh, a phrase characteristic of the Hebrew prophets, typically referring to a divine pronouncement, judgment, or statement of purpose that the prophet delivers in his God's name. (2) The preincarnate Jesus (John 1:1–3). *See* Logos.

Writings *See* Kethuvim.

Xerxes I Thought to be the biblical Ahasuerus, emperor of Persia (486–465 B.C.E.) (Esther; Ezra 4:6).

Yahweh A translation of the sacred name of Israel's god, represented almost 7000 times in the canonical Hebrew Bible by the four consonants of the Tetragrammaton (YHWH). According to Exodus 6:2–4, it was revealed for the first time to Moses at the burning bush; according to J, it was used from the time of Enosh before the Flood (Gen. 4:26). Scholars have offered various interpretations of the origin and meaning of the divine name. According to one accepted theory, it is derived from the Hebrew verb "to be" and means "he is" or "he causes to be," implying that Yahweh is the maker of events and shaper of history.

Yahwist The name scholars give the anonymous writer or compiler who produced the J document, the oldest stratum in the Pentateuch (c. 850 B.C.E.).

YHWH English letters transliterating the four Hebrew consonants (the Tetragrammaton) denoting the sacred personal name of Israel's God, Yahweh.

Yom Kippur *See* Day of Atonement.

Zadok A priest officiating during the reigns of David and Solomon who supported the latter's claim to the throne and was rewarded by being made chief priest at the Temple (2 Sam. 15:24–29; 17:15; 19:11; 20:25; 1 Kings 1:7–8; 32–39; 45; 2 Kings 35; 1 Chron. 6:4–15, 50–52; 12:28). Ezekiel regarded Zadok's descendants as the only legitimate priests (Ezek. 40:46; 43:19; 44:15; 48:11). After the exile, they apparently enjoyed a monopoly in the second Temple (1 Chron. 24:2–19; 27:17; 29:22).

Zaphenath-paneah According to Genesis 41:45, the Egyptian name given Joseph, son of Jacob. It has been variously translated as "says the God: he will live," "revealer of secrets," and "minister of agriculture."

Zarephath According to 1 Kings 17:8–24, a Phoenician town near Sidon where Elijah befriended a widow during a famine and resuscitated her son (Luke 4:25–27).

Zealots An extremely nationalistic party in first-century Judaism dedicated to freeing Judea from foreign domination, by armed revolt if necessary. Their militarism and fanatical patriotism generated several uprisings, culminating in the great rebellion against Rome (66–73 C.E.). According to Flavius Josephus' possibly biased account, their intransigence led to the destruction of Jerusalem and the Temple. The Simon of Luke 6:15 and Acts 1:13 is called a "zealot."

Zebedee A Galilean fisherman, husband of Salome, father of the apostles James and John (Matt. 27:56; Mark 1:19–20; 3:17; 14:33; 15:40).

Zebulun (1) The sixth son of Jacob and Leah, full brother of Reuben, Simeon, Levi, Judah, and Issachar (Gen. 30:20; 35:23). (2) The tribe of Zebulun, represented in Jacob's blessing (Gen. 49:13) as a seagoing group located near the Phoenician port of Sidon, actually settled in a landlocked farming area of northern Palestine (Josh. 19:10–16), although they were on a main trading route with coastal cities. Except for their failure to expel the Canaanites from their allotted territory and their joining Barak and Deborah against Sisera (Judg. 1:27–30; 4:10–16; 5:18), they are seldom mentioned in the Hebrew Bible.

Zechariah

1. The son of Jehoiada the priest, Zechariah was stoned to death for denouncing Judah's idolatry (late ninth century B.C.E.) (2 Chron. 25:20–22; he is usually identified with Zacharias in Matt. 23:35 and Luke 11:51).

2. The son of Jeroboam II and the last king of Jehu's dynasty in Israel, who reigned only six months (c. 746/745 B.C.E.) before he was murdered (2 Kings 10:30).

3. The son of Berechiah or the priest Iddo (Zech. 1:1, 8; Ezra 5:1; Neh. 12:16), a Judean prophet whose message is contained in the book of the Minor Prophets bearing his name.

   The latter, a contemporary of Haggai (c. 520–515 B.C.E.), urged the returned exiles to rebuild Yahweh's Temple in Jerusalem. Although Judah was then part of the Persian Empire ruled by Darius, he apparently regarded the Jewish governor, Zerubbabel, a descendant of David, as a potential messianic king (Zech. 4:6–15; 6:9–14). His work is characterized by strange imagery and apocalyptic visions. Chapters 9–14 of the Book of Zechariah are thought to have been appended by a later author.

4. A Judean priest married to Elisabeth, a descendant of Aaron, whose long, childless marriage was blessed in his old age by the birth of the future John the Baptist (Luke 1:5–25, 57–80;

3:2). A vision foretelling the birth rendered him temporarily paralyzed, but he recovered his speech in time to name the child and to utter a prayer of thanksgiving — the Benedictus (Luke 1:67–79).

5. A Jewish martyr mentioned in Jesus' phrase "from Abel to Zecharias" (Matt. 23:35; Luke 11:51), usually identified with Zechariah, son of Jehoiada in 2 Chronicles 24:20–24.

Zedekiah   The last king of Judah (c. 597–587 B.C.E.), Zedekiah reigned as a tribute-paying vassal of Nebuchadnezzar (2 Chron. 36:13; Jer. 29:3–7; Ezek. 17:15–18). A weak ruler, he consulted the prophet Jeremiah (Jer. 21:1–7) but acceded to his advisers' pressures to seek help from Egypt in throwing off Babylon's yoke (Jer. 27:12–22; 37:6–21; 38:7–28). When he rebelled against Babylon, Nebuchadnezzar laid siege to and destroyed Jerusalem (587 B.C.E.). Zedekiah tried to escape but was captured, tried, and condemned to having his sons slain before his eyes and his own eyes put out, after which he was imprisoned in Babylon, where he died (2 Kings 24:17–25:7; 2 Chron. 36:10–21; Jer. 39:6–14; 52:1–27).

Zephaniah   (1) Son of Maaseiah and second-ranking priest under King Zedekiah who acted as go-between for the king in his consultations with Jeremiah (2 Kings 25:18; Jer. 21:1; 29:25–32; 37:3–4; 52:24–27). After Jerusalem's fall, he was executed by the Babylonians. (2) A seventh-century Judean prophet whose pronouncements of judgment are collected in the book bearing his name (Zeph. 1:1). Virtually nothing is known of his life.

Zerubbabel   A son of Shealtiel or Salathiel (Ezra 3:2, 8; Hag. 1:1; Matt. 1:12) or of Pedaiah (1 Chron. 3:19), Zerubbabel (meaning "begotten in Babylon") was a grandson of Jehoiachin, the king of Judah imprisoned in Babylon (1 Chron. 3:17), and therefore a legitimate heir to the Davidic throne. Appointed governor of the restored Jewish community in Jerusalem (Ezra 3; Hag. 1:1, 14), he returned from Babylon with the first group of exiles and, with Joshua, the High Priest, set up an altar to Yahweh and made arrangements to rebuild the Temple. Between the time the work began and the Temple's dedication in 515 B.C.E. (Ezra 6), however, Zerubbabel disappeared from history. The prophets Haggai and Zechariah, who had urged the rebuilding, had both regarded him as a potential messianic king (Hag. 2:20–23; Zech. 4:6b–10a; 6:9–15 — the latter passage reworked by later scribes). When these political expectations failed to materialize, hopes were focused on a priestly hierarchy represented by Joshua (Zech. 3:1–4; 6:11–12).

Zeus   In Greek mythology, the son of Cronus and Rhea, king of the Olympian gods, and patron of civic order. A personification of storm and other heavenly powers, he ruled by wielding the lightning bolt. The Romans identified him with Jupiter (Jove). Some people of Lystra compared Barnabas to Zeus and Paul to Hermes (Acts 14:12). The erection of his statue in the Jerusalem Temple courts helped spark the Maccabean revolt (c. 168 B.C.E.).

ziggurat   A characteristic architectural form of Sumerian and Babylonian temples, the ziggurat was a multileveled tower resembling a stepped or recessed pyramid consisting of succeedingly smaller platforms built one atop the other. At its apex was a chapel dedicated to a major civic god. Broad ceremonial staircases used for liturgical processions led to the ziggurat's summit, to which it was believed the gods invisibly descended. The story of the Tower of Babel in Genesis 11:1–9 is probably based on a misunderstanding of the ziggurat's function.

Zilpah   The handmaid of Leah by whom Jacob begot Gad and Asher (Gen. 29:24; 30:9–13, 35:26).

Zimri   A chariot captain who murdered King Elah and seized Israel's throne, which he held for only seven days (876 B.C.E.). When Omri, leader of the military, attacked him at Tirzah, Zimri set the palace on fire and perished in the ruins, after which Omri became king (1 Kings 16:8–20).

Zion   The name, probably meaning "citadel," for a rocky hill in old Jerusalem, it was originally a Jebusite acropolis that David captured and on which he built his palace and housed the Ark of the Covenant (Judg. 19:11–12; 2 Sam. 5:6–12; 6:12–17; 1 Chron. 11:5–8). David purchased a threshing floor in Zion (2 Sam. 24:18–25) on which Solomon later built the Temple. In time, the term referred either to the hill on which the Temple stood or to the surrounding city of Jerusalem (Pss. 2:6; 9:11; 76:2; 127:3; Isa. 1:26–27; 10:24; 30:19; 64:10; Jer. 31:6; Amos 1:2; Mic. 3:12).

Zipporah   A daughter of Jethro, a Midianite shepherd and priest, Zipporah became Moses' wife (Exod. 2:11–22) and bore him at least two sons, Gershom (Exod. 2:22) and Eliezer (Exod. 18:3–4), saving the latter from Yahweh's wrath by circumcising him with a flint stone (Exod. 4:18–26).

Zoar   One of the five "cities of the plain" on the eastern shore of the Dead Sea (Gen. 13:10; 14:2, 8) that Lot reached as Sodom was being destroyed (Gen. 19:20–23). Because it is referred to by the prophets, it may have survived the catastrophe (Isa. 15:5; Jer. 48:34).

Zoroastrianism   The official religion of imperial Persia, it was founded in about the sixth century B.C.E. by the east Iranian prophet Zoroaster. According to his followers, the universe is dualistic, composed of parallel worlds of matter and spirit in which legions of good and evil spirits contend. In a final cosmic battle, Ahura Mazda, god of light and righteousness, will totally defeat Ahriman, embodiment of darkness and chaos. Historians believe that many biblical concepts of angelology and demonology, including the character of Satan, ultimately derive from Zoroastrian influence.

Zophar   A Naamathite, one of Job's three companions (Job 2:11; 11:1; 20:1; 42:9).

Selected Bibliography

This bibliography provides a representative list of important scholarly works on the Hebrew Bible and New Testament. Many additional references on specific topics and individual biblical books are included in the lists of Recommended Readings that appear throughout the text.

Bible Commentaries, Dictionaries, and Hebrew Bible Introductions

Achtemeier, Paul J., ed. *Harper's Bible Dictionary*, San Francisco: Harper & Row, 2nd ed., 1996. An excellent one-volume dictionary.

Ackroyd, P. R., et al., eds. *The Cambridge Bible Commentary*. Cambridge, Eng.: Cambridge University Press, 1979.

Anderson, Bernard. *Understanding the Old Testament*, 4th ed. Englewood Cliffs, N.J.: Prentice-Hall, 1986. An abridged edition was issued in 1998.

Brown, Raymond E.; Fitzmeyer, Joseph A.; and Murphy, Roland E. *The New Jerome Biblical Commentary*, 2nd ed. Englewood Cliffs, N.J.: Prentice-Hall, 1990.

Campbell, Antony F., and O'Brien, M. A. *Sources of the Pentateuch: Texts, Introductions, Annotations*. Minneapolis: Fortress Press, 1993. Prints separate narratives of J, E, and P with interpretive commentary; a major resource.

Dorsey, David A. *The Literary Structure of the Old Testament: A Commentary on Genesis-Malachi*. Grand Rapids, Mich.: Baker Books, 1999. Examines major themes of each biblical book.

Freedman, David Noel., ed., *The Anchor Bible Dictionary*, Vols. 1–6. New York: Doubleday, 1992. Indispensable resource.

———, ed. *Eerdmans Dictionary of the Bible*. Grand Rapids, Mich.: Wm. B. Eerdmans, 2000. Superb one-volume reference.

Friedman, Richard Elliott. *Commentary on the Torah with a New English Translation*. San Francisco: HarperSanFrancisco, 2001. An important study by a leading scholar.

Gottwald, Norman K. *The Hebrew Bible: A Socio-Literary Introduction*. Philadelphia: Fortress Press, 1985.

Humphreys, W. Lee. *Crisis and Story: Introduction to the Old Testament*, 2nd ed. Mountain View, Calif.: Mayfield, 1990.

Keck, Leander E., ed. *The New Interpreter's Bible*. Nashville: Abingdon Press, 1994. The complete biblical text in twelve volumes with scholarly commentary. (Vols. 1, 2, 3, 5, 6, 7, 8, 9, and 12 currently available.)

Lasor, William S., et al., *Old Testament Survey. The Message, Form, and Background of the Old Testament*, 2nd ed. Grand Rapids, Mich.: Wm. B. Eerdmans, 1996. A meticulously detailed, conservative approach.

Metzger, B. M., and Coogan, M. D., eds. *The Oxford Companion to the Bible*. New York: Oxford University Press, 1993.

Soggin, J. Alberto. *Introduction to the Old Testament*, 3rd ed. Translated by J. Bowden. Louisville, Ky: John Knox Press, 1989.

Suggs, M. J.; Sakenfeld, K. D.; and Mueller, J. R., eds. *The Oxford Study Bible*. New York: Oxford University Press, 1992.

Wigoder, Geoffrey, ed. *The Encyclopedia of Judaism*. New York: Macmillan, 1989.

Ancient Texts Relating to the Hebrew Bible (Tanak)

Beyerlin, Walter, ed. *Near Eastern Religious Texts Relating to the Old Testament.* Translated by J. Bowden. Philadelphia: Westminster Press, 1978.

Coogan, Michael David. *Stories from Ancient Canaan.* Philadelphia: Westminster Press, 1978. A paperback collection of Canaanite myths and their biblical parallels.

Cross, Frank M. *Canaanite Myth and Hebrew Epic, Essays in the History of the Religion of Israel.* Cambridge, Mass.: Harvard University Press, 1973.

Dalley, Stephanie. *Myths from Mesopotamia: Creation, the Flood, Gilgarmeds and Others.* New York: Oxford University Press, 1989.

Foster, Benjamin R. *Before the Muses: An Anthology of Akkadian Literature.* 2 vols. Bethesda, Md.: CDL Press, 1993. A valuable collection of Near Eastern texts.

Gardner, John, and Maier, John. *Gilgamesh.* New York: Knopf, 1984. A recent translation with scholarly annotations.

Halls, William W., ed. *The Context of Scripture.* Vol. 1, *Canonical Compositions from the Biblical World.* Leiden: Brill, 1997.

Lichtheim, Miriam. *Ancient Egyptian Literature: A Book of Readings.* 3 vols. Berkeley: University of California Press, 1973–1980.

Maier, John, ed. *Gilgamesh: A Reader.* Wauconda, Ill.: Bolohazy-Carducci, 1997.

Matthews, Victor H., and Benjamin, Don C. *Old Testament Parallels: Documents from the Ancient Near East.* Mahwah, N.J.: Paulist Press, 1991.

Parker, Simon B. *Stories in Scripture and Inscriptions: Comparative Studies on Northwest Semitic Inscriptions and the Hebrew Bible.* New York: Oxford University Press, 1997.

Pritchard, James B. *The Ancient Near East: An Anthology of Texts and Pictures.* Princeton, N.J.: Princeton University Press, 1965. A text that contains excerpts from the following two books:

———. *The Ancient Near East in Pictures Relating to the Old Testament.* Princeton, N.J.: Princeton University Press, 1965.

———, ed. *Ancient Near Eastern Texts Relating to the Old Testament,* 3rd ed. supp. Princeton, N.J.: Princeton University Press, 1969. Translations of relevant Egyptian, Babylonian, Canaanite, and other ancient literatures — the standard work.

Roth, Martha T. *Law Collections from Mesopotamia and Asia Minor.* Atlanta: Scholars Press, 1997.

Sanders, N. K. *The Epic of Gilgamesh.* Baltimore: Penguin Books, 1972. A readable paraphrase of the *Epic of Gilgamesh* with a scholarly introduction.

———. *Poems of Heaven and Hell from Ancient Mesopotamia.* London and New York: Penguin Books, 1971.

Biblical Archaeology

Aharoni, Yohanan, and Avi-Yonah, Michael. *The Macmillan Bible Atlas,* 3rd ed. New York; Macmillan, 1993. Oriented toward specific biblical texts.

Ahlström, Gösta W. *The History of Ancient Palestine.* Minneapolis: Fortress Press, 1993. A comprehensive study of the archaeological record in Canaan.

Báez-Camargo, Gonzalo. *Archaeological Commentary on the Bible.* Garden City, N.Y.: Doubleday, 1984. A book-by-book study of archaeology's contribution to understanding biblical literature.

Dever, William G. *What Did Biblical Writers Know and When Did They Know It? What Archaeology Can Tell Us about the Reality of Ancient Israel.* Grand Rapids, Mich.: Wm. B. Eerdmans, 2001. A spirited argument defending the historicity of preexilic Israel and the Davidic Monarchy.

Drinkard, Joel F., Jr., et al., eds. *Benchmarks in Time and Culture: An Introduction to the History and Methodology of Syro-Palestinian Archaeology.* Atlanta: Scholars Press, 1988.

Finegan, Jack. *The Archaeology of the New Testament,* rev. ed. Princeton, N.J.: Princeton University Press, 1992.

Harris, Roberta L. *The World of the Bible.* London: Thames & Hudson, 1995.

King, Philip J. and Stager, Lawrence E. *Life in Biblical Israel.* Louisville, Ky.: Westminster John Knox Press, 2001. An authoritative compendium of current biblical and archaeological scholarship.

Magnusson, Magnus. *Archaeology of the Bible.* New York: Simon & Schuster, 1977.

Mazzar, Amihai. *Archaeology of the Land of the Bible, 10,000–586.* New York: Doubleday, 1990.

Moscati, Sabatino. *The Face of the Ancient Orient.* Garden City, N.Y.: Doubleday/Anchor Books, 1962.

Negev, Auraham, ed. *The Archaeological Encyclopedia of the Holy Land,* rev. ed. Nelson, 1986.

Pritchard, James B. *The Harper Atlas of the Bible.* New York and San Francisco: Harper & Row, 1987. Includes beautifully illustrated discussions of archaeological sites.

Stern, Ephraim, et al., eds. *The New Encyclopedia of Archaeological Excavations in the Holy Land.* 4 vols. Israel Exploration Society, 1993.

Wright, George E. *Biblical Archaeology,* rev. ed. Philadelphia: Westminster Press, 1966.

Hebrew Bible History, Theology, and Interpretation

Ackroyd, Peter R. *Exile and Restoration: A Study of Hebrew Thought in the Sixth Century B.C.E.* Philadelphia: Westminster Press, 1968.

Ahlström, Gosta W. *Who Were the Israelites?* Winona Lake, Ind.: Eisenbrauns, 1986.

Albrektson, Bertil. *History and the Gods.* Lund, Sweden: Gleerup, 1967.

Albertz, Rainier. *A History of Israelite Religion in the Old Testament Period*, 2 vols. Translated by John Bowden. Louisville, Ky.: Westminster John Knox Press, 1994. Analyzes growth of the Hebrew Bible in its socio-historical context.

Alt, Albrecht. *Essays on Old Testament History and Religion.* Translated by R. A. Wilson. New York: Doubleday, 1967.

Alter, Robert, and Kermode, Frank, eds. *The Literary Guide to the Bible.* Cambridge, Mass.: Harvard University Press, 1987. Scholarly essays on the critical interpretation of biblical literature.

Anderson, Bernhard W., ed. *Creation in the Old Testament.* Philadelphia: Fortress Press, 1984.

Anderson, G. W., ed. *Tradition and Interpretation.* Oxford, Eng.: Clarendon Press, 1979.

Birch, Bruce, et al. *A Theological Introduction to the Old Testament.* Nashville: Abingdon Press, 1999. Thoughtful essays on evolving ideas in the biblical texts.

Bright, John. *A History of Israel,* 4th ed. Lousiville, Ky.: Westminster John Knox Press, 2000. A standard reference.

Brueggemann, Walter. *Theology of the Old Testament: Testimony, Dispute, Advocacy.* Minneapolis: Fortress Press, 1997. A superb study of the biblical God and his troubled relationship with Israel.

Coogan, Michael D., ed. *The Oxford History of the Biblical World.* New York: Oxford University Press, 1998. Provides up-to-date information on the cultural/historical environment in which the Bible originated.

Coote, Robert B., and Coote, Mary P. *Power, Politics and the Making of the Bible.* Minneapolis: Augsburg Fortress Press, 1990.

Cross, Frank M. *The Ancient Library of Qumran and Modern Biblical Studies.* Garden City, N.Y.: Doubleday, 1961.

Crüsemann, Frank. *The Torah: Theology and Social History of Old Testament Law.* Minneapolis: Fortress Press, 1996.

Eichrodt, Walther. *Theology of the Old Testament,* Vol. 1. Translated by J. A. Baker. Philadelphia: Westminster Press, 1961.

———. *Theology of the Old Testament,* Vol. 2. Translated by J. A. Baker. Philadelphia: Westminster Press, 1967.

Eliade, Mircea. *Cosmos and History: The Myth of the Eternal Return.* New York: Harper Torchbooks, 1954.

———. *The Sacred and the Profane: The Nature of Religion.* New York: Harper Torchbooks, 1961.

Ellis, Peter. *The Yahwist: The Bible's First Theologian.* Notre Dame, Ind.: Fides, 1968.

Fohrer, Georg. *History of Israelite Religion.* Translated by D. Green. Nashville: Abingdon Press, 1972. Traces the development of Israel's characteristic religious concepts and traditions.

Friedman, Richard E. *Who Wrote the Bible?* San Francisco: Harper & Row, 1987. A superb analysis of theories about biblical authorship, including the suggestion that J (the Yahwist) was a woman.

———. *The Hidden Book in the Bible.* San Francisco: HarperSanFrancisco, 1998.

Gabel, John B. *The Bible as Literature: An Introduction,* 3rd ed. New York: Oxford University Press, 1996.

Gaster, Theodor H. *Thespis: Ritual, Myth, and Drama in the Ancient Near East.* New York: Abelard-Schuman, 1950.

———. *Myth, Legend, and Custom in the Old Testament.* New York: Harper & Row, 1969.

———. *The Dead Sea Scriptures in English Translation.* Garden City, N.Y.: Doubleday, 1976.

Gordon, Cyrus H., and G. A. Rendsburg. *The Bible and the Ancient Near East,* 4th ed. 1998.

Gottwald, Norman K. *The Tribes of Yahweh: A Sociology of the Religion of Liberated Israel, 1250–1050 B.C.E.* Maryknoll, N.Y.: Orbis Books, 1979.

Gray, John. *Near Eastern Mythology.* New York: Peter Bedrick Books, 1982.

Hadley, Judith M. *The Cult of Asherah in Ancient Israel and Judah: Evidence for a Hebrew Goddess.* Cambridge, Eng.: Cambridge University Press, 2000. Examines the biblical and archaeological case for Asherah as Yahureh's divine consort.

Halpern, Baruch. *The First Historians: The Hebrew Bible and History.* San Francisco: Harper & Row, 1988.

Hillers, Delbert R. *Covenant: The History of a Biblical Idea.* Baltimore: Johns Hopkins University Press, 1969.

Klein, Ralph W. *Textual Criticism of the Old Testament: The Septuagint After Qumram.* Philadelphia: Fortress Press, 1974.

Koch, Klaus. *The Growth of the Biblical Tradition: The Form-Critical Method.* Translated by S. M. Cupitt. New York: Scribner, 1969.

———. *The Prophets.* Vol. 1, *The Assyrian Age.* Translated by M. Kohl. Philadelphia: Fortress Press, 1982.

Kugel, James L. *The Bible as It Was.* Cambridge, Mass.: The Belknap Press of Harvard University Press, 1997. Examines the earliest extant interpretations of the biblical narratives.

Lang, Bernhard. *The Hebrew God: Portrait of an Ancient Deity.* New Haven: Yale University Press, 2002. Shows that Yahweh incorporates multiple roles of older Near Eastern gods.

Levenson, Jon D. *Sinai and Zion: An Entry into the Jewish Bible.* San Francisco: HarperSanFrancisco, 1985. A concise but incisive analysis of the sometimes conflicting covenants associated with Moses and David.

———. *Creation and the Persistence of Evil.* San Francisco: Harper & Row, 1988.

Mays, James L., ed. *Harper's Bible Commentary.* San Francisco: Harper & Row, 1988. Provides clear, scholarly discussions of each book in the Hebrew Bible and New Testament Aprocrypha.

McCurley, Foster R. *Ancient Myths and Biblical Faith: Scriptural Transformations*. Philadelphia: Fortress Press, 1983.

McKenzie, John L. *A Theology of the Old Testament*. Garden City, N.Y.: Doubleday, 1974.

Mendenhall, George. *Law and Covenant in Israel and the Ancient Near East*. Pittsburgh: Biblical Colloquium, 1955.

———. "Biblical History in Transition." In G. E. Wright, ed., *The Bible and the Ancient Near East*. New York: Doubleday/Anchor Books, 1965.

———. *The Tenth Generation: The Origins of the Biblical Tradition*. Baltimore: Johns Hopkins University Press, 1973.

Miller, Patrick D. *The Religion of Ancient Israel*. Louisville, Ky.: Westminster John Knox Press, 2000. An important study of the biblical concept of God.

Niditch, Susan. *Ancient Israelite Religion*. New York: Oxford Press, 1997. Helpful introductory survey.

Noth, Martin. *The History of Israel*. New York: Harper & Row, 1960.

———. *A History of Pentateuchal Traditions*. Englewood Cliffs, N.J.: Prentice-Hall, 1972.

Redford, Donald B. *Egypt, Canaan, and Israel in Ancient Times*. Princeton, N.J.: Princeton University Press, 1992.

Robertson, David. *The Old Testament and the Literary Critic*. Guides to Biblical Scholarship. Philadelphia: Fortress Press, 1977.

Sanders, James A. *Torah and Canon*. Philadelphia: Fortress Press, 1972. A concise and helpful introduction to canon information.

Shanks, Hershel, ed. *Ancient Israel: A Short History from Abraham to the Roman Destruction of the Temple*, rev. ed., Washington, D.C.: Biblical Archaeology Society, 1999.

———, ed. *Understanding the Dead Sea Scrolls*. New York: Random House, 1992.

Smith, Morton, and Hoffman, R. Joseph, eds. *What the Bible Really Says*. Buffalo: Prometheus Books, 1989. A collection of essays on key biblical topics, for the nonspecialist.

Soulen, Richard N. *Handbook of Biblical Criticism*. Atlanta: John Knox Press, 1976.

Tucker, Gene M. *Form Criticism of the Old Testament*. Guides to Biblical Scholarship. Philadelphia: Fortress Press, 1971.

von Rad, Gerhard. *Old Testament Theology*. Vol. 1, *The Theology of Israel's Historical Traditions*. Translated by M. G. Stalker. New York: Harper & Row, 1962.

———. *Old Testament Theology*. Vol. 2, *The Theology of Israel's Prophetic Traditions*. Translated by M. G. Stalker. New York: Harper & Row, 1965.

———. *God at Work in Israel*. Translated by J. Marks. Nashville: Abingdon Press, 1980.

Westermann, Claus, ed. *Essays on Old Testament Hermeneutics*. Translated and edited by J. L. Mays. Richmond, Va.: John Knox Press, 1963.

———. *The Promises to the Fathers: Studies on the Patriarchal Narratives*. Translated by D. E. Green. Philadelphia: Fortress Press, 1980.

Wolff, Hans W. *Anthropology of the Old Testament*. Translated by M. Kohl. Philadelphia: Fortress Press, 1981.

———. *Confrontations with Prophets*. Philadelphia: Fortress Press, 1983.

Wright, G. Ernest. *The Old Testament and Theology*. New York: Harper & Row, 1969.

Zimmerli, Walther. *Man and His Hope in the Old Testament: Studies in Biblical Theology*, 2nd series. Naperville, Ill.: Allenson, 1968.

———. *Old Testament Theology in Outline*. Translated by D. E. Green. Atlanta: John Knox Press, 1978.

Old Testament Apocrypha, Pseudepigrapha, and Apocalyptic Writings

Becker, Joachim. *Messianic Expectation in the Old Testament*. Translated by D. E. Green. Philadelphia: Fortress Press, 1980.

Charles, R. H., ed. *The Apocrypha and Pseudepigrapha of the Old Testament in English*, Vols. 1 and 2. New York: Oxford University Press, 1963 (1913).

Charlesworth, J. H., ed. *The Old Testament Pseudepigrapha*. Vol. 1, *Apocalyptic Literature and Testaments*. Garden City, N.Y.: Doubleday/Anchor Books, 1983.

———, ed. *The Old Testament Pseudepigrapha*. Vol. 2, *Expansions of the "Old Testament" and Philosophical Literature, Prayers, Psalms, and Odes, Fragments of Lost Judeo-Hellenistic Works*. Garden City, N.Y.: Doubleday/Anchor Books, 1985.

Cohen, Shaye J. D. *From the Maccabees to the Mishnah*. Philadelphia: Westminster Press, 1987.

Collins, John J., ed. *The Encyclopedia of Apocalypticism*, Vol. 1, *The Origins of Apocalypticism in Judaism and Christianity*. New York: Continuum, 1998.

Hanson, Paul D. *The Dawn of Apocalyptic: The Historical and Sociological Roots of Jewish Eschatology*. Philadelphia: Fortress Press, 1979.

Mowinckel, Sigmund. *He That Cometh*. Translated by G. W. Anderson. Nashville: Abingdon Press, 1956.

Nickelsburg, George W. E. *Jewish Literature Between the Bible and the Mishnah: A Historical and Literary Introduction*. Philadelphia: Fortress Press, 1981.

Ringgren, Helmer. *The Messiah in the Old Testament: Studies in Biblical Theology*, no. 18. Chicago: Allenson, 1956.

Rost, Leonard. *Judaism Outside the Hebrew Canon: An Introduction to the Documents*. Nashville: Abingdon Press, 1976.

Russell, D. S. *The Method and Message of Jewish Apocalyptic: 200 B.C.–A.D. 100*. Philadelphia: Westminster Press, 1964. A useful review of apocalyptic literature of the Greco-Roman period.

———. *Apocalyptic: Ancient and Modern*. Philadelphia: Fortress Press, 1978.

New Testament Introductions, Theology, Criticism, and Interpretation

Boring, M. E.; Berger, Klaus; and Culpe, Carsten, eds. *Hellenistic Commentary to the New Testament.* Nashville: Abingdon Press, 1995.

Brown, Raymond E. *An Introduction to the New Testament.* New York: Doubleday, 1997. A masterful compendium of current scholarly research.

Duling, Dennis C., and Perrin, Norman. *The New Testament: Proclamation and Parenesis, Myth and History,* 3rd ed. New York: Harcourt Brace, 1994.

Ehrman, Bart D. *The New Testament and Other Early Christian Writings: A Reader.* New York: Oxford University Press, 1998. Integrates canonical New Testament texts with apocryphal books, illustrating the theological range of early Christianity.

Evans, Craig A. and Porter, Stanley E., eds. *Dictionary of New Testament Background.* Downers Grove, Ill.: InterVarsity Press, 2000. Provides socio-historical setting of early Christian thought.

Ferguson, Everett. *Backgrounds of Early Christianity,* 2nd ed. Grand Rapids, Mich.: Wm. B. Eerdmans, 1993.

Funk, R. W. *New Gospel Parallels.* Vols. 1 and 2. Philadelphia: Fortress Press, 1985. A major achievement in New Testament scholarship; Volume 1 provides parallels to the three Synoptic Gospels, and Volume 2 assembles parallels to the Gospels of John, Thomas, and Peter, the Infancy Gospel of Thomas, the Protoevangelium of James, the Acts of Pilate, and various manuscript fragments.

Funk, Robert W.; Hoover, Roy W.; and the Jesus Seminar. *The Five Gospels: The Search for the Authentic Words of Jesus.* San Francisco: HarperSanFrancisco, 1993. A translation that color-codes Jesus' sayings according to the translators' belief in their relative authenticity.

Funk, Robert W., and the Jesus Seminar. *The Acts of Jesus: What Did Jesus Really Do?* San Francisco: HarperSan Francisco, 1998.

Goppelt, Leonhard. *Theology of the New Testament,* Vols. 1 and 2. Translated by J. E. Alsup. Edited by J. Roloff. Grand Rapids, Mich.: Wm. B. Eerdmans, 1981.

Guthrie, Donald. *New Testament Theology.* Downers Grove, Ill.: InterVarsity Press, 1981.

Hahn, Ferdinand. *Historical Imagination and New Testament Faith: Two Essays.* Philadelphia: Fortress Press, 1983.

Harris, Stephen L. *The New Testament: A Student's Introduction,* 4th ed. Boston: McGraw-Hill, 2002.

Kee, Howard C. *Understanding the New Testament,* 5th ed. Englewood Cliffs, N.J.: Prentice-Hall, 1993. A scholarly, analytical approach to New Testament study.

Koester, Helmut. *Ancient Christian Gospels: Their History and Development.* Philadelphia: Trinity Press International, 1990.

———. *Introduction to the New Testament,* Vol. 1. *History, Culture, and Religion of the Hellenistic Age,* 2nd. ed. New York: Walter de Gruyter, 1995.

———, Vol. 2. *History and Literature of Early Christianity,* 2nd ed. New York: Walter de Gruyter, 2000.

Kummel, W. G. *Introduction to the New Testament.* Translated by H. C. Kee. Nashville: Abingdon Press, 1975.

Ladd, George Eldon. *A Theology of the New Testament.* Grand Rapids, Mich.: Wm. B. Eerdmans, 1974.

McGrath, Alister E. *Christian Theology: An Introduction.* Oxford: Blackwell, 1994.

Miller, Robert J. *The Complete Gospels,* 2nd ed. San Francisco: HarperSanFrancisco, 1994. Contains both canonical and all extant noncanonical gospels.

Pfeiffer, Robert. *History of the New Testament Times: With an Introduction to the Apocrypha.* New York: Harper & Brothers, 1949. Covers Roman rule from Pompey's conquest (63 B.C.E.) to the outbreak of the Jewish revolt (66 C.E.).

Birth, Trial, and Resurrection Narratives

Brown, Raymond E. *The Birth of the Messiah: A Commentary on the Infancy Narratives in Matthew and Luke.* New York: Doubleday, 1977. A comprehensive analysis of the historicity and theological implications of the infancy narratives.

———. *The Death of the Messiah,* Vols. 1 and 2. New York: Anchor Doubleday, 1994.

Brown, Raymond E.; Donfried, K. P.; Fitzmyer, S. J.; and Reumann, John, eds. *Mary in the New Testament: A Collaborative Assessment by Protestant and Roman Catholic Scholars.* Philadelphia: Fortress Press, 1978.

Catchpole, David R. *The Trial of Jesus.* Leiden, Netherlands: Brill, 1971. Argues that Jesus was executed for religious offenses.

Crossan, John Dominic. *The Historical Jesus.* San Francisco: HarperSanFrancisco, 1991.

Denielou, Jean. *The Infancy Narratives.* Translated by R. Sheed. New York: Herder & Herder, 1968. Attempts to discern the historical worth of the birth stories.

Fuller, Reginald H. *The Formation of the Resurrection Narratives.* Philadelphia: Fortress Press, 1980.

Funk, Robert W., and Hoover, Roy W. *Five Gospels, One Jesus.* Sonoma, Calif.: Polebridge Press, 1992. Includes the Gospel of Thomas and the four canonical Gospels, with the probable words of the historical Jesus printed in red or pink.

Marxsen, Willi. *The Resurrection of Jesus of Nazareth.* Translated by M. Kohl. Philadelphia: Fortress Press, 1970.

Meier, John P. *A Marginal Jew: Rethinking the Historical Jesus.* 3 vols. New York: Doubleday, 1991.

Perrin, Norman. *The Resurrection According to Matthew, Mark, and Luke.* Philadelphia: Fortress Press, 1977.

Rivkin, Ellis. *What Crucified Jesus? The Political Execution of a Charismatic.* Nashville: Abingdon Press, 1984. Presents Jesus as a victim of "the system," a Roman-Jewish establishment devoted to preserving the political status quo.

Sanders, E. P. *The Historical Figure of Jesus.* New York: Viking Press, 1994.

Sawicki, Marianne. *Seeing the Lord: Resurrection and Early Christian Practices.* Minneapolis: Fortress Press, 1994.

Theissen, Gerd, and Merz, Annette. *The Historical Jesus: A Comprehensive Guide.* Minneapolis: Fortress Press, 1996. Provides systematic analysis of current Jesus research.

Winter, Paul. *On the Trial of Jesus.* Berlin: Walter de Gruyter, 1977. Emphasizes the political charges against Jesus.

Women and the Bible

Daly, Mary. *Beyond God the Father: Toward a Philosophy of Women's Liberation.* New York: Harper & Row, 1980.

Frymer-Kensky, Tikva. *In the Wake of the Goddesses: Women, Culture, and the Biblical Transformation of Pagan Myth.* New York: Free Press, 1992. A superb scholarly study of biblical religion's relation to older Near Eastern pantheons.

Gerstenberger, Erhard S., and Schrage, Wolfgang. *Woman and Man.* Translated by D. W. Scott. Nashville: Abingdon Press, 1982.

Jeunsonne, Sharon P. *The Women of Genesis, from Sarah to Potiphar's Wife.* Minneapolis: Augsburg Fortress Press, 1990.

LaCocque, André. *The Feminine Unconventional: Four Subversive Figures in Israel's Tradition.* Minneapolis: Augsburg Fortress Press, 1990.

Laffrey, Alice L. *An Introduction to the Old Testament: A Feminist Perspective.* Philadelphia: Fortress Press, 1988. Addresses specifically feminist issues in the context of the Hebrew Bible.

Mullenkott, Virginia R. *The Divine Feminine: The Biblical Image of God as Female.* New York: Crossroads Press, 1983.

Myers, Carol. *Discovering Eve: Ancient Israelite Women in Context.* Oxford: Oxford University Press, 1988.

Newsom, Carol A., and Ringe, S. H., eds. *The Women's Bible Commentary.* Louisville, Ky.: Westminster John Knox Press, 1992. Examines both the Hebrew Bible and the New Testament from women's perspective.

Otwell, John H. *And Sarah Laughed.* Philadelphia: Westminster Press, 1977.

Ruether, Rosemary R. *Sexism and God-Talk.* New York: Harper & Row, 1982.

Schüssler Fiorenza, Elizabeth. *In Memory of Her: A Feminist Theological Reconstruction of Christian Origins.* New York: Crossroads Press, 1983.

———. *Bread Not Stone: The Challenge of Feminist Biblical Interpretation.* Boston: Beacon Press, 1985.

———. *But She Said: Feminist Practices of Biblical Interpretation.* Boston: Beacon Press, 1992.

Wolkenstein, Diane, and Kramer, Samuel N. *Inanna, Queen of Heaven and Earth.* New York: Harper & Row, 1980.

Credits

Text Credits

Excerpts from *The New English Bible.* Copyright © 1961, 1970 Oxford University Press and Cambridge University Press. Reprinted with permission from the publisher. Excerpts from *The Jerusalem Bible.* Copyright © 1966 by Darton, Longman & Todd, Ltd. and Doubleday, a division of Random House, Inc. Reprinted by permission.

Photo Credits

Chapter 1 **1.2,** Courtesy of the British Library, no. 43725 *f* 260; **1.3,** Reproduced by courtesy of the Director and University Librarian, The John Rylands University Library of Manchester.

Chapter 2 **2.2,** © The British Museum; **2.3,** Courtesy of the University Museum, University of Pennsylvania, Neg. #S8-139343; **2.4,** Courtesy of the University Museum, University of Pennsylvania, Neg. #S5-23215; **2.5,** Courtesy of the Ashmolean Museum, Oxford; **2.6,** © The British Museum; **2.7, 2.8, 2.9,** © Réunion des Musées Nationaux/Art Resource, NY; **2.10,** © Alinari/Art Resource, NY; **2.11,** © Egyptian Museum/PhotoEdit; **2.13,** Courtesy of NASA.

Chapter 3 **3.1 left,** © Erich Lessing/Art Resource, NY; **3.1 right,** Courtesy Nicolas Wyatt/Edinburgh Ras Shamra Project/University of Edinburgh.

Chapter 4 **4.1,** © Hirmer Fotoarchiv; **4.3,** Courtesy of the University Museum, University of Pennsylvania, Neg. #S4-142836; **4.4,** Courtesy of the Oriental Division, The New York Public Library, Astor, Lenox and Tilden Foundations; **4.5,** © Erich Lessing/Art Resource, NY; **4.7,** © Alan Oddie/PhotoEdit; **4.8,** © Zev Radovan/PhotoEdit.

Chapter 5 **5.1,** © The British Museum; **5.2,** © PhotoEdit; **5.3,** © Erich Lessing/Art Resource, NY; **5.8,** © Réunion des Musées Nationaux/Art Resource, NY; **5.9,** © The British Museum; **5.10,** © Réunion des Musées Nationaux/Art Resource, NY; **5.11,** © The British Museum.

Chapter 6 **6.2,** © Oriental Institute Museum, University of Chicago; **6.3,** © The British Museum; **6.4,** Courtesy of Vorderasiatisches Museum, Berlin; **6.5,** © Oriental Institute Museum, University of Chicago; **6.7, 6.8,** © The British Museum.

Chapter 7 **7.1,** © The British Museum; **7.2,** Courtesy of the University Museum, University of Pennsylvania, Neg. #S8-68052b; **7.3,** Courtesy of the Bible Lands Museum Jerusalem. Photo Credit: Dietrich Widmer; **7.4,** © Oriental Institute Museum, University of Chicago; **7.6,** Courtesy of Vorderasiatisches Museum, Berlin; **7.7,** © Erich Lessing/Art Resource, NY; **7.8,** Courtesy of the Israel Antiquities Authority.

Chapter 8 **8.2,** © Alinari/Art Resource, NY; **8.4,** © Erich Lessing/Art Resource, NY; **8.5,** © Hirmer Fotoarchiv; **8.6,** © Réunion des Musées Nationaux/Art Resource, NY; **8.7,** © Alinari/Art Resource, NY; **8.8,** © Israel Museum/PhotoEdit.

Chapter 9 **9.2,** © Erich Lessing/Art Resource, NY; **9.3,** © Erich Lessing/PhotoEdit; **9.5,** Courtesy of the American Numismatic Society Photographic Services, NY; **9.6, 9.7, 9.8,** © The British Museum; **9.9,** © Corbis; **9.10,** © Foto Marburg/Art Resource, NY; **9.11,** © Archaeological Receipts Fund; **9.12,**

Index